AN INTRODUCTION TO THE
STUDY OF INSECTS

AN INTRODUCTION TO THE STUDY OF INSECTS

fourth edition

DONALD J. BORROR
PROFESSOR OF ENTOMOLOGY / THE OHIO STATE UNIVERSITY

DWIGHT M. DELONG
EMERITUS PROFESSOR OF ENTOMOLOGY / THE OHIO STATE UNIVERSITY

CHARLES A. TRIPLEHORN
PROFESSOR OF ENTOMOLOGY / THE OHIO STATE UNIVERSITY

Holt, Rinehart and Winston
New York, Chicago, San Francisco, Atlanta, Dallas, Montreal, Toronto, London, Sydney

Library of Congress Cataloging in Publication Data

Borror, Donald Joyce, 1907–
An introduction to the study of insects.

Includes bibliographies and index.
1. Entomology. 2. Insects—United States.
I. De Long, Dwight Moore, 1892– joint author.
II. Triplehorn, Charles A., joint author.
III. Title.
QL463.B69 1971b 595.7 75-26620
ISBN 0-03-088406-3

Printed in the United States of America
9 8 7 6 032 1 2 3 4 5 6 7 8 9

Art Supervisor: Renee Davis Art Studio: Vantage Art Designer: Scott Chelius

PREFACE

The importance of the role played by insects in the world of living things is becoming more appreciated each year, not only because of the attention given to the species which act as pests, but because of the increasing realization that many species are extremely valuable to man. The study of insects is an important part of the training of every agriculturalist, biology teacher, and student of nature.

Many books are already available to the student or teacher interested in insects; some give special emphasis to the biological or economic aspects, and others emphasize the taxonomic phase of entomology, but few combine emphasis on both insect study—working with insects—and identification. This book is intended to serve as a text for a beginning course in college entomology, and as a guide for teachers and others interested in the study of insects; it might also serve as a text for an advanced course in systematic entomology, as it contains keys for the identitication of all the families of insects occurring in North America north of Mexico, and keys to some subfamilies.

The discussions of morphology and physiology in this book may not be as complete as in some other books; our aim has been to present enough material on these phases of entomology to enable the student to use the keys and to understand something of the general biology of the insects he encounters. An attempt has been made to make the keys as workable as possible by illustrating most of the key characters. No attempt has been made to present keys to immature forms.

Insects should be observed and studied in the field as well as in the classroom and laboratory, and this book is designed to serve as a text for entomology courses which involve both field and laboratory work. We realize that field work is difficult or impossible in some courses, due to the season in which the course is given, the location of the school, or other factors, but many insects can be maintained indoors in cages or aquaria, and the study of such living material can be substituted for field observations.

We have drawn on many sources of information in the preparation of this book, some of which are listed in the bibliographies at the end of each chapter. These bibliographies are far from complete; rather than striving for completeness, we have tried to list references which can serve as a starting point for the student interested in going further. In our treatment of the various orders we have generally followed the most recent or accepted classification; in some cases we have used a somewhat simplified classification because it seemed more suitable in a book of this type. Concepts of insect relationships and classification change as our knowledge of insects increases, and no arrangement of orders and families is likely to be permanent.

There have been several major changes in the fourth edition. A new chapter has been added on insect behavior. The two separate chapters on the phylum Arthropóda have been combined into one chapter. The chapters on collecting and preserving insects and activities and projects in insect study have also been combined into a new chapter. Many of the keys have been revised, new illustrations have been added and some old ones deleted, and the reference lists have been updated. The classification in a few orders has been updated, with the addition of a few new families to the list for North America. General revisions have been made throughout the book, in some cases by minor changes in rewording, in other cases by completely rewriting a section or adding new material. We have added a third coauthor for this edition, Dr. Charles A. Triplehorn, whose contributions have included the revision of Chapters 25 and 34.

Many people have made valuable suggestions or criticisms regarding particular parts of this book, or have helped with taxonomic problems or in other ways, but we are particularly indebted to the following people for assistance in preparing this edition: Dwight Bennett, Glen Berkey, N. Wilson Britt, Harley P. Brown, Leland R. Brown, Horace R. Burke, Donald S. Chandler, Frank W. Fisk, Donald F. J. Hilton, Roger Hoopingarner, C. Dennis Hynes, Albin T. Khouw, Alice B. Kolbe, Robert J. Lavigne, John F. Lawrence, Kingston L. H. Leong, William F. Lyon, Carl R. Mappes, Frank W. Mead, Arnold Menke, Carl Mohr, Ian Moore, Martin H. Muma, Milledge Murphy, Joseph C. Schaffner, Charles L. Selman, Robbin W. Thorp, J. R. Vockeroth, Tsing Cheng Wang, and Richard E. White.

D. J. B.
D. M. DeL.
C. A. T.

Columbus, Ohio
November, 1975

ACKNOWLEDGMENTS

Throughout previous editions a great many people have made valuable suggestions and criticisms regarding specific portions of this book, or have helped solve problems of taxonomy in various orders. We would like to acknowledge their help in the past.

FIRST EDITION

J. Gordon Edwards, T. H. Hubbell, Maurice T. James, Clarence H. Kennedy, Josef N. Knull, Karl V. Krombein, John E. Lane, A. W. Lindsey, Harlow B. Mills, C. F. W. Muesebeck, Alvah Peterson, E. S. Ross, H. H. Ross, Marion R. Smith, Kathryn M. Sommerman, Louis J. Stannard, Edward S. Thomas, and E. M. Walker.

The majority of the original drawings in this book was made by or under the direction of the senior author. The following persons have assisted in the preparation of these drawings: Richard D. Alexander, Calvin E. Beckelheimer, Arthur C. Borror, G. Mallory Boush, William C. Costello, Edward W. Huffman, John E. Lane, Paul D. Ludwig, George W. Murphy, Robert F. Ruppel, and Celeste W. Taft. The original photographs were made principally by the junior author, assisted by Oscar Metze.

Many entomologists and a few editors have assisted with the loan of illustrations or permission to use certain illustrations previously printed in their publications. In each case where a borrowed illustration is used its source is indicated. Special credit, we believe, should be given the following persons: James S. Ayars, Stanley F. Bailey, Richard M. Bohart, Hazel E. Branch, A. W. A. Brown, H. E. Burke, Barnard D. Burks, R. W. Burrell, C. P. Clausen, Ralph H. Davidson, Donald DeLeon, Lafe R. Edmunds, Richard C. Froeschner, B. B. Fulton, Robert Glenn, Ashley B. Gurney, David G. Hall, Philip H. Harden, M. J. Hayell, William R. Horsfall, H. B. Hungerford, Maurice T. James, B. J. Kaston, George F. Knowlton, J. N. Knull, J. W. Leonard, Philip Luginbill, E. A. McGregor, Luis F. Martorell, John Moser, Claud R. Neiswander, Harry L. Parker, Alvah Peterson, Edward S. Ross, Herbert H. Ross, John G. Shaw, Herbert H. Smith, Kathryn M. Sommerman, R. W. Strandtmann, George R. Struble, Edwin Way Teale, C. A. Triplehorn, G. Stuart Walley, E. M. Walker, and Mrs. Blanche P. Young. To all organizations and individuals who have loaned illustrations, we wish to express our sincere thanks for permission to use their material.

SECOND EDITION

Richard D. Alexander, Ross H. Arnett, Jr., Arthur C. Borror, Osmond P. Breland, Theodore J. Cohn, Paul H. Freytag, Theodore H. Hubbell, F. P. Ide, D. E. Johnston, Josef N. Knull, Michael Kosztarab, Alan Stone, Charles A. Triplehorn, Barry Valentine, and Richard E. White. The following have assisted with the loan of illustrations or permission to use illustrations previously printed in their publications: Richard D. Alexander, Arthur C. Borror, Adrien Robert, Charles A. Triplehorn, and Richard E. White.

THIRD EDITION

Richard D. Alexander, Donald M. Anderson, Ross H. Arnett, Jr. (particularly for the loan of a number of illustrations of beetles), N. Wilson Britt, Barnard D. Burks, George W. Byers, Donald R. Davis, W. Donald Duckworth, J. Gordon Edwards, Frank W. Fisk, Oliver S. Flint, Richard H. Foote, Raymond J. Gagné, Robert C. Graves, Ashley B. Gurney, Robert W. Hamilton, Ronald W. Hodges, F. P. Ide, Donald E. Johnston, Josef N. Knull, L. V. Knutson, Karl V. Krombein, John D. Lattin, Paul M. Marsh, Frank W. Mead, Frank J. Moore, Thomas E. Moore, C. F. W. Muesebeck, Lois B. O'Brien, Kellie O'Neill, Vincent D. Roth, Louise M. Russell, Curtis W. Sabrosky, Howard A. Schneiderman, F. Elizabeth Sims, David R. Smith, Thomas E. Snyder, Paul J. Spangler, Ted J. Spilman, George C. Steyskal, Alan Stone, William H. Telfer, Charles A. Triplehorn, Barry D. Valentine, Luella M. Walkley, Richard E. White, Willis W. Wirth, J. Porter Woodring, and David A. Young.

CONTENTS

MEASUREMENT TABLES

ENGLISH TO METRIC

LENGTH

1 in = 2.54001 cm = 25.4001 mm
1 yd = 0.9144 m
1 mi = 1.60935 km

AREA

1 in^2 = 6.452 cm^2
1 yd^2 = 0.8361 m^2
1 acre = 0.40469 hectares

VOLUME

1 in^3 = 16.387 cm^3
1 yd^3 = 0.765 m^3
1 qt = 0.9463 liter

WEIGHT

1 oz = 28.3495 g
1 lb = 453.5924 g = 0.45359 kg

METRIC TO ENGLISH

LENGTH

1 mm = 0.03937 in
1 m = 39.37 in = 1.0936 yd
1 km = 0.62137 mi

AREA

1 mm^2 = 0.00155 in^2
1 m^2 = 10.76387 ft^2 = 1.195986 yd^2
1 hectare = 2.471 acres

VOLUME

$1\ cm^3 = 0.0610\ in^3$
$1\ m^3 = 35.315\ ft^3 = 1.3080\ yd^3$
1 liter = 1.05671 qt

WEIGHT

1 g = 0.03527 oz
1 kg = 2.2046 lb

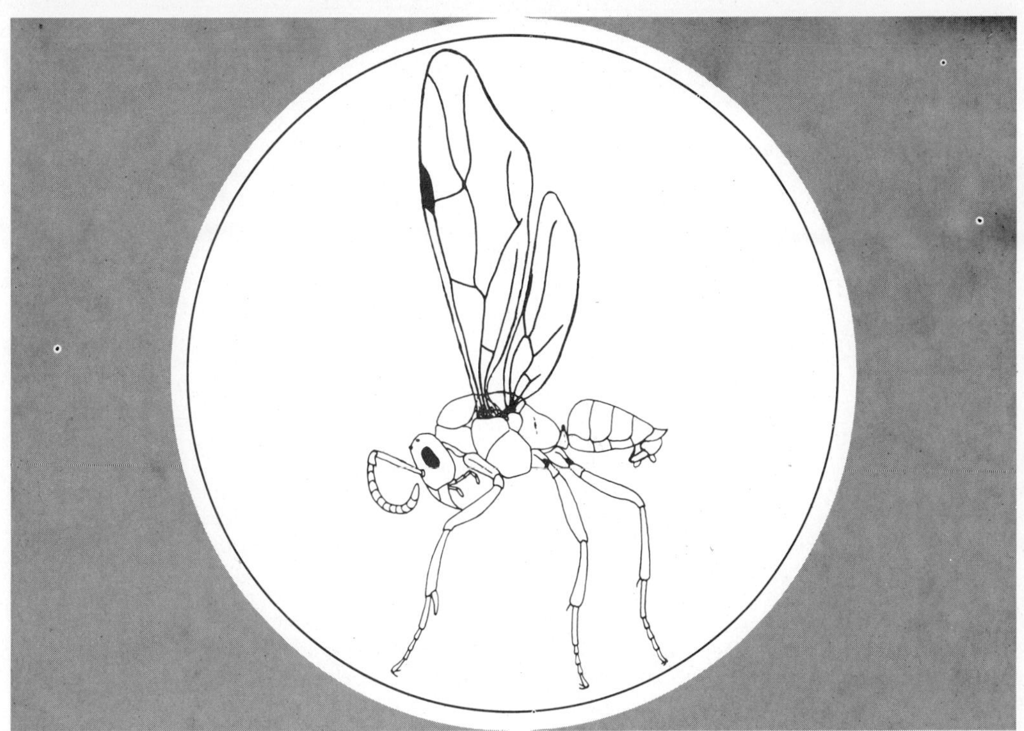

1: INSECTS AND THEIR WAYS

Insects are the dominant group of animals on the earth today. They far surpass all other terrestrial animals in numbers, and they occur practically everywhere. Several hundred thousand different kinds have been described—three times as many as there are in the rest of the animal kingdom—and there are probably as many more that are still undescribed. Over a thousand kinds may occur in a fair-sized backyard, and their populations often number many millions to the acre.

A great many insects are extremely valuable to man, and human society could not exist in its present form without them. By their pollinating activities they make possible the production of many agricultural crops, including many orchard fruits, clovers, vegetables, cotton, and tobacco; they provide us with honey, beeswax, silk, and other products of commercial value; they serve as the food of many birds, fish, and other useful animals; they perform valuable services as scavengers; they help to keep harmful animals and plants in check; they have been useful in medicine and in scientific research; and they are looked upon as interesting animals by people in all walks of life. A few insects are harmful and cause enormous losses each year in agricultural crops, stored products, and the health of man and animals.

Insects have lived on the earth for about 350 million years—compared with less than 2 million for man—and during this time they have evolved in many directions to become adapted to life in almost every type of habitat, and have developed many unusual, picturesque, and even amazing features. Let us examine briefly some of the interesting things to be found in the world of insects.

STRUCTURE

Compared with ourselves, insects are peculiarly constructed animals. They might be said to be inside out because their skeleton is on the outside, or upside down because their nerve cord extends along the lower side of the body and the heart lies above the alimentary canal. They have no lungs, but breathe through a number of tiny holes in the body wall—all behind the head—and the air entering these holes is distributed over the body and directly to the tissues through a multitude of tiny branching tubes. The heart and blood are unimportant in the transport of oxygen to the tissues. They smell with their antennae, some taste with their feet, and some hear with special organs in the abdomen, front legs, or antennae.

In an animal whose skeleton is on the outside of the body, the mechanics of support and growth are such that the animal is limited to a relatively small size. Most insects *are* relatively small; probably three fourths or more are less than $\frac{1}{4}$ inch (6 mm) in length. Their small size enables them to live in places that would not be available to larger animals. This fact, plus the fact that there are a great many different kinds of places where they can live, is in part responsible for the large number of different kinds of insects.

Insects range in size from about 1/100 to 13 inches (0.25 to 330 mm) in length, and from about 1/50 inch to nearly a foot (0.5 to 300 mm) in wingspread; one fossil dragonfly had a wingspread of over $2\frac{1}{2}$ feet (760 mm)! Some of the largest insects are very slender (the 13-inch (330 mm) insect is a walking stick occurring in Borneo), but some beetles have a body nearly as large as one's fist. The largest insects in North America are some of the moths, with a wingspread of about 6 inches (150 mm), and the walking sticks, with a body length of about 6 inches (150 mm).

The insects are the only invertebrates with wings, and these wings have had an evolutionary history different from that of the wings of vertebrates. The wings of flying vertebrates (birds, bats, and others) are modifications of one of the pairs of paired limbs; those of insects are structures *in addition to* the paired "limbs," and might be likened to the wings of the mythical Pegasus (flying horse). The wings of insects are certainly one of the features responsible for the dominant position insects hold on the earth. With wings, insects can leave a habitat when it becomes unsuitable; aquatic insects, for example, have wings when adult, and if their habitat dries up they can fly to another habitat. Fish and other aquatic forms usually perish under similar adverse conditions.

Insects range in color from the very drab to the very brilliant; there are no other animals on the earth more brilliantly colored than some of the insects. Some insect colors are glittering and iridescent, and the insects possessing them are like living jewels. Their colors have made many insects the patterns for much in art and design.

Some insects have structures that are amazing when we consider them in relation to structures possessed by vertebrates. The bees and wasps and some of the ants have their ovipositor or egg-laying organ developed into a poison dagger (sting) which serves as an excellent means of offense and defense. Some ichneumons have a hairlike ovipositor 4 inches long that can penetrate wood. Some snout beetles have the front of the head drawn out into a slender structure longer than the rest of the body, with tiny jaws at the end. Some stalk-eyed flies have their eyes situated at the ends of long slender stalks, which in one South American species are as long as the wings. Some of the stag beetles have jaws half as long as the body, and branched like the antlers of a stag. Certain individuals in some of the honey ants become so engorged with food that their abdomens become greatly distended, and they serve as living storehouses of food which they regurgitate "on demand" to other ants in the colony.

PHYSIOLOGY

A feature of insect physiology that enables these animals to survive adverse climatic conditions is their cold-bloodedness; their body temperature follows very closely the temperature to which they are exposed. When the environmental temperature drops, their body temperature also drops, and their physiological processes slow down. Many insects can withstand short periods of freezing temperatures, and some can withstand long periods of freezing or subfreezing temperatures. During the winter they are quiescent and their metabolic rate is extremely low; during these adverse conditions when food is not available, they can survive without it.

Insect sense organs are often peculiar compared with those of man and other vertebrates. Some insects have two kinds of eyes—two or three simple eyes located on the upper part of the face, and a pair of compound eyes on the sides of the head; the compound eyes are often very large, occupying most of the head, and may consist of thousands of individual eye units. Some insects hear by means of eardrums, while others hear by means of very sensitive hairs on the antennae or elsewhere on their bodies; an insect possessing eardrums may have them on the sides of the body at the base of the abdomen (short-horned grasshoppers), or on the front legs below the "knee" (long-horned grasshoppers and crickets).

The reproductive powers of insects are often tremendous; most people do not realize just how great they are. The capacity of any animal to build up its numbers through reproduction depends on three characteristics of that animal—the number of eggs laid by each female (which in insects may vary from one to many thousands), the length of a generation (which may vary from a few days to several years), and the proportion of each generation that are females and will produce the next generation (in some insects there are no males).

An example that might be cited to illustrate insects' reproductive powers is *Drosóphila,* the pomace flies, that have been studied so much by geneticists. These flies develop rapidly, and under ideal conditions may produce 25 generations in a year. Each female lays up to 100 eggs, of which about half will hatch into males and half into females. Now, suppose we started with a pair of these flies and allowed them to reproduce under ideal conditions, with no checks on increase, for a year—with the original and each succeeding female laying 100 eggs before she dies, and each egg hatching and growing to maturity and reproducing again. The number of flies that would be produced in the twenty-fifth generation is staggering, about 10^{41}. If this many flies were packed tightly together, 1000 to a cubic inch, they would form a ball of flies *96 million miles* in diameter, or a ball extending nearly from the earth to the sun!

Throughout the animal kingdom an egg usually develops into a single individual. In man and some other animals an egg occasionally develops into two individuals (for example, identical twins in man), or on rare occasions three or four. Some insects carry this phenomenon of polyembryony (more than one young from a single egg) much further; some platygasterid wasps have as many as 18, some dryinid wasps as many as 60, and some encyrtid wasps have *over a thousand* young developing from a single egg. A few insects have another unusual method of reproduction—paedogenesis (reproduction by larvae); this occurs in the gall gnat genus *Miástor* and in the beetle genera *Micromálthus, Phengòdes,* and *Thylódrias.*

DEVELOPMENT

In the nature of their development and life cycle, insects run the gamut from the very simple to the complex and even amazing. Many insects undergo very little change as they develop, with the young and adults having similar habits, and differing principally in size. Most insects, on the other hand, undergo in their development rather remarkable changes, both in appearance and in habits. Most people are familiar with the metamorphosis of insects and possibly think of it as commonplace—which, as a matter of fact, it is—but in comparison with the development of a vertebrate it is indeed fantastic. Consider the development of a butterfly: an egg hatches into a wormlike caterpillar; this caterpillar eats ravenously and every week or two sheds its skin; after a time it becomes a pupa, hung from a leaf or branch like a ham in a meat shop; and finally a beautiful winged butterfly emerges from this "ham." If this sort of thing happened in a bird, it would be like an eagle developing from a snake—an event that would indeed be fantastic.

The majority of the insects have a life cycle like that of a butterfly; the eggs hatch into wormlike larvae, which grow by periodically shedding their outer skin (together with the linings of the foregut, hindgut, and breathing tubes), finally transforming into an inactive pupal stage from which the winged adult emerges. A fly grows from a maggot; a beetle grows from a grub; and a bee, wasp, or ant grows from a maggotlike larval stage. When these insects become adult they stop growing; a little fly (in the winged stage) does not grow into a bigger one.

An insect with this sort of development (complete metamorphosis) may live as a larva in a very different sort of place from that in which it lives as an adult. One fly that is a common household pest spends its larval life in garbage or some other filth; another very similar fly may have spent its larval life eating the insides out of a grub or caterpillar. The junebug that beats against the screens at night spent its larval life in the ground; and a long-horned beetle one may see on a flower spent its larval life in the wood of a tree or log.

BEHAVIOR

Many insects have unusual features of structure, physiology, or life cycle, but probably the most interesting things about insects are what they do. One may find many instances where the behavior of an insect seems to surpass in intelligence the behavior of man. Some insects seem to show an amazing foresight, especially as regards laying eggs with a view to the future needs of the young. Insects have very varied food habits, they have some interesting means of defense, many have what (compared with vertebrates) might be considered fantastic strength, and many have "invented" things which we may think of as strictly human accomplishments. Complex and fascinating social behavior has been developed in some groups of insects.

Insects feed on an almost endless variety of foods, and they feed in many different ways. Thousands of species feed on plants, and practically every kind of plant (on land, or in fresh water) is fed upon by some kind of insect. The plant feeders may feed on almost any part of the plant; caterpillars, leaf beetles, and leafhoppers feed on the leaves, aphids may feed on the stems, white grubs feed on the roots, certain weevil and moth larvae feed on the fruits, and so on. These insects may feed on the outside of the plant, or they may burrow into it. Thousands of insects are carnivorous, feeding on other animals; some are predators, and some are parasites. Many insects that feed on vertebrates are blood-sucking; some of these, such as mosquitoes, lice, fleas, and certain bugs, are not only annoying pests because of their bites, but may serve as disease vectors. Some insects feed on dead wood; others feed on stored foods of all types; some feed on various fabrics; and many feed on decaying materials. Drugstore beetles are capable of feeding on almost everything from face powder to mustard plasters.

The digger wasps have an interesting method of preserving food collected and stored for their young. These wasps dig burrows in the ground, provision them with a certain type of prey (usually other insects or spiders), and then lay their eggs (usually on the body of a prey animal). If the prey animals were killed before being put into the burrows, they would dry up and be of little value as food by the time the wasp eggs hatched. These prey animals are not killed; they are stung and paralyzed, and thus "preserved" in good condition for the young wasps when they hatch.

Insects often have interesting and effective means of defense against intruders and enemies. Many insects "play dead," either by dropping to the ground and remaining motionless, or "freezing" in a characteristic position. Many insects are masters of the art of camouflage, being so colored that they blend with the background and are very inconspicuous; some very closely resemble objects in their environment—dead leaves, twigs, thorns, or even bird droppings. Some insects become concealed by covering themselves with debris. Some insects that do not have any special means of defense very closely resemble another that does, and presumably are afforded some protection because of this resemblance. Many moths have the hind wings (which at rest are generally concealed beneath the front wings) brightly or strikingly colored—sometimes with spots resembling the eyes of a larger animal (for example, giant silkworm moths; see Figure 426)—and when disturbed display these hind wings; the effect may sometimes be enough to scare off a potential intruder. Some of the sound-producing insects (for example, cicadas, some beetles, and others) will produce a characteristic sound when attacked, and this sound often scares off the attacker.

Many insects utilize a "chemical warfare" type of defense. Some insects secrete foul-smelling substances when disturbed; stink bugs, broad-headed bugs, lacewings, and some beetles might well be called the skunks of the insect world, as they have a very unpleasant odor. A few of the insects utilizing such defensive mechanisms are able to eject the substance as a spray, in some cases even aiming it at an intruder. Some insects, such as the milkweed butterflies, ladybird beetles, and net-winged beetles, apparently have distasteful or mildly toxic body fluids, and are avoided by predators.

Many insects will inflict a painful bite when handled; the bite may be simply a severe pinch by powerful jaws, or it may be what amounts to a hypodermic injection by needlelike mouth parts. The bites of mosquitoes, fleas, black flies, assassin bugs, and many others are much like hypodermic injections, and the irritation caused is due to the saliva injected at the time of the bite.

Other means of defense include the stinging hairs possessed by some caterpillars (for example, the saddleback caterpillar and the larva of the io moth), body fluids that are irritating (for example, blister beetles, death feigning (many beetles, and some insects in other orders), and warning displays, often including eye spots on the wings (many moths and mantids) or other bizarre or grotesque structures or patterns.

One of the most effective means of defense possessed by insects is a sting, which is developed in the wasps, bees, and some ants. The sting is a modified egg-laying organ, hence only females sting. It is located at the posterior end of the body, so the "business" end of a stinging insect is the rear.

Insects often perform what—compared with man—are near impossible feats of strength. It is not unusual for an insect to be able to lift 50 or more times its own weight, and some beetles rigged with a special harness have been found able to lift over 800 times their own weight; in comparison with such beetles, a man could lift some 60 tons, and an elephant could lift a fair-sized building! When it comes to jumping, many insects put our best olympic athletes to shame; many grasshoppers can easily jump a distance of three feet, which would be comparable to a man broad-jumping the length of a football field, and a flea jumping several inches up in the air would be comparable to a man jumping over a 30-story building!

Many insects do things which we might consider strictly an activity of civilized man, or a product of our modern technology. Caddisfly larvae were probably the first organisms to use nets to capture aquatic organisms. Dragonfly nymphs, in their intake and expulsion of water to aerate the gills in the rectum, were among the first to use jet propulsion. Honey bees were air-conditioning their "hives" long before man even appeared on the earth. The hornets were the first animals to make paper from wood pulp. Long before man began building crude shelters many insects were constructing shelters of clay, stone, or "logs" (Figure 352), and some even induce plants to make shelters (galls) for them. Long before the appearance of man on the earth the insects had "invented" cold light and chemical warfare, and had solved many complex problems of aerodynamics and celestial navigation. Many insects have elaborate communication systems, involving chemicals (sex, alarm, trail-following, and other pheromones), sound (cicadas, many Orthoptera, and others), behavior (for example, honey bee dance "language"), light (fireflies), and possibly other mechanisms.

These are only a few of the ways in which insects have become adapted to life in the world about us. Some of the detailed stories about these animals are fantastic and almost incredible. In the following chapters we have tried to point out many of the interesting and often unique features of insect biology—methods of reproduction, obtaining food, depositing eggs, rearing young, and features of life history—as well as the more technical phases that deal with morphology and taxonomy.

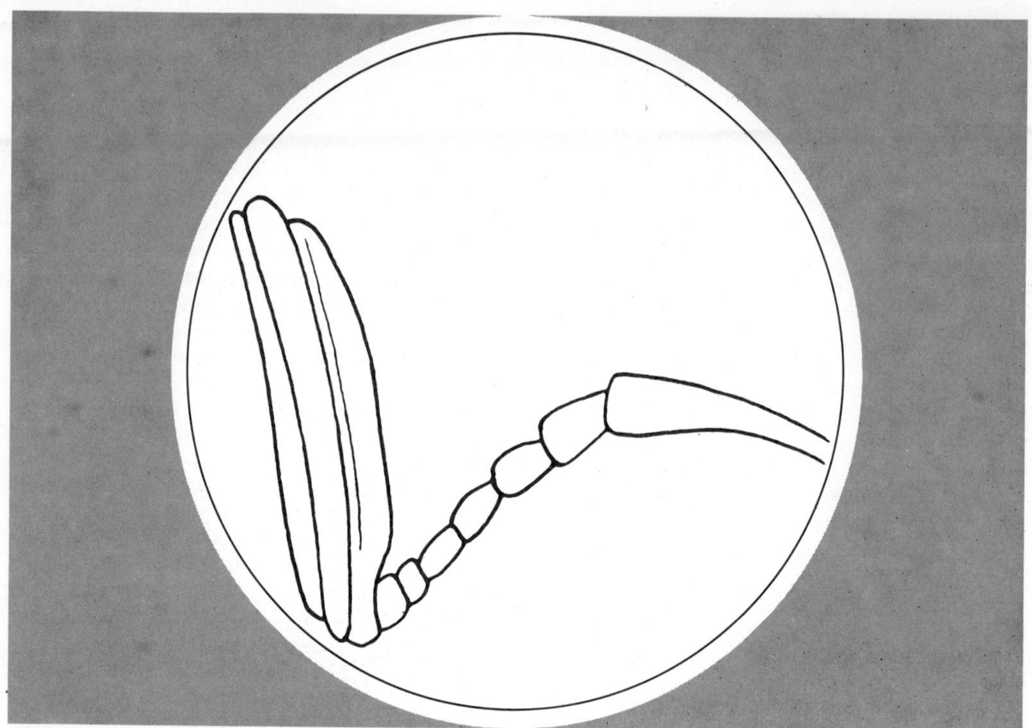

2: THE ANATOMY OF INSECTS

A knowledge of the anatomy of insects is essential to an understanding of how insects live and how they can be distinguished from one another and from other animals.

THE GENERAL STRUCTURE OF AN INSECT

Insects are generally more or less elongate and cylindrical in form and are bilaterally symmetrical, that is, the right and left sides of the body are essentially alike. The body is segmented, and the segments are grouped into three distinct regions—head, thorax, and abdomen (Figure 1). The head bears the eyes, antennae, and mouth parts; the thorax bears the legs and wings (when these are present); the abdomen usually bears no locomotor appendages, but often has some appendages at its apex. Most of the appendages of an insect are segmented.

THE BODY WALL

In man and other vertebrates the skeleton or supporting framework is on the inside of the body and is spoken of as an endoskeleton; in insects and other arthropods the skeleton is, for the most part, on the outside and is called an exoskeleton. The insect's body wall thus serves not only as the outer covering of the body but also as a supporting structure, and it is to the body wall that most of the muscles are attached.

The body wall of an insect (Figure 2) is composed of three principal layers: an outer cuticle (*cut*) that contains a characteristic chemical compound called chitin, proteins, and often pigments; a cellular layer, the epidermis (*ep*) that lies beneath and secretes the cuticle; and a thin noncellular layer beneath the epidermis, called the basement membrane (*bm*). The body wall completely covers the insect and bends inward at various points to form supporting ridges and braces. The tracheae (breathing tubes) and the anterior and posterior ends of the digestive tract are invaginations of the body wall and are lined with cuticle.

formula $(C_8H_{13}NO_5)_n$, is a characteristic constituent of the procuticle; it is most abundant in the softer parts of the procuticle, and is entirely absent from the epicuticle. Chitin is a very resistant substance; it is insoluble in water, alcohol, dilute acid, and alkalis, and is not attacked by the digestive enzymes of mammals; it is broken down by snails, certain insects (for example, cockroaches), and certain bacteria. Treatment with alkali removes the coloring and hardening substances and "clears" the cuticle, but produces no visible change in its essential structure.

The hardness of the cuticle is due to the presence in the exocuticle of a horny substance called sclerotin. The process of hardening is spoken of as sclerotization. Sclerotin is formed from the protein component of the cuticle by the action

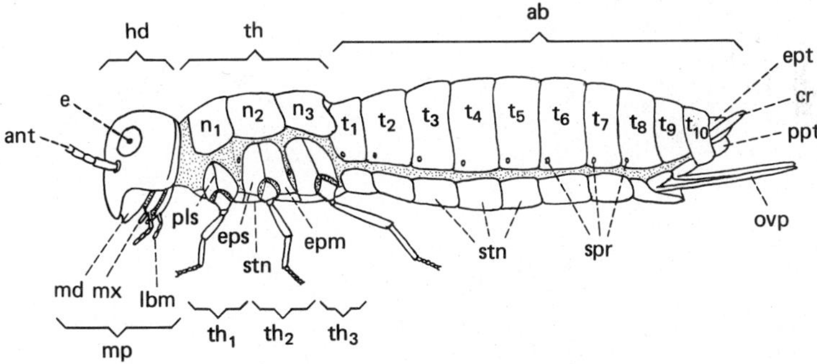

Figure 1. General structure of an insect. *ab,* abdomen; *ant,* antenna; *cr,* cercus; *e,* compound eye; *epm,* epimeron; *eps,* episternum; *ept,* epiproct; *hd,* head; *lbm,* labium; *md,* mandible; *mp,* mouth parts; *mx,* maxilla; *n,* nota of thorax; *ovp,* ovipositor; *pls,* pleural suture; *ppt,* paraproct; *spr,* spiracles; t_{1-10}, terga; *th,* thorax; th_1, prothorax; th_2, mesothorax; th_3, metathorax. (Modified from Snodgrass by permission of McGraw-Hill Book Company, Inc.)

The cuticle is made up of two principal parts, the epicuticle (*epi*) and the procuticle; the outer half or third of the procuticle is often darker and harder than the rest, and is called exocuticle (*exo*); the unchanged inner part is called the endocuticle (*end*). The epicuticle is a very thin layer, about 1 micron thick; it usually has two layers, an inner lipoprotein or cuticulin layer and an outer wax layer. The endocuticle and exocuticle are generally composed of horizontal layers (*lct*), and are traversed by "pore canals" (*pcn*), which are minute, usually helical channels extending from the epidermal cells to the epicuticle. When the epicuticle is first formed, the pore canals extend through it; various substances (including waxes) exude from the pore canals to coat and waterproof the epicuticle.

Chitin, a nitrogenous polysaccharide with the

of quinones. A few insects (for example, some Díptera larvae and puparia) and many crustaceans have calcium salts as the hardening material in the cuticle, but sclerotin is harder than these calcium salts; the mandibles of some insects are so hard that they can bite through metal (see page 000). Certain areas of the cuticle contain an elastic protein called resilin, which provides the elasticity of the cuticle and forms the elastic tendons for most muscles.

The color of an insect may be due to pigment in the body wall, usually in the exocuticle. Metallic or iridescent colors are the result of refraction of the light by many minute vanelike structures or ridges on the surface of the epicuticle; these tiny ridges are usually visible under extremely high magnification (for example, with an electron microscope). The cuticular pigment in

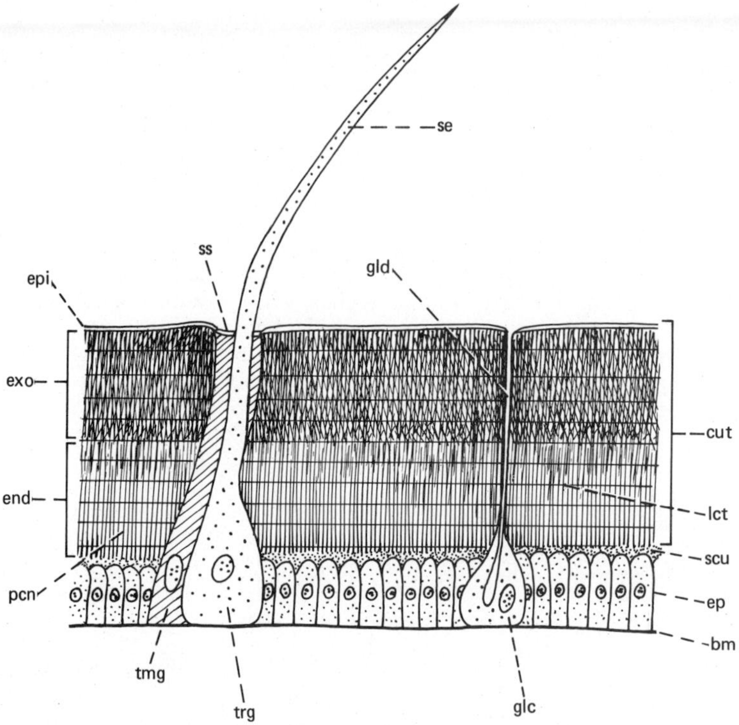

Figure 2. Structure of body wall (diagrammatic). *bm,* basement membrane; *cut,* cuticle; *end,* endocuticle; *ep,* epidermis; *epi,* epicuticle; *exo,* exocuticle; *glc,* gland cell; *gld,* duct of gland cell; *lct,* layer of the cuticle; *pcn,* pore canal; *scu,* subcuticle; *se,* seta; *ss,* setal socket; *tmg,* tormogen cell (which forms the setal socket); *trg,* trichogen cell (which forms the seta). The exocuticle and endocuticle together make up the procuticle.

the adult is usually deposited shortly after the final molt; newly emerged adults are generally rather pale (teneral). This deposition of pigment occurs within a few hours after the molt in most insects, but in some cases (for example, most Odonàta) may require a week or more. Some pigments may undergo chemical change after death; many pigments are changed by substances used to kill or preserve insects. Pigment production in an insect is usually genetically controlled, but it (and hence the color of the insect) may be affected by various environmental conditions; some pigments are synthesized by the insect, while others are obtained from the food.

The surface of the insect body consists of a number of hardened plates, or sclerites, which are separated by sutures or membranous areas. Sutures are seamlike lines marking an infolding of the body wall (the suture at the left in Figure 3; these lines are sometimes called sulci), lines where two sclerites formerly separated have come together, or lines of softer cuticle (the suture at the right in Figure 3). The membranous areas permit movement of the various parts of the body and its appendages. The sclerites and sutures are named, and are made considerable use of for descriptive purposes. The principal dorsal sclerites of the abdomen are called terga (singular, tergum), and those of the thorax are called nota (singular, notum); subdivisions of a tergum are called tergites, and subdivisions of the thoracic nota have special names (see below, under "The Thorax"). The principal sclerite on the ventral surface of a body segment is called the sternum (plural, sterna), and subdivisions of it are called sternites. If sclerites are present between the dorsal and ventral sclerites (such sclerites are usually present only on the thorax), they are called pleurites; the lateral area of a segment is often called the pleuron (plural, pleura).

The body wall bears numerous external and internal processes. The external processes include

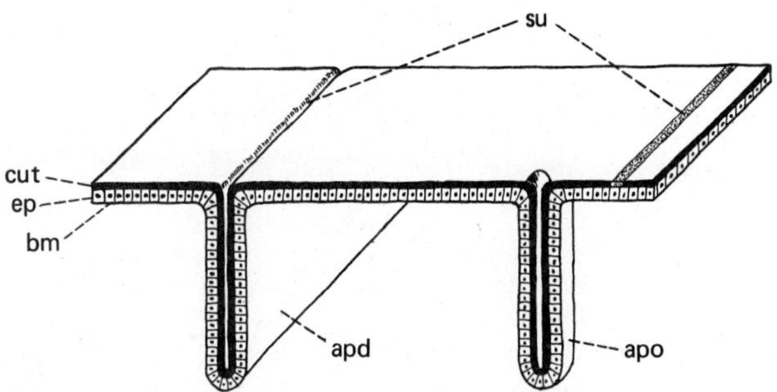

Figure 3. Diagram of external and internal features of body wall. *apd,* apodeme; *apo,* apophysis; *bm,* basement membrane; *cut,* cuticle; *ep,* epidermis; *su,* sutures.

setae, spines, scales, and the like; some of these are solid cuticle, while others contain all three body-wall layers. Some external processes, such as setae, are outgrowths of individual epidermal cells; others are of multicellular origin. The internal processes of the body wall may be ridgelike (Figure 3, *apd*) or spinelike (Figure 3, *apo*); these infoldings strengthen the body wall and serve as the place of attachment of muscles.

BODY SEGMENTATION

The body segmentation of an insect is most evident in the abdomen, where the segments have their simplest structure. Each abdominal segment typically consists of two sclerites, a dorsal tergum and a ventral sternum (Figure 4); these are connected laterally by a membranous area, the pleural membrane, and successive terga and sterna are connected by an intersegmental membrane. These membranous areas make movement possible. At the anterior end of each tergum and sternum is an infolding of the body wall, forming a ridge internally and a suture externally; the internal ridge is called the antecosta, and the external suture the antecostal suture. The narrow anterior flange of the tergum, in front of the antecostal suture, is called the acrotergite, and the corre-

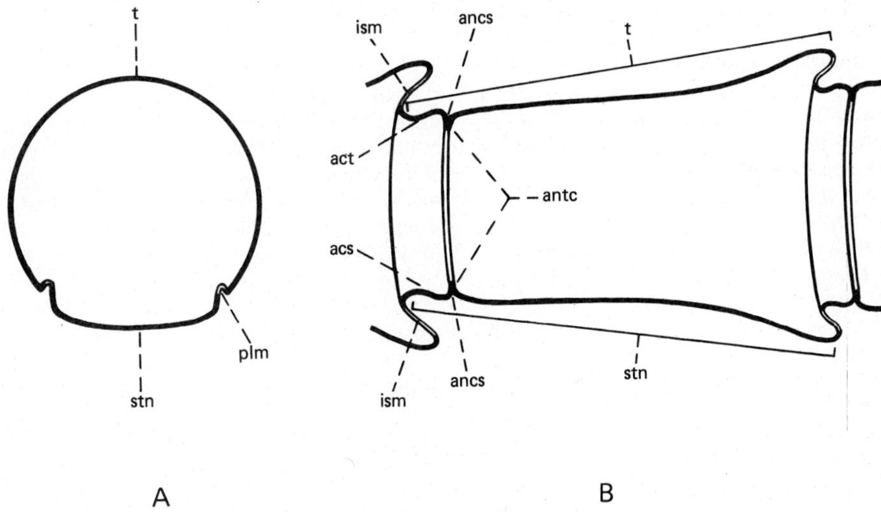

Figure 4. Structure of typical abdominal segment (diagrammatic). A, cross section; B, sagittal section. *acs,* acrosternite; *act,* acrotergite; *ancs,* antecostal suture; *antc,* antecosta; *ism,* intersegmental membrane; *plm,* pleural membrane; *stn,* sternum; *t,* tergum.

sponding anterior piece of the sternum is called the acrosternite. The antecostae provide places for muscle attachments. There are sometimes small sclerites in the pleural membrane; these usually represent detached portions of the terga or sterna, and are called laterotergites or laterosternites.

The segmentation of the thorax is somewhat modified as compared to that of the abdomen, and these modifications are associated with the presence on the thorax of the locomotor organs (legs and wings). Each thoracic segment, in addition to the main dorsal and ventral sclerites, has pleural sclerites, and the dorsal and ventral sclerites are generally more complex than those of the abdomen. The pleural sclerites are believed to have evolved from subcoxal sclerites, and in pterygote insects each pleuron bears a suture (the pleural suture) extending upward from the base of the leg; this suture marks an infolding of the pleural wall that forms a ridge (the pleural ridge) internally. Additional infoldings usually occur on the mesonotum and metanotum and on the sterna, and the external sutures thus formed set off subdivisions of these areas. In winged insects the antecostae of the first abdominal segment and the last two thoracic segments are enlarged, forming what are called phragmata (singular, phragma) (Figure 25, *ph*), and the acrotergites of the metathorax and first abdominal segment enlarge to form the postnota of the segment just anterior to them.

THE HEAD

The head is the anterior capsulelike body region that bears the eyes, antennae, and mouth parts. The shape of the head varies considerably in different insects, but it is usually heavily sclerotized (that is, the wall of the head is quite hard).

Most insects have a pair of relatively large compound eyes, located dorsolaterally on the head. The surface of each compound eye is divided into a number of circular or hexagonal areas called facets; each facet is the lens of a single eye unit or ommatidium. In addition to compound eyes, most insects also possess three simple eyes, the ocelli, located on the upper part of the head between the compound eyes.

The head is divided by sutures into a number of more or less distinct sclerites; these vary somewhat in different insects. Typically (Figure 5), there is a transverse suture extending across the lower part of the face just above the base of the mouth parts; the medial or anterior part of this suture is called the epistomal suture (*es*), and the lateral portions, above the mandibles and maxillae, the subgenal sutures (*sgs*). There is usually a pair of sutures extending upward from near the anterior articulation of the mandible to the base of the antenna or the compound eye; these may be called frontogenal sutures, but are more often called subantennal (*sas*) or subocular (*sos*), depending on the location of their upper ends. The anterior sclerite of the head, above the epistomal suture and between the frontogenal sutures, and usually including the median ocellus, is the frons (*fr*). The areas laterad of the frontogenal sutures, between the compound eye and the subgenal suture, are the genae (singular, gena) (*ge*). The area above the frons, on the dorsal part of the head between the compound eyes, is the vertex (*ver*). Below the epistomal suture is a flaplike structure composed of two sclerites; the upper sclerite is the clypeus (*clp*), and the lower one is the upper lip or labrum (*lbr*). Behind the labrum are the mandibles (*md*), a pair of heavily sclerotized jaws; behind the mandibles are the maxillae (*mx*), segmented mouth-part structures that bear feelerlike palps (*p*); and behind the maxillae is the lower lip or labium (*lbm*), which also bears palps. These mouth-part structures will be discussed in more detail later. The vertex and genae are limited posteriorly by the occipital suture (*os*); behind the occipital suture dorsally is the occiput (*ocp*), and behind it on the sides (or rear) of the head are the postgenae (*pg*). The occiput and postgenae are limited posteriorly by the postoccipital suture (*pos*), behind which is a narrow ringlike sclerite, the postocciput (*po*), which forms the posterior rim of the head and surrounds the foramen magnum or occipital foramen (*for*).

There is sometimes present in the adult insect traces of an inverted **Y**-shaped ecdysial suture, marking the lines along which the head wall splits at the time of molting. The basal part of this **Y** extends along the middorsal line of the head, and is sometimes called the coronal suture (*cs*); the arms of the **Y** extend ventrolaterally from the anterior end of the coronal suture toward the epistomal suture, between the median and lateral ocelli, and are called frontal sutures (*fs*).

The points on the head where the arms of the tentorium (a set of internal braces in the head; see page 27) meet the head wall are usually marked by pits: the anterior tentorial pits are at the lateral ends of the epistomal suture (Figure 5, *atp*), and the posterior tentorial pits are at the lower ends of the postoccipital suture (Figure 5, *ptp*).

There is considerable variation in the development of the head sutures and the shape of the various head sclerites, and some of the above-

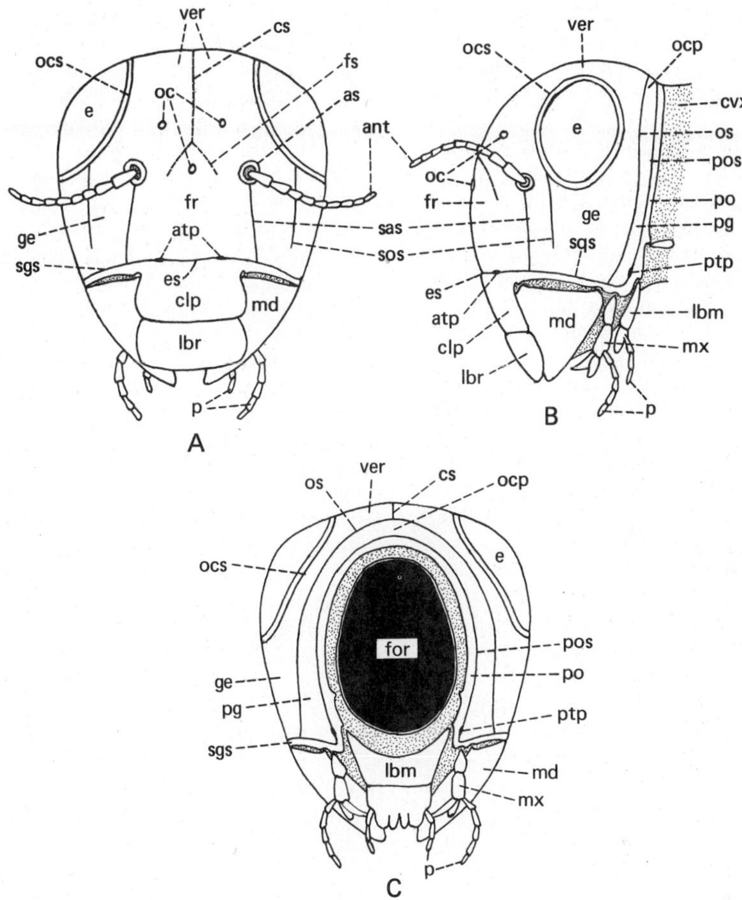

Figure 5. Typical structure of an insect head. A, anterior view; B, lateral view; C, posterior view. *ant,* antenna; *as,* antennal suture; *atp,* anterior tentorial pit; *clp,* clypeus; *cs,* coronal suture; *cvx,* cervix, e, compound eye; *es,* epistomal suture; *for,* foramen magnum; *fr,* frons; *fs,* frontal suture; *ge,* gena; *lbm,* labium; *lbr,* labrum; *md,* mandible; *mx,* maxilla; *oc,* ocelli; *ocp,* occiput; *ocs,* ocular suture; *os,* occipital suture; *p,* palps; *pg,* postgena; *po,* postocciput; *pos,* postoccipital suture; *ptp,* posterior tentorial pit; *sas,* subantennal suture; *sgs,* subgenal suture; *sos,* subocular suture; *ver,* vertex. (Modified from Snodgrass by permission of McGraw-Hill Book Company, Inc.)

mentioned sutures may be absent. There are usually sutures closely paralleling the compound eyes (*ocs*) and surrounding the bases of the antennae (*as*). The head sclerites posterior to the occipital suture are usually on the posterior side of the head.

The posterior surface of the head, between the foramen and the labium, is membranous in most insects (Figure 5 C), but in a few the region between the foramen and the labium is sclerotized. This sclerotization may be the result of the hypostomal areas (areas below the subgenal sutures posterior to the mandibles) extending ventrally and toward the midline to form what is called a hypostomal bridge (Figure 8 C and D, *hbr*), or (particularly in prognathous insects) the result of the postoccipital sutures extending forward onto the ventral side of the head, with a sclerite developing between these sutures and the foramen. In the latter case the anterior extensions of the postoccipital sutures are called gular sutures, and the sclerite between them the gula (Figure 243, *gs* and *gu*).

The number of segments making up the head is not apparent in the adult insect, as the head sutures rarely coincide with the sutures between the original segments. Entomologists do not agree on the number of segments in the insect head, but most agree that it is composed of a preoral region and four postoral segments. The preoral region bears the compound eyes, ocelli, antennae, and the facial areas (including the labrum); Snodgrass (1935), Butt (1960), and others believe that this region represents a single body segment, while others (for example, Manton, 1960) believe it represents two or three segments. The first postoral segment is greatly reduced and bears no appendages (this segment bears the chelicerae in chelicerate arthropods); the second, third, and fourth postoral segments bear the mandibles, maxillae, and labium, respectively.

THE ANTENNAE

The antennae are paired segmented appendages located on the head, usually between or below the compound eyes. The basal segment is called the scape, the second segment the pedicel, and the remainder the flagellum (Figure 6 N). The "segments" of the flagellum lack individual muscles (as the scape and pedicel have), and are sometimes called flagellomeres. An antenna arises from an antennal socket that is membranous but is surrounded by a ringlike antennal sclerite that often bears a small process called the antennifer, on which the scape pivots. The antennae are sensory in function, and act as tactile organs, organs of smell, and in some cases organs of hearing.

Insect antennae vary greatly in size and form, and are much used in classification. The following terms are used in describing the form of the antennae.

Setaceous—bristlelike, the segments becoming more slender distally; for example, dragonfly (Figure 6 A), damselfly, leafhopper

Filiform—threadlike, the segments nearly uniform in size, and usually cylindrical; for example, ground beetle (Figure 6 B), tiger beetle

Moniliform—like a string of beads, the segments similar in size and more or less spherical in shape; for example, wrinkled bark beetle (Figure 6 C)

Serrate—sawlike, the segments, particularly those in the distal half or two thirds of the antenna, more or less triangular; for example, click beetle (Figure 6 G)

Pectinate—comblike, most segments with long, slender, lateral processes; for example, fire-colored beetle (Figure 6 H)

Clubbed—the segments increasing in diameter distally (Figure 6 D–F, L, M). If the increase is gradual, the condition is termed **clavate** (Figure 6 D, E); if the terminal segments are rather suddenly enlarged, the condition is termed **captitate** (Figure 6 F); if the terminal segments are expanded laterally to form rounded or oval platelike lobes, the condition is termed **lamellate** (Figure 6 M); where the terminal segments have long, parallel-sided, sheetlike, or tonguelike lobes extending laterally, the condition is termed **flabellate** (Figure 6 L)

Geniculate—elbowed, with the first segment long and the following segments small and going off at an angle to the first; for example, stag beetle, ant, chalcid (Figure 6 N)

Plumose—feathery, most segments with whorls of long hair; for example, male mosquito (Figure 6 I)

Aristate—the last segment usually enlarged and bearing a conspicuous dorsal bristle, the arista; for example, house fly, syrphid fly (Figure 6 J)

Stylate—the last segment bearing an elongate terminal stylelike or fingerlike process, the style; for example, robber fly, snipe fly (Figure 6 K)

THE MOUTH PARTS

Insect mouth parts typically consist of a labrum, a pair each of mandibles and maxillae, a labium, and a hypopharynx. These structures are variously modified in different insect groups and are often used in classification and identification. The type of mouth parts an insect has determines how it feeds and (in the case of most injurious species) what sort of damage it does. It is important, therefore, that the student have some knowledge of the structure of insect mouth parts.

THE MOUTH PARTS OF A CRICKET

The most generalized condition of the mouth parts is found in chewing insects, such as a cricket. The cricket is said to have "chewing" mouth parts because it has heavily sclerotized mandibles that move sideways and can bite off and chew particles of food. These mouth-part structures are most easily seen and studied by removing them from the insect one at a time and studying them under a lens or microscope.

The **labrum,** or upper lip (Figure 5, *lbr;* Figure 7 E), is a broad flaplike lobe situated below the clypeus on the anterior side of the head, in front of

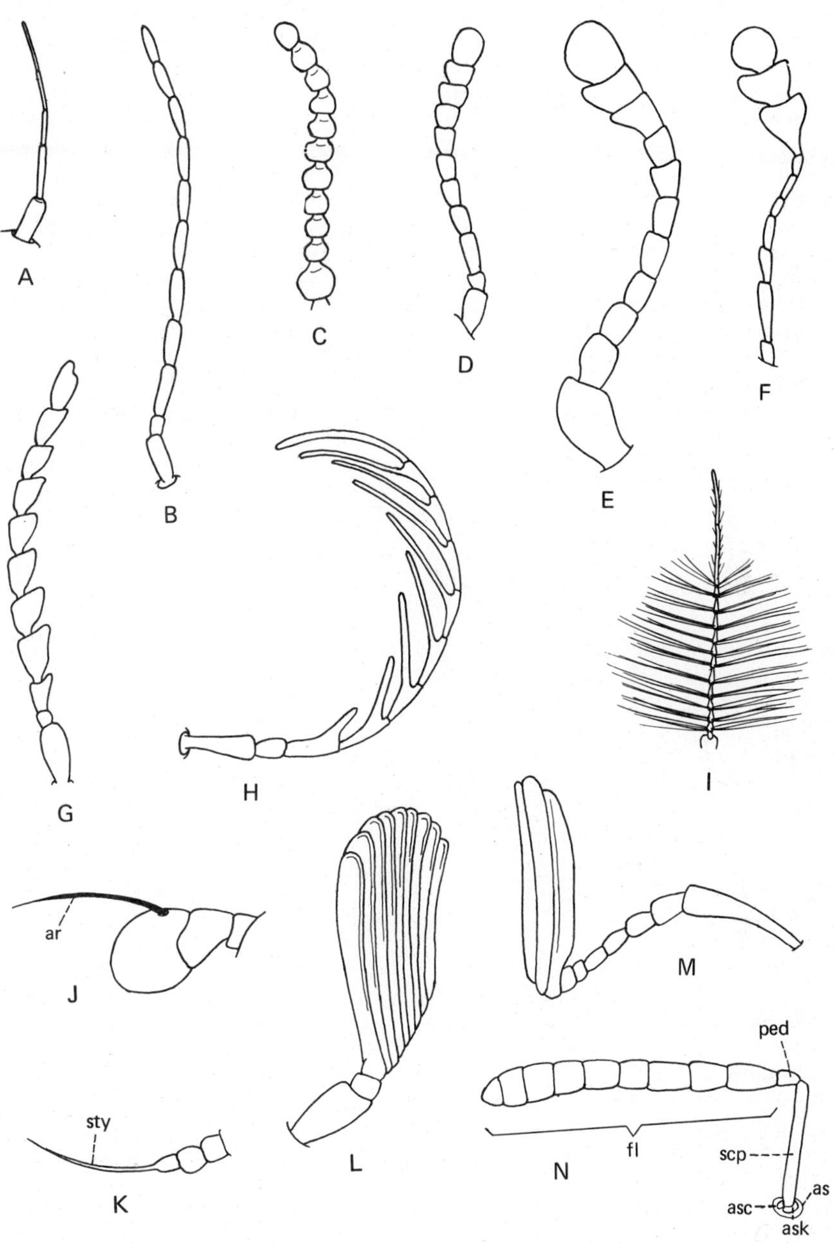

Figure 6. Types of antennae. A, setaceous (dragonfly); B, filiform (ground beetle); C, moniliform (wrinkled bark beetle); D, clavate (darkling beetle); E, clavate (ladybird beetle); F, capitate (sap beetle); G, serrate (click beetle); H, pectinate (fire-colored beetle); I, plumose (male mosquito); J, aristate (syrphid fly); K, stylate (snipe fly); L, flabellate (cedar beetle); M, lamellate (June beetle); N, geniculate (chalcid). Antennae such as those in D–F, L, and M are also called clubbed. *ar*, arista; *as*, antennal suture; *asc*, antennal sclerite; *ask*, antennal socket; *fl*, flagellum; *ped*, pedicel; *scp*, scape; *sty*, style.

the other mouth-part structures. On the ventral or posterior side of the labrum is a swollen area, the epipharynx.

The **mandibles** (Figure 5, *md;* Figure 7 D) are the paired, heavily sclerotized, unsegmented jaws lying immediately behind the labrum. They articulate with the head capsule at two points, one anterior and one posterior, and move laterally. The mandibles of different chewing insects vary somewhat in structure; in some insects (including the cricket) they bear both cutting and grinding ridges, while in others (such as certain predaceous beetles) they are long and sicklelike.

The **maxillae** (Figure 7 A) are paired structures lying behind the mandibles; they are segmented, and each maxilla bears a feelerlike organ, the palp (*mxp*). The basal segment of the maxilla is the cardo (*cd*); the second segment is the stipes (*stp*). The palp is borne on a lobe of the stipes called the palpifer (*plf*). The stipes bears at its apex two lobelike structures: the lacinia (*lc*), an elongate jawlike structure, and the galea (*g*), a lobelike structure. Variations in the maxillae in different chewing insects involve chiefly the palps and the terminal lobes.

The **labium,** or lower lip (Figure 5, *lbm;* Figure 7 C), is a single structure (though it probably evolved from two maxillalike structures fusing along the midline) lying behind the maxillae. It is divided by a transverse suture (*ls*) into two portions, a basal postmentum (*pmt*) and a distal prementum (*prmt*). The postmentum in the cricket is divided into a basal submentum (*smt*) and a distal mentum (*mn*). The prementum bears a pair of palps (*lp*) and a group of apical lobes which constitute the ligula (*lg*). All the muscles of the labium have their insertions distad of the labial suture. The labial palps are borne on lateral lobes of the

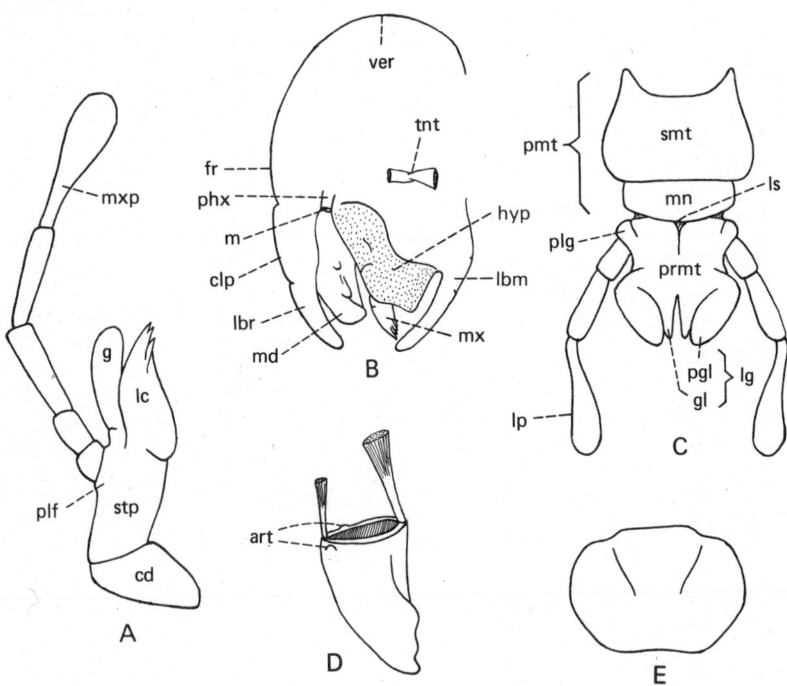

Figure 7. Mouth parts of a cricket (*Gryllus*). A, maxilla; B, median vertical section of head, showing relation of hypopharynx (*hyp*) to other mouth parts (somewhat diagrammatic); C, labium; D, mandible, showing muscle attachments and points of articulation; E, labrum. *art,* points of articulation of mandible; *cd,* cardo; *clp,* clypeus; *fr,* frons; *g,* galea; *gl,* glossa; *hyp,* hypopharynx; *lbm,* labium; *lbr,* labrum; *lc,* lacinia; *lg,* ligula; *lp,* labial palp; *ls,* labial suture; *m,* mouth; *md,* mandible; *mn,* mentum; *mx,* maxilla; *mxp,* maxillary palp; *pgl,* paraglossa; *phx,* pharynx; *plf,* palpifer; *plg,* palpiger; *pmt,* postmentum; *prmt,* prementum; *smt,* submentum; *stp,* stipes; *tnt,* tentorium; *ver,* vertex.

prementum, called palpigers (*plg*). The ligula consists of a pair of small mesal lobes, the glossae (*gl*), and a pair of larger lateral lobes, the paraglossae (*pgl*). The variations in labial structure in chewing insects involve principally the structure of the ligula and the sclerotization of the basal portion of the labium.

If the mandible and maxilla on one side are removed, one may see the **hypopharynx** (Figure 7 B, *hyp*), a short tonguelike structure located immediately in front of or above the labium and between the maxillae. In most insects the ducts from the salivary glands open on or near the hypopharynx. Between the hypopharynx, mandibles, and labrum lies the preoral food cavity, which leads dorsally to the mouth (*m*).

VARIATIONS IN INSECT MOUTH PARTS

Insect mouth parts are of two general types, mandibulate (chewing) and haustellate (sucking). In mandibulate mouth parts the mandibles move sideways, and the insect is usually able to bite off and chew its food. Insects with haustellate mouth parts do not have mandibles of this type and cannot chew food; their mouth parts are in the form of a somewhat elongated proboscis or beak through which liquid food is sucked. The mandibles in haustellate mouth parts either are elongate and styletlike or are lacking. Both mandibulate and haustellate mouth parts are subject to considerable variation in different insects; an outline of some of these variations is given below.

MANDIBULATE MOUTH PARTS This is the more primitive type and occurs in adult Thysanùra, Diplùra, Collémbola, Orthóptera, Dermáptera, Psocóptera, Mallóphaga, Odonàta, Plecóptera, Isóptera, Neuróptera, Mecóptera, Trichóptera, Coleóptera, and Hymenóptera, as well as in the larval stages of many insects. The variations in the different mouth-part structures were noted briefly in the discussion of the mouth parts of a cricket (page 12).

A few mandibulate insects obtain their food in liquid form by sucking it through a channel of some sort in the mouth parts; such mouth parts are sometimes described as chewing-sucking and are found in bees and in some larvae. In the bees (Figure 8) the labium and maxillae are modified into a tonguelike structure through which liquid food is sucked; modifications of the tongue provide useful taxonomic characters in the bees. The larvae of some Neuróptera (for example, antlions and owlflies, Figure 241) have the mandibles and maxillae elongate, and suck up the body fluids of their prey through a channel between the mandibles and maxillae. The larvae of some beetles (for example, predaceous diving beetles, Figure 261) suck the body fluids of their prey through channels in the mandibles.

HAUSTELLATE MOUTH PARTS Some of or all the various parts are elongate or styletlike in these mouth parts. There are eight principal variations in haustellate mouth parts: those occurring in (1) thrips, (2) Hemíptera and Homóptera, (3) "lower" Díptera, (4) robber flies, (5) "higher" Díptera, (6) fleas, (7) sucking lice, and (8) Lepidóptera.

1. The Mouth Parts of Thrips (Figure 9): The proboscis in thrips is a short, stout, asymmetrical, conical structure located ventrally at the rear of the head. The labrum forms the front of the proboscis, the basal portions of the maxillae form the sides, and the labium forms the rear. There are three stylets: the left mandible (the right mandible is rudimentary) and two maxillary stylets. Both maxillary and labial palps are present, but short; the hypopharynx is a small median lobe in the proboscis. The mouth parts of thrips have been termed "rasping-sucking," but it is probable that the stylets pierce rather than rasp the tissues fed upon; the food ingested is generally in liquid form, but very minute spores are sometimes ingested.

2. The Mouth Parts of Hemíptera and Homóptera (Figure 10): The beak is elongate, usually segmented, and arises from the front (Hemíptera) or rear (Homóptera) of the head. The external segmented structure of the beak is the labium, which is sheathlike and encloses four piercing stylets: the two mandibles and the two maxillae. The labrum is a short lobe at the base of the beak on the anterior side, and the hypopharynx is a short lobe within the base of the beak. The labium does no piercing, but folds up as the stylets enter the tissue fed upon. The inner stylets in the beak, the maxillae, fit together in such a way as to form two channels, a food channel and a salivary channel. The palps are lacking.

3. The Mouth Parts of the Biting Lower Díptera: The biting lower Díptera include the mosquitoes (Figure 11), sand flies, punkies, black flies, horse flies, and snipe flies. These insects have six piercing stylets: the labrum, the mandibles, the maxillae, and the hypopharynx; the labium usually serves as a sheath for the stylets. The stylets may be very slender and needlelike (mosquitoes) or broader and knifelike (the other groups). The max-

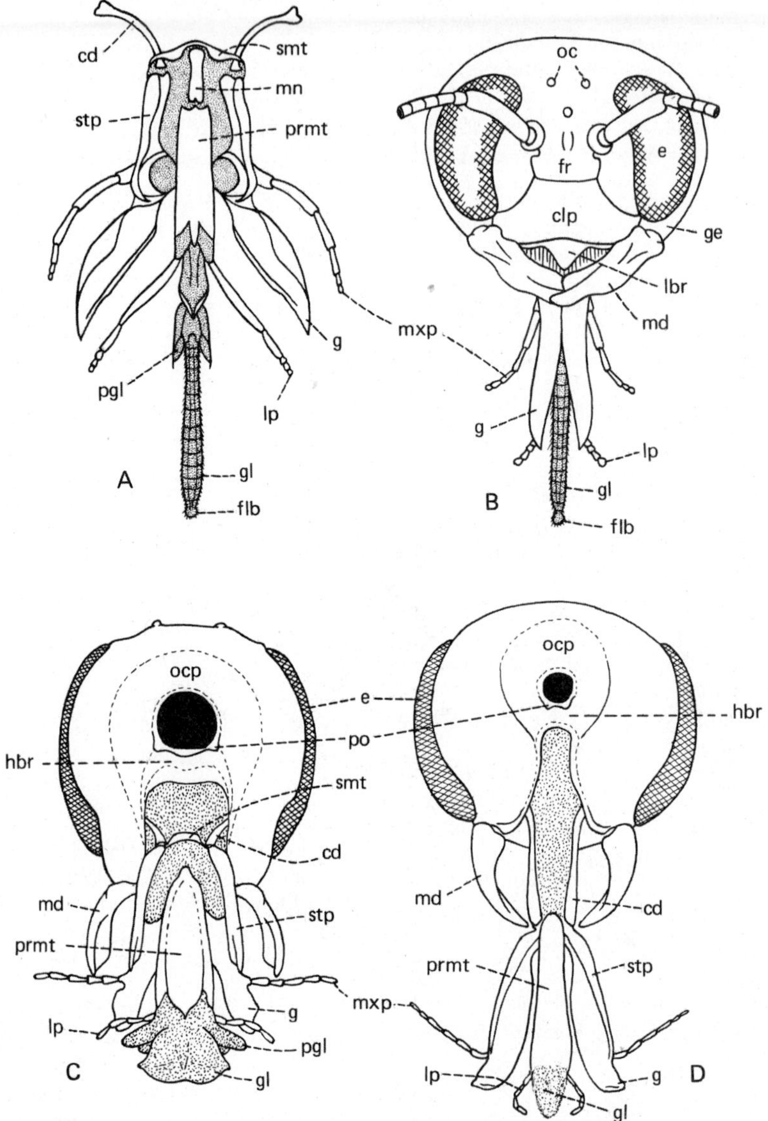

Figure 8. Head and mouth part structure in bees. A, mouth parts of *Xylocòpa* Àpidae, Xylocopìnae), posterior view; B, same, anterior view; C, mouth parts of *Hylaèus* (Collètidae, Hylaeìnae), posterior view; D, mouth parts of *Sphecòdes* (Halíctidae), posterior view. *cd,* cardo; *clp,* clypeus; e, compound eye; *flb,* flabellum; *fr,* frons; *g,* galea; *ge,* gena; *gl,* glossa; *hbr,* hypostomal bridge; *lbr,* labrum; *lp,* labial palp; *md,* mandible; *mn,* mentum; *mxp,* maxillary palp; *oc,* ocelli; *ocp,* occiput; *pgl,* paraglossa; *po,* postocciput; *prmt,* prementum; *smt,* submentum; *stp,* stipes.

illary palps are well developed, but labial palps are lacking (some dipterists regard the labellar lobes as labial palps). The salivary channel is in the hypopharynx, and the food channel is between the grooved labrum and the hypopharynx (for example, mosquitoes) or between the labrum

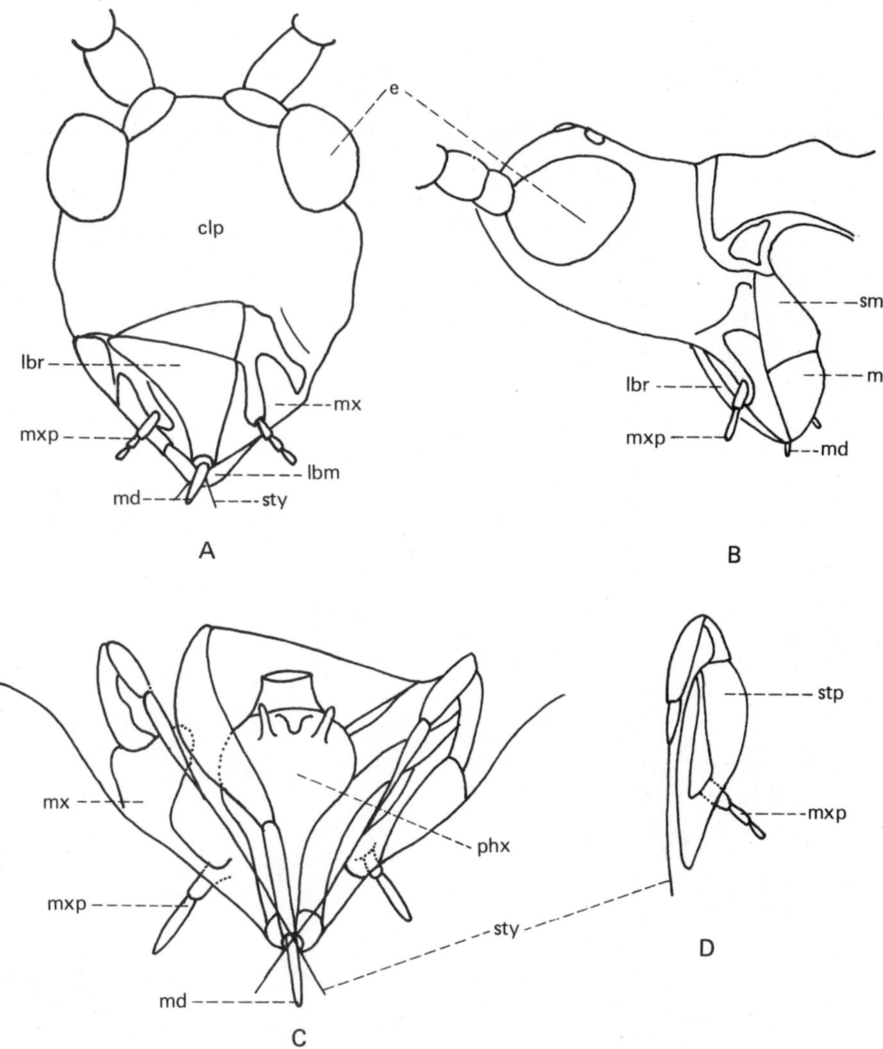

Figure 9. Mouth parts of a thrips. A, head, ventro-anterior view; B, head, lateral view; C, mouth parts; D, a maxilla. *clp,* clypeus; *e,* compound eye; *lbm,* labium; *lbr,* labrum; *md,* left mandible; *mn,* mentum; *mx,* maxilla; *mxp,* maxillary palp; *phx,* pharynx; *smt,* submentum; *stp,* stipes; *sty,* maxillary stylet. (Redrawn from Peterson, 1915.)

and the mandibles (for example, punkies and horse flies). The labium does no piercing and folds up or back as the stylets enter the tissue pierced.

4. The Mouth Parts of Robber Flies (Asìlidae): The mouth parts of these insects (Figure 12) are similar to those of the preceding group, but there are no mandibles and the principal piercing organ is the hypopharynx. There are four stylets: the labrum, maxillae, and hypopharynx. The salivary channel is in the hypopharynx, and the food channel is between the labrum and the hypopharynx. The robber flies feed on other insects or spiders, and only rarely bite man.

5. The Mouth Parts of the Higher Díptera: By "higher" Díptera is meant the flies belonging to the Cyclòrrhapha (see pages 588–606). The man-

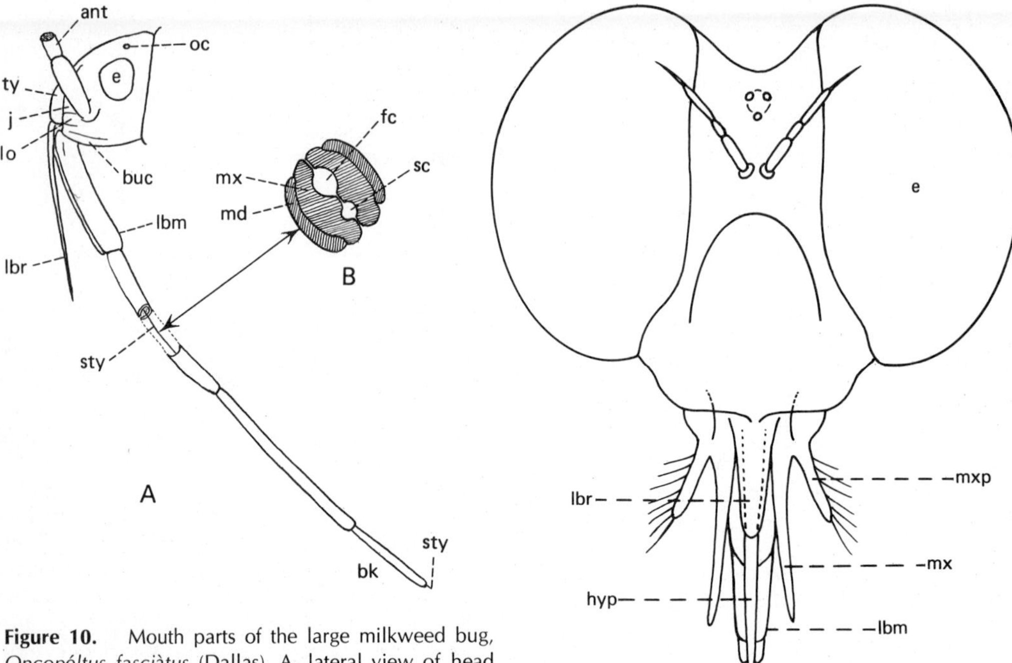

Figure 10. Mouth parts of the large milkweed bug, *Oncopéltus fasciàtus* (Dallas). A, lateral view of head showing beak, with labrum detached from front of beak; B, cross section of stylets (somewhat diagrammatic). *ant,* antenna; *bk,* beak; *buc,* buccula; *e,* compound eye; *fc,* food channel; *j,* jugum; *lbm,* labium; *lbr,* labrum; *lo,* lorum; *md,* mandible; *mx,* maxilla; *oc,* ocellus; *sc,* salivary channel; *sty,* stylets; *ty,* tylus.

Figure 12. Head and mouth parts of a robber fly. e, compound eye; *hyp,* hypopharynx; *lbm,* labium; *lbr,* labrum; *mx,* maxillary stylet; *mxp,* maxillary palp.

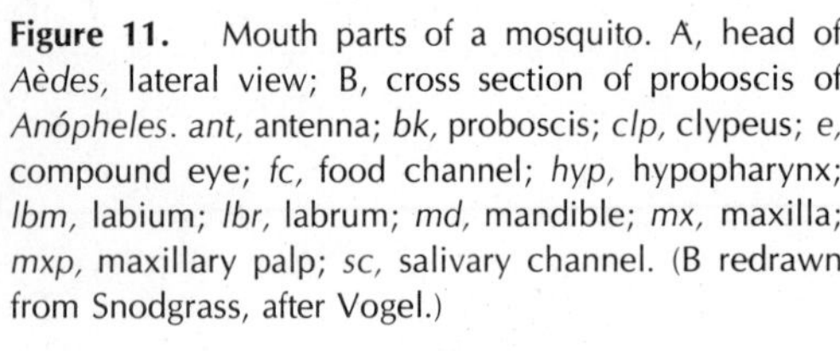

Figure 11. Mouth parts of a mosquito. A, head of *Aèdes,* lateral view; B, cross section of proboscis of *Anópheles. ant,* antenna; *bk,* proboscis; *clp,* clypeus; *e,* compound eye; *fc,* food channel; *hyp,* hypopharynx; *lbm,* labium; *lbr,* labrum; *md,* mandible; *mx,* maxilla; *mxp,* maxillary palp; *sc,* salivary channel. (B redrawn from Snodgrass, after Vogel.)

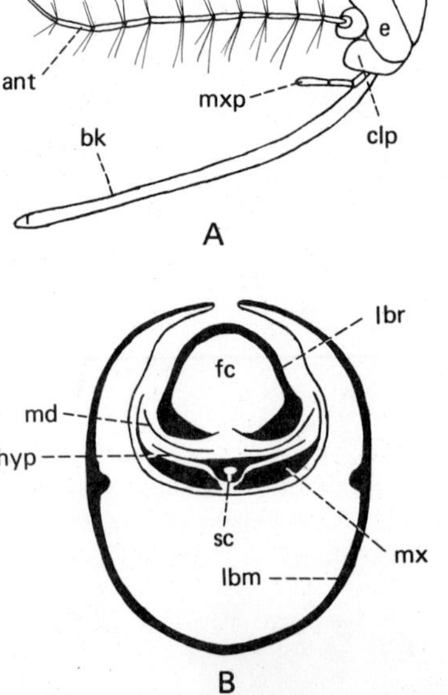

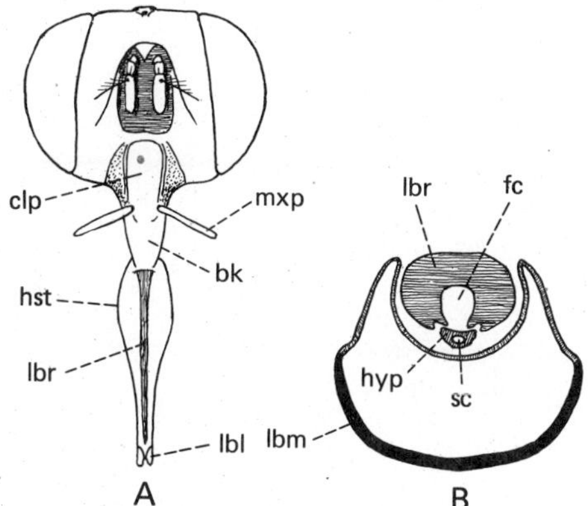

Figure 13. Mouth parts of the stable fly, *Stomóxys cálcitrans* (L). A, anterior view of head; B, cross section through haustellum. *bk,* rostrum; *clp,* clypeus; *fc,* food channel; *hst,* haustellum; *hyp,* hypopharynx; *lbl,* labellum; *lbm,* labium; *lbr,* labrum; *mxp,* maxillary palp; *sc,* salivary channel. (Redrawn from various sources; somewhat diagrammatic.)

dibles in these flies are lacking, and the maxillae are represented by the palps (maxillary stylets are usually lacking). The proboscis consists of the labrum, hypopharynx, and labium. There are two modifications of the mouth parts in these flies: (a) a piercing type, and (b) a sponging or lapping type.

a. The higher Díptera with piercing mouth parts include the stable fly (Figure 13), tsetse fly, horn fly, and the louse flies. The principal piercing structure in these flies is the labium; the labrum and hypopharynx are slender and stylet-like, and lie in a dorsal groove of the labium. The labium terminates in a pair of small hard plates, the labella, which are armed with teeth. The salivary channel is in the hypopharynx, and the food channel is between the labrum and hypopharynx. The proboscis in the louse flies (Hippobóscidae) is somewhat retracted into a pouch on the ventral side of the head when not in use.

b. The higher Díptera with sponging or lapping mouth parts include the nonbiting Cyclórrhapha such as the house fly (Figure 14), blow flies, and fruit flies. The mouth-part structures are suspended from a conical membranous projection of the lower part of the head called the rostrum. The maxillary palps arise at the distal end of the rostrum, and that part of the proboscis beyond the palps is termed the haustellum. The labrum and hypopharynx are slender and lie in an anterior groove of the labium, which forms the bulk of the haustellum. The salivary channel is in the hypopharynx, and the food channel lies between the labrum and the hypopharynx. At the apex of the labium are the labella, a pair of large, soft, oval lobes. The lower surface of these lobes bears numerous transverse grooves which serve as food channels. The proboscis can usually be folded up against the lower side of the head or into a cavity on the lower side of the head. These flies lap up liquid food; this food may be already in liquid form, or it may first be liquefied by salivary secretions of the fly.

6. The Mouth Parts of Fleas (Figure 15): Adult fleas feed on blood, and their mouth parts contain three piercing stylets: the epipharynx and the

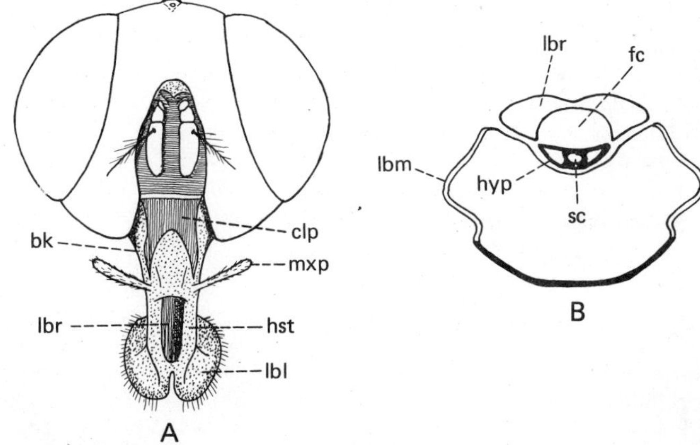

Figure 14. Mouth parts of the house fly, *Músca doméstica* (L.) A, anterior view of head; B, cross section through haustellum. *bk,* rostrum; *clp,* clypeus; *fc,* food channel; *hst,* haustellum; *hyp,* hypopharynx; *lbl,* labellum; *lbm,* labium; *lbr,* labrum; *mxp,* maxillary palp; *sc,* salivary channel. (Redrawn from Snodgrass, by permission of McGraw-Hill Book Company, Inc.)

laciniae of the maxillae. The labrum is a very small lobe on the lower surface of the head, in front of the base of the epipharynx; it is the epipharyngeal portion of the labrum that is prolonged into a piercing stylet. The maxillae consist of large plates or lobes, each of which bears a piercing lacinia and a large palp. The labium is short and slender and bears short palps; the labium and its palps serve to guide the stylets. The hypopharynx is a small lobelike structure lying within the base of the beak. The food channel lies between the epipharynx and the maxillary stylets, and the salivary channel lies between the edges of the maxillary stylets.

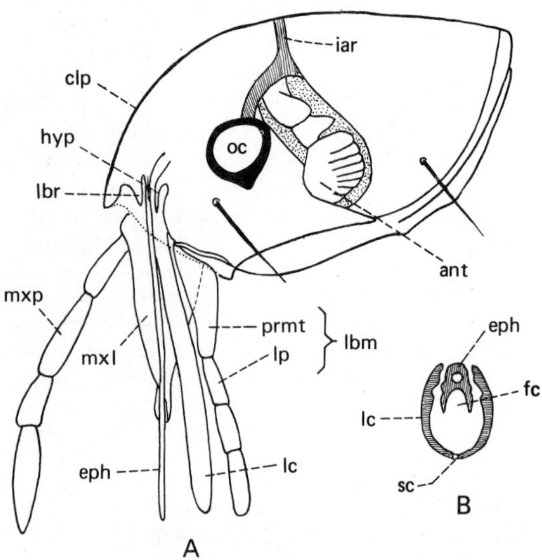

Figure 15. Mouth parts of a flea. A, lateral view of head, somewhat diagrammatic, with stylets separated and left maxilla not shown; B, cross section through stylets. *ant*, antenna; *clp*, clypeus; *eph*, epipharynx; *fc*, food channel; *hyp*, hypopharynx; *iar*, interantennal ridge; *lbm*, labium; *lbr*, labrum; *lc*, lacinia; *lp*, labial palp; *mxl*, maxillary lobe; *mxp*, maxillary palp; *oc*, ocellus; *prmt*, prementum; *sc*, salivary channel. (A modified from Snodgrass; B redrawn from Matheson, by permission of Comstock Publishing Co.)

internally with small recurved teeth. The stylets are about as long as the head and, when not in use, are withdrawn into a long saclike structure lying below the alimentary tract. The dorsal stylet probably represents the fused maxillae; its edges are curved upward and inward to form a tube that serves as a food channel. The intermediate stylet is very slender and contains the salivary channel; this stylet is probably the hypopharynx. The ventral stylet is the principal piercing organ; it is a trough-shaped structure and is probably the labium. There are no palps.

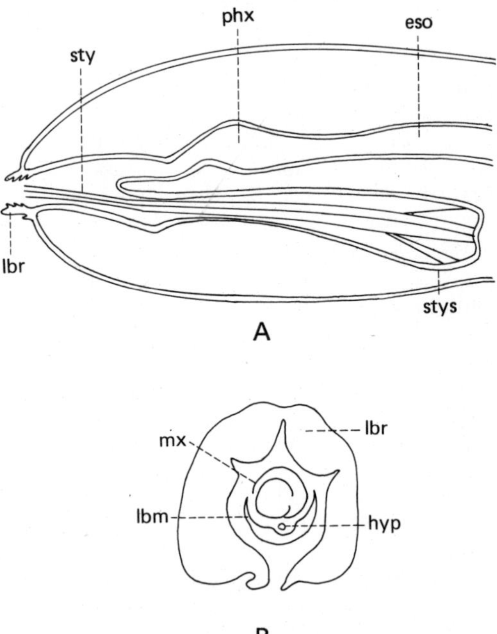

Figure 16. Mouth parts of a sucking louse. A, sagittal section of head; B, cross section through rostrum. *eso*, esophagus; *hyp*, intermediate stylet (probably hypopharynx); *lbm*, ventral stylet (probably labium); *lbr*, rostrum (probably labrum); *mx*, dorsal stylet (probably fused maxillae); *phx*, pharynx; *sty*, stylets; *stys*, stylet sac. (Redrawn from Snodgrass.)

7. The Mouth Parts of the Sucking Lice (Figure 16): The mouth parts of these insects are highly specialized and difficult to homologize with those of other sucking insects. There is a short rostrum (probably the labrum) at the anterior end of the head, from which the three piercing stylets are protruded; the rostrum is eversible and is armed

8. The Mouth Parts of Lepidóptera (Figure 17): The proboscis of adult Lepidóptera is usually long and coiled and is formed of the two galeae of the maxillae; the food channel is between the galeae. The labrum is reduced to a narrow transverse band across the lower margin of the face, and the mandibles and hypopharynx are lacking. The

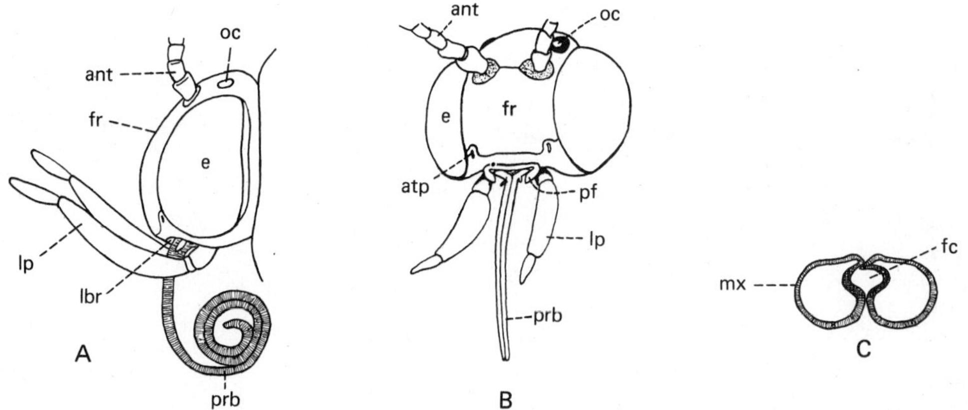

Figure 17. Mouth parts of a moth. A, lateral view of head; B, anterior view of head; C, cross section through proboscis. *ant,* antenna; *atp,* anterior tentorial pit; *e,* compound eye; *fc,* food channel; *fr,* frons; *lbr,* labrum; *lp,* labial palp; *mx,* maxilla (galea); *oc,* ocellus; *pf,* pilifer, *prb,* proboscis. (Redrawn from Snodgrass, by permission of McGraw-Hill Book Company, Inc.)

maxillary palps are usually reduced or absent, but the labial palps are usually well developed. There is no special salivary channel. This type of mouth-part structure is sometimes called siphoning-sucking, for there is no piercing and the insect merely sucks or siphons liquids up through the proboscis. When used, the proboscis is uncoiled by blood pressure; it recoils by its own elasticity.

THE THORAX

The thorax is the middle region of the body and bears the legs and wings (in some adult insects there are no wings, and in many immature and a few adult insects there are no legs). The thorax is composed of three segments: the prothorax, mesothorax, and metathorax. Each thoracic segment typically bears a pair of legs, and the wings (when present) are borne by the mesothorax and the metathorax. If there is only one pair of wings present, they are usually borne by the mesothorax. The prothorax never bears wings.

The thorax is connected to the head by a membranous neck region, the cervix (Figure 18, *cvx*). There are usually one or two small sclerites (*cvs*) on each side of the neck, which link the head with the episterna of the prothorax.

Each thoracic segment is composed of four groups of sclerites: the notum dorsally, the pleura laterally, and the sternum ventrally. Any thoracic sclerite may be located on a particular segment by using the appropriate prefix, either pro-, meso-, or meta-; for example, the notum of the prothorax, which in insects such as a grasshopper or cricket is a large and conspicuous saddlelike plate between the head and the base of the wings, is called the pronotum. The thoracic segment of any given sclerite is indicated in our illustrations by a subscript numeral; for example, the pronotum is indicated by n_1, the episternum of the mesothorax by eps_2, and the epimeron of the metathorax by epm_3.

The nota of the mesothorax and metathorax are often divided by sutures into two or more sclerites each. In a rather generalized winged insect there are two principal notal sclerites, the alinotum (*AN*), which occupies most of the notum, and the postnotum (*PN*), at the posterior margin of the notum. The alinotum is often divided into two sclerites, an anterior scutum (*sct*) and a posterior scutellum (*scl*); in some insects there are additional sutures on the alinotum. Each pleuron is typically divided into two sclerites by a pleural suture (*pls*), which extends dorsoventrally between the base of the leg and the base of the wing; the anterior sclerite is the episternum (*eps*), and the posterior sclerite is the epimeron (*epm*). The pleuron in a wing-bearing segment is produced into a pleural wing process (*pwp*) at the upper end of the pleural suture; this process serves as a fulcrum for the movement of the wing. There are usually one or two small sclerites, the epipleurites (*epp*), in the membranous area between the pleuron and the base of the wing; these are impor-

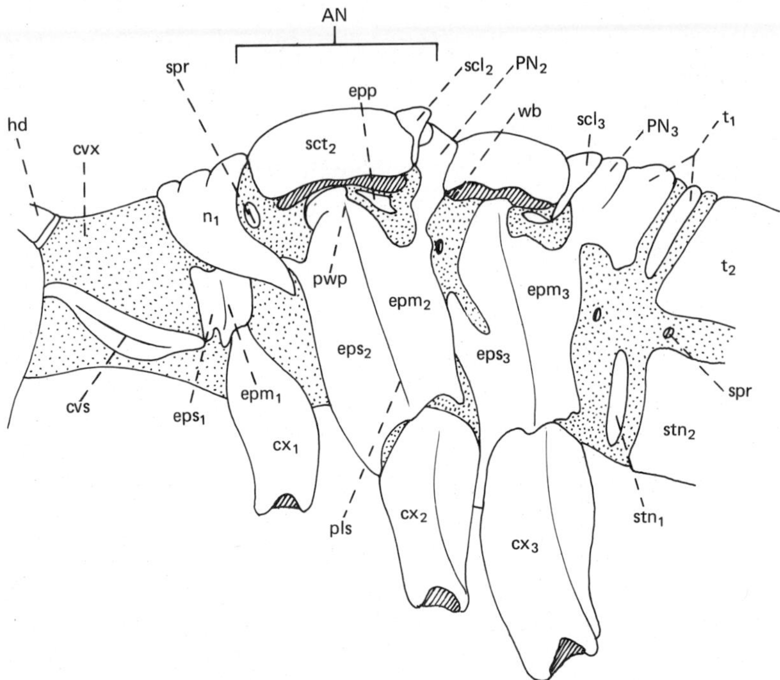

Figure 18. Thorax of *Panórpa*, lateral view. *AN*, alinotum; *cvs*, cervical sclerite; *cvx*, cervix; *cx*, coxa; *epm*, epimeron; *epp*, epipleurite; *eps*, episternum; *hd*, head; n_1, pronotum; *pls*, pleural suture; *PN*, postnotum; *pwp*, pleural wing process; *scl*, scutellum; *sct*, scutum; *spr*, spiracle; *stn*, abdominal sternum; *t*, abdominal tergum; *wb*, base of wing. (Redrawn from Ferris and Rees.)

tant to the wing movements, for certain muscles that move the wings are attached to them. Each sternum may be divided into two or more sclerites.

On each side of the thorax are two slitlike openings, one between the prothorax and mesothorax, and the other between the mesothorax and metathorax. These are the spiracles (*spr*), the external openings of the respiratory system (which will be discussed later).

THE LEGS

The legs of insects (Figure 19) typically consist of the following segments: the coxa (*cx*), the basal segment; the trochanter (*tr*), a small segment (rarely two segments) following the coxa; the femur (*fm*), the first long segment of the leg; the tibia (*tb*), the second long segment of the leg; the tarsus (*ts*), a series of small segments beyond the tibia; and the pretarsus (*ptar*), consisting of the tarsal claws and other structures at the end of the tarsus. A true leg segment (the six listed above) is a subdivision with its own musculature; the subdivisions of the tarsus, though commonly referred to as "segments," do not have their own musculature and hence are not true leg segments. They might more properly be called subsegments or tarsomeres, but for simplicity they are referred to as segments in this book. The number of tarsal segments in different insects varies from one to five. The pretarsus usually consists of a pair of claws (*tcl*) and often one or more padlike structures between or at the base of the claws; a pad or lobe between the claws is usually called an arolium (*aro*), and pads located at the base of the claws are called pulvilli (*pul*).

The legs may be variously modified in different insects, and the characters of the legs are made considerable use of in identification. The different segments of the leg may vary in size, shape, or spination, and the number of tarsal segments varies in different insects. The crickets and long-horned grasshoppers have an eardrum or tympanum at the basal end of the front tibiae (Figure 19 D, *tym*).

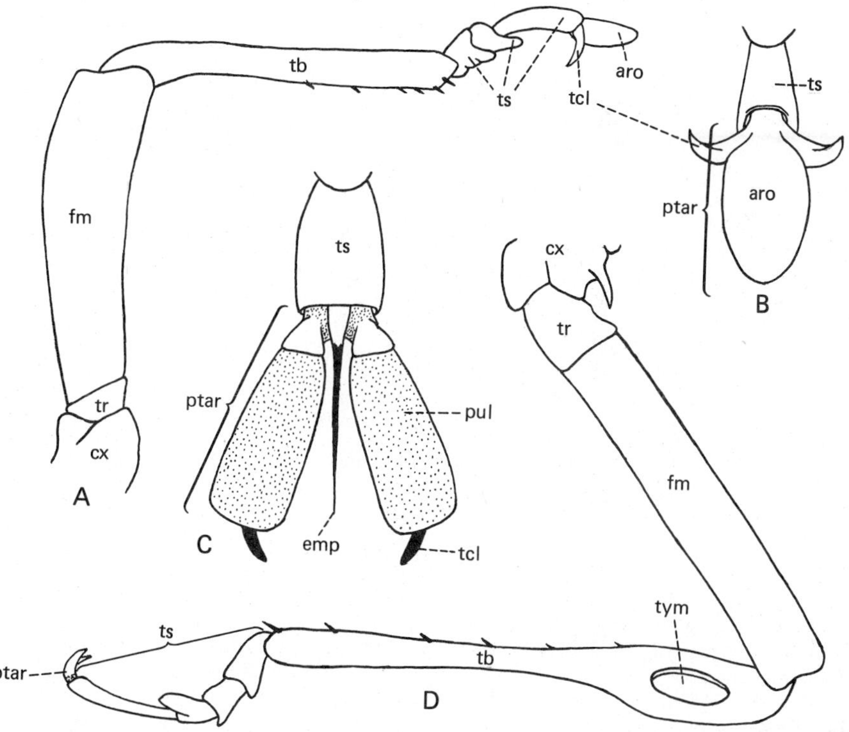

Figure 19. Leg structure in insects. A, middle leg of a short-horned grasshopper (*Melánoplus*); B, last tarsal segment and pretarsus of *Melánoplus;* C, last tarsal segment and pretarsus of a robber fly; D, front leg of a long-horned grasshopper (*Scuddèria*). *aro,* arolium; *cx,* coxa; *emp,* empodium; *fm,* femur; *ptar,* pretarsus; *pul,* pulvillus; *tb,* tibia, *tcl,* tarsal claw; *tr,* trochanter; *ts,* tarsus; *tym,* tympanum.

THE WINGS

The wings of insects are outgrowths of the body wall located dorsolaterally between the nota and pleura. They arise as saclike outgrowths, but in the adult insect they are solid structures, with the only cavities being those of the wing veins. The base of the wing is membranous, but contains certain small sclerites (the axillary sclerites) which are important in the wing movements. Most of the muscles that move the wings are attached to sclerites in the thoracic wall rather than to the wings directly, and the movements are produced by changes in the shape of the thorax; the only muscle attached to the wing directly (at least in most insects) is attached to one of the sclerites in the membranous wing base.

The wings of insects vary in number, size, shape, texture, venation, and in the position at which they are held at rest. Most adult insects have two pairs of wings, borne by the mesothorax and metathorax, but some have only one pair (usually borne by the mesothorax), and some are wingless. In most insects the wings are membranous (like cellophane) and may bear tiny hairs or scales; in some insects the front wings are thickened, leathery, or hard and sheathlike. Most insects are able to fold the wings over the abdomen when at rest, but the dragonflies, damselflies, and mayflies cannot do this and hold the wings either outstretched or together above the body when at rest.

The wing articulations and muscles are discussed in the following chapter (page 57).

WING VENATION

The wings of most insects are membranous and bear a framework of thickened lines, the veins. The number and arrangement of the veins is of great taxonomic value in many insect groups. There is considerable variation in the wing vena-

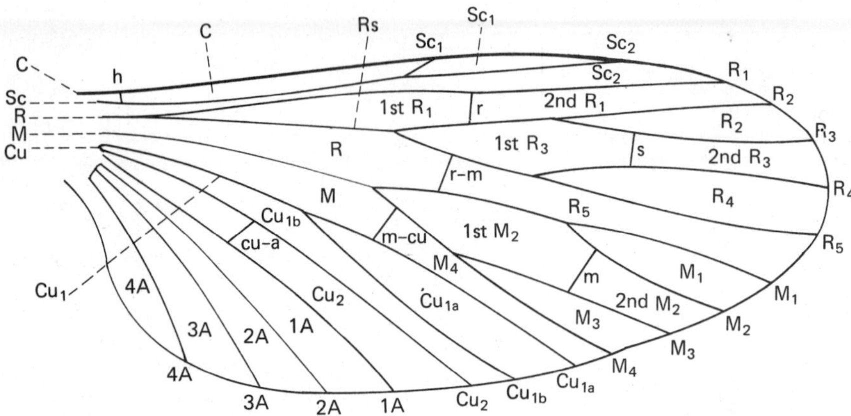

Figure 20. Generalized wing venation, according to Comstock; for a key to the lettering, see accompanying text. In some orders, the vein here labeled Cu_1 is called Cu by Comstock (and its branches Cu_1 and Cu_2), and the remaining veins anal veins.

tion of different insects, but a system of terminology (based on venational homologies) has been developed that is applicable to all insects; this is the Comstock (or Comstock–Needham) system, and is outlined below.

The principal veins of the insect wing (with their abbreviations in parentheses) are as follows:

Longitudinal veins
- Costa (C)
- Subcosta (Sc)
- Radius (R)
- Radial Sector (Rs)
- Media (M)
- Cubitus (Cu)
- Anal veins (A)

Cross veins
- Humeral (h)
- Radial (r)
- Sectorial (s)
- Radio-medial (r-m)
- Medial (m)
- Medio-cubital (m-cu)
- Cubito-anal (cu-a)

The longitudinal veins vary somewhat in their method of branching in different insects, but the basic or hypothetical primitive arrangement is as follows (Figure 20). The costa is an unbranched vein that usually forms the anterior (or costal) margin of the wing. The subcosta is forked distally. The branches of the longitudinal veins are numbered from anterior to posterior around the wing by means of subscript numerals; the two branches of the subcosta are designated Sc_1 and Sc_2. The radius gives off a posterior branch, the radial sector, usually near the base of the wing; the anterior branch of the radius is R_1; the radial sector forks twice, with four branches reaching the wing margin. The media forks twice, with four branches reaching the wing margin. The cubitus, according to the Comstock–Needham system, forks once, the two branches being Cu_1 and Cu_2; according to some other authorities, Cu_1 forks again distally, the two branches being Cu_{1a} and Cu_{1b}. The anal veins, which are typically unbranched, are designated from anterior to posterior as the first anal (1A), second anal (2A), and so on.

The cross veins are named according to their location in the wing or the longitudinal veins they connect. The humeral cross vein is located near the base of the wing, between the costa and the subcosta. The radial cross vein connects R_1 and the anterior branch of the radial sector. The sectorial cross vein connects R_3 and R_4. The radio-medial cross vein connects the posterior branch of the radius and the anterior branch of the media. The medial cross vein connects M_2 and M_3. The medio-cubital cross vein connects the posterior branch of the media and the anterior branch of the cubitus. The cubito-anal cross vein connects the posterior branch of the cubitus and the first anal vein.

The wing venation of any particular insect may differ from the basic arrangement just described in that it may have fewer veins or more veins. If the venation is reduced, either one or more veins are lacking, two or more veins are fused, or one or more veins fail to branch. A fused or unbranched vein is named on the basis of its component parts;

for example, the anterior branch of the radial sector is R_{2+3}, and it sometimes fails to branch. Other similar veins are R_{4+5}, M_{1+2}, and Cu + 2A. Extra veins may be either extra cross veins or extra branches of the longitudinal veins. Extra cross veins may be designated by number (for example, first radial and second radial) if they are not too numerous, or they may have special names based on their location (for example, the antenodal cross veins in the Odonata), or they may be unnamed. Extra longitudinal veins are usually additional branches of the principal veins, called accessory veins; such veins, if they are not too numerous and are constant in number and position, are named after the vein from which they branch; a single accessory vein branching from M_1, for example, is designated as M_{1a}. If there are two or more accessory veins branching from M_1 (or any other principal vein), they are usually simply called M_1 accessories. Other types of extra longitudinal veins may have special names, such as the intercalary veins of mayflies and the supplements of dragonflies.

The spaces in the wing between the veins are called cells. Cells may be open (extending to the wing margin) or closed (completely surrounded by veins). The cells are named according to the longitudinal vein on the anterior side of the cell; for example, the open cell between R_2 and R_3 is the R_2 cell. The cells at the base of the wing are usually named after the basal or unbranched part of the longitudinal vein on the anterior side of the cell; for example, the cells R, M, and Cu. Where two cells separated by a cross vein would ordinarily have the same name, they are individually designated by number; for example, the medial cross vein divides the M_2 cell into two cells, the basal one of which is designated as the first M_2 cell and the distal one as the second M_2 cell. Where a cell is bordered anteriorly by a fused vein (for example, R_{2+3}), it is named after the posterior component of that fused vein (cell R_3). In some insects certain cells may have special names; for example, the triangles of the dragonfly wing and the discal cell of Lepidóptera.

OTHER INTERPRETATIONS

Not all entomologists agree with Comstock's idea of the generalized venation of the insect wing; the principal points of difference are as follows: (1) Sc is basically unbranched; (2) Rs is a principal longitudinal vein, and not a basal branch of R; (3) M is basically 2-branched, with the anterior branch lost in most present-day insects and only the posterior branch retained; and (4) the interpretation of the veins behind M. The generalized arrangement of the veins behind M, according to some authorities, is somewhat as follows:

- I The first vein behind M, which is often forked
- II The second vein behind M, which arises independently, or very close to the first
- III The third vein behind M, which arises independently
- IV The remaining veins (usually three or four), which arise from a common base that articulates with the third axillary sclerite

Comstock calls I the cubitus and the others anal veins in some orders, but in other orders he calls I, Cu_1 (and its two branches Cu_{1a} and Cu_{1b}), he calls II, Cu_2, and he calls the rest anal veins. Snodgrass (1952) calls I the cubitus, II and III postcubitus veins, and IV vannal veins. Hamilton (1972, Part II) calls I the cubitus, II the plical vein, III the empusal vein, and IV anal veins.

In this book we follow Comstock's terminology in most orders, using his interpretation in some groups and a different interpretation in others, depending on the practice of most current workers in the groups concerned.

THE ABDOMEN

The insect abdomen is typically 11-segmented, but the eleventh segment is usually much reduced and is represented only by appendages so that the maximum number of segments rarely appears to be more than ten. In many insects this number is reduced, either by a fusion of segments or by a telescoping of the terminal segments.

Each abdominal segment generally consists of two sclerites, a dorsal tergum (*t*) and a smaller ventral sternum (*stn*); the pleural region is membranous and seldom contains sclerotized areas (Figure 1). Most segments bear a pair of laterally located spiracles.

The pregenital abdominal segments (segments 1–7) bear appendages in various immature insects and in adult Apterygòta and male Odonàta. The abdominal appendages of immature insects may consist of gills (for example, in mayfly nymphs, Figure 93), lateral filaments (for example, in certain Neuróptera larvae, Figure 237), or prolegs (for example, in Lepidóptera larvae, Figure 357). The abdominal appendages in Apterygòta consist of styli or other appendages (see Chapter 9), and in male Odonàta they consist of the copulatory structures (Figure 97 A, *gen*).

The genital segments (8 and 9, Figures 21 and 22) may bear structures associated with the external openings of the genital ducts; in the male these structures (which are believed to develop from segment 10) have to do with copulation and the transfer of sperm to the female, and in the female (where they develop from segments 8 and 9) they are concerned primarily with oviposition. These structures are the external genitalia, though they may be partly or entirely withdrawn into the abdomen when not in use, and are often (especially in the male) not visible without dissection.

The external genitalia of the male are extremely variable and are often quite complex; they are frequently of considerable taxonomic value. In a leafhopper (Figure 21) they are contained in a genital chamber that is formed by a dorsolaterally located pygofer (*pgf*) and a pair of ventrally located plates (*pla*); these structures are portions of the ninth segment. The genitalia within this chamber consist of a pair of latero–ventral processes, the styles (*sty*), a median basal connective (*con*), and a central structure, the aedeagus (*aed*). The aedeagus, through which the sperms are discharged during mating, is often provided with various processes. When the male leafhopper mates, the genital chamber is completely opened; the pygofer is pushed dorsally and the plates are deflected, and the aedeagus and styles are exposed directly to the base of the female ovipositor.

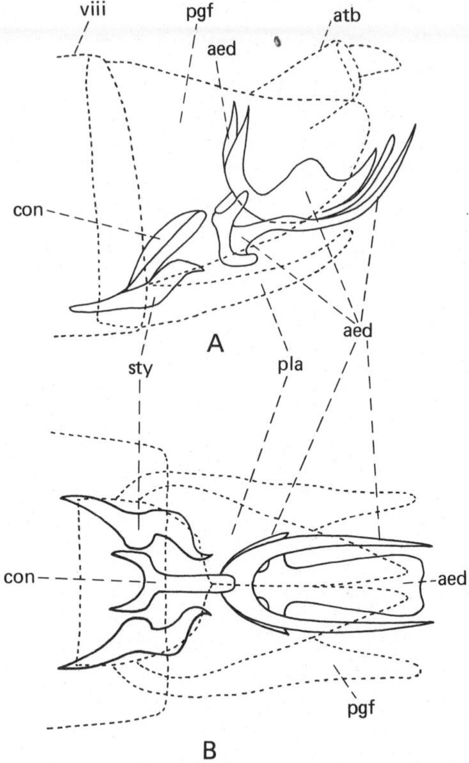

Figure 21. Male genitalia of the leafhopper, *Draeculacéphala ántica* (Walker). A, lateral view; B, ventral view. External structures are shown by dotted lines, internal structures by solid lines. *aed,* aedeagus; *atb,* anal tube; *con,* connective; *pgf,* pygofer; *pla,* plate; *sty,* style; *VIII,* eighth abdominal segment.

The female genitalia consist of an ovipositor, which is formed by the appendages (gonopods) of segments 8 and 9 (Figure 22). A gonopod characteristically consists of a basal portion (the coxopodite) that bears a more or less elongate process (the gonapophysis), and sometimes also a style, posteriorly. The ovipositor consists of a pair of basal plates, the valvifers (*vf*), and up to three pairs of elongate structures, the valvulae (*vlv*). The valvifers are formed by the coxopodites of the gonopods of segments 8 and 9, and the valvulae are formed by the gonapophyses of these gonopods (the first and second valvulae) and by a posterior prolongation of the ninth coxopodite (the third valvulae). The ovipositor is generally used to pierce and insert the eggs into something, such as plant or animal tissue; one or more of the pairs of valvulae serve as the shaft of the ovipositor and do the actual piercing; one of the pairs of valvulae, usually the third, may serve as a sheath for the shaft and may not function as a piercing structure.

An appendicular ovipositor (such as described above) is present only in the Thysanùra (Figure 90, *ovp*), Thysanóptera (suborder Terebrántia), Odonàta (except the Gómphidae and Libellulòidea), Orthóptera, Homóptera (suborder Auchenorrhýncha), and Hymenóptera. The ovipositor varies considerably in form in different insects; in a damselfly it is located on the ventral side of segments 9 and 10, and gives the end of the abdomen a swollen appearance (Figures 97 E and 108 D); in a long-horned grasshopper it is a long sword-shaped structure (Figures 120 C, 121 B, 122); in ichneumons (Figure 562 A) it appears as three long hairlike structures, often as long as or longer than the body. (The median structure here is the shaft and consists of the first two pairs of valvulae fused together; the lateral structures are the third valvulae, which function as a sheath for the shaft.) In bees and wasps the ovipositor is modified into a

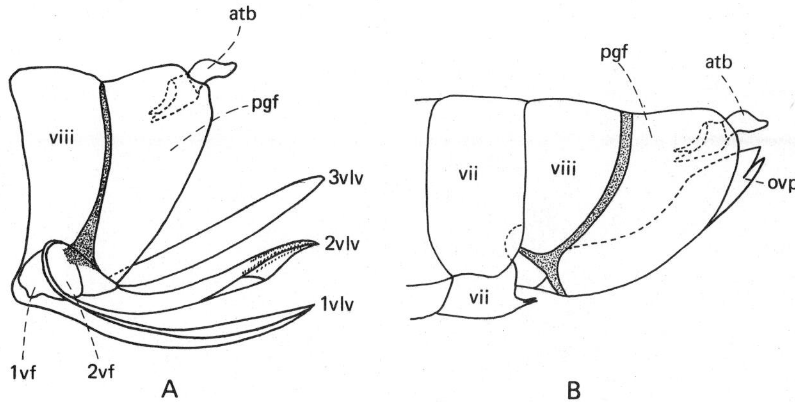

Figure 22. Ovipositor of a leafhopper. A, lateral view, with parts of ovipositor spread out; B, lateral view of terminal segments of abdomen, with ovipositor in a normal or resting position. *atb*, anal tube; *ovp*, ovipositor; *1 vf, 2 vf*, first and second valvifers; *1 vlv, 2 vlv, 3 vlv*, first, second, and third valvulae. The first and second valvulae form the shaft, or piercing part of the ovipositor, the third valvulae serve as a sheath for the shaft.

sting and is withdrawn into the abdomen when not in use.

Many insects that lack an appendicular ovipositor have the terminal abdominal segments capable of being extended in a long telescoping tube; this is the case in many Díptera, Mecóptera, Lepidóptera, and some other insects. Odonàta that lack an ovipositor have the sternum of the eighth segment more or less prolonged distally, usually into a trough-shaped structure (the vulvar lamina) that serves as an egg guide; these dragonflies generally lay their eggs by flying low over the surface of the water and washing the eggs off into the water. Many insects have no special structural modifications for egg laying.

The appendages at the apex of the abdomen, which arise from segment 10 (when ten complete segments are present), consist of the cerci (singular, cercus), the epiproct, and the paraprocts. The cerci are a pair of structures arising from the dorsal part of the last abdominal segment (Figure 1, *cr*); they may be clasperlike (Figures 97 and 145), feelerlike (Figures 125, 130, 131), or absent. The epiproct arises just above the anus; it may be filamentous (the median caudal filament of mayflies, Figure 93), somewhat clasperlike (the inferior appendage of male Anisóptera, Figure 97, *ept*), a small and inconspicuous lobe, or lacking. The paraprocts are located lateroventrally from the anus, and may appear as small, more or less rounded lobes (Figure 97 A, B, E, *ppt*), leaflike structures (the lateral gills of Zygóptera nymphs, Figure 103), clasperlike structures (the inferior appendages of male Zygóptera, Figure 97 C, D, *iap*), or may be lacking.

THE INTERNAL ANATOMY OF INSECTS

The general arrangement of the internal organs of an insect is shown in Figure 23. These organs, plus some not shown in this figure, are discussed in the following sections.

ENDOSKELETON

The principal skeleton of an insect is an exoskeleton located on the outside of the body, but there are various invaginations of this exoskeleton that serve to strengthen the body wall and provide points for the attachment of muscles; these invaginations constitute an endoskeleton. The elements of the endoskeleton may take various forms; the ridgelike invaginations are usually called apodemes, and the spinelike or armlike processes, apophyses (Figure 3).

The head is braced internally by a group of apophyses forming the tentorium (Figure 24, *ttb, ata, dta*). The tentorium is usually **H**-shaped, **X**-shaped, or is shaped like the Greek letter π (pi) with the principal arms in a more or less horizontal plane and extending from the lower part of the

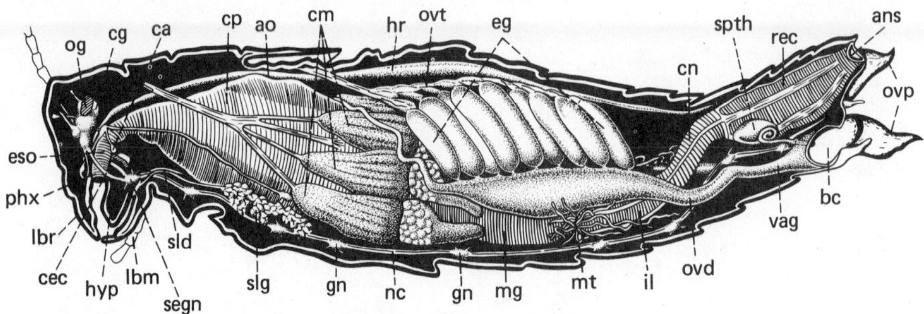

Figure 23. Internal organs of a grasshopper, shown in longitudinal section (somewhat diagrammatic). *ans,* anus; *ao,* dorsal aorta; *bc,* bursa copulatrix; *ca,* corpus allatum; *cec,* circumesophageal connective; *cg,* cerebral ganglion (part of the brain); *cm,* gastric caeca; *cn,* colon; *cp,* crop; eg, eggs; *eso,* esophagus; *gn,* ganglia of ventral nerve cord; *hr,* heart; *hyp,* hypopharynx; *il,* ileum; *lbm,* labium; *lbr,* labrum; *mg,* midgut or mesenteron; *mt,* Malpighian tubules; *nc,* ventral nerve cord; *og,* optic ganglion (part of the brain); *ovd,* oviduct; *ovp,* ovipositor; *ovt,* ovarian tubules; *phx,* pharynx; *rec,* rectum; *segn,* subesophageal ganglion; *slg,* salivary gland; *sld,* salivary duct; *spth,* spermatheca; *vag,* vagina. (Redrawn from Matheson, by permission of the Comstock Publishing Co.)

rear of the head to the face. The points where the anterior arms of the tentorium meet the face are marked externally by the anterior tentorial pits (*atp*), which are located in the epistomal suture between the frons and the clypeus. The posterior arms of the tentorium meet the head wall at the posterior tentorial pits (*ptp*), which are located at the lower ends of the postoccipital sutures. Some insects have dorsal arms on the tentorium (*dta*), which extend to the upper part of the face near the antennal bases.

Each thoracic segment is usually braced internally by a group of apophyses and apodemes consisting of the phragmata, the furca, and the pleural apophyses (Figure 25). The phragmata represent greatly enlarged antecostae, and they serve as points of attachment for the dorsal longitudinal muscles; they are usually notched medially, and the dorsal aorta lies in this notch. The phragmata are best developed in the wing-bearing segments. The furca is a **Y**-shaped sternal apophysis, or a pair of apophyses; most of the ventral longitudinal muscles attach to it. The pleural apophyses extend inward and downward from the pleural suture to the furca; they serve as the points of attachment for various muscles.

MUSCULAR SYSTEM

The muscular system of an insect is rather complex and consists of from several hundred to a few thousand individual muscles. All are composed of striated muscle cells, even those around the alimentary canal and the heart. The skeletal muscles, which attach to the body wall, move the various parts of the body, including the appendages; they usually attach to the cuticle by means of fine connective fibrils called tonofibrillae, which break down and are reformed at each molt. The locations of the points of attachment of the skeletal muscles are sometimes useful in determining the homologies of various body parts. The visceral muscles, which surround the heart, the alimentary canal, and the ducts of the reproductive system, produce the peristaltic movements that move materials along these tracts; they usually consist of longitudinal and circular muscle fibers.

The muscles moving the appendages are arranged segmentally, generally in antagonistic pairs. Some appendage parts (for example, the galea and lacinia of the maxillae, and the pretarsus) have only flexor muscles; extension of these is usually brought about by blood pressure. Each segment of an appendage normally has its own muscles; the tarsal and flagellar "segments," which are not true segments, do not have their own muscles.

DIGESTIVE SYSTEM

Insects feed upon almost every organic substance found in nature, and their digestive systems exhibit considerable variation—but all have certain features in common. The alimentary canal is a tube, usually somewhat coiled, which extends from the mouth to the anus (Figure 23). It is dif-

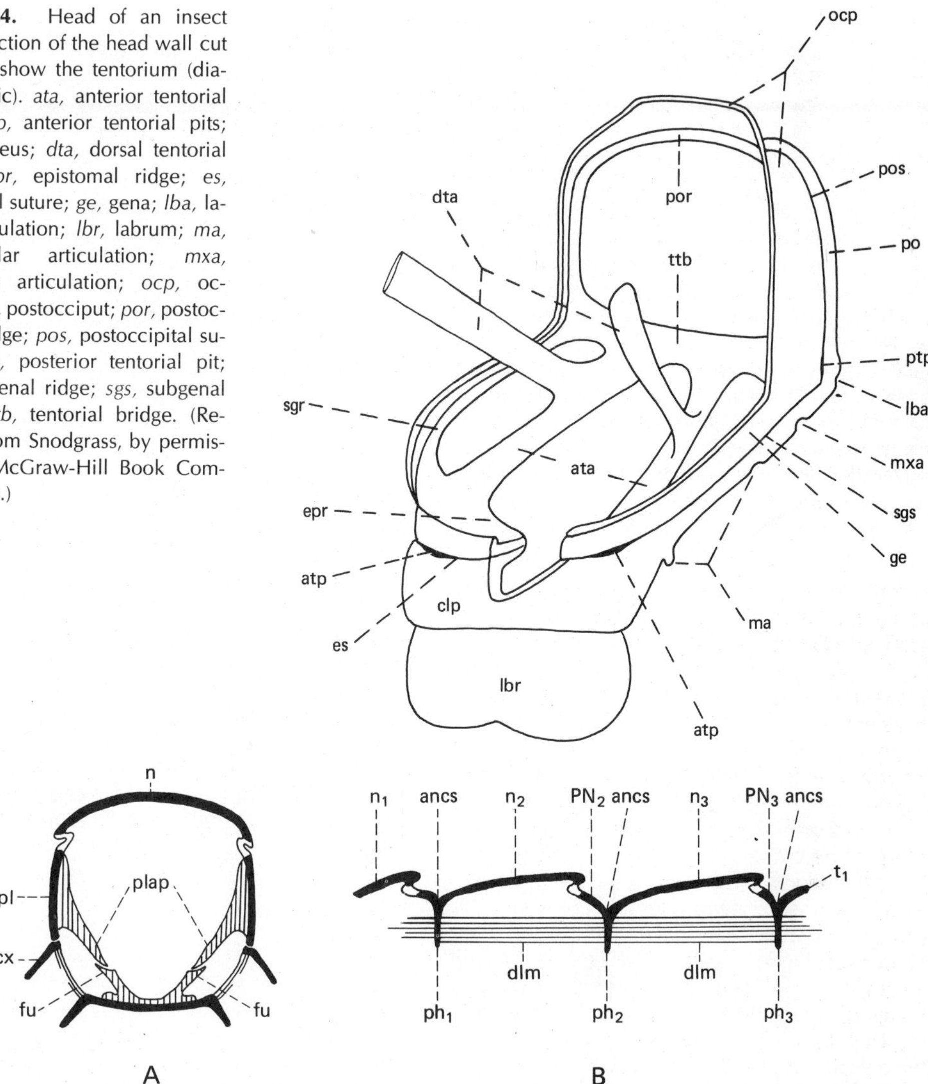

Figure 24. Head of an insect with a section of the head wall cut away to show the tentorium (diagrammatic). *ata,* anterior tentorial arms; *atp,* anterior tentorial pits; *clp,* clypeus; *dta,* dorsal tentorial arms; *epr,* epistomal ridge; *es,* epistomal suture; *ge,* gena; *lba,* labial articulation; *lbr,* labrum; *ma,* mandibular articulation; *mxa,* maxillary articulation; *ocp,* occiput; *po,* postocciput; *por,* postoccipital ridge; *pos,* postoccipital suture; *ptp,* posterior tentorial pit; *sgr,* subgenal ridge; *sgs,* subgenal suture; *ttb,* tentorial bridge. (Redrawn from Snodgrass, by permission of McGraw-Hill Book Company, Inc.)

Figure 25. Endoskeleton of thorax (diagrammatic). A, cross section of a thoracic segment; B, longitudinal section of thoracic dorsum. *ancs,* antecostal suture; *cx,* coxa; *dlm,* dorsal longitudinal muscles; *fu,* sternal apophyses or furca; *n,* notum; n_1, pronotum; n_2, mesonotum; n_3, metanotum; *ph,* phragmata; *pl,* pleuron; *plap,* pleural apophyses; PN_2, mesopostnotum; PN_3, metapostnotum; t_1, first abdominal tergum. (Redrawn from Snodgrass, by permission of McGraw-Hill Book Company, Inc.)

ferentiated into three main regions: the foregut, or stomodaeum; the midgut, or mesenteron; and the hindgut, or proctodaeum. Each of these three regions may be differentiated into two or more subregions. Valves and sphincters between these regions regulate the passage of food from one region to another.

LABIAL GLANDS Most insects possess a pair of glands lying below the anterior part of the alimentary canal (Figure 23, *sgl*). The ducts from these glands extend forward and unite into a common duct that opens near the base of the labium or hypopharynx. These glands are generally called salivary glands, but they do not always secrete saliva; they are perhaps better referred to as labial glands. There is often an enlargement of the duct from each gland that serves as a reservoir for the secretion. The labial glands in the larvae of the Lepidóptera and Hymenóptera secrete silk, which is used in making cocoons and shelters.

THE FOREGUT, OR STOMODAEUM The foregut is usually differentiated into a pharynx (immediately inside the mouth), esophagus (a slender tube extending posteriorly from the pharynx), crop (an enlargement of the posterior end of the esophagus), and the proventriculus; at its posterior end is the stomodaeal valve, which regulates the passage of food and digestive juices between the foregut and midgut. The foregut is lined with a relatively thick layer of cuticle called the intima; the intima is often provided with short hairs or spicules, and in the proventriculus may bear an armature of teeth. Just outside the intima is an epithelial layer; the intima and epithelium are often thrown into longitudinal folds. Outside the epithelium is an inner layer of longitudinal muscles and an outer layer of circular muscles; the longitudinal muscles sometimes have insertions on the intima. The anterior part of the foregut is provided with dilator muscles, which have their origins on the walls and apodemes of the head and thorax, and their insertions on the stomodaeal muscle layers, epithelium, or intima. These are best developed in the pharyngeal region in sucking insects, where they make the pharynx into a sucking pump.

THE MIDGUT, OR MESENTERON The midgut is usually an elongate sac of rather uniform diameter; sometimes it is differentiated into two or more parts. It often bears diverticula (the gastric caeca, Figure 23, *cm*), usually near its anterior end. The midgut does not have a cuticle (though portions of the intima shed from the foregut may be present), nor does it have mucus to lubricate the food and protect the epithelial cells. Instead, the epithelial cells secrete a thin membrane (of chitin and protein) called the peritrophic membrane, which prevents the food from coming into direct contact with the epithelial cells. This membrane is permeable, permitting the exchange of both digestive enzymes and the digestive products that are ready for absorption. It envelops the food and is voided with the excrement. The epithelium of the midgut is thicker than in other parts of the alimentary canal; its inner surface is usually irregular, and it often has fingerlike groups of cells extending into the lumen. Outside the epithelial layer is a muscle layer, similar to that in the foregut but thinner.

THE HINDGUT, OR PROCTODAEUM The hindgut extends from the pyloric valve, which lies between the midgut and hindgut, to the anus; posteriorly it is supported by muscles extending to the abdominal wall. The hindgut is generally differentiated into at least two regions, the anterior intestine and the rectum; the anterior intestine may be a simple tube, or it may be subdivided into an anterior ileum and a posterior colon. The Malpighian tubules, which are excretory in function, arise at the anterior end of the hindgut. The walls of the hindgut have a structure similar to those of the foregut, but the cuticle is thinner and is permeable to water.

THE FILTER CHAMBER Most Homóptera have a peculiar modification of the alimentary canal known as the filter chamber, which serves to extract water from the food reaching the midgut. It consists of two, ordinarily distant, parts of the alimentary tract held close together by connective tissue, the anterior part of the midgut and the anterior part of the hindgut. The midgut in these insects is differentiated into three regions, an anterior enlargement behind the stomodaeal valve (which is enclosed in the filter chamber), a croplike sac behind this, and a long tubular section, which turns anteriorly to reenter the filter chamber.

CIRCULATORY SYSTEM

The circulatory system of an insect is an open one, as compared to the closed system of a vertebrate. The only blood vessel is a tube located dorsal to the alimentary tract and extending through the thorax and abdomen; elsewhere the blood flows through the body cavity. The posterior part of the dorsal vessel, which is divided by valves into a series of chambers, is the heart (Figure 23, *hr*), and the slender anterior part is the dorsal aorta (Figure 23, *ao*). Extending from the lower surface of the heart to the lateral portions of the terga are pairs of sheetlike muscle bands; these constitute a dorsal diaphragm more or less completely separating the region around the heart from the main body cavity. The heart is provided with paired lateral openings called ostia, one pair per heart chamber, through which the blood enters the heart. The number of ostia varies in different insects; in some cases there may be as few as two pairs.

The blood is usually a clear fluid in which are suspended a number of cells (the hemocytes); it is often greenish or yellowish, but is seldom red (it is red in some midge larvae, due to the presence of hemoglobin). It makes up from 5 to 40 percent of the body weight (usually 25 percent or less).

Pulsations of the heart produce the circulation by pumping the blood forward and out of the aorta in the neck region; from here it moves posteriorly through the body cavity. The body cavity lacks the epithelial lining of a true coelome, and serves as a chamber for the circulating blood, and may be called a hemocoele. Most of the organs and tissues of the insect are thus exposed to and bathed by the circulating blood.

TRACHEAL SYSTEM

The intake of oxygen, its distribution to the tissues, and the removal of carbon dioxide are accomplished in most insects by means of an intricate system of tubes called the tracheal system (Figure 26). The principal tubes of this system, the tracheae, open externally at the spiracles (*spr*); internally they branch variously, extend throughout the body, and terminate in very fine branches called tracheoles, which permeate the various tissues. The tracheae are lined with a thin layer of cuticle, which is thickened to form helical rings (the taenidia) that give the tracheae rigidity. The tracheoles (also lined with cuticle) are minute intracellular tubes with thin walls and often contain fluid; they are usually a micron or less in diameter.

The spiracles are located laterally and vary in number from one to ten pairs. There is typically a pair on the anterior margin of the mesothorax, another pair on the anterior margin of the metathorax, and a pair on each of the first eight (or fewer) abdominal segments. They vary in size and shape, and are usually provided with some sort of valvelike closing device.

Tracheal systems may be open or closed. Open tracheal systems have spiracles that can open; such systems occur in most insects. Closed tracheal systems have the spiracles permanently closed, but have a network of tracheae just under the integument—either widely distributed over the body or particularly below certain surfaces (the tracheal gills). Closed systems are found in some aquatic and parasitic insects; some of the special respiratory adaptations occurring in such insects are discussed in Chapter 3, page 42.

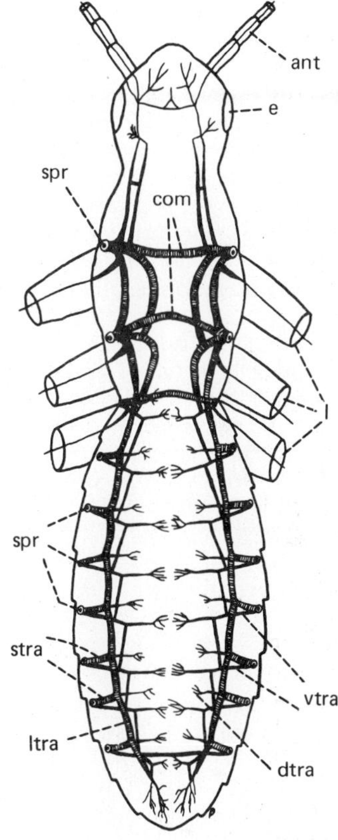

Figure 26. Diagram of a horizontal section of an insect showing the arrangement of the principal tracheae. *ant,* antenna; *com,* commissural tracheae; *dtra,* dorsal trachea; *e,* compound eye; *l,* legs; *ltra,* main longitudinal tracheal trunk; *spr,* spiracles; *stra,* spiracular tracheae; *vtra,* ventral tracheae. (Modified from Fernald and Shepard, after Kolbe, by permission of McGraw-Hill Book Company, Inc.)

EXCRETORY SYSTEM

The excretory system consists of a group of tubes, the Malpighian tubules (Figure 23, *mt*), which arise as evaginations at the anterior end of the hindgut. These tubules vary in number from one or two to over a hundred, and their distal ends are closed. Waste products are taken up from the blood by these tubules and pass out by way of the hindgut and anus.

Glands in the rectum may also be considered as a part of the insect's excretory system, as these glands may remove water and salts from the material reaching the rectum (see page 42).

REPRODUCTIVE SYSTEM

Reproduction in insects is nearly always sexual, and the sexes are separate.[1] Parthenogenesis occurs in many species, and in some of these no males are known. Adult workers of many social insects are unable to reproduce because their sex organs are undeveloped.

The gonads of insects (ovaries in the female and testes in the male) are located in the abdomen; ducts from the gonads open to the outside near the posterior end of the abdomen.

FEMALE REPRODUCTIVE SYSTEM The reproductive system of the female (Figure 27 A) consists of a pair of ovaries, a system of ducts through which the eggs pass to the outside, and some associated structures. Each ovary generally consists of a group of ovarioles (*ovl*); these lead into the oviduct posteriorly, and anteriorly unite in a suspensory ligament (*sl*) that usually attaches to the body wall or to the dorsal diaphragm. The number of ovarioles per ovary varies from 1 to 200 or more, but is usually 4–8. Eggs arise in the upper part of the ovarioles, and become mature as they pass down toward the oviduct. In many insects, all or most of the eggs mature before any are laid, and the egg-swollen ovaries may occupy a large part of the body cavity and may even distend the abdomen. The two oviducts (*ovd*) usually unite posteriorly to form a single duct (*covd*), which enlarges posteriorly into a genital chamber or vagina (*vag*); the vagina extends to the outside. Associated with the vagina are usually a saclike structure called the spermatheca (*spth*), in which sperm are stored, and often various glands (*acg*),

[1] The cottony cushion scale, *Icérya púrchasi* Maskell, is normally hermaphroditic; both sexes are present in one individual, and the eggs of this individual may be fertilized by its sperm.

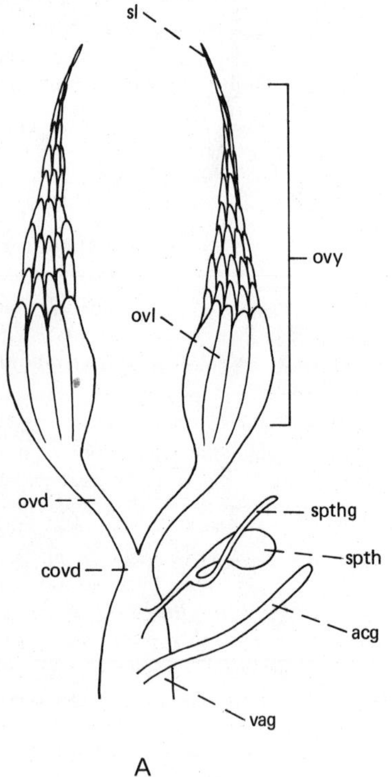

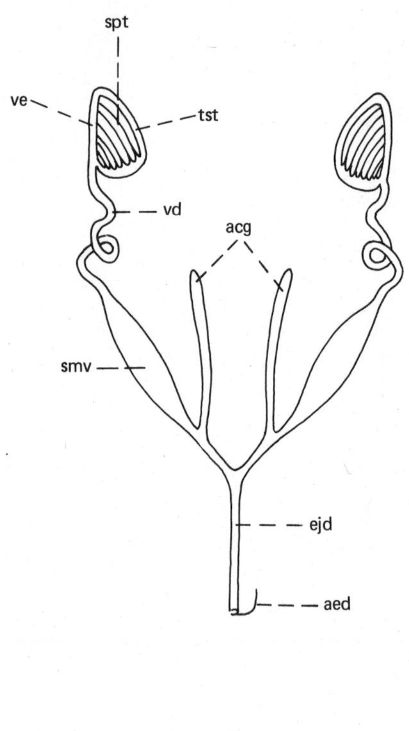

Figure 27. Reproductive systems of an insect. A, female reproductive system; B, male reproductive system. *acg*, accessory gland; *aed*, aedeagus; *covd*, common oviduct; *ejd*, ejaculatory duct; *ovd*, oviduct; *ovl*, ovariole; *ovy*, ovary; *sl*, suspensory ligament; *smv*, seminal vesicle; *spt*, sperm tube; *spth*, spermatheca; *spthg*, spermathecal gland; *tst*, testis; *vag*, genital chamber or vagina; *vd*, vas deferens; *ve*, vas efferens. (Redrawn from Snodgrass, by permission of McGraw-Hill Book Company, Inc.)

which may secrete an adhesive material used to fasten the eggs to some object or provide material that covers the egg mass with a protective coating.

MALE REPRODUCTIVE SYSTEM The reproductive system of the male (Figure 27 B) is similar to that of the female; it consists of a pair of testes (*tst*), ducts to the outside, and accessory glands. Each testis consists of a group of sperm tubes or follicles (*spt*), in which the sperm develop, surrounded by a peritoneal sheath; each sperm tube attaches to the vas deferens by a stalklike vas efferens (*ve*). The vas deferens (*vd*) is the tube leading posteriorly from each testis; the two vasa deferentia unite posteriorly to form an ejaculatory duct (*ejd*), which opens to the outside on a penis or an aedeagus. In some insects there is an enlargement on each vas deferens in which sperm are stored; these enlargements are called seminal vesicles (*smv*). The accessory glands (*acg*) secrete a liquid that serves as a carrier for the sperm or which hardens about them to form a sperm-containing capsule called a spermatophore.

The above accounts describe the generalized condition; many variations occur in the features of these two systems. A few groups have paired genital openings to the outside, with the ducts from the gonads not meeting to form a common duct. In the female, variations occur in the number and shape of the ovarioles, the way the developing eggs are nourished, the form of the oviducts, the number and character of the accessory glands, and in the form of the spermatheca; variations in the spermatheca are sometimes used as taxonomic characters. Comparable variations occur in the male system, but the principal variations in the male that are of taxonomic value are those of the external genitalia (see page 26).

THE FAT BODY

The fat body is an aggregation of cells located in the body cavity; its location and degree of compactness varies in different insects. It serves as a food-storage reservoir and is an important site of intermediate metabolism. It is best developed in the late nymphal or larval instars. By the end of metamorphosis it is often depleted. Some adult insects that do not feed retain their fat body in adult life and "live off it."

NERVOUS SYSTEM

The central nervous system of an insect consists of a brain located in the head above the esophagus, a subesophageal ganglion[2] connected to the brain by two commissures that extend around each side of the esophagus (Figures 23 and 28, *cec*), and a ventral nerve cord extending posteriorly from the subesophageal ganglion. The brain (Figure 28) consists of three pairs of lobes, the protocerebrum, deutocerebrum, and tritocerebrum. The protocerebrum innervates the compound eyes and ocelli, and the deutocerebrum innervates the antennae; the tritocerebrum innervates the labrum and foregut, and the circumesophageal connectives connect it with the subesophageal ganglion. The two lobes of the tritocerebrum are separated by the esophagus, and are connected by a commissure that passes under the esophagus. The ventral nerve cord is typically double and contains segmentally located ganglia; occasionally some of these ganglia fuse, and there may be fewer ganglia than segments.

The size of the brain in relation to body size varies considerably in different insects; it is generally larger in those insects having more complex behavior. Some sample ratios of brain volume to total body volume are 1:4200 in a predaceous diving beetle, 1:460 in an ichneumon, and 1:174 in a bee.

SENSE ORGANS

The sense organs of insects are located mainly in the body wall, and most of them are microscopic in size; each is usually excited by only a specific stimulus. Insects have sense organs receptive to mechanical, chemical, auditory, visual, and other types of stimuli.

THE CHEMICAL SENSES

The chemical senses are those of taste and smell; the principal differences between these two is that taste is detected by contact and smell is detected from a distance. The sensilla involved are subject to some variation but generally consist of a group of sensory nerve cells whose distal processes form a bundle extending to the body surface (Figure 29 C). The endings of the sensory processes may be in a thin-walled peglike structure (Figure 29 C, *scn*); the peglike process may be sunk in a pit, or the sensory processes may end in a thin cuticular plate set over a cavity in the cuticle. In some cases the endings of the sensory processes may lie in a pit in the body wall and not be covered by cuticle.

[2] This ganglion is sometimes located below the pharynx.

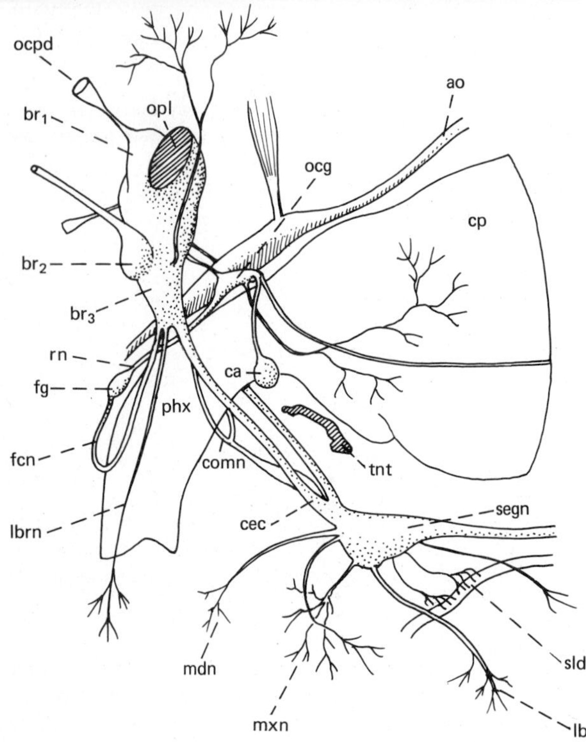

Figure 28. Anterior part of the nervous system of a grasshopper. *ao,* dorsal aorta; *br*$_1$*,* protocerebrum; *br*$_2$*,* deutocerebrum; *br*$_3$*, tritocerebrum; ca,* corpus allatum; *cec,* circumesophageal connective; *comn,* tritocerebral commissure; *cp,* crop; *fcn,* frontal ganglion connective; *fg,* frontal ganglion; *lbn,* labial nerve; *lbrn,* labral nerve; *mdn,* mandibular nerve; *mxn,* maxillary nerve; *ocg,* occipital ganglion; *ocpd,* ocellar pedicel; *opl,* optic lobe, *phx,* pharynx; *rn,* recurrent nerve; *segn,* subesophageal ganglion; *sld,* salivary duct; *tnt,* tentorium. (Redrawn from Snodgrass, by permission of McGraw-Hill Book Company, Inc.)

The organs of taste are located principally on the mouth parts, but some insects (for example, ants, bees, and wasps) also have taste organs on the antennae, and some (for example, butterflies, moths, and flies) have taste organs on the tarsi. The organs of smell are located principally on the antennae (in some cases also on the palps, and possibly the tarsi). The chemical senses of insects are often extremely keen, much more so than those of man; many insects can detect odors at very great distances (in some instances a few miles).

THE MECHANICAL SENSES

The sense organs receptive to mechanical stimuli (touch, pressure, vibration, etc.) are of three principal types: hair sensilla, campaniform sensilla, and scolopophorous organs. The simplest type of tactile receptor is a hair sensillum, or a seta provided with a nerve cell (Figure 29 A). A process from the nerve cell extends to the base of the seta, and movements of the seta initiate impulses in the nerve cell. A campaniform sensillum is similar to a hair sensillum, but there is no seta; the nerve ending lies just under a domelike area of the cuticle (Figure 29 B). Scolopophorous organs are more complex sensilla and consist of a bundle of sensory cells whose endings are attached to the body wall; they are sensitive to movements of the body (including pressure and vibration). These organs are widely distributed over the body, and are of various sorts; they include subgenual organs (usually located at the proximal end of the tibia), Johnston's organ (in the second antennal segment, and sensitive to movements of the antennae), and the tympanal organs (involved in hearing; see "Auditory Organs").

AUDITORY ORGANS

Insects detect airborne sounds by means of two types of sense organs, hair sensilla and tympanal organs; vibrations of the substrate are detected by subgenual organs (see "The Mechanical Senses").

Many insects apparently have hair sensilla by which they detect sound, but the particular hairs having this function are not always known. In some of the Díptera (for example, mosquitoes), however, it is known that the hairs of the antennae are involved in hearing (the sensilla being Johnston's organ, in the second antennal segment).

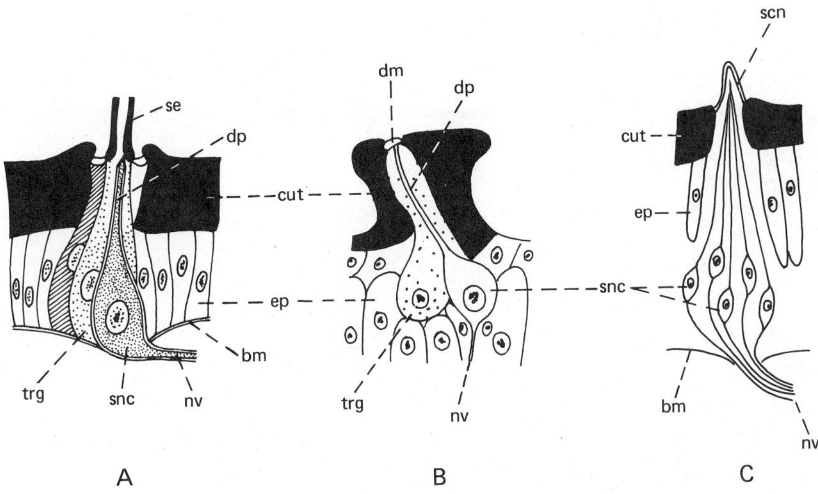

Figure 29. Insect sensilla. A, hair sensillum; B, campaniform sensillum; C, chemoreceptor. *bm,* basement membrane; *cut,* cuticle; *dm,* domelike layer of cuticle over nerve ending; *dp,* distal process of sensory cell; *ep,* epidermis; *nv,* nerve; *scn,* sense cone; *se,* seta; *snc,* sensory cell; *trg,* trichogen cell. (Redrawn from Snodgrass, by permission of McGraw-Hill Book Company, Inc.)

Tympanal organs are scolopophorous organs in which the sensory cells are attached to (or very near to) tympanic membranes. The number of sensory cells involved ranges from one or two (for example, in the tympanal organs of certain moths) up to several hundred. The tympanic membrane (or tympanum) is a very thin membrane with air on both sides of it.

Tympanal organs are present in certain Orthóptera, Homóptera, and Lepidóptera. The tympana of short-horned grasshoppers (Acrídidae) are located on the sides of the first abdominal segment; those of long-horned grasshoppers (Tettigonìidae) and crickets (Grýllidae), when present, are located at the proximal end of the front tibiae (Figure 19, *tym*). Some moths have tympana on the dorsal surface of the metathorax. The tympana of cicadas are located on the first abdominal segment (Figure 206, *tym*).

ORGANS OF VISION

An organ of vision is one sensitive to light rays. Some of the sensilla described above may be sensitive to light and function as light receptors if the cuticular part of the sensillum is translucent; such photoreceptors apparently occur in many larvae, but are not generally called "eyes." An essential feature of an eye is a transparency of the overlying cuticle (forming a cornea). The sense cells of insect eyes differ from those in other sensilla in lacking terminal processes, and the receptive part of each cell consists of fine striations on the surface of the cell (resolved by the electron microscope as closely packed microvilli). The striated parts of two or more adjacent cells are usually united to form an optic rod, or rhabdom.

The eyes of insects are of two general types, simple and compound. Simple eyes are usually called ocelli, but the ocelli of the adult ("dorsal" ocelli, located more or less dorsally on the head) are a little different from the "lateral" ocelli (or stemmata) of larvae. Simple eyes are present in some larvae and nymphs and in many adults; most adult insects have compound eyes.

Simple eyes have a single corneal lens that is somewhat elevated or domelike; beneath the lens are two cell layers, the corneagenous cells and the retina (Figure 30 A). The cornea is usually thickened to form a convex lens. The corneagenous cells, which secrete the cornea, are transparent. The rhabdoms of the retinal cells are in the outer part of the retina; the basal portions of the retinal cells are often pigmented. The lateral ocelli of larvae differ from the dorsal ocelli of adults in having a crystalline lens beneath the corneal lens (Figure 30 B, *crl*). The ocelli apparently do not perceive form, but are sensitive to light intensity.

A compound eye is composed of many (up to several thousand) individual units called omma-

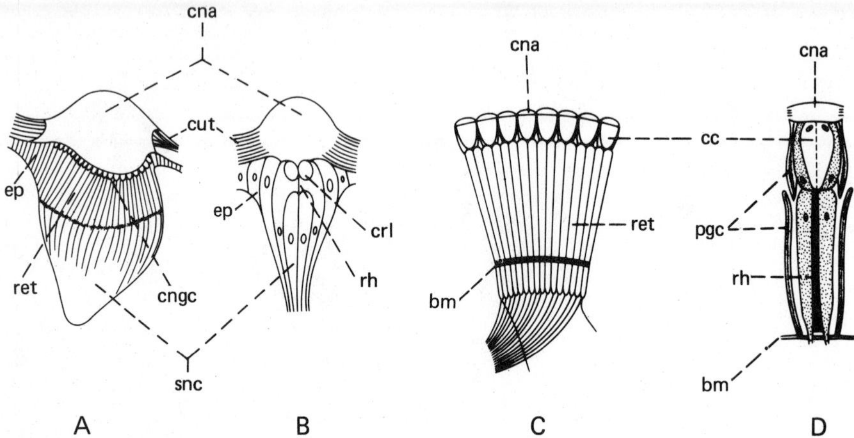

Figure 30. Eye structure in insects (diagrammatic). A, dorsal ocellus of an ant; B, lateral ocellus of a caterpillar; C, vertical section of part of a compound eye; D, ommatidium of a compound eye. *bm,* basement membrane; *cc,* crystalline cone; *cna,* cornea; *cnge,* corneagenous cells; *crl,* crystalline lens; *cut,* cuticle; *ep,* epidermis; *pgc,* pigment cells; *ret,* retina; *rh,* rhabdom; *snc,* sensory cells of retina. (A–C redrawn from Snodgrass, by permission of McGraw-Hill Book Co., Inc.; D redrawn from Matheson, by permission of Comstock Pub. Co.)

tidia (Figure 30 C, D). Each ommatidium is an elongate group of cells capped externally by a hexagonal corneal lens. Beneath the corneal lens is usually a crystalline cone of four cells surrounded by two pigmented corneagenous cells, and beneath the crystalline cone is a group of elongate sensory cells (usually eight in number) surrounded by a sheath of epidermal pigment cells. The striated portions of the sensory cells form a central or axial rhabdom in the ommatidium. The corneal lenses are usually convex externally, forming the facets of the eye.

The ommatidia in most diurnal insects are generally surrounded by pigment; only light rays perpendicular to the lens reach the rhabdom, the oblique rays being absorbed by the pigmented sheath of the ommatidium (apposition eye). The picture obtained by the insect is thus a sort of mosaic. In nocturnal insects the pigment is limited to the basal portions of the ommatidia, and oblique light rays entering the cornea may reach rhabdoms of neighboring ommatidia (superposition eye). In some insects the pigment may move outward or inward, depending on the light intensity.

OTHER SENSE ORGANS

Insects usually have a well-developed temperature sense; the sense organs involved are distributed all over the body, but are more numerous on the antennae and legs. It is probable that these organs are specialized thermal receptors. Some insects have a well-developed humidity sense, but little is known of the sensory mechanism involved.

References on the Anatomy of Insects

Butt, F. H. 1960. Head development in the arthropods. *Biol. Rev.*, 35(1):43–91; 15 f.

Chapman, R. F. 1971. *The Insects, Structure and Function.* New York: American Elsevier, xii + 819 pp., 541 f.

Comstock, J. H. 1940 (9th ed.). *An Introduction to Entomology.* Ithaca, N.Y.: Comstock Publ., xix + 1064 pp., 1228 f.

DuPorte, E. M. 1957. The comparative morphology of the insect head. *Ann. Rev. Ent.*, 2(1):55–70; 7 f.

Essig, E. O. 1942. *College Entomology.* New York: Macmillan, vii + 900 pp., 305 f.

Hamilton, K. G. A. 1971–1972. The insect wing. Part I: Origin and development of wings from notal lobes. *J. Kan. Ent. Soc.*, 44(4):421–433; 18 f. (1971). Part II: Vein homology and the archetypal wing. *Ibid.*,

45(1):54–58; 5 f. (1972). Part III: Venation of the orders. *Ibid.*, 45(2):145–162; 29 f. (1972). Part IV: Venational trends and the phylogeny of the winged orders. *Ibid.*, 45(3):295–308; 35 f. (1972).

Imms, A. D. 1957 (9th ed., revised by O. W. Richards and R. G. Davies). *A General Textbook of Entomology*. New York: E. P. Dutton, x + 886 pp., 609 f.

Manton, S. M. 1960. Concerning head development in the arthropods. *Biol. Rev.*, 35(2):265–282; 3 f.

Matsuda, R. 1958. On the origin of the external genitalia of insects. *Ann. Ent. Soc. Amer.*, 51(1):84–94.

Matsuda, R. 1963. Some evolutionary aspects of the insect thorax. *Ann. Rev. Ent.*, 8:59–76; 3 f.

Matsuda, R. 1970. Morphology and evolution of the insect thorax. *Mem. Ent. Soc. Canada*, No. 76; 431 pp., 172 f.

Peterson, A. 1915. Morphological studies on the head and mouthparts of the Thysanoptera. *Ann. Ent. Soc. Amer.*, 8(1):20–67; 7 pl.

Richards, A. G. 1951. *The Integument of Arthropods*. Minneapolis: Univ. Minnesota Press, xvi + 411 pp., 65 f.

Ross, H. H. 1965 (3rd ed.). *A Textbook of Entomology*. New York: Wiley, ix + 539 pp., 401 f.

Schmitt, J. B. 1962. The comparative anatomy of the insect nervous system. *Ann. Rev. Ent.*, 7:137–156; 1 f.

Scudder, G. G. E. 1961. The comparative morphology of the insect ovipositor. *Trans. Roy. Ent. Soc. London*, 113(2):25–40; 10 f.

Scudder G. G. E. 1971. Comparative morphology of insect genitalia. *Ann. Rev. Ent., 16:379–406*.

Snodgrass, R. E. 1935. *Principles of Insect Morphology*. New York: McGraw-Hill, x + 667 pp., 319 f.

Snodgrass, R. E. 1952. *A Textbook of Arthropod Anatomy*. Ithaca, N.Y.: Comstock Publ., viii + 363 pp., 88 f.

Snodgrass, R. E. 1957. A revised interpretation of the external reproductive organs of male insects. *Smiths. Misc. Coll.*, 135(6):1–60; 15 f.

Snodgrass, R. E. 1960. Facts and theories concerning the insect head. *Smiths. Misc. Coll.*,142(1):1–61; 21 f.

Tillyard, R. J. 1926. *The Insects of Australia and New Zealand*. Sydney, Australia: Angus & Robertson, xi + 560 pp.; illus.

Waterhouse, D. F. *et al.* 1970. *Insects of Australia*. Canberra: Melbourne Univ. Press. xiii + 1029 pp.; illus. (especially Ch. 1–2, pp. 3–71; 71 f.).

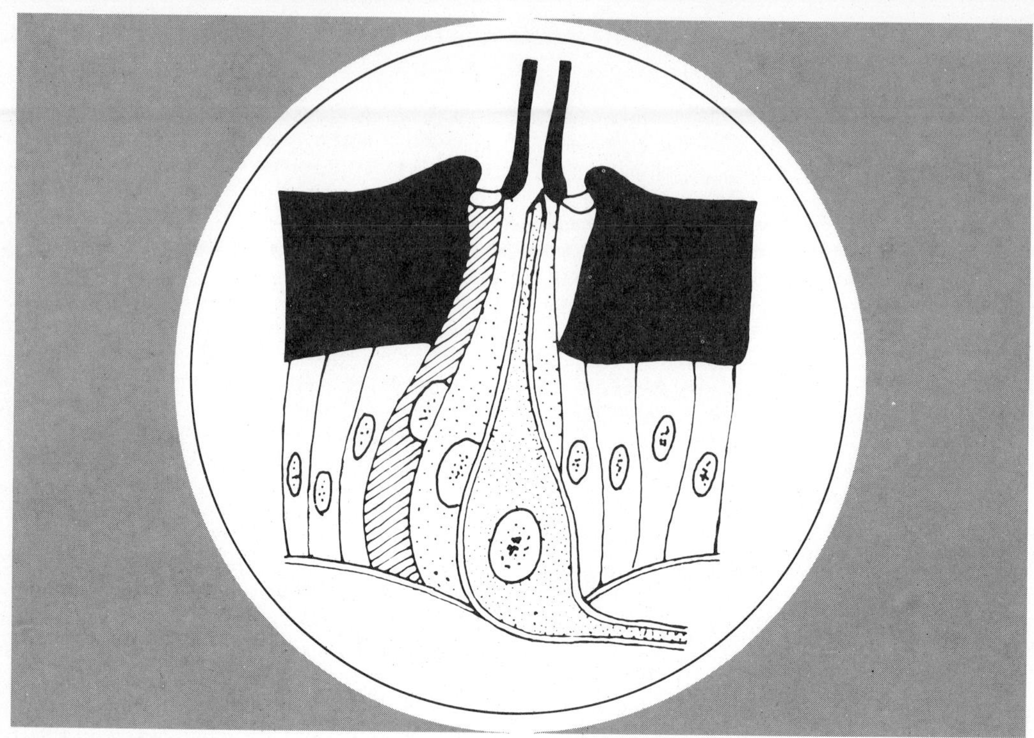

3: THE PHYSIOLOGY OF INSECTS

In the preceding chapter we were concerned primarily with the structure of insects; here we are concerned with how these structures function, how the insect carries on its various life processes. An understanding of insect physiology is essential to an understanding of how these insects live, and how they can be controlled.

Various aspects of insect physiology are treated in this chapter under separate headings, but it should be understood that all these phenomena are interrelated and interdependent, and our organization of this discussion is a purely arbitrary one.

Since insects are living animals, their life processes are much like those of other animals; the peculiarities of *insect* physiology, as compared to the physiology of other animals, are correlated with the particular structures (organs) that insects have (outlined in the preceding chapter). The major peculiarities of insect physiology have to do with their possession of an exoskeleton, which affects the way they grow and the way they carry on various physiological processes.

THE BODY WALL

FUNCTIONS

The body wall of an insect has three major functions: (1) protection, (2) reception of external stimuli, and (3) service as an exoskeleton. As the outer covering of the insect it surrounds and protects the internal organs, and its hardness serves as an armor against shock and abrasions; it also serves as a barrier to the entrance of inimical organisms or substances, and as a barrier to water loss by evaporation. It acts as the insect's contact with its external environment and contains most of the animal's sense organs. As an exoskeleton, it not only provides support but also serves as an element of the locomotor mechanisms, as muscles are attached to it. The properties of the body wall have effects on many aspects of insect biology.

PENETRATION OF SUBSTANCES THROUGH THE BODY WALL

WATER The small size of insects means that the ratio of body surface to volume is higher than in larger animals; hence the potential for water loss by evaporation from the body surface is greater than in larger animals. Water may be lost through the tracheal system, but the insect can minimize this by closing its spiracles. The epicuticular layer of the body wall offers a considerable resistance to water loss by evaporation, due principally to the thin layer of lipids (chiefly waxes) on its surface. High temperatures (which change the character of these lipids) or abrasions of the epicuticle increase the rate of evaporation from the body surface.

Some insects and other arthropods are capable of absorbing water vapor from the air when the relative humidity is fairly high (90 percent or higher). The absorption is apparently through the cuticle; the cuticle may be somewhat hygroscopic, but the absorption is thought to depend upon the activity of the epidermal cells.

The insect cuticle is generally not easily wetted by water. A small insect coming in contact with a water surface will be supported by the surface film; many insects can walk around on the surface of water without breaking this film, or can hang from it with the body submerged (for example, mosquito larvae). If an insect covered with short thick pubescence submerges, it will carry with it a thin film of air in this pubescence. If one wants to get an insect wet (for example, with an insect spray that acts as a contact poison), it is generally necessary to add a wetting agent (such as a detergent) to the spray.

GASES It is obvious that the cuticular surface overlying chemoreceptors and respiratory surfaces must be permeable to some gases; otherwise these structures could not function. Most gases enter or leave the body via the tracheal system, but there may be some diffusion through the body wall.

OTHER SUBSTANCES These include many things, such as salts, nonelectrolytes, and insecticides. Different substances penetrate the cuticle at different rates; lipid-soluble substances usually penetrate better than substances that are not lipid-soluble, wetting agents speed up the penetration of water-soluble substances, and mixtures sometimes penetrate faster than the components of the mixture would penetrate if by themselves. Penetration is faster through some areas of the cuticle, such as articular membranes, cuticular sensilla, and (generally) areas where the cuticle is thinner.

CONSEQUENCES OF THE POSSESSION OF AN EXOSKELETON

The possession of an exoskeleton has certain consequences for insects and other arthropods; it is in many ways an advantageous arrangement, but on the other hand it imposes certain limitations. It may be of interest to consider briefly some of the consequences of possessing an exoskeleton.

An exoskeleton—a supporting structure on the outside of the body—must have a certain amount of rigidity; hence it serves not only as support but also as protection. External armor (body hardness) is well developed in most insects that lack other specialized means of protection; it is less developed in insects with protective coloration or chemical means of defense, and in insects that live in protected situations. It is perhaps best developed in the beetles, and is undoubtedly one of the reasons why beetles are such a successful group (more than 40 percent of all the species of insects are beetles).

An exoskeleton is inherently stronger than an endoskeleton. A hollow cylinder is stronger, sometimes much stronger, than a solid cylinder made of the same amount of material. The area of an exoskeleton on which muscles can be attached is much greater than that of an endoskeleton, and this greater area permits a more advantageous placement of the muscles with respect to their leverages.

The exoskeleton is a factor making possible aerial life in insects, in that it protects the insect from injury in collision. Insects may often crash into an obstacle with a force that would completely wreck a vertebrate, and take off again unharmed. This protection against shock, afforded by the exoskeleton, is in part due to the strength of the exoskeleton itself and in part to the insect's small size. The deforming force of a crash is the product of the speed of the animal and its weight, and hence decreases as the weight decreases; the smaller the insect, the greater the protective power of its exoskeleton.

The surface of a body varies with the square of its radius, while the volume or mass varies with the cube of the radius. As a body decreases in size, the surface/volume ratio increases, and in a terrestrial animal such as an insect this increased surface/volume ratio increases the likelihood of water loss by evaporation from the body surface. The exoskeleton counteracts this effect because it is relatively impervious and serves as a protection against desiccation.

The presence of an exoskeleton (with very limited powers of expansion and no ability to grow once it is formed) means that the growth of the animal must be discontinuous, that is, accompanied by periodic shedding and renewal of the exoskeleton. The process of molting is described below (page 77), but an important point to note here is that immediately after the molt the exoskeleton is quite soft. A land arthropod preserves its shape at this critical period by the strength of its soft tissues or (in some larger insects) by the inflation of air spaces. This mechanism works all right for a small animal, but a larger animal would collapse at the time of the molt. The largest arthropods (some crustaceans), which approach or surpass many vertebrates in size, molt in water, which provides them with a considerable amount of support. Terrestrial animals that periodically shed their exoskeleton are thus restricted to small size.

Restriction to small size has a number of effects. A small animal can live in situations not available to larger animals, and since such situations are innumerable and very diverse, there can be a great many different kinds of small animals. Small size usually means a shorter life span, which means more opportunity for mutation and hence a greater potential for evolutionary change. On the other hand, small size means less space for complex organ systems; a small nervous system limits the complexity of behavior, and limits it largely to instinctive behavior.[1] Small size generally restricts an animal to coldbloodedness, which prevents activity in cold weather; insects in temperate or arctic climates are dormant a large part of the time.

Periodic ecdysis has made possible the evolution of metamorphosis in insects. Metamorphosis, especially of the complete type (see Chapter 5), has two general effects: it means that one stage can be specialized for feeding and another for reproduction and dispersal (thereby increasing efficiency), and it enables the insect to utilize different habitats in the course of its life cycle.

The presence of an exoskeleton has also had an effect on the nature and efficiency of the sense organs developed. Organs of smell can be on practically any part of the body, and being on the body surface they can be more effective than such organs located internally; insects generally have extremely sensitive organs of smell. On the other hand, their organs of hearing and sight are probably less efficient than those of a vertebrate; highly discriminating ears and eyes require relatively great morphological complexity and size .

DIGESTION AND NUTRITION

Digestion is the process of changing food chemically so that it may be absorbed and supply nutriment to various parts of the body. This process may begin even before the food is ingested, but usually occurs as the ingested materials pass through the digestive tract. Solid foods are broken down by various mechanical means (chiefly the mouth parts and the teeth in the proventriculus), and all foods are subjected to a battery of enzymes as they pass through the digestive tract.

Insects feed on a great variety of living, dead, and decomposing animals and plants, and on plant and animal products; in some cases, blood or plant juices may constitute their entire food supply. The digestive system varies considerably with the different kinds of foods utilized. The food habits may vary greatly in a given order; larvae and adults usually have entirely different food habits and different types of digestive systems, and some adults do not feed at all.

Most insects take food into the body through the mouth. Some larvae that live endoparasitically in a host animal are able to absorb food through the surface of their bodies from host tissues. Many insects have chewing mandibles and maxillae that cut, crush, or macerate food materials and force them into the pharynx. In sucking insects the pharynx functions as a pump that brings liquid foods through the beak into the esophagus. Food

[1] It is interesting to note that those insects having more complex behavior generally have a relatively larger brain (see page 33); the brain in some social insects is relatively larger than that in some vertebrates.

is moved along the alimentary canal by peristaltic action.

Saliva is usually added to the food, either as it enters the alimentary canal or before, as in the case of many sucking insects that inject it into the fluids they siphon up as foods. Saliva is generally produced by the labial glands. The labial glands of many insects produce amylase; in certain bees these glands secrete invertase, which is later taken into the body with nectar. In blood-sucking insects such as mosquitoes, the saliva generally contains no digestive enzymes but contains a substance that prevents coagulation of the blood and the consequent mechanical plugging of the food channel; it is this saliva that causes the irritation produced by the bite of a blood-sucking insect.

Many insects eject digestive enzymes upon food, and partial digestion may occur before the food is ingested. Flesh fly larvae discharge proteolytic enzymes onto their food, and aphids inject amylase into the plant tissues and thus digest starch in the food plant. Extraintestinal digestion also occurs in the prey of larvae of antlions and predaceous diving beetles and in the case of bugs that feed on dry seeds.

After ingestion the food passes through the esophagus into the posterior part of the foregut; this latter region often serves as a crop where food is stored and in which partial digestion may take place. The foregut is lined with cuticle, and very little absorption (except possibly of fats) takes place here. The proventriculus, at the posterior end of the foregut and the entrance to the midgut, may be supplied with large or sharp teeth; when the food consists of coarse particles these teeth serve as separators or may even break up the particles into smaller pieces.

The midgut is lined with epithelial cells; no cuticle is present in this part of the alimentary tract (though the food here is surrounded by a peritrophic membrane in chewing insects; see page 30). Some of the epithelial cells produce enzymes, and others absorb digested food; sometimes secretion and absorption are carried out by the same cells. Enzymes may be released into the lumen of the midgut by the disintegration of the secretory cells (holocrine secretion), or may diffuse through the cell membrane into the lumen (merocrine secretion). Most of the absorption takes place in the midgut.

The types of digestive enzymes produced are associated to a large degree with the insect's food habits. In some cases, such as the clothes moths that digest keratin or hair, the enzymes produced are very specific for these substances. Omnivorous insects usually produce a more general group of enzymes, including lipases (fat-digesting enzymes), carbohydrases (enzymes digesting starch and sugars), and proteolytic (protein-digesting) enzymes. The enzymes produced by blood-sucking insects are mostly proteolytic.

After the food is digested and for the most part absorbed, the residue passes into the hindgut, where some absorption may take place. Water absorption occurs in the midgut and hindgut (particularly in the rectum of the hindgut), especially in insects feeding on stored grain or living in very dry conditions, where water is conserved and reused. In such cases the fecal pellets are dry and are compressed and expelled by the heavy muscles of the rectum.

Only a few species of insects produce enzymes that digest cellulose, but some are able to utilize cellulose as food because of a fauna of microorganisms present in their digestive tracts. These microorganisms, usually bacteria or flagellated protozoans, can digest the cellulose, and the insect can utilize the cellulose digestion products. Such microorganisms are present in many termites and wood-boring beetles, sometimes in considerable numbers; they are often housed in special organs adjacent to the gut.

Insects feeding on blood, plant juices, or other liquid foods are equipped with various special arrangements for extracting a large percentage of the water from the food before it comes in contact with the digestive enzymes. In the blood-sucking Hemíptera the blood meal is temporarily stored in the crop; the water is absorbed through the crop wall into the blood and passes to the hindgut by way of the Malpighian tubules. In the case of the Homóptera, in which large quantities of plant juices are taken into the body, the excess water is extracted by a filter chamber (see page 30); the presence of this filter chamber is one feature that distinguishes most Homóptera from the Hemíptera.

The nutritional requirements of insects include the same ten amino acids that are essential for man (arginine, histidine, isoleucine, leucine, lysine, methionine, phenylalanine, threonine, tryptophane, and valine), a number of B vitamins, sterols (such as cholesterol or stigmasterol), some nucleic acid derivatives, and several minerals. Insects are unable to synthesize some amino acids (the ten listed above) and sterols, and must obtain them from their food. Most insects require several vitamins of the B group (for example, thiamin, riboflavin, pyridoxine, and nicotinic acid); in some cases the essential vitamins are furnished by symbiotic organisms. The minerals required include calcium, potassium, phosphorus, iron, copper, cobalt, and many others. The quantity and quality of the food has considerable effect on the growth rate of the insect and sometimes on reproductive processes.

A mosquito larva is generally unable to store enough protein nutrient for subsequent egg production when it becomes an adult female. Most female mosquitoes must feed on blood to get these nutrients before they can lay any eggs. *Anópheles* and *Aèdes* mosquitoes have produced eggs after feeding on a diet of egg albumen and skimmed milk, or on one composed of amino acids, dextrose, fructose, and a salt mixture. No eggs are produced by females of *Anópheles quadrimaculàtus* Say or *Aèdes aegýpti* (L.) that are fed a diet of sugar alone, although these females will remain alive and vigorous for long periods on such a diet. The males, which do not suck blood, produce sperm on a diet of carbohydrates alone.

The water requirements are very different in different types of insects, although the water and salt content of the blood is essentially the same in all. Leaf-feeding insects obtain great quantities of water with their food, and the body water loss is usually high. Aquatic insects such as mosquito larvae must excrete water and conserve salts. On the other hand, insects feeding on stored grain obtain little water with their food and conserve practically all of it, while excess salts are excreted. In some cases the water is so completely extracted in the rectum that the excrement consists of dry pellets. Water in some cases may be obtained chiefly through the metabolic processes, such as the oxidation of foods. Insects such as the mealworm are able under conditions of high humidity to absorb moisture from the air (see page 39).

RESPIRATION

We are concerned here with gas transport—the uptake of oxygen from the environment and its distribution to the tissues, and the elimination of carbon dioxide. Gas transport in insects is a function of the tracheal system; the circulatory system usually plays no significant role in this process.

In insects with an open tracheal system (one having the spiracles functional) air enters the body through the spiracles, passes through the tracheae to the tracheoles, and oxygen ultimately enters the cells of the body by diffusion; carbon dioxide leaves the body in a similar fashion. The spiracles may be partly or completely closed for extended periods in some insects; water loss through the spiracles may be minimized in this way. The movement of air through the tracheal system is by simple diffusion in many small insects, but in most larger insects this movement is augmented by active ventilation, chiefly by abdominal muscles (for example, in a grasshopper); the movements of the internal organs, or of the legs and wings, may also aid ventilation. Where ventilation occurs, air may move in and out of each spiracle, but generally enters through the anterior spiracles and leaves through the posterior ones. Valves in the spiracles regulate the passage of air through these openings. Sections of the main tracheal trunks are often dilated to form air sacs which assist in ventilation and give buoyancy to a flying insect.

In insects with a closed tracheal system, gases enter and leave the body by diffusion through the body wall between the tracheae and the environment, and the movement of gases through the tracheal system is by diffusion.

RESPIRATION IN AQUATIC INSECTS

A great many insects (nymphs, larvae, and adults) live in water; these insects get their oxygen from one (rarely both) of two sources, the oxygen dissolved in the water and atmospheric air.

Gaseous exchange in many small, soft-bodied aquatic nymphs and larvae (and possibly in some adults) occurs by diffusion through the body wall, usually into and out of a tracheal system. The body wall in some cases is unmodified except perhaps for having a fairly rich tracheal network just under the integument; in other cases there are special thin extensions of the body wall that have a rich tracheal supply and through which the gaseous exchange occurs. These latter structures are called tracheal gills, and may be of various forms and located on various parts of the body. The gills in mayfly nymphs are in the form of leaflike structures on the sides of the first seven abdominal segments (Figure 93); in dragonfly nymphs (Anisóptera) they are in the form of folds in the rectum, and water is moved through the anus into and out of the rectum and over these folds; in damselfly nymphs the gills are in the form of three leaflike structures at the end of the abdomen (Figure 103) as well as folds in the rectum; in stonefly nymphs the gills are fingerlike or branched structures located around the bases of the legs or on the basal abdominal segments (Figure 140 B). Gaseous exchange may occur through the general body surface in these insects, and in some cases (for example, damselfly nymphs) the exchange through the body surface may be more important than that through the tracheal gills.

Insects that live in water and get their oxygen from atmospheric air (some larvae, many nymphs, and all adults) get this air in one of three general ways: from the air spaces in the submerged parts of certain aquatic plants, through spiracles placed at the water surface (with the body of the insect submerged), or from a film of air held somewhere on the surface of the body while the insect is submerged. A few larvae (for example, those of the beetle genus *Donàcia* and the mosquito genus *Mansònia*) have their spiracles in spines at the posterior end of the body, and these spines are inserted into the air spaces of submerged aquatic plants. Many aquatic insects (for example, waterscorpions, rattailed maggots, and the larvae of culicine mosquitoes) have a breathing tube at the posterior end of the body, which is extended to the surface; hydrophobic hairs around the end of this tube enable the insect to hang from the surface film, and they prevent water from entering the breathing tube. Other aquatic insects (for example, backswimmers and the larvae of anopheline mosquitoes) get air through posterior spiracles that are placed at the water surface; they do not have an extended breathing tube.

The insects that get their oxygen from atmospheric air at the water surface do not spend all their time at the surface; they can submerge and remain under water for a considerable period, getting oxygen from an air store either inside or outside the body. The air stores in the tracheae of a mosquito larva, for example, enable the larva to remain under water for a considerable period.

Many aquatic bugs and beetles carry a thin film of air somewhere on the surface of the body when they submerge; this film is usually under the wings or on the ventral side of the body. This air film acts like a physical gill, and the insect may obtain several times as much oxygen from it as was originally in it as a result of the gaseous exchanges between the air film and the surrounding water. A few insects (for example, elmid beetles) have a permanent layer of air around the body surface, held there by a body covering of thick fine hydrophobic hairs; such a layer is sometimes called a gaseous plastron. The air reservoirs of aquatic insects not only play a role in gaseous exchange, but may also have a hydrostatic function (like the swim bladder of fishes); the two crescent-shaped air sacs in *Chaóborus* larvae (Figure 466 A) are apparently used to regulate this insect's specific gravity: to hold it perfectly motionless in the water or to enable it to go up or down.

Parasitic insects that live inside the body of their host get oxygen from the body fluids of the host by diffusion through their body surface, or (for example, in tachinid fly larvae) their posterior spiracles may be extended to the body surface of the host or attach to one of its tracheal trunks.

THE BLOOD AND CIRCULATION

FUNCTIONS

The principal function of the blood is the transportation of materials; it transports salts, hormones, the products of digestion, and metabolic products from one part of the body to another. The blood also has a homeostatic function, that is, the maintenance of the water and salt balance in the body; this function involves certain other organs, particularly the Malpighian tubules and the rectum. The blood plays a role in molting (in enabling the insect to get out of the old exoskeleton) and in the expansion of the wings after the last molt. Blood is also important as a storage tissue (for example, for proteins and water during metamorphosis).

BLOOD CONSTITUENTS

The blood consists of plasma and hemocytes. There is a great deal of variation—in different insects, and in the same insect at different times—in the substances dissolved in the plasma; insect blood contains very little oxygen, and generally contains 20 or more times as much of the amino acids as mammalian blood. Except in those midge larvae whose blood contains dissolved hemoglobin, the blood plays only a very minor role in the transport of oxygen. The plasma generally has a relatively high content of uric acid, as compared with mammalian blood. The hemocytes are of a number of different types; they vary considerably in number, but average about 50,000 per cubic millimeter (a somewhat higher count than the leucocytes of mammals). The functions of the various types of hemocytes are not well known, but some of them encapsulate foreign bodies in the blood, some migrate to wounds and play a role in healing, and some appear to be capable of phagocytosis.

CIRCULATION

The movement of the blood is brought about by pulsations of the heart, and is aided in other parts of the body by various accessory pulsatile organs. The heartbeat is a peristaltic wave that moves forward; blood enters the heart through the ostia, which are closed during the systolic phase of the heartbeat. The rate of the heartbeat varies greatly; observed rates in different insects range from 14 to about 160 beats per minute. There is usually an increase in this rate during increased activity. The pulsations of the heart may be initiated within the heart muscle, or they may be under nervous control. A reversal of the beat (moving the blood backward instead of forward) occasionally occurs in some insects.

The heartbeat moves the blood forward through the dorsal aorta and out of the anterior end of the aorta in the head region. Accessory pulsatile organs in the thorax aid in moving the blood into the wings, and similar organs near the base of the antennae and in the legs aid in moving the blood through these appendages. The blood generally moves out into the wings through the veins in the anterior part of the wing, and back through the posterior veins. From the anterior part of the body the blood percolates slowly back through the body cavity. Eventually it gets into the pericardial sinus and reenters the heart through the ostia.

Very little pressure is developed in the general flow of blood through the body; the blood pressure may be sometimes less than atmospheric pressure. It can be increased by compression of the body wall or by dilation of the alimentary tract (produced by swallowing air); it is by such means that pressure is developed to break out of the old exoskeleton at the time of molting and to inflate the wings following the final molt.

HOMEOSTASIS

Homeostasis is the maintenance of a relatively constant condition of water content, pH, salt content, or some other factor. The blood contains buffer systems that serve to maintain a relatively constant pH (generally between 6.0 and 7.5), but the maintenance of water and salt balance involves other body tissues in addition to the blood. Some materials pass between the blood and body cells by simple diffusion, from regions of high concentration to regions of lower concentration, but other materials move against a diffusion gradient as a result of activity of the cells concerned.

An insect's small size makes it readily susceptible to water loss by evaporation from the body surface; if it lives in a situation of low humidity or where moisture is scarce, it must have some means of conserving water. On the other hand, if it lives in water or has a high water intake, it must have a means of eliminating the excess water. The insect's body wall provides protection against water loss by evaporation; water loss may also be reduced by the absorption of water from the rectum, and some water is available from the end products of metabolism. Water balance in aquatic insects, and in insects taking in large amounts of water in their food, is maintained largely by the Malpighian tubules. Aquatic insects are able to take up salts from the water even when these salts are present in very low concentration. The few insects that live in saline water are able (by means of the Malpighian tubules) to get rid of excess salt.

EXCRETION

The excretory organs of an insect (the Malpighian tubules and rectal glands) function in removing nitrogenous wastes and in regulating the balance of water and various salts in the body fluids. The Malpighian tubules extract water, salts, and nitrogenous wastes from the blood; these materials pass from the tubules to the hindgut and out of the body through the anus. The principal nitrogenous waste is uric acid. Some reabsorption, especially of water and salts, may occur in the lower sections of the Malpighian tubules or in the rectum. The taking in of water at the distal ends of the tubules and losing it at the proximal ends helps move the fluid through the tubules.

The Malpighian tubules are usually provided with muscles that produce movements of the tubules; these movements probably increase the absorption of materials from the blood and aid in moving these materials to the hindgut. The tubules in some insects contain yellow pigment, some of which represents vitamins of the B group.

A few insects (for example, Thysanùra and Collémbola) lack Malpighian tubules; other structures take over the excretory functions in such insects. Tubular glands in the head of Thysanùra and Collémbola are believed to be excretory in function; in other cases the alimentary tract may serve as an excretory organ. Collémbola get rid of uric acid in the molted skin, and continue molting after becoming adult. Some insects may store metabolic wastes, generally in the fat body (as uric acid) or in pigments.

THE SENSES

An insect receives information about its environment through its sense organs. The structure of these organs was described briefly in the preceding chapter; here we are concerned with the function of these structures.

CHEMORECEPTION

Chemoreceptors are very important components of an insect's sensory system, as they are involved in many types of behavior. The patterns of behavior in feeding, mating, habitat selection, and parasite–host relations, for example, are often mediated through the insect's chemical sense. The responses of insects to man-made attractants and repellents involve these receptors.

The exact mechanism by which a particular substance initiates a nerve impulse in the sensory cells of the chemoreceptors is not known. The substance may penetrate to the sensory cells and stimulate them directly, or it may react with something in the receptor to produce one or more other substances that stimulate the sensory cells. In any event, an insect's sensitivity to different substances varies; two substances very similar chemically (such as the dextro and laevo forms of a particular sugar) may be quite different in their stimulating effect. Some scents (for example, the sex-attractant substance produced by a female) can be detected by one sex (in this case, the male) but not by the other. The sensitivity of chemoreceptors to some substances is very high; many insects can detect certain odors at very great distances (up to a few miles).

Chemical stimuli play an important role in insects in triggering various activities such as feeding and egg laying; some chemicals have a repelling effect. It is of interest to note that while a chemoresponse such as feeding usually results in the insect's feeding on a suitable food, substances with no food value (or even some toxic substances) will sometimes trigger a feeding response.

MECHANORECEPTION

Insect sense organs sensitive to mechanical stimuli (hair sensilla, campaniform sensilla, and scolopophorous organs) react to touch, pressure, or vibration and provide the insect with information that may guide orientation, general movements, feeding, flight from enemies, reproduction, and other activities. Mechanical stimuli act by displacement, that is, they displace certain structures in relation to others. The stimuli may come from outside the insect (for example, touch and hearing) or from inside it (stimuli resulting from position or movement). The mechanical stimuli initiate a series of nerve impulses, the character of which is determined by the stimulus; in some cases the nerve impulses may be transmitted at frequencies as high as several hundred impulses per second.

THE TACTILE SENSE

The sense of touch in insects operates mainly through hair sensilla; the character of the nerve impulses initiated is determined by the rate and direction of the hair deflection. This sense is generally quite acute, as very little hair deflection may be necessary to initiate a series of impulses in the sensory nerve.

SENSITIVITY TO GRAVITY AND PRESSURE

Many insects show a response to gravity, for example, in the surfacing of aquatic insects and in the vertical constructions (burrows in the ground, combs in a bee hive, etc.) some insects make. Insects generally do not have organs of equilibrium comparable to the statocysts of certain crustaceans, though the air bubbles carried on the body surface by certain aquatic insects when they submerge may act like a statocyst; the forces of gravity and pressure are detected by other means.

Many joints in insects are provided with tactile hairs that register any movement of the joint, thus providing the insect with information on the position of these joints. Pressure on the body wall, whether produced by gravity or other forces, is usually detected by the campaniform sensilla; pressure on the legs may be detected by subgenual organs or by sensitive hairs on the tarsi.

SENSITIVITY TO MOVEMENT

An insect detects movements of the surrounding medium (air or water currents) chiefly by various tactile hairs. It receives information on its own movements by both mechanoreceptors and by visual cues. Many insects show definite reactions to water and air currents; insects living in rapidly flowing streams often orient to face upstream, and a row of dragonflies sitting on a fence will generally all face into the wind. Movements of air or water past an insect (whether the insect is stationary and the medium is moving, or the insect is moving) are detected largely by the antennae or by sensory hairs on the body. The antennae appear to be the most important detectors of such movements in the Díptera and Hymenóptera; in other insects, sensory hairs on the head or neck may be the most important receptors. The halteres of the Díptera play an important role in maintaining equilibrium in flight; they move through an arc of nearly 180 degrees at rates up to several hundred times per second, and any change in direction by the insect produces a gyroscopic effect that is detected by campaniform sensilla at the base of the halteres.

HEARING

The ability to detect sound (vibrations in the substrate or the surrounding medium) is developed in many insects, and sound plays a role in many types of behavior; the sense of hearing is perhaps best developed in the insects that produce sound. The organs involved in hearing are various hair sensilla, Johnston's organ (in the second segment of the antennae), and tympanal organs.

Vibrations in the substrate may be initiated in the substrate directly or may be induced (through resonance) by airborne sound vibration. The detection of substrate vibrations is mainly by subgenual organs. The frequency range to which these organs are sensitive varies in different insects, but is mainly from about 200 to 3000 hertz. Some insects (for example, bees) may be largely insensitive to airborne sound, but can detect sound vibrations reaching them through the substrate.

Airborne sound is detected in many insects by means of sensory hairs; in some cases the particular hairs involved are not known, while in other cases it is known that the hairs involved are located on a particular part of the body (for example, on the antennae in certain Díptera, on the cerci in certain Orthóptera). These hairs are generally sensitive to relatively low frequencies (a few hundred hertz or less; rarely, a few thousand). Probably the most efficient auditory organs in insects are the tympanal organs developed in certain moths, Orthóptera, and Homóptera. These are often sensitive to frequencies extending well into the ultrasonic range (up to 100,000 or more hertz),[2] but their discriminatory ability is to amplitude modulation rather than to frequency modulation. An insect's response (its behavior, and the nerve impulses initiated in the auditory nerves) are unaffected by differences in the frequency of the sound, as long as these frequencies are within the detectable range; an insect thus does not detect differences in the pitch of a sound, at least in the higher frequencies. On the other hand, tympanal organs are very sensitive to amplitude modulation, that is, the rhythmic features of the sound; the rhythmic features of an insect's "song" are its most important features as far as another insect is concerned. Airborne sound can be localized very well by all types of sound receptors; an insect with paired tympana can locate a sound even with one tympanum rendered inoperative (but can do it better if both tympana are functional).

The principal roles played by sound in insect behavior are to alert the insect to an environmental condition, to enable it to locate something in the environment, and to allow communication. Many insects respond to sound by reduced or increased activity (for example, by "freezing" or by flight). Noctuid moths can detect the very high-pitched echolocating sounds emitted by hunting bats, and thus take evasive action. Predaceous insects (for example, backswimmers) sometimes locate their prey by sound. Whirligig beetles swimming on the surface of the water are able to avoid obstacles if their antennae are intact, but bump into things if the antennae are removed; they appear to be the only insect using echos to detect obstacles (a type of behavior well developed in most bats, porpoises, and some other vertebrates). Sound plays a very important role in sexual behavior (see page 65).

VISION

Four types of photoreceptors occur in insects: dermal receptors, dorsal ocelli, lateral ocelli, and compound eyes. Many larvae that lack ocelli and compound eyes are able to respond to light, but the exact nature and location of the receptors involved are generally unknown. The structure of dorsal ocelli is such that they apparently do not form perceptible images (the light is focused *below* the retina); they are organs that react to differences in light intensity. The lateral ocelli form images on the light-sensitive regions of the retinal cells; they are probably capable of at least rudimentary form perception and color vision.

The best developed and most complex light receptors in insects are the compound eyes, which are composed of many ommatidial units. The light-sensitive elements in the compound eyes are the rhabdoms, which are composed of the sensitive areas of the retinal cells in the ommatidium (usually eight in number), forming an axial rod in the ommatidium. The visual unit in the compound eyes is assumed to be the rhabdom, but there is some evidence that the individual retinal cells may constitute the units.

The structure of an ommatidium (page 35 and Figure 30) is such that its visual angle is usually small, and the light reaching a rhabdom comes through just the one ommatidium; the image the

---

[2] The upper limit of hearing in man is generally about 15,000 hertz.

insect gets is thus a mosaic, and such an eye is spoken of as an apposition eye. When the pigment does not extend as far into the ommatidium, light from adjacent ommatidia may reach the rhabdom; such an eye is spoken of as a superposition eye. In some insects that fly by day or night, such as moths, the amount of light reaching a rhabdom may be varied by the migration of the pigment (outward at night, for maximum light penetration, inward in daytime to form an apposition type of eye).

The flicker-fusion frequency in insects (the rate of flicker at which the light appears continuous) is much higher than in man (45–53 per second in man, up to 250 or more per second in some insects), which means that they can perceive form even when in rapid flight and that they are very sensitive to motion. Some insects have a certain amount of depth or distance perception, which appears to depend on binocular vision; if one compound eye of a dragonfly nymph is rendered inoperative, the nymph is unable to judge the position of its prey accurately.

The range in wavelength to which insect eyes are sensitive is from about 2540 to 7000 Å, compared with about 4000 to 8000 Å in man; insects can see farther into the ultraviolet than man. Some wavelengths (especially the shorter ones: blue-green to ultraviolet) appear more stimulating. In the eyes of some insects, different retinal cells appear to differ in their spectral sensitivity, that is, some cells are sensitive to certain wavelengths and others are sensitive to other wavelengths. Some insects (for example, the honey bee) are able to analyze polarized light; from the pattern of polarization in a small patch of sky, they can determine the position of the sun.

Many insects appear to be color blind, but some can distinguish colors, including ultraviolet. The honey bee, for example, can see blue and yellow but not red. Just how an insect distinguishes different colors is not clear; there is some evidence that it may be the result of different retinal cells being sensitive to light of different wavelengths.

REPRODUCTION

EGG PRODUCTION

Eggs are developed in the ovarioles of the ovary; development begins in follicles at the upper ends of the ovarioles and continues as the follicles pass downward. The egg cells, or oocytes, are nourished during development by cells in the wall of the ovariole or by special cells called trophocytes; the oocytes increase greatly in volume, largely by the addition of yolk. Yolk consists of protein bodies (largely derived from blood proteins), lipid droplets, and glycogen. Many insects harbor microorganisms in their bodies, and in some cases these microorganisms may get into the egg during its development, usually through the follicle cells. The maturation divisions of the oocyte may occur at about the end of the yolk-forming period or after insemination, resulting in eggs with the haploid number of chromosomes. The oocyte membrane becomes surrounded by the vitelline membrane, and the chorion (a secretion of the follicle cells) is added. The chorion gives the eggs their final appearance, which varies greatly in different insects (see page 72). The mature eggs may remain in the body for a time before passing to the outside, either in the lower ends of the ovarioles or in an egg chamber (or egg calyx) in the oviduct or vagina.

Egg development is usually completed about the time the adult stage is reached; in some cases it is completed later, and in some cases it is completed earlier. In those aphids in which the female gives birth to living young parthenogenetically, the eggs are matured and development begins before the adult stage is reached. In the beetle genus *Micromálthus* (see page 369) the eggs are matured and begin their development (without fertilization) in the ovaries of the larvae, and are passed to the outside (either as eggs or larvae) in this stage. In the cecidomyid genus *Miástor* (see page 579), egg development is also completed in the larval stage, but in this case the young larvae (which have developed parthenogenetically) break out of the ovaries into the body cavity and develop there; they eventually rupture the cuticle of the mother larva and escape to the outside. This production of eggs or young by a preadult stage is called paedogenesis.

Egg production appears to be controlled in most insects by one or more hormones from the corpora allata (Figure 28) that act by controlling yolk deposition. Removal of the corpora allata prevents normal egg formation, and their reimplantation (from either a male or a female) induces ovarian activity again. Strangely enough these gonadotrophic hormones appear to be identical with the juvenile hormone (see page 51). The corpora allata have nerve connections with the brain, and nerve impulses affect their activity. It is also believed that (at least in some cases) neurosecretory cells in the brain may produce a hormone that affects the activity of the corpora allata. Many external factors (for example, photoperiod and temperature) affect egg production, and these factors probably act through the corpora allata. Egg development in some insects (for example, many mosquitoes) is not completed until the adult has eaten certain types of food (see page 42); the corpora allata play a role in this effect. In a few insects (for example, certain species of *Anópheles*), egg development is not completed until after mating; the mechanism in these cases involves impulses from the genital apparatus of the female to the brain and thence to the corpora allata, which then produce the hormones necessary for the completion of egg development.

SPERM FORMATION

The sperm begin their development in the outer ends of the sperm tubes of the testes and continue development as they pass toward the vas efferens. The maturation divisions that produce the haploid number of chromosomes in the sperm usually occur in the sperm tube, and the resulting spermatids develop into mature sperm that migrate to the seminal vesicles. Sperm development is usually complete by the time the insect reaches the adult stage, or is completed very shortly thereafter. The fluid (semen) in which the sperm are discharged, and the sperm cases (spermatophores) produced by some insects, are secreted by accessory glands. The corpora allata do not appear to be involved in sperm development, but may be involved in the activity of the accessory glands.

IMPREGNATION

Many factors are involved in getting the sexes together and inducing copulation—particular scents, sounds, body color patterns or shapes, special behavior patterns, and the like. These factors are generally much more responsible for the rarity of interspecific hybridization in insects than the possible physical incompatability of the genitalia. The gonads appear to have no effect on mating behavior; many insects will mate before their gonads are fully developed, and copulation may take place after castration.

At the time of copulation, sperm are usually deposited in the vagina of the female. In many insects, particularly in the lower orders, the sperm are encased in small capsules called spermatophores; these are transferred to the female at the time of copulation or are deposited on the substrate and are picked up by the female and placed in her vagina; the sperm are forced out of the spermatophores (sometimes through special channels) by vaginal pressure. The case of the spermatophore may be absorbed by the female, or she may eat it (she may sometimes eat it instead of placing it in her vagina).

Once in the female the sperm are usually stored in the spermatheca, and in some insects may remain viable there for long periods. When the eggs reach the opening of the spermathecal duct, sperm leave the spermatheca and enter the eggs through the micropyle.

OVIPOSITION

Insect eggs may be laid singly or in batches; most insects lay more than one egg at a time. Many insects have their eggs enclosed in an egg case or ootheca, which is secreted by the accessory glands. Each species normally lays its eggs in a particular type of situation; it is guided to these sites by various cues (visual, chemical, or other types). Many insects insert their eggs into something, such as animal or plant tissue, or into the soil by means of an ovipositor (see page 26). Where no ovipositor is developed, a telescopic extension of the terminal abdominal segments may operate like one, a sort of egg guide may be developed (such as the vulvar lamina of certain Odonàta, a more or less scoop-shaped structure formed by a posterior extension of the eighth abdominal sternum), or there may be no special external structures involved in egg laying.

SEX DETERMINATION

The chromosomes of insects usually occur in pairs, but in one sex the members of one pair do not match or are represented by one chromosome only. The chromosomes of this odd pair are called sex chromosomes; those of the other pairs, autosomes. In most insects the male has just one X (sex) chromosome and the female has two; the male condition is generally referred to as XO (only one chromosome in this pair) or XY (the Y chromosome being different from the X chromosome) and the female as XX (two X chromosomes).[3]

The eggs and sperm are haploid, that is, they contain only one chromosome of each pair. Each egg (in insects other than Lepidóptera) thus contains an X chromosome, but half the sperm contain an X chromosome and the other half lack an X chromosome. Sex is thus determined at the time of fertilization by the sex chromosome content of the

[3] This situation is reversed in most Lepidóptera, where it is the male that has the sex chromosomes paired.

sperm: an XO or XY condition in the zygote becomes a male and an XX condition becomes a female.

The autosomes appear to contain genes for maleness, while the X chromosomes contain genes for femaleness; the sex is determined by the balance between these two groups of genes. With two autosomes of each pair and only one X chromosome, the genes for maleness predominate and the animal becomes a male; with two autosomes of each pair and two X chromosomes, the genes for femaleness predominate and the animal becomes a female.

Sex is determined a little differently in the Hymenóptera and a few other insects; in these insects the males are generally haploid (only very rarely diploid) and the females are diploid. The males develop from unfertilized eggs and the females develop from fertilized eggs. Just how a haploid condition produces a male and a diploid condition produces a female is less well understood, but it is believed that sex in these insects depends on a series of multiple alleles (Xa, Xb, Xc, etc.); haploids and homozygous diploids (Xa/Xa, Xb/Xb, etc.) are males, while heterozygous diploids (Xa/Xb, Xc/Xd, etc.) are females.

Parthenogenetic development producing females occurs in many insects; in some of these the males are relatively rare or are unknown. These insects usually have the XO or XY male and XX female sex-determining mechanism, which means that either the eggs fail to undergo meiosis and are diploid or if they do undergo meiosis then two cleavage nuclei fuse to restore the diploid condition. Some insects (for example, aphids and gall wasps) produce both males and females parthenogenetically (at certain seasons); the production of a male apparently involves the loss of an X chromosome, and the production of a female involves either a fusion of two cleavage nuclei to restore the diploid condition or diploid eggs arising from tetraploid ovarian tissue.

Individual insects sometimes develop with aberrant sex characters. Individuals having some tissues male and other tissues female are called gynandromorphs; such individuals sometimes occur in the Hymenóptera and Lepidóptera. In the Hymenóptera, where the sex-determining mechanism is haploidy = male and diploidy = female, a gynandromorph may develop from a binucleate egg in which only one of the nuclei is fertilized or when an extra sperm enters the egg and undergoes cleavage to produce haploid (male) tissue in an otherwise female individual. Individuals with a sexual condition intermediate between maleness and femaleness are called intersexes; these usually result from genetic imbalance, particularly in polyploids (for example, a triploid *Drosóphila* with an XXY sex chromosome content is an intersex and is sterile).

MUSCLE ACTION

STRENGTH AND ACTIVITY

Insect muscles seem to be very strong; many insects can lift 20 or more times their body weight, and jumping insects can often jump distances equal to many times their own length. These feats appear very remarkable when compared to what man can do; they are possible not because the muscles of insects are inherently stronger but because of the insects' smaller size. The power of a muscle varies with the size of its cross section, or with the square of one dimension; what the muscle moves (the mass of the body) varies with the cube of the linear dimension. As the body becomes smaller, the muscles become *relatively* more powerful.

Insect muscles are often capable of extremely rapid contraction. Wing stroke rates of a few hundred per second are fairly common in insects, and rates up to 1000 or more per second are known. In insects with relatively slow wing stroke rates (for example, up to about 50 per second) it is probable that a nerve impulse induces each muscle contraction, but in insects with faster wing strokes, the muscle contractions occur more frequently than the impulses reaching them, and are the result of properties of the muscles themselves.

The fact that insect muscles often have an extremely rapid contraction frequency, which is sometimes maintained for a more or less prolonged period, means that the muscles are very efficient. Such action requires an efficient oxygen supply, which the tracheal system provides. The available figures on energy output in insect muscles (in terms of the amount of energy per unit of muscle weight per unit of time) indicate that insect muscles may have a much higher energy output than the muscles of any bird or mammal.

ENERGY SOURCE

The ultimate source in the insect of the energy released at muscle contraction is food, and observations of the respiratory quotient of insect muscles indicate that the principal food source for muscle contraction is carbohydrate. This is confirmed by the fact that the glycogen stores in an insect become depleted after prolonged muscular activity. Between the glycogen and the actual muscle contraction, many chemical reactions take place, but the end products are carbon dioxide and water and the release of energy. Some of these reactions may occur in the absence of oxygen, while others utilize oxygen. Organic phosphates, particularly ATP (adenosine triphosphate), are involved in the breakdown of glycogen; the reactions of ATP with the muscle proteins appear to be the immediate source of the energy required for the contraction process.

BODY TEMPERATURE

Insects are generally considered to be cold-blooded or poikilothermous, that is, their body temperature rises and falls with the environmental temperature. This is the case with most insects, particularly if they are not very active, but the action of the thoracic muscles in flight usually raises the insect's temperature above that of the environment. The cooling of a small object is fairly rapid, and the body temperature of a small insect in flight is very close to that of the environment; in insects such as butterflies and grasshoppers the body temperature in flight may be 5 or 10°C above the environmental temperature, and in such insects as moths and bumble bees (which are insulated with scales and/or hair), the metabolism during flight may raise the temperature of the flight muscles 20 or 30°C above the environmental temperature.

With most flying insects, the temperature of the flight muscles must be maintained above a certain point in order to produce the power necessary for flight. Many larger insects may actively increase the temperature of their flight muscles prior to flight by a "shivering" or a vibration of the wing muscles.

Honey bees remain in the hive during the winter, but do not go into a state of dormancy at the onset of cold weather (as most other insects do). When the temperature gets down to about 14°C they form a cluster in the hive, and by the activity of their thoracic muscles maintain the temperature of the cluster well over 14° (as high as 34–36°C when they are rearing brood).

COORDINATION

If a living organism is to function as a unit, it must have some means of coordinating the activities of its various parts. Insects have two mechanisms serving this function, the nervous system and the endocrine system. The nervous system is concerned principally with rapid adjustments to environmental change; the endocrine system regulates slower and longer-lasting changes (growth, development, and the like).

NERVOUS SYSTEM

The functional units of the nervous system are the nerve cells, of which there are three principal types; sensory, internuncial, and motor. The cell bodies of sensory cells generally lie close to the body surface, where they are arranged singly or grouped into sense organs. From each cell body a more or less elongate axon extends to a ganglion of the central nervous system. Motor cells have the cell body in a ganglion and have a more or less elongate axon extending to an effector (muscle or gland). Internuncial cells are association cells through which incoming "messages" (nerve impulses) are channeled into appropriate motor nerve cells. The connections between nerve cells are called synapses; they are places where the branching processes of one nerve cell come into close association (but do not fuse) with the processes of one or more other nerve cells.

Nerve impulses are changes in electric potential that pass along the nerve cell. Variations may occur in the number of impulses per unit of time and in their rate of travel; the maximum number of impulses observed in an insect nerve fiber is about 800 per second, and the maximum rate of travel over the fiber is about 10 meters per second. "Interpretation" of nerve impulses by the central nervous system is based on the fibers over which they travel and on the number of impulses per unit of time. When a nerve impulse reaches a synapse, it does not itself cross the synapse but causes the liberation of some chemical substance that sets off a new nerve impulse in the succeeding neurone. The nature of the synapses and of the internuncial cells determines the direction(s) of outgoing (motor) impulses initiated by incoming (sensory) ones. Synapses are one-way gates; consequently, nerve impulses normally travel in only one direction.

The ganglia of the central nervous system (brain, subesophageal ganglion, and the segmental ganglia of the ventral nerve cord) serve as the coordinating centers. Each of these ganglia has a certain amount of autonomy, that is, each may coordinate the impulses involved in various activities. Activities involving the entire body may be coordinated by impulses from the brain, but many of these activities can occur with the brain absent.

ENDOCRINE SYSTEM

The endocrine system consists of glands that produce hormones. Hormones are chemical substances that are introduced into the blood, which carries them to other parts of the body where they produce some effect on physiological processes. Several organs in an insect are known to produce hormones, the principal functions of which are the control of reproductive processes, molting, and metamorphosis. The gonads of insects apparently do not produce sex hormones (as they do in vertebrates).

The neurosecretory cells in the brain produce one or more hormones that play a role in growth, metamorphosis, and reproductive activities. One of these, commonly called the *brain hormone,* plays an important role in molting by stimulating a pair of glands in the prothorax to produce a hormone (ecdysone) that causes molting. Other hormones produced by the brain may have other functions; for example, it is believed that a brain hormone plays a role in caste determination in termites (see page 82) and in breaking diapause in some insects.

The prothoracic glands secrete a hormone called *ecdysone* (a steroid with the empirical formula $C_{27}H_{44}O_6$), which initiates growth and development and causes molting.[4] Some authorities believe that this hormone acts on cell nuclei, activating particular chromosomal regions and bringing about a variety of reactions that culminate in molting. These glands generally cease their secretory activity at the time of pupation.

The corpora allata (Figure 28, *ca*) produce a hormone called the *juvenile hormone,* the effect of which is the inhibition of metamorphosis. The chemical nature of this hormone has recently been discovered: it is an epoxy derivative of tridecadiene. Various substances, particularly terpenes like farnesol ($C_{15}H_{26}O$), show considerable juvenile hormone activity. Secretions of the corpora allata have effects on other processes besides the inhibition of metamorphosis, and it is likely that several hormones may be produced by these structures. The hormones of the corpora allata affect egg production in the female and the development of the accessory glands of the male (see pages 47–48), and various metabolic processes.

Substances chemically related to ecdysone and juvenile hormone occur in certain plants and make these plants toxic to insects. Chemical analogs of ecdysone and juvenile hormone are now being studied to see whether they can function as new kinds of insecticides.

PHEROMONES

Pheromones are substances that serve as chemical signals between members of the same species; they are secreted to the outside of the body and cause specific reactions by other individuals of the species. They are sometimes called "social hormones," as they act in a group of individuals somewhat like hormones in an individual animal, or they might be considered as a chemical communication system. Some animals produce only a few pheromones, while others produce many. Pheromone systems are the most complex in some of the social insects.

Chemical communication differs from that by sight or sound in several ways. Transmission is slow (the chemicals are usually airborne), but the signal is slow-fading and is sometimes effective over a very long range (a mile (2 km) or more). Localization of the signal by the receiver is generally poorer than localization of a sound or visual stimulus, and is usually effected by the animal moving upwind in response to it, or by moving in the direction of a higher concentration. Repertoires are usually very limited, compared with those possible in communication by visual or acoustic means, but some pheromones may convey different meanings depending on their concentration, or when presented in combination.

Pheromones play a role in various activities of the insects possessing them. Some act as alarm substances, some play a role in individual and group recognition, some serve as sex attractants, some play a role in the formation of aggregations, some are involved in trail-laying, and some may play a role in caste determination. Alarm substances in ants are usually produced by mandibular or anal glands; some may elicit responses by more than one species. Sex attractants are usually produced by the female, and serve to attract the male. Trail-marking substances are usually discharged from the sting or anus (in ants). Pheromones involved in caste determination include the "queen substance" produced by queen honey bees (see page 82), and somewhat similarly acting substances produced by termites (see page 82) and ants, and must generally be ingested to be effective.

The chemical composition of many insect pheromones is known; some are quite specific (that is, isomers are inactive), and some appear to

---

[4] This hormone occurs in all insect groups that have been studied, in crustaceans, and in arachnids, and is probably the molting hormone of all arthropods.

be complex mixtures containing specific quantities of each chemical. Closely related species may use the same chemicals, but different ratios or isomers; such small differences, for example in sex pheromones, give sexual isolation between species.

Some insect pheromones have been used in insect control. For example, if an area is "saturated" with a sex-attractant type of pheromone, the males responding to it (usually by traveling upwind) very often fail to find a female, and mating is much less likely to occur.

References on Insect Physiology

Barton-Browne, L. B. 1964. Water regulation in insects. *Ann. Rev. Ent.*, 9:63–82.

Bullock, T. H., and G. A. Horridge. 1965. *Structure and Function in the Nervous System of Invertebrates.* San Francisco: Freeman, 2 vols., xx + 1719 pp.; illus.

Chapman, R. F. 1971. *The Insects, Structure and Function.* New York: American Elsevier, xii + 819 pp.; illus.

Craig, R. 1960. The physiology of excretion in the insect. *Ann. Rev. Ent.*, 5:53–68.

Davey, K. G. 1965. *Reproduction in the Insects.* San Francisco: Freeman, x + 96 pp., 21 f.

Dethier, V. G. 1963. *The Physiology of Insect Senses.* New York: Wiley, ix + 266 pp., 99 f.

Engelmann, F. 1968. Endocrine control of reproduction in insects. *Ann. Rev. Ent.*, 13:1–26; 2 f.

Heinrich, B. 1974. Thermoregulation in endothermic insects. *Science*, 185(4153):747–756; 8 f.

House, H. L. 1961. Insect nutrition. *Ann. Rev. Ent.*, 6:13–26.

Imms, A. D. 1957 (9th ed., revised by O. W. Richards and R. G. Davies). *A General Textbook of Entomology.* New York: E. P. Dutton, x + 886 pp., 609 f.

Jacobson, M. 1972. *Insect Sex Pheromones.* New York: Academic Press, xii + 382 pp.; illus.

Lipke, H., and G. Fraenkle. 1956. Insect nutrition. *Ann. Rev. Ent.*, 1:17–44.

Mazokhin-Porshniakov, G. A. 1969. *Insect Vision.* New York: Plenum Press (translated from Russian), xiv + 306 pp., 125 f.

Menn, J. J., and M. Beroza (Eds). 1972. *Insect Juvenile Hormones. Chemistry and Action.* New York: Academic Press, xv + 341 pp.; illus.

Rockstein, M. (Ed.). 1973–1974 (2nd ed.). *The Physiology of Insecta.* 6 vol.; illus. Vol. 1 (1973): *Physiology of Ontogeny—Biology, Development, and Aging;* 544 pp. Vol. 2 (1974): *Part A: The Insect and the External Environment.* I. Environmental aspects. *Part B:* The *Insect and the External Environment.* II. Reaction and interaction; 608 pp. Vol. 3 (1974): *Part A: The Insect and the External Environment.* II. Reaction and interaction. *Part B: The Insect and the External Environment.* III. Locomotion; 540 pp. Vol. 4 (1974): *The Insect and the External Environment—Homeostasis—I;* 476 pp. Vol. 5 (1974): *The Insect and the External Environment—Homeostasis—II;* 682 pp. Vol. 6 (1974): *The Insect and the External Environment—Homeostasis—III;* (in preparation). New York: Academic Press.

Rodriguez, J. G. (Ed.). 1972. *Insect and Mite Nutrition.* New York: American Elsevier, 701 pp.

Roeder, K. D. (Ed.). 1953. *Insect Physiology.* New York: Wiley, xiv + 1100 pp., 257 f.

Roeder, K. D. 1963. *Nerve Cells and Insect Behavior.* Cambridge, Mass.: Harvard Univ. Press, 188 pp., frontis. + 47 f.

Romoser, W. S. 1973. *The Science of Entomology.* New York: Macmillan, xi + 449 pp.; illus.

Ross, H. H. 1965 (3rd ed.). *A Textbook of Entomology.* New York: Wiley, ix + 539 pp., 401 f.

Waterhouse, D. F. 1957. Digestion in insects. *Ann. Rev. Ent.*, 2:1–18.

Waterhouse, D. F. *et al.* 1970. *Insects of Australia.* Canberra: Melbourne Univ. Press. xiii + 1029 pp.; illus. (especially Ch. 2, pp. 29–71; 40 f.).

Wigglesworth, V. B. 1973 (7th ed.). *The Principles of Insect Physiology.* London: Methuen, ix + 827 pp., illus.

Wigglesworth, V. B. 1970. *Insect Hormones.* San Francisco: Freeman, ix + 159 pp.; illus.

Wigglesworth, V. B. 1974 (7th ed.). *Insect Physiology.* London: Methuen, x + 176 pp., illus.

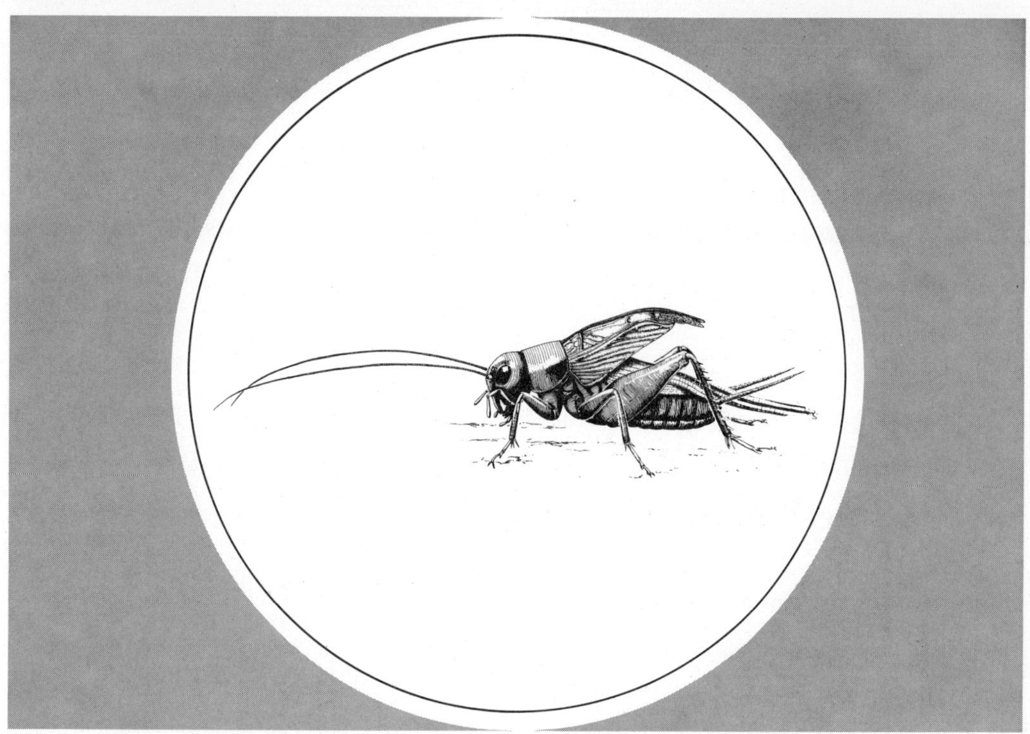

4: INSECT BEHAVIOR

The importance of insects is determined largely by what they do—or by their behavior. In the preceding chapter we were concerned with the function (or behavior) of various organ systems in the insect; here we will be concerned with the activities of the entire animal. Many examples of insect behavior are given later in this book, in the accounts of the various insect groups; our purpose in this chapter is to discuss some of the general types of behavior that occur in insects.

BASIC ASPECTS OF INSECT BEHAVIOR

The behavior of insects consists of responses to stimuli. The stimuli may be internal (for example, a particular physiological state) or external (an environmental factor), and they set up impulses that travel over the nervous system to effectors; the response is determined by the pattern of pathways over which the impulses travel, and by the physiological state of the insect.

The fact that the response in any given case may be advantageous to the insect does not indicate that any thinking or reasoning is involved. It is unsafe to assume that a mental process such as liking or disliking something has anything to do with an insect's response. The nerve pathways involved in insect behavior are largely hereditary, hence the responses are largely automatic and not learned.

DIRECTED RESPONSES

Many insect responses to stimuli consist of orientation and movement toward or away from the stimulus. These directed responses may be positive (toward the stimulus) or negative (away from the stimulus); responses consisting of orientation with respect to the stimulus are usually called tropisms, and movements toward or away from the stimulus are called taxes. The stimulus producing a directed response may be light, temperature, water, chemicals, touch or contact, the force of gravity, or currents of air or water.

Many insects have very definite responses to light; some, such as house flies, go toward a light, while others, such as bed bugs, avoid it. Night-flying insects respond positively to a source of light, especially one of high intensity, but not to a diffuse light. The intensity, duration, or wavelength (color) of the light may influence the response. Positive responses to certain chemicals often result in the insect's locating its food, a mate, or a site for oviposition; a chemical producing a negative response is called a repellent. Insects react negatively to many tactile stimuli, that is, they move away when touched; on the other hand, a positive response to certain tactile stimuli may result in an insect like a cockroach squeezing into a small opening or crevice. A group of dragonflies sitting on a fence, all headed into the wind, show a positive orientation response to air currents. Many aquatic insects head or swim upstream, thus exhibiting a positive response to water currents.

The nature of an insect's response to a specific stimulus is often modified by other stimuli. Honey bees respond positively to a bright light at high temperatures (for example, they leave the hive), but respond negatively to the same light intensity at low temperatures (for example, they remain in the hive). House flies move upward at night, but do not exhibit this response (to gravity) during the day. The responses of many insects to gravity are influenced by temperature, being negative at high temperature (that is, the insect moves upward) and positive at low temperatures. The physiological state of the insect, as affected by its food or its state of development or by other factors, often influences its response to a given stimulus. An insect that is well fed often does not respond to a chemical stimulus to which it will respond when it is not well fed, and the larval and adult stages (or adults of different age) of the same species often react differently to a given stimulus.

Some insect responses to stimuli are not as simple as they may at first appear. For example, many moths are attracted to a candle flame—but more males are attracted to such a flame than females, and these moths will not fly to the flame of a bunsen burner or to the light output of a campfire. It has been shown that some moths emit infrared signals (from the thorax) that are very similar to some of the emissions of a candle flame, and that they can detect such emissions (probably by sense organs on the antennae). Some moths have been observed attempting to mate with a candle flame. It is believed that these infrared signals may serve as a means of getting the sexes together, and the infrared of the candle flame is a confusing mimic of the moth's infrared signal, and triggers the response of the moth to the flame.

A knowledge of insect responses has many practical applications. Such knowledge may be used to locate insects or to predict where they will go or what they will do under certain conditions. Directed responses make it possible to trap and destroy undesirable insects or to avoid the damage they do by repelling them. Many control measures depend for their effectiveness upon the reaction of the insect to particular stimuli.

COMPLEX BEHAVIOR

Much of the behavior of insects involves more than orientation or movement with respect to a particular stimulus. Activities such as mating, nest-building, egg laying, and capturing prey commonly involve a series of different acts. For example, many insects have rather elaborate egg-laying habits; the cicada slits the bark of a twig and lays an egg in each slit; lacewings lay their eggs at the ends of long slender stalks; certain carrion beetles excavate beneath carcasses and bury them, and lay their eggs in them; most parasitic insects lay their eggs in or on the body of their host. This behavior often appears purposive or intelligent; for example, the activities of a wasp in building a nest, capturing and stinging prey, storing that prey in a cell in the nest, laying an egg in the cell, and then sealing up the cell seem to show a remarkable foresight on the part of the wasp.

When carefully examined, however, this behavior is generally found to be automatic. These activities are performed in a characteristic manner by all the members of a species; they do not have to be learned and are performed about as well the first time as after practice, and the various individual acts involved are performed in a characteristic sequence. This type of behavior is generally spoken of as instinctive, and does not involve volition or learning. Such behavior has persisted during the course of evolution because of its survival value. Individuals whose behavior patterns are not beneficial tend to die out, whereas those whose behavior favors survival persist in greater numbers and pass the hereditary elements of this behavior on to their offspring.

Many types of behavior in insects show definite rhythms that are correlated with rhythmic variations in environmental factors. Insects that live in the open (as contrasted with insects living in concealed situations, in constant darkness) commonly exhibit diurnal rhythms of activity, for example, being active during the day and inactive at night. Such rhythms (commonly called circadian rhythms) appear to be controlled by environmental factors (particularly light), but in some cases may be controlled by internal factors. Some insects that show diurnal rhythms of activity continue this rhythmicity for a while when placed in continuous light or darkness.

The mating behavior of insects is often very complex and varies greatly in different species. The factors that bring the sexes together may be chemical (sex attractants), sound signals (as in many Orthóptera), or visual signals (light flashing in fireflies, the dances and other courtship maneuvers in many flies), and the high degree of specificity in this behavior acts as an isolating mechanism to prevent the mating of different species.

Whether or not insects can be said to be intelligent depends on how intelligence is defined. There is some difference of opinion as to just what intelligence is, but the term usually implies a capacity to modify behavior as a result of experience (that is, the capacity to learn), and possibly the ability to think or reason. There is abundant evidence that insects possess some limited capacity to learn, but little or no evidence that they can think.

Examples of learning in insects are found in the facts that conditioned responses can be developed, maze running can be improved, and nest-building insects that forage away from the nest can find their way back to the nest. Conditioned responses—situations where a previously ineffective stimulus comes to elicit a response after having being repeatedly associated with an effective stimulus—has been developed in many insects. Maze tests show that cockroaches and ants can "learn" a maze. Ants do much better than cockroaches, but both are very inferior to rats. The ability of many insects to "home" to a nest indicates some sort of memory of visual, chemical, or other stimuli. The proverbial "bee line" of a homing honey bee is learned after preliminary flights and appears to be based on the recognition of various landmarks and the direction of the sun. The homing of ants commonly involves following odor trails, but the direction of the sun may also serve in orientation.

Whether such learning involves any thinking or reasoning is impossible to say. Entomological literature abounds in descriptions of insect behavior that appears intelligent, especially in social insects, but a careful study of such behavior shows it to be largely automatic. Insects might be said to possess a certain amount of intelligence, but the gap between the intelligence of insects and that of man is enormous.

LOCOMOTION

Mobility is an important attribute of any animal, and locomotor abilities are well developed in insects. Insects are basically terrestrial animals, but many live in water and many are capable of flight. The insects have developed effective mechanisms for locomotion on land, in water, and in the air.

TERRESTRIAL LOCOMOTION

The basic equipment of insects for locomotion on land consists of the legs. The particular movements of which any leg is capable depends on its musculature and the nature of the leg joints. Leg joints may be dicondylic, with two points of articulation, or monocondylic, with one point of articulation (Figure 31); the movement at a dicondylic joint is largely limited to one plane, while that in a monocondylic joint (which is like a ball-and-socket joint) can be more varied. The joint between the coxa and the thoracic wall may be monocondylic or dicondylic; if dicondylic, the axis is more or less vertical and the movement is forward and backward. The coxo-trochanteral, trochantero-femoral, and femoro-tibial joints are usually dicondylic; the movement at the trochantero-femoral joint is forward and backward (with the axis vertical), and that at the coxo-trochanteral and femoro-tibial is up and down (with the axis horizontal). The tibio-tarsal joint is usually monocondylic, permitting more varied movements.

CREEPING The movement of legless larvae and caterpillars might best be described as creeping locomotion. Legless larvae move by means of peristaltic movements of the body, with the waves of contraction moving in the direction of locomotion. Most caterpillars move by waves of body contractions that progress in the direction of locomotion; the posterior prolegs are raised and

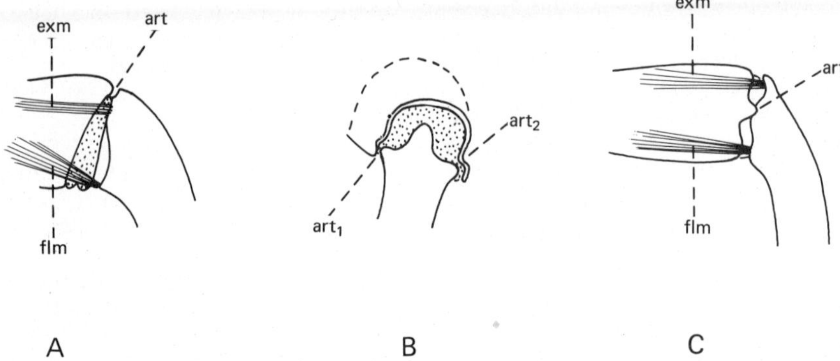

Figure 31. Articular mechanisms in insect legs. A, monocondylic joint; B and C, end view and side view of a dicondylic joint. *art,* points of articulation; *exm,* extensor muscle; *flm,* flexor muscle. (Redrawn from Snodgrass, by permission of McGraw-Hill Book Company, Inc.)

moved forward, and a wave of movements of this sort passes forward along the body; two or three segments are usually involved in the wave, and the two legs of each segment are moved together. Loopers (larvae of Geométridae and some Noctùidae), in which the prolegs are reduced in number and located posteriorly (Figure 408), move by bringing the posterior legs forward (looping the body in the process) and then moving the anterior part of the body forward.

WALKING Any distinction between walking and running in insects would have to be based on speed, and would be rather arbitrary; running in man or other mammals involves moments when all the legs are off the ground, and if this should occur in the terrestrial locomotion of an insect, we would call it jumping.

The most common pattern of leg movements in the walking of insects involves three legs being moved forward while the other three are on the ground; the front and hind legs on one side and the middle leg on the other side move together. This is probably the most common pattern of leg movements, but other patterns occur; the pattern may vary in the same insect when moving at different speeds, or in different insects. In some insects, four or five legs may be on the ground at any one moment.

JUMPING The best-known jumpers among the insects are the grasshoppers, hoppers (Homóptera), fleas, flea beetles, and springtails. In all of these except the springtails, the hind legs provide the propulsion for the jump; the springtails use a special structure, the furcula (see page 152). When a grasshopper jumps, the front of the body is elevated by means of the front and middle legs, and the hind legs are suddenly extended. The principal muscles involved in this process are those in the hind femora, which extend the tibiae; the herringbone arrangement of these muscles makes possible a maximum pull, and the leverage at the femoro-tibial joint makes it possible for the insect to develop a great deal of propulsion.

SWIMMING

Many insects live in water, at least during part of their lives, and there is quite a bit of variation in the nature and efficiency of their swimming techniques. The best swimmers (for example, some of the beetles) have the body streamlined and have a very efficient swimming mechanism.

AQUATIC BEETLES The best swimmers among the aquatic beetles are the Dytíscidae, Gyrìnidae, and Hydrophílidae. The middle and hind legs in these groups are the chief means of propulsion; the front legs are used in grasping prey and in steering. The propelling legs of dytiscids and hydrophilids are elongate and flattened (this modification involves chiefly the tarsi), and generally have a dense fringe of hairs. These swimming hairs are very important, as up to three fourths of the total thrust may be due to them. The middle and hind legs of gyrinids are short and greatly flattened.

The two legs on a given segment move together in dytiscids and alternately in hydrophilids; the middle and hind legs alternate in the dytiscids. The leg stroke rate varies from 3 to 10 per second in *Acílius* (Dytíscidae) and from about 50 to 60 per second in *Gyrìnus* (Gyrìnidae). *Acílius* can develop a speed of about 35 cm per second; *Gyrìnus* (swimming on the surface) may reach a speed of 100 cm per second. The legs are "feathered" (rotated) on the backstroke; the swimming hairs simply fold on the backstroke. The mechanism in *Gyrìnus* is a very efficient one; the resistance of the water to the backstroke is only about one fortieth that of the power stroke.

AQUATIC BUGS The most proficient swimmers among the aquatic bugs are certain of the Hydrocorìzae. The swimming mechanism in the Belostomátidae and Naucòridae is much like that in the aquatic beetles, and these animals are more or less streamlined. In the Coríxidae and Notonéctidae the hind legs are elongated, flattened, and provided with swimming hairs; these legs provide the propulsion.

AQUATIC NYMPHS AND LARVAE These insects have various methods of swimming. Forms such as the larvae of the Ceratopogónidae, which are elongate and snakelike in shape, swim by body undulations. Damselfly nymphs swim in much the same way, but the leaflike gills at the end of their abdomen provide added propulsion, much like the tail of a fish. Nymphs or larvae that have lateral abdominal appendages generally use these as paddles in swimming. Many dipterous larvae (midges, mosquitoes, and the like) swim by whiplike motions of the body, which is not a very efficient method. Dragonfly nymphs are jet propulsed by drawing water into the rectum and forcibly expelling it; they can sometimes move very rapidly by this method.

FLIGHT

Flight is a distinctive attribute of most insects, one that to a large extent has been responsible for their success as a group. It is involved in an insect's search for food, a mate, oviposition sites, and the like, and it has hastened the dispersal of insects over the earth. It is often an important means of escape for an insect threatened by a predator (or man). Many insects have powers of flight that exceed those of all other flying animals; they can steer accurately, hover, and go sideways or backward. Only the hummingbirds approach insects in their ability to maneuver on the wing.

The wings of flying vertebrates (birds and bats) are moved by muscles that attach directly to the wings; flight in insects is accomplished principally by muscles that do not attach directly to the wings but move the wings indirectly by changing the shape of the thorax.

WING STRUCTURE AND ARTICULATIONS The wings of insects arise as saclike outgrowths of the body wall; when fully developed they are flattened and flaplike, and are strengthened by a series of veins. The veins are thickened and more heavily sclerotized than the rest of the wing, and are hollow; their cavities contain tracheae, nerves, and blood. The veins are generally thicker and closer together in the anterior part of the

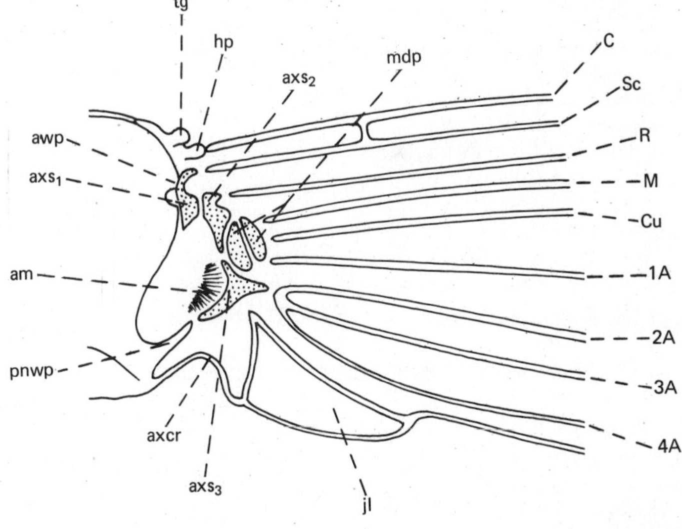

Figure 32. Diagram showing the articulation of the wing with thoracic notum. *am,* axillary muscles; *awp,* anterior notal wing process; *axcr,* axillary cord; *axs,* axillary sclerites 1–3; *hp,* humeral plate; *jl,* jugal lobe; *mdp,* median plates; *n,* notum; *pnwp,* posterior notal wing process; *tg,* tegula. The letters at the right side of the figure indicate the veins. (Redrawn from Snodgrass, by permission of McGraw-Hill Book Co., Inc.)

wing. Much taxonomic use is made of variations in wing venation, but little is known of the functional significance of these variations.

The movements of the wings are made possible by the nature of their articulation with the thorax; the basal articulations of the wing are shown in Figure 32. The base of the wing is membranous, and in this membranous region are several articular sclerites: a humeral plate (*hp*) at the base of the costa, three (sometimes four) axillary sclerites (*axs*), and two median plates (*mdp*). The first axillary sclerite (axs_1) articulates between the anterior wing process of the thoracic notum (*awp*), the base of the subcosta, and the second axillary sclerite; the second axillary sclerite (axs_2) articulates between the first and third axillary sclerites, and has a process associated with the base of the radius; the third axillary sclerite (axs_3) articulates between the second axillary sclerite and the posterior wing process of the thoracic notum (*pnwp*), and has a process associated with the base of the anal veins; the median plates (*mdp*) are at the base of the veins in the medio-cubital area. The membranous line between the two median plates forms an upward-projecting fold when the wing is flexed (folded back over the body).

WING MUSCLES The wings in most insects are moved by five paired groups of muscles (Figure 33): (1) tergosternal muscles (*tsm*), extending from the notum to the sternum; (2) dorsal longitudinal muscles (*dlm*), which extend between the phragmata; (3) basalar muscles (*bms*), arising on the coxa and episternum and inserted on the basalare (the epipleurite above the episternum); (4) subalar muscles (*sbm*), arising on the coxa and epimeron and inserted on the subalare (the epipleurite above the epimeron); and (5) axillary muscles (*am*), extending from the pleuron to the third axillary sclerite.

The tergosternal and dorsal longitudinal muscles are sometimes referred to as the indirect wing muscles because they produce their effects (upward and downward movements of the wings) indirectly by changing the shape of the thorax. Contraction of the tergosternal muscles depresses the

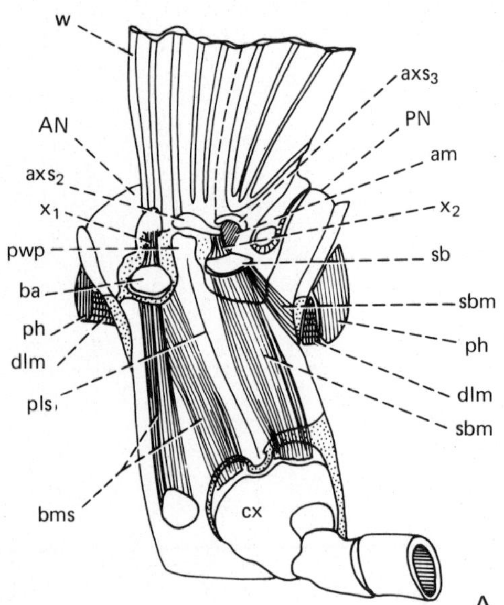

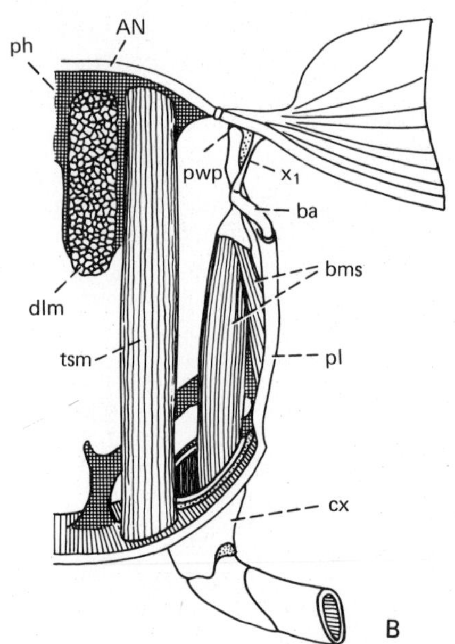

Figure 33. Diagrams of wing muscles of an insect. A, lateral view; B, cross section of a wing-bearing segment. *am*, axillary muscles, *AN*, alinotum; axs_2 and axs_3, second and third axillary sclerites; *ba*, basalare; *bms*, basalar muscles; *cx*, coxa; *dlm*, dorsal longitudinal muscles; *ph*, phragma; *pl*, pleuron; *pls*, pleural suture; *PN*, postnotum; *pwp*, pleural wing process; *sb*, subalare; *sbm*, subalar muscles; *tsm*, tergosternal muscles; x_1 and x_2, connections between epipeurites (basalare and subalare) and wing base; *w*, wing. (Redrawn from Snodgrass, by permission of McGraw-Hill Book Company, Inc.)

notum and produces an upward movement of the wings, the pivotal points being the pleural wing processes; contraction of the dorsal longitudinal muscles produces an upward arching of the notum, resulting in a downward movement of the wings. The basalar muscles produce a downward movement of the basalare, which in turn (because of its connection with the costal margin of the wing, x_1) results in a depression of the costal wing margin and/or an extension (forward movement) of the wing. The subalar muscles extend the wing or depress the rear edge of it. The axillary muscles move the wing backward and flex it by revolving the third axillary dorsally and inward.

RELATIVE ACTION OF FRONT AND HIND WINGS Most insects have two pairs of wings, and the two wings on each side may be overlapped at the base or hooked together in some way so that they move together as one wing, or they may be capable of independent movement. In some of the primitive orders (for example, the Orthóptera and Odonàta) the front and hind wings are neither overlapped at the base nor hooked together, and can move independently. The approximately equal size of the two pterothoracic segments in these orders suggests that the front and hind wings are equally important in flight. In many Odonàta there is a phase difference in the movements of the two pairs of wings, that is, when one pair is moving up the other pair is moving down; in other Odonàta, and in most Orthóptera, there is a less pronounced phase difference in the wing movements, with the front wings moving a little ahead of the hind wings.

In the Coleóptera it is the hind wings that are largely responsible for flight. The elytra are extended during flight,[1] but are not actively moved up and down; they play a role in the aerodynamics of flight by providing fixed lift-generating surfaces.

WING MOVEMENTS IN FLIGHT When an insect is held so that its feet are in contact with a resting surface, it will usually remain quiet; if this surface is removed, the insect usually moves its wings as in flight, and studies of the wing movements can be made while the insect is held suspended. By attaching a tiny metallic object such as a piece of foil to the wing tip, one may follow the movements of the wing. A graphic record of the wing movements can be made by attaching a tiny bristle to the wing tip and allowing it to make a line on a rotating drum (kymograph) as the wings are moved. The character of the wing movements is probably best studied by means of high-speed motion pictures or by means of a stroboscope.[2]

The movements of the wings during active flight are quite complex and involve upward and downward movements, movements forward and backward, movements of the wing on its longitudinal axis, and changes in the wing shape by twisting, folding, and buckling. The movements are usually in the form of a figure eight; the angle of the figure-eight movements and the pitch of the wings (the amount of deflection of the front or rear edge) determine the direction and speed of flight.

An insect's wing movements in forward flight produce the same mechanical effect as the revolution of an airplane propeller. Each wing acts as a propeller, drawing air from above and in front and driving it backward; this produces a region of low pressure above and in front of the insect and a high pressure region behind it, causing lift and forward movement. The wing action during hovering is much like that of a helicopter rotor except that the wing movements are oscillatory rather than rotary (with the action of the oscillation horizontal).

Data on the wingstroke rate in insects can be obtained by kymograph records, high-speed motion pictures, the use of a stroboscope, or by acoustic methods. Most observations have been made by acoustic methods (for example, Sotavalta, 1947), and with modern acoustic equipment such observations can be quite acurate. The pitch of the fundamental in the wing sound (this sound generally contains many harmonics), in hertz, represents the number of wingstrokes per second; pitch determinations of wing sounds thus give data on wingstroke rates.

The wingstroke rate in insects varies considerably; some butterflies move their wings only a few times a second, many dragonflies have a wingstroke rate of about 40 per second, and many Díptera have wingstroke rates of 200 to 400 per sec-

[1] There are a few beetles (for example, certain scarabs in the subfamily Cetoniìnae) which do not extend their elytra in flight, but extend their hind wings out from under the elytra at points where there is a broad shallow emargination on the lateral edge of the elytra (see also page 387).

[2] A stroboscope is a device that emits very short flashes of light at controllable rates. If the flash rate is the same as the wingstroke rate (or an integral multiple of it) the wings appear to stand still, but if the flash rate is a little different from the wingstroke rate, the wings will appear to move slowly and the character of their movements can be studied.

ond; midges in the genus *Forcipomỳia* have a wingstroke rate of about 1000 per second.

The speed at which insects fly is often difficult to measure because few insects fly very far in a straight line. It will be obvious to any collector that many insects can fly faster than he can run, and some can fly faster than he can swing an insect net. Reliable figures on the flight speed of insects generally range up to about 35 miles (56 km) per hour; many insects can doubtlessly exceed this speed on occasion.

A flight speed of 10 miles (16 km) per hour (a maximum for many insects) may not seem very fast when compared with the speeds obtained by some land animals, many birds, or such man-made vehicles as jet planes—but in terms of body lengths per second it may be quite remarkable. A man running at top speed covers about 5 body lengths per second, a horse about 6, a cheetah (probably the fastest land animal) about 18, a peregrine falcon (doing 180 miles (290 km) per hour in a power dive) about 175, and a jet plane flying at three times the speed of sound about 100; a blow fly 10 mm in length flying at a speed of 3 meters per second (a normal flight speed for such a fly, and equivalent to about 6.8 miles (11 km) per hour) covers 300 times its length per second.

Insects maintain their equilibrium while in flight by active control of the wing movements. The information necessary to maintain equilibrium comes from several sense organs, particularly the eyes and the antennae. In the Díptera the halteres probably serve as the principal sense organs, enabling the insect to maintain its equilibrium; these structures vibrate with the wings and act as gyroscopic sense organs in detecting changes of direction.

INSECT MIGRATIONS

The term "migration" usually brings to mind the spring and fall flights of birds, where most or all of the individuals of a species fly over a considerable distance from nesting grounds to wintering grounds, or vice versa. Somewhat similar mass movements occur in some species of insects, but with insects the movements are nearly always one-way, that is, the migrating individuals do not make a return flight; the return flight, if made, is made by a subsequent generation.

One of the best known of the migratory insects is the monarch butterfly, *Dánaus plexíppus* (L.), which occurs throughout most of the United States and southern Canada, and in some other parts of the world as well. The movements of this species have been studied by tagging; the tag is a small piece of paper fastened to the front edge of the front wing, and each tag bears an identifying number and some information on whom to notify if the tag is recovered. Thousands of monarchs have been tagged, most of them by Dr. F. A. Urquhart, of the Royal Ontario Museum of Zoology and Paleontology, and his associates, and enough of these have been subsequently recovered to give an idea of their movements. In late summer the individuals that have developed during the summer in the north begin to fly south; the farther south they go, the more numerous they become, and in some parts of the country enormous aggregations of monarchs are seen on their southward migration. One area famous for its aggregations of monarchs is Pacific Grove, California. Most of these migrating monarchs probably go as far south as the southern United States or northern Mexico; the longest flight known for a tagged individual is 1870 miles (2896 km)—from Ontario to San Luis Potosi, Mexico, from September 18, 1957, to January 25, 1958. In the south, and on their northward flight in the spring, the monarchs reproduce, and most (if not all) of the individuals reaching the northern part of the breeding range are not the same ones that left there at the end of the preceding summer.

Another butterfly that undergoes rather spectacular migratory flights in some parts of the world is the painted lady, *Cýnthia cárdui* (L.), which is almost worldwide in distribution. In North America these butterflies apparently overwinter south of the Mexican border, and in the spring fly northward over a broad front. They breed in the United States and Canada, the larvae feeding on thistles. There does not appear to be a mass migration south in late summer in North America, but such movements have been observed in the Old World.

There are a number of insects that have a permanent breeding area in the southern part of the United States and undergo mass movements northward in the spring and early summer. The insects making these flights breed in the north but do not overwinter there, and in most cases die out at the onset of cold weather. Such movements are known to occur in some of the noctuid moths and leafhoppers, for example, the black witch, *Érebus òdora* (L.), the cotton leafworm, *Alabáma argillàcea* (Hübner), the potato leafhopper, *Empoásca fàbae* (Harris), and the beet leafhopper, *Circùlifer tenéllus* (Baker). In the case of the beet leafhopper, when the food supply in the north becomes unfavorable in late summer a mass movement south may occur (but not involving the same individuals that migrated north in the spring).

Mass migrations of short-horned grasshoppers have been known since biblical times, the migrating hordes often containing millions and millions of individuals, and eating everything in sight during the stopovers on the flight. Migration in these insects seems to be induced by a combination of certain weather conditions and a buildup in numbers. Such flights are seldom seen in this country any more, but a hundred years ago such flights occurred in the Plains States; one such flight was estimated to contain 124 billion individuals, and another was estimated to be half a mile high, 100 miles (160 km) wide, and 300 miles (480 km) long.

FEEDING BEHAVIOR

All animals must eat, or they will eventually starve. Much of the activity of many animals is concerned with feeding—locating the food and eating it. Food is a very important factor in determining an animal's abundance, and where it can live (hence, its distribution). The feeding behavior of an insect—what it eats and how it feeds—generally determines that insect's economic importance.

PHYTOPHAGOUS INSECTS

Phytophagous (or herbivorous) insects feed on plants and probably outnumber those feeding on other things. There are very few terrestrial or freshwater plants that are not fed upon by some insects, and these insects feed in different ways and on different parts of the plants. Phytophagous insects that feed on plants used by man often cause considerable economic losses.

The feeding of chewing insects on foliage results in leaves that are skeletonized, riddled with holes, eaten around the edges, or entirely consumed. The smaller insects eat between the veins of the leaf and skeletonize it; the larger ones consume a part or all of the leaf. The principal insects that feed this way are grasshoppers, the larvae of various butterflies, moths, and sawflies, and beetles. When abundant, such insects can completely defoliate large areas of crops or forest.

Other insects feed on plants by sucking sap from the leaves or other parts of the plant. Leaf-feeding by sucking insects produces a characteristic spotting or browning of the leaves, or a curling and wilting (Figure 218 B); such feeding on stems or twigs may cause dwarfing or wilting. The damage to the plant is caused by the removal of the sap and by an actual injury to the plant tissues. The principal insects that feed this way are scale insects, aphids, leafhoppers, froghoppers, and various bugs. Scale insects are usually quite minute, but may occur in such numbers as to encrust the bark of a tree or the twigs or stems of a plant; they are able to kill orchard or shade trees. Aphids produce a curling of the leaves, and when feeding on fruit may leave the fruit stunted or misshapen.

Many types of insects feed inside plant tissues, as miners in the leaves, or as borers in the stems, roots, or fruits. Leaf miners tunnel and feed between the two surfaces of the leaf; their mines are of various sorts, but each leaf-mining species produces a characteristic type of mine in a particular species of plant. There are over 750 leaf-mining species of insects in the United States, representing the orders Lepidóptera (about 400 species in 17 families), Díptera (300 species in 4 families), Hymenóptera (principally sawflies), and Coleóptera (about 50 species in the families Chrysomélidae, Bupréstidae, and Curculiónidae).

Many insects, chiefly the larvae of certain moths and beetles, bore into stems; such stems are usually killed, resulting in a stunted or misshapen plant. Other insects, chiefly the larvae of various moths, flies, and beetles, burrow into fruit. Many insects bore into the wood or cambium of living trees, weakening, deforming, or sometimes killing the trees. The most important phloem and wood borers are various beetles (chiefly in the families Cerambýcidae, Bupréstidae, Scolýtidae, and Curculiónidae), certain moths (Cóssidae and Sesìidae), horntails, carpenter ants, and termites.

Many insects that feed on plants inject a chemical into the plant that causes it to grow abnormally and produce a gall. Galls may be produced on various parts of a plant, but each species of gall insect produces a characteristic gall on a certain part of a particular type of plant. Each gall may harbor one to many gall insects. The stimulus to the formation of the gall is usually provided by the feeding stage of the insect; in a few cases the ovipositing female provides the stimulus when she lays her eggs in the plant. A plant gall may have an opening to the outside (for example, the galls of Homóptera and mites), or they may be entirely closed (galls of larval insects). Five orders of insects contain gall-making species: Díptera (principally Cecidomyìidae, Tephrítidae, and Agromỳzidae), Hymenóptera (Cynípidae, some

Chalcidòidea, and some Tenthredínidae), Coleóptera (certain Curculiónidae, Buprèstidae, and Cerambýcidae), Lepidóptera (for example, the goldenrod gall moth), and Homóptera (various aphids, psyllids, and coccids). Other plant galls are caused by mites, roundworms, or fungi.

Some insects that feed on plants live in the soil and feed on the underground parts of the plant; it is usually the larval or nymphal stage of the insect that feeds in this way. Root-feeding insects are principally wireworms (Elatéridae), white grubs (Scarabaèidae), some mealy bugs, cicada nymphs, various aphids, and some fly larvae.

Perhaps the most interesting behavior to be found among the phytophagous insects is that of the few insects that grow their own plant food (a fungus). Such "fungus gardens" are produced and tended by certain ants, ambrosia beetles, and some termites. The fungus-growing ants in this country belong to the genera *Átta* and *Trachymýrmex;* one species of *Átta, A. texàna* (Buckley), occurs in the South and Southwest, and *Trachymýrmex* ants occur as far north as Canada. *Átta* ants nest in the ground, where they excavate a complex system of galleries and chambers. They cut circular pieces of leaves and carry them—parasol-like—back to their nests; they are commonly called leaf-cutting or parasol ants. The leaves are taken to special chambers in the nest, chewed up, and "seeded" with a fungus. The resulting fungus garden is tended by certain workers, which weed out any foreign fungi that may be brought in with the leaves, and it is this fungus that serves as the food of the colony. Queens that start a new colony take with them a bit of this fungus (carrying it in their mouths), to start the fungus gardens in the new colony.

ZOOPHAGOUS INSECTS

Zoophagous (or carnivorous) insects are those that feed on other animals; these other animals may be of various types, but the majority of the zoophagous insects feed on other insects, and hence might be termed entomophagous. Entomophagous insects play an important role in keeping down the populations of pest species.

Entomophagous insects are of two general sorts, predators and parasites. The distinction between these two is sometimes not very sharp, but in general predators feed on smaller or weaker insects, usually using one or more for a single meal; they live apart from their prey and often seek insects in different places for different meals. Predators are usually active, powerful insects. Parasites live in or on the bodies of their host, and live continually with their host during at least a part of their life cycle; they obtain successive meals from this host, and their feeding is at the expense of their host. Parasites are smaller than their hosts, and often more than one parasite may live in or on the same host.

Entomophagous insect parasites often operate a little differently than those parasitizing larger animals such as vertebrates, and some authorities use the term "parasitoid" for these insects. A parasite of a larger animal usually does not kill its host or consume a large part of its tissues, while an entomophagous insect parasite (a "parasitoid") consumes all or most of the host's tissues and eventually kills it.

A great many insects are predaceous on other insects. Dragonflies and damselflies are predaceous during both nymphal and adult stages; the nymphs feed on a variety of aquatic insects (and other small aquatic animals), and the adults feed on mosquitoes, small moths, and other insects. The more important predators among the beetles are the ground and tiger beetles (which feed, both as larvae and adults, on a variety of insects), and the ladybird beetles (which are important predators of aphids). Wasps (the Pompílidae, Véspidae, and Sphécidae) prey on a variety of insects and spiders, but the prey is used as food for the wasp young, and is usually not eaten by the wasp that caught it. Most of the Neuróptera are predaceous; lacewings (Chrysòpidae) are important predators of aphids. A number of groups of bugs (Hemíptera) are predaceous; for example, some of the stink bugs feed on caterpillars, and many of the aquatic bugs feed on mosquito larvae and other aquatic animals. The important predators among the flies (Díptera) are the robber flies, long-legged flies, dance flies, and syrphid flies (the latter only in the larval stage).

The majority of the entomophagous insect parasites are parasitic only during the larval stage; the adult stage is usually active and free-living, and generally locates the host and lays its eggs in, on, or near it. When the parasite eggs are laid entirely apart from the host, the host may be located and attacked by an active larval stage of the parasite, the larva may "hitch a ride" to the host on another animal (entomologists call this "phoresy"), or the eggs may be eaten by the host. Parasitic insects may feed internally or externally on their host, depending on the species; they may pupate in the host, on the outside of it, or entirely apart from it.

Some entomophagous insects are hyperparasites, that is, they parasitize another parasite. In such cases the parasite of a nonparasitic species is termed a primary parasite, and the hyperparasite a secondary parasite. There are occasionally tertiary parasites, which attack another hyperparasite.

Most of the entomophagous insect parasites belong to the orders Díptera and Hymenóptera. Among the Díptera the most important parasites are the tachinid flies; other families containing entomophagous parasites are the Sarcophágidae, Pyrgòtidae, Pipuncùlidae, Acrocéridae, and Bombylìidae. The principal parasitic Hymenoptera are the Ichneumonòidea, Chalcidòidea, Proctotrupòidea, Pelecinòidea, and Scoliòidea; these groups contain hundreds of species that parasitize other insects. Only a few insects in other orders are entomophagous parasites, for example, the Strepsiptera, and the Melòidae and Rhipiphòridae among the beetles.

The term "parasite" is sometimes applied to those insects which live in the nests of other species. The exact relationships between some of these and the members of the host species are not well understood, but many are treated as guests or inquilines, and some—which feed on the food stored by the host individuals for their own young—are called cleptoparasites.

Many insects live as parasites in or on the bodies of vertebrates, and some of these are serious pests of man or domestic animals. Most of them are external parasites, chiefly the lice (Anoplùra and Mallóphaga) and fleas. Some fly larvae (for example, bot fly larvae) are internal parasites of vertebrates, producing a condition called myiasis. Some insects and mites live as external parasites of other insects, at least during part of their life cycle, and do relatively little damage to their host; for example, some of the Ceratopogónidae live on the wings of dragonflies, many mites are ectoparasites of beetles, and water mites are ectoparasites of other insects during a part of their life cycle.

SAPROPHAGOUS INSECTS

Saprophagous insects are those feeding on dead or decaying plant or animal materials, such as carrion, dung, leaf litter, dead logs, and the like. These materials often support large insect populations. Not all the insects present in decaying material feed on it; some, such as the flies that feed in decaying fruit, may feed principally on the microorganisms present rather than on the decaying fruit, and some others, such as some of the rove beetles found around carrion, may feed on other insects there rather than on the carrion.

Saprophagous insects are found in many orders, but probably the most important are in the orders Orthóptera (cockroaches), Isóptera (termites), Coleóptera (many families), and Díptera (many families, chiefly muscoids). The most common carrion feeders are carrion beetles (Sílphidae), skin beetles (Derméstidae and Trogìnae), and the larvae of various flies (especially blow flies). The most common dung feeders are certain dung beetles (Scarabaèidae, Histéridae, and others) and the larvae of various flies (chiefly muscoids).

It is convenient to classify insect feeding behavior in three categories—phytophagous, zoophagous, and saprophagous—but it should be understood that not all insects belong exclusively to one of these categories. Many insects are rather varied feeders and may feed on either living or dead plants or animals.

DEFENSIVE BEHAVIOR

Every species of animal is subject to attack by various enemies, and if it is to survive it must have some means of defense. Many types of defense are to be found among insects; some rely on their appearance or location to avoid attack, some attempt to escape, some attack the predator, and some rely on what amounts to chemical warfare.

PASSIVE MEANS OF DEFENSE

Most insects will attempt to escape when attacked or threatened—by flying, running, jumping, swimming, or diving—and many are extremely quick. Insect collectors, like fishermen, may often speak of the "one that got away" because they didn't swing the net quite fast enough, or because the insect could fly faster than the collector could run.

Many insects "play dead" when disturbed. Some beetles fold up their legs and fall to the ground and remain motionless, often resembling a bit of dirt. Many caterpillars "freeze," often in a peculiar position; some of the inchworms hold the body out like a twig, holding on by means of prolegs at the posterior end of the body; some hawk moth larvae elevate the front part of the body and assume a sphinxlike position (it is because of this behavior that these moths are sometimes called sphinx moths); and larvae of the handmaid moths elevate both ends of the body, holding on with the prolegs in the middle of the body.

THE USE OF SHELTERS

A great many insects live in situations where enemies have difficulty in attacking them; many burrow into plant or animal tissues, under rocks, or into the soil, and others construct and live in cases or shelters. Such devices are often less effective against parasites than against predators; many parasites (especially some of the Hymenóptera) have long ovipositors with which they can reach hosts in seemingly protected situations, and sometimes these parasites are able to thrust their ovipositor through material as hard as wood to reach a host.

Many insect larvae construct cases of one sort or another, which they carry about with them, and in which they eventually pupate; the best known of these are the caddisflies, certain moth larvae, and a few beetle larvae. Caddisfly larvae construct their cases of bits of leaves, twigs, sand grains, pebbles, or other materials (Figure 352), which are fastened together with silk or may be cemented together. Each species builds a characteristic sort of case, and when a case is outgrown another is built (in some instances the cases of young larvae are different from those made by older larvae). A common case-making caterpillar is the bagworm, whose cases are made of bits of leaves and twigs tied together with silk (Figure 406). The larvae of the case-making leaf beetles construct a case composed largely of the insect's excrement.

Many lepidopterous larvae, and a few insects in other orders (for example, leaf-rolling grasshoppers and sawflies), live in a shelter made of leaves tied together with silk. In some cases a single leaf is folded or rolled up to serve as a shelter, and in some cases two or more leaves are involved; some of the gregarious caterpillars, such as the webworms, make a large shelter involving many leaves, or even entire branches.

The adults of most wasps and bees construct nurseries for their young in protected nests of various sorts—in the soil, in stems, or in natural cavities. Most social insects (termites, ants, wasps, and bees) construct fairly elaborate nests, usually in the soil. The larvae of many insects with complete metamorphosis, after completing their feeding and growth, construct a cocoon or other type of case in which they pupate.

CAMOUFLAGE

Many insects are so colored that they blend perfectly with their background; many grasshoppers are colored like the ground on which they alight, many moths are colored like the bark of a tree, and many beetles, bugs, flies, and bees are colored like the flowers they visit. Many insects resemble objects in their environment, in both color and shape; walking sticks and inchworms resemble twigs, so much so that it sometimes takes a keen eye to detect them when they remain motionless; certain treehoppers resemble thorns; some of the butterflies resemble dead leaves; some of the beetles resemble bits of bark; and some caterpillars resemble bird droppings.

Some insects are rendered inconspicuous by covering themselves with debris or excrement. The larvae of tortoise beetles (Figure 322 A) attach bits of debris and excrement to a pair of spines at the posterior end of the body and hold this material over their body like a parasol. Many dragonfly nymphs become covered with silt and debris as they rest on the bottom of a pond. The masked hunter (an assassin bug) becomes covered with lint and looks nothing more than a mass of fuzz. The larvae of some lacewings cover themselves with debris, which affords them concealment.

One of the most remarkable types of mimicry to be found in insects is Batesian mimicry, where an insect without special means of defense resembles another that has a sting or some other effective defense mechanism. This resemblance may be in behavior, as well as in size, shape, and color. Some of the robber flies, hawk moths, and syrphid flies mimic bumble bees, and many syrphid flies, thick-headed flies, clear-winged moths, and beetles mimic wasps; this mimicry is often very striking, and only a trained observer will notice that these insects are not wasps, and will neither bite nor sting. Some butterflies apparently have distasteful body fluids and are seldom attacked by predators; other species, without such body fluids, may mimic them very closely. The mimicry of the monarch by the viceroy (cf. Figures 436 A and 439 A) is an example of this type of mimicry.

CHEMICAL DEFENSES

Chemical defenses may involve body fluids that are apparently distasteful to predators, the use of repellent secretions, or the injection of poisons into an attacker. Most insects using such defenses are brightly or strikingly colored, advertising the fact that they are dangerous; one experience with such an insect, by another animal or by man, is usually sufficient to cause that type of insect to be avoided in the future—and its bright coloration makes it easily recognized.

A few insects, such as the monarch butterfly and ladybird beetles, are seldom attacked by predators, as they apparently have distasteful body fluids. Some insects give off foul-smelling substances when disturbed; stink bugs, broad-headed bugs, green lacewings, swallowtail larvae, and others might be called the skunks of the insect world, as some of these have a very unpleasant odor. A few of the insects utilizing such defensive mechanisms are able to eject the substance as a spray, in some cases even aiming it at an intruder. Bombardier beetles give off from the anus a liquid that quickly volatilizes and looks like a puff of smoke; some ants eject a very irritating liquid (mostly formic acid) from the anus; and some earwigs can squirt a foul-smelling liquid from glands on the dorsal side of the abdomen. Most of these substances appear to act as repellents, though some may be mildly toxic.

The larvae of the monarch butterfly obtain certain substances from the milkweed plants on which they feed, and these substances become especially concentrated in the wings of the adults. Birds that feed on these butterflies do not die, but vomit violently, and soon learn to avoid monarchs (and any other butterfly that resembles them). The larvae of some pine sawflies (Dipríonidae), when disturbed, discharge from the mouth an oily material that is an effective deterrent to predators. This material is similar chemically to a resin of the host plant (pine), and during feeding is stored in pouches in the insect's foregut. These represent cases of plant-feeding insects utilizing protective chemicals of the host plants.

While some insects have developed foul-smelling secretions that may repel their enemies, others have developed more potent means of chemical defense—the use of poisons that kill or injure the attacker. These may have an irritative effect on the skin of the attacker (for example, the exudations of some blister beetles), or they may be injected into the attacker by means of special poison hairs, by the bite of the insect, or by a sting. The effect of these poisons on a human being depends primarily on that person's sensitivity to the poison and on the insects involved; some people are more sensitive than others to these poisons, and some insects are much more toxic than others.

A few species of caterpillars have stinging hairs or spines which may cause severe skin irritation; the most common are the larvae of the io moth (Figure 425 D), the saddleback caterpillar (Figure 390 B), and the puss caterpillar. The io larva is a spiny greenish caterpillar, about 2 inches (50 mm) long when full grown, with a narrow lateral reddish stripe that is edged below with white. The saddleback caterpillar (Figure 390 B) is smaller and is greenish with a brown saddlelike mark on the back. The puss caterpillar, *Megalopỳge opercularis* (J. E. Smith) (family Megalopỳgidae), is densely covered with soft brown hair, but beneath the hair are numerous poison spines that can cause severe skin irritation.

Many insects will bite when handled, and some will bite if given the opportunity, whether handled or not. The bite may simply be a severe pinch by means of powerful jaws, as in certain ants and beetles, or it may be a piercing by needlelike mouth parts. Bites by mandibulate insects do not ordinarily involve any injection of poison, but the bites of sucking insects are very much like hypodermic injections, and the irritation they cause is due to the saliva injected by the insect. The bites of some sucking insects (for example, mosquitoes and bed bugs) are not particularly painful, but may cause considerable subsequent irritation; the bites of some others (for example, some of the assassin bugs and creeping water bugs) are quite painful. Centipedes, spiders, and ticks are other arthropods that inject venom when they bite.

Of all the chemical defenses used by insects, the use of a sting is probably the most effective; the effect is immediate and often severe. The only stinging insects are certain Hymenóptera (bees, wasps, and some ants), and since the sting is a modified egg-laying organ, only females sting. Some people are particularly sensitive to insect stings, and for such people a sting can be fatal; it may be of interest to note that more people are killed each year in the United States by insect bites and stings than by poisonous snakes.

ACOUSTIC BEHAVIOR

One of the most interesting types of behavior in insects is that which occurs in relation to sound. A great many insects (probably as many as all other animals combined) produce sound by means of special structures, but only a few, such as the crickets, grasshoppers, and cicadas, are heard by most people. The sounds produced by many insects are very soft or very high-pitched, and are seldom if ever heard by man. Sound in many insects plays an important role in behavior.

A serious problem encountered by early students of insect sounds was accurate description based on aural observations. The human ear is not a very good sound-analyzing instrument; many features of insect sounds, including some of those most important to the insects themselves, cannot be detected by the human ear, and a given insect sound often sounds different to different people due to differences in their hearing ability. The advent of such electronic aids as the tape recorder and some sound-analyzing instruments have opened up the modern field of bioacoustics. With the tape recorder we can "capture" a sound for future study, and can play it back to the insect (and observe the insect's reaction to it). Modern sound-analyzing instruments make it possible to determine characteristics of frequency (pitch) and rhythm with considerable accuracy. Instruments such as the sound spectrograph give a graph of the sound (for example, Figures 111 and 112), making possible an objective description; the minute details shown by these graphs enable us to detect features not apparent to the ear.

SOUND-PRODUCING MECHANISMS

Insects produce sound in several ways: (1) by stridulation, (2) by the vibration of special membranes called tymbals, (3) by striking some part of the body against the substrate, (4) by forcibly ejecting air or liquid from some body opening, (5) by the vibration of their wings or other body parts, and (6) by such general activities as moving about or feeding. The sounds produced by the last two methods are similar in that they are incidental sounds produced by general activity. All these sounds, at least in some insects, may have communicative significance.

Stridulation involves the rubbing of one body part against another; one part is generally sharp-edged, and the other is more or less filelike. Stridulatory structures are developed in a great many insect orders, and involve almost all parts of the body. Some of the best-known singers (males of the crickets and long-horned grasshoppers) stridulate with the two front wings (see page 185); some of the short-horned grasshoppers rub the hind femora (which bear a row of peglike processes) over the front wings (see page 187 and Figure 113 L). Some long-horned beetles (*Priònus*) stridulate by rubbing the hind legs along the edges of the elytra. Other beetles stridulate by rubbing hardened tubercles on the dorsal side of the abdomen against the hind wings (Passálidae) or against filelike ridges on the underside of the elytra (some Curculiónidae). Many long-horned beetles stridulate by rubbing the rear edge of one thoracic segment (usually the pronotum) against the front edge of the segment behind it; in some Hymenóptera (ants, mutillid wasps) the edges of adjacent abdominal segments are rubbed together. Some aquatic bugs stridulate by rubbing the legs against the head. Stridulatory structures have been reported on various other body parts.

Sound production by the vibration of tymbals is best known in the cicadas (see page 295), but some of the leafhoppers also produce sound in this way. A few insects tap or drum on the substrate with their head (death watch beetles), feet (some grasshoppers), or the tip of the abdomen (some cockroaches). The wing movements of most insects produce a humming or buzzing sound, but in some insects the thorax is also involved in the production of this sound; a bumble bee held by the wings will still buzz (by vibrations of the thorax).

Sound production by the expulsion of air or liquid from some body opening (the common method of sound production in birds and mammals) is relatively rare in insects. The bombardier beetles produce a popping sound when they expel a glandular fluid from the anus (see page 370); the death's-head sphinx moth, *Acheróntia átropos* (L.), expels air forcibly from the pharynx to produce a whistling sound; and certain cockroaches (for example, *Gromphadorhìna*) produce a hissing sound by expelling air from certain spiracles. These sounds are usually produced in response to disturbance.

THE CHARACTER OF INSECT SOUNDS

Most insect sounds are noiselike, that is, they contain many nonharmonically related frequencies and cannot be assigned a definite pitch; relatively few are musical or capable of being assigned a definite pitch. The principal musical sounds are those produced by wing vibration (in which case the fundamental of the sound represents the wing-stroke rate) and those produced by cricket stridulation. The musical character of cricket sounds is apparently the result of the membranous structure of the wings; the pitch appears to be determined by the toothstrike rate. The pitch of most insect sounds (stridulating sounds, sounds produced by vibrating tymbals) is usually constant throughout the sound; in only a few cases are there pitch changes through the sound. Judging by the sensitivity of the auditory organs in these insects (see page 46), it is unlikely that the insects detect any pitch changes that may occur.

The principal differences in the sounds produced by related species are in their rhythm. In the tree cricket genus *Oecánthus*, for example, the pulses of the sound (a "pulse" is the sound produced by one stroke of the scraper across the file) may be produced for relatively long periods (continuous trills), with the songs of different species differing in the pulse rate, or they may be produced in groups (bursts or chirps); the songs of different species having the pulses grouped may differ in the pulse rate in the groups, and/or in group length and rate. The insects themselves are very sensitive to these differences in rhythm; the discrimination occurs in the central nervous system.

SOUND PRODUCTION BEHAVIOR

Many insects, such as the crickets, grasshoppers, and cicadas, produce sounds more or less continuously through certain periods. Some insects "sing" only during the day (cicadas), some sing only at night (most long-horned grasshoppers, some tree crickets), and some sing both day and night (field crickets). These periods of song are probably determined largely by light intensity, temperature, and possibly other factors. In many species of singing insects, neighboring individuals synchronize their songs; when the first individual begins to sing, others near by chime in very quickly, synchronizing their pulses or chirps. This synchronization occurs in spite of other species singing in the same area, indicating that the individuals involved must be able to recognize the song of their own species very quickly. The singing of crickets, grasshoppers, and cicadas is done almost entirely by the males.

The rhythmic features of insect songs are affected by temperature; pulse rates, chirp rates, and the like rise or fall with temperature. The rate in one species may rise with temperature to a rate occurring in another species at a lower temperature, but it is still recognized by a female of this species if she is at the same temperature as the male; if she is at a different temperature, she may not respond to the male's song.

THE ROLE OF SOUND IN BEHAVIOR

Many insects respond to sound by flight or evasive behavior. Some moths have auditory organs capable of detecting the ultrasonic sounds emitted by bats; when they hear these sounds they go into a tumbling or erratic flight and head for the ground. Many insects produce what might be called a "disturbance" sound when disturbed, captured, or handled; these sounds are believed to have some survival value in possibly discouraging a predator. Song in the field cricket plays a role in the maintenance of territory. A male will remain on his territory and sing for long periods, thereby advertising the fact that it is *his* territory. When another male enters this territory, the song of the resident male changes to what might be termed an aggressive song, which usually serves to drive off the intruding male (if it doesn't, there may be a fight).

The principal role played by sound in many insects is to bring the sexes together. The common song of the male attracts the female; in a few cases the singing of the male may cause the female to produce a sound that enables the male to locate her. In some species (for example, crickets) the male sings a somewhat different song (often called a "courtship" song) in the presence of a female. Male mosquitoes are attracted to the female by the wing sounds she produces; wing sounds act similarly in other Díptera. While sound plays an important role in bringing together the sexes of many species, once they are in close proximity then other stimuli (different sounds, odors, visual stimuli, and the like) may be involved in bringing about copulatory activity.

Because the songs of different species of singing insects are different, and because the females respond only to the songs of their own species, song plays a role in species isolation and evolution. It often provides good taxonomic characters, which in some cases (for example, in the cricket genus *Grýllus*) are more diagnostic than morphological characters.

BIOLUMINESCENCE

Bioluminescence, the production of light, occurs in relatively few insects; it is known to occur in a few Collémbola, Díptera, and Coleóptera. The early interest in bioluminescence was principally in how the light was produced; current studies are more concerned with the function of the light and its role in communication. Bioluminescence has probably been most studied in the beetle family Lampýridae.

Little is known about the luminescence of Collémbola, but apparently a few of the Podùridae are able to emit light. In some the glow is continuous, while others emit light only when stimulated (from the entire body surface, for a period of 5 to 10 seconds).

The only Díptera known to be luminescent are the larvae of certain fungus gnats (Mycetophílidae), in the genera *Keroplàtus, Orfèlia,* and *Arachnocámpa.* These larvae occur only in deeply shaded areas or caves, where they spin silken webs; their luminescence attracts small insects, which are trapped in the webs and eaten by the mycetophilid larvae. The light produced by *Orfèlia fúltoni* (Fisher) (Figure 479) is continuous and light bluish, and is produced by organs in the anterior 4 or 5 segments and at the posterior end of the body; the luminous bodies are along main tracheal trunks. In a New Zealand species (*Arachnocámpa*) that spins webs on the ceilings of caves, the luminous organs are the enlarged tips of the Malpighian tubules, at the posterior end of the body; the light in this species can be turned on and off. The exact mechanism by which light is produced in these larvae is not known.

The best known luminous insects are beetles in the families Elatéridae, Phengòdidae, and Lampýridae. In *Pyróphorus* (Elatéridae), which occurs in Florida and Texas and throughout tropical America, the luminescent organs are two spots on the hind corners of the pronotum (which emit a greenish light) and areas on the first abdominal segment (which emit an orange light); the light appears slowly, persists a few seconds, and then fades out. The larvae of the Phengòdidae, often called glowworms, have pairs of luminous spots on several body segments, and when these are glowing the insect looks like a railroad car at night.

The Lampýridae (lightningbugs or fireflies) are the best known of the luminous insects; many species have well-developed light-producing organs. These organs are located just under the body wall (which is transparent) on the ventral side of the terminal abdominal segments; they consist of a layer of light-producing cells or photocytes, backed by another cell layer that acts as a reflector. These organs have a rich tracheal supply, and are supplied with nerves that generally follow the tracheae; the nerve endings are in the tracheolar cells. The light is produced by the oxidation of a substance called luciferin, catalyzed by the enzyme luciferinase, in the presence of ATP (adenosine triphosphate) and magnesium ions. The luciferinase presumably exists in an inhibited form; a nerve impulse reaching the organ releases acetylcholine, which in turn leads to the synthesis of pyrophosphate (PP); this PP reacts with the inhibited luciferinase to give free luciferinase and ATP, and the free luciferinase reacts with the luciferin in the presence of oxygen to produce light (and some by-products). Practically 100 percent of the energy released in this reaction is light.

The light signals emitted by Lampýridae serve as a means of communication and function primarily in getting the sexes together. The flashing of each species is distinctive, chiefly in its timing or rhythmic features, and a firefly can apparently recognize a member of its own species by its flashing. In *Photìnus pyràlis* (L.), for example, the male flashes as it flies about, and if a female (usually in vegetation) flashes in response (after a very specific time interval) he flies to her. These insects can be attracted to artificial lights if the lights are flashed at the proper rhythm. The female of some species of *Photùris* sometimes mimics the flashes of the females of other species and attracts males of these species—which she eats. In some lampyrids (for example, *Pteróptyx*) occurring in southeastern Asia large numbers of males flash in unison; both males and females are attracted to aggregations of synchronously flashing males.

GREGARIOUS AND SOCIAL BEHAVIOR

Many insects occur in groups, and these groups differ in the factors responsible for bringing the individuals together and in the nature of the interactions between individuals.

AGGREGATIONS

Some insect groups are simply the result of a positive reaction by many individuals to the same stimulus, for example, the insects attracted to a light or to a dead animal. Others may result from the simultaneous emergence of many adults, for example, emerging mayflies. The larvae of many Lepidóptera, which hatch from a given egg mass, may remain together during most of their larval life as a result of their reaction to a common food supply and/or to each other. Other aggregations where some mutual attraction, as well as a common reaction to the same stimulus, is involved in keeping the aggregation together include hibernating aggregations (for example, of ladybird beetles), sleeping aggregations (for example, monarch butterflies), and others.

INSECT SOCIETIES

Ants and termites, and some of the bees and wasps, live in much more integrated aggregations called societies, and these groups have some features of special interest.

CHARACTERISTICS OF AN INSECT SOCIETY An insect society is basically a family group (and undoubtedly evolved from a family group) in which the parents (or at least the female parent) remains with the young; the young and adults are associated, and the adults care for the young.

A series of stages leading to a full-fledged society can be found in some groups of Hymenóptera —from strictly solitary species where the only provision for the young by the adult is the preparation and stocking with food of some sort of shelter (cell or nest), through a subsocial situation in which there is some association of young and adults and progressive provisioning (as in the bembicine wasps).

An insect society, though composed of many individual insects, operates as a unit and is in many ways comparable to a single individual; it grows, it carries on various life processes as a unit, and reproduces itself. There are mechanisms by which the activities of different individuals (like the cells and tissues of an individual organism) are coordinated, and also mechanisms for keeping the individuals together.

A distinctive feature of an insect society is the polymorphism (caste differentiation) of its members; along with this polymorphism are differences in behavior. There is thus a division of labor in the society, which makes for greater efficiency. In hymenopterous societies there are at least three castes, queen, males (drones), and workers. The queen generally starts the colony and raises the first brood, and thereafter is concerned principally or entirely with producing eggs; the males (or one of them) fertilize the queen; the workers carry on various activities, and the different things done by different workers may be associated with the workers' age or with the particular environmental factors to which they are exposed. In the honey bee, for example, the worker engages in cell cleaning the first two days after it emerges; from 3 to 6 days of age it feeds older larvae with honey and pollen; from about 6 to 12 days of age, when its pharyngeal glands are most active, it feeds the younger larvae with a mixture of honey and saliva; from about 12 to 18 days of age, when the wax glands are most active, it works in the hive building combs and storing nectar, and may make some preliminary flights outside the hive; thereafter it is mainly concerned with foraging outside the hive, gathering nectar and pollen. The workers in some ant colonies are of different sizes, and the activities of these different-sized workers may differ; the larger ones act as soldiers, fighting and protecting the colony, and are fed by other workers; the intermediate-sized workers do most of the foraging, and regurgitate food to other workers; the smaller workers are concerned chiefly with tending the brood, nest construction, and the like.

SOME ACTIVITIES OF SOCIAL INSECTS The coordination of different body parts in an individual insect is accomplished largely by the nervous system, which serves as a means of communication between different body parts. Looking upon the insect society as a unit comparable to an individual insect, one would expect to find a means of communication between the individuals in a society, as a mechanism of coordinating the activities of different individuals. Social insects *do* have means of communication, but such communication does not operate to the extent that the nervous system does for the individual. Observations of the nest-building activities of a group of ants, or of the activities of a group during a raid, might lead one to suspect that the coordination of the activities of the different individuals was accomplished by "commands from a leader," but this is probably not the case; different individuals are simply responding to particular conditions as the situation changes. The chief means of communication in ants is by means of pheromones (see page 51). A honey bee worker, upon returning to the hive after finding a nectar source, communicates information about this source to the other workers by means of characteristic dances (see page 698).

Social insects have a home base, the nest (or in such insects as the army ants, at least a temporary bivouac), and the individuals that forage away from the nest must be able to find their way back. Some of the factors involved in this homing ability have been discussed above (page 55).

Social insects form new colonies in one of two ways: by swarming or by parental forms leaving and starting a new colony. Swarming is the method used by the honey bee and some ants; the queen, along with a group of workers, leaves and establishes a new colony somewhere else, and a new queen is developed in the group that did not leave. A queen ant, after mating, begins a new nest and raises a brood of workers; thereafter she generally does little except lay eggs, with the workers taking over other activities. In some cases (for example, certain wasps) the queen may do some foraging (in addition to egg laying) after the first group of workers appears.

Insect societies often have associated with them various other organisms: other insects, mites, other animals, and sometimes fungi. Some of these may be parasites or predators, attacking various members of the colony; some may be commensals or scavengers, tolerated by the members of the society and feeding on refuse; some may be "guests," not only tolerated but actually fed by the host insects. Many social insects cultivate fungi upon which they feed, and might be called insect farmers. Many ants "tend" aphids, and feed on the honeydew excreted by them (see page 310).

A characteristic activity in insect societies is the interchange of materials (food, secretions, etc.) between individuals (trophallaxis). Workers frequently lick one another, and many workers regurgitate food for another individual. These interchanges are apparently important in keeping the group together. Another feature common to insect societies is the ability to recognize members of one's own group, and members of another group. This is a matter of nest odor; an individual (even of the same species) entering another nest, with an odor different from that of its own nest, is generally attacked.

There are some interesting differences between the societies of termites and those of Hymenóptera. Termites have a "child labor" society in that the young, from about the second instar on, must take care of themselves; the nymphs are thus the workers and, except for those that become soldiers or reproductives, remain workers the rest of their lives. They live a shut-in existence in their nests and rarely leave. The hymenopterous society is one built on adult labor; the relatively helpless young are protected from an adverse outside environment and cared for by adults. The adults, with their perfected adult structures and abilities, perform the various activities that maintain the colony, and regularly forage outside the nest.

References on Insect Behavior

Alexander, R. D. 1967. Acoustical communication in arthropods. *Ann. Rev. Ent.*, 12:495–526.

Askew, R. R. 1971. *Parasitic Insects*. New York: American Elsevier, xx + 316 pp., 124 f.

Brues, C. T. 1946. *Insect Dietary*. Cambridge, Mass.: Harvard Univ. Press, xxvi + 466 pp., 68 f., 22 pl.

Chapman, R. F. 1971. *The Insects, Structure and Function*. New York: American Elsevier, xii + 819 pp.; illus.

Clausen, C. P. 1940. *Entomophagous Insects*. New York: McGraw-Hill, x + 688 pp., 257 f.

DeLong, D. M. 1971. The bionomics of leafhoppers. *Ann. Rev. Ent.*, 16:179–210.

Dethier, V. G., and E. Stellae. 1964 (2nd ed.). *Animal Behavior*. Englewood Cliffs, N.J.: Prentice-Hall, viii + 118 pp.; illus.

Eisner, T. E. 1970. Chemical defense against predators in arthropods. In *Chemical Ecology*, E. Sondheimer and J. B. Simeone (Eds.). New York: Academic Press, pp. 157–217.

Eisner, T. E., and Y. C. Meinwald. 1966. Defensive secretions of arthropods. *Science*, 153:1341–1350.

Frisch, K. von. 1967. *The Dance Language and Orientation of Bees*. Belknap Press of Harvard Univ. Press, xv + 566 pp.; illus.

Frisch, K. von. 1971 (rev. ed.). *Bees, Their Vision, Chemical Senses, and Language*. Ithaca, N.Y.: Cornell Univ. Press, xviii + 157 pp., 76 f.

Haskell, P. T. 1974. Sound Production. In *The Physiology of Insects*, 2nd ed., Morris Rockstein (Ed.). New York: Academic Press, Vol. 2, pp. 353–410.

Hutchins, R. E. 1966. *Insects*. Englewood Cliffs, N.J.: Prentice-Hall, xii + 324 pp.; illus.

Johnsgard, P. A. 1967. *Animal Behavior*. Dubuque, Iowa: Wm. C. Brown, ix + 156 pp., 6 f.

Lindauer, M. 1967. Recent advances in bee communication and orientation. *Ann. Rev. Ent.*, 12:439–470; 15 f.

Lloyd, J. E. 1971. Bioluminescent communication in insects. *Ann. Rev. Ent.*, 16:97–122; 40 f.

Michener, C. D. 1974. *The Social Behavior of Bees. A Comparative Study*. Cambridge, Mass.: Belknap Press of Harvard Univ. Press, xii + 404 pp.; illus.

Michener, C. D., and M. H. Michener. 1951. *American Social Insects*. New York: Van Nostrand, xiv + 267 pp., 109 f.

Nachtigall, W. 1974. *Insects in Flight*. (Translated from German by H. Oldroyd, R. H. Abbott, and M. Biederman-Thorson.) New York: McGraw-Hill, 153 pp., 32 pl., 59 f.

Pringle, J. W. S. 1957. *Insect Flight*. Cambridge: Cambridge Univ. Press, vii + 132 pp., 52 f.

Rettenmeyer, C. W. 1970. Insect Mimicry. *Ann. Rev. Ent.*, 15:43-74.

Romoser, W. S. 1973. *The Science of Entomology*. New York: Macmillan, xi + 449 pp.; illus.

Scott, J. P. 1958. *Animal Behavior*. Chicago: Univ. Chicago Press, xi + 281 pp., 33 f.

Sotavalta, O. 1947. Wingstroke frequency. *Acta Ent. Fennica*, 4:1–117.

Van der Kloot, W. G. 1968. *Behavior*. New York: Holt, Rinehart & Winston, ix + 166 pp.; illus.

Wallace, R. A. 1973. *The Ecology and Evolution of Animal Behavior*. Pacific Palisades, Calif.: Goodyear, viii + 342 pp.; illus.

Waterhouse, D. F., *et al*. 1970. *Insects of Australia*. Canberra: Melbourne Univ. Press. xiii + 1029 pp.; illus. (especially Ch. 5, pp. 107–140; 45 f.).

Wigglesworth, V. B. 1972. *The Life of Insects*. New York: Universe Books, 360 pp.; illus.

Williams, C. B. 1958. *Insect Migration*. London: Collins. xiii + 236 pp., illus.

Wilson, E. O. 1965. Chemical communication in the social insects. *Science,* 149(3688):1064–1070; 4 f.

Wilson, E. O. 1971. *The Insect Societies*. Cambridge, Mass.: Harvard Univ. Press, x + 548 pp.; illus.

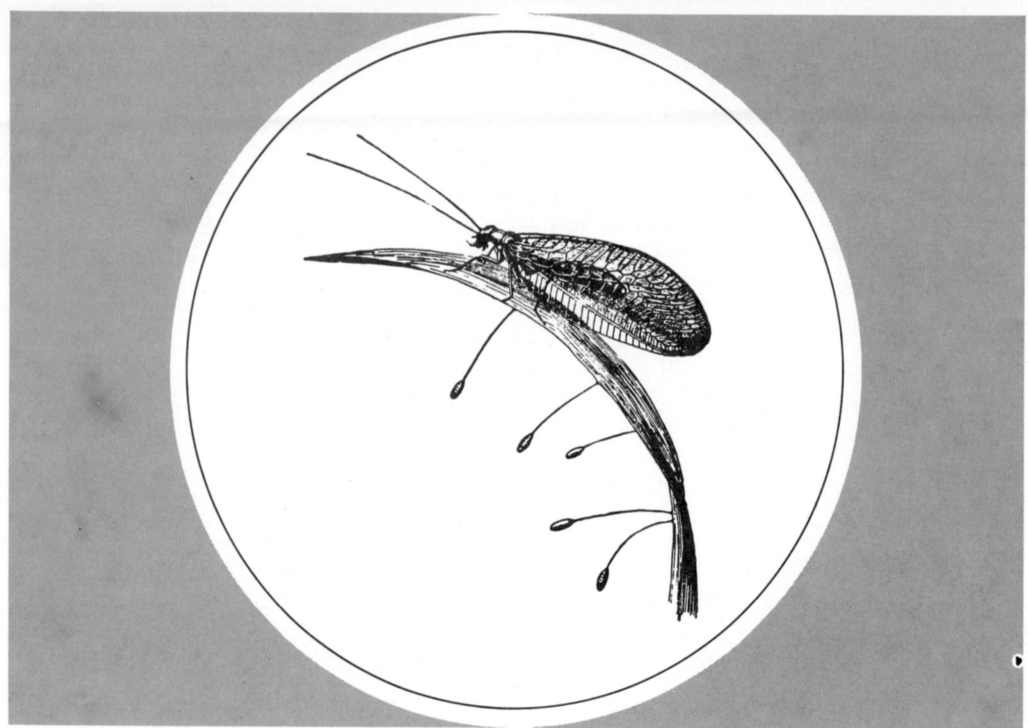

5: THE DEVELOPMENT AND METAMORPHOSIS OF INSECTS

All insects develop from eggs. Most insects are oviparous, that is, the young hatch from the eggs after they have been laid; in a few insects the eggs develop within the body of the female, and living young are produced.

INSECT EGGS

The eggs of different insects vary greatly in appearance (Figures 34 and 35). Most eggs are spherical, oval, or elongate (Figure 34 B, C, G), but some are barrel-shaped (Figure 35), some are disc-shaped, and others are of other shapes. The egg is covered with a shell that varies in thickness, sculpturing, and color; many eggs are provided with characteristic ridges, spines, or other processes, and some are brightly colored.

Most insect eggs are laid in a situation where they are afforded some protection or where the young on hatching will have suitable conditions for development. Many insects enclose their eggs in some sort of protective material; cockroaches, mantids, and other insects enclose their eggs in an egg case or capsule; the tent caterpillar covers its eggs with a shellaclike material; the gypsy moth lays its eggs in a mass of its body hairs. Grasshoppers, June beetles, and other insects lay their eggs in the ground; tree crickets insert their eggs in plant tissues (Figure 34 E). Most plant-feeding insects lay their eggs on the food plant of the young. Insects whose immature stages are aquatic usually

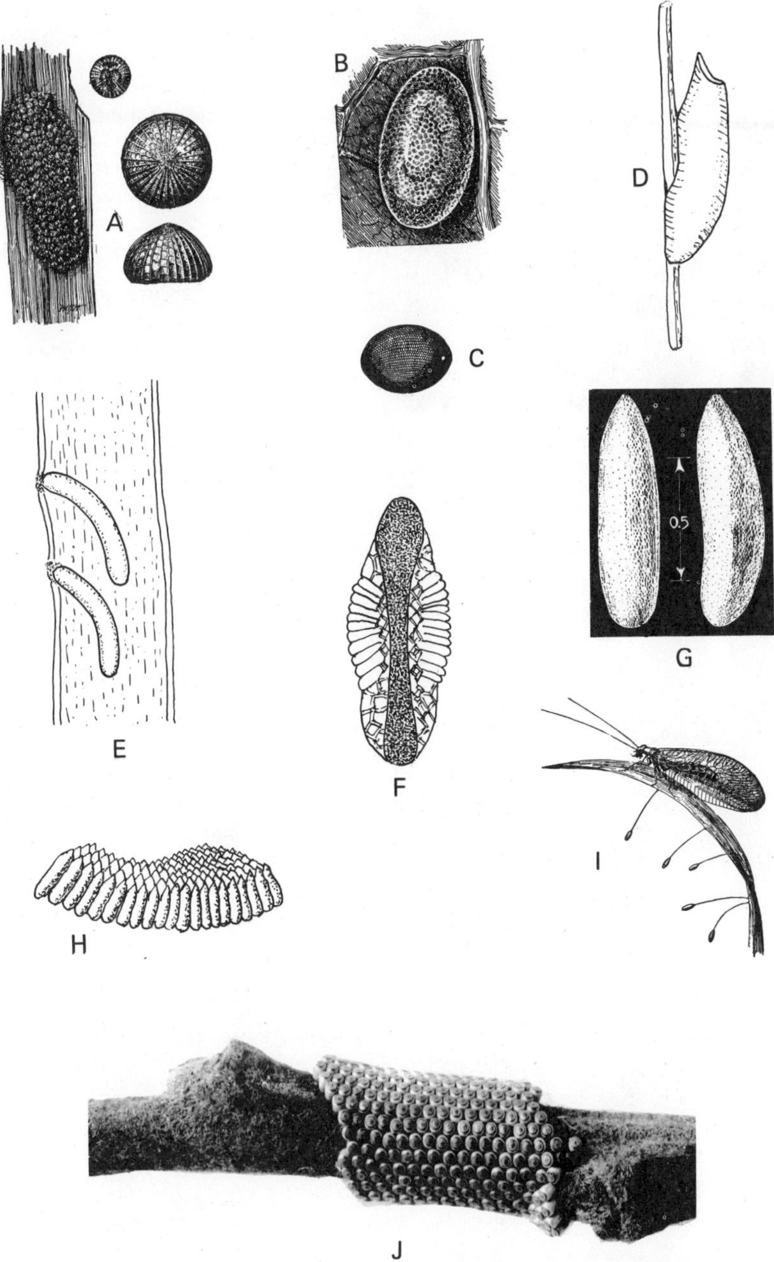

Figure 34. Insect eggs. A, fall armyworm, *Spodóptera frugipérda* (J. E. Smith); B, grape leaffolder, *Désmia funeràlis* (Hübner); C, southern corn rootworm, *Diabrótica undécimpunctàta howardi* Barber; D, horse bot fly, *Gasteróphilus intestinàlis* (De Geer); E, snowy tree cricket, *Oecánthus fúltoni* Walker; F, *Anópheles* mosquito G, seedcorn maggot, *Hylemỳa platùra* (Meigen); H. *Cùlex* mosquito, egg raft; I, lacewing, *Chrysòpa* sp.; J, fall cankerworm, *Alsóphila pometària* (Harris). (A–C, G, and I, courtesy of USDA; J, courtesy of Ohio Agricultural Research and Development Center.)

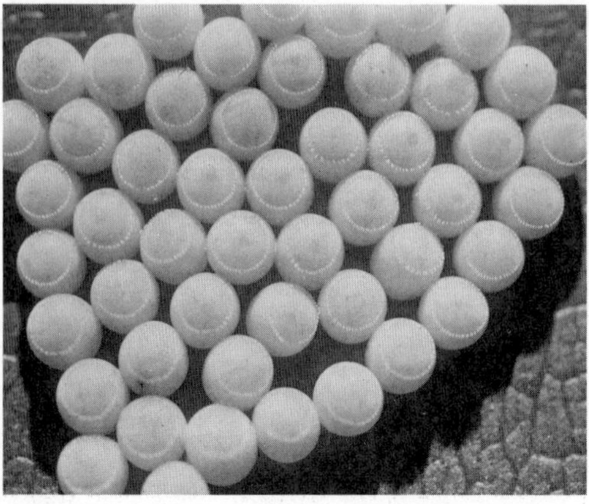

Figure 35. Eggs of a stink bug. (Courtesy of Ohio Agricultural Research and Development Center.)

lay their eggs in water, often attaching them to objects in the water. Parasitic insects usually lay their eggs in or on the body of the host. Some insects deposit their eggs singly, while others lay their eggs in characteristic groups or masses (Figures 34 H, J and 35). The number laid varies from one in certain aphids to many thousands in some of the social insects; most insects lay from 50 to a few hundred eggs.

EMBRYONIC DEVELOPMENT

The egg of an insect is a cell with two outer coverings, a thin vitelline membrane surrounding the cytoplasm, and an outer chorion; the chorion, which is the hard outer shell of the egg, has a minute pore or set of pores (the micropyle) at one end, through which sperm enter the egg (Figure 36 A). Just inside the vitelline membrane is a layer of

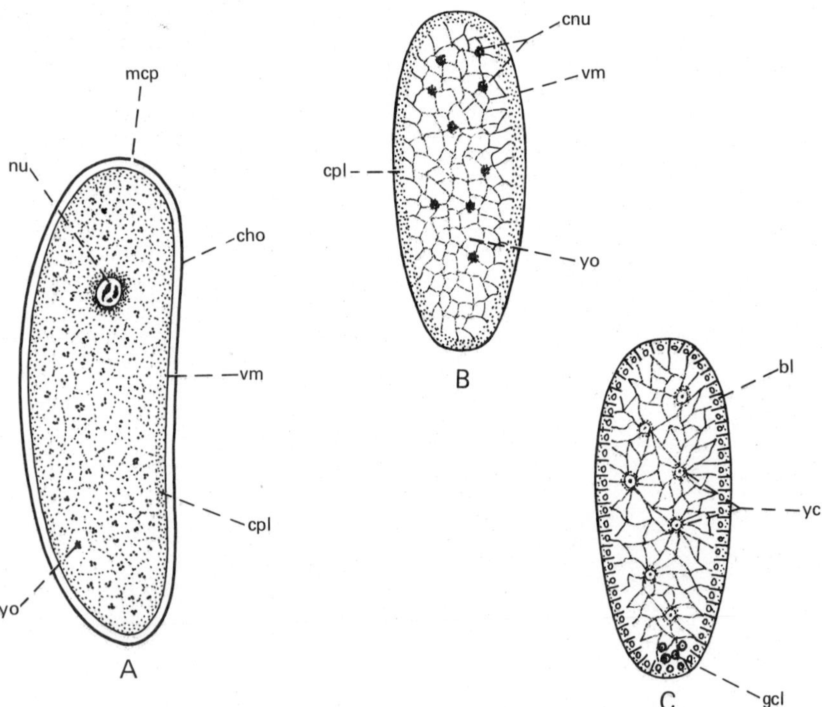

Figure 36. A, diagram of a typical insect egg; B, early cleavage; C, peripheral blastoderm layer formed. *bl,* blastoderm; *cho,* chorion; *cnu,* cleavage nuclei; *cpl,* cortical cytoplasm; *gcl,* germ cells; *mcp,* micropyle; *nu,* nucleus; *vm,* vitelline membrane; *yc,* yolk cells; *yo,* yolk. (Redrawn from Snodgrass, by permission of McGraw-Hill Book Company, Inc.)

cortical cytoplasm; the central portion of the egg, inside the cortical cytoplasm, is largely yolk.

Most insect eggs undergo meroblastic cleavage. The early cleavages involve only the nucleus, giving rise to daughter nuclei scattered through the cytoplasm (Figure 36 B); eventually these nuclei migrate to the periphery of the egg (to the layer of cortical cytoplasm). After nuclear migration the peripheral cytoplasm becomes subdivided into cells, usually each with one nucleus, forming a cell layer, the blastoderm (Figure 36 C, *bl*). This is the blastula stage. Within the blastoderm, in the mass of yolk material, are a few cells that do not take part in the formation of the blastoderm; these consist mainly of yolk cells.

The blastoderm cells on the ventral side of the egg enlarge and thicken, forming a germ band or ventral plate that will eventually form the embryo; the remaining cells of the blastoderm become the serosa and (later) the amnion. The germ band becomes differentiated into a median area or middle plate and two lateral areas, the lateral plates (Figure 37 A). The gastrula stage begins when the mesoderm is formed from the middle plate in one of three ways: by an invagination of this plate (Figure 37 B, C), by the lateral plates growing over it (Figure 37 D, E), or by a proliferation of cells from the inner surface of it (Figure 37 F). Cells proliferate from each end of the mesoderm and eventually grow around the yolk; these cells represent the beginnings of the endoderm, and they form the lining of what will be the midgut of the insect (Figure 38). From the three germ layers—ectoderm, mesoderm, and endoderm—the various organs and tissues of the insect develop; the ectoderm gives rise to the body wall, tracheal system, nervous system, the Malpighian tubules, and the anterior and posterior ends of the alimentary tract; the mesoderm gives rise to the muscular system, heart, and gonads.

The alimentary tract is formed by invaginations from each end of the embryo, which extend to and unite with the primitive midgut (Figure 38). The anterior invagination becomes the foregut, the posterior invagination becomes the hindgut, and the central part (lined with endoderm) becomes the midgut. The cells lining the foregut and hindgut are ectodermal in origin and secrete cuticle.

Body segmentation becomes evident fairly early in embryonic development; it appears first in the anterior part of the body. It involves ectoderm and mesoderm, but not endoderm, and is reflected in the segmental arrangement of the struc-

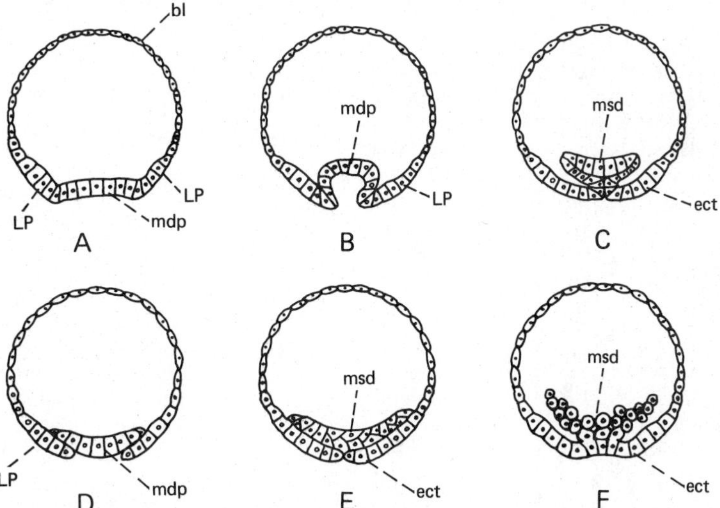

Figure 37. Cross-section diagrams showing mesoderm formation in insects. A, germ band differentiated into middle and lateral plates; B and C, stages in mesoderm formation by invagination of middle plate; D and E, stages in mesoderm formation by lateral plates growing over middle plate; F, mesoderm formation by internal proliferation from middle plate. *bl*, blastoderm; *ect*, ectoderm; *mdp*, middle plate; *LP*, lateral plate; *msd*, mesoderm. (Redrawn from Snodgrass, by permission of McGraw-Hill Book Company, Inc.)

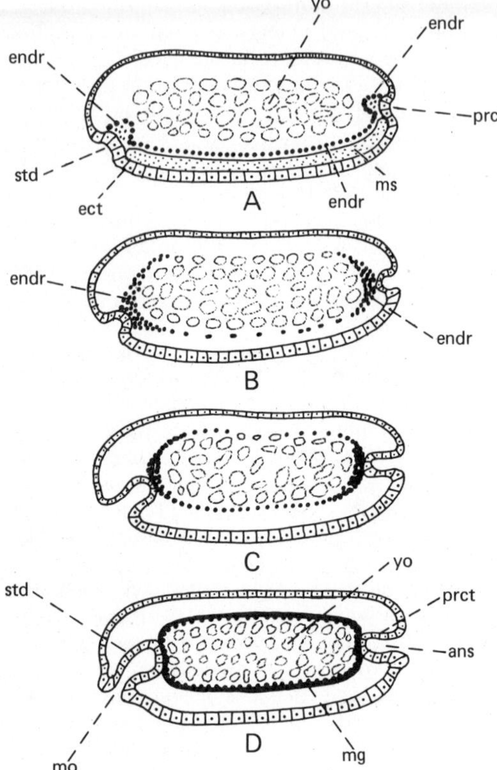

Figure 38. Diagrams showing the formation of the alimentary canal. A, early stage in which endoderm is represented by rudiments; B and C, development of endoderm around yolk; D, completion of alimentary canal. *ans,* anus; *ect,* ectoderm; *end,* endoderm; *endr,* endodermal rudiments; *mg,* midgut; *mo,* mouth; *ms,* mesoderm; *prct,* proctodaeum; *std,* stomodaeum or foregut; *yo,* yolk. (Redrawn from Snodgrass, by permission of McGraw-Hill Book Company, Inc.)

tures developing from these germ layers (nervous system, heart, tracheal system, and the appendages). The appendages appear soon after segmentation becomes evident; typically, each segment begins to develop a pair of appendages, but most of these are resorbed and do not develop further.

At some time early in its development the embryo becomes surrounded by two membranes, an inner amnion and an outer serosa; later it acquires a cuticular membrane secreted by the epidermis. The formation of the amnion and serosa sometimes involves a reversal of position of the embryo in the egg; the embryo turns tail first into the yolk, away from the blastoderm. This turning carries part of the extraembryonic blastoderm into the yolk, and when the turning is complete, the opening into the embryonic cavity is closed; the extraembryonic blastoderm thus forms a lining (the amnion) around the embryonic cavity, and the outer part of the blastoderm, which surrounds the egg, becomes the serosa. The embryo later returns to its original position on the ventral side of the egg. In other cases the amnion and serosa are formed by folds of the blastoderm, which grow out from the edge of the germ band and unite beneath it. These membranes usually disappear before the embryo is ready to leave the egg. Cuticular coverings of the embryo (sometimes called pronymphal membranes) occur in insects with simple metamorphosis and in a few with complete metamorphosis; these are shed by a process akin to molting before or very shortly after hatching.

A young insect may escape from the egg in various ways. Most insects with chewing mouth parts chew their way out of the egg. Many insects possess what are called egg-bursters—spinelike, knifelike, or sawlike processes on the dorsal side of the head—which are used in breaking through the egg shell. The egg shell is sometimes broken along weakened lines, either by the wriggling of the insect within, or by the insect taking in air and rupturing the shell by internal pressure. The hatching of the egg is sometimes called eclosion.

POLYEMBRYONY

Polyembryony is the development of two or more embryos from a single egg; it occurs in some of the parasitic Hymenóptera. In the embryonic development of such an insect, the dividing nucleus forms cell clusters, each of which develops into an embryo. The number of embryos that grow to maturity in a given host depends on the relative size of the parasite larvae and the host; in some cases there are more parasite larvae than the food supply (the body contents of the host) will support, and some of them die and may be eaten by the surviving larvae.

Polyembryony occurs in four families of parasitic Hymenóptera, the Bracónidae (species of *Macrocéntrus*), Encýrtidae (many genera), Platygastéridae (species of *Platygáster*), and Dryínidae (in *Aphelòpus thèliae* Gahan). The number of young from a single egg varies in *Macrocéntrus* from 16 to 24, but in *M. ancylívorus* Rohwer only one parasite larva leaves the host. In *Platygáster* from 2 to 18 larvae develop from a single egg, and in *Aphelòpus* from 40 to 60 develop from a single egg; in some of the Encýrtidae over 1500 young develop from a single egg.

POSTEMBRYONIC GROWTH

The fact that an insect possesses an exoskeleton presents a problem as far as growth is concerned. To function as an exoskeleton, the insect's body wall must be relatively rigid; if it is relatively rigid, it cannot expand very much. Therefore, as the insect grows or increases in size, this exoskeleton must be periodically shed and replaced with a larger one. This process of shedding and renewing the exoskeleton is called molting, or ecdysis.

The molt involves not only the cuticle of the body wall, but also the cuticular linings of the tracheae, foregut, and hindgut, and the endoskeletal structures. The tracheal linings usually remain attached to the body wall when it is shed; the linings of the foregut and hindgut usually break up, and the pieces are passed out through the anus; the tentorium usually breaks into four pieces, which are withdrawn through the tentorial pits during the molt. The cast skins (exuviae) often retain the shape of the insects from which they were shed.

Prior to the actual shedding process, a new cuticle (secreted by the epidermal cells) begins to form under the old one. Secretion of a fluid by the epidermal cells (the molting fluid) first separates the epidermis from the old cuticle, then the new cuticle is deposited, outer layers first. The molting fluid contains enzymes that digest the endocuticle (but do not affect the epicuticle or the sclerotin of the exocuticle), and the digestion products are absorbed through the new cuticle and are used in forming the new cuticle. Once the new cuticle is formed, the insect is ready to shed or break out of the old one. The shedding process begins with a splitting of the old cuticle along lines of weakness, usually in the midline of the dorsal side of the thorax. The rupturing force is pressure of the blood (and sometimes air or water), forced into the thorax by contraction of the abdominal muscles. This split in the thorax grows, and the insect eventually wriggles its way out of the old cuticle.

When it first emerges from the old cuticle, the insect is pale in color and its cuticle is soft; within an hour or two the exocuticle begins to harden and darken. During this brief period the insect enlarges to the size of the next stage, usually by taking in air or water. The wings (if present) are expanded (after the last molt) by forcing blood into their veins. The alimentary tract often serves as a reservoir of the air used in this expansion; if the crop of a cockroach, for example, is punctured with a needle, the insect does not expand but collapses; if the wing tips of an emerging dragonfly are cut off, blood escapes from the cut ends and the wings fail to expand.

The number of molts varies in most insects from four to eight, but some of the Odonàta undergo 10 or 12 molts, and some of the Epheméroptera may undergo as many as 28 molts. A few insects, such as the bristletails, may continue to molt after reaching the adult stage, but most insects neither molt nor increase in size once the adult stage is reached.

The stage of the insect between molts is called an instar; the first instar is between hatching and the first larval or nymphal molt, the second instar is between the first and second molts, and so on.

The increase in size at each molt varies in different species and in different body parts, but in many insects the increase follows a geometric progression. The increase in the width of the larval head capsule, for example, is usually by a factor of 1.2–1.4 at each molt (Dyar's rule). In species where the individual molts are not actually observed, Dyar's rule can be applied to head capsule measurements of a series of different-sized larvae to determine the number of instars.

METAMORPHOSIS

Most insects change in form during postembryonic development, and the different instars are not all alike; this change is called metamorphosis. Some insects undergo very little change in form, and the young and adults are very similar except for size (Figure 39); in other cases the young and adults are quite different, in habits as well as in form (Figure 41).

There is quite a bit of variation in the metamorphosis occurring in different insect groups, but these variations can be grouped in two general types, simple metamorphosis and complete metamorphosis. In simple metamorphosis the wings (if any) develop externally during the immature stages, and there is ordinarily no "resting" stage preceding the last molt (Figures 39 and 40). In complete metamorphosis the wings (if any) develop internally during the immature stages, and there is a "resting" or pupal stage preceding the last molt (Figure 41). The pupal stage is a "resting" stage in that the insect at this time ordinarily does

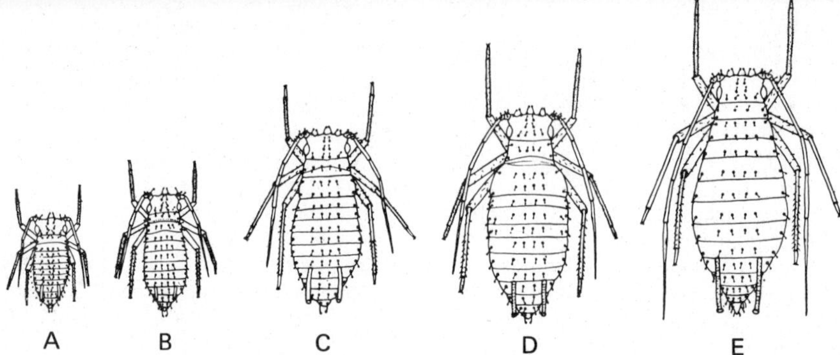

Figure 39. Stages in the development of the strawberry aphid, *Chaetosìphon fragaefòlii* (Cockerell). A, first instar; B, second instar; C, third instar; D, fourth instar; E, adult female. (Courtesy of Baerg and Arkansas Agricultural Experiment Station.)

not move around, but a very considerable amount of change (to the adult) is taking place in this stage.

SIMPLE METAMORPHOSIS

The young of insects with this type of metamorphosis are called nymphs, and are usually very similar to the adults. Compound eyes are present in the nymph if they are present in the adult. If the adults are winged, the wings appear as budlike outgrowths in the early instars (Figure 40) and increase in size only slightly up to the last molt; after the last molt the wings expand to their full adult size. Simple metamorphosis occurs in orders 1–18 (see list, page 137).

There are differences in the kind and amount of change occurring in the insects with simple metamorphosis, and many entomologists recognize three types of metamorphosis in these insects, ametabolous, paurometabolous, and hemimetabolous. Ametabolous insects (with "no" metamorphosis) are wingless as adults, and the principal difference between nymphs and adults is in size. This type of development occurs in the apterygote orders (Protùra, Collémbola, Diplùra, and Thysanùra), and in most wingless members of the other orders with simple metamorphosis. In hemimetabolous insects (with "incomplete" metamorphosis) the nymphs are aquatic and gill-breathing, and differ considerably from the adults in appearance; this type of development occurs in the

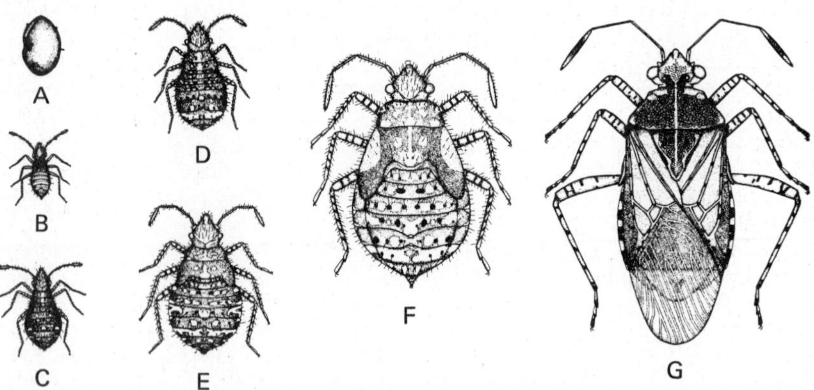

Figure 40. Stages in the development of the grass bug, *Arhýssus sìdae* (Fabricius). A, egg; B, first instar; C, second instar; D, third instar; E, fourth instar; F, fifth instar; G, adult female. (Courtesy of Readio and the Entomological Society of America.)

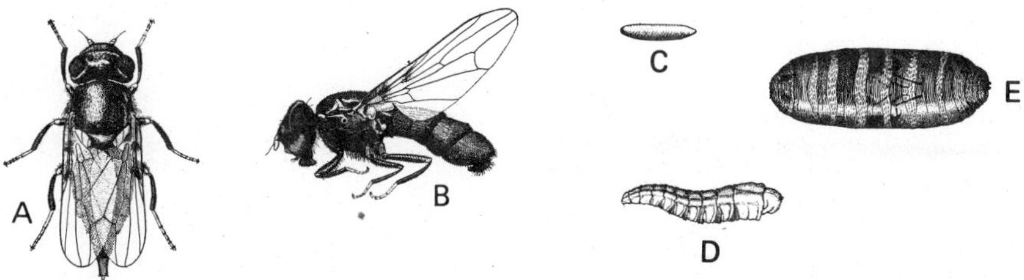

Figure 41. Stages in the development of the sugarbeet root maggot, *Tétanops myopaefòrmis* (Röder). A, adult female; B, adult male; C, egg; D, larva; E, puparium (pupa inside). (Courtesy of Knowlton and the Utah Agricultural Experiment Station.)

Ephemeróptera, Odonàta, and Plecóptera, and the young of these insects are sometimes called naiads. Paurometabolous insects (with "gradual" metamorphosis) include the remaining insects with simple metamorphosis. The adults are winged, the nymphs and adults live in the same habitat, and the principal changes during growth are in size, body proportions, the development of the ocelli, and occasionally in the form of other structures.

COMPLETE METAMORPHOSIS

The immature and adult stages of insects that undergo complete metamorphosis are usually quite different in form, often live in different habitats, and have very different habits. The early instars are more or less wormlike, and the young in this stage are called larvae (Figures 41 D and 42). The different larval instars are usually similar in form but differ in size. The wings, when they are present in the adult, develop internally during the larval stage and are not everted until the end of the last larval instar. Larvae do not have compound eyes, they may or may not have thoracic legs, and they sometimes possess leglike appendages (the prolegs) on the abdomen. Larvae generally have chewing mouth parts, even in those orders in which the adults have sucking mouth parts.

Following the molt of the last larval instar, the insect transforms into a stage called the pupa (Figures 41 E and 43). The insect does not feed in this stage and is usually inactive. Pupae are often covered by a cocoon or some other protective material, and many insects pass the winter in the pupal stage. The final molt occurs at the end of the pupal stage, and the last stage is the adult. The adult is usually pale in color when it first emerges from the pupa, and its wings are short, soft, and wrinkled. In a short time, from a few minutes to several hours or more, depending on the species, the wings expand and harden, the pigmentation develops, and the insect is ready to go on its way. This type of metamorphosis occurs in orders 19–27 and is often called holometabolous (see list, page 137).

INTERMEDIATE TYPES OF METAMORPHOSIS

Insects with simple metamorphosis have the wings (if present) developing externally, they have compound eyes in the nymphal stages if such eyes are present in the adult, and although the insect may be quiescent prior to the final molt, this quiescence usually does not last through the entire penultimate instar; this instar is generally not referred to as a pupa. Insects with complete metamorphosis have the wings (if present) developing internally during the early (larval) instars, and the wings do not appear externally until the penultimate instar, which is usually quiescent and is called a pupa; the larva lacks compound eyes and is usually quite different from the adult in body form and habits.

Not all insects have a type of metamorphosis that can be readily classified as simple or complete; some have a metamorphosis that is somewhat intermediate between these two types. Such intermediate metamorphosis is found in thrips (page 251), whiteflies (page 309), and in male scale insects (page 314).

METAMORPHOSIS IN THRIPS The first two instars are wingless and active, and are usually called larvae. The next two instars (the next three in the suborder Tubulífera) are inactive, with external wings; the first of these (the first two in the Tubulífera) is called a prepupa and the second a pupa; the final instar is the adult. Apparently at least some of the wing development is internal during the first two instars. This metamorphosis resembles complete metamorphosis in that at least some of the wing development is internal, and an inactive ("pupa") stage precedes the adult; it is similar to simple metamorphosis in that the early instars have compound eyes, and external wings are present in more than one preadult instar.

METAMORPHOSIS IN WHITEFLIES These insects have five instars, the last of which is the adult. The first instar is active and wingless, while the next three instars are inactive, sessile, and scalelike, with the wings developing internally. The fourth instar is called the pupa, and it has external wings. The first three instars are usually called larvae. The molt from the last larval instar to the pupa takes place inside the last larval skin, which forms a puparium. This metamorphosis is essentially complete, though most other members of this order (Homóptera) have simple metamorphosis.

METAMORPHOSIS IN MALE SCALE INSECTS These insects have a type of metamorphosis that is very similar to that in whiteflies. The first instar (Figure 224 B), the "crawler," is active and wingless, but the remaining preadult instars are sessile and inactive; the last preadult instar, which has external wings, is called the pupa. The development of the wings is at least partly internal.

THE CONTROL OF METAMORPHOSIS

The metamorphosis of insects is controlled by three hormones: a brain hormone, a molting hormone called ecdysone, and the juvenile hormone (see page 51). The brain hormone stimulates the prothoracic glands to produce ecdysone, which promotes growth and induces molting. The juvenile hormone promotes larval or nymphal development and prevents metamorphosis. If ecdysone is injected into an isolated insect abdomen, this abdomen will molt. Removal of the juvenile hormone from a larva or nymph (by removing the corpora allata) will cause the larva to pupate and the nymph to molt to an adult when ecdysone is present. Injection of ecdysone into a pupa (in the presence of the juvenile hormone) will cause the pupa to molt to a second pupa. Injection of the juvenile hormone into a last instar nymph or larva will cause another nymphal or larval stage to be produced at the next molt. The corpora allata are active during the early instars, and usually cease secreting the juvenile hormone in the last preadult instar; its absence in this instar results in metamorphosis.

HISTOLOGICAL CHANGES IN METAMORPHOSIS

The changes from instar to instar in insects with simple metamorphosis are generally relatively slight and gradual, being most marked at the final molt to the adult, but in insects with complete metamorphosis there is considerable reorganization within the insect in the pupal stage. Some structures in the larva, such as the heart, nervous system, and tracheal system, change very little at metamorphosis; some adult structures are present in a rudimentary form in the larva and remain so during successive larval instars; then, more or less suddenly, they develop to their adult form in the pupal stage. Still other adult structures are not represented in the larva and must be developed at the time of metamorphosis.

The changes during metamorphosis are accomplished by two processes, histolysis and histogenesis. Histolysis is a process whereby larval structures are broken down into material that can be used in the development of adult structures; histogenesis is the process of developing the adult structures from the products of histolysis. The chief sources of material for histogenesis are the blood, fat body, and histolyzed tissues such as the larval muscles.

These changes begin in the last larval instar, before the molt to the pupa. The first change appears in the epidermis, which secretes the pupal cuticle; the other changes begin in the prepupal stage of the last larval instar, and continue through the pupal stage.

TYPES OF LARVAE

The larvae of the various insects that undergo complete metamorphosis differ considerably in form, and several types may be recognized.

Eruciform – caterpillarlike (Figure 42 G); body cylindrical, the head well developed but with very short antennae, and with both thoracic legs and abdominal prolegs. This type occurs in the Lepidóptera, Mecóptera, and some Hymenóptera (suborder Sýmphyta).

Scarabaeiform – grublike (Figure 42 B); usually curved, the head well developed, with thoracic legs but without abdominal prolegs, and relatively inactive and sluggish. This type occurs in certain Coleóptera (for example, Scarabaèidae).

Campodeiform – resembling diplurans in the genus *Campòdea* (Figure 89 A); body elongate and somewhat flattened, the cerci and antennae usually well developed, the thoracic legs well de-

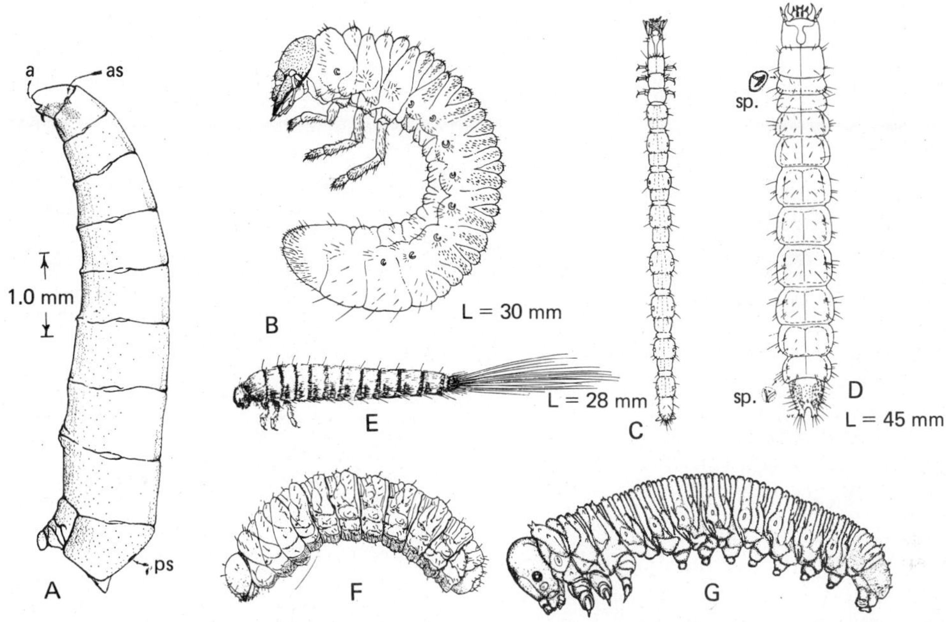

Figure 42. Insect larvae. A, maggot or vermiform larva of *Hylemỳa platùra* (Meigen) (Díptera, Anthomyìidae); B, grub or scarabaeiform larva of *Phyllóphaga rugòsa* (Melsheimer) (Coleóptera, Scarabaèidae); C, elateriform larva of *Cardióphorus* sp. (Coleóptera, Elatéridae); D, elateriform larva of *Álaus oculàtus* (L.) (Coleóptera, Elatéridae); E, larva of *Attagènus megátoma* (Fabricius) (Coleóptera, Derméstidae); F, vermiform larva of *Cỳlas formicàrius elegántulus* (Summers) (Coleóptera, Curculiónidae); G, eruciform larva of *Caliròa aèthiops* (Fabricius) (Hymenóptera, Tenthredínidae). *a*, antenna; *as*, anterior spiracle; *L*, length; *ps*, posterior spiracle; *sp*, spiracle. (A and E–G, courtesy of USDA; B–D, courtesy of Peterson. Reprinted by permission.)

veloped, and the larvae usually active. This type occurs in the Neuróptera, Trichóptera, and many Coleóptera.

Elateriform—wirewormlike (Figure 42 C, D); body elongate, cylindrical, and hard-shelled, the legs short, and the body bristles reduced. This type occurs in certain Coleóptera (for example, Elatéridae).

Vermiform—maggotlike (Figure 42 A, F); body elongate and wormlike, legless, and with or without a well-developed head. This type occurs in the Díptera, Siphonáptera, most Hymenóptera (suborder Apócrita), and in some Coleóptera and Lepidóptera.

TYPES OF PUPAE

The pupae of insects with complete metamorphosis vary, and three principal types may be recognized.

Obtect—with the appendages more or less glued to the body (Figure 43 A, B). This type occurs in the Lepidóptera and some Díptera (suborder Nematócera). The pupa in many Lepidóptera is covered by a silken cocoon formed by the larva before it molts to the pupal stage.

Exarate—with the appendages free and not glued to the body (Figure 43 C–E). Such a pupa looks much like a pale, mummified adult, and is usually not covered by a cocoon. This type occurs in most insects with complete metamorphosis, except the Díptera and most Lepídoptera.

Coarctate—essentially like an exarate pupa, but remaining covered by the hardened exuviae of the next to the last larval instar, which is called a puparium (Figure 43 F). This type occurs in the Díptera (suborders Brachýcera and Cyclórrhapha).

HYPERMETAMORPHOSIS

Hypermetamorphosis is a type of complete metamorphosis in which the different larval instars are not of the same type; the first instar is active and

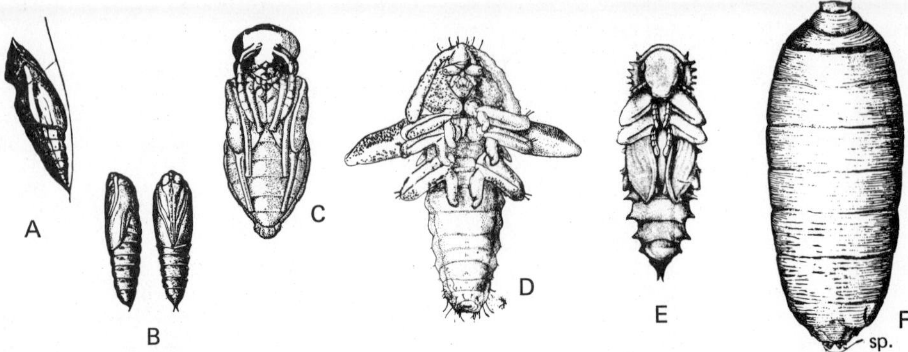

Figure 43. Insect pupae. A, chysalis of the sulphur butterfly, *Còlias eurýtheme* Boisduval (Lepidóptera, Piéridae); B, fall armyworm, *Spodóptera frugipérda* (J. E. Smith) (Lepidóptera, Noctùidae); C, clover seed chalcid, *Bruchóphagus platýptera* (Walker) (Hymenóptera, Eurytómidae); D, sweetpotato weevil Cỳlas formicà*rius elegántulus* (Summers) (Coleóptera, Curculiónídae); E. sawtoothed grain beetle, *Oryzaéphilus surinaménsis* (L.) (Coleóptera, Cucùjidae); F, seedcorn maggot, *Hylemỳa platùra* (Meigen) (Díptera, Anthomyìidae). A and B are obtect pupae, C–E are exarate pupae, and F is a coarctate pupa. *sp,* spiracle. (Courtesy of USDA.)

usually campodeiform, and the subsequent larval instars are vermiform or scarabaeiform. Hypermetamorphosis occurs in parasitic insects; the first instar seeks out the host, and once in the host, molts into a less active type of larva. This type of complete metamorphosis occurs in the Melòidae (Figure 312) and Rhipiphòridae (Coleóptera), the Mantíspidae (Neuróptera), the Strepsíptera, and in a few Díptera and Hymenóptera.

CASTE DETERMINATION

A characteristic feature of social insects is a differentiation of castes (queens, drones, soldiers, workers, etc.), and in some of these castes (workers, soldiers) the reproductive organs are not fully developed and the individuals do not reproduce. Caste in the honey bee and many other social insects is determined in part by fertilization (unfertilized eggs becoming males, or drones) and in part by the food fed to the larvae (female larvae destined to become queens are fed a "royal jelly"). Honey bee workers normally have undeveloped ovaries and do not lay eggs, but under certain conditions the ovaries may become functional. This ovarian development occurs when the queen is removed, suggesting that the queen, when present, in some way inhibits ovarian development in the workers.

Recent studies have shown that this inhibition of ovarian development in honey bee workers by the queen is accomplished through a "queen substance" which the workers lick from the queen's body. In the absence of a queen (and this "queen substance") there is not only a development of the ovaries in the workers, but also a change in the workers' behavior. They set about changing a worker larval cell into a queen larval cell, and feed this larva the type of food that will result in its becoming a queen. The queen substance (a pheromone) contains two chemicals; together they inhibit ovarian development in the workers, and one inhibits the queen-rearing behavior. Just how these chemicals act to inhibit ovarian development in the worker is not known, but it is probably through the corpora allata.

A somewhat similar caste-influencing mechanism occurs in termites. The reproductives (king and queen) of *Kalotérmes* produce a substance that inhibits ovarian development in certain workers; in the absence of this substance, these workers become capable of reproduction.

VARIATIONS IN LIFE HISTORY

The length of a generation and the way it is fitted to the different seasons vary quite a bit in different insects. Most insects in temperate regions have what is called a heterodynamic life cycle, that is, the adults appear for a limited time during a particular season, and some life stage passes the winter in a state of dormancy. The overwintering stage may be the egg (for example, most Orthóptera and Homóptera), nymph (for example, most Odonàta and many Orthóptera), larva (for example, many Lepidóptera), or adult (for example, most Hemíptera and many Coleóptera and Hymenóptera). Many insects, particularly those living in the tropics, have a homodynamic life cycle, that is, development is continuous and there is no regular period of dormancy.

Most insects in the United States have a single generation a year. Some require two or more years to complete their life cycle; this is usually the case with large insects occurring in the northern part of the country. Some of the larger beetles, dragonflies, and moths in the northern states and Canada regularly require two or three years to complete their development. Perhaps the longest life cycle of any insect is that of some of the periodical cicadas (*Magicicàda* spp.), which lasts 17 years (see page 296).

Many insects have more than one generation a year. In some cases the number of generations in a year is constant throughout the range of the species; in other cases the species may have more generations per year in the southern part of its range. A few insects, usually rather small species that can complete their life cycle in a few weeks, have many generations a year; such insects continue to reproduce through the season as long as weather conditions are favorable. Insects of tropical origin, such as those of the household and those which attack stored products, may continue breeding throughout the entire 12 months.

A more or less prolonged period of quiescence, or dormancy, occurs in the life cycle of many insects; visible activity ceases during this period, and physiological processes occur at greatly reduced rates. Any stage in the life cycle may be involved. The length of this period of dormancy may vary from a few days to several months, or even years.

Many types of insects are subject to a period of dormancy in their annual cycle. A period of winter dormancy in temperate or arctic regions is usually called hibernation, and a period of dormancy during high temperature is called aestivation. The period of hibernation may be from several weeks to several months; generally only one stage (egg, larva, pupa, or adult, depending on the species) will hibernate, but in some species two or more stages may undergo a period of winter dormancy.

Dormancy in insects is controlled by two sorts of factors, environmental and genetic. Most insects enter a period of dormancy when some environmental factor (for example, temperature) becomes unfavorable, and resume their activity when conditions become favorable again. The Mexican bean beetle, for example, will breed continuously throughout the year if conditions are favorable, but will hibernate (as an adult) for several months if subjected to low temperatures (3° C or lower). Other species will not breed continuously throughout the year, even under favorable conditions, but at a certain time will go into dormancy *before* conditions become unfavorable. Such dormancy (which is different from hibernation and is usually called diapause) is normally broken only when the insect is subjected to a period of low temperature (for weeks or months) and then returned to a temperature favorable for development. The larvae of the second generation of the codling moth in Ohio, for example, will remain as larvae in silk-lined cells under the bark of apple trees unless subjected to a short period (some three weeks) of low temperatures (0° C or lower); when returned to normal developmental temperatures, they pupate and complete their development.

The chief factor initiating diapause is photoperiod (day length). Many species enter diapause at the time of the year when the day reaches a certain length; this differs in different species. Studies of hornworm larvae (Sphíngidae) have shown that in a culture of the larvae, all individuals that enter the soil for pupation before a certain date will complete their development and emerge as moths and reproduce, but individuals entering the soil after this date go into diapause and do not complete their development until the following spring. This factor of day length apparently operates similarly in the case of the codling moth; individuals of the first generation pupate and emerge as adults in the summer, but individuals of the second generation (in autumn) do not. In some cases (for example, *Antheraèa,* family Saturnìidae), day length may also control emergence from diapause. The effect of day length is usually direct, on the insect itself, but may occasionally be indirect by its effect on the food eaten by the insect.

Most birds and mammals, as well as many other vertebrates, have a type of life history sometimes spoken of as iteroparous, that is, adults may live several years and reproduce two or more times during their lifetime—once or more each year or (for example, some rodents) at fairly regular intervals through a year. Natural populations of such animals normally contain individuals of different age. Insects, on the other hand, are generally semelparous, that is, they reproduce only once during their lifetime. Natural populations of such animals usually consist of individuals about the same age, and there is little or no overlapping of successive generations.

A number of insects reproduce parthenogenetically (see page 49), and in some of these the life cycle involves an alternation of bisexual and parthenogenetic reproduction; this is the case, for example, in many aphids (see pages 309–310) and gall wasps (see page 666). The adults of the bisexual and parthenogenetic generations of such insects may be different in appearance and may occur on different host plants. Males are unknown in some insects, and parthenogenesis is the only known type of reproduction; this is the case, for example, in the whitefringed beetle, *Graphógnathus leucolòma* (Boheman) (see page 434).

Paedogenesis, or reproduction by larval stages, occurs in a few insects; such insects may produce a series of generations in this way, or paedogenesis may alternate with normal reproduction. Paedogenesis occurs in the beetle *Micromálthus debilis* LeConte (see page 369) and in the gall gnat *Miástor metralòas* Meinert (see page 579).

References on Development and Metamorphosis

Agrell, I. 1964. Physiological and biochemical changes during insect development. In *Physiology of Insects*, Morris Rockstein (Ed.). New York: Academic Press, Vol. 1, pp. 91–148; 10 f.

Anderson, D. T. 1973. *Embryology and Phylogeny in Annelids and Arthropods*. New York: Pergamon Press, xiv + 495 pp., 164 f.

Campbell, F. L. (Ed.). 1959. *Physiology of Insect Development*. Chicago: Univ. Chicago Press, xiv + 167 pp., 13 f.

Chapman, R. F. 1971. *The Insects, Structure and Function*. New York: American Elsevier, xii + 819 pp., 541 f.

Cole, L. C. 1954. The population consequences of life history phenomena. *Quart. Rev. Biol.*, 29(2):103–137; 10 f.

Comstock, J. H. 1940 (9th ed.). *An Introduction to Entomology*. Ithaca, N.Y.: Comstock Publ., xix + 1064 pp., 1228 f. (especially Ch. 4).

Essig, E. O. 1942. *College Entomology*. New York: Macmillan, vii + 900 pp., 305 f. (especially Ch. 1).

Gilbert, L. I. 1964. Physiology of growth and development: endocrine aspects. In *The Physiology of Insects*, Morris Rockstein (Ed.). New York: Academic Press, Vol. 1, pp. 149–225; 5 f.

Imms, A. D. 1957 (9th ed., revised by O. W. Richards and R. G. Davies). *A General Textbook of Entomology*. New York: E. P. Dutton, x + 886 pp., 609 f. (especially Part II).

Johannsen, O. A., and F. H. Butt. 1941. *Embryology of Insects and Myriapods*. New York: McGraw-Hill, xi + 462 pp., 370 f.

Matheson, R. 1951 (2nd ed.). *Entomology for Introductory Courses*. Ithaca, N.Y.: Comstock Publ., xiv + 629 pp., 500 f. (especially Ch. 5).

Peterson, A. 1948. *Larvae of Insects*. Part I. *Lepidoptera and Hymenoptera*. Ann Arbor, Mich.: Edwards Bros., 315 pp., 84 f.

Peterson, A. 1951. *Larvae of Insects*. Part II. *Coleoptera, Diptera, Neuroptera, Siphonaptera, Mecoptera, Trichoptera*. Ann Arbor, Mich.: Edwards Bros., v + 416 pp., 104 f.

Schneiderman, H. A., and L. I. Gilbert. 1964. Control of growth and development in insects. *Science*, 143(3604):325–333; 1 f.

Sharplin, J. 1965. Replacement of the tentorium of *Periplaneta americana* (Linnaeus) during ecdysis. *Can. Ent.*, 97(9):947–951.

Snodgrass, R. E. 1954. Insect metamorphosis . *Smiths. Misc. Coll.*, 122(9):iii + 1–124 pp.; 17 f.

Waterhouse, D. F., *et al*. 1970. *Insects of Australia*. Canberra: Melbourne Univ. Press, xiii + 1029 pp.; illus. (especially Ch. 4, pp. 107–140; 45 f.).

Wigglesworth, V. B. 1954. *The Physiology of Insect Metamorphosis*. Cambridge: Cambridge Univ. Press, vii + 151 pp.; illus.

Wigglesworth, V. B. 1959. *The Control of Growth and Form*. Ithaca, N.Y.: Cornell Univ. Press, 140 pp.; illus.

6: CLASSIFICATION, NOMENCLATURE, AND IDENTIFICATION

CLASSIFICATION

There are upwards of a million different kinds of animals in the world, and a systematic study of the animal kingdom necessitates some scheme of arranging them into groups, or classifying them. Animals might be classified in various ways, but the classification followed by zoologists is one based primarily on *structural* characters; those animals with certain structures in common are classified into one group, and those with other structures into other groups. Thus, the animal kingdom is divided into a dozen or so major groups called *phyla* (singular, *phylum*); each phylum has a name, and its members have certain structural characters in common.

On the basis of degree of complexity, and probable evolutionary sequence, the animal phyla are usually arranged in a series from the "lower" phyla to the "higher" ones. The principal phyla of the animal kingdom are as follows:

Phylum **Protozòa**—single-celled animals
Phylum **Porífera**—sponges
Phylum **Coelenteràta**—jellyfish, hydroids, corals, sea anemones
Phylum **Platyhelmínthes**—flatworms: planarians, flukes, tapeworms
Phylum **Nemathelmínthes**—roundworms
Phylum **Trochelmínthes (Rotatòria)**—rotifers
Phylum **Brachiópoda**—brachiopods
Phylum **Bryozòa**—moss animals

Phylum **Mollúsca**—molluscs: clams, snails, octopi
Phylum **Echinodérmata**—starfish, sea urchins, crinoids, sea cucumbers
Phylum **Annélida**—earthworms, marine worms, leeches
Phylum **Onychóphora**—onychophorans: *Peripatus* and its allies
Phylum **Arthrópoda**—crayfish, millipedes, centipedes, spiders, INSECTS
Phylum **Chordàta**—fishes, amphibians, reptiles, birds, mammals

The classification of animals does not stop with phyla; each phylum is further subdivided, on the basis of structural characters, into groups called *classes;* each class has a name and certain structural characters in common. Classes are further divided into *orders,* orders into *families,* families into *genera* (singular, *genus*), and genera into *species*. The main categories (taxa) in animal classification are phylum, class, order, family, genus, and species, but frequently intermediate categories are used. The categories commonly used, arranged in order of rank, may be listed as follows:

Phylum
  Subphylum
    Class
      Subclass
        Order
          Suborder
            Superfamily
              Family
                Subfamily
                  Tribe
                    Genus
                      Subgenus
                        Species
                          Subspecies

The basic category in this scheme of classification (and perhaps the only "real" entity) is the *species*. A species is a group of individuals or populations in nature that are (1) capable of interbreeding and producing fertile offspring, (2) reproductively isolated from (that is, ordinarily not interbreeding with) other such groups, and (3) fundamentally similar in structure. It is often impossible to determine whether or not two groups of animals will interbreed. Hence, one may have to rely on morphological or other characters to determine specific limits; this must be done with some caution, since there are "good" species (groups reproductively isolated) that cannot be distinguished by morphological characters. A subspecies is a geographic subdivision of a species. The differences between the subspecies of a given species are usually not clear-cut, but are intergrading, particularly where adjacent subspecies come in contact.

Any scheme of classification that is developed for a group of animals will be affected by the particular characters used and by the relative weight they are given; if different people use different characters or different "weighting" of a series of characters, they will arrive at different schemes of classification. Numerical methods (for example, see Sokal, 1963, and Sneath and Sokal, 1973) usually yield schemes that give good phenetic affinity, but may not give good phyletic affinity; zoologists attempting to develop a classification generally strive for one that shows phylogenetic relationships.

Modern workers, in developing a scheme of classification, use not only structural characters (including characters of the internal organs), but also data from physiology (for example, Stephen, 1961), behavior (for example, Alexander, 1962), life history and immature stages (for example, van Emden, 1957), cytology (for example, White, 1957), and other fields.

Since the delimitation of taxa (phyla, classes, orders, and so on, except possibly species) is more or less arbitrary, different workers often arrive at different schemes of classification. Any biologists who use schemes of classification (as we do in this book) generally have several from which to choose; the schemes we follow in this book are the ones that we believe best represent the relationships of the animals concerned, or are the ones most widely used.

NOMENCLATURE

Animals have two types of names, scientific and common. Scientific names are the ones used by scientists; they are used throughout the world, and every animal taxon has one. Common names are vernacular names; they are often less precise than scientific names (some common names are used for more than one taxon, and a given animal taxon may have several common names), and many animals lack them because they are small or seldom encountered.

SCIENTIFIC NOMENCLATURE

The scientific naming of animals follows certain rules, which are outlined in the *International Code of Zoological Nomenclature* (Stoll *et al.*, 1964). Scientific names are latinized, but may be derived from any language or from the names of people or places; most names are derived from Latin or Greek words, and usually refer to some characteristic of the animal or group named.

The names of groups above genus are latinized nouns in the nominative plural; names of genera and subgenera are latinized nouns in the nominative singular. Specific and subspecific names may be adjectives, the present or past participles of verbs, or nouns; adjectives and participles must agree in gender with the genus name, and nouns are in either the nominative or genitive case.

The scientific name of a species is a binomial, that is, it consists of two words (the genus name and a specific name); that of a subspecies is a trinomial (the genus name, the specific name, and a subspecific name). These names are always printed in *italics* (if written or typewritten, italics are indicated by underlining). Names of species and subspecies are followed by the name of the author, the person who described the species or subspecies; authors' names are not italicized. The names of genera and higher categories always begin with a capital letter; specific and subspecific names do not. If the author's name is in parentheses, it means that he described the species (or subspecies, in the case of a subspecies name) in some genus other than the one in which it is now placed. For example,

Papílio glaùcus Linnaeus[1]—the tiger swallowtail. The species *glaùcus* was described by Linnaeus in the genus *Papílio*.

Leptinotársa décemlineàta (Say)—the Colorado potato beetle. The species *décemlineàta* was described by Say in some genus other than *Leptinotársa*, and this species has since been transferred to the genus *Leptinotársa*.

Argia fumipénnis (Burmeister). The species *fumipénnis* was described by Burmeister in some genus other than *Árgia*, and has subsequently been transferred to the genus *Árgia*. There are three subspecies of this species in the eastern United States: a northern subspecies (*violàcea*) with clear wings and considerable violet coloration, a southern subspecies (*fumipénnis*) with smoky wings and considerable violet coloration, and a subspecies in peninsular Florida (*átra*) with very dark wings and dark brownish (not violet) coloration. These three subspecies would be listed as *Árgia fumipénnis violàcea* (Hagen), *Árgia fumipénnis fumipénnis* (Burmeister), and *Árgia fumipénnis átra* Gloyd. Hagen's name in parentheses means that *violàcea* was described in a genus other than *Árgia*, but there is no way of knowing from this name whether *violàcea* was originally described as a species, as a subspecies of *fumipénnis*, or as a subspecies of some other species. Gloyd's name not in parentheses means that *átra* was originally described in the genus *Árgia*, but there is no way of knowing from this name whether *átra* was originally described as a species of *Árgia*, as a subspecies of *fumipénnis*, or as a subspecies of another species of *Árgia*. (Actually, Hagen originally described *violàcea* as a species of *Ágrion*, and Gloyd originally described *átra* as a subspecies of *Árgia fumipénnis*.)

[1] Throughout this book Linnaeus is abbreviated "L."

Some entomologists have used trinomials for what they have called "varieties" (for example, *A-us b-us*, var. *c-us*). Such names, if published before 1961, are assumed to be names of subspecies, in which case the "var." in the name is dropped, or if they are shown to designate an individual variant, they are considered "infra" categories, which are not covered by the Rules of Zoological Nomenclature; such names published after 1960 are considered to designate individual variants ("infra" categories), not covered by the rules. The taxonomic categories listed on page 86 apply to *populations* and not to individual variants such as color forms, sexual forms, and seasonal forms.

A species referred to but not named is often designated simply by "sp." For example, "*Gómphus* sp." refers to a species of *Gómphus*. More than one species may be designated by "spp."; for example, "*Gómphus* spp." refers to two or more species of *Gómphus*.

The names of categories from tribe through superfamily have standard endings, and hence can always be recognized as referring to a particular category. These can be illustrated by some taxa of bees, as follows:

Superfamily names end in *-oidea*; for example, *Apòidea*, bees

Family names end in *-idae*; for example, *Àpidae*, euglossine bees, bumble bees, and honey bees

Subfamily names end in *-inae*; for example, *Apìnae*, honey bees

Tribe names end in *-ini*; for example, *Xylocopìni*, large carpenter bees.

TYPES Whenever a new taxon (from subspecies to superfamily) is described, the describer is supposed to designate a *type,* which is used as a reference if there is ever any question what the taxon includes, and it serves to anchor the name. The type of a species or subspecies is a specimen (the *type,* or *holotype*), the type of a genus or subgenus is a species (the *type species*), and the type of a taxon from tribe through superfamily is a genus (the *type genus*). Names of taxa from tribe through superfamily (see examples above) are formed by adding the appropriate ending to the root of the name of the type genus (for the type genus *Àpis* in the examples above, the stem is *Ap-*). If a species is divided into subspecies, the particular subspecies that includes the holotype of the species has the same subspecific as specific name (for example, *Árgia fumipénnis fumipénnis*). Similarly, if a genus is divided into subgenera, the subgenus that includes the type species of the genus has the same subgenus name as genus name, for example, *Formìca (Formìca) rùfa* L. (the name in parentheses in the subgenus).

PRIORITY All zoological names begin with the publication of the 10th edition of Linnaeus' *Systema Naturae;* the date is taken as 1 January 1758. It often happens that a particular taxon is described independently by two or more people, and hence may have more than one name. In such cases the first name used from 1758 on (provided the describer has followed certain rules) is the correct name, and any other names become synonyms. A particular name will often be used for a long time before it is discovered that another name has priority over it.

Sometimes a person describing a new taxon will give it a name that has previously been used for another taxon; if the taxa involved are at the same taxonomic level, the names are termed homonyms, and all but the oldest must be discarded and the taxa renamed. There cannot be two (or more) species or subspecies with the same name in a given genus (except that the name of the type-containing subspecies has the same name as the specific name). There cannot be two (or more) genera or subgenera in the animal kingdom with the same name (except that the subgenus containing the type-species of the genus has the same name as the genus). Neither can there be two (or more) taxa in the family group of categories (tribe through superfamily) with the same name (though the names of the typical subdivisions will be the same except for their endings). Homonymy is not involved if the taxa with the same name are in different category levels; for example, the same name *can* be used for both a genus and a species, or for both a genus and an order.

Because of the large number of animal taxa and the vast amount of zoological literature, errors in naming (homonyms and synonyms) are not easy to discover. As they are discovered it becomes necessary to change names, not only of genera and species, but also of families and even orders. The problems of priority in scientific nomenclature are often very intricate, and it is sometimes difficult to determine just what name is the correct one. Name changes may also result from increased knowledge; this added knowledge may indicate that groups should be split or combined, which would result in name changes for some of the groups involved.

In cases where two or more names for a group have been in fairly wide use, we have listed first in this book what we believe to be the correct name, and have listed other names in parentheses.

PRONUNCIATION

The pronunciation of some of the technical names and terms used in entomology may be found in a good dictionary or glossary, but very few texts or references give the pronunciation of the vast bulk of technical names (genera and species). There *are* rules for the pronunciation of these names, but few entomologists are familiar with them and many names are pronounced differently by different people. We have therefore listed below some of the general rules for the pronunciation of the technical names and terms used in zoology, and throughout this book have indicated the accent in scientific names by the use of a grave or acute accent over the vowel of the accented syllable.

We realize that not all entomologists will agree with our pronunciation of some names. There are two reasons for such disagreement: (1) a given pronunciation, whether it follows the rules or not, may become established through usage as the "correct" pronunciation, and we may be unaware of some of these; and (2) the correct pronunciation of many scientific names depends on the derivation of the name and the vowel sound in the source language, and it is difficult or impossible to determine the derivation of some scientific names. Hence there will always be a question as to their correct pronunciation.

The principal rules for the pronunciation of scientific names and terms are outlined below.

VOWELS All vowels in scientific names are pronounced. Vowels are generally either long or short, and in the examples that follow (and elsewhere in this book), a long vowel sound is indicated by a grave accent (ì) and a short vowel sound by an acute accent (í); for example, *màte, mát, mète, mét, bìte, bít, ròpe, rót, cùte, cút, bỳ, sýmmetry*. A vowel at the end of a word has the long sound, except when it is *a*; a final *a* has the *uh* sound, as in *idea*. The vowel in the final syllable of a word has the short sound, except *es*, which is pronounced *ease*.

DIPHTHONGS A diphthong consists of two vowels written together and pronounced as a single vowel. The diphthongs are *ae* (pronounced è, rarely é), *oe* (usually pronounced è, rarely é), *oi* (pronounced as in *oil*), *eu* (pronounced ù), *ei* (pronounced ì), *ai* (pronounced à), and *au* (pronounced as in *August*).

CONSONANTS *Ch* has the *k* sound, except in words derived from a language other than Greek. When c is followed by *ae, e, oe, i,* or *y*, it has the soft (*s*) sound; when it is followed by *a, o, oi,* or *u*, it has the hard (*k*) sound. When g is followed by *ae, e, i, oe,* or *y*, it has the soft (*j*) sound; when it is followed by *a, o, oi,* or *u*, it has the hard sound (as in *go*). In words beginning with *ps, pt, ct, cn, gn,* or *mn*, the initial letter is not pronounced, but when these letters appear together in the middle of a word, the first letter is pronounced (for example, the *p* is not pronounced in the word *pteromorph*, but it is pronounced in the word *Orthoptera*). An *x* at the beginning of a word is pronounced as *z*, but as *ks* when it appears elsewhere in a word. When a double *c* is followed by *e, i,* or *y*, it is pronounced as *ks*.

ACCENT The pronunciation of technical names and terms in this book is indicated by a grave or acute accent on the vowel of the accented syllable. When the accented syllable contains a diphthong, the accent mark is placed over the vowel that gives the diphthong its sound (for example, *aè, oè, eù, eì, ài*), or over the first vowel of the diphthong (for example, *òi, àu*). The accented syllable is either the penult or the antepenult (in very long words there may be a secondary accent on a syllable near the beginning of the word). The principal rules governing the syllable accented and the vowel sound (whether long or short) are as follows:

1. The accent is on the penult syllable in the following cases:
   a. When the name contains only two syllables; for example, *Àpis, Bómbus*
   b. When the penult contains a diphthong; for example, *Culicòides, Hemileùca, Lygaèus*
   c. When the vowel in the penult is followed by x or z; for example, *Coríxa, Prodóxus, Agromỳza, Triòza*
   d. When the vowel of the penult is long. Whether the penult vowel is long or short often depends on the derivation of the word and the vowel sound in the source language. The vowel e in a word derived from the Greek is long if the vowel in the Greek word is eta (η), but short if it is epsilon (ϵ); for example, in words derived from the Greek μηρος, meaning *thigh*, the e is long (*Diápheromèra, epimèron*), while in those derived from the Greek μεσος, meaning *part*, the e is short (Heterómera). Similarly, the vowel *o* in a word derived from the Greek is long if the vowel in the Greek word is omega (ω), but short if it is omicron (ο); for example, in words derived from the Greek ςωμα, meaning *body*, the *o* is long (*Calosòma, Malacosòma*), while in those derived from the Greek ςτομα, meaning *mouth*, it is short (*Melanóstoma, Belóstoma, epístoma*). The penult vowel is long in subfamily names (for example, *Sphecìnae*) and tribe names (for example, *Sphecìni*); in tribe names, the final *i* is also long. The penult vowel is usually long in the following cases:
      (1) Words derived from the Latin past participle and ending in *-ata, -atus,* or *-atum*; for example, *maculàta*. (The penult vowel is short in such Greek plurals as *Echinodérmata*).
      (2) Latin adjectives ending in *-alis* (masculine and feminine) or *-ale* (neuter); for example, *orientàlis, orientàle, verticàlis, verticàle*
      (3) Words ending in *-ina;* for example, *carolìna, Ceratìna, Glossìna*
      (4) Words ending in *-ica*; for example, *Formìca, Myrmìca*
      (5) Words ending in *-ana, -anus,* or *-anum*; for example, *americàna, Tabànus, mexicànum*
      (6) Words ending in *-ura*; for example, *Thysanùra, Xìphosùra*
      (7) Words ending in *-odes*; for example, *Sabulòdes, Sphecòdes*

(8) Words ending in *-otes*; for example, *Epiròtes*
(9) Words ending in *-ates*; for example, *Aceràtes, Hippelàtes*
(10) Words ending in *-ales*; for example, the names of plant orders, such as *Graminàles*
(11) Words ending in *-osis*; for example, *pediculòsis, trichinòsis*; there are a few exceptions in modern usage, for example, *metamórphosis*
(12) Words ending in *-soma*; for example, *Calosòma, Eriosòma*
(13) Words ending in *-pogon*; for example, *Heteropògon, Lasiopògon*
(14) Words ending in *-chlora*; for example, *Augochlòra*
(15) Words in which the vowel of the penult is *u*, except when the *u* is followed by *l*; for example, *Fenùsa, Ctenùcha*; exceptions, *Libéllula, Bétula*
(16) When the vowel is followed by *z*; for example, *Agromỳza, Triòza*

e. When the vowel of the penult is short and followed by two consonants, except a mute followed by *l* or *r*; for example, *Pseudocóccus, pulchélla, Pterophýlla, Vanéssa, Chlorotéttix, Latrodéctus, Enallágma, Gryllotálpa, Adélges, Hemerocámpa, Microbémbex, Philánthus, Monárthrum, Leptinotársa, Schistocérca, Sapérda, Polyérgus, Osmodérma, Panórpa, Pyromórpha, Chionáspis, Cordulegáster, Derméstes, Mantíspa, Prionoxýstus, Macrópsis.* When the vowel of the penult is followed by a mute (*b*, hard *c*, *d*, *g*, *k*, *p*, *q*, *t*, *ch*, *ph*, or *th*) and *l* or *r*, the accent is on the antepenult; for example, *Cutérebra, Geómetra, Ánabrus, Ránatra, Éphydra, Grýllacris, Melánoplus, Stenóbothrus, élytra.*

2. In other cases the antepenult is accented.
   a. The vowel of the antepenult is long in the following cases:
      (1) When it is followed by another vowel; for example, *Anthomỳia, Epèolus, Hepìalus, Llavèia, Sìalis.* This includes family names that have a vowel immediately preceding the *-idae*: *Danàidae, Canacèidae, Citheronìidae, Melòidae, Grùidae, Melandrỳidae*
      (2) When it is *a*, *e*, *o*, or *u*, followed by a single consonant and two vowels, the first of which is *e*, *i*, or *y*; for example, *Aràneus, Callosàmia, Citherònia, Climàcia, Cordùlia, Lecànium, Làsius, Nemòbius, Orthèzia, Plòdia, Redùvius, Rhàgium, Tèlea, Xylòmya*
      (3) When it is *u* followed by a single consonant; for example, *Libellùlidae, Linguatùlida*
      (4) When it is *y* followed by *z*; for example, *Agromỳzidae, Anthomỳzidae*
      (5) In family names when this vowel is long in the name of the type genus; for example, *Aleyròdidae, Asìlidae, Beròthidae, Chrysòpidae, Gyròpidae, Hèbridae, Isometòpidae, Nàbidae, Nèpidae, Phylloxèridae,* names ending in *-mỳzidae*, names ending in *-psòcidae*, names ending in *-sòmidae*.
   b. The vowel of the antepenult is short in other cases. This includes all family names in which the antepenult vowel is followed by a consonant (except when the vowel is *u* followed by a single consonant or *y* followed by *z*); for example, *Belostomátidae, Elatéridae, Chrysópidae.* The following names, and others with similar endings, have the antepenult vowel short: *Heterócera, Geócoris, Conocéphalus, Tiphódytes, Chauliógnathus, Pantógrapha, Chirónomus, Mallóphaga, Drosóphila, Anthóphora, Orthóptera, Micrópteryx, Chilópoda, Triátoma.*

COMMON NAMES OF INSECTS

Because there are so many species of insects, and because so many of them are very small or poorly known, relatively few have common names. Those that do are generally particularly showy insects or insects of economic importance. American entomologists recognize as "official" the common names in a list published every few years in the *Bulletin of the Entomological Society of America* (the most recent such list is that of Blickenstaff, 1970), but this list does not include all species of insects (and other arthropods) to which common names have been applied. The common names used in this book for individual species have been taken from this list in cases where the species was included in the list; our common names for other species have been obtained from various sources.

Many common names of insects refer to groups such as subfamilies, families, suborders, or orders, rather than to individual species. The name "tortoise beetle," for example, refers to all species in the subfamily Cassidìnae of the family Chrysomélidae (about 3000 world species and 24 in North America); the name "leaf beetle" applies to all species in the family Chrysomélidae (about 25,000 world species, and nearly 1400 in North America); the name "beetle" applies to all species in the order Coleóptera (some 300,000 world species, and about 30,000 in North America); the name "damselfly" applies to the entire suborder Zygóptera, of which there are hundreds of species; the name "narrow-winged damselfly" applies to all species in the family Coenagriónidae (87 species in North America).

Most common names of insects that consist of a single word refer to entire orders (for example, beetle, bug, caddisfly, stonefly, and termite); some (for example, bee, damselfly, grasshopper, cockroach, and lacewing) refer to suborders or groups of families; only a few (for example, ants and mantids) refer to families. Most common names applying to families consist of two or more words, the last being the name of the larger group, and the other(s) descriptive (for example, brown lacewings, click beetles, soldier flies, and small winter stoneflies).

The members of a group are often referred to by an adjectival form of the group name; for example, insects in the order Hymenóptera might be called hymenopterans, the wasps in the superfamily Sphecòidea are called sphecoid wasps, those in the Sphécidae are called sphecid wasps, and those in the subfamily Nyssonìnae might be called nyssonine wasps. It is standard practice to use an adjectival form of the family name as a common name.

The names "fly" and "bug" are used for insects in more than one order, and the way the names of these insects are written may indicate the order to which the insect belongs. For example, when a fly belongs to the order Díptera, the "fly" of the name is written as a separate word (for example, black fly, horse fly, and blow fly); when it belongs to another order the "fly" of the name is written together with the descriptive word (for example, dragonfly, butterfly, and sawfly). When a bug belongs to the order Hemíptera, the "bug" of the name is written as a separate word (for example, damsel bug, stink bug, and lace bug); when it belongs to another order the "bug" of the name is written together with the descriptive word (for example, mealybug, ladybug, junebug, and sowbug).

THE IDENTIFICATION OF INSECTS

When one encounters an insect, one of the first questions that will be asked is, "What kind of insect is it?" One of the principal aims of the beginning student in any field of biology is to become able to identify the organisms he is studying. The identification of insects differs from the identification of other types of organisms only in that it is likely to be somewhat more difficult, for there are more kinds of insects than anything else.

Four things complicate the problem of insect identification. In the first place, there are so many different kinds (species) of insects that the beginner may be discouraged at the outset at ever becoming proficient in insect identification. In the second place, most insects are small, and the identifying characters are often difficult to see. In the third place, many insects are little known, and when finally identified, the student may have only a technical name (which he may not understand) and no very specific common name. In the fourth place, many insects go through very different stages in their life history, and one may come to know insects in one stage of their life cycle and still know very little about those same insects in another stage.

There are about six ways a student may identify an unknown insect: (1) by having it identified for him by an expert, (2) by comparing it with labeled specimens in a collection, (3) by comparing it with pictures, (4) by comparing it with descriptions, (5) by the use of an analytical key, or (6) by a combination of two or more of these procedures. Of these six methods, obviously the first is the simplest, but this method is not always available; similarly, the second method may not always be available. In the absence of an expert or a labeled collection, the next best method is usually the use of a key. In the case of particularly striking or well-known insects, the identification can often be made by the third method mentioned above, but in many groups this method is unsatisfactory. No book can illustrate all kinds of insects and still sell for a price a student can afford to pay. Where an unknown insect cannot be definitely identified by means of illustrations, the best procedure is to use an analytical key, and then to check the identification by as many of the other methods mentioned as possible. Identification from pictures is often unsafe, as there are many instances in the insect world where one type of insect looks a great deal like another.

As a general rule in this book, identification will be carried only to family; to go further usually requires specialized knowledge and is beyond the scope of this book. Identifying insects only to family reduces the number of names from many thousand to several hundred, and of these probably only 200 or less are likely to be encountered by the average student. We reduce the problem still further by being concerned largely with *adults*. Thus, insect identification becomes less formidable.

THE KEYS IN THIS BOOK

Analytical keys are devices used to identify all sorts of things, plants as well as animals. Different keys may be arranged somewhat differently, but all involve the same general principles. One runs an insect (or other organism) through a key in steps; at each step he is faced with two (rarely more) alternatives, one of which should apply to the specimen at hand. In our keys there is either a number or a name following the alternative that fits the specimen; if a number, the next step is the couplet with this number. Thus, each step leads to another step and its alternatives until a name is reached.

The couplets of alternatives in our keys are numbered 1 and 1′, 2 and 2′, and so on. In each couplet after the first is a number in parentheses; this is the number of the couplet from which that couplet is reached, and it enables the student to work backward in the key if he discovers he has made a mistake somewhere along the line. This method of numbering also serves as a check on the accuracy of the organization of the key. In a few large keys, certain couplets may be reached from more than one previous couplet; this fact is indicated by two or more numbers in parentheses.

The keys in this book have been prepared from three principal sources: other published keys, descriptions, and from an examination of specimens of the groups concerned. Many are taken largely from previously published keys (generally with some changes in wording or organization), but some represent a new approach. Our aim with each key has been to prepare something that is *workable* and which will work for practically every species (or specimen) in the groups covered. Most of these keys have been tested by student use over a number of years. In many of the insect orders (particularly the larger ones), some groups key out in more than one place; this is the case in two types of situations: (1) where there is significant variation within the group, and (2) with borderline cases where the specimen might seem to fit both alternatives of a couplet. In the latter situation a specimen should key out correctly from either alternative. While we hope that these keys will work for every specimen, we realize that there are species or specimens in many groups that are erratic in their characters; an attempt has been made to include as many as possible of these atypical forms in our keys, but it is possible that a few may not key out correctly. We believe that our keys should work for 95 percent or more of the North American insects. We believe that the user of our keys is more likely to reach an impasse because of an inability to see or interpret a character than because of a discrepancy in the key.

When a determination is reached in the key, the student should check the specimen against any illustrations or descriptions available. If these do not fit the specimen, then he has either made a mistake somewhere in the key or the specimen is one that will not work out correctly in the key. In the latter event, the specimen should be saved until it can be shown to an expert; it may be something rare or unusual.

One's success in running an insect through a key depends largely on an understanding of the characters used. In many cases in this book the key characters are illustrated. Often several characters are given in each alternative; in case one character cannot be seen or interpreted, the student can use the other characters. If at any point in the key the student cannot decide which way to go, he should try following up both alternatives, and then check further with illustrations and descriptions when he reaches a name.

A great many families of insects are very unlikely to be encountered by the general collector because they contain small or minute forms that may be overlooked, because they are quite rare, or because they have a very restricted geographic range. Such families are indicated in most of our keys by an asterisk, and couplets containing such groups can often be skipped by the beginning student.

Most measurements under about 1½ inches are given in this book in millimeters; most measurements over 1½ inches are given in both inches and millimeters.

It should be understood that analytical keys are made for people who do not know the identity of a specimen they have. Once a specimen has been identified with a key, subsequent identifications of this same insect may often be based on such characters as general appearance, size, shape, and color, without reference to minute characters.

It will be apparent very early during the student's work in identifying insects that a good hand lens, and preferably a binocular microscope, is necessary to see many of the characters of the insect. Most insects, once the student knows what to look for, can be identified by means of a good hand lens (about 10 ×).

The mere identifying and naming of insects should not be the student's final objective in insect study; there is much more of interest in insects than just identifying them. The student should go further and learn something of the habits, distribution, and importance of insects.

GEOGRAPHICAL COVERAGE OF THIS BOOK

The taxonomic treatment in this book of the various insect orders and the other groups of arthropods applies particularly to the fauna of North America north of Mexico. A few insects occurring in other parts of the world are mentioned, but the characters given for each group (and the keys) apply to North American species and may not apply to all other species occuring outside of North America. The terms "North America" and "North American" refer to that portion of the continent north of Mexico. Where the geographic range of a group in North America is more or less limited, information on this range is given; groups for which there is no information on range are widely distributed in North America.

References on Classification, Nomenclature, and Identification

Alexander, R. D. 1962. The role of behavior study in cricket classification. *Syst. Zool.*, 11(2):53–72; 19 f.

Blackwelder, R. E. 1967. *Taxonomy. A Text and Reference Book.* New York: Wiley, xiv + 698 pp.; illus.

Blickenstaff, C. C. 1970. Common names of insects. *Ent. Soc. Amer.*; 36 pp. This list is revised every few years.

Borror, D. J. 1960. *Dictionary of Word Roots and Combining Forms.* Palo Alto, Calif.: National Press Books (now Mayfield Publ.), v + 134 pp.

Calman, W. T. 1949. *The Classification of Animals.* London: Methuen, vii + 54 pp.

Chamberlin, W. J. 1946 (2nd ed.). *Entomological Nomenclature and Literature.* Ann Arbor, Mich.: J. W. Edwards, Publ., xvi + 135 pp.

Crowson, R. A. 1970. *Classification and Biology.* New York: Atherton Press, 350 pp.

Ferris, G. F. 1928. *The Principles of Systematic Entomology.* Stanford, Calif.: Stanford Univ. Press, 169 pp., 11 f.

Hennig, W. 1965. Phylogenetic systematics. *Ann. Rev. Ent.*, 10:97–116; 4 f.

Mayr, E. 1969. *Principles of Systematic Zoology.* New York: McGraw-Hill, xi + 428 pp.; illus.

Melander, A. L. 1940. *Source Book of Biological Terms.* New York: Dept. Biol., City College of New York, vi + 157 pp.

Ross, H. H. 1973. *Biological Systematics.* Reading, Mass.: Addison-Wesley, vi + 346 pp.; illus.

Schenk, E. T., and J. H. McMasters. 1956 (3rd ed.). *Procedure in Taxonomy.* Stanford, Calif.: Stanford Univ. Press, vii + 119 pp.

Simpson, G. G. 1961. *Principles of Animal Taxonomy.* New York: Columbia Univ. Press, 247 pp.; illus.

Sneath, P. H. A., and R. R. Sokal. 1973. *Numerical Taxonomy.* San Francisco: W. H. Freeman, xvi +574 pp., 81 f.

Sokal, R. R. 1963. The principles and practice of numerical taxonomy. *Taxon,* 12:190–199; 2 f.

Stephen, W. P. 1961. Phylogenetic significance of blood proteins among some orthopteroid insects. *Syst. Zool.*, 10(1):1–9.

Stoll, N. R., R. Ph. Dollfus, J. Forest, N. D. Riley, C. W. Sabrosky, C. W. Wright, and R. V. Melville (Editorial Committee). 1964. *International Code of Zoological Nomenclature Adopted by the XV International Congress of Zoology.* London: International Trust for Zoological Nomenclature, xx + 176 pp.

Van Emden, F. I. 1957. The taxonomic significance of the characters of immature insects. *Ann. Rev. Ent.*, 2:91–106; 1 f.

Waterhouse, D. F., *et al.* 1970. *Insects of Australia.* Canberra: Melbourne Univ. Press, xiii + 1029 pp.; illus. (especially Ch. 6, pp. 141–151; 2 f.).

White, M. J. D. 1957. Cytogenetics and systematic entomology. *Ann. Rev. Ent.*, 2:71–90.

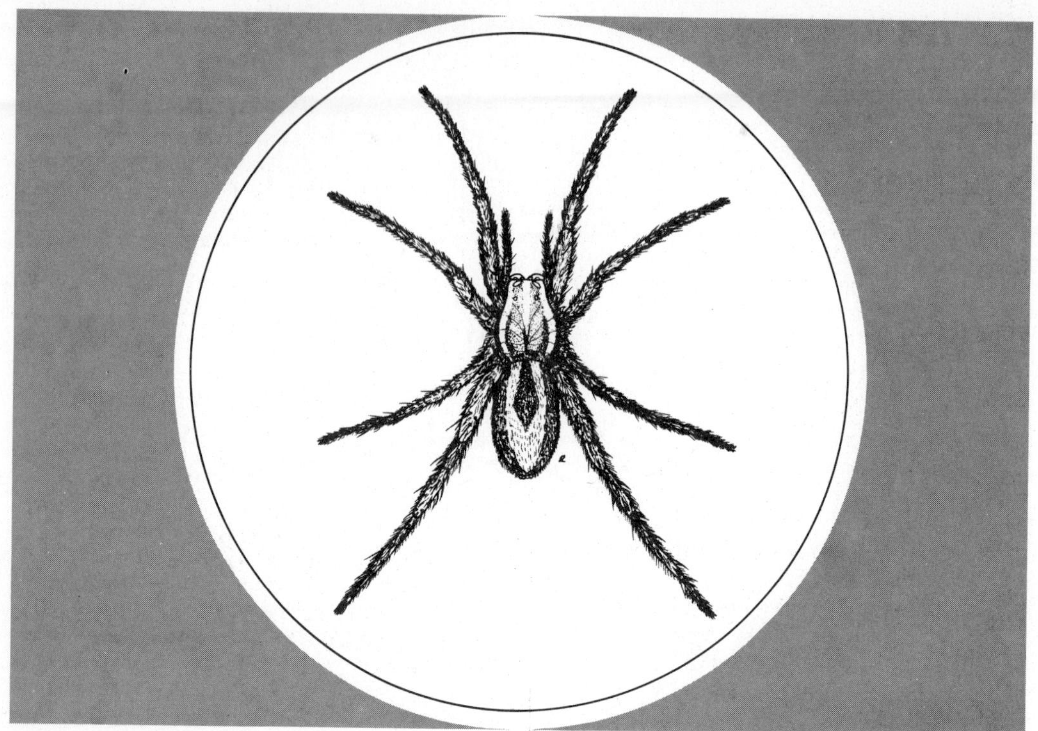

7: PHYLUM ARTHRÓPODA[1]

ARTHROPODS

We are concerned in this book primarily with insects, but it is appropriate to point out the place of insects in the animal kingdom, and to include some account of the animals most closely related to – and sometimes confused with – the insects.

The insects belong to the phylum Arthrópoda, the principal characters of which are as follows:

1. Body segmented, the segments usually grouped in two or three rather distinct regions
2. Paired segmented appendages (from which the phylum gets its name)
3. Bilateral symmetry
4. A chitinous exoskeleton, which is periodically shed and renewed as the animal grows
5. A tubular alimentary canal, with mouth and anus
6. The circulatory system an open one, the only blood vessel usually being a tubular structure dorsal to the alimentary canal with lateral openings in the abdominal region
7. The body cavity a blood cavity or hemocoele, the coelome reduced
8. The nervous system consisting of an anterior ganglion or brain located above the alimentary canal, a pair of connectives extending ventrally from the brain around the alimentary canal, and paired ganglionated nerve cords located below the alimentary canal
9. The skeletal muscles striated
10. Excretion usually by means of tubes (the Malpighian tubules) that empty into the alimen-

[1] Arthrópoda: *arthro,* joint or segment; *poda,* foot or appendage.

tary canal, the excreted materials passing to the outside by way of the anus

11. Respiration by means of gills, or tracheae and spiracles.

The phyla most closely related to the Arthrópoda are the Annélida and Onychóphora. Annelids (earthworms, marine worms, and leeches) differ from arthropods in lacking segmented appendages and a chitinous exoskeleton, and in lacking a tracheal system; they have a closed circulatory system, excretion is usually by means of ciliated tubes called nephridia, and their muscles are not striated. Some insect larvae lack appendages and superficially resemble certain annelids; they can be recognized as insects by their internal organization (different types of circulatory and excretory systems, and the presence of tracheae). Onychophorans (*Perípatus* and its allies) are probably more closely related to the arthropods than are the annelids (some authorities consider them arthropods), but they have ciliated nephridia (as in annelids), their only segmented appendages are the antennae, and their muscles are not striated; they have a chitinous exoskeleton that is periodically shed and renewed, an open circulatory system, and a tracheal system.

CLASSIFICATION OF THE ARTHRÓPODA

The various arthropod groups are classified somewhat differently by different authorities, but the classification followed in this book is as follows:

Phylum ARTHRÓPODA
- Subphylum **Trilóbita**—trilobites (known only from fossils)
- Subphylum **Cheliceràta**
  - Class **Xìphosùra**—horseshoe crabs
  - Class **Euryptérida**—eurypterids (known only from fossils)
  - Class **Pyncnogónida**—sea spiders
  - Class **Aráchnida**—arachnids
- Subphylum **Mandibulàta**
  - Class **Crustàcea**—crustaceans
  - Class **Diplópoda**—millipedes
  - Class **Chilópoda**—centipedes
  - Class **Paurópoda**—pauropods
  - Class **Sýmphyla**—symphylans
  - Class **Insécta**—INSECTS

The trilobites lived during the Paleozoic era (see Table 2, page 139), but were most abundant during the Cambrian and Ordovician periods. They are generally considered to be very primitive arthropods; they had a pair of antennae, with the remaining appendages similar and leglike. The body had three rather distinct longitudinal divisions, and the anterior part of the body (the preoral region and the first four postoral segments) was covered by a carapace. These animals were marine.

Present-day arthropods appear to fall in two fairly distinct groups, the Cheliceràta and Mandibulàta, which differ in several respects. The Cheliceràta lack antennae, the first postoral segment bears a pair of appendages called chelicerae, and the next five postoral segments (the next six in the Pycnogónida) bear leglike appendages. The body of a chelicerate usually has two distinct divisions, an anterior region called the prosoma or cephalothorax (which bears the chelicerae and the leglike appendages), and a posterior region called the opisthosoma or abdomen. The genital ducts open to the outside near the anterior end of the opisthosoma. Most chelicerates have an extra leg segment, the patella, between the femur and tibia. The Mandibulàta have antennae, and the second postoral segment bears a pair of mandibles; the first postoral segment either bears a second pair of antennae (Crustàcea), or is much reduced and bears no appendages (the other mandibulate groups). The number of legs varies greatly in the Mandibulàta; Crustàcea have from 3 to 70 or more pairs, Paurópoda have 9 pairs, Sýmphyla have 10 to 12 pairs, Chilópoda and Diplópoda have 13 or more (usually more) pairs, and Insécta have 3 pairs.

The Crustàcea are quite different from the other groups we have placed in the Mandibulàta, and some authorities consider them to represent a separate subphylum. The myriapod groups (Diplópoda, Chilópoda, Paurópoda, and Sýmphyla) are similar in being many-legged and more or less wormlike in form; some authorities place these groups together in the superclass Myriápoda. The Insécta are a little more like the myriapod groups than the Crustàcea (some authorities put insects and myriapods into the subphylum Uniràmia), but have three fairly distinct body regions, only three pairs of legs, and often possess wings. The Diplópoda, Paurópoda, and Sýmphyla are progoneate, that is, the genital ducts open to the outside anteriorly; the Chilópoda and Insécta are opisthogoneate, with the genital ducts opening to the outside near the posterior end of the body.

Most adults of the present-day classes of arthropods may be separated by the following key.

Key to the Classes of Arthrópoda

1. With antennae 2
1′. Without antennae 7
2(1). With 2 pairs of antennae (one of which may be small); body usually with 2 distinct divisions, cephalothorax and abdomen; the cephalothorax with a variable number of leglike appendages, the abdomen with or without appendages (if with appendages, they are usually not leglike) (Figures 66–72); some appendages biramous (consisting of a basal segment bearing 2 terminal branches); mostly aquatic and gill-breathing, rarely with tracheae .... **Crustàcea** p. 122
2′. With only 1 pair of antennae; body regions and number of legs variable; appendages not biramous; aquatic or terrestrial, nearly always with a tracheal system 3
3(2′). With only 3 pairs of legs and often with 1 or 2 pairs of wings; 3 body regions fairly distinct: head, thorax, and abdomen, the abdomen without legs (but often with some terminal appendages); body shape variable .... **Insécta** p. 136
3′. With 9 or more pairs of legs, the legs on most body segments back of the head; head distinct from rest of body; wings absent; body elongate and wormlike 4
4(3′). Legs evenly spaced on the body, usually 1 pair per segment (Figures 75 and 77) 5
4′. Legs arranged in double pairs, most segments with 2 pairs (Figure 73) .... **Diplópoda** p. 128
5(4). Genital ducts opening near posterior end of body; body flattened; usually not minute, and with 15 or more pairs of legs (Figure 75) ... **Chilópoda** p. 131
5′. Genital ducts opening near anterior end of body; body usually cylindrical; minute forms with 9–12 pairs of legs (Figure 77) 6
6(5′). Antennae branched; 9 pairs of legs (Figure 77 A) .... **Paurópoda** p. 133
6′. Antennae not branched; 10–12 pairs of legs (Figure 77 B) ..... **Sýmphyla** p. 134
7(1′). Usually 7 pairs of appendages, with 5 pairs of legs; first pair of legs small, used by male in holding eggs; abdomen rudimentary; marine, spiderlike forms .... **Pycnogónida** p. 97
7′. Six (rarely fewer) pairs of appendages, with 4 (rarely 5) pairs of legs; abdomen usually well developed and constituting a distinct body region, occasionally fused with cephalothorax 8
8(7′). Abdomen with book gills; large (up to $1\frac{1}{2}$ feet (460 mm) in length) marine forms, the body oval and covered with a hard shell, and with a long spinelike tail (Figure 44) .... **Xìphosùra** p. 97
8′. Abdomen without book gills; smaller forms, rarely over 3 inches (76 mm) in length, the body not as above (Figures 45–56, 61–65) .... **Aráchnida** p. 97

SUBPHYLUM CHELICERÀTA[2]

The Cheliceràta differ from the Mandibulàta primarily in the character of their appendages, and to some extent in body form. The Cheliceràta have no antennae, and usually possess 6 pairs of appendages: a pair of fanglike chelicerae, a pair of leglike structures (usually called pedipalps) behind the chelicerae, and 4 (5, or rarely 6, in the Pycnogónida) pairs of legs behind the pedipalps. Most Cheliceràta have an extra leg segment, the patella, between the femur and tibia. Chelicerates usually have two distinct body divisions, the cephalothorax (prosoma) and abdomen (opisthosoma), and are seldom wormlike in form. There are three present-day classes of Cheliceràta, the Xìphosùra, Pycnogónida, and Aráchnida.

[2] Chelicerata: meaning with chelicerae.

CLASS XÌPHOSÙRA[3] – KING CRABS OR HORSESHOE CRABS

The horseshoe crabs are marine forms and are quite common along the Atlantic Coast from Maine to the Gulf of Mexico. They are found in shallow water and along sandy or muddy shores where they spawn. They feed chiefly on marine worms. Horseshoe crabs are easily recognized by the characteristic oval shell and the long spinelike tail (Figure 44).

[3] Xìphosùra: *xipho*, sword; *ura*, tail.

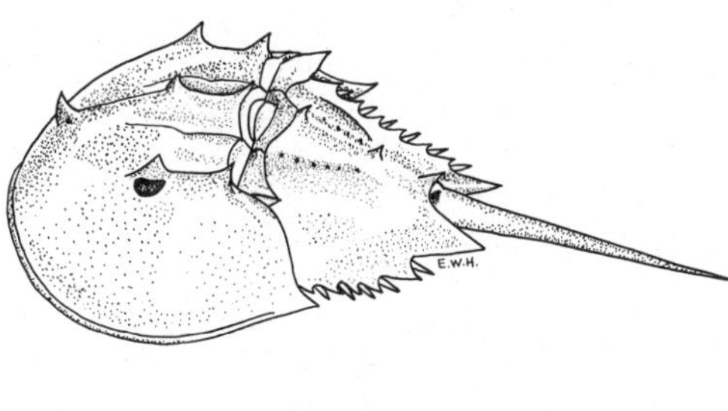

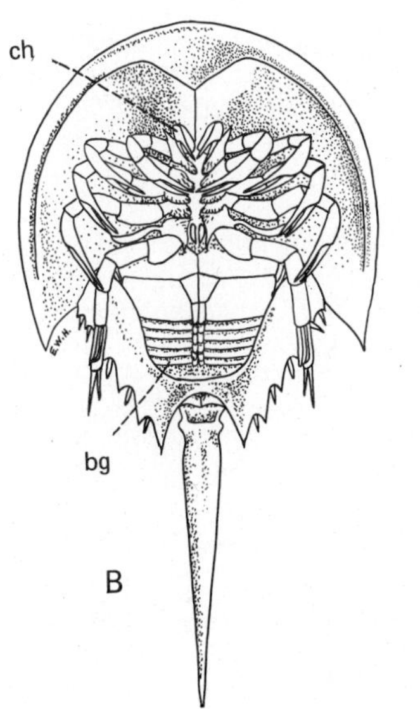

Figure 44. A horseshoe crab, *Límulus* sp. (class Xiphosùra). A, dorsolateral view; B, ventral view. *bg*, book gills; *ch*, chelicera.

CLASS PYCNOGÓNIDA[4] – SEA SPIDERS

The pycnogonids are marine, spiderlike forms with long legs; they are occasionally found under stones near the low-tide mark, but usually occur in deep water. They are predaceous and have a sucking proboscis. The body consists principally of cephalothorax; the abdomen is very small. The sea spiders vary in length from one to several centimeters; little is known of their habits, for they are not common.

CLASS ARÁCHNIDA[5] – ARACHNIDS

This is by far the largest class of the Cheliceràta, and a person studying insects will probably encounter more of them than of any other noninsect class. Its members occur almost everywhere, often in considerable numbers.

Most authorities recognize eleven orders of the Aráchnida (all represented in our area), but not all agree on the names to be used for these orders. Our arrangement is as follows (with other names and arrangements in parentheses):

Scòrpiónida (Scorpiònes) – scorpions
Pseudoscorpiónida (Pseudoscorpiònes, Chelonéthida) – pseudoscorpions
Phalángida (Opiliònes) – harvestmen, daddy-long-legs
Àcari (Acarìna, Acàrida) – mites and ticks
Thelyphónida (Uropỳgi; Pedipálpida in part) – whip-scorpions
Schizómida (Tartárides, Schizopéltida; Pedipálpida in part) – short-tailed whip-scorpions
Amblypỳgida (Amblypỳgi; Pedipálpida in part) – tailless whip-scorpions
Palpigràda (Palpigràdi, Microthelyphónida) – micro-whip-scorpions
Ricinulèida (Ricinùlei, Meridogástra, Podogòna) – ricinuleids
Solpùgida (Solifùgae) – sun-scorpions, wind-scorpions
Aranèida (Arràneae) – spiders

[4] Pycnogónida: *pycno*, thick or dense; *gonida*, off-spring (referring to the eggs).

[5] Aráchnida: from the Greek, meaning a spider.

Key to the Orders of Aráchnida

1. Opisthosoma (abdomen) unsegmented, or if segmented then with spinnerets posteriorly on ventral side of opisthosoma 2

1′. Opisthosoma distinctly segmented, without spinnerets 3

2(1). Opisthosoma petiolate (Figures 57, 62–65) .... **Aranèida** p. 107

2′. Opisthosoma broadly joined to prosoma and not petiolate (Figures 48–55) .... **Àcari** p. 100

3(1′). Opisthosoma with a taillike prolongation that is either thick and terminating in a sting (Figure 45), or slender and more or less whiplike without a sting (Figure 56 A, B); mostly tropical 4

3′. Opisthosoma without a taillike prolongation, or with a very short leaflike appendage 7

4(3). Opisthosoma ending in a sting (Figure 45); first pair of legs not greatly elongated; second ventral segment of opisthosoma with a pair of comblike organs .... **Scorpiónida** p. 99

4′. Opisthosoma not ending in a sting; first pair of legs longer than the other pairs (Figure 56 A, B); second ventral segment of opisthosoma without comblike organs 5

5(4′). Pedipalps slender, similar to the legs (Figure 56 A); minute forms, 5 mm in length or less .... **Palpigràda** p. 106

5′. Pedipalps much stouter than any of the legs (Figure 56 B); moderate-sized to large forms 6

6(5′). With 2 median eyes on a tubercle anteriorly, and a group of 3 eyes on each lateral margin; tail long, filiform, and many-segmented; prosoma (cephalothorax) undivided; 2 pairs of book lungs, on second and third opisthosomal segments .... **Thelyphónida** p. 106

6′. Eyes lacking, or with only 1 pair of eyes or eye spots; tail short, 1- to 4-segmented; prosoma divided by a transverse membranous suture in caudal third; 1 pair of book lungs, on second opisthosomal segment; females .... **Schizómida** p. 106

7(3′). Pedipalps chelate (pincerlike) (Figure 46); opisthosoma not petiolate; body flattened and usually less than 5 mm in length .... **Pseudoscorpiónida** p. 99

7′. Pedipalps raptorial or leglike, not chelate; body not particularly flattened; opisthosoma and size variable 8

8(7′). Front legs very long, with long tarsi; opisthosoma strongly constricted at base; mainly tropical 9

8′. Front legs similar to the others, and not unusually long; opisthosoma not strongly constricted at base 10

9(8). Prosoma longer than wide, the lateral margins nearly parallel, and with a transverse membranous suture in caudal third; opisthosoma with a very short terminal appendage; 4.5–7.5 mm in length; males .... **Schizómida** p. 106

9′. Prosoma wider than long, the lateral margins rounded or arched, and without a transverse suture; opisthosoma without a terminal appendage; size variable, to about 2 inches (51 mm) in length .... **Amblypỳgida** p. 106

10(8′). Legs extremely long and slender (Figure 47); body usually short and oval; common and widely distributed animals .... **Phalángida** p. 100

10′. Legs at most only moderately long; body usually elongate; southwestern United States 11

11(10′). Orange-red to brown arachnids about 3 mm in length; chelicerae concealed under a broad flap at anterior end of prosoma; base of opisthosoma narrowed; recorded from the Rio Grande valley of Texas ... **Ricinulèida** p. 107

11′. Color usually pale yellow to brownish, and length over 10 mm; chelicerae very large, extending forward, and easily visible (Figure 56 C); opisthosoma slightly narrowed at base; mainly nocturnal desert forms, occurring in the arid regions of western United States .... **Solpùgida** p. 107

ORDER **Scorpiónida**[6] — Scorpions: The scorpions are well-known animals that occur in the southern and western parts of the United States. They are fair-sized arachnids, varying in length up to 4 or 5 inches (102 or 127 mm). The abdomen is broadly joined to the cephalothorax and is differentiated into two portions, a broad 7-segmented anterior portion, and a much narrower 5-segmented posterior portion that terminates in a sting (Figure 45). The pedipalps are large and clawlike.

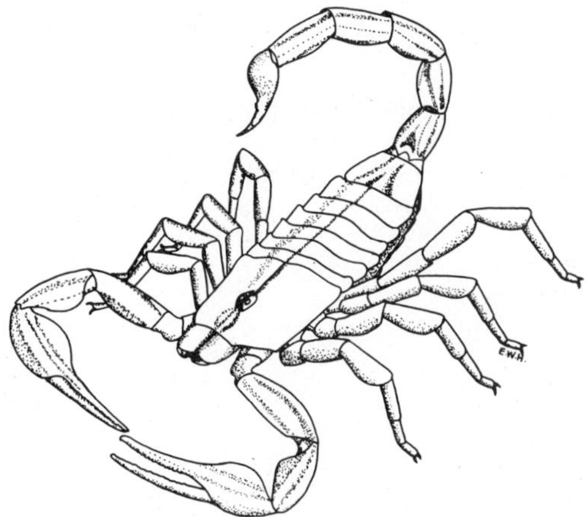

Figure 45. A scorpion; 2 ×.

Scorpions are largely nocturnal in habit, and during the day remain concealed in various protected places. When they run, the pedipalps are held forward and the posterior end of the abdomen is usually curved upward. Scorpions feed largely on insects and spiders, which they capture with their pedipalps and kill with their sting. The young are born alive, and for a time after their birth are carried on the body of the mother. Scorpions grow slowly, and some species require several years to reach maturity.

The effect of a scorpion sting depends primarily on the species of scorpion involved. The sting of most species is painful and is usually accompanied by local swelling and discoloration, but is not dangerous. Of the forty-odd species of scorpions in the United States, only one — *Centruròides sculpturàtus* Ewing — is very venomous and its sting may be fatal. This species is slender and rarely exceeds 2½ inches (64 mm) in length; it varies in color from almost entirely yellowish to yellowish brown with two irregular black stripes down the back; there is a slight dorsal protuberance at the base of the sting. As far as known, this species occurs only in Arizona.

Scorpions do not ordinarily attack man, but will sting quickly if disturbed. In areas where scorpions occur, one should be careful in picking up boards, stones, and similar objects, and a scorpion found crawling on one's body should be brushed off rather than swatted.

ORDER **Pseudoscorpiónida**[7] — Pseudoscorpions or Book Scorpions: The pseudoscorpions are small arachnids, seldom over 5 mm in length, and resemble the true scorpions in having large clawlike pedipalps, but the abdomen is short and oval and there is no sting (Figure 46); the body is very flat. Pseudoscorpions are found under bark, between the boards of buildings, between the pages of books, in moss, under leaves, and in similar situations. They often cling to and are carried about by large insects. They feed chiefly on small insects. They possess silk glands, the ducts from which open on the chelicerae; the silk is used in making a cocoon in which the animal overwinters. This group is small but is widely distributed.

[6] Scorpiónida: from the Latin, meaning a scorpion.

[7] Pseudoscorpiónida: *pseudo*, false; *scorpionida*, scorpion.

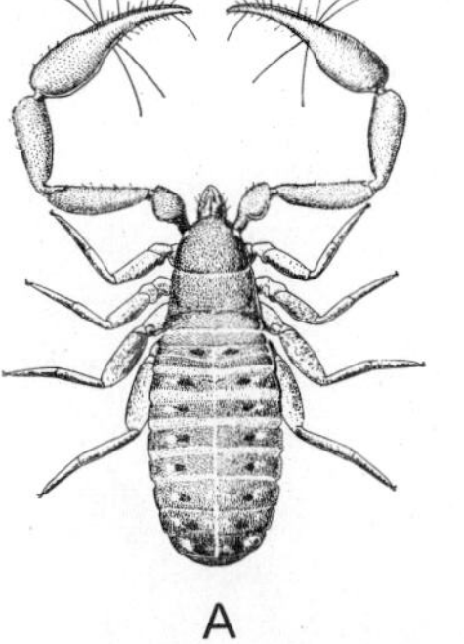

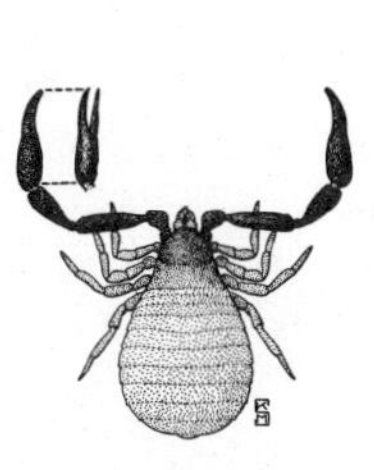

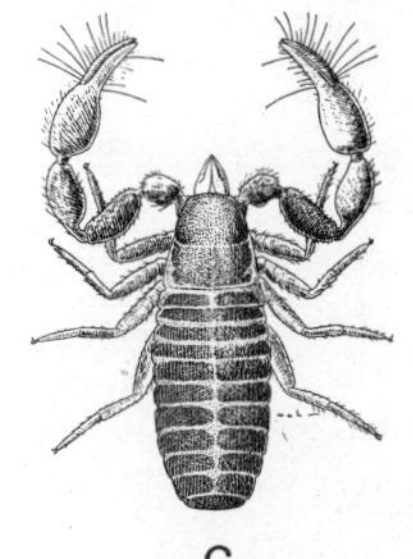

A B C

Figure 46. Pseudoscorpions. A, *Dactylochélifer copiòsus* Hoff; B, *Lárca granulàta* (Banks); C, *Pselaphochérnes párvus* Hoff. (Courtesy of Hoff and Illinois Natural History Survey.)

ORDER **Phalángida**[8]—Harvestmen or Daddy-Long-Legs: These animals, which are perhaps better known by the name daddy-long-legs, are common in most parts of the country. They are easily recognized by the oval compact body and the extremly long slender legs (Figure 47). Harvestmen feed chiefly on plant juices or dead insects, but some species apparently feed chiefly on living insects. In the North, most species overwinter in the egg stage, but in the South the adults usually overwinter. The eggs are laid in the ground, underneath stones, or in crevices in wood.

[8] Phalángida: from the Greek, meaning a finger or toe.

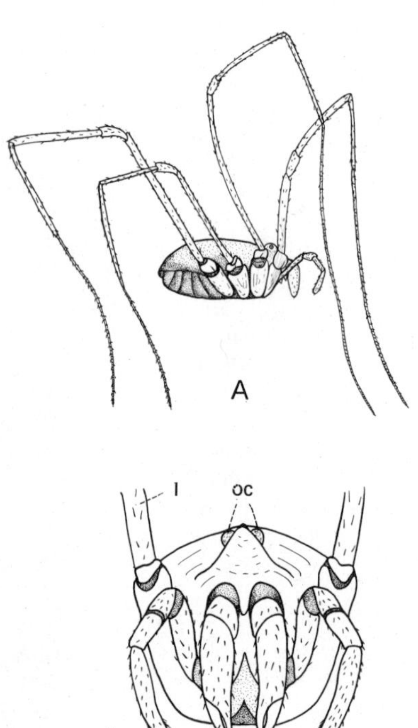

Figure 47. A harvestman or daddy-longlegs (order Phalángida). A, lateral view; B, anterior view. *ch,* chelicera; *l,* front leg; *oc,* eyes or ocelli; *pdp,* pedipalp. The harvestmen typically have two eyes located on a tubercle, and the chelicerae clawlike, as shown in B.

ORDER **Àcari**[9]—Mites and Ticks: The Àcari constitute a very large group consisting principally of small to minute animals. The body may be oval and compact, with little or no differentiation of the two body regions (prosoma or cephalothorax, and opisthosoma or abdomen) (Figures 51–55), or these two body regions may be evident (Figure 48). Newly hatched young, called larvae, have only three pairs of legs (Figures 54 B and 55 A) and acquire the fourth pair after the first molt. Instars between larva and adult are called nymphs.

The Àcari rival the insects in number of species and in the variety of habits exhibited. The group includes both terrestrial and aquatic forms, and the aquatic forms occur in both salt and fresh water. They are abundant in soil and organic debris, where they usually outnumber other arthropods. Many are parasitic, at least during a part of the life cycle, and both vertebrates and invertebrates serve as hosts; most of the parasitic forms are external parasites of their hosts. Many of the free-living forms are predaceous, many are phytophagous, and many are scavengers. This group is one of considerable biological interest and economic importance.

The groups in the order Àcari have been arranged differently by different authorities. The arrangement followed in this book is as follows:

- Order Àcari—mites and ticks
  - Group I—Opílioacarifórmes (Notostigmàta)
  - Group II—Parasítifórmes
    - Suborder Holothyrìna
    - Suborder Mesostigmàta—gamasid mites and others
    - Suborder Ixódides—ticks
  - Group III—Àcarifórmes
    - Suborder Acarídei—cheese, mange, itch, feather, and other mites
    - Suborder Tarsonemìni
    - Suborder Tetrapódili—gall mites
    - Suborder Prostigmàta—spider, harvest, water, and other mites
    - Suborder Endeostigmàta
    - Suborder Oribátei—oribatid mites

GROUP I—**Opílioacarifórmes:** The members of this group (Figure 49) live under stones and in organic debris and are predaceous. The legs are

[9] Àcari: from the Greek, meaning a mite. Many acarologists consider this group a subclass rather than an order, but because there is no uniform agreement on the relationships of the other arachnid "orders," we are treating the Àcari as an order.

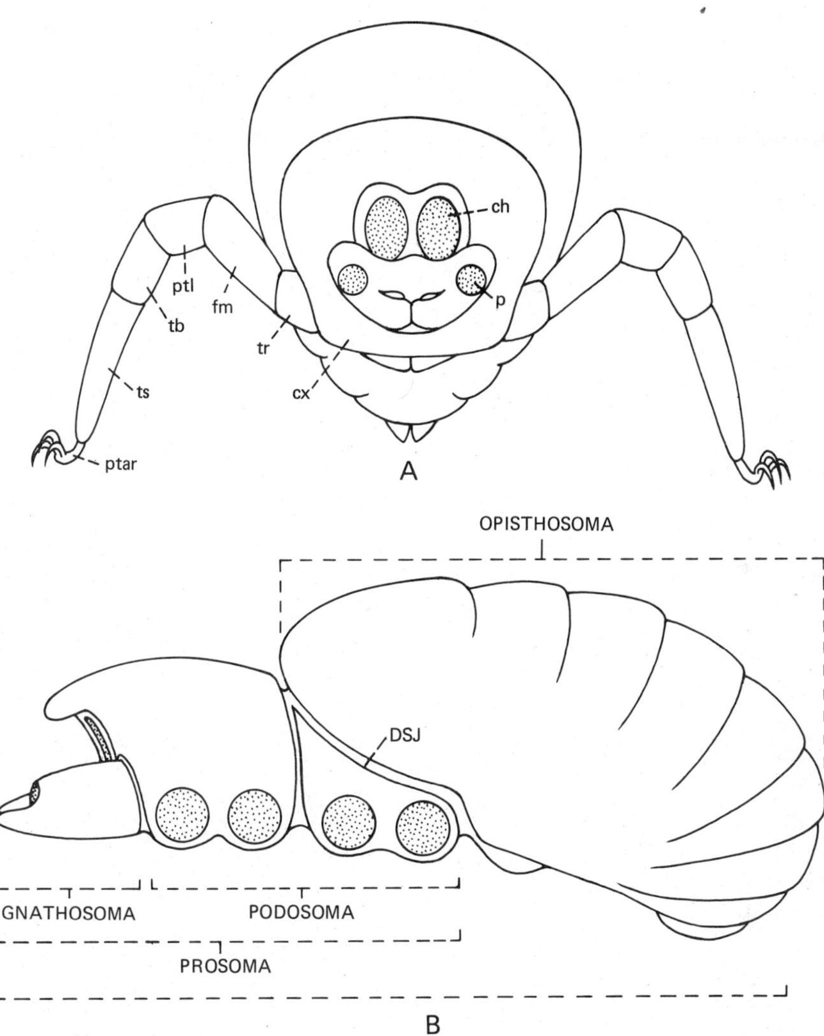

Figure 48. Generalized acariform mite. A, anterior view; B, lateral view. *ch*, socket of chelicera; *cx*, coxa; *DSJ*, disjugal furrow; *fm*, femur; *p*, socket of palp; *ptar*, pretarsus; *ptl*, genu (or patella); *tb*, tibia; *tr*, trochanter; *ts*, tarsus. (Courtesy of Johnston.)

long and slender, and these mites are superficially somewhat similar to the harvestmen. This group contains a single family, the Opílioacàridae.

GROUP II—SUBORDER **Holothyrìna:** This is a little-known group found mainly on islands in the Indian Ocean and in the Australian region; they are presumed to be predaceous. This suborder contains a single family, the Holothỳridae.

SUBORDER **Mesostigmàta:** This is the largest suborder in the Parasítifórmes and includes predaceous, scavenging, and parasitic forms. Members of this suborder are usually the dominant predaceous mites in leaf litter and soil. The gamasid mites are common representatives of this group. The parasitic mites in this group attack birds, bats, small mammals, snakes, insects, and rarely man. One parasitic species, the chicken mite, *Der-*

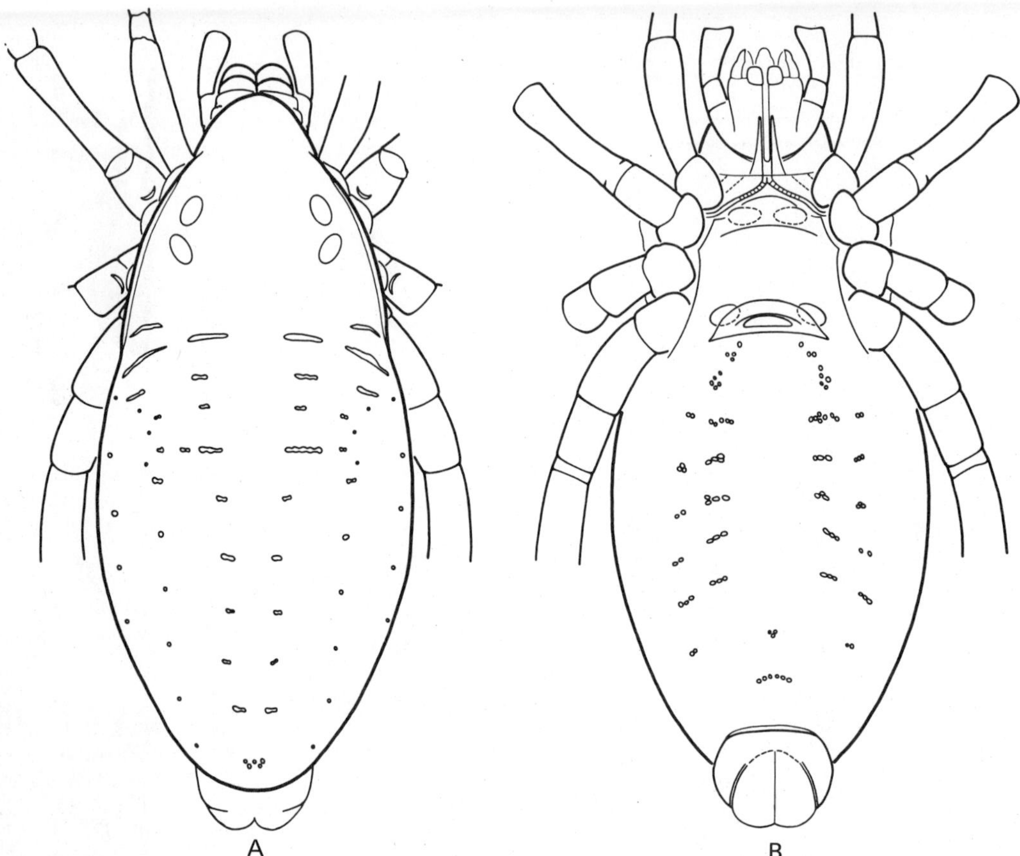

Figure 49. Female opilioacariform mite. A, dorsal view; B, ventral view. (From Johnston, redrawn from van der Hammen.)

manýssus gállinae (De Geer), is a serious pest of poultry; it hides during the day and attacks poultry and sucks their blood at night; this species also causes a dermatitis in man.

SUBORDER **Ixódides**—Ticks: Two families of ticks occur in North America: the Ixódidae or hard ticks, and the Argásidae or soft ticks. Ticks are larger than most other Àcari and are parasitic, attacking chiefly mammals, birds, and reptiles. From man's point of view, they are annoying pests, and some species serve as the vectors of disease. Certain ticks, particularly engorging females feeding on the neck or near the base of the skull of their host (man or animals), inject a venom that produces paralysis; this paralysis may be fatal if the tick is not removed. The most important tick-borne diseases are spotted fever, relapsing fever, tularemia, and Texas cattle fever.

Ticks lay their eggs in various places, but not on their host; the young seek out a host after hatching. The hard ticks take only one blood meal in each of their three instars; they remain on the host several days while feeding, but usually drop off to molt. The soft ticks usually hide in crevices during the day and feed on their host at night; each instar may feed several times. The hard ticks usually have only two or three hosts during their development, while the soft ticks may have many hosts; the cattle tick that transmits Texas cattle fever feeds on the same host individual during all three instars, and the protozoan that causes the disease is transmitted transovarially, that is, through the eggs to the tick's offspring. The hard ticks (Figure 50) possess a hard dorsal plate called the scutum, and they have the mouth parts protruding anteriorly and visible from above; the soft ticks (Figure 51) lack a scutum and are soft-

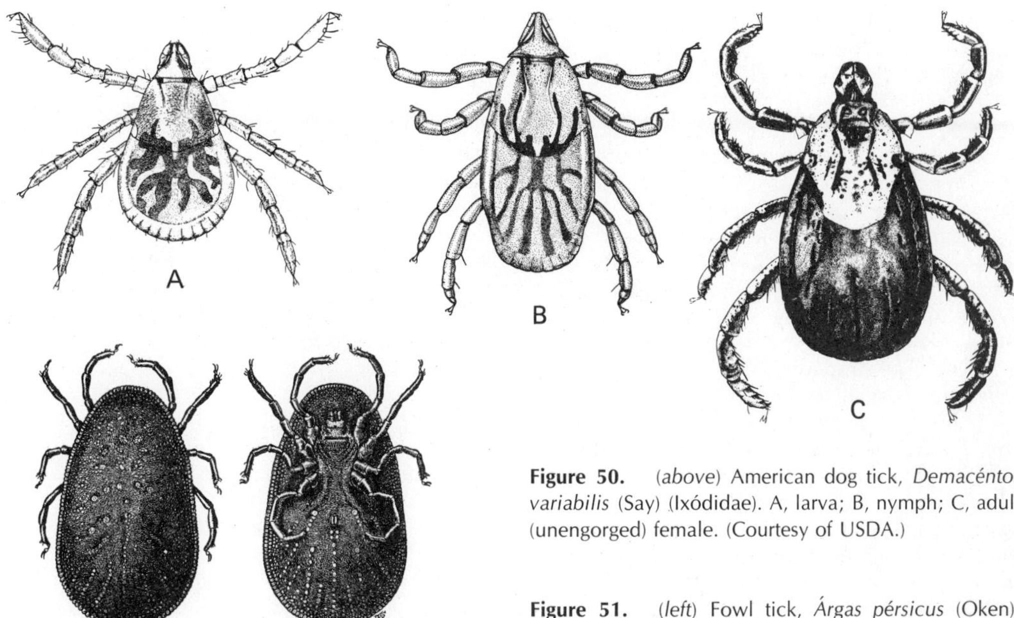

Figure 50. (*above*) American dog tick, *Demacéntor variabilis* (Say) (Ixódidae). A, larva; B, nymph; C, adult (unengorged) female. (Courtesy of USDA.)

Figure 51. (*left*) Fowl tick, *Árgas pérsicus* (Oken), adult female (Argásidae). A, dorsal view; B, ventral view. (Courtesy of USDA.)

bodied, and the mouth parts are ventrally located and not visible from above.

GROUP III – SUBORDER **Acarídei:** This group includes the cheese, mange, itch, feather, and other mites, the most important of which are probably those that cause dermatitis in man or animals (the itch and mange mites). The most important mites causing dermatitis belong to three families: the Acàridae (=Tyroglỳphidae), Sarcóptidae, and Psoróptidae. The family Acàridae is a very large group whose members are widely distributed; they live on all kinds of organic substances and often infest cheese, dried meats, flour, and seeds. They not only damage or contaminate these materials, but also often get on man and cause a dermatitis called grocer's itch or miller's itch. The Sarcóptidae include the itch or scab mites, which attack man and other animals and burrow into the skin; these mites cause severe irritation, and the resulting scratching often causes additional injury or leads to secondary infection. One of the best treatments for scabies (infection by these mites) is the application of a solution of benzyl benzoate. The Psoróptidae include the mange mites, which attack various domestic animals (Figure 52). Spe-

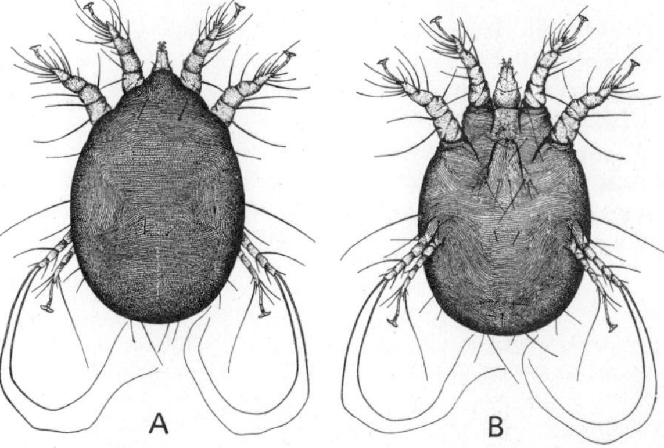

Figure 52. Sheep scab mite, *Psoróptes òvis* (Hering), female. A, dorsal view; B, ventral view. (Courtesy of USDA.)

cies of *Dermatophagòides* (family Acàridae) are common inhabitants of houses, and have been implicated in house-dust allergies.

SUBORDER **Tarsonemìni:** This group includes small mites associated with plants and some that are free-living or associated with insects. *Pyemòtes ventricòsus* (Newport) often causes a dermatitis known as "hay itch" in man, and sometimes occurs in grocery stores around discarded cereals. *Acaràpis woodi* (Rennie) causes "Isle of Wight" disease in honey bees.

SUBORDER **Tetrapódili**—Gall Mites: The gall mites are elongate and wormlike and have only two pairs of legs (Figure 53). A few species form small pouchlike galls on leaves, but the majority feed on leaves without forming galls and produce a rusting of the leaves; some attack buds, and one forms the conspicuous witch's broom twig gall on hackberry. Many are serious pests of orchard trees or other cultivated plants. This suborder contains a single family, the Eriophyidae.

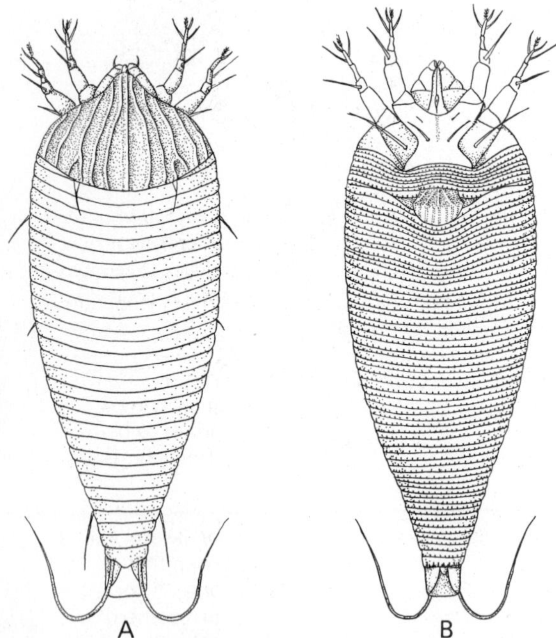

Figure 53. A gall mite, *Phyllocóptes variábilis* Hodgkiss, a species attacking sugar maple; 460 ×. A, dorsal view; B, ventral view. (Redrawn from Hodgkiss.)

SUBORDER **Prostigmàta:** This is a large group containing predaceous, scavenging, plant-feeding, and parasitic forms; the best known mites in this group are the spider mites, harvest mites, and water mites.

The spider mites, or red mites (Tetranýchidae), are plant feeders, and some species do serious damage to orchard trees, field crops, and greenhouse plants. They feed on the foliage or fruit and attack a variety of plants; they are widely distributed and sometimes occur in tremendous numbers. The eggs are laid on the plant, and during the summer hatch in four or five days; there are four instars (Figure 54), and growth from egg to adult usually requires about three weeks. Most species overwinter in the egg stage. The immature instars are usually yellowish or pale in color, and the adults are yellowish or greenish (seldom red). Sex in these mites is determined by the fertilization of the egg; males develop from unfertilized eggs and females from fertilized eggs.

The harvest mites (also called chiggers or redbugs) (Trombicùlidae) are ectoparasites of vertebrates in the larval stage, whereas the nymphs and adults are free-living and predaceous on small arthropods and arthropod eggs. Harvest mites lay their eggs among vegetation; the larvae, on hatching, crawl over the vegetation and attach to a passing host. They insert their mouth parts into the outer layer of the skin, and their saliva partly digests the tissues beneath. The larvae remain on the host for a few days, feeding on tissue fluid and digested cellular material, and then drop off. These mites are small (Figure 55 A) and are seldom noticed; their bites, however, cause considerable irritation, and the itching persists for some time after the mites have left. On man, the mites seem to prefer areas where the clothing is tight. A person going into an area infested with chiggers can avoid being attacked by using a good repellent, such as dimethyl phthallate or diethyl toluamide; this material can be put on the clothing, or the clothing can be impregnated with it. A good material to reduce the itching caused by chiggers is tincture of benzyl benzoate. In the Orient, southern Asia, the Southwest Pacific, and Australia, certain harvest mites serve as vectors of scrub typhus or tsutsugamushi disease; this disease caused over 7000 casualties in the United States armed forces during World War II.

The water mites include a number of common and widely distributed freshwater species and a few marine forms; a few species occur in hot springs. The larvae are parasitic on aquatic in-

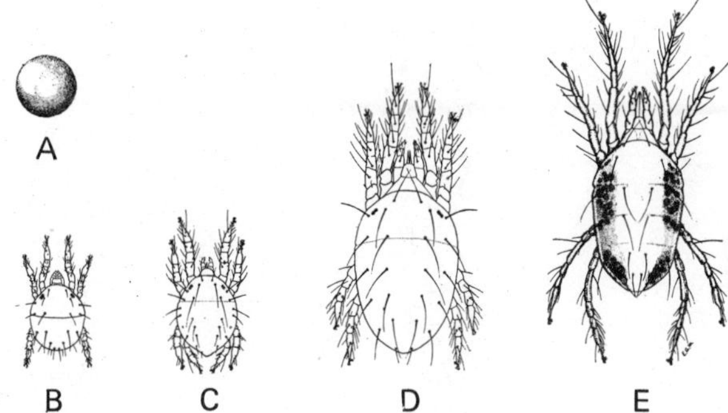

Figure 54. Fourspotted spider mite, *Tetránychus canadénsis* (McGregor). A, egg; B, first instar, or larva; C, second instar, or protonymph; D, third instar, or deutonymph; E, fourth instar, adult female. (Courtesy of USDA, after McGregor and McDunough.)

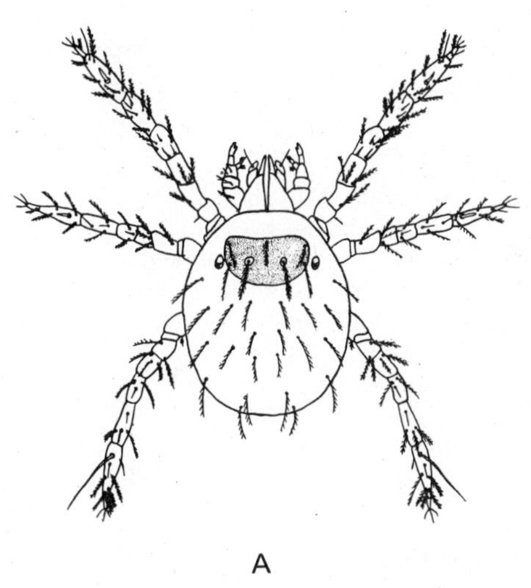

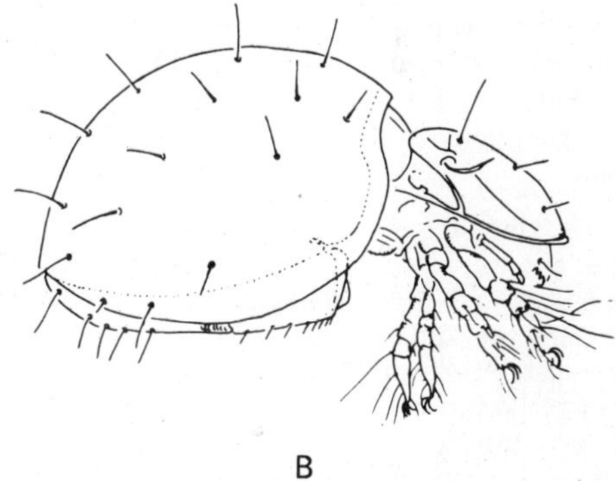

Figure 55. A, a chigger, the larva of *Eutrombícula alfreddùgesi* (Oudemans); 215 ×. B, an oribatid mite of the box-mite type (family Euphthiracàridae). (A redrawn from a U.S. Public Health Service release; B, courtesy of the Institute of Acarology.)

sects, and most nymphs and adults are predaceous. Water mites are small, round-bodied, usually brightly colored (red or green), and are often quite common in ponds; they crawl about over the bottom and over aquatic vegetation, and lay their eggs on the undersides of leaves or on aquatic animals (mainly freshwater mussels). Water mite larvae (usually in the genus *Arrenùrus*) are often abundant on the bodies of dragonflies and damselflies; they crawl from the nymph to the adult when the latter emerges, and may remain there a couple of weeks, feeding on the body fluids of the insect and eventually dropping off and developing into the adult if they happen to get into a suitable aquatic habitat.

SUBORDER **Endeostigmàta:** This is a small group of small to medium-sized free-living mites that are considered by some authorities to be very primitive. One species is known from the Devonian of England.

SUBORDER **Oribátei**—Oribatid or Beetle Mites: This is a large and very diverse group that exhibits a great deal of variation in form; it includes some of the most primitive and also some of the most specialized of the mites. Many of the higher oribatids superficially resemble small beetles (Figure 55 B). Some species have winglike lateral extensions of the notum; in a few species these extensions, or pteromorphs, are hinged, contain

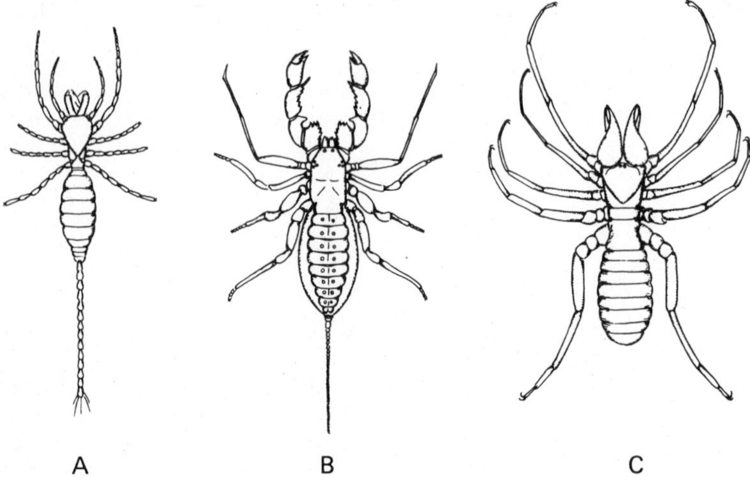

Figure 56. Arachnids. A, micro-whip-scorpion (order Palpigràda); B, whip-scorpion (order Thelyphónida); C, wind-scorpion (order Solpùgida). (Courtesy of the Institute of Acarology.)

"veins," and are provided with muscles. Oribatid mites are found in leaf litter, under bark and stones, in moss and freshwater plants, and in the soil; they are apparently scavengers. They comprise a large percentage of the soil fauna, and are important in promoting soil fertility through breaking down the organic matter. A number of species in this group have been found to serve as the intermediate hosts of certain tapeworms that infest sheep, cattle, and other ruminants.

ORDER **Thelyphónida**[10] — Whip-Scorpions: The whip-scorpions are mainly tropical, and in the United States occur only in the southern states. They range in length up to about 4 or 5 inches (100–130 mm). They are somewhat scorpionlike in appearance, but lack a sting at the end of the abdomen and have a long whiplike tail (Figure 56 B). The whip-scorpions are nocturnal and predaceous; they are generally found under logs or other objects, or burrowing in sand. These arachnids are sometimes greatly feared, but they do not have poison glands. Some species when irritated give off a vinegarlike odor, and are called vinegarroons. Our only species of whip-scorpion is *Mastigopróctus gigánteus* (Lucas), which occurs in Florida and the Southwest.

[10] Thelyphónida: *thely,* female; *phonida,* kill.

ORDER **Schizómida**[11] — Short-Tailed Whip-Scorpions: These animals are similar to the Thelyphónida, but the terminal appendage is short, and not long and whiplike. A few species are known from Florida and California; they have the fourth legs modified for jumping, and in the field superficially resemble small crickets. *Trithỳreus pentapéltis* (Cook), which occurs in the desert regions of southern California, is 4.5–7.5 mm in length, yellowish to reddish brown in color, and occurs under rocks and in leaf litter.

ORDER **Amblypỳgida**[12] — Tailless Whip-Scorpions: These are relatively large spiderlike arachnids, the largest about 2 inches (51 mm) in length; they have 8 eyes, the prosoma (cephalothorax) is wider than long with the sides rounded, and the front tarsi are long, slender, and many-segmented. Our few species occur in Florida and southern California.

ORDER **Palpigràda**[13] — Micro-Whip-Scorpions: These arachnids are tiny animals, 5 mm in length or less, with a long segmented tail; they are

[11] Schizómida: *schizo,* split (referring to the transverse suture on the prosoma.

[12] Amblypỳgida: *ambly,* blunt; *pygida,* rump.

[13] Palpigràda: *palpi,* palp or feeler; *grada,* walk (referring to the leglike character of the pedipalps).

usually found under stones or in the soil. They are similar to the whip-scorpions (Thelyphónida) in general form (Figure 56 A). This group is represented in the United States by only a few species occurring in the South and Southwest.

ORDER **Ricinulèida**[14]: This is a small group of extremely rare tropical arachnids. They superficially resemble spiders, but the abdomen is segmented and not petiolate, eyes are lacking, and they have a movable flap at the anterior end of the prosoma that extends over the chelicerae. One species, *Cryptocéllus doròtheae* Gertsch and Mulaik, has been reported from the Rio Grande valley of Texas; this arachnid is about 3 mm in length, orange-red to brown in color, and occurs under rocks or slabs in sandy areas.

ORDER **Solpùgida**[15] — Sun-Scorpions or Wind-Scorpions: These arachnids occur chiefly in desert regions; the one species that is found in the eastern United States, *Ammotrechélla stímponi* (Putnam), occurs in Florida. The body of a solpugid may be an inch or more in length and is somewhat constricted in the middle, and the chelicerae are very large (Figure 56 C). The large chelicerae give these animals a ferocious appearance, but they are relatively harmless; they do not possess venom glands. On each hind leg there are five racquet organs — short, broad, **T**-shaped structures (attached by the base of the **T**). Solpugids are nocturnal in habit and fast-moving; they are predaceous on other small animals.

ORDER **Aranèida**[16] — Spiders: The spiders are a large, distinct, and widespread group; they occur in many types of habitats and are often very abundant. Many people have the idea that spiders are very venomous, but although they all have venom glands, they very rarely bite man; only a few species in the United States are dangerously venomous.

The body of a spider is divided into two regions, the cephalothorax and abdomen; the abdomen is unsegmented (in our species) and attached to the cephalothorax by a slender pedicel (Figures 57 A, B and 61–65). The cephalothorax bears the eyes, mouth parts, and legs, and the abdomen bears the genital structures, spiracles, anus, and spinnerets.

The cephalothorax is covered dorsally by the carapace and ventrally by the sternum; anterior to the sternum is a small sclerite called the labium (Figure 57 B, *lbm*). The eyes are simple and are located on the anterior end of the carapace (Figure 60); most spiders have eight eyes, but some have fewer; the number and arrangement of the eyes provide characters useful in distinguishing different families.[17] The area between the anterior row of eyes and the edge of the carapace is the clypeus.

The chelicerae are located at the anterior end of the cephalothorax, below the eyes, and are usually directed downward; they are 2-segmented, with the basal segment stout and the distal segment fanglike. Spiders have poison glands, and the ducts from these glands open near the tips of the chelicerae. The fangs move laterally in most spiders (suborder Labidógnatha), but move vertically in the tarantulas and trapdoor spiders (suborder Orthógnatha). The basal segment of the chelicerae sometimes bears a small, rounded lateral prominence (the boss) at its base. Some spiders have a filelike ridge on the lateral surface of the chelicerae; such spiders stridulate by stroking this ridge with the pedipalp to produce a soft sound.

The pedipalps, which are located behind the chelicerae and in front of the legs, are somewhat leglike or palplike; the basal segment, the endite (Figure 57 B, *cx*), is enlarged and functions as a crushing jaw. The labium lies between the two endites. The pedipalps are clubbed in male spiders; the terminal segment is modified into a copulatory organ (Figure 57 C).

The legs are 7-segmented (coxa, trochanter, femur, patella, tibia, metatarsus, and tarsus; Figure 57 E), and usually bear two or three claws at their apex. If there are three claws, two are paired and the third is a median claw; the median claw, when present, is usually small and difficult to see. The tip of the tarsus is usually provided with numerous hairs and bristles, which may obscure the claws. Bristles here that are thick, serrated, and somewhat clawlike are called spurious claws.

---

[14] Ricinulèida: *ricin,* a kind of mite or tick; *uleida,* small (a diminutive suffix).

[15] Solpùgida: from the Latin, meaning a venomous ant or spider.

[16] Aranèida: from the Latin, meaning a spider.

[17] The anterior row of eyes is referred to in the key as the *first* row. An eye pattern described as 4-2-2 (for example, Figure 60 C) would mean 4 eyes in the anterior row, 2 in the second row, and 2 in the posterior row.

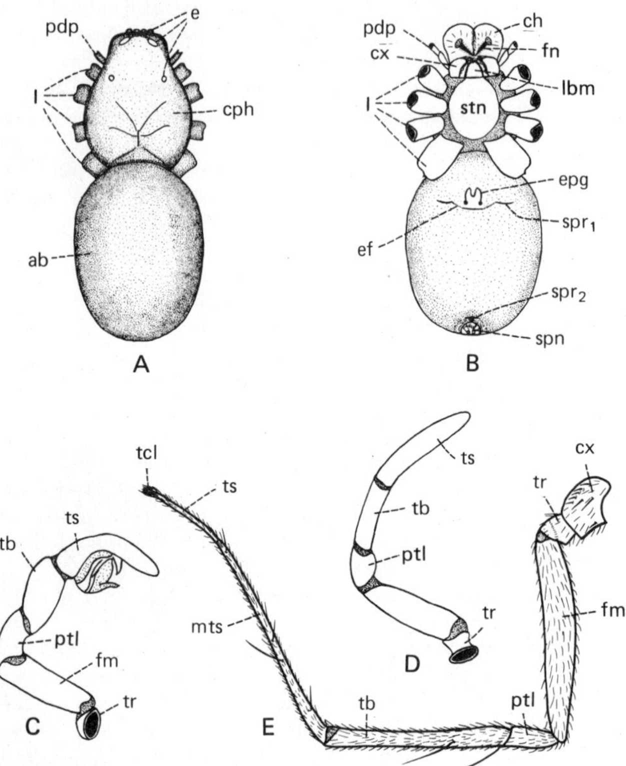

Figure 57. Structural characters of spiders. A, dorsal view (generalized); B, ventral view (generalized); C, male pedipalp; D, female pedipalp; E, leg. *ab,* opisthosoma or abdomen; *ch,* chelicera; *cph,* prosoma or cephalothorax; *cx,* coxa (the coxa of the pedipalp, shown in B, is expanded to form the endite); *e,* eyes; *ef,* epigastric furrow; *epg,* epigynum; *fm,* femur; *fn,* fang of chelicera; *l,* coxae of legs; *lbm,* labium; *mts,* metatarsus; *pdp,* pedipalp; *ptl,* patella; *spn,* spinnerets; spr_1, book lung spiracle; spr_2, tracheal spiracle; *stn,* sternum; *tb,* tibia; *tcl,* tarsal claws; *tr,* trochanter; *ts,* tarsus.

Many spiders with only two claws have a dense tuft of hairs below the claws; this is the claw tuft (Figure 59 D, *clt*). The legs are often provided with hairs or bristles that are useful in separating families. The fine vertical hairs on the tarsi and metatarsi are called trichobothria (Figure 59 B, *trb*); these hairs are probably sensory in function. Spiders with a cribellum (a structure on abdomen; see following paragraph) also have on the metatarsi of the hind legs a close-set series of heavy bristles, the calamistrum (Figure 59 B, *clm*); the calamistrum plays a part in the formation of the ribbonlike bands of silk spun by these spiders.

Near the anterior end of the abdomen on the ventral side is a transverse groove called the epigastric furrow (Figure 57 B, *ef*); the openings of the book lungs (Figure 57 B, spr_1) are located at the lateral ends of this furrow (book lungs are lacking in the Caponìidae), and the genital opening is located at the middle of this furrow. The book lungs are breathing organs consisting of saclike invaginations containing a series of sheetlike leaves. A few spiders have a second pair of book lungs, the openings of which are located laterally behind the epigastric furrow. Spiders also have tracheae, and there is usually a single spiracle, located on the midventral line of the abdomen anterior to the spinnerets (Figure 57 B, spr_2); this spiracle is often difficult to see.

Adult female spiders have a sclerotized structure, the epigynum, usually somewhat conical in shape, at the genital opening (Figure 57 B, *epg*); this structure varies considerably in different species and often provides good taxonomic characters. At the posterior end of the abdomen on the ventral side are six (rarely two or four) fingerlike structures, the spinnerets, from which the silk of the spider is spun (Figures 57 B, *spn* and 58 B–E); at the apex of each spinneret are many (sometimes a hundred or more) spinning tubes from which the silk emerges. Above (posterior to) the spinnerets is a small, variously developed tubercle, the anal tubercle, in which the anus is located. A few families of spiders (those in the section Cribellàtae) have a sievelike structure, called the cribellum, just anterior to the spinnerets (Figure 58 B *crb*);

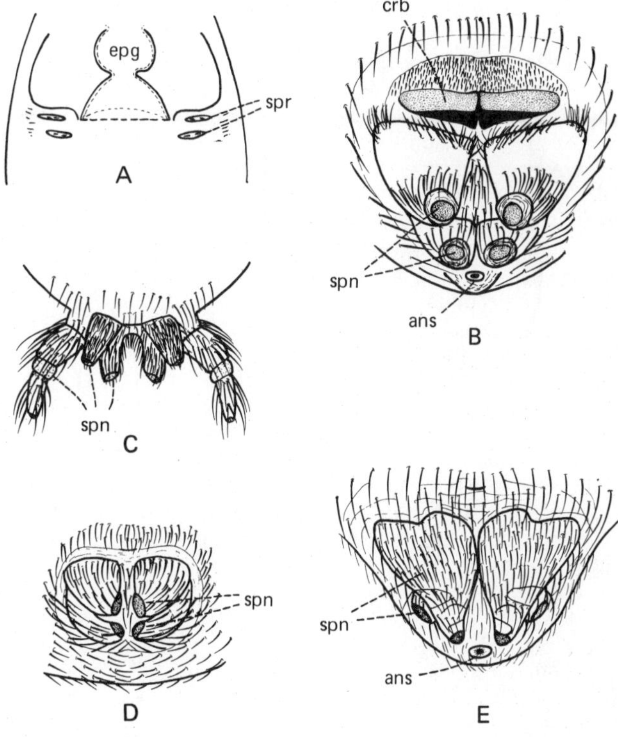

Figure 58. Abdominal characters of spiders. A, base of abdomen of *Dýsdera* (Dysdéridae), showing the two pairs of spiracles; B–E, spinnerets, ventral view; B, *Amauròbius* (Amaurobìidae); C, *Tegenària* (Agelénidae); D, *Lycòsa* (Lycòsidae); E, *Therídion* (Theridìidae). *ans,* anus; *crb,* cribellum; *epg,* epigynum; *spn,* spinnerets; *spr,* spiracle.

this is an accessory silk-spinning organ. A few spiders that lack a cribellum have a small conical appendage, the colulus, between the bases of the anterior spinnerets; the function of this structure is not known.

Spiders undergo very little metamorphosis during their development; when hatched they usually look like miniature adults. If legs are lost during development, they can usually be regenerated. Spider eggs are generally laid in a silken sac; these egg sacs vary in their construction and are deposited in all sorts of places. Some are attached to leaves or twigs or bark, some are placed in crevices, some are placed in or near the web, and some are carried about by the female. The eggs usually hatch soon after they are laid, but if the eggs are laid in the fall, the young spiders may remain in the sac until the following spring. The young spiders are sometimes cannibalistic, and fewer young may escape from the sac than there were eggs originally.

The two sexes of a spider often differ considerably in size, with the female being larger than the male. Mating is sometimes preceded by a more or less elaborate courtship performance, and in many cases is followed by the female's killing and eating the male (hence the name black "widow" for one species of spider).

All spiders are predaceous and feed mainly on insects; some of the larger spiders may occasionally feed on small vertebrates. The prey is usually killed by the poison injected into it by the bite of the spider. Different spiders capture their prey in different ways; the wolf spiders and jumping spiders forage for and pounce on their prey, the crab spiders lie in wait for their prey on flowers—feeding on bees, flies, and other insects that frequent the flowers; the majority of spiders capture their prey in nets or webs. A few spiders are commensals; that is, they live in the web of a larger spider and feed on small insects not eaten by the larger spider.

Various types of silk are spun by spiders. Many spin a strand of silk almost wherever they go, the strand serving as a dragline. Some silk is covered with minute drops of a very sticky material to which the spider's victims stick; in an orb web the spiral strands are viscous, and the radiating strands are simple silk. Many spiders wrap up in silk the insects caught in their web. Some silk, such as that of the hackled-band spiders, consists of flattened strands.

The webs built by spiders are of several principal types; each species of spider constructs a characteristic web that is often as distinctive as the spider itself. The house spider and others build irregular nets, with the strands of silk extending in almost every direction. The sheet-web spiders make a closely woven, sheetlike, and usually horizontal web. The web of the funnel-web spiders is somewhat sheetlike, but is shaped like a funnel. Many spiders build orb webs consisting of radiating and spiral strands. The trap-door spiders and some of the wolf spiders construct tunnels. Some spiders construct leaf nests. Many spiders have a retreat of some sort close to or adjoining the web; they spend most of their time in this retreat and come out onto the web when it has caught something. The stimulus that brings out the spider is apparently the vibration of the web caused by the insect that is caught; a vibrating tuning fork held against the web will usually produce the same reaction by the spider.

Although spiders do not have wings, small ones often "fly." They get on top of a rock or post and spin out some silk. The wind catches this silk, and off "flies" the spider. If the wind is particularly strong, the silk may be torn off the spider; when many spiders are trying to fly on a windy day, large quantities of this silk ("gossamer") may be blown over the landscape. This flying of spiders is sometimes called "ballooning" or "parachuting," and it is usually young spiders that are involved.

Spiders play an important role in the general economy of nature, for they are quite numerous and their predatory habits serve to keep many other animals, particularly insects, in check. They are in turn preyed upon by various other animals, particularly wasps. Spider silk is used in the preparation of the cross hairs in certain optical instruments. Many people dislike having spiders in the house because their webs are a nuisance (or simply because they dislike spiders), but spiders do not damage anything in the house and they may perform a service by destroying noxious insects. As we pointed out above, the venomous nature of spiders is generally greatly exaggerated. Most spiders will not bite if handled carefully.

The order Aranèida is usually divided into two suborders, the Orthógnatha (Aviculariòidea) and the Labidógnatha (Argiopòidea), primarily on the basis of the structure of the chelicerae. The suborder Labidógnatha is divided into two sections, the Cribellàtae and Ecribellàtae; the Cribellàtae have a cribellum and calamistrum, which are lacking in the Ecribellàtae. The majority of our spiders belong to the Ecribellàtae.

Key to the Familes of Spiders

The groups in this key marked with an asterisk are relatively rare or are unlikely to be taken by the general collector.

1. Fangs of the chelicerae moving vertically or forward and backward; 2 pairs of book lungs; no cribellum; stout-bodied spiders, mostly western and tropical (suborder Orthógnatha) 2

1′. Fangs of the chelicerae moving laterally or in and out; usually only 1 pair of book lungs (if with 2, then a cribellum is present) (suborder Labidógnatha) 7

2(1). Anal tubercle well separated from spinnerets; abdomen with 1–3 sclerotized terga 3

2′. Anal tubercle immediately adjacent to spinnerets; abdomen without sclerotized terga 5

3(2). Endites well developed; labium fused to sternum; carapace with a transverse pit; widely distributed .... **Atýpidae** p. 116

3′. Endites weakly developed; labium not fused to sternum; carapace with a longitudinal pit or groove; mostly western United States 4*

4(3′). Chelicerae with a group of apical teeth on mesal margin; labium about as long as wide; 4 spinnerets, the last segment of posterior pair a little longer than preceding segment .... **Antrodiaètidae*** p. 116

4′. Chelicerae without such teeth on mesal margin; labium much wider than long; 6 spinnerets, the last segment of posterior pair nearly twice as long as preceding segment .... **Mecicobothrìidae*** p. 116

5(2′). Tarsi with 2 claws and with claw tufts; large (40 mm or more in length), robust, hairy spiders, occurring in the South and West ... **Theraphòsidae** p. 116

5′. Tarsi with 3 claws and without claw tufts; less than 30 mm in length ... 6

6(5′). Chelicerae with a group of apical teeth on mesal margin; anterior portion of carapace higher than posterior portion; anterior spinnerets separated by less than their own length; basal segment of posterior spinnerets as long as or longer than remaining segments combined; 15–28 mm in length .... **Ctenìzidae** p. 116

6′. Chelicerae without such teeth on mesal margin; carapace flattened, the anterior part no higher than posterior portion; anterior spinnerets separated by at least their own length; the 3 segments of posterior spinnerets of about equal length; about 15 mm in length .... **Diplùridae** p. 116

7(1′). With 2 pairs of book lungs, or with 1 pair of book lungs and a pair of spiracles behind the book lungs, or without book lungs and with 2 pairs of spiracles 8*

7′. With 1 pair of book lungs, and a single spiracle (or none) between epigastric furrow and spinnerets 12

8(7). Book lungs lacking, and with 2 pairs of tracheal spiracles; 2 or 8 eyes; rare southwestern spiders .... **Caponìidae***

8′. One or 2 pairs of book lungs present; not more than 1 pair of tracheal spiracles 9*

9(8′). Eight eyes; 2 pairs of book lungs, the posterior pair about halfway between epigastric furrow and spinnerets; cribellum present; 5–10 mm in length; in southern mountains .... **Hypochìlidae*** p. 116

9′. Six eyes or none; 1 pair of book lungs and a pair of spiracles (Figure 58 A); cribellum absent 10*

10(9′). Median eyes larger than lateral ones; minute spiders, about 1 mm in length .... **Oonópidae*** p. 116

10′. Median eyes not larger than lateral ones (Figure 60 F); 7–13 mm in length 11*

11(10′). Third legs directed backward; cephalothorax and legs reddish orange, abdomen dirty white; 12–13 mm in length; eastern United States .... **Dysdéridae*** p. 116

11′. Third legs directed forward; color brownish; 7–10 mm in length; widely distributed .... **Segestrìidae*** p. 116

12(7′). With a cribellum (Figure 58 B, *crb*) and a calamistrum (Figure 59 B, *clm*); if the cribellum and calamistrum are rudimentary (males of *Filastàta*), the eyes are all on a single raised tubercle and the pedipalps are longer than the body 13

12′. With neither a cribellum nor a calamistrum; eyes and pedipalps not as above 19

13(12). Anal tubercle large, 2-segmented, and fringed with long hair; 8 eyes in a compact group, the posterior median eyes triangular or irregular in shape; 2–4 mm in length .... **Oecobìidae*** p. 116

13′. Anal tubercle small, unsegmented, and without a conspicuous fringe of hair; arrangement of eyes variable, the posterior median eyes round ... 14

14(13′). Tarsi with 2 claws and with claw tufts; cribellum divided; eyes in 2 rows; rare southwestern spiders .... **Zorópsidae*** p. 116

14′. Tarsi with 3 claws and usually without claw tufts; cribellum and eyes variable 15

15(14′). Chelicerae fused together at base, each with an apical tooth, which with the fang forms a sort of claw; tracheal spiracle considerably anterior to spinnerets; labium fused to sternum; the 8 eyes in a compact group; 9–18 mm in length; southern United States .... **Filastátidae*** p. 116

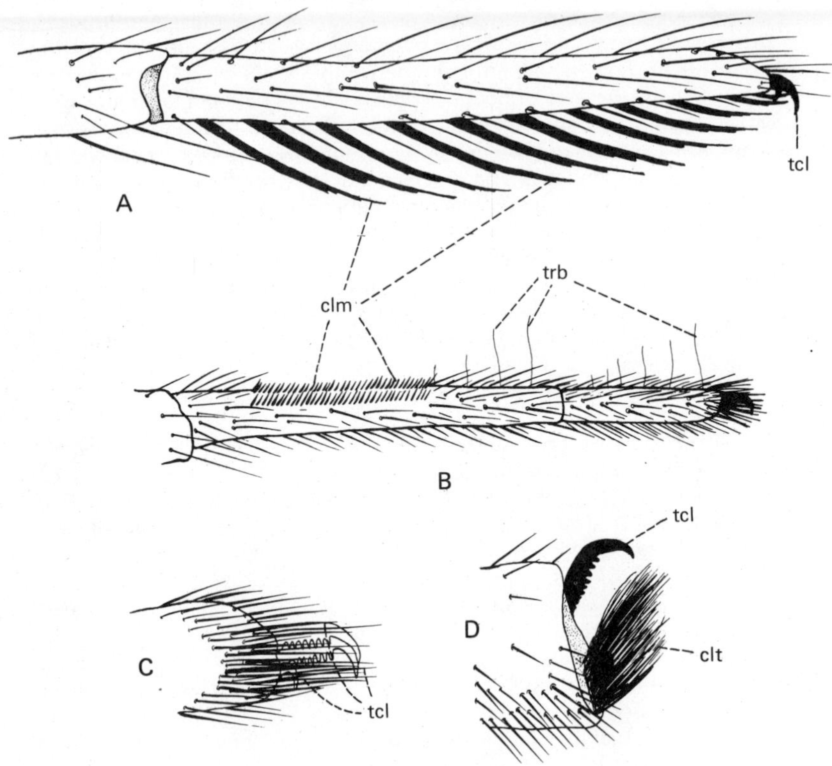

Figure 59. Leg characters of spiders. A, hind tarsus of *Therídion* (Theridìidae); B, hind tarsus of *Amauròbius* (Amaurobìidae); C, tip of tarsus of a lycosid; D, tip of tarsus of a salticid. *clm,* calamistrum; *clt,* claw tuft; *tcl,* tarsal claws; *trb,* trichobothria.

15′. Chelicerae not fused together at base, and without an apical tooth; tracheal spiracle close to spinnerets; labium not fused to sternum 16

16(15′). Eight eyes, all light-colored (Figure 60 E); tarsi with trichobothria; cribellum divided; 4.5–12.0 mm in length .... **Amaurobìidae** p. 116

16′. Six or 8 eyes (if with 8, then some or all are dark-colored); tarsi usually without trichobothria; 1.7–8.0 mm in length 17

17(16′). Eight eyes, all dark-colored 18

17′. Either 8 eyes and only the anterior median ones dark, or 6 eyes and all pearly white; 1.7–6.0 mm in length .... **Dictỳnidae** p. 116

18(17). Femora with trichobothria; eyes in 2 recurved rows; 2.4–8.0 mm in length .... **Ulobóridae** p. 116

18′. Femora without trichobothria; eyes in 2 or 3 rows, the first row of 4 eyes; posterior eyes often large .... **Dinòpidae*** p. 116

19(12′). Tibiae and metatarsi of first and second legs with a series of long spines and a series of shorter spines between each 2 long ones; 5–8 mm in length .... **Mimètidae** p. 120

19′. Spines on first and second tibiae and metatarsi not as above 20

20(19′). With 6 spinnerets; widely distributed 21

20′. With 2 spinnerets (*Lùtica,* recorded from Oregon) .... **Zodarìidae***

21(20). Chelicerae fused together at base, each with an apical tooth, which with

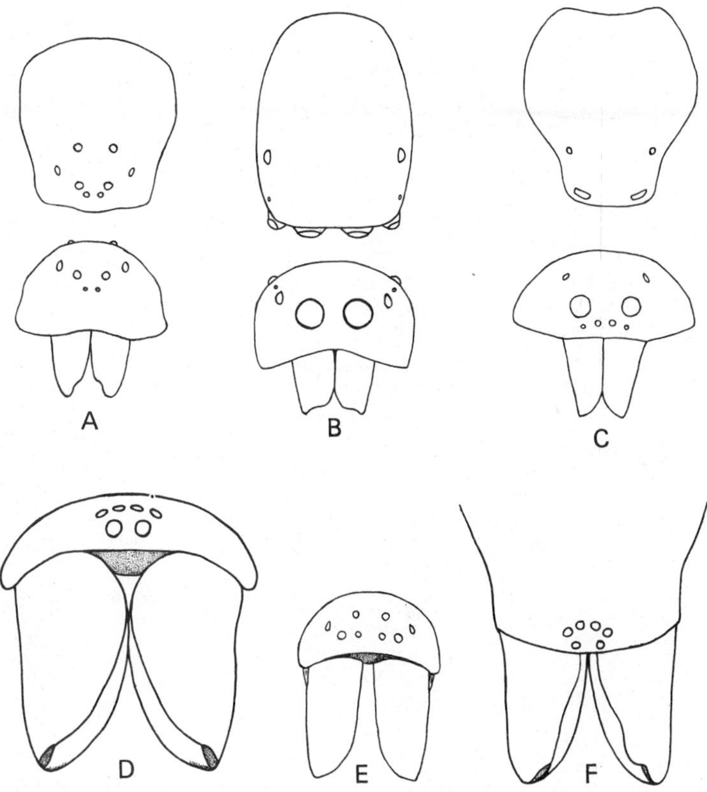

Figure 60. Chelicerae and eye patterns of spiders. In A, B, and C the upper figure is a dorsal view and the lower figure is an anterior view. A, Oxyópidae; B, Saltícidae; C, Lycòsidae; D, Dysdéridae (anterior view); E, Amaurobìidae (anterior view); F, Dysdéridae (dorsal view).

the fang forms a sort of claw 22

21′. Chelicerae not fused together at base, and without an apical tooth ... 26

22(21). Tarsi long, flexible, and with many pseudosegments; spiracle lacking; labium broader than long; 2–6 mm in length .... **Phólcidae** p. 117

22′. Tarsi not greatly elongated, and without pseudosegments; spiracle present, and at least one sixth the distance from epigastric furrow to spinnerets; labium longer than broad; mostly western spiders 23

23(22′). Eight eyes, in 2 rows; labium not fused to sternum; 3 tarsal claws; about 12.5 mm in length; western and southwestern United States .... **Plectreùridae***

23′. Six eyes, in three groups of 2 each; labium fused to sternum; 2–3 tarsal claws 24

24(23′). Anterior row of eyes in a nearly straight line; carapace only two-thirds as wide as long; 3 tarsal claws; 5.6–9.5 mm in length; western United States .... **Diguétidae***

24′. Median pair of eyes distinctly anterior to lateral eyes; carapace more than two thirds as wide as long; 2 or 3 tarsal claws; 3.5–15.0 mm in length; widely distributed 25

25(24′). Carapace flat, with a conspicuous median furrow in posterior portion; sternum pointed posteriorly; tarsi with 2 claws; 6.0–8.8 mm in length; southern and western United States .... **Loxoscélidae** p. 117

25′. Carapace much arched posteriorly and without a conspicuous median furrow; tarsi with 3 claws; 3.5–15.0 mm in length; widely distributed .... **Scytòdidae** p. 117

26(21′). Tarsi with 2 claws and with or without claw tufts 27

26′. Tarsi with 3 claws and without claw tufts (Figure 59 C); spurious claws sometimes present 39

27(26). Tracheal spiracle immediately in front of spinnerets 28

27′. Tracheal spiracle well anterior to spinnerets, at least one third the distance to epigastric furrow; 3–7 mm in length .... **Anyphaènidae** p. 117

28(27). Claw tufts present (Figure 59 D) 29

28′. Claw tufts absent 38

29(28). Eight eyes in 2 rows, 6 in first row; body flat; tropical spiders .... **Selenópidae***

29′. Eyes in 2–4 rows; 2 or 4 in first row 30

30(29′). The anterior median eyes dark-colored; the other eyes light-colored ... 31

30′. All eyes dark-colored 32

31(30). Eyes in 2 rows of 4 each; tarsi with a dense row of short hairs beneath; anterior spinnerets normal; 4–15 mm in length .... **Gnaphòsidae** p. 117

31′. Eyes in 3 rows, of 4, 2, and 2; tarsi (except possibly the front tarsi) without a dense row of short hairs beneath; anterior spinnerets long and brushlike; southern United States .... **Prodidómidae***

32(30′). Hind coxae widely separated by the rounded sternum; a pair of spurious claws present; southwestern United States .... **Homalonýchidae***

32′. Hind coxae approximated; sternum oval or elongate; no spurious claws; widely distributed 33

33(32′). At least the first 2 pairs of legs laterograde, that is, turned so that the morphological dorsal surface is posterior and the anterior surface appears to be dorsal (Figure 62) 34

33′. Legs normal, not as above 35

34(33). Length 20 mm or more; colulus absent; apex of metatarsi with a soft trilobate membrane; southern United States .... **Sparássidae** p. 117

34′. Length 15 mm or less; colulus present but small; apex of metatarsi sclerotized, without a soft trilobate membrane; widely distributed .... **Thomísidae** p. 117

35(33′). Eyes in 4 rows of 2 each, the anterior eyes much larger than the others, and the eyes of the third row minute; 5–8 mm in length; southern and southeastern United States .... **Lyssománidae*** p. 117

35′. Eyes in 2 or 3 rows 36

36(35′). Eyes in 3 rows (4-2-2), the anterior median eyes much larger than the others, the 2 eyes of the second row very small, and the 2 eyes in the third row medium-sized (Figure 60 B); body usually with scales ... **Saltícidae** p. 117

36′. Eyes not as above 37

37(36′). Eyes in 2 rows of 4 each; 3–15 mm in length .... **Clubiónidae** p. 117

37′. Eyes in 3 rows, usually 2-4-2, the eyes of the first row smaller than the eyes of the second row .... **Ctènidae** p. 117

38(28′). At least the first 2 pairs of legs laterograde (see couplet 33) .. **Thomísidae** p. 117

38′. Legs normal, not laterograde (see also couplet 51′) .... **Zodarìidae***

39(26′). Spinnerets in a more or less transverse row; tracheal spiracle considerably anterior to spinnerets; 3.5 mm in length or less .... **Hahnìidae** p. 118

39′. Spinnerets not in a single transverse row (Figure 58 C–E); size and location of tracheal spiracle variable 40

40(39′). Hind tarsi with a ventral row of strong, curved, serrated bristles forming a comb (Figure 59 A); 1–12 mm in length; spiders hanging in an inverted position in irregular webs .... **Theridìidae** p. 119

40′. Hind tarsi without such a row of bristles 41

41(40′). Eyes in a hexagonal group, the anterior row recurved and the posterior row procurved (Figure 60 A); abdomen pointed apically (Figure 64 A); legs with prominent spines; 4–20 mm in length .... **Oxyòpidae** p. 119

41′. Eyes not as above 42
42(41′). Tarsi with serrated bristles, forming at least 1 pair of spurious claws; tarsi usually without trichobothria 43
42′. Tarsi without serrated bristles, or at least none in the shape of spurious claws; tarsi usually with trichobothria 48
43(42). Labium with a thickened anterior edge; 8 eyes (rarely 6 or none); widely distributed 44
43′. Labium not as above; 6 eyes in a compact group; legs with short spines; cave spiders; western United States .... **Leptonètidae***
44(43). All eyes the same color; clypeus usually narrower than height of median ocular area (the area with the 4 median eyes); mostly builders of orb webs 45
44′. All eyes not the same color; clypeus usually as wide as, or wider than height of median ocular area; mostly not building orb webs 46
45(44). Femora with trichobothria (at least 1 at base of first and second femora); boss on chelicerae rudimentary or absent; chelicerae usually large and powerful; 3.5–9.0 mm in length .... **Tetragnáthidae** p. 120
45′. Femora without trichobothria; boss on chelicerae usually present; chelicerae not unusually large; 1.5–30.0 mm in length .... **Aranèidae** p. 120
46(44′). Sternum broadly truncate posteriorly; anterior femora about three times as thick as posterior femora; legs without spines; pedipalp of female without a claw; chelicerae without a stridulating area; 1.6–2.7 mm in length; orb web weavers .... **Theridiosomátidae** p. 120
46′. Without the above combination of characters; web not an orb but an irregular net or modified sheet; lateral surface of chelicerae often with a stridulating area 47
47(46′). Hind tibiae usually with 2 dorsal spines or bristles; tibiae of male pedipalp without an apophysis (a subapical pointed process); female pedipalp usually with a claw at apex of tarsus; 1.5–8.0 mm in length; sheet web spiders .... **Linyphìidae** p. 120
47′. Hind tibiae with a single dorsal spine or bristle, or with none; tibiae of male pedipalp with at least 1 apophysis; female pedipalp without a claw; mostly less than 2 mm in length, and usually living in debris .... **Micryphántidae** p. 121
48(42′). Chelicerae with a distinct boss 49
48′. Chelicerae without a boss 51*
49(48). Trochanters with a curved notch along distal edge on ventral side; trichobothria numerous and in 2 rows or irregularly distributed; hind spinnerets not particularly lengthened (Figure 58 D); spiders not generally building webs 50
49′. Trochanters not notched; tarsi with a single row of trichobothria; hind spinnerets very long (Figure 58 C); body with plumose hairs; spiders living in funnel webs; 2.5–20.0 mm in length .... **Agelènidae** p. 118
50(49). Posterior row of eyes so strongly recurved that it might be considered as 2 rows, the 2 eyes in the middle row (or in the middle of the second row) usually much larger than the others (Figure 60 C); body hairs usually simple; anterior plate on pedicel rounded behind; 2.5–35.0 mm in length; egg sac carried attached to spinnerets, and young carried on back of mother .... **Lycòsidae** p. 119
50′. Posterior row of eyes only slightly recurved, the median eyes in this row little if any larger than the others; body with plumose hairs; anterior plate on pedicel emarginate or transverse behind; 9–26 mm in length; egg sac held under cephalothorax, and young not carried about by mother .... **Pisaùridae** p. 118
51(48′). Body flat; posterior spinnerets very long; legs long and slender; anterior

portion of carapace marked off by grooves and elevated above rest of carapace; rare tropical spiders, occurring in Texas .... **Hersilìidae***

51′. Body not flat; posterior spinnerets much shorter than anterior ones, often minute; hind legs normal or stout; carapace not as above (*Storèna*, recorded from Georgia) .... **Zodarìidae***

SUBORDER **Orthógnatha:** These spiders have large and powerful chelicerae that move in a plane more or less parallel to the median plane of the body; most species are heavy-bodied and stout-legged. The group is largely tropical; most United States species occur in the South and Southwest, but a few occur as far north as Massachusetts. The family **Ctenìzidae** includes the trapdoor spiders, so called because they construct burrows in the ground that are closed by a door hinged with silk. The door fits snugly and is usually camouflaged on the outside. The tunnels may be simple or branched, or they may contain side chambers that are closed off from the main tunnel by hinged doors. These spiders occur in the South and West. The family **Theraphòsidae (Aviculariidae)** includes the tarantulas, the largest of our spiders; these spiders are often greatly feared, but the United States species are actually less venomous than the much smaller black widow spider and the brown recluse. Some species have a dense covering of special hairs on the abdomen that cause intense skin irritation in man; the effect is apparently mechanical, and not chemical. The **Diplùridae** includes the funnel-web tarantulas, so called because of the type of web they construct. The **Atýpidae** includes the purse-web spiders, whose webs are tubes of silk at the base of tree trunks and extending down into the ground; these spiders occur in the Northeast and in Florida. The **Antrodiaètidae,** which occur from Ohio west to the Pacific Coast, burrow in the ground, and their burrows are closed by double doors that meet in the middle of the opening. The **Mecicobothrìidae,** which occur along the West Coast, construct sheet webs similar to those of the funnel-web tarantulas.

SUBORDER **Labidógnatha:** This group includes the vast majority of the spiders occurring in the United States. They differ from the Orthógnatha in having the chelicerae moving laterally, or in and out, rather than in a vertical plane, and they are generally smaller. This suborder is divided into two sections, the Cribellàtae and the Ecribellàtae, on the basis of the presence or absence of a cribellum.

SECTION **Cribellàtae**—Hackled Band Spiders: These spiders have a cribellum in front of the spinnerets (Figure 58 B, *crb*) and a calamistrum on the hind legs (Figure 59 B, *clm*). Their webs contain ribbonlike bands of silk, but the ribbonlike nature of these bands is usually visible only with considerable magnification. The family **Hypochìlidae,** or four-lunged spiders (so called because they have two pairs of book lungs), make irregular webs on the underside of overhanging ledges, usually along streams; these spiders occur in the mountains of the southeastern states. The **Amaurobìidae,** or white-eyed spiders, are widely distributed over the United States; they construct irregular webs under stones, in rock crevices, and in debris. The **Ulobóridae** construct orb webs or sectors of orbs; this group is widely distributed. The largest family in this section is the **Dictỳnidae,** most species of which construct irregular webs on vegetation or on the ground. The other families in this section are the **Oecobìidae** (widely distributed), **Filastátidae** (southern states west to the Pacific Coast), **Zorópsidae** (rare spiders in the Southwest), and **Dinòpidae.**

SECTION **Ecribellàtae:** These spiders lack a cribellum and calamistrum. This group includes the majority of our spiders; it contains a large number of families, only the more important of which can be mentioned here.

Family **Dysdéridae:** The dysderids are medium-sized spiders, 12–13 mm in length, with two pairs of spiracles at the base of the abdomen (Figure 58 A). They live under bark or stones, where they construct a retreat of silk and hunt their prey from this retreat. These spiders occur from New England west to Nebraska and south to Georgia.

Family **Oonópidae**—Minute Jumping Spiders: These spiders are only about a millimeter in length, and are most commonly found in buildings; they can often be recognized by their jumping habits. The oonopids occur in the eastern states.

Family **Segestrìidae:** The segestriids have the three anterior pairs of legs directed forward and the hind pair directed backward. They are brownish in color, and 7–10 mm in length. They construct tubular retreats in crevices, under bark and stones, and in similar situations.

Family **Lyssománidae:** These spiders are pale green in color, with some black around the eyes and some red scales on the anterior part of the carapace, and are 5–8 mm in length. They are usually found in low bushes, from the southeastern states west to Texas.

Family **Scytòdidae**—Spitting Spiders: The spitting spiders do not construct snares, but capture their prey by spitting out a mucilaginous substance that engulfs and traps the prey. These spiders generally occur in shaded places and in the dark corners of buildings.

Family **Loxoscélidae**—Recluse Spiders: These are small, light-colored spiders, 6.0–8.8 mm in length, which have only 6 eyes and have the colulus large and conspicuous. The group is mainly western, and some species are quite venomous. The brown recluse spider, *Loxósceles reclùsus* Gertsch and Mulaik, is a venomous species occurring in the East; it varies in color from grayish brown to deep reddish brown, and has a dark fiddle-shaped mark on the anterior part of the cephalothorax (Figure 61). It usually occurs out of doors in sheltered places (under rocks and bark, and in similar places), but may sometimes occur indoors in basements, attics, storage places, and barns; it frequently occurs in clothing left hanging in a barn or outbuilding.

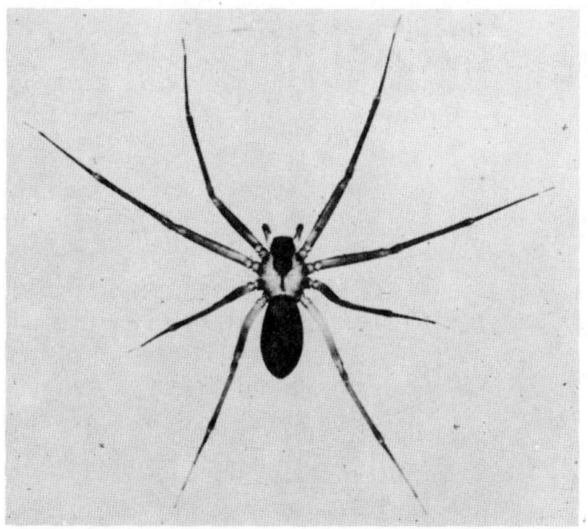

Figure 61. Brown recluse spider, *Loxósceles reclùsus* Gertsch and Mulaik. (Courtesy U.S. Public Health Service.)

Family **Gnaphòsidae (Drássidae)**—Hunting Spiders: These spiders are 4–15 mm in length; most species are uniformly dark-colored, but some species have a pattern of lines or spots. They construct a tubular retreat under stones and in debris, and hunt from this retreat.

Family **Phólcidae**—Long-Legged Spiders: The pholcids are small (2–6 mm in length), with very long and slender legs; the tarsi are long and flexible, with many pseudosegments. They construct sheetlike or irregular webs, and usually hang upside down on the under side of the web. The egg sac is held by the female in her chelicerae.

Family **Clubiónidae**—Two-Clawed Hunting Spiders: The clubionids are relatively common spiders, 3–15 mm in length, and occur on foliage or on the ground. They do not spin webs for the capture of prey, but construct a tubular retreat under stones or in rolled-up leaves or folds of grasses. One species, *Chiracànthium inclùsum* (Hentz), is quite venomous; this spider is about 8 mm in length, greenish white in color, and occurs throughout the United States.

Family **Anyphaènidae:** These hunting spiders are somewhat similar to the clubionids, but have the tracheal spiracle well anterior to the spinnerets, and the hairs of the claw tufts are somewhat flattened. They usually occur on foliage.

Family **Ctènidae**—Wandering Spiders: The wandering spiders are somewhat similar to the clubionids, but have the eyes in three rows instead of two. They usually occur on foliage and are more common in the southern states.

Family **Sparássidae (Heteropódidae)**—Giant Crab Spiders: These spiders are similar to the thomisids, but are larger and occur only in the southern states.

Family **Thomísidae**—Crab Spiders: The crab spiders are somewhat crablike in shape, and walk sideways or backward; the two anterior pairs of legs are usually stouter than the two posterior pairs (Figure 62). These spiders spin no webs, but forage for their prey or lie in ambush for it. Many species lie in wait for their prey on flowers, and are able to capture flies or bees much larger than themselves. One of the most common species in this group is the goldenrod spider, *Misùmena vàtia* (Clerck), which is white or yellow with a light-red band on either side of the abdomen; this species can change color (over a period of several days), depending on the color of the flower.

Family **Saltícidae (Áttidae)**—Jumping Spiders: These spiders are medium to small in size, stout-

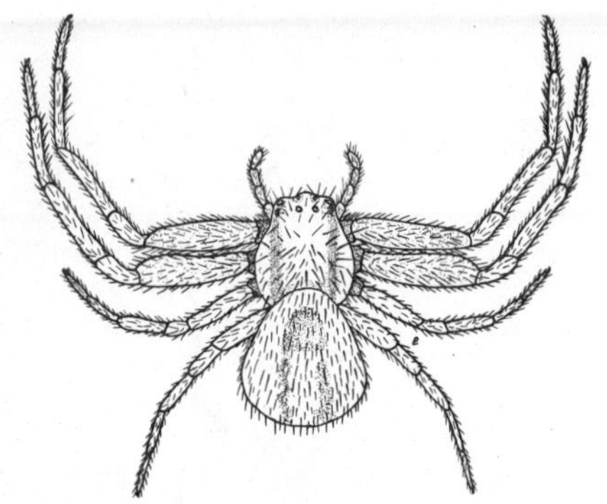

Figure 62. A crab spider, *Misùmenops* sp. (Thomísidae).

bodied, and short-legged (Figure 63 A), with a distinctive arrangement of the eyes (Figure 60 B). The body is rather hairy and is often brightly colored or iridescent; some species are antlike in appearance. These spiders are hunters and pursue their prey; they construct silken retreats under stones and in debris.

Family **Agelènidae**—Grass and Funnel-Web Spiders: These spiders build sheetlike webs in grass, under rocks and boards, and in debris; the webs are somewhat funnel-shaped and have a tubular retreat leading down into the material in which the web is built. They are often very common, a fact that is most evident in the early morning when their webs are covered with dew.

Family **Hahnìidae:** The hahniids are small spiders, 1.5–3.2 mm in length, that spin funnel webs similar to those of the Agelènidae but without the funnel-like retreats. The webs are located on or near the ground, usually in damp places, and are delicate and difficult to see unless covered with dew.

Family **Pisaùridae**—Nursery-Web and Fishing Spiders: The egg sac in these spiders is carried by the female under her cephalothorax and held by the chelicerae and pedipalps; before the eggs hatch, the female attaches the sac to a plant and ties leaves around it. The pisaurids are wandering spiders, and make webs only for the young. The female stands guard near this nursery web after the young hatch. Some spiders in this group, particularly the fishing spiders in the genus *Dolómedes,* are quite large, and may have a leg spread of 3 inches (Figure 64 B). The *Dolómedes* spiders

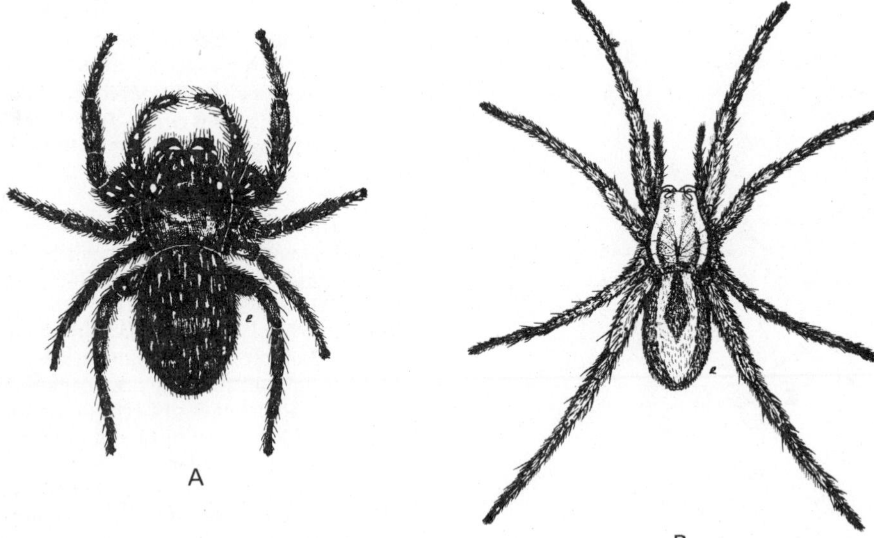

Figure 63. A, a jumping spider, *Phidíppus àudax* (Hentz) (Saltícidae); B, a wolf or ground spider, *Lycòsa* sp. (Lycòsidae).

live near water; they may walk over the surface or dive beneath it, and occasionally capture aquatic insects and even small fish.

Family **Theridìidae**—Comb-Footed Spiders: The webs of these spiders are an irregular network in which the spider usually hangs upside down; many live in buildings and other protected places. The cephalothorax is usually small, the abdomen large and rounded (some have the abdomen oddly shaped), and the legs are usually bent. The common name of the group is derived from the comb of serrated bristles on the hind tarsi (Figure 59 A); these combs are used in wrapping the prey in silk. One of the most important species in this group is the black widow spider, *Latrodéctus máctans* Fabricius, the most venomous spider in the United States; its bite is sometimes fatal. The female is about 12 mm in body length, black and shining, with a reddish-orange spot shaped like an hour glass on the ventral side of the abdomen (Figure 65 A). The male, which is less often seen because it is usually killed by the female after mating, is about 6 mm in length and is marked like the female, but also has four pairs of reddish-orange stripes along the sides of the abdomen. Black widows are found under stones, about stumps, in holes in the ground, about outbuildings, and in similar places; they are widely distributed over the United States, but are more common in the southern states. Two other species of *Latrodéctus* that occur in the United States are quite venomous: the brown or gray widow, *L. geométricus* Koch,

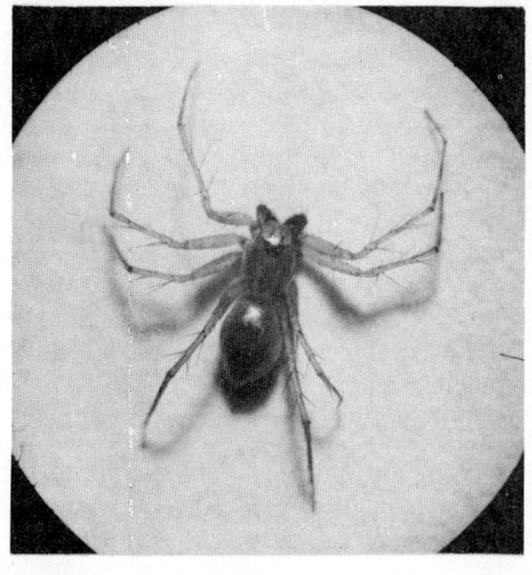

A

B

Figure 64. A, a lynx spider, *Oxyòpes sálticus* Hentz; B, a fishing spider, *Dolómedes tenebròsus* Hentz (the darker lines are 1 inch apart). (Courtesy of R. L. Snouffer.)

Family **Lycòsidae**—Wolf Spiders or Ground Spiders: The wolf spiders are hunting spiders that chase their prey, and some are relatively large. Most of them are dark brown in color. The members of this group can usually be recognized by the characteristic arrangement of the eyes; four small eyes in the first row, two very large eyes in the second row, and two small or medium-sized eyes in the third row (Figure 60 C). The egg sac is carried about by the female, attached to her spinnerets; when the young hatch, they are carried about on the back of the female for a time. The lycosids are a large and widely distributed group, and many species are fairly common.

Family **Oxyòpidae**—Lynx Spiders: These spiders can usually be recognized by the arrangement of the eyes in a hexagonal group (Figure 60 A). The abdomen usually tapers to a point posteriorly (Figure 64 A). These spiders chase their prey over foliage with great rapidity; many can jump, and some ambush their prey at flowers. The lynx spiders do not construct a web or a retreat; they occur among low vegetation and attach their egg sacs to foliage. These spiders are more common in the southern states.

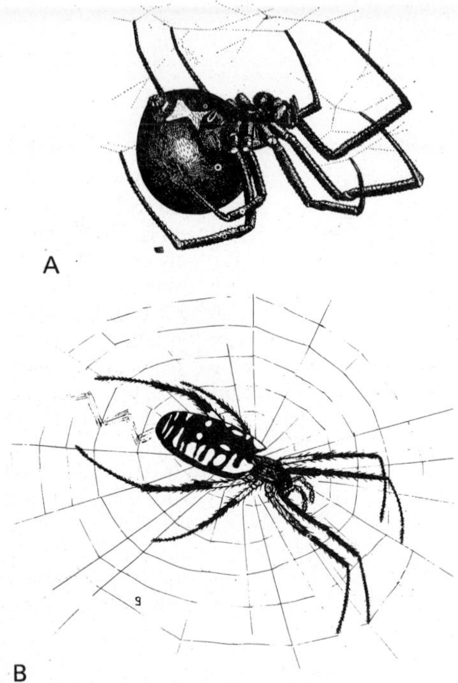

Figure 65. A, black widow spider, *Latrodéctus máctans* (Fabricius), female, hanging from its web; B, a garden spider, *Argiòpe aurántia* Lucas. (A, courtesy of Utah Agricultural Experiment Station.)

which occurs in southern Florida and southern California, and *L. bíshopi* Kaston, which occurs in southern Florida. Another common species in this family is the house spider, *Therídion tepidariòrum* (Koch).

Family **Mimètidae**—Spider-Hunting Spiders: These spiders can generally be recognized by the spination of the tibiae and metatarsi of the first two pairs of legs; the larger spines are separated by a row of smaller spines. These spiders appear to feed largely, if not entirely, on other spiders; they do not construct a web for the capture of prey.

Family **Aranèidae (Argiópidae, Epeìridae)**—Orb-Weavers: This is a very large and widely distributed group, and nearly all its members construct an orb web. There is a great deal of variation in size, color, and shape in this family, and the family is divided into several subfamilies, some of which are mentioned here.

The Gasteracanthìnae, or spiny-bellied spiders, are so called because of the spiny protuberances on the abdomen. These small spiders are usually found in woods, where their small orb web is suspended between two trees several feet apart.

The Nephilìnae, or silk spiders, are so called because of the large amount and great strength of their silk, which is sometimes used in the manufacture of fabrics. This group is largely tropical, but one species, *Néphila clávipes* (L.), is fairly common in the southern states. Females are about 22 mm in length, the carapace is dark brown, the abdomen is dark greenish with several pairs of small light spots, and there are conspicuous tufts of hair on the femora and tibiae of the first, second, and fourth legs.

The Metìnae is a small group, and its members live in caves, ravines, and other dark places; some species are brightly colored.

The Argiopìnae, or garden spiders, are common in grassy places; they are often brightly colored, black and yellow or black and red (Figure 65 B). The web is constructed in grass and consists of an orb with a dense net of silk extending through the middle; the spider usually rests head downward in the center of its web.

The largest subfamily is the Araneìnae, or typical orb-weavers; the members of this group vary greatly in size and color.

Family **Tetragnáthidae**—Four-Jawed Spiders: These spiders have very large and protruding chelicerae, especially in the males. Most species are brownish in color and rather long and slender, and the legs, especially the front pair, are very long. These spiders are usually found in marshy places.

Family **Theridiosomátidae**—Ray Spiders: These small spiders (less than 3 mm in length) are usually found near streams or in other damp situations. The web is peculiar in that the radii unite in groups of three or four, and each group is connected to the center by a single thread. The web is drawn into a conical shape by a thread from the center to a nearby twig, where it is held taut by the spider; when an insect gets into the web the spider releases its line, allowing the web to spring back and entangle the insect.

Family **Linyphìidae** – Sheet-Web Spiders: These are fairly common spiders, but they are small (mostly less than 7 mm in length) and are not often seen. The webs, however, are often conspicuous, particularly when covered with dew; they are flat and sheetlike, sometimes bowl-shaped or dome-shaped, and usually with an irregular mesh of silk around or above the sheetlike part. The spider is usually found on the underside of the web.

Family **Micryphántidae (Erigónidae)** – Dwarf Spiders: This is a very large group of small spiders, most of which are less than 2 mm in length. They are usually found on the ground in leaf litter and debris, and are seldom seen except by a careful collector.

COLLECTING AND PRESERVING CHELICERATES

To obtain a large collection of chelicerates, one needs primarily to collect in as many different types of habitats as possible. Chelicerates are frequently very abundant, often as abundant as insects or more so. The general collector of insects is likely to encounter more spiders and mites than any other types of chelicerates, so the following suggestions are concerned primarily with these groups.

Chelicerates occur in a great variety of situations and can often be collected with the same techniques and equipment used in collecting insects. Many may be taken by sweeping vegetation with an insect net; many may be obtained with beating equipment, that is, using a sheet or beating umbrella beneath a tree or bush and beating the bush to knock off the specimens. The ground forms may be found running on the ground or under stones, boards, bark, or other objects. Many are to be found in the angles of buildings and similar protected places. Many of the smaller forms can be found in debris, soil litter, or moss, and are best collected by means of sifting equipment such as a Berlese funnel (Figure 616). Many are aquatic or semiaquatic and may be collected in marshy areas with aerial collecting equipment or in water with aquatic equipment. The parasitic species (various mites and ticks) must usually be looked for on their hosts.

Many chelicerates are nocturnal, and collecting at night may prove more successful than collecting during the day. Very few are attracted to lights, but may be spotted at night with a flashlight; the eyes of many spiders will reflect the light, and with a little experience one may locate a good many spiders at night by the use of a flashlight.

Chelicerates should be preserved in fluids rather than on pins or points; many forms, such as the spiders, are very soft-bodied and shrivel when dry. They are usually preserved in 70–90 percent alcohol; there should be plenty of alcohol in the bottle in relation to the specimen, and it is often desirable to change the alcohol after the first few days. Many workers preserve mites in Oudeman's fluid, which consists of 87 parts of 70 percent alcohol, 5 parts of glycerine, and 8 parts of glacial acetic acid; the chief advantage of this fluid is that the mites die with their appendages extended so that subsequent examination is easier. Alcohol is not suitable for preserving gall mites; such mites are best collected by wrapping infested plant parts in soft tissue paper and allowing them to dry. This dried material can be kept indefinitely, and the mites can be recovered for study by warming the dried material in Kiefer's solution (50 grams of resorcinal, 20 grams of diglycolic acid, 25 milliliters of glycerol, enough iodine to produce the desired color, and about 10 milliliters of water). Specialists on mites prefer specimens in fluid, rather than mounted on permanent microscope slides, so that all aspects and structures can be studied.

Chelicerates may be collected by means of a net, forceps, vial, or a small brush, or they may be collected by hand. In the case of biting or stinging forms, it is safer to use some method other than collecting them in the fingers. Specimens collected with a net can be transferred directly to a vial of alcohol, or they may be collected in an empty vial and later transferred to alcohol. Since some species are quite active, it is sometimes preferable to put them first into a cyanide bottle and transfer them to alcohol after they have been stunned and are quiet. Specimens collected from the ground or from debris may be picked up with forceps or coaxed into a bottle, or the smaller specimens (and this applies to small specimens found in any sort of situation) may be picked up with a small brush moistened with alcohol.

Spider webs that are flat and not too large may be collected and preserved between two pieces of glass. One piece of glass is pressed against the web (which will usually stick to the glass because of the viscous material on some of the silk strands) and then the other piece of glass is applied to the

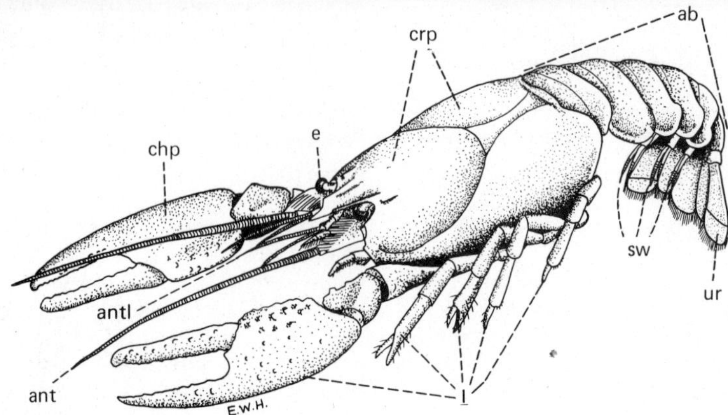

Figure 66. A crayfish (*Cámbarus* sp.), natural size. *ab,* abdomen; *ant,* antenna; *antl,* antennule; *chp,* cheliped; *crp,* carapace; *e,* eye; *l,* legs (including cheliped); *sw,* swimmerets; *ur,* uropod.

first; it is often desirable to have the two pieces of glass separated by thin strips of paper around the edge of the glass. Once the web is between the two pieces of glass, the glass is bound together with lanternslide binding tape. Spider webs are best photographed when they are covered with moisture (dew or fog) or dust; they may often be photographed dry if illuminated from the side and photographed against a dark background.

SUBPHYLUM MANDIBULÀTA[18]

The Mandibulàta differ from the Cheliceràta in having antennae, a pair of mandibles (on the second postoral segment, corresponding to the pedipalps of chelicerates), and a variable arrangement of appendages behind the mandibles; most mandibulates have mouth parts on the anterior segments, and the number of legs varies greatly. There is no patella in the legs. Many mandibulates are elongate and wormlike in form. This group contains six classes, the Crustàcea, Diplópoda, Chilópoda, Paurópoda, Sýmphyla, and Insécta.

[18] Mandibulàta: from the Latin, meaning with mandibles.

CLASS CRUSTÀCEA[19] – CRUSTACEANS

The crustaceans form a rather heterogeneous group, but nearly all are aquatic and breathe by means of gills. The head and thoracic portions of the body are often fused into a cephalothorax; the cephalothorax in many crustaceans is partly or entirely covered by a shieldlike portion of the body wall called the carapace. The appendages vary in number, but there are two pairs of antennae, a pair of appendages on each segment of the cephalothorax, and (in the subclass Malacóstraca) appendages on the abdominal segments. Most of the appendages in the Crustàcea are biramous, that is, they consist of a basal segment bearing two terminal branches. One of the two branches may be lost in some specialized appendages.

Most present students of this group recognize five major subclasses of the Crustàcea; four of these (the Cirripèdia, Branchiópoda, Ostrácoda, and Copépoda) are sometimes placed in a single subclass, the Entomóstraca. The five subclasses may be separated by the following key.

[19] Crustàcea: from the Latin, referring to the crustlike exoskeleton possessed by many of these animals.

Key to the Subclasses of Crustàcea

1. All body segments except the last (the telson) bearing appendages, 7–8 pairs on the thorax, and 6 (rarely more) on the abdomen (Figures 66 and 70–72); mostly over 5 mm in length .... **Malacóstraca** p. 125

1′. All body segments except the last few (the abdomen) bearing appendages,

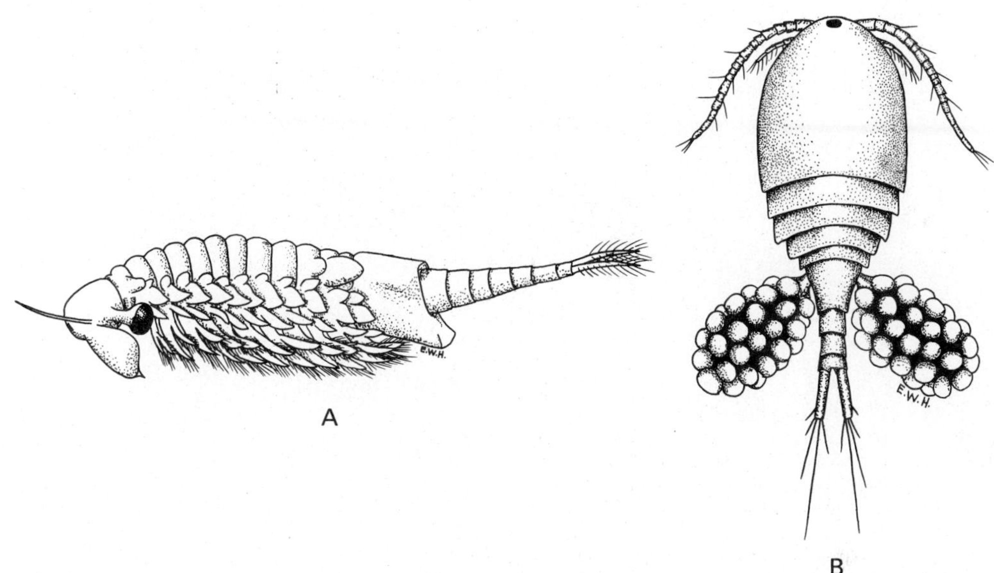

Figure 67. Crustaceans. A, a fairy shrimp, *Eubránchipus* (subclass Branchiópoda, order Anóstraca), 6 ×; B, a female copepod, *Cỳclops* sp., 50 ×, with two egg sacs at posterior end of body.

the number of appendages variable (Figures 67–69); size variable, but mostly less than 5 mm in length 2

2(1′). Free-swimming, or parasitic on fish; marine and freshwater forms 3

2′. Sessile forms, with the body enclosed in a shell (Figure 69), or parasitic on decapods or molluscs; marine .... **Cirripèdia** p. 125

3(2). Thoracic appendages flattened, often leaflike (Figures 67 A and 68 A); mostly freshwater forms .... **Branchiópoda** p. 123

3′. Thoracic appendages slender and cylindrical (Figures 67 B and 68 B, C); marine and freshwater forms 4

4(3′). Body short, unsegmented, and covered by a bivalved carapace; 4 pairs of head appendages and 3 pairs of thoracic legs (Figure 68 B, C)... **Ostrácoda** p. 125

4′. Body elongate and distinctly segmented, not covered by a bivalved carapace; 5 pairs of head appendages and 4–6 pairs of thoracic legs (Figure 67 B) .... **Copépoda** p. 125

The smaller crustaceans, particularly those in the subclasses Branchiópoda, Copépoda, and Ostrácoda, are abundant in both salt and fresh water. The chief importance of most species lies in the fact that they serve as food for larger animals and thus are an important link in the food chains leading to fish and other larger aquatic animals. A few species are parasitic on fish and other animals, and the barnacles are often a nuisance when they encrust pilings, boat bottoms, and other surfaces. Many of the small crustaceans can be easily maintained in indoor aquaria, and are frequently reared as food for other aquatic animals.

SUBCLASS BRANCHIÓPODA[20]

Most members of this subclass occur in fresh water. Males are uncommon in many species, and parthenogenesis is a common method of reproduction. Both unisexual (parthenogenetic) and bisexual reproduction occurs in many species, and the factors controlling the production of males are not well understood.

There are differences of opinion regarding the classification of these crustaceans, but four fairly

[20] Branchiópoda: *branchio,* gill; *poda,* foot or appendage.

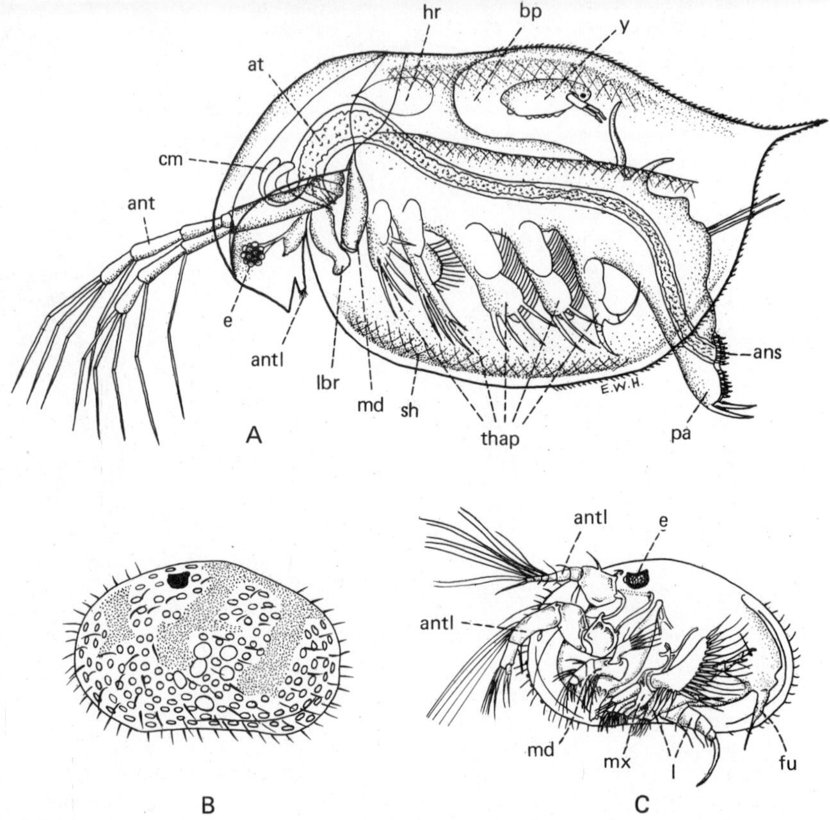

Figure 68. Crustaceans. A, a water flea or cladoceran, *Dáphnia* sp., 25 ×; B, an ostracod, *Cypridópsis* sp., lateral view; C, same, but with left valva of carapace removed. *ans,* anus; *ant,* antenna; *antl,* antennule; *at,* alimentary tract; *bp,* brood pouch; *cm,* caecum; *e,* compound eye; *fu,* furca; *hr,* heart; *l,* first and second thoracic legs; *lbr,* labrum; *md,* mandible; *mx,* maxilla; *pa,* postabdomen; *sh,* bivalved shell; *thap,* thoracic appendages; *y,* developing young. (C modified from Kesling.)

distinct groups are usually recognized, the Anóstraca, Notóstraca, Conchóstraca, and Cladócera. The first two or three of these are sometimes placed in a group called the Phyllópoda.

The Anóstraca,[21] or fairy shrimps (Figure 67 A), have the body elongate and distinctly segmented, without a carapace, with 11 pairs of swimming legs, and the eyes are stalked; the fairy shrimps are often abundant in temporary pools. The Notóstraca,[22] or tadpole shrimps, have an oval convex carapace covering the anterior part of the body, 35–71 pairs of thoracic appendages, and two long filamentous caudal appendages; these animals range in size from about $\frac{1}{2}$ to 2 inches (13 to 51 mm), and are restricted to the western states. The Conchóstraca,[23] or clam shrimps, have the body somewhat flattened laterally and entirely enclosed in a bivalved carapace, and have 10–32 pairs of legs; most species are 10 mm in length or less. The Cladócera,[24] or water fleas (Figure 68 A), have a bivalved carapace, but the head is not enclosed in the carapace; there are 4–6 pairs of thoracic legs. The water fleas are 0.2–3.0 mm in length and are very common in freshwater pools.

There are three groups of small crustaceans occuring in fresh water that have a bivalved carapace, and these groups are likely to be confused.

[21] Anóstraca: *an,* without; *ostraca,* shell.

[22] Notóstraca: *not,* back; *ostraca,* shell.

[23] Conchóstraca: *conch,* shell or shellfish; *ostraca,* shell.

[24] Cladócera: *clado,* branch: *cera,* horn (referring to the antennae).

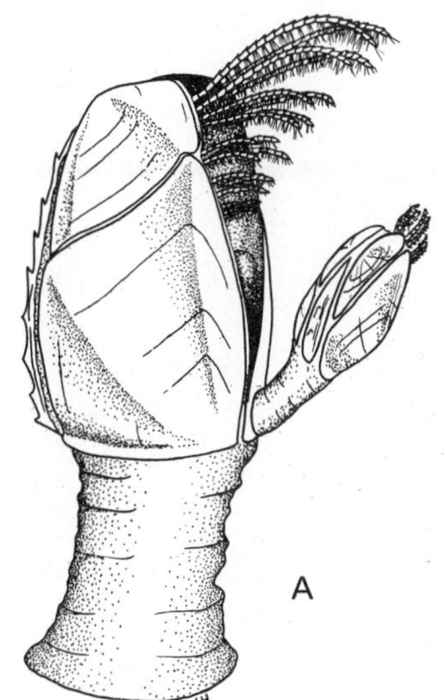

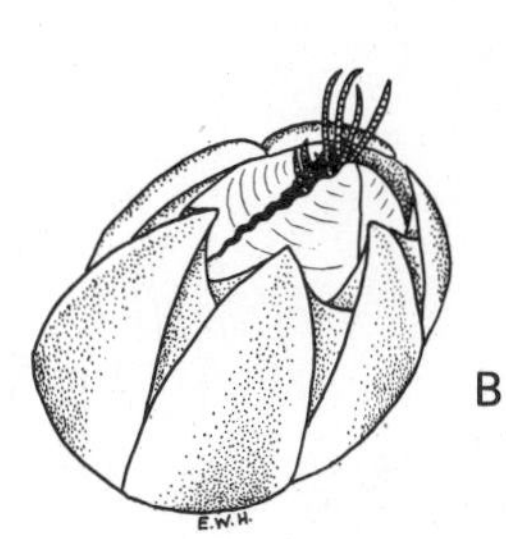

Figure 69. Barnacles. A, a goose barnacle, *Lèpas* sp., 3 ×; B, a rock barnacle, *Balànus* sp., 2 ×. The basal stalk or peduncle of the goose barnacle is at the animal's anterior end; the biramous appendages protruding from the shell at the top of the figure are the posterior thoracic legs; a second small individual is shown attached to the first.

The Ostrácoda (Figure 68 B, C) and Conchóstraca have the body completely enclosed in the carapace, whereas in the Cladócera (Figure 68 A) the head is outside the carapace. The Ostrácoda have only three pairs of thoracic legs; the Conchóstraca have 10–32 pairs.

SUBCLASS COPÉPODA[25]

Some of the copepods are free swimming and others are parasitic on fish; the parasitic forms are often peculiar in body form and quite unlike the free-swimming forms in general appearance. This group includes both marine and freshwater forms. The female of most copepods carries her eggs in two egg sacs located laterally near the end of the abdomen (Figure 67 B). The parasitic copepods are often called fish lice, and they live on the gills or skin or burrow into the flesh of their host; when numerous they may seriously injure the host. Some species serve as an intermediate host of certain human parasites (for example, the fish tapeworm, *Diphyllobóthriumlátum* L.).

SUBCLASS OSTRÁCODA[26]

The ostracods have a bivalved carapace that can be closed by a muscle, and when the valves are closed the animal looks like a miniature clam (Figure 68 B, C). When the valves of the carapace are open the appendages are protruded and propel the animal through the water. Many species are parthenogenetic. Most of the ostracods are marine, but there are also many common freshwater species.

SUBCLASS CIRRIPÈDIA[27]

The best known members of this group are the barnacles, the adults of which live attached to rocks, pilings, seaweeds, boats, or marine animals, and which are enclosed in a calcareous shell. A few species are parasitic, usually on crabs or molluscs. Most of the members of this group are hermaphroditic, that is, each individual contains both male and female organs. Some barnacles, such as the goose barnacle (Figure 69 A), have the shell attached to some object by means of a stalk; others, such as the rock barnacles (Figure 69 B), are sessile and do not have stalks.

SUBCLASS MALACÓSTRACA[28]

This subclass includes the larger and better known crustaceans; they differ from the preceding subclasses in having appendages (swimmerets) on the abdomen. There are typically 19 pairs of appendages, the first 13 being cephalothoracic and the last six abdominal. The leglike appendages on the cephalothorax are often clawlike. Only the more

[25] Copépoda: *cope*, oar; *poda*, foot or appendage.

[26] Ostrácoda: from the Greek, meaning shell-like (referring to the clamlike character of the carapace).

[27] Cirripèdia: *cirri*, a curl of hair; *pedia*, foot or appendage.

[28] Malacóstraca: *malac*, soft; *ostraca*, shell.

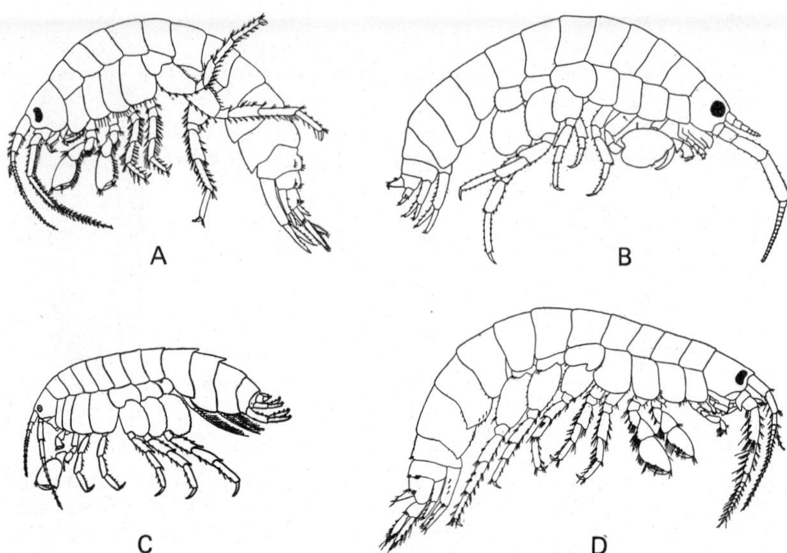

Figure 70. Amphípoda. A, a common freshwater scud, *Dikerogámmarus fasciàtus* (Say), 10–15 mm in length; B, a sand flea or beach flea, *Orchéstia ágilis* Smith, abundant underneath seaweed along the coast near the high-tide mark; C, a common freshwater scud, *Hyalélla knickerbóckeri* (Bate), about 7 mm in length; D, a sea scud, *Gámmarus annulàtus* Smith, a common coastal form, about 15 mm in length. (Courtesy of Kunkle and the Connecticut State Geology and Natural History Survey; C, after Smith.)

common orders in this group can be mentioned here.

ORDER **Amphípoda[29]:** The body of an amphipod is elongate and more or less compressed, there is no carapace, and seven (rarely six) of the thoracic segments are distinct and bear leglike appendages; the abdominal segments are often more or less fused, and hence the six or seven thoracic segments make up most of the body length (Figure 70). This group contains both marine and freshwater forms. Many of them, such as the beach fleas (Figure 70 B), live on the beach, where they occur under stones or in decaying vegetation. Most of the amphipods are scavengers.

ORDER **Isópoda[30]:** The isopods are similar to the amphipods in lacking a carapace, but are dorsoventrally flattened. The last seven thoracic segments are distinct and bear leglike appendages; the abdominal segments are more or less fused, and hence the thoracic segments (with their seven pairs of legs) make up most of the body length (Figure 71). The anterior abdominal appendages of the aquatic forms usually bear gills; the terminal abdominal appendages are often enlarged and feelerlike. Most of the isopods are small marine animals living under stones or among seaweed; away from the seacoast the most common species are the sowbugs—blackish, gray, or brownish animals usually found under stones, boards, or bark. Some of the sowbugs (often called pillbugs) are capable of rolling up into a ball. In some areas, sowbugs are important pests of cultivated plants.

ORDER **Stomatópoda[31]:** The stomatopods are marine forms that can be recognized by the large abdomen, which is broader than the cephalothorax. There are three pairs of legs, in front of which are five pairs of maxillipeds, one pair of which is very large and clawlike. The carapace does not cover the posterior thoracic segments. The stomatopods occur principally along our southern coasts; some are used as food.

ORDER **Decápoda[32]:** This order contains the largest and probably the best known of the crustaceans, the lobsters, crayfish (Figure 66), crabs

[29] Amphípoda: *amphi,* on both sides, double; *poda,* foot or appendage.

[30] Isópoda: *iso,* equal; *poda,* foot or appendage.

[31] Stomatópoda: *stomato,* mouth; *poda,* foot or appendage.

[32] Decápoda: *deca,* ten; *poda,* foot or appendage.

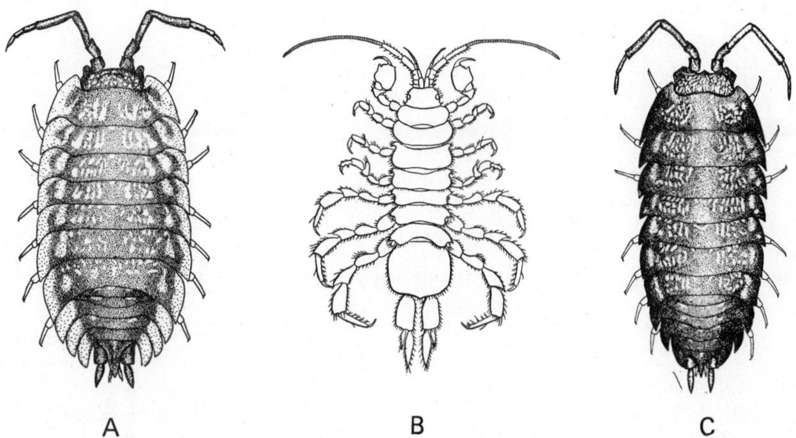

Figure 71. Isópoda. A, *Oníscus aséllus* L., a common sowbug; B, *Aséllus commùnis* Say, a common freshwater isopod; C, *Cylísticus convéxus* (De Geer), a pillbug capable of rolling itself into a ball. (Courtesy of the Connecticut State Geology and Natural History Survey. A and C, courtesy of Kunkle; after Paulmier. B, courtesy of Kunkle; after Smith.)

(Figure 72), and shrimps. The carapace of a decapod covers the entire thorax; five pairs of the cephalothoracic appendages are leglike, and the first pair of these usually bears a large claw. The abdomen may be well developed (lobsters and crayfish), or it may be very much reduced (crabs). This is a very important group, for many of its members are used as food, and their collection and distribution provides the basis of a large coastal industry.

COLLEÇTING AND PRESERVING CRUSTÀCEA

The aquatic crustaceans must be collected by various types of aquatic collecting equipment. Most of them can be collected by a dip net. A white enameled dipper is the best means of collecting many of the smaller forms; the dipper is simply dipped into the water, and any small animals in the dipper can be easily seen. Forms so

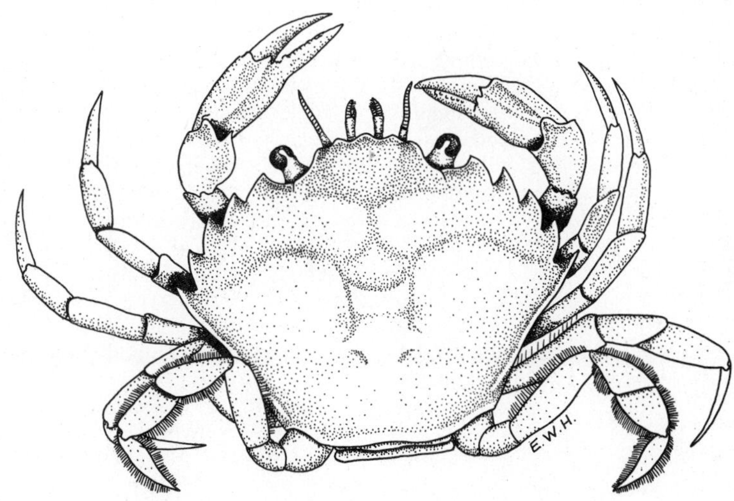

Figure 72. A green crab, *Carcínides* sp., 1½ ×.

collected can be removed by means of an eye dropper or (if they are fairly large) by forceps. The smaller forms in ponds, lakes, and the ocean are often collected by means of a fine-mesh net called a plankton net, towed by a boat. Many of the larger forms are collected by traps; such traps (or "pots") are the standard means of collecting lobsters and crabs. The shore-dwelling and terrestrial forms can be collected by hand or forceps, or possibly (for example, beach fleas) with an aerial insect net. The larger forms with well-developed claws should be handled with care, for the claw may inflict serious injury. The safest way to pick up a large crayfish or lobster is from above, grasping the animal at the back of the carapace.

One must collect in a variety of places to obtain a variety of Crustàcea. When collecting in water, one should investigate every possible aquatic niche; some crustaceans are free-swimming, some burrow in the mud of the bottom, some occur under stones, and many are to be found on aquatic vegetation. The shore-dwelling forms are usually found under stones, debris, or decaying vegetation along the shore.

Crustaceans should be preserved in fluids (for example, 70–95 percent alcohol). Most of the smaller forms must be mounted on microscope slides for detailed study. Some of the smaller Malacóstraca can be preserved dry (for example, pinned), but specimens preserved in fluid are more satisfactory for study.

CLASS DIPLÓPODA[33] — MILLIPEDES

The millipedes are elongate, wormlike animals with many legs (Figure 73). Most millipedes have 30 or more pairs of legs, and most body segments bear two pairs. The body is cylindrical or slightly flattened, and the antennae are short and usually 7-segmented. The external openings of the reproductive system are located at the anterior end of the body, between the second and third pairs of legs; one or both pairs of legs on the seventh segment of the male are usually modified into gonopods, which function in copulation. Compound eyes are usually present, each consisting of a group of ocelli. The first tergum behind the head is usually large and is called the collum (Figure 74 A).

The head in most millipedes is convex above, with a large epistomal area, and flat beneath; the bases of the mandibles form a part of the side of the head. Beneath the mandibles, and forming the flat ventral surface of the head, is a characteristic liplike structure called the gnathochilarium (Figure 74 B). The gnathochilarium is usually divided by sutures into several areas: a median more or less triangular plate, the mentum (*mn*); two lateral lobes, the stipites (*stp*); two median distal plates, the laminae linguales (*ll*); and usually a median transverse basal sclerite, the prebasalare (*pbs*), and two small laterobasal sclerites, the cardines (*cd*). The size and shape of these different areas differ in different groups of millipedes, and the gnathochilarium often provides characters by which the groups are recognized.

Millipedes are usually found in damp places—under leaves, in moss, under stones or boards, in rotting wood, or in the soil. Many species are able to give off an ill-smelling fluid through openings along the sides of the body; this fluid is sometimes strong enough to kill insects that are placed in a jar with the millipede, and it has been shown (in some cases at least) to contain hydrogen cyanide. Millipedes do not bite man. Most millipedes are scavengers and feed on decaying plant material, but a few attack living plants and sometimes do serious damage in greenhouses and gardens, and a few are predaceous. These animals overwinter as adults in protected situations, and lay their eggs during the summer. Some construct nestlike cavities in the soil in which they deposit their eggs; others lay their eggs in damp places without constructing any sort of nest. The eggs are usually white and hatch within a few weeks. Newly hatched millipedes have only three pairs of legs; the remaining legs are added at subsequent molts.

There are a number of arrangements of orders and families in this group; we follow the arrangement of Chamberlin and Hoffman (1958), which is outlined below (with alternate names or arrangements in parentheses).

Subclass Pselaphógnatha
- Order Polyxénida

Subclass Chilógnatha
- Superorder Pentazònia (Opisthándria)
  - Order Glomérida
- Superorder Helminthomórpha (Ológnatha, Eùgnatha)
  - Order Polydésmida (Proterospermóphora)
  - Order Chordeùmida (Nematóphora)

[33] Diplópoda: *diplo*, two, or double; *poda*, foot or appendage (referring to the fact that most body segments bear two pairs of legs).

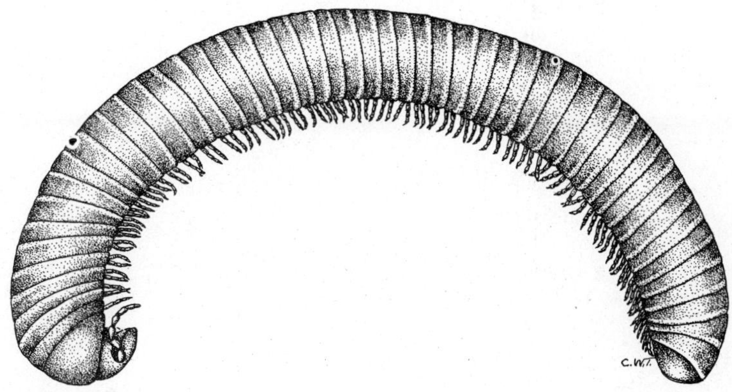

Figure 73. A common millipede, *Nárceus* sp. (order Spirobólida), 1½ ×.

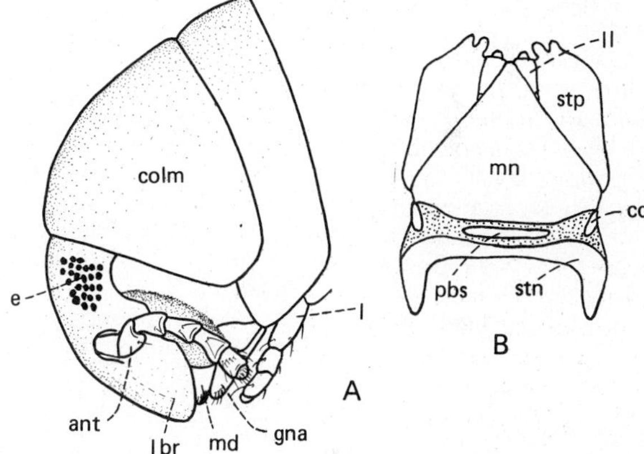

Figure 74. Head structure in a millipede (*Nárceus*, order Spirobólida). A, lateral view of head; B, gnathochilarium. *ant*, antenna; *cd*, cardo; *colm*, collum, tergite of first body segment; *e*, eye; *gna*, gnathochilarium; *l*, first leg; *lbr*, labrum; *ll*, lamina lingualis; *md*, mandible; *mn*, mentum; *pbs*, prebasalare; *stn*, sternum of first body segment; *stp*, stipes.

Order Jùlida (Opisthospermóphora in part)
Order Spirobólida (Opisthospermóphora in part)
Order Spirostréptida (Opisthospermóphora in part)
Order Cambálida (Opisthospermóphora in part)
Superorder Colobógnatha
Order Polyzonìida
Order Platydésmida

Key to the Orders of Diplópoda

1. Adults with 13 pairs of legs; integument soft; body hairs forming long lateral tufts; 2–4 mm in length .... **Polyxénida** p. 130
1′. Adults with 28 or more pairs of legs; integument strongly sclerotized; body hairs not forming long tufts; larger millipedes 2
2(1′). Body with 14–16 segments and with 11–13 tergites; male gonopods at caudal end of body, modified from last 2 pairs of legs; southern and western United States .... **Glomérida** p. 130
2′. Body with 19 or more segments; male gonopods modified from legs of seventh segment 3
3(2′). Body more or less flattened, or with lateral carinae; the number of body segments variable 4

3′. Body cylindrical or nearly so, without lateral carinae, and containing 26 or more segments 6
4(3). Body with 18–22 segments; eyes absent; head and mouth parts of normal size .... **Polydésmida** p. 130
4′. Body with 30–60 (rarely 20, 26, or 28) segments; eyes usually present; head small, the mandibles usually much reduced 5
5(4′). Tergites with a median groove; gnathochilarium with most of the typical parts .... **Platydésmida** p. 131
5′. Tergites without a median groove; gnathochilarium consisting of a single plate, or several indistinctly defined plates .... **Polyzonìida** p. 131
6(3′). Terminal segment of body with 1–3 pairs of setae-bearing papillae; collum not overlapping head; sternites not fused with pleurotergites .... **Chordeùmida** p. 130
6′. Terminal segment of body without such papillae; collum large, hoodlike, usually overlapping head; sternites usually fused with pleurotergites .. 7
7(6′). Stipites of gnathochilarium broadly contiguous along midline behind laminae linguales .... **Jùlida** p. 131
7′. Stipites of gnathochilarium not contiguous, but widely separated by mentum and laminae linguales (Figure 74 B) 8
8(7′). Fifth segment with 2 pairs of legs; third segment open ventrally, the fourth and following segments closed 9
8′. Fifth segment with 1 pair of legs; third segment closed ventrally .... **Spirobólida** p. 131
9(8). Laminae linguales completely separated by mentum; both anterior and posterior pairs of gonopods present and functional, the posterior pair usually with long flagella .... **Cambálida** p. 131
9′. Laminae linguales usually not separated by mentum; posterior pair of gonopods rudimentary or absent, the anterior pair elaborate .... **Spirostréptida** p. 131

Order **Polyxénida**[34]**:** These millipedes are minute (2–4 mm in length) and soft-bodied, with the body very bristly. They are widely distributed, but are not common, and are usually found under bark. The order contains a single genus *Polỳxenus,* in the family Polyxénidae.

ORDER **Glomérida**[35]**:** Males of this group have the gonopods at the caudal end of the body, modified from the last two pairs of legs, which are clasperlike; the appendages of the seventh segment are not modified. These millipedes are relatively large, and the body can be contracted into a ball; they occur in southern and southeastern United States and in California. The United States members of this order are in the family Gloméridae.

ORDER **Polydésmida**[36]**:** The polydesmids are rather flattened millipedes, with the body keeled laterally, and the eyes much reduced or absent. The tergites are divided by a transverse groove a little anterior to the middle of the segment, into an anterior prozonite and a posterior metazonite; the metazonite is extended laterally as a broad lobe. The first and last two body segments are legless, segments 2–4 have a single pair of legs, and the remaining segments each bear two pairs of legs. The anterior pair of legs on the seventh segment of the male are modified into gonopods. The diplosomites (segments bearing two pairs of legs) are continuously sclerotized rings; there are no sutures between tergites, pleurites, and sternites. *Óxidus grácilis* (Koch), a dark-brown to black millipede, 19–22 mm in length and 2.0–2.5 mm wide, is a common pest in greenhouses. This order is divided into ten families, and its members occur throughout the United States.

ORDER **Chordeùmida**[37]**:** The last tergite of these millipedes bears two or three pairs of hair-tipped papillae (spinnerets). The body is usually cylindri-

[34] Polyxénida: *poly,* many; *xenida,* stranger or guest.

[35] Glomérida: from the Latin, meaning a ball of yarn (referring to the way these animals coil themselves into a ball).

[36] Polydésmida: *poly,* many; *desmida,* bands.

[37] Chordeùmida: from the Greek, meaning a sausage.

cal, and composed of 30 or more segments; the head is broad and free and not overlapped by the collum. One or both pairs of legs on the seventh segment of the male may be modified into gonopods.

Three suborders of Chordeùmida occur in the United States. The suborder Chordeumídea, with nine families (in some classifications these millipedes are placed in a single family, the Craspedosomátidae), are small (mostly 4–15 mm in length), soft-bodied millipedes with 32 or fewer segments and no keels on the metazonites, and without scent glands; they are not very common. The suborder Lysiopetalídea, with one family, the Lysiopetálidae (= Callipódidae), contains larger millipedes with 40 or more body segments that are usually keeled; these millipedes can coil the body into a spiral. The secretions of the scent glands are milky white and very odoriferous. The suborder Striariídea, with one family (the Striarìidae), have 32 or fewer body segments, no scent glands, the anal segment three-lobed, and a high mid-dorsal carina on the metazonites; these millipedes are mostly southern and western in distribution.

ORDER **Jùlida**[38]**:** This order, together with the succeeding three, is combined by some authorities in the order Opisthospermóphora. The millipedes in these groups have the body cylindrical, with 40 or more segments; the collum is large and hoodlike and overlaps the head; either both pairs of legs on the seventh segment of the male are modified into gonopods or one pair is absent; scent glands are present; and the diplosomites are not differentiated into prozonite and metazonites. The millipedes in the order Jùlida have the stipites of the gnathochilarium broadly contiguous along the midline behind the laminae linguales. Segment 3 and the terminal segment are legless; segments 1, 2, and 4 have one pair of legs each; and the remaining segments (diplosomites) have two pairs of legs. The Jùlida are represented in the United States by five families arranged in two suborders.

ORDER **Spirobólida**[39]**:** The millipedes in this order differ from the Jùlida in that they have the stipites of the gnathochilarium separated (Figure 74 B), and from the succeeding two orders in having one pair of legs each on segments 1–5. This group includes some of the largest millipedes in the United States; *Nárceus americànus* (Beauvois), which is dark brown and narrowly ringed with red, may reach a length of 4 inches (102 mm) (Figure 73).

ORDER **Spirostréptida**[40]**:** The members of this order have one pair of legs each on segments 1–4, and the posterior pair of gonopods on the seventh segment of the male is rudimentary or absent; the stipites of the gnathochilarium are separated, but the laminae linguales are usually contiguous. This order is represented in the United States by two families; most species occur in the western and southern United States.

ORDER **Cambálida**[41]**:** These millipedes are very similar to the Spirostréptida, but have the laminae linguales separated by the mentum, and both pairs of legs on the seventh segment of the male are modified into gonopods. This order is represented in the United States by two families. One species in this group, *Cámbala annulàta* (Say), is known to be predaceous.

SUPERORDER COLOBÓGNATHA[42]

The members of this group have the head small and the mouth parts suctorial, and the body is somewhat flattened with 30–60 segments. The first pair of legs on the seventh segment of the male is not modified into gonopods. This superorder contains two orders, the **Platydésmida**[43] and **Polyzonìida,**[44] which may be separated by the characters given in the key. They are represented in the United States by one and two families, respectively. *Polyzònium bivirgàtum* (Wood), which reaches a length of about 20 mm, occurs in rotten wood.

CLASS CHILÓPODA[45] – CENTIPEDES

The centipedes are elongate, flattened, wormlike animals with 15 or more pairs of legs (Figure 75). Each body segment bears a single pair of legs; the last two pairs are directed backward and are often different in form from the other pairs. The antennae consist of 14 or more segments. The genital openings are located at the posterior end of the body, usually on the next to the last segment. Eyes may be present or absent; if present, they usually

[38] Jùlida: from the Greek, meaning a centipede.

[39] Spirobólida: *spiro,* spiral; *bolida,* throw.

[40] Spirostréptida: *spiro,* spiral; *streptida,* twisted.

[41] Cambálida: derivation unknown.

[42] Colobógnatha: *colobo,* shortened; *gnatha,* jaws.

[43] Platydésmida: *platy,* flat; *desmida,* bands.

[44] Polyzonìida: *poly,* many; *zoniida,* belt or girdle.

[45] Chilópoda: *chilo,* lip; *poda,* foot or appendage (referring to the fact that the poison jaws are modified legs).

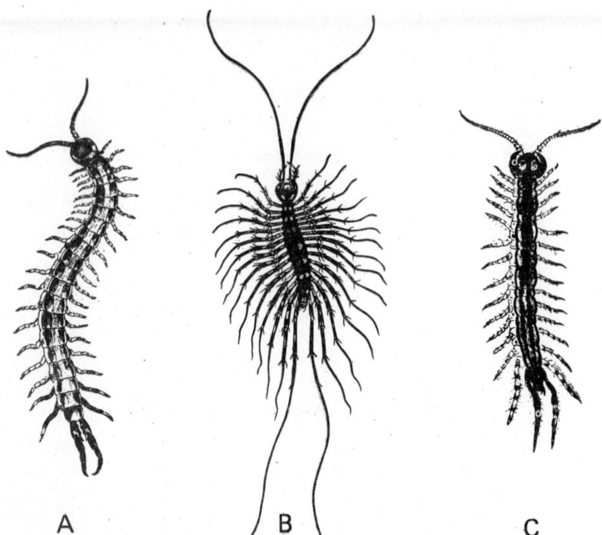

Figure 75. Typical centipedes. A, a large centipede, *Scolopéndra obscùra* Newport, about ¼ natural size; B, a house centipede, *Scutígera coleoptràta* (L.), about ½ natural size; C, a small centipede, *Lithòbius erythrocéphalus* Koch, about natural size. (Courtesy of USDA.)

consist of numerous ocelli. The head bears a pair of mandibles and two pairs of maxillae; the second pair of maxillae may be somewhat leglike in form, or short with the basal segments of the two maxillae fused together. The appendages of the first body segment behind the head are clawlike and function as poison jaws (Figure 76).

Centipedes are found in a variety of places, but usually occur in a protected situation such as in the soil, under bark, or in rotten logs. They are very active, fast-running animals, and are predaceous; they feed on insects, spiders, and other small animals. All centipedes possess poison jaws with which they paralyze their prey; the smaller centipedes of the northern states are harmless to man, but the larger ones of the South and the tropics are able to inflict a painful bite. Centipedes overwinter as adults in protected situations and lay their eggs during the summer. The eggs are usually sticky and become covered with soil, and are deposited singly; in some species the male will eat the egg before the female can get it covered with soil.

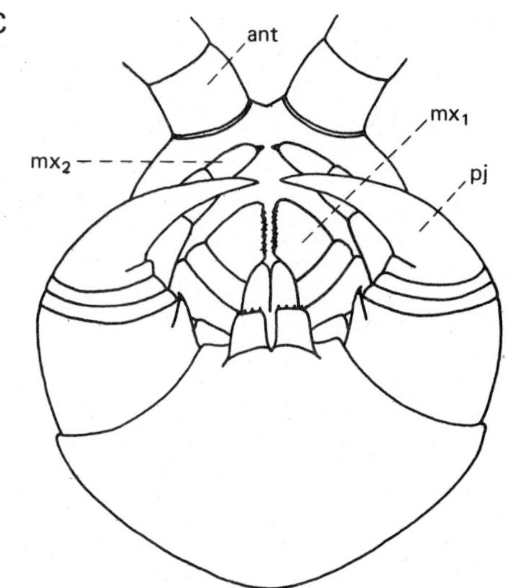

Figure 76. Head of a centipede (*Scolopéndra,* order Scolopendromórpha), ventral view. *ant,* antenna; mx_1, first maxilla; mx_2, second maxilla; *pj,* poison jaw or toxicognath, a modified leg.

Key to the Orders of Chilópoda

1. Adults with 15 pairs of legs, the newly hatched young with 7 pairs (subclass Anamórpha) 2

1′. Adults and newly hatched young with 21 or more pairs of legs (subclass Epimórpha) 3

2(1). Spiracles unpaired, 7 in number, located on mid-dorsal line near posterior margin of tergites; antennae long and many-segmented; legs long (Figure 75 B); eyes compound .... **Scutigeromórpha** p. 133

2′.	Spiracles paired and located laterally; antennae and legs relatively short (Figure 75 C); eyes not compound, but consisting of single ocelli or groups of ocelli, or absent .... **Lithòbiomórpha**	p. 133
3(1′).	Antennae with 17 or more segments; 21–23 pairs of legs; usually 4 or more ocelli on each side .... **Scolopéndromórpha**	p. 133
3′.	Antennae 14-segmented; 29 or more pairs of legs; ocelli absent .... **Geophilomórpha**	p. 133

ORDER **Scutigeromórpha[46]:** This group includes the common house centipede, *Scutígera coleoptràta* (L.) (Figure 75 B), which is found throughout the eastern United States and Canada. Its natural habitat is under stones and in similar places, but it frequently enters houses where it feeds on flies, spiders, and the like. In houses it often frequents the vicinity of sinks and drains; it is harmless to man. This order contains a single family, the Scutigéridae.

ORDER **Lithòbiomórpha[47]:** These are short-legged, usually brownish centipedes with 15 pairs of legs in the adults (Figure 75 C); they vary in length from 4 to about 25 mm. Some members of this order are quite common, usually occurring under stones or logs, under bark, and in similar situations. The order contains two families, the Henicópidae (4–11 mm in length, and the eyes consisting of a single ocellus each, or absent) and the Lithobìidae (10–25 mm in length, and the eyes usually consisting of many ocelli).

ORDER **Scolopéndromórpha[48]:** The scolopendrids are mainly tropical, and in the United States occur principally in the southern states. This group contains our largest centipedes, which reach a length of about 6 inches (152 mm) (Figure 75 A); some tropical species in this group are a foot or so in length. These are the most venomous of the centipedes; the bite of the larger species is quite painful. Two families in this order occur in the United States, the Scolopéndridae (each eye with four ocelli) and the Cryptópidae (each eye with one ocellus).

ORDER **Geophilomórpha[49]:** The members of this order are slender, with 29 or more pairs of short legs and large poison jaws, usually whitish or yellowish in color, and they usually occur in the soil, in rotten logs, or in debris. Most species are small, but some reach a length of 4 inches (101 mm). Five families occur in the United States; they are separated principally by the structure of the mandibles.

[46] Scutigeromórpha: *scuti,* shield; *gero,* bear or carry; *morpha,* form.

[47] Lithòbiomórpha: *litho,* stone; *bio,* life; *morpha,* form.

[48] Scolopéndromórpha: *scolopendro,* centipede; *morpha,* form.

[49] Geophilomórpha: *geo,* earth; *philo,* loving; *morpha,* form.

CLASS PAURÓPODA[50]—PAUROPODS

Pauropods are minute, usually whitish myriapods, 1.0–1.5 mm in length. The antennae bear three apical branches; the nine pairs of legs are not grouped in double pairs as in the millipedes; the head is small and is sometimes covered by the tergal plate of the first body segment (Figure 77 A).

[50] Paurópoda: *pauro,* small; *poda,* food or appendage.

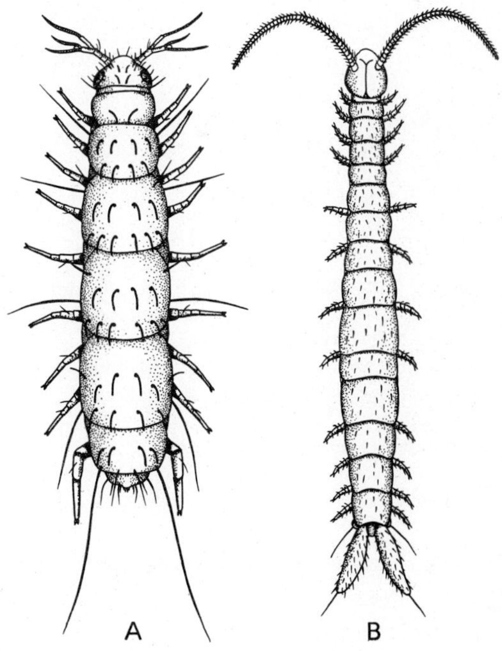

Figure 77. A, a pauropod, *Pàuropus* sp., 95 ×; B, a symphylan, *Scolopendrélla* sp., 16 ×. (A, redrawn from Lubbock; B, redrawn from Comstock, after Latzel.)

The genital ducts open near the anterior end of the body. Pauropods occur under stones, in leaf litter, and in similar places.

CLASS SÝMPHYLA[51] — SYMPHYLANS

The symphylans are slender, whitish myriapods, 1–8 mm in length, with 15–22 (usually 15) body segments and 10–12 pairs of legs (Figure 77 B). The antennae are slender and many-segmented, and the head is well developed and distinct. The genital openings are located near the anterior end of the body. The symphylans occur in humus soil, under stones, in decaying wood, and in other damp situations; one species, *Scutigerélla immaculàta* (Newport) is occasionally a pest in greenhouses.

[51] Sýmphyla: from the Greek, meaning a growing together.

COLLECTING AND PRESERVING MYRIAPODS

Myriapods may be killed in a cyanide bottle, but such specimens often become coiled or distorted; these animals are best killed and preserved in alcohol (about 75 percent) or in alcohol and glycerine (ten parts of alcohol to one part of glycerine). Millipedes may be picked up by hand or with forceps; except in the case of the smaller specimens, it is well to handle centipedes with forceps, as the larger specimens can inflict a painful bite.

CLASS INSÉCTA — INSECTS

This class is included here merely to indicate its position in the phylum; since the bulk of this book is concerned with insects, we need say no more about them here.

References on the Arthropods

GENERAL REFERENCES

Anderson, D. T. 1973. *Embryology and Phylogeny in Annelids and Arthropods*. New York: Pergamon Press, xiv + 495 pp., 164 f.

Borradale, L. A., F. A. Potts, L. E. S. Eastam, and J. T. Saunders. 1963 (4th ed., rev. by G. A. Kerkert). *The Invertebrata*. Cambridge: Cambridge Univ. Press, xvi + 820 pp.; illus.

Clarke, K. U. 1973. *The Biology of the Arthropoda*. New York: American Elsevier, x + 270 pp.; illus.

Cloudsley-Thompson, J. L. 1958. *Spiders, Scorpions, Centipedes, and Mites*. New York: Pergamon Press, xiv + 228 pp., 41 f.

Eddy, S., and A. C. Hodson. 1950. *Taxonomic Keys to the Common Animals of the North Central States Exclusive of the Parasitic Worms, Insects, and Birds*. Minneapolis: Burgess Publ., 123 pp., 608 f.

Manton, S. M. 1964. Mandibular mechanisms and the evolution of the arthropods. *Phil. Trans. Roy. Soc. B*, 247:1–183; 1 pl., 66 f.

Pimentel, R. A. 1967. *Invertebrate Identification Manual*. New York: Reinhold Publ., 150 pp.; illus.

Snodgrass, R. E. 1935. *Principles of Insect Morphology*. New York: McGraw-Hill, ix + 677 pp., 319 f.

Snodgrass, R. E. 1952. *A Textbook of Arthropod Anatomy*. Ithaca, N.Y.: Comstock Publ., viii + 363 pp., 88 f.

Tiegs, O. W., and S. M. Manton. 1958. The evolution of the Arthropoda. *Biol. Rev.*, 33:255–337; 18 f.

REFERENCES ON THE CHELICERATES

Arthur, D. R. 1959. *Ticks. A Monograph of the Ixodoidea. Part V. The Genera Dermacentor, Anocentor, Cosmiomma, Boophilus, and Margaropus*. Cambridge: Cambridge Univ. Press, xviii + 251 pp., 4 pl., 510 f.

Atkins, J. A., C. W. Wingo, W. A. Sodeman, and J. E. Flynn. 1958. Necrotic arachnidism. *Amer. J. Trop. Med. and Hyg.*, 7(2): 165–184; 17 f.

Baker, E. W., T. M. Evans, D. J. Gould, W. B. Hull, and H. L. Keegan. 1956. *A Manual of Parasitic Mites of Medical or Economic Importance*. New York: National Pest Control Assn., vi + 170 pp., 59 f.

Baker, E. W., and G. W. Wharton. 1952. *An Introduction to Acarology*. New York: Macmillan, xiii + 465 pp., 377 f., 3 pl.

Bishop, S. C. 1949. The Phalangida (Opiliones) of New York, with special reference to the species in the Edmund Niles Huyck Preserve, Rensselaerville, N.Y. *Proc. Rochester Acad. Sci.*, 9(3):159–235; 8 pl., 2 textf.

Bristowe, W. S. 1939–1941. *The Comity of Spiders*. London: The Ray Society. Two volumes: Vol. 1, 1939, x + 228 pp., 19 pl., 16 textf.; Vol. 2, 1941, x + 229-560 pp., 3 pl., 81 textf.

Bristowe, W. S. 1958. *The World of Spiders*. London: Collins, xiii + 304 pp., 36 pl., 116 f.

Chamberlin, J. C. 1931. The arachnid order Chelonethida. *Stanford Univ. Publ. Biol. Ser.*, 7(1):1–284; 71 f.

Chamberlin, R. V., and W. Ivie. 1944. Spiders of the Georgia region of North America. *Bull. Univ. Utah,* 35(9):1–267; 217 f.

Comstock, J. H., and W. J. Gertsch. 1940. *The Spider Book.* New York: Doubleday, xi + 729 pp., 770 f.

Evans, G. O., J. G. Sheals, and D. Macfarlane. 1961. *The Terrestrial Acari of the British Isles. An Introduction to their Morphology, Biology, and Classification.* Vol. 1. *Introduction and Biology.* London: British Museum, vii + 219 pp., frontis. + 216 f.

Ewing, H. E. 1928. Scorpions of the western part of the United States, with notes on those occurring in northern Mexico. *Proc. U.S. Natl. Mus.,* 73(9):1–24; 2 pl.

Ewing, H. E. 1929. A synopsis of the order Ricinulei. *Ann. Ent. Soc. Amer.,* 22(4):583–600; 9 f.

Gertsch, W. J. 1949. *American Spiders.* New York: Van Nostrand, xiii + 285 pp.; illus.

Gertsch, W. J., and S. Mulaik. 1939. Report on a new ricinuleid from Texas. *Amer. Mus. Novitat.,* No. 1037; 5 pp., 10 f.

Gorham, J. R., and T. B. Rheney. 1968. Envenomation by the spiders *Chiracanthium inclusum* and *Argiope aurantia.* Observations on arachnidism in the United States. *J. Amer. Med. Assn.,* 206(9):1958–1962; 3 f.

Hoff, C. C. 1949. The pseudoscorpions of Illinois. *Ill. Nat. Hist. Surv. Bull.,* 24(4):411–498; 51 f.

Hoff, C. C. 1958. List of the pseudoscorpions of North America north of Mexico. *Amer. Mus. Novitat.,* No. 1875; 50 pp.

Johnson, J. D., and D. M. Allred. 1972. Scorpions of Utah. *Gr. Basin Nat.,* 32(3):157–170; 24 f.

Johnston, D. E. 1968. *An Atlas of Acari. I. The Families of Parasitiformes and Opilioacariformes.* Columbus, Ohio: Acarology Laboratory, Ohio State Univ., x + 110 pp., 110 pl.

Kaston, B. J. 1948. Spiders of Connecticut. *Conn. State Geol. and Nat. Hist. Surv. Bull.,* 70:1–874; 6 textf., 144 pl.

Kaston, B. J., and E. Kaston. 1953. *How to Know the Spiders.* Dubuque, Iowa: Wm. C. Brown, vi + 220 pp., 552 f.

King, P. E. 1974. *Pycnogonids.* New York: St. Martin's, 144 pp.; illus.

Muma, M. H. 1943. *Common Spiders of Maryland.* Baltimore: Natural History Society of Maryland, 173 pp., 15 pl.

Muma, M. H. 1951–1962. The arachnid order Solpugida in the United States. *Bull. Amer. Mus. Nat. Hist.,* 97:31–141; 316 f. (1951). Supplement 1 (1962), *Amer. Mus. Novitat.,* No. 2902; 44 pp., 75 f.

Parrish, H. M. 1959. Deaths from bites and stings of venomous animals and insects. *A.M.A. Arch. Internal Med.,* 104:198–207.

Pritchard, A. E., and E. W. Baker. 1955. A revision of the spider mite family Tetrancychidae. *Mem. Pac. Coast Ent. Soc.,* 2:1–472; 391 f., 1 col. pl.

Tuttle, D. M., and E. W. Baker. 1968. *Spider Mites of Southwestern United States and Revisions of the Family Tetranychidae.* Tucson: Univ. Arizona Press, 150 pp., 125 f.

Wingo, C. W. 1960. Poisonous spiders. *Univ. Missouri Agric. Ext. Serv. Bull.,* 738; 11 pp.; illus.

REFERENCES ON THE CRUSTACEANS

Crowder, W. 1931. *Between the Tides.* New York: Dodd, Mead, 461 pp., 451 f., 34 pl.

Edmondson, W. T. (Ed.). 1959. *Fresh-Water Biology.* New York: Wiley, xx + 1248 pp.; illus.

Green, J. 1961. *A Biology of the Crustacea.* Chicago: Quadrangle Books, xv + 180 pp., 58 f.

Klots, E. B. 1966. *The New Book of Freshwater Life.* New York: G. P. Putnam's, 398 pp.; illus.

Miner, R. W. 1950. *Field Book of Seashore Life.* New York: G. P. Putnam's, xv + 888 pp., 251 pl.

Pennak, R. W. 1953. *Fresh-Water Invertebrates of the United States.* New York: Ronald, ix + 769 pp., 470 f.

REFERENCES ON THE MYRIAPODS

Bailey, J. W. 1928. The Chilopoda of New York state, with notes on the Diplopoda. *N. Y. State Mus. Bull.,* 276:5–50; 15 f.

Chamberlin, R. V., and R. L. Hoffman. 1958. Checklist of the millipedes of North America. *U.S. Natl. Mus. Bull.,* 212; 236 pp.

Eason, E. H. 1964. *Centipedes of the British Isles.* London: Frederick Warne, x + 294 pp., 4 pl., 495 f.

Johnson, B. M. 1954. The millipedes of Michigan. *Pap. Mich. Acad. Sci.,* 39(1953):241–252; 7 pl.

Keeton, W. T. 1960. A taxonomic study of the millipede family Spirobolidae (Diplopoda, Spirobolida). *Mem. Ent. Soc. Amer.,* No. 17; ii + 146 pp., 268 f.

Wood, H. C. 1865. On the Myriapoda of North America. *Trans. Amer. Phil. Soc.,* 13(7):137–248; 61 f., 3 pl.

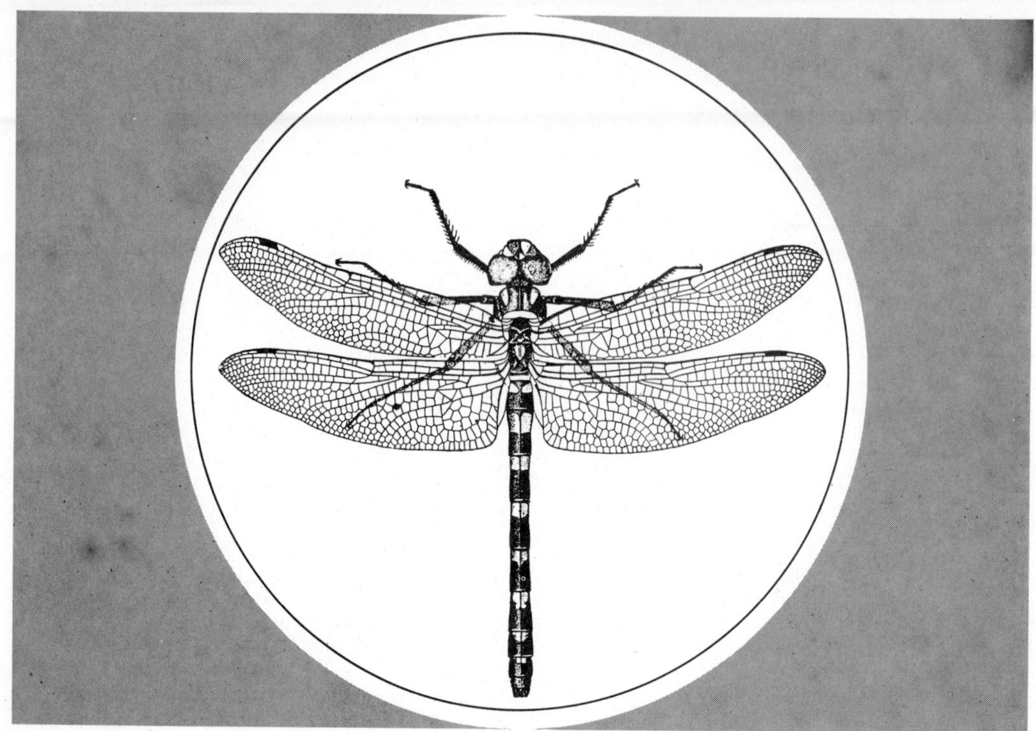

8: CLASS INSÉCTA[1]

INSECTS

CHARACTERS OF THE INSÉCTA

The distinguishing characters of the Insécta may be listed briefly as follows:

Body

1. Body with three distinct regions: head, thorax, and abdomen.

Head

2. One pair of antennae (rarely no antennae)
3. One pair of mandibles
4. One pair of maxillae
5. A hypopharynx
6. A labium

Thorax

7. Three pairs of legs, one pair per thoracic segment (a few insects are legless, and some larvae possess additional leglike appendages—such as prolegs—on the abdominal segments)
8. Often one or two pairs of wings, borne by the second and/or third of the three thoracic segments

Abdomen

9. The gonopore at the posterior end of the abdomen
10. No locomotor appendages on the abdomen of the adult (except in some primitive insects); the abdominal appendages, if present, are at the apex of the abdomen and consist of a pair of cerci, an epiproct, and a pair of paraprocts

[1] Insécta: *in*, in or into; *sect*, cut (referring to the fact that the body is "cut into" by the segmentation).

CLASSIFICATION OF THE INSÉCTA

The class Insécta is divided into orders on the basis of the structure of the wings and mouth parts, the metamorphosis, and on various other characters. There are differences of opinion among entomologists regarding the limits of some of the orders and the names that should be used for them; a few of the groups that we treat as a single order are divided into two or more orders by some authorities, and there are cases where two groups that we recognize as separate orders are combined into a single order by some authorities. A few of the groups that we treat as orders of insects are sometimes considered as separate classes of arthropods.

A synopsis of the orders of insects, as recognized in this book, is given below; other names or arrangements are given in parentheses. The relative sizes of the various insect orders are shown in Table 1.

Subclass Apterygòta—primitively wingless insects
1. Protùra (Myrientómata)—proturans
2. Collémbola—springtails
3. Diplùra (Entógnatha, Entótrophi, Áptera)—diplurans
4. Thysanùra (Ectógnatha, Ectótrophi; including Microcorýphia)—bristletails

Subclass Pterygòta—winged and secondarily wingless insects

Division Exopterygòta—pterygotes with simple metamorphosis
5. Ephemeróptera (Ephemérida, Plectóptera)—mayflies
6. Odonàta—dragonflies and damselflies
7. Orthóptera (including Dictyóptera, Blattària, and Grylloblattòdea)—grasshoppers, crickets, walking sticks, mantids, cockroaches, and rock crawlers
8. Dermáptera (Euplexóptera)—earwigs
9. Isóptera—termites
10. Embióptera (Embiidìna)—webspinners
11. Plecóptera—stoneflies
12. Zoráptera—zorapterans
13. Psocóptera (Corrodéntia)—psocids
14. Mallóphaga (Phthiriáptera in part)—chewing lice
15. Anoplùra (Siphunculàta; Phthiriáptera in part)—sucking lice
16. Thysanóptera (Physápoda)—thrips
17. Hemíptera (Heteróptera)—bugs
18. Homóptera (Hemíptera in part)—cicadas, hoppers, psyllids, whiteflies, aphids, and scale insects

Division Endopterygòta—pterygotes with complete metamorphosis
19. Neuróptera (including Megalóptera and Raphidiòdea)—alderflies, dobsonflies, fishflies, snakeflies, lacewings, antlions, and owlflies
20. Coleóptera—beetles
21. Strepsíptera (Coleóptera in part)—twisted-winged parasites
22. Mecóptera (including Neomecóptera)—scorpionflies
23. Trichóptera—caddisflies
24. Lepidóptera (including Zeuglóptera)—butterflies and moths
25. Díptera—flies
26. Siphonáptera—fleas
27. Hymenóptera—sawflies, ichneumons, chalcids, ants, wasps, and bees.

PHYLOGENY OF THE INSÉCTA

Data on the phylogeny of insects are found chiefly in the fossil record and in comparative studies of present-day insects. Insect fossils are not abundant, but enough have been found to give us a general idea of insect history on the earth; a brief summary of the fossil record is given in Table 2. The data from comparative studies are sometimes interpreted differently by different people, who may attribute different degrees of importance to particular features, but certain general relationships are evident and can be outlined here.

The fossil record for precambrian time is quite scanty, but by the Cambrian period marine arthropods were present, consisting of trilobites, crustaceans, and xiphosurans. The first terrestrial arthropods—scorpions and millipedes—appeared later, in the Silurian period, and the first insects appeared in the Devonian. Relatively few insect fossils are known from the Devonian, but many are known from the Carboniferous and later periods.

The insects are believed to have arisen from a myriapod ancestor that had paired leglike appendages on each body segment. The change to the insect condition involved a specialization of the anterior body segments to form the head and mouth parts, a modification of the next three segments as locomotor segments, and the loss or reduction of most of the appendages on the remaining body segments. The first insects were undoubtedly wingless (apterygotes).

Not all entomologists agree on the number of apterygote orders that should be recognized. The

Table 1 RELATIVE SIZE OF THE VARIOUS INSECT ORDERS, AS SHOWN BY THE NUMBER OF SPECIES AND FAMILIES OCCURRING IN DIFFERENT GEOGRAPHIC AREAS

	Number of Species					
Order	*North Carolina*[a]	*Mt. Desert, Maine*[b]	*New York*[c]	*N.A. North of Mexico*[d]	*World*[d]	*Families in N.A. North of Mexico*[e]
Protùra	0	0	1	18	118	3
Collémbola	169	1	200	314	2,000	5
Diplùra	1	1	2	25	400	3
Thysanùra	6	1	5	25	370	4
Ephemeróptera	121	44	61	585	2,100	15
Odonàta	148	81	159	423	4,950	11
Orthóptera	258	50	136	1,025	23,000	19
Dermáptera	7	0	4	18	1,100	4
Isóptera	5	0	1	41	2,100	4
Embióptera	0	0	0	9	149	3
Plecóptera	94	31	59	400	1,600	6
Zoráptera	1	0	0	2	22	1
Psocóptera	37	25	36	150	1,100	11
Mallóphaga	164	180	53	318	2,675	6
Anoplùra	11	6	11	62	250	3
Thysanóptera	68	9	71	600	4,700	5
Hemíptera	568	179	727	4,600	23,500	44
Homóptera	759	224	864	6,700	33,000	32
Neuróptera	68	35	61	338	4,700	15
Coleóptera	3,336	1,175	4,546	30,000	300,000	112
Strepsíptera	11	2	2	60	300	4
Mecóptera	27	5	20	85	400	4
Trichóptera	161	96	174	975	4,500	17
Lepidóptera	1,428	1,479	2,439	10,100	113,000	78
Díptera	2,595	1,626	3,615	17,000	90,000	107
Siphonáptera	14	10	26	250	1,600	7
Hymenóptera	2,463	1,107	2,300	17,100	108,000	71
Total	12,520	6,367	15,573	91,223	725,634	594

[a]From Wray, D. L. 1967. *Insects of North Carolina,* Third Supplement. N. Carolina Dept. Agriculture, Division of Entomology. 181 pp.

[b]From Procter, W. 1946. *Biological Survey of the Mt. Desert Region.* Part VIII. The Insect Fauna. Wistar Institute Press. 566 pp.

[c]Mainly from Leonard, M. D. 1928. *A List of the Insects of New York.* Cornell University Agricultural Experiment Station, Mem. 101; 1121 pp.

[d]From various sources, chiefly the U.S.D.A. Yearbook for 1952, p. 6; the figures in most cases are approximate.

[e]The number recognized in this book.

Protúra and Collémbola are very distinct groups (some authorities would put these in separate classes, and not in the Inséсta), while the Diplùra and Thysanùra may be a little more closely related. The Protùra and Collémbola probably represent early offshoots of the hexapod line, and the type that gave rise to winged insects was more like present-day Thysanùra.

The insects are unique among flying animals in that their wings are *in addition to* their legs, and not modified legs (as is the case in flying vertebrates). A question thus arises, from *what* did the wings of insects evolve? They obviously arose from flaps located dorsoventrally on the thorax, but there are differences of opinion as to what the original function of these flaps might have been. Many entomologists believe that they originally functioned as gliders, and later developed basal articulations (and the necessary musculature) and became functional wings. Other entomologists

Table 2 AN OUTLINE OF THE FOSSIL RECORD

Era	*Millions of years ago*[a]	*Periods*		*Forms of Life*	
		Pleistocene		First man	
Cenozoic	70	Tertiary	Pliocene Miocene Oligocene Eocene Paleocene	Age of mammals and flowering plants; rise of modern insect genera; insects in amber	
Mesozoic	135 180 225	Cretaceous Jurassic Triassic		 First birds First mammals	Age of reptiles; first flowering plants; most modern orders of insects present; extinction of fossil insect orders
Paleozoic	270	Permian		Rise of most modern insect orders; extinction of many fossil orders	
	350	Carboniferous		First winged insects (in several orders, most now extinct; some very large insects in this period); appearance of primitive reptiles	
	400	Devonian		First insects (apterygotes); first land vertebrates (amphibians); age of fishes	
	440	Silurian		First land animals (scorpions and millipedes); rise of fishes	
	500	Ordovician		First vertebrates (ostracoderms)	
	600	Cambrian		First arthropods (trilobites, xiphosurans, and branchiopods)	
Precambrian				Primitive invertebrates	

[a]From the beginning of the era.

believe that these flaps functioned originally in sexual display (as they still do in many Orthóptera)—one point of evidence for this being their restriction to the adult stage—and later developed into organs of flight. Whatever their original function may have been, wings apparently developed in insects in the Devonian period; by the Carboniferous many types of winged insects were present.

The earliest winged insects were probably ephemeroid in character, something like present-day Ephemeróptera. From these earliest winged forms two major lines developed, which have been termed Paleóptera and Neóptera; these two lines differ (among other ways) in their ability to flex their wings—the Paleóoptera cannot flex their wings over the abdomen, while the Neóptera can. There were several orders of Paleóptera present in the late Paleozoic, but the only ones that have survived to the present are the Ephemeróptera and Odonàta.

The earliest Neóptera were probably cockroachlike, and from these early Neóptera there were three major lines of development, which may be referred to as the orthopteroid, hemipteroid, and endopterygote lines. Representatives of all three of these were present by the Permian period.

The orthopteroid groups are characterized by simple metamorphosis, mandibulate mouth parts, a large anal lobe in the hind wing, cerci, and numerous Malpighian tubules. They include the present orders Orthóptera, Dermáptera, Isóptera, and Embióptera. Some authorities would include the Zoráptera and Psocóptera among the orthopteroids, but other authorities believe these

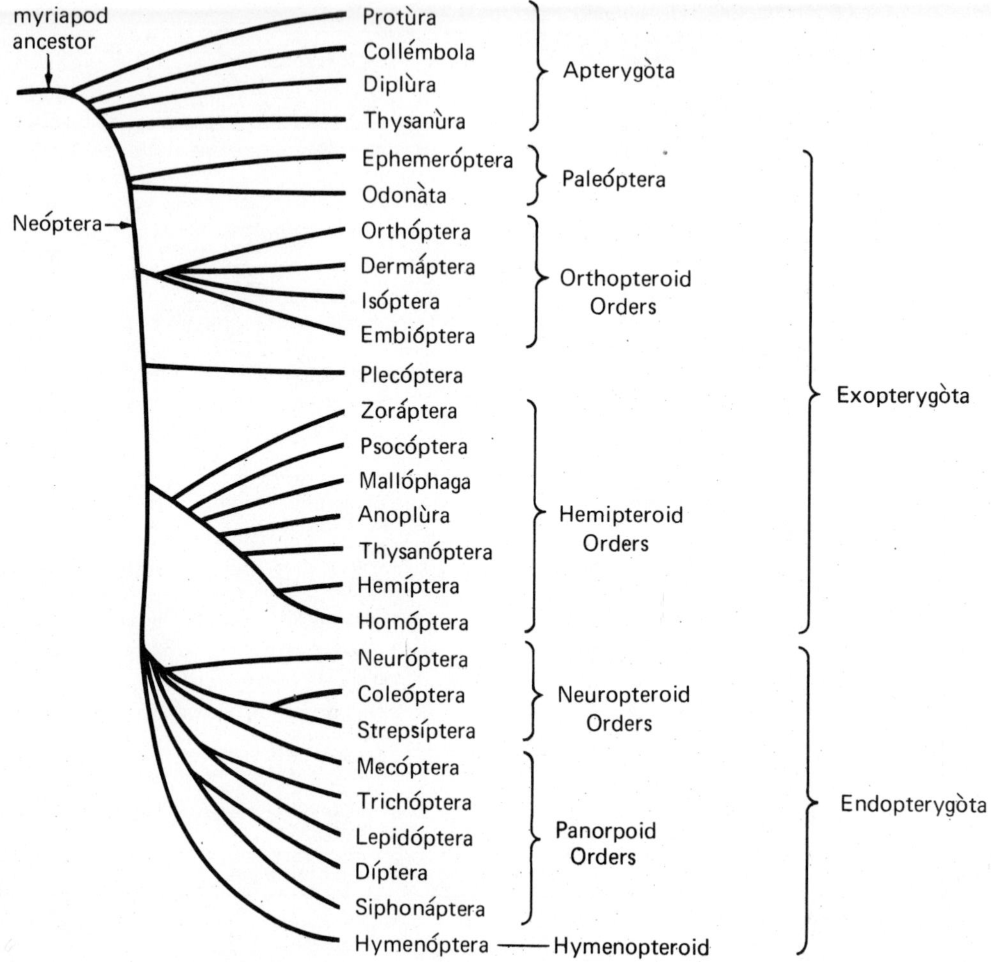

Figure 78. Phylogeny of the insect orders.

groups to be closer to the hemipteroid line. The Plecóptera are believed to be an early offshoot from near the base of the hemipteroid–endopterygote line.

The hemipteroid groups are characterized by simple metamorphosis, a trend toward haustellate mouth parts, no large anal lobe in the hind wing and the venation somewhat reduced, no cerci, and relatively few Malpighian tubules. This group certainly includes the Thysanóptera, Hemíptera, and Homóptera, and probably also includes the Psocóptera; the Zoráptera may belong here, or may represent a position somewhat intermediate between the orthopteroids and hemipteroids. The Mallóphaga and Anoplùra are probably also representatives of the hemipteroid line.

Complete metamorphosis appeared with the endopterygote orders. The earliest of these were probably near present-day Neuróptera, and from these there arose the other endopterygote orders, in about five major lines: (1) Coleóptera and Strepsíptera, (2) Mecóptera, (3) Trichóptera and Lepidóptera, (4) Díptera and Siphonáptera, and (5) Hymenóptera.

The above concepts of the phylogeny of the insect orders are summarized in the diagram in Figure 78, which also shows the sequence in which the orders are treated in this book.

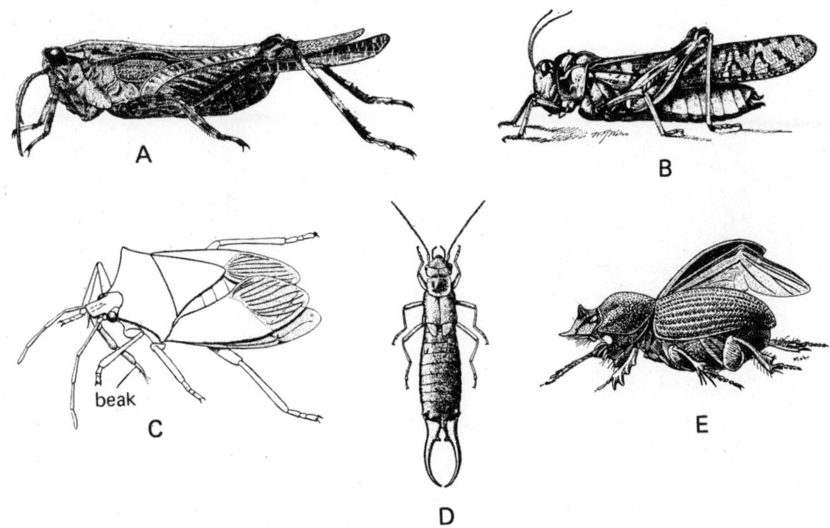

Figure 79. Insects with front wings thickened and hind wings membranous. A, a pygmy grasshopper (Orthóptera); B, a band-winged grasshopper (Orthóptera); C, a stink bug (Hemíptera); D, an earwig (Dermáptera); E, a dung beetle (Coleóptera). (A, C, and E, courtesy of Illinois Natural History Survey; B, courtesy of USDA; D, courtesy of Knowlton and the Utah Agricultural Experiment Station.)

Key to the Orders of Insects

The following key is based on adults, but will work for some nymphs. The groups marked with an asterisk are unlikely to be encountered by the general collector.

1. With well developed wings 2

1′. Wingless, or with the wings vestigial or rudimentary 28

2(1). Wings membranous (like cellophane), not hardened or leathery 3

2′. Front wings hardened or leathery, at least at base (Figure 79); hind wings, if present, usually membranous 24

3(2). With only 1 pair of wings 4

3′. With 2 pairs of wings 10

4(3). Body grasshopperlike; pronotum extending back over abdomen, and pointed apically; hind legs enlarged (Figures 79 A and 114) (pygmy grasshoppers, family Tetrígidae) .... **Orthóptera** p. 185

4′. Body not grasshopperlike; pronotum not as above; hind legs not so enlarged 5

5(4′). Antennae with at least one segment bearing a long lateral process; front wings minute, the hind wings fanlike (Figure 340 A–D); minute insects (male twisted-winged parasites) .... **Strepsíptera** p. 442

5′. Not exactly fitting the above description 6

6(5′). Abdomen with 1–3 threadlike or stylelike tails; mouth parts vestigial .. 7

6′. Abdomen without threadlike or stylelike tails; mouth parts nearly always well developed, mandibulate or haustellate 8

7(6). Antennae long and conspicuous; abdomen terminating in a long style (rarely 2 styles); wings with only a single forked vein (Figure 224 A); hal-

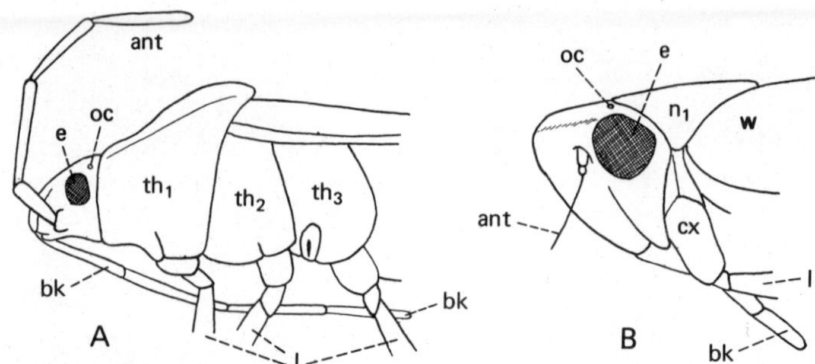

Figure 80. Lateral view of anterior part of the body of A, a lygaeid bug (Hemíptera), and B, a froghopper (Homóptera). *ant*, antenna; *bk*, beak; *cx*, front coxa; *e*, compound eye; *l*, legs; n_1, pronotum; *oc*, ocellus; $th_{1\text{-}3}$, thoracic segments; *w*, *front wing*.

teres present and usually terminating in a hooklike bristle; minute insects, usually less than 5 mm in length (male scale insects) ..... **Homóptera*** p. 286

7′. Antennae short, bristlelike, and inconspicuous; abdomen terminating in 2 or 3 threadlike tails; wings with numerous veins and cells; halteres absent; usually over 5 mm in length (mayflies). .... **Ephemeróptera** p. 159

8(6′). Tarsi nearly always 5-segmented; mouth parts haustellate; hind wings reduced to halteres (Figure 81 A, *hal*); very common insects (flies) .... **Díptera** p. 536

8′. Tarsi 2- or 3-segmented; mouth parts variable; hind wings reduced or absent, not halterelike 9

9(8′). Mouth parts mandibulate (some psocids) .... **Psocóptera*** p. 235

9′. Mouth parts haustellate (some planthoppers) .... **Homóptera** p. 286

10(3′). Wings largely or entirely covered with scales; mouth parts usually in the form of a coiled proboscis; antennae many-segmented (Figure 81 B) (butterflies and moths) .... **Lepidóptera** p. 463

10′. Wings not covered with scales; mouth parts not in the form of a coiled proboscis; antennae variable 11

11(10′). Wings long and narrow, veinless or with only 1 or 2 veins, and fringed with long hairs (Figure 83 A); tarsi 1- or 2-segmented, the last segment swollen; minute insects, usually less than 5 mm in length (thrips) .... **Thysanóptera** p. 251

11′. Wings not as above, or if wings are somewhat linear then tarsi have more than 2 segments 12

12(11′). Front wings relatively large and triangular, hind wings small and rounded, the wings at rest held together above body; wings usually with many cross veins and cells; antennae short, bristlelike, and inconspicuous; abdomen with 2 or 3 threadlike tails (Figure 82); delicate, soft-bodied insects (mayflies) .... **Ephemeróptera** p. 159

12′. Not exactly fitting the above description 13

13(12′). Tarsi 5-segmented 14

13′. Tarsi with 4 or fewer segments 17

14(13). Front wings noticeably hairy; mouth parts usually much reduced except for the palps; antennae generally as long as body or longer; rather soft-bodied insects (caddisflies) .... **Trichóptera** p. 451

14′. Front wings not hairy, at most with only microscopic hairs; mandibles well developed; antennae shorter than body 15

15(14′) Rather hard-bodied, wasplike insects, the abdomen often constricted at base; hind wings smaller than front wings, and with fewer veins; front

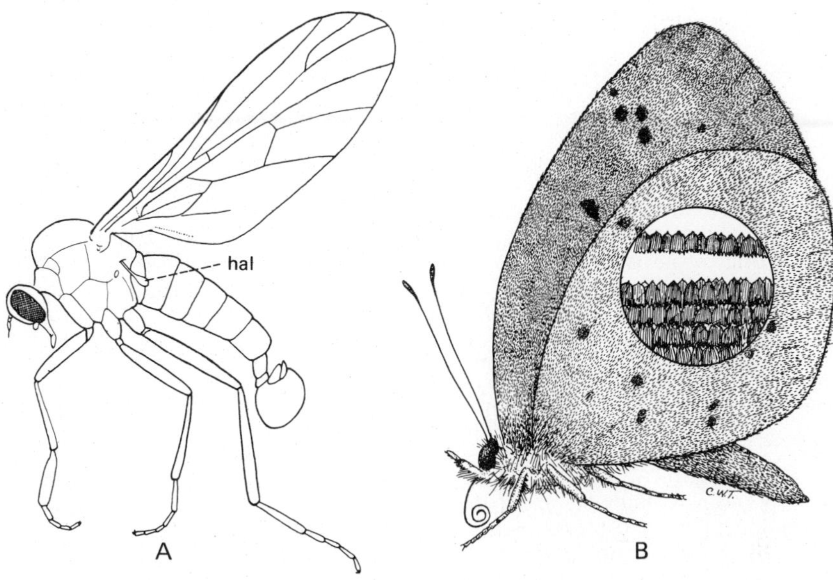

Figure 81. A, a dance fly (Diptera); B, a butterfly (Lepidóptera), with a section of wing enlarged to show scales. *hal,* halter.

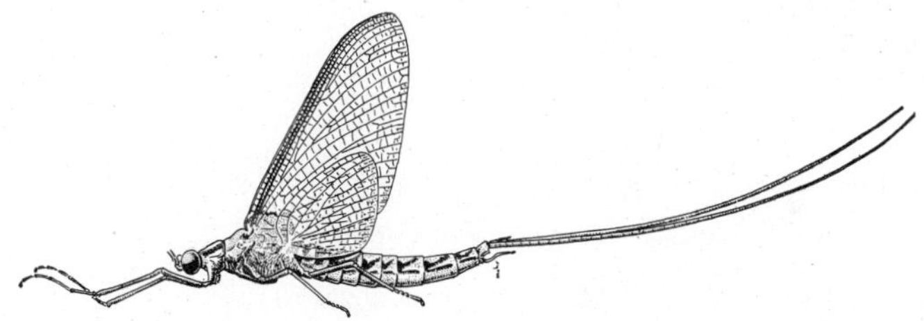

Figure 82. A mayfly (Ephemeróptera). (Courtesy of Illinois Natural History Survey.)

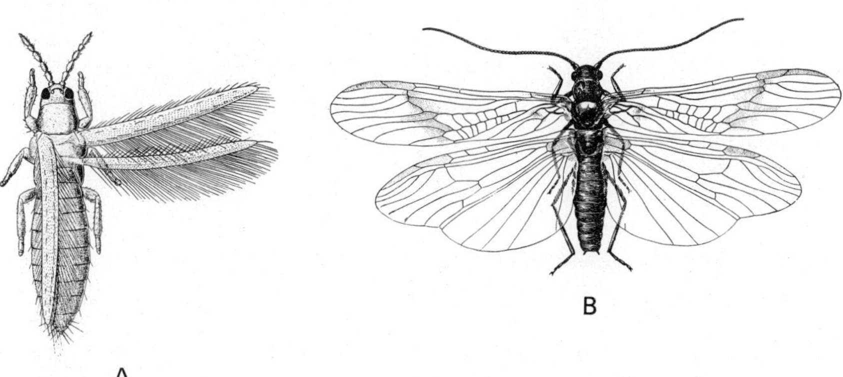

Figure 83. A, a thrips (Thysanóptera); B, a stonefly (Plecóptera). (A, courtesy of Illinois Natural History Survey; B, courtesy of USDA.)

wings with 20 or fewer cells (sawflies, ichneumons, chalcids, ants, wasps, and bees) .... **Hymenóptera** p. 617

15′. Soft-bodied insects, not wasplike, the abdomen not constricted at base; hind wings about same size as front wings, and usually with about as many veins; front wings often with more than 20 cells 16

16(15′). Costal area of front wing nearly always with numerous cross veins (Figure 84 B), or if not (Coniopterýgidae, Figure 233 A) then hind wings shorter than front wings; mouth parts not prolonged into a beak (fishflies, dobsonflies, lacewings, and antlions) .... **Neuróptera** p. 323

16′. Costal area of front wings with not more than 2 or 3 cross veins (Figure 84 A); mouth parts prolonged ventrally to form a beaklike structure (Figures 341 and 342) (scorpionflies) .... **Mecóptera** p. 446

17(13′). Hind wings as long as front wings, and of the same shape or wider at base, the wings at rest held above body or outstretched (never held flat over abdomen); wings with many veins and cells; antennae short, bristlelike, and inconspicuous; abdomen long and slender (Figure 85); tarsi 3-segmented; $\frac{3}{4}$ to $3\frac{1}{4}$ inches (19 to 83 mm) in length (dragonflies and damselflies) .... **Odonàta** p. 169

17′. Not exactly fitting the above description 18

18(17′). Mouth parts haustellate 19

18′ Mouth parts mandibulate 20

19(18). Beak arising from front part of head (Figures 80 A and 183 B) (gnat bugs) .... **Hemíptera** p. 257

19′. Beak arising from hind part of head (Figure 80 B) (cicadas, some hoppers, aphids, some psyllids, and whiteflies) .... **Homóptera** p. 286

20(18′). Tarsi 4-segmented; front and hind wings similar in size, shape, and venation (Figure 133); cerci minute or absent (termites) .... **Isóptera** p. 214

20′. Tarsi with 3 or fewer segments; hind wings usually shorter than front wings 21

21(20′). Hind wings with anal area nearly always enlarged and forming a lobe, which is folded fanwise at rest; venation varying from normal to very dense, front wings usually with several cross veins between Cu_1 and M and between Cu_1 and Cu_2 (Figure 83 B); cerci present and often fairly long; mostly 10 mm or more in length; nymphs aquatic, and the adults usually found near water (stoneflies) .... **Plecóptera** p. 225

21′. Hind wings without an enlarged anal area and not folded at rest; venation normal or reduced, with no extra cross veins; cerci present (but short) or absent; mostly 10 mm in length or less; nymphs not aquatic, the adults not necessarily near water 22

22(21′). Tarsi 3-segmented, the basal segment of front tarsi enlarged (Figure 139) (webspinners) .... **Embióptera*** p. 222

22′. Tarsi 2- or 3-segmented, the basal segment of front tarsi not enlarged 23

23(22′). Cerci present; tarsi 2-segmented; wing venation reduced (Figure 148 A); antennae moniliform and 9-segmented (zorapterans) .... **Zoráptera*** p. 233

23′. Cerci absent; tarsi 2- or 3-segmented; wing venation not particularly reduced (Figure 151 A–E); antennae not moniliform, usually long and hairlike, and with 13 or more segments (Figure 150) (psocids) .... **Psocóptera** p. 235

24(2′). Mouth parts haustellate, the beak elongate and usually segmented (Figure 80) 25

24′. Mouth parts mandibulate 26

25(24). Beak arising from front of head (Figure 80 A); front wings usually thickened at base and membranous at tip, the tips generally overlapping at rest (Figure 79 C) (bugs) .... **Hemíptera** p. 257

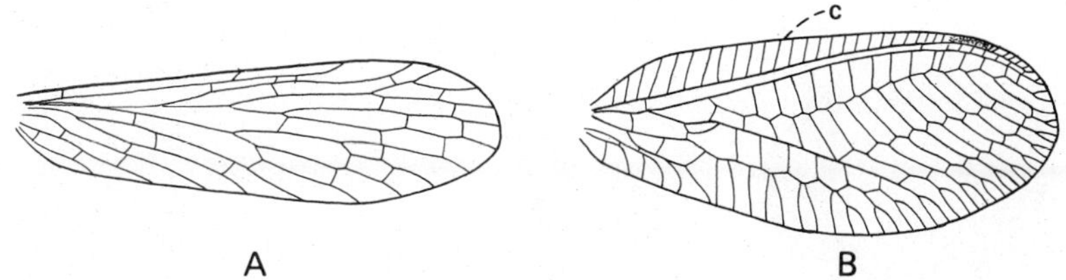

Figure 84. A, front wing of a scorpionfly (Mecóptera); B, front wing of a lacewing (Neuróptera).

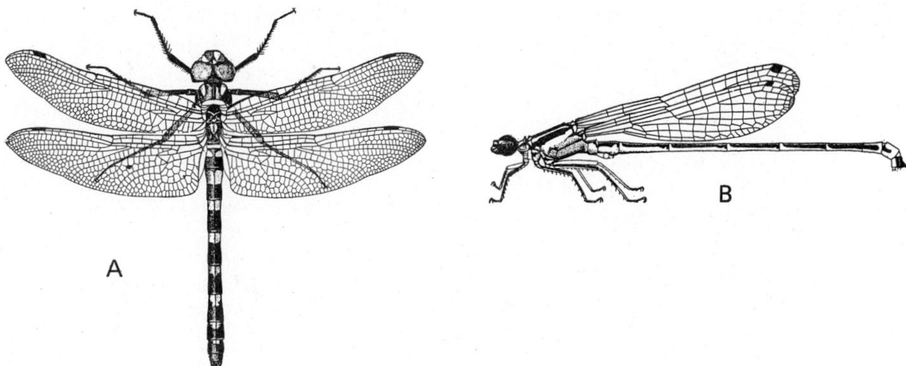

Figure 85. Odonàta. A, a dragonfly; B, a damselfly. (Courtesy of Kennedy and the U.S. National Museum.)

25′.	Beak arising from hind part of head, often appearing to arise at base of front legs (Figure 80 B); front wings of uniform texture throughout, the tips not, or but slightly, overlapping at rest (hoppers, some psyllids) ... **Homóptera**	p. 286
26(24′).	Abdomen with forcepslike cerci (Figure 79 D); front wings short, leaving most of abdomen exposed; tarsi 3-segmented (earwigs) .... **Dermáptera**	p. 176
26′.	Abdomen without forcepslike cerci, or if cerci appear forcepslike then front wings cover most of abdomen; tarsi variable 27	
27(26′).	Front wings without veins, and usually meeting in a straight line down middle of back; antennae generally with 11 or fewer segments; hind wings narrow, usually longer than front wings when unfolded, and with few veins (Figure 79 E) (beetles) .... **Coleóptera**	p. 335
27′.	Front wings with veins, and either held rooflike over abdomen or overlapping over abdomen when at rest; antennae generally with more than 12 segments; hind wings broad, usually shorter than front wings, and with many veins (Figure 118), usually folded fanwise at rest (grasshoppers, crickets, cockroaches, and mantids) .... **Orthóptera**	p. 185
28(1′).	Body insectlike, with a more or less distinct head and segmented legs .. 29	
28′	Body not insectlike, without a distinct head or legs, and usually incapable of locomotion 55	
29(28).	Front wings present but rudimentary; hind wings absent or represented by halteres; tarsi nearly always 5-segmented (some flies) .... **Díptera***	p. 536
29′.	Wings entirely absent, or with 4 rudimentary wings and no halteres; tarsi variable 30	

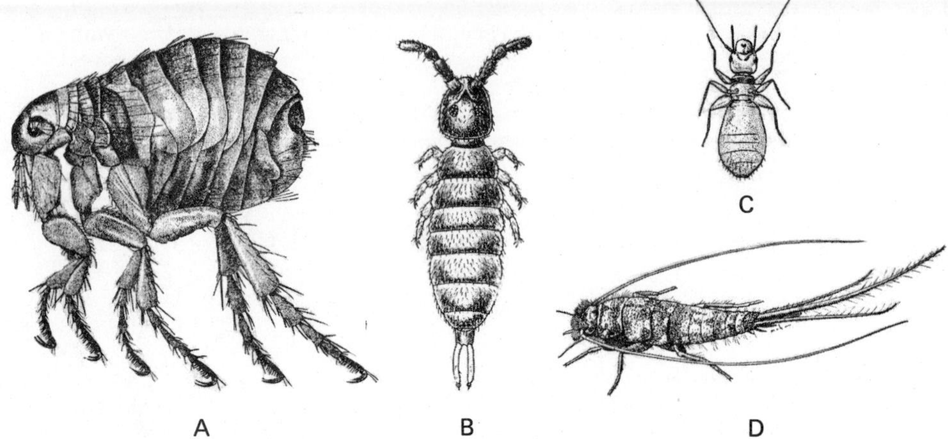

Figure 86. Wingless insects. A, human flea (Siphonáptera); B, springtail (Collémbola); C, psocid (Psocóptera); D, bristletail (Thysanùra). (A and C, courtesy of USDA; B, courtesy of Folsom and the U.S. National Museum; D, courtesy of Illinois Natural History Survey.)

30(29′).	Antennae present; size variable 31	
30′.	Antennae absent; length 1.5 mm or less (proturans) .... **Protùra***	p. 150
31(30).	Ectoparasites of birds, mammals, or honey bees, and usually found on the host; body more or less leathery, and usually flattened dorsoventrally or laterally 32	
31′.	Free-living (not ectoparasites), terrestrial or aquatic 36	
32(31).	Tarsi 5-segmented; antennae short and usually concealed in grooves on head; mouth parts haustellate 33	
32′	Tarsi with fewer than 5 segments; antennae and mouth parts variable 34	
33(32).	Body flattened laterally; usually jumping insects, with legs relatively long (Figure 86 A) (fleas) .... **Siphonáptera**	p. 608
33′.	Body flattened dorsoventrally; not jumping insects, the legs usually short (louse flies, bat flies, and bee lice) .... **Díptera***	p. 536
34(32′).	Antennae distinctly longer than head; tarsi 3-segmented (bed bugs and bat bugs) .... **Hemíptera**	p. 257
34′.	Antennae not longer than head; tarsi 1-segmented (lice) 35	
35(34′).	Head as wide as or wider than prothorax; mouth parts mandibulate; parasites of birds (with 2 tarsal claws) and mammals (with 1 small tarsal claw) (chewing lice) .... **Mallóphaga**	p. 243
35′.	Head usually narrower than prothorax; mouth parts haustellate; parasites of mammals, with 1 large tarsal claw (sucking lice) .... **Anoplùra**	p. 247
36(31′).	Abdomen distinctly constricted at base; antennae usually elbowed; hard-bodied, antlike insects (ants and wingless wasps) .... **Hymenóptera**	p. 617
36′.	Abdomen not particularly constricted at base; antennae not elbowed... 37	
37(36′).	Abdomen with 3 long threadlike tails, and with stylelike appendages on some abdominal segments (Figure 86 D); mouth parts mandibulate, but often more or less retracted into head; body nearly always covered with scales (bristletails) .... **Thysanùra**	p. 150
37′.	Abdomen with only 2 tails (or terminal appendages), or with none; other characters variable 38	
38(37′).	Body covered with scales; mouth parts haustellate, and usually in the form of a coiled tube (wingless moths) .... **Lepidóptera**	p. 463

38′. Body usually not covered with scales; mouth parts not as above 39

39(38′). Mouth parts usually withdrawn into head and not apparent; abdomen with stylelike appendages on some segments, or with a forked appendage near end of abdomen; usually less than 7 mm in length 40

39′. Mouth parts usually distinct, mandibulate or haustellate; abdomen without appendages such as described above; size variable 41

40(39). Antennae long and many-segmented; abdomen with at least 9 segments, and with stylelike appendages on ventral side of some segments; without a forked appendage near end of abdomen, but with well developed cerci (Figure 89) (diplurans) .... **Diplùra** p. 150

40′. Antennae short, with 6 or fewer segments; abdomen with 6 or fewer segments, and usually with a forked appendage near posterior end (Figure 86 B) (springtails) .... **Collémbola** p. 150

41(39′). Tarsi 5-segmented 42

41′. Tarsi with 4 or fewer segments 46

42(41). Mouth parts haustellate; antennae often with 3 or fewer segments (wingless flies) .... **Díptera*** p. 536

42′. Mouth parts mandibulate; antennae with several to many segments .. 43

43(42′). Body larviform, the thorax and abdomen not differentiated (larviform female beetles) .... **Coleóptera*** p. 335

43′. Body not larviform, the thorax and abdomen differentiated 44

44(43′). Mouth parts prolonged ventrally into a snoutlike structure (Figure 346); body more or less cylindrical, and usually less than 8 mm in length (wingless scorpionflies) .... **Mecóptera*** p. 446

44′. Mouth parts not as above; body shape and size variable 45

45(44′). Antennae 5-segmented; might occur in Texas (some female twisted-winged parasites: Mengèidae) .... **Strepsíptera*** p. 442

45′. Antennae with more than 5 segments; widely distributed (rock crawlers, and some cockroaches and walking sticks) .... **Orthóptera** p. 185

46(41′). Cerci forcepslike; tarsi 3-segmented 47

46′. Cerci absent, or if present not forcepslike; tarsi variable 48

47(46). Antennae more than half as long as body; cerci short; western United States (Tímémidae) .... **Orthóptera*** p. 185

47′. Antennae usually less than half as long as body; cerci long (Figure 79 D); widely distributed (earwigs) .... **Dermáptera** p. 176

48(46′). Mouth parts haustellate, with beak elongate and extending backward from head, or cone-shaped and directed ventrad 49

48′. Mouth parts mandibulate 51

49(48). Body elongate and more or less parallel-sided; tarsi 1- or 2-segmented and often without claws; beak cone-shaped; minute insects, usually less than 5 mm in length (thrips) .... **Thysanóptera** p. 251

49′. Body usually more or less oval; tarsi 2- or 3-segmented, with well developed claws; size variable 50

50(48′). Beak arising from front part of head; antennae 4- or 5-segmented; abdomen without cornicles; tarsi usually 3-segmented (wingless bugs) .. **Hemíptera** p. 257

50′. Beak arising from rear of head; antennae usually with more than 5 segments; abdomen often with a pair of cornicles (Figure 201 C); tarsi usually 2-segmented (aphids and others) .... **Homóptera** p. 286

51(48′). Tarsi 3-segmented, the basal segment of front tarsi enlarged (Figure 139) (webspinners) .... **Embióptera*** p. 222

51′. Tarsi 2- to 4-segmented, the basal segment of front tarsi not enlarged... 52

52(51′). Grasshopperlike insects, with hind legs enlarged and fitted for jumping; length over 15 mm (wingless grasshoppers) .... **Orthóptera** p. 185

52′. Not grasshopperlike, the hind legs usually not as above; length less than 10 mm 53

53(52'). Tarsi 4-segmented; pale, soft-bodied, wood- or ground-inhabiting insects (termites) .... **Isóptera** p. 214

53'. Tarsi 2- or 3-segmented; color and habits variable 54

54(53'). Cerci present, 1-segmented, and terminating in a long bristle; antennae 9-segmented and moniliform (Figure 148 B–D); compound eyes and ocelli absent; tarsi 2-segmented (zorapterans) .... **Zoráptera*** p. 233

54'. Cerci absent; antennae with 13 or more segments and usually hairlike (Figure 86 C); compound eyes and 3 ocelli usually present; tarsi 2- or 3-segmented (psocids) .... **Psocóptera** p. 235

55(28'). Sessile, plant-feeding; body covered by a scale or waxy material; mouth parts haustellate, long and threadlike (female scale insects)... **Homóptera** p. 286

55'. Endoparasites of other insects; body not covered by a scale or waxy material; mouth parts not as above (female twisted-winged parasites) .... **Strepsíptera*** p. 442

References on the Insécta

Alexander, R. D., and W. L. Brown, Jr. 1963. Mating behavior and the origin of insect wings. *Occ. Pap. Mus. Zool. Univ. Mich.*, No. 628; 19 pp., 1 f.

Borror, D. J., and R. E. White. 1970 (paperback edition, 1974). *A Field Guide to the Insects of America North of Mexico*. Boston: Houghton Mifflin, xi + 404 pp.; illus. (incl. 16 color pl.).

Brues, C. T., A. L. Melander, and F. M. Carpenter. 1954. Classification of insects. *Harvard Univ., Mus. Compar. Zool. Bull.* 73; v + 917 pp., 1219 f.

Chinery, M. 1974. *A Field Guide to the Insects of Britain and Northern Europe*. Boston: Houghton Mifflin, 352 pp., illus. (incl. 60 col. pl.).

Chu, P. 1949. *How to Know the Immature Insects*. Dubuque, Iowa: Wm. C. Brown, 234 pp.; illus.

Comstock, J. H. 1940 (9th ed.). *An Introduction to Entomology*. Ithaca, N.Y.: Comstock Publ., xix + 1064 pp., 1228 f.

Essig, E. O. 1958. *Insects and Mites of Western North America*. New York: Macmillan, xiii + 1050 pp., 766 f.

Grassé, P. P. (Ed.). 1949. *Traité de Zoologie; Anatomie, Systématique, Biologie*. Vol. 9. *Insectes: Paleontologie, Géonémie, Aptérygotes, Ephéméroptères, Odonatoptères, Blattoptéroïdes, Orthoptéroïdes, Dermaptéroïdes, Coléoptères*. Paris: Masson, 1117 pp., 752 f.

Grassé, P. P. (Ed.). 1951. *Traité de Zoologie; Anatomie, Systématique, Biologie*. Vol. 10. *Insectes Supérieurs et Hemiptéroïdes*. Part I, Neuroptéroïdes, Mecoptéroïdes, Hemiptéroïdes; pp. 1–975, f. 1–905. Part II, Hymenoptéroïdes, Psocoptéroïdes, Hemiptéroïdes, Thysanoptéroïdes; pp. 976–1948, f. 906–1648. Paris: Masson.

Hamilton, K. G. A. 1972. The insect wing, Part IV. Venational trends and the phylogeny of the winged orders. *J. Kan. Ent. Soc.*, 45(3):295–308; 35 f.

Imms, A. D. 1947. *Insect Natural History*. New York: William Collins, xviii + 317 pp., 40 textf., 32 pl. in black and white, 40 pl. in color.

Imms, A. D. 1957 (9th ed., revised by O. W. Richards and R. G. Davies). *A General Textbook of Entomology*. New York: E. P. Dutton, x + 886 pp., 609 f.

Jaques, H. E. 1947 (2nd ed.). *How to Know the Insects*. Dubuque, Iowa: Wm. C. Brown, 205 pp., 411 f.

Linsenmaier. W. 1972. *Insects of the World*. (Translated from the German by L. E. Chadwick.) New York: McGraw-Hill, 392 pp., 384 f. (many in color).

Lutz, F. E. 1935. *Field Book of Insects*. New York: G. P. Putnam's, ix + 510 pp., 100 pl.

Martynov, A. V. 1925. Über zwei Grundtypen der Flügel bei den Insekten und ihre Evolution. *Z. Morph. Ökol. Tiere*, 4:465-501; 24 f.

Martynova, O. 1961. Palaeoentomology. *Ann. Rev. Ent.*, 6:285–294.

Matheson, R. 1951 (2nd ed.). *Entomology for Introductory Courses*. Ithaca, N.Y.: Comstock Publ., xiv + 629 pp., 500 f.

Oldroyd, H. 1970. *Elements of Entomology; An Introduction to the Study of Insects*. London: Weidenfield & Nicolson, ix + 312 pp., 24 pl.

Pennak, R. W. 1953. *Fresh-Water Invertebrates of the United States*. New York: Ronald Press, ix + 769 pp., 470 f.

Peterson, A. 1939. Keys to the orders of immature insects (exclusive of eggs and pronymphs) of North American insects. *Ann. Ent. Soc. Amer.*, 32(2):267–278.

Peterson, A. 1948. *Larvae of Insects. Part I. Lepidoptera and Plant Infesting Hymenoptera*. Ann Arbor, Mich.:

Edwards Bros., 315 pp. 84 f.

Peterson, A. 1951. *Larvae of Insects. Part II. Coleoptera, Diptera, Neuroptera, Siphonaptera, Mecoptera, Trichoptera.* Ann Arbor, Mich.: Edwards Bros., v + 416 pp., 104 f.

Romoser, W. S. 1973. *The Science of Entomology.* New York: Macmillan, xi + 449 pp.; illus.

Ross, H. H. 1955. Evolution of the insect orders. *Ent. News,* 66:197–208.

Ross, H. H. 1965 (3rd ed.). *A Textbook of Entomology.* New York: Wiley, ix + 539 pp., 401 f.

Smart, J. 1963. Explosive evolution and the phylogeny of insects. *Proc. Linn. Soc. London,* 174:125–126; 1 chart.

Swain, R. B. 1948. *The Insect Guide.* New York: Doubleday, xlvi + 261 pp.; illus.

Swan, L. A., and C. S. Papp. 1972. *The Common Insects of North America.* New York: Harper & Row, xiii + 750 pp.; illus. (part color).

Usinger, R. L. (Ed.). 1956. *Aquatic Insects of California, with Keys to North American Genera and California Species.* Berkeley, Calif.: Univ. Calif. Press, ix + 508 pp.; illus.

9: SUBCLASS APTERYGÒTA

PROTÙRA, COLLÉMBOLA, DIPLÙRA, AND THYSANÙRA

The subclass Apterygòta contains small, primitive, wingless insects with simple metamorphosis. Some of the Pterygòta lack wings, but this wingless condition is a secondary one; the wingless Pterygòta are believed to have evolved from winged ancestors.

The two subclasses of insects differ in the structure of the thorax and in the development of abdominal appendages; certain features of thoracic structure in the Pterygòta are correlated with the development of wings and are present even in the wingless members of this subclass. In the Pterygòta, each thoracic pleuron (with rare exceptions) is divided by a pleural suture into an episternum and an epimeron, and the thoracic wall is strengthened internally by furcae and phragmata; in the Apterygòta there is no pleural suture, and furcae and phragmata are not developed. The Apterygòta usually have stylelike appendages on some of the pregenital abdominal segments; such appendages are lacking in adult Pterygòta.

There are some differences between the Thysanùra and the other Apterygòta. The Thysanùra are ectognathous (the mouth parts more or less protruding), the segments of the antennal flagellum are without muscles, the tarsi are 3- to 5-segmented, compound eyes are usually present, and the tentorium is fairly well developed. The other Apterygòta are entognathous (mouth parts withdrawn into the head), the segments of the antennal flagellum (when present) have muscles, the tarsi are 1-segmented, compound eyes are usually absent, and the tentorium is rudimentary.

There are differences of opinion regarding the status of the groups of apterygote insects; our arrangement is outlined below.

Order Protùra – proturans
- Eosentómidae
- Protentómidae (including Hesperentómidae)
- Acerentómidae

Order Collémbola – springtails
- Suborder Arthroplèona – elongate-bodied springtails
  - Podùridae
  - Onychiùridae (Podùridae in part)
  - Isotómidae (Entomobrỳidae in part)
  - Entomobrỳidae
- Suborder Symphyplèona – globular springtails
  - Sminthùridae (including Neélidae)

Order Diplùra – diplurans
- Campodèidae
- Anajapýgidae
- Japýgidae

Order Thysanùra – bristletails
- Lepidotríchidae – primitive bristletails
- Nicoletìidae – nicoletiids
- Lepismátidae – silverfish
- Machílidae – jumping bristletails

ORDER PROTÙRA[1] – PROTURANS

The proturans are minute whitish insects, 0.6–1.5 mm in length. The head is somewhat conical, with the mouth parts suctorial and largely withdrawn into the head, and there are no eyes or antennae (Figure 87). The first pair of legs is principally sensory in function and is carried in an elevated position like antennae. Styli are present on the three basal abdominal segments. The proturans undergo only three molts; at hatching there are nine abdominal segments, and another is added at each molt; the abdomen of the adult contains 12 segments.

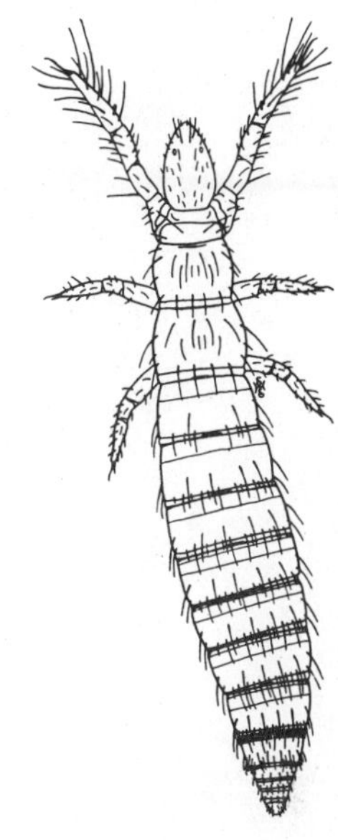

Figure 87. Dorsal view of a proturan, *Aceréntulus bárberi bárberi* Ewing. (Courtesy of Ewing and the Entomological Society of America.)

These insects live in moist soil or humus, in leaf mold, under bark, and in decomposing logs; they feed on decomposing organic matter.

[1] Protùra: *prot,* first; *ura,* tail.

Key to the Families of Protùra

1.	Tracheae present, with 2 pairs of spiracles on thorax; abdominal appendages with a terminal vesicle	**Eosentómidae**	p. 152
1′.	Tracheae and spiracles absent; abdominal appendages with or without a terminal vesicle	2	
2(1′).	At least 2 pairs of abdominal appendages with a terminal vesicle	**Protentómidae**	p. 152
2′.	Only the first pair of abdominal appendages with a terminal vesicle	**Acerentómidae**	p. 152

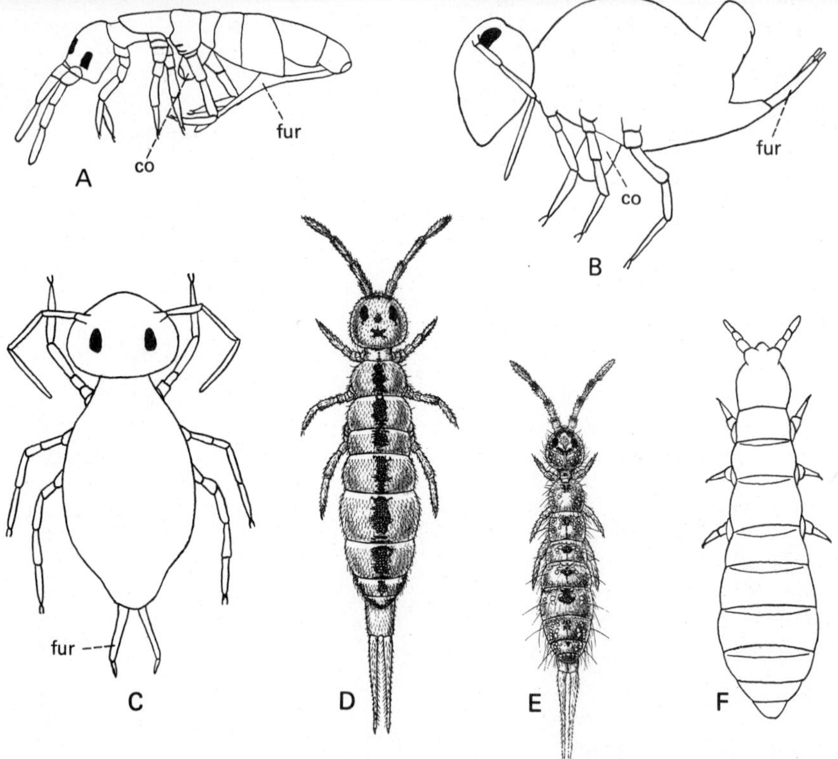

Figure 88. Springtails. A, *Orchesélla* (Entomobrỳidae); B, *Bourletiélla* (Sminthùridae), lateral view; C, same, dorsal view; D, *Isotomùrus palústris* (Müller) (Isotómidae); E, *Isótoma víridis* (Bourlet) (Isotómidae); F, *Anùrida maritíma* (Guérin) (Podùridae). *co,* collophore; *fur,* furcula. (A–C redrawn from Maynard, by permission of Comstock Publishing Co.; D–E, courtesy of Folsom and the U.S. National Museum; F, redrawn from Lubbock.)

The **Eosentómidae** contains eight North American species, all belonging to the genus *Eosentomon.* The **Protentómidae** includes three rather rare North American species, one recorded from Maryland, another from Iowa, and a third from California. The **Acerentómidae** is a widely distributed group, with seven North American species.

ORDER **Collémbola**[2] – Springtails: Springtails are minute insects that get their name from the fact that most of them have a forked structure or furcula with which they jump. The furcula arises on the ventral side of the fourth abdominal segment, and when at rest is folded forward under the abdomen, where it is held in place by a clasplike structure on the third abdominal segment called the tenaculum. The insect jumps by extending the furcula downward and backward; a springtail 5 or 6 mm in length may be able to jump 3 or 4 inches (76 or 102 mm).

Springtails vary in coloration; many are white, gray, or yellow; others are orange, metallic green, lavender, red, or some other color, and some are patterned or mottled. The mouth parts are somewhat elongate and styletlike, and are concealed within the head. These insects possess a tubelike structure, the collophore, on the ventral side of the first abdominal segment; at the apex of the collophore is a bilobed eversible vesicle. It was originally believed that the collophore in some way enabled the insect to cling to the surface on which it walked (hence the order name), but it is now believed that this structure may play a role in water uptake.

[2] Collémbola: *coll,* glue; *embola,* a bolt or wedge (referring to the collophore).

Springtails are usually very common and abundant insects, but they are seldom observed because of their small size and the fact that most of them live in concealed situations. Most species live in the soil or in such habitats as leaf mold, under bark, in decaying logs, and in fungi; some species may be found on the surface of freshwater pools or along the seashore, some occur on vegetation, and a few live in termite nests, caves, or snow fields. Springtail populations are often very high—up to 100,000 per cubic meter of surface soil, or many millions per acre.

Most soil-inhabiting springtails feed on decaying plant material, fungi, and bacteria; others feed on arthropod feces, pollen, algae, and other materials. A few species may occasionally cause damage in gardens, greenhouses, or mushroom cellars.

Key to the Families of Collémbola

1. Body elongate (Figure 88 A, D–F), the abdomen with 6 distinct segments (suborder Arthroplèona) 2
1′. Body oval or globular (Figure 88 B, C), the abdomen with the 4 basal segments fused, and segments 5 and 6 forming a small apical papilla (suborder Symphyplèona) .... **Sminthùridae** p. 154
2(1). Prothorax well developed and visible from above, and with bristles or setae dorsally 3
2′. Prothorax reduced and usually not visible from above, and without bristles or setae dorsally 4
3(2). Eyes usually present; third antennal segment with papillalike sense organs only, the fourth segment with large retractile terminal vesicles; integument without regularly distributed pores .... **Podùridae** p. 153
3′. Eyes absent; third antennal segment with 2 or 3 conelike sense organs in addition to the papillalike structures (often more or less concealed by the latter), the fourth segment without or with only minute terminal vesicles; integument with regularly distributed pores on at least some segments .... **Onychiùridae** p. 153
4(2′). Fourth abdominal segment at least twice as long as third along middorsal line (Figure 88 A); body scaly or with clavate setae; furcula always well developed .... **Entomobrỳidae** p. 154
4′. Third and fourth abdominal segments about the same length along middorsal line (Figure 88 D, E); body not scaly, and with only simple setae; furcula often reduced .... **Isotómidae** p. 153

Family **Podùridae:** The members of this family are minute insects that are usually gray or black and have short appendages. The snow flea, *Achorùtes nivícolus* (Fitch), is a dark-colored species often found in winter on the surface of the snow. The armored springtail, *Achorùtes armàtus* (Nicolet), is a widely distributed species occurring in leaves, rotting wood, and similar places; the young are whitish and the adults are slate-colored. The seashore springtail, *Anùrida maritíma* (Guérin), is a slate-colored species that is sometimes extremely abundant along the seashore between the tidemarks, where it is found on the surface of small pools, under stones, and crawling over the shore; these springtails cluster in air-filled pockets under submerged rocks at high tide. Another aquatic springtail, *Podùra aquática* L., occurs on the surface of the water along the edges of ponds and streams.

Family **Onychiùridae:** The members of this family are very similar to the Podùridae. *Tullbérgia granulàta* Mills is a common species that is usually found in abundance in agricultural soils. *Onychiùrus horténsis* Gisin is a species known to reproduce parthenogenetically.

Family **Isotómidae:** Most members of this family are brownish or whitish in color, but some are mottled. The marsh springtail, *Isotomùrus palústris* (Müller), is a common species occurring in moist woodlands, under leaves, and in moist soil, and it may sometimes be found on the surface of freshwater pools. *Isótoma propínqua* Axel-

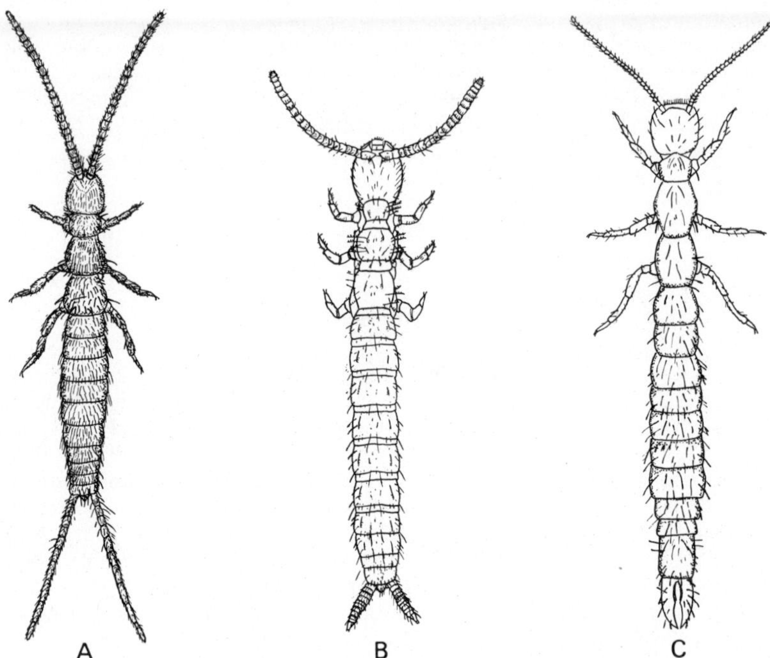

Figure 89. Diplurans. A, *Campòdea fòlsomi* Silvestri (Campodèidae); B, *Anajápyx vesiculòsus* Silvestri (Anajapýgidae); C, *Jápyx diversiúngis* Silvestri (Japýgidae). (Redrawn from Essig, by permission of Macmillan Company.)

son is one of several species that exhibit a phenomenon known as ecomorphosis; individuals developing at abnormally high temperatures differ considerably in form from those developing at lower temperatures, so much so that some have been described as belonging to different genera.

Family **Entomobrỳidae:** These springtails are very similar to the Isotómidae. *Orchesélla hexfasciàta* Harvey is a common yellow species with purple markings, and is found in leaf litter and under bark. *Tomócerus flavéscens* (Tullberg) is a common large species with long antennae that can be coiled; it occurs under bark, in leaf litter, and in sphagnum moss.

Family **Sminthùridae:** These springtails are minute, oval-bodied, usually yellowish insects with black eyes; they commonly occur on vegetation and are sometimes quite abundant. *Bourletiélla horténsis* (Fitch), the garden springtail, is blackish with some yellow, and occurs on various flowers and vegetables; it frequently causes considerable damage. The lucerne flea, *Sminthùrus víridis* (L.), is an important pest of alfalfa in Australia. *Pténothrix ùnicolor* (Harvey) is dull red to purplish, and is common in woodland litter.

ORDER **Diplùra**[3] – Diplurans: The diplurans are similar to the bristletails, but lack a median caudal filament and have only two caudal filaments or appendages, the body is not covered with scales, compound eyes are absent, and the tarsi are 1-segmented; the mouth parts are mandibulate, but are more or less withdrawn into the head. These insects are small (generally less than 7 mm in length) and usually pale-colored. They are found in damp places in the soil, under bark, under stones or logs, in rotting wood, in debris, and in similar situations.

---

[3] Diplùra: *dipl*, two; *ura*, tail.

Key to the Families of Diplùra

1. Cerci (of adults) 1-segmented and forcepslike (Figure 89 C) .... **Japýgidae** p. 155
1′. Cerci with more than 1 segment, and not forcepslike (Figure 89 A, B)... 2
2(1′). Cerci many-segmented, and as long as the antennae (Figure 89 A); styli on abdominal segments 2–7; palps absent; 4 mm or more in length .... **Campodèidae** p. 155
2′. Cerci shorter than antennae and with fewer segments (Figure 89 B); styli on abdominal segments 1–7; palps present; less than 4 mm in length .... **Anajapýgidae** p. 155

Family **Campodèidae:** This is the most commonly encountered family of diplurans; most are about 6 mm in length. A fairly common member of this family is *Campòdea staphylìnus* Westwood.

Family **Anajapýgidae:** This family is represented in the United States by a single rare species, *Anajápyx hermòsus* Smith, known only from California.

Family **Japýgidae:** This group is widely distributed, but its members are not often encountered; they can be recognized by the forcepslike cerci (Figure 89 C). Some tropical species reach a length of 20 mm.

ORDER **Thysanùra**[4] — Bristletails: The bristletails are moderate-sized to small insects, usually elongate in shape, with three taillike appendages at the posterior end of the abdomen and with stylelike appendages on some abdominal segments. The tarsi are 3- to 5-segmented. The paired caudal appendages are the cerci, and the third is the median caudal filament. The abdomen is 11-segmented, but the last segment is often much reduced. The mouth parts are of the chewing type. The body is nearly always covered with scales.

[4] Thysanùra: *thysan,* bristle or fringe; *ura,* tail.

Key to the Families of Thysanùra

1. Compound eyes large and usually contiguous; middle and hind coxae with styli; abdominal styli on segments 2–9; tarsi 3-segmented; jumping insects (Figure 90) .... **Machílidae** p. 157
1′. Compound eyes small and widely separated, or absent; middle and hind coxae without styli; abdominal styli variable; tarsi 3- to 5-segmented; running insects 2
2(1′). Ocelli present; body not covered with scales; tarsi 5-segmented; northern California .... **Lepidotríchidae** p. 155
2′. Ocelli absent; body usually covered with scales; tarsi 3- or 4-segmented 3
3(2′). Compound eyes present; body always covered with scales; widely distributed .... **Lepismátidae** p. 156
3′. Compound eyes absent; body with (Atelurìnae) or without (Nicoletiìnae) scales; Florida and Texas .... **Nicoletìidae** p. 155

Family **Lepidotríchidae** — Primitive Bristletails: This family is represented in the United States by a single species, *Tricholepídion gértschi* Wygodzinsky, which occurs under decaying bark and in rotten wood of fallen Douglas firs in northern California (Wygodzinsky, 1961). It is closely related to a species known only from Baltic amber (*Lépidothrix*). This species has a maximum body length of 12 mm, with the antennae reaching a length of 9 mm and the caudal appendages 14 mm.

Family **Nicoletìidae:** Most of our nicoletiids (Nicoletiìnae) are slender, 7 – 19 mm in length, and lack scales; others (Atelurìnae) are oval and have

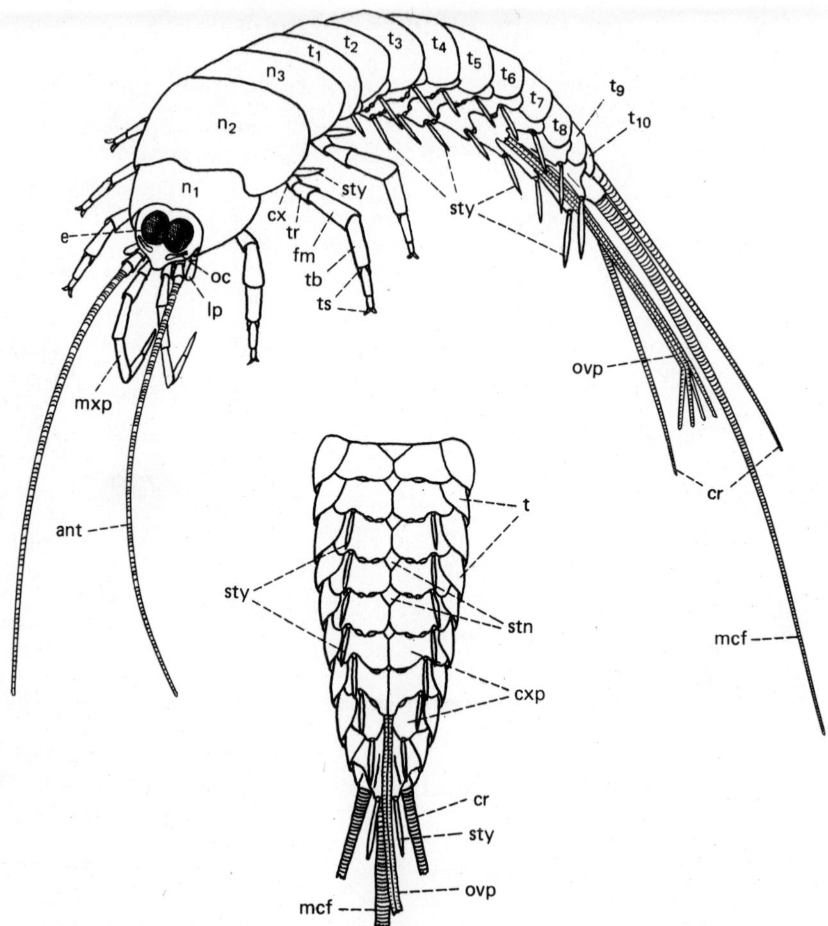

Figure 90. A jumping bristletail, *Máchilis* sp., female. Lower figure, ventral view of abdomen. *ant,* antenna; *cr,* cerci; *cx,* coxa; *cxp,* coxopodite of abdominal appendages; *e,* compound eye; *fm,* femur; *lp,* labial palp; *mcf,* median caudal filament; *mxp,* maxillary palp; n_{1-3}, thoracic nota; *oc,* ocellus; *ovp,* ovipositor (in the upper figure the gonapophyses forming the ovipositor are shown separated at the apex); *stn,* abdominal sternites; *sty,* styli; *t,* terga; *tb,* tibia; *tr,* trochanter; *ts,* tarsus.

the body covered with scales. The Nicoletiìnae occur in caves and mammal burrows, and the Atelurìnae occur in ant and termite nests. Four species have been reported from Florida and Texas, and all are quite rare.

Family **Lepismátidae:** The best known members of this family are the silverfish, *Lepísma saccharìna* L., and the firebrat, *Thermòbia doméstica* (Packard), which are domestic species inhabiting buildings. They feed on all sorts of starchy substances and frequently become pests. In libraries they feed on the starch in books, bindings, and labels; in dwellings they feed on starched clothing, curtains, linens, silks, and the starch paste in wallpaper; in stores they feed on paper, vegetables, and foods that contain starch. The silverfish is gray in color, a little less than half an inch in length, and is found in cool, damp situations. The firebrat (Figure 91) is tan or brown in color, about the same size as the silverfish, and frequents the warm situations around furnaces, boilers, and steampipes. Both species are quite active and can run rapidly. The lepismatids that occur outside buildings are found in caves, debris, under stones and leaves, and in ant nests.

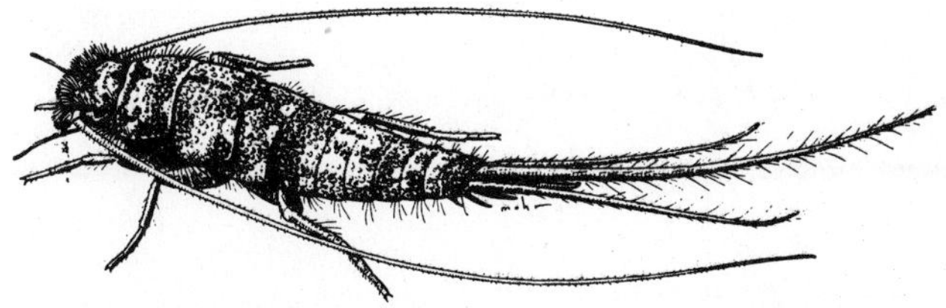

Figure 91. Firebrat, *Thermòbia doméstica* (Packard). (Courtesy of the Illinois Natural History Survey.)

Family **Machílidae**—Jumping Bristletails: These insects live in grassy and wooded areas under leaves, under bark or stones, in dead wood, and in similar habitats. The largest members of the group are about 15 mm in length. These insects are more cylindrical than the Lepismátidae. They are quite active and jump when disturbed.

This family is believed to represent a separate evolutionary line from the other Thysanùra. Styli are present on the coxae, which some authorities relate to the biramous appendages of the Crustàcea, and the mandibles have a single articulation with the head capsule (other Thysanùra, and all the Pterygòta, have two articulations).

COLLECTING AND PRESERVING APTERYGÒTA[5]

Indoor species like the silverfish and firebrat can be trapped (see page 727), or they may be collected with forceps or with a moistened brush. Most outdoor species can be collected by sifting debris or by looking under bark or stones and in fungi. Soil, leaf litter, or other material that may contain these insects can be sifted onto a white surface and the insects can be picked up with a moistened brush or an aspirator; many forms are easily collected by means of a Berlese funnel (see page 726). The springtails that occur on vegetation can be collected by "sweeping" the vegetation with a white enameled pan held at about a 30 degree angle to the ground; the insects falling or jumping into the pan can be easily seen and collected. The aquatic springtails can be collected with a dipper or tea strainer.

These insects should be preserved in 80–95 percent alcohol; it is necessary to mount the smaller forms on microscope slides for detailed study.

[5] See also Chapter 34.

References on the Apterygòta

Bellinger, P. F. 1954. Studies of soil fauna with special reference to the Collembola. *Bull. Conn. Agric. Expt. Sta.*, No. 583; 67 pp., 18 f.

Christiansen, K. 1964. Bionomics of Collembola. *Ann. Rev. Ent.*, 9:147–178.

Ewing, H. E. 1940. The Protura of North America. *Ann. Ent. Soc. Amer.*, 33(3):495–551; 32 f.

Folsom, J. W. 1913. North American springtails of the subfamily Tomocerinae. *Proc. U.S. Natl. Mus.*, 46(2037):451–472; pl. 40–41.

Folsom, J. W. 1916. North American collembolous insects of the subfamilies Achoreutinae, Neanurinae, and Podurinae. *Proc. U.S. Natl. Mus.*, 50(2134):477–525; pl. 7–25.

Folsom, J. W. 1917. North American collembolous insects of the subfamily Onychiurinae. *Proc. U.S. Natl. Mus.*, 53(2222):637–659; pl. 68–79.

Folsom, J. W. 1937. Nearctic Collembola, or springtails, of the family Isotomidae. *U.S. Natl. Mus. Bull.*, 168; 144 pp., 460 f.

Gisin, H. 1944. Hilfstabellen zum Bestimmen der holarktischen Collembolen. *Verhandl. Naturforsch. Ges. Basel*, 55:1–130.

Gisin, H. 1960. *Collembolenfauna Europas*. Geneva: Museum d'Histoire Naturelle. 312 pp., 554 f.

Guthrie, J. E. 1903. The Collembola of Minnesota. *Minn. Geol. and Nat. Hist. Survey*, Ser. 4; 110 pp., 16 pl.

Lubbock, J. 1873. Monograph of the Collembola and Thysanura. *Roy. Soc. London*, x + 276 pp., 78 pl.

MacGillivray, A. D. 1893. North American Thysanura. *Can. Ent.*, 25(5, 7, 9, 12): 127–128, 173–174, 218–220, 313–318.

Maynard, E. A. 1951. *A Monograph of the Collembola, or Springtail Insects of New York State*. Ithaca, N.Y.:

Comstock Publ., xxiv + 339 pp., 669 f.

Mills, H. B. 1934. *A Monograph of the Collembola of Iowa*. Ames, Iowa: Iowa State College Press, Monog. 3, Iowa State College, 143 pp., 12 pl., 183 f.

Paclt, J. 1956. *Biologie der primär flügellosen Insekten*. Jena, Germany: Gustav Fischer Verlag, vii + 258 pp., 138 f.

Paclt, J. 1963. Thysanura, family Nicoletiidae. *Genera Insectorum,* Fasc. 216e; 58 pp., 36 f.

Remington, C. L. 1954. The suprageneric classification of the order Thysanura (Insecta). *Ann. Ent. Soc. Amer.,* 47(2):277–286.

Richards, W. R. 1968. Generic classification, evolution, and biogeography of the Sminthuridae of the world (Collembola). *Mem. Ent. Soc. Can.,* 53:1–54.

Salmon, J. T. 1964–1965. An index to the Collembola. *Bull. Roy. Soc. New Zealand,* No. 7; Vol. 1, 1964, pp. 1–144; Vol. 2, 1964, pp. 145–644; Vol. 3, 1965, pp. 645–651.

Scott, H. G. 1961. Collembola: pictorial keys to the nearctic genera. *Ann. Ent. Soc. Amer.,* 54(1):104–113; illus.

Slabaugh, R. E. 1940. A new thysanuran, and a key to the domestic species of Lepismatidae (Thysanura) found in the United States. *Ent. News,* 51(4):95–98; 1 pl.

Smith, E. L. 1970. Biology and structure of some California bristletails and silverfish (Apterygota: Microcoryphia, Thysanura). *Pan-Pac. Ent.,* 46(3):212–225, 5 f.

Smith, L. M. 1960. The family Projapygidae and Anajapygidae (Diplura) in North America. *Ann. Ent. Soc. Amer.,* 53(5):575–583; 25 f.

Tuxen, S. L. 1959. The phylogenetic significance of entognathy in entognathous apterygotes. *Smiths. Misc. Coll.,* 137:379–416; 22 f.

Tuxen, S. L. 1964. *The Protura. A Revision of the Species of the World with Keys for Determination*. Paris: Hermann, 360 pp., 567 f.

Wygodzinsky, P. 1961. On a surviving representative of the Lepidotrichidae (Thysanura). *Ann. Ent. Soc. Amer.,* 54(5):621–627; 54 f.

Wygodzinsky, P. 1972. A revision of the silverfish (Lepismatidae, Thysanura) of the United States and the Caribbean area. *Amer. Mus. Novit.,* No. 2481; 26 pp., 10 f.

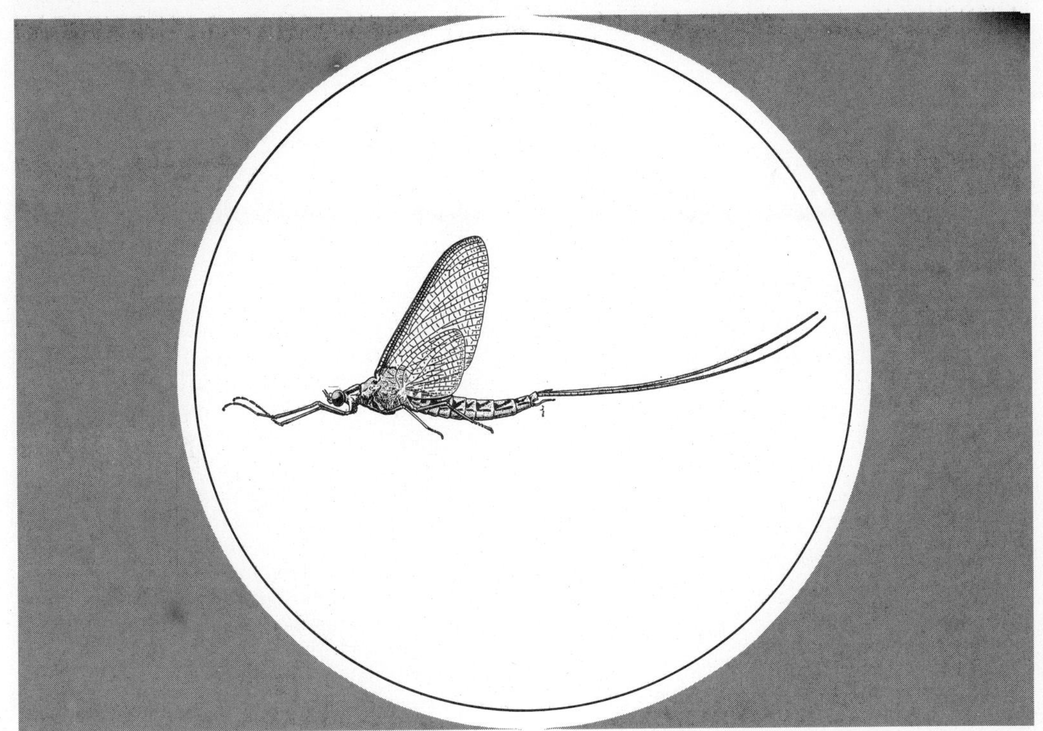

10: ORDER EPHEMERÓPTERA[1]

MAYFLIES

Mayflies are small to medium-sized, elongate, very soft-bodied insects with two or three long threadlike tails; they are often very common about ponds or streams. The adults (Figure 92) have membranous wings with numerous veins; the front wings are large and triangular, and the hind wings are small and rounded; in some species the hind wings are vestigial or absent. The wings at rest are held together above the body. The antennae are small, bristlelike, and inconspicuous. The immature stages are aquatic, and the metamorphosis is simple.

[1] Ephemeróptera; *ephemero,* for a day, short-lived; *ptera,* wings (referring to the short life of the adults).

Mayfly nymphs may be found in a variety of aquatic habitats. Some are streamlined in form and very active; others are burrowing in habit. They can usually be recognized by the leaflike or plumose gills along the sides of the abdomen and the three (rarely two) long tails (Figure 93); stonefly nymphs are similar (Figures 140 B and 141), but have only two tails (the cerci), and the gills are on the thorax (only rarely on the abdomen) and are not leaflike. When ready to transform to the winged stage, the nymph rises to the surface of the water, molts, and the winged form flies a short distance to the shore where it usually alights on the vegetation. This insect, which is usually dull in appearance and more or less pubescent, is not the

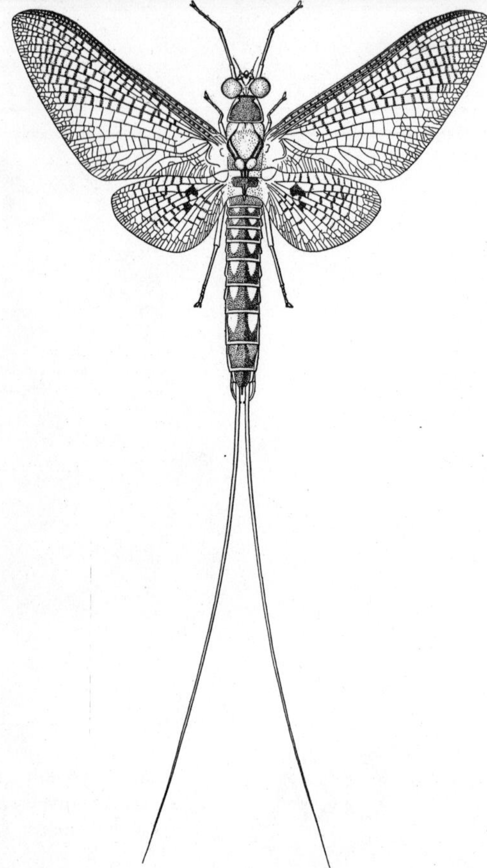

Figure 92. A mayfly, *Hexagènia bilineàta* (Say) (Ephemèridae). (Courtesy of Needham and the Bureau of Fisheries.)

adult stage, and is called a subimago; it molts once more, usually the next day, to become the adult. The adult is usually smooth and shining, and has longer tails and legs than the subimago. The mayflies are the only insects that molt after the wings become functional. The aquatic stages require a year or more to develop, but the adults, which have vestigial mouth parts and do not feed, seldom live more than a day or two.

Adult mayflies often engage in rather spectacular swarming flights during which mating takes place. The individuals in a swarm are usually all males, and they often fly up and down in unison. Sooner or later females will enter the swarm, and a male will seize a female and fly away with her.

The eggs are laid on the surface of the water or are attached to vegetation or stones in the water. In cases where the eggs are laid on the surface of the water, they may simply be washed off the end of the abdomen a few at a time, or they may be all laid in one clump. Each species has characteristic egg-laying habits.

Mayflies often emerge in enormous numbers from lakes and rivers, and sometimes may pile up along the shore or on nearby roads and streets. Piles as deep as four feet have been observed on roads in Illinois (Burks, 1953), causing serious traffic problems; such enormous emergences are often a considerable nuisance. Up until about the middle fifties, mass emergences of this sort occurred along the shores of Lake Erie, but changes in the lake (increased pollution) in recent years have greatly reduced the numbers of these insects (and also the numbers of many fish), and their emergences now are not as striking as they used to be.

The chief importance of mayflies lies in their value as food for fish; both adults and nymphs are an important food for many freshwater fish, and many artificial flies used by fishermen are modeled after these insects. Mayflies also serve as food for many other animals, including birds, amphibians, spiders, and many predaceous insects. Most species of mayflies are restricted in the nymphal stages to particular types of aquatic habitats, hence the mayfly fauna of an aquatic habitat may serve as an indicator of the ecological characteristics (including degree of pollution) of that habitat.

CLASSIFICATION OF THE EPHEMERÓPTERA

Needham, Traver, and Hsu (1935) recognize only three families of Ephemeróptera, but most present workers recognize more families. We follow here the classification of Edmunds (1962a), who classifies the North American species in 5 superfamilies and 15 families, based on characters of both adults and nymphs. This classification is outlined below, with other names or arrangements in parentheses.

Superfamily Heptageniòidea
- Siphlonùridae (Siphlùridae; Baètidae in part)
  - Siphlonurìnae (6 genera)
  - Isonychiìnae (1 genus: *Isonýchia*)
- Baètidae (Baetìnae of Baètidae) (9 genera)

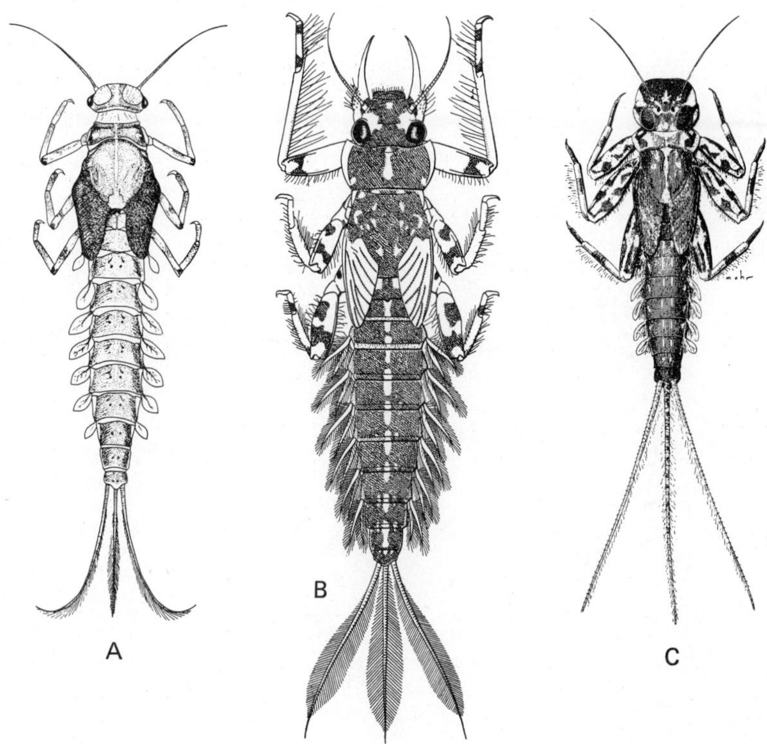

Figure 93. Mayfly nymphs. A, *Baètis hiemàlis* Leonard (Baètidae); B, *Potamánthus* sp. (Potamánthidae); C, *Heptagènia diabàsia* Burks (Heptagenìidae). (A, courtesy of Leonard and the Entomological Society of America; B, courtesy of Needham and the Bureau of Fisheries; C, courtesy of Burks and the Entomological Society of America.)

Oligoneurìidae (2 genera: *Homoeoneùria, Lachlània*)
Heptagenìidae (Ecydùridae, Ecydonùridae; Ametrópidae in part)
Heptageniìnae (6 genera)
Anepeorìnae (1 genus: *Anepeòrus*)
Arthropleìnae (1 genus: *Arthróplea*)
Pseudironìnae (1 genus: *Pseudìron*)
Ametropódidae (Ametrópidae; Baètidae in part)
Ametropodìnae (1 genus: *Amétropus*)
Metretopodìnae (2 genera: *Metrétopus, Siphloplécton*)
Superfamily Leptophlebiòidea
Leptophlebìidae (Baètidae in part) (7 genera)
Ephemeréllidae (Baètidae in part) (1 genus: *Ephemerélla*)
Tricorýthidae (Caènidae in part, Ephemeréllidae in part) (2 genera: *Leptohỳphes, Tricorythòdes*)
Superfamily Caenòidea
Neoephemèridae (Ephemèridae in part) (1 genus: *Neoemphémera*)
Caènidae (Baètidae in part) (2 genera: *Brachycércus, Caènis*)
Superfamily Prosopistomatòidea
Baetíscidae (Baètidae in part) (1 genus: *Baetísca*)

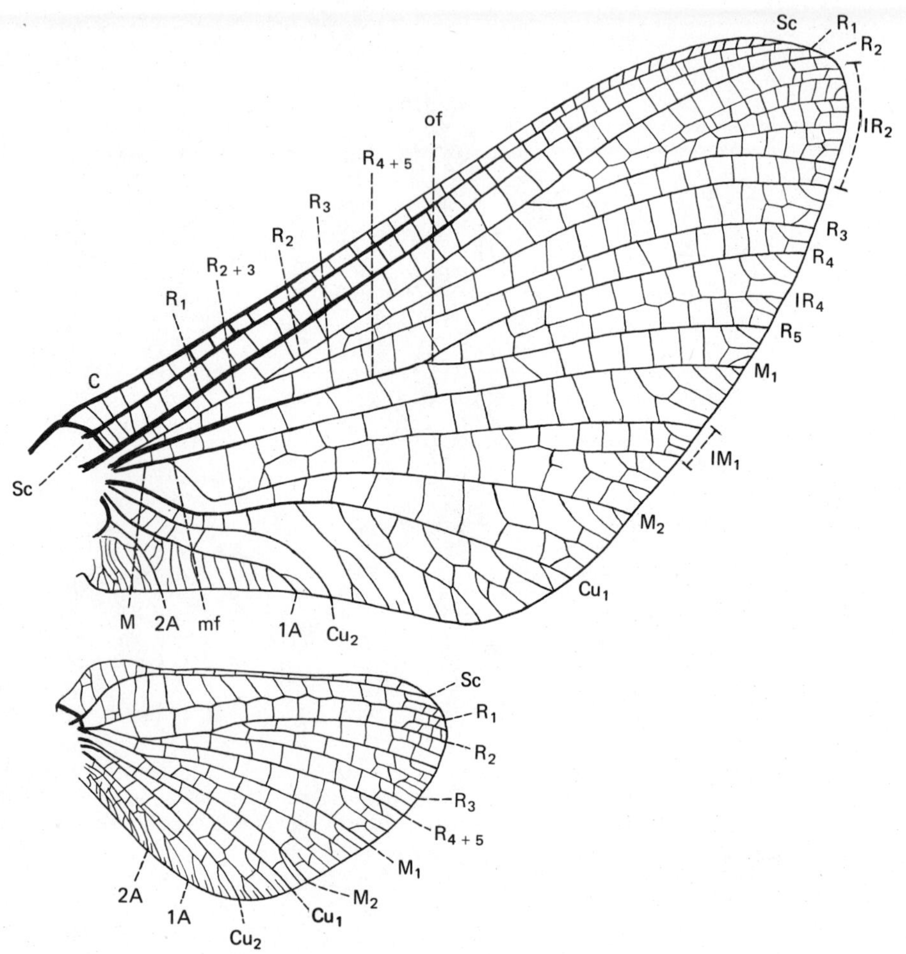

Figure 94. Wings of *Pentagènia* (Epheméridae). *mf,* fork of M; *of,* outer fork.

Superfamily Ephemeroìdea
- Potamánthidae (Epheméridae in part) (1 genus: *Potamánthus*)
- Behningìidae (1 genus: *Dolània*)
- Epheméridae (Ephemerìnae) (3 genera: *Ephémera, Hexagènia, Pentagènia*)
- Polymitárcidae (Epheméridae in part)
  - Polymitarcìnae (1 genus: *Éphoron*)
  - Campsurìnae (2 genera: *Campsùrus, Tórtopus*)

Key to the Families of Epheméroptera

This key includes all the families of North American mayflies except the Behningìidae, which is known in North America only from nymphs. The venational terminology is that of Needham, Traver, and Hsu (1935), which is illustrated in Figure 94. Keys to mayfly nymphs are given by Edmunds, Allen, and Peters (1963).

1. Veins M and Cu_1 in front wing strongly divergent at base, with M_2 bent strongly toward Cu_1 basally (Figure 94); outer fork in hind wing lacking; hind tarsi 4-segmented 2

1′. Veins M and Cu_1 in front wing not very divergent at base, and M_2 (M rarely is unbranched) not strongly bent toward Cu_1 basally (Figures 95 A, B, and 96 B–E); outer fork in hind wing present or absent; hind tarsi 3- to 5-segmented 6

2(1). M_1 and M_2 in hind wing separating beyond middle of wing; hind wing with an acute costal projection near base (Figure 95 C); 3 tails in both sexes .... **Neoepheméridae** p. 166

2′. M_1 and M_2 in hind wing separating proximad of middle of wing (Figure 94); hind wing usually without a costal projection; 2 or 3 tails 3

3(2′). Sc and R_1 in front wing curved backward at apex and continuing around apical angle of wing (Figure 95 D); marginal veinlets wanting; middle and hind legs reduced or atrophied beyond trochanters (Campsurìnae) .... **Polymitárcidae** p. 167

3′. Sc and R_1 in front wing straight at apex, not continuing around apical angle of wing (Figure 94); marginal veinlets present; middle and hind legs not reduced or atrophied 4

4(3′). Cubital intercalaries in front wing straight, not attached at base to Cu_1 (Figure 95 E, *ICu*); marginal veinlets in front wing very numerous (Polymitarcìnae) .... **Polymitárcidae** p. 167

4′. Cubital intercalaries in front wing sinuate, attached at base to Cu_1 (Figure 94); marginal veinlets in front wing relatively few in number 5

5(4′). 1A in front wing forked near margin of wing (Figure 96 A) ... **Potamánthidae** p. 167

5′. 1A in front wing not forked (Figure 94) .... **Epheméridae** p. 167

6(1′). Hind tarsi 5-segmented; cubital intercalaries in front wing in 2 parallel pairs, long and short alternately (Figure 95 A); venation never greatly reduced, outer fork in hind wing usually present .... **Heptagenìidae** p. 166

6′. Hind tarsi 3- or 4-segmented; cubital intercalaries in front wing usually not in 2 parallel pairs (Figure 95 B); venation sometimes greatly reduced, outer fork in hind wing present or absent 7

7(6′). Lateral ocelli very large, about half as large as compound eyes; hind wings absent; 3 tails 8

7′. Lateral ocelli smaller, not more than one fourth as large as compound eyes; hind wings present or absent; 2 or 3 tails 9

8(7). Front wing with very few cross veins and with medial intercalary extending to wing base; male genital forceps 1-segmented .... **Caènidae** p. 166

8′. Front wing with a number of cross veins and with medial intercalary not extending to wing base; male genital forceps 3-segmented ... **Tricorýthidae** p. 166

9(7′). Sc in front wing absent or fused with R; M unbranched (Figure 96 B) .... **Oligoneurìidae** p. 166

9′. Sc in front wing distinct, extending to apex of wing; M usually branched 10

10(9′). Cubital intercalaries of front wing absent (Figure 96 C); cross veins near middle of front wing weak and netlike; 1A in front wing extending to outer margin of wing; 2 tails .... **Baetíscidae** p. 167

10′. Cubital intercalaries of front wing present (Figure 96 D, E); cross veins near middle of front wing not netlike; 1A in front wing ending in hind margin of wing; 2 or 3 tails 11

11(10′). Front wing with 1 or 2 long intercalaries between M_2 and Cu_1 (Figure 96 D), *IM*$_2$) .... **Ephemeréllidae** p. 166

11′. Front wing without long intercalaries between M_2 and Cu_1 12

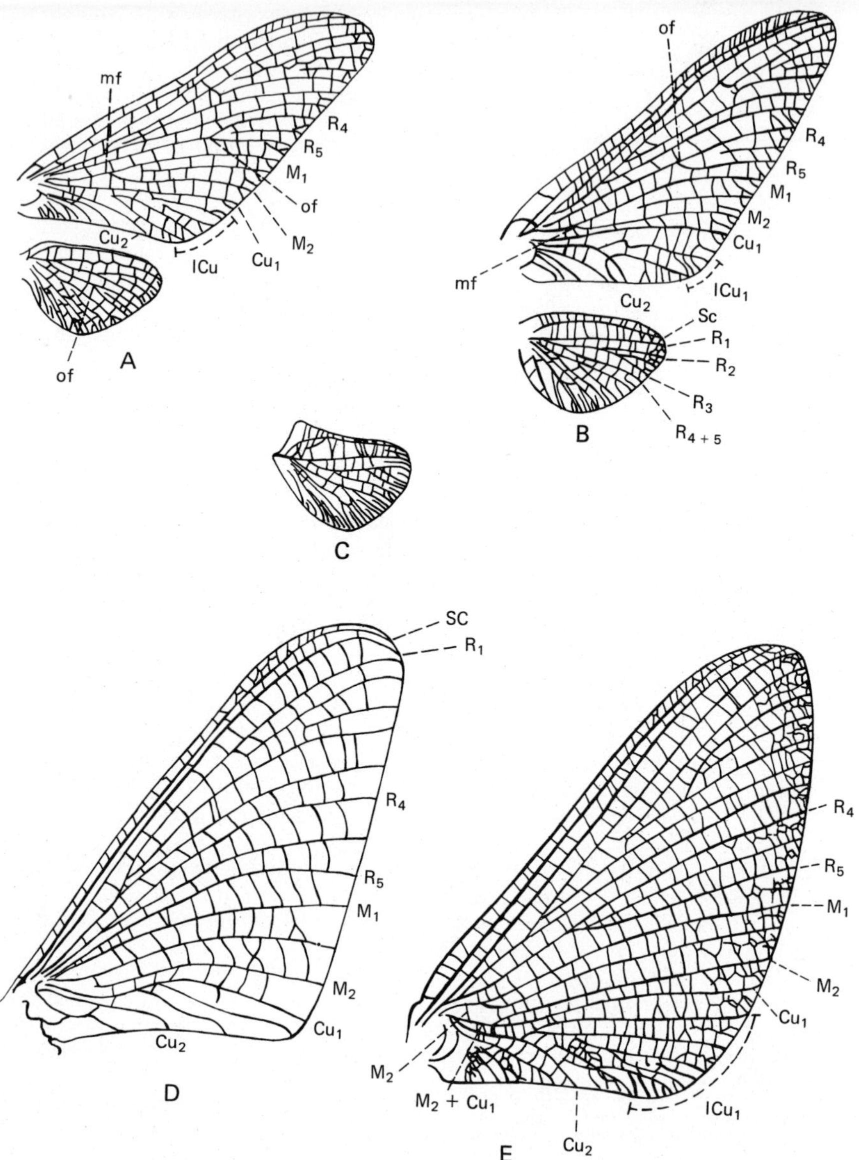

Figure 95. Wings of Ephemeróptera. A, a heptageniid; B, *Leptophlèbia* (Leptophlebìidae); C, hind wing of *Neoephémera* (Neoepheméridae); D, front wing of *Tórtopus* (Campsurìnae, Polymitárcidae); E, front wing of *Ephoron* (Polymitarcìnae, Polymitárcidae). *mf,* fork of M; *of,* outer fork. (C–E, redrawn from Burks.)

12(11′). Cu_2 in front wing angularly bent toward hind margin of wing (Figure 95 B); 3 tails, the median one often smaller .... **Leptophlebìidae** p. 166

12′. Cu_2 in front wing straight or evenly curved; 2 or 3 tails 13

13(12′). Cubital intercalaries of front wing consisting of 1 or 2 pairs of long parallel veins (Figure 96 E); no free marginal veinlets; hind wings always present 14

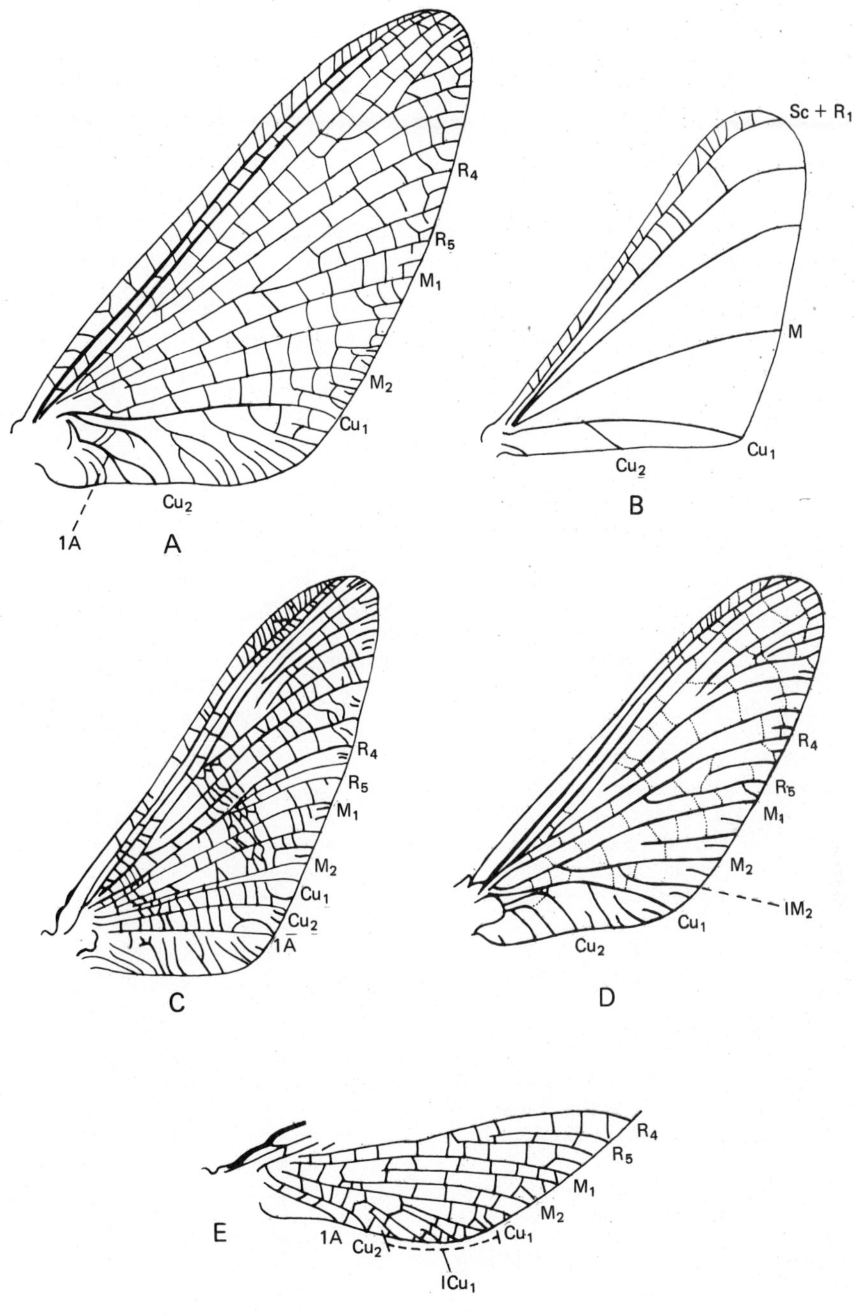

Figure 96. Wings of Ephemeróptera. A, front wing of *Potamánthus* (Potamánthidae); B, front wing of *Oligoneùria* (Oligoneurìidae); C, front wing of *Baetísca* (Baetíscidae); D, front wing of *Ephemerélla* (Ephemeréllidae); E, hind part of front wing of *Siphloplécton* (Ametropódidae). (Redrawn from Burks.)

13′. Cubital intercalaries of front wing either a series of short, slightly sinuate veins extending from Cu_1 to hind margin of wing, or 1 or 2 long basally detached veins and free marginal veinlets; hind wings present or absent ... 15

14(13). First segment of tarsi of male only about three fourths as long as second segment; ninth abdominal sternum of female extended caudad, and with a pronounced median notch on posterior margin (*Pseudìron*) .... **Heptagenìidae** p. 166

14′. First segment of front tarsi of male slightly longer than second segment; ninth abdominal sternum of female not extended caudad, and without a median notch on posterior margin .... **Ametropódidae** p. 166

15(13′). M_2 in front wing detached at base from stem of M; hind wings reduced or lacking; hind tarsi 3-segmented .... **Baètidae** p. 166

15′. M_2 in front wing not detached at base from stem of M; hind wings well developed; hind tarsi 4-segmented .... **Siphlonùridae** p. 166

Family **Siphlonùridae:** The nymphs of these mayflies are streamlined in form, and occur principally in rapidly flowing streams and rivers; at least some are predaceous. The adults have the compound eyes large and more or less two-parted; the Siphlonurìnae have M in the hind wing unforked, or forked in the basal half, while the Isonychiìnae have M in the hind wing forked near the outer margin of the wing. This is a fairly large group (82 North American species), and its members are widely distributed.

Family **Baètidae:** This is the largest family of mayflies in our area, with 140 North American species; its members are common and widely distributed, and the nymphs occur in a variety of aquatic habitats. The adults are small, and have the hind wings reduced or lacking; the compound eyes are large and two-parted in the male, and simple and small in the female.

Family **Oligoneurìidae:** The nymphs of this group occur in shallow, rapid streams with sandy bottoms. The adults have a reduced wing venation; the front wings lack Sc and have M unbranched, and there are few or no cross veins in the hind wings (Figure 96 B). The group is small (4 North American species) but widely distributed.

Family **Heptagenìidae:** The nymphs of these mayflies are sprawling forms, usually dark-colored, with the head and body flattened (Figure 93 C). Most species occur on the underside of stones in streams, but some occur in sandy rivers and boggy ponds. The adults are medium-sized, usually without spots on the wings. This is the second largest mayfly family, with 128 North American species.

Family **Ametropódidae:** These mayflies have a wing venation very similar to that in the Heptagenìidae (Figure 96 E), but have the hind tarsi 4-segmented; the front tarsi of the males are three to five times as long as the front tibiae. The nymphs are mostly stream forms.

Family **Leptophlebìidae:** The mayflies in this family have the venation fairly complete, and can usually be recognized by the form of Cu_2 in the front wings (bent sharply caudad at about midlength; see Figure 95 B). The nymphs occur in standing water or in water with a reduced current. This group is widely distributed, with 61 North American species.

Family **Ephemeréllidae:** These mayflies are small to medium-sized, and usually brownish; the adults live three or four days, and are strong fliers. The nymphs generally occur under rocks or debris in cool, clear, rapid streams or small clear lakes. The group is widely distributed, but is more common in the northern and western parts of the United States.

Family **Tricorýthidae:** This is a small but widely distributed group whose nymphs occur in streams and rivers. The nymphs are sprawling forms, flattened and hairy, with the body tapering caudad, and with the lateral margins of segments 2–9 produced into flattened spines or plates. The adults are small (6–7 mm in length), whitish to brownish black in color, with large lateral ocelli, three tails, and with the hind wings lacking.

Family **Caènidae:** These mayflies are very similar to the Tricorýthidae. The adults of these two families may be separated by the characters given in the key (couplet 8).

Family **Neoephemèridae:** These mayflies are similar to the ephemerids, but have the costal cross veins in the front wing somewhat reduced and have an acute costal projection near the base of the hind wing (Figure 95 C). The nymphs occur in small streams and rivers, and are somewhat similar to those of the Tricorýthidae. Four species, in the genus *Neoephémera,* occur in the eastern United States.

Family **Baetíscidae:** These mayflies have only two tails, and there are no cubital intercalaries in the front wings; the wings are hyaline or tinged with reddish or orange, and the outer margin of the front wings is slightly scalloped. This group is widely distributed but is more common in the eastern United States; the nymphs occurs in cool, fairly rapid streams.

Family **Potamánthidae:** The nymphs of this group (Figure 93 B) occur on sandy or silty stream bottoms. Our eight species (in the genus *Potamánthus*) occur principally in the eastern United States.

Family **Behningìidae:** This group is represented in North America by a single species, *Dolània americàna* Edmunds and Traver, which is known only from the nymph. A few nymphs of this species have been taken in South Carolina, where they burrow in the sand at the bottom of large rivers.

Family **Epheméridae:** The nymphs of these mayflies have long mandibles and plumose gills, and are usually burrowing in habit; the adults are usually large insects with numerous cross veins in the wings (Figure 92). The nymphs occur in large streams and lakes; the adults sometimes emerge in large numbers. The wings are spotted in *Ephémera* and clear or nearly so in *Hexagènia* and *Pentagènia.*

Family **Polymitárcidae:** These mayflies are similar to the ephemerids; they may be recognized (and the two subfamilies separated) by the characters given in the key. The nymphs are burrowing in habit, and burrow into the mud or clay at the bottoms of large rivers and lakes.

COLLECTING AND PRESERVING EPHEMEROPTERA

Adult mayflies may be captured by simply picking them up with the fingers, or they may be collected with a net. Nets are useful in capturing mayflies from swarms and in sweeping vegetation for them. The adults are extremely fragile and must be handled with considerable care. They should be preserved in 70–80 percent alcohol; specimens that are pinned or preserved in envelopes often shrivel and are easily broken.

Nymphs may be collected in various types of aquatic habitats by the usual methods of collecting aquatic insects. They should be preserved in 70–80 percent alcohol.

References on the Ephemeróptera

Berner, L. 1950. *The Mayflies of Florida.* Gainesville: Univ. Florida Press, xii + 267 pp., 24 pl., 88 f., 19 maps.

Britt, N. W. 1962. Biology of two species of Lake Erie mayflies, *Ephoron album* (Say) and *Ephemera simulans* Walker. *Bull. Ohio Biol. Survey* (New Series), 1(5):1–70; 28 f.

Burks, B. D. 1953. The mayflies, or Ephemeroptera, of Illinois. *Ill. Nat. Hist. Surv. Bull.,* 26(1):1–216; 395 f.

Day, W. C. 1956. Ephemeroptera. In *Aquatic Insects of California,* R. L. Usinger (Ed.). Berkeley: Univ. California Press, pp. 79–105; 28 f.

Edmunds, G. F., Jr. 1959. Ephemeroptera. In *Freshwater Biology,* W. T. Edmondson (Ed.). New York: Wiley, pp. 908–916; 39 f.

Edmunds, G. F., Jr. 1962a. The principles applied in determining the hierarchic level of the higher categories of Ephemeroptera. *Syst. Zool.,* 11(1):22–31; 1 f.

Edmunds, G. F., Jr. 1962b. The type localities of the Ephemeroptera of North America north of Mexico. *Univ. Utah Biol. Ser.,* 12(5):viii + 1–39.

Edmunds, G. F., Jr. 1972. Biogeography and evolution of the Ephemeroptera. *Ann. Rev. Ent.,* 17:21–42; 1 f.

Edmunds, G. F., Jr., and R. K. Allen. 1957. A checklist of the Ephemeroptera of North America north of Mexico. *Ann. Ent. Soc. Amer.,* 50(4):317–324.

Edmunds, G. F., Jr., R. K. Allen, and W. L. Peters. 1963. An annotated key to the nymphs of the families and subfamilies of mayflies (Ephemeroptera). *Univ. Utah Biol. Ser.,* 13(1):1–49; 20 pl.

Edmunds, G. F., Jr., L. Berner, and J. R. Traver. 1958. North American mayflies of the family Oligoneuridae. *Ann. Ent. Soc. Amer.,* 51(4):375–382; 31 f.

Edmunds, G. F., Jr., and J. R. Traver. 1954a. An outline of a reclassification of the Ephemeroptera. *Proc. Amer. Ent. Soc.,* 56:236–240.

Edmunds, G. F., Jr., and J. R. Traver. 1954b. The flight mechanics and evolution of the wings of Ephemeroptera, with notes on the archetype wing. *J. Wash. Acad. Sci.*, 44(12):390–400; 14 f.

Edmunds, G. F., Jr., and J. R. Traver. 1959. The classification of the Ephemeroptera. I. Ephemeroidea: Behningiidae. *Ann. Ent. Soc. Amer.*, 52(1):43–51; 32 f.

Needham, J. G. 1920. Burrowing mayflies of our larger lakes and streams. *Bull. U. S. Bur. Fish.*, 36:269–292; 73 f.

Needham, J. G., J. R. Traver, and Y.-C. Hsu. 1935. *The Biology of Mayflies, With a Systematic Account of North American Species.* Ithaca, N.Y.: Comstock Publ., xiv + 759 pp., 168 f., 40 pl.

Pennak, R. W. 1953. *Fresh-Water Invertebrates of the United States.* New York: Ronald Press, ix + 769 pp., 470 f.

Peters, W. L., and G. F. Edmunds, Jr. 1970. Revision of the generic classification of the eastern hemisphere Leptophlebiidae (Ephemeroptera). *Pacific Insects*, 12(1):157–240; 356 f.

Thew, T. B. 1960. Revision of the genera of the family Caenidae (Ephemeroptera). *Trans. Amer. Ent. Soc.*, 86:187–205; 3 f.

Traver, J. R. 1932–1933. Mayflies of North Carolina. *J. Elisha Mitchell Sci. Soc.*, 47(1):85–161, pl. 5–12 (1932); 47(2):163–236 (1932); 48(2):141–206, pl. 15 (1933).

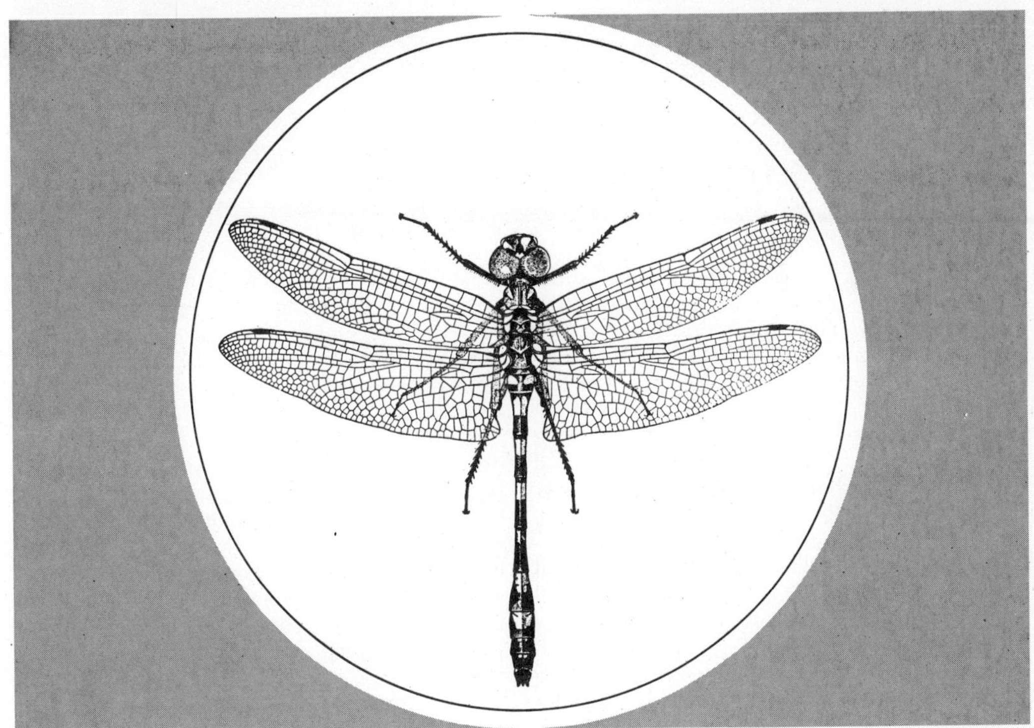

11: ORDER ODONÀTA[1]
DRAGONFLIES AND DAMSELFLIES

The Odonàta are relatively large and often beautifully colored insects that spend a large part of their time on the wing. The immature stages are aquatic, and the adults are usually found near water. All stages are predaceous and feed on various insects and other organisms, and from man's point of view, are generally very beneficial. The adults are harmless to man, that is, they do not bite or sting.

Adult dragonflies and damselflies are easily recognized (Figures 106–109): the four wings are elongate, many-veined, and membranous; the compound eyes are large and many-faceted, and often occupy most of the head; the thorax is relatively small and compact (the prothorax is always small, and the other two thoracic segments make up most of the thorax), and the dorsal surface of the pterothorax, between the pronotum and the base of the wings, is formed by pleural sclerites. The antennae are very small and bristlelike. The abdomen is long and slender; the cerci are 1-segmented and function as clasping organs in the male. The mouth parts are of the chewing type, and the metamorphosis is simple.

Present-day Odonàta vary in length from about $\frac{3}{4}$ inch to over 5 inches (19–127 mm); the largest dragonfly known,[2] which lived about 250 million years ago and is known only from fossils, had a

[1] Odonàta: from the Greek, meaning tooth (referring to the teeth on the mandibles).

[2] *Meganeùra mònyi* Brongniart, usually placed in the extinct order Megasecóptera.

wing spread of about $2\frac{1}{2}$ feet (640 mm)! The largest dragonflies in this country are about $3\frac{1}{4}$ inches (83 mm) in length, though they often look much larger when seen on the wing.

Odonàta nymphs are aquatic and breathe by means of gills. The gills of damselfly nymphs (Zygóptera) are in the form of three leaflike structures at the end of the abdomen (Figure 103); these nymphs swim by body undulations, the gills functioning like the tail of a fish. The gills of dragonfly nymphs (Anisóptera) (Figures 105 and 106 A, B) are in the form of ridges in the rectum; when a dragonfly nymph breathes, it draws water into the rectum through the anus and then expels it. If the insect is "in a hurry," this expulsion of water from the anus is the chief means of locomotion, and the insect moves by "jet" propulsion.

The nymphs vary somewhat in habits, but all are aquatic and feed on various sorts of small aquatic organisms. They usually lie in wait for their prey, either on a plant or more or less buried in the mud. The prey is generally small, but some of the larger nymphs (particularly Aéshnidae) occasionally attack tadpoles and small fish. The nymphs have the labium modified into a peculiar segmented structure with which the prey is captured. The labium is folded under the head when not in use; when used, it is thrust forward, usually very quickly, and the prey is grabbed by two movable clawlike lobes (the lateral lobes or palps) at the tip of the labium (Figure 104). The labium, when extended, is usually at least a third as long as the body (Figure 106 B).

When a nymph is fully grown, it crawls up out of the water, usually on a plant stem or rock (and usually early in the morning), and undergoes its final molt; the nymphs of some species wander many yards from the water before molting. Once out of the last nymphal skin, the adult expands to its full size in about half an hour. The flight of newly emerged adults is relatively feeble, and they are very easy to catch, but they make poor specimens. They are not yet fully colored, and they are very soft-bodied. It is usually a few days before the insect's full powers of flight are developed, and it may be a week or two before the color pattern is fully developed. Many Odonàta have quite a different color or color pattern the first few days of their adult life than they will have after a week or two. Newly emerged, pale, soft-bodied adults are usually spoken of as *teneral* individuals.

The two sexes in the suborder Anisóptera are usually similarly colored, though the colors of the male are frequently brighter. In some of the Libellùlidae the two sexes differ in the color pattern on the wings. The two sexes are differently colored in most of the Zygóptera, and the male is usually the more brightly colored. In most of the Coenagriónidae the two sexes have a different color pattern. Some damselflies have two or more different color phases in the female; for example, most females of *Ischnùra verticàlis* (Say) have a color pattern that is different from that of the male, and are either orange and black (newly emerged) or rather uniformly bluish (older individuals), but a few females have a color pattern that is similar to that of the male.

Some species of Odonàta are on the wing for only a few weeks each year, whereas others may be seen throughout the summer or over a period of several months. Observations of marked individuals indicate that the average damselfly probably has a maximum adult life of three or four weeks, and some dragonflies may live six or eight weeks. Most species have a single generation a year, with the egg or nymph (usually the nymph) overwintering. A few of the larger darners are known to spend two or three years in the nymphal stage.

Dragonflies and damselflies are peculiar among insects in having the copulatory organs of the male located at the anterior end of the abdomen, on the ventral side of the second abdominal segment; the male genitalia of other insects are located at the posterior end of the abdomen. Before mating, the male dragonfly must transfer sperm from the genital opening on the ninth segment to the structures on the second segment; this is done by bending the abdomen downward and forward.

The two sexes frequently spend considerable time "in tandem," with the male clasping the female by the back of the head or the prothorax with the appendages at the end of his abdomen. Copulation, with the female bending her abdomen downward and forward and contacting the second segment genitalia of the male, usually occurs in flight.

Odonàta lay their eggs in or near water, and may do so while in tandem or when alone. In some species where the female detaches from the male before beginning oviposition, the male will remain nearby "on guard" while the female is ovipositing, and will chase off other males that come near. An unprotected female, after she begins ovipositing, may be interrupted by another male, who may grab her and fly off in tandem with her.

Females of the Gómphidae, Macromìidae, Cordulìidae, and Libellùlidae do not have an ovipositor, and the eggs are generally laid on the

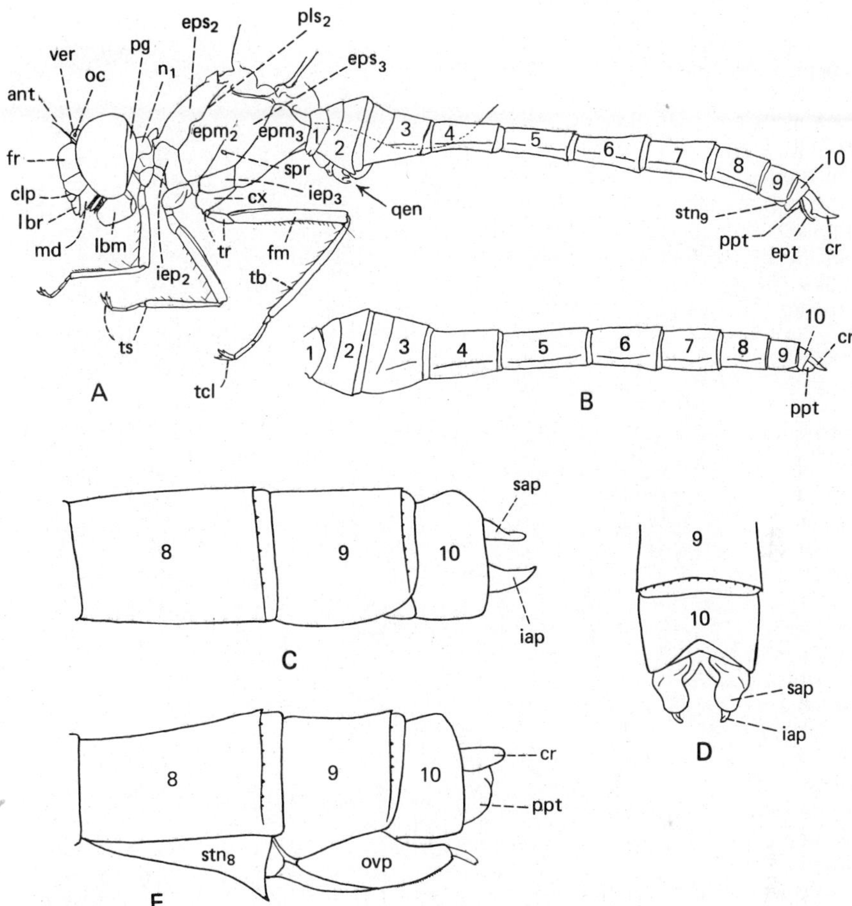

Figure 97. Structural characters of Odonàta. A, lateral view of *Sympètrum intérnum* Montgomery, male; B, lateral view of abdomen of *S. intérnum,* female; C, terminal abdominal segments of *Enallágma hágeni* (Walsh), male, lateral view; D, same, dorsal view; E, terminal abdominal segments of *E. hágeni,* female, lateral view. *ant,* antenna; *clp,* clypeus; *cr,* cerci or superior appendages; *cx,* coxa; e, compound eye; epm_2, mesepimeron; epm_3, metepimeron; eps_2, mesepisternum; eps_3, metepisternum; *ept,* epiproct or inferior appendage; *fm,* femur; *fr,* frons; *gen,* male copulatory apparatus; *iap,* inferior appendage; iep_2, mesinfraepisternum; iep_3, metinfraepisternum; *lbm,* labium; *lbr,* labrum; *md,* mandible; n_1, pronotum; *oc,* ocellus; *ovp,* ovipositor; *pg,* postgena; pls_2, mesopleural or humeral suture; *ppt,* paraproct; *sap,* superior appendage or, cercus; *spr,* spiracle; *stn,* sternum; *tb,* tibia; *tcl,* tarsal claws; *tr,* trochanter; *ts,* tarsus; *ver,* vertex; *1–10,* abdominal segments.

surface of the water by the female flying low and dipping her abdomen in the water and washing off the eggs; the females of most species in these groups are alone when ovipositing. A somewhat rudimentary ovipositor is developed in the Cordulegástridae, which oviposit by hovering above shallow water with the body in a more or less vertical position, and repeatedly jabbing the abdomen into the water and laying the eggs in the bottom. The females of the other groups (Aéshnidae, Petalùridae, and all Zygóptera) have a well-developed ovipositor (Figure 97 E), and insert their eggs in plant tissues (in many species while still in tandem with the male). The eggs are usually inserted just below the surface of the water, no farther than the female can reach, but in a few cases (for example, some species of *Léstes*) the eggs are laid in plant stems above the water line, and in a

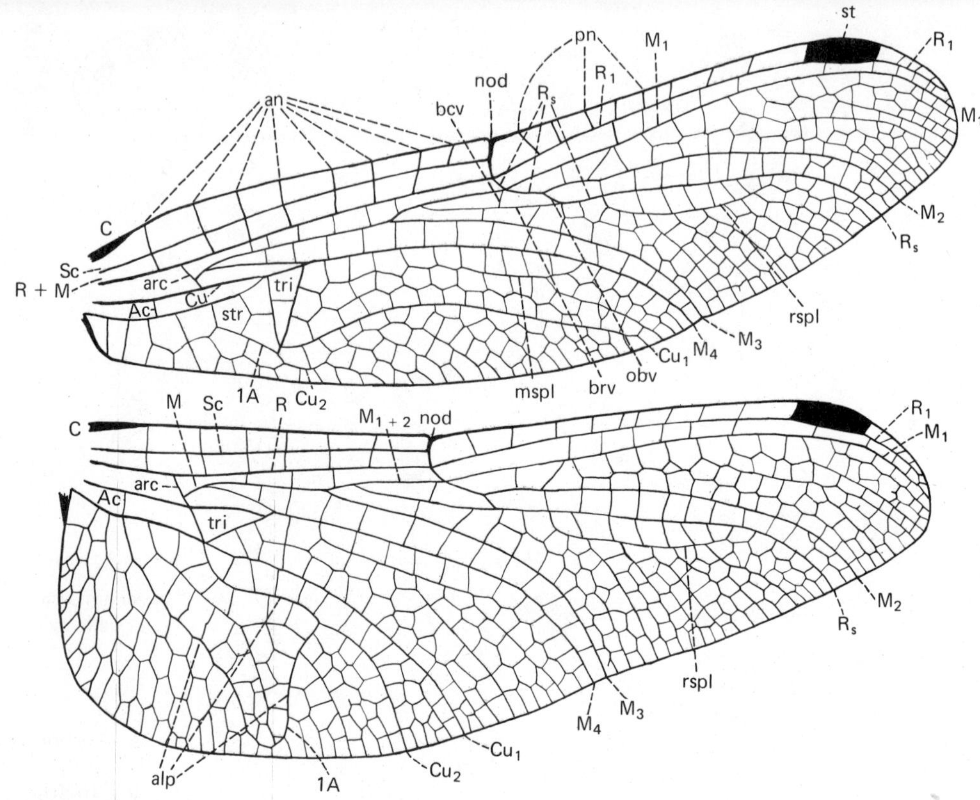

Figure 98. Wings of *Sympètrum rubicùndulum* (Say) (Libellùlidae), showing the Comstock–Needham system of terminology. *Ac,* anal crossing (A branching posteriorly from Cu; often called the cubitoanal cross vein); *alp,* anal loop (foot-shaped in this species); *an,* antenodal cross veins; *arc,* arculus (the upper part is M, the lower part is a cross vein); *bcv,* bridge cross vein; *brv,* bridge vein; *mspl,* median supplement; *nod,* nodus; *obv,* oblique vein; *pn,* postnodal cross veins; *rspl,* radial supplement; *st,* stigma; *str,* subtriangle (3-celled in this wing); *tri,* triangle (2-celled in front wing, 1-celled in hind wing). The usual symbols are used for other venational characters.

few other cases (for example, some species of *Enallágma*) the female may climb down a plant stem and insert her eggs into the plant a foot or more below the surface of the water. The eggs usually hatch in one to three weeks, but in some species (for example, *Léstes*) overwinter and hatch the following spring.

Most species of Odonàta have characteristic habits of flight. The flight of most common skimmers (Libellùlidae) is very erratic; they fly this way and that, often hovering in one spot for a few moments, and they seldom fly very far in a straight line. Many stream species fly relatively slowly up and down the stream, often patrolling a stretch of a hundred yards or more; these dragonflies fly at a height and speed that is characteristic for the species. Some of the gomphids, when flying over open land areas, fly with a very undulating flight, each undulation covering 4–6 feet (1.2–1.8 m) vertically and 2–3 feet (0.6–0.9 m) horizontally. Many of the corduliids and aeshnids fly from 6–20 feet (1.8–6.1 m) or more above the ground, and their flight seems tireless; many of the smaller damselflies fly only an inch or two above the surface of the water.

Most dragonflies feed on a variety of small insects that are caught on the wing in a basketlike arrangement of the legs. The dragonfly may alight and eat its prey or may eat it on the wing. The prey is chiefly small flying insects such as midges, mosquitoes, and small moths, but the larger dragonflies often capture bees, butterflies, or other dragonflies. Odonàta normally take only moving prey, but if captured will eat or chew on almost anything that is put into their mouth—even their own abdomen!

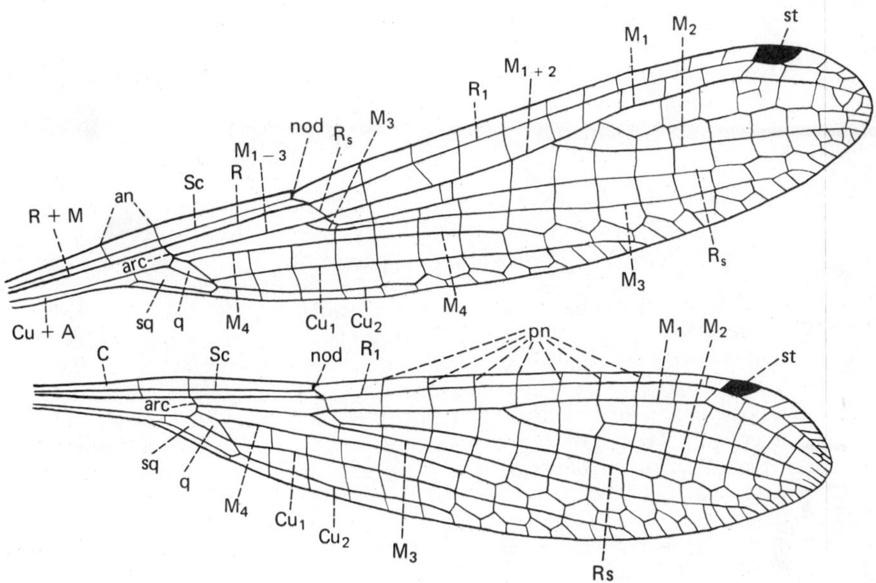

Figure 99. Wings of *Enallágma hágeni* (Walsh) (Coenagriónidae), showing the Comstock–Needham system of terminology, *an,* antenodal cross veins; *arc,* arculus; *nod,* nodus; *pn,* postnodal cross veins; *q,* quadrangle; *sq,* subquadrangle; *st,* stigma. The usual symbols are used for the other venational characters.

Many pond species are frequently found with large numbers of small, rounded, usually reddish bodies attached to the under side of the thorax or abdomen; these bodies are larval water mites. The mite larvae attach to the dragonfly nymph, and when the nymph emerges, move onto the adult. The mites spend two or three weeks on the dragonfly, feeding on its blood and increasing in size, and eventually leave it; if they get back into water, they develop into adult mites, which are free-living and predaceous. The mite larvae do not appear to do a great deal of damage to the dragonflies; it is not unusual to find dragonflies with dozens of mite larvae on them.

CLASSIFICATION OF THE ODONÀTA

A synopsis of the Odonàta occurring in North America north of Mexico is given below; synonyms and alternate spellings are given in parentheses.

- Suborder Anisóptera—dragonflies
  - Superfamily Aeshnòidea
    - Petalùridae—graybacks
    - Aéshnidae (Aéschnidae)—darners
    - Gómphidae—clubtails
  - Superfamily Cordulegastròidea (Aeshnòidea in part)
    - Cordulegástridae (Cordulegastéridae)—biddies
  - Superfamily Libellulòidea
    - Macromìidae (Epophthalmìidae)—belted skimmers and river skimmers
    - Cordulìidae—green-eyed skimmers
    - Libellùlidae—common skimmers
- Suborder Zygóptera—damselflies
  - Calopterýgidae (Agriónidae, Agrìidae)—broad-winged damselflies
  - Léstidae—spread-winged damselflies
  - Protoneùridae (Coenagriónidae in part)—protoneurid damselflies
  - Coenagriónidae (Coenagrìidae, Agriónidae)—narrow-winged damselflies

The separation of the families of Odonàta is based primarily on characters of the wings. There are two major interpretations of the wing venation in this order; we use the Comstock–Needham interpretation (which includes a number of special terms not used in other orders), illustrated in Figures 98 and 99. The separation of genera and species is based on wing venation, color pattern, the structure of the genitalia, and other characters. Many species of Odonàta can be recognized in the field by their characteristic size, shape, color, or habits.

Key to the Familes of Odonàta

1. Front and hind wings similar in shape and both narrowed at base (Figures 99, 100 D, E, G); wings at rest held either together above body or slightly divergent; head transversely elongate; males with 4 appendages at end of abdomen (Figure 97 C, D) (damselflies, suborder Zygóptera) 2

1′. Hind wings wider at base than front wings (Figures 98, 100 A–C); wings at rest held horizontally or nearly so; head not usually transversely elongate, but more rounded; males with 3 appendages at end of abdomen (Figure 97 A) (dragonflies, suborder Anisóptera) 5

2(1). Ten or more antenodal cross veins (Figure 100 D); wings not stalked, and often with black or red markings .... **Calopterýgidae** p. 181

2′. Two (rarely 3) antenodal cross veins (Figures 99, 100 E, G); wings stalked at base, and either hyaline or lightly tinged with brownish (only rarely blackish) 3

3(2′). M_3 arising nearer arculus than nodus (Figure 100 E); wings usually divergent above body at rest .... **Léstidae** p. 181

3′. M_3 arising nearer nodus than arculus (Figure 99), usually arising below nodus; wings usually held together above body at rest 4

4(3′). Cu_2 rudimentary or absent, Cu_1 short, forming the anterior border of only 3 or 4 cells distal to arculus (Figure 100 G); reddish or brownish damselflies; southern Texas .... **Protoneùridae** p. 181

4′. Cu_1 and Cu_2 well developed, both extending several cells distal to arculus (Figure 99); color variable; widely distributed .... **Coenagriónidae** p. 181

5(1′). Triangles in front and hind wings similar in shape and about equidistant from arculus (Figure 100 A); most of costal and subcostal cross veins not in line; usually a brace vein (an oblique cross vein, Figure 100 F, *bvn*) behind proximal end of stigma 6

5′. Triangles in front and hind wings usually not similar in shape, the triangle in front wing farther distad of arculus than triangle in hind wing (Figures 98 and 100 B, C); most of costal and subcostal cross veins in line; no brace vein behind proximal end of stigma 9

6(5). A brace vein behind proximal end of stigma (Figure 100 F, *bvn*) 7

6′. No brace vein behind proximal end of stigma .... **Cordulegástridae** p. 178

7(6). Compound eyes in contact for a considerable distance on dorsal side of head (Figure 102 B) .... **Aéshnidae** p. 178

7′. Compound eyes separated on dorsal side of head (Figure 102 A), or meeting at a single point only 8

8(7′). Median lobe of labium notched (Figure 101 A); stigma at least 8 mm in length .... **Petalùridae** p. 178

8′. Median lobe of labium not notched (Figure 101 B); stigma less than 8 mm in length .... **Gómphidae** p. 178

9(5′). Hind margin of compound eyes slightly lobed (Figure 102 D); males with a small lobe on each side of second abdominal segment, and with inner margin of hind wing somewhat notched; anal loop rounded (Figure 100 B) or elongate, if foot-shaped with little development of "toe" (Figure 100 C) 10

9′. Hind margin of compound eyes straight or with a very small lobe (Figure 102 C); males without a small lobe on side of second abdominal segment, and with inner margin of hind wing rounded; anal loop usually foot-shaped, with "toe" well developed (Figure 98) .... **Libellùlidae** p. 179

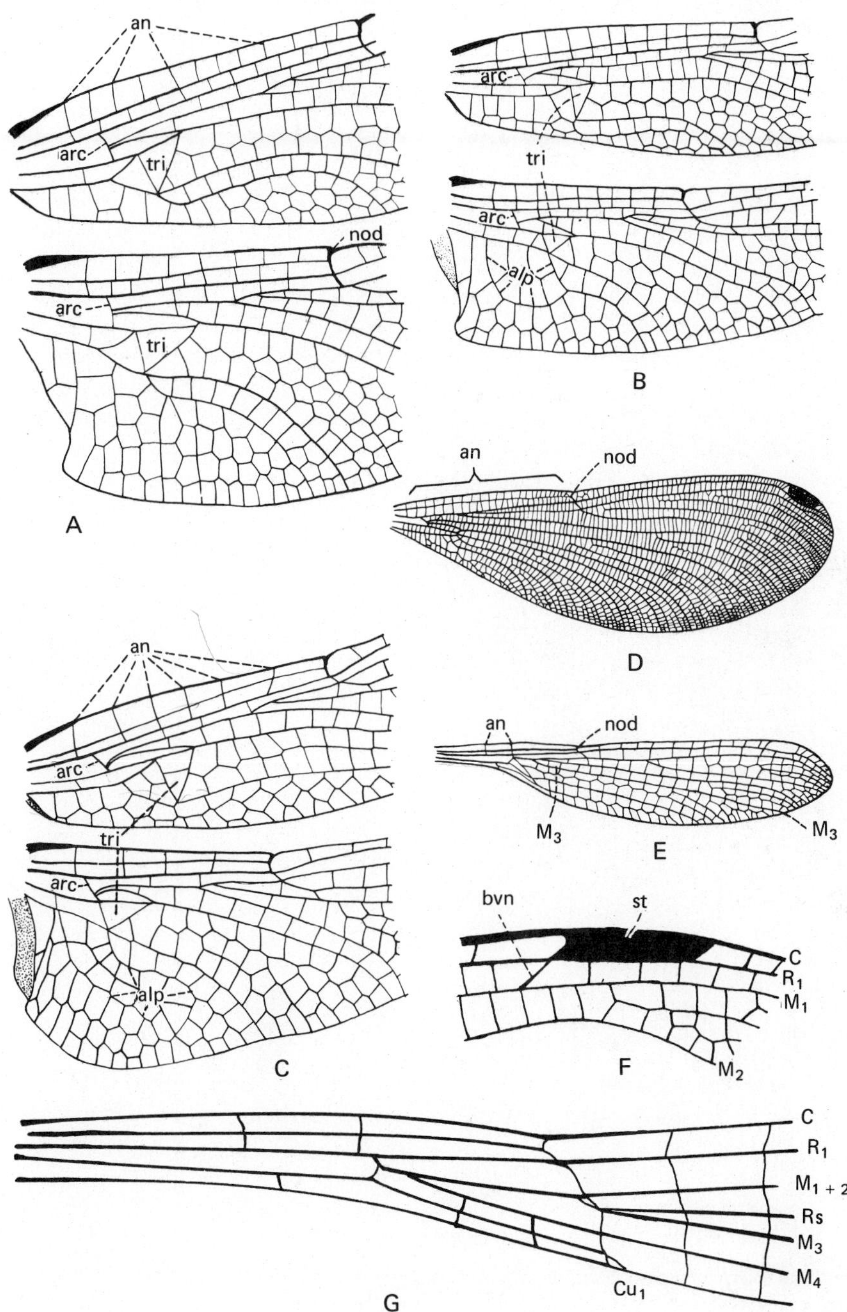

Figure 100. Wings of Odonàta. A, base of wings of *Gómphus* (Gómphidae); B, base of wings of *Dídymops* (Macromìidae); C, base of wings of *Epithèca* (Cordulìidae); D, front wing of *Calópteryx* (Calopterýgidae); E, front wing of *Léstes* (Léstidae); F, stigmal area of wing of *Aéshna* (Aéshnidae); G, base of front wing of *Protoneùra* (Protoneùridae). *alp,* anal loop; *an,* antenodal cross veins; *arc,* arculus; *bvn,* brace vein; *nod,* nodus; *st,* stigma; *tri,* triangle.

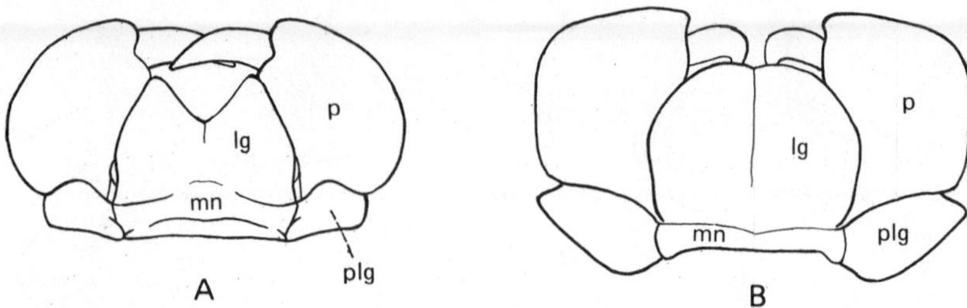

Figure 101. Labia of adult dragonflies. A, *Tachópteryx* (Petalùridae); B, *Aéshna* (Aéshnidae). *lg*, ligula or median lobe; *mn*, mentum; *p*, palp or lateral lobe; *plg*, palpiger or squama.

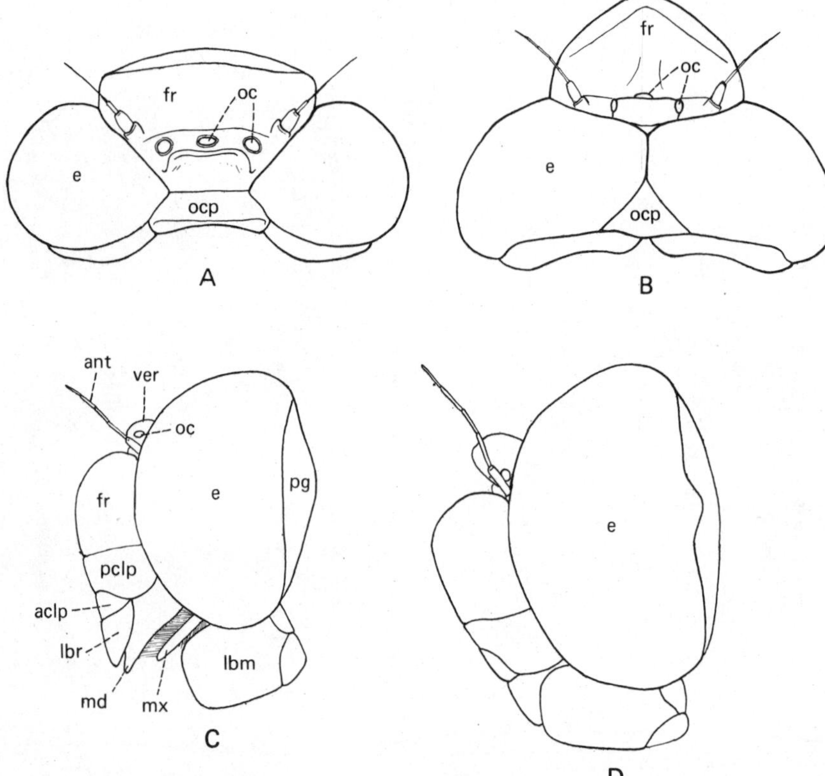

Figure 102. Head structure in dragonflies. A, *Gómphus éxilis* Selys (Gómphidae), dorsal view; B, *Basiaéschna janàta* (Say) (Aéshnidae), dorsal view; C, *Sympètrum* (Libellùlidae), lateral view; D, *Epithèca* (Cordulìidae), lateral view. *aclp*, anteclypeus; *ant*, antenna; *e*, compound eye; *fr*, frons; *lbm*, labium; *lbr*, labrum; *md*, mandible; *mx*, maxilla; *oc*, ocellus; *ocp*, occiput; *pclp*, postclypeus; *pg*, postgena; *ver*, vertex.

10(9). Anal loop rounded, without a bisector (Figure 100 B); triangle in hind wing distad of arculus; 3 or more cu-a cross veins in hind wing .. **Macromìidae** p. 179

10′. Anal loop elongate, with a bisector (Figure 100 C); triangle in hind wing opposite arculus or nearly so; 1–2 cu-a cross veins in hind wing .... **Cordulìidae** p. 179

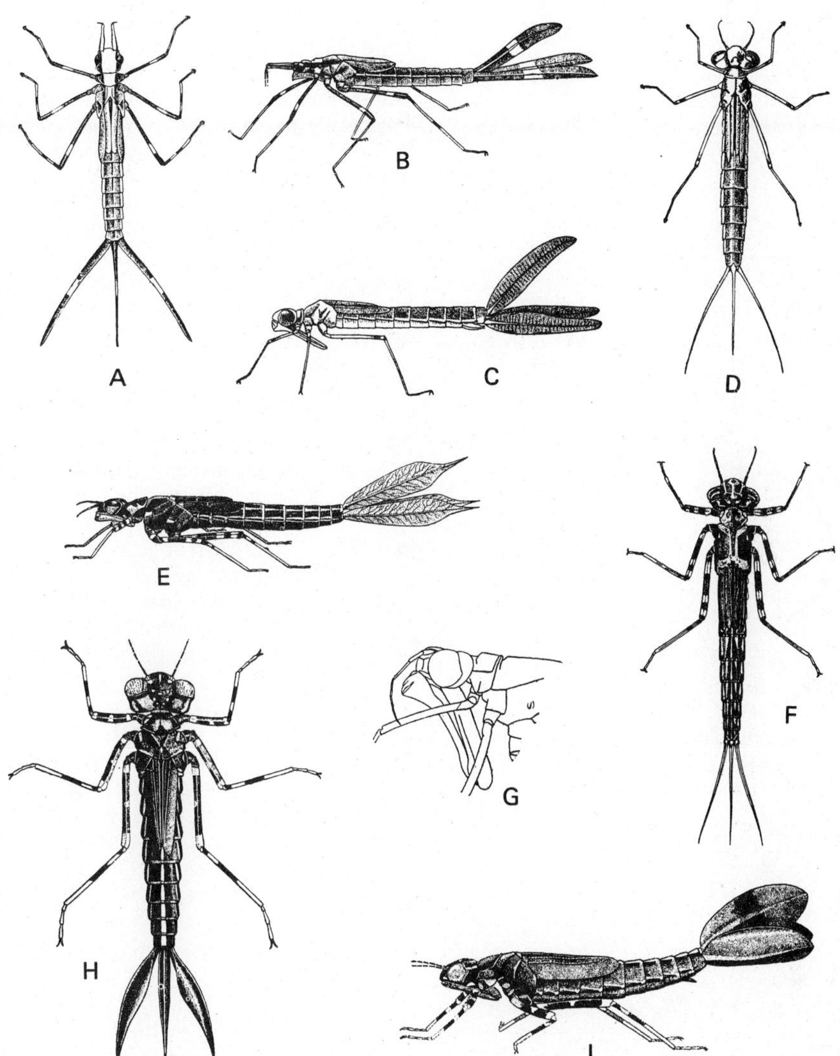

Figure 103. Nymphs of damselflies (Zygóptera), dorsal and lateral views. A and B, *Calópteryx aequábilis* (Say) (Calopterýgidae); C and D, *Léstes drỳas Kirby* (Léstidae); E and F, *Ischnùra cervùla* Selys (Coenagriónidae); G, head of *Léstes drỳas* Kirby, lateral view; H and I, *Argia émma* Kennedy (Coenagriónidae). (Courtesy of Kennedy and the U.S. National Museum.)

SUBORDER **Anisóptera**—Dragonflies: Dragonflies have the hind wings wider at the base than the front wings, and the wings are held horizontal (or nearly so) at rest. The hind wings of the male in all but the Libellùlidae are somewhat notched at the anal angle (Figure 100 A–C), while the hind wings of all Libellùlidae and the females of the other families have the anal angle rounded (Figure 98). The head is somewhat rounded, and is seldom transversely elongate. The males have 3 appendages at the apex of the abdomen, 2 superior appendages (the cerci) and an inferior appendage (the epiproct). The females of some groups have a well developed ovipositor, while those of other groups either have the ovipositor poorly developed or entirely absent (with the sternum of segment 8 more or less prolonged posteriorly to form an egg guide called the vulvar lamina). The

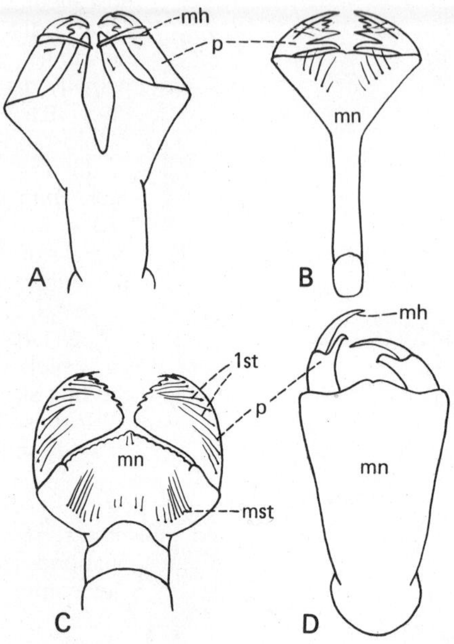

Figure 104. Labia of nymphal Odonàta. A, *Calópteryx* (Calopterýgidae); B, *Léstes* (Léstidae); C, *Plathèmis lýdia* (Drury) (Libellùlidae); D, *Ànax* (Aéshnidae). *lst,* lateral setae; *mh,* movable hook of palp; *mn,* mentum; *mst,* mental setae; *p,* palp or lateral lobe. (Redrawn from Garman.)

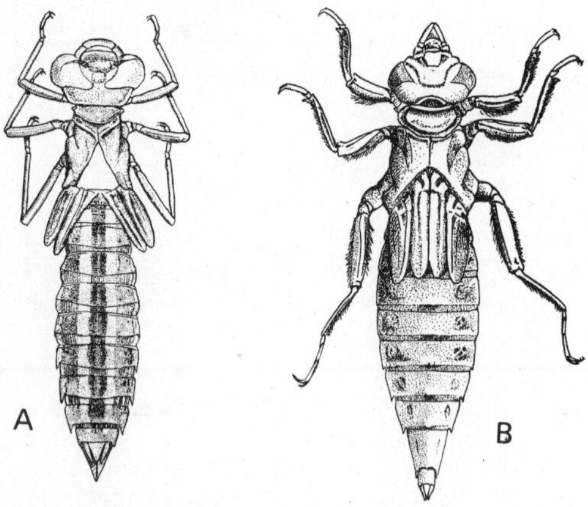

Figure 105. Nymphs of Aeshnòidea. A, *Aéshna verticàlis* Hagen (Aéshnidae); B, *Gómphus quadricòlor* Walsh (Gómphidae), (Courtesy of Walker and *The Canadian Entomologist.*)

nymphs have short appendages at the apex of the abdomen, and have the gills in the rectum.

Family **Petalùridae**—Graybacks: Two species in this family occur in North America: *Tachópteryx thòreyi* (Hagen) in the eastern United States, and *Tanýpteryx hágeni* (Selys) in the Northwest (California and Nevada to southern British Columbia). Adults of *T. thòreyi* are grayish brown and about 3 inches (76 mm) in length; they usually occur along small streams in wooded valleys, where they often alight on tree trunks. Adults of *T. hágeni* are a little smaller and blackish, and are found at high elevations; the nymphs of this species occur in wet moss.

Family **Gómphidae**—Clubtails: This is a fairly large group, and most of its members occur along streams or lake shores. The clubtails are 2–3 inches (51–76 mm) in length, dark-colored, usually with yellowish or greenish markings. They generally alight on a bare flat surface. Many species have the terminal abdominal segments swollen; hence the common name for the group. The largest genus in the family is *Gómphus.*

Family **Aéshnidae**—Darners: This group includes the largest and most powerful of the dragonflies; most of them are about 3 inches (76 mm) in length. The green darner, *Ànax jùnius* (Drury), a common and widely distributed species that occurs about ponds, has a greenish thorax and a bluish abdomen, and a targetlike mark on the upper part of the face. The genus *Aéshna* contains a number of species, most of which are to be found near marshes in the latter part of the summer; they are dark-colored with blue or greenish markings on the thorax and abdomen. One of the largest species in this family is *Epiaéschna hèros* (Fabricius), an early-summer species about $3\frac{1}{4}$ inches (83 mm) in length, and dark brown with indistinct greenish markings on the thorax and abdomen.

Family **Cordulegástridae**—Biddies: The biddies are large, brownish-black dragonflies with yellow markings; they differ from the other Aeshnòidea in lacking a brace vein at the proximal end of the stigma. These dragonflies are usually found along small, clear, woodland streams. The adults fly slowly up and down the stream, a foot or two above the water, but if disturbed can fly very rapidly. The group is a small one, and all the species in the United States belong to the genus *Cordulegáster.*

Family **Macromìidae** — Belted Skimmers and River Skimmers: The members of this group can be distinguished from the Cordulìidae, with which they were formerly classified, by the rounded anal loop that lacks a bisector (Figure 100 B). Two genera occur in the United States, *Dídymops* and *Macròmia*. The belted skimmers (*Dídymops*) are light brown in color, with light markings on the thorax; they occur along boggy pond shores. The river skimmers (*Macròmia*) are large species that occur along lake shores and large streams; these dragonflies are dark brown with yellowish markings on the thorax and abdomen (Figure 106 C, D), and are extremely fast fliers. The eyes of the Macromìidae are greenish in life (in *Macròmia*, usually a brilliant green).

Family **Cordulìidae** — Green-Eyed Skimmers: These skimmers are mostly black or metallic in color, and seldom have conspicuous light markings; the eyes of most species are brilliant green in life. The flight is usually direct, in many species interrupted by periods of hovering. Most members of this group are more common in the northern United States and Canada than in the south.

The genus *Epithèca* contains principally dark-colored dragonflies about $1\frac{1}{2}$ to $1\frac{3}{4}$ inches (38 to 45 mm) in length, often with brownish color at the base of the hind wing; they occur chiefly around ponds and swamps. The royal skimmer, *Epithèca prínceps* (Hagen), is the only corduliid in the Northeast with black spots beyond the base of the wing. It is about 3 inches (76 mm) in length, with 3 blackish spots in each wing — basal, nodal, and apical — and occurs about ponds. The largest genus in this group is *Somátochlora*, which includes the bog skimmers. Most of the bog skimmers are metallic in color and over 2 inches (51 mm) in length, and they usually occur along small wooded streams or in bogs.

Family **Libellùlidae** — Common Skimmers: Most of the species in this group occur about ponds and swamps, and many species are quite common.

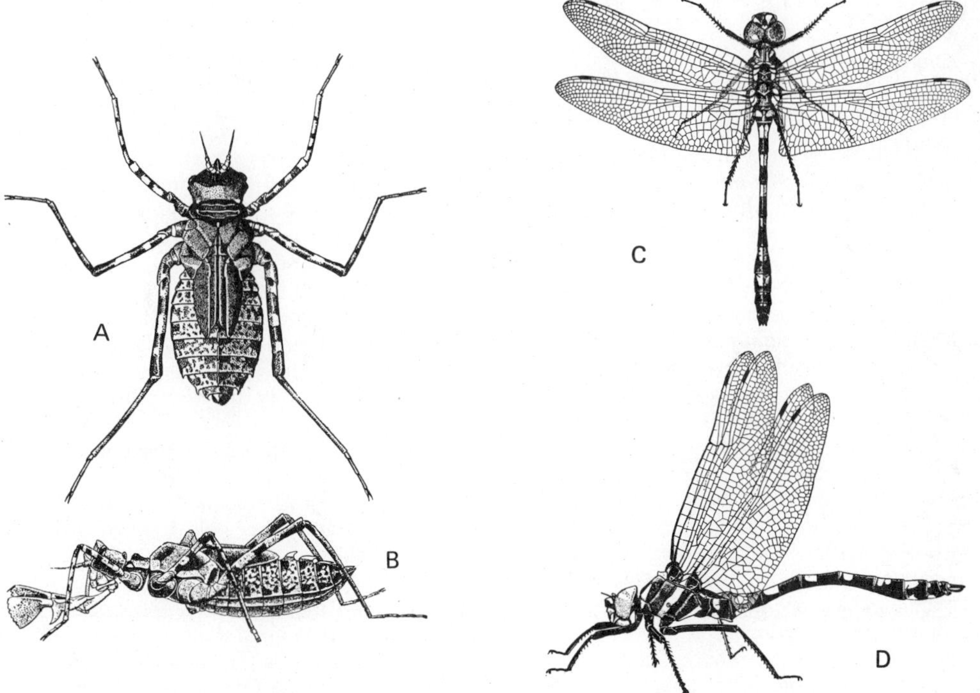

Figure 106. *Macròmia magnífica* MacLachlan (Macromìidae). A, nymph, dorsal view; B, nymph, lateral view, with labium extended; C, adult, dorsal view; D, adult, lateral view. (Courtesy of Kennedy and the U.S. National Museum.)

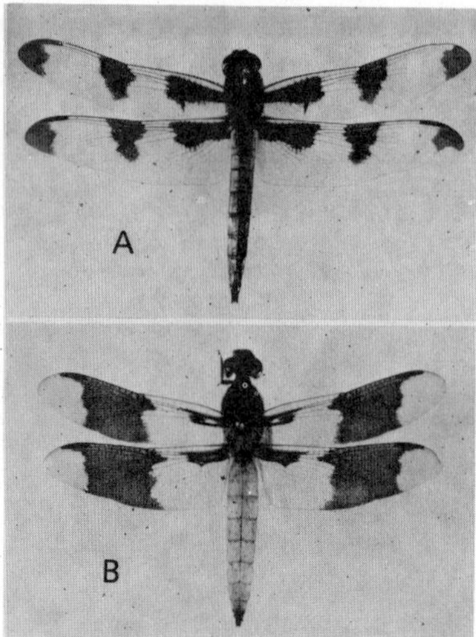

Figure 107. Common pond dragonflies (Libellùlidae). A, *Libéllula pulchélla* Drury, male; B, *Plathèmis lýdia* (Drury), male.

These dragonflies vary in length from about $\frac{3}{4}$ to 3 inches (19 to 76 mm), and many species have the wings marked with spots or bands. The flight is usually rather erratic. This is a large group, and only a few of the more common genera and species can be mentioned here.

The smallest libellulid in the United States is the dwarf skimmer, *Nannothèmis béla* (Uhler), which is about 19 mm in length and occurs in bogs in the eastern states. The males are bluish with clear wings, and the females are patterned with black and yellow and have the basal third or more of the wings yellowish brown. The large dragonflies that are common about ponds and have black or black and white spots on the wings are mostly species in the genus *Libéllula*. The tenspot skimmer, *L. pulchélla* Drury (Figure 107 A), with a wingspread of about $3\frac{1}{2}$ inches (89 mm), has three black spots (basal, nodal, and apical) on each wing, and the males have white spots between the black spots. The widow skimmer, *L. luctuòsa* Burmeister, which is slightly smaller, has the basal third or so of each wing blackish brown, and the males have a white band beyond the basal dark coloring of the wing.

The white-tailed skimmer, *Plathèmis lýdia* (Drury) has a wingspread of about $2\frac{1}{2}$ inches (64 mm). The male has a broad dark band across the middle of each wing and the dorsal side of the abdomen nearly white (Figure 107 B); the females have the wings spotted as in the females of *L. pulchélla,* and do not have a white abdomen. Spotted skimmers (*Celithèmis*) are medium-sized (wingspread of about 2 inches (51 mm)), mostly reddish or brownish with darker markings, and with reddish or brownish spots on the wings.

The amber-winged skimmer, *Perithèmis ténera* (Say), with a wingspread of about $1\frac{1}{2}$ inches (38 mm), has the wings amber-colored in the male and clear with brownish spots in the female. The dragonflies of the genus *Sympètrum* are medium-sized, late-summer, marsh-inhabiting insects; their color varies from yellowish brown to a bright brownish red, and the wings are usually clear except for a small basal spot of yellowish brown. The white-faced skimmers (*Leucorrhínia*) have a wingspread of about $1\frac{1}{2}$ inches (38 mm) and are dark-colored, with a conspicuous white face; the most common species in the East is *L. intácta* Hagen, which has a yellow spot on the dorsal side of the seventh abdominal segment.

The blue pirate, *Pachydíplax longipénnis* (Burmeister), is a common pond species, particularly in the central and southern United States. It varies in color from a patterned brown and yellow to a uniform bluish, and the wings are often tinged with brownish; it has a long cell just behind the stigma and has a wingspread of $2–2\frac{1}{2}$ inches (51 to 64 mm). The green-jacket skimmer, *Erythèmis simplicicóllis* (Say), is a little larger than *P. longipènnis;* it has clear wings, and the body color varies from light green patterned with black to a uniform light blue. The skimmers in the genera *Pantàla* and *Tràmea* are medium-sized to large (wingspread 3–4 inches (76 to 102 mm)), wide-ranging insects and have the base of the hind wings very broad; those in *Pantàla* are yellowish brown with a light yellowish or brownish spot at the base of the hind wing; those of *Tràmea* are largely black or dark-reddish brown, with a black or dark brown spot at the base of the hind wing.

SUBORDER **Zygóptera**—Damselflies: Damselflies have the front and hind wings similar in shape, with both narrowed at the base, and the wings at rest are either held together above the body or slightly divergent; the wings of the two sexes are similar in shape. The head is transversely elongate. The males have 4 appendages at the apex of the abdomen, a pair of superior appendages (the cerci) and a pair of inferior appendages (the paraprocts). The females have an ovipositor, which usually gives the end of the abdomen a somewhat swollen appearance. The nymphs have 3 leaflike gills at the apex of the abdomen (Figure 103).

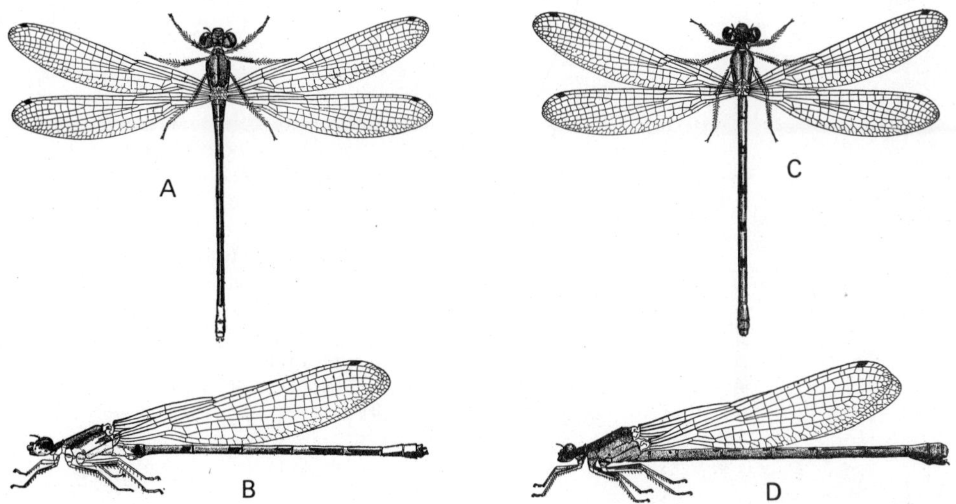

Figure 108. *Árgia émma* Kennedy (Coenagriónidae). A and B, male; C and D, female. (Courtesy of Kennedy and the U.S. National Museum.)

Family **Calopterýgidae**—Broad-Winged Damselflies: The members of this group are relatively large damselflies that have the base of the wings gradually narrowed, not stalked as in other families of Zygóptera; these insects occur along streams. Two genera occur in the United States, *Calópteryx* (=*Ágrion*) and *Hetaerìna*. The common eastern species of *Calópteryx* is the black-winged damselfly, *C. maculàta* (Beauvois). The wings of the male are black, and those of the female are dark gray with a white stigma; the body is metallic greenish black. The most common species of *Hetaerìna* is the American ruby-spot, *H. americàna* (Fabricius), which is reddish in color, with a red or reddish spot in the basal third or fourth of the wings.

The majority of the damselflies in the United States belong to the remaining families. Nearly all have clear wings that are stalked at the base and have only two antenodal cross veins. Most of them are between 1 and 2 inches (25 and 51 mm) in length.

Family **Léstidae**—Spread-Winged Damselflies: The members of this group occur chiefly in swamps, but the adults occasionally wander some distance from swamps. When alighting, these damselflies hold the body vertical, or nearly so, and the wings partly outspread; they usually alight on plant or grass stems. Most of the species in this group belong to the genus *Léstes*.

Family **Protoneùridae:** Two species in this tropical group, *Neoneùra àaroni* Calvert and *Protoneùra càra* Calvert, occur in southern Texas. They are reddish or brownish in color, 32–37 mm in length, and occur along streams.

Family **Coenagriónidae**—Narrow-Winged Damselflies: This family is a large one, with many genera and species. These damselflies occur in a variety of habitats; some occur chiefly along streams, and others about ponds or swamps. Most of them are rather feeble fliers, and when alighting, usually hold the body horizontal and the wings together over the body. The two sexes are differently colored in most species, with the males more brightly colored than the females. Many of these damselflies are beautifully colored, but the color usually fades after the insect dies.

The dancers (*Árgia*, Figure 108) are chiefly stream species, and can be recognized by the long, close-set spines on the tibiae. The males of the violet dancer, *Árgia fumipénnis violàcea* (Hagen), a common species occurring along streams and pond shores, are a beautiful violet color. The green damsels (*Nehalénnia*) are small, slender, bronzy-green insects usually found in bogs and swamps. The bicolored bog damsel, *Amphiágrion sàucium* (Burmeister), is a small, stout-bodied, red and black damselfly usually found in bogs. The largest genus in this family is *Enallágma*, which includes the bluets; most spe-

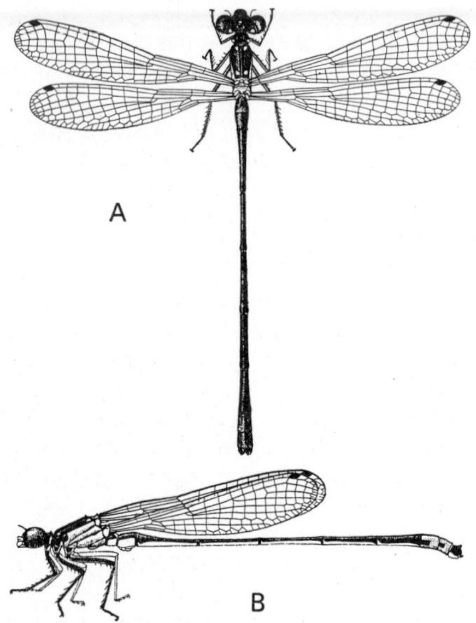

Figure 109. *Ischnùra cervùla* Selys, male (Coenagriónidae). A, dorsal view; B, lateral view. (Courtesy of Kennedy and the U.S. National Museum.)

cies are light blue with black markings. Several species of *Enallágma* may be found about the same pond or lake. The common fork-tail, *Ischnùra verticàlis* (Say), is a very common species in the East and occurs nearly everywhere that any damselfly is to be found. The males are dark-colored, with green stripes on the thorax and blue on the tip of the abdomen; most of the females are bluish green with faint dark markings (older individuals), or brownish orange with black markings (recently emerged individuals); a very few of the females are colored like the males.

COLLECTING AND PRESERVING ODONÀTA

Many of the Odonàta are powerful fliers, and their capture often presents a challenge to the collector. Many are so adept on the wing that they can easily dodge a net, even when the net is swung as one would swing a baseball bat. If one wishes to catch these fast-flying insects, he must study their flight habits. Many species have particular beats along which they fly at rather regular intervals, or have perches on which they frequently alight; if one is familiar with the insect's flight habits, he can often anticipate where it will fly and can be prepared for it. One should swing at a flying dragonfly from behind; if swung at from in front, the insect can see the net coming and can usually dodge it. In stalking a specimen, one should use only the slowest motions until the final swing; movements of the legs and feet should be covered by vegetation as much as possible, for dragonflies often see motion below them better than that on a level with them.

The net used to capture Odonàta should be an open-mesh net with little air resistance so that it can be swung rapidly. The rim size and handle length may depend on the collector, but for many species it is desirable to have a relatively large rim (12–15 inches (305–381 mm) in diameter) and a net handle at least 3 feet (1 m) long.

Dragonflies beyond the reach of a net (many specimens will fall in this category) may often be collected with a sling shot loaded with sand, or with a gun loaded with dust shot. Many specimens so collected may be slightly damaged, but a slightly damaged specimen is usually better than none at all.

Odonàta occur in a great variety of habitats, and to obtain a large number of species, one should visit as many different habitats as possible. Two habitats that appear similar often contain different species, or the same habitat may harbor different species in different seasons. Many species have a short seasonal flight range, and one must be in the field at just the right season to collect them. Most species will be found near aquatic habitats—ponds, streams, marshes, and the like—but many are wide-ranging and may be found in meadows, woodlands, and the hillsides above aquatic habitats.

It is practically impossible to collect many Odonàta without wading, for they often fly at some distance (beyond net reach) out from the shores of a pond or stream. Many species, particularly damselflies, can be obtained by sweeping in the vegetation along and near the shores of ponds and marshes; others patrol along the edge of the emergent vegetation, where the water is a few feet deep. Stream species, which are usually rare in collections and are often locally distributed, are best collected by wading streams (if the streams are small enough to wade); this often means wading for considerable distances.

Killing jars for Odonàta should be relatively large and wide-mouthed, and should contain several pieces of cleansing tissue. Specimens should be removed from the killing jars as soon as they are killed, since they may become discolored if left in too long. Mating pairs or pairs in tandem should be pinned together before they are put into the killing jar, so they can be associated later. Specimens collected in the field should be placed in envelopes, with the wings folded above the body; ordinary letter envelopes will do for this, and the collecting data can be written on the outside. After returning from the field, the contents of the envelopes can be sorted and mounted.

Most of the bright colors of the Odonàta fade after the insect dies; these colors are most likely to be retained if the specimens are dried rapidly—in the sun, under a lamp, or in an oven. If one collects Odonàta in any numbers, they are best kept in triangular paper envelopes (Figure 618), one or two specimens to an envelope (never two species in the same envelope). If specimens are pinned, they may be pinned with the wings outspread, with the help of a spreading board, or they may be pinned sideways. It is usually preferable to pin the specimen sideways, with the pin passing through the thorax at the base of the wings and the left side of the insect uppermost. Some specimens, particularly dragonflies, will usually have to be placed in an envelope for a few days before they are pinned, so that the wings will stay together above the body. It is often necessary to support the abdomen of a pinned specimen either with crossed insect pins under the abdomen, a strip of narrow cardboard on the pin under the insect, or by bristling (a heavy bristle or a very slender insect pin shoved through the fresh specimen from frons to anus).

The nymphs of Odonàta may be collected by the various types of aquatic collecting equipment and methods described in Chapter 34. Nymphs should be preserved in 70–75 percent alcohol. Newly emerged adults and their exuviae should be preserved together in a pillbox, an envelope, or (preferably) in alcohol. If full-grown nymphs are collected in the field, they may be brought back to the laboratory (preferably wrapped in wet cloth or grass) and reared out in a fish-free balanced aquarium. A stick must be provided for the nymphs to crawl out of the water, and the aquarium should be covered with a screen or cloth.

References on the Odonàta

Borror, D. J. 1945. A key to the New World genera of Libellulidae (Odonata). *Ann. Ent. Soc. Amer.*, 38(2):168–194; 72 f.

Byers, C. F. 1927. Key to the North American species of *Enallagma*, with a description of a new species (Odonata: Zygoptera). *Trans. Amer. Ent. Soc.*, 53:249–260; 1 f.

Byers, C. F. 1930. A contribution to the knowledge of Florida Odonata. *Univ. Fla. Publ. Biol. Ser.*, No. 1; 327 pp., 115 f.

Calvert, P. 1901–1909. Odonata. *Biologia Centrali Americana: Insecta Neuroptera*. London: Dulau & Co. Pp. v–xxx, 17–342, Suppl. pp. 324–420; illus.

Corbet, P. S. 1963. *A Biology of Dragonflies*. Chicago: Quadrangle Books, xvi + 247 pp., frontis. (color), 115 f., 6 pl.

Fraser, F. C. 1957. *A Reclassification of the Order Odonata*. Sydney: Roy. Soc. Zool. New South Wales, 133 pp., 62 f.

Garman, P. 1917. The Zygoptera, or damselflies, of Illinois. *Ill. State Lab. Nat. Hist. Bull.*, 12(4):411–587; pl. 58–73.

Garman, P. 1927. The Odonata or dragonflies of Connecticut. *Conn. State Geol. and Nat. Hist. Surv. Bull.* 39; 331 pp., 67 f., 22 pl.

Gloyd, L. K., and M. Wright. 1959. Odonata. In *Fresh-Water Biology*, W. T. Edmondson (Ed.). New York: Wiley, pp. 917–940; 86 f.

Howe, R. H. 1917–1923. Manual of the Odonata of New England. *Mem. Thoreau Mus. Nat. Hist.*, 2:1–138; illus. Suppl. 1921, pp. 1–14.

Johnson, C. 1972. The damselflies (Zygoptera) of Texas. *Bull. Fla. State Mus. Biol. Sci.*, 16(2):55–128; 18 f.

Johnson, C., and M. J. Westfall, Jr. 1970. Diagnostic keys and notes on the damselflies (Zygoptera) of Florida. *Bull. Fla. State Mus.*, 15(2):45–89; 18 f.

Kennedy, C. H. 1915. Notes on the life history and ecology of the dragonflies of Washington and Oregon. *Proc. U.S. Natl. Mus.*, 49:259–345; 201 f.

Kennedy, C. H. 1917a. Notes on the life history and ecology of the dragonflies of central California and Nevada. *Proc. U.S. Natl. Mus.*, 52:483–635; 404 f.

Kennedy, C. H. 1917b. The dragonflies of Kansas. *Bull. Kan. Univ.*, 18:127–145; 7 pl.

Montgomery, B. E. 1962. The classification and nomenclature of calopterygine dragonflies (Odonata: Calopterygoidea). *Verh. XI int. Kongr. Ent. Wien, 1960*, 3(1962):281–284.

Munz, P. A. 1919. A venational study of the suborder Zygoptera (Odonata), with keys for the identification of genera. *Mem. Amer. Ent. Soc.*, No. 3; 78 pp., 20 pl.

Musser, R. J. 1962. Dragonfly nymphs of Utah (Odonata: Anisoptera). *Univ. Utah Biol. Ser.*, 12(6):viii + 1–66; 5 pl., 1 f.

Muttkowski, R. A. 1910. Catalogue of the Odonata of North America. *Milwaukee Pub. Mus. Bull.,* 1(1):1–207.

Needham, J. G., and E. Broughton. 1927. The venation of the Libellulidae. *Trans. Amer. Ent. Soc.,* 53:157–190; 4 f.

Needham, J. G., and E. Fisher. 1936. The nymphs of North American Libelluline dragonflies (Odonata). *Trans. Amer. Ent. Soc.,* 62:107–116; pl. 6–7.

Needham, J. G., and H. B. Heywood. 1929. *A Handbook of the Dragonflies of North America.* Springfield, Ill.: Charles C. Thomas, viii + 378 pp.; illus.

Needham, J. G., and M. J. Westfall, Jr. 1955. *A Manual of the Dragonflies of North America (Anisoptera).* Los Angeles: Univ. California Press, xii + 615 pp., frontis. + 341 f.

Pennak, R. W. 1953. *Fresh-Water Invertebrates of the United States.* New York: Ronald Press, ix + 769 pp., 470 f.

Ris, F. 1909–1919. *Collections Zoologiques du Baron Edm. de Selys Longchamps.* Bruxelles: Hayez, Impr. des Academies, Fasc. IX–XVI, Libellulinen 4–8. 1278 pp., 692 f., 8 col. pl.

Robert, A. 1963. *Les Libellules du Quebec.* Bull. 1, Serv. de la Faune, Ministère du Tourisme, de la Chasse et de la Pèche, Prov. Quebec, viii + 223 pp., 278 f.

Smith, R. F., and A. E. Pritchard. 1956. Odonata. In *Aquatic Insects of California,* R. L. Usinger (Ed.). Berkeley, Calif.: Univ. California Press, pp. 106–153; 92 f.

Tillyard, R. J. 1917. *The Biology of Dragonflies.* Cambridge: The University Press, xii + 396 pp., 188 f., 4 pl.

Walker, E. M. 1912. North American dragonflies of the genus *Aeshna. Univ. Toronto Studies, Biol. Ser.,* No. 11. 214 pp., 28 pl.

Walker, E. M. 1925. The North American dragonflies of the genus *Somatochlora. Univ. Toronto Studies, Biol. Ser.,* No. 26. 202 pp., 35 pl.

Walker, E. M. 1953. *The Odonata of Canada and Alaska.* Vol. 1. *General, the Zygoptera—Damselflies.* Toronto: Univ. Toronto Press, xi + 292 pp., 42 pl.

Walker, E. M. 1958. *The Odonata of Canada and Alaska.* Vol. 2. *The Anisoptera—Four Families.* Toronto: Univ. Toronto Press, xi + 318 pp., 64 pl.

Wright, M., and A. Peterson. 1944. A key to the genera of anisopterous dragonfly nymphs of the United States and Canada (Odonata, suborder Anisoptera). *Ohio J. Sci.,* 44(4):151–166; illus.

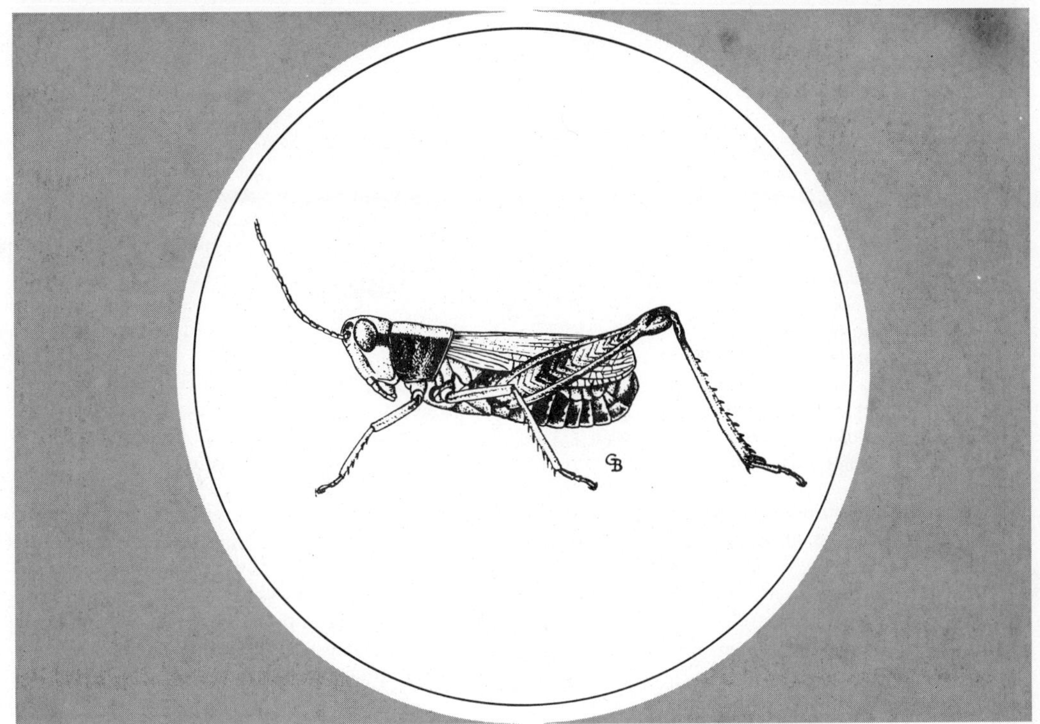

12: ORDER ORTHÓPTERA[1]

GRASSHOPPERS, CRICKETS, WALKING STICKS, MANTIDS, COCKROACHES, AND ROCK CRAWLERS

The order Orthóptera contains a great many large and well-known insects. Most of them are plant feeders, and some are very destructive to vegetation; a few are predaceous, and a few are somewhat omnivorous in food habits.

The Orthóptera may be winged or wingless, and the winged forms usually have four wings. The front wings are generally long and narrow, many-veined, and somewhat thickened, and are usually referred to as tegmina (singular, tegmen). In the family Tetrígidae the front wings are reduced to small scalelike structures. The hind wings are membranous, broad, many-veined, and when at rest, are usually folded fanwise beneath the front wings. The body is elongate, and the cerci are usually well developed. Many species have a long ovipositor, often as long as the body. The mouth parts are of the chewing type, and the metamorphosis is simple.

SOUND PRODUCTION IN THE ORTHÓPTERA

A great many types of insects "sing," but some of the best known insect songsters (grasshoppers and crickets) are in the order Orthóptera. The songs of these insects are produced chiefly by stridulation, that is, by rubbing one body part against another. The singing Orthóptera usually possess auditory

[1] Orthóptera: *ortho,* straight; *ptera,* wings.

Figure 110. Field cricket singing (note elevated position of the front wings). (Courtesy of R. D. Alexander.)

organs—oval eardrums or tympana, located on the sides of the first abdominal segment (short-horned grasshoppers) or at the base of the front tibiae (long-horned grasshoppers and crickets; Figure 113 C, *tym*). These tympana are relatively insensitive to changes in pitch, but are capable of responding to rapid and abrupt changes in intensity. The songs of grasshoppers and crickets play an important role in their behavior, and the songs of different species are usually different; the significant differences are in rhythm.

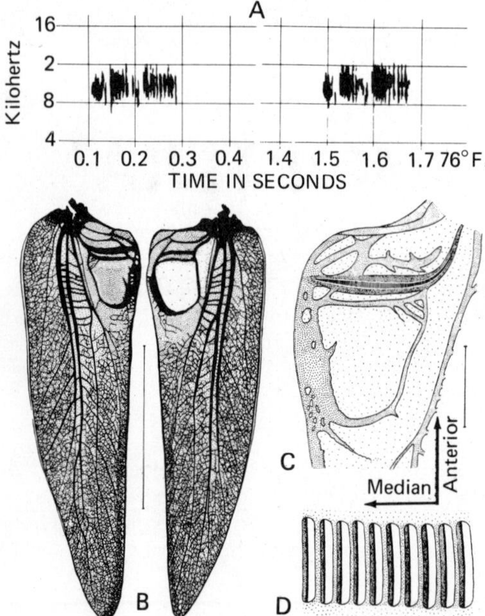

Figure 111. Song and song-producing structures of the big green pine-tree katydid, *Hubbéllia marginífera* (Walker) (Tettigonìidae, Tettigoniìnae). A, audiospectrograph of two pulses of the song (4 kHz is approximately the pitch of the top note of a piano); B, front wings, dorsal view (line = 10 mm); C, ventral surface of basal portion of left front wing showing the file (line = 1 mm); D, several teeth of file (line = 0.1 mm). (Courtesy of R. D. Alexander.)

The crickets (Grýllidae) and long-horned grasshoppers (Tettigonìidae) produce their songs by rubbing a sharp edge (the scraper) at the base of one front wing along a filelike ridge (the file) on the ventral side of the other front wing (Figure 111 B–D). The bases of the front wings at rest lie one above the other; the left one is usually uppermost in the long-horned grasshoppers, and the right is usually uppermost in the crickets. Both front wings possess a file and scraper, but the file is usually longer in the upper wing and the scraper is better developed in the lower wing. In the long-horned grasshoppers the lower (right) front wing usually contains more membranous area than the upper one. The file on the lower front wing and the scraper on the upper one are usually nonfunctional.

When the song is produced, the front wings are elevated (Figure 110) and moved back and forth; generally, only the closing stroke of the wings produces a sound. The sound produced by a single stroke of the front wings is called a pulse; each pulse is composed of a number of individual tooth strikes of the scraper on the file. The pulse rate in a given insect varies with temperature, being faster at higher temperatures; in different species it varies from 4 or 5 per second to over 200 per second.

The songs of different species differ in the character of the pulses, the pulse rate, and in the way the pulses are grouped. The pulses of crickets are relatively musical, that is, they can usually be assigned a definite pitch (the pitch in hertz, which varies in different crickets from about 1500 to 10,000, corresponds to the tooth strike rate). Those of the long-horned grasshoppers (Figure 111 A) are more noiselike (that is, they contain a wide band of frequencies), clicking, or lisping, and cannot be assigned a definite pitch. The principal frequencies in the songs of some Orthóptera are quite high, between 10,000 and 20,000 hertz, and may be nearly or quite inaudible to some people. The pulses may be delivered at a regular rate for a considerable period, producing a more or less prolonged trill or buzz (some tree crickets and cone-headed grasshoppers); they may be delivered in short bursts, a second or less in length, separated by silent intervals of a second or more (some tree crickets); the pulses may be delivered in short series of a few pulses each, producing chirps (most field crickets; see Figure 112, the calling songs); they may be delivered in regularly alternating series of fast and slow pulses (meadow grasshoppers), or the pulse rhythm may be more complex.

The band-winged grasshoppers (Oedipodìnae) usually make their noises by snapping their hind wings in flight; the noises so produced are crackling or buzzing. The slant-faced grasshoppers (Acridìnae) "sing" by rubbing the hind legs against the front wings, producing a soft rasping sound; the hind femora of these insects are usually provided with a series of short peglike structures that function something like a file (Figure 113 L, *strp*).

The females of a few Orthóptera may make a few soft noises, but most of the singing is done by the males. The short-horned grasshoppers usually move about while singing; the crickets and long-horned grasshoppers are usually stationary. Many Orthóptera, particularly some of the crickets and long-horned grasshoppers, are capable of producing two or more different types of songs (Figure 112); each type is produced under certain circumstances, and each produces a characteristic reaction by other individuals. The loudest and most commonly heard song (the "calling" song, Figure 112) serves primarily to attract the female; the female, if she is at the same temperature as the singing male, is able to recognize the song of her species, and moves toward the male. The males of some species produce a "fighting" or "aggressive" song in the presence of another male; this determines the dominance of an individual. Most crickets produce a special "courtship" song in the presence of a female; this usually leads to copulation. Some insects produce "alarm" or "disturbance" sounds when disturbed or threatened with injury.

Some of the Orthóptera (for example, most katydids) sing only at night; many (for example, most crickets) sing both day and night; a few (for example, band-winged grasshoppers) sing only in the daytime. Many species (for example, some of the cone-headed grasshoppers and tree crickets) often "chorus," that is, two or more individuals sing simultaneously, their pulses synchronized, or their chirps or phrases alternating and producing a pulsating sound.

CLASSIFICATION OF THE ORTHÓPTERA

There are differences of opinion regarding the taxonomic position of the insects that we include in the order Orthóptera. All authorities agree that the suborders Caelífera and Ensífera should be placed in the Orthóptera, but some believe the other suborders should be treated as orders. There are also differences of opinion regarding the number of families to be recognized in some suborders, and on the status (whether family or subfamily) to be given certain groups.

A synopsis of the North American Orthóptera, as treated in this book, is given below. Other names, arrangements, and spellings are given in parentheses. The groups marked with an asterisk are relatively rare or are unlikely to be taken by a general collector.

Suborder Caelífera
- Superfamily Acridòidea
  - Tetrígidae (Acrydìidae; Acrídidae in part)—pygmy grasshoppers or grouse locusts
  - *Eumastácidae (Acrídidae in part)—monkey grasshoppers
  - *Tanaocéridae (Eumastácidae in part)—desert long-horned grasshoppers
  - Acrídidae (Locústidae)—short-horned grasshoppers
    - Romaleìnae (Cyrtacanthacridìnae in part)—lubber grasshoppers
    - Cyrtacanthacridìnae (including Catantopìnae)—spur-throated grasshoppers
    - Acridìnae (Truxalìnae, Tryxalìnae; including Gomphocerìnae)—slant-faced grasshoppers
    - Oedipodìnae—band-winged grasshoppers

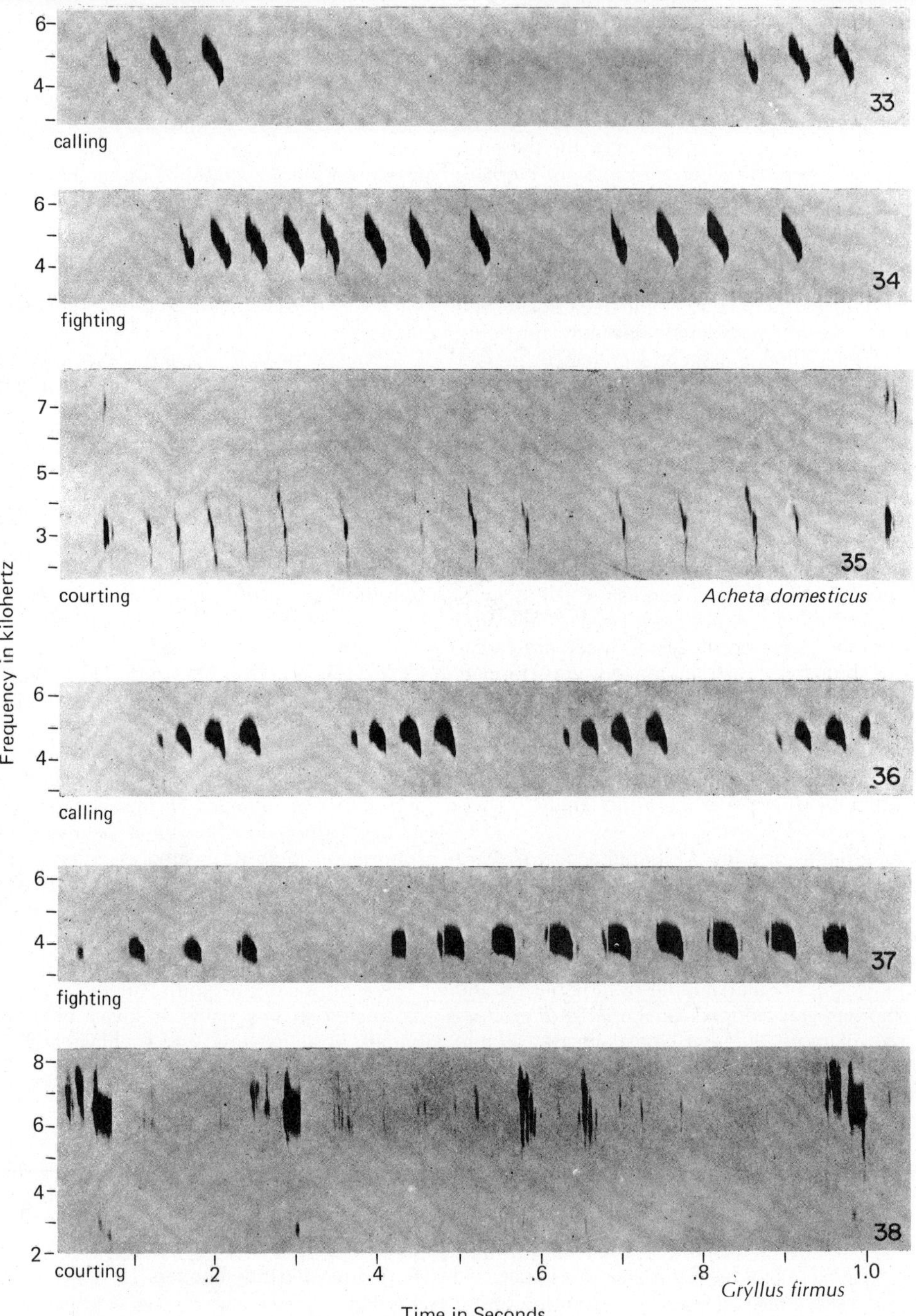

Figure 112. Audiospectrographs of the calling, fighting, and courting songs of the house cricket, *Achèta domésticus* (L.) (three upper graphs), and of the beach cricket, *Grýllus fírmus* Scudder (transferred from *Achèta* to *Grýllus* since this figure was prepared) (three lower graphs). (Courtesy of R. D. Alexander.)

Superfamily Tridactylòidea
Tridactýlidae (Grýllidae in part, Gryllotálpidae in part)—pygmy mole crickets
Suborder Ensífera
Tettigonìidae—long-horned grasshoppers
Phaneropterìnae—bush and round-headed katydids
Copiphorìnae—cone-headed grasshoppers
Pseudophyllìnae—true katydids
*Listroscelìnae (Decticìnae in part)—listrosceline grasshoppers
Conocephalìnae—meadow grasshoppers
Decticìnae—shield-backed grasshoppers
*Tettigoniìnae—pine-tree katydids
*Prophalangópsidae (Tettigonìidae in part)—hump-winged crickets
Gryllacrídidae (Gryllácridae; Stenopelmátidae in part, Tettigonìidae in part)—wingless long-horned grasshoppers
*Gryllacridìnae (Gryllacrìnae)—leaf-rolling grasshoppers
Rhaphidophorìnae (Ceuthophilìnae)—cave or camel crickets
Stenopelmatìnae—Jerusalem, sand, or stone crickets
Grýllidae—crickets
Oecanthìnae—tree crickets
Eneopterìnae—bush crickets
Trigonidiìnae—sword-bearing or sword-tailed crickets
*Mogoplistìnae—short-winged crickets
*Myrmecophilìnae—ant-loving crickets
Nemobiìnae (Gryllìnae in part)—ground crickets
Gryllìnae—house and field crickets
*Brachytrupìnae (Gryllìnae in part)—short-tailed crickets
Gryllotálpidae (Grýllidae in part)—mole crickets
Suborder Phasmatòdea (Phasmòidea, Phasmòdea, Phásmida, Pharmatóptera)
Phasmátidae (Phásmidae)—walking sticks
*Timémidae (Phasmátidae in part)—timemas
Suborder Dictyóptera (Oothecària)
Superfamily Mantòidea (Mantòdea)
Mántidae—mantids
Superfamily Blattòidea (Blattòdea, Blattària, Bláttidae)—cockroaches
*Cryptocércidae—brown-hooded cockroach
Bláttidae—oriental cockroach, American cockroach, and others
*Polyphágidae—sand cockroaches and others
Blattéllidae—German cockroach, wood cockroaches, and others
*Blabéridae—giant cockroaches and others
Suborder Grylloblattòdea (Notóptera)
*Gryllobláttidae—rock crawlers

Key to the Families of Orthóptera

Adults (and some nymphs) of North American Orthóptera may be identified as to family by means of the following key. Families marked with an asterisk are relatively rare or are unlikely to be taken by a general collector.

1. Hind femora more or less enlarged (Figures 110, 114, 116–118, 120–125); tarsi with 4 or fewer segments; usually jumping insects 2

1′. Hind femora not enlarged (Figures 127–129); tarsi nearly always 5-segmented; running or walking insects 11

2(1). Front legs enlarged and fitted for digging (Figure 126); tarsi with 3 or fewer segments 3

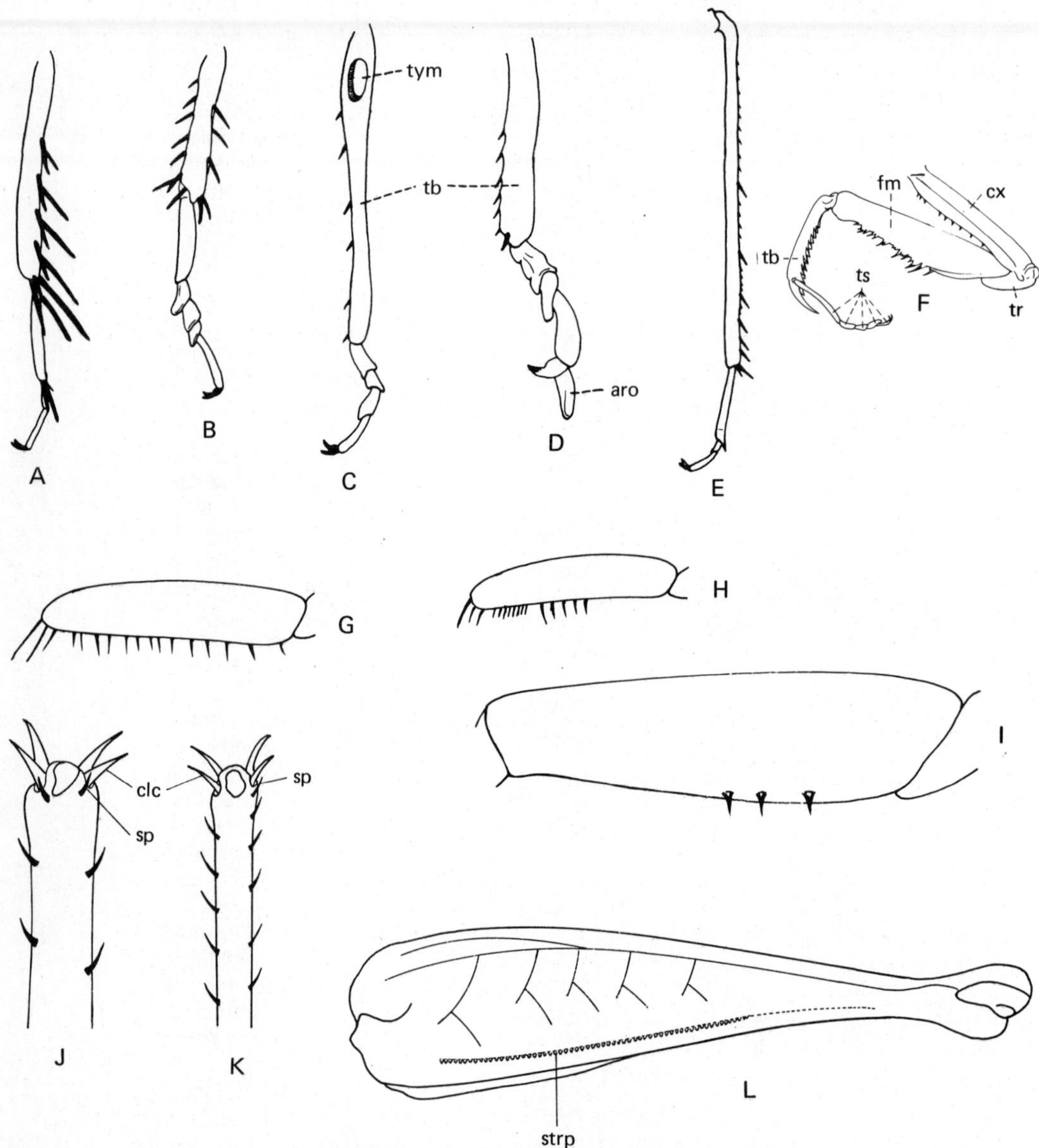

Figure 113. Leg structure in Orthóptera; A–E, tibiae and tarsi; F, front leg; G–I, front femora; J–K, apical portion of left hind femur, dorsal view; L., hind femur, mesal view. A, *Nemòbius* (Nemobiìnae, Grýllidae), hind leg; B, *Periplanèta* (Bláttidae), front leg; C, *Scuddèria* (Phaneropterìnae, Tettigonìidae), front leg; D, *Schistocérca* (Cyrtacanthacridìnae, Acrídidae), front leg; E, *Oecánthus* (Oecanthìnae, Grýllidae), hind leg; F, *Tenódera* (Mántidae), front leg; G, *Periplanèta* (Bláttidae); H, *Parcoblátta* (Blattéllidae); I, *Bláberus* (Blabéridae); J, *Romàlea* (Romaleìnae, Acrídidae); K, *Melánoplus* (Cyrtacanthacridìnae, Acrídidae); L, Acridìnae, (Acrídidae). *aro,* arolium; *clc,* movable spines or calcaria; *cx,* coxa; *fm,* femur; *sp,* immovable spines; *strp,* stridulatory pegs; *tb,* tibia; *tr,* trochanter; *ts* tarsus; *tym,* tympanum.

2′. Front legs not enlarged and fitted for digging (Figures 110, 114, 116–118, 120–125), or if somewhat enlarged (Stenopelmatìnae) then tarsi are 4-segmented; tarsi 2- to 4-segmented 4

3(2). Front and middle tarsi 2-segmented, hind tarsi 1-segmented or absent; antennae 11-segmented; 3 small ocelli; hind femora greatly enlarged; body not pubescent; length less than 10 mm .... **Tridactýlidae*** p. 197

3′. Tarsi 3-segmented; antennae with more than 11 segments; 2 large ocelli; hind femora not greatly enlarged; body pubescent or hairy; length 18 mm or more (Figure 126) .... **Gryllotálpidae** p. 204

4(2′). Antennae usually short, seldom more than half as long as body (Figures 114, 116–118); auditory organs (tympana), if present, on sides of first abdominal segment; hind tarsi 3-segmented, front and middle tarsi 2- or 3-segmented; ovipositor short 5

4′. Antennae long, usually as long as body or longer (Figures 110 and 120–125); auditory organs, if present, at base of front tibiae (Figure 113 C, *tym*); tarsi 3- or 4-segmented; ovipositor usually elongate 8

5(4). Pronotum prolonged backward over abdomen, and tapering posteriorly (Figure 114); front wings vestigial; no arolia; front and middle tarsi 2-segmented, hind tarsi 3-segmented .... **Tetrígidae** p. 193

5′. Pronotum not prolonged backward over abdomen (Figures 116–118); front wings usually well developed if hind wings are present; arolia present (Figure 113 D); all tarsi 3-segmented 6

6(5′). Antennae shorter than front femora; wings absent; 8–25 mm in length; occurring in the chaparral country of southwestern United States .... **Eumastácidae*** p. 193

6′. Antennae longer than front femora; wings nearly always present; size variable, but usually over 15 mm in length; widely distributed 7

7(6′). Wings and tympana nearly always present; antennae not unusually long; males without a file on third abdominal tergum; widely distributed .... **Acrídidae** p. 194

7′. Wings and tympana absent; antennae very long, in males longer than body; males with a file on third abdominal tergum; southwestern United States .. .. **Tanaocéridae*** p. 194

8(4′). At least middle tarsi, and usually all tarsi, 4-segmented (Figures 113 C and 119 E); ocelli usually present; ovipositor sword-shaped 9

8′. All tarsi 3-segmented (Figure 113 A, B); ocelli present or absent; ovipositor usually cylindrical or needle-shaped .... **Grýllidae** p. 201

9(8). Wings present (but sometimes very small), and with fewer than 8 principal longitudinal veins; males with stridulatory structures on front wings (Figure 111 B–D); front tibiae with tympana; color variable, but often green 10

9′. Wings usually absent, but if present then with 8 or more principal longitudinal veins; males lacking stridulatory structures on front wings; front tibiae with or without tympana; color usually gray or brown .... **Gryllacrídidae** p. 201

10(9). Antennal sockets located about halfway between espistomal suture and top of head; wings reduced, broad in male, minute in female; ovipositor extremely short; hind femora extending to about tip of abdomen; northwestern United States and southwestern Canada .... **Prophalangópsidae*** p. 201

10′. Antennal sockets located near top of head; wings and ovipositor variable; hind femora usually extending beyond tip of abdomen; widely distributed .... **Tettigonìidae** p. 197

11(1′). Prothorax much longer than mesothorax (Figure 127); front legs modified for grasping prey (Figure 113 F) .... **Mántidae** p. 205

11′. Prothorax not greatly lengthened; front legs not modified for grasping prey 12

12(11′). Cerci 1-segmented; body elongate, often very slender; wings usually lacking 13

12′. Cerci with 8 or more segments; body and wings variable 14

13(12). Tarsi 5-segmented; body and legs very slender (Figure 128); widely distributed .... **Phasmátidae** p. 204

13′. Tarsi 3-segmented; body more robust and legs relatively short; Pacific Coast states .... **Timémidae*** p. 204

14(12′). Body flattened and oval, head more or less concealed from above by pronotum (Figure 129); ocelli usually present; wings usually present, but sometimes short; widely distributed 15

14′. Body elongate and cylindrical, head not concealed from above by pronotum; ocelli and wings absent; northwestern United States and western Canada .... **Gryllobláttidae*** p. 207

15(14). Length 3 mm or less; found in ant nests (*Attáphila*) .... **Polyphágidae*** p. 207

15′. Length over 3 mm; almost never found in ant nests 16

16(15′). Middle and hind femora with numerous spines on ventroposterior margin 17

16′. Middle and hind femora without spines on ventroposterior margin, or with hairs and bristles only, or 1 or 2 apical spines 21*

17(16). Pronotum and front wings densely covered with silky pubescence; length 27 mm or more (tropical species accidental in the United States) (*Nyctibòra*) .... **Blattéllidae*** p. 207

17′. Pronotum and front wings glabrous or only very sparsely pubescent... 18

18(17′). Ventroposterior margin of front femora with a row of spines that either decrease gradually in size and length distally or are of nearly equal length throughout (Figure 113 G) 19

18′. Ventroposterior margin of front femora with a row of heavy spines proximally and more slender and shorter spines distally (Figure 113 H) .. 20

19(18). Length 18 mm or more; female subgenital plate divided longitudinally (Figure 115 E); male styli similar, slender, elongate, and straight (Figure 115 G) .... **Bláttidae** p. 206

19′. Length variable, but usually less than 18 mm; female subgenital plate entire, not divided longitudinally (Figure 115 F); male styli variable, often modified, asymmetrical, or unequal in size (Figure 115 H) (*Supélla, Cariblátta, Symplòce, Pseùdomops, Blattélla*) .... **Blattéllidae** p. 207

20(18′). Front femora with only 1 apical spine; supra-anal plate weakly bilobed; glossy light brown, with sides and front of pronotum and basal costal part of front wings yellowish; 15–20 mm in length; Florida Keys (*Phoetàlia* = *Leuroléstes*) .... **Blabéridae*** p. 207

20′. Front femora with 2 or 3 apical spines; supra-anal plate not bilobed; size and color variable; widely distributed (*Ectòbius, Latiblattélla, Ischnóptera, Parcoblátta, Euthlastoblátta, Aglaópteryx*) .... **Blattéllidae** p. 207

21(16′). Distal portion of abdomen (usually including cerci) covered by the produced seventh dorsal and sixth ventral abdominal sclerites, and subgenital plate absent; wingless, body almost parallel-sided, shining reddish brown, finely punctate, 23–29 mm in length; widely distributed, usually found in rotting logs .... **Cryptocércidae*** p. 206

21′. Distal portion of abdomen not so covered, the subgenital plate present; wings usually well developed (absent in some females); usually oval in shape; size and color variable; mostly southern United States 22*

22(21′). Hind wings with an apical portion (an intercalated triangle or an appendicular area) that folds over when the wings are in a resting position (Figure 115 D, *it*); 8.5 mm in length or less, and glossy yellowish in color, often beetlelike in appearance; southeastern United States (*Chorisoneùra, Plectóptera*) .... **Blattéllidae*** p. 207

22′. Hind wings not as above 23*

23(22′). Front femora with 1 to 3 spines on ventroposterior margin and 1 at tip (Figure 113 I); length over 40 mm; arolia absent; southern Florida (*Bláberus, Hemiblábera*) .... **Blabéridae*** p. 207

23′. Front femora without spines on ventroposterior margin, and with 1 or a few at tip; size variable; arolia present or absent; eastern and southern United States 24*

24(23′). Wings well developed, the anal area of hind wings folded fanwise at rest; frons flat, not bulging; length over 16 mm, or (some *Panchlòra*) pale green in color (*Panchlòra, Pycnoscèlus, Nauphoèta, Leucophaèa*) .... **Blabéridae*** p. 207

24′. Anal area of hind wings flat, not folded fanwise at rest (some females are wingless); frons thickened and somewhat bulging; usually (except some *Arenivàga*) less than 16 mm in length, and never green (*Holocómpsa, Eremoblátta, Compsòdes, Arenivàga*). .... **Polyphágidae*** p. 207

SUBORDER **Caelífera:** The Caelífera are jumping Orthoptera, with the hind femora more or less enlarged; they include the short-horned grasshoppers and the pygmy mole crickets. The antennae are nearly always relatively short, and the tarsi contain 3 or fewer segments. The tympana, if present, are located on the sides of the first abdominal segment. The species that stridulate usually do so by rubbing the hind femora over the tegmina or abdomen, or snapping the wings in flight. All have the cerci and ovipositor short.

Family **Tetrígidae**—Pygmy Grasshoppers or Grouse Locusts: The pygmy grasshoppers may be recognized by the characteristic pronotum, which extends backward over the abdomen and is narrowed posteriorly (Figure 114). Most species are between 13 and 19 mm in length; the females are usually larger and heavier bodied than the males. These are among the few grasshoppers that winter as adults, and the adults are most often encountered in the spring and early summer. The pygmy grasshoppers are not of very much economic importance.

Family **Eumastácidae**—Monkey Grasshoppers: The members of this group occur on bushes in the chaparral country of the Southwest. They are wingless and remarkably agile; their common name refers to their ability to progress through small trees and shrubs. Adults are slender, 8–25 mm in length, and usually brownish in color; the face is somewhat slanting and the vertex is pointed, and the antennae are very short (not reaching the rear edge of the pronotum). Monkey grasshoppers do not have a stridulatory organ on the sides of the third abdominal segment, as do the Tanaocéridae. This group is principally tropical, and only six species occur in the United States; they occur from central California, south-

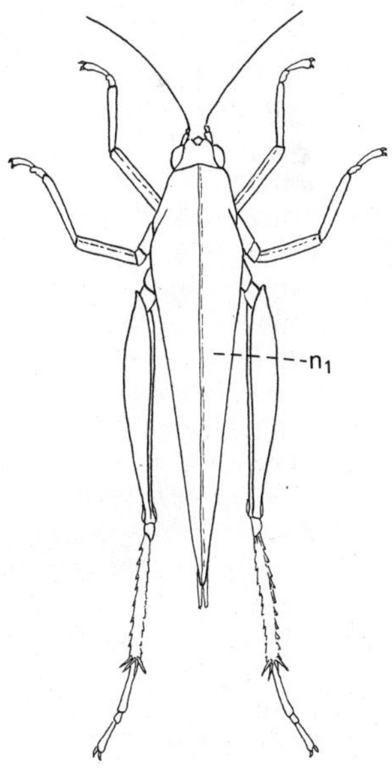

Figure 114. A pygmy grasshopper, *Tettigídea lateràlis* (Say), $3\frac{1}{2}\times$ n_1, pronotum.

ern Nevada, and southwestern Utah south to southern California and southeastern Arizona.

Family **Tanaocéridae** — Desert Long-Horned Grasshoppers: The members of this family resemble the monkey grasshoppers in being wingless and very active, and they occur in the deserts of the Southwest. They are grayish to blackish in color, relatively robust, and 8–25 mm in length; the face is less slanting than in the monkey grasshoppers, and the vertex is rounded. The antennae are long and slender, longer than the body in the male, and shorter than the body in the female. Males have a stridulatory organ on the sides of the third abdominal segment. These grasshoppers are very seldom encountered; they are nocturnal, and are likely to be found early in the season. Only two species occur in the United States (in the genera *Tanaócerus* and *Mohavácris*); they occur from southern Nevada to southern California.

Family **Acrídidae** — Short-Horned Grasshoppers: This family includes most of the grasshoppers that are so common in meadows and along roadsides from midsummer until fall. The antennae are usually much shorter than the body, the auditory organs (tympana) are located on the sides of the first abdominal segment, the tarsi are 3-segmented, and the ovipositor is short. Most are gray or brownish in color, and some have brightly colored hind wings. These insects are plant feeders and are often very destructive to vegetation. Most species pass the winter in the egg stage, the eggs being laid in the ground; a few overwinter as nymphs, and a very few overwinter as adults.

Many males in this group sing (during the day), either by rubbing the inner surface of the hind femur against the lower edge of the front wing, or by snapping the hind wings in flight. Males in the former group (most slant-faced grasshoppers) have a row of tiny stridulatory pegs on the inner surface of the hind femur (Figure 113 L, *strp*), and the sound produced is usually a low buzzing sound; in the latter group (band-winged grasshoppers) the song is a sort of crackling sound.

Key to the Subfamilies of Acrídidae

There are differences of opinion regarding the number of subfamilies in this family. We follow Rehn and Grant (1961), who recognize four subfamilies in our fauna. Most genera of these subfamilies may be separated by the following key.

1. Hind tibiae with both inner and outer immovable spines at tip (Figure 113 J); prosternum usually with a median spine or tubercle ..... **Romaleìnae** p. 195

1′. Hind tibiae with only the inner immovable spine at tip, the outer one absent (Figure 113 K); prosternum with or without a median spine or tubercle .. 2

2(1′). Prosternum with a median spine or tubercle (Figure 115 A, *tub*); hind wings usually hyaline; hind femora of males without a row of stridulatory pegs .. .. **Cyrtacanthacridìnae** p. 195

2′. Prosternum without a median spine or tubercle; color of hind wings variable, but if hyaline then hind femora of males usually with a row of stridulatory pegs (Figure 113 L, *strp*) 3

3(2′). Face vertical or nearly so; pronotum with a strong median ridge, and caudal margin produced backward and angulate mesally (Figure 115 C); hind wings usually colored; antennae slender and cylindrical, not flattened; wings long, reaching or surpassing tip of abdomen; grasshoppers that often stridulate in flight; hind femora of males without a row of stridulatory pegs .... **Oedipodìnae** p. 197

3′. Face usually slanting backward, sometimes very strongly so; pronotum flat or with a low median ridge; caudal margin of pronotum truncate or rounded, and not angulate mesally (Figure 115 B); hind wings usually hyaline; antennae usually slightly flattened, sometimes strongly so; wings variable in length, sometimes short and not reaching tip of abdomen; grasshoppers that do not stridulate in flight, but usually have a row of stridulatory pegs on hind femora of male (Figure 113 L, *strp*), which are rubbed against the tegmina when the insect is at rest .... **Acridìnae** p. 196

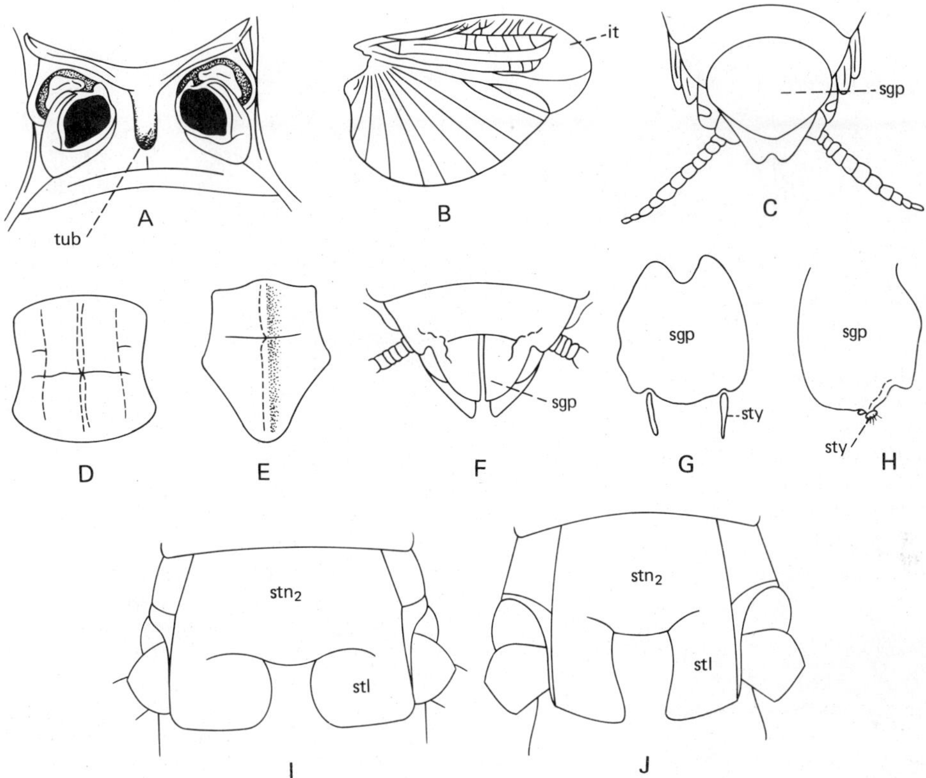

Figure 115. A, prothorax of *Melánoplus* (Cyrtacanthacridìnae, Acrídidae), ventral view; B, hind wing of *Chorisoneùra* (Blattéllidae); C, apex of abdomen of a female cockroach (Blattéllidae), ventral view; D, pronotum of *Sýrbula* (Acridìnae, Acrídidae), dorsal view; E, pronotum of *Chortóphaga* (Oedipodìnae, Acrídidae), dorsal view; F, apex of abdomen of a female cockroach (Bláttidae), ventral view; G, subgenital plate of a male cockroach (Bláttidae), ventral view; H, same (Blattéllidae); I, mesothorax of *Melánoplus* (Cyrtacanthacridìnae, Acrídidae), ventral view); J, same, *Schistocérca* (Cyrtacanthacridìnae, Acrídidae). *it,* intercalated triangle; *sgp,* subgenital plate; *stl,* mesosternal lobe; *stn*$_2$, mesosternum; *sty,* stylus; *tub,* prosternal tubercle.

Subfamily **Romaleìnae**—Lubber Grasshoppers: The only species in this group that normally occurs east of the Mississippi River is *Romàlea micróptera* (Palisot de Beauvois), which occurs in the southeastern states; it is a large robust insect, 2–2½ inches (51–64 mm) in length, and the hind wings are red with a black border. The other species in this group, which are medium-sized to large grasshoppers, occur in the West.

Subfamily **Cyrtacanthacridìnae**—Spur-Throated Grasshoppers: Most grasshoppers in this group can be recognized by the presence of a median spine or tubercle on the prosternum. Most of them have the face vertical or nearly so, but a few, such as the slender grasshopper, *Leptýsma marginicóllis* (Serville), have the face very slanting and may be confused with some Acridìnae. The males lack a row of stridulatory pegs on the inner surface of the hind femur, while most Acridìnae have such pegs.

Uvarov (1966) places the grasshoppers that we here treat as Cyrtacanthacridìnae in two subfamilies, the Cyrtacanthacridìnae and Catantopìnae, which differ in the shape of the mesosternal lobes: rounded and about as long as wide in the Catantopìnae (Figure 115 I), and somewhat rectangular, longer than wide, in the Cyrtacanthacridìnae (Figure 115 J). Uvarov puts the genus *Schistocérca* in the Cyrtacanthacridìnae,

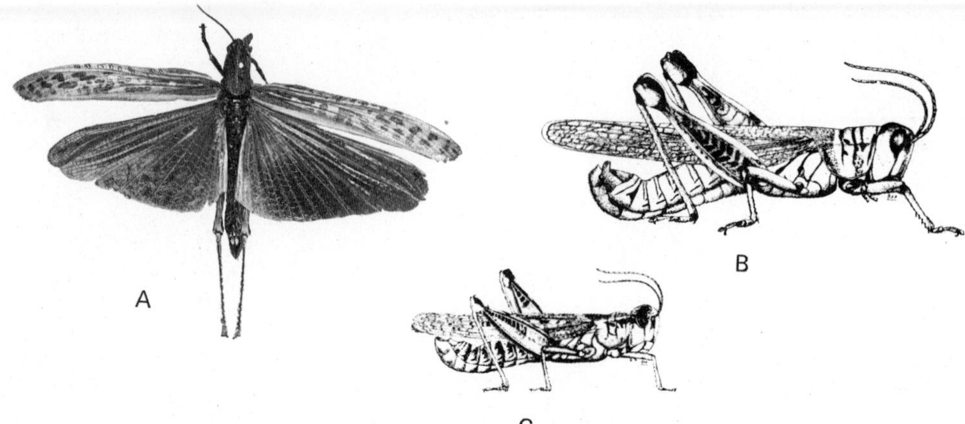

Figure 116. Spur-throated grasshoppers. A, *Schistocérca americàna* (Drury), with wings outspread; B, *Melánoplus differentiàlis* (Thomas); C, *Melánoplus sanguínipes* (Fabricius). (A, courtesy of the Ohio Agricultural Research and Development Center; B–C, courtesy of USDA.)

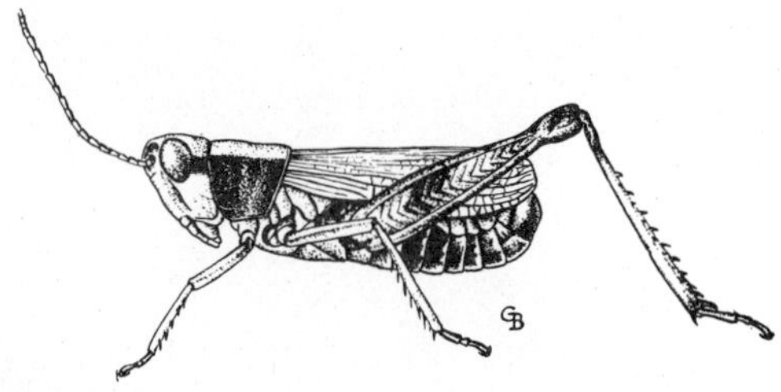

Figure 117. A slant-faced grasshopper, *Chloeáltis conspérsa* Harris. (Courtesy of Institut de Biologie Générale, Université de Montréal.)

and most other genera in our area in the Catantopìnae. The species in the genus *Schistocérca* are large and often brightly colored (Figure 116 A).

The largest genus in this subfamily is *Melánoplus,* and here belong our most common grasshoppers—and the ones that are the most destructive. Most of the damage to crops in this country by spur-throated grasshoppers is caused by four species of *Melánoplus,* the migratory grasshopper, *M. sanguínipes* (Fabricius) (Figure 116 C), the differential grasshopper, *M. differentiàlis* (Thomas) (Figure 116 B), the twostriped grasshopper, *M. bivittàtus* (Say), and the redlegged grasshopper, *M. femurrùbrum* (De Geer).

Some species of spur-throated grasshoppers occasionally increase to tremendous numbers and migrate considerable distances, causing damage of catastrophic proportions. The migrating hordes of these insects may contain millions upon millions of individuals, and literally darken the sky. From 1874 to 1877 great swarms of migratory grasshoppers appeared in the plains east of the Rocky Mountains and migrated to the Mississippi valley and to Texas, destroying crops wherever they stopped in their flight. One migrating swarm during this period was estimated to contain 124 billion insects. This migratory behavior follows a tremendous buildup in numbers, resulting from a combination of favorable environmental conditions; when the numbers decrease, the insects remain stationary.

Subfamily **Acridìnae**—Slant-Faced Grasshoppers: The slanting face of these grasshoppers (Figure 117) will distinguish them from most other Acrídidae, except the very slender grasshoppers in the Cyrtacanthacridìnae. Males of most genera have a row of tiny stridulatory pegs on the inner surface of the hind femur (Figure 113 L, *strp*); these pegs are lacking in the other subfamilies in our area. The Acridìnae usually lack a prosternal spine or tubercle, and the hind wings are usually hyaline.

Uvarov (1966) places the grasshoppers that we here treat as Acridìnae in two subfamilies, the Acridìnae and Gomphocerìnae, which differ in the presence of stridulatory pegs on the hind femur of the males (present in Gomphocerìnae and absent in Acridìnae); Uvarov puts the genus *Radinonòtum* (very slender grasshoppers occurring in the southeastern states) in the Acridìnae, and most other genera in our area in the Gomphocerìnae.

The Acridìnae are not as abundant as the Cyrtacanthacridìnae and Oedipodìnae, and are most likely to be found along the borders of marshes, in wet meadows, and in similar places. They are rarely numerous enough to do much damage to vegetation.

Subfamily **Oedipodìnae**—Band-Winged Grasshoppers: These insects have the hind wings brightly colored, and they generally frequent areas of sparse vegetation. They often alight on bare ground, with the hind wings concealed and the front wings blending with the background. These insects are quite conspicuous in flight, owing to the bright colors of the hind wings, and the crackling sound sometimes made by the wings. The Oedipodìnae are the only short-horned grasshoppers that stridulate while flying (the stridulation producing the crackling sound).

One of the more common species in this group is the Carolina grasshopper, *Dissosteìra carolìna* (L.), in which the hind wings are black with a pale border (Figure 118 A). The clearwinged grasshopper, *Cámnula pellùcida* (Scudder), is an important pest species in this group; it has clear wings.

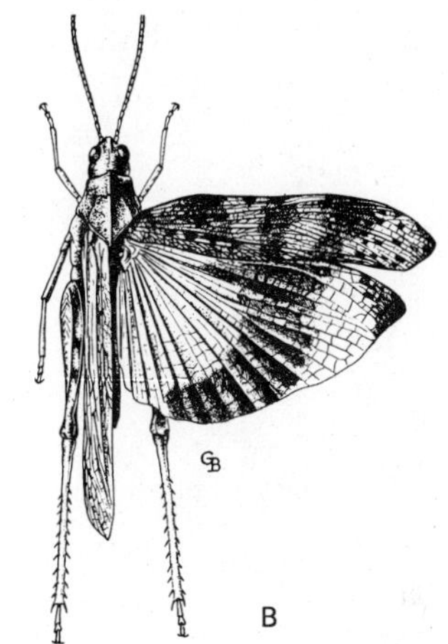

Figure 118. Band-winged grasshoppers. A, *Dissosteìra carolìna* (L.); B, *Spharágemon bólli* Scudder. (B, courtesy of Institut de Biologie Générale, Université de Montréal.)

Family **Tridactýlidae**—Pygmy Mole Crickets: These insects are less than 10 mm in length and can jump actively. They burrow into the ground, but are often found jumping about on the surface of the ground. They occur principally in moist sandy situations along the shores of streams and lakes. The males do not sing.

SUBORDER **Ensífera** The Ensífera are jumping Orthoptera, with the hind femora more or less enlarged; they include the long-horned grasshoppers and crickets. The antennae are nearly always long and hairlike, and the tarsi are 3- or 4-segmented. The tympana, if present, are located on the upper ends of the front tibiae. The species that stridulate do so by rubbing the edge of one front wing over a filelike ridge on the ventral side of the other front wing. Nearly all have the ovipositor relatively long, either sword-shaped or cylindrical.

Family **Tettigonìidae**—Long-Horned Grasshoppers and Katydids: The members of this family can usually be recognized by the long hairlike antennae, the 4-segmented tarsi, the auditory organs (when present) located at the base of the front tibiae, and the laterally flattened bladelike ovipositor. Most species have well developed stridulating organs and are noted songsters; each species has a characteristic song. The winter is usually passed in the egg stage, and in many species the eggs are inserted into plant tissues. Most species are plant feeding, but a few prey on other insects.

Key to the Subfamilies of Tettigonìidae

1. Dorsal surface of first tarsal segment laterally grooved (Figure 119 E); prosternal spines usually present (Figure 119 D); front wings about as long as or longer than hind wings 2

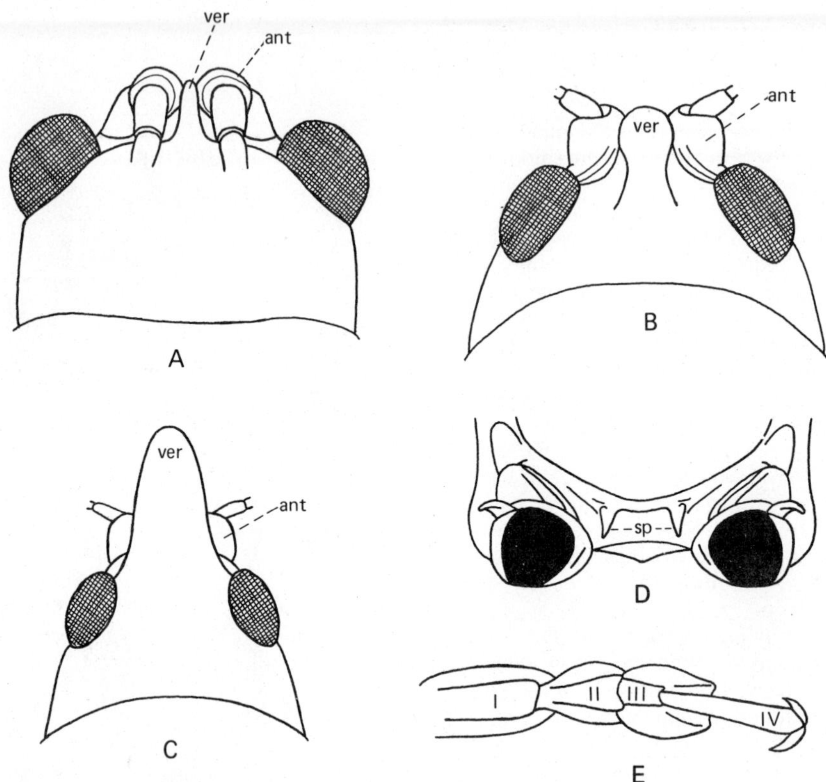

Figure 119. Characters of Tettigonìidae. A, head of *Réhnia* (Listroscelìnae), dorsal view; B, head of *Orchélimum* (Conocephalìnae), dorsal view; C, head of *Neoconocéphalus* (Copiphorìnae), dorsal view; D, prothorax of *Orchélimum* (Conocephalìnae), ventral view; E, hind tarsus of *Neoconocéphalus* (Copiphorìnae), dorsal view. *ant,* base of antenna; *sp,* prosternal spine; *ver,* vertex; *I–IV,* tarsal segments.

1′. Dorsal surface of first tarsal segment smoothly rounded; prosternal spines absent; hind wings longer than front wings, or front wings obliquely truncate at apex .... **Phaneropterìnae** p. 199

2(1). Pronotum about as long as wide, and with 2 transverse grooves; front wings usually broadly oval and convex; mesal margins of antennal sockets elevated and ridgelike, and extending nearly or quite to dorsal surface of vertex .... **Pseudophyllìnae** p. 200

2′. Pronotum longer than wide, and with only 1 transverse groove or none; front wings variable, but usually not broadly oval and convex; mesal margins of antennal sockets not particularly ridgelike, and rarely approaching dorsal part of vertex 3

3(2′). Anterior portion of vertex conical, sometimes acuminate, and extending well beyond basal antennal segment (Figure 119 C, *ver*)... **Copiphorìnae** p. 199

3′. Anterior portion of vertex usually not conical or acuminate and not extending beyond basal antennal segment (Figure 119 A, B, *ver*) 4

4(3′). Anterior portion of vertex laterally compressed, much less than half as wide as basal antennal segment (Figure 119 A, *ver*); southwestern United States

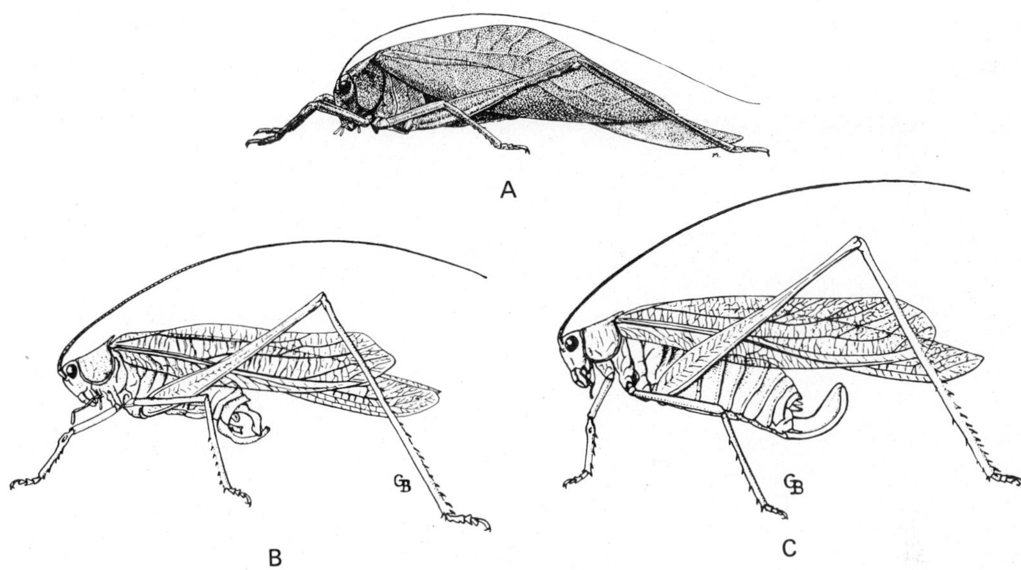

Figure 120. Bush katydids. A, *Microcéntrum rhombifòlium* (Saussure); B, *Scuddèria furcàta* Brunner, male; C, *S. furcàta* Brunner, female. (A, courtesy of Hebard and the Illinois Natural History Survey; B and C, courtesy of Institut de Biologie Générale, Université de Montréal.)

	.... **Listroscelìnae**	p. 200
4′.	Anterior portion of vertex variable, but always more than half as wide as basal antennal segment; widely distributed 5	
5(4′).	One or more spines on dorsal surface of front tibiae 6	
5′.	No spines on dorsal surface of front tibiae .... **Conocephalìnae**	p. 200
6(5).	Pronotum extending back to abdomen (except in a few long-winged forms); wings usually greatly reduced; front wings usually gray, brown, or spotted; prosternal spines present or absent; widely distributed .. **Decticìnae**	p. 200
6′.	Pronotum never extending back to abdomen; wings always well developed; front wings green, rarely spotted with brown; prosternal spines present; southeastern United States .... **Tettigoniìnae**	p. 201

Subfamily **Phaneropterìnae**—Bush and Round-Headed Katydids: The members of this and the next subfamily are commonly called katydids and are well known for their songs, which are usually heard in the evening and at night. The katydids belonging to this subfamily can be recognized by the absence of spines on the prosternum. The bush katydids (*Scuddèria* and *Microcéntrum*, Figure 120) have the wings rather long and narrow, and the vertex is narrowed anteriorly; the round-headed katydids (*Amblycòrypha*) have the wings elongate-oval in shape and have the vertex broad and rounded anteriorly. The katydids are normally green, but pink forms occasionally occur, especially in *Amblycòrypha*; these color forms are not distinct species.

Subfamily **Copiphorìnae**—Cone-Headed Grasshoppers: The cone-heads are long-bodied grasshoppers that have the head conical (Figure 121) and the ovipositor long and swordlike. They occur in two color phases, green and brown. They are generally found in high grass or weeds and are rather sluggish; their jaws are very strong, and a person handling these insects carelessly may receive a healthy nip. The eastern species in this group belong to genus *Neoconocéphalus*.

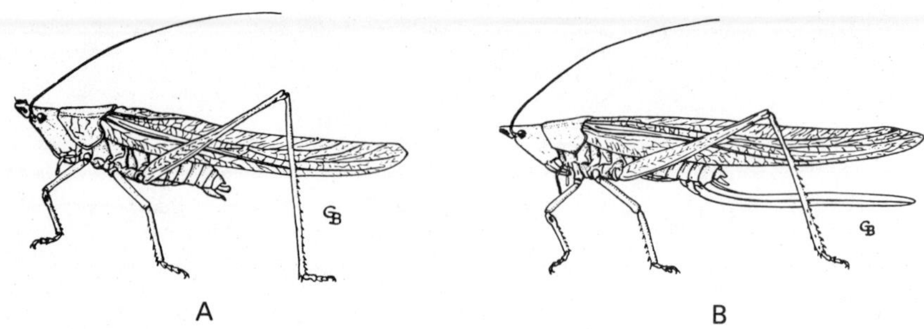

Figure 121. A cone-headed grasshopper, *Neoconocéphalus énsiger* (Harris). A, male; B, female. (Courtesy of Institut de Biologie Générale, Université de Montréal.)

Subfamily **Pseudophyllìnae**—True Katydids: These katydids are principally arboreal in habit, living in the foliage of trees and shrubs. The northern true katydid, *Pterophýlla caméllifòlia* (Fabricius), is the insect whose "katy did, katy didn't" song is so commonly heard on summer evenings in the Northeast; its song contains from two to five pulses. The southern representatives of this katydid sing a somewhat longer and faster song, containing up to about a dozen pulses.

Subfamily **Listroscelìnae:** These grasshoppers are very similar to the Decticìnae, and the United States genera (*Neobarréttia* and *Réhnia*) were formerly placed in the Decticìnae. This subfamily is principally tropical in distribution and is represented in this country by a few species in the South Central States, from Texas north to Kansas.

Subfamily **Conocephalìnae**—Meadow Grasshoppers: These are small to medium-sized, slender bodied, usually greenish grasshoppers (Figure 122) that are found principally in wet grassy meadows and along the margins of ponds and streams. Two genera are common in the eastern United States, *Orchélimum* (usually over 18 mm in length) and *Conocéphalus* (usually less than 17 mm in length).

Subfamily **Decticìnae**—Shield-Backed Grasshoppers: These insects are brownish to black, short-winged, usually an inch or more in length, and have the pronotum extending back to the abdomen; most species are cricketlike in appearance. The eastern species, most of which belong to the genus *Atlánticus,* occur in dry upland woods. The majority of the Decticìnae occur in the West, where they may occur in fields or woods. Some of the western species often do serious damage to field crops; the Mormon cricket, *Ánabrus símplex* Haldeman, is a serious pest in the Great Plains states, and the coulee cricket, *Peránabrus scabricóllis* (Thomas), often does considerable damage in the arid regions of

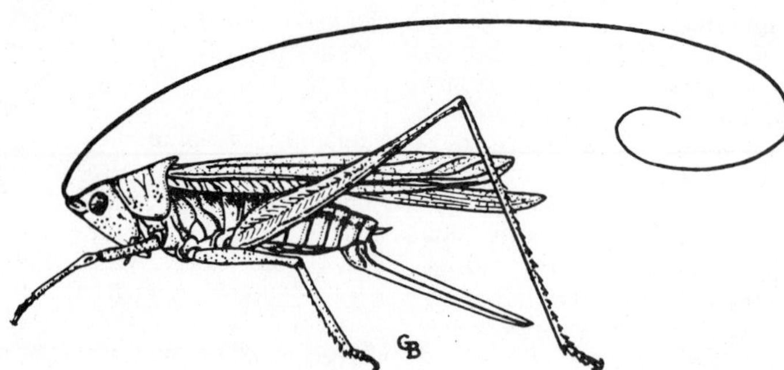

Figure 122. A meadow grasshopper, *Conocéphalus fasciàtus* (De Geer), female. (Courtesy of Institut de Biologie Générale, Université de Montréal.)

the Pacific Northwest. The work of gulls in checking an outbreak of the Mormon crickets in Utah is now commemorated by a monument to the gull in Salt Lake City.

Subfamily **Tettigoniìnae:** This group includes a single United States species, *Hubbéllia marginífera* (Walker), the big green pine-tree katydid, which occurs in the southeastern states. The song and song-producing structures of this katydid are illustrated in Figure 111.

Family **Prophalangópsidae**—Hump-Winged Crickets: This family is represented in North America by two species of *Cyphodérris,* which occur in the mountains of the northwestern United States and southwestern Canada. Adults are brownish with light markings, relatively robust, and about 25 mm in length. In the Tettigonìidae the left front wing is uppermost, and its file is the functional one; in this group either front wing may be uppermost, and the males may switch the position of the wings while singing. The song of *C. monstròsa* Uhler is a loud, very high-pitched (12–13 kHz) trill about two seconds in length or less, which has a slight pulsating quality that is apparently due to the switching of the positions of the front wings during the song.

Family **Gryllacrídidae**—Wingless Long-Horned Grasshoppers: The members of this family are brown or gray in color and lack auditory organs; the wings are vestigial or completely lacking. The three subfamilies occurring in the United States may be separated by the following key.

1. Antennae at base contiguous or nearly so .... **Rhaphidophorìnae** p. 201
1′. Antennae at base separated by a distance equal to or greater than the length of the first antennal segment 2
2(1′). Tarsi lobed and more or less flattened dorsoventrally; hind femora extending beyond apex of abdomen; eastern United States ..... **Gryllacridìnae** p. 201
2′. Tarsi not lobed, and more or less flattened laterally; hind femora not extending beyond apex of abdomen; western United States .... **Stenopelmatìnae** p. 201

Subfamily **Gryllacridìnae**—Leaf-Rolling Grasshoppers: This group is represented in the East by a single species, *Camptonòtus carolinénsis* (Gerstaecker), which seldom occurs north of New Jersey and Indiana. This insect is about 15 mm in length and nests in a leaf that it rolls up and ties with silk; it is nocturnal in habit, and feeds chiefly on aphids.

Subfamily **Rhaphidophorìnae**—Cave or Camel Crickets: These insects are brownish and rather humpbacked in appearance (Figure 123), and are found in caves, hollow trees, under logs and stones, and in other dark moist places. The antennae are often extremely long. Most of the species in this group belong to the genus *Ceuthóphilus.*

Subfamily **Stenopelmatìnae**—Jerusalem, Sand, or Stone Crickets: This group occurs in the West, principally along the Pacific Coast. The sand crickets are large brown insects with big heads, and they usually occur under stones in loose soil.

Family **Grýllidae**—Crickets: The crickets resemble the long-horned grasshoppers in having long tapering antennae, stridulating organs on the front wings of the male, and the auditory organs on the front tibiae, but differ from them in having not more than three tarsal segments, the ovipositor usually needlelike or cylindrical rather than flattened, and the front wings bent down rather sharply at the sides of the body. Many of these insects are well-known songsters, and each species has a characteristic song. Most species overwinter as eggs, laid generally in the ground or in vegetation. This family is represented in the United States by eight subfamilies, which may be separated by the following key.

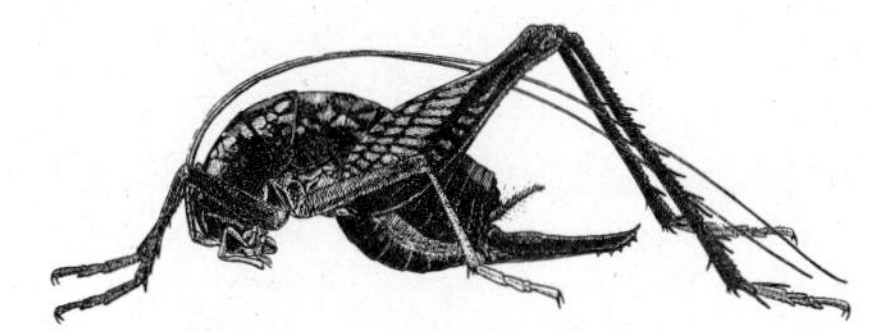

Figure 123. A cave cricket, *Ceuthóphilus maculàtus* (Harris), female. (Courtesy of Hebard and the Illinois Natural History Survey.)

Key to the Subfamilies of Grýllidae

1.	Second tarsal segment somewhat expanded laterally and flattened dorsoventrally 2	
1′.	Second tarsal segment small and flattened laterally (Figure 113 A, E) ... 3	
2(1).	Hind tibiae with teeth between the spines; ovipositor cylindrical and nearly straight .... **Eneopterìnae**	p. 203
2′.	Hind tibiae without teeth between the spines; ovipositor compressed and distinctly upcurved .... **Trigonidiìnae**	p. 203
3(1′).	Hind femora very broad and oval; small, rounded, wingless insects living in ant nests .... **Myrmecophilìnae**	p. 203
3′.	Hind femora more slender; usually large, elongate, free-living insects...4	
4(3′).	Wings vestigial or lacking; hind tibiae without spines but with 3 pairs of apical spurs; body covered with scales; southern United States .... **Mogoplistìnae**	p. 203
4′.	Wings usually well developed; hind tibiae usually with 2 series of spines (Figure 113 A, E); body not covered with scales; widely distributed ... 5	
5(4′).	Ocelli present; head short, vertical (Figures 110 and 125); hind tibiae without teeth between the spines (Figure 113 A); black or brown insects 6	
5′.	Ocelli absent; head elongate, horizontal (Figure 124); hind tibiae usually with minute teeth between the spines (Figure 113 E); usually pale green insects .... **Oecanthìnae**	p. 202
6(5).	Spines of hind tibiae long and movable (Figure 113 A); last segment of maxillary palps at least twice as long as preceding segment; body usually less than 12 mm in length .... **Nemobiìnae**	p. 203
6′.	Spines of hind tibiae stout and immovable; last segment of maxillary palps only slightly longer than preceding segment; body usually over 14 mm in length 7	
7(6′).	Ocelli arranged in a nearly transverse row; ovipositor very short, often not visible; southeastern United States .... **Brachytrupìnae**	p. 203
7′.	Ocelli arranged in an obtuse triangle; ovipositor at least half as long as hind femora; widely distributed .... **Gryllìnae**	p. 203

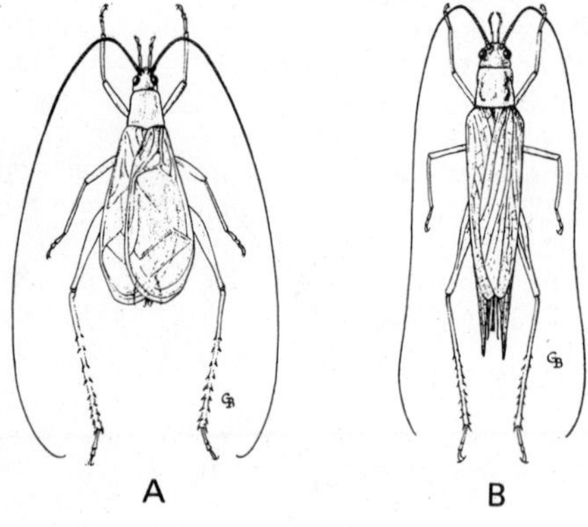

Figure 124. A tree cricket, *Oecánthus quadrimaculàtus* Beutenmüller. A, male; B, female. (Courtesy of Institut de Biologie Générale, Université de Montréal.)

Subfamily **Oecanthìnae**—Tree Crickets: Most tree crickets are slender, whitish or pale-green insects (Figure 124); all are excellent singers. Some species occur in trees and shrubs, others occur in weedy fields. The snowy tree cricket, *Oecánthus fúltoni* Walker, a shrub inhabitant, chirps; its chirping is at a very regular rate, which varies with temperature; 40 added to the number of its chirps in 15 seconds gives a good approximation of the temperature in degrees Fahrenheit. Most species of tree crickets deliver loud trills; some of the tree-inhabiting species have songs consisting of short bursts of pulses. Most of our tree crickets belong to the genus *Oecánthus*; the two-spotted tree cricket, *Neoxàbea bipunctàta* (De Geer), differs from *Oecánthus* in lacking teeth on the hind tibiae, in having the hind wings much longer than the front wings, and in its buffy coloration. Tree crickets lay their eggs in bark or on stems (Figure 34 E) and often seriously damage twigs by their egg laying.

Subfamily **Eneopterìnae**—Bush Crickets: The crickets in this group are medium-sized, slender, and usually brownish in color; they are generally found in bushes or trees. The jumping bush cricket, *Orócharis saltàtor* Uhler, is a common eastern species.

Subfamily **Trigonidiìnae**—Sword-Bearing Crickets: These small (4.0–8.5 mm in length) crickets are usually found on bushes or weeds near ponds or streams; they are fairly common, but are secretive and not often seen. Say's bush cricket, *Anàxipha exígua* (Say), is a common, brownish eastern species; the handsome bush cricket, *Phyllopàlpus pulchéllus* (Uhler), another eastern species, is a pretty black and red insect.

Subfamily **Mogoplistìnae**—Short-Winged Crickets: The members of this group are small, wingless or with very short wings, slender-bodied, flattened insects that are chiefly tropical in distribution; they occur on bushes or beneath debris in sandy localities near water. The body is covered with translucent scales that are easily rubbed off. The members of this group occurring in the southern states are 5–13 mm in length.

Subfamily **Myrmecophilìnae**—Ant-Loving Crickets: These crickets are small (3–5 mm in length) and oval, with greatly dilated hind femora; they occur in ant nests. One species, *Myrmecóphila pergándei* Bruner, occurs in the eastern states.

Subfamily **Nemobiìnae**—Ground Crickets: These crickets (Figure 125 A) are common insects in pastures, meadows, along roadsides, and in wooded areas. They are less than 13 mm in length, and are usually brownish in color. The songs of most species are soft, high-pitched, and often pulsating trills or buzzes.

Subfamily **Gryllìnae**—House and Field Crickets: These crickets are very similar to the ground crickets, but are generally larger (over 13 mm in length), and they vary in color from brownish to black. The field crickets (Figure 110) are very common insects in pastures, meadows, and along roadsides, and some enter houses. The several native species of *Grýllus* are very similar morphologically and were formerly considered to represent a single species; now several species are recognized, which differ chiefly in habits, life history, and song. The most common of these species in the East is probably the northern field cricket, *Grýllus pennsylvánicus* Burmeister (Figure 125 C). The house cricket, *Achèta domésticus* (L.), a species introduced into this country from Europe and which often enters houses, differs from the native species of *Grýllus* in having the head light-colored, with dark crossbars (Figure 125 B). Most of the field crickets chirp, and they sing both day and night.

Subfamily **Brachytrupìnae**—Short-Tailed Crickets: These crickets get their common name from the fact that their ovipositor is very short and often not visible, not long and slender as in most other crickets. The short-tailed crickets are burrowing in habit and usually occur in colonies, their burrows going a foot or more into the ground. They spend most of the time during the day in their burrows, and generally come out only at night. A single species of short-tailed cricket

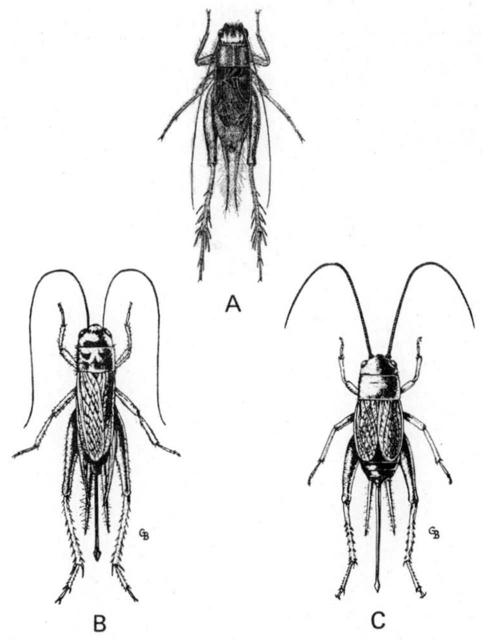

Figure 125. A, ground cricket, *Allonemòbius fasciàtus* (De Geer), male; B, the house cricket, *Achèta doméstic*us (L.); C, a field cricket, *Grýllus pennsylvánicus* Burmeister. (A, courtesy of Hebard and the Illinois Natural History Survey; B and C, courtesy of Institut de Biologie Générale, Université de Montréal.)

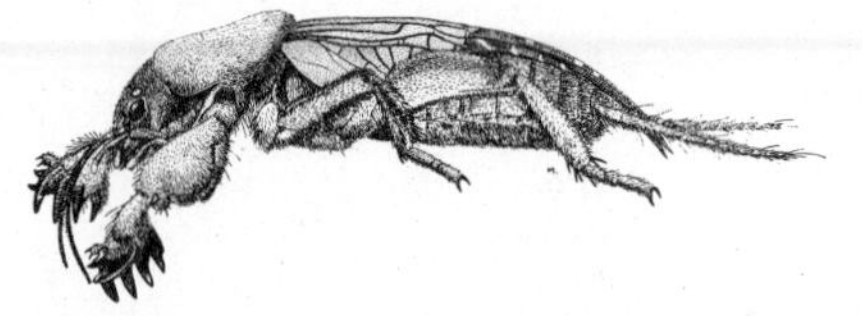

Figure 126. Northern mole cricket, *Gryllotálpa hexadáctyla* Perty. (Courtesy of Hebard and the Illinois Natural History Survey.)

occurs in the southeastern states, *Anurogrýllus mùticus* (De Geer); this insect is 12 to 17 mm in length and yellowish brown in color.

Family **Gryllotálpidae**—Mole Crickets: Mole crickets are brownish insects, very pubescent, and an inch (25 mm) or more in length; they have short antennae, and the front legs (tibia and basal tarsal segment) are very broad and spadelike (Figure 126). They burrow in moist places, usually 6 to 8 inches (152–203 mm) below the surface. The most common eastern species is *Gryllotálpa hexadáctyla* Perty, and the only species in the West is *G. cúltriger* Uhler.

SUBORDER **Phasmatòdea:** The Phasmatòdea are cursorial Orthóptera; the hind femora are not enlarged, and the tarsi are usually 5-segmented (3-segmented in the Timémidae). The body is usually elongate and sticklike, with the pronotum shorter than either the mesonotum or metanotum. Tympana and stridulatory structures are absent. The wings (in our species) are either much reduced or entirely absent. The cerci are short, and 1-segmented.

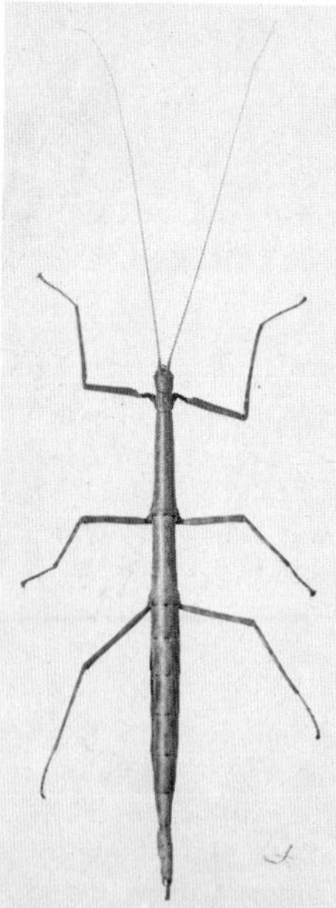

Figure 127. A walking stick. (Courtesy of the Ohio Agricultural Research and Development Center.)

Family **Phasmátidae**—Walking Sticks: The insects in this family are particularly striking in their resemblance to twigs and leaves. Some of the tropical species look very much like leaves, and are often called leaf-insects; the species in the United States are very elongate and twiglike, and are called walking sticks (Figure 127).

The walking sticks are slow-moving herbivorous insects that are usually found on trees or shrubs. They are very similar to twigs in appearance; this mimicry probably has protective value. Walking sticks are able to emit a foul-smelling substance from glands in the thorax; this behavior serves as a means of defense. Unlike most insects, the walking sticks are able to regenerate lost legs, at least in part. These insects are usually not sufficiently numerous to do much damage to cultivated plants, but when numerous may do serious damage to trees.

The eggs are not laid in any particular situation, but are simply scattered on the ground. There is a single generation a year, with the egg stage overwintering. The eggs often do not hatch the following spring, but hatch the second year after they are laid; for this reason walking sticks are generally abundant only in alternate years. The young are usually greenish in color, and the adults are brownish.

The walking sticks are widely distributed, but the group is principally tropical, and is better represented in the southern states. The common walking stick in the northern states is *Diápheromèra femoràta* (Say). All walking sticks in this country are wingless except *Áplopus mày-eri* Caudell, which occurs in southern Florida; this species has short oval front wings, and the hind wings project 2 or 3 mm beyond the front wings. This group contains the longest insect in the United States, *Megaphásma déntricus* (Stål), which reaches a length of 6 or 7 inches (152–178 mm); it occurs in the South and Southwest. Some tropical walking sticks get to be a foot or so long.

Family **Timémidae**—Timemas: These insects resemble walking sticks but are a little stouter and look a little like some earwigs, and the tarsi are 3-

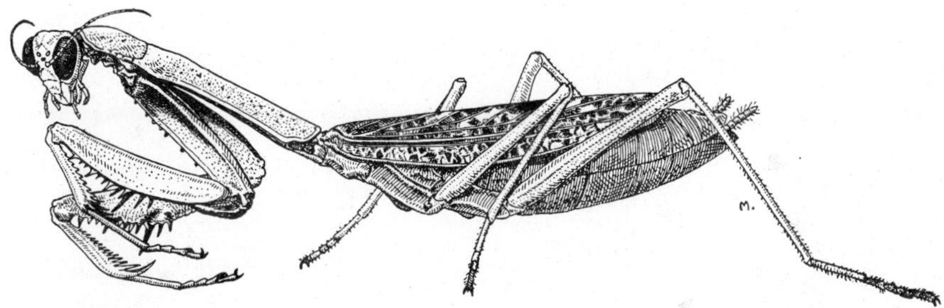

Figure 128. Carolina mantid, *Stagmomántis carolìna* (L.). (Courtesy of Hebard and the Illinois Natural History Survey.)

segmented. They are 14–22 mm in length, greenish to pink in color, and occur in deciduous trees in the Pacific Coast states. Our few species belong to the genus *Tímema*.

SUBORDER **Dictyóptera:** These are cursorial Orthóptera; the hind femora are not enlarged, and the tarsi are 5-segmented. The body is much elongated in the Mantòidea, and oval and flattened in the Blattòidea; the pronotum is usually longer than either the mesonotum or metanotum. Tympana and stridulatory structures are absent. The wings are generally present, though in some cases they are reduced. The cerci are many-segmented, and are usually fairly long.

Family **Mántidae**—Mantids: Mantids are large, elongate, rather slow-moving insects that are striking in appearance due to their peculiarly modified front legs (Figures 113 F and 128). The prothorax is greatly lengthened, the front coxae are very long, and the front femora and tibiae are armed with strong spines and fitted for grasping prey. The head is highly movable; mantids are the only insects that can "look over their shoulders." These insects are highly predaceous and feed on a variety of insects (including other mantids). They usually lie in wait for their prey with the front legs in an upraised position; this position has given rise to the common names "praying mantid" and "soothsayer" that are often applied to these insects.

Mantids overwinter in the egg stage, and the eggs are deposited on twigs or grass stems in a papier-mâchélike egg case or ootheca; each egg case may contain 200 or more eggs.

Mantids are chiefly tropical in distribution. The Carolina mantid, *Stagmomántis carolìna* (L.), which is about 2 inches (51 mm) in length (Figure 128), is the most common of several species of mantids occurring in the southern states. The large mantid (3–4 inches (76–102 mm) in length) which is locally common in the northern states is an introduced species, the Chinese mantid, *Tenódera aridifòlia sinénsis* Saussure; this species was introduced in the vicinity of Philadelphia about 70 years ago and has since become rather widely distributed through the transportation of egg masses. The European mantid, *Mántis religiòsa* L., a pale-green insect about 2 inches (51 mm) in length, was introduced in the vicinity of Rochester, New York, about 70 years ago, and now occurs throughout most of the eastern states. No males are known for *Brunnéria boreàlis* Scudder, a fairly common species in the South and Southwest.

SUPERFAMILY **Blattòidea**—Cockroaches or Roaches: Cockroaches can usually be recognized by their oval flattened shape, the head concealed under the pronotum, and the long hairlike antennae (Figure 129). The wings may be well developed, reduced, or absent; the females of many species have shorter wings than the males. These insects are rather general feeders. The eggs are enclosed in capsules or oothecae, which may be deposited immediately after they are formed or may be carried about on the end of the abdomen of the female until they hatch.

Cockroaches are primarily tropical insects, and most of our species occur in the southern part of the country. Some tropical species are occasionally brought into the North in shipments of bananas or other tropical fruits. The most commonly encountered cockroaches in the North are those that invade houses, where they are often serious pests. None is known to be a specific vector of disease, but they feed on all sorts of things in a house; they contaminate food, they have an unpleasant odor, and their presence is often very annoying.

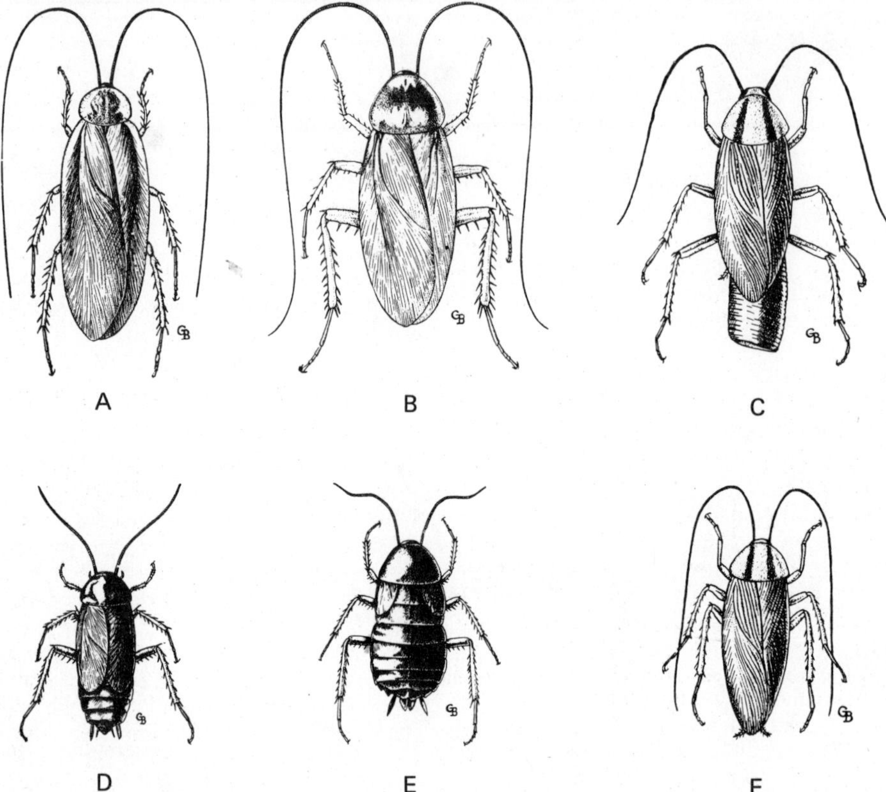

Figure 129. Some common cockroaches. A, wood cockroach, *Parcoblátta pennsylvánica* (De Geer) (Blattéllidae); B, American cockroach, *Periplanèta americàna* (L.) (Bláttidae); C, German cockroach, *Blattélla germánica* (L.), female (Blattéllidae); D, oriental cockroach, *Blátta orientàlis* (L.), male (Bláttidae); E, oriental cockroach, female; F, German cockroach, male. A, slightly enlarged; B, D, and E, about natural size; C and F, 2 ×. (Courtesy of Institut de Biologie Générale, Université de Montréal.)

There is much difference of opinion regarding the classification of cockroaches. The 40-odd major groups are variously treated as tribes, subfamilies, or families by different authorities. We follow here the classification of McKittrick (1964), who groups the 50 or so North American species in five families.

Family **Cryptocércidae:** The only cryptocercid in this country is the brown-hooded cockroach, *Cryptocércus punctulàtus* Scudder, which occurs in hilly or mountainous areas from New York to Georgia in the East and from Washington to California in the West. This cockroach is wingless, 23–29 mm in length, shining reddish brown with the dorsal surface finely punctured, and is somewhat elongate and parallel-sided; it occurs in decaying logs, particularly oak logs.

Family **Bláttidae:** The cockroaches in this group are relatively large insects (most are an inch or more in length) with numerous spines on the ventroposterior margin of the femora; several species are important household pests. One of the most common pest species in this group is the oriental cockroach, *Blátta orientàlis* L., which is about an inch long, dark brown, and broadly oval with short wings (Figure 129 D, E). Several species of *Periplanèta* also invade houses, one of the most common being the American cockroach, *P. americàna* (L.) (Figure 129 B); this species is about 27–35 mm in length and reddish brown with well-developed wings. One blattid occurring in Florida, *Eurycòtis floridàna* (Walker) (brown to black with very short wings, and 30–39 mm in length), which occurs under various sorts of cover out-of-doors, emits a very smelly liquid and is sometimes called the stinking cockroach.

Family **Polyphágidae:** These are mostly small cockroaches that have the pronotum rather hairy; the winged forms have the anal area of the hind wings flat at rest (not folded fanwise). They occur in the southern states, from Florida to California. Most species occurring in the Southwest (*Arenivàga* and *Eremoblátta*) occur in desert areas (some of these burrow in the sand like moles), and have the females wingless; some *Arenivàga* are nearly an inch in length. Other species are 6.5 mm in length or less; a species of *Attáphila* that occurs in southern Texas in the nests of leaf-cutting ants is 3 mm in length or less.

Family **Blattéllidae:** This is a large group of small cockroaches, most of them 12 mm in length or less. Several species invade houses; one of the most important of these is the German cockroach, *Blattélla germánica* (L.) (Figure 129 C, F), light brown with two longitudinal stripes on the pronotum; another is the brown-banded cockroach, *Supélla longipálpa* (Fabricius). A number of species in this group occur out-of-doors; the most common such species in the North are the wood cockroaches, *Parcoblátta* spp. (Figure 129 A), which live in litter and debris in woods. Most of the species in this group occur in the South, where they may be found in litter and debris out-of-doors, under signs on trees, and in similar situations.

Family **Blabéridae:** This group is principally tropical, and our species are nearly all restricted to the southern states. The group includes our largest cockroaches (*Bláberus* and *Leucophaèa*), which may reach a length of 2 inches (50 mm). Most species are brownish, but one occurring in southern Texas, *Panchlòra nívea* (L.), is pale green. Most members of this group are found out-of-doors in litter or debris; a few get into houses occasionally: for example, the Surinam cockroach, *Pycnoscèlus surinaménsis* (L.), and the Madeira cockroach, *Leucophaèa madérae* (Fabricius). The Madeira cockroach ($1\frac{1}{2}$–2 inches (38–51 mm) in length) is able to stridulate, and it gives off an offensive odor.

SUBORDER **Grylloblattòdea,** *Family* **Gryllobláttidae**—Rock Crawlers: These insects are slender and elongate, 15–30 mm in length, yellowish brown to grayish in color, and are wingless. The antennae are long and filiform with 28–50 segments, the cerci are long and 8-segmented, and the ovipositor is sword-shaped.

Rock crawlers occur in Japan, Siberia, the northwestern United States, and western Canada. They occur at high elevations under rocks, at the edges of snow fields or crawling about on the snow, in ice caves, and in moss. They are active at rather low temperatures, and are probably predaceous or scavengers. Five species occur in North America.

COLLECTING AND PRESERVING ORTHÓPTERA

Many of the Orthóptera, because they are relatively large and numerous, are fairly easy to collect. The best time for collecting most species is from midsummer to late fall, though a few species should be looked for in early summer, and others (such as the house-infesting roaches) may be collected at almost any time of the year. The more conspicuous forms, such as the grasshoppers and crickets, are most easily collected with a net, either by sweeping vegetation or by aiming for particular individuals. Some of the more secretive species may be collected at night by listening for their songs and then locating them with a flashlight, or by means of various sorts of baited traps. Some forms can be caught by putting molasses or a similar material in the bottom of a trap like that shown in Figure 617 B; the insects so collected can simply be picked out of the trap.

Most nymphs and some soft-bodied adult specimens should be preserved in alcohol, but most adults can be pinned. Grasshoppers should be pinned through the right side of the rear part of the pronotum; crickets, roaches, and mantids should be pinned through the right tegmen, in about the middle (from front to rear) of the body. If the specimen is very soft-bodied, the body should be supported by a piece of cardboard or by pins; otherwise, it will sag at either end. In the case of grasshoppers, it is desirable to spread the wings, at least on one side (as in Figure 118 A), in order that the color and venation of the hind wing can be seen. It is sometimes desirable to eviscerate some of the larger grasshoppers before they are pinned to facilitate drying and preservation. This may be done by making a short incision on the right or left side of the body near the base of the abdomen and removing as much as possible of the viscera.

References on the Orthóptera

Alexander, R. D. 1957a. Sound production and associated behavior in insects. *Ohio J. Sci.*, 57(2):101–113; 1 textf., 4 pl.

Alexander, R. D. 1957b. The taxonomy of the field crickets of the eastern United States (Orthoptera: Gryllidae: *Acheta*). *Ann. Ent. Soc. Amer.*, 50(6):584–602; 19 f.

Alexander, R. D., and D. J. Borror. 1956. The songs of insects. A 12-inch long-play phonograph record, published by Cornell Univ. Press, Ithaca, N.Y.

Alexander, R. D., and T. J. Walker. 1962. Two introduced field crickets new to eastern United States (Orthoptera: Gryllidae). *Ann. Ent. Soc. Amer.*, 55(1):90–94. (Includes a discussion of the status of the names *Gryllus* and *Acheta*.)

Ball, E. D., E. R. Tinkham, R. Flock, and C. T. Vorheis. 1942. The grasshoppers and other Orthoptera of Arizona. *Ariz. Agr. Expt. Sta. Tech. Bull.*, No. 93; pp. 257–373; 11 f., 4 pl.

Blatchley, W. S. 1920. *Orthoptera of Northeastern America*. Indianapolis: Nature Publ. Co., 785 pp., 246 f.

Brooks, A. R. 1958. Acridoidea of southern Alberta, Saskatchewan, and Manitoba (Orthoptera). *Can. Ent. Suppl.*, 9:1–92; 128 f., 38 maps.

Brusven, M. A. 1967. Differentiation, ecology, and distribution of immature slant-faced grasshoppers (Acridinae) in Kansas. *Kan. Agric. Exp. Sta. Tech. Bull.*, No. 149; 59 pp., 12 pl., 36 f.

Cantrell, I. J. 1968. An annotated list of the Dermaptera, Dictyoptera, Phasmatoptera, and Orthoptera of Michigan. *Mich. Ent.*, 1(9):299–346; 142 f.

Chopard, L. 1938. *La Biologie des Orthoptères*. Paris: Lachevalier, 541 pp., 4 pl.

Froeschner, R. C. 1954. The grasshoppers and other Orthoptera of Iowa. *Iowa State Coll. J. Sci.*, 29(2):163–354; 123 f.

Grant, H. J., Jr., and D. Rentz. 1967. Biosystematic review of the family Tanaoceridae, including a comparative study of the proventriculus (Orthoptera: Tanaoceridae). *Pan-Pac. Ent.*, 43(1):65–74; 9 f.

Gurney, A. B. 1948. The taxonomy and distribution of the Grylloblattidae. *Proc. Ent. Soc. Wash.*, 50(4):86–102; 3 pl.

Gurney, A. B. 1951. Praying mantids of the United States. *Smiths. Inst. Rept.*, 1950:339–362.

Hebard, M. 1917. The Blattidae of North America north of the Mexican boundary. *Mem. Amer. Ent. Soc.*, 2:1–284; illus.

Hebard, M. 1934. The Dermaptera and Orthoptera of Illinois. *Ill. Nat. Hist. Surv. Bull.*, 20(3):iv + 125–179; 167 f.

Helfer, J. R. 1963. *How to Know the Grasshoppers, Cockroaches, and Their Allies*. Dubuque, Iowa: W. C. Brown, v + 353 pp., 579 f.

Hubbell, T. H. 1936. A monographic revision of the genus *Ceuthophilus* (Orthoptera, Gryllacrididae, Rhaphidophorinae). *Univ. Fla. Pub. Biol. Sci. Ser.*, 2(1):1–551; frontis. + 38 pl.

Jago, N. D. 1971. A revision of the Gomphocerinae of the world with a key to the genera (Orthoptera, Acrididae). *Proc. Acad. Nat. Sci. Phila.*, 123(8):205–343; 404 f.

Kamp, J. W. 1963. Descriptions of two new species of Grylloblattidae and of the adult of *Grylloblatta barberi*, with an interpretation of their geographical distribution. *Ann. Ent. Soc. Amer.*, 56(1):53–68; 9 pl.

Kamp, J. W. 1973. Numerical classification of the orthopteroids, with special reference to the Grylloblattodea. *Can. Ent.*, 105(9):1235–1249.

McKittrick, F. A. 1964. Evolutionary studies of cockroaches. *Cornell Univ. Agric. Expt. Sta. Mem.*, 389; 197 pp., 6 textf., 205 f.

Morse, A. P. 1920. Manual of the Orthoptera of New England. *Proc. Boston Soc. Nat. Hist.*, 35(6):197–556; 99 f., pl. 10–29.

Princis, K. 1960. Zur Systematik der Blattarien. *Eos, Revista Espanol de Entomologia*, 36(4):427–449; 15 f.

Rehn, J. W. H. 1950. A key to the genera of North American Blattaria, including established adventives. *Ent. News*, 61(3):64–67.

Rehn, J. W. H. 1951. Classification of the Blattaria as indicated by their wings (Orthoptera). *Mem. Amer. Ent. Soc.*, No. 14; ii + 134 pp., 5 textf., 1 diag., 141 f.

Rehn, J. A. G., and H. J. Grant, Jr. 1961. A monograph of the Orthoptera of North America (north of Mexico), Vol. 1. *Acad. Nat. Sci. Phil. Monog.*, No. 12; 257 pp., 401 f., 8 pl., 36 maps.

Rehn, J. A. G., and M. Hebard. 1918. A study of the North American Eumastacidae (Orthoptera; Acrididae). *Trans. Amer. Ent. Soc.*, 44:223–250; pl. XI–XVI.

Rentz, D., and J. D. Burchim. 1968. Revisionary studies of nearctic Decticinae. *Mem. Pac. Coast Ent. Soc.*, 3:1–173; 37 f.

Strohecker, H. F., W. W. Middlekauff, and D. C. Rentz. 1968. The grasshoppers of California. *Bull. Calif. Insect Surv.*, 10:1–177; f. I–IV, 1–175, 107 maps.

Uvarov, B. P. 1928. *Locusts and Grasshoppers*. London: Imperial Bureau of Entomology, xiii + 352 pp., 118 f., 9 pl.

Uvarov. B. P. 1966. *Grasshoppers and Locusts. A Handbook of General Acridology*. Vol 1. *Anatomy, Physiology and Development, Phase Polymorphism, In-*

troduction to Taxonomy. Cambridge: Cambridge Univ. Press, xi + 481 pp., frontis. (color), 1 pl., 244 f.

Vickerey, V. R., and D. E. Johnstone. 1970. Generic status of some Nemobiinae (Orthoptera: Gryllidae) in northern North America. *Ann. Ent. Soc. Amer.*, 63(6):1740–1749; 29 f.

Vickerey, V. R., and D. E. Johnstone. 1973. The Nemobiinae (Orthoptera: Gryllidae) of Canada. *Can. Ent.*, 105(4):623–645; 48 f., 5 maps.

Waldon, B. H. 1911. The Euplexoptera and Orthoptera of Connecticut. *Conn. State Geol. and Nat. Hist. Surv. Bull.*, 16:39–169; 66 textf., 11 pl.

Walker, E. M. 1931–1938. On the anatomy of *Grylloblatta campodeiformis* Walker. *Ann. Ent. Soc. Amer.*, 24(3):519–536, 4 pl. (1931); 26(2):309–344, 7 pl. (1933); 31(4):588–640, 40 f. (1938).

Walker, T. J. 1962. The taxonomy and calling songs of the United States tree crickets (Orthoptera: Gryllidae: Oecanthinae). I. The genus *Neoxabea* and the *niveus* and *varicornis* groups of the genus *Oecanthus*. *Ann. Ent. Soc. Amer.*, 55(3):303–322; 17 f.

Walker, T. J. 1963. The taxonomy and calling songs of the United States tree crickets (Orthoptera: Gryllidae: Oecanthinae). II. The *nigricornis* group of the genus *Oecanthus*. *Ann. Ent. Soc. Amer.*, 56(6):772–789; 18f.

Walker, T. J. 1966. Annotated checklist of the Oecanthinae (Orthoptera: Gryllidae) of the world. *Fla. Ent.*, 49:265–277.

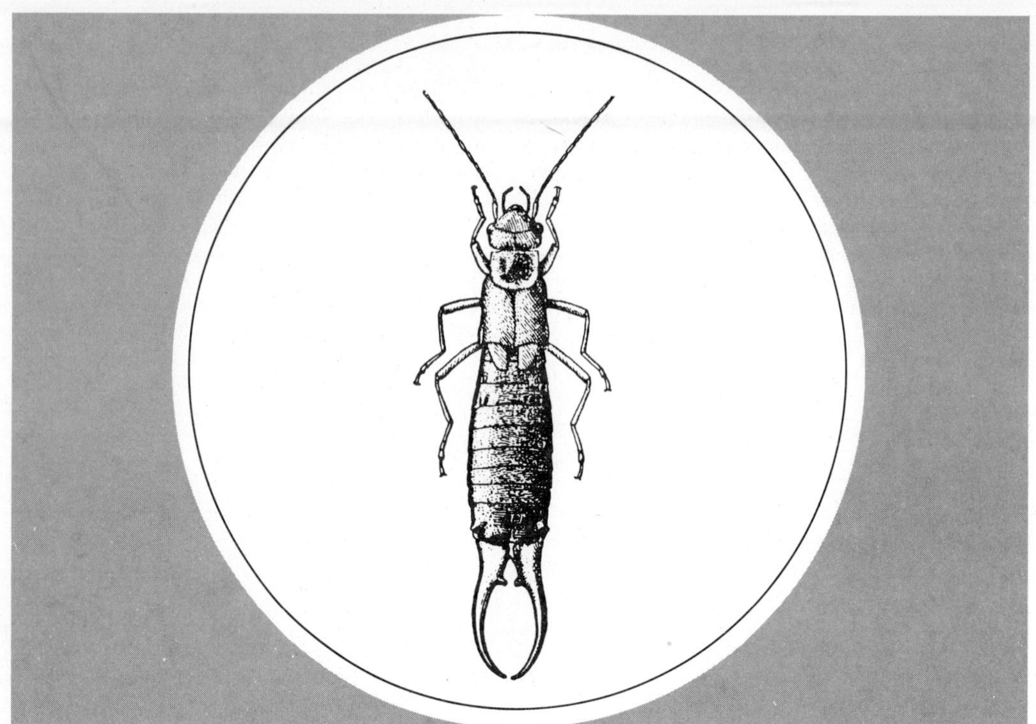

13: ORDER DERMÁPTERA[1]

EARWIGS

Earwigs are slender insects that resemble rove beetles but have large forcepslike cerci (Figures 130, 132). The adults usually have four wings. The front wings are short, leathery, and veinless, the hind wings (when present) are membranous and rounded with radiating veins, and when at rest are folded up under the front wings. The tarsi are 3-segmented. The mouth parts are of the chewing type, and the metamorphosis is simple.

Earwigs are largely nocturnal in habit and hide during the day in cracks, crevices, under bark, and in similar places. They are mainly scavengers, but are occasionally herbivorous. The eggs are laid in burrows in the ground and are carefully guarded by the female until they hatch. Earwigs overwinter in the adult stage.

Some species of earwigs have scent glands opening on the dorsal side of the third and fourth abdominal segments, and from these glands they can squirt a foul-smelling, yellowish-brown fluid some 3 or 4 inches (76 or 102 mm); this serves as a means of protection.

The name "earwig" is derived from an old superstition that these insects enter people's ears; this belief is entirely without foundation. Earwigs do not bite, but if handled will attempt to pinch with their cerci, and the abdomen is quite maneuverable; the larger earwigs, especially the males, can inflict a painful pinch.

The order Dermáptera is divided into three suborders, the Arixenìna, Diploglossàta, and For-

[1] Dermáptera: *derma,* skin; *ptera,* wings (referring to the texture of the front wings).

ficulìna. The Arixenìna and Diploglossàta have the cerci small and not forcepslike; the Arixenìna are Malayan ectoparasites of bats, and the Diploglossàta are South African ectoparasites of rodents. The Forficulìna is the only suborder occurring in this country, where it is represented by four families; these families may be separated by the following key.

Key to the Families of Dermáptera

1.	Second tarsal segment lobed beneath and prolonged distally beneath base of third segment (Figure 131 D); antennae with 12–16 segments 2		
1′.	Second tarsal segment cylindrical, not prolonged distally beneath base of third segment (Figure 131 C); antennae with 10–24 segments 3		
2(1).	Apical lobe of second tarsal segment narrow, and with a brush of long hairs beneath; antennae 12-segmented; California	**Chelisóchidae**	p. 213
2′.	Apical lobe of second tarsal segment wide (Figure 131 D), with very short pubescence beneath; antennae with 12–16 segments; widely distributed	**Forficùlidae**	p. 211
3(1′).	Antennae with 14–24 segments, segments 4–6 together rarely longer than first segment (Figure 131 B)	**Labidùridae**	p. 211
3′.	Antennae with 10–16 segments, segments 4–6 together longer than first segment (Figure 131 A)	**Labìidae**	p. 211

Family **Labidùridae:** This family includes three common genera: *Anisólabis, Euboréllia,* and *Labidùra*. The adults of *Anisólabis* and *Euboréllia* differ from those of *Labidùra* in being wingless, and the cerci of the male are asymmetrical (the right one curved more than the left one); these two genera are placed in a separate family (the Psalídidae) by some authorities. The seaside earwig, *A. maritíma* Géné, which occurs on both the Atlantic and Pacific coasts, is brownish black and 18–25 mm in length, and has 24-segmented antennae. The ringlegged earwig, *E. annùlipes* (Lucas), which occurs in the southern states, is brownish black and 9–11 mm in length, and has 15 or 16 antennal segments. The striped earwig, *L. bìdens* (Olivier), which occurs in the southern states, is light brown and 18–26 mm in length. *L. ripària* (Pallas) is known to be predaceous.

Family **Labìidae:** This family contains several species, the most common of which is the little earwig, *Làbia mìnor* (L.), 4–5 mm in length and introduced into this country from Europe (Figure 132 B). The handsome earwig, *Prolàbia pulchélla* (Serville), which is fairly common in the southern states, is 6.0–6.5 mm in length and dark brown in color. The toothed earwig, *Spongovóstox apicedentàtus* (Caudell), is fairly common among dead leaves and cacti in the desert regions of the Southwest.

Family **Forficùlidae:** The most common member of this family is the European earwig, *Forfícula auriculària* L., a brown insect 10–15 mm in

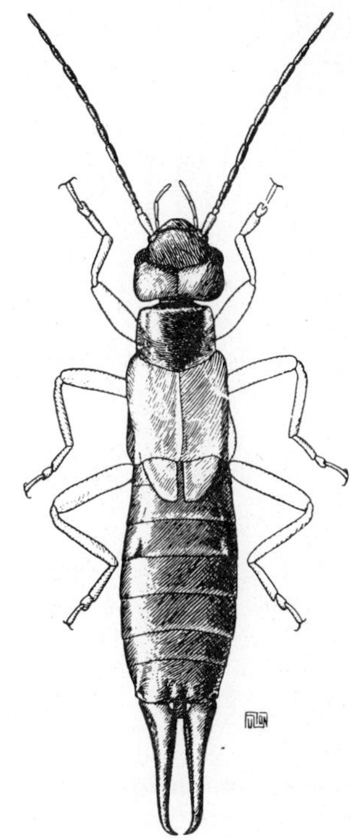

Figure 130. European earwig. *Forfícula auriculària* L., female. About 4 times natural size. (Courtesy of Fulton and the Oregon Agricultural Experiment Station.)

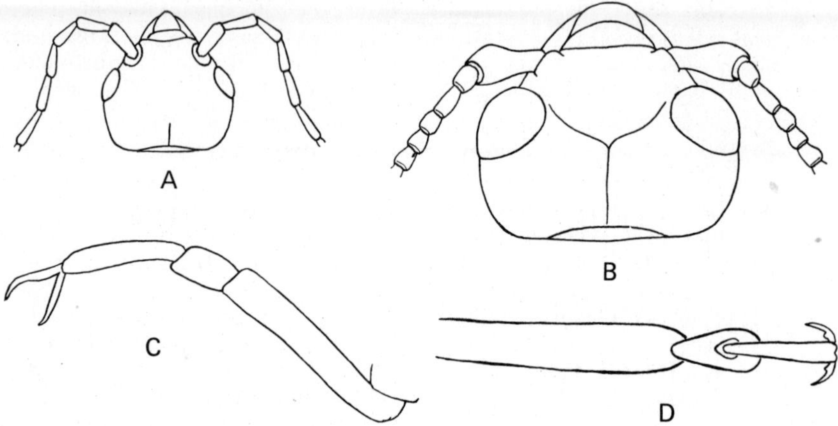

Figure 131. Characters of Dermáptera. A, head of *Làbia mìnor* (L.), dorsal view; B, head of *Labidùra ripària* Pallas, dorsal view; C, tarsus of *Labidùra;* D, tarsus of *Forfícula*.

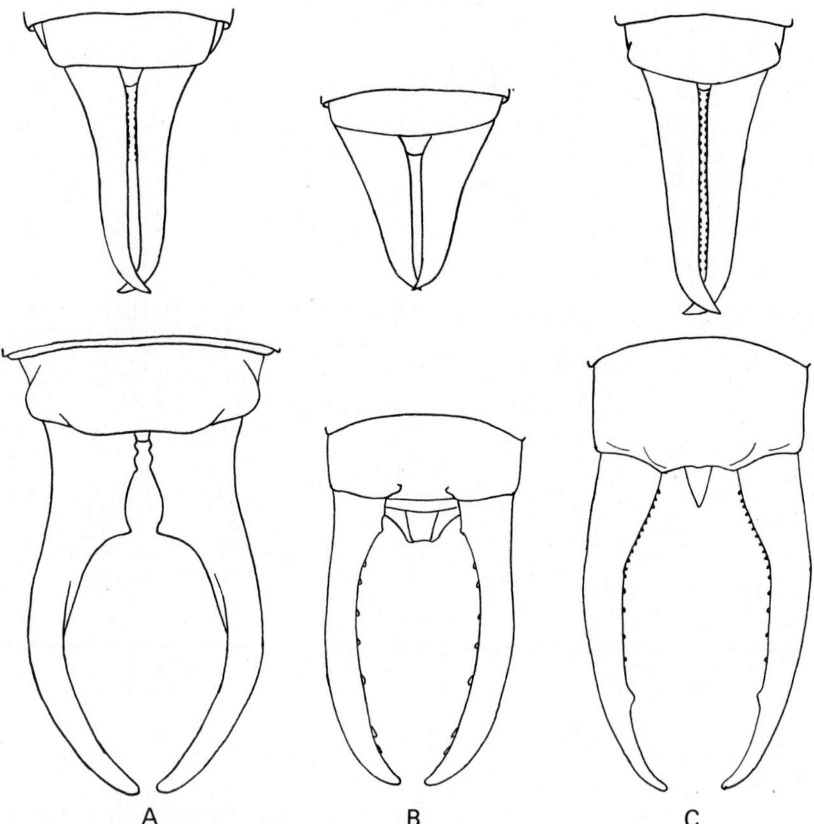

Figure 132. Anal forceps of Dermáptera. A, *Forfícula auriculària* L.; B, *Làbia mìnor* (L.); C, *Dòru lineàre* (Escholtz). Upper figures, forceps of female; lower figures, forceps of male.

length with 14–15 antennal segments (Figure 130). This species is widely distributed, and sometimes attacks vegetable crops, fruit trees, and ornamental plants. The spine-tailed earwig, *Dòru aculeàtum* (Scudder) is 7.5–11.0 mm in length with 12-segmented antennae.

Family **Chelisóchidae:** This family is represented in the United States by a single species, *Chelísoches mòrio* (Fabricius), a black tropical earwig 16–20 mm in length and occurring in California.

COLLECTING AND PRESERVING DERMÁPTERA

Earwigs must generally be looked for in various protected places—in debris, in cracks and crevices, or under bark; they are not often collected with a net. Some may be taken in pitfall traps (Figure 617 A). They are normally preserved dry, either on pins or points. If pinned, they are pinned through the right elytron, as in beetles.

References on the Dermáptera

Blatchley, W. S. 1920. *Orthoptera of Northeastern America.* Indianapolis: Nature Publ. Co., 784 pp., 246 f.

Brindle, A. 1966. A revision of the subfamily Labidurinae (Dermaptera: Labiduridae). *Ann. Mag. Nat. Hist.* (13), 9:239–269; illus.

Cantrell, I. J. 1968. An annotated list of the Dermaptera, Dictyoptera, Phasmatoptera, and Orthoptera of Michigan. *Mich. Ent.,* 1(9):299–346; 142 f.

Eisner, T. 1960. Defense mechanisms of arthropods. II. The chemical and mechanical weapons of an earwig. *Psyche,* 67(3):62–70; 1 textf., 2 pl.

Giles, E. T. 1963. The comparative external morphology and affinities of the Dermaptera. *Trans. Roy. Ent. Soc. London,* 115:95–164; 66 f.

Hebard, M. 1934. The Dermaptera and Orthoptera of Illinois. *Ill. Nat. Hist. Surv. Bull.,* 20(3):iv + 125–179; 167 f.

Hinks, W. D. 1955–1959. *A Systematic Monograph of the Dermaptera of the World Based on the Material in the British Museum (Natural History).* Part I. *Pygidicranidae, Subfamily Diplatyinae;* ix + 132 pp., 167 f. (1955). Part II. *Pygidicranidae Excluding Diplatyinae;* x + 218 pp., 214 f. (1959). London: British Museum (Natural History).

Popham, E. J. 1965. A key to the Dermaptera subfamilies. *Entomologist,* 98:126–136.

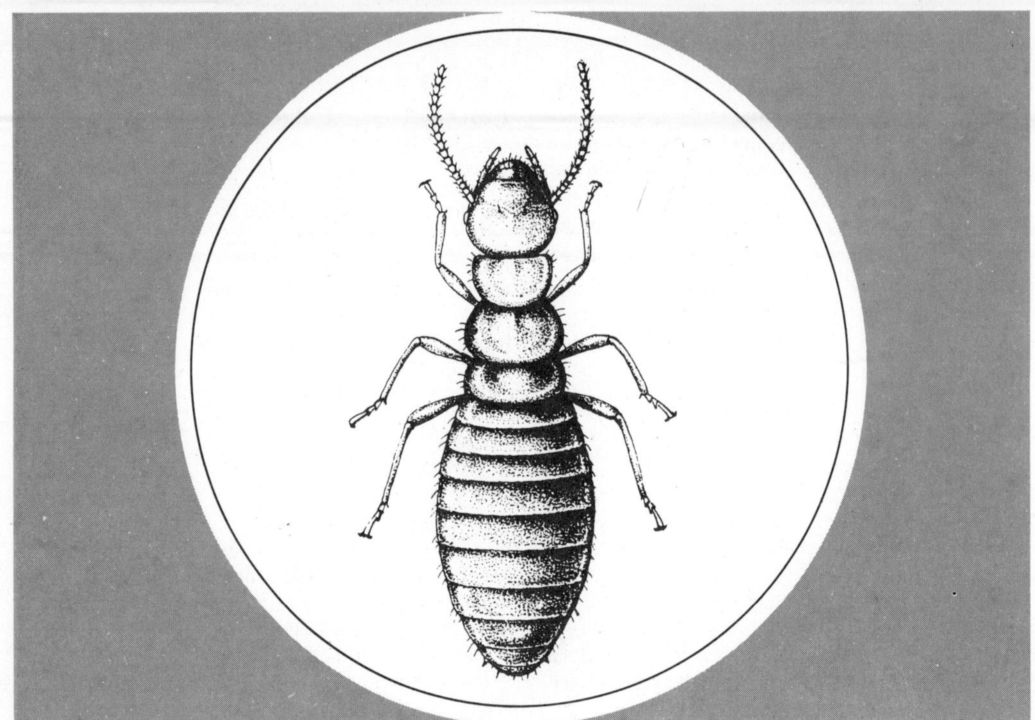

14: ORDER ISÓPTERA[1]

TERMITES

Termites are small to medium-sized insects that live in social groups and have a highly developed caste system. Both winged and wingless individuals occur in a colony, and some individuals may be short-winged. The wings, when present, are four in number, membranous, with a somewhat reduced venation, but often with numerous vein-like wrinkles. The front and hind wings are the same size and shape in American species (hence the order name), and when at rest are held flat over the body and extend beyond the tip of the abdomen (Figure 133). The mouth parts are of the chewing type, and the metamorphosis is simple.

Termites are sometimes called white ants, but they differ from the ants in several ways. Termites are very soft-bodied and usually light-colored, while ants are hard-bodied and usually dark-colored; the front and hind wings of a termite are similar in size and venation and are held flat over the abdomen at rest, but in ants the hind wings are smaller than the front wings and have fewer veins, and the wings at rest are usually held above the body. The abdomen in termites is broadly joined to the thorax, whereas in ants it is constricted at the base and connected to the thorax by a narrow petiole. The antennae of a termite are moniliform or filiform, while those of ants are elbowed. The caste system differs somewhat in the two types of insects; termite workers and soldiers consist of individuals of both sexes, with all nymphs acting as workers; in ants the individuals of these castes are all adult females.

There are differences of opinion regarding the systematic position of the termites. They appear to

[1] Isóptera: *iso,* equal; *ptera,* wings.

be closely related to the cockroaches, and some authorities would place them in the same order as the cockroaches. One Australian species of termite, *Mastotérmes darwiniénsis* Froggatt, which has an anal lobe in the hind wing, and has an egg mass like the ootheca of cockroaches, is looked upon as a sort of connecting link between the termites and the cockroaches.

TERMITE CASTES

The reproductives (kings and queens) are the most highly developed individuals sexually. They have fully developed wings, compound eyes, and are usually heavily pigmented. The males are often small, and in some species the queens may become very large (3 inches (76 mm) or more in length in some tropical species); the queens sometimes live for several years, laying thousands of eggs. The kings and queens are usually produced in large numbers at certain seasons; they leave the colony in a swarm, mate, and individual pairs establish new colonies. This swarming occurs at different times of the year in different species; in the most common eastern species, *Reticulitérmes flávipes* (Kollar), it occurs in the spring; in many western species, it occurs in late summer. The reproductives shed their wings, usually after mating; the wings break off along a weakened line at the base, leaving only a stub (the *scale*) attached to the thorax.

The supplementary reproductives have short wings and are less heavily pigmented than the reproductives, and usually have smaller eyes. They sometimes carry on extensive reproduction in the nest and may supplement the queen in building the colony. In some species there may be a second group of supplementary reproductives, sometimes referred to as the third form adults; these are similar to the workers in appearance, but are able to reproduce.

The worker caste consists of nymphs and sterile adults; they are pale in color, wingless, and usually lack compound eyes; the mandibles are relatively small. These individuals perform most of the work of the colony; they collect food and feed the queens, soldiers, and newly hatched young; they construct and care for the fungus gardens; and they build nests, passageways, tunnels, and galleries.

The soldier caste consists of sterile adults that have greatly enlarged heads and mandibles. The mandibles may in some cases be so large that the insect is unable to secure its own food and must be fed by the workers. The soldiers are usually slightly larger than the workers; they may or may not have compound eyes. When the colony is disturbed, the soldiers attack the intruders; if a small hole is punctured in the wall of the gallery, they attempt to plug it with their heads; if the intruder is an insect, they will grasp it with their mandibles. The termites in the genus *Anoplotérmes* lack a soldier caste.

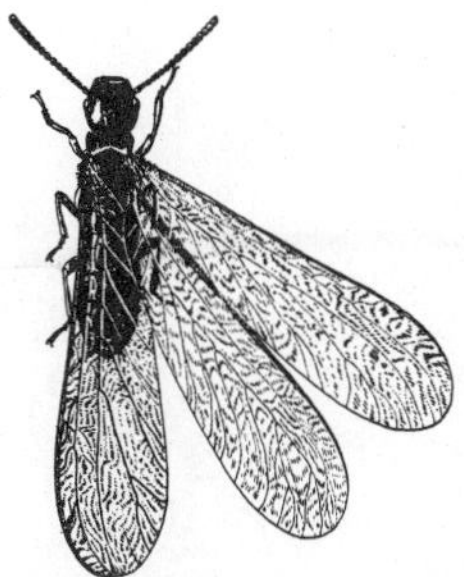

Figure 133. A winged termite. (Courtesy of USDA.)

In some species there is another caste, the nasutus (Figure 134 B). These individuals have the head prolonged anteriorly into a narrow snout through which a sticky secretion is exuded or squirted at an intruder. The nasuti function like the soldier caste in serving to defend the colony. They usually have well-developed palps, but their mandibles are reduced.

In some of the primitive species of termites, only two castes are developed, the reproductives and soldiers; the work of the colony is done by the immature individuals of these two castes.

HABITS OF TERMITES

Termites frequently groom each other with their mouth parts, probably as a result of the attraction of secretions that are usually available on the body. The food of termites is composed of the cast skins and feces of other individuals, dead individuals, and plant materials such as wood and wood products.

Some termites live in moist subterranean habitats and others live in dry habitats above ground. The subterranean forms normally live in wood buried beneath or in contact with the soil; they may enter wood remote from the soil, but must maintain a passageway or connecting gallery to the soil, from which they obtain moisture. Some species construct earthen tubes between the soil and wood above ground; these tubes are made of

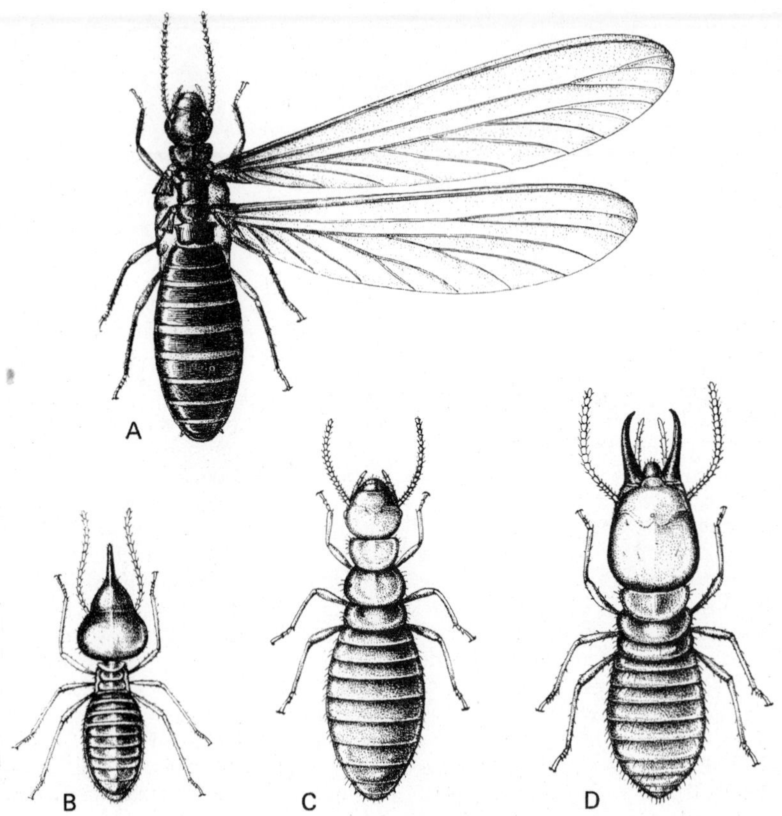

Figure 134. Castes of termites. A, sexual winged adult, *Amitérmes tubifórmans* (Buckley), 10 × (Termítidae); B, nasutus of *Tenuiróstritérmes tenuiróstris* (Desneux), 15 × (Termítidae); C, worker, and D, soldier, of *Prorhinotérmes símplex* (Hagen), 10 × (Rhinotermítidae). (Courtesy of Banks and Snyder and the U.S. National Museum.)

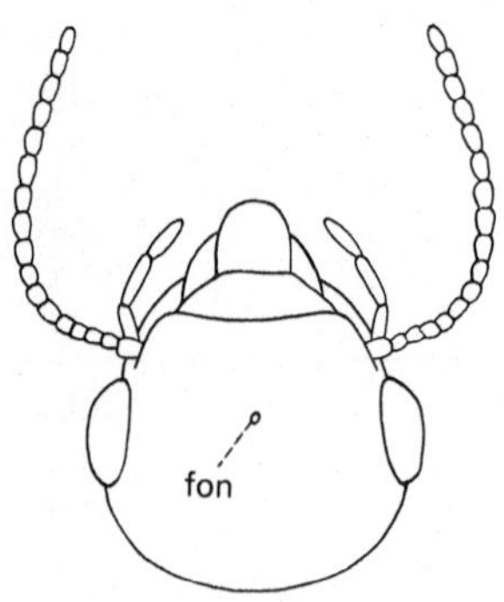

Figure 135. Head of *Prorhinotérmes,* dorsal view, showing fontanelle (*fon*). (Modified from Banks and Snyder.)

dirt mixed with a secretion from a pore on the front of the head (the fontanelle). The nests may be entirely subterranean, or they may protrude above the surface; some tropical species have nests (termitaria) 30 feet (9 m) high. The dry-wood termites, which live above ground (without a contact with the ground) live in posts, stumps, trees, and buildings constructed of wood; their chief source of moisture is metabolic water (water resulting from the oxidation of food).

The cellulose in a termite's food is digested by myriads of flagellated protozoans living in the termite's digestive tract. A termite from which these protozoans have been removed will continue to feed, but will eventually starve to death because its food is not digested. This association is an excellent example of symbiosis, or mutualism. Some termites harbor bacteria rather than Protozoa. Ter-

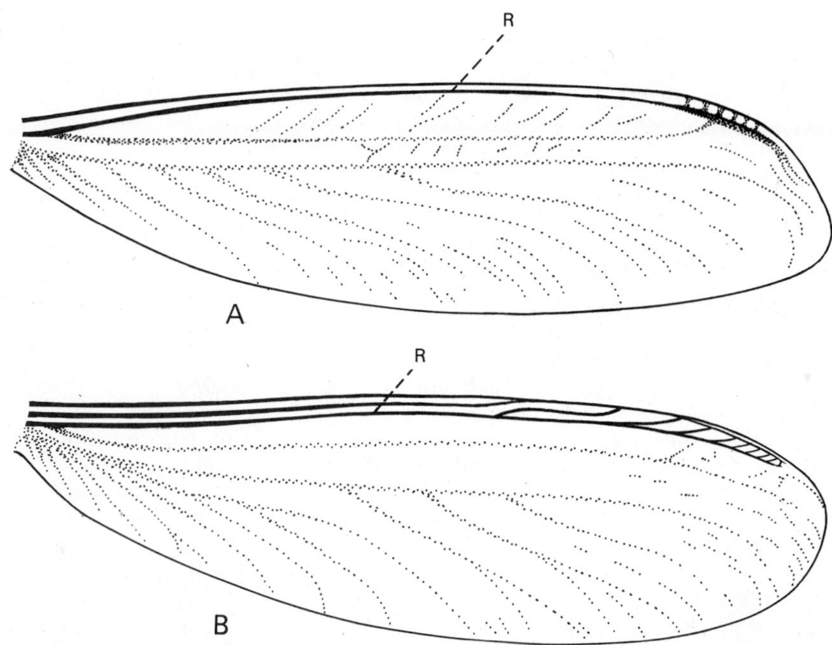

Figure 136. Wings of termites. A, Rhinotermítidae; B, Kalotermítidae.

mites engage in a unique form of anal liquid exchange (trophallaxis), and it is by this means that intestinal microorganisms are transmitted from one individual to another. Many wood- and plant-eating animals harbor in their digestive tract microorganisms that aid in digestion; even in man, much of the digestion is brought about by bacteria.

Key to the Families of Isóptera (Winged Adults)

1. Fontanelle usually present (Figure 135, *fon*); wings with only 2 heavy veins in anterior part of wing beyond scale, and R usually without anterior branches (Figure 136 A) 2

1′. Fontanelle absent; wings with 3 or more heavy veins in anterior part of wing beyond scale, and R with 1 or more anterior branches (Figure 136 B) 3

2(1). Scale of front wing longer than pronotum; pronotum flat; cerci 2-segmented; widely distributed .... **Rhinotermítidae** p. 218

2′. Scale of front wing shorter than pronotum; pronotum saddle-shaped; cerci 1- or 2-segmented; southwestern United States .... **Termítidae** p. 219

3(1′.). Ocelli present; shaft of tibiae without spines; antennae usually with 23 or more segments; Florida and western United States .... **Kalotermítidae** p. 218

3′. Ocelli absent; shaft of tibiae usually with spines; antennae usually with less than 22 segments; western United States .... **Hodotermítidae** p. 218

Key to the Families of Isóptera (Soldiers)

1. Mandibles vestigial, the head produced anteriorly into a long noselike projection (nasuti, Figure 134 B) .... **Termítidae** p. 219

1′.	Mandibles normal, head not as above 2	
2(1′).	Head longer than broad (Figure 134 D); mandibles with or without prominent marginal teeth 3	
2′.	Head short, hollowed out; mandibles without marginal teeth; southern United States (powderpost termites) .... **Kalotermítidae**	p. 218
3(2).	Mandibles with one or more prominent marginal teeth; southern and western United States 4	
3′.	Mandibles without marginal teeth (Figure 134 D); widely distributed .... **Rhinotermítidae**	p. 218
4(3).	Mandibles with only 1 prominent marginal tooth; head narrowed anteriorly .... **Termítidae**	p. 219
4′.	Mandibles with more than 1 prominent marginal tooth; head not narrowed anteriorly 5	
5(4′).	Third antennal segment modified; hind femora swollen .. **Kalotermítidae**	p. 218
5′.	Third antennal segment not modified; hind femora variable 6	
6(5′).	Hind femora swollen; antennae with at least 23 segments; shaft of tibiae with spines .... **Hodotermítidae**	p. 218
6′.	Hind femora not, or only slightly, swollen; antennae with fewer than 23 segments; shaft of tibiae without spines .... **Kalotermítidae**	p. 218

Family **Kalotermítidae:** This family is represented in the United States by 16 species and includes drywood, dampwood, and powderpost termites. These termites have no worker caste, and the young of the other castes perform the work of the colony. The kalotermitids lack a fontanelle and do not construct earthen tubes.

The drywood termites (*Incisitérmes, Pterotérmes,* and *Marginitérmes*) attack dry sound wood and do not have a ground contact. Most infestations are in buildings, but furniture, utility poles, and piled lumber may also be attacked. Adults are cylindrical in shape and about 13 mm in length, and the reproductives are pale brown in color. *Incisitérmes mìnor* (Hagen) and *Marginitérmes húbbardi* (Banks) are important species in the southwestern states.

The dampwood termites in this family (*Neotérmes* and *Paraneotérmes*) attack moist dead wood, tree roots, and the like; they occur in Florida and the western United States.

The powderpost termites (*Cryptotérmes* and *Calcaritérmes*) usually attack dry wood (without a soil contact), and reduce it to powder; they occur in the southern United States. *Cryptotérmes brévis* (Walker) is probably the only introduced species of termite in the United States. It occurs along the Gulf Coast near Tampa and New Orleans, and has been found as far north as Tennessee; it was probably introduced in furniture. It attacks furniture, books, stationery, dry goods, and building timbers; it frequently does a great deal of damage. It is found in buildings, never out-of-doors; where it is found, its colonies are numerous but small.

Family **Hodotermítidae**—Dampwood Termites: This group includes three species of *Zootermópsis,* which occur along the Pacific Coast. The adults are 13 mm or more in length, somewhat flattened, and lack a fontanelle; there is no worker caste. These termites attack dead wood, and although they do not require a ground contact, some moisture in the wood is required. They generally occur in dead, damp, rotting logs, but frequently damage buildings, utility poles, and lumber, particularly in coastal regions where there is considerable fog.

The most common species in this group are *Z. nevadénsis* Banks and *Z. angusticóllis* (Hagen). *Z. nevadénsis* is a little over 13 mm long, and lives in relatively dry habitats (especially dead tree trunks). The wingless forms are pale with a darker head, and the winged forms are dark brown with the head chestnut or orange. *Z. angusticóllis* is larger (about 18 mm long), and generally occurs in damp dead logs; adults are pale with a brown head.

Family **Rhinotermítidae:** This group is represented in the United States by eight species, and includes the subterranean termites (*Reticulitérmes* and *Heterotérmes*) and the dampwood termites in the genus *Prorhinotérmes* (Figure 134 C, D); the subterranean termites are widely distributed, but the dampwood termites occur only in Florida. These termites are small (adults are about 6–8 mm long); wingless forms are very pale (soldiers have a pale brown head), and winged forms are black; there is a fontanelle on the front of the head (Figure 135, *fon*). The members of this group always maintain a contact with the soil; they often construct earthen tubes to wood not in contact with the soil. The eastern subterranean termite, *Reticulitérmes flávipes* (Kollar) (Figure 137), is probably the most destructive species in the order, and is the only termite occurring in the Northeast.

Family **Termítidae:** This group is represented in the United States by 14 species, which occur in the Southwest. It includes the soldierless termites (*Anoplotérmes*), desert termites (*Amitérmes* and *Gnáthamitérmes*), and the nasutiform termites (*Nasutitérmes* and *Tenuiróstritérmes*). The soldierless termites burrow under logs or cow chips, and are not of economic importance. The desert termites are subterranean, and occasionally damage the wood of buildings, poles, and fence posts. The nasutiform termites have a nasutus caste (Figure 134 B); they attack trees or other objects on the ground, and maintain a ground contact.

Figure 137. A group of workers of the eastern subterranean termite, *Recticulitérmes flávipes* (Kollar); note the soldier in the right central portion of the picture. (Courtesy of Davidson.)

ECONOMIC IMPORTANCE OF TERMITES

Termites hold two positions from the economic point of view. They may be very destructive, since they feed upon and often destroy various structures or materials that man utilizes (wooden portions of buildings, furniture, books, utility poles, fence posts, many fabrics, and the like), but on the other hand, they are beneficial in that they assist in the conversion of dead trees and other plant products to substances that can be utilized by plants.

Reticulitérmes flávipes (Kollar) is the common termite throughout the eastern United States. This species occurs in buried wood, fallen trees, and logs; it must maintain a ground connection to obtain moisture. It cannot initiate a new colony in the wood in a house; the nest in the soil must be established first. Once the soil nest is established, these termites may enter buildings from the soil in one of five ways: (1) through timbers that are in direct contact with the soil, (2) through openings in rough stone foundations, (3) through openings or cracks in concrete-block foundations, (4) through expansion joints or cracks in concrete floors, or (5) by means of earthen tubes constructed over foundations or in hidden cracks and crevices in masonry.

Infestations of the subterranean termite in a building may be recognized by the swarming of the reproductives in the spring in or about the building, by mud protruding from cracks between boards or beams or along basement joists, by the earthen tubes extending from the soil to the wood, or by the hollowness of the wood in which the insects have been tunneling. A knife blade can easily be pushed into a timber hollowed out by termites, and such wood readily breaks apart.

Subterranean termites in buildings are controlled by two general methods: by proper construction of the buildings to render them termite-proof, or by the use of chemicals. The former involves construction in which no wood is in contact with the ground and in which the termites cannot reach the wooden part of the building through outside steps, sills, or through the foundation. Control by chemicals involves the use of such materials as aldrin, heptachlor, chlordane, lindane, or pentachlorophenol applied to the wood or the soil. Utility poles and fence posts, which must be in contact with the ground, may be rendered termite-proof by chemical treatment.

The best method of eliminating drywood termites is by fumigation; for such termites in buildings this involves the use of a large tent of plastic or other impervious material placed over the entire building, and is a rather expensive procedure. Dry-wood termites may also be eliminated by drilling holes in infested timbers, forcing a small amount of a poison dust (arsenic, fluorine, or other material) into the holes, and then plugging up the holes. Termites constantly groom one another, and once a few individuals get this dust on themselves, the other individuals of the colony will eventually obtain it and be killed.

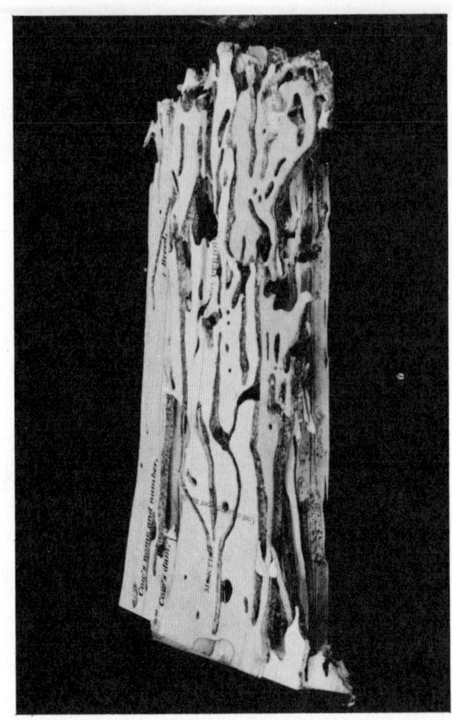

Figure 138. Termite damage. (Courtesy of Davidson.)

COLLECTING AND PRESERVING ISÓPTERA

Termites can be found by turning over dead logs or by digging into dead stumps; they may be collected with forceps or a moistened brush, or they may be shaken out of infested timbers onto a paper. Termites should be preserved in 70–80 percent alcohol; most individuals are very soft-bodied and shrivel or become distorted if mounted on pins or points. It is often necessary to mount these insects on microscope slides for detailed study.

References on the Isóptera

Banks, N., and T. E. Snyder. 1920. A revision of the nearctic termites, with notes on their biology and geographic distribution. *Bull. U.S. Natl. Mus.*, No. 108; viii + 228 pp., 35 pl., 70 textf.

Berger, B. G. 1947. How to recognize and control termites in Illinois. *Ill. Nat. Hist. Surv. Circ.*, No. 41; 44 pp., 32 f.

Ebeling, W. 1968. Termites: identification, biology, and control of termites attacking buildings. *Calif. Agric. Expt. Sta. Extension Service Manual* 38. 68 pp.

Kofoid, C. A., et al. 1934. *Termites and Their Control.* Berkeley, Calif.: Univ. California Press, xxv + 734 pp., 182 f.

Krishna, K. 1961. A generic revision and phylogenetic study of the family Kalotermitidae (Isoptera). *Bull. Amer. Mus. Nat. Hist.*, 122(4):307–408; 81 f.

Krishna, K., and F. M. Weesner (Eds.). 1969–1970. *Biology of Termites.* New York: Academic Press, Vol. 1 (1969), xiv + 600 pp.; illus. Vol. 2 (1970), 600 pp.; illus.

Lüscher, M. 1961. Social control of polymorphism in termites. *Sym. Roy. Ent. Soc. London,* 1:57–67; 5 f.

Skaife, S. H. 1961. *Dwellers in Darkness.* New York: Doubleday, xi + 180 pp., 26 f., 16 pl.

Snyder, T. E. 1935. *Our Enemy the Termite.* Ithaca, N.Y.: Comstock Publ., 196 pp., 56 f.

Snyder, T. E. 1949. Catalogue of the termites (Isoptera) of the world. *Smiths. Inst. Misc. Coll.*, 112(3953):1–490.

Snyder, T. E. 1954. *Order Isoptera—the Termites of the United States and Canada*. New York: Nat. Pest Control Assn., 64 pp., 27 f.

Snyder, T. E. 1956. Annotated, subject-heading bibliography of termites, 1350 B.C. to A.D. 1954. *Smiths. Inst. Misc. Coll.*, 130(4258):iii + 305 pp.

Weesner, F. M. 1960. Evolution and biology of the termites. *Ann. Rev. Ent.*, 5:153–170.

Weesner, F. M. 1965. *The Termites of the United States. A Handbook*. Elizabeth, N.J.: Natl. Pest Control Assn., 70 pp., 21 f.

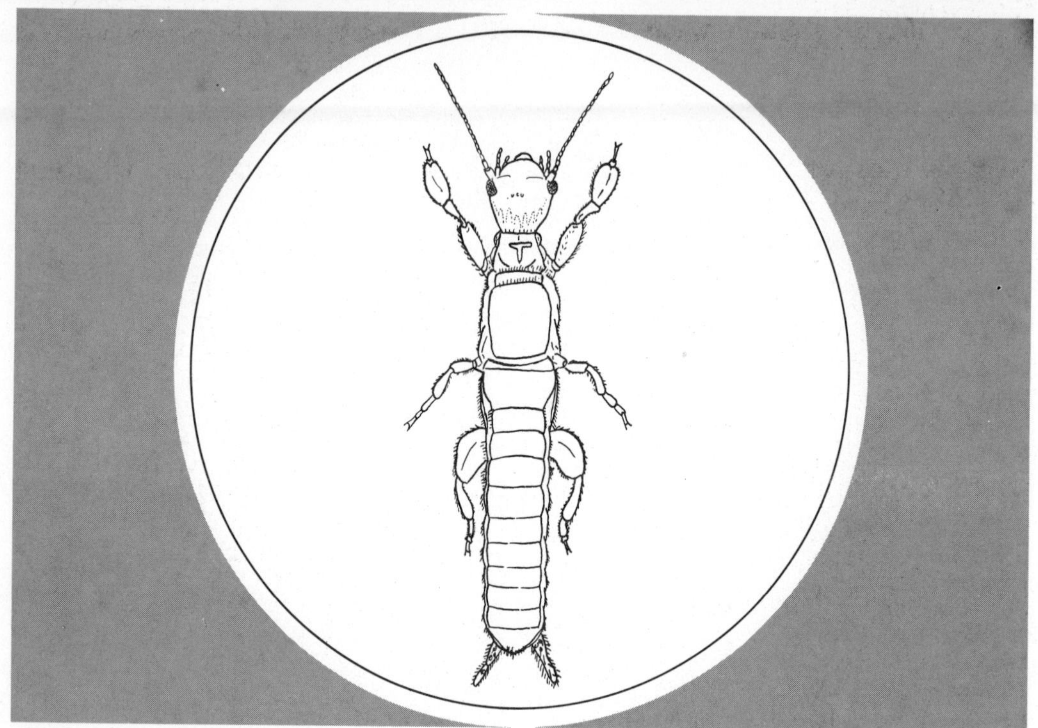

15: ORDER EMBIÓPTERA[1]

WEBSPINNERS

The webspinners are small, slender insects that are chiefly tropical in distribution; a few species occur in the southern United States. The body is somewhat flattened in the males and more or less cylindrical in the females and young; most species are between 4 and 7 mm in length. The antennae are filiform, ocelli are lacking, and the mouth parts are of the chewing type; the head is prognathous. The legs are short and stout, and the hind femora are thickened; the tarsi are 3-segmented, with the basal segment of the front tarsi enlarged and containing silk glands and hollow spinning hairs. The males of most species are winged, though some are wingless or have vestigial wings; the front and hind wings are similar in size and venation, and the venation is somewhat reduced (Figure 139 A). Both winged and wingless males may occur in the same species. The females are always wingless. The abdomen is 10-segmented and bears a pair of cerci that are generally 2-segmented; in certain genera the adult male has the left cercus 1-segmented. The terminal abdominal appendages are generally asymmetrical in the male and always so in the female. The webspinners undergo simple metamorphosis. At least one species is parthenogenetic.

These insects live in silken galleries spun in debris, in cracks in the soil, under stones, on or under bark, or among epiphytic plants, mosses, or lichens. In most silk-producing insects the silk is spun from modified salivary glands that open in the mouth, but in the webspinners the silk glands and spinnerets are located in the basal segment of the front tarsi. All stages of these insects, even the

[1] Embióptera; *embio*, lively; *ptera*, wings.

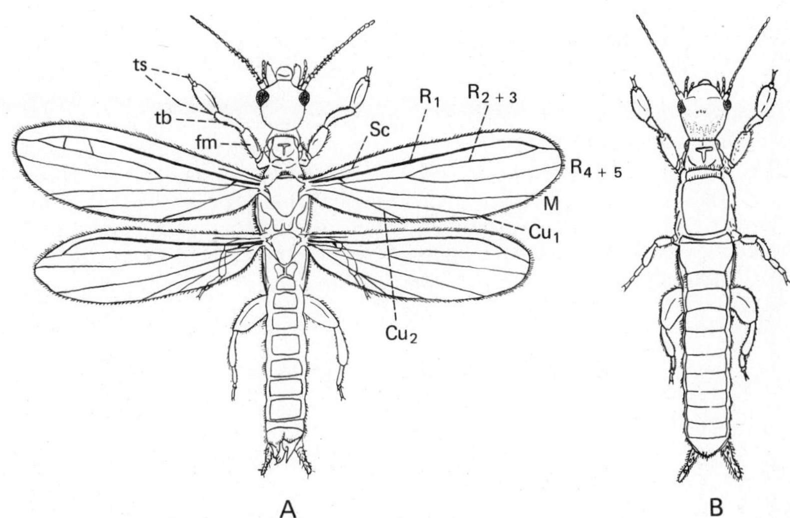

Figure 139. A webspinner, *Oligótoma saundérsii* (Westwood). A, winged male; B, wingless female. *fm*, femur; *tb*, tibia; *ts*, tarsus. (Redrawn from Essig, by permission of Macmillan Company.)

first instar young, are able to spin silk. Most species live in colonies. The webspinners often feign death when disturbed, but on occasion can move very rapidly, usually running backward. The eggs are large and cylindrical, are laid in the galleries, and are often covered with chewed food particles; the eggs are attended by the females. Webspinners feed on various plant materials, principally dead grass and leaves, moss, lichens, and bark.

Key to the Families of Embióptera

1. R_{4+5} in wings of male forked; left cercus 2-segmented ..... **Teratembìidae** p. 223

1′. R_{4+5} in wings of male not forked (Figure 139 A); if wings are absent, then left cercus is 1-segmented 2

2(1′). Mandibles without apical teeth; tenth tergite of male completely divided by a median membranous area that reaches ninth tergite; left cercus of male usually with peglike spines on mesal side of basal segment .... **Anisembìidae** p. 223

2′. Mandibles with distinct apical teeth; tenth tergite of male incompletely divided by a median membranous area that does not extend to ninth tergite; left cercus of male smooth on mesal side .... **Oligotómidae** p. 223

Family **Anisembìidae:** The Anisembìidae are represented in the United States by two species, *Anisémbia texàna* (Melander) of eastern Texas, Louisiana, Mississippi, and Arkansas, and *Chelicérca rùbra* (Ross) of the Southwest. Both winged and wingless males occur in colonies of *A. texàna*.

Family **Teratembìidae (Oligembìidae):** The Teratembìidae are represented in the United States by four species: *Oligémbia húbbardi* (Hagen) of southern Florida, *O. vandỳkei* Ross (an arboreal species) of the southeastern states, *O. melanùra* Ross (another arboreal species) of southern Louisiana and the Gulf Coast of Texas, and *O. lobàta* Ross of the Brownsville region of Texas.

Family **Oligotómidae:** The Oligotómidae are represented in the United States by three species, two of which have been introduced from the Old

World. The introduced species are *Oligótoma saundérsii* (Westwood) of the Southeast, and *O. nìgra* Hagen of the Southwest.

COLLECTING AND PRESERVING EMBIÓPTERA

The males, which are generally more easily identified than the females, are best collected at lights. In their normal habitat these insects are perhaps most readily collected during and following the rainy season, while the soil is damp. Many specimens collected at this time may be immatures, but they can be reared to maturity (males and females) in jars containing some dried grass and leaves that are kept somewhat moist.

Webspinners should be preserved in 70 percent alcohol. For detailed study it may be desirable to clear the specimens in KOH and mount them on microscope slides (see Ross, 1940, page 634).

References on the Embióptera

Davis, C. 1940. Family classification of the order Embioptera. *Ann. Ent. Soc. Amer.*, 33(4):677–682.

Ross, E. S. 1940. A revision of the Embioptera of North America. *Ann. Ent. Soc. Amer.*, 33(4):629–676; 50 f.

Ross, E. S. 1944. A revision of the Embioptera, or webspinners, of the New World. *Proc. U.S. Natl. Mus.*, 94(3175):401–504; f. 6–156, pl. 18–19.

Ross, E. S. 1970. Biosystematics of the Embioptera. *Ann. Rev. Ent.*, 15:157–172.

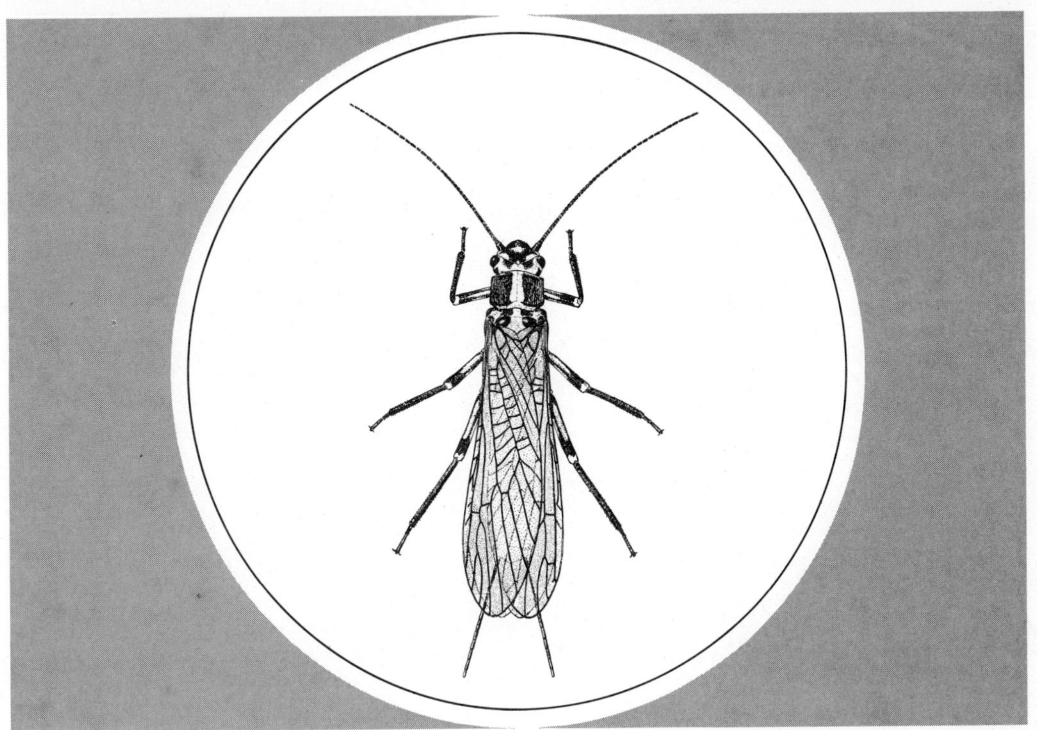

16: ORDER PLECÓPTERA[1]

STONEFLIES

Stoneflies are mostly medium-sized or small, somewhat flattened, soft-bodied, rather drab-colored insects found near streams or rocky lake shores. They are poor fliers, and are seldom found far from water. Most species have four membranous wings (Figure 142); the front wings are elongate and rather narrow and usually have a series of cross veins between M and Cu_1 and between Cu_1 and Cu_2; the hind wings are slightly shorter than the front wings, and usually have a well-developed anal lobe that is folded fanwise when the wings are at rest. A few species of stoneflies have the wings reduced or absent in the male. Stoneflies at rest hold the wings flat over the abdomen (Figure 140 A). The antennae are long, slender, and many-segmented. The tarsi are 3-segmented. Cerci are present and may be long or short. The mouth parts are of the chewing type, though in many adults (which do not feed) they are somewhat reduced. The stoneflies undergo simple metamorphosis, and the nymphal stages of development are aquatic.

Stonefly nymphs (Figures 140B and 141) are somewhat elongate flattened insects with long antennae, long cerci, and with branched gills on the thorax and about the bases of the legs. They are very similar to mayfly nymphs, but lack a median caudal filament (that is, they have only two tails, while mayfly nymphs nearly always have three), and the gills are different; mayfly nymphs have leaflike gills along the sides of the abdomen (Figure 93). Stonefly nymphs are often found under

[1] Plecóptera: *pleco,* folded or plaited; *ptera,* wings (referring to the fact that the anal region of the hind wings is folded when the wings are at rest).

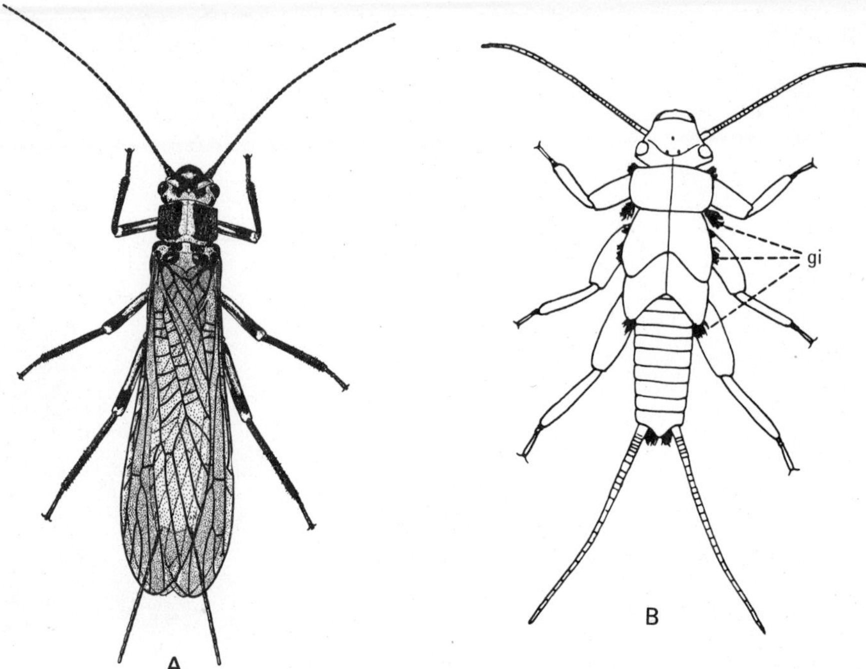

Figure 140. A, an adult stonefly, *Isopérla confùsa* Frison (Perlòdidae); B, a stonefly nymph. *gi*, gills. (Courtesy of Frison and the Illinois Natural History Survey; B, redrawn from Frison.)

stones in streams or along lake shores (hence the common name of these insects), but may occasionally be found anywhere in a stream where food is available. A few species are known to live in underground water; nymphs of these sometimes appear in wells or other drinking water supplies. Some species are plant feeders in the nymphal stage, and others are predaceous or omnivorous.

Some species of stoneflies emerge, feed, and mate during the fall and winter months. The nymphs of these species are generally plant feeders, and the adults feed chiefly on blue-green algae and are diurnal in feeding habits. The species that emerge during the summer vary in nymphal feeding habits; many do not feed as adults.

CLASSIFICATION OF THE PLECÓPTERA

The classification followed here is that of Gaufin *et al.* (1972), who recognize six families in two suborders; this arrangement is given below, with alternate names of arrangements in parentheses.

Suborder Filipálpia (Hológnatha)
- Peltopérlidae—roachlike stoneflies
- Nemoùridae (including Leùctridae, Capnìidae, and Taeniopterýgidae)
  - Nemourìnae—spring stoneflies
  - Leuctrìnae—rolled-winged stoneflies
  - Capniìnae—small winter stoneflies
  - Taeniopterygìnae—winter stoneflies
- Pteronárcidae—giant stoneflies

Suborder Setipálpia (Subulipálpia, Systellógnatha)
- Perlòdidae (including Isopérlidae)—perlodid stoneflies
- Chloropérlidae—green stoneflies
- Pérlidae—common stoneflies

The two suborders differ principally in the form of the labium. The Filipálpia have the glossae and paraglossae about the same size, whereas the glossae in the Setipálpia are quite small, appearing almost as a basal lobe of the paraglossae. The Filipálpia are principally plant feeders, both as nymphs and adults, while the Setipálpia are mostly carnivorous as nymphs and are usually nonfeeding as adults.

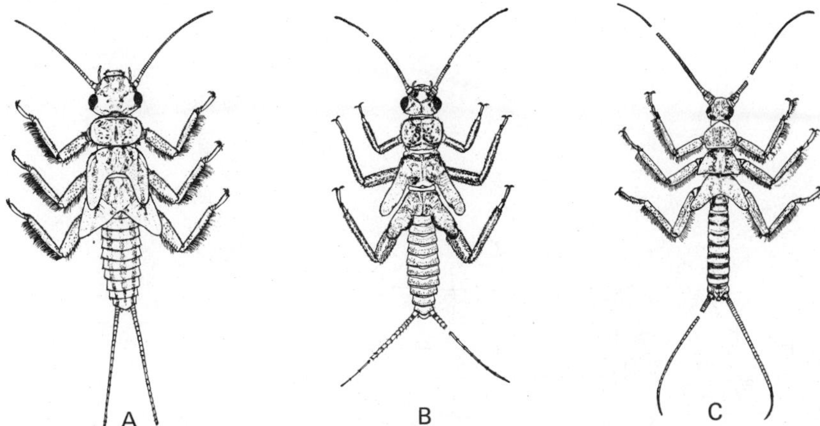

Figure 141. Stonefly nymphs. A, *Isopérla transmàrina* (Newman) (Perlòdidae); B, *Nemoùra trispinòsa* Claassen (Nemoùridae); C, *Taeniópteryx glaciàlis* (Newport) (Taeniopterygìnae). (Courtesy of Harden and the Entomological Society of America.)

The principal characters used to separate families are wing venation, the characters of the tarsi, and gill remnants. The gill remnants are usually shriveled and difficult to see in pinned and dried specimens; their location on the thorax is shown in Figure 147. The characters of the gill remnants are much easier to study in specimens that are preserved in alcohol.

Key to the Families of Plecóptera

1. Anal area of front wings with 2 or more rows of cross veins (Figure 143 A); large stoneflies, usually over 25 mm in length .... **Pteronárcidae** p. 231

1′. Anal area of front wings without cross veins, or with only 1 row (Figures 142 and 143 B–E); size variable 2

2(1′). Cerci short, no longer than greatest width or pronotum 3

2′. Cerci long, much longer than greatest width of pronotum 4

3(2). With 2 ocelli (Figure 145 A); front wings with 10 or more costal cross veins; no forked vein arising from basal anal cell in front wing; form somewhat cockroachlike .... **Peltopérlidae** p. 228

3′. With 3 ocelli; front wings usually with less than 10 costal cross veins, and with a forked vein coming from basal anal cell (Figure 143 B, D); form not cockroachlike .... **Nemoùridae** p. 228

4(2′). First tarsal segment about as long as third (Figure 144 D); front wings with few or no median and cubital cross veins (Figure 143 E) (*Capniìnae*) .... **Nemoùridae** p. 228

4′. First tarsal segment much shorter than third; front wings with several to many median and cubital cross veins (Figure 142) 5

5(4′). Rs in front wings usually with more than 2 branches, the posterior branch usually arising at or near anterior end of first r-m cross vein (Figure 142); cu-a in front wings (if present) usually opposite basal anal cell, or distad of it by no more than its own length; remnants of branched or filamentous gills on sides or venter of thorax (Figure 147) .... **Pérlidae** p. 231

5′. Rs in front wings with a variable number of branches, but if with more than 2 then the posterior branch usually arises distinctly distad of anterior end

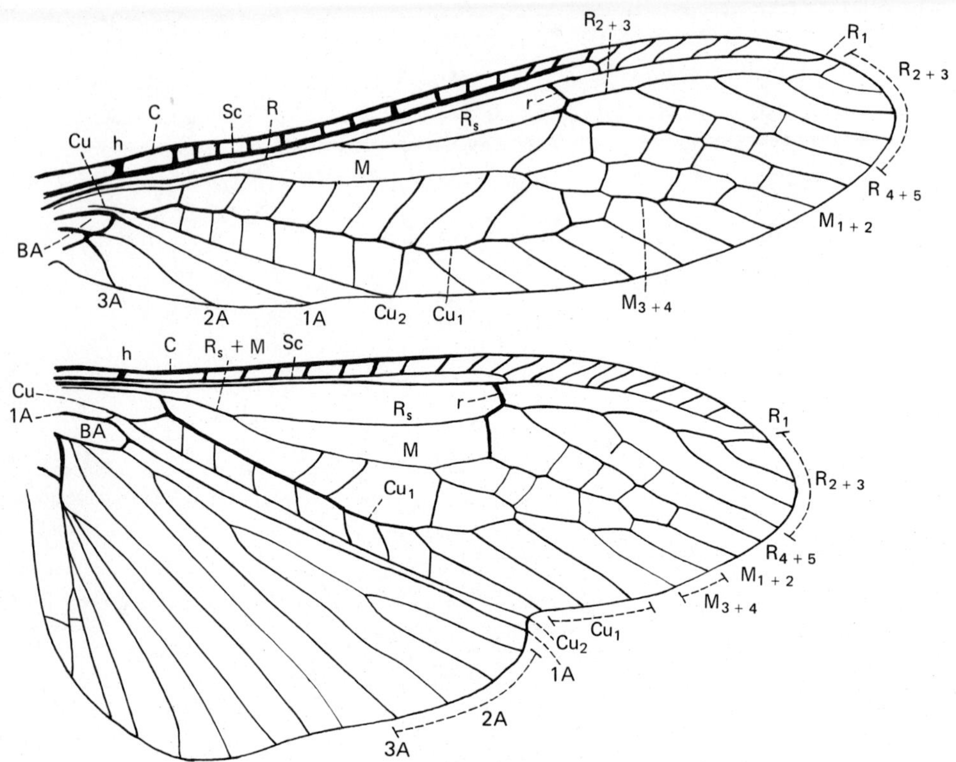

Figure 142. Wings of a perlid stonefly. *BA,* basal anal cell.

of first r-m cross vein; cu-a in front wings (if present) usually distad of basal anal cell by more than its own length; usually no remnants of branched gills on thorax (if any gill remnants are present they are unbranched and fingerlike) 6

6(5′). Anal lobe of hind wing reduced (rarely absent), usually with no more than 3 veins reaching wing margin behind 1A; Rs in front wings usually with only 2 branches; sometimes a forked vein arising from basal anal cell in front wings; pronotum more or less oval, with the corners rounded (Figure 145 C); length 15 mm or less .... **Chloropérlidae** p. 231

6′. Anal lobe of hind wings well developed, with 5 or more veins reaching wing margin behind 1A; Rs in front wings variable; no forked vein arising from basal anal cell in front wings; pronotum rectangular, the corners acute or narrowly rounded (Figure 145 B, D); length 6–25 mm .... **Perlòdidae** p. 231

Family **Peltopérlidae**—Roachlike Stoneflies: Most of these stoneflies are western and northern in distribution. The nymphs are somewhat roachlike in appearance. This group contains only one North American genus, which is *Peltopérla;* two brownish species occurring in the eastern United States are *P. arcuàta* Needham (14–18 mm in length) and *P. zìpha* Frison (12 mm in length).

Family **Nemoùridae:** This group contains four subfamilies, which are considered as families by some authorities; these subfamilies may be separated by the following key.

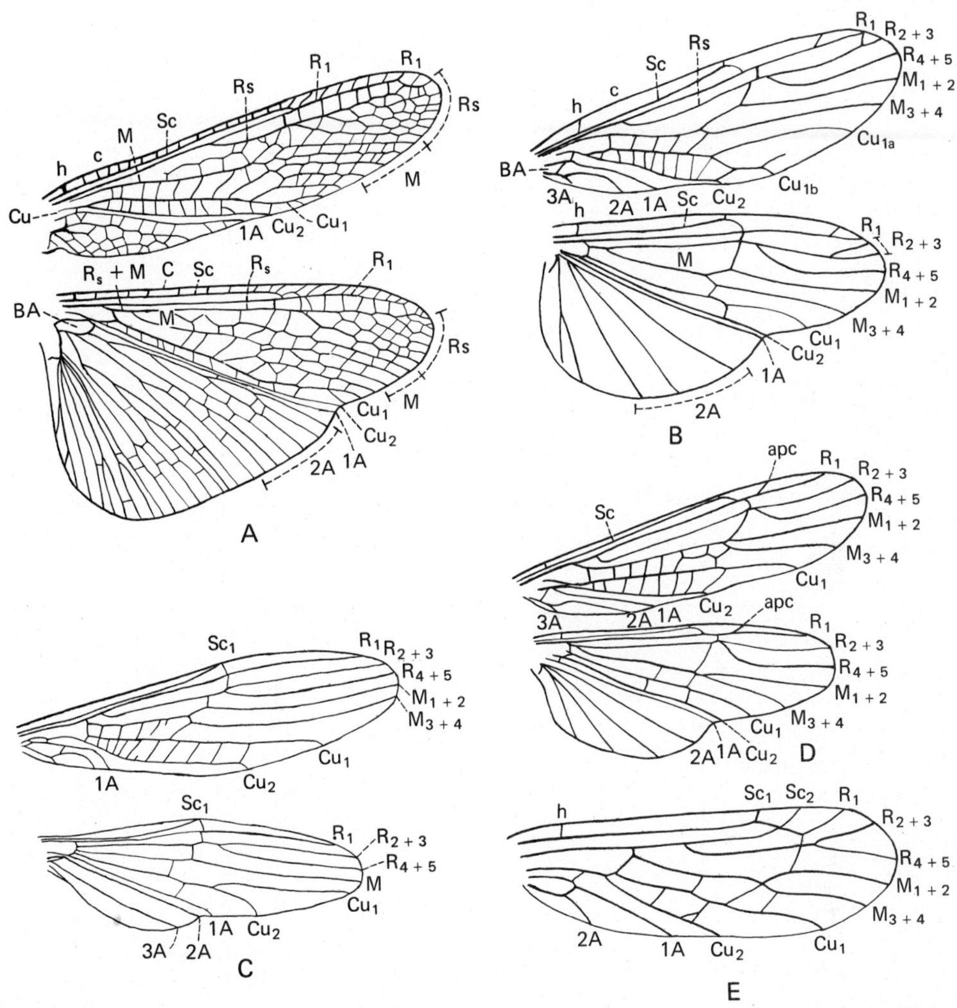

Figure 143. Wings of Plecóptera. A, *Pteronárcys* (Pteronárcidae); B, *Brachyptera* (Taeniopterygínae); C, *Leùctra* (Leuctrìnae); D, *Nemoùra* (Nemoùridae); E, front wing of a capniine. *apc*, apical cross vein; *BA*, basal anal cell.

1	Second tarsal segment about as long as the other segments (Figure 144 A) .... **Taeniopterygìnae**	p. 231
1′.	Second tarsal segment much shorter than the other segments (Figure 144 B–D) 2	
2(1′).	Cerci short, 1-segmented; front wings usually with 4 or more cubital cross veins (Figure 143 C, D) 3	
2′.	Cerci long, with at least 4 segments; front wings with only 1 or 2 cubital cross veins (Figure 143 E) .... **Capniìnae**	p. 231
3(2).	Front wings flat at rest, and with an apical cross vein (Figure 143 D, *apc*) .... **Nemourìnae**	p. 231
3′.	Front wings at rest bent down around sides of abdomen, and without an apical cross vein (Figure 143 C) .... **Leuctrìnae**	p. 231

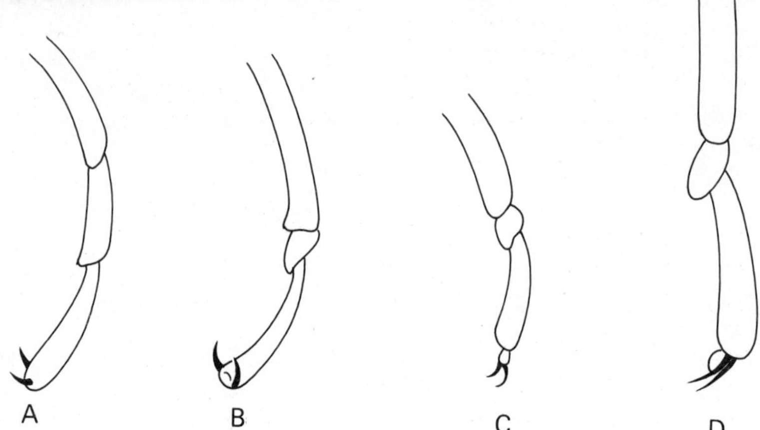

Figure 144. Hind tarsi of Plecóptera. A, *Taeniópteryx* (Taeniopterygìnae); B, *Leùctra* (Leuctrìnae); C, *Nemoùra* (Nemoùridae); D, *Allocápnia* (Capniìnae).

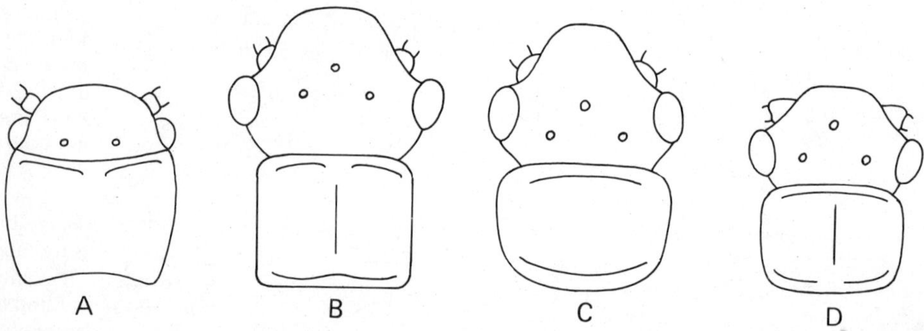

Figure 145. Head and pronotum of Plecóptera. A, *Peltopérla* (Peltopérlidae); B, *Isogènus* (Perlòdidae); C, *Chloropérla* (Chloropérlidae); D, *Isopérla* (Perlòdidae). (Redrawn from Frison, courtesy of the Illinois Natural History Survey.)

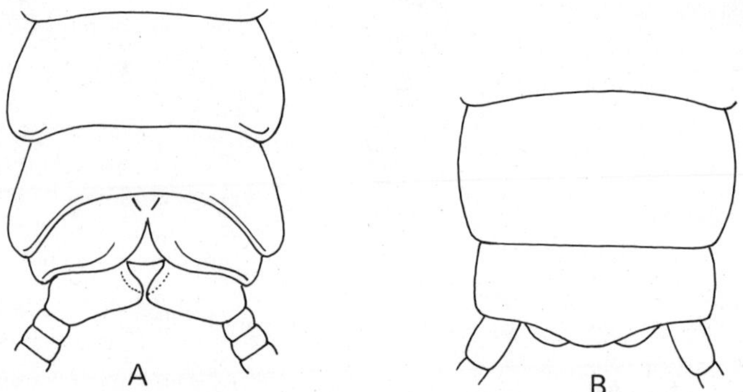

Figure 146. Terminal abdominal segments of male Plecóptera, dorsal view. A, *Isogènus* (Perlòdidae); B, *Isopérla* (Perlòdidae). (Redrawn from Frison, courtesy of the Illinois Natural History Survey.)

Subfamily **Nemourìnae**—Spring Stoneflies: The adults of this group, which appear from April to June, are 15 mm in length or less and brownish or blackish in color. The nymphs (Figure 141 B) are phytophagous and usually occur in small streams with sandy bottoms. The single North American genus, *Nemoùra,* contains about two dozen species.

Subfamily **Leuctrìnae**—Rolled-Winged Stoneflies: These stoneflies are for the most part 10 mm in length or less and brownish or blackish in color; the wings at rest are bent down over the sides of the abdomen. These insects are most common in hilly or mountainous regions, and the nymphs usually occur in small streams. The adults appear from February to June (in December in the South). The eastern species belong to the genus *Leùctra.*

Subfamily **Capniìnae**—Small Winter Stoneflies: These stoneflies are blackish in color, mostly 10 mm in length or less, and emerge during the winter months. The wings are short or rudimentary in some males. Most of the small winter stoneflies occurring in the East belong to the genus *Allocápnia.*

Subfamily **Taeniopterygìnae**—Winter Stoneflies: The members of this group are dark brown to blackish insects, generally 13 mm or less in length, which emerge from January to April. The nymphs (Figure 141 C) are phytophagous and occur in large streams and rivers; some adults are flower feeders. Two common eastern species in this group are *Taeniópteryx maùra* (Pictet), 8–12 mm in length, which emerges from January to March, and *Brachýptera fasciàta* (Burmeister), 10–15 mm in length, which emerges during March and April.

Family **Pteronárcidae**—Giant Stoneflies: This group includes the largest insects in the order; females of a common eastern species, *Pteronárcys dorsàta* (Say), may sometimes reach a length (measured to the wing tips) of $2\frac{1}{2}$ inches (64 mm). The nymphs are plant feeders and occur in medium-sized to large rivers. The adults are nocturnal in habit and often come to lights; they do not feed. They appear in late spring and early summer.

Family **Perlòdidae:** The most common members of this group (*Isopérla,* Figure 140 A) usually have the wings greenish and the body yellowish or greenish, and are 6–15 mm in length; the adults are chiefly pollen feeders and diurnal in habit. Other less common species are brownish or blackish in color and 10–25 mm in length. The habits of the nymphs vary.

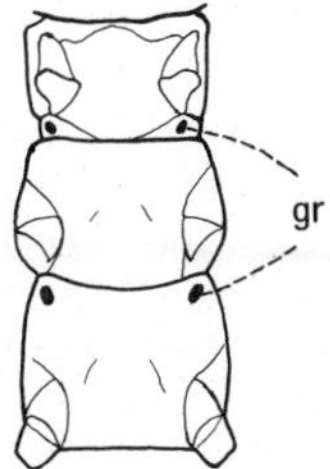

Figure 147. Thorax of *Acroneùria* (Pérlidae), ventral view. *gr,* gill remnants. (Redrawn from Frison, courtesy of the Illinois Natural History Survey.)

Family **Chloropérlidae**—Green Stoneflies: The adults of this family are 6–15 mm in length and yellowish or greenish in color; they appear in the spring. *Hastapérla brévis* (Banks), a common eastern species, is 6–9 mm in length and bright green in color, and has no anal lobe in the hind wing. The stoneflies belonging to the genus *Allopérla,* of which there are several eastern species, are 8–15 mm in length, and have a small anal lobe in the hind wing.

Family **Pérlidae**—Common Stoneflies: This family is the largest in the order, and its members are the stoneflies most often collected. The adults are nonfeeding spring and summer forms, and most of them are 20–40 mm in length. The nymphs are generally carnivorous.

Two eastern species in this group have only two ocelli, *Atopérla éphyre* (Newman) and *Neopérla clýmene* (Newman). Both are about 12 mm in length, brownish, with somewhat brownish wings; *N. clýmene* has the ocelli close together, and *A. éphyre* has them far apart. *Perlinélla drỳmo* (Newman), 10–20 mm in length, is brownish, with two black spots on the yellow head, and it has a row of cross veins in the anal area of the front wing. *Perlésta plácida* (Hagen), 9–14 mm in length and nocturnal in habit, and *Neophasganóphora capitàta* (Pictet), 16–24 mm in length and diurnal in habit, have the costal edge of the front wing yellowish. One of the largest and most common genera is *Acroneùria;* the adults are relatively large (20–40 mm in length), and the males have a disclike structure in the middle of the posterior portion of the ninth abdominal sternum.

COLLECTING AND PRESERVING PLECÓPTERA

During the warmer days in the fall, winter, and spring, adults of the winter species may be found resting on bridges, fence posts, and other objects near the streams in which the nymphs develop. Many species may be collected by sweeping the foliage along the banks of streams. Bridges are a favorite resting place for many species throughout the year. Many of the summer forms are attracted to lights. The nymphs are to be found in streams, usually under stones or in the bottom debris.

Both adult and nymphal stoneflies should be preserved in alcohol; pinned adults often shrink so that some characters, particularly those of the genitalia and the gill remnants, are difficult to make out.

References on the Plecóptera

Claassen, P. W. 1931. Plecoptera nymphs of America (north of Mexico). *Thomas Say Foundation Publ.* 3; 199 pp., 35 pl.

Frison, T. H. 1929. Fall and winter stoneflies, or Plecoptera, of Illinois. *Ill. Nat. Hist. Surv. Bull.,* 18(2):340–409; 77 f.

Frison, T. H. 1935. The stoneflies, or Plecoptera, of Illinois. *Ill. Nat. Hist. Surv. Bull.,* 20(4):281–471; 344 f.

Frison, T. H. 1942. Studies of North American Plecoptera, with special reference to the fauna of Illinois. *Ill. Nat. Hist. Surv. Bull.,* 22(2):231–355; 126 f.

Gaufin, A. R., A. V. Nebeker, and J. Sessions. 1966. The stoneflies (Plecoptera) of Utah. *Univ. Utah Biol. Ser.,* 14:9–89; illus.

Gaufin, A. R., W. E. Ricker, M. Moner, P. Milan, and R. A. Hays. 1972. The stoneflies (Plecoptera) of Montana. *Trans. Amer. Ent. Soc.,* 98(1):1–161; 308 f.

Illies, J. 1965. Phylogeny and zoogeography of the Plecoptera. *Ann. Rev. Ent.,* 10:117–140; 8 f.

Jewett, S. G., Jr. 1956. Plecoptera. In *Aquatic Insects of California,* Robert L. Usinger (Ed.). Berkeley: Univ. California Press, pp. 155–181; 52 f.

Jewett, S. G., Jr. 1959. The stoneflies (Plecoptera) of the Pacific Northwest. *Ore. State Monog.,* No. 3; iv + 95 pp., 33 f.

Nebeker, A. V., and A. R. Gaufin. 1967. Geographical and seasonal distribution of the family Capniidae of western North America (Plecoptera). *J. Kan. Ent. Soc.,* 40(3):415–421.

Nebeker, A. V., and A. R. Gaufin. 1968. The winter stoneflies of the Rocky Mountains (Plecoptera: Capniidae). *Trans. Amer. Ent. Soc.,* 94(1):1–24; 126 f.

Needham, J. G., and P. W. Claassen. 1925. A monograph of the Plecoptera or stoneflies of America north of Mexico. *Thomas Say Foundation Publ.,* 2; 397 pp., 29 f., 50 pl.

Pennak, R. W. 1953. *Fresh-Water Invertebrates of the United States.* New York: Ronald Press, ix + 769 pp., 470 f.

Ricker, W. E. 1943. Stoneflies of southwestern British Columbia. *Indiana Univ. Pub. Sci. Ser.,* No. 12; 143 pp., 129 f.

Ricker, W. E. 1950. Some evolutionary trends in Plecoptera. *Proc. Indiana Acad. Sci.,* 59:197–209.

Ricker, W. E. 1952. Systematic studies in Plecoptera. *Indiana Univ. Stud., Sci. Ser.,* 18:1–200; 154 f.

Ricker, W. E. 1959. Plecoptera. In *Fresh-water Biology,* W. T. Edmondson (Ed.). New York: Wiley, pp. 941–957, 10 f.

Ross, H. H., and W. E. Ricker. 1971. The classification, evolution, and dispersal of the winter stonefly genus *Allocapnia. Ill. Biol. Monog.,* No. 43; 240 pp., 111 f.

Zwick, P. 1971. Notes on the genus *Perlinella* and a generic synonymy in North American Perlidae (Plecoptera). *Fla. Ent.,* 54(4):315–320; 9 f.

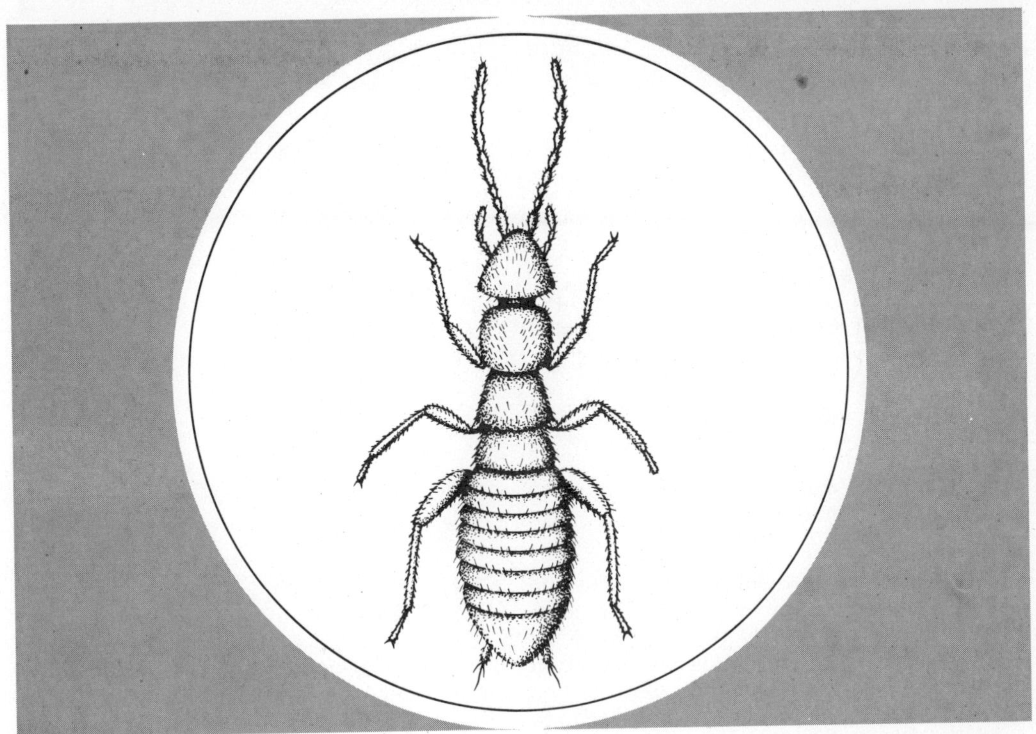

17: ORDER ZORÁPTERA[1]

ZORAPTERANS

The zorapterans are minute insects, 3 mm in length or less, and may be winged or wingless. The winged forms are generally dark-colored, and the wingless forms are pale. The zorapterans are a little like termites in general appearance, and are gregarious.

Both winged and wingless forms occur in both sexes. The wings are four in number, membranous, with a much reduced venation and with the hind wings smaller than the front wings (Figure 148 A). The wings of the adult are eventually shed, as in ants and termites, leaving stubs attached to the thorax. The antennae are moniliform and 9-segmented. The wingless forms (Figure 148 D) lack both compound eyes and ocelli, but the winged forms have compound eyes and three ocelli. The tarsi are 2-segmented, and each tarsus bears two claws. The cerci are short and unsegmented and terminate in a long bristle. The abdomen is short, oval, and 10-segmented. The mouth parts are of the chewing type, and the metamorphosis is simple.

The order Zoráptera contains a single family, the **Zorotýpidae,** and a single genus, *Zorótypus*. There are 22 known species of zorapterans, of which two occur in the United States. *Z. húbbardi* Caudell has been taken in a number of localities

---

[1] Zoráptera: *zor,* pure; *aptera,* wingless. Only wingless individuals were known when this order was described, and the wingless condition was thought to be a distinctive feature of the order.

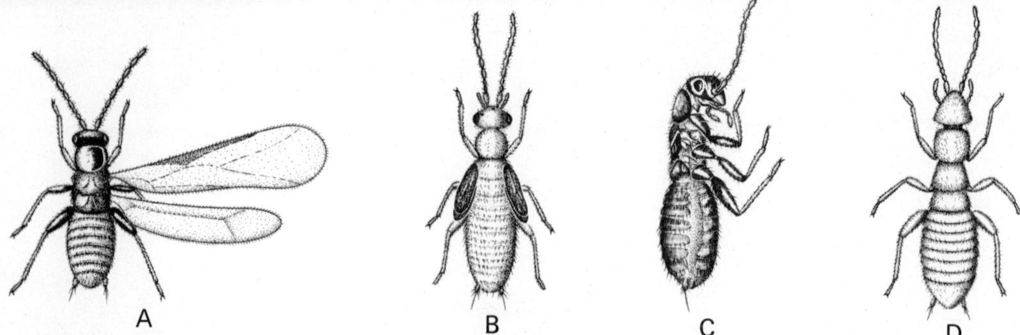

Figure 148. *Zorótypus húbbardi* Caudell, female. A, winged adult; B, nymph of winged form; C, dealated winged adult, lateral view; D, wingless adult. (Courtesy of Caudell.)

in the southeastern United States, from Maryland and southern Pennsylvania westward to southern Iowa, and southward to Florida and Texas; *Z. snỳderi* Caudell occurs in Florida and Jamaica. *Z. húbbardi* is commonly found under slabs of wood buried in piles of old sawdust; colonies are also found under bark and in rotting logs. The principal food of zorapterans appears to be fungus spores, but they are known to eat small dead arthropods.

COLLECTING AND PRESERVING ZORÁPTERA

Zorapterans are to be looked for in the habitats indicated above, and are generally collected by sifting debris or by means of a Berlese funnel (Figure 616). They should be preserved in 70 percent alcohol, and may be mounted on microscope slides for detailed study.

References on the Zoráptera

Caudell, A. N. 1918. *Zorotypus hubbardi,* a new species of the order Zoraptera from the United States. *Can. Ent.,* 50(11):375–381.

Caudell, A. N. 1920. Zoraptera not an apterous order. *Proc. Ent. Soc. Wash.,* 22(5):84–97; pl. 6.

Caudell, A. N. 1927. *Zorotypus longiceratus,* a new species of Zoraptera from Jamaica. *Proc. Ent. Soc. Wash.,* 29(6):144–145; 2 f.

Gurney, A. B. 1938. A synopsis of the order Zoraptera, with notes on the biology of *Zorotypus hubbardi* Caudell. *Proc. Ent. Soc. Wash.,* 40(3):57–87; 56 f.

Gurney, A. B. 1959. New distribution records for *Zorotypus hubbardi* Caudell (Zoraptera). *Proc. Ent. Soc. Wash.,* 61(4):183–184.

Riegel, G. T. 1963. The distribution of *Zorotypus hubbardi* (Zoraptera). *Ann. Ent. Soc. Amer.,* 56(6):744–747; 3 f.

Riegel, G. T., and M. B. Ferguson. 1960. New state records of Zoraptera. *Ent. News,* 71(8):213–216.

St. Amand, W. 1954. Records of the order Zoraptera from South Carolina. *Ent. News,* 65(5):131.

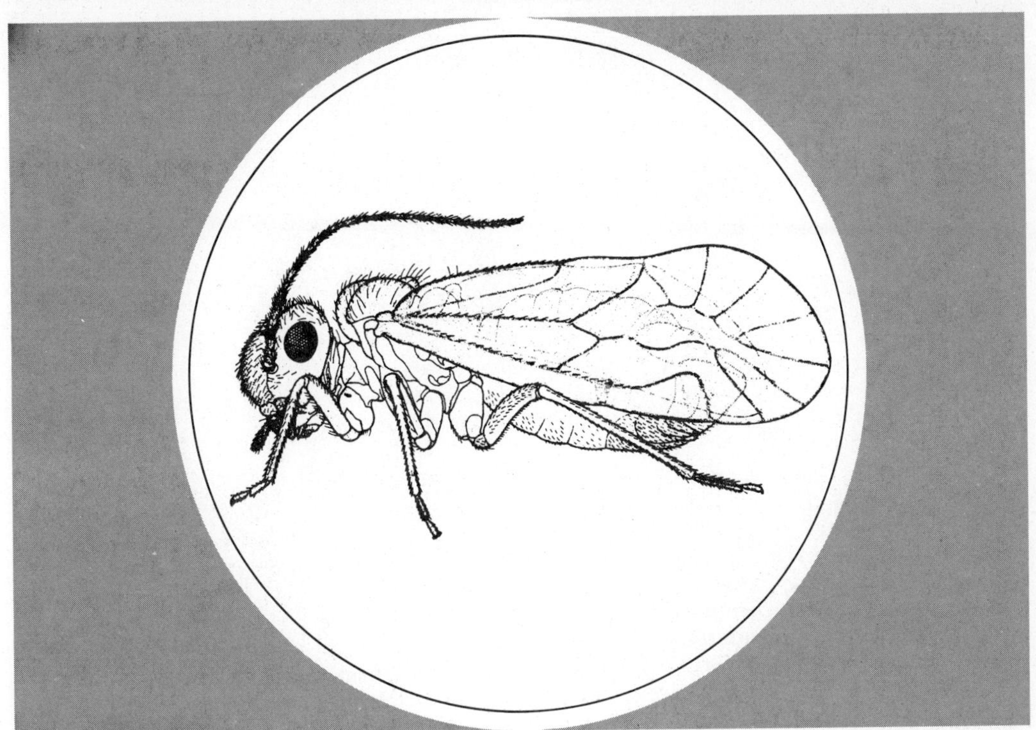

18: ORDER PSOCÓPTERA[1]

PSOCIDS

The psocids are small, soft-bodied insects, most of which are less than 6 mm in length. Wings may be present or absent, and both long-winged and short-winged individuals occur in some species. The winged forms have four membranous wings (rarely two, with the hind wings vestigial); the front wings are a little larger than the hind wings, and the wings at rest are usually held rooflike over the abdomen. The antennae are generally fairly long, the tarsi are 2- or 3-segmented, and cerci are lacking. Psocids have chewing mouth parts, and the clypeus is large and somewhat swollen. The metamorphosis is simple (Figure 149).

[1] Psocóptera: *psoco,* rub small: *ptera,* wings (referring to the gnawing habits of these insects).

Some 40 genera and nearly 150 species of psocids are known from the United States, but most people see only a few species that occur in houses or other buildings. Most of the species found in buildings are wingless, and because they often live among books or papers, are usually called booklice. The majority of the psocids are outdoor species with well-developed wings, and occur on the bark or foliage of trees and shrubs or under bark or stones; these psocids are sometimes called barklice.

The psocids feed on molds, fungi, cereals, pollen, fragments of dead insects, and similar materials. The term "lice" in the names "booklice" and "barklice" is somewhat misleading, for none of these insects is parasitic, and relatively few are

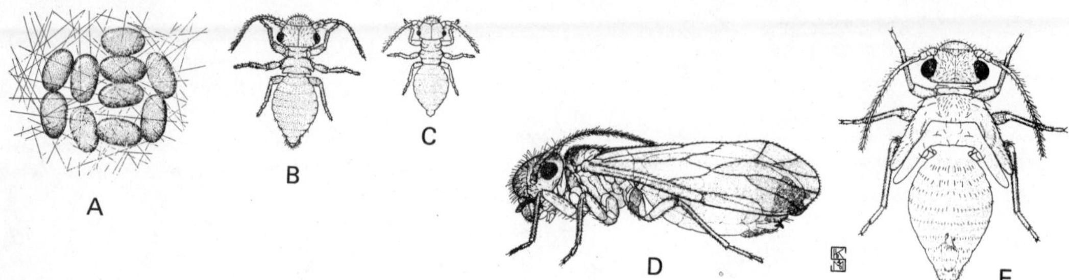

Figure 149. Developmental stages of the psocid, *Ectopsòcus pùmilis* (Banks) (Pseudocoecilìidae). A, eggs; B, third instar; C, first instar; D, adult female; E, sixth instar. (Courtesy of Sommerman.)

louselike in appearance. The species occurring in buildings rarely cause much damage, but are frequently a nuisance.

The eggs of psocids are laid singly or in clusters and are sometimes covered by silk or debris. Most species pass through six nymphal instars. Some species are gregarious, living under thin silken webs; one southern species, *Archipsòcus nòmas* Gurney, often makes unsightly webs on tree trunks and branches.

Certain psocids (species of *Liposcèlis* and *Rhyopsòcus*) have recently been found capable of acting as the intermediate hosts of the fringed tapeworm of sheep, *Thysanosòma ostiniòides* Diesing.

CLASSIFICATION OF THE PSOCÓPTERA

The classification of this order is in a somewhat confused state; different authorities have different ideas of the groupings within the order, and there have been many shiftings of species and genera from one genus or family to another. Three classifications of the Psocóptera are those of Banks (1929), Pearman (1936), and Roesler (1944); we follow here the arrangement of Roesler.

A synopsis of the Psocóptera occurring in the United States is given below. The names in parentheses following a particular family name represent other families in which members of this family have been classified by some authorities. The groups starred are seldom encountered.

Suborder Trogiomórpha
- Trogìidae (Atrópidae, Psoquíllidae)
- *Lepidopsòcidae (Lepidíllidae)
- *Psyllipsòcidae (Psocathrópidae = Psocatrópidae, Empherìidae)

Suborder Troctomórpha
- *Pachytróctidae
- Liposcèlidae (Tróctidae, Embidopsòcidae, Atrópidae)

Suborder Eupsòcida
- *Epipsòcidae
- *Myopsòcidae (Psòcidae)
- Psòcidae
- *Mesopsòcidae (Philotársidae, Elipsòcidae)
- Pseudocaecilìidae (Archipsòcidae, Pterodèlidae, Peripsòcidae, Trichopsòcidae, Embidopsòcidae, Caecilìidae, Psòcidae, Empherìidae)
- *Polypsòcidae (Caecilìidae, Psòcidae)

Key to the Families of Psocóptera

This key is modified from Roesler (1944). The families marked with an asterisk are small and are not likely to be encountered by the general collector.

1. Tarsi 2-segmented; labial palps 1-segmented 2

1′. Tarsi 3-segmented; labial palps 1- or 2-segmented 5

2(1). Labial palps broadly triangular (Figure 153 C); lacinia uniformly conical toward tip, acuminate, usually without definite teeth (Figure 153 G); lateral gonapophyses absent; Cu_{1b} in front wing very short or absent, Cu_{1a} ending in distal margin of wing .... **Polypsòcidae*** p. 241

2′. Labial palps short and appressed, sometimes semicircular (Figure 153 B); lacinia broad and oblique at end or distinctly toothed (Figure 153 H, I);

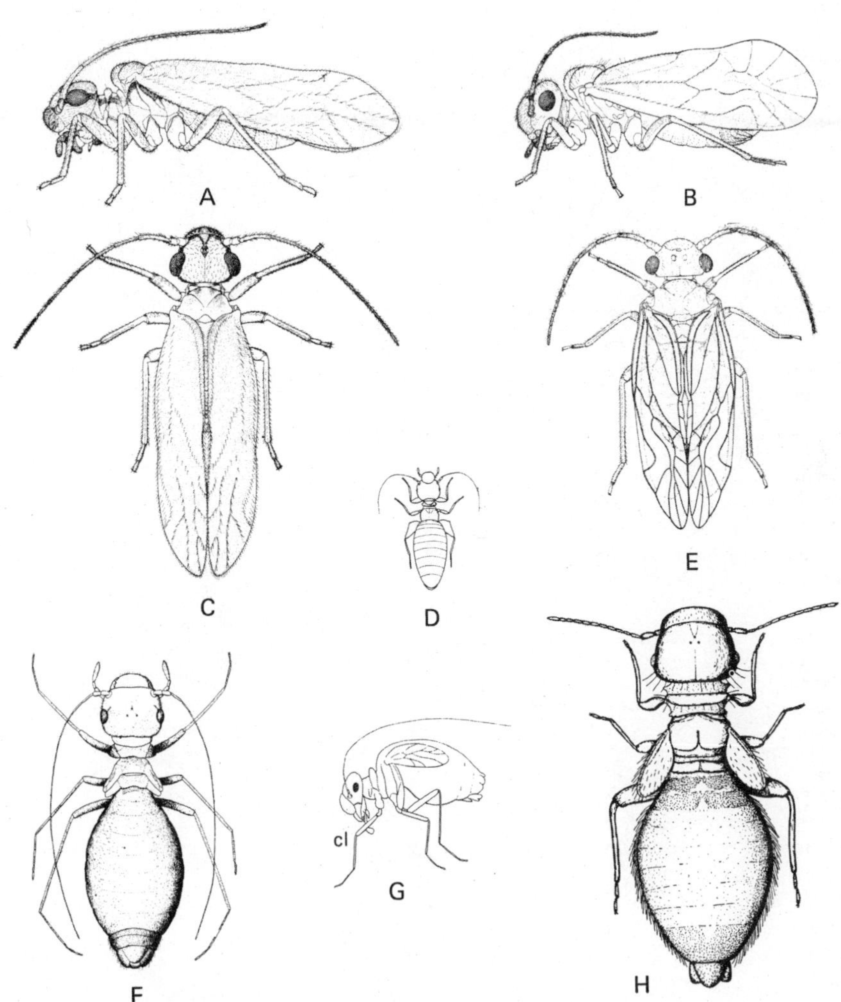

Figure 150. Psocids. A, *Caecílius mánteri* Sommerman, female, lateral view (Polypsòcidae); B, *Anomopsòcus amábilis* (Walsh), female, lateral view (Pseudocaecilìidae); C, *Caecílius mánteri* Sommerman, female, dorsal view (Polypsòcidae); D, *Liposcèlis divinatòrius* (Müller), dorsal view (Liposcèlidae); E, *Anomopsòcus amábilis* (Walsh), male, dorsal view (Pseudocaecilìidae); F, *Psyllipsòcus rambùrii* Selys, short-winged female, dorsal view (Psyllipsòcidae); G, *Psocathròpus* sp., lateral view (Psyllipsòcidae); H, *Archipsòcus nòmas* Gurney, short-winged female, dorsal view (Pseudocaecilìidae). (A–C and E, courtesy of Sommerman; D and F–H, courtesy of Gurney; D and G reprinted by permission of Pest Control Technology, National Pest Control Association; A, courtesy of Psyche; B–C and E–F, courtesy of the Entomological Society of America; H, courtesy of the Washington Academy of Science.)

lateral gonapophyses of female clothed with hairs, or if lateral gonapophyses are absent then dorsal gonapophyses with hairs; Cu_1 variable . 3

3(2′). Labrum with 2 internal sclerotized ridges that are often united anteriorly (Figure 153 D); lacinia broad at end with many small teeth (Figure 153 H); head long (Figure 152 C); tarsal claws straight (Figure 154 D) .... **Epipsòcidae*** p. 241

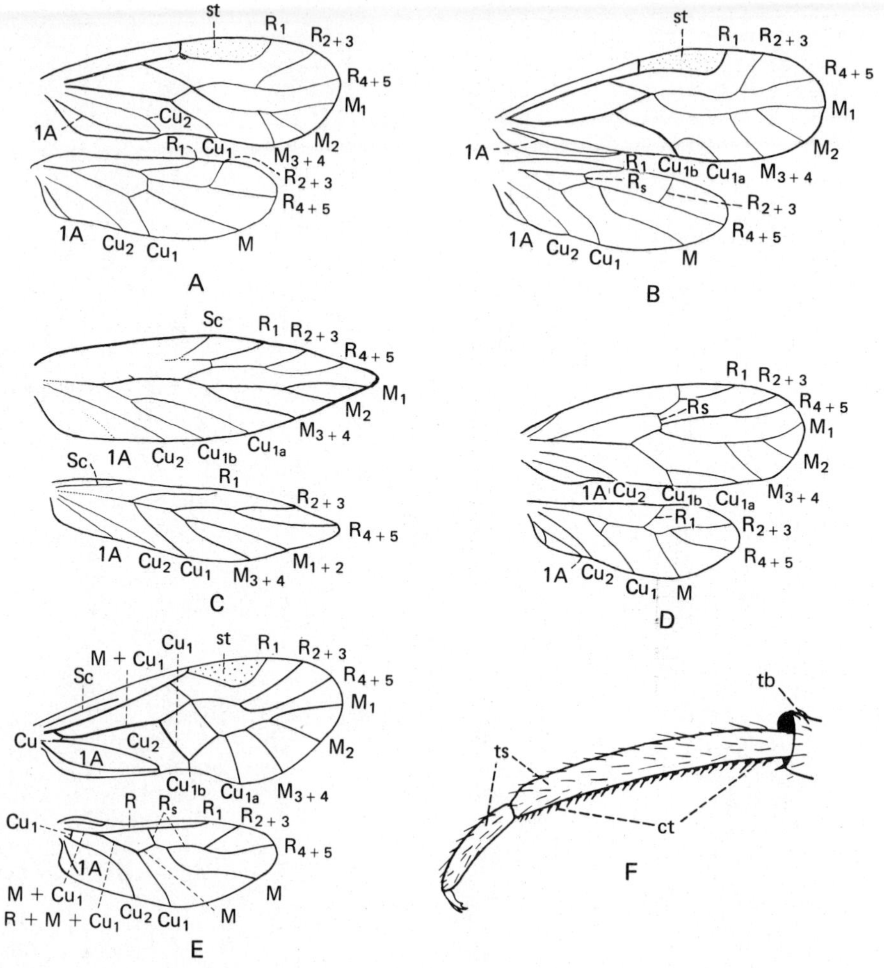

Figure 151. Wings (A–E) and hind tarsus (F) of Psocóptera. A, *Ectopsòcus pùmilis* (Banks) (Pseudocaecilìidae); B, *Lachesílla pediculària* (L.) (Pseudocaecilìidae); C, Lepidopsòcidae; D, *Psyllipsòcus rambùrii* Selys (Psyllipsòcidae); E, *Psòcus* (Psòcidae); F, *Psòcus* (Psòcidae). *ct,* ctenidia; *st,* stigma; *tb,* tibia; *ts,* tarsal segments. (A, B, D, and E redrawn from Gurney, courtesy of the National Pest Control Association.)

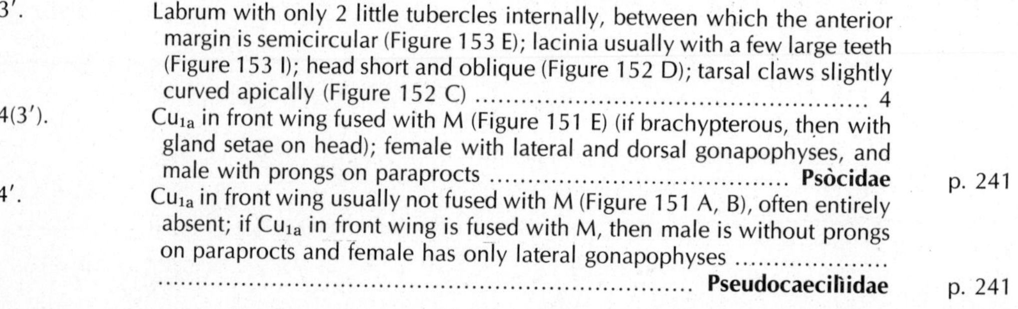

3′. Labrum with only 2 little tubercles internally, between which the anterior margin is semicircular (Figure 153 E); lacinia usually with a few large teeth (Figure 153 I); head short and oblique (Figure 152 D); tarsal claws slightly curved apically (Figure 152 C) 4

4(3′). Cu_{1a} in front wing fused with M (Figure 151 E) (if brachypterous, then with gland setae on head); female with lateral and dorsal gonapophyses, and male with prongs on paraprocts .... **Psòcidae** p. 241

4′. Cu_{1a} in front wing usually not fused with M (Figure 151 A, B), often entirely absent; if Cu_{1a} in front wing is fused with M, then male is without prongs on paraprocts and female has only lateral gonapophyses .... **Pseudocaecilìidae** p. 241

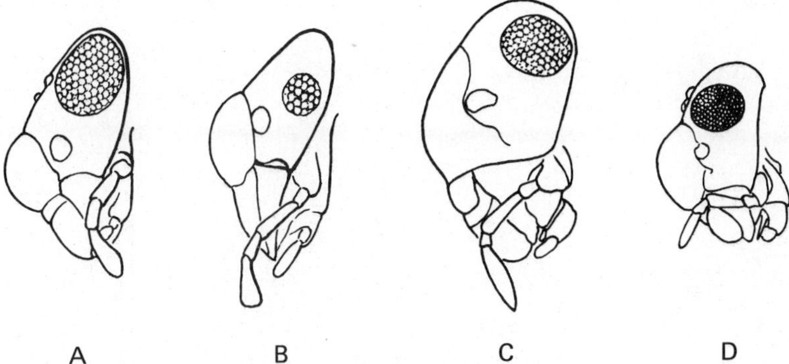

Figure 152. Heads of Psocóptera, lateral view. A, Lepidopsòcidae; B, Psyllipsòcidae (*Psocáthropus*); C, Epipsòcidae (*Epipsòcus*); D, Psòcidae (*Psòcus*). (Drawn by Kathryn M. Sommerman.)

5(1′). Antennae long, with more than 20 segments, which are generally not secondarily ringed (Figure 150 F, G); labial palps 2-segmented (Figure 153 A) (suborder Trogiomórpha) 6

5′. Antennae shorter, usually 13-segmented, sometimes with 15–17 segments, in which case the segments from 7 distad are secondarily ringed; labial palps 1- or 2-segmented 8

6(5). Head short and oblique (Figure 152 A); winged forms with Cu_2 and 1A in front wing ending separately at wing margin (Figure 151 C); a sense peg on inner side of second segment of maxillary palps (Figure 153 F) 7

6′. Head long and perpendicular (Figure 152 B); Cu_2 and 1A in front wing usually meeting at wing margin (Figure 151 D); no sense peg on inner side of second segment of maxillary palps (except in the genus *Speléketor,* cave-inhabiting forms occurring in Arizona) .... **Psyllipsòcidae*** p. 241

7(6). Tarsal claws with a preapical tooth (Figure 154 B); body and wings densely covered with scales. .... **Lepidopsòcidae*** p. 240

7′. Tarsal claws simple (Figure 154 A); body and wings not covered with scales; front wings either broadly rounded apically, knobby, or lacking . ... **Trogìidae** p. 240

8(5′). Labial palps 2-segmented (as in Figure 153 A); if antennae contain more than 13 segments, then the segments from 7 distad are secondarily ringed; hind tarsi of winged forms lacking ctenidia (suborder Troctomórpha) ... 9

8′. Labial palps 1-segmented (Figure 153 B, C); antennal segments not secondarily ringed; hind tarsi of winged forms usually with ctenidia (Figure 151 F) (suborder Eupsòcida, in part) 10

9(8). Body short and arched; legs long and slender, the hind femora not broadened; if winged, then the eyes are composed of many facets .... **Pachytróctidae*** p. 241

9′. Body elongate and flat; legs very short, the hind femora flat and very broad (Figure 150 D); if winged, then the eyes are composed of 2–8 facets .... **Liposcèlidae** p. 241

10(8′). Cu_{1a} in front wing fused with M (if brachypterous then with gland setae on head); subgenital plate with posterior points .... **Myopsòcidae*** p. 241

10′. Cu_{1a} in front wing usually not fused with M, often entirely absent; if Cu_{1a} in front wing is fused with M, then subgenital plate has 2 posterior points . ... **Mesopsòcidae*** p. 241

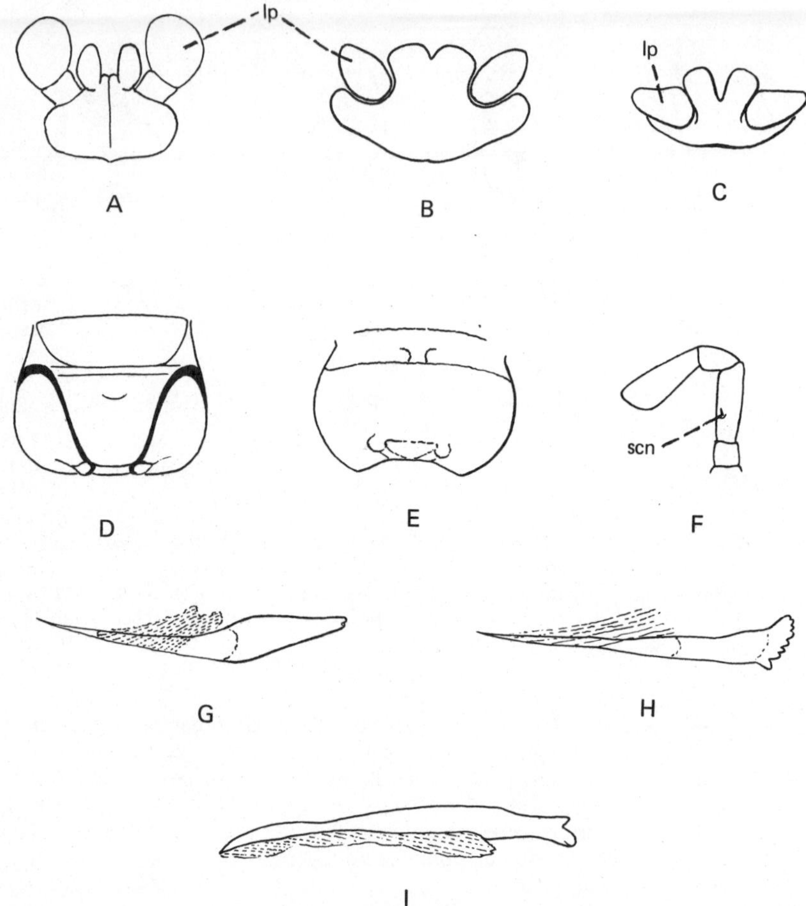

Figure 153. Mouth parts of Psocóptera. A, labium of *Trògium* (Trogìidae); B, labium of *Epipsòcus* (Epipsòcidae); C, labium of *Polypsòcus* (Polypsòcidae); D, labrum of *Epipsòcus* (Epipsòcidae); E, labrum of *Psòcus* (Psòcidae); F, maxillary palpus of *Lepidopsòcus* (Lepidopsòcidae); G, lacinia (tip at right) of *Polypsòcus* (Polypsòcidae); H, lacinia of *Epipsòcus* (Epipsòcidae); I, lacinia of *Psòcus* (Psòcidae). *lp*, labial palp; *scn*, sense peg. (Drawn by Kathryn M. Sommerman.)

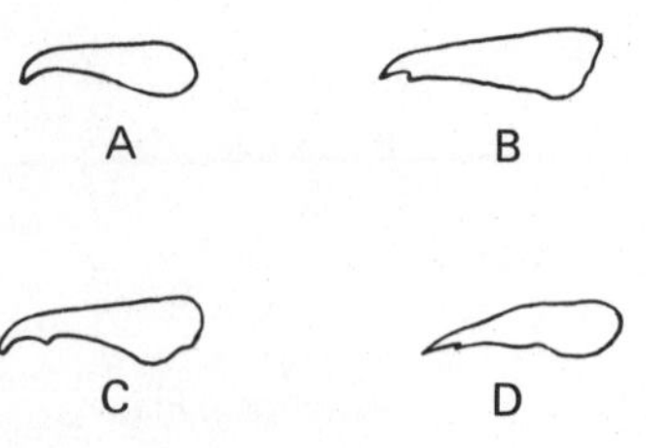

Figure 154. Tarsal claws of Psocóptera. A, *Trògium* (Trogìidae); B, Lepidopsòcidae; C, *Psòcus* (Psòcidae); D, *Epipsòcus* (Epipsòcidae). (Drawn by Kathryn M. Sommerman.)

SUBORDER **Trogiomórpha:** The members of this suborder have more than 20 antennal segments, the labial palps are 2-segmented, and the tarsi are 3-segmented.

Family **Trogìidae:** The trogiids are either wingless or have the wings reduced. A few species occur in buildings. *Lepinòtus inquilìnus* Heyden is often found in granaries; *Trògium pulsatòrium* (L.) occurs in houses, barns, and granaries, and is one of the more common species of booklice.

Family **Lepidopsòcidae:** These are rather small psocids that occur out of doors and have the wings and body covered with scales. This is a small group, with only three species occurring in the United States, and they are not common.

Family **Psyllipsòcidae:** The psyllipsocids are pale-colored, and occur principally in damp, dark places such as cellars and caves; a few species occasionally occur in buildings. *Psyllipsòcus rambùrii* Selys commonly occurs in cellars about the openings of wine and vinegar barrels. Both long- and short-winged individuals occur in some species; in others, one or both pairs of wings may be reduced.

SUBORDER **Troctomórpha:** The members of this suborder usually have fewer than 20 antennal segments, the labial palps are 2-segmented, the tarsi are 3-segmented, and there are no ctenidia (Figure 151 F, *ct*) in winged forms.

Family **Pachytróctidae:** Only two species in this family occur in the United States, and they are relatively rare.

Family **Liposcèlidae:** This group includes the booklouse *Liposcèlis divinatòrius* (Müller) (Figure 150 D), which is perhaps the most common psocid occurring in buildings. It occurs in dusty places where the temperature and humidity are fairly high, on shelves, in the cracks of window sills, behind loose wallpaper, and in similar situations; it feeds principally on molds. It is a minute psocid that can be recognized by the enlarged hind femora.

SUBORDER **Eupsòcida:** The antennae in these psocids usually contain fewer than 20 segments, the labial palps are 1-segmented, and the tarsi are 2- or 3-segmented, with ctenidia usually present in the winged forms. Most winged psocids belong to this suborder.

Families **Epipsòcidae** and **Myopsòcidae:** These are small groups, with two and four North American species, respectively; they are seldom encountered.

Family **Psòcidae:** This is the largest family in the order, with over 40 North American species. Most of the common barklice belong to this group. None of them is of economic importance.

Families **Mesopsòcidae** and **Polypsòcidae:** These are small groups, with 6 and 13 North American species; these barklice occur principally out of doors.

Family **Pseudocaecilìidae:** This is a large group, with nearly 40 species occurring in this country; a few occasionally occur indoors, particularly in granaries. *Lachesílla pediculària* (L.) is often common in buildings where there are cereals, straw products, or fresh plant materials; *Archipsòcus nòmas* Gurney sometimes makes unsightly silken webs on tree trunks and branches in the southern states from Texas to Florida.

COLLECTING AND PRESERVING PSOCÓPTERA

The psocids living out-of-doors can often be collected by sweeping or by beating the branches of trees and shrubs; some species are found under bark or stones. Indoor species can be trapped or collected with an aspirator or moistened brush. The best method of preserving psocids is in alcohol (about 80 or 90 percent); when specimens are mounted on pins or points, they shrivel and are usually unsatisfactory for study. The smallest specimens are generally mounted on microscope slides for detailed study.

References on the Psocóptera

Banks, N. 1929. A classification of the Psocidae. *Psyche,* 36(4): 321–325.

Chapman, P. J. 1930. Corrodentia of the United States of America. I. Suborder Isotecnomera. *J. N.Y. Ent. Soc.,* 38(3–4):219–290, 319–403; pl. 12–21.

Gurney, A. B. 1950. Corrodentia. In *Pest Control Technology, Entomological Section.* New York: National Pest Control Assn., pp. 129–163, f. 61–63.

Lee, S. S., and I. W. B. Thornton. 1967. The family Pseudocaeciliidae (Psocoptera)—a reappraisal based on the discovery of new Oriental and Pacific species. *Pacific Insects Monog.,* No. 16; 114 pp., 187 f.

Mockford, E. L. 1951. The Psocoptera of Indiana. *Proc. Ind. Acad. Sci.,* 60:192–204.

Mockford, E. L. 1955a. Notes on some eastern North American psocids with descriptions of two new species. *Amer. Midl. Nat.,* 53(2):436–441; 9 f.

Mockford, E. L. 1955b. Studies on the reuterelline psocids (Psocoptera). *Proc. Ent. Soc., Wash.,* 57(3):97–108; 17 f.

Mockford, E. L. 1963. The species of Embidopsocinae of the United States (Psocoptera: Liposcelidae). *Ann. Ent. Soc. Amer.,* 56(1):25–37; 68 f.

Mockford, E. L., and A. B. Gurney. 1956. A review of the

psocids, or book-lice and bark-lice, of Texas (Psocoptera). *J. Wash. Acad. Sci.*, 46:353–368; 53 f., 1 map.

Pearman, J. V. 1936. The taxonomy of the Psocoptera; preliminary sketch. *Proc. Roy. Ent. Soc. London, Ser. B*, 5(3):58–62.

Roesler, R. 1944. Die Gattungen der Copeognathen. *Stn. Ent. Ztg.*, 105:117–166.

Sommerman, K. M. 1943. Bionomics of *Ectopsocus pumilis* (Banks) (Corrodentia, Caeciliidae). *Psyche*, 50(3–4):53–63; 7 f.

Sommerman, K. M. 1944. Bionomics of *Amapsocus amabilis* (Walsh) (Corrodentia, Psocidae). *Ann. Ent. Soc. Amer.*, 37(3):359–364; 5 f.

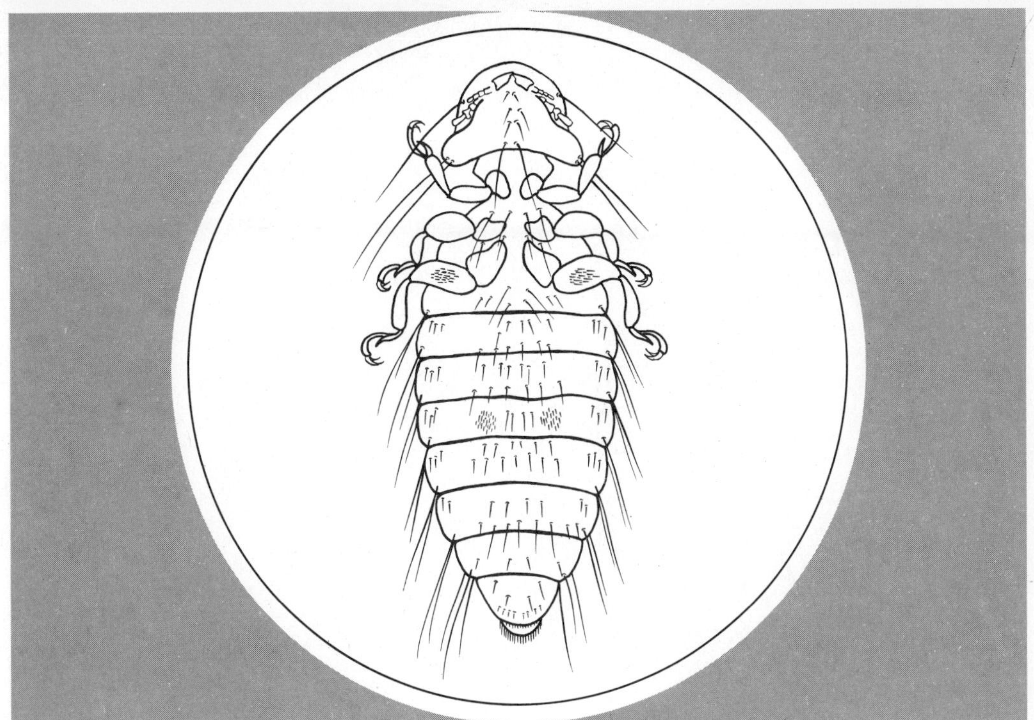

19: ORDER MALLÓPHAGA[1]

CHEWING LICE

The chewing lice are small, usually flattened, wingless external parasites of birds and mammals; most of them are parasitic on birds, and the lice of this order are often referred to as the bird lice. They have chewing mouth parts and feed on bits of hair, feathers, or skin of the host. The young resemble the adults, and all stages are passed on the host. Transmission from one host to another is usually accomplished when two hosts come in contact, as in the nest; these lice are unable to survive long away from the host. Most species occur on only one or a few species of hosts. None of the Mallóphaga is known to attack man; persons handling birds or other animals infested with these lice may occasionally get the lice on themselves, but the lice do not stay long on man.

[1] Mallóphaga: *mallo,* wool; *phaga,* eat.

Many chewing lice are important pests of domestic animals, particularly poultry. The lice cause considerable irritation, and heavily infested animals appear run-down and emaciated, and if not actually killed by the lice, are rendered easy prey for various diseases. Different species of lice attack different types of poultry and domestic mammals, and each species usually infests a particular part of the host's body. The control of chewing lice usually involves treatment of the infested animal with a suitable dust or dip.

CLASSIFICATION OF THE MALLÓPHAGA

Six families of Mallóphaga, in two suborders, occur in our area; they are separated primarily on

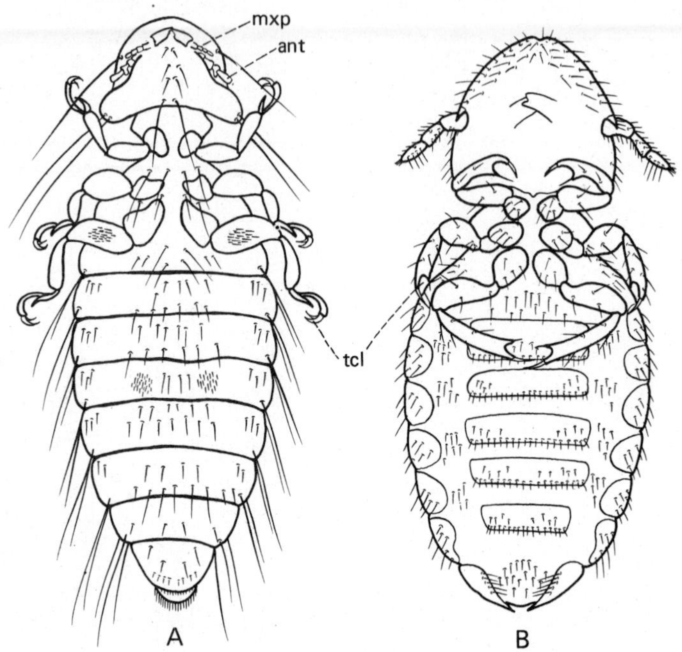

Figure 155. A, shaft louse of chickens, *Ménopon gállinae* (L.) (Menopónidae), ventral view of female; B, cattle biting louse, *Bovícola bòvis* (L.) (Trichodéctidae), ventral view of female. *ant,* antenna; *mxp,* maxillary palp; *tcl,* tarsal claws.

the basis of the structure of the antennae, head shape, mouth parts, and tarsal claws. These groups are as follows:

Suborder Amblýcera
- Gyrópidae—lice of guinea pigs
- Menopónidae—lice of birds
- Laemobothrìidae—lice of birds
- Ricínidae—lice of birds

Suborder Ischnócera
- Philoptéridae—lice of birds
- Trichodéctidae—lice of mammals

Key to the Families of Mallóphaga

1. Antennae more or less clubbed, and usually concealed in grooves; maxillary palps present (Figures 155 A and 156) (suborder Amblýcera) 2

1′. Antennae filiform and exposed; maxillary palps absent (Figures 155 B and 157) (suborder Ischnócera) 5

2(1). Tarsi with 1 claw or none; parasitic on guinea pigs .... **Gyrópidae** p. 245

2′. Tarsi with 2 claws; parasitic on birds 3

3(2′). Antennae lying in grooves on sides of head; head broadly triangular and expanded behind the eyes (Figure 155 A) .... **Menopónidae** p. 245

3′. Antennae lying in cavities that open ventrally; head not broadly triangular and expanded behind the eyes (Figure 156) 4

4(3′). Sides of head with a conspicuous swelling in front of eye at base of antennae (Figure 156 A) .... **Laemobothrìidae** p. 245

4′. Sides of head without such swellings (Figure 156 B) .... **Ricínidae** p. 246

5(1′). Tarsi with 2 claws; antennae 5-segmented (Figure 157); parasitic on birds .... **Philoptéridae** p. 246

5′. Tarsi with 1 claw; antennae usually 3-segmented (Figure 155 B); parasitic on mammals .... **Trichodéctidae** p. 246

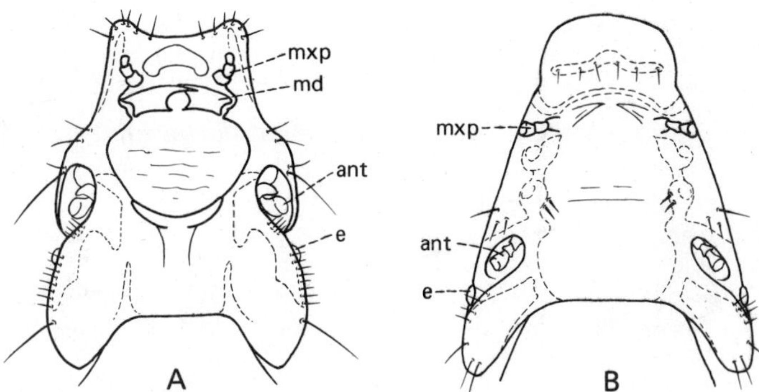

Figure 156. A, head of *Laemobòthrion* (Laemobothrìidae), ventral view; B, head of a ricinid (Ricínidae), ventral view. *ant,* antenna; e, eye; *md,* mandible; *nxp,* maxillary palp.

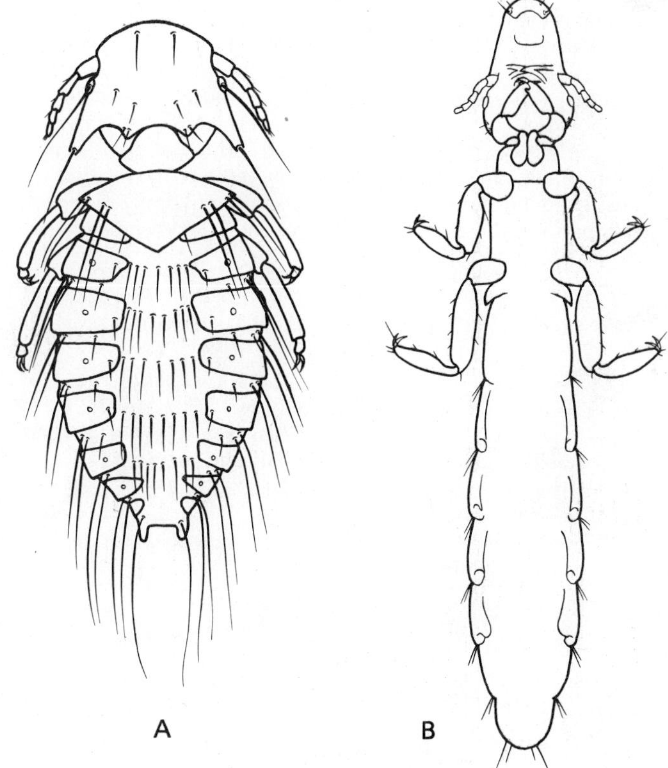

Figure 157. Philoptéridae. A, large turkey louse, *Chelopístes meleágridis* (L.), dorsal view; B, *Esthiópterum crassicòrne* (Scopoli), a louse of the blue-winged teal, ventral view.

Family **Gyrópidae:** The members of this group are chiefly confined to Central and South America. Two species occur in the United States on guinea pigs.

Family **Menopónidae:** This is a large group whose members attack birds. Two important pests of poultry in this group are the chicken body louse, *Menacánthus stramíneus* (Nitzsch), and the shaft louse, *Ménopon gállinae* (L.) (Figure 155 A).

Family **Laemobothrìidae:** This is a small group whose members are parasitic on water birds and on birds of prey.

Family **Ricínidae:** This is a small group whose members are parasitic on birds, chiefly on sparrows and other passerine birds, and on hummingbirds.

Family **Philoptéridae:** This is the largest family in the order, and contains species parasitizing a wide variety of birds. Two important pests of poultry in this group are the chicken head louse, *Cuclotogáster heterógrapha* (Nitzsch), and the large turkey louse, *Chelopístes meleágridis* (L.) (Figure 157 A).

Family **Trichodéctidae:** The trichodectids are parasites of mammals. Some important pest species in this group are the cattle biting louse, *Bovícola bòvis* (L.) (Figure 155 B), the horse biting louse, *B. équi* (Denny), and the dog biting louse, *Trichodéctes cànis* (De Geer).

COLLECTING AND PRESERVING MALLÓPHAGA

Mallóphaga are seldom off the host; hence, to collect them, one must examine the host. Hosts other than domestic animals usually must be shot or trapped; Mallóphaga may occasionally be found still attached to museum skins of birds or mammals. Small host animals collected in the field to be examined later should be placed in a bag and the bag tightly closed; any lice that fall or crawl off the host can then be found in the bag.

All parts of the host should be examined; different species of lice often occur on different parts of the same host. The best way to locate lice is to go over the host carefully with forceps; a comb can often be used to advantage. The lice will sometimes fall off if the host is shaken over a paper. Lice may be picked up with forceps or with a camel's-hair brush moistened with alcohol.

Lice should be preserved in alcohol (70–75 percent), along with collection and host data. A different vial should be used for the lice from each host, and the collection data (on a penciled label inside the vial) should include the host species, date, locality, and the name of the collector.

Lice must be mounted on microscope slides for detailed study; specimens preserved on pins or points are usually unsatisfactory. Specimens to be mounted are first cleared for a few hours in cold potassium hydroxide; it is sometimes desirable to stain the specimen before mounting it on a slide.

References on the Mallóphaga

Emerson, K. C. 1964. *Checklist of the Mallophaga of North America (North of Mexico)*. Proving Ground, Dugway, Utah, 275 pp.

Ewing, H. E. 1924. Taxonomy, biology, and distribution of the Gyropidae. *Proc. U.S. Natl. Mus.*, 63(20):1–42.

Ferris, G. F. 1924. The mallophagan family Menoponidae. *Parasitology*, 16(1):55–66; 5 f.

Harrison, L. 1916. The genera and species of Mallophaga. *Parasitology*, 9(1):1–156.

Hopkins, G. H. E., and T. Clay. 1952. *A Check List of the Genera and Species of Mallophaga*. London: British Museum, 362 pp.

Kellogg, V. L. 1899. A list of Mallophaga taken from birds and mammals of North America. *Proc. U.S. Natl. Mus.*, 22(1183):39–100.

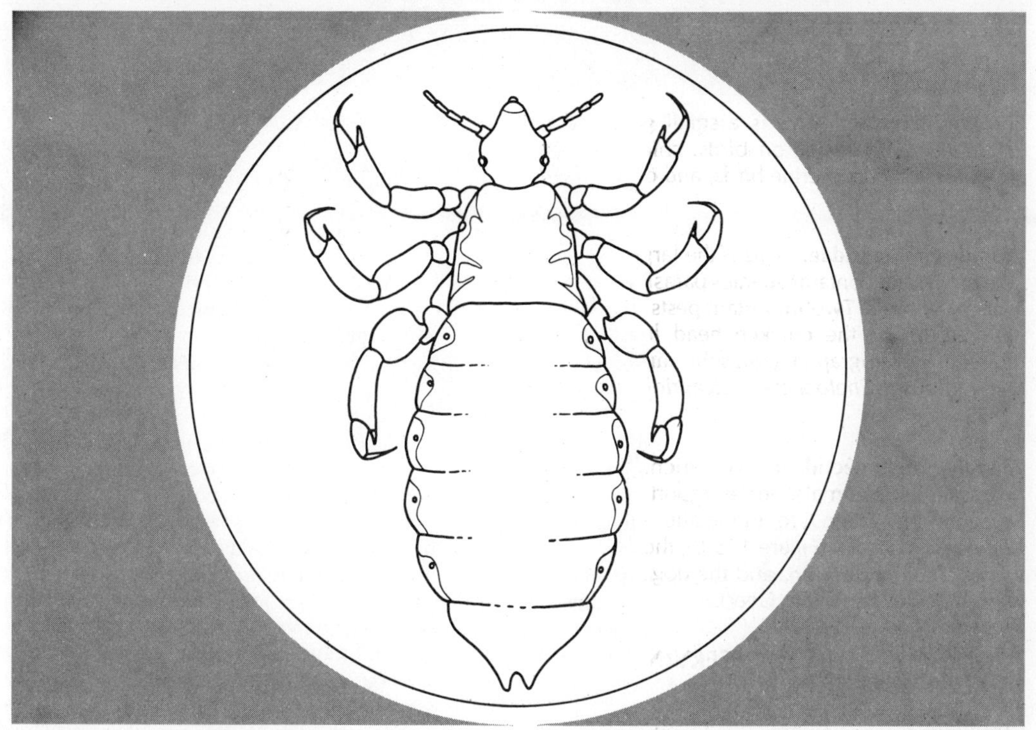

20: ORDER ANOPLÙRA[1]

SUCKING LICE

The sucking lice are small wingless external parasites that feed by sucking blood. They differ from the chewing lice (Mallóphaga) in that they have sucking rather than chewing mouth parts, and the head is narrower than the thorax. The Anoplùra are parasites of mammals, while the Mallóphaga are parasites of birds and mammals. The order Anoplùra contains several species parasitic on domestic animals, and two species that attack man; these insects are irritating pests, and some of them are important vectors of disease. Most species are restricted to one or a few types of hosts. The metamorphosis is simple.

The mouth parts of a sucking louse consist of three piercing stylets that are normally carried withdrawn into a stylet sac in the head (Figure 16). When a louse feeds, the stylets are everted through a rostrum at the front of the head; the rostrum is provided with tiny hooks with which the louse attaches to its host while feeding.

The tarsi of the sucking lice are 1-segmented and provided with a single large claw that usually fits against a thumblike process at the end of the tibia; this forms an efficient mechanism for hanging to the hairs of the host.

[1] Anoplùra: *anopl,* unarmed; *ura,* tail.

Key to the Families of Anoplùra

1.	Body thickly beset with short stout spines, or with spines and scales; parasitic on marine mammals .... **Echinophthirìidae**	p. 248
1′.	Body with spines or hairs, but never with scales; parasitic on land mammals 2	
2(1′).	Eyes or eye tubercles present (Figure 159); parasitic on man and other primates .... **Pedicùlidae**	p. 248
2′.	Eyes lacking (Figure 159); parasitic on mammals other than man and other primates .... **Haematopínidae**	p. 248

Family **Echinophthirìidae:** The lice in this group are spiny or scaly, and attack marine mammals such as seals, sea lions, and walruses. At least some species burrow into the skin of their host.

Family **Haematopínidae:** The family Haematopínidae is a fairly large group and contains the sucking lice of horses, cattle, hogs, sheep, and other animals. The control of these lice usually involves treating the host with dusts, sprays, or dips.

Family **Pedicùlidae:** This group includes the only lice that attack man—the crab louse, head louse, and body louse. All these are irritating pests, and the body louse acts as a disease vector.

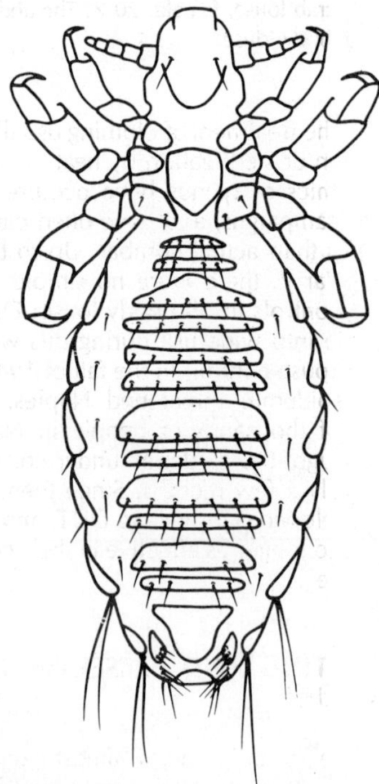

Figure 158. Spined rat louse, *Pólyplax spinulòsa* (Burmeister), female, ventral view (Haematopínidae).

The crab louse, *Pthírus pùbis* (L.) (Figure 159 B), is broadly oval and somewhat crab-shaped, with the claws of the middle and hind legs very large, the head much narrower than the thorax, and with lateral lobes on the abdominal segments; adults are 1.5–2.0 mm in length. This louse occurs chiefly in the pubic region, but in hairy individuals may occur almost anywhere on the body. The eggs (nits) are attached to body hairs.

The head and body lice are usually considered as varieties of a single species, *Pedículus humànus* L. These lice (Figure 159 A) are narrower and more elongate than crab lice; the head is but little narrower than the thorax, and the abdomen lacks lateral lobes; adults are 2.5–3.5 mm in length.

The head and body lice have a similar life history, but differ somewhat in habits. The head louse occurs chiefly on the head, and its eggs are attached to the hair; the body louse occurs chiefly on the body, and its eggs are laid on the clothing, chiefly along the seams. The eggs hatch in about a week, and the entire life cycle from egg to adult requires about a month. Lice feed at frequent intervals, and individual feedings last a few minutes. Body lice usually hang onto clothing while feeding and often remain on the clothing when it is removed. The head louse is transmitted from person to person largely through the promiscuous use of combs, hair brushes, and caps; the body louse is transmitted by clothing and bedding, and at night may migrate from one pile of clothes to another.

The body louse (also called "cootie" or "seam squirrel") is an important vector of human disease. The most important disease it transmits is epidemic typhus, which frequently occurs in epidemic proportions and may have a mortality rate as high as 70 percent. Body lice become infected by feeding on a typhus patient and are able to infect another person a week or so later. Infection results from scratching the feces of the louse, or the crushed louse itself, into the skin; this disease

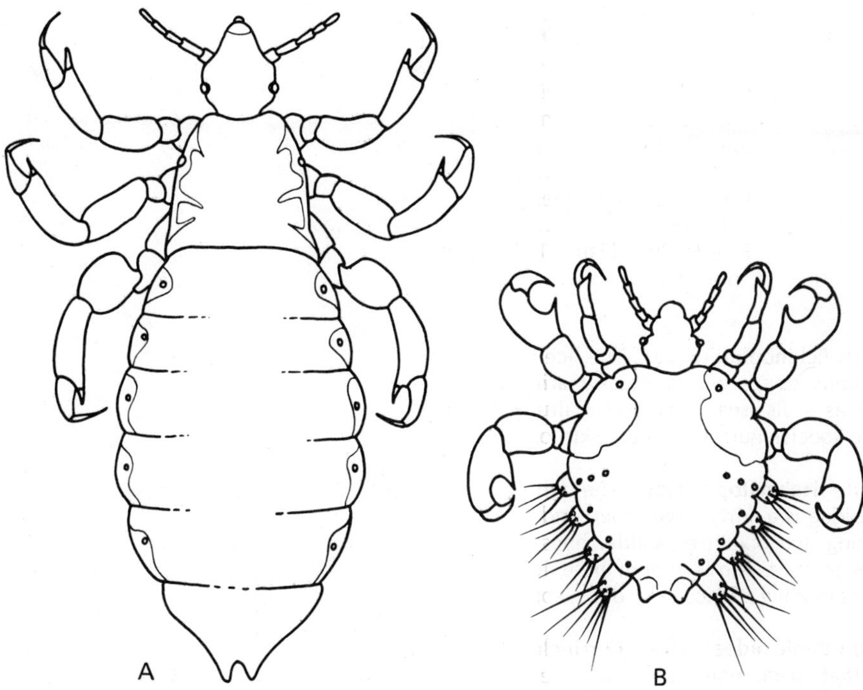

Figure 159. Human lice (Pedicùlidae). A, body louse, female; B, crab louse, female, 20 ×. The abdominal projections in B are a feature that distinguishes the crab louse from the body louse.

is not transmitted by the bite of the louse. Another important louse-borne disease is a type of relapsing fever; this disease is transmitted by the infected louse being crushed and rubbed into the skin; neither the feces nor the bite of the louse is infective. A third louse-borne disease is trench fever; this disease occurred in epidemic proportions during World War I, but since then has not been very important.

People who bathe and change clothes regularly seldom become infested with lice, but when they go for long periods without bathing or changing clothes and live in crowded conditions, lousiness is likely to be prevalent. The latter conditions are often common during wartime, when living quarters are crowded, sanitation facilities are at a minimum, and people go for long periods without a change of clothes. If a louse-borne disease such as typhus ever gets started in a population that is heavily infested with body lice, it can quickly spread to epidemic proportions.

The control of body lice usually involves dusting individuals with an insecticide; clothing must also be treated, for the eggs are laid on it, and adult lice often cling to clothing when it is removed. The treatment of clothing usually involves fumigation or sterilization by heat.

Epidemics of typhus have occurred in many military campaigns, and have often caused more casualties than actual combat. Up to the time of World War II, there were no simple and easily applied controls for the body louse; DDT, which first came into wide use during this war, proved ideal for louse control. In the fall of 1943, when a typhus epidemic threatened Naples, Italy, the dusting of thousands of people in Naples with DDT brought the epidemic under complete control in only a few months. Since then, body lice have developed resistance to DDT, and this insecticide is no longer as effective in their control as it used to be.

COLLECTING AND PRESERVING ANOPLÙRA

These lice are to be found almost exclusively on their host, and the methods suggested for collecting and preserving Mallóphaga (page 246) will apply also to the Anoplùra.

References on the Anoplùra

Clay. T. 1940. Anoplura. In *The Scientific Reports of the British Graham Land Expedition,* 1:295–318.

Ferris, G. F. 1951. The sucking lice. *Pacific Coast Ent. Soc. Mem.,* 1:x + 320 pp.; 124 f.

Hopkins, G. H. E. 1949. The host associations of the lice of mammals. *Proc. Zool. Soc. London,* 119:387–604.

Matthysse, J. G. 1946. Cattle lice, their biology and control. *Cornell Univ. Agric. Expt. Sta. Bull.,* 823; 67 pp.

21: ORDER THYSANÓPTERA[1]

THRIPS

The thrips are minute, slender-bodied insects 0.5–5.0 mm in length (some tropical species are nearly 13 mm in length). Wings may be present or absent; the wings when fully developed are four in number, very long and narrow with few or no veins, and fringed with long hairs. The fringe of hairs on the wings gives the order its name. The mouth parts (Figure 9) are of the sucking type, and the proboscis is a stout, conical, asymmetrical structure located posteriorly on the ventral surface of the head; there are three stylets: one mandible (the left one; the right mandible is vestigial) and the laciniae of the two maxillae. The antennae are short and 4- to 9-segmented. The tarsi are 1- or 2-segmented, with one or two claws, and are bladderlike at the tip. An ovipositor is present in some thrips; in others, the tip of the abdomen is tubular and an ovipositor is lacking.

The metamorphosis of thrips is somewhat intermediate between simple and complete (Figure 160). The first two instars have no wings externally and are usually called larvae; in at least some cases, the wings are developing internally during these two instars. In the suborder Terebrántia, the third and fourth instars (only the third instar in *Franklínothrips*) are inactive, do not feed, and have external wings; the third instar is called the prepupa and the fourth the pupa. The pupa is sometimes enclosed in a cocoon. In the suborder Tubulífera, the third and fourth instars are prepupae (the third does not have external wings), and the fifth instar is the pupa. The stage following the

[1] Thysanóptera: *thysano,* fringe; *ptera,* wings.

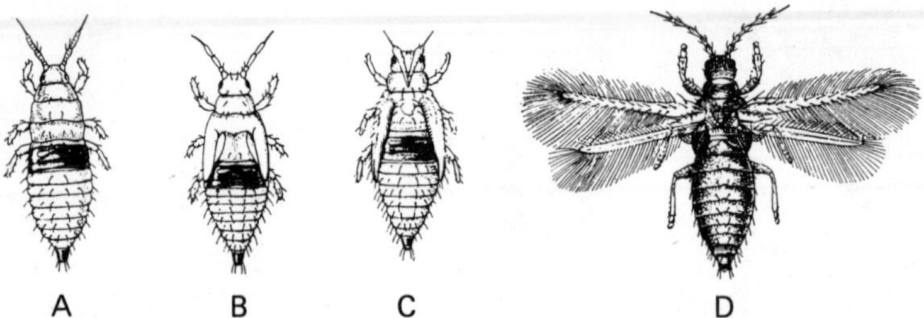

Figure 160. Redbanded thrips, *Sélenothrips rubrocínctus* (Giard) (Thrípidae). A, full-grown larva; B, prepupa; C, pupa; D, adult female. (Courtesy of USDA.)

pupa is the adult. This type of metamorphosis resembles simple metamorphosis in that more than one preadult instar (except in *Franklínothrips*) has external wings; it resembles complete metamorphosis in that at least some of the wing development is internal, and there is a quiescent (pupal) instar preceding the adult.

The two sexes of thrips are similar in appearance, but the males are usually smaller. Parthenogenesis occurs in many species. Those thrips that have an ovipositor usually insert their eggs in plant tissues; the thrips that lack an ovipositor usually lay their eggs in crevices or under bark. Young thrips are relatively inactive. Generally there are several generations a year.

A great many of the thrips are plant feeders, attacking flowers, leaves, fruit, twigs, or buds; they feed on a great many types of plants. They are particularly abundant in the flower heads of daisies and dandelions. They destroy plant cells by their feeding, and some species act as vectors of plant disease; many species are serious pests of cultivated plants. A few thrips feed on fungus spores, and a few are predaceous on other small arthropods. These insects sometimes occur in enormous numbers, and a few species may bite man.

CLASSIFICATION OF THE THYSANÓPTERA

This order is divided into two suborders, the Terebrántia and the Tubulífera, which differ in the shape of the last abdominal segment and the development of the ovipositor. The Terebrántia have the last abdominal segment more or less conical or rounded, and the females usually have a well-developed ovipositor; the Tubulífera have the last abdominal segment tubular, and the females lack an ovipositor. Five families of thrips occur in North America, four of them in the suborder Terebrántia; these families may be separated by the key below. The families of Terebrántia are separated largely by characters of the antennae, particularly the number of antennal segments and the nature of the sensoria on the third and fourth segments. These sensoria are circular or oval areas near the apex of the segments, or are in the form of simple or forked sense cones.

Key to the Families of Thysanóptera

1. Last abdominal segment tubular (Figures 161 C and 163 C), the female without an ovipositor; front wings, if present, either veinless or with a short median vein that does not extend to wing tip, and membrane without microscopic hairs; antennae 4- to 8-segmented (suborder Tubulífera) .... **Phlaeothrípidae** p. 256

1′. Last abdominal segment broadly rounded or conical (Figures 161 A, B, and 163 A, B, D–G), the female usually with a sawlike ovipositor (Figure 161 A, B); front wings, if present, with 1 or 2 longitudinal veins, and membrane with microscopic hairs; antennae 4- to 9-segmented (suborder Terebrántia) 2

2(1′). Antennae 9-segmented, the sensoria on the third and fourth segments in the form of longitudinal flat areas (Figure 162 A, *sa*); ovipositor curved

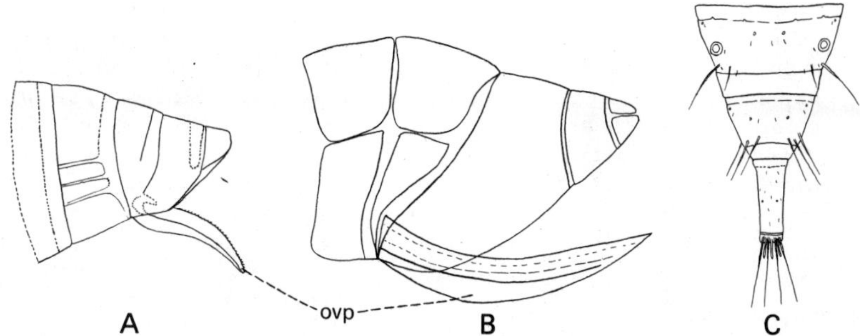

Figure 161. Abdominal structures of Thysanóptera. A, apex of abdomen of the pear thrips, *Taèniothrips incónsequens* (Uzel) (Thrípidae), lateral view, showing the decurved ovipositor; B, apex of abdomen of *Mélanothrips* (Aeolothrípidae), lateral view, showing up-curved ovipositor; C, apex of abdomen of *Háplothrips hispánicus* Priesner (Phlaeothrípidae), dorsal view. *ovp*, ovipositor. (Modified from Pesson.)

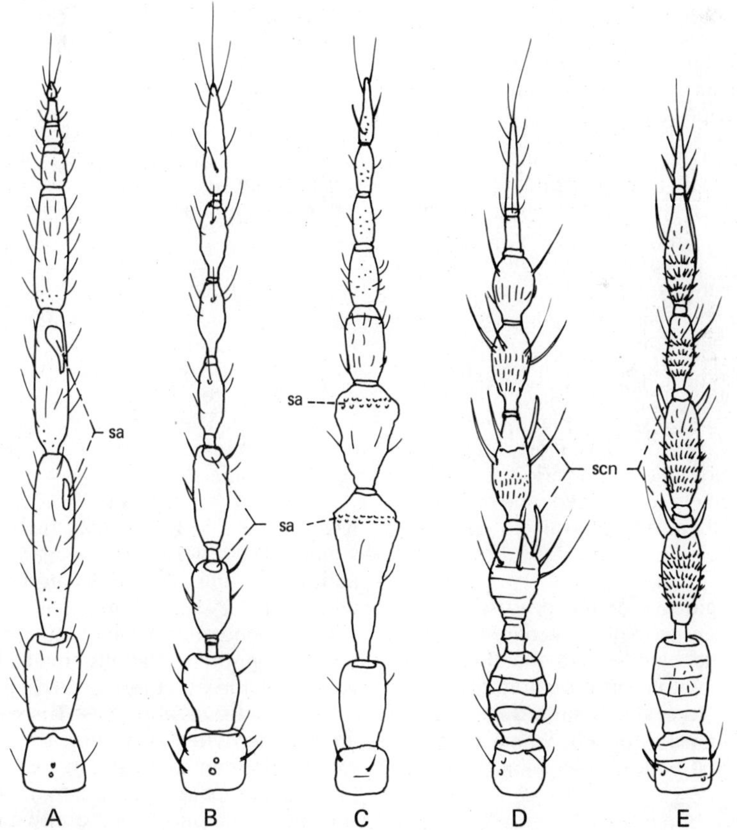

Figure 162. Antennae of Thysanóptera. A, *Aeólothrips* (Aeolothrípidae); B, *Mèrothrips* (Merothrípidae); C, *Héterothrips* (Heterothrípidae); D, *Cáliothrips* (Thrípidae); E, *Thríps* (Thrípidae). *sa*, sensoria; *scn*, sense cone. (Redrawn from Stannard, courtesy of the Illinois Natural History Survey.)

upward (Figure 161 B); front wings relatively broad, with tips rounded .... **Aeolothrípidae** p. 254

2′. Antennae 6- to 9-segmented, the sensoria on the third and fourth segments in the form of flat areas that are not longitudinal (Figure 162 B, C, *sa*) or protruding as simple or forked sense cones (Figure 162 D, E, *scn*); ovipositor, when developed, curved downward (Figure 161 A); front wings narrower, usually pointed at tip 3

3(2′). Sensoria of third and fourth antennal segments in the form of slender, simple, or forked sense cones located preapically (Figure 162 D, E, *scn*) .... **Thrípidae** p. 254

3′. Sensoria of third and fourth antennal segments in the form of flat areas encircling apex of segment (Figure 162 B, C, *sa*), or a short blunt sense cone at outer tip of segment 4

4(3′). Antennae 8-segmented, the sensoria of third and fourth segments in the form of a flat apical area (Figure 162 B, *sa*); color light yellowish brown; ovipositor weakly developed; pronotum with a longitudinal suture on each side; front and hind femora thickened (Figure 163 G) **Merothrípidae** p. 254

4′. Antennae 9-segmented, the sensoria of third and fourth segments forming a band of small, flat, circular areas around apex of segment (Figure 162 C, *sa; Héterothrips,* widely distributed), or in the form of a short, blunt sense cone at outer tip of segment (*Òligothrips,* California and Oregon) .... **Heterothrípidae** p. 254

Family **Aeolothrípidae**—Broad-Winged or Banded Thrips: The front wings in this group are relatively broad, with two longitudinal veins extending from the base of the wing nearly to the tip, and usually with several cross veins. The adults are dark-colored, and often have the wings banded or mottled (Figure 163 E). The most common species in this group is the banded thrips, *Aeólothrips fasciàtus* (L.). The adult is yellowish to dark brown, with three white bands on the wings; the larvae are yellowish, shading into orange posteriorly. The adults are about 1.6 mm in length. This species occurs on various plants and is often common in the flower heads of clover; it feeds on other thrips, aphids, mites, and various other small insects. It is widely distributed and occurs in Europe, Asia, Africa, and Hawaii as well as in North America.

Family **Merothrípidae**—Large-Legged Thrips: The members of this group may be recognized by the enlarged front and hind femora and by the two longitudinal sutures on the pronotum. The only common species in this family is *Mérothrips mòrgani* Hood (Figure 163 G), which occurs in the eastern United States under bark, in debris, and in fungi.

Family **Heterothrípidae:** Two genera in this small family occur in North America, *Héterothrips* (widely distributed, Figure 163 F) and *Òligothrips* (California and Oregon). The several species of *Héterothrips* occur on various trees (buckeye, oak, and willow) and flowers (azalea, wild rose, and jack-in-the-pulpit), and in the buds of wild grape; our only species of *Òligothrips, O. oreìos* Moulton, occurs in the blossoms of madrone and manzanita.

Family **Thrípidae**—Common Thrips: This family is the largest in the order and contains most of the species that are of economic importance. The wings are narrower than in the Aeolothrípidae and are more pointed at the tip; the antennae are 6- to 9-segmented. These thrips are mostly plant feeders, and a number of species are serious pests of cultivated plants.

The pear thrips, *Taèniothrips incónsequens* (Uzel) (Figure 163 B) attacks the buds, blossoms, young leaves, and fruit of pears, plums, cherries, and other plants. The adults are brown with pale wings and 1.2–1.3 mm in length. This species has a single generation a year and overwinters as a pupa in the soil. The adults emerge in early spring and attack the fruit trees, and oviposit on the petioles of the leaves and fruits. The young feed until about June, when they drop to the ground and remain dormant until about October, at which time they pupate and go into hibernation. This species occurs on the east and west coasts of the United States.

The gladiolus thrips, *Taèniothrips símplex* (Morison), is a serious pest of gladiolus, injuring the leaves and greatly reducing the size, develop-

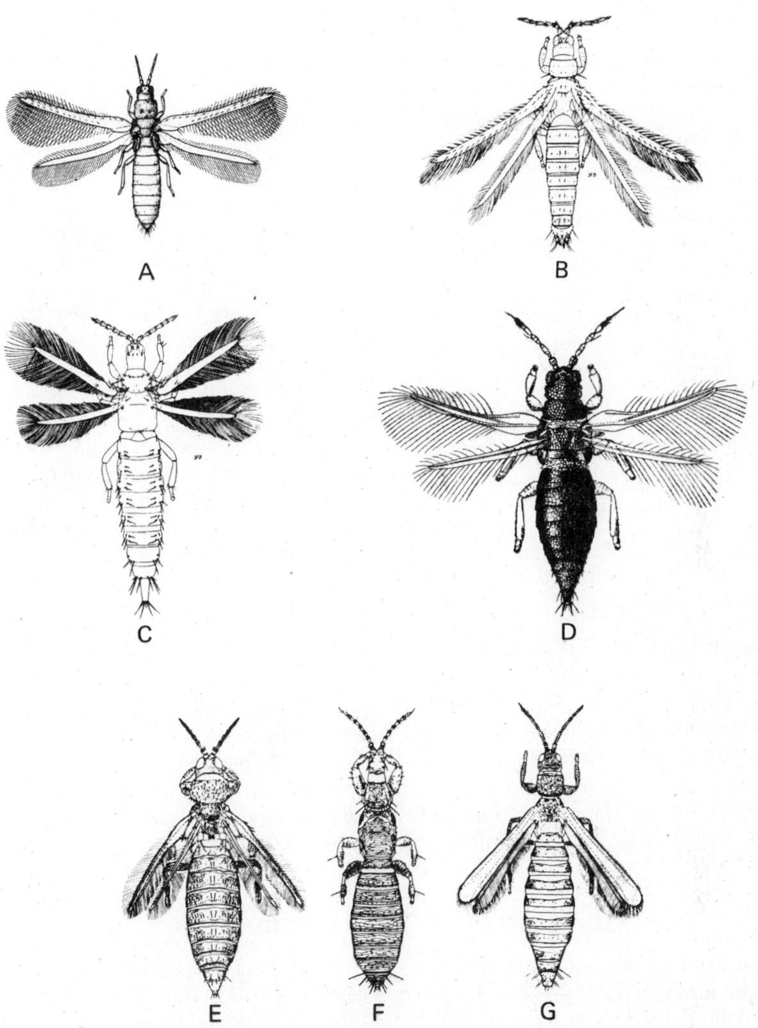

Figure 163. Thrips. A, gladiolus thrips, *Taèniothrips símplex* (Morison) (Thrípidae); B, pear thrips, *Taéniothrips incónsequens* (Uzel) (Thrípidae); C, lily bulb thrips, *Lìothrips vanèeckei* Priesner (Phlaeothrípidae); D, greenhouse thrips, *Hèliothrips haèmorrhoidàlis* (Bouché) (Thrípidae); E, a banded thrips, *Stòmatothrips crawfordi* Stannard (Aeolothrípidae); F, *Héterothrips sálicis* (Shull) (Heterothrípidae); G, a large-legged thrips, *Mèrothrips mòrgani* Hood. (A, courtesy of the Utah Agricultural Experiment Station; B, courtesy of Bailey and the University of California Experiment Station; C, courtesy of Bailey and the California Department of Agriculture; D, courtesy of USDA; E–G, courtesy of Stannard and the Illinois Natural History Survey.)

ment, and color of the flowers; it is very similar to the pear thrips in appearance (Figure 163 A). The onion thrips, *Thríps tabàci* Lindeman, is a widely distributed species that attacks onions, tobacco, beans, and many other plants; it is a pale yellowish or brownish insect 1.0–1.2 mm in length. It transmits the virus that causes spotted wilt disease in tomatoes and other plants. The greenhouse thrips, *Hèliothríps haèmorrhoidàlis* (Bouché) (Figure 163 D), is a tropical species that occurs out-of-doors in the warmer parts of the world and is a serious pest in greenhouses in the North; the male of this species is very rare. The flower thrips, *Frankliniélla trítici* (Fitch), is a common and widely distributed pest of grasses, grains, truck crops, weeds, trees, and shrubs; it is a slender yellow and orange insect 1.2–1.3 mm in length. The six-spotted thrips, *Scòlothrips sexmaculàtus* (Pergande), is a little less than a millimeter in length and is yellow with three black spots on each front wing; it is predaceous on plant-feeding mites. The grain thrips, *Lìmothrips cereàlium* (Haliday), is a dark-brown to black thrips, 1.2–1.4 mm in length, that feeds on various cereals and grasses; it is sometimes quite abundant and may bite man.

Family **Phlaeothrípidae:** The family Phlaeothrípidae is a rather large group, most species of which are larger and stouter bodied than the thrips in the suborder Terebrántia. One Australian species, *Idólothrips marginàtus* Haliday, is 10–14 mm in length. These thrips are mostly dark brown or black, often with light-colored or mottled wings. Most of them are spore feeders; some are predaceous, feeding on small insects and mites; a few are plant feeders, and some of these may be of economic importance. The lily bulb thrips, *Lìothrips vanèeckei* Priesner, is a dark-colored species about 2 mm in length (Figure 163 C) which feeds on lilies and injures the bulbs. The black hunter, *Léptothrips máli* (Fitch), is a fairly common predaceous species. *Aleuródothrips fasciapénnis* Franklin, which is common in Florida, is predaceous on whiteflies. *Háplothrips leucánthemi* (Schrank) is a black thrips that is common in daisy flowers.

COLLECTING AND PRESERVING THYSANÓPTERA

Thrips may be found on flowers, foliage, fruits, bark, fungi, and in debris. The species occurring on vegetation are most easily collected by sweeping; they may be removed from the net by stunning the entire net contents and sorting out the thrips later, or the net contents may be shaken out onto a paper and the thrips picked up with an aspirator or with a moistened camel's-hair brush; dark species are best seen on a light paper, and the light species on a dark paper. If host data are desired, the specimens should be collected directly from the host plant; the best way to collect flower-frequenting species is to collect the flowers in a paper bag and examine them later in the laboratory. The species that occur in debris and in similar situations are usually collected by means of a Berlese funnel (Figure 616) or by sifting the material in which they occur. Bark- and branch-inhabiting species can be collected with a beating umbrella.

Thrips should be preserved in liquid and mounted on microscope slides for detailed study; they may be mounted on points, but specimens so mounted are usually not very satisfactory. The best killing solution is AGA, which contains 8 parts of 95 percent alcohol, 5 parts of distilled water, 1 part of glycerine, and 1 part of glacial acetic acid. After a few weeks, specimens should be transferred from this solution to alcohol (about 80 percent) for permanent preservation.

References on the Thysanóptera

Bailey, S. F. 1940. The distribution of injurious thrips in the United States. *J. Econ. Ent.*, 33(1):133–136.

Bailey, S. F. 1951. The genus *Aeolothrips* Haliday in North America. *Hilgardia*, 21(2):43–80; 73 f.

Bailey, S. F. 1957. The thrips of California, Part 1: Suborder Terebrantia. *Bull. Calif. Insect Survey*, 4(5):143–220; 55 f.

Cott, H. E. 1956. *Systematics of the Suborder Tubulifera (Thysanoptera) in California*. Berkeley: Univ. California Press, 216 pp., 4 pl.

Hinds, W. E. 1902. Contribution to a monograph of the insects of the order Thysanoptera inhabiting North America. *Proc. U.S. Natl. Mus.*, 26(1310):79–242; 11 pl.

Lewis, T. 1973. *Thrips, Their Biology, Ecology and Economic Importance*. New York: Academic, 366 pp.

Moulton, D. 1911. Synopsis, catalogue, and bibliography of North American Thysanoptera. *U.S.D.A. Bur. Ent. and Plant Quarantine, Tech. Ser.*, No. 21; 56 pp., 6 pl.

O'Neill, K., and R. S. Bigelow. 1964. The *Taeniothrips* of Canada. *Can. Ent.*, 96(9):1219–1239; 44 f.

Peterson, A. 1915. Morphological studies on the head and mouthparts of the Thysanoptera. *Ann. Ent. Soc. Amer.*, 8(1):20–67; 7 pl.

Priesner, H. 1926–1928. *Die Thysanopteren Europas*. Wien: Verlag Fritz Wagner, Abh. I–II, 1926, 342 pp., 4 pl., 2 textf.; Abh. III, 1927, pp. 343–570, 2 pl.; Abh. IV, 1928, pp. 571–755, 10 textf.

Priesner, H. 1949. Genera Thysanopterorum. Keys for the identification of the genera of the order Thysanoptera. *Bull. Soc. Fouad Ier Ent.*, 33:31–157.

Stannard, L. J., Jr. 1957. The phylogeny and classification of the North American genera of the suborder Tubulifera (Thysanoptera). *Ill. Biol. Monog.*, No. 25; vii + 200 pp., 144 f.

Stannard, L. J., Jr. 1968. The thrips, or Thysanoptera, of Illinois. *Ill. Nat. Hist. Surv. Bull.*, 29(4):vi + 215–552; 310 f.

Watson, J. R. 1923. Synopsis and catalogue of the Thysanoptera of North America. *Univ. Fla. Agric. Expt. Sta. Bull.*, 168; 100 p.

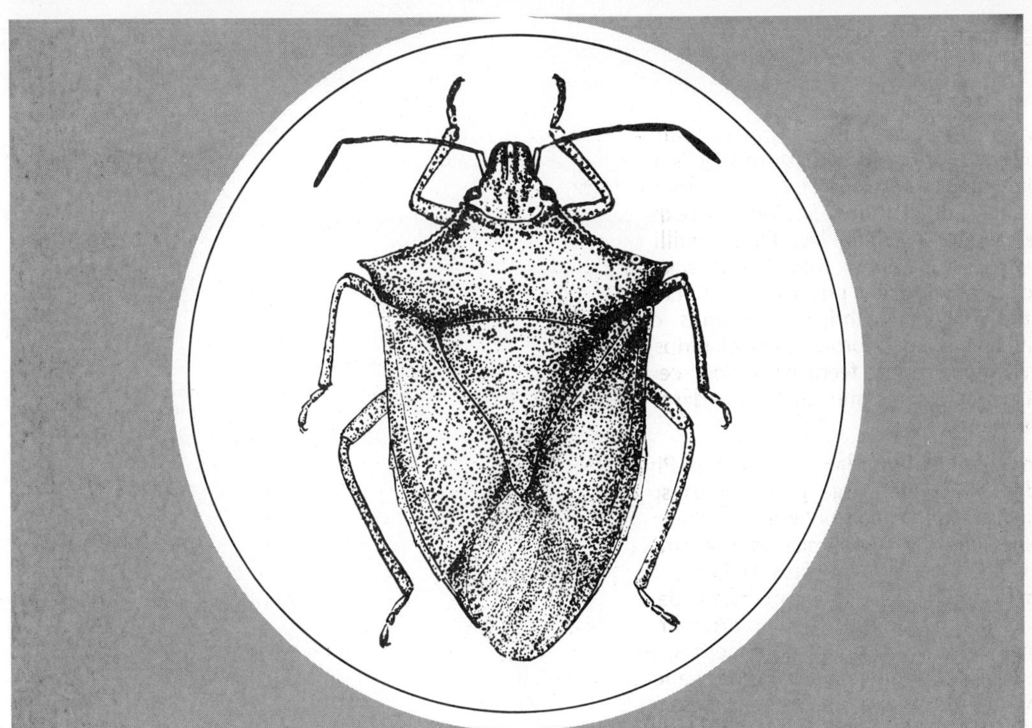

22: ORDER HEMÍPTERA[1]

BUGS

The term "bug" is used by the general public for a great many different animals, and by entomologists for occasional insects in other orders (for example, mealybugs, lightningbugs): When used for an insect in the order Hemíptera, the "bug" of the name is written as a separate word. The Hemíptera are sometimes called the "true" bugs, to distinguish them from the occasional insects in other orders to which the term "bug" is applied.

One of the most distinctive features of the Hemíptera, and one from which the order gets its name, is the structure of the front wings. In most Hemíptera the basal portion of the front wing is thickened and leathery, and the apical portion is membranous; this type of wing is called a hemelytron (plural, hemelytra). The hind wings are entirely membranous and are slightly shorter than the front wings. The wings at rest are held flat over the abdomen, with the membranous tips of the front wings overlapping.

The mouth parts of the Hemíptera are of the piercing-sucking type and are in the form of a slender segmented beak that arises from the front part of the head and usually extends back along the ventral side of the body, sometimes as far as the base of the hind legs (Figure 164 B, *bk*). The segmented portion of the beak is the labium, which serves as a sheath for the four piercing stylets (two mandibles and two maxillae). The maxillae fit together in the beak to form two channels, a food channel and a salivary channel (Fig-

[1] Hemíptera: *hemi,* half; *ptera,* wings (referring to the fact that the front wings usually have the basal portion thickened and the distal portion membranous.

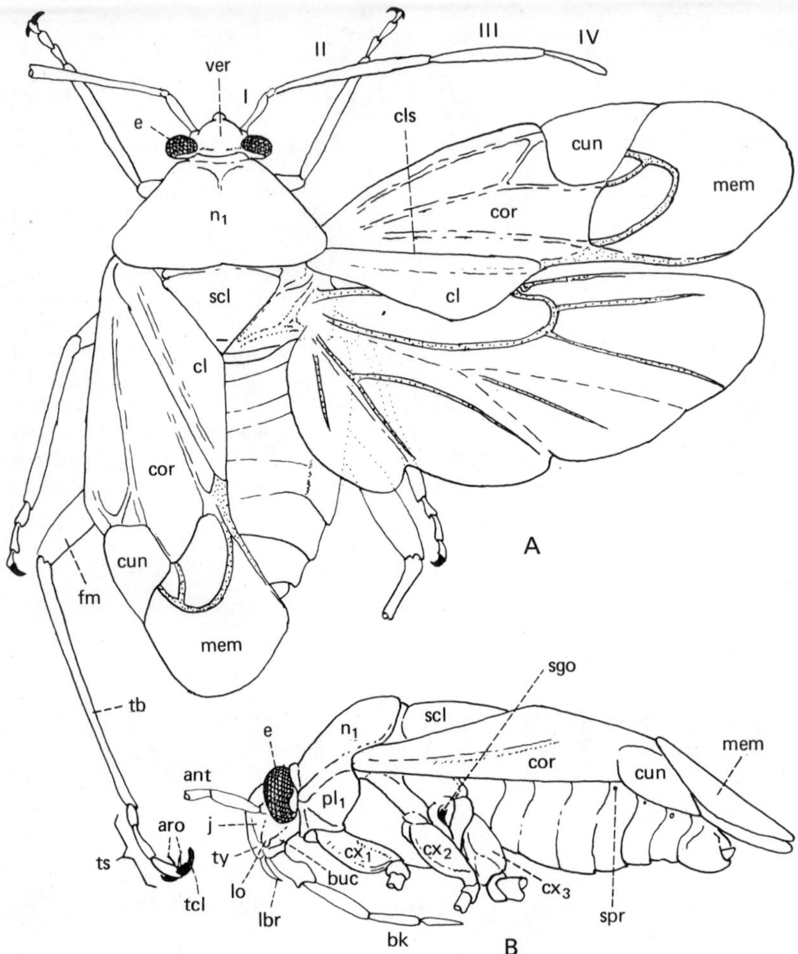

Figure 164. Structure of a bug, *Lỳgus oblineàtus* (Say), family Míridae. A, dorsal view; B, lateral view. *ant,* antenna; *aro,* arolia; *bk,* beak; *buc,* buccula; *cl,* clavus; *cls,* claval suture; *cor,* corium; *cun,* cuneus; *cx,* coxa; e, compound eye; *fm,* femur; *j,* jugum; *lbr,* labrum; *lo,* lorum; *mem,* membrane; n_1, pronotum; pl_1, propleuron; *scl,* scutellum; *sgo,* scent gland opening; *spr,* spiracle; *tb,* tibia; *tcl,* tarsal claw; *ts,* tarsus; *ty,* tylus; *ver,* vertex; *I-IV,* antennal segments.

ure 10). There are no palps, though certain tiny lobelike structures on the beak of some aquatic bugs are thought by some authorities to represent palps.

The Hemíptera and the Homóptera are very similar in many respects and are grouped by some authorities in a single order, the Hemíptera, with the two groups as the suborders Homóptera and Heteróptera (the latter including the true bugs). The two groups differ principally in the structure of the wings and in the location of the beak. The front wings in the Homóptera have a uniform texture throughout, either leathery or membranous (hence the name: *homo,* uniform; *ptera,* wings); in the Hemíptera the basal portion of the front wings is usually thickened. The beak in the Hemíptera arises from the front part of the head, whereas in the Homóptera it arises from the posterior part of the head (Figure 80).

The antennae are fairly long in most of the Hemíptera and consist of four or five segments. The compound eyes are nearly always well developed, but the ocelli (two in number) may be present or absent (always absent in nymphs). Many Hemíptera have scent glands, usually opening on the side of the thorax (Figure 164 B, *sgo*), and give off a characteristic odor, particularly when disturbed; this odor is often unpleasant to man. Most of the Hemíptera have well-developed wings, but some species are wingless, some are brachypterous (wings short, the front wings usually lacking the membrane), and in some species both long-winged and brachypterous forms occur. The members of this order undergo simple metamorphosis.

The Hemíptera are a large and widely distributed group of insects. Most species are terrestrial, but many are aquatic. Many feed on plant juices, and some of these are serious pests of cultivated plants; others are predaceous, and some of these are very beneficial to man; still others attack man and other animals and suck blood, and a few of these act as disease vectors.

CLASSIFICATION OF THE HEMÍPTERA

We follow the classification of China and Miller (1959) in dividing this order into three suborders, but differ slightly from this classification in the families we recognize. The three suborders are separated principally by antennal structure, trichobothria (special sensory hairs on the head), and habits. The presence or absence of trichobothria is sometimes difficult to determine, and we have not used this character in our key.

A synopsis of the Hemíptera occurring in North America north of Mexico is given below; synonyms and other arrangements are given in parentheses. Groups marked with an asterisk are rare or are unlikely to be taken by a general collector.

Suborder Hydrocorìzae (Cryptocérata)—aquatic bugs
- Coríxidae—water boatmen
- Notonéctidae—backswimmers
- *Plèidae (Notonéctidae in part)—pleid water bugs
- Naucòridae (including Aphelocheìridae)—creeping water bugs
- Belostomátidae (Belostómidae)—giant water bugs
- Nèpidae—waterscorpions
- Gelastocòridae (Galgùlidae)—toad bugs
- *Ochtéridae (Pelogónidae, Pelogonìidae)—velvety shore bugs

Suborder Amphibicorìzae (Gymnocérata in part)—semiaquatic or shore-inhabiting bugs
- Gérridae (Hydrobátidae)—water striders
- Velìidae—broad-shouldered water striders or ripple bugs
- Hydrométridae (Limnobátidae)—water measurers
- *Mesovelìidae—water treaders
- *Macrovelìidae (Mesovelìidae in part, Velìidae in part)—macroveliid shore bugs
- *Hèbridae (Naeogaèidae)—velvet water bugs
- Sáldidae (Acanthìidae)—shore bugs
- *Leptopódidae—spiny shore bugs

Suborder Geocorìzae (Gymnocérata in part)—terrestrial bugs
- *Schizoptéridae (Cryptostemmátidae in part)—jumping ground bugs
- *Dipsocòridae (Cryptostemmátidae, Ceratocómbidae)—jumping ground bugs
- *Thaumastocòridae (Thaumastotherìidae)—royal palm bugs
- *Polycténidae—bat bugs
- Cimícidae (Acanthìidae, Clinocòridae)—bed bugs
- Anthocòridae—minute pirate bugs
- *Microphỳsidae—microphysid bugs
- *Isometòpidae—jumping tree bugs
- Míridae (Cápsidae; including Termatophỳlidae)—plant bugs or leaf bugs
- Nàbidae—damsel bugs
- *Enicocephálidae (Henicocephálidae)—gnat bugs
- Reduvìidae (including Ploiarìidae)—assassin bugs
- Phymátidae (Macrocephálidae)—ambush bugs
- Tíngidae (Tingídidae, Tingítidae)—lace bugs
- Arádidae—flat bugs
- *Piesmátidae (Piésmidae)—ash-gray leaf bugs

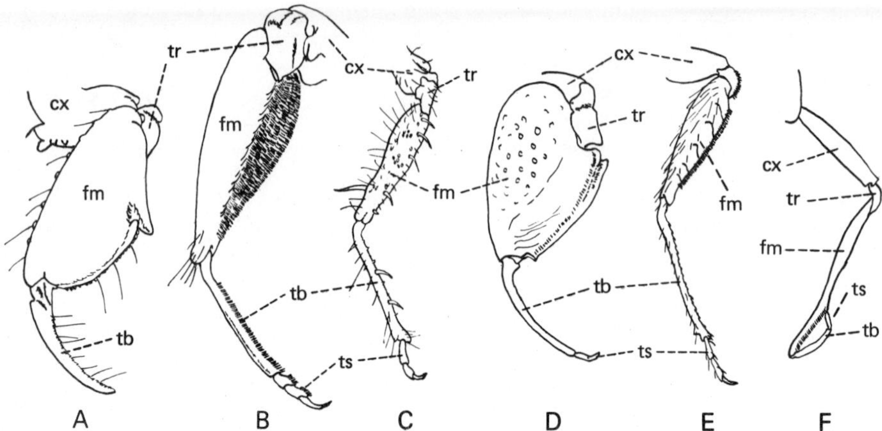

Figure 165. Raptorial front legs of Hemíptera. A, *Phýmata* (Phymátidae); B, *Lethócerus* (Belostomátidae); C, *Sìnea* (Reduvìidae); D, *Pelócoris* (Naucòridae); E, *Nàbis* (Nàbidae); F, *Ránatra* (Nèpidae). *cx*, coxa; *fm*, femur; *tb*, tibia; *tr*, trochanter; *ts*, tarsus.

Lygaèidae (Myodóchidae) – seed bugs
Berýtidae (Neídidae) – stilt bugs
Lárgidae (Euryphthalmìnae of Pyrrhocòridae) – largid bugs
Pyrrhocòridae – red bugs or stainers
Corèidae – leaf-footed bugs
Rhopálidae (Corìzidae) – scentless plant bugs
Alỳdidae (Coríscidae) – broad-headed bugs
Scutelléridae (Pentatómidae in part) – shield-backed bugs
*Podópidae (Graphosomátidae; Pentatómidae in part) – terrestrial turtle bugs
Pentatómidae – stink bugs
Cýdnidae – burrower bugs
Corimelaènidae (Thyreocòridae; Cýdnidae in part) – negro bugs

CHARACTERS USED IN IDENTIFYING HEMÍPTERA

The principal characters used in separating the families of the Hemíptera are those of the antennae, beak, legs, and wings. The antennae may be either 4- or 5-segmented; they are very short and concealed in grooves under the head in the Hydrocorìzae and are fairly long and conspicuous in the Amphibicorìzae and Geocorìzae. The beak is usually 3- or 4-segmented and in some groups fits into a groove in the prosternum when not in use.

The front legs in most of the predaceous Hemíptera are more or less modified into grasping structures and are spoken of as being raptorial. A raptorial leg (Figure 165) usually has the femur enlarged and armed with large spines on the ventroposterior margin; the tibia fits tightly against this armed surface, and often it, too, bears conspicuous spines.

The Hemíptera generally have two or three tarsal segments, the last of which bears a pair of claws. The claws are apical in most of the Hemíptera, but in the water striders (Gérridae and Velìidae) they are anteapical, that is, they arise slightly proximad of the tip of the last tarsal segment (Figure 166 C, D). Many Hemíptera have arolia, or lobelike pads, one at the base of each tarsal claw (Figure 166 A, *aro*).

The hemelytra are subject to considerable modification in different groups of bugs, and special names are given to the different parts of a hemelytron (Figure 167). The thickened basal part of the hemelytron consists of two sections, the corium (*cor*) and clavus (*cl*), which are separated by the claval suture (*cls*); the thin apical part of the hemelytron is the membrane (*mem*). In some Hemíptera a narrow strip of the corium along the costal margin is set off from the remainder of the corium by a suture; this is the embolium (Figure

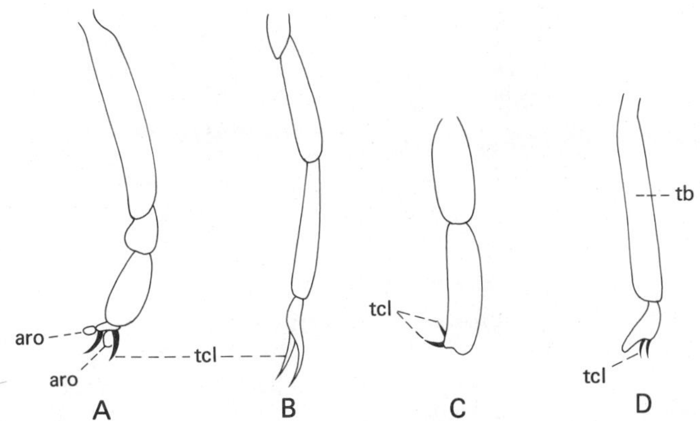

Figure 166. Tarsi of Hemíptera. A, hind tarsus of *Lygaèus* (Lygaèidae); B, hind tarsus of *Nàbis* (Nàbidae); C, front tarsus of *Gérris* (Gérridae); D, front tarsus and tibia of *Rhagovèlia* (Velìidae). *aro,* arolia; *tb,* tibia; *tcl,* tarsal claws.

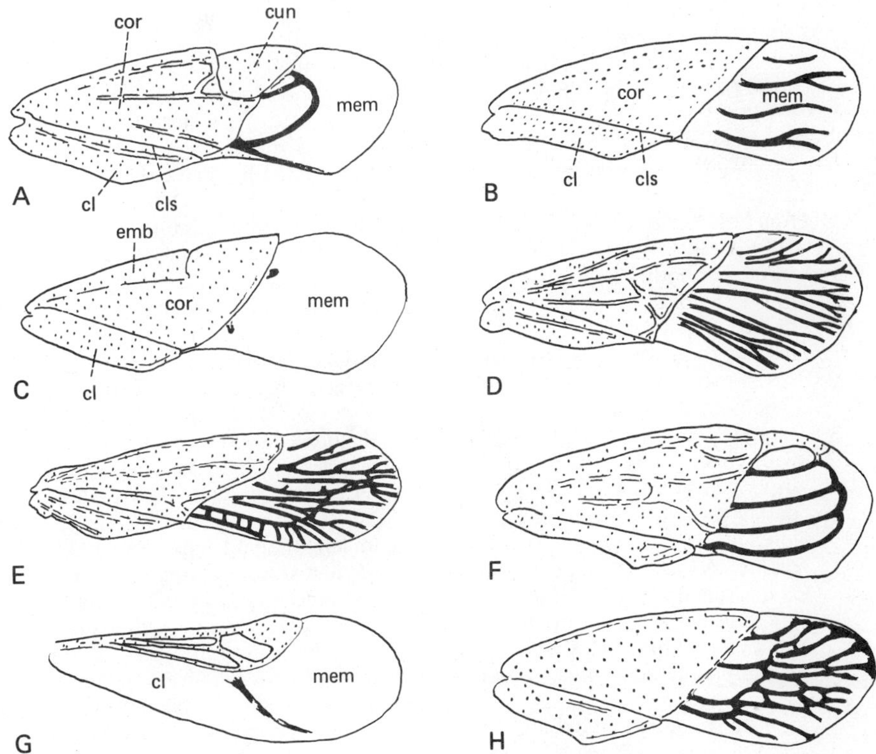

Figure 167. Hemelytra of Hemíptera. A, *Lỳgus* (Miridae); B, *Ligyrócorus* (Lygaèidae); C, *Òrius* (Anthocòridae); D, *Leptócoris* (Rhopálidae); E, *Nàbis* (Nàbidae); F, *Sáldula* (Sáldidae); G, *Mesovèlia* (Mesovelìidae); H, *Lárgus* (Lárgidae). *cl,* clavus; *cls,* claval suture; *cor,* corium; *cun,* cuneus; *emb,* embolium; *mem,* membrane.

167 C, *emb*). In a few Hemíptera a cuneus (Figure 167 A, *cun*) is set off by a suture in the apical part of the corium. The membrane usually contains veins, the number and arrangement of which often serve to separate different families.

The principal difficulties likely to be encountered in using the key are those involving the interpretation of certain characters and those due to the small size of some specimens. If the front femora are thicker than the other femora, the front legs are usually considered to be raptorial. In counting the antennal segments, the minute segments between the larger segments are not counted. It is often necessary to use much magnification to determine the number of segments in the beak, particularly in small specimens.

Key to the Families of Hemíptera

Families that are rare or unlikely to be taken by a general collector are indicated by an asterisk; couplets containing these families may often be skipped over when running a specimen through the key. Some brachypterous forms may not key out in this key.

1.	Antennae shorter than head, usually (except Ochtéridae*) hidden in cavities beneath eyes (Figure 168 A); no arolia; aquatic or semiaquatic (suborder Hydrocorìzae) 2	
1′.	Antennae as long as or longer than head, usually free and visible from above; arolia present or absent; habits variable 9	
2(1).	Ocelli present (Figure 168 B); length 10 mm or less; shore species ... 3	
2′.	Ocelli absent; size variable; aquatic species 4	
3(2).	Antennae hidden; front legs raptorial, shorter than middle legs; eyes strongly protuberant (Figure 176); beak short, concealed by front femora .... **Gelastocòridae**	p. 269
3′.	Antennae exposed; front legs cursorial, as long as middle legs; eyes not strongly protuberant; beak long, extending at least to hind coxae .... **Ochtéridae***	p. 269
4(2′).	Front tarsi 1-segmented, and modified into a scoop-shaped structure (Figure 169); beak very short and hidden, and apparently unsegmented; dorsal surface of body usually with fine transverse lines .... **Coríxidae**	p. 267
4′.	Front tarsi not as above; beak segmentation clearly evident; dorsal surface of body not as above 5	
5(4′).	Front legs not raptorial; hind tarsi usually without claws; body strongly convex above; aquatic bugs swimming upside down, with dorsal side of body usually light-colored 6	
5′.	Front legs raptorial, with femora thickened (Figure 165 B, D, F); hind tarsi with claws, body flattened or only slightly convex above; aquatic bugs usually swimming right side up, with dorsal side of body as dark as or darker than ventral side 7	
6(5).	Elongate, wedge-shaped, 5 mm or more in length; hind legs long and oarlike, without tarsal claws, and with tibiae flattened .... **Notonéctidae**	p. 267
6′.	Oval, strongly convex, 3 mm in length or less; hind legs short, with 2 distinct tarsal claws, and the tibiae cylindrical .... **Plèidae***	p. 268
7(5′).	Membrane of hemelytra with veins; length 20 mm or more 8	
7′.	Membrane of hemelytra without veins (Figure 174 B); length 5–16 mm .... **Naucòridae**	p. 268
8(7).	Tarsi 1-segmented; apical abdominal appendages forming a long, slender, nonretractile breathing tube; hind legs cylindrical, fitted for walking (Figure 175) .... **Nèpidae**	p. 269
8′.	Tarsi 2-segmented (front tarsi 3-segmented in *Lethócerus*); apical abdominal appendages short, flat, retractile; hind legs flattened and fringed, fitted for swimming (Figure 174 A) .... **Belostomátidae**	p. 269

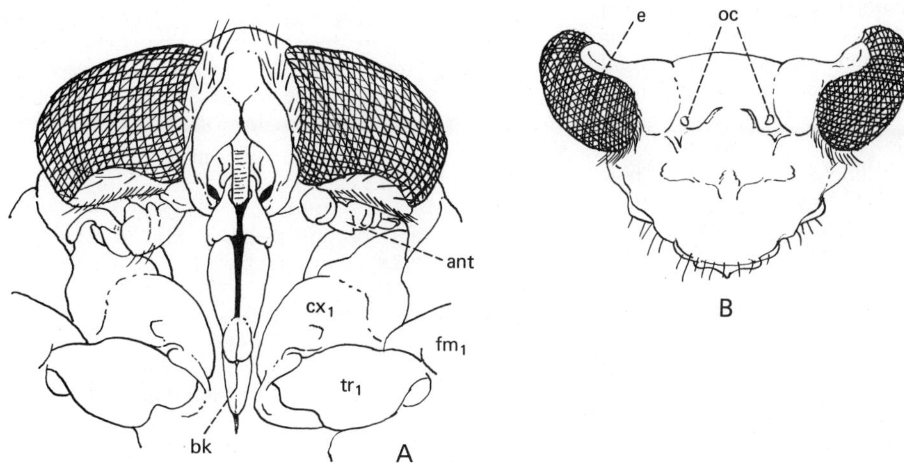

Figure 168. Head structure in Hydrocorìzae. A, *Lethócerus* (Belostomátidae), ventro-anterior view; B, *Gelastócoris* (Gelastocòridae), dorso-anterior view. *ant,* antenna; *bk,* beak; *cx*$_1$, coxa; e, compound eye; *fm,* femur; *oc,* ocelli; *tr,* trochanter.

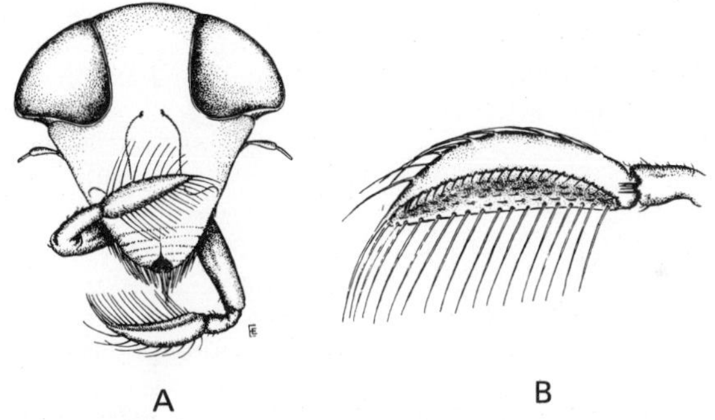

Figure 169. *Coríxa* (Coríxidae). A, head, anterior view; B, front leg. (Courtesy of Hungerford.)

9(1′). Compound eyes present 10

9′. Compound eyes absent; ectoparasites of bats, 3.5–5.0 mm in length; western United States .... **Polycténidae*** p. 272

10(9). Tarsal claws (especially on front legs) anteapical (Figure 166 C, D); tip of last tarsal segment more or less cleft; aquatic, surface-inhabiting 11

10′. Tarsal claws apical; tip of last tarsal segment entire 12

11(10). Middle legs arising closer to hind legs than to front legs; hind femora extending well beyond apex of abdomen (Figure 177 A); all tarsi 2-segmented; ocelli present but small; usually over 5 mm in length... **Gérridae** p. 270

11′. Middle legs usually arising about midway between front and hind legs; if middle legs arise closer to hind legs than to front legs (*Rhagovèlia*), then front tarsi are 1-segmented (Figure 177 B); hind femora extending little if any beyond apex of abdomen; tarsi 1-, 2-, or 3-segmented; ocelli absent; 1.6–5.5 mm in length .... **Velìidae** p. 270

12(10′). Body linear, head as long as entire thorax, and legs very slender (Figure 178); aquatic or semiaquatic bugs .... **Hydrométridae** p. 270

12′. Body of various forms, but if linear, then head is shorter than thorax and the insect is terrestrial 13

13(12′). Antennae 4-segmented 14

13′. Antennae 5-segmented 42

14(13). Body and wings areolate or with reticulate sculpturing (Figures 186 and 188); tarsi 1- or 2-segmented; beak 4-segmented; small flattened bugs, usually less than 5 mm in length 15

14′. Body and wings not so sculptured; tarsi, beak, and size variable... 16

15(14). Ocelli present; juga extending considerably beyond tylus; membrane of hemelytra not reticulate; pronotum not extending backward over scutellum (Figure 188) .... **Piesmátidae*** p. 276

15′. Ocelli absent; juga not, or but slightly, longer than tylus; hemelytra entirely reticulate; pronotum with a triangular process that extends backward over scutellum (Figure 186) .... **Tíngidae** p. 276

16(14′). Antennae with the two basal segments short and thick, and the third and fourth very slender (Figure 170 A); tarsi and beak 3-segmented; ocelli present; 3.5 mm in length or less 17*

16′. Not exactly fitting the above description 19

17(16). Head including eyes, pronotum, front wings, and front legs very spiny; third and fourth antennal segments not hairy; front femora thickened; 3.5 mm in length; California .... **Leptopódidae*** p. 272

17′. Body not spiny; third and fourth antennal segments hairy (Figure 170 A); 1–2 mm in length; widely distributed 18*

18(17′). Eyes projecting outward, not overlapping front angles of pronotum; head and tibiae with strong bristles .... **Dipsocòridae*** p. 272

18′. Eyes projecting outward and backward, overlapping front angles of pronotum; head and tibiae without strong bristles .... **Schizoptéridae*** p. 272

19(16′). Ocelli present 20

19′. Ocelli absent 36

20(19). Middle and hind tarsi with 2 or fewer segments; small or minute bugs 21*

20′. Middle and hind tarsi 3-segmented; size variable 24

21(20). Clavus and membrane of hemelytra similar in texture (as in Figure 167 G) (some are brachypterous); body densely clothed with short velvety hairs; small, stout-bodied, semiaquatic bugs (*Merragàta*) .... **Hèbridae*** p. 272

21′. Clavus and membrane of hemelytra different in texture; body not as above 22*

22(21′). Hemelytra with a cuneus; shining black, 1.2 mm in length; recorded from Maryland and the District of Columbia .... **Microphỳsidae*** p. 273

22′. Hemelytra without a cuneus 23*

23(22′). Front legs enlarged, raptorial; beak 4-segmented; pronotum divided into 3 lobes; hemelytra entirely membranous; color variable, but usually not yellowish with red eyes; 3–4 mm in length (Figure 183 B); widely distributed .... **Enicocephálidae*** p. 274

23′. Front legs not enlarged, not raptorial; beak 3-segmented; pronotum not divided into 3 lobes; hemelytra thickened at base, with only the inner apical portion membranous, the corium extending to the wing tip; pale yellowish with red eyes, 2.0–2.5 mm in length; Florida .... **Thausmastocòridae*** p. 272

24(20′). Hemelytra with a cuneus; small bugs, 1.2–5.0 mm in length, usually 2–3 mm 25

24′. Hemelytra without a cuneus; size variable 26

25(24). Beak 3-segmented (Figure 180 B) .... **Anthocòridae** p. 272

25′. Beak 4-segmented (Figure 181) .... **Isometòpidae*** p. 273

26(24′). Beak 3-segmented 27

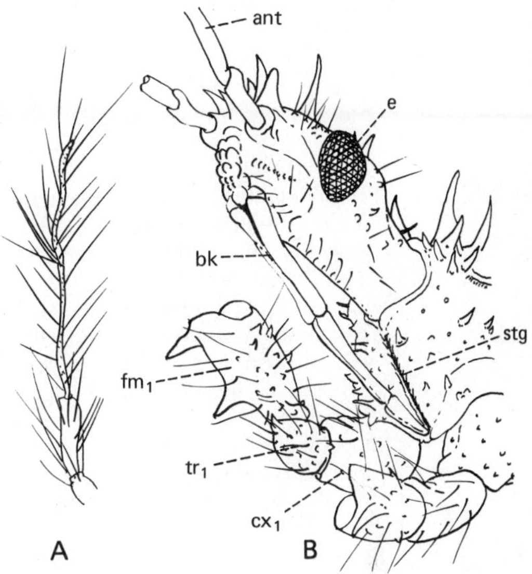

Figure 170. A, antenna of *Cryptostemmátida* (Dipsocòridae); B, head of *Sìnea* (Reduvìidae). *ant*, antenna; *bk*, beak; *cx*, coxa; *e*, compound eye; *fm*, femur; *stg*, prosternal groove; *tr*, trochanter.

26′. Beak 4-segmented 30

27(26). Front legs usually more or less enlarged, raptorial (Figure 165 A, C); beak short, fitting into a groove in prosternum (Figure 170 B); head cylindrical; arolia usually present 28

27′. Front legs not raptorial; beak long, not fitting into a groove in prosternum; head usually not cylindrical; arolia absent 29

28(27). Antennae with last segment swollen; front femora greatly enlarged (Figures 165 A and 185); head without a transverse suture near eyes .... **Phymátidae** p. 276

28′. Antennae with last segment not swollen; front femora not more than moderately enlarged (Figure 165 C); head usually with a transverse suture near eyes .... **Reduvìidae** p. 275

29(27′). Membrane of hemelytra with 4 or 5 long closed cells (Figure 167 F) .... **Sáldidae** p. 272

29′. Membrane of hemelytra without veins, and more or less confluent with the membranous clavus (Figure 167 G) .... **Mesovelìidae*** p. 270

30(26′). Bugs resembling mesoveliids in general appearance (Figure 179 A), but with 6 closed cells in hemelytra and pronotum with a median backward-projecting lobe that covers scutellum; western United States .... **Macrovelìidae*** p. 272

30′. Without the above combination of characters 31

31(26′). Arolia absent (Figure 166 B); front legs enlarged, raptorial (Figure 165 E); hemelytra (when well developed) with numerous marginal veins (Figure 167 E) (Nabìnae) .... **Nàbidae** p. 273

31′. Arolia present (Figure 166 A); front legs and hemelytra variable 32

32(31′). Body and appendages long and slender; first segment of antennae long and enlarged apically, the last segment spindle-shaped; femora clavate (Figure 191) .... **Berýtidae** p. 278

32′. Body shape variable; antennae and femora not as above 33

33(32′). Membrane of hemelytra with only 4 or 5 veins (Figure 167 B) ... **Lygaèidae** p. 276

33′. Membrane of hemelytra with many veins (Figure 167 D) 34

34(33′). Usually dark-colored and over 10 mm in length; scent glands present, their openings between middle and hind coxae (Figure 164 B, *sgo*) 35

34′. Usually pale-colored and less than 10 mm in length; scent glands absent .... **Rhopálidae** p. 278

35(34). Head narrower and shorter than pronotum (Figure 193 A–C); hind coxae more or less rounded or quadrate .... **Corèidae** p. 278

35′. Head nearly as wide and as long as pronotum (Figure 193 D); hind coxae more or less transverse .... **Alỳdidae** p. 280

36(19′). Tarsi 1-segmented; beak 3-segmented; front legs raptorial, the front femora slightly swollen; elongate, slender, 4.5–5.0 mm in length; yellowish or greenish yellow, with a red bar across middle of wings; eastern United States, New York to Florida (Carthasìnae) .... **Nàbidae*** p. 273

36′. Not exactly fitting the above description 37

37(36′). Beak short, 3-segmented, and fitting into a groove in prosternum (Figure 170 B); front femora more or less enlarged, raptorial; head more or less cylindrical, usually with a transverse suture near eyes (Emesìnae and Saicìnae) .... **Reduvìidae** p. 275

37′. Beak longer, 3- or 4-segmented, and not fitting into a groove in prosternum; front femora and head variable 38

38(37′). Beak 3-segmented; wings vestigial (Figure 180 A); ectoparasites of birds and mammals .... **Cimícidae** p. 272

38′. Beak 4-segmented; wings usually well developed 39

39(38′). Hemelytra with a cuneus, the membrane with 1 or 2 closed cells and rarely with other veins (Figure 167 A); rarely (for example, *Hálticus,* Figure 182 A) membrane absent, in which case the cuneus is lacking and the hind femora are enlarged; meso- and metasternum formed of more than 1 sclerite .... **Míridae** p. 273

39′. Hemelytra without a cuneus, and membrane not as above; meso- and metasternum formed of a single sclerite 40

40(39′). Tarsi 2-segmented, without arolia; body very flat; usually dull-colored, gray, brown, or black (Figure 187) .... **Arádidae** p. 276

40′. Tarsi 3-segmented, with arolia; body not particularly flattened; often brightly colored 41

41(40′). Shining black bugs, 7–9 mm in length; front femora moderately swollen and armed beneath with 2 rows of teeth (*Cnemòdus*) .... **Lygaèidae** p. 276

41′. Color variable, but usually not shining black; 8–18 mm in length; front femora not swollen and usually not armed with teeth 42

42(41′). Pronotum margined laterally; sixth visible abdominal sternum entire in both sexes .... **Pyrrhocòridae** p. 278

42′. Pronotum rounded laterally; sixth visible abdominal segment of female cleft to base .... **Lárgidae** p. 278

43(13′). Front legs raptorial; shining black bugs, 5–7 mm in length; second antennal segment about one fifth as long as third (Prostemmìnae) .... **Nàbidae*** p. 273

43′. Front legs not raptorial; size and color variable; antennae usually not as above 44

44(43′). Tarsi 2-segmented; body densely clothed with velvety pubescence; hemelytra with clavus and membrane similar in texture and without veins; the two basal antennal segments thicker than the others; semiaquatic bugs, 3 mm in length or less (*Hèbrus,* Figure 179 B) .... **Hèbridae*** p. 272

44′. Not exactly fitting the above description 45

45(44′). Tibiae armed with strong spines (Figure 171 A); color usually shining black, and length 8 mm or less 46

45′. Tibiae not armed with strong spines (Figure 171 B); color rarely shining black; usually over 8 mm in length 47

46(45). Scutellum very large, broadly rounded posteriorly, and covering most of abdomen (Figure 197 A); length usually 3–4 mm .... **Corimelaènidae** p. 283

46′. Scutellum more or less triangular, and not extending to apex of abdomen (Figure 197 B); length up to about 8 mm .... **Cýdnidae** p. 283

47(45′). Scutellum very large, broadly rounded posteriorly, and covering most of abdomen (Figure 194); corium of hemelytra narrow, not extending to anal margin of wing 48

47′. Scutellum shorter, usually narrowed posteriorly and more or less triangular (Figures 195 and 196), if large and broadly rounded posteriorly (*Stíretrus*, subfamily Asopìnae) the colors are bright and contrasting; corium of hemelytra broad, extending to anal margin of wing .... **Pentatómidae** p. 281

48(47). Sides of pronotum with a prominent tooth or lobe in front of humeral angle (Figure 194 B); length 3.5–6.5 mm .... **Podópidae*** p. 281

48′. Sides of pronotum without such teeth or lobes (Figure 194 A); length 8–10 mm .... **Scutelléridae** p. 280

SUBORDER **Hydrocorìzae:** The Hydrocorìzae are aquatic (rarely shore-inhabiting), and have the antennae shorter than the head and usually concealed in grooves on the underside of the head; trichobothria are absent.

Family **Coríxidae**—Water Boatmen: These insects are aquatic and have the hind legs elongate and oarlike (Figure 172). The body is oval, somewhat flattened, and usually dark gray in color; the dorsal surface of the body is often finely cross lined. The water boatmen are common insects in freshwater ponds and lakes; they occasionally occur in streams, and a few species occur in the brackish pools just above the high-tide mark along the seashore. As do all other aquatic bugs, they lack gills and get air at the surface of the water; they frequently carry a bubble of air under water, either on the surface of the body or under the wings. They can swim rapidly, but often cling to vegetation for long periods.

Most of the water boatmen feed on algae and other minute aquatic organisms, which they scoop up with their spatulate front tarsi (Figure 169 B). A few species are predaceous, feeding on midge larvae and other small aquatic animals. Unlike most of the other aquatic bugs, water boatmen will not bite man.

The eggs of water boatmen are usually attached to aquatic plants. In some parts of the world (for example, certain parts of Mexico) water boatmen eggs are used as food; they are collected from aquatic plants, dried, and later ground into flour. Water boatmen are an important item of food for many aquatic animals.

Family **Notonéctidae**—Backswimmers: The backswimmers are so named because they swim upside down. They are very similar to the water boatmen in shape (Figure 173), but have the dorsal side of the body more convex and usually

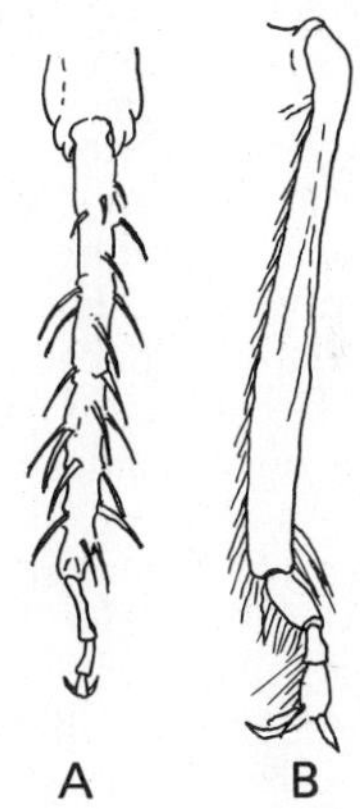

Figure 171. A, tibia of *Pangaèus* (Cýdnidae); B, tibia of *Murgántia* (Pentatómidae).

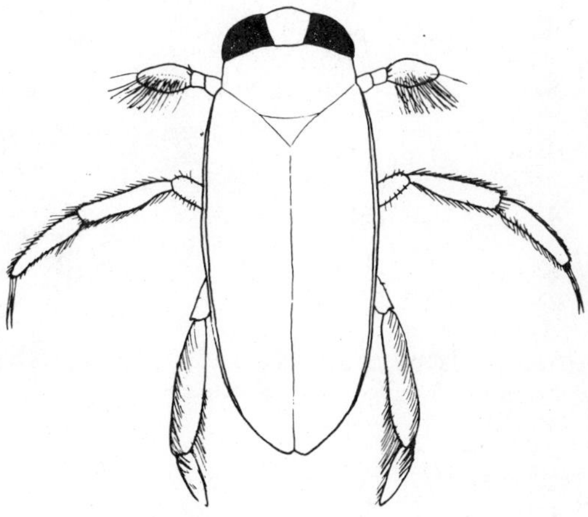

Figure 172. A water boatman, *Sígara atropodónta* Hungerford, 7 ×.

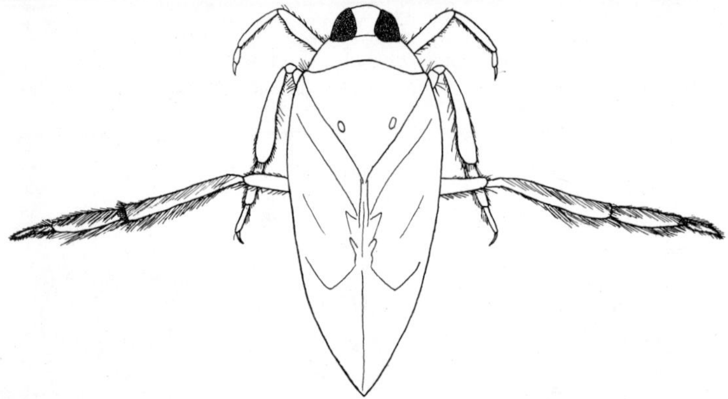

Figure 173. A backswimmer, *Notonécta undulàta* (Say), 7 ×.

light-colored. They frequently rest at the surface of the water, with the body at an angle and the head down, and with the long hind legs extended. They can swim rapidly, using the hind legs like oars.

Backswimmers are predaceous, feeding on other insects and occasionally on tadpoles and small fish. They frequently attack animals larger than themselves and feed by sucking the body juices from their prey. A common method of capturing prey is to drift up under it after releasing hold of submerged plants to which they have been clinging. These insects will bite man when handled, and the effect is much like a bee sting. Backswimmer eggs are deposited in the tissues or glued to the surface of aquatic plants.

Two genera of backswimmers occur in North America, *Notonécta* and *Buénoa*. *Notonécta* includes the largest and most common species (Figure 173), which have the hemelytra pubescent and are 8–17 mm in length; the species of *Buénoa* are smaller, 5–9 mm in length, and more slender.

Family **Plèidae**—Pleid Water Bugs: These bugs are similar to the backswimmers in habits, but are very small (1.6–2.3 mm in length) and have the dorsal surface of the body strongly arched.

Family **Naucòridae**—Creeping Water Bugs: These bugs are brownish in color, broadly oval, and somewhat flattened, generally about 13 mm in length, and the front femora are greatly thickened (Figure 174 B). They live in quiet water and swim or creep about slowly through submerged vegetation in search of food; they feed on various small aquatic animals. They bite quite readily—and painfully—when handled. This family is a small one, with only a little over a dozen species occurring in North America; the two species occurring in the East belong to the genus *Pelócoris*.

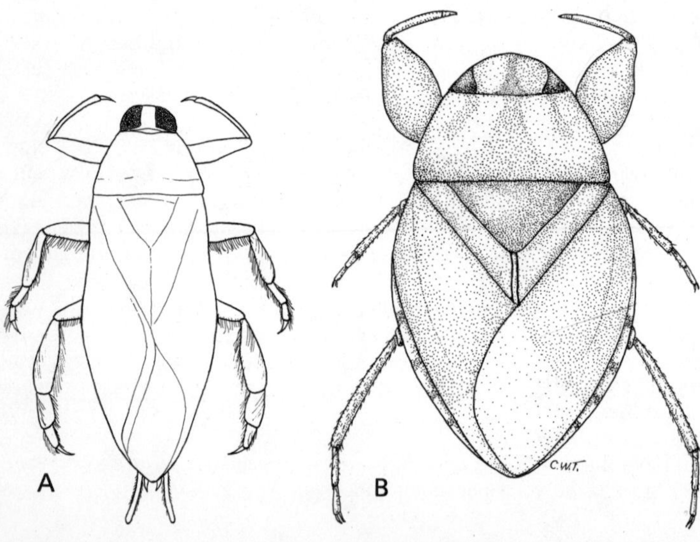

Figure 174. A, a giant water bug, *Lethócerus gríseus* (Say), slightly reduced; B, a creeping water bug, *Pelócoris femoràtus* (Beauvois), 5 ×.

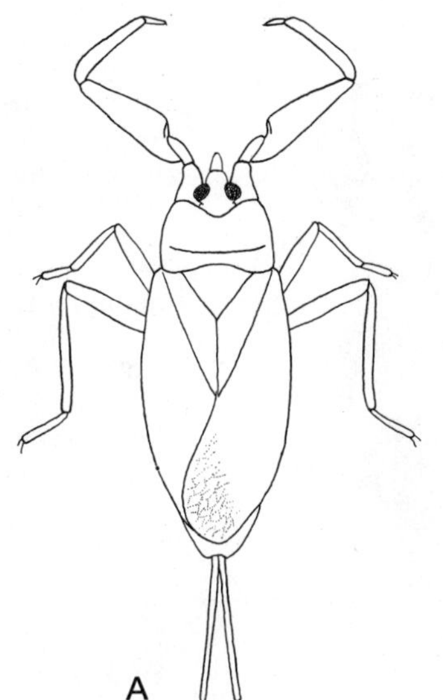

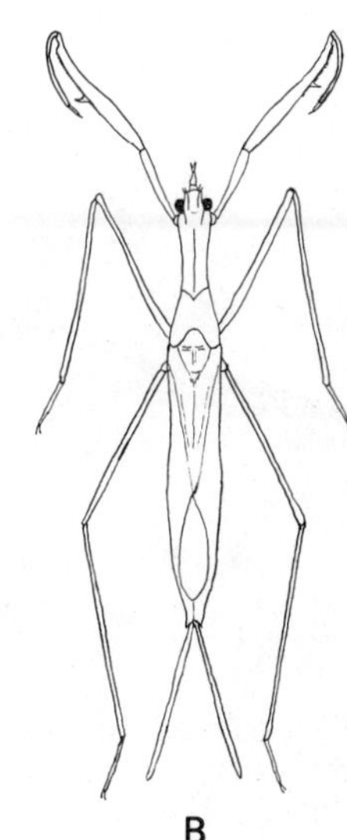

Figure 175. Waterscorpions. A, *Nèpa apiculàta* Uhler, 2½ ×; B, *Ránatra fúsca* Beauvois, about natural size.

Family **Belostomátidae**—Giant Water Bugs: This family contains the largest bugs in the order, some of which (in the United States) may reach a length of over 2 inches (51 mm); one species occurring in South America is over 4 inches (102 mm) in length. The giant water bugs are brownish in color, oval, and somewhat flattened, with the front legs raptorial (Figure 174 A). These insects are fairly common in ponds and lakes, where they feed on other insects, snails, tadpoles, and even small fish. They frequently leave the water and fly about, and because they are often attracted to lights, they are sometimes called electric-light bugs. Giant water bugs can inflict a painful bite if handled carelessly. In some species (*Belóstoma* and *Ábedus*), the eggs are laid on the back of the male, which carries them about until they hatch; other species lay their eggs at the bottom of ponds or attached to aquatic vegetation. Three genera of giant water bugs occur in the United States; *Lethócerus* (including *Bénacus*), *Belóstoma*, and *Ábedus*. The first two are widely distributed, while *Ábedus* occurs in the South and West. The species of *Lethócerus* are large bugs, usually 1½ inches (38 mm) or more in length (Figure 174 A), whereas the species of *Belóstoma* and *Ábedus* are smaller.

Family **Nèpidae**—Waterscorpions: The waterscorpions are predaceous aquatic bugs with raptorial front legs and with a long caudal breathing tube formed by the cerci. The breathing tube is often almost as long as the body, and is thrust up to the surface as the insect crawls about on aquatic vegetation. These insects move slowly and prey on various types of small aquatic animals, which they capture with their front legs. Waterscorpions can inflict a painful bite when handled. They have well-developed wings, but seldom fly. The eggs are inserted into the tissues of aquatic plants.

Three genera and 12 species of waterscorpions occur in the United States: the 9 species of *Ránatra* are slender and elongate with very long legs, and are somewhat similar to walking sticks in appearance (Figure 175 B); our only species of *Nèpa*, *N. apiculàta* Uhler, has the body oval and somewhat flattened (Figure 175 A); the body shape in *Curícta* is somewhat intermediate between those of *Ránatra* and *Nèpa*. Our most common waterscorpions belong to the genus *Ránatra;* *N. apiculàta* is less common, and occurs in the eastern states; the two species of *Curícta* are relatively rare, and occur in the Southwest.

Family **Gelastocòridae**—Toad Bugs: These bugs superficially resemble small toads, both in appearance and hopping habits. They are short and broad and have large projecting eyes (Figure 176), and are usually found along the moist margins of ponds and streams; one has to examine them closely to be certain they are not toads. Toad bugs feed on other insects; they capture their prey by leaping on it and grasping it in their front legs. The eggs are laid in the sand, and the adults often spend a portion of their life down in the sand.

Family **Ochtéridae**—Velvety Shore Bugs: These are oval-bodied insects 4–5 mm in length which

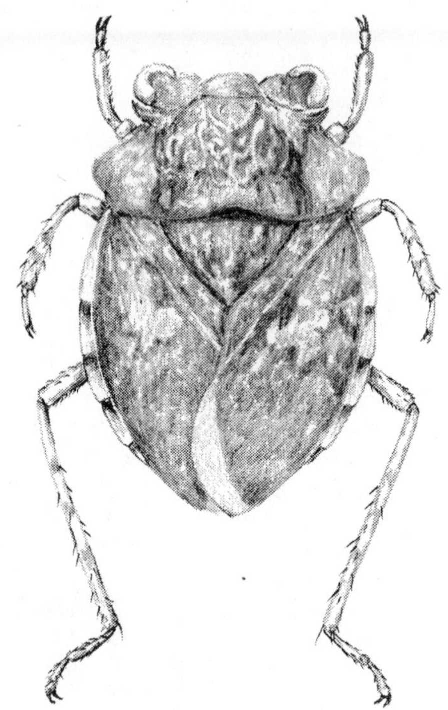

Figure 176. A toad bug, *Gelastócoris oculàtus* (Fabricius), 7½ ×.

occur along the shores of quiet streams and ponds, but are uncommon. They are velvety bluish or black in color, and are predaceous. Seven species occur in the United States.

SUBORDER **Amphibicorìzae:** The Amphibicorìzae are semiaquatic or shore-inhabiting, they have conspicuous antennae, and they have three pairs of trichobothria on the head.

Family **Gérridae**—Water Striders: The water striders are long-legged insects (Figure 177 A) that live on the surface of the water, running or skating over the surface and feeding on insects that fall onto the surface. The front legs are short and are used in capturing food, and the middle and hind legs are long and are used in locomotion. Most species are black or dark-colored, and the body is long and narrow.

The tarsi of water striders are clothed with fine hairs and are difficult to wet; this tarsal structure enables a water strider to skate around on the surface of the water. If the tarsi become wet, the insect can no longer stay on the surface film and will drown unless it can crawl up on some dry surface; when the tarsi dry again, they function normally.

These insects are common on quiet water in small coves or protected places; they often occur in large numbers. Species inhabiting small intermittent streams burrow down in the mud or under stones when the stream dries up, and remain dormant until the stream fills with water again; the adults hibernate in such situations. Except for one genus, the water striders are restricted to fresh water; the species in the genus *Halóbates* live on the surface of the ocean, often many miles from land. Winged and wingless adults occur in many species, and the insect moves from one aquatic situation to another when in the winged stage. The eggs are laid at the surface of the water on floating objects.

Family **Velìidae**—Broad-Shouldered Water Striders or Ripple Bugs: These water striders are small (1.6–5.5 mm in length), brown or black in color and often with silvery markings, and they usually occur in or near the ripples (or riffles) of small streams. They are gregarious, and a single sweep of a dip net sometimes yields up to 50 or more specimens. The body is usually widest near the bases of the middle and hind legs, with the abdomen narrower (Figure 177 B). They feed on small insects and other aquatic animals. Three widely distributed genera occur in the United States: *Vèlia, Microvèlia,* and *Rhagovèlia.*

Family **Hydrométridae**—Water Measurers or Marsh Treaders: These bugs are small (about 8 mm in length), usually grayish in color, and very slender; they resemble tiny walking sticks (Figure 178). The head is very long and slender, with the eyes conspicuously bulging laterally. These insects are usually wingless. They occur in shallow water among vegetation and feed on minute organisms; they frequently walk very slowly over surface vegetation or over the surface of the water. The eggs, which are elongate and about one fourth as long as the adult, are laid singly and glued to objects near the water.

Family **Mesovelìidae**—Water Treaders: These bugs are usually found crawling over floating vegetation at the margins of ponds or pools, or on logs projecting from the water; when disturbed they run rapidly over the surface of the water. They are small (5 mm in length or less), slender, and usually greenish or yellowish green in color (Figure 179 A); within a species, some adults are winged and some are wingless. These insects feed on small

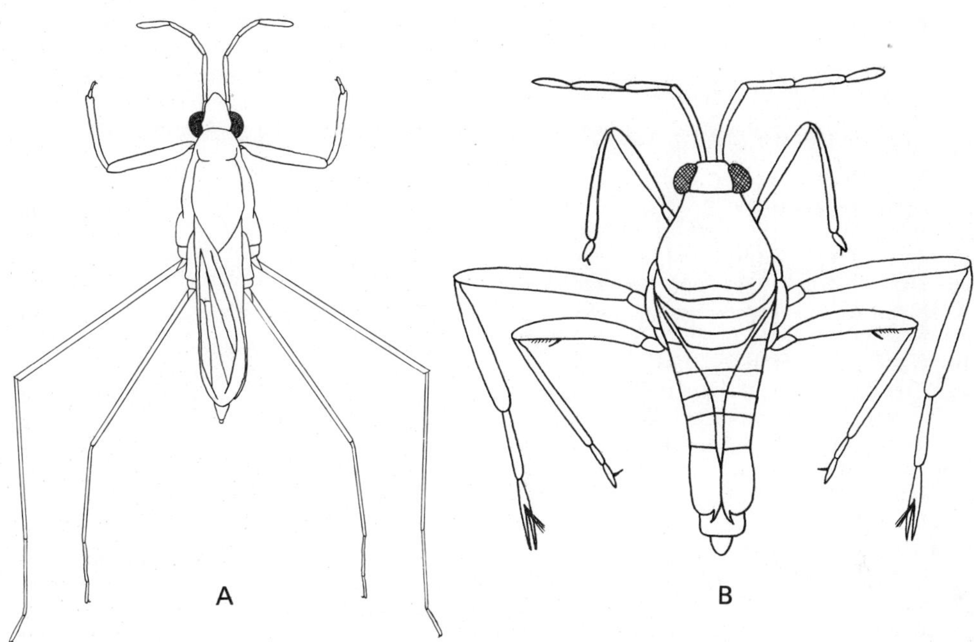

Figure 177. Water striders. A, *Gérris marginàtus* (Say) (Gérridae), 5 ×; B, *Rhagovèlia* sp. (Velìidae), 10 ×.

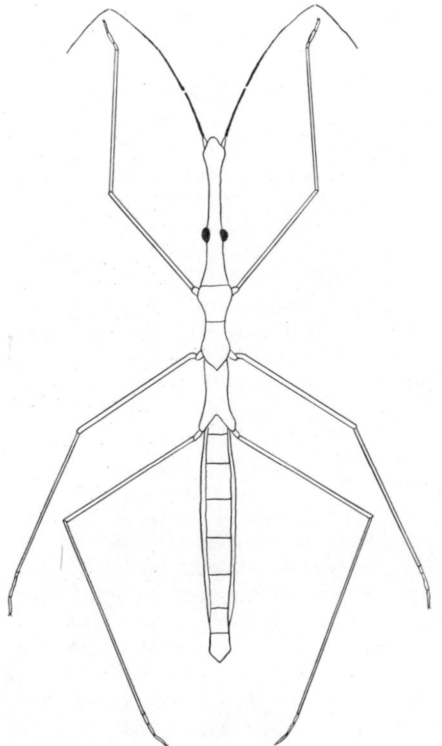

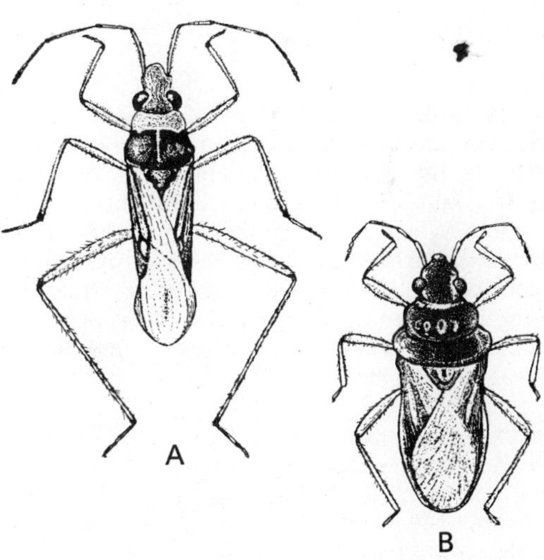

Figure 178 *(left).* A water measurer, *Hydrómetra mártini* Kirkaldy, 7½ ×.

Figure 179 *(above).* A, a water treader, *Mesovèlia mulsánti* White, 9 ×; B, a velvet water bug, *Hèbrus sobrìnus* Uhler, 16 ×. (Courtesy of Froeschner and *The American Midland Naturalist.*)

aquatic organisms on and just beneath the surface of the water.

Family **Macroveliidae:** This group is represented in North America by a single species, *Macrovèlia hornii* Uhler, which occurs in the West. It has been variously classified, but China and Miller included it in the Mesoveliidae. *M. hornii* resembles a mesoveliid in appearance (see Figure 179 A), but differs from the Mesoveliidae in having 6 closed cells in the hemelytra, and the pronotum has a backward-projecting lobe that covers the scutellum. The family Macroveliidae was erected for this species by McKinstry (1942). *M. hornii* occurs along the shores of springs and streams, usually in moss or other protected places; it does not run about on the water surface, but it has never been taken more than a few feet from the water's edge.

Family **Hèbridae**—Velvet Water Bugs: The hebrids are small oblong bugs with a broad-shouldered appearance (Figure 179 B), and the entire body is covered with velvety hairs that prevent the insect from becoming wet when it runs or walks on the surface of the water. The hebrids are all less than 3 mm in length. They occur in shallow pools where there is an abundance of aquatic vegetation. The group is a small one, and only 7 species are known in the United States.

Family **Sáldidae**—Shore Bugs: The shore bugs are small, oval, flattened, usually brownish bugs that are often common along the shores of streams, ponds, or the ocean; some are burrowing in habit. When disturbed, they fly quickly for a short distance and then scurry under vegetation or into a crevice. They are predaceous on other insects. The shore bugs can usually be recognized by the four or five long closed cells in the membrane of the hemelytra (Figure 167 F).

Family **Leptopódidae**—Spiny Shore Bugs: This is an Old World group, one species of which, *Patàpius spinòsus* (Rossi), has been introduced into California; it may be found from Butte County southward to Los Angeles County.

SUBORDER **Geocorìzae:** The Geocorìzae are terrestrial, they almost always have conspicuous antennae, and they lack trichobothria.

Families **Schizoptéridae** and **Dipsocóridae**—Jumping Ground Bugs: These are minute oval bugs, 1.0–1.5 mm in length, which live in moist places on the ground, beneath dead leaves, or in moist soil. They jump actively when disturbed. Only seven species in these two families occur in the United States, and they are principally southern in distribution and uncommon.

Family **Thaumastocòridae**—Royal Palm Bugs: This group is represented in the United States by a single species, *Xylastódoris lutèolus* Barber, which occurs in Florida. This insect is 2.0–2.5 mm in length, flattened, oblong-oval, and pale yellowish with reddish eyes; it feeds on the royal palm.

Family **Polycténidae**—Bat Bugs: Only two rare species of bat bugs occur in the United States: one in Texas and the other in California. These bugs, which are ectoparasites of bats, are wingless and lack compound eyes and ocelli; the front legs are short, with the femora thickened, and the middle and hind legs are long and slender.

Family **Cimícidae**—Bed Bugs: The bed bugs are flat, broadly oval, wingless bugs about 6 mm in length (Figure 180 A), and feed by sucking blood from birds and mammals. The group is a small one, but some of the species are widely distributed and well known. The common bed bug that attacks man is *Cìmex lectulàrius* L.; this species is frequently a serious pest in houses, hotels, barracks, and other living quarters; it also attacks animals other than man. A tropical species, *Cìmex hemípterus* (Fabricius), also bites man. Other species in this family attack bats and various birds.

The common bed bug is largely nocturnal, and during the day hides in cracks in a wall, under the baseboard, in the springs of a bed, under the edge of a mattress, under wallpaper, and in similar places. Its flatness makes it possible for it to hide in very small crevices. Bed bugs may be transported from place to place on clothing, in luggage or furniture, or they may migrate from house to house. They lay their eggs, 100–250 per female, in cracks; development to the adult stage requires about two months in warm weather. The adults may live for several months and can survive long periods without food. Bed bugs are important primarily because of their irritating bites; they are apparently unimportant as disease vectors.

Family **Anthocòridae**—Minute Pirate Bugs: The commoner species in this group are usually found on flowers, but some species occur under loose bark, in leaf litter, and in decaying fungi. Most species are black with white markings (Figure 180 B) and 3–5 mm in length. The anthocorids feed on small insects and insect eggs.

Family **Microphỳsidae:** This family includes a single eastern species, *Mallochìola gagàtes* (McAtee and Malloch), which has been recorded from Maryland and the District of Columbia. This bug is broadly oval, somewhat flattened, shiny black, and 1.2 mm in length.

Family **Isometòpidae**—Jumping Tree Bugs: The members of this group are flattened oval bugs 2.0–2.6 mm in length; they are similar to the leaf bugs in having a cuneus, but differ in having ocelli (Figure 181). They are found on bark and dead twigs, and jump quickly when disturbed. This group is a small one, with only five rare species occurring in the eastern United States.

Family **Míridae**—Plant Bugs or Leaf Bugs: This family is the largest in the order, and its members are to be found on vegetation almost everywhere; some are very abundant. Practically all the leaf bugs feed on the juices of plants, often causing serious damage; a few are predaceous on other insects.

The leaf bugs are the only common bugs possessing a cuneus, and they can be readily recognized by this character (Figures 164 and 167 A); most of them have two closed cells at the base of the membrane. The antennae and beak are 4-segmented, and ocelli are lacking. Most leaf bugs are small (rarely over 10 mm in length), usually elongate and soft bodied, and they may be variously colored; many species are strikingly marked with red, orange, green, or white (Figure 182).

Several species in this family attack cultivated plants. One of the most serious pests among the Míridae is the tarnished plant bug, *Lýgus lineolàris* (Palisot de Beauvois) (Figure 182 C). This insect is 5–6 mm in length and varies in color from pale brown to almost black. It feeds on a great variety of wild and cultivated plants. Another fairly common species is the fourlined plant bug, *Poecilocápsus lineàtus* (Fabricius), a yellowish or yellowish-green bug with four longitudinal black lines on the body (Figure 182 E); this species feeds particularly on currants and gooseberries, and inserts its eggs into the stems of these plants. In some fruit-growing areas the apple red bug, *Lygídea méndax* Reuter, a red-and-black bug about 6 mm in length (Figure 182 B), is a serious pest in apple orchards.

The garden fleahopper, *Hálticus bractàtus* (Say), is a common leaf bug that is usually brachypterous (Figure 182 A); it is a shining black, jumping bug 1.5–2.0 mm in length, which feeds on many cultivated plants. The front wings usually lack a membrane and are much like the elytra of a beetle.

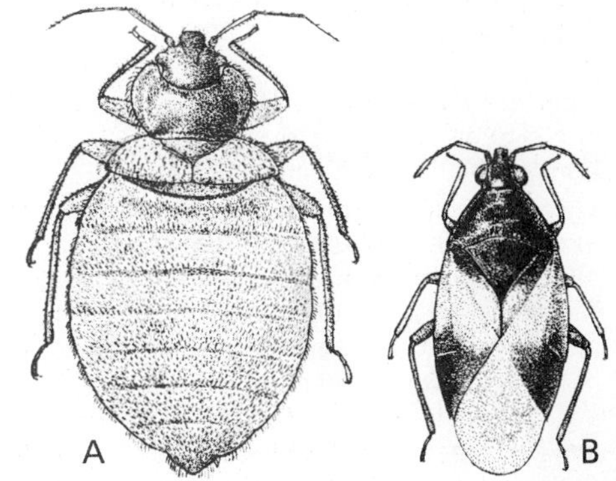

Figure 180. A, common bed bug, *Cìmex lectulàrius* L., 7 ×; B, a minute pirate bug, *Òrius insidiòsus* (Say), 16 ×. (Courtesy of Froeschner and *The American Midland Naturalist*.)

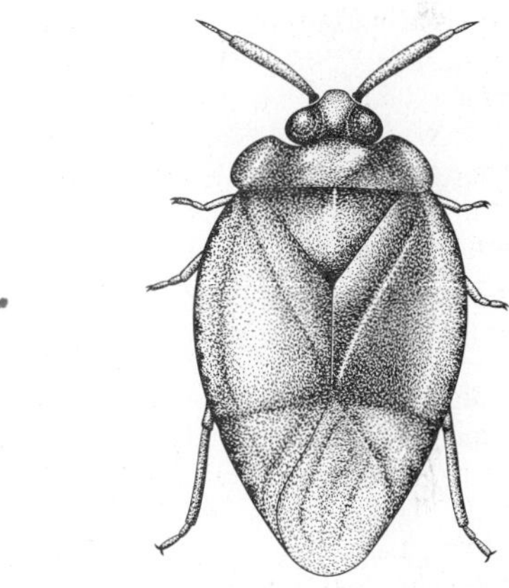

Figure 181. A jumping tree bug, *Teratòdia emoritùra* Bergroth, 22 ×. (Redrawn from Froeschner.)

Family **Nàbidae**—Damsel Bugs: The nabids are small bugs with the body somewhat narrowed anteriorly and the front femora slightly enlarged and raptorial; the membrane of the hemelytra has a number of small cells around the margin (Figures 167 E and 183 A). The damsel bugs are predaceous on many different types of insects, including aphids and small caterpillars.

There are two common types of damsel bugs, a yellowish-brown type about 8 mm in length with well-developed wings, and a shining black type

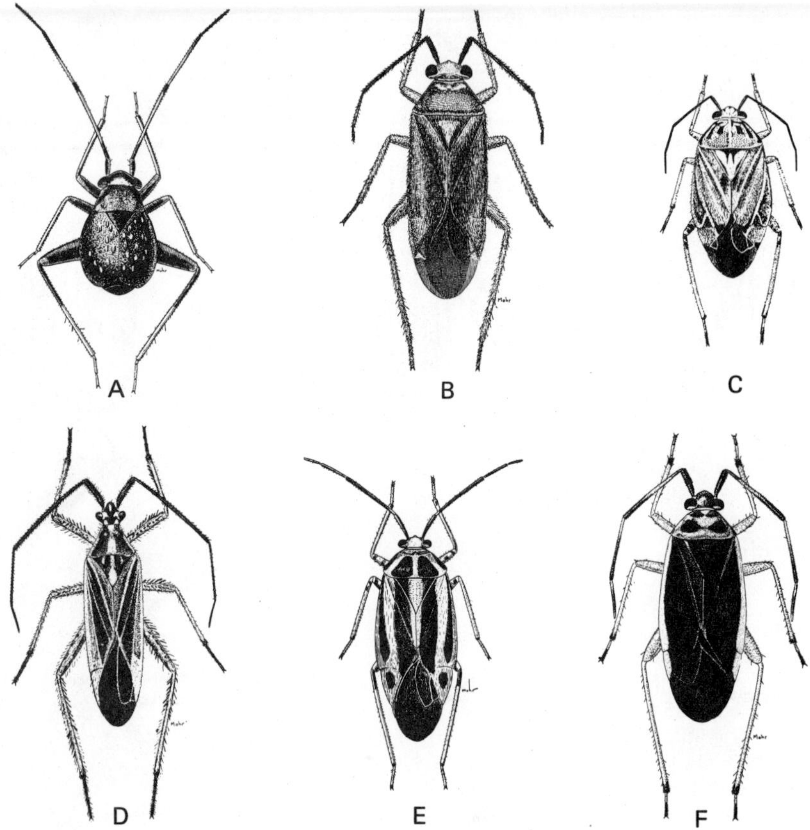

Figure 182. Plant bugs (Miridae). A, garden fleahopper, *Hálticus bractàtus* (Say), female, 10 ×; B, apple red bug, *Lygídea méndax* Reuter, female, 5 ×; C, tarnished plant bug, *Lỳgus lineolàris* (Palisot de Beauvois), 4 ×; D, meadow plant bug, *Leptoptérna dolobràta* (L.), male, 4 ×; E, fourlined plant bug, *Poecilocápsus lineàtus* (Fabricius), 4 ×; F rapid plant bug, *Adelphócoris rápidus* (Say), 4 ×. (Redrawn from the Illinois Natural History Survey.)

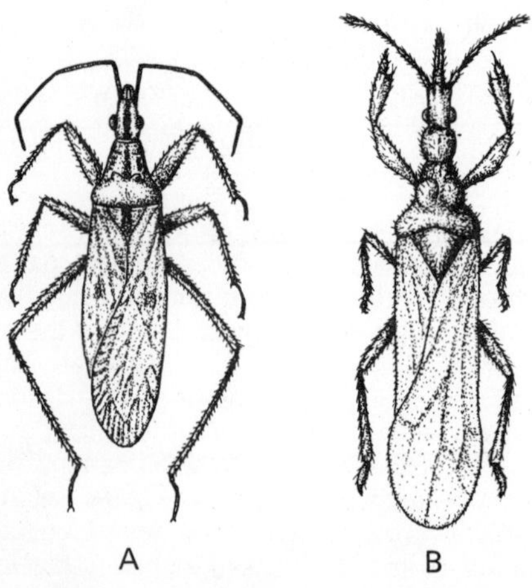

Figure 183. A, a damsel bug, *Nábis fèrus* (L.), 5 ×; B, a gnat bug, *Systellóderes bìceps* (Say), 15 ×. (Redrawn from Froeschner and *The American Midland Naturalist.*)

that is a little larger and usually has very short wings. The most common species of the first type is *Nàbis fèrus* (L.) (Figure 183 A), and a fairly common representative of the second is *Nàbis subcoleoptràtus* (Kirby). The latter species occurs in both long-winged and short-winged forms, but the short-winged form is more common.

Family **Enicocephálidae**—Gnat Bugs: These are small (3–4 mm in length), slender, predaceous bugs that have the head elongate and constricted behind the eyes, and the front wings entirely

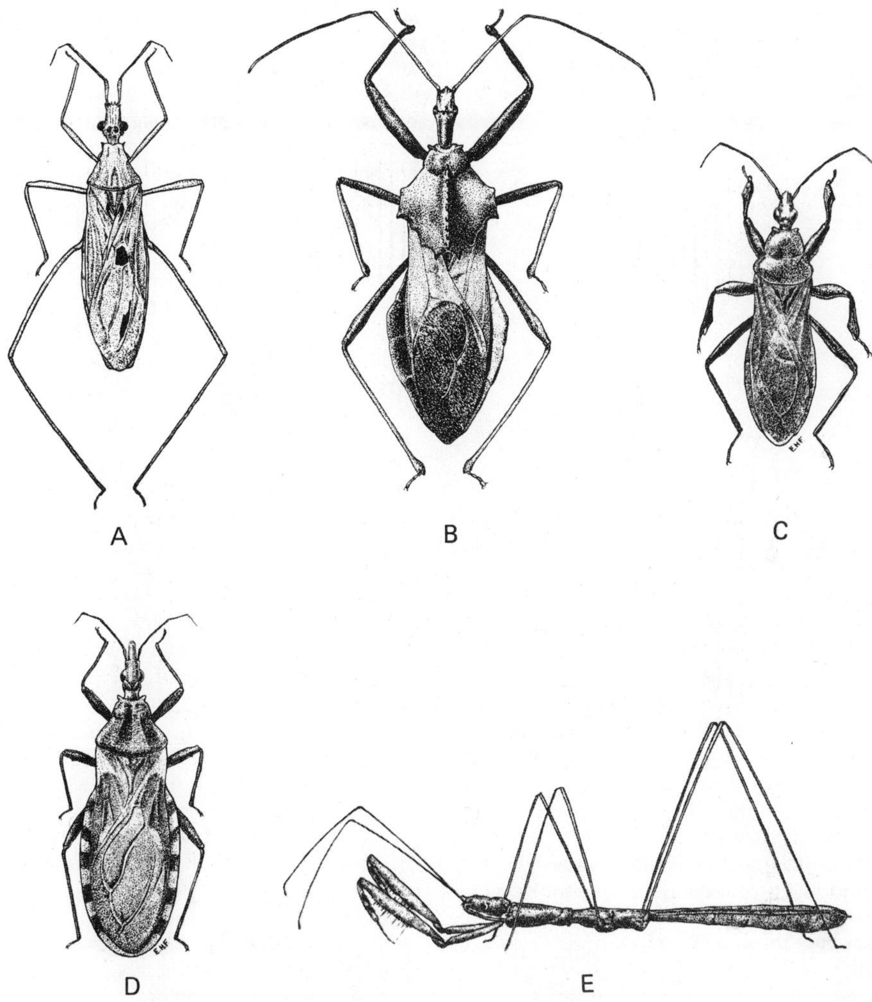

Figure 184. Assassin bugs. A, *Narvèsus carolinénsis* Stål, 2½ ×; B, wheel bug, *Àrilus cristàtus* (L.), 1½ ×; C, *Melanoléstes pìcipes* (Herrick-Schäffer), 2 ×; D, bloodsucking conenose, *Triátoma sanquisùga* (LeConte), 2 ×; E, a thread-legged bug, *Metápterus ùhleri* (Banks), 5½ ×. (Courtesy of Froeschner and *The American Midland Naturalist.*)

membranous (Figure 183 B); they are sometimes called unique-headed bugs. Several species occur in the United States, but they are rarely collected.

Family **Reduvìidae**—Assassin Bugs: The members of this group are medium-sized to large, usually black or brownish bugs (Figure 184), and some species are fairly common. The head is narrow and elongate with the part behind the eyes necklike; the beak is 3-segmented, usually curved, and its tip fits into a groove in the prosternum (Figure 170 B). The abdomen is often widened at the middle, exposing the margins of the segments beyond the wings. Most of the assassin bugs are predaceous on other insects, but a few are blood-sucking and frequently bite man. Many species will inflict a painful bite if carelessly handled.

One of the most curious species in this group is the wheel bug, *Árilus cristàtus* (L.), a black bug about 25 mm long, with a semicircular crest on the pronotum that terminates in spurs and resembles a cogwheel (Figure 184 B); this species is fairly common. The masked hunter, *Redùvius per-*

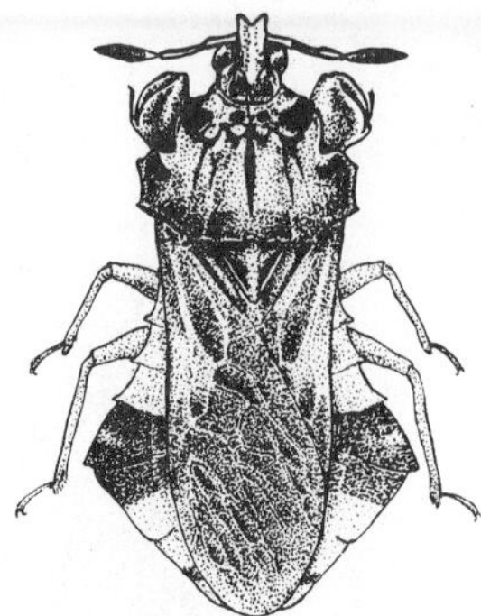

Figure 185. An ambush bug, *Phýmata fasciàta georgiénsis* Melin, 4½ ×. (Courtesy of Froeschner and *The American Midland Naturalist.*)

sonàtus (L.), is a brownish-black bug that is often found in houses; it feeds on bed bugs, but will also bite man. It has a habit of accumulating lint on its head and thus becomes "masked." The assassin bugs in the genus *Triátoma* also invade houses and bite man; *T. sanguisùga* (LeConte) (Figure 184 D), sometimes called the bloodsucking conenose, can inflict an extremely painful bite. The bugs in the genus *Triátoma* are in some areas called kissing bugs (because of their tendency to bite about the mouth) or Mexican bed bugs. In South America species of this genus serve as vectors of a trypanosome disease of man known as Chagas' disease (several cases of this disease have recently been found in the United States); certain species in the southwestern United States act as vectors of a trypanosome disease of wood and pack rats.

The thread-legged bugs (Emesìnae) are very slender and long-legged, and resemble small walking sticks (Figure 184 E). They occur in old barns, cellars, dwellings, or out-of-doors beneath loose bark and in grass tufts, where they catch and feed on other insects.

Family **Phymátidae**—Ambush Bugs: The phymatids are small stout-bodied bugs with raptorial front legs (Figure 185); the front femora are short and at least half as broad as long, and the tibiae are small and curved (Figure 165 A). Most of the ambush bugs are about 13 mm in length or less, yet they are able to capture insects as large as fair-sized bumble bees. They lie in wait for their prey on flowers, particularly goldenrod, where they are excellently concealed by their greenish yellow color. They feed principally on relatively large bees, wasps, and flies.

Family **Tíngidae**—Lace Bugs: These bugs are easily recognized by the sculptured lacelike pattern of the upper surface of the body (Figure 186); the head, lateral expansions of the thorax, and wings usually present a pattern of elevated ridges and sunken membranous oval areas. This lacelike appearance is found only in the adults; the nymphs are usually spiny. The lace bugs are small, usually whitish insects (the nymphs are black), 5–6 mm in length. They feed chiefly on the leaves of trees and shrubs; their feeding first causes a yellow spotting of the leaf, but with continued feeding the leaf becomes entirely brown and falls off. The eggs are usually laid on the underside of the leaves. *Corythùca ciliàta* (Say) (Figure 186 B) is a common species that feeds on sycamore.

Family **Arádidae**—Flat Bugs or Fungus Bugs: These small, usually dark-brownish, very flat bugs (Figure 187) are found under loose bark or in crevices of dead or decaying trees. They feed on the sap of fungi or the moisture in bark or decaying wood. The wings are well developed but small and do not cover the entire abdomen; the antennae and beak are 4-segmented, the tarsi are 2-segmented, and there are no ocelli.

Family **Piesmátidae**—Ash-Gray Leaf Bugs: These bugs are similar to the lace bugs, but are more slender and do not have so much lacelike sculpturing on the dorsal side of the body (Figure 188 B). They feed on the foliage of various weeds and trees.

Family **Lygaèidae**—Seed Bugs: This family is a relatively large one, and many of its members are common bugs. Most of them, including the species having the front femora enlarged and appearing raptorial, feed on seeds; the Blissìnae (which includes the chinch bug) feed on the sap of the host plant, and the big-eyed bugs (Geocorìnae; Figure 190 C) occasionally feed on other insects.

Seed bugs have the beak and antennae 4-segmented, ocelli are nearly always present, and there are four or five simple veins in the membrane of the hemelytra (Figure 167 B). They differ from the leaf bugs (Míridae) in lacking a cuneus and in possessing ocelli, and they are harder bodied; they differ from the Corèidae, Rhopálidae, and Alỳdidae in that they have only a few veins in the membrane of the wing. Lygaeids are small bugs, the largest being only about 13 mm or so in length; they vary somewhat in shape (Figures 189 and 190). Many species are conspicu-

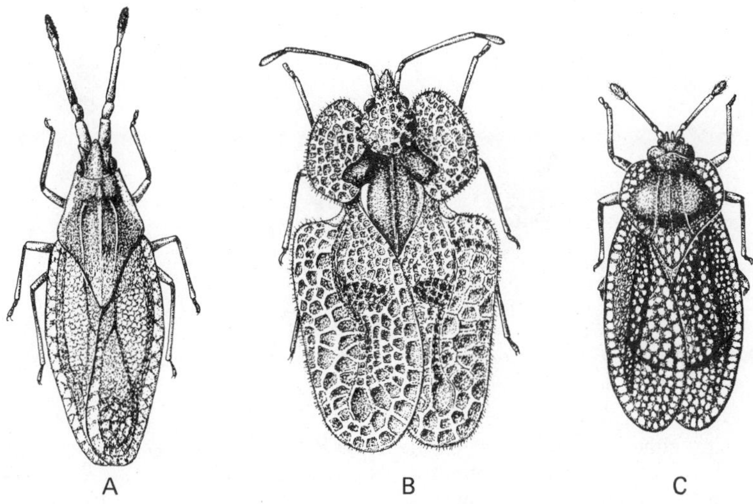

Figure 186. Lace bugs. A, *Atheas miméticus* Heidemann, 18 ×; B, sycamore lace bug, *Corythùca ciliàta* (Say), 13 ×; C, *Acalýpta lilliànis* Bueno, 14 ×. (A and B, redrawn from Froeschner and *The American Midland Naturalist*, C, redrawn from Osborn and Drake and the Ohio Biological Survey.)

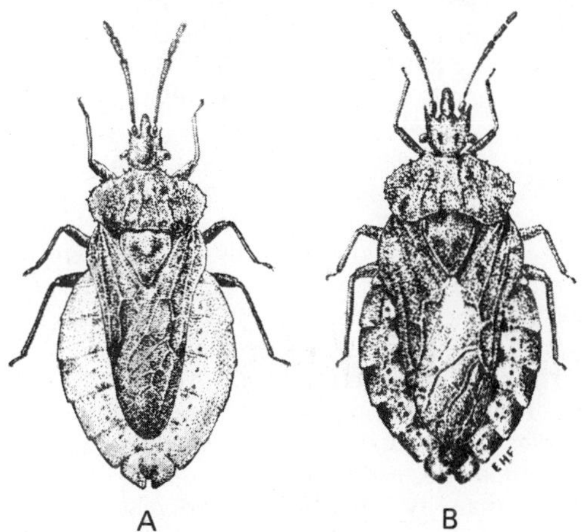

Figure 187. Flat bugs (Arádidae). A, *Áradus inornàtus* Uhler, 4½ ×; B, *Áradus acùtus* (Say), 5½ ×. (Redrawn from Froeschner and *The American Midland Naturalist*.)

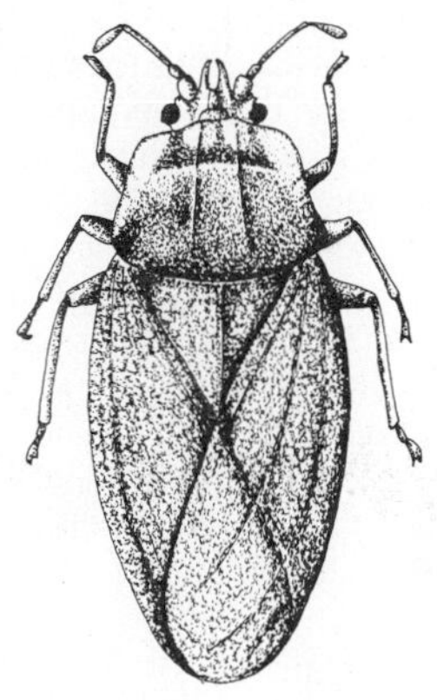

Figure 188. An ash-gray leaf bug, *Piésma cinèrea* (Say), 15 ×. (Redrawn from Froeschner and *The American Midland Naturalist*.)

ously marked with spots or bands of red, white, or black.

The chinch bug (Figure 189) is probably the most injurious bug in this family, attacking wheat, corn, and other cereals; sometimes it becomes a serious pest of turf grasses. It is about 3.5 mm in length and is black with white front wings; each front wing has a black spot near the middle of the costal margin. Both long-winged and short-winged forms occur in this species (Figure 189 C, D). Chinch bugs overwinter as adults in grass clumps, fallen leaves, fence rows, and other protected places, and emerge about the middle of April and begin feeding on small grains. The eggs

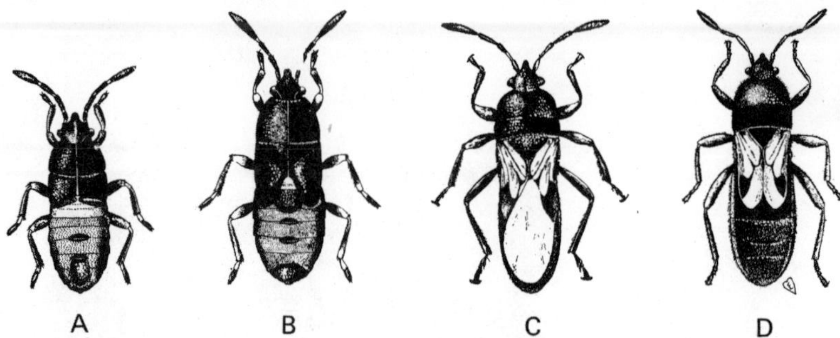

Figure 189. Chinch bug, *Blíssus leucópterus leucópterus* (Say). A, fourth-instar nymph; B, fifth-instar nymph; C, adult; D, short-winged adult. (Courtesy of USDA.)

are laid during May, either in the ground or in grass stems near the ground, and hatch about a week or ten days later; each female may lay several hundred eggs. The nymphs feed on the juices of grasses and grains and reach maturity in four to six weeks. By the time these nymphs become adult, the small grains (wheat, rye, oats, and barley) are nearly mature and no longer succulent, and the adults (along with nymphs nearly adult) migrate to other fields of more succulent grain, usually corn. They migrate on foot, often in great numbers. The females lay eggs for a second generation on the corn, and this generation reaches maturity in late fall and then seeks out places of hibernation. When chinch bugs are abundant, whole fields of grain may be destroyed.

Several species in this group are brightly marked with red and black. The small milkweed bug, *Lygaèus kálmii* Stål (Figure 190 A), has a red **X**-shaped area on the hemelytra and a broad red band across the base of the pronotum; the large milkweed bug, *Oncopéltus fasciàtus* (Dallas), is broadly banded with red and black.

Family **Berýtidae**—Stilt Bugs: The stilt bugs are slender, long-legged bugs (Figure 191) that feed on plants. They are 5-9 mm in length and are usually brownish in color; they are rather sluggish insects, and are generally found in dense herbaceous vegetation.

Family **Lárgidae:** The members of this group are medium-sized to large, elongate-oval bugs that are usually brightly marked with red and black (Figure 192). They resemble the lygaeids, but lack ocelli and have more branched veins and cells in the membrane of the hemelytra (Figure 167 H). Some of the largids, such as *Arhaphe carolìna* (Herrich-Schäffer), are very antlike in appearance and have short hemelytra (Figure 192 A). The largids are plant feeders and occur principally in the southern states.

Family **Pyrrhocòridae**—Red Bugs and Stainers: These bugs are similar to the largids in appearance and habits. An important pest species in this family is the cotton stainer, *Dysdércus suturéllus* (Herrich-Schäffer), which is a serious pest of cotton in the southern states; it stains the cotton fibers by its feeding and greatly reduces their value. The members of this group feed chiefly on seeds, and are principally southern in distribution.

Family **Corèidae**—Leaf-Footed Bugs: The members of this group are mostly large, dark-colored bugs with well-developed scent glands (opening on the side of the thorax between the middle and hind coxae; see Figure 164 B, *sgo*) and with the head narrower and shorter than the pronotum (Figure 193 A–C). Some species have the hind tibiae dilated and leaflike (Figure 193 A), hence the common name for this group. Most species give off a distinct odor (sometimes pleasant, sometimes not so) when handled.

The majority of the Corèidae are plant feeders, but a few are predaceous. The squash bug, *Ánasa trístis* (De Geer) (Figure 193 C), a serious pest of cucurbits, is dark brown in color and about 13 mm in length; it has one generation a year, and passes the winter in the adult stage in debris or other sheltered places.

Family **Rhopálidae**—Scentless Plant Bugs: These bugs differ from the Corèidae in lacking scent glands; they are usually light-colored and smaller than the Corèidae (Figure 193 E–F). They occur principally on weeds and similar vegetation and are plant feeders; they are more common in late summer and early fall. The boxelder bug, *Leptócoris trivittàtus* (Say), a common species in this

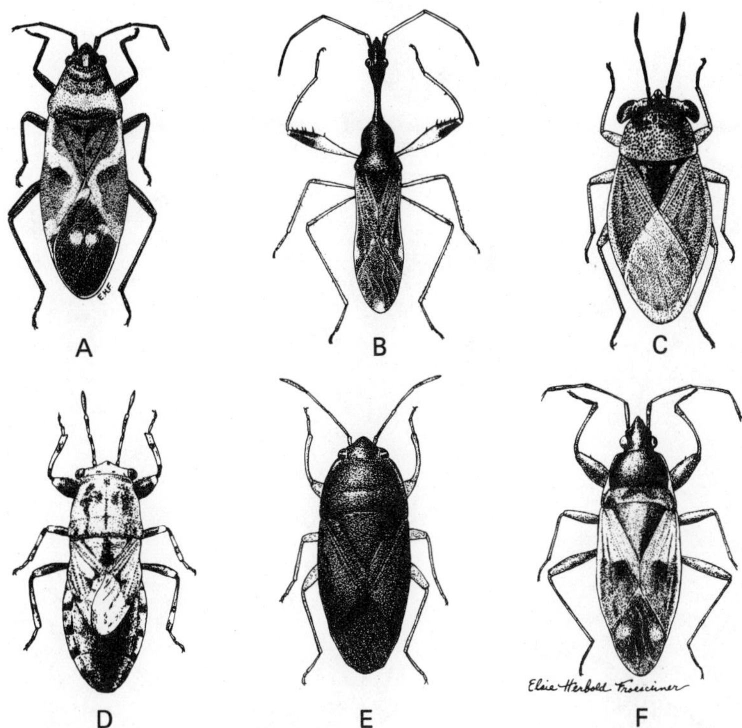

Figure 190. Seed bugs (Lygaèidae). A, small milkweed bug, *Lygaèus kálmii* Stål, 3 ×; B, *Myódocha sérripes* Olivier, 4 ×; C, a big-eyed bug, *Geócoris púnctipes* (Say), 8 ×; D, *Phlégyas abbreviàtus* (Uhler), 8 ×; E, *Aphànus illuminàtus* (Distant), 6 ×; F, *Eremócoris fèrus* (Say). (Courtesy of Froeschner and *The American Midland Naturalist.*)

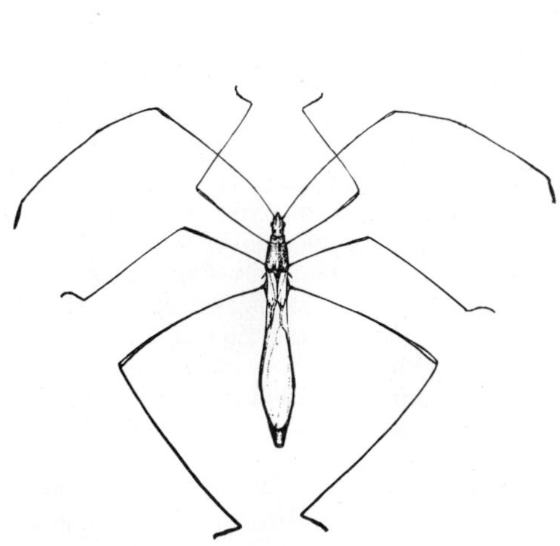

Figure 191. A stilt bug, *Jálysus wíckhami* Van Duzee, 3½ ×. (Courtesy of Froeschner and *The American Midland Naturalist.*)

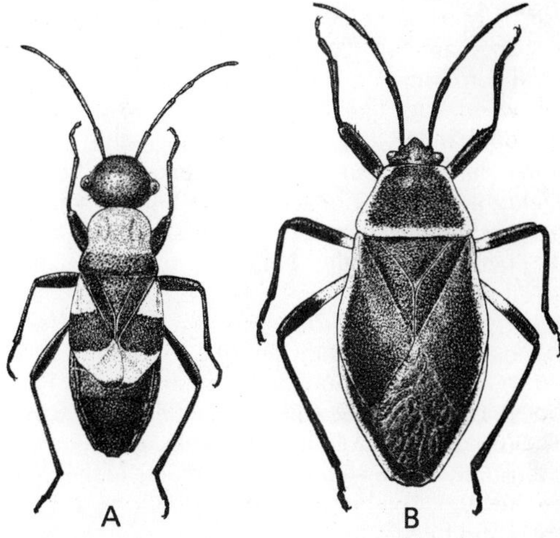

Figure 192. Largid bugs. A, *Árhaphe carolìna* (Herrick-Schäffer), 4 ×; B, *Lárgus succínctus* (L.), 3 ×. (Courtesy of Froeschner and *The American Midland Naturalist.*)

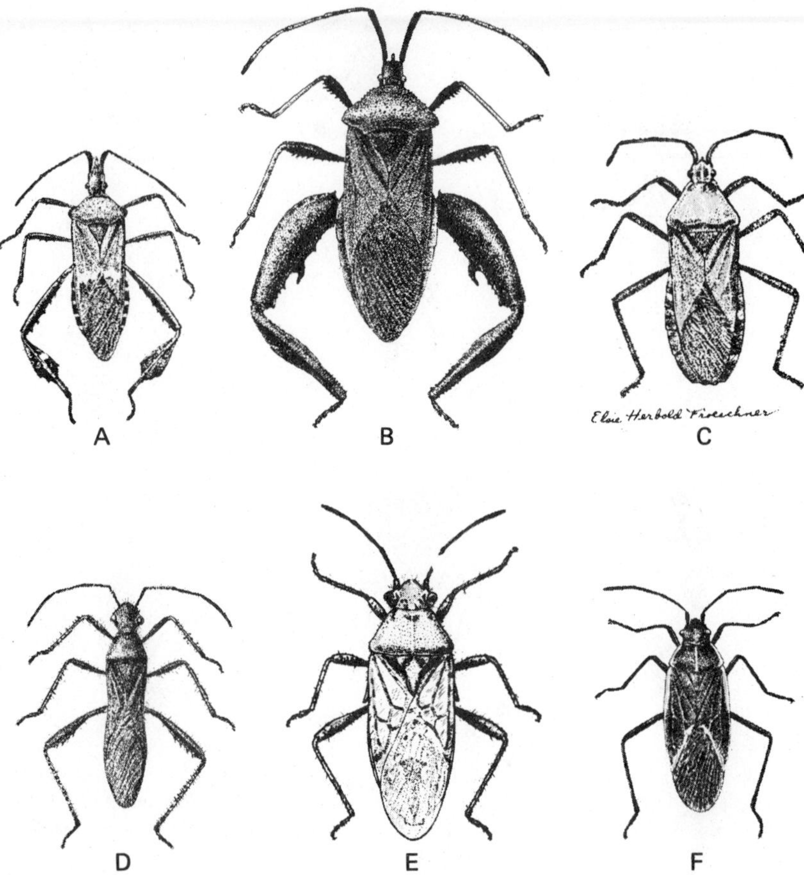

Figure 193. A, a leaf-footed bug, *Leptoglóssus clypeàlis* (Heidemann), 1½ ×; B, *Acanthocéphala femoràta* (Fabricius), male (Corèidae), 1½ ×; C, squash bug, *Ánasa trístis* (De Geer), 2 ×; D, a broad-headed bug, *Alỳdus eurìnus* (Say), 2 ×; E, a scentless plant bug, *Arhýssus lateràlis* (Say), 5 ×; F, boxelder bug, *Leptócoris trivittàtus* (Say), 2 ×. (Redrawn from Froeschner.)

group, is blackish with red markings and 11–14 mm in length (Figure 193 F). It often enters houses and other sheltered places in the fall, sometimes in considerable numbers; it feeds on box elder and occasionally other trees.

Family **Alỳdidae**—Broad-Headed Bugs: These bugs are similar to the Corèidae, but the head is broad and nearly as long as the pronotum, and the body is usually long and narrow (Figure 193 D). They might well be called stink bugs, as they often "stink" much worse than the members of the Pentatómidae (to which the name "stink" bug is usually applied); they give off an odor reminiscent of someone with a bad case of halitosis. The openings of the scent glands are conspicuous oval openings between the middle and hind coxae. These bugs are fairly common on the foliage of weeds and shrubs along roadsides and in woodland areas. Most broad-headed bugs are either yellowish brown or black; some of the black species have a red band across the middle of the dorsal side of the abdomen. A common brown species in the Northeast is *Pròtenor belfrágei* Haglund; it is 12–15 mm in length. Some of the black species (for example, *Alỳdus,* Figure 193 D) look very much like ants in their nymphal stage, and the adults in the field look much like some of the spider wasps.

Family **Scutellèridae**—Shield-Backed Bugs: These look much like stink bugs (Pentatómidae), but have the scutellum very large and extending to the apex of the abdomen; the wings are visible only at the edge of the scutellum (Figure 194 A). Most of these bugs are brownish and 8–10 mm in

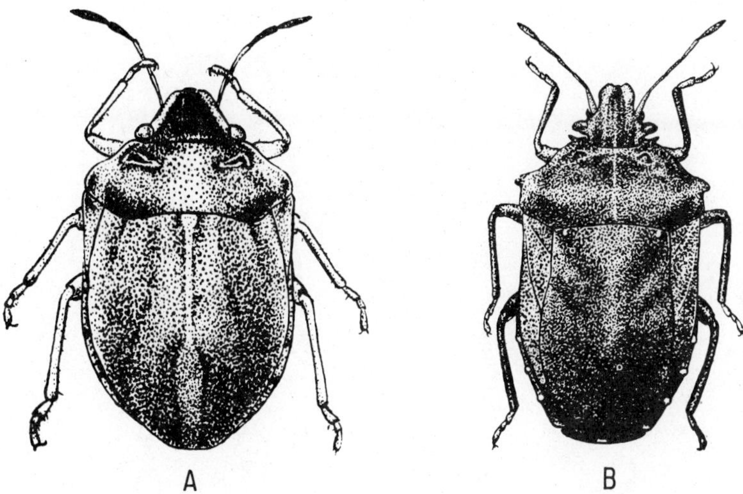

Figure 194. A, a shield-backed bug, *Homaèmus párvulus* (Germar), 8 ×; B, a terrestrial turtle bug, *Pòdops cínctipes* (Say), 8 ×. (Courtesy of Froeschner and *The American Midland Naturalist.*)

length. They are seldom abundant, but may be found on woodland vegetation; they are plant feeders.

Family **Podópidae**—Terrestrial Turtle Bugs: These are small brownish bugs, similar to the Scutelléridae in appearance but smaller (3.5–6.5 mm in length) (Figure 194 B); they are relatively rare.

Family **Pentatómidae**—Stink Bugs: This is a large and well-known group, and its members are easily recognized by their shieldlike shape and 5-segmented antennae; they can be separated from other bugs that have 5-segmented antennae by the characters given in the key. Stink bugs are the most common and abundant of the bugs that produce a disagreeable odor,

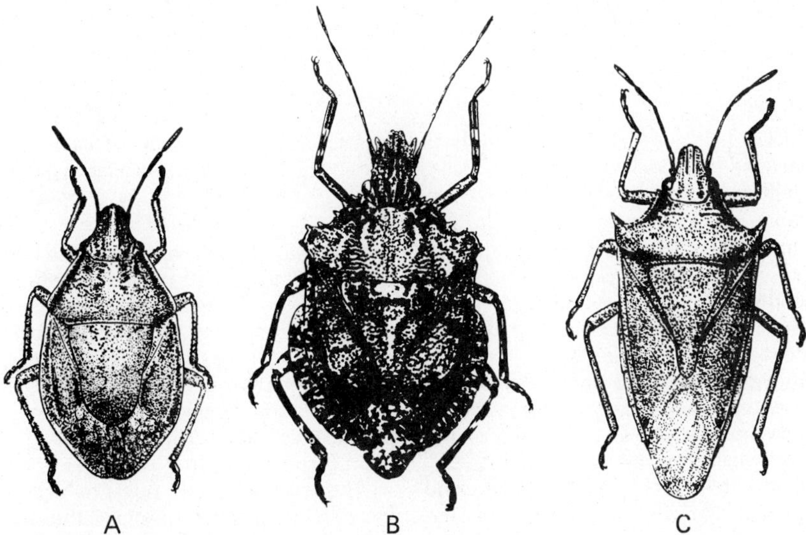

Figure 195. Stink bugs (subfamily Pentatomìnae). A, *Coènus dèlius* (Say), 3½ ×; B, *Brochýmena arbòrea* (Say), 3 ×; C, *Solùbea púgnax* (Fabricius), 4½ ×. (Courtesy of Froeschner and *The American Midland Naturalist.*)

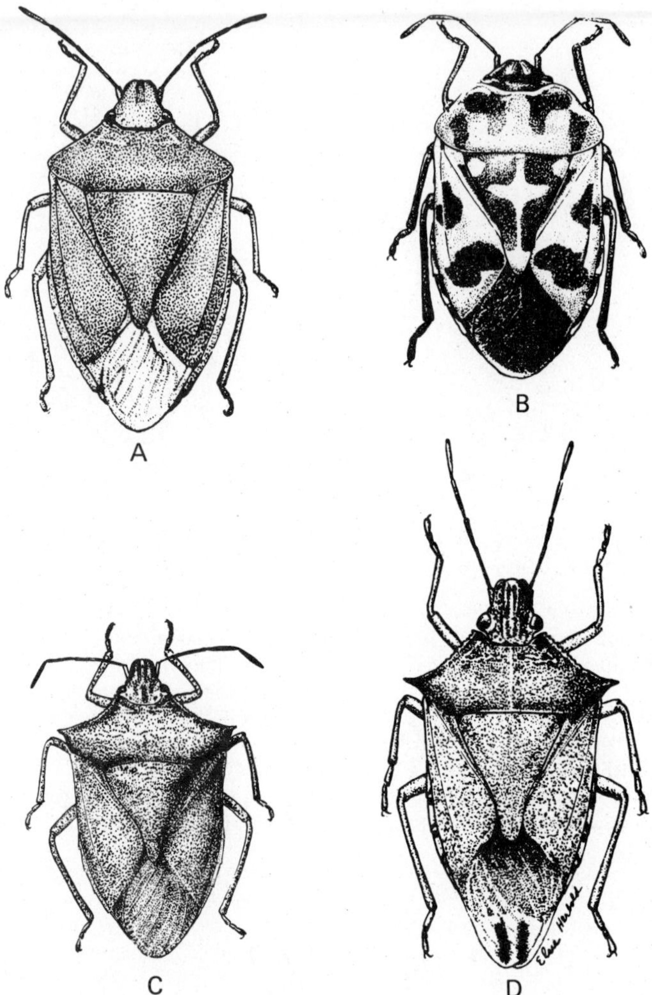

Figure 196. Stink bugs. A, *Thyánta custàtor* (Fabricius), 4½ ×; B, harlequin bug, *Murgántia histriónica* (Hahn), 4 ×; C, onespot stink bug, *Euschístus variolàrius* (Palisot de Beauvois), 3 ×; D, spined soldier bug, *Pódisus maculivéntris* (Say), 4½ ×. A–C, Pentatomìnae; D, Asopìnae. (Courtesy of Froeschner and *The American Midland Naturalist.*)

but some other bugs (particularly the broad-headed bugs; see page 280) produce an odor that is stronger and more disagreeable than that produced by stink bugs. Many species are brightly colored or conspicuously marked.

The family Pentatómidae is divided into three subfamilies, Acanthosomatìnae, Asopìnae, and Pentatomìnae, which differ in characters of the tarsi, head, and beak. The Acanthosomatìnae differ from the other two subfamilies in having the tarsi 2-segmented; the Pentatomìnae have the basal segment of the beak slender, and at rest lying between the bucculae, which are parallel; the Asopìnae have the basal segment of the beak short and thick, with only the base lying between the bucculae, which converge behind the beak.

Some stink bugs are plant feeders, some feed on other insects, and some feed on both plant and insect food. Some of the predaceous species will feed on plants if insect prey is not easily found. The Acanthosomatìnae and Asopìnae are mostly predaceous, and the Pentatomìnae are mostly plant feeders.

The eggs of stink bugs, which are usually barrel-shaped and some have the upper end ornamented with spines, are usually laid in groups, like so many little brightly colored barrels lined up side by side (Figure 35).

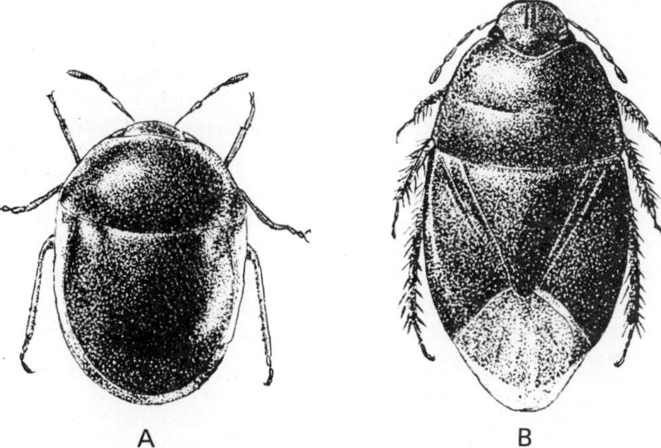

Figure 197. A, a negro bug, *Allócoris pulicària* (Germar), 6½ ×; B, a burrower bug, *Pangaèus bilineàtus* (Say), 7½ ×. (Courtesy of Froeschner and *The American Midland Naturalist.*)

One rather important pest species in this group is the harlequin bug, *Murgántia histriónica* (Hahn) (Figure 196 B). This brightly colored insect is often very destructive to cabbage and other cruciferous plants, particularly in the southern part of the country. The other stink bugs that are plant feeders (Figures 195 and 196 A, C) usually attack grasses or other plants and are not of very great economic importance. The spined soldier bug, *Pódisus maculivéntris* (Say) (Figure 196 D), is predaceous on lepidopterous larvae.

Family **Cýdnidae**—Burrower Bugs: These bugs are a little like stink bugs in general appearance and antennal structure, but are a little more oval and have the tibiae spiny; most are black and less than 8 mm in length. They are usually found beneath stones or boards, in sand, or in the mold about the roots of grass tufts; many come to lights at night.

Family **Corimelaènidae**—Negro Bugs: These bugs are small (mostly 3–6 mm in length), broadly oval, strongly convex, shining black bugs that are somewhat beetlelike in appearance (Figure 197 A); the scutellum is very large and covers most of the abdomen and wings. These insects are common on grasses, weeds, berries, and flowers.

COLLECTING AND PRESERVING HEMÍPTERA

The aquatic bugs can be collected by means of the aquatic collecting equipment and methods described in Chapter 34. A few aquatic species, particularly water boatmen and giant water bugs, may often be collected at lights. One should examine a variety of aquatic habitats, as different species occur in different types of situations. Terrestrial forms may be collected with a net (particularly by sweeping vegetation), at lights, or by examining such specialized habitats as leaf litter, under bark, and in fungi.

The best type of killing bottle for most Hemíptera is a small vial such as that shown in Figure 614 A, which should be partly filled with small pieces of cleansing tissue or lens paper. One should have several such vials, since large and heavy-bodied specimens should not be put into the same killing vial with small and delicate specimens. After the specimens have been killed, they should be taken from the vial and placed in pillboxes that are partly filled with cleansing tissue or cellucotton.

Most Hemíptera are preserved dry on pins or points. The larger specimens should be pinned through the scutellum, and the smaller specimens through the right hemelytron; care must be taken in pinning a bug not to destroy structures on the ventral side of the thorax that will be used in identification. Most Hemíptera less than 10 mm in length should be mounted on points. Specimens mounted on points should be mounted so that the beak, legs, and ventral side of the body are not embedded in glue; the best way to mount a small bug on a point is to bend the tip of the point down and glue the bug to the point by the right side of the thorax. If a specimen is mounted dorsal side up on the tip of a point (Figure 624 A), the point should not extend beyond the middle of the ventral side of the insect.

References on the Hemíptera

Blatchley, W. S. 1926. *Heteroptera or True Bugs of Eastern North America, with Special Reference to the Faunas of Indiana and Florida.* Indianapolis: Nature Publ. Co., 1116 pp., 215 f., 12 pl.

Britton, W. E., *et al.* 1923. The Hemiptera or sucking insects of Connecticut. Guide to the insects of Connecticut. Part IV. *Conn. State Geol. and Nat. Hist. Surv.,* 807 pp., pl. I–XX, 168 f.

Brooks, A. R., and L. A. Kelton. 1967. Aquatic and semiaquatic Heteroptera of Alberta, Saskatchewan, and Manitoba (Hemiptera). *Mem. Ent. Soc. Canada,* 51:1–92; 138 f.

Carvalho, J. C. de Melo. 1957–1960. A catalogue of the Miridae of the world (1758–1956), Pts. I–IV, V—Bibliography and general index. General Catalogue of the Hemiptera, Fasc. 7. *Archos Mus. Nat. Rio de Janeiro,* 44:1–158 (1957), 45:1–216 (1958), 47:1–161 (1958), 48:1–384 (1959), 51:1–194 (1960).

China, W. E., and N. C. E. Miller. 1959. Check-list and keys to the families and subfamilies of the Hemiptera-Heteroptera. *Bull. Brit. Mus. (Nat. Hist.), Entomology,* 8(1):1–45; 1 f.

DeCoursey, R. M. 1971. Keys to the families and subfamilies of the nymphs of North American Hemiptera-Heteroptera. *Proc. Ent. Soc. Wash.,* 73(4):413–428; 23 f.

Drake, C. J., and N. T. Davis. 1960. The morphology, phylogeny, and higher classification of the family Tingidae, including the descriptions of a new genus and species of the subfamily Vianaidinae (Hemiptera Heteroptera). *Ent. Amer.,* 39:1–100; 75 f.

Drake, C. J., and F. A. Ruhoff. 1960. Lace-bug genera of the world (Hemiptera: Tingidae). *Proc. U. S. Natl. Mus.,* 112:1–105; 9 pl., 5 f.

Drake, C. J., and F. A. Ruhoff. 1965. Lacebugs of the world. A Catalogue (Hemiptera: Tingidae). *Bull. U. S. Natl. Mus.,* 243:viii + 634 pp., 56 pl.

Fracker, S. B. 1913. A systematic outline of the Reduviidae of North America. *Proc. Iowa Acad. Sci.,* 19:217–247.

Froeschner, R. C. 1941–1961. Contributions to a synopsis of the Hemiptera of Missouri. Part I, 1941; Scutelleridae, Podopidae, Pentatomidae, Cydnidae, Thyreocoridae; *Amer. Midl. Nat.,* 26(1):122–146; f. 1–36. Part II, 1942; Coreidae, Aradidae, Neididae; *ibid.,* 27(3):591–609; f. 37–55. Part III, 1944; Lygaeidae, Pyrrhocoridae, Piesmidae, Tingidae, Enicocephalidae, Phymatidae, Ploiariidae, Reduviidae, Nabidae; *ibid.,* 31(3):638–683; f. 56–88. Part IV, 1949; Hebridae, Mesoveliidae, Cimicidae, Anthocoridae, Cryptostemmatidae, Isometopidae, Miridae; *ibid.,* 42(1):123–188; f. 89–123. Part V, 1961; Hydrometridae, Gerridae, Veliidae, Saldidae, Ochteridae, Gelastocoridae, Naucoridae, Belostomatidae, Nepidae, Notonectidae, Pleidae, Corixidae; *ibid.,* 67(1):208–240; pl. 11–13.

Froeschner, R. C. 1960. Cydnidae of the Western Hemisphere. *Proc. U. S. Natl. Mus.,* 111:337–680; 13 pl.

Hart, C. A., and J. R. Malloch. 1919. Pentatomoidea of Illinois with keys to nearctic genera. *Ill. Nat. Hist. Surv. Bull.,* 13(7):157–223; pl. 16–21.

Herring, J. L., and P. D. Ashlock. 1971. A key to the nymphs of the families of Hemiptera (Heteroptera) of America north of Mexico. *Fla. Ent.,* 54(3):207–213; 13 f.

Hoffman, R. L. 1971. The insects of Virginia. No. 4. Shield bugs (Hemiptera; Scutelleroidae: Scutelleridae, Corimelaenidae, Cydnidae, Pentatomidae). *Res. Div. Bull.,* 67, Virginia Polytechnic Inst. and State Univ.; 61 pp., 17 f.

Hungerford, H. B. 1948. The Corixidae of the Western Hemisphere (Hemiptera). *Univ. Kan. Sci. Bull.,* 32:1–827; 19 f., 112 pl.

Hungerford, H. B. 1959. Hemiptera. In *Fresh-Water Biology,* W. T. Edmundson (Ed.). New York: Wiley, pp. 958–972; 5 f.

Knight, H. H. 1941. The plant bugs or Miridae of Illinois. *Ill. Nat. Hist. Surv. Bull.,* 22(1):1–234; 181 f.

Knight, H. H. 1968. Taxonomic review; Miridae of the Nevada test site and the western United States. *Brigham Young Univ. Sci. Bull., Biol. Ser.,* 9(3):1–282; frontis. (color) + 318 f.

Lawson, F. A. 1959. Identification of the nymphs of common families of Hemiptera. *J. Kan. Ent. Soc.,* 32(2):88–92; 15 f.

McKinstry, A. P. 1942. A new family of the Hemiptera-Homoptera, proposed for *Macrovelia hornii* Uhler. *Pan-Pac. Ent.,* 18(2):90–96; 4 f.

Miller, N. C. E. 1956. *Biology of the Heteroptera.* London: Methuen, 172 pp. (Reprinted 1971, by Entomological Reprint Specialists, Los Angeles.)

Parshley, H. M. 1925. *A Bibliography of the North American Hemiptera-Heteroptera.* Northampton, Mass.: Smith College, ix + 252 pp.

Pennak, R. W. 1953. *Fresh-Water Invertebrates of the United States.* New York: Ronald Press, ix + 769 pp., 470 f.

Readio, P. A. 1927. Studies on the biology of the Reduviidae of America north of Mexico. *Univ. Kan. Sci. Bull.,* 17:1–248; 21 pl.

Schaefer, C. W. 1964. The morphology and higher classification of the Coreoidae (Hemiptera-Heteroptera). Parts I and II. *Ann. Ent. Soc. Amer.,* 57(6):670–684; 12 f.

Schaefer, C. W. 1965. The morphology and higher classification of the Coreoidae (Hemiptera-Heteroptera).

Part III. The families Rhopalidae, Alydidae, and Coreidae. *Misc. Pub. Ent. Soc. Amer.*, 5(1):1–76; 15 pl.

Scudder, G. G. E. 1963. Adult abdominal characters of the Lygaeoid-Coreoid complex of the Heteroptera, and a classification of the group. *Can. J. Zool.*, 41(1):1–14; 9 f.

Slater, J. A. 1964. *A Catalogue of the Lygaeidae of the World.* Vols. I and II. Storrs, Conn.: Univ. Connecticut, xviii + 1668 pp.

Slater, J. A., T. E. Woodward, and M. H. Sweet. 1962. A contribution to the classification of the Lygaeidae, with the description of a new genus from New Zealand (Hemiptera: Heteroptera). *Ann. Ent. Soc. Amer.*, 55(5):597–605; 17 f.

Stoner, D. 1920. The Scutelleroidea of Iowa. *Iowa Univ. Stud. Nat. Hist.*, 8(4):1–140; 7 pl.

Sweet, M. H. 1960. The seed bugs: a contribution to the feeding habits of the Lygaeidae (Hemiptera: Heteroptera). *Ann. Ent. Soc. Amer.*, 53(3):317–321.

Torre-Bueno, J. R. de la. 1939–1941. A synopsis of the Hemiptera-Heteroptera of America north of Mexico. *Ent. Amer.*, 19:141–304; 4 pl. (1939); 21:41–122 (1941).

Usinger, R. L. 1943. A revised classification of the Reduviidae with a new subfamily from South America (Hemiptera). *Ann. Ent. Soc. Amer.*, 36(4):602–618; 3 f.

Usinger, R. L. 1956. Aquatic Hemiptera. In *Aquatic Insects of California*, R. L. Usinger (Ed.). Berkeley, Calif.: Univ. California Press, pp. 182–228; 43 f.

Usinger, R. L. 1966. Monograph of the Cimicidae (Hemiptera-Heteroptera). *Thomas Say Foundation Publ.*, 7:1–585; illus.

Van Duzee, E. P. 1917. Catalogue of the Hemiptera of America north of Mexico, excepting the Aphididae, Coccidae, and Aleyrodidae. *Calif. Univ. Publ., Tech. Bull. Ent. II*, xiv + 902 pp.

23: ORDER HOMÓPTERA[1]

CICADAS, HOPPERS, PSYLLIDS, WHITEFLIES, APHIDS, AND SCALE INSECTS

This order contains a large and diverse group of insects closely related to the Hemíptera. They exhibit considerable variation in body form, and many species are rather degenerate structurally. The life history of some Homóptera is very complex, involving bisexual and parthenogenetic generations, winged and wingless individuals and generations, and sometimes regular alternations of food plants. All the Homóptera are plant feeders, and many species are serious pests of cultivated plants; some species transmit plant diseases. A few Homóptera are beneficial and serve as a source of shellac, dyes, or other materials.

[1] Homóptera: *homo,* alike, uniform; *ptera,* wings (referring to the fact that the front wings are uniform in texture throughout).

The mouth parts are similar to those of the Hemíptera; they are sucking, with four piercing stylets (the mandibles and maxillae). The beak arises from the back of the head, in some cases appearing to arise between the front coxae; in the Hemíptera the beak arises from the front of the head. In some adults the mouth parts are vestigial or lacking.

Winged Homóptera usually have four wings; the front wings have a uniform structure throughout, either membranous or slightly thickened, and the hind wings are membranous. The wings at rest are usually held rooflike over the body, with the inner margins overlapping slightly at the apex. In some groups one or both sexes may be wingless, or both winged and wingless individuals may occur in the same sex. Male scale insects have only one pair of wings, on the mesothorax.

The members of this group usually undergo simple metamorphosis; the development in whiteflies and male scale insects resembles complete metamorphosis in that the last nymphal instar is quiescent and pupalike.

The antennae are very short and bristlelike in some Homóptera and longer and usually filiform in others. Ocelli may be present or absent; if present, there are either two or three. The compound eyes are usually well developed.

CLASSIFICATION OF THE HOMÓPTERA

Some authorities consider the insects here treated as Homóptera to represent a suborder of the Hemíptera, with the insects we treat as Hemíptera representing another suborder (the Heteróptera) of this order. We believe there are enough differences between the Homóptera and Hemíptera (Heteróptera) to warrant their recognition as separate orders.

The order Homóptera is divided into two suborders, the Auchenorrhýncha and Sternorrhýncha, each of which is further divided into superfamilies and families. There are differences of opinion regarding the taxonomic status that should be given the various groups in this order; some of the groups that we treat as superfamilies (especially the Fulgoròidea, Aphidòidea, and Coccòidea) are regarded as families by some entomologists; other entomologists regard as superfamilies some of the groups that we treat as families (especially the families of Cicadòidea). The arrangement followed in this book is outlined below.

- Suborder Auchenorrhýncha—cicadas and hoppers
  - Superfamily Cicadòidea
    - Cicàdidae—cicadas
    - Membràcidae—treehoppers
    - Cercòpidae—froghoppers, spittlebugs
    - Cicadéllidae (Jássidae)—leafhoppers
  - Superfamily Fulgoròidae—planthoppers
    - Delphácidae (Areopódidae)—delphacid planthoppers
    - Dérbidae—derbid planthoppers
    - Cixìidae—cixiid planthoppers
    - Kinnàridae—kinnarid planthoppers
    - Dictyophàridae—dictyopharid planthoppers
    - Fulgòridae—fulgorid planthoppers
    - Achìlidae—achilid planthoppers
    - Tropidùchidae—tropiduchid planthoppers
    - Flàtidae—flatid planthoppers
    - Acanalonìidae (Amphiscépidae)—acanaloniid planthoppers
    - Íssidae—issid planthoppers
- Suborder Sternorrhýncha (Gularóstria)
  - Superfamily Psyllòidea
    - Psýllidae (Psyllìidae, Chérmidae)—psyllids or jumping plantlice
  - Superfamily Aleyrodòidea
    - Aleyròdidae (Aleuròdidae)—whiteflies
  - Superfamily Aphidòidea
    - Aphídidae (Àphidae)—aphids or plantlice
    - Eriosomátidae (Aphídidae in part)—woolly and gall-making aphids
    - Chérmidae (Adélgidae; Phylloxèridae in part)—pine and spruce aphids
    - Phylloxèridae (Chérmidae in part)—phylloxerans
  - Superfamily Coccòidea—scale insects
    - Margaròdidae (Monophlébidae)—giant coccids, ground pearls, cottony cushion scales
    - Orthezìidae—ensign coccids
    - Diaspídidae—armored scales
    - Cóccidae (Lecanìidae)—soft scales, wax scales, tortoise scales
    - Aclérdidae—aclerdid scales
    - Lacciféridae (Tachardìidae)—lac insects

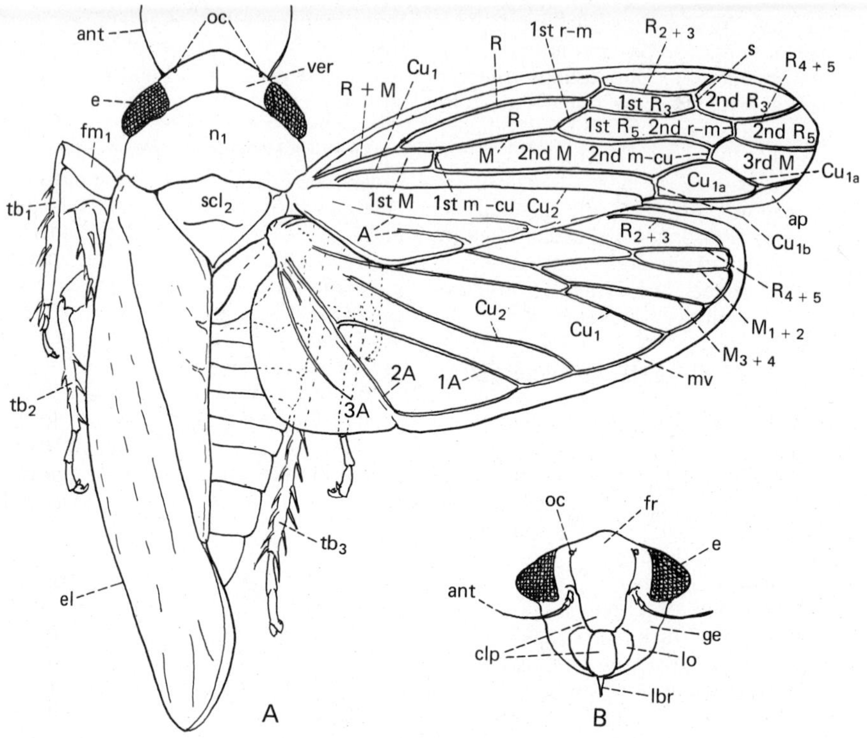

Figure 198. Structure of a leafhopper, *Paraphlépsius irroràtus* (Say). A, dorsal view; B, anterior view of head. *ant*, antenna; *ap*, appendix; *clp*, clypeus; *e*, compound eye; *el*, elytron or front wing; *fm*, femur; *fr*, frons; *ge*, gena; *lbr*, labrum; *lo*, lorum; *mv*, marginal vein; n_1, pronotum; *oc*, ocelli; scl_2, mesocutellum; *tb*, tibia; *ver*, vertex. The venational terminology follows the Comstock–Needham system, except for the veins posterior to the media. Students of the leafhoppers usually use a different terminology for the venational characters of the front wing; a comparison of their terminology with that used here is given in the following table.

Veins		**Cells**	
Terms in This Figure	*Other Terms*	*Terms in This Figure*	*Other Terms*
R + M	first sector	R	discal cell
R	outer branch of first sector	1st R_3	outer anteapical cell
M	inner branch of first sector	2nd R_3	first apical cell
Cu_1	second sector	1st R_5	anteapical cell
Cu_2	claval suture	2nd R_5	second apical cell
A	claval veins	2nd M	inner anteapical cell
1st m-cu	first crossvein	3rd M	third apical cell
2nd m-cu	apical crossvein	Cu_{1a}	fourth apical cell
s	apical crossvein		
1st r-m	crossvein between sectors		
2nd r-m	apical crossvein		

Asterolecanìidae — pit scales
Pseudocóccidae — mealybugs
Eriocóccidae (Conchaspídidae; Pseudocóccidae in part) — eriococcid scales
Dactylopìidae (Cóccidae) — cochineal insects
Kérmidae (Kermésidae, Hemicóccidae) — gall-like coccids

The superfamilies and families of the Auchenorrhýncha are separated principally on the basis of the character of the ocelli, the position of the antennae, the form of the pronotum, and the spination of the legs. The superfamilies of the Sternorrhýncha are separted on the basis of the number of antennal and tarsal segments, the structure and venation of the wings, and other characters. The families of scale insects are separated on the basis of characters of the female.

Key to the Families of Homóptera

The student should have no particular difficulty in running winged specimens through this key, but he may have trouble with some of the wingless forms. The separation of the families of scale insects is based on females (unless otherwise indicated), which generally must be mounted on microscope slides in order to run them through the key. Some wingless Aphidòidea can be separated only if one is familiar with their life history.

1. Tarsi 3-segmented; antennae very short and bristlelike; beak arising from back of head; active insects (suborder Auchenorrhýncha) 2

1′. Tarsi 1- or 2-segmented (when legs are present); antennae usually long and filiform; beak, when present, arising between front coxae; usually not active insects (suborder Sternorrhýncha) 16

2(1). Antennae arising on front of head between eyes (Figures 198 B and 200 B), or at least anterior to eyes (Figure 200 A); middle coxae short and close together; tegulae usually absent; no **Y** vein in anal area of front wing (Figure 198 A and 199 A) (superfamily Cicadòidae) 3

2′. Antennae arising on sides of head beneath eyes (Figure 200 C); middle coxae elongated and separated; tegulae usually present; 2 anal veins in front wing usually meeting apically to form a **Y** vein (Figure 202 A, B) (superfamily Fulgoròidae) 6

3(2). Three ocelli (Figure 200 B); large insects with front wings membranous (Figure 205); males usually with sound-producing organs ventrally at base of abdomen (Figure 206); not jumping insects .... **Cicàdidae** p. 293

3′. Two (rarely 3) ocelli (Figure 198 B) or none; smaller insects, sometimes with front wings thickened; sound-producing organs present or absent; usually jumping insects 4

4(3′). Pronotum extending backward over abdomen (Figure 207)... **Membràcidae** p. 297

4′. Pronotum not extending backward over abdomen (Figures 208 and 210) 5

5(4′). Hind tibiae with 1 or 2 stout spines, and usually a circlet of spines at apex (Figure 201 B); hind coxae short and conical .... **Cercòpidae** p. 297

5′. Hind tibiae with 1 or more rows of small spines (Figure 201 A); hind coxae transverse .... **Cicadéllidae** p. 300

6(2′). Hind tibiae with a broad movable apical spur (Figure 202 C, *sp*); a large group of small to minute forms, many dimorphic (with wings well developed or short), the sexes often very different .... **Delphácidae** p. 306

6′. Hind tibiae without a broad movable apical spur 7

7(6′). Anal area of hind wings reticulate, with many cross veins... **Fulgòridae** p. 306

7′. Anal area of hind wings not reticulate, without cross veins 8

8(7′). Second segment of hind tarsi with 2 apical spines (one on each side), and with apex usually rounded or conical (Figure 202 D) 9

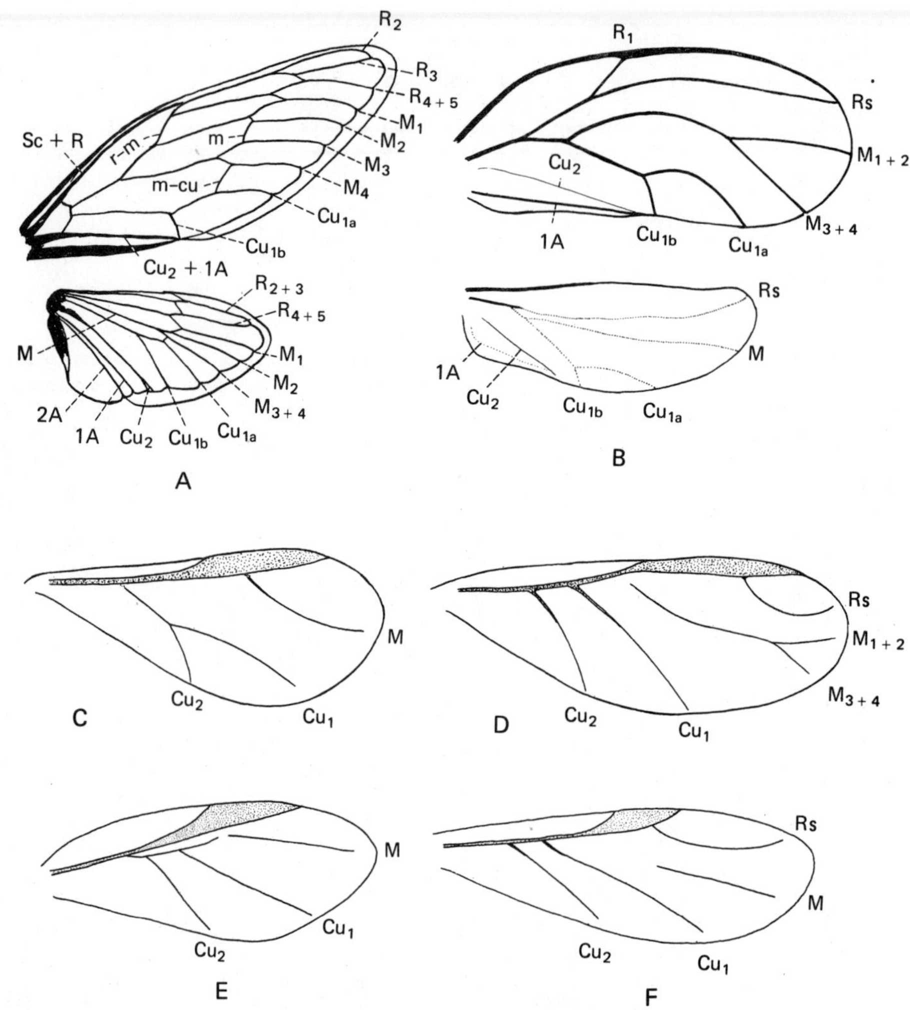

Figure 199. Wings of Homóptera. A, Cicàdidae (*Magicicàda*); B, Psýllidae (*Psýlla*); C, Phylloxèridae (*Phylloxèra*); D, Aphídidae (*Macrosìphum*); E, Chérmidae (*Adélges*); F, Eriosomátidae (*Cólopha*). C–F, front wings.

8′. Second segment of hind tarsi with a row of apical spines, and with apex truncate or emarginate 12

9(8). Front wings with numerous costal cross veins, longer than body, and at rest held almost vertically at sides of body (Figure 212 F); clavus with numerous small pustulelike tubercles .... **Flàtidae** p. 308

9′. Front wings without numerous costal cross veins (except sometimes apically), variable in size and position at rest; clavus without numerous small pustulelike tubercles 10

10(9′). Front wings longer than abdomen, with a series of cross veins between costal margin and apex of clavus separating off an apical more densely veined portion of the wing; slender, greenish or yellowish to brownish, 7–9 mm

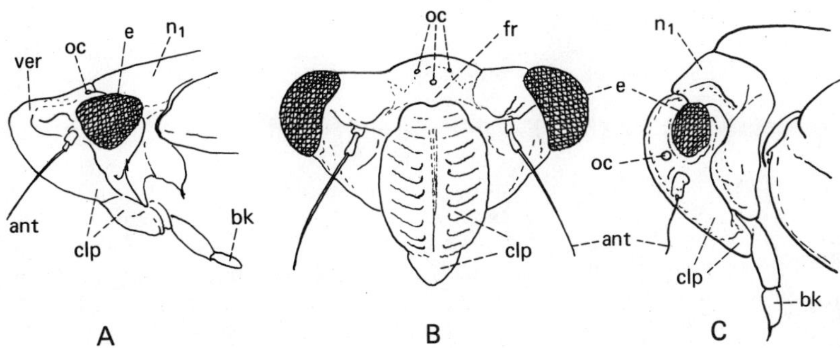

Figure 200. Head structure in Homóptera. A, froghopper (*Philaènus*), lateral view; B, cicada (*Magicicàda*), anterior view; C, planthopper (*Anórmenis*) lateral view. *ant*, antenna; *bk*, beak; *clp*, clypeus; *e*, compound eye; *fr*, frons; n_1, pronotum; *oc*, ocelli; *ver*, vertex.

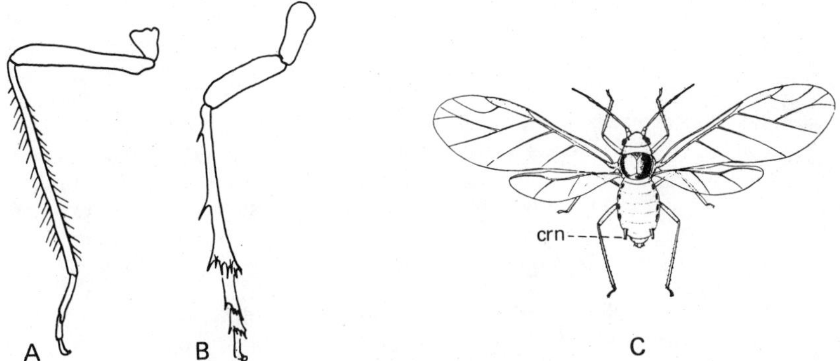

Figure 201. A, hind leg of a leafhopper (Cicadéllidae); B, hind leg of a froghopper (Cercòpidae); C, a winged aphid (Aphídidae). *crn*, cornicle. (C, courtesy of USDA.)

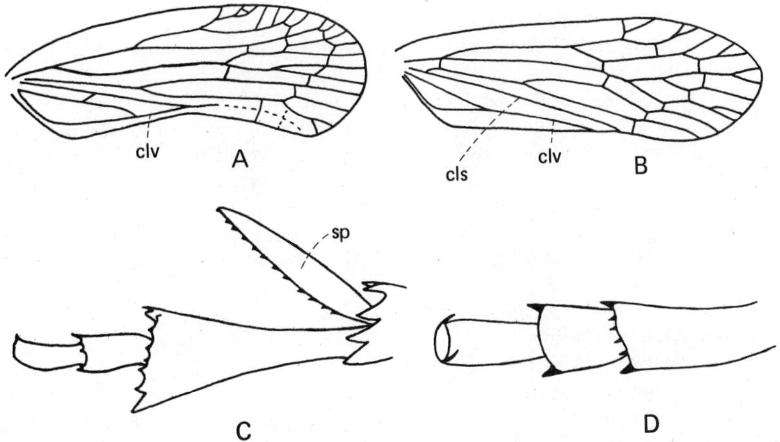

Figure 202. Characters of Fulgoròidea. A, front wing of *Epíptera* (Achìlidae); B, front wing of *Cíxius* (Cixìidae); C, hind tarsus of a delphacid; D, hind tarsus of *Anórmenis* (Flàtidae). *cls*, claval suture; *clv*, claval vein; *sp*, apical spur of hind tibia.

in length; southeastern United States, Florida to Mississippi .... **Tropidùchidae** p. 307

10′. Front wings without a differentiated apical portion as described above, and variable in length 11

11(10′). Front wings very broad, with costal margin rounded and venation reticulate, longer than body, and at rest held almost vertically at sides of body (Figure 212 E); hind tibiae without spines except at apex .... **Acanalonìidae** p. 308

11′. Front wings variable in size and shape, often shorter than abdomen, but if longer than abdomen then usually oval; hind tibiae usually with spines on sides, in addition to apical ones .... **Íssidae** p. 308

12(8′). Terminal segment of beak short, not more than 1½ times as long as wide .... **Dérbidae** p. 306

12′. Terminal segment of beak longer, at least twice as long as wide... 13

13(12′). Front wings overlapping at apex (Figure 212 C); claval vein extending to apex of clavus (Figure 202 A, *clv*); body somewhat flattened... **Achìlidae** p. 307

13′. Front wings usually not overlapping at apex; claval vein not reaching apex of clavus (Figure 202 B, *clv*); body not particularly flattened 14

14(13′). Head prolonged in front (Figure 212 G–I), or if not then frons bears 2 or 3 carinae, or the tegulae are absent and the claval suture is obscure; no median ocellus .... **Dictyophàridae** p. 306

14′. Head not prolonged in front (Figure 212 A, D), or only moderately so; frons either without carinae or with a median carina only; tegulae present; claval suture distinct; median ocellus usually present 15

15(14′). Abdominal terga 6–8 chevron-shaped, sometimes sunk below rest of terga; 3–4 mm in length; western United States .... **Kinnàridae** p. 306

15′. Abdominal terga 6–8 rectangular; size variable; widely distributed .... **Cixìidae** p. 306

16(1′). Tarsi 2-segmented, with 2 claws; winged forms with 4 wings; mouth parts usually well developed in both sexes, with the beak long 17

16′. Tarsi 1-segmented, with a single claw (when legs are present); female wingless and often legless, scalelike, or grublike and wax-covered; male with only 1 pair of wings, and without a beak (superfamily Coccòidae) 22

17(16). Antennae with 5–10 (usually 10) segments; front wings often thicker than hind wings; jumping insects .... **Psýllidae** p. 308

17′. Antennae with 3–7 segments; wings membranous or opaque whitish; not jumping insects 18

18(17′). Wings usually opaque, whitish, and covered with a whitish powder; hind wings nearly as large as front wings; no cornicles .... **Aleyròdidae** p. 309

18′. Wings membranous and not covered with a whitish powder; hind wings much smaller than front wings (Figure 201 C); cornicles often present (superfamily Aphidòidae) 19

19(18′). Front wings with 4 or 5 (rarely 6) veins behind stigma extending to wing margin (Rs present) (Figure 199 D, F); cornicles usually present (Figure 201 C); antennae generally 6-segmented; sexual females oviparous, parthenogenetic females viviparous 20

19′. Front wings with only 3 veins behind stigma extending to wing margin (Rs absent) (Figure 199 C, E); cornicles absent; antennae 3- to 5-segmented; all females oviparous 21

20(19). Cornicles nearly always present and conspicuous; M in front wing branched (Figure 199 D); females, and usually also males, with functional mouth parts; without abundant wax glands .... **Aphídidae** p. 309

20′. Cornicles indistinct or lacking; M in front wing not branched (Figure 199 F); sexual forms with mouth parts atrophied and not functional; wax glands usually abundant .... **Eriosomátidae** p. 312

21(19′). Wings at rest held rooflike over body; Cu_1 and Cu_2 in front wing separated at base (Figure 199 E); apterous parthenogenetic females covered with waxy flocculence; on conifers .... **Chérmidae** p. 314

21′. Wings at rest held horizontal; Cu_1 and Cu_2 in front wing stalked at base (Figure 199 C); apterous parthenogenetic females not covered with waxy flocculence (at most, covered with a powdery material) .. **Phylloxèridae** p. 314

22(16′). Abdominal spiracles present (Figure 204 A, *spr*); male usually with compound eyes and ocelli 23

22′. Abdominal spiracles absent (Figure 203 B); male with ocelli only 24

23(22). Anal ring distinct and flat, bearing many pores and 6 long setae (Figure 204 A) .... **Orthezìidae** p. 315

23′. Anal ring reduced, without pores and setae .... **Margaròdidae** p. 315

24(22′). Terminal segments of female fused into a pygidium (Figure 203, *py*); female with a removable scale; antennae rudimentary; legs absent; beak 1-segmented .... **Diaspídidae** p. 315

24′. Pygidium absent; legs and antennae present or absent; beak with more than 1 segment 25

25(24′). Posterior end of body cleft (Figure 204 D); openings of wax glands rarely 8-shaped (shaped like the figure 8) 26

25′. Posterior end of body not cleft, or if slightly so then some of the wax gland openings are 8-shaped (Figure 204 C, *mpo*) 27

26(25). Anus covered by a single dorsal plate .... **Aclérdidae** p. 318

26′. Anus covered by 2 dorsal plates (Figure 204 D, *anp*) (rarely with no plates) .... **Cóccidae** p. 318

27(25′). Abdomen narrower posteriorly, or produced into an anal tube; body enclosed in a resinous cell. .... **Lacciféridae** p. 319

27′. Abdomen not narrowed posteriorly or produced into an anal tube, or if so then with 8-shaped pores (see couplet 25); body not in a resinous cell 28

28(27′). Wax gland openings (mostly along margin of dorsum) 8-shaped, usually in rows (Figure 204 C, *mpo*); legs vestigial or absent; usually on oak .... **Asterolecanìidae** p. 319

28′. Wax gland openings on dorsum not 8-shaped 29

29(28′). Anal ring present (as in Figure 204 A) 30

29′. Anal ring absent 32

30(29). Anal ring with 2 setae, and never cellular; on palms .... **Diaspídidae** p. 315

30′. Anal ring with 4 or more setae, and often cellular 31

31(30′). Dorsal ostioles and usually 1–4 ventral circuli present (Figure 204 B, *do* and *vc*); insect in life covered with a white powdery secretion .... **Pseudocóccidae** p. 319

31′. Dorsal ostioles and ventral circuli absent; insect in life usually naked, not covered with a white powdery secretion .... **Eriocóccidae** p. 319

32(29′). Ducts of wax glands minute, arising from center of a cluster of sessile pores; setae stout and cut off at end; on cactus .... **Dactylopìidae** p. 320

32′. Ducts of wax glands not as above; on oaks .... **Kérmidae** p. 320

SUBORDER **Auchenorrhýncha:** The members of this suborder (cicadas and hoppers) are active insects, being good fliers or jumpers. Their tarsi are 3-segmented, and their antennae are very short and bristlelike. The cicadas are relatively large insects, with membranous wings and three ocelli. The hoppers are small to minute insects, with the front wings usually more or less thickened, and they usually have two ocelli (or none). The males of many Auchenorrhýncha are able to produce sound, but except for the cicadas these sounds are very weak and are seldom heard.

Family **Cicàdidae**—Cicadas: The members of this family can usually be recognized by their characteristic shape and their large size (Figure 205). This group contains the largest Homóptera in the United States, some of which reach a length of about 2 inches (50 mm); the smallest cicadas are a little less than 25 mm in length.

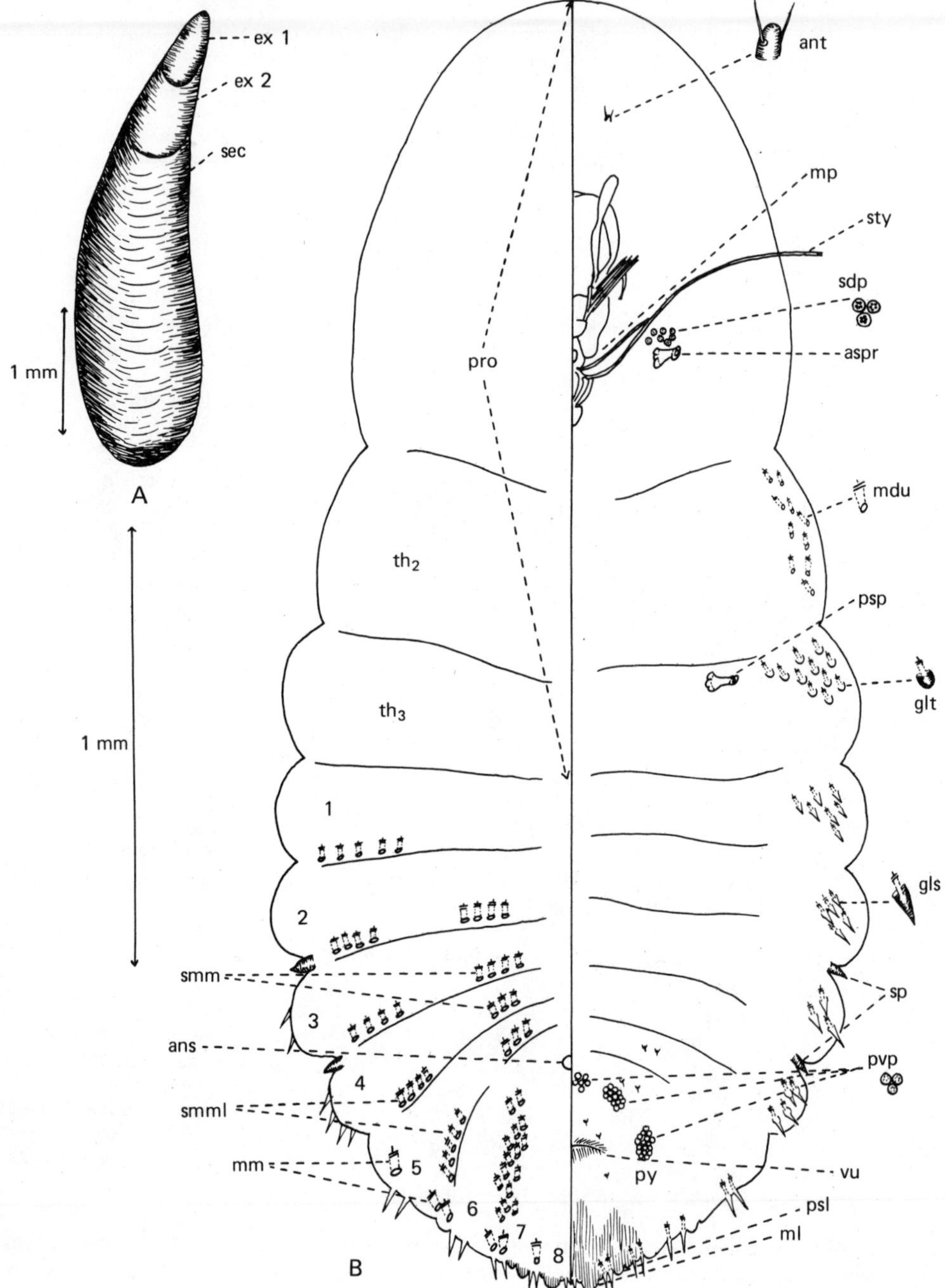

Figure 203. Characters of scale insects. A, scale of female; B, diagrammatic drawing of a female armored scale. The left side of B represents a dorsal view, and the right side a ventral view. *ans,* anus; *ant,* antenna; *aspr,* anterior spiracle; *ex* 1, first exuvia; *ex* 2, second exuvia; *gls,* gland spines; *glt,* gland tubercle; *mdu,* microduct; *ml,* median lobe; *mm,* marginal macroduct, *mp,* mouth parts; *pro,* prosoma; *psl,* paired second lobe; *psp,* posterior spiracle; *pvp,* perivulvar pores; *py,* pygidium; *sdp,* spiracular disc pore; *sec,* secretion of adult; *smm,* submedian macroduct; *smml,* submarginal macroducts; *sp,* spur; *sty,* stylets; th_2, mesothorax; th_3 metathorax; *vu,* vulva. (Figure prepared by Dr. Michael Kosztarab.)

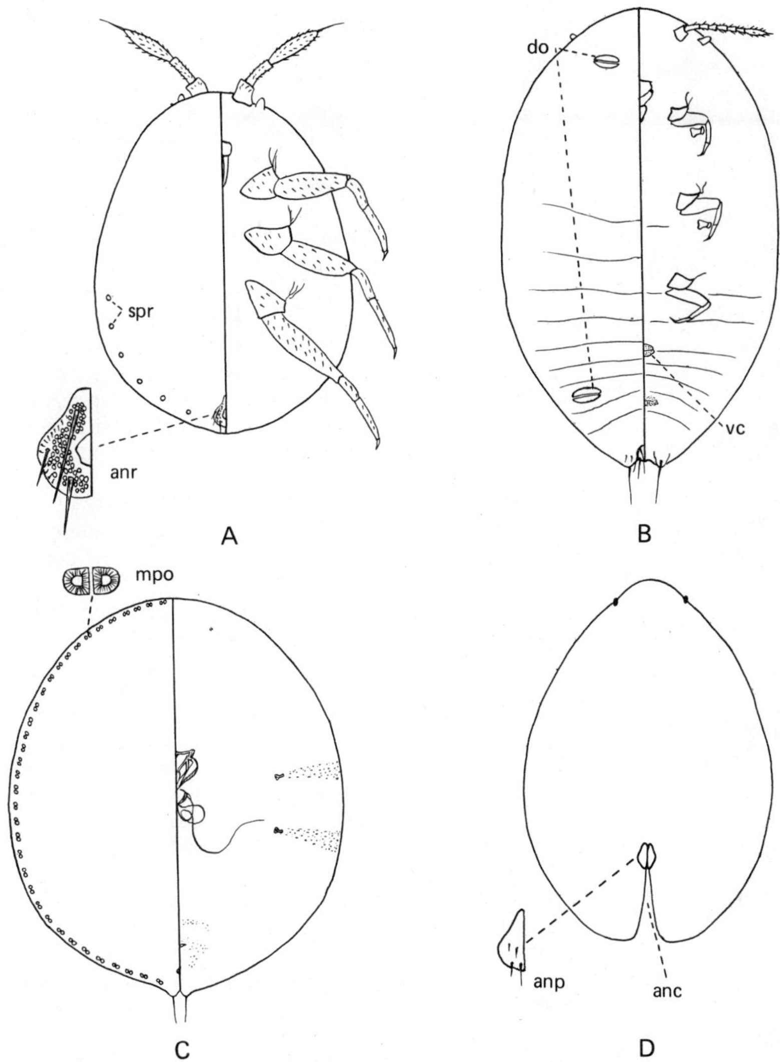

Figure 204. Characters of female scale insects (diagrammatic). A, Ortheziidae; B, Pseudocóccidae; C, Asterolecaniidae; D, Cóccidae. In A–C, the left side represents a dorsal view, and the right side a ventral view. *anc*, anal cleft; *anp*, anal plate; *anr*, anal ring; *do*, dorsal ostioles; *mpo*, marginal 8-shaped pores; *spr*, abdominal spiracles; *vc*, ventral circulus. (Figure prepared by Dr. Michael Kosztarab.)

A conspicuous characteristic of cicadas is their ability to produce sound. Other Homóptera (for example, leafhoppers) can produce sounds, but their sounds are very weak; the sounds produced by cicadas are generally quite loud. The sounds are produced by the males, and each species has a characteristic song; one familiar with these songs can identify the species by song alone. Each species also produces a somewhat different sound (a disturbance squawk or "protest" sound) when handled or disturbed, and some species have a special song (termed a "courtship" song) that is produced by a male approaching a female.

Cicada sounds are produced by a pair of tymbals located dorsally at the sides of the basal abdominal segment (Figure 206, *tmb*). The tymbals consist of a posterior plate and several riblike bands lying in a membrane, and are sometimes

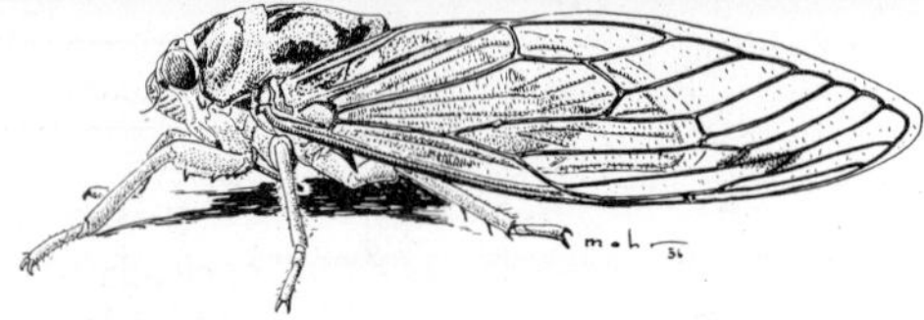

Figure 205. A dog-day cicada, *Tibìcen pruinòsa* (Say), about natural size. (Courtesy of Carl Mohr and the Illinois Natural History Survey.)

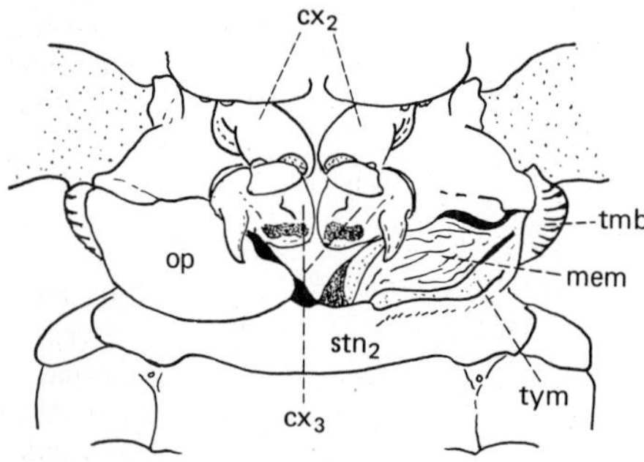

Figure 206. Thorax of a cicada (*Magicicàda*), ventral view, showing the sound-producing organs; the operculum at the right has been removed. *cx*, coxa; *mem*, membrane; *op*, operculum; *stn*, abdominal sternum; *tmb*, tymbal; *tym*, tympanum.

completely exposed above; in the dog-day cicadas (*Tibìcen* spp.) they are covered above by an abdominal flap. The hearing organs, or tympana (*tym*), lie posteriorly in a ventral cavity through which the tymbals or tymbal spaces are exposed below. This space often has a yellowish membrane (*mem*) connecting anteriorly to the thorax, and is covered over ventrally by a pair of thoracic flaps called opercula (*op*). Internally, the last thoracic segment and up to five abdominal segments are nearly entirely filled by a large tracheal air sac that functions as a resonance chamber. A pair of large muscles runs through this air sac from above the tympana to the large plate of the tymbals, and their contractions cause the ribs to bend suddenly and produce the sounds. The air sacs and general body tension, plus other structures, control the volume and quality of the sounds. There are also stridulating and wingbanging groups of cicadas, which produce their characteristic sounds by these other means.

Two common types in this family are the dog-day cicadas (various species) (Figure 205) and the periodical cicadas (*Magicicàda*). The dog-day cicadas are mostly large blackish insects, usually with greenish markings, that appear each year in July and August; the periodical cicadas, which occur in the eastern United States, differ from other eastern species in that they have the eyes and wing veins reddish, they are smaller than most other eastern species, and the adults appear in late May and early June. The life cycle of dog-day cicadas is unknown, but two Japanese woodland species are known to require seven years to mature. The shortest known cicada life cycle is four years, for a grassland species. In dog-day cicadas, even with long life cycles, the broods overlap so that some adults appear each year. The life cycle of the periodical cicadas lasts 13 or 17 years, and in any given area adults are not present each year.

There are at least 13 broods of 17-year cicadas and five of 13-year cicadas; these broods emerge in different years, and have different geographic ranges. The 17-year cicadas are generally northern and the 13-year cicadas southern, but there is considerable overlap, and both life-cycle types may occur in the same woods (but would emerge together only once every 221 years). The emergence of some of the larger broods is a very striking event, as the insects in these broods may be extremely numerous. The large broods of 17-year cicadas that have occurred in central and southern Ohio in recent years appeared in 1970 (Brood X), 1973 (Brood XIII), and 1974 (Brood XIV).

There are six species of periodical cicadas, three with a 17-year cycle and three with a 13-year cycle. The three species in each life-cycle group differ in size, color, and song (see Table 3); each 17-year species has a similar or sibling species with a 13-year cycle, from which it can be separated only by differences in life cycle and distribution. Most broods of each life-cycle type contain more than one species, and many contain all three.

Cicadas deposit their eggs in the twigs of various trees and shrubs. The twigs are usually so severely injured by this egg laying that the terminal part of the twig dies. The eggs generally hatch in a month or so (some species overwinter as eggs) and the nymphs drop to the ground, enter the soil, and feed on roots, particularly of perennial plants. The nymphs remain in the ground until they are ready to molt the last time; in the case of the periodical cicadas, this period is 13–17 years. When the last nymphal instar digs its way out of the ground, it climbs up on some object, usually a

Table 3 SUMMARY OF THE PERIODICAL CICADAS *(Magicicàda)*[a]

Characteristics	*17-Year cycle*	*13-Year cycle*
Body length 27–33 mm Propleura and lateral extensions of pronotum between eyes and wing bases reddish Abdominal sterna primarily reddish brown or yellow Song: "Phaaaaaroah," a low buzz, 1–3 seconds in length, with a drop in pitch at the end	Linnaeus' 17-year cicada, *M. septéndecim* (L.)	Riley's 13-year cicada, *M. trédecim* Walsh and Riley
Body length 20–28 mm Propleura and lateral extensions of pronotum between eyes and wing bases black Abdominal sterna all black, or a few with a narrow band of reddish brown or yellow on apical third, this band often constricted or interrupted medially Last tarsal segment with apical half or more black Song: 2–3 seconds of ticks alternating with 1–3 second buzzes that rise and then fall in pitch and intensity	Cassin's 17-year cicada, *M. cássini* (Fisher)	Cassin's 13-year cicada, *M. tredecássini* Alexander and Moore
Body length 19–27 mm Propleura and lateral extensions of pronotum between eyes and wing bases black Abdominal sterna black basally, with a broad apical band of reddish yellow or brown on posterior half of each sternum, this band not interrupted medially Last tarsal segment entirely brownish or yellowish, or at most, the apical third black Song: 20–40 short high-pitched phrases, each like a short buzz and tick delivered together, at the rate of 3–5 per second, the final phrases shorter and lacking the short buzz	The Little 17-year cicada, *M. septendécula* Alexander and Moore	The Little 13-year cicada, *M. tredécula* Alexander and Moore

[a]Data from Alexander and Moore (1962).

tree, fastens its claws in the bark, and the final molt then takes place. The adult stage lasts a month or more.

The principal damage done by cicadas is caused by the egg laying of the adults. When the adults are numerous, as in years when the periodical cicadas emerge, they may do considerable damage to young trees and nursery stock.

Family **Membràcidae**—Treehoppers: The members of this group can be recognized by the large pronotum that covers the head, extends back over the abdomen, and often assumes various peculiar shapes (Figure 207). Many species appear more or less humpbacked; others have various spines, horns, or keels on the pronotum, and some species are shaped like thorns. The wings are largely concealed by the pronotum. These insects are rarely over 10 or 12 mm in length.

Treehoppers feed chiefly on trees and shrubs, and most species feed only on specific types of host plants. Some species feed on grass and herbaceous plants in the nymphal stage. The treehoppers have one or two generations a year and usually pass the winter in the egg stage.

Only a few species in this group are considered of economic importance, and most of their damage is caused by egg laying. The buffalo treehopper, *Stictocéphala bubàlus* (Fabricius) (Figure 207 C), is a common pest species that lays its eggs in the twigs of apple and several other trees. The eggs are placed in slits cut in the bark, and the terminal portion of the twig beyond the eggs often dies. The eggs overwinter and hatch in the spring, and the nymphs drop to herbaceous vegetation where they complete their development, returning to the trees to lay their eggs.

Family **Cercòpidae**—Froghoppers or Spittlebugs: Froghoppers are small hopping insects, rarely over

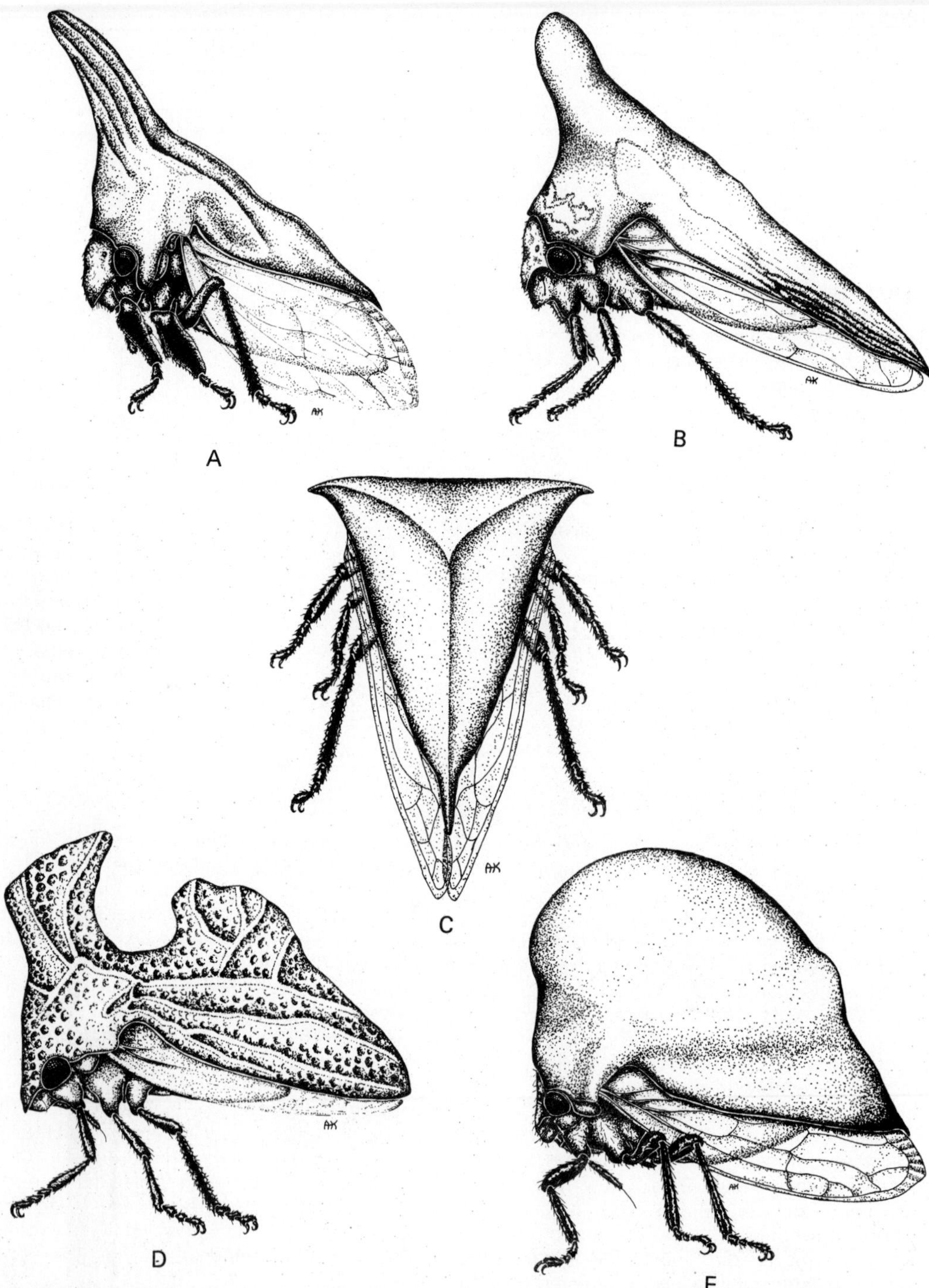

Figure 207. Treehoppers. A, *Campylénchia látipes* (Say); B, *Thèlia bimaculàta* (Fabricius); C, *Stictocéphala bubàlus* (Fabricius); D, *Entỳlia concìsa* Walker; E, *Archàsia galeàta* (Fabricius). A, B, D, and E, lateral views; C, dorsal view.

13 mm in length, some species of which vaguely resemble tiny frogs in shape (Figure 208). They are very similar to the leafhoppers, but can be distinguished by the spination of the hind tibiae (Figure 201 A, B). They are usually brown or gray in color; some species have a characteristic color pattern.

These insects feed on shrubs and herbaceous plants, the different species feeding on different food plants. The nymphs surround themselves with a frothy spittlelike mass (Figure 209), and are usually called spittlebugs. These masses of spittle are sometimes quite abundant in meadows; each mass contains one or more greenish or brownish spittlebugs. After the last molt the insect leaves the spittle and moves about actively.

The spittle is derived from fluid voided from the anus and from a mucilaginous substance excreted by the epidermal glands on the seventh and eighth abdominal segments. Air bubbles are introduced into the spittle by means of the caudal appendages of the insect. A spittlebug usually rests head downward on the plant, and as the spittle forms, it flows down over and covers the insect; it lasts some time, even when exposed to heavy rains, and provides the nymph with a moist habitat. The adults do not produce spittle.

The most important economic species of spittlebug in the eastern states is *Philaènus spumàrius* (L.) (Figure 208), a meadow species that causes serious stunting, particularly to clovers. This insect lays its eggs in late summer in the stems or sheaths of grasses and other plants, and the eggs hatch the following spring; there is one generation a year. There are several color forms of this species. Most of the spittlebugs attack grasses and herbaceous plants, but a few attack trees; *Aphróphora parállela* (Say) and *A. saratogénsis* (Fitch) are important pests of pine.

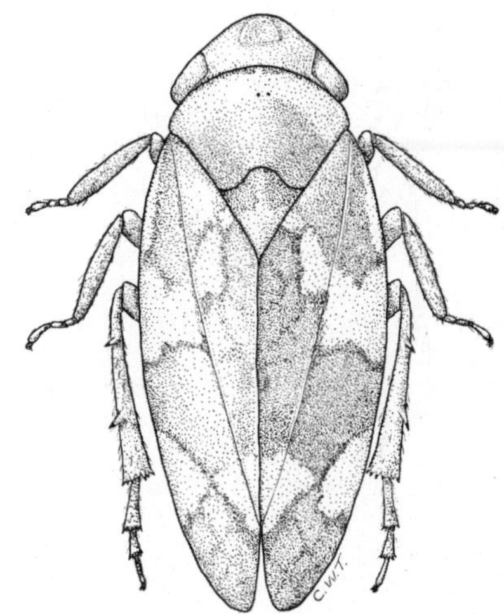

Figure 208. A froghopper, *Philaènus spumàrius* (L.).

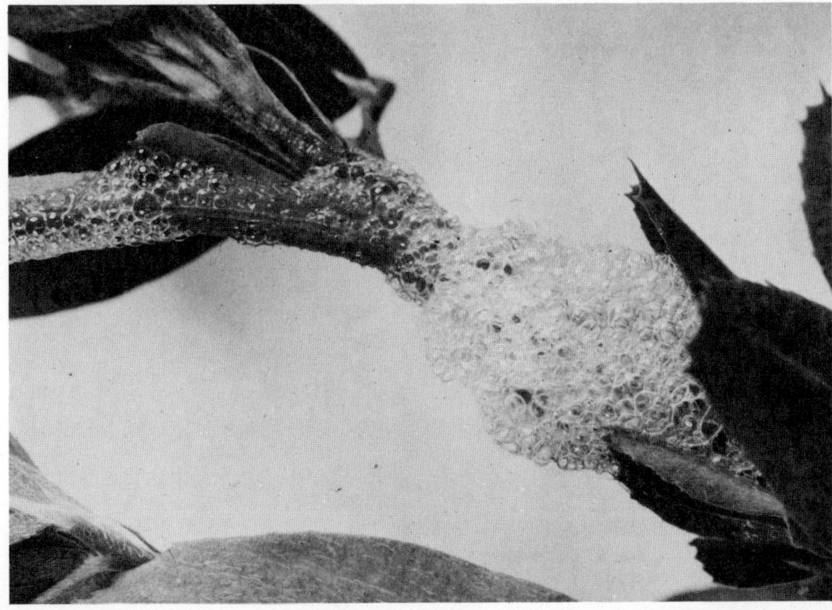

Figure 209. Spittle mass of the spittlebug, *Philaènus spumàrius* (L.). (Courtesy of the Illinois Natural History Survey.)

Family **Cicadéllidae**—Leafhoppers: The leafhoppers constitute a very large group (about 2500 North American species), and they are of various forms, colors, and sizes (Figure 210). They are similar to froghoppers but have one or more rows of small spines extending the length of the hind tibiae. They rarely exceed 13 mm in length, and many are only a few millimeters in length; many are marked with a beautiful color pattern.

Leafhoppers occur on almost all types of plants, including forest, shade, and orchard trees, shrubs, grasses, flowers, and many field and garden crops; they feed principally on the leaves of their food plant. The food of most species is quite specific, and the habitat is therefore well defined. In many cases a specialist in this group can examine a series of specimens taken in a given habitat, and can describe that habitat, and often determine the general region of the country from which the specimens came.

Most leafhoppers have a single generation a year, but a few have two or three. The winter is usually passed in either the adult or the egg stage, depending on the species.

There are many economically important pest species in this group, and they cause five major types of injury to plants. (1) Some species remove excessive amounts of sap and reduce or destroy the chlorophyll in the leaves, causing the leaves to become covered with minute white or yellow spots; with continued feeding the leaves turn yellowish or brownish. This type of injury is produced on apple leaves by various species of *Erythroneùra, Typhlocỳba,* and *Empoásca.* (2) Some species interfere with the normal physiology of the plant, for example, by mechanically plugging the phloem and xylem vessels in the leaves so that transport of food materials is impaired; a browning of the outer portion of the leaf, and eventually of the entire leaf, results. The potato

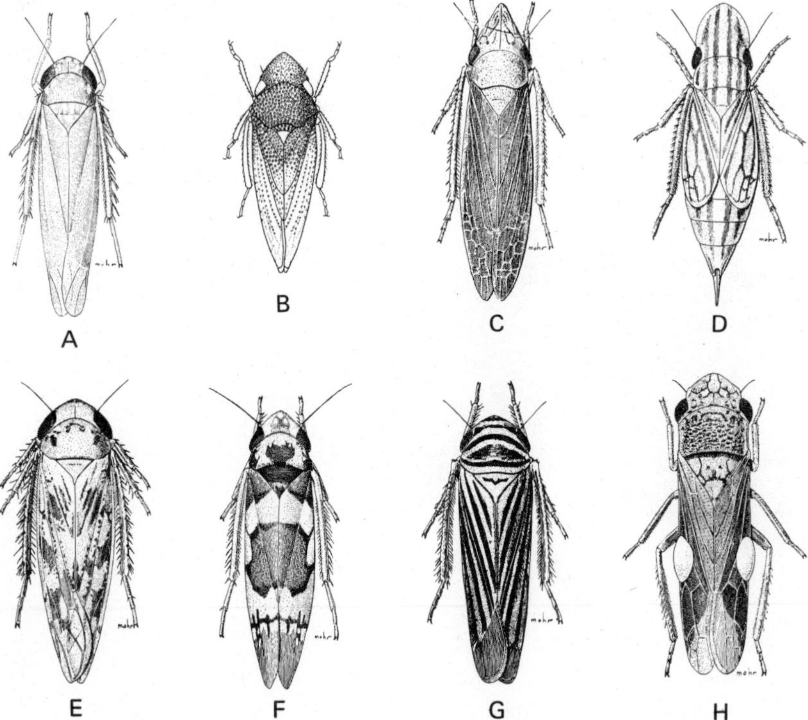

Figure 210. Leafhoppers. A, potato leafhopper, *Empoásca fàbae* (Harris) (Typholocybìnae); B, *Xerophloèa màjor* Baker (Ledrìnae); C, *Draeculacéphala móllipes* (Say) (Cicadellìnae); D, *Hécalus lineàtus* (Uhler), female (Hecalìnae); E, beet leafhopper, *Circùlifer tenéllus* Baker (Deltocephalìnae); F, *Erythroneùra vìtis* (Harris) (Typhlocybìnae); G, *Tylozỳgus bìfidus* (Say) (Cicadellìnae); H, *Oncometòpia undàta* (Fabricius) (Cicadellìnae). (Courtesy of the Illinois Natural History Survey.)

leafhopper, *Empoásca fàbae* (Harris) (Figure 210 A), causes this type of injury. (3) A few species injure plants by ovipositing in green twigs, often causing the terminal portion of the twigs to die. Various species of *Gyponàna* cause damage of this sort; their egg punctures are similar to those of the buffalo treehopper, but are smaller. (4) Many species of leafhoppers act as vectors of the organisms that cause plant diseases; aster yellows, corn stunt, phloem necrosis of elm, Pierce's disease of grape, phony peach, potato yellow dwarf, curly top in sugar beets, and other plant diseases (see Table 5, Chapter 33) are transmitted by leafhoppers, chiefly species in the subfamilies Agalliínae, Cicadellìnae, and Deltocephalìnae. (5) Some species cause stunting and leaf curling due to the inhibition of growth on the undersurface of the leaves where the leafhoppers feed; the potato leafhopper, *Empoásca fàbae* (Harris), produces injury of this type.

Many species of leafhoppers emit from the anus a liquid called honeydew; this is composed of unused portions of plant sap to which are added certain waste products of the insect.

Many of the leafhoppers (as well as some of the other hoppers) are known to produce sound (Ossiannilsson, 1949). These sounds are all quite weak; some can be heard if the insect is held close to one's ear, while others can only be heard when amplified. These sounds are produced by the vibration of tymbals located dorsolaterally at the base of the abdomen (on the first or second segment); the tymbals are thin-walled areas of the body wall, and are not very conspicuous from an external view. The sounds produced by leafhoppers of the genus *Empoásca* (Shaw *et al.*, 1974) are of up to five types (depending on the species): one or two types of "common" sounds, disturbance sounds, courtship sounds, and sounds by the female. Most of these sounds are different in different species, and are believed to play a role in species recognition by the insects.

Metcalf (1962–1967) considers the leafhoppers to represent a superfamily (the Cicadellòidea), and divides them into a number of families. The differences between these families are not as great as those between the families of Fulgoròidea, and most leafhopper specialists prefer to treat the leafhoppers as a single family divided into subfamilies. There are differences of opinion as to the leafhopper subfamilies to be recognized, and the names to be given them; the arrangement followed in this book is outlined below, with other names and arrangements in parentheses. Following each subfamily is a list of the genera in that group mentioned in this book.

Family Cicadéllidae
- Ledrìnae (Xerophloeìnae)—*Xerophloèa*
- Dorycephalìnae (Dorydiìnae in part)—*Dorycéphalus*
- Hecalìnae (Dorydiìnae in part)—*Hécalus, Parábolocràtus*
- Megophthalmìnae (Ulopìnae; Agalliìnae in part)
- Agalliìnae—*Aceratagállia, Agállia, Agalliàna, Agallиópsis*
- Macropsìnae—*Macrópsis*
- Idiocerìnae—*Idiócerus*
- Gyponìnae—*Gyponàna*
- Iassìnae (including Bythoscopìnae)
- Penthimiìnae—*Penthímia*
- Koebeliìnae—*Koebèlia*
- Coelidiìnae (Jassìnae)—*Tinobrégmus*
- Nioniìnae—*Niònia*
- Aphrodìnae—*Aphròdes*
- Xestocephalìnae—*Xestocéphalus*
- Neocoelidiìnae—*Paracoelídia*
- Cicadellìnae (Tettigellìnae, Tettigoniellìnae; including Evacanthìnae)—*Carneocéphala, Cuérna, Draeculacéphala, Friscànus, Graphocéphala, Helochàra, Homalodísca, Hórdnia, Keonólla, Neokólla, Oncometòpia, Pagarònia, Sibòvia, Tylozỳgus*
- Typhlocybìnae (Cicadellìnae)—*Empoásca, Erythroneùra, Kunzeàna, Typhlocỳba*
- Deltocephalìnae (Athysanìnae, Euscelìnae; including Balcluthìnae)—*Acinópterus, Chlorotéttix, Circùlifer, Colladònus, Dálbulus, Éndria, Euscelídius, Eùscelis, Excultànus, Fieberiélla, Graminélla, Macrósteles, Norvellìna, Paraphlépsius, Paratànus, Pseudotéttix, Scaphòideus, Scaphytòpius, Scleroràcus, Texanànus*

Key to the Subfamilies of Cicadéllidae

1. Front wings without cross veins basad of apical cross veins (Figure 211 F); longitudinal veins indistinct basally; ocelli often absent; apex of first segment of hind tarsus sharp-tipped; slender, fragile leafhoppers .... **Typhlocybìnae** p. 306

1′. Front wings with cross veins basad of apical cross veins (Figure 211 H); longitudinal veins distinct basally; ocelli present; apex of first segment of hind tarsus truncate; usually relatively robust leafhoppers 2

2(1′). Episterna of prothorax easily visible in anterior view, not largely concealed by genae (Figure 211 A, eps_1) 3

2′. Episterna of prothorax largely or entirely concealed by genae in anterior view (Figure 211 B–E, G) 4

3(2). Ocelli on crown, remote from eyes and from anterior margin of crown (Figure 211 L); dorsum covered with rounded pits (Figure 210 B)... **Ledrìnae** p. 304

3′. Ocelli on lateral margins of head, just in front of eyes (Figure 211 J, K); dorsum not covered with rounded pits .... **Dorycephalìnae** p. 304

4(2′). Ocelli on crown (usually disc of crown), the frontal sutures extending over margin of crown nearly to ocelli; clypellus broad above and narrowed below; clypeus usually swollen (Figure 211 E) .... **Cicadellìnae** p. 305

4′. Without the above combination of characters 5

5(4′). Frontal sutures terminating at or slightly above antennal pits, or ocelli near disc of crown and remote from eyes, or both 6

5′. Frontal sutures extending beyond antennal pits to or near ocelli, the ocelli never on disc of crown 11

6(5). Lateral margins of pronotum carinate and moderately long; ledge or carina above antennal pits transverse or nearly so 7

6′. Lateral margins of pronotum short, and not or but feebly carinate; ledge above antennal pits, if present, oblique 8

7(6). Face in profile concave; front wings with appendix very large, and first (inner) apical cell large (equal in area to second and third apical cells combined) .... **Penthimiìnae** p. 305

7′. Face in profile not concave, usually distinctly convex; front wings with appendix normal or small, and first apical cell not enlarged 10

8(6′). Hind wings always present and with 3 apical cells (Figure 211 I, *AP*); pronotum extending forward beyond anterior margins of eyes; distance between ocelli usually greater than twice the distance from ocellus to eye .... **Macropsìnae** p. 304

8′. Hind wings present or absent, if present with 4 apical cells (Figure 211 M, *AP*); pronotum not extending forward beyond anterior margins of eyes; distance between ocelli not more than twice the distance from ocellus to eye 9

9(8′). Face with carinae replacing frontal sutures above antennal pits; western United States .... **Megophthalmìnae** p. 304

9′. Face without such carinae; widely distributed .... **Agalliìnae** p. 304

10(7′). Ocelli on crown, usually remote from anterior margin of head .... **Gyponìnae** p. 305

10′. Ocelli on anterior margin of crown .... **Iassìnae** p. 305

11(5′). Dorsum with circular pits; pronotum extending forward beyond anterior margins of eyes; shining black leafhoppers .... **Nioniìnae** p. 305

11′. Dorsum without such pits; pronotum not extending forward beyond anterior margins of eyes 12

12(11′). Distance between ocelli less than the distance between antennal pits, or clypellus much wider distally than basally and extending to or beyond apex of genae 13

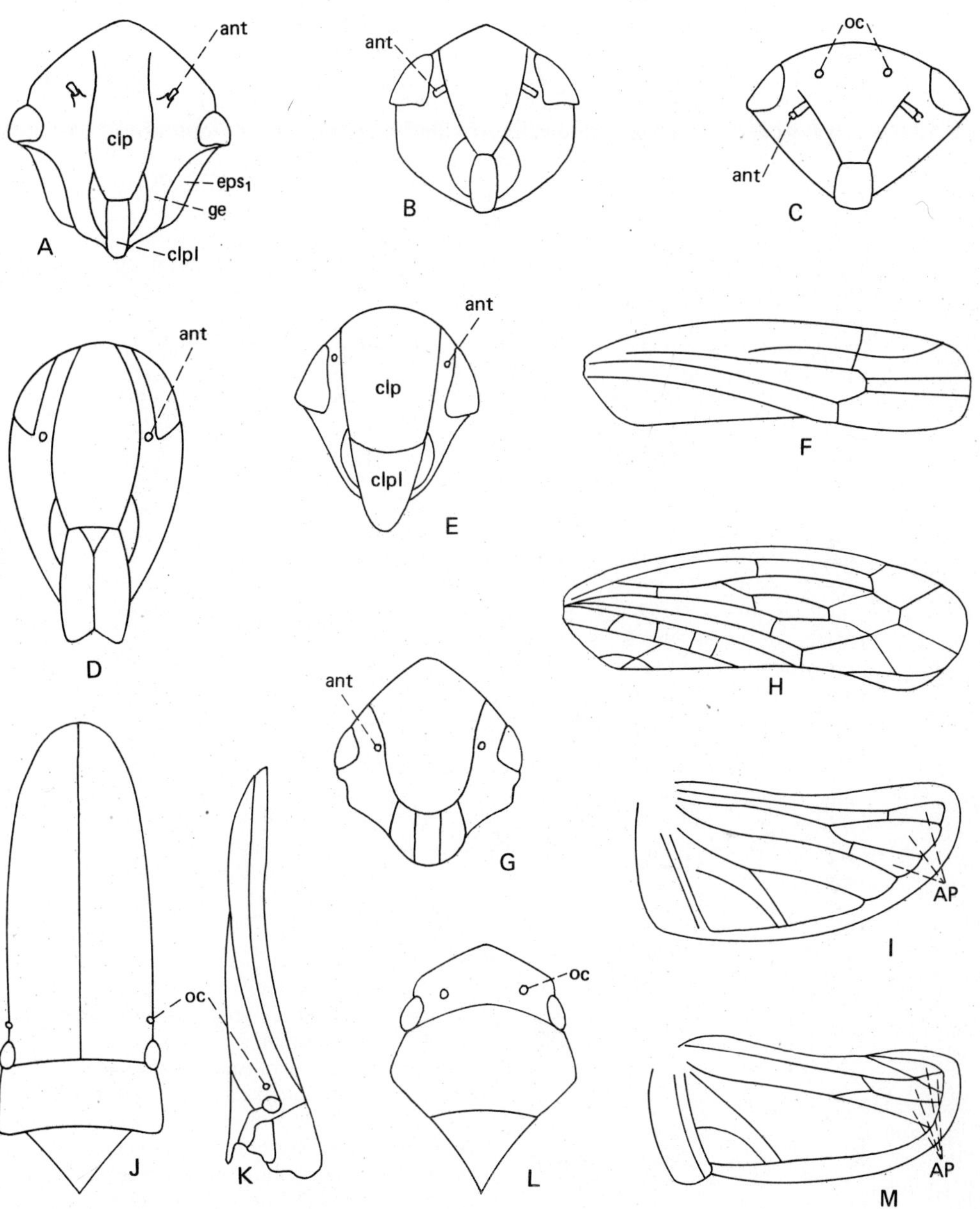

Figure 211. Characters of leafhoppers. A, face of *Xerophloèa víridis* (Fabricius) (Ledrìnae); B, face of *Paraphlépsius irroràtus* (Say) (Deltocephalìnae); C, face of *Idiócerus alternàtus* (Fitch) (Idiocerìnae); D, face of *Tinobrégmus viridéscens* DeLong (Coelidiìnae); E, face of *Sibòvia occatòria* (Say) (Cicadellìnae); F, front wing of *Kunzeàna marginélla* (Baker) (Typhlocybìnae); G, face of *Parabolocràtus víridis* (Uhler) (Hecalìnae); H, front wing of *Éndria inímica* (Say) (Deltocephalìnae); I, hind wing of *Macrópsis víridis* (Fitch) (Macropsìnae); J, head, pronotum, and scutellum of *Dorycéphalus platyrhýnchus* Osborn, dorsal view (Dorycephalìnae); K, same, lateral view; L, head, pronotum, and scutellum of *Xerophloèa víridis* (Fabricius), dorsal view (Ledrìnae); M, hind wing of *Aceratagállia sanguinolénta* (Provancher) (Agalliìnae). *ant,* antenna; *AP,* apical cells; *clp,* clypeus; *clpl,* clypellus; *eps*$_1$, episternum of prothorax; *ge,* gena; *oc,* ocellus.

12′. Distance between ocelli equal to or greater than the distance between antennal pits, or clypellus parallel-sided and usually not extending to apex of genae 14

13(12). Clypeus long and narrow, of nearly uniform width (Figure 211 D); crown not wider than an eye; costal margin of hind wings of macropterous forms expanded for a short distance near base; head narrower than pronotum .... **Coelidìinae** p. 305

13′. Clypeus short and broad, wider above (Figure 211 C); crown wider than an eye; costal margin of hind wings not expanded basally; head usually wider than pronotum .... **Idiocerìnae** p. 305

14(12′). Ocelli on face .... **Koebelìinae** p. 305

14′. Ocelli on or near margin of head 15

15(14′). Clypeus extended laterally over bases of antennae, thus forming relatively deep antennal pits; small leafhoppers with the head rounded, eyes small, clypeus ovate, antennae near margin of eyes, and ocelli distant from eyes .... **Xestocephalìnae** p. 305

15′. Clypeus not extended laterally over bases of antennae to form antennal pits; variable leafhoppers, but not having the above combination of characters 16

16(15′). A distinct ledge or carina above each antennal pit 17

16′. Without a ledge or carina above each antennal pit 18

17(16). The ledge above each antennal pit oblique; face strongly convex (viewed from above) .... **Neocoelidìinae** p. 305

17′. The ledge above each antennal pit transverse; face broad and relatively flat .... **Aphrodìnae** p. 305

18(16′). Lower margins of genae sinuate (Figure 211 G); body usually elongate and somewhat flattened, the crown flat or nearly so and strongly produced, with anterior margin acute or foliacious; lateral margins of pronotum carinate, and as long as or longer than width of eye in dorsal view .... **Hecalìnae** p. 304

18′. Lower margins of genae not sinuate, or if so then head not produced and body not flattened; lateral margins of pronotum short, and if carinate usually only feebly so .... **Deltocephalìnae** p. 306

Subfamily **Ledrìnae:** This group is represented in our area by about 8 species of *Xerophloèa;* they are grass feeders, and sometimes become pests of forage crops. They have the dorsum covered with numerous pits, and the ocelli are on the disc of the crown (Figure 210 B).

Subfamily **Dorycephalìnae:** This is another small group (about 9 North American species) of grass feeders, and they are chiefly southern in distribution. They are elongate and somewhat flattened, and have the head long and with the margin thin and foliacious (Figure 211 J, K).

Subfamily **Hecalìnae:** These leafhoppers (Figure 210 D) are similar to the Dorycephalìnae, but have the episterna of the prothorax largely or entirely concealed in anterior view; they feed chiefly on grasses.

Subfamily **Megophthalmìnae:** The members of this small group (7 North American species) are known only from California; their food plants are unknown.

Subfamily **Agallìinae:** This is a fairly large group (about 70 North American species) in which the head is short, the ocelli are on the face, and the frontal sutures terminate at the antennal pits. The food habits of these leafhoppers are rather varied. A few species in this group act as vectors of plant diseases; for example, species of *Aceratagállia, Agállia,* and *Agalliópsis* serve as vectors of potato yellow dwarf.

Subfamily **Macropsìnae:** In this group (over 50 North American species) the head is short and broad, and the ocelli are on the face; the anterior margin of the pronotum extends forward beyond the anterior margins of the eyes. The dorsal surface, from the crown to the scutellum, is somewhat roughened—rugulose, punctate, or striate. These leafhoppers feed on trees and shrubs.

Subfamily **Idiocerìnae:** This is a moderate-sized group (about 75 North American species) whose members are similar to the Macropsìnae, but the pronotum does not extend forward beyond the anterior margins of the eyes; these leafhoppers also feed on trees and shrubs.

Subfamily **Gyponìnae:** This is a large group (over 140 North American species) of relatively robust and somewhat flattened leafhoppers, which have the ocelli on the crown remote from the eyes and back from the anterior margin of the head; the crown is variable in shape, and may be produced and foliacious, or short and broadly rounded in front. Some species feed on herbaceous plants, and others feed on trees and shrubs. One species, *Gyponàna hásta* DeLong, acts as a vector of aster yellows, and another, *G. lámina* DeLong, acts as a vector of peach X-disease.

Subfamily **Iassìnae:** These leafhoppers are relatively robust and somewhat flattened, with the head short and the ocelli on the anterior margin of the crown, about midway between the eyes and the apex of the head. The group is a small one (23 North American species), and its members occur chiefly in the West; little is known about their food plants, but some species are known to feed on shrubs.

Subfamily **Penthimiìnae:** This group is represented in our area by only two species of *Penthímia,* which occur in the East. They are short, oval, and somewhat flattened. The ocelli are located on the crown about halfway between the eyes and the midline, and the front wings are broad with a large appendix. Their food plants are not known.

Subfamily **Koebeliìnae:** This group is represented in the United States by four species of *Koebèlia,* which occur in the West and feed on pine. The head is wider than the pronotum, and the crown is flat with a foliacious margin and a broad shallow furrow in the midline; the ocelli are on the face.

Subfamily **Coelidiìnae:** This is a small group (10 North American species) of relatively large and robust leafhoppers. The clypeus is long and narrow and of nearly uniform width (Figure 211 D; in most other leafhoppers the clypeus is wider dorsally); the head is narrower than the pronotum, with the eyes large and the crown small, and the ocelli are on the anterior margin of the crown. This group is mainly neotropical, and its known food plants are shrubs and herbaceous plants.

Subfamily **Nioniìnae:** This group is represented in our area by a single species, *Niònia pálmeri* (Van Duzee), which occurs in the southern states; its food plants are not known. This leafhopper is shining black, with the crown short and broad, and with the ocelli on the anterior margin and distant from the eyes. The anterior margin of the pronotum extends forward beyond the anterior margins of the eyes, and the anterior part of the dorsum bears numerous circular pits.

Subfamily **Aphrodìnae:** This is a small group (6 North American species), but its members are common and widely distributed. They are short, broad, and somewhat flattened, with the ocelli on the anterior margin of the crown; the head and pronotum are rugulose or coarsely granulate. Species of *Aphròdes* are known to act as vectors of aster yellows, clover stunt, and clover phyllody.

Subfamily **Xestocephalìnae:** This is a small (14 species of *Xestocéphalus*) but widely distributed group whose members are small and robust, with the head and eyes small; the crown is rounded anteriorly, with the ocelli on the anterior margin.

Subfamily **Neocoelidiìnae:** This is a small group (26 North American species), and many of its members are rather elongate in form. The face is strongly convex, and the ocelli are on the crown near the anterior margin and the eyes. Some species (*Paracoelídia*) occur on pine.

Subfamily **Cicadellìnae:** This is a fairly large group (nearly a hundred North American species), with many common species; most species are relatively large, and some are rather robust. The ocelli are on the crown, and the frontal sutures extend over the margin of the head nearly to the ocelli. Some members of this group are very strikingly colored; one of our largest and most common species is *Graphocéphala coccínea* (Foerster), which is similar in size and shape to *Draeculacéphala móllipes* (Say) (Figure 210 C), but has the wings reddish striped with bright green; the nymphs of this species are bright yellow. This species is often found on forsythia and other ornamental shrubs. Many species in this group serve as vectors of plant disease: species of *Carneocéphala, Cuérna, Draeculacéphala, Friscànus, Graphocéphala, Helochàra, Homalodísca, Neokólla, Oncometòpia,* and *Pagarònia* serve as vectors of Pierce's disease of grape; and species of *Draeculacéphala, Graphocéphala, Homalodísca,* and *Oncometòpia* serve as vectors of phony peach.

Subfamily **Typhlocybìnae:** This is a large group (over 700 North American species, more than half of which are in the genus *Erythroneùra)* of small, fragile, and often brightly colored leafhoppers (Figure 210 A, F). The ocelli may be present or absent, and the venation of the front wings is somewhat reduced—with no cross veins except in the apical portion. The food plants are varied. This group includes a number of pest species in the genera *Empoásca, Erythroneùra,* and *Typhlocỳba.*

Subfamily **Deltocephalìnae:** This is the largest subfamily of leafhoppers (over 1150 North American species), and its members are variable in form and food plants. The ocelli are always on the anterior margin of the crown, and there is no ledge above the antennal pits. Many members of this group are important vectors of plant diseases: aster yellows is transmitted by species of *Scaphytòpius, Macrósteles, Paraphlépsius,* and *Texanànus;* curly top of sugar beets is transmitted by *Circùlifer tenéllus* Baker; phloem necrosis of elm is transmitted by *Scaphòideus luteòlus* Van Duzee; clover phyllody is transmitted by species of *Macrósteles, Chlorotéttix, Colladònus,* and *Eùscelis;* and corn stunt is transmitted by species of *Dálbulus* and *Graminélla.*

SUPERFAMILY **Fulgoròidea**—Planthoppers: This is a large group, but its members are seldom as abundant as the leafhoppers or froghoppers. The species in the United States are seldom over 10 or 12 mm in length, but some tropical species reach a length of 2 inches (50 mm) or more. Many of the planthoppers have the head peculiarly modified, with that part in front of the eyes greatly enlarged and more or less snoutlike (Figure 212, especially G–I).

The planthoppers can be separated from the leafhoppers and froghoppers by the spination of the hind tibiae and the location of the antennae and ocelli. The planthoppers differ from the leafhoppers in having only a few large spines on the hind tibiae, and from both the leafhoppers and froghoppers in having the antennae arising below the compound eyes; the ocelli are usually located immediately in front of the eyes, on the side (rather than the front or dorsal surface) of the head (Figure 200 C). There is often a sharp angle separating the side of the head (where the compound eyes, antennae, and ocelli are located) and the front.

The food plants of these insects range from trees and shrubs to herbaceous plants and grasses. The planthoppers feed on the plant juices and, like many other Homóptera, produce honeydew. Many of the nymphal forms are ornamented with wax filaments. Very few planthoppers cause economic damage to cultivated plants.

Family **Delphácidae:** This is the largest family of planthoppers, and its members can be recognized by the large flattened spur at the apex of the hind tibiae (Figure 202 C, *sp*); most species are small, and many have reduced wings. The sugarcane leafhopper, *Perkinsiélla sacchàrida* Kirkaldy, which at one time was a very destructive pest in Hawaii, is a member of this family.

Family **Dérbidae:** These planthoppers are principally tropical and feed on woody fungi; most species are elongate with long wings and are rather delicate in build (Figure 212 K).

Family **Cixìidae:** This is one of the larger families of planthoppers; its members are widely distributed, but most species are tropical. Some species are subterranean feeders on the roots of grasses during their nymphal stage. The wings are hyaline and frequently ornamented with spots along the veins (Figure 212 A, D).

Family **Kinnàridae:** These planthoppers resemble the Cixìidae, but are quite small and have no dark spots on the wings. Our six species (*Oeclídius*) occur in the Southwest, but some West Indies species might occur in southern Florida.

Family **Dictyophàridae:** The members of this group are chiefly grass feeders, and are generally found in meadows. The most common eastern members of this group (*Scòlops;* Figures 212 G–I) have the head prolonged anteriorly into a long slender process; other dictyopharids have the head somewhat triangularly produced anteriorly, or not at all produced.

Family **Fulgòridae:** This group contains some of the largest planthoppers, some tropical species having a wingspread of about 6 inches (150 mm); our largest fulgorids have a wingspread of a little over 25 mm and a body length of about 13 mm. Some tropical species have the head greatly inflated anteriorly, producing a peanutlike process; this was believed to be luminous, thereby giving rise to the name "lanternflies" for these insects. Most of our species (for example, Figure 212 M) have the head short. The members of this family can generally be recognized by the reticulated anal area of the hind wings.

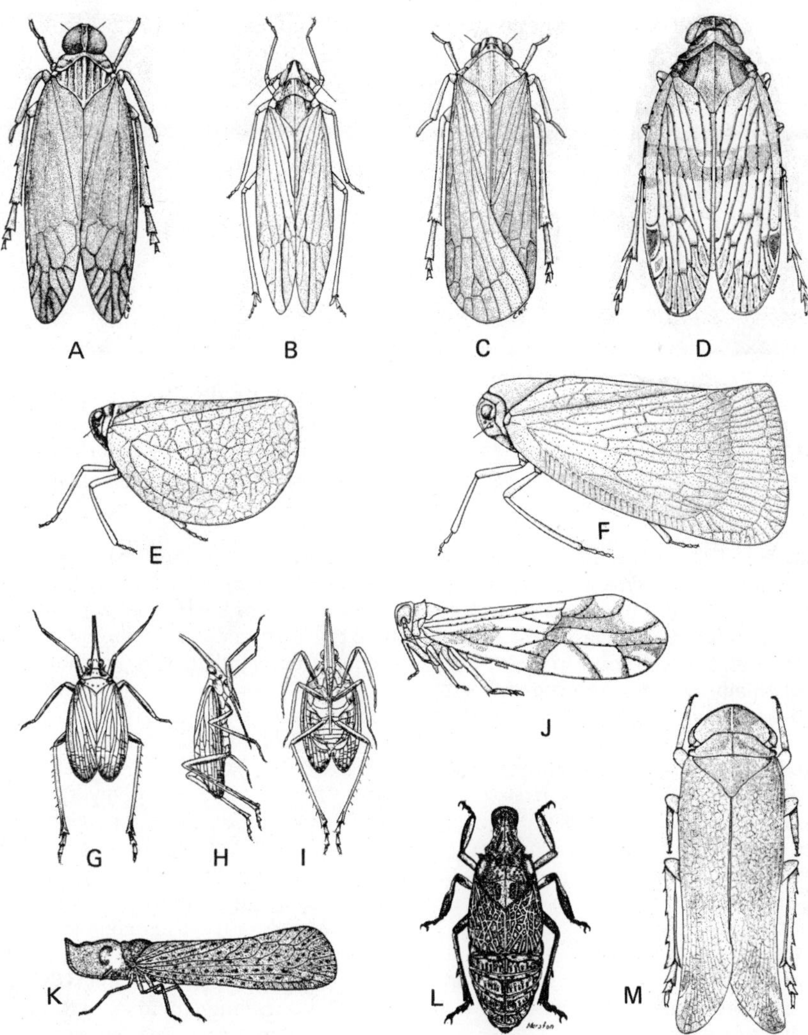

Figure 212. Planthoppers. A, *Oècleus boreàlis* Van Duzee (Cixìidae); B, *Stenocrànus dorsàlis* Fitch (Delphácidae); C, *Catònia impunctàta* (Fitch) (Achìlidae); D, *Cíxius angustàtus* Caldwell (Cixìidae); E, *Acanalònia bivittàta* (Say) (Acanalonìidae); F, *Anórmenis septentrionàlis* (Spinola) (Flàtidae); G, H, and I, *Scòlops pérdix Uhler* (Dictyophàridae), dorsal, lateral and ventral views; J, *Liburnílla ornàta* (Stål) (Delphácidae); K, *Apáche degeèrii* (Kirby) (Dérbidae); L, *Fitchiélla róbertsoni* (Fitch) (Issidae); M, *Cyrpóptus belfrágei* Stål (Fulgòridae). (Courtesy of Osborn and the Ohio Biological Survey.)

Family **Achìlidae:** These planthoppers can usually be recognized by their overlapping front wings (Figure 212 C); most species are brownish, and vary in length from about 4 to 10 mm. The nymphs usually live under loose bark or in a depression in dead wood.

Family **Tropidùchidae:** This is a tropical group, but three species have been found in Florida; the most common is probably *Pelitròpis rotulàta* Van Duzee, which has three longitudinal keels on the vertex, pronotum, and scutellum, those on the scutellum meeting anteriorly.

A

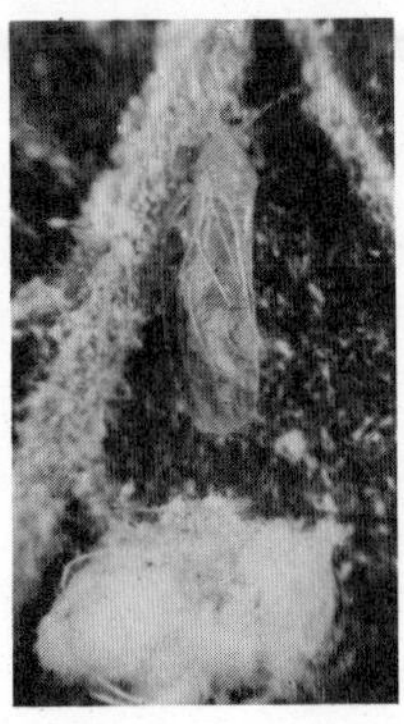
B

Figure 213. Alder psyllid, *Psýlla floccòsa* (Patch). A, groups of nymphs on alder (these groups form white cottony masses on the twigs, particularly at the base of leaf petioles); B, a newly emerged adult; below the adult is the cast skin of the nymph, still covered with the cottony secretions characteristic of the nymphs of this species.

Family **Flàtidae:** These planthoppers have a wedge-shaped appearance when at rest (Figure 212 F), and there are usually numerous cross veins in the costal area of the front wings. Most species are either pale green or dark brown in color. They appear to feed chiefly on vines, shrubs, and trees, and are usually found in wooded areas.

Family **Acanalonìidae:** These planthoppers are somewhat similar to the Flàtidae, but have a little different shape (Figure 212 E), and they do not have a lot of cross veins in the costal area of the front wings. These planthoppers are usually greenish, with brown markings dorsally.

Family **Íssidae:** This is a large and widely distributed group; most of them are dark-colored and rather stocky in build, and some have short wings and a weevil-like snout (Figure 212 L).

SUBORDER **Sternorrhýncha:** The members of this suborder are for the most part relatively inactive insects, and some (for example, most scale insects) are quite sedentary. The tarsi are 1- or 2-segmented, and the antennae (when present) are usually long and filiform. Many members of this suborder are wingless, and some scale insects lack legs and antennae and are not very insectlike in appearance.

Family **Psýllidae**—Jumping Plantlice or Psyllids: These insects are small, 2–5 mm in length, and usually resemble miniature cicadas in form (Figures 213 B, 214, and 215 B). They are somewhat similar to the aphids, but have strong jumping legs and relatively long antennae. The adults of both sexes are winged, and the beak is short and 3-segmented. The nymphs of many species produce large amounts of a white waxy secretion, causing them to superficially resemble the woolly aphids. The jumping plantlice feed on plant juices, and as in the case of most of the Homóptera, the food–plant relationships are quite specific.

Two important pest species in this group, the pear psylla, *Psýlla pyrícola* Foerster, and the apple sucker, *Psýlla máli* (Schmidberger), have been imported from Europe. A western species, the potato or tomato psyllid, *Paratriòza cockerélli* (Sulc) (Figure 214), transmits a virus that causes psyllid yellows in potatoes, tomatoes, peppers, and eggplants; this disease causes a reduction in yield due to the dwarfing and discoloration of the plant.

The cottony alder psyllid, *Psýlla floccòsa* (Patch), is a common member of this group occurring in the Northeast. The nymphs feed on alder and produce large amounts of wax, and groups of the nymphs on alder twigs resemble masses of cotton (Figure 213 A). These insects may sometimes be confused with the woolly alder aphid, *Procíphilus tessellàtus* (Fitch); the psyllid is to be

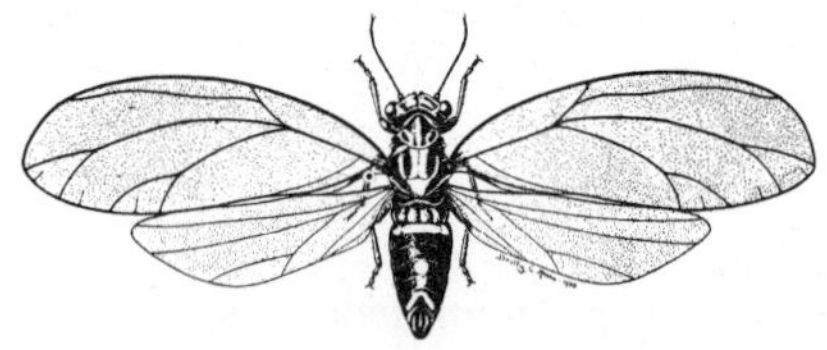

Figure 214. Potato psyllid *Paratriòza cockerélli* (Sulc). (Courtesy of Knowlton and Janes and the Entomological Society of America.)

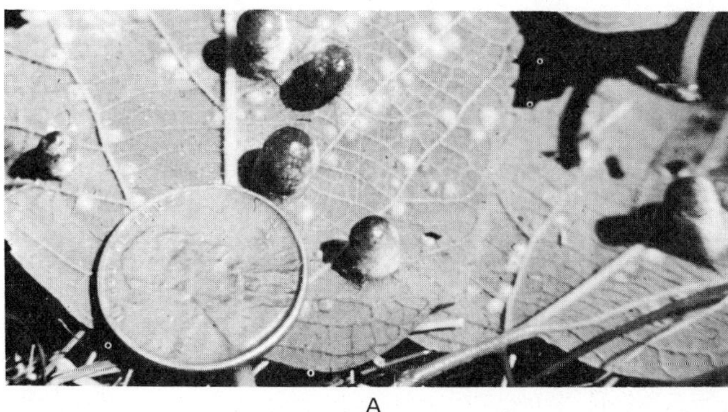

Figure 215. A, galls of *Pachypsýlla celtidismámma* (Riley) on hackberry; B, adult of *Pachypsýlla* sp., 20 × (A, courtesy of Moser; B, courtesy of Ohio Agricultural Research and Development Center.)

found on the alder only during the early part of the summer, while the aphid occurs up until fall. The adults of the cottony alder psyllid (Figure 213 B) are pale green in color.

A few of the psyllids are gall-making forms; species of *Pachypsýlla* produce small galls on the leaves of hackberry (Figure 215).

Family **Aleyròdidae**—Whiteflies: The whiteflies are minute insects, rarely over 2 or 3 mm in length, which resemble tiny moths. The adults of both sexes are winged, and the wings are covered with a white dust or waxy powder. The adults are usually active whitish insects that feed on leaves.

The metamorphosis of whiteflies is somewhat different from that of most other Homóptera. The first-instar young are active, but subsequent immature instars are sessile and look like scales; the scalelike covering is a waxy secretion of the insect and has a rather characteristic appearance (Figure 216). The wings develop internally during metamorphosis, and the early instars are usually called larvae; the next to the last instar is quiescent and is usually called a pupa. The wings are everted at the molt of the last larval instar.

The whiteflies are most abundant in the tropics and subtropics, and the most important pest species in this country are those that attack citrus trees and greenhouse plants. The damage is done by sucking sap from the leaves. One of the most serious pests in this group is *Aleurocánthus wóglumi* Ashby, which attacks citrus trees and is well established in the West Indies and Mexico. An objectionable sooty fungus often grows on the honeydew excreted by whiteflies and interferes with photosynthesis; this fungus is more prevalent in the South and in the tropics than in the North.

Family **Aphídidae**—Aphids or Plantlice: The aphids constitute a large group of small, soft-bodied insects that are frequently found in large numbers sucking the sap from the stems or leaves of plants. Such aphid groups often include individuals in all stages of development. The members of this family can usually be recognized by their characteristic pearlike shape, a pair of cornicles at

Figure 216. "Pupae" of mulberry whiteflies, *Tetraleuròdes mòri* (Quaintance). (Courtesy of the Ohio Agricultural Research and Development Center.)

the posterior end of the abdomen, and the fairly long antennae; winged forms can usually be recognized by the venation and the relative size of the front and hind wings (Figure 201 C). The wings at rest are generally held vertically above the body.

The cornicles of aphids are tubelike structures arising from the dorsal side of the fifth or sixth abdominal segment; they secrete a defensive fluid. In some species the body is more or less covered with white waxy fibers, secreted by dermal glands. Aphids also excrete honeydew, which is emitted from the anus; the honeydew consists mainly of excess sap ingested by the insect, to which are added excess sugars and waste material. This honeydew may be produced in sufficient quantities to cause the surface of objects beneath to become sticky. Honeydew is a favorite food of many ants, and some species (for example, the corn root aphid, *Àphis maidirádicis* Forbes) are tended like cows by certain species of ants.

The life cycle of many aphids is rather unusual and complex (Figure 217). Most species overwinter in the egg stage, and these eggs hatch in the spring into females that reproduce parthenogenetically and give birth to living young. Several generations may be produced during the season in this way, with only females being produced and the young being born alive. The first generation or two usually consist of wingless individuals, but eventually winged individuals appear; in many species these winged forms migrate to a different host plant, and the reproductive process continues. In the latter part of the season the aphids migrate back to the original host plant, and a generation consisting of both males and females appears. The individuals of this bisexual generation mate, and the females lay the eggs, which overwinter.

Enormous populations of aphids can be built up in a relatively short time by this method of reproduction. The aphids would be a great deal more destructive to vegetation were it not for their numerous parasites and predators. The principal parasites of aphids are braconids and chalcids, and the most important predators are ladybird beetles, lacewings, and the larvae of certain syrphid flies.

The members of this family are very similar to the Eriosomátidae, but differ in having the cornicles nearly always well developed, the wax glands much less abundant, the sexual female

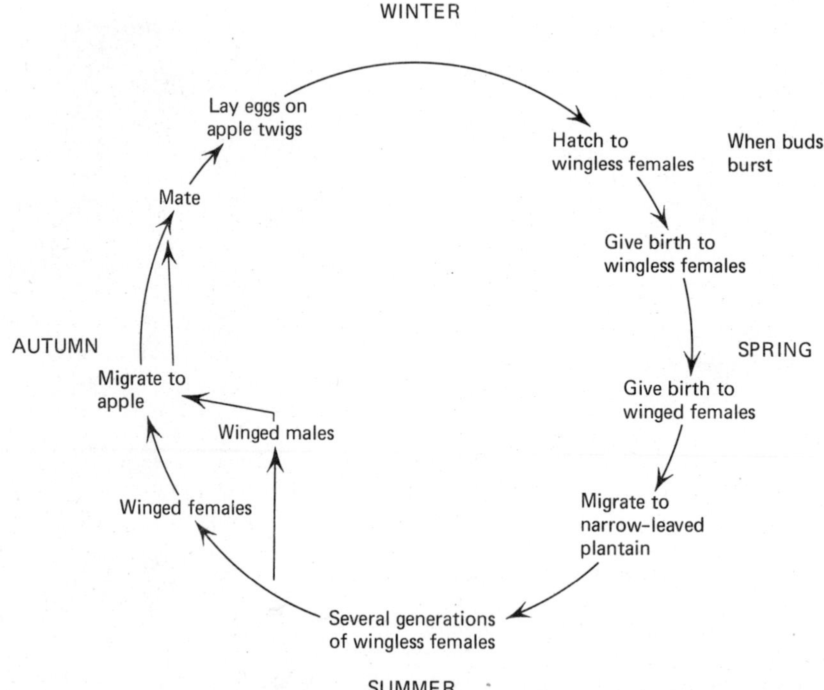

Figure 217. Diagram of the life history of the rosy apple aphid, *Dysàphis plantagínea* (Passerini).

A

B

Figure 218. Plant injury by aphids. A, injury by an infestation of the rusty plum aphid, *Hysteroneùra setàriae* (Thomas); B, curling of the leaves of wild sunflower caused by *Àphis debilicórnis* (Gillette and Palmer). (Courtesy of the Illinois Natural History Survey.)

(and usually also the male) with functional mouth parts, and the ovipositing female producing more than one egg.

This family contains a number of serious pests of cultivated plants. Aphids cause a curling or wilting of the food plant by their feeding (Figure 218 B), and they serve as vectors of a number of important plant diseases. Several virus diseases are transmitted by aphids, including the mosaics of beans, sugar cane, and cucumbers, by species of *Àphis, Macrosìphum,* and *Mỳzus,* beet mosaic by *Àphis rùmicis* L., and cabbage ring spot, crucifer mosaic, and potato yellow dwarf by *Mỳzus pérsicae* (Sulzer) (see Table 5, Chapter 33).

The rosy apple aphid, *Dysàphis plantagínea* (Passerini), overwinters on apple and related trees and passes the early summer generations there, then migrates to the narrow-leaved plantain as the secondary host; later in the season migration back to the apple takes place (Figure 217). The apple grain aphid, *Rhopalosìphum fítchii* (Sanderson), has the apple as its primary host plant, and migrates in early summer to various grasses, including wheat and oats. Other species of importance are the apple aphid, *Àphis pòmi* De Geer, the cotton aphid, *A. gossýpii* Glover, the potato aphid, *Macrosìphum euphòrbiae* (Thomas), the rose aphid, *M. ròsae* (L.), the pea aphid, *Acyrthosìphon pìsum* (Harris), and the cabbage aphid, *Brevicòryne brássicae* (L.). The largest aphid in the East is the giant bark aphid, *Longistígma càryae* (Harris), 6 mm in length, which feeds on hickory, sycamore, and other trees (Figure 219).

The corn root aphid, *Àphis màidirádicis* Forbes, is sometimes a serious pest of corn, and it has an interesting relationship with ants. The eggs of this aphid pass the winter in the nests of certain

Figure 219. A colony of apterous viviparous females and nymphs of the giant bark aphid, *Longistígma càryae* (Harris). (Courtesy of the Illinois Natural History Survey.)

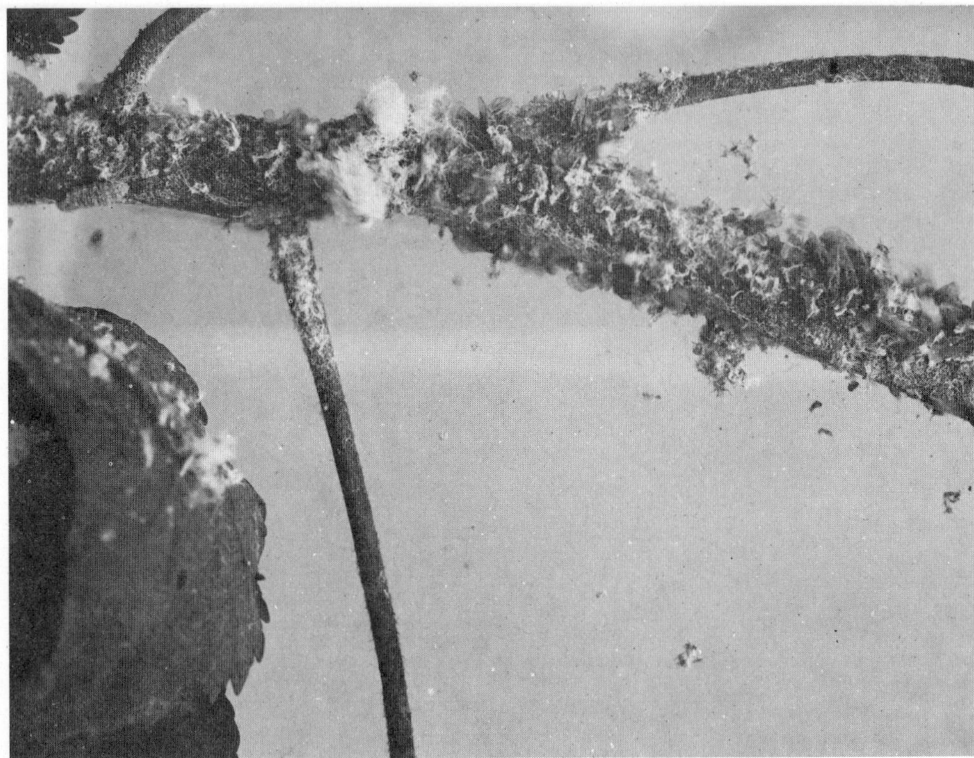

Figure 220. A colony of woolly apple aphids, *Eriosòma lanígerum* (Hausman). (Courtesy of the Ohio Agricultural Research and Development Center.)

field ants, chiefly those in the genus *Làsius*. In the spring, the ants carry the young aphids to the roots of smartweed and other weeds, where the aphids feed; later in the season, the ants transfer the aphids to the roots of corn. When the aphid eggs are laid in the fall, they are gathered by the ants and stored in their nest for the winter. All during the season the aphids are tended by the ants, which transfer them from one food plant to another; the ants feed on the honeydew produced by the aphids.

Family **Eriosomátidae**—Woolly and Gall-Making Aphids: The cornicles are reduced or absent in this group, and wax glands are abundant; the sexual forms lack mouth parts, and the ovipositing female produces only one egg. Nearly all members of this family alternate between host plants, with the primary host (on which the overwintering eggs are laid) usually a tree or shrub, and the secondary host a herbaceous plant. These aphids may feed either on the roots of the host plant or on the part of the plant above the ground. Many species produce galls or malformations of the tissues of the primary host, but usually do not produce galls on the secondary host.

The woolly apple aphid, *Eriosòma lanígerum* (Hausmann) (Figure 220), is a common and important example of this group. This species feeds principally on the roots and bark and can be recognized by the characteristic woolly masses of wax on its body. These aphids usually overwinter on the elm, and the first generations of the season are spent on that host; in early summer, winged forms appear and migrate to apple, hawthorn, and related trees. Later in the season some of these migrate back to the elm, where the bisexual generation is produced and the overwintering eggs are laid; other individuals migrate from the branches of the apple tree to the roots, where they produce gall-like growths. The root-inhabiting forms may remain there a year or more, passing

Figure 221. Aphid galls. A, elm cockscomb gall, caused by *Cólopha ulmícola* (Fitch); B, spiny bud gall of witch hazel, caused by *Hamamelístes spinòsus* Shimer; C, leaf petiole gall of poplar, caused by *Pémphigus populitransvérsus* Riley; D, vagabond gall of poplar, caused by *Pémphigus vagabúndus* Walsh. (A–C, courtesy of the Illinois Natural History Survey; D, courtesy of the Ohio Agricultural Research and Development Center.)

through several generations. This aphid transmits perennial canker.

The woolly alder aphid, *Procíphilus tessellàtus* (Fitch) is often found in dense masses on the branches of alder and maple. All the generations may be passed on alder, or the species may overwinter on maple and migrate to the alder in the summer and then back to maple in the fall, where the sexual forms are produced. The species may overwinter in either the egg or nymphal stages.

Some of the more common gall-making species in this group are *Cólopha ulmícola* (Fitch), which causes the cockscomb gall on elm leaves (Figure 221 A); *Hormàphis hamamélidis* (Fitch), which causes the cone gall on the leaves of witch hazel; *Hamamelístes spinòsus* Shimer, which forms a spiny gall on the flower buds of witch

Figure 222. Eastern spruce gall, caused by *Adélges abìetis* (L.). (Courtesy of the Ohio Agricultural Research and Development Center.)

hazel (Figure 221 B); and *Pémphigus pópuli-transvérsus* Riley, which forms a marble-shaped gall on the stems of poplar leaves (Figure 221 C).

Family **Chérmidae**—Pine and Spruce Aphids: The members of this group feed only on conifers; they live on the needles, twigs, or in galls. Most species alternate in their life history between two different conifers, forming galls only on the primary host tree. All the females are oviparous. The antennae are 5-segmented in the winged forms, 4-segmented in the sexual forms, and 3-segmented in the wingless parthenogenetically reproducing females. The body is often covered with waxy threads, and the wings at rest are held rooflike over the body. Cu_1 and Cu_2 in the front wing are separated at the base (Figure 199 E).

The eastern spruce gall aphid, *Adélges abìetis* (L.), is a fairly common species attacking spruce in the northeastern part of the country and forming pineapple-shaped galls on the twigs (Figure 222). It has two generations a year, and both generations consist entirely of females; there is no bisexual generation. Both generations occur on spruce. Partly grown nymphs pass the winter attached to the base of the spruce buds. The nymphs mature into females the following April or May and lay their eggs at the base of the buds. The feeding of these females on the needles of the new shoots causes the needles to swell. The eggs hatch in about a week, and the nymphs settle on the needles that have become swollen by the feeding of the mother; the twig-swelling continues and a gall is formed, and the nymphs complete their development in cavities in the gall. Later in the summer, winged females emerge from the galls and lay their eggs on the needles of nearby branches; these eggs hatch and the nymphs overwinter.

Family **Phylloxèridae**—Phylloxerans: The antennae in this group are 3-segmented in all forms, and the wings at rest are held flat over the body. Cu_1 and Cu_2 in the front wing are stalked at the base (Figure 199 C). These insects do not produce waxy threads, but some species are covered with a waxy powder. The phylloxerans feed on plants other than conifers, and the life history is often very complex.

The grape phylloxera, *Phylloxèra vitifòliae* (Fitch), is a common and economically important species in this group. This minute form attacks both the leaves and the roots of the grape, forming small galls on the leaves (Figure 223) and gall-like swellings on the roots. The European grapes are much more susceptible to the attacks of this insect than are the native American grapes.

SUPERFAMILY **Coccòidea**—Scale Insects: This group is a large one and contains forms that are minute and highly specialized; many are so modified that they look very little like other Homóptera. The females are wingless and usually legless and sessile, and the males have only a single pair of wings (rarely, the males, too, are wingless); the males lack mouth parts and do not feed, the abdomen terminates in one (rarely two) long stylelike process (Figure 224 A), and the hind wings are reduced to small halterlike processes that usually terminate in a hooked bristle. The antennae of the female may be lacking or may have up to 11 segments; the antennae of the male have 10–25 segments. Male scale insects look very much like small gnats, but can usually be recognized by the absence of mouth parts and the presence of a stylelike process at the end of the abdomen.

The development of scale insects varies somewhat in different species, but in most cases it is rather complex. The first instar nymphs have legs and antennae and are fairly active insects; they are often called crawlers. After the first molt, the legs and antennae are often lost and the insect becomes sessile, and a waxy or scalelike covering

Figure 223. Galls on grape leaves caused by the grape phylloxera, *Phylloxèra vitifòliae* (Fitch). (Courtesy of the Ohio Agricultural Research and Development Center.)

is secreted and covers the body. In the armored scales (Diaspídidae), this covering is often separate from the body of the insect. The females remain under the scale covering when they become adult, and produce their eggs or give birth to their young there. The males develop much like the females, except that the last instar preceding the adult is quiescent and is often called a pupa; the wings develop externally in the pupa.

Family **Orthezìidae**—Ensign Coccids: These scales occur on the roots of plants. The females are distinctly segmented, elongate-oval, with 4- to 9-segmented antennae, and are covered with hard, white, waxy plates (Figure 225 A); some have a wax egg sac at the posterior end of the body. *Orthèzia insígnis* Browne is a common and important greenhouse pest; it is native to the tropics, but has become widely distributed throughout the world on ornamental plants.

Family **Margaròdidae**—Giant Coccids and Ground Pearls: The females in this group are large and rounded and have the body segmented; the legs may be well developed or reduced. This family is small but is worldwide in distribution. It contains some of the largest species in the superfamily; some in the genera *Llavèia* and *Callipáppus* may reach a length of about 25 mm. An interesting species occurring in Mexico, *Llavèia áxin* (Llave), is used by the natives as a source of substances used in making varnish. Beads are made from tropical ground pearls that are metallic bronze or gold in color; these ground pearls are the wax cysts of females of the genus *Margaròdes,* which live on the roots of plants. The cottony cushion scale, *Icérya púrchasi* Maskell, is an important pest of citrus in the West. A few other species in this group occur in the southern United States.

Family **Diaspídidae**—Armored Scales: This is the largest family of scale insects and contains a number of very important pest species. The females are very small and soft-bodied, and are concealed under a scale covering that is usually free from the body of the insect beneath. The scale covering is formed of wax secreted by the insect, together with the cast skins of the early instars. The scales vary in different species; they may be circular or elongate, smooth or rough, and variously colored; the scales of the male are usually smaller and more elongate than those of the female. The adult females have the body small, flattened, and disclike, and the segmentation is frequently obscure; they have neither eyes nor legs, and the antennae are absent or vestigial; the males are winged and have well-developed legs and antennae.

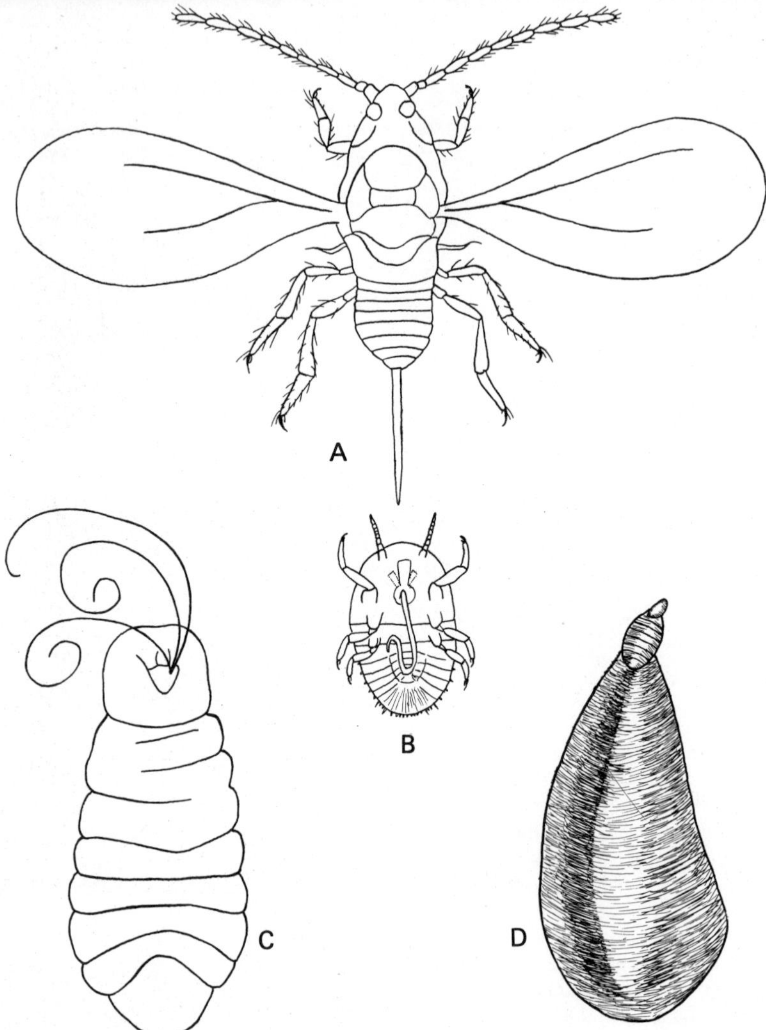

Figure 224. Stages of the oystershell scale, *Lepidósaphes úlmi* (L.). A, adult male; B, newly hatched young, or crawler; C, adult female; D, scale of female. (Redrawn from various sources.)

Reproduction may be bisexual or parthenogenetic; some species are oviparous, and others give birth to living young. The eggs are laid under the scale. The first instar young, or crawlers, are active insects and may travel some distance; they are able to live several days without food. A species is spread in this crawler stage, either by the locomotion of the crawler itself or by the crawlers' being transported on the feet of birds or by other means. Eventually the crawlers settle down, insert their mouth parts into the host plant, and the females remain sessile the remainder of their lives.

These insects injure plants by sucking sap, and when numerous may kill the plant. The armored scales feed principally on trees and shrubs and may sometimes heavily encrust the twigs or branches. Several species are important pests of orchard and shade trees.

The San Jose scale, *Quadraspidiòtus perniciòsus* (Comstock) (Figure 226), is a very serious pest. It first appeared in California about 1880, probably from the Orient, and has since spread throughout the country. It attacks a number of different trees and shrubs, including orchard trees,

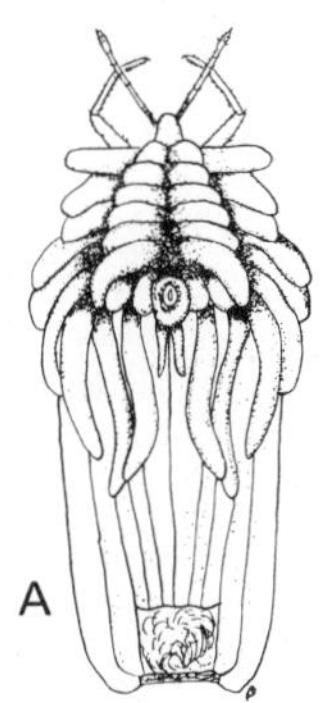

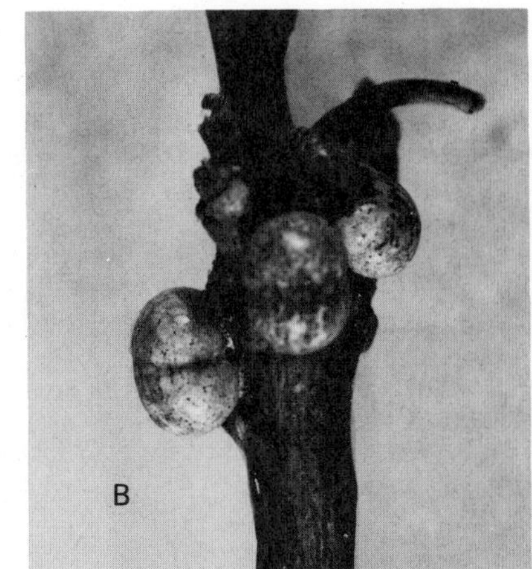

Figure 225. A, an ensign coccid, *Orthèzia solidáginis* (Sanders), female; B, bur oak gall-like coccid, *Kérmes pubéscens* (Bogue). (A, redrawn from Sanders; B, courtesy of the Ohio Agricultural Research and Development Center.)

Figure 226. San Jose scale, *Quadraspidiòtus perniciòsus* (Comstock). (Courtesy of the Ohio Agricultural Research and Development Center.)

shade trees, and ornamental shrubs, and when numerous may kill the host plant. The scale is somewhat circular in shape. This species gives birth to living young.

The oystershell scale, *Lepidósaphes úlmi* (L.), is another important species; it is so named because of the shape of its scale (Figure 227). This widely distributed species attacks a number of plants, including most fruit trees and many ornamental trees and shrubs. Plants heavily infested are often killed. The oystershell scale lays eggs which overwinter under the scale of the female.

A number of other armored scales are somewhat less important than the two just mentioned. The scurfy scale, *Chionáspis fúrfura* (Fitch), is a common whitish scale that attacks a number of trees and shrubs. The rose scale, *Aulacáspis ròsae* (Bouché), is a reddish insect with a white scale and attacks various types of berries and roses;

Figure 227. Oystershell scale, *Lepidósaphes úlmi* (L.). (Courtesy of the Ohio Agricultural Research and Development Center.)

Figure 228. Terrapin scale, *Lecànium nigrofasciàtum* Pergande (Cóccidae).

heavily infested plants look as though they have been whitewashed. The pine needle scale, *Phenacáspis pinifòliae* (Fitch), is common throughout the country on pine, and sometimes attacks other evergreens.

Several tropical or subtropical species in this group attack citrus or greenhouse plants. The California red scale, *Aonidiélla aurántii* (Maskell), is an important pest of citrus in California; the female has a circular scale slightly larger than that of the San Jose scale.

Family **Aclérdidae:** This is a small family, most of the members of which attack grasses; these scales usually occur beneath the leaf sheaths or are crowded among the crowns of the roots. A few species occur on orchids and species of Cyperàceae and Combretàceae.

Family **Cóccidae**—Soft Scales, Wax Scales, and Tortoise Scales: The females in this group are flattened elongate-oval insects with a hard smooth exoskeleton, or are covered with wax; legs are present or absent, and the antennae are either absent or much reduced. The males may be winged or wingless. The female of many species is somewhat tortoise-shaped.

This family contains a number of injurious species. The black scale, *Saissètia òleae* (Bernard), is a tropical species that is widely distributed; it is an important pest of citrus and other plants in the South. The hemispherical scale, *S. cóffeae* (Walker), is a common pest of ferns and other plants in homes and greenhouses. Several species attack various shade and fruit trees; the tuliptree scale, *Toumeyélla liriodéndri* (Gmelin), is one of the largest scale insects in this country, the adult female being about 8 mm in length; the cottony maple scale, *Pulvinària innumerábilis* (Rathvon) is a relatively large species (about 6 mm in length) in which the eggs are laid in a large cottony mass that protrudes from the end of the scale (Figure 229). Soft scales belonging to the genus *Lecànium* (Figure 228) attack a variety of plants and often become pests in greenhouses.

The Chinese wax scale, *Ericèrus pèla* Chavannes, is an interesting and important oriental species. The males secrete large amounts of a pure white wax, which is used in making candles. Wax is also produced by the wax scales of the genus *Ceroplástes*; the Indian wax scale, *C. cerîferus* An-

Figure 229. Cottony maple scale, *Pulvinària innumerábilis* (Rathvon). (Courtesy of the Ohio Agricultural Research and Development Center.)

derson, produces a wax that is used for medicinal purposes.

Family **Lacciféridae**—Lac Insects: The females in this group are globular in form, legless, and have minute 3- or 4-segmented antennae. These insects live in cells of resin, and most of them are tropical or subtropical. The Indian lac insect, *Láccifer lácca* (Kern), is the most important species in this group, and one of great commercial value. It occurs on fig, banyan, and other plants in India, Indo-China, Formosa, Ceylon, and the Philippine Islands. The bodies of the females become covered with heavy exudations of wax or lac, and are sometimes so numerous that the twigs are coated with lac to a thickness of 6 to 13 mm. The twigs are cut and the lac is melted off, refined, and used in the preparation of shellac and varnishes. About 4 million pounds of this material are produced yearly. A few species in the genus *Tachardiélla* occur in the southwestern United States, where they feed on cactus and other desert plants. They all produce lac, some of which is highly pigmented.

Family **Asterolecanìidae**—Pit Scales: The pit scales are small, elongate-oval coccids in which the body of the female may be covered by a tough waxy film or embedded in a waxy mass; the legs are vestigial or absent, eyes are lacking, and the antennae are short and 4- to 9-segmented. The oak wax scale, *Cerocóccus quércus* Comstock, is completely encased in a mass of wax; this species occurs on oak in California and Arizona, and was once used as chewing gum by the Indians.

Family **Pseudocóccidae**—Mealybugs: The name mealybug is derived from the mealy or waxy secretions that cover the bodies of these insects. The body of the female is elongate-oval, segmented, and has well-developed legs (Figure 230). Some species lay eggs, and others give birth to living young; when eggs are laid, they are placed in loose cottony wax. Mealybugs may be found on almost any part of the host plant. The most important pest species in this group are the citrus mealybug, *Planocóccus cítri* (Risso), the citrophilus mealybug, *Pseudocóccus frágilis* Brain, and the longtailed mealybug, *Pseudocóccus longispìnus* (Targioni-Tozzetti). *P. cítri* and *P. frágilis* are serious pests of citrus and also attack greenhouse plants; *P. longispìnus* is often found in greenhouses, where it attacks a variety of plants.

Family **Eriocóccidae**—Mealybugs: These insects are similar to the pseudococcids, but the body of the immature stages is bare or only slightly covered with wax. This is a widely distributed group. The European elm scale, *Gossypària spùria* (Modeer), is a common pest of elms in North America and Europe. This family contains the tamarisk manna scale, *Trabutìna mannípara* (Ehrenberg), which probably produced the manna for the Children of Israel. This species feeds on

Figure 230. Citrus mealybug, *Planocóccus cítri* (Risso). (Courtesy of the Ohio Agricultural Research and Development Center.)

plants in the genus *Támarix*, and the females excrete large quantities of honeydew; in arid regions the honeydew solidifies on the leaves and accumulates in thick layers to form a sweet sugar-like material called manna.

Family **Dactylopìidae**—Cochineal Insects: These insects resemble the mealybugs in appearance and habits. The females are red in color, elongate-oval in shape, and distinctly segmented, and the body is covered with white waxy plates; the legs and antennae are short. This family contains only two genera, *Epicóccus* and *Dactylòpius*. The cochineal insect, *D. cóccus* Costa, feeds on opuntia (prickly pear) cacti and is important as the source of a crimson dye produced by the natives of Mexico. The females, when mature, are brushed from the cacti, dried, and the pigments are extracted from the dried bodies. These insects were commercially important until about 1875, when aniline dyes were introduced.

Family **Kérmidae**—Gall-like Coccids: The females in this group are spherical, hemispherical, or oval; legs are absent in the adult, and the antennae are 4- to 6-segmented. Members of the genus *Kérmes* live on the twigs of oak; they are spherical in shape and resemble tiny galls (Figure 225 B).

COLLECTING AND PRESERVING HOMÓPTERA

The methods of collecting and preserving Homóptera vary with the group concerned. The active species are collected and preserved much like other insects, but special techniques are used for such forms as the aphids and scale insects.

Most of the active species of Homóptera are best collected by sweeping. Different species occur on different types of plants, and one should collect from as many different types of plants as possible to secure a large number of species. The smaller hopping species may be removed from the net with an aspirator, or the entire net contents can be stunned and sorted later. Forms that are not too active can be collected from foliage or twigs directly into a killing jar, without using a net. Some of the cicadas, which spend most of their time high in trees, may be collected with a long-handled net; they may be dislodged with a long stick in the hope that they will land within net range, or they may be shot. A slingshot loaded with sand or fine shot, or a rifle or shotgun loaded with dust shot, may be used to collect cicadas that are out of reach of a net.

Cicadas, the various hoppers, whiteflies, and psyllids are usually mounted dry, either on pins or points; whiteflies and psyllids are sometimes preserved in fluids and mounted on microscope slides for study. Aphids that are pinned or mounted on points usually shrivel; these insects should be preserved in fluids and mounted on microscope slides for detailed study.

Scale insects may be preserved in two general ways: the part of the plant containing the scales may be collected, dried, and mounted (pinned or in a Riker mount), or the insect may be specially treated and mounted on a microscope slide. No special techniques are involved in the first method; this is satisfactory if one is interested only in the form of the scale; the insects themselves must be mounted on microscope slides for detailed study. The best way to secure male scale insects is to rear them; very few are ever collected with a net.

In mounting a scale insect on a microscope slide, the scale is removed and the insect is cleared, stained, and mounted. Some general suggestions for mounting insects on microscope slides are given on pages 737–738; the following procedures are specifically recommended for mounting scale insects.

1. Place the dry scale insect, or fresh specimens that have been in 70 percent alcohol for at least 2 hours, in 10 percent potassium hydroxide until the body contents are soft.
2. While the specimen is still in the potassium hydroxide, remove the body contents by making a small hole in the body (at the anterior end or at the side where no taxonomically important characters will be damaged) and pressing the insect.
3. Transfer the specimen to acetic acid alcohol for 20 minutes or more. Acetic acid alcohol is made by mixing 1 part of acetic acid, 1 part of distilled water, and 4 parts of 95 percent alcohol.
4. Stain in acid fuchsin for 10 minutes or more; then transfer to 70 percent alcohol for 5 to 15 minutes, to wash out excess stain.
5. Transfer the specimen to 95 percent alcohol for 5 to 10 minutes.
6. Transfer the specimen to 100 percent alcohol for 5 to 10 minutes.
7. Transfer the specimen to clove oil for 10 minutes or more.
8. Mount in balsam.

Aphids should be preserved in 80 or 85 percent alcohol and can often be collected from the plant directly into a vial of alcohol. Winged forms are usually necessary for specific identification and should be mounted on microscope slides.

References on the Homóptera

Alexander, R. D., and T. E. Moore. 1962. The evolutionary relationships of 17-year and 13-year cicadas, and three new species (Homoptera, Cicadidae, *Magicicada*). *Misc. Pub. Mus. Zool. Univ. Mich.*, No. 121; 59 pp., frontis (color) + 10 f.

Beirne, B. P. 1956. Leafhoppers (Homoptera: Cicadellidae) of Canada and Alaska. *Can. Ent. Suppl.*, 2:1–180; 1277 f.

Britton, W. E. *et al.* 1923. The Hemiptera or sucking insects of Connecticut. *Conn. State Geol. and Nat. Hist. Surv. Bull.*, 34; 807 pp., 169 f., 20 pl.

Caldwell, J. S. 1938. The jumping plant-lice of Ohio (Homoptera: Chermidae). *Ohio Biol. Surv. Bull.*, 6(5):229–281; 11 pl.

Crawford, D. L. 1914. Monograph of the jumping plant lice or Psyllidae of the New World. *U.S. Natl. Mus. Bull.*, 85; 186 pp., 30 pl.

DeLong, D. M. 1948. The leafhoppers, or Cicadellidae, of Illinois (Eurymelinae-Balcluthinae). *Ill. Nat. Hist. Surv. Bull.*, 24(2):91–376; 514 f.

DeLong, D. M. 1971. The bionomics of leafhoppers. *Ann. Rev. Ent.*, 16:179–210.

DeLong, D. M., and P. H. Freytag. 1967. Studies of the world Gyponinae (Homoptera, Cicadellidae). A synopsis of the genus *Ponana*. *Contrib. Amer. Ent. Inst.*, 1(7):1–86; 257 f.

Doering, K. 1930. Synopsis of North American Cercopidae. *J. Kan. Ent. Soc.*, 3(3–4):53–64, 81–108; 6 pl.

Dozier, H. L. 1926. The Fulgoridae or plant-hoppers of Mississippi, including those of possible occurrence. *Miss. Agric. Expt. Sta. Tech. Bull.*, 14; 151 pp., 34 f.

Evans, J. W. 1946a. A natural classification of leafhoppers (Jassoidea, Homoptera). Part I. External morphology and systematic position. *Trans. Roy. Ent. Soc. London*, 96(3):47–60; 25 f.

Evans, J. W. 1946b. A natural classification of leafhoppers (Jassoidea, Homoptera). Part 2. Aetalionidae, Hyticidae, Eurymelidae. *Trans. Roy. Ent. Soc. London*, 97(2):39–54; 3 f.

Evans, J. W. 1947. A natural classification of leafhoppers (Jassoidae, Homoptera). Part 3. Jassidae. *Trans. Roy. Ent. Soc. London*, 98(6):105–271; 36 f.

Evans, J. W. 1963. The phylogeny of the Homoptera. *Ann. Rev. Ent.*, 8:77–94; 1 f.

Fennah, R. G. 1956. Homoptera: Fulgoroidea. *Insects of Micronesia* (Bishop Museum, Honolulu), 6(3):iv + 72 pp., 64 f.

Ferris, G. F. 1937–1955. *Atlas of the Scale Insects of North America*. Stanford, Calif.: Stanford Univ. Press, 7 vol. illus.

Funkhouser, W. D. 1917. Biology of the Membracidae of the Cayuga Lake Basin. *N.Y. (Cornell) Agric. Expt. Sta. Mem.*, 11:177–445; f. 34–43, pl. 23–44.

Hanna, M., and T. H. Moore. 1966. The spittlebugs of Michigan. *Pap. Mich. Acad. Sci.*, 51:39–73; illus.

Hottes, F. C., and T. H. Frison. 1931. The plant lice, or Aphididae, of Illinois. *Ill. Nat. Hist. Surv. Bull.*, 19(3):121–447; 47 f., 10 pl.

Kennedy, J. S., and H. L. G. Stroyan. 1959. Biology of aphids. *Ann. Rev. Ent.*, 4:139–160.

Kramer, J. P. 1966. A revision of the New World leafhoppers of the subfamily Ledrinae (Homoptera: Cicadellidae). *Trans. Amer. Ent. Soc.*, 92:469–502; illus.

Kramer, J. P. 1971. A taxonomic study of the North American leafhoppers of the genus *Deltocephalus* (Homoptera: Cicadellidae: Deltocephalinae). *Trans. Amer. Ent. Soc.*, 97(3):413–439; 107 f.

Lambers, D. H. R. 1966. Polymorphism in Aphididae. *Ann. Rev. Ent.*, 11:47–78, 4 f.

Linnavuori, R. 1959. Revision of the neotropical Deltocephalinae and some related subfamilies (Homoptera). *Ann. Zool. Soc., "Vanamo,"* 20(1):1–370; 144 f.

MacGillivray, A. D. 1921. *The Coccidae*. Urbana, Ill.: Scarab, vi + 502 pp.

McKenzie, H. L. 1967. *The Mealybugs of California*. Berkeley: Univ. California Press, 525 pp.; illus.

Metcalf, Z. P. 1923. Fulgoridae of eastern North America. *J. Elisha Mitchell Sci. Soc.*, 38:139–230; pl. 39–69 (Res. Bull. No. 1).

Metcalf, Z. P. 1945. *A Bibliography of the Homoptera (Auchenorrhyncha)*. Raleigh, N.C.: Dept. Zool. & Ent., North Carolina State College. Vol. 1. Authors' list, A–Z; 886 pp. Vol. 2. List of journals and topical index; 186 pp.

Metcalf, Z. P. 1954–1960. *General Catalogue of the Homoptera*. Raleigh, N.C.: North Carolina State College. Fasc. IV, Fulgoroidea. Part 11, Tropiduchidae, 1954, 176 pp.; part 12, Nogodinidae, 1954, 84 pp.; part 13, Flatidae and Hypochthonellidae, 1957, 574 pp.; part 14, Acanaloniidae, 1954, 64 pp.; part 15, Issidae, 1958, 570 pp.; part 16, Ricaniidae, 1955, 208 pp.; part 17, Lophopidae, 1955, 84 pp.; part 18, Eurybrachidae and Gengidae, 1956, 90 pp.

Metcalf, Z. P. 1960–1962. *General Catalogue of the Homoptera*. Raleigh, N.C.: North Carolina State College. Fasc. VII, Cercopoidea. A bibliography of the Cercopoidea, 1960, 266 pp.; part 1, Macherotidae, 1960, 56 pp.; part 2, Cercopidae, 1961, 616 pp.; part 3, Aphrophoridae, 1962, 608 pp.; part 4, Clastopteridae, 1962, 66 pp.

Metcalf, Z. P. 1962–1963. *General Catalogue of the Homoptera*. Raleigh, N.C.: North Carolina State College. Fasc. VIII, Cicadoidea. A bibliography of the Cicadoidea, 1962, 234 pp.; part 1, Cicadidae, 1963, 492 pp.; part 2, Tibicinidae, 1963, 919 pp.

Metcalf, Z. P. 1962–1967. *General Catalogue of the Homoptera*. USDA, ARS. Fasc. VI. Cicadelloidea. Part

1, Tettigellidae, 1965, 730 pp.; part 2, Hylicidae, 1962, 18 pp.; part 3, Gyponidae, 1962, 229 pp.; part 4, Ledridae, 1962, 147 pp.; part 5, Ulopidae, 1962, 101 pp.; part 6, Evacanthidae, 1963, 63 pp.; part 7, Nirvanidae, 1963, vi + 35 pp.; part 8, Aphrodidae, 1963, 268 pp.; part 9, Hecalidae, 1963, 123 pp.; part 10, Euscelidae, 1967, Section 1, v + 1077 pp., Section 2, pp. 1078–2074, Section 3, pp. 2075–2695; part 11, Coelidiidae, 1964, 182 pp.; part 12, Eurymelidae, 1965, 43 pp.; part 13, Macropsidae, 1966, 261 pp.; part 14, Agalliidae, 1966, vi + 173 pp.; part 15, Iassidae, 1966, 229 pp.; part 16, Idioceridae, 1966, 237 pp.; part 17, Cicadellidae, 1968, 1513 pp.

Metcalf, Z. P., and V. Wade. 1966. General catalogue of the Homoptera. A supplement to fascicle 1—Membracidae of the General Catalogue of the Hemiptera. A catalogue of fossil Homoptera (Homoptera: Auchenorrhyncha). *N. C. Agric. Expt. Sta. Pap.*, No. 2049; v + 245 pp.

Moore, T. E. 1966. The cicadas of Michigan (Homoptera: Cicadidae). *Pap. Mich. Acad. Sci.*, 51:75–96; illus.

Morrison, H., and A. V. Renk. 1957. A selected bibliography of the Coccoidea. *USDA Agric. Res. Serv., Misc. Pub.*, No. 734; 222 pp.

Oman, P. W. 1949. The nearctic leafhoppers (Homoptera: Cicadellidae), a generic classification and check list. *Ent. Soc. Wash. Mem.*, No. 3; 253 pp., 44 pl.

Osborn, H. 1938. The Fulgoridae of Ohio. *Ohio Biol. Surv. Bull.*, 6(6):283–349; 42 f.

Osborn, H. 1940. The Membracidae of Ohio. *Ohio Biol. Surv. Bull.*, 7(2):51–101; 31 f.

Ossiannilsson, F. 1949. Insect drummers. A study of the morphology and function of the sound-producing organs of Swedish Homoptera, Auchenorrhyncha. *Opusc. Ent. Suppl.*, 10:1–146; illus.

Shaw, K. C., A. Vargo, and O. V. Carlson. 1974. Sounds and associated behavior of *Empoasca* (Homoptera: Cicadellidae). *J. Kan. Ent. Soc.*, 47(3):284–307; 8 f.

Smith, C. F. 1972. Bibliography of the Aphididae of the world. *N.C. Agric. Expt. Sta. Tech. Bull.*, 216; 717 pp.

Wade, V. 1966. General Catalogue of the Homoptera. Species index of the Membracoidea and fossil Homoptera (Homoptera: Auchenorrhyncha). A supplement to fascicle 1—Membracidae of the General Catalogue of the Hemiptera. *N. C. Agric. Expt. Sta. Pap.*, No. 2160(2); 40 pp.

Way, M. J. 1963. Mutualism between ants and honeydew-producing Homoptera. *Ann. Rev. Ent.*, 8:307–344.

Williams, M. L., and M. Kosztarab. 1972. Morphology and systematics of the Coccidae of Virginia, with notes on their biology (Homoptera: Coccoidae). *Va. Polytech. Inst. and State Univ., Res. Div. Bull.*, 74; 215 pp.; illus.

Young, D. A. 1968. Taxonomic study of the Cicadellinae (Homoptera: Cicadellidae). Part I. Proconiini. *Smiths. Inst. Bull.*, 261; 287 pp., 261 f.

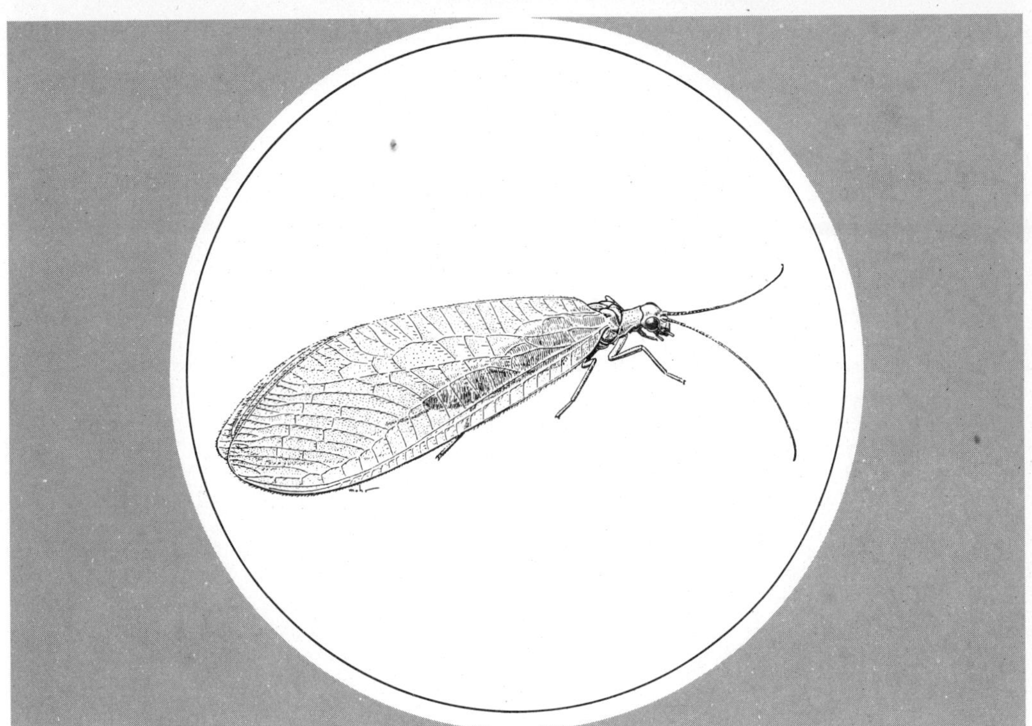

24: ORDER NEURÓPTERA[1]

ALDERFLIES, DOBSONFLIES, FISHFLIES, SNAKEFLIES, LACEWINGS, ANTLIONS, AND OWLFLIES

The Neuróptera are soft-bodied insects with four membranous wings that usually have a great many cross veins and extra branches of the longitudinal veins (hence the order name); there are generally a number of cross veins along the costal border of the wing, between C and Sc. The radial sector often bears a number of parallel branches. The front and hind wings in our species are similar in shape and venation, and are usually held rooflike over the body at rest. The mouth parts are of the mandibulate type, the antennae are generally long and many-segmented, the tarsi are 5-segmented, and cerci are absent.

[1] Neuróptera: *neuro,* nerve (referring to the wing veins); *ptera,* wings.

These insects undergo complete metamorphosis. The larvae are generally campodeiform, with mandibulate mouth parts. Most larvae are predaceous, but those of the Sisýridae feed on freshwater sponges, and those of the Mantíspidae are parasitic in the egg sacs of spiders. The mandibles of Megalóptera and Raphidiòdea larvae are relatively short, while those of Planipénnia larvae are long and sicklelike; in the Planipénnia the feeding is done by sucking the body fluids of the victim through a narrow channel formed between the mandibles and maxillae. The pupae are naked in the Megalóptera and Raphidiòdea, but in the Planipénnia pupation occurs in a silken cocoon; the silk is produced by the Malpighian tubules, and is spun from the anus.

Adult Neuróptera are found in a variety of situations, but those whose larvae are aquatic (Siálidae, Corydálidae, and Sisýridae) generally occur near water. The adults are rather weak fliers. Most adults are predaceous; some take only relatively weak prey, and adults of the Megalóptera probably feed little or not at all.

CLASSIFICATION OF THE NEURÓPTERA

The insects here included in the order Neuróptera are by some authorities divided into three orders, Megalóptera, Raphidiòdea, and Neuróptera; some authorities would include the Raphidiòdea in the Megalóptera. We are treating these three groups as suborders.

An outline of the groups in the order is given below; alternate names or spellings are given in parentheses, and groups that are rare or unlikely to be taken by the general collector are marked with an asterisk.

Suborder Megalóptera (Sialòdea)
- Siálidae—alderflies
- Corydálidae—dobsonflies and fishflies

Suborder Raphidiòdea (Raphidiòidea)—snakeflies
- Raphidìidae—raphidiid snakeflies
- Inocellìidae—inocelliid snakeflies

Suborder Planipénnia (Neuróptera in the narrow sense)
- Superfamily Coniopterygòidea
  - *Coniopterýgidae—dusty-wings
- Superfamily Ithonòidea
  - *Ithònidae—ithonid lacewings
- Superfamily Hemerobiòidea
  - Mantíspidae—mantidflies
  - Hemerobìidae (including Sympherobìidae)—brown lacewings
  - Chrysòpidae—common lacewings, green lacewings
  - *Dilàridae—pleasing lacewings
  - *Beròthidae—beaded lacewings
  - *Polystoechòtidae—giant lacewings
  - Sisýridae—spongillaflies
- Superfamily Myrmeleontòidea
  - Myrmeleóntidae—antlions
  - Ascaláphidae—owlflies

Two slightly different interpretations of the wing venation are encountered in this order. Most present workers, particularly those studying the Raphidiòdea and Planipénnia—following Martynov (1928), Carpenter (1936 and 1940), and others—believe that an anterior branch of the media (labeled MA in our figures) persists in this order, branching from M near the base of the wing and usually fusing with Rs for a short distance. These workers look upon the "basal cross vein" (the basal r-m of Comstock) as the base of MA, and upon what Comstock considers the basal branch of Rs as the distal part of MA. What Comstock calls M_{1+2} and M_{3+4} they refer to as MP_{1+2} and MP_{3+4} (MP = posterior media). Some workers refer to what Comstock calls Cu_1 and Cu_2 as CuA (the anterior cubitus) and CuP (the posterior cubitus). We have followed Comstock's interpretation in labeling our figures of the wings of the Megalóptera, Coniopterýgidae, Chrysòpidae, and Myrmeleontòidea, and the interpretation of Carpenter and others in labeling our figures of other wings in this order.

Key to the Families of Neuróptera

The families marked with an asterisk in this key are relatively rare or are unlikely to be encountered by the general collector. Keys to larvae are given by Peterson (1951).

1. Hind wings broader at base than front wings, and with an enlarged anal area that is folded fanwise at rest (Figure 231 A, B); longitudinal veins usually not forking near wing margin; larvae aquatic (suborder Megaloptera) 2

1′. Front and hind wings similar in size and shape, the hind wings without an enlarged anal area that is folded fanwise at rest (Figures 231 C, D, 232–234) 3

2(1). Ocelli present; fourth tarsal segment cylindrical; body usually 25 mm or more in length; wings hyaline or with smoky areas .... **Corydálidae** p. 329

2′. Ocelli absent; fourth tarsal segment dilated and deeply bilobed; body usually less than 25 mm in length; wings usually smoky (Figure 235) .... **Siálidae** p. 329

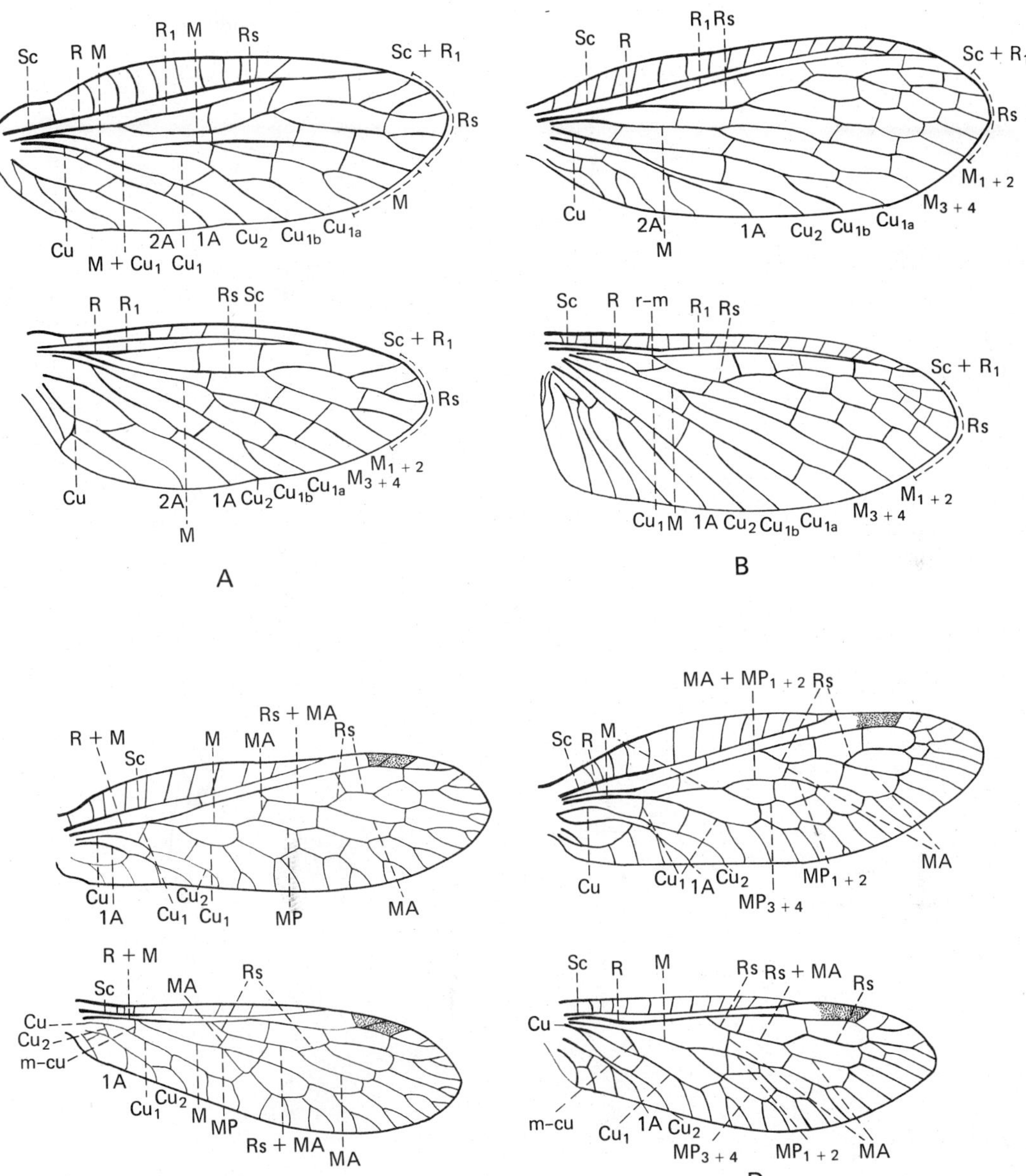

Figure 231. Wings of Neuróptera. A, *Sìalis* (Siálidae); B, *Nigrònia* (Corydálidae); C, *Agúlla* (Raphidìidae); D, *Inocéllia* (Inocellìidae). The venation in A and B is labeled with the interpretation of Comstock, and that in C and D with the interpretation of Carpenter (1936) and others. *MA*, anterior media; *MP*, posterior media; *st*, stigma.

3(1′). Wings with relatively few veins, Rs with only 2 branches (Figure 233 A); wings covered with a whitish powder; minute insects .... **Coniopterýgidae*** p. 331

3′. Wings with many veins, Rs usually with more than 2 branches (Figures 231 C, D, 232, 233 B, 234); wings not covered with a whitish powder; size

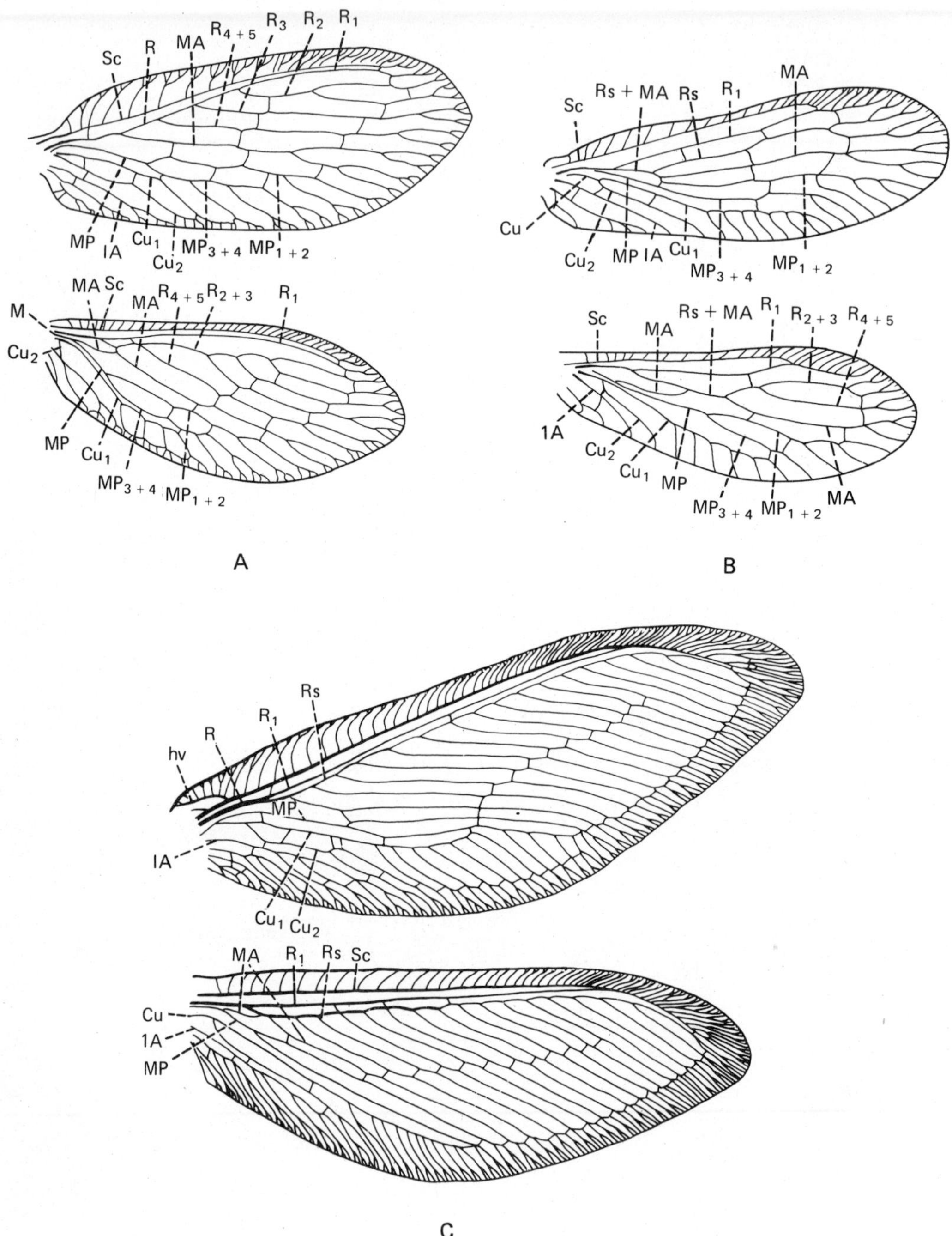

Figure 232. Wings of Neuróptera. A, *Ameromicròmus* (Hemerobìidae); B, *Climàcia* (Sisýridae); C, *Polystoechòtes* (Polystoechòtidae). The venation is labeled with the interpretation of Carpenter (1940) and others. *hv,* humeral or recurrent vein; *MA,* anterior media; *MP,* posterior media.

variable, but usually not minute 4

4(3′). Prothorax elongate (Figure 238) 5

4′. Prothorax of normal size, not elongate 7

5(4). Front legs raptorial and arising from anterior end of prothorax (Figure 238 B); mantidlike insects, widely distributed .... **Mantíspidae** p. 331

5′. Front legs not raptorial, and arising from posterior end of prothorax (Figure 238 A); western United States (suborder Raphidiòdea) 6

6(5′). Ocelli present; front wings with a stigma bordered proximally by a cross vein; hind wings with Cu_2 and 1A fused for a short distance, and basal m-cu transverse (Figure 231 C) .... **Raphidìidae** p. 329

6′. Ocelli absent; front wings with stigma not bordered proximally by a cross vein; hind wings with Cu_1 and 1A separate, and basal m-cu oblique (Figure 231 D) .... **Inocellìidae** p. 330

7(4′). Antennae clubbed or knobbed; insects with the abdomen long and slender, and resembling dragonflies or damselflies in general appearance (Figure 240) (superfamily Myrmeleontòidea) 8

7′. Antennae filiform, moniliform, or pectinate, not clubbed or knobbed; usually not particularly resembling dragonflies or damselflies in appearance 9

8(7). Antennae about as long as head and thorax together (Figure 240); truss cell (the cell behind the point of fusion of Sc and R_1, Figure 234, *trc*), very long, several times as long as wide (Figure 234 A) .... **Myrmeleóntidae** p. 332

8′. Antennae nearly or quite as long as body; truss cell short, not more than 2 or 3 times as long as wide (Figure 234 B, *trc*) .... **Ascaláphidae** p. 333

9(7′). At least some costal cross veins forked (Figure 232 A, C) 10

9′. All costal cross veins simple (Figures 232 B and 233 B) 13

10(9). Front wings with apparently 2 or more radial sectors (Figure 232 A) .... **Hemerobìidae** p. 331

10′. Front wings with only 1 radial sector, which has 2 or more branches (Figure 232 C) 11*

11(10′). Front wings with a recurrent humeral vein (Figure 232 C, *hv*); front wings 16–34 mm in length 12*

11′. Front wings without a recurrent humeral vein, and 9–13 mm in length .... **Beròthidae*** p. 332

12(11). Sc and R_1 in front wing fused distally; Rs in front wing with many branches, the cross veins between them forming a fairly distinct gradate vein; free basal portion of MA in hind wing longitudinal (Figure 232 C); widely distributed .... **Polystoechòtidae*** p. 332

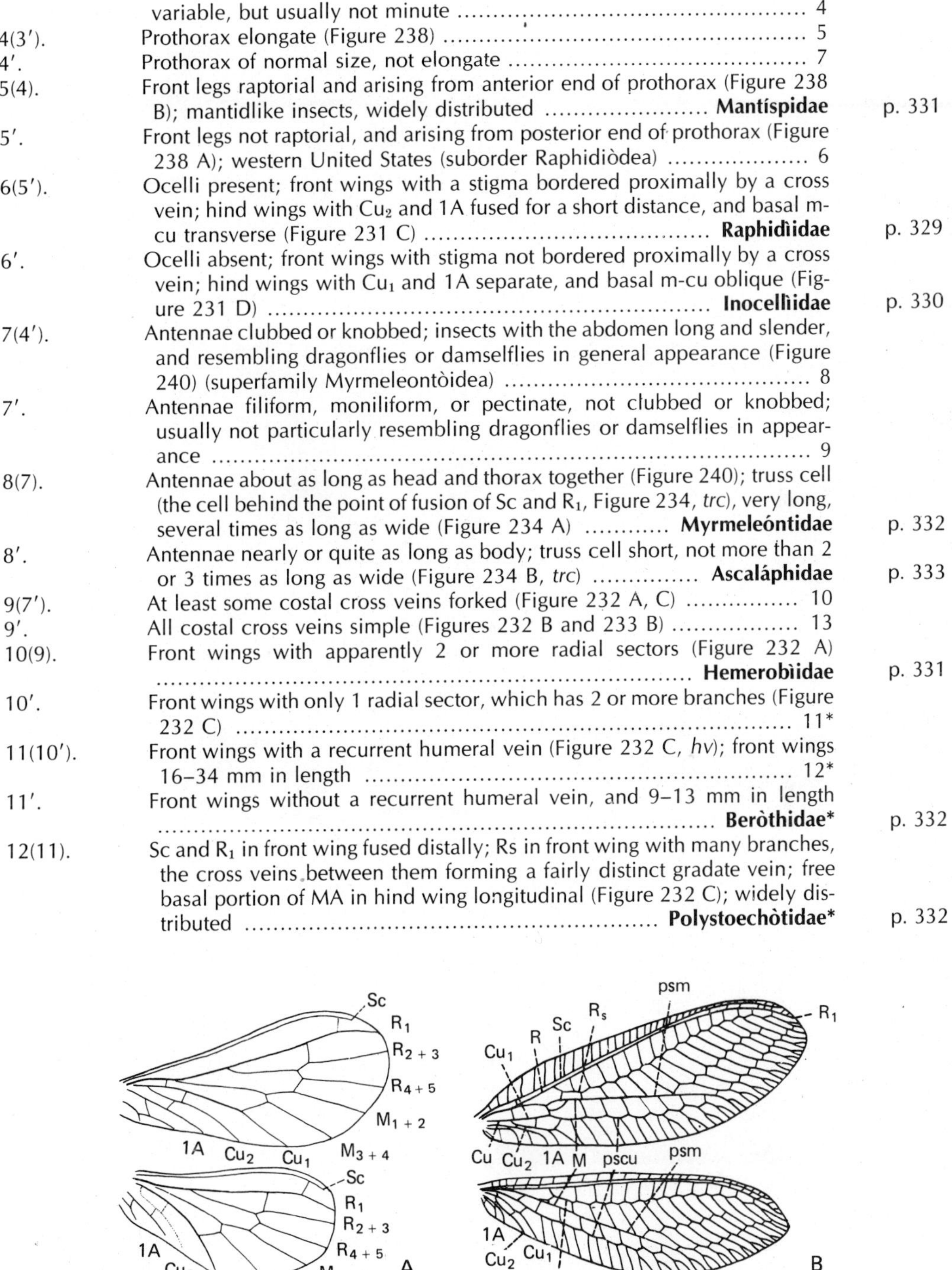

Figure 233. Wings of Neuróptera. A, *Coniópteryx* (Coniopterýgidae); B, *Chrysòpa* (Chrysòpidae). The venation is labeled with the interpretation of Comstock.

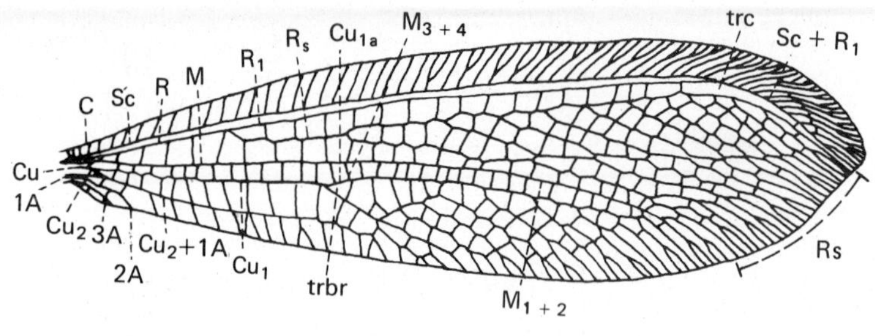

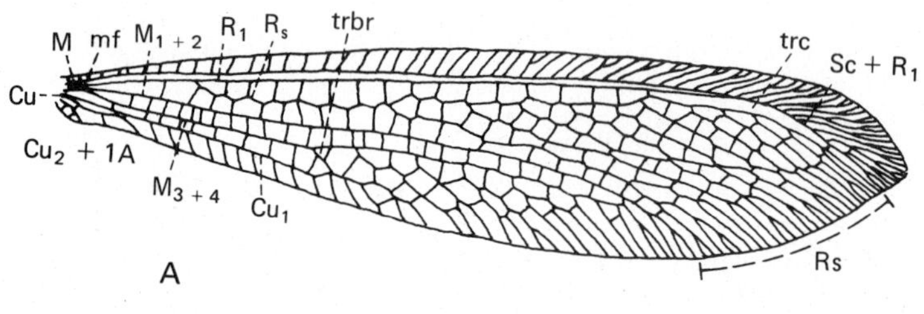

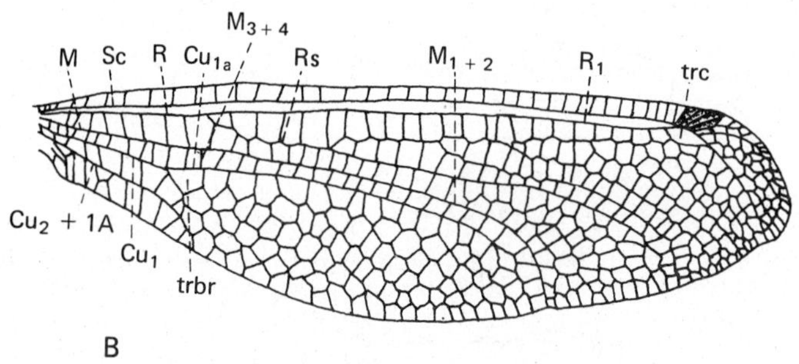

Figure 234. Wings of Myrmeleontòidea. A, *Dendròleon* (Myrmeleóntidae); B, an ascalaphid (front wing). The venation is labeled with the interpretation of Comstock. *trbr,* trigonal brace; *trc,* truss cell.

12′. Sc and R_1 in front wing not fused distally; Rs in front wing with only a few branches, the cross veins between them scattered and not forming a distinct gradate vein; free basal part of MA in hind wing short and oblique; southern California .... **Ithònidae*** p. 331

13(9′). Sc and R_1 in front wing not fused near wing tip, and Rs appearing unbranched (Figure 233 B); wings, at least in life, often greenish; very common insects .... **Chrysòpidae** p. 332

13′. Sc and R_1 in front wing fused or separate apically, and Rs appearing branched (Figure 232 B); wings not greenish; uncommon insects 14

14(13′). Antennae pectinate in male and filiform in female; female with an exserted ovipositor about as long as body; hind wing with free basal part of MA absent; front wing more or less triangular in shape, very hairy, hind wing about as long as front wing in male, about two thirds as long as front wing in female; front wing 3.0–5.5 mm in length .... **Dilàridae*** p. 332

14′. Antennae filiform in both sexes; female without an exserted ovipositor; hind wing with free basal part of MA present, longitudinal (Figure 232 B); wings elongate-oval, hind wing nearly as long as front wing, front wing 3.5–7.0 mm in length .... **Sisýridae** p. 332

SUBORDER **Megalóptera:** The members of this suborder have the hind wings broader at the base than the front wings, and this enlarged anal area is folded fanwise at rest. The longitudinal veins do not have branches near the wing margin, as do many of the other insects in this order. Ocelli may be present or absent. The larvae are aquatic, with lateral abdominal gills, and with normal jaws (not elongate and sicklelike, as in the Planipénnia); the pupae are not in cocoons.

Family **Siálidae**—Alderflies: The alderflies (Figure 235) are dark-colored insects, about 25 mm in length or less, and are usually found near water. The larvae are aquatic and are usually found under stones in streams; they are predaceous on small aquatic insects. The larvae of alderflies (Figure 237 C) differ from those of the Corydálidae in that they have a terminal filament, seven pairs of lateral filaments, and no hooked anal prolegs. *Sìalis infumàta* Newman is a common eastern species; it is about 19 mm in length and has smoky wings.

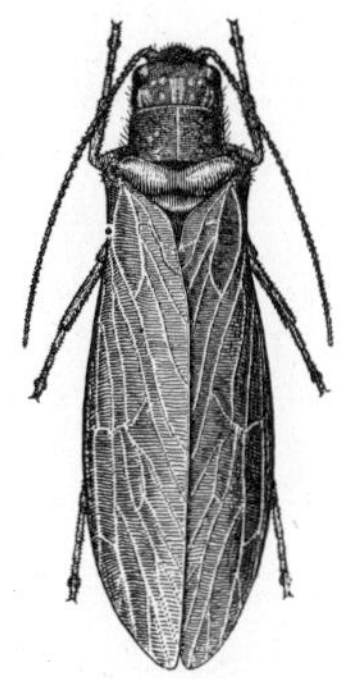

Figure 235. An alderfly, *Sìalis mòhri* Ross. (Courtesy of the Illinois Natural History Survey.)

Family **Corydálidae**—Dobsonflies and Fishflies: These insects are similar to the alderflies, but are in general larger (usually over 25 mm in length) and have ocelli. They are soft-bodied, have a rather fluttery flight, and are usually found near water. Some species are attracted to lights, and may be found some distance from water. The larvae (Figure 237 A, B) are aquatic and usually occur under stones in streams; they differ from alderfly larvae in that they have a pair of hooked anal prolegs, no terminal filament, and eight pairs of lateral filaments. These larvae are sometimes called hellgrammites and are frequently used as bait by fishermen; the jaws can inflict a painful nip.

The largest insects in this group are the dobsonflies (*Corýdalus* and *Dysmicohérmes*), which have the front wings 2 inches (50 mm) or more in length. A common eastern species (Figure 236) has a wingspread of about 5 inches (130 mm) and the males have extremely long mandibles. The smaller species in this group (front wings less than 2 inches (50 mm) in length) are called fishflies; most of them belong to the genera *Chauliòdes, Neohérmes,* and *Nigrònia.* Dobsonflies and some of the fishflies have clear wings; other fishflies (species of *Nigrònia*) have the wings black or smoky with a few small clear areas. Fishflies in the genera *Chauliòdes* and *Nigrònia* have the antennae serrate or pectinate.

SUBORDER **Raphidiòdea:** These insects, the snakeflies, are peculiar in having the prothorax elongate, somewhat as in the Mantíspidae, but the front legs are similar to the other legs and are borne at the posterior end of the prothorax (Figure 238 A). These insects can raise the head above the rest of the body, much like a snake preparing to strike. The adults are predaceous, but are capable of catching only small and weak prey. The female (which has a long ovipositor) lays her eggs in clusters in crevices in bark, and the larvae are usually found under bark. The larvae feed principally on small insects such as aphids and caterpillars. The snakeflies are restricted to the western states.

Family **Raphidìidae:** This family is represented in the United States by 17 species of *Agúlla,* which are widely distributed through the West, occurring from Arizona and California north to British Columbia and Alberta. They vary in size from a front

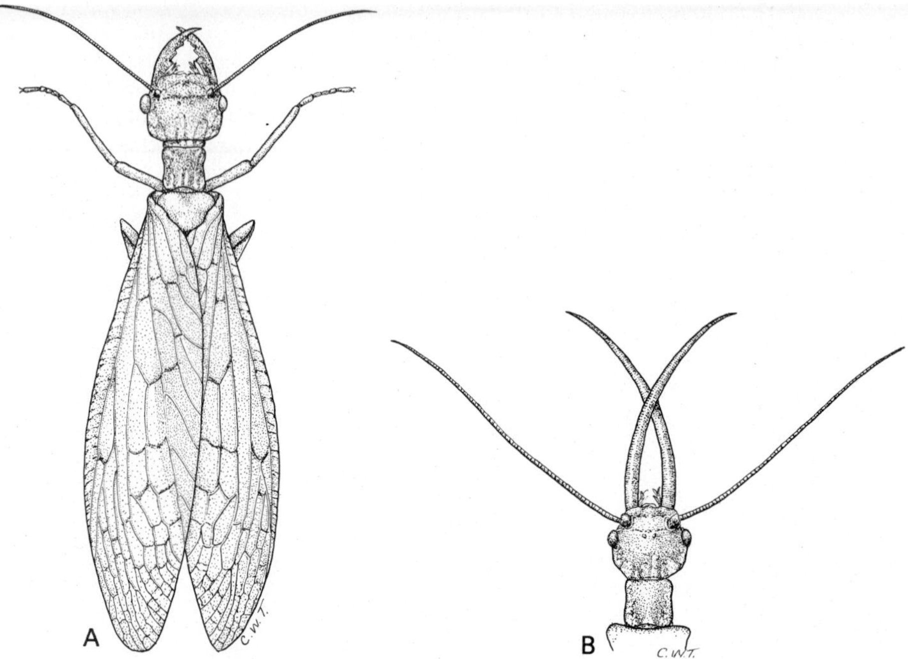

Figure 236. Dobsonfly, *Corýdalus cornùtus* (L.). A, female; B, head of male showing the greatly enlarged mandibles; about natural size.

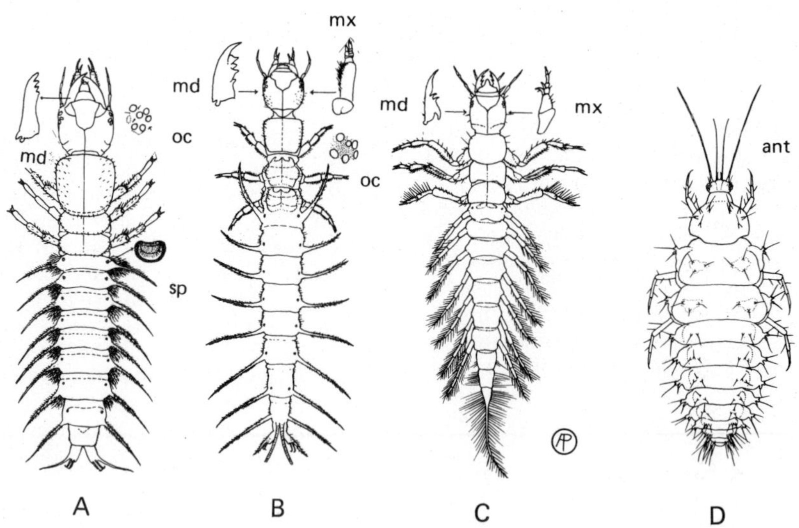

Figure 237. Larvae of aquatic Neuróptera. A, *Corýdalus* (Corydálidae); B, *Chauliòdes* (Corydálidae); C, *Sìalis* (Siálidae); D, *Climàcia* (Sisýridae). *ant,* antenna; *md,* mandible; *mx,* maxilla; *oc,* ocelli; *sp,* spiracle. (Courtesy of Peterson. Reprinted by permission.)

wing length of 6 to 17 mm (females are usually a little larger than males).

Family **Inocellìidae:** This group is represented in our area by two species of *Inocéllia,* which occur

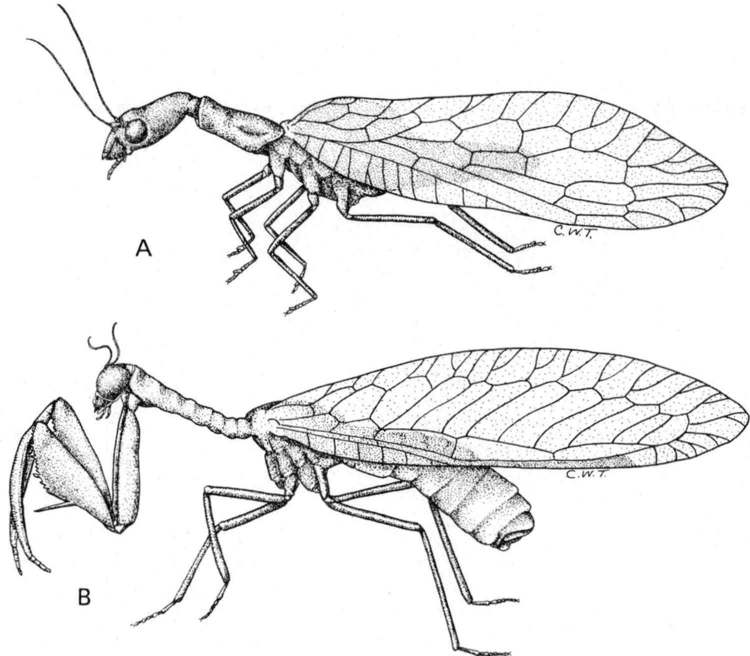

Figure 238. A, a snakefly, *Agúlla adníxa* (Hagen); B, a mantispid, *Mantíspa cincticórnis* Banks.

from California and Nevada north to British Columbia; they are larger than most raphidiids, with the front wing varying in length from 11 to 17 mm.

SUBORDER **Planipénnia:** This suborder includes the dusty-wings, lacewings, antlions, and owlflies; some authorities include only these insects in the order Neuróptera. The adults lack ocelli, the front and hind wings (in our species) are similar in size and shape, and the longitudinal veins in the wings often have branches near the wing margin. The larvae have long sicklelike mandibles, and the food is sucked up through a channel formed between the mandible and maxilla. Pupation occurs in a silken cocoon.

Family **Coniopterýgidae**—Dusty-Wings: These are minute insects, 3 mm in length or less, and are covered with a whitish powder. The group is a small one, and its members are relatively rare. The larvae feed on small insects and insect eggs.

Family **Ithònidae:** This family is represented in the United States by a single very rare species, *Oliárces clàra* Banks, which has been taken in southern California. This insect has a wingspread of 35–40 mm and resembles a small polystoechotid.

Family **Mantíspidae**—Mantidflies: These insects resemble mantids in having the prothorax lengthened and the front legs enlarged and fitted for grasping prey (Figure 238 B); they have a wing spread of 25 mm or so. The adults are predaceous, and the larvae are parasitic in the egg sacs of ground spiders. Mantidflies undergo hypermetamorphosis; the first instar larvae are active and campodeiform, and the subsequent larval instars are scarabaeiform. These insects are more common in the South.

Family **Hemerobìidae**—Brown Lacewings: These insects resemble common lacewings (Chrysòpidae), but are brownish instead of green, generally smaller, and have a different wing venation (compare Figures 232 A and 233 B). Some species have a recurved and branched humeral vein in the front wing. Most of the brown lacewings appear to have three or more radial sectors; two genera that appear to have only two (*Pséctra* and *Sympheròbius*) are placed by some authorities in a separate family, the Sympherobìidae. Brown lacewings are generally found in wooded areas, and they are much less common than the Chrysòpidae; the larvae, which often pile debris on their backs and carry it around, are predaceous.

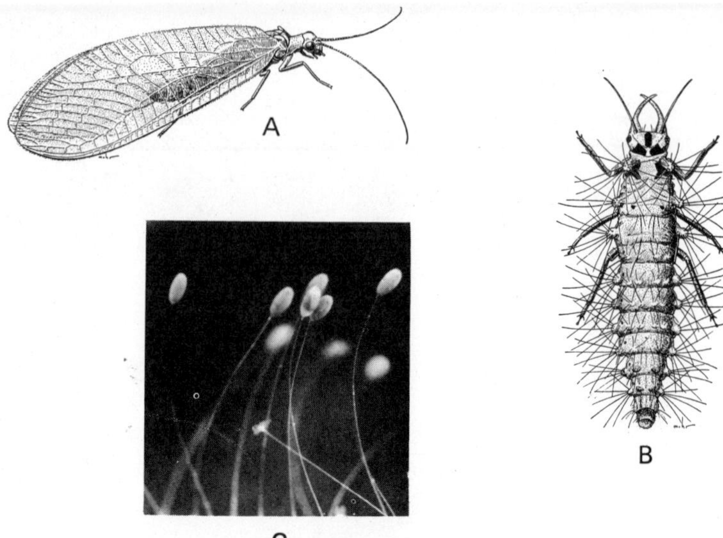

Figure 239. Adult (A), larva (B), and eggs (C) of a common lacewing (*Chrysòpa* sp.). (A and B, courtesy of the Illinois Natural History Survey.)

Family **Chrysòpidae**—Common Lacewings: These insects are quite common in grass and weeds and on the foliage of trees and shrubs. Most of them are greenish in color with golden or copper-colored eyes (Figure 239 A); some of them give off a rather disagreeable odor when handled. The larvae are predaceous, chiefly on aphids, and are often called aphidlions (Figure 239 B). The eggs are usually laid on foliage, and each egg is laid at the end of a tiny stalk (Figure 239 C). The larvae pupate in silken cocoons that are generally attached to the underside of leaves. Most of our species belong to the genus *Chrysòpa*.

Family **Dilàridae**—Pleasing Lacewings: This group contains two very rare North American species: *Nalláchius americànus* (MacLachlan) and *N. pulchéllus* (Banks). *N. americànus,* which has MP in the front wing forked near the wing margin, has been recorded from several eastern states, from Michigan to Georgia; *N. pulchéllus,* which has MP in the front wing forked near its base, has been recorded from Cuba and Arizona. Unlike most Neuróptera, these insects commonly rest with the wings outspread, and resemble small moths. The female has an ovipositor that is a little longer than the body. The eggs are laid in crevices or under bark, and the larvae are predaceous.

Family **Beròthidae**—Beaded Lacewings: This group is represented in North America by ten rather rare species in the genus *Lomamỳia*. Adults are frequently attracted to lights at night, and resemble slender caddisflies. In some species the outer margin of the front wing is somewhat indented just behind the apex, and the females of some species have scales on the wings and thorax. The eggs are stalked, and the larvae are predaceous.

Family **Polystoechòtidae**—Giant Lacewings: These lacewings have a wing spread of 40–75 mm. They are quite rare, and only two species are known in North America; the larvae are terrestrial and predaceous.

Family **Sisỳridae**—Spongillaflies: The spongillaflies look very much like tiny, brownish lacewings. They are usually found near ponds or streams, for the larvae (Figure 237 D) are aquatic and feed on freshwater sponges. When full grown, the larvae emerge from the water and pupate in silken cocoons attached to objects near the water; these cocoons are constructed inside hemispherical lacelike cocoon covers. Two genera of spongillaflies occur in the United States, *Climàcia* and *Sísyra*.

Family **Myrmeleóntidae**—Antlions: The adults of this group are very similar in general appearance to damselflies, with long, narrow, many-

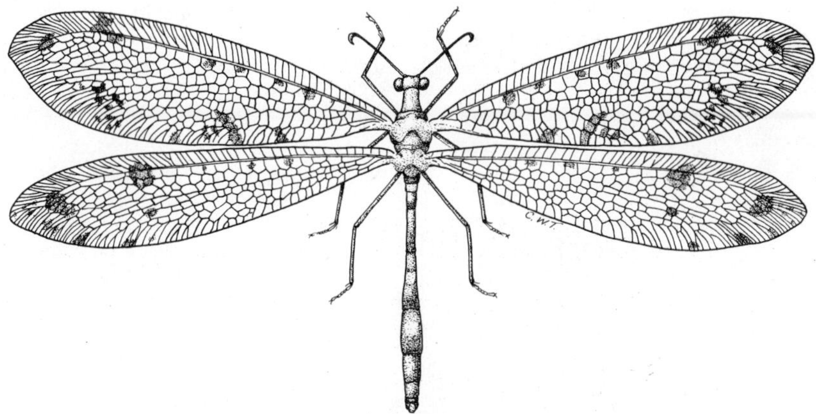

Figure 240. An adult antlion, *Dendròleon obsolètum* (Say).

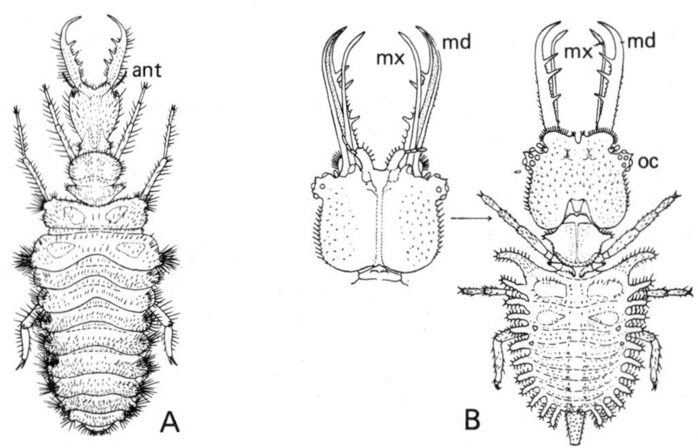

Figure 241. A, larva of *Myrméleon immaculàtus* De Geer (Myrmeleóntidae); B, larva of *Ascalóptynx appendiculàtus* (Fabricius) (Ascaláphidae). *ant,* antenna; *md,* mandible; *mx,* maxilla; *oc,* ocelli. (Courtesy of Peterson. Reprinted by permission.)

veined wings and a long slender abdomen (Figure 240). They differ from damselflies in being very softbodied, in having relatively long clubbed antennae, and in having a quite different wing venation (compare Figures 234 A and 99). They are rather feeble fliers and are often attracted to lights. The wings are clear in some species and irregularly spotted in others.

Antlion larvae, or doodlebugs, are queer-looking creatures with long, sicklelike jaws (Figure 241 A). Some species have an interesting method of capturing their prey; they conceal themselves at the bottom of a small conical pit, made in dry sand or dust, and feed on ants and other insects that fall down into this pit. The pits are generally 1½ to 2 inches (38 to 50 mm) across, and an inch or two (25 or 50 mm) deep. It is not always easy to dig one of these larvae from its pit because, when disturbed, the larva usually remains motionless. If it is dug out, it is covered with a layer of dust or sand and is easily overlooked. Pupation occurs in the soil in a cocoon of sand and silk.

Antlions are much more common in the South and Southwest than in the northeastern part of the country. The pits of the larvae are usually found in dry situations such as under overhanging cliffs or under buildings.

Family **Ascaláphidae**—Owlflies: The owlflies are large, dragonflylike insects with long antennae;

they are fairly common in the South and Southwest, but are quite rare in the northern states. The larvae (Figure 241 B) are similar to the larvae of the antlions, but do not dig pits; they lie in ambush for their prey on the surface of the ground, often more or less covered with debris, and attack small insects that pass by.

COLLECTING AND PRESERVING NEURÓPTERA

Most Neuróptera can be collected with an insect net by sweeping vegetation. Adults of the Siálidae, Corydálidae, and Sisýridae are generally to be found near the aquatic habitats (ponds and streams) in which the larvae live. The best way to collect many Neuróptera, particularly representatives of the less common groups, is at lights.

Adult Neuróptera are preserved in alcohol, on pins or points, or in envelopes. All are relatively soft-bodied, and pinned specimens often sag or shrivel and become distorted; many pinned specimens need some support for the abdomen, at least until the insect has dried. Very small forms can be mounted on points, but preservation in alcohol is better. Large elongate forms, such as dobsonflies and antlions, can be preserved in envelopes.

References on the Neuróptera

Adams, P. A. 1956. New ant-lions from the southwestern United States (Neuroptera: Myrmeleontidae). *Psyche*, 63(2):82–108; 46 f.

Banks, N. 1906. A revision of the nearctic Coniopterygidae. *Proc. Ent. Soc. Wash.*, 8(3–4): 77–86; pl. vi–vii.

Banks, N. 1927. Revision of nearctic Myrmeleontidae. *Bull. Mus. Comp. Zool., Harvard Univ.*, 68:1–84; 4 pl.

Bickley, W. E., and E. G. MacLeod. 1956. A synopsis of the nearctic Chrysopidae with a key to the genera (Neuroptera). *Proc. Ent. Soc. Wash.*, 59(4):177–202; illus.

Carpenter, F. M. 1936. Revision of the nearctic Raphidiodea (recent and fossil). *Proc. Amer. Acad. Arts Sci.*, 71(2):89–157; 25 f., 13 textf.

Carpenter, F. M. 1940. A revision of the nearctic Hemerobiidae, Berothidae, Sisyridae, Polystoechotidae, and Dilaridae (Neuroptera). *Proc. Amer. Acad. Arts Sci.*, 74(7):193–280; 103 f.

Carpenter, F. M. 1951. The structure and relationships of *Oliarces* (Neuroptera). *Psyche*, 58:32–41; 3 f.

Chandler, H. P. 1956. Megaloptera. In *Aquatic Insects of California*, Robert L. Usinger (Ed.). Berkeley, Calif.: Univ. California Press, pp. 229–233; 7 f.

Davis, K. C. 1903. Sialididae of North and South America. *N.Y. State Mus. Bull.*, 68:442–486; pl. li–lii.

Froeschner, R. C. 1947. Notes and keys to the Neuroptera of Missouri. *Ann. Ent. Soc. Amer.*, 40(1):123–136; 20 f.

Gurney, A. B. 1947. Notes on Dilaridae and Berothidae, with special reference to the immature stages of the nearctic genera (Neuroptera). *Psyche*, 54(3):145–169; 22 f.

Gurney, A. B., and S. Parfin. 1959. Neuroptera. In *Freshwater Biology*, W. T. Edmondson (Ed.). New York: Wiley, pp. 973–980; 4 f.

Martynov, A. 1928. Permian fossil insects of northeast Europe. *Trav. Mus. Geol. Acad. Sci. USSR*, 4:1–117.

Parfin, S. 1952. The Megaloptera and Neuroptera of Minnesota. *Amer. Midl. Nat.*, 47(2):421–434.

Parfin, S. and A. B. Gurney. 1956. The spongillaflies, with special reference to those of the western hemisphere (Sisyridae, Neuroptera). *Proc. U.S. Natl. Mus.*, 105(3360):421–529; 24 f., 3 pl.

Peterson, A. 1951. *Larvae of Insects*. Part II. *Coleoptera, Diptera, Neuroptera, Siphonaptera, Mecoptera, Trichoptera*. Ann Arbor, Mich.: Edwards Bros., v + 416 pp., 104 f.

Rehn, J. W. H. 1939. Studies in North American Mantispidae (Neuroptera). *Trans. Amer. Ent. Soc.*, 65:237–263; 22 f.

Smith, R. C. 1922. The biology of the Chrysopidae. *N.Y. (Cornell) Agric. Expt. Sta. Mem.*, 58:1285–1377; f. 154–163, pl. 85–88.

Stange, L. A. 1970. Revision of the ant-lion tribe Brachyneurini of North America (Neuroptera: Myrmeleontidae). *Univ. Calif. Pub. Ent.*, 55:1–192; 231 f., 31 maps.

Tauber, C. A. 1969. Taxonomy and biology of the lacewing genus *Meleoma* (Neuroptera: Chrysopidae). *Univ. Calif. Pub. Ent.*, 58:1–94; 67 f., 7 pl.

Throne, A. L. 1971a. The Neuroptera—suborder Planipennia of Wisconsin. Part I—Introduction and Chrysopidae. *Mich. Ent.*, 4(3):65–78; 15 f.

Throne, A. L. 1971b. The Neuroptera—suborder Planipennia of Wisconsin. Part II—Hemerobiidae, Polystoechotidae, and Sisyridae. *Mich. Ent.*, 4(3):79–87; 18 f.

Withycombe, C. L. 1925. Some aspects of the biology and morphology of the Neuroptera. With special reference to the immature stages and their phylogenetic significance. *Trans. Ent. Soc. London*, 1924(XV):303–411; 2 textf., pl. XXXIX–XLIV.

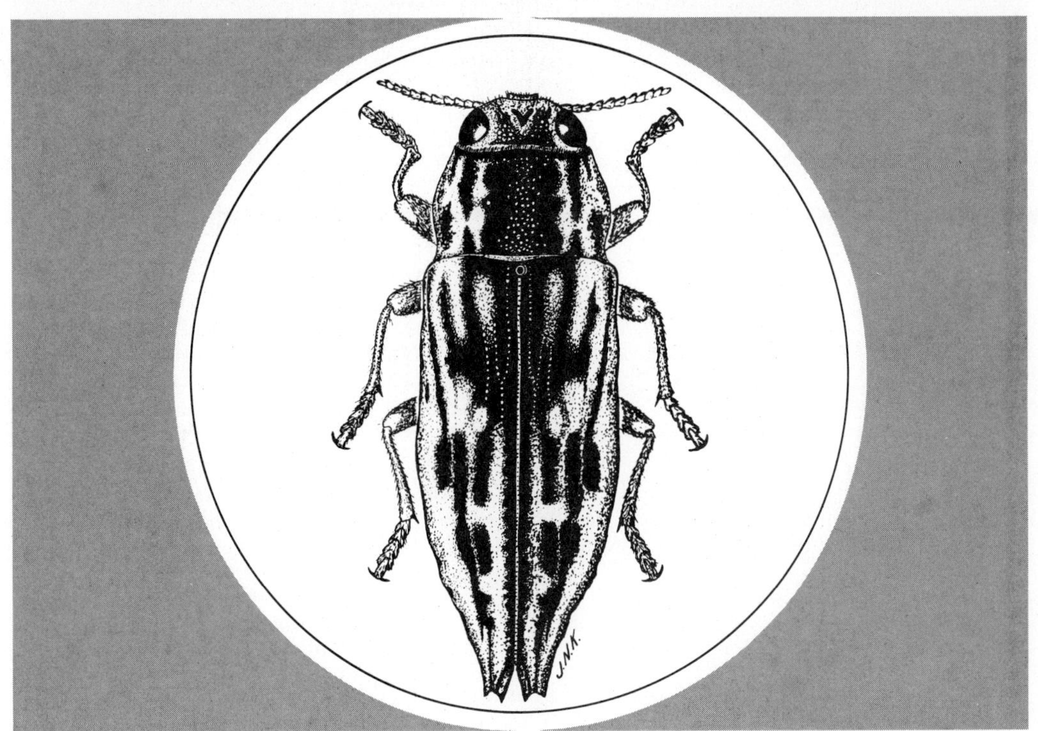

25: ORDER COLEÓPTERA[1]

BEETLES

The order Coleóptera is the largest order of insects and contains about 40 percent of the known species in the class Insécta. Over a quarter of a million species of beetles have been described, and about 30,000 of this number occur in the United States. These insects vary in length in this country from less than a millimeter up to about 3 inches (76 mm), and some tropical species reach a length of 4 or 5 inches (100 or 130 mm). The beetles vary considerably in habits, and are to be found almost everywhere; many species are of great economic importance.

One of the most distinctive features of the Coleóptera is the structure of the wings. Most beetles have four wings, with the front pair thickened, leathery, or hard and brittle, and usually meeting in a straight line down the middle of the back and covering the hind wings (hence the order name). The hind wings are membranous, usually longer than the front wings, and when at rest, are usually folded up under the front wings. The front wings of a beetle are called elytra (singular, elytron). The elytra normally serve only as protective sheaths; the hind wings are the only ones ordinarily used for flight. The front and/or hind wings are greatly reduced in a few beetles.

The mouth parts in this order are of the chewing type, and the mandibles are well developed. The mandibles of many beetles are stout and are used in crushing seeds or gnawing wood; in others they are slender and sharp. In the snout

[1] Coleóptera: *coleo,* sheath; *ptera,* wings (referring to the elytra).

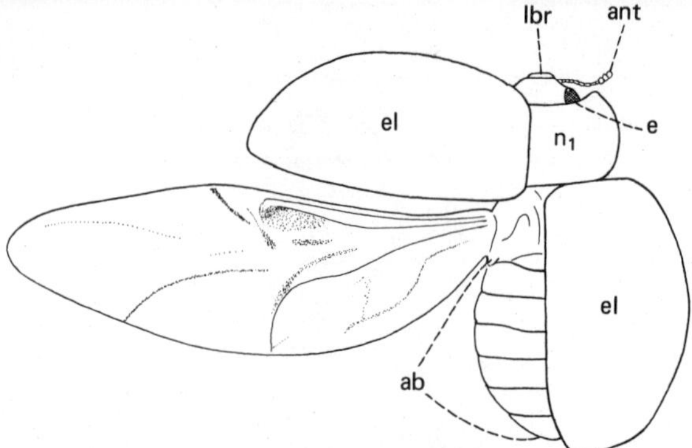

Figure 242. Dorsal view of a ladybird beetle (*Adàlia* sp.), with the left wings extended. *ab,* abdomen; *ant,* antenna; *e,* compound eye; *el,* elytron; *lbr,* labrum; n_1, pronotum.

beetles the front of the head is drawn out into a more or less elongated snout, with the mouth parts at the end.

The beetles undergo complete metamorphosis. The larvae vary considerably in form in different families; most beetle larvae are campodeiform or scarabaeiform, but some are platyform, some are elateriform, and a few are vermiform.

Beetles may be found in almost every type of habitat in which any insect is found, and they feed on all sorts of plant and animal materials. Many are phytophagous, many are predaceous, some are scavengers, others feed on mold or fungi, and a very few are parasitic. Some are subterranean in habit, many are aquatic or semiaquatic, and a few live as commensals in the nests of social insects. Some of the phytophagous species are free feeders on foliage, some bore into the wood or fruit, some are leaf miners, some attack the roots, and some feed on parts of the blossoms; any part of a plant may be fed upon by some type of beetle. Many beetles feed on stored plant or animal products, including many types of foods, clothing, and other organic materials. One species is remarkable for its ability to bore through the lead sheathing of telephone cables in California. Many beetles are of value to man because they destroy injurious insects or act as scavengers.

The life cycle in this order varies in length from four generations a year to one generation in several years; most species have one generation a year. The winter may be passed in any of the life stages, depending on the species. Many overwinter as partly grown larvae, many overwinter as pupae in chambers in the soil or in wood or in other protected situations, and many overwinter as adults; relatively few species overwinter as eggs.

CLASSIFICATION OF THE COLEÓPTERA

There are differences of opinion among coleopterists with regard to the relationships of the various groups of beetles, the groups that should be given family status, and their arrangement into superfamilies. The arrangement of suborders, superfamilies, and families followed in this book is taken from various sources, principally Crowson (1955), Arnett (1968), and the unpublished work of John F. Lawrence. Many authorities give family status to more groups than we do in this book.

An outline of the groups in the order Coleòptera, as they are treated in this book, is given below. Names in parentheses represent different spellings, synonyms, or other treatments of the group. Families marked with an asterisk are relatively rare, or are not very likely to be taken by the general collector. Most of the common names of families are those given by Arnett (1968).

Suborder Archostémata
- *Cupédidae (Cupésidae, Cùpidae, Ommátidae) – reticulated beetles
- *Micromálthidae – micromalthid beetles

Suborder Adéphaga
- Rhysòdidae (Rhyssòdidae) – wrinkled bark beetles

Cicindèlidae—tiger beetles
Carábidae (including Pàussidae and Omophrónidae)—ground beetles
*Amphizòidae—trout-stream beetles
Halíplidae—crawling water beetles
Dytíscidae—predaceous diving beetles
*Notéridae (Dytíscidae in part)—burrowing water beetles
Gyrìnidae—whirligig beetles

Suborder Myxóphaga
*Sphaèridae (Sphaerìidae)—minute bog beetles
*Hydroscáphidae (Hydrophílidae in part)—skiff beetles

Suborder Polýphaga
Superfamily Hydrophilòidea
Hydrophílidae (including Hydróchidae and Sperchèidae)—water scavenger beetles
*Hydraènidae (Limnebìidae; Hydrophílidae in part)—minute moss beetles
*Georýssidae—minute mud-loving beetles
Superfamily Histeròidea
Histéridae—hister beetles
*Sphaerìtidae—false clown beetles
Superfamily Staphylinòidea
Staphylìnidae (including Micropéplidae and Brathìnidae)—rove beetles
Pseláphidae (including Clavigéridae)—short-winged mold beetles
Ptilìidae (Ptílidae, Trichopterýgidae)—feather-winged beetles
*Limulòdidae (Ptilìidae in part plus Staphylìnidae in part)—horseshoe crab beetles
*Dasycéridae (Lathridìidae in part)—dasycerid beetles
*Leptìnidae (including Platypsýllidae)—mammal-nest beetles and beaver parasites
*Leiòdidae (Liòdidae, Anisotómidae, Leptodíridae, Catópidae; Sílphidae in part)—round fungus beetles
Sílphidae—carrion beetles
*Scydmaènidae—antlike stone beetles
Scaphidìidae—shining fungus beetles
Superfamily Dascillòidea
*Eucinètidae (Dascíllidae in part)—plate-thigh beetles
*Clámbidae—fringe-winged beetles
Helòdidae (Cyphónidae; Dascíllidae in part)—marsh beetles
Dascíllidae (Dascýllidae; including Karumìidae)—soft-bodied plant beetles
Rhipicéridae (Sandálidae in part)—cedar beetles
Superfamily Scarabaeòidea
Lucànidae—stag beetles
Passálidae—bess beetles
Scarabaèidae (including Acanthocéridae, Geotrùpidae, and Trógidae)—scarab beetles
Superfamily Byrrhòidea
Býrrhidae—pill beetles
Superfamily Dryopòidea
Psephènidae—water-penny beetles
Ptilodactýlidae (Dascíllidae in part)—ptilodactylid beetles
*Chelonarìidae—chelonariid beetles
*Artematópidae (Eurypogónidae; Dascíllidae in part: Macropogonìni)—artematopid beetles
*Callirhípidae (Rhipicéridae in part, Sandálidae in part)—callirhipid beetles
*Brachypséctridae (Dascíllidae in part)—the Texas beetle
Heterocéridae—variegated mud-loving beetles
*Limníchidae (Dryópidae in part)—minute marsh-loving beetles
Dryópidae (Párnidae)—long-toed water beetles
Élmidae (Hélmidae)—riffle beetles
Superfamily Buprestòidea
Bupréstidae (including Schizópidae)—metallic wood-boring beetles

Superfamily Elateròidea
- *Cebriónidae – cebrionid beetles
- Elatéridae (including Plastocéridae) – click beetles
- Thróscidae (Trixágidae) – throscid beetles
- *Cerophýtidae – cerophytid beetles
- *Perothópidae (Eucnèmidae in part) – perothopid beetles
- Eucnèmidae (Melásidae) – false click beetles

Superfamily Cantharòidea
- *Telegeùsidae – telegeusid beetles
- *Phengòdidae – glow-worms
- Lampýridae – lightningbugs, fireflies
- Canthàridae – soldier beetles
- Lỳcidae – net-winged beetles

Superfamily Dermestòidea
- *Derodóntidae – tooth-necked fungus beetles
- *Nosodéndridae – wounded-tree beetles
- Derméstidae (including Thoríctidae) – dermestid or skin beetles

Superfamily Bostrichòidea
- Anobìidae – anobiid beetles
- Ptìnidae (including Gnóstidae) – spider beetles
- Bostríchidae (Bostrýchidae, Apátidae; including Psòidae) – branch and twig borers
- Lýctidae (Bostríchidae in part) – powder-post beetles

Superfamily Cleròidea
- Trogosítidae (Ostómidae, Ostomátidae, Temnochìlidae) – bark-gnawing beetles
- Cléridae (including Corynètidae=Korynètidae) – checkered beetles
- Melýridae (Malachìidae plus Dasýtidae) – soft-winged flower beetles

Superfamily Lymexylonòidea
- Lymexylónidae (Lymexýlidae) – ship-timber beetles

Superfamily Cucujòidea
- Nitidùlidae (including Smicripìnae) – sap beetles
- Rhizophágidae (Nitidùlidae in part; including Monotómidae) – root-eating beetles
- *Sphíndidae – dry-fungus beetles
- Cucùjidae (including Silvànidae and Prostómidae) – flat bark beetles
- Cryptophágidae (including Biphýllidae=Diphýllidae) – silken fungus beetles
- Languriidae – lizard beetles
- Erotýlidae (including Dácnidae) – pleasing fungus beetles
- Phalácridae – shining flower beetles
- Cerylónidae (Murmidìidae; Colydìidae in part) – cerylonid beetles
- Corylóphidae (Orthopéridae) – minute fungus beetles
- Coccinéllidae – ladybird beetles
- Endomýchidae (including Mycetaèidae) – handsome fungus beetles
- Lathridìidae (including Merophysìidae) – minute brown scavenger beetles
- Bytùridae (Derméstidae in part) – fruitworm beetles
- Mycetophágidae (Tritómidae) – hairy fungus beetles
- Cìidae (Císidae, Ciòidae) – minute tree-fungus beetles

Superfamily Tenebrionòidea (Heterómera in part)
- Monómmidae (Monommátidae) – monommid beetles
- Colydìidae (including Adiméridae, Monoèdidae, Bothridéridae) – cylindrical bark beetles
- *Cephalòidae – false longhorn beetles
- Tenebriónidae (including Zophéridae) – darkling beetles
- Lagrìidae – long-jointed beetles
- Allecùlidae (Cistèlidae) – comb-clawed beetles
- Salpíngidae (including Pýthidae, Aegialìtidae=Eurystéthidae, and Bòridae) – narrow-waisted bark beetles
- Pyrochròidae – fire-colored beetles

*Othnìidae (Elacátidae) — false tiger beetles
*Inopéplidae (Cucùjidae in part, Staphylinidae in part) — inopeplid beetles
Myctéridae (including Cononòtidae and Hemipéplidae) — mycterid beetles
Oedeméridae — false blister beetles
Melandrỳidae (including Synchròidae, Tetratómidae, Scraptìidae, Anaspídidae, and Serropálpidae) — false darkling beetles

Superfamily Meloòidea (Heterómera in part)
Mordéllidae — tumbling flower beetles
Rhipiphòridae — wedge-shaped beetles
Melòidae (Lýttidae; including Tetraonýchidae) — blister beetles
Anthícidae — antlike flower beetles
Pedìlidae (Anthícidae in part) — pedilid beetles
*Euglénidae (Adéridae, Hylophílidae, Xylophílidae; Anthícidae in part) — antlike leaf beetles

Superfamily Chrysomelòidea
Cerambýcidae (including Distenìidae, Parándridae, and Spondýlidae) — long-horned beetles
Brùchidae (Mylábridae, Acanthoscélidae, Larìidae) — seed beetles
Chrysomélidae — leaf beetles

Superfamily Curculionòidea
Anthríbidae (Platystómidae, Bruchélidae, Chorágidae, Platyrrhínidae) — fungus weevils
Bréntidae (Brénthidae) — straight-snouted weevils
Curculiónidae (including Ithycéridae=Bélidae, Nemonýchidae=Rhinomacéridae, Rhynchítidae, Attelábidae, Oxycorýnidae, Apiónidae, Cyládidae, and Rhynchophòridae) — snout beetles or weevils
Platypódidae — pin-hole borers
Scolýtidae (including Ípidae) — bark or engraver beetles, and ambrosia or timber beetles

CHARACTERS USED IN THE IDENTIFICATION OF BEETLES

The principal characters of beetles used in identification are those of the head, antennae, thoracic sclerites, legs, elytra, and abdomen; occasionally, characters such as size, shape, and color are used. In most cases the ease of recognizing these characters depends on the size of the beetle. Some characters require careful observation, often at high magnification, for accurate interpretation.

HEAD CHARACTERS The principal head character used involves the development of a snout. In the Curculionòidea the head is more or less prolonged forward into a snout; the mouth parts are reduced in size and are located at the tip of the snout, and the antennae usually arise on the sides of it. The basal antennal segment often fits into a groove (the *scrobe;* Figure 244, *agr*) on the side of the snout. In many cases (Figure 244) the snout is quite distinct and occasionally may be as long as the body or longer; in other cases (for example, the Scolýtidae and Platypódidae) the snout is poorly developed and not very evident as such. The families in the Curculionòidea are sometimes placed in a separate suborder, the Rhynchóphora. These beetles differ from most of the other members of the order in having the gular sutures fused (Figure 244 C). There is some development of a snout in a few beetles outside this superfamily, but such beetles have the gular sutures separated (Figure 243, *gs*).

ANTENNAE The antennae of beetles are subject to considerable variation in different groups, and these differences are used in identification. The term "clubbed," as used in the key, refers to any condition in which the terminal segments are larger than the segments preceding them, including *clavate* (the terminal segments enlarging gradually and only slightly, as in Figure 6 D, E); *capitate* (the terminal segments abruptly enlarged, as in Figure 249 F–I); *lamellate* (the terminal segments expanded on one side into rounded or oval plates, as in Figure 250 A, C–G); and *flabellate* (the terminal segments expanded on one side into long, thin, parallel-sided, tonguelike processes, as in Figure 250 B). The distinction between some of these antennal variations (for example, between filiform and slightly clubbed, or between filiform and serrate) is not very sharp, and some conditions might be interpreted in different ways; this fact is taken into account in the key, as specimens

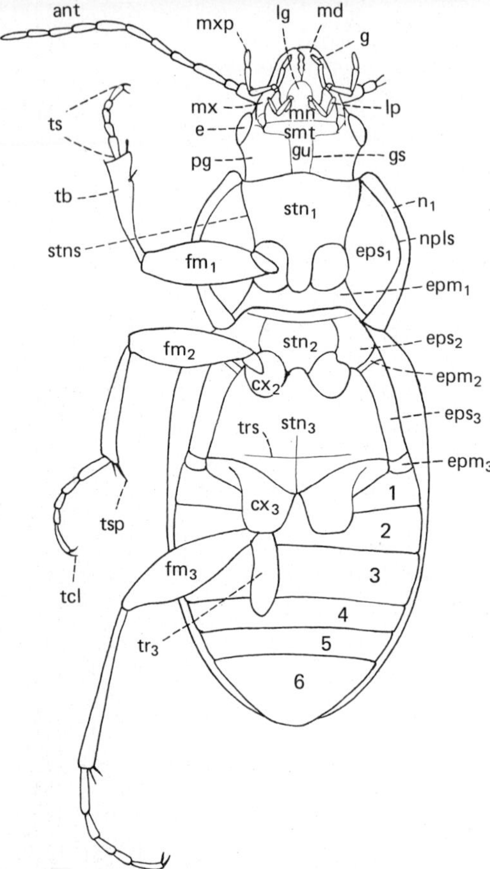

Figure 243. Ventral view of a ground beetle (*Omàseus* sp.). *ant,* antenna; *cx,* coxa; *e,* compound eye; *epm_1,* proepimeron; *epm_2,* mesepimeron; *epm_3,* metepimeron; *eps_1,* proepisternum; *eps_2,* mesepisternum; *eps_3,* metepisternum; *fm,* femur; *g,* galea; *gs,* gular suture; *gu,* gula; *lg,* ligula; *lp,* labial palp; *md,* mandible; *mn,* mentum; *mx,* maxilla; *mxp,* maxillary palp; *n_1,* pronotum; *npls,* notopleural suture; *pg,* postgena; *smt,* submentum; *stn_1,* prosternum; *stn_2,* mesosternum; *stn_3,* metasternum; *stns,* prosternal suture; *tb,* tibia; *tcl,* tarsal claws; *tr,* trochanter; *trs,* transverse suture on metasternum; *ts,* tarsus; *tsp,* tibial spurs; *1–6,* abdominal sterna.

will key out correctly from either alternative at many places in the key.

The number of terminal antennal segments that form the club (in clubbed antennae) often serves as a key character. The antennal segments between the scape (the basal segment) and the club are often referred to as the funiculus (or funicle).

THORACIC CHARACTERS The pronotum and scutellum are normally the only thoracic areas visible from above; the other thoracic areas are usually visible only in a ventral view. The pronotum, when viewed from above, may vary greatly in shape, and its posterior margin may be straight, convex, or sinuate (Figure 245 E–G). Laterally, the pronotum may be margined (with a sharp keel-like lateral edge) or rounded. The surface of the pronotum may be bare or pubescent, and it may

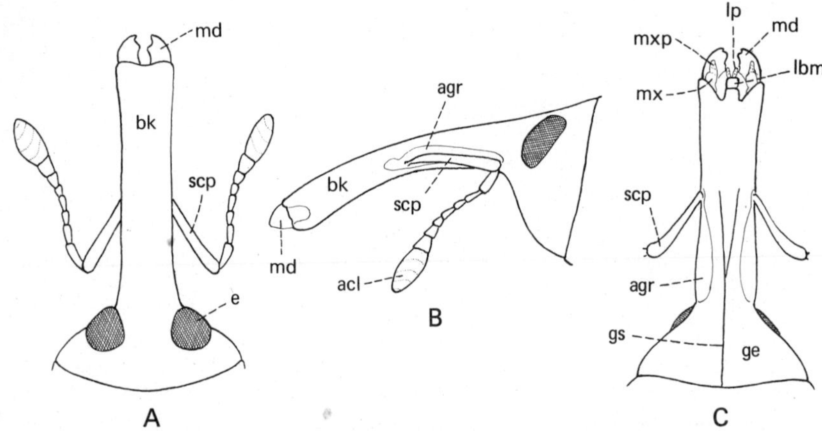

Figure 244. Head of a snout beetle (*Pissòdes,* Curculiónidae). A, dorsal view; B, lateral view; C, ventral view. *acl,* antennal club; *agr,* scrobe, the groove in beak for reception of antennal scape; *bk,* beak or snout; *e,* compound eye; *ge,* gena; *gs,* gular suture; *lbm,* labium; *lp,* labial palp; *md,* mandible; *mx,* maxilla; *mxp,* maxillary palp; *scp,* scape of antenna.

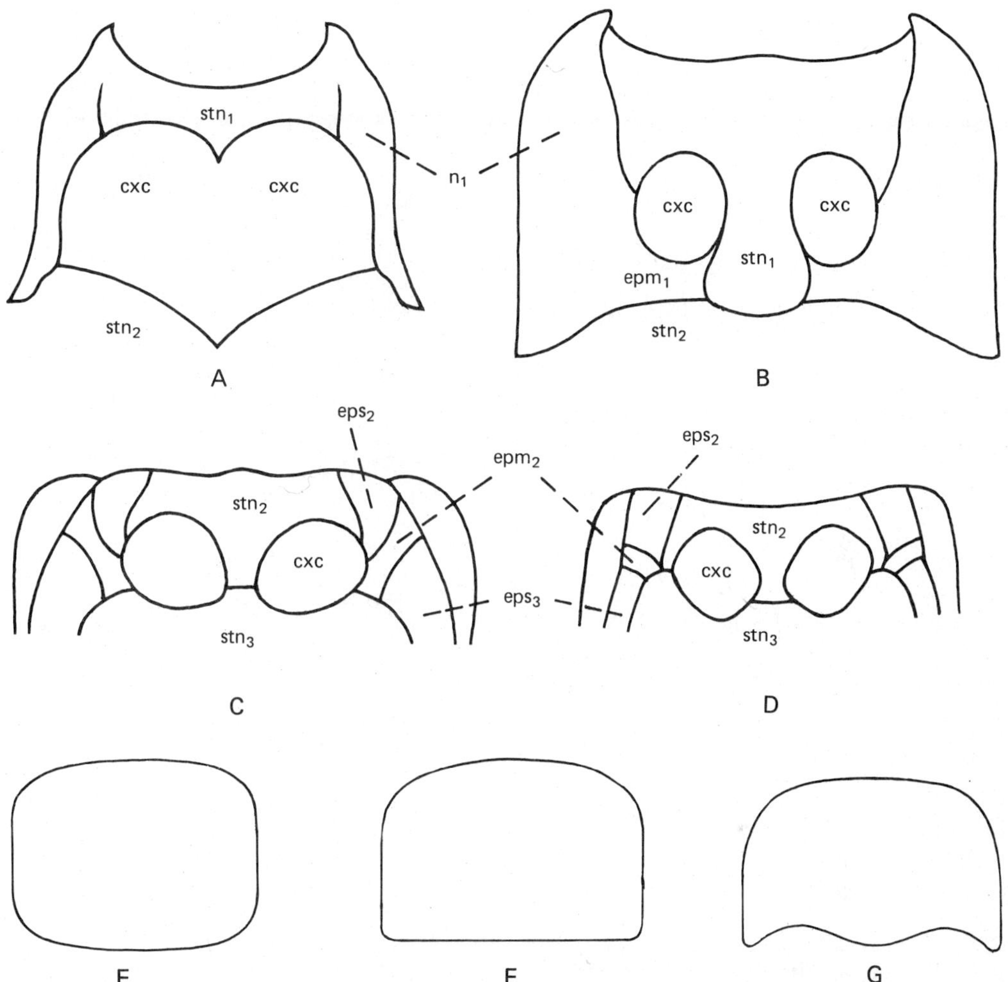

Figure 245. Thoracic structure in Coleóptera. A and B, prosterna showing open (A) and closed (B) coxal cavities; C and D, mesosterna showing open (C) and closed (D) coxal cavities; E–G, pronota with posterior margin convex (E), straight (F), or sinuate (G). *cxc,* coxal cavity; *epm*$_1$, proepimeron; *epm*$_2$, mesepimeron; *eps*$_2$, mesepisternum; *eps*$_3$, metepisternum; *stn*$_1$, prosternum; *stn*$_2$, mesosternum; *stn*$_3$, metasternum.

be smooth or with various punctures or dents, ridges, grooves, tubercles, or other features. The scutellum (the mesoscutellum) is usually visible as a small triangular sclerite immediately behind the pronotum, between the bases of the elytra; only occasionally is it rounded or heart-shaped, and sometimes it is concealed.

The chief thoracic characters apparent in a ventral view that are of importance in identification are the various sutures, the shape of certain sclerites, and the particular sclerites that are adjacent to the front and middle coxae. A few beetles (the Adéphaga, Myxóphaga, and Cupédidae) have notopleural sutures (Figure 243 *npls*), which separate the pronotum from the propleura; most beetles have prosternal sutures (Figure 243, *stns*), which separate the prosternum from the rest of the prothorax. The anterior margin of the prosternum is usually straight; when it is somewhat convex (as in Figure 254 A), it is said to be "lobed." The prosternum often has a process or lobe extending backward between the front coxae; sometimes (for example, in click beetles, Figure 254 A) this process is spinelike.

When the sclerites of the prothorax extend around the front coxae, these coxal cavities are said to be "closed" (Figure 245 B); when the sclerite immediately behind the front coxae is a sclerite of the mesothorax, these cavities are said to be "open" (Figure 245 A). When the middle coxae are surrounded by sterna and are not touched by any pleural sclerite, these coxal cavities are said to be "closed" (Figure 245 D); when at least some of the pleural sclerites reach the middle coxae, these coxal cavities are said to be "open" (Figure 245 C).

LEG CHARACTERS The coxae of beetles vary greatly in size and shape. In some cases they are globose or rounded and project only slightly; when they are more or less elongate laterally without projecting very much, they are said to be *transverse;* sometimes they are more or less conical, and project ventrad noticeably. A few beetles have a small sclerite, the trochantin, located in the anterolateral portion of the coxal cavity (Figure 246 B, *tn*).

Many beetles when disturbed draw their appendages in close to the body and "play dead"; such beetles often have grooves in the body or in certain leg segments into which the appendages fit when so retracted. Beetles with retractile legs usually have grooves in the coxae (particularly the middle and/or hind coxae) into which the femora fit when the legs are retracted, and may have grooves in other leg segments.

The trochanters of most beetles do not lie directly between the coxae and the femora, but a little to one side. In the Adéphaga (Figures 243 and 248 A) the hind trochanters are relatively large and strongly offset toward the midline, and the femora may appear to touch the coxae. The trochanters of most beetles are small and somewhat triangular, with the trochanter–femur union slanting and not at a right angle to the long axis of the body (Figure 246 A, B, D). A few beetles have the trochanters more or less quadrate (sometimes longer than wide), with the trochanter—femur union at right angles to the long axis of the leg (Figure 246 E); such trochanters are sometimes described as "interstitial."

The number and relative size and shape of the tarsal segments are very important characters for the identification of beetles; it is necessary to examine the tarsi of almost any beetle one wishes to run through the key. The number of tarsal segments in most beetles varies from three to five; it is usually the same on all tarsi, but some groups have one less segment in the hind tarsi than in the middle and front tarsi, and others have fewer segments in the front tarsi. The tarsal formula is an important part of any group description, and is given as 5-5-5, 5-5-4, 4-4-4, 3-3-3, and so on, indicating the number of tarsal segments on the front, middle, and hind tarsi, respectively. Most Coleóptera have a 5-5-5 tarsal formula.

In a few groups, including some very common beetles, the next to the last tarsal segment is very small and inconspicuous. In such cases this segment may be very difficult to see unless very carefully examined under high magnification. These tarsi thus appear to have one segment less than they actually have, and are so described in the key; for example, a 5-segmented tarsus such as that shown in Figure 251 A is described in the key as "apparently 4-segmented."

A few groups have the basal tarsal segment very small (Figure 251 D) and visible only if the tarsus is properly oriented.

If the tarsi of a beetle appear to be 4-segmented and the third segment is relatively large and more or less **U**-shaped (Figure 251 A), they are generally 5-segmented, with the fourth segment very small. If the tarsi appear to be 4-segmented and the third segment is slender and not greatly different from the terminal segment, then they are either actually 4-segmented, or are 5-segmented with the basal segment very small.

The tarsal claws of beetles are subject to some variation; in most cases they are simple, that is, without branches or teeth, but in some cases they are toothed, cleft, or pectinate (Figure 247).

THE ELYTRA The elytra normally meet in a straight line down the middle of the body; this line of union of the elytra is called the suture. The suture may extend to the tips of the elytra, or the tips may be slightly separated. The antero-lateral angles of the elytra are called the humeri. The elytra usually slope gradually from the suture to the outer edge; when they are abruptly bent down laterally, the bent-down portion is called the epipleura (plural, epipleurae).

The elytra vary principally in shape, length, and texture. They are usually parallel-sided anteriorly and tapering posteriorly; sometimes they are more or less oval or hemispherical. The elytra of some beetles are truncate at the apex. The elytra in some groups are variously sculptured, with ridges, grooves or striae, punctures, tubercles, and the like; in other cases they are quite smooth. If the elytra appear hairy under low or medium mag-

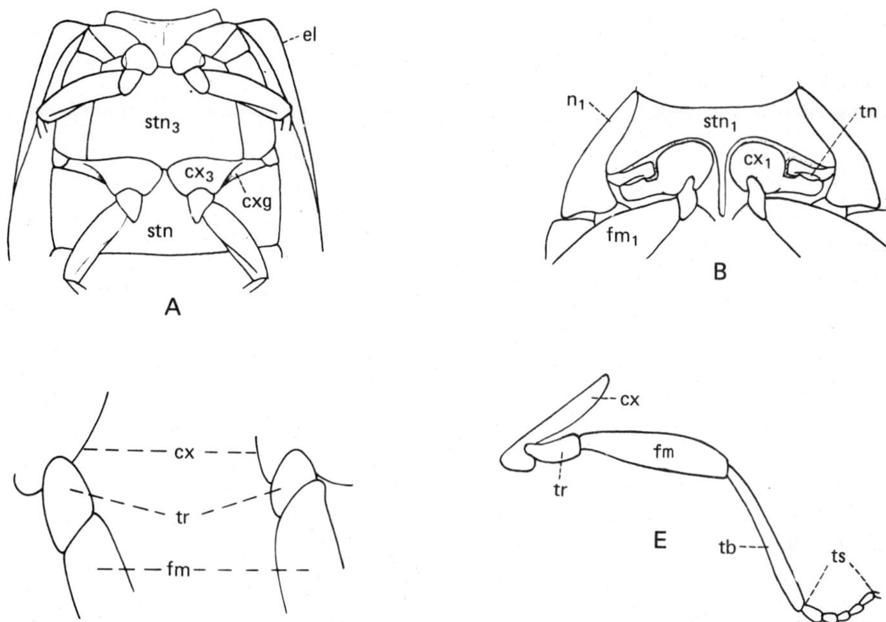

Figure 246. Leg structure in Coleóptera. A, thorax of *Derméstes* (Derméstidae), ventral view, showing grooved hind coxae; B, prothorax of *Psephènus* (Psephènidae), ventral view, showing trochantin; C, base of hind leg of *Àpion* (Curculiónidae); D, base of hind leg of *Conotrachèlus* (Curculiónidae); E, hind leg of *Trichodésma* (Anobìidae), showing interstitial trochanter. *cx*, coxa; *cxg*, groove in coxa; *el*, elytron; *fm*, femur; n_1, pronotum; *stn*, sternum of first abdominal segment; stn_1, prosternum; stn_3, metasternum; *tb*, tibia; *tn*, trochantin; *tr*, trochanter; *ts*, tarsus.

nification, they are said to be pubescent. The elytra of some beetles are quite hard and stiff, and curve around the sides of the abdomen to some extent; in others they are soft and pliable, and lie loosely on top of the abdomen without firmly embracing it.

THE ABDOMEN The structure of the first abdominal segment serves to separate the two principal suborders of the Coleóptera. In the Adéphaga the hind coxae extend backward and bisect the first abdominal sternum so that instead of extending completely across the body this sternum is divided and consists of two lateral pieces separated by the hind coxae (Figures 243 and 248 A). In the Polýphaga the hind coxae extend backward a different distance in different groups, but the first abdominal sternum is never completely divided, and its posterior edge extends completely across the body.

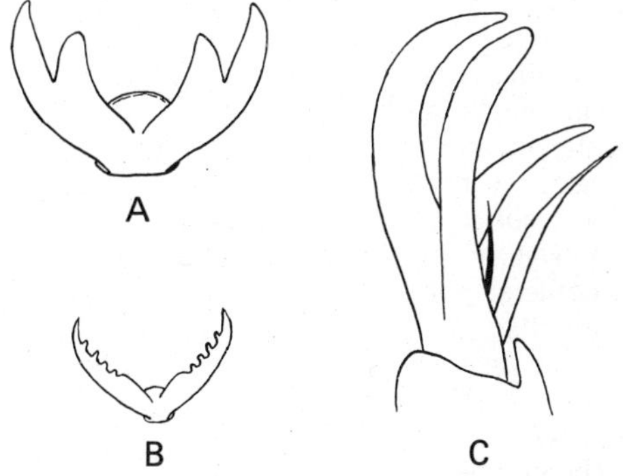

Figure 247. Tarsal claws of Coleóptera. A, toothed (coccinellid); B, pectinate (alleculid); C, cleft (meloid).

The number of visible abdominal sterna varies in different groups and is repeatedly used in the key. In a few cases (for example, the Bupréstidae)

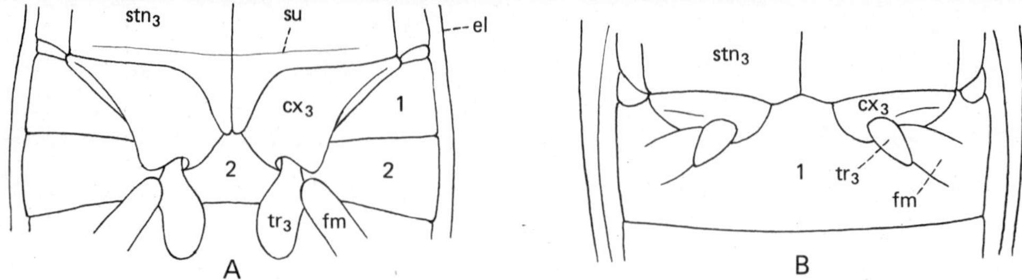

Figure 248. Base of abdomen, ventral view, showing difference between Adéphaga and Polýphaga. A, tiger beetle (Adéphaga); B, pleasing fungus beetle (Polýphaga). cx_3, hind coxa; *el*, elytron; *fm*, hind femur; stn_3, metasternum; *su*, transverse metasternal suture; tr_3, hind trochanter; *1, 2*, abdominal sterna.

the first two visible sterna are more or less fused together, and the suture between them is much less distinct than the other abdominal sutures (Figure 254 B). If the sutures between the abdominal sterna are all equally distinct, then no segments are said to be fused.

The last abdominal tergum is often called the pygidium, and is sometimes exposed beyond the tips of the elytra.

OTHER CHARACTERS Characters such as size, shape, or color should not prove particularly difficult. The term "base" is used to distinguish the two ends to various body parts; when speaking of an appendage, the base is that end nearest the body; the base of the head or pronotum is the posterior end, and the base of the elytra or abdomen is the anterior end. The segments of the tarsi or antennae are numbered from the base distad.

Key to the Families of Coleóptera

The following key is rather long, not only because this is the largest order of insects, but also because there is quite a bit of variation in many families. The key is constructed to take this variation into account, and also to provide for specimens whose characters are somewhat borderline; many specimens will key out correctly from either alternative at certain points in the key. Groups marked with an asterisk are relatively rare, or are not very likely to be taken by the general collector. This key is to adults; keys to larvae are given by Peterson (1951), and Brues, Melander, and Carpenter (1954).

1. Form beetlelike, the elytra present 2

1′. Larviform, the elytra and hind wings absent (females) 234

2(1). Hind coxae expanded into large plates that conceal most of the abdomen (Figure 259 B); antennae 11-segmented and filiform; small aquatic beetles, 5 mm in length or less .... **Halíplidae** p. 371

2′. Hind coxae not so expanded; other characters variable 3

3(2′). First visible abdominal sternum divided by the hind coxae, the posterior margin of the sternum not extending completely across abdomen; hind trochanters large and offset toward midline, the femora almost touching the coxae (Figure 248 A); prothorax usually with notopleural sutures (Figure 243, *npls*); tarsi nearly always 5-5-5; antennae usually filiform (suborder Adéphaga) 4

3′. First visible abdominal sternum not divided by hind coxae, the posterior margin of the sternum extending completely across abdomen, and/or hind trochanters small (Figure 248 B); prothorax usually without notopleural sutures; tarsi and antennae variable 11

4(3). Aquatic beetles, the hind legs fringed with hairs and more or less flattened, fitted for swimming; metasternum without a transverse suture in front of hind coxae 5

4′. Usually terrestrial beetles, the hind legs not fringed or modified for swimming; metasternum usually with a transverse suture just in front of hind coxae (Figure 243, *trs*) 8

5(4). Two pairs of compound eyes, one dorsal and one ventral (Figure 252 C); antennae very short and stout (Figure 249 E); oval, blackish beetles (Figure 262), 3–15 mm in length .... **Gyrìnidae** p. 373

5′. One pair of compound eyes; antennae long and slender 6

6(5′). Scutellum exposed; length 1–40 mm .... **Dytíscidae** p. 371

6′. Scutellum not visible; size variable 7

7(6′). Hind tarsi with 2 curved claws of equal length; abdomen with 5 visible sterna; front coxal cavities closed behind; length 1.2–5.5 mm... **Notéridae*** p. 373

7′. Hind tarsi with a single straight claw; abdomen with 6 visible sterna; front coxal cavities open behind; length usually over 5 mm .... **Dytíscidae** p. 371

8(4′). Metasternum with a transverse suture just in front of hind coxae (Figure 243, *trs*); antennae usually slender, most segments much longer than broad 9

8′. Metasternum without a transverse suture in front of hind coxae; antennae short and thick, or moniliform 10

9(8). Antennae arising from front of head, above mandibles; clypeus produced laterally beyond bases of antennae; mandibles long, sickle-shaped, and toothed; elytra without grooves or rows of punctures; head, including eyes, usually as wide as or wider than pronotum (Figure 257); mostly 10–24 mm in length .... **Cicindèlidae** p. 370

9′. Antennae arising more laterally, on sides of head between eye and base of mandible; clypeus not produced laterally beyond bases of antennae; mandibles usually not as above; elytra often with longitudinal grooves or rows of punctures; head, including eyes, usually narrower than pronotum (Figure 258); length 4–35 mm .... **Carábidae** p. 370

10(8′). Body slender and elongate, 5.5–7.5 mm in length (Figure 256); pronotum with at least 3 longitudinal grooves; terrestrial beetles, widely distributed... .... **Rhysòdidae** p. 369

10′. Body oval and blackish, 11–16 mm in length; pronotum not as above; occurring in mountain streams in western United States .... **Amphizòidae*** p. 371

11(3′). Prothorax with notopleural sutures (as in Figure 243) 12*

11′. Prothorax without notopleural sutures 14

12(11). Tarsi 5-5-5; elongate, parallel-sided, covered with scales, and 7–11 mm in length; elytra covering entire abdomen, and with several longitudinal ridges between which are rows of large square punctures; antennae filiform; widely distributed .... **Cupédidae*** p. 369

12′. Tarsi 3-3-3; oval in shape, and 1.5 mm in length or less; elytra not as above, sometimes short; antennae usually clubbed; western United States . 13*

13(12′). Abdomen with 3 visible sterna, the second short; antennae 11-segmented, with a 3-segmented club; hind coxae large and contiguous; elytra completely covering abdomen; length 0.5–0.75 mm (see also couplet 45) .... **Sphaèridae*** p. 375

13′. Abdomen with 6 or 7 visible sterna; antennae 9-segmented, with a 1-segmented club; hind coxae small and separated; elytra short, exposing about 3 abdominal segments; length about 1.5 mm .. **Hydroscáphidae*** p. 375

14(11′). Palps very short, generally rigid and not visible; prosternal sutures usually lacking; labrum nearly always lacking; head often prolonged into a beak or snout, with the antennae arising far in front of eyes on snout (Figures 244, 328 A, 330–336); tarsi 5-5-5, often appearing 4-4-4; antennae filiform or clubbed, often elbowed and clubbed 15

14′. Palps longer, flexible, and usually evident; prosternal sutures nearly always present (Figure 243, *stns*); head rarely prolonged into a beak (if it is, the

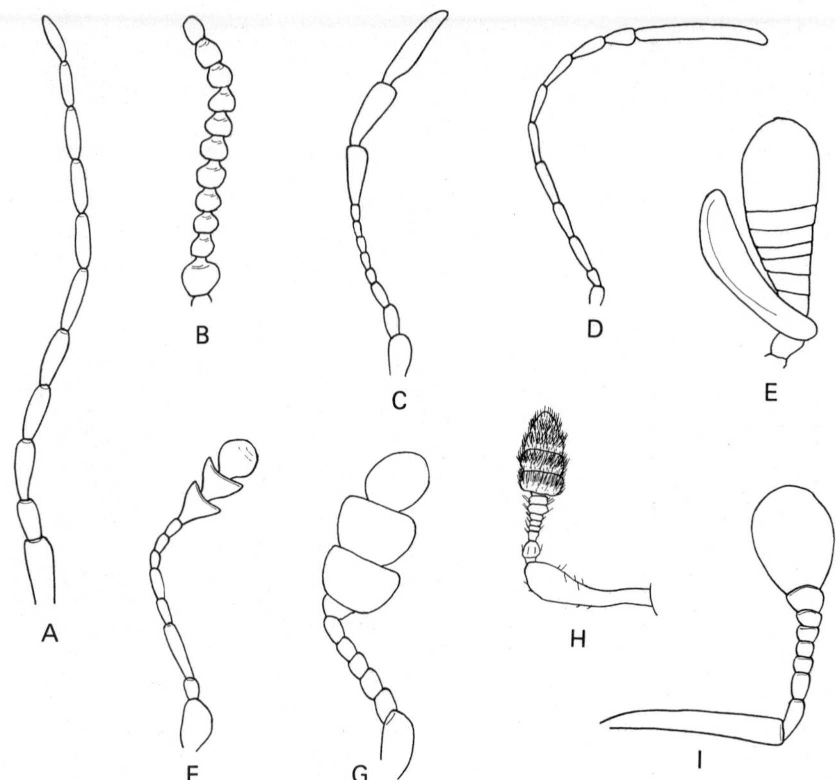

Figure 249. Antennae of Coleóptera. A, *Hárpalus* (Carábidae); B, *Rhysòdes* (Rhysòdidae); C, *Trichodésma* (Anobìidae); D, *Arthromàcra* (Lagrìidae); E, *Dineùtes* (Gyrìnidae); F, *Lobìopa* (Nitidùlidae); G, *Derméstes* (Derméstidae); H, *Hylurgópinus* (Scolýtidae); I, *Hololépta* (Histéridae). (H, redrawn from Kaston.)

antennae arise near the eyes and are not elbowed); labrum usually present; tarsi variable 17

15(15). Antennae filiform or moniliform; head prolonged into a beak extending straight forward (Figure 329 G, H); body parallel-sided or nearly so (Figure 328 A) .... **Bréntidae** p. 425

15′. Antennae clubbed, sometimes also elbowed; beak, if developed, usually more or less decurved; shape variable 16

16(15′). Head prolonged into a distinct beak or snout (Figure 244); basal segment of antennae often received in grooves on snout; antennae often reaching base of pronotum or beyond; tarsi apparently 4-4-4; front tibiae usually without a series of teeth externally or prolonged distally into a stout spur; size and shape variable .... **Curculiónidae** p. 425

16′. Head broad and short beyond eyes, not prolonged into a distinct snout; basal segment of antennae not received in grooves; antennae short, scarcely extending beyond anterior edge of pronotum; tarsi 5-5-5, sometimes appearing 4-4-4; front tibiae with a series of teeth externally, or prolonged distally into a stout spur; antennae with a large compact club; length 9 mm or less 116

17(14′). Elytra short, leaving one or more complete abdominal segments exposed 18

17′. Elytra covering tip of abdomen, or leaving only a part of the last abdominal segment exposed 40

18(17). Tarsi with apparently 3 or fewer segments 19

18′. Tarsi with more than 3 segments 23

19(18). Elytra very short, leaving 3 or more abdominal segments exposed 20

19′. Elytra longer, leaving only 1 or 2 abdominal segments exposed 22

20(19). Antennae 2-segmented; tarsi 3-3-3, the first 2 segments very small; tarsi with 1 claw; head and pronotum much narrower than elytra; brownish-yellow beetles, 2.5 mm in length or less, living in ant nests (Clavigerìnae) .... **Pseláphidae*** p. 377

20′. Not exactly fitting the above description 21

21(20′). Abdomen with 5 or 6 visible sterna, and usually more or less oval; antennae abruptly clubbed; length less than 6 mm .... **Pseláphidae** p. 377

21′. Abdomen with 6 or 7 visible sterna, and usually parallel-sided; antennae moniliform or slightly clavate; size variable .... **Staphylìnidae*** p. 377

22(19′). Last visible abdominal sternum very long; hind wings without a fringe of hair; body elongate and parallel-sided; antennae 10-segmented, with a 2-segmented club; southern United States (*Smícrips*) .... **Nitidùlidae*** p. 400

22′. Last visible abdominal sternum not unusually long; hind wings with a fringe of hair, or absent; body more or less oval; antennae 9-to 11-segmented, with a 2- or 3-segmented club 47

23(18′). Antennae elbowed and clubbed (Figure 249 I); tarsi 5-5-5 (rarely 5-5-4); shiny, hard-bodied, usually black beetles, 0.5–10.0 mm in length (Figure 265). .... **Histéridae** p. 376

23′. Antennae not elbowed 24

24(23′). Tarsi 5-5-5, 5-4-4, or 4-4-4 25

24′. Tarsi 5-5-4 151

25(24). Tarsi apparently 4-4-4 26

25′. Tarsi 5-5-5 or 5-4-4 29

26(25). Third tarsal segment very small and concealed in a notch of second; hind wings with a fringe of hairs; abdomen with 6 visible sterna, the first very long; oval convex beetles, 5 mm in length or less .... **Corylóphidae** p. 404

26′. Third tarsal segment not as above; hind wings without a fringe of hairs .. 27

27(26′). Antennae filiform, moniliform, serrate, or slightly clavate 28

27′. Antennae with an abrupt club 35

28(27). Head somewhat prolonged into a broad quadrate muzzle; antennae usually filiform or serrate; elytra pubescent; brownish or yellowish, more or less oval beetles, with only tip of abdomen exposed (Figure 320), generally less than 5 mm in length .... **Brùchidae** p. 417

28′. Head not as above; antennae filiform to slightly clavate; elytra pubescent or bare; size, shape, color, and length of elytra variable 183

29(25′). Maxillary palps very long, nearly as long as antennae, the last segment very long and straplike; antennae filiform; elytra short, exposing more than half of abdomen; hind wings not folded, and extending beyond elytra; slender brownish beetles, 4–6 mm in length; Arizona and California .... **Telegeùsidae*** p. 394

29′. Not exactly fitting the above description 30

30(29′). Small, oval, somewhat flattened, louselike insects, 2–4 mm in length; found in nests of small mammals or ground-nesting bees, or on beavers; abdomen with 6 visible sterna; eyes reduced or lacking ..... **Leptìnidae*** p. 378

30′. Not exactly fitting the above description 31

31(30′). Body very flat, the dorsal and ventral surfaces flat and parallel; pronotum somewhat triangular, much narrowed basally; front coxae rounded; gen-

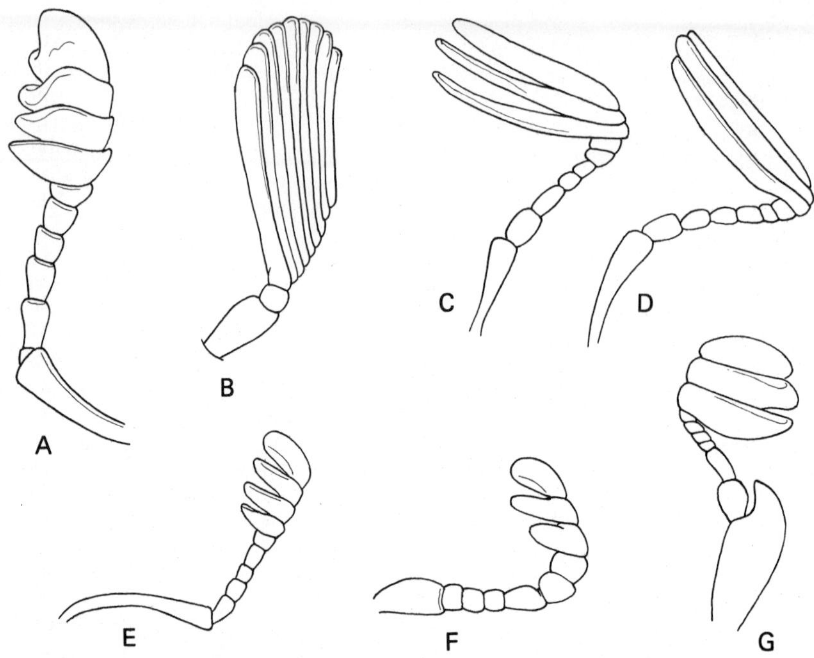

Figure 250. Antennae of Coleóptera. A, *Nicróphorus* (Sílphidae); B, *Sándalus,* male (Rhipicéridae); C, *Phylló-phaga* (Scarabaèidae), terminal segments expanded; D, same, terminal segments together forming a club; E, *Lucànus* (Lucànidae); F, *Popílius* (Passálidae); G, *Tróx* (Scarabaèidae).

erally less than 6 mm in length (*Inopéplus*) .... **Inopéplidae*** p. 409

31′. Body not unusually flattened, or pronotum not as above 32

32(31′). Antennae lamellate (Figure 250 A, C, D) or with an abrupt club.. 33

32′. Antennae filiform, moniliform, serrate, pectinate, or slightly clavate .. 36

33(32). Antennae lamellate, the terminal segments expanded on one side to form a lopsided club; usually over 10 mm in length 34

33′. Antennae not lamellate, the club symmetrical 35

34(33). The terminal antennal segments expanded laterally into rounded lobes not capable of being united to form a compact ball (Figure 250 A); elytra usually black or orange and black; length 15–35 mm (*Nicróphorus,* Figure 268 B) .... **Sílphidae** p. 378

34′. The 3 or 4 terminal antennal segments expanded laterally into oval or elongate lobes capable of being united into a compact ball (Figure 250 C, D); color and size variable .... **Scarabaèidae** p. 381

35(27′, 33′). Antennae 10-segmented with a 1- or 2-segmented club; first and fifth visible abdominal sterna longer than the others; third tarsal segment short, the fourth as long as or longer than the first 3 combined; length 3 mm or less 80

35′. Antennae 11-segmented, with a 3-segmented club; abdominal sterna not as above; length variable, but usually over 3 mm .... **Nitidùlidae** p. 400

36(32′). Small, elongate, dark-colored beetles, 1.7–2.2 mm in length, with yellow legs and antennae; first 2 antennal segments large, the antennae filiform or moniliform, and scarcely extending beyond head; head wider than pronotum; pronotum narrowed posteriorly; 3 or 4 abdominal segments exposed beyond elytra .... **Micromálthidae*** p. 369

36′. Not exactly fitting the above description 37

37(36′). Abdomen with 7 or 8 visible sterna 38

37′. Abdomen with 5 or 6 visible sterna 39

38(37). Antennae moniliform or clavate, rarely filiform; at least 4 abdominal segments exposed beyond elytra; pronotum usually margined laterally; length 1–20 mm .... **Staphylìnidae** p. 377

38′. Antennae filiform, serrate, or pectinate; other characters variable 192

39(37′). Elytra bare and shining, truncate, exposing 1 or 2 abdominal segments; antennae clavate; last abdominal segment sharply pointed (Figure 269); length 2–7 mm .... **Scaphidìidae** p. 379

39′. Elytra pubescent, their length variable; antennae clavate or filiform; last abdominal segment not sharply pointed; length 5–20 mm 231

40(17′). Terminal segments of antennae enlarged, forming a club of various sorts (Figures 249 C, F–I, and 250) 41

40′. Antennae not clubbed, but filiform, moniliform, serrate, pectinate, or gradually and only very slightly enlarged distally 150

41(40). Maxillary palps long and slender, usually as long as antennae or longer (Figure 264) 42

41′. Maxillary palps much shorter than antennae 43

42(41). Abdomen with 5 visible sterna; antennae with last 3 segments pubescent; length 1–40 mm .... **Hydrophílidae** p. 375

42′. Abdomen with 6 or 7 visible sterna; antennae with last 5 segments pubescent; length 2 mm or less .... **Hydraènidae*** p. 376

43(41′). All tarsi with apparently 4 or fewer segments 44

43′. Tarsi 5-5-5, 5-5-4, or 5-4-4 104

44(43). Tarsi apparently 3-3-3, 2-3-3, or 2-2-3 45

44′. Some or all tarsi apparently 4-segmented; second tarsal segment dilated and spongy pubescent beneath, third slender and much shorter than fourth (see also 44″) 51

44″. Some or all tarsi apparently 4-segmented, but second and third segments not as in 44′ 55

45(44). Body oval, convex, shining, blackish, and 0.5–0.75 mm in length; abdomen short and appearing 3-segmented: the first segment a triangular piece between hind coxae, the second a narrow transverse band, and the third occupying most of abdomen; antennae short, not extending beyond middle of pronotum, and 11-segmented; western United States .... **Sphaèridae*** p. 375

45′. Not exactly fitting the above description 46

46(45′). Hind wings fringed with hairs that often project beyond elytra; length usually less than 2 mm 47

46′. Hind wings not fringed with hairs; length usually over 2 mm... 49

47(22′, 46). Minute (mostly less than 1 mm in length) convex beetles, shaped a little like a horseshoe crab, with the abdomen tapering posteriorly; compound eyes and hind wings absent; tarsi 2-segmented, or 3-segmented with the first segment minute and concealed in apex of tibia; antennae short and retractile into grooves on underside of head, with a 2-segmented club; prosternal process broad and long, extending backward under mesosternum; abdomen with 5–7 visible sterna; living in ant nests .... **Limulòdidae*** p. 378

47′. Not exactly fitting the above description 48

48(47′). Antennae 11-segmented, with whorls of long hairs, and the 2 basal segments not enlarged; first visible abdominal sternum not unusually long; fringe on hind wings long; length 1 mm or less .... **Ptilìidae** p. 377

48′. Antennae 9- to 11-segmented, without whorls of long hairs, and the 2 basal segments enlarged; first abdominal segment very long; fringe on hind wings short; length usually over 1 mm .... **Corylóphidae** p. 404

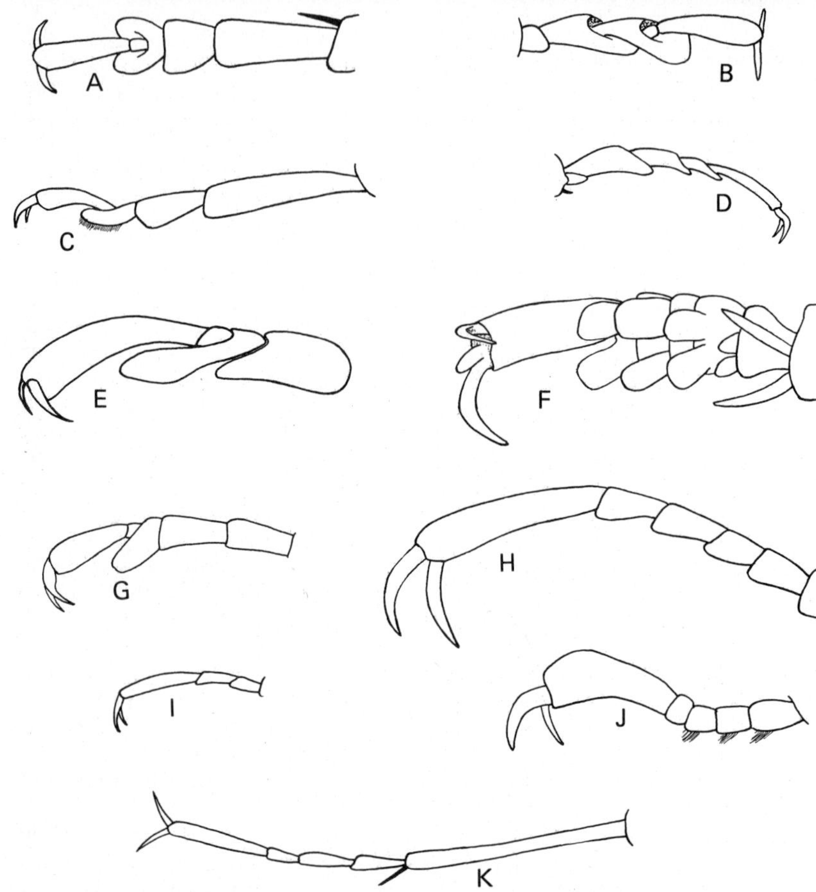

Figure 251. Tarsi of Coleóptera. A, *Megacyllène* (Cerambýcidae); B, *Necròbia* (Cléridae); C, *Nacérda* (Oedeméridae), hind leg; D, *Trichòdes* (Cléridae); E, *Chilócorus* (Coccinéllidae); F, *Sándalus* (Rhipicéridae); G, *Scólytus* (Scolýtidae); H, *Psephènus* (Psephènidae); I, a lathridiid; J, *Párandra* (Cerambýcidae); K, *Plátypus* (Platypódidae).

49(46′). Pronotum margined laterally, its base as wide as base of elytra; head much narrower than pronotum, and usually not visible from above; antennal club 3- to 5-segmented; oval, convex, shiny beetles, usually capable of tucking head and prothorax under body and rolling into a ball .... **Leiòdidae*** p. 378

49′. Not exactly fitting the above description 50

50(49′). Second tarsal segment dilated; tarsi actually 4-segmented, but third segment minute, fused to base of fourth, and difficult to see (Figure 251 E); oval, convex beetles, often brightly colored 51

50′. Second tarsal segment not dilated; color and shape variable 52

51(44′, 50). Tarsal claws toothed at base (Figure 247 A); antennae short, the antennae and head often hidden from above; anterior margin of pronotum straight or nearly so, not extended forward at sides; first visible abdominal sternum with curved coxal lines .... **Coccinéllidae** p. 404

51′. Tarsal claws simple; head and antennae easily visible from above; anterior margin of pronotum broadly excavated, and produced forward at sides; first visible abdominal sternum without curved coxal lines .... **Endomýchidae** p. 404

52(50′). Elytra covering the entire abdomen 53

52′. Elytra truncate, exposing the last abdominal segment 80

53(52). First visible abdominal sternum long, often as long as next 3 sterna combined; the first 3 abdominal sterna more or less fused together; front coxae globular, and widely separated; elytra shiny, with sparse pubescence; length usually more than 3 mm .... **Colydìidae** p. 406

53′. First visible abdominal sternum not unusually long, and all the sterna freely movable; front coxae somewhat conical, contiguous or separated; elytra usually pubescent; length 3 mm or less (see also 53″) 54

53″. First visible abdominal sternum not unusually long, and all the sterna more or less fused and immovable; front coxae globular, usually slightly separated; elytra pubescent; length 0.5–11.0 mm .... **Anthríbidae** p. 424

54(53′). Front coxal cavities open; front coxae contiguous .... **Dasycéridae*** p. 378

54′. Front coxal cavities closed, or if open then front coxae are separated .... **Lathridìidae** p. 405

55(44″). First tarsal segment broad, flat, and oval, with a dense pad of short hairs beneath, the second and third segments minute, the second arising from upper surface of first near its base, the fourth large, long; head and pronotum of about equal width, parallel-sided; elytra parallel-sided, about one third wider than pronotum; reddish yellow or tawny, with black antennae and scutellum, and with 5 elongate black marks on each elytron; 2 mm in length; Florida (*Monoèdus*) .... **Colydìidae*** p. 406

55′. Not exactly fitting the above description 56

56(55′). Tibiae dilated and very spiny; body broad and flat, the mandibles and labrum projecting forward prominently; first and fourth tarsal segments much longer than second and third; the last 7 antennal segments forming a long serrate club; semiaquatic, mud-inhabiting beetles, 4.0–6.5 mm in length (Figure 283 A) .... **Heterocéridae** p. 389

56′. Not exactly fitting the above description 57

57(56′). Stout, cylindrical or slightly oval beetles, 1–9 (usually 5 or less) mm in length (Figure 338); antennae short, scarcely reaching beyond front of pronotum, with a large solid club (Figure 249 H); front tibiae with a series of teeth externally, or produced distally into a stout spur; eyes oval, emarginate, or divided .... **Scolýtidae** p. 438

57′. Not exactly fitting the above description 58

58(57′). Front tarsi with a different number of segments than middle and hind tarsi 59

58′. All tarsi apparently 4-4-4 60

59(58). Tarsi 3-4-4; elytra pubescent; elongate-oval, somewhat flattened beetles, 1.5–6.0 mm in length, often brightly patterned (males) (Figure 305 A) .... **Mycetophágidae** p. 405

59′. Tarsi 4-3-3; elytra bare; oval, convex, brownish or black beetles (see also couplet 49) (males of *Aglyptìnus*) .... **Leiòdidae*** p. 378

60(58′). Elytra bare or with a few scattered hairs 61

60′. Elytra pubescent 85

61(60). Third tarsal segment more or less lobed beneath 62

61′. Third tarsal segment slender or small, not lobed beneath 66

62(61). Body elongate and usually very flat; length 4 mm or less (Silvanìnae) .... **Cucùjidae** p. 401

62′. Body not unusually flattened; size and shape variable 63

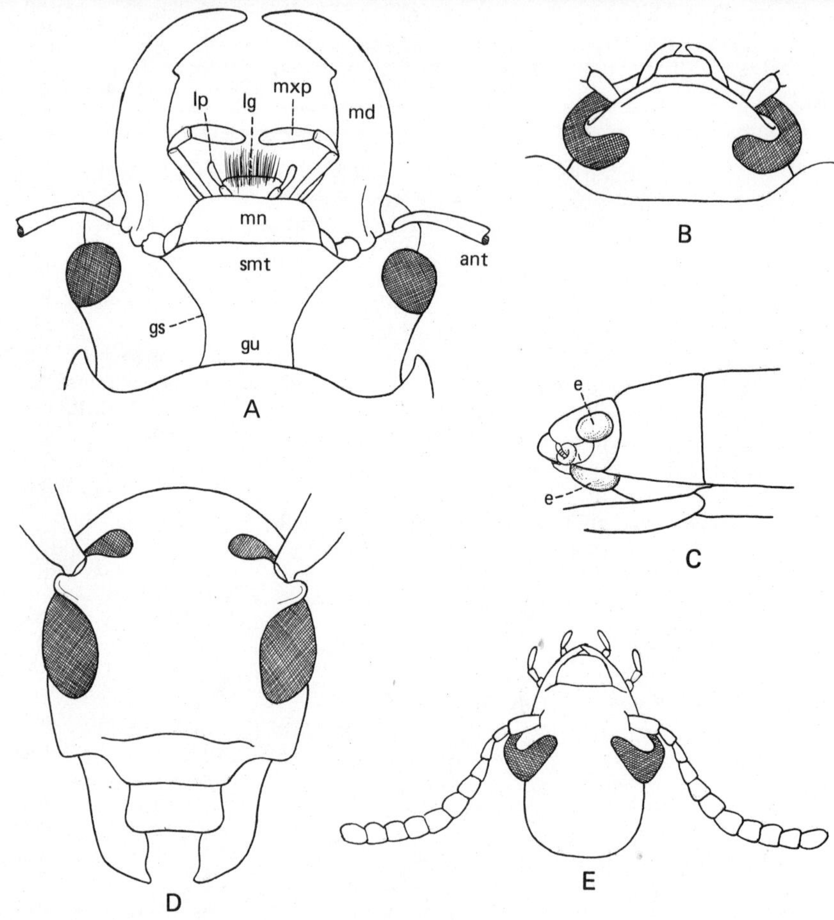

Figure 252. Heads of Coleóptera. A, *Lucànus* (Lucànidae), ventral view; B, *Diapèris* (Tenebriónidae), dorsal view; C, *Dineùtes* (Gyrìnidae), lateral view; D, *Sapérda* (Cerambýcidae), anterior view; E, *Brùchus* (Brùchidae), dorsal view. *ant,* base of antenna; *e,* compound eye; *gs,* gular suture; *gu,* gula; *lg,* ligula; *lp,* labial palp; *md,* mandible; *mn,* mentum; *mxp,* maxillary palp; *smt,* submentum.

63(62′). Elongate, somewhat cylindrical beetles, 5.5–12.0 mm in length, usually with pronotum yellow or red and elytra black (Figure 302 D) .... **Languriìdae** p. 402

63′. Body shape and color variable, usually not as above 64

64(63′). Antennal club not very abrupt, the segments gradually enlarging distally, and the club usually consisting of more than 3 segments 65

64′. Antennal club abrupt, 3-segmented (Figure 249 F); oval, convex beetles, less than 5 mm in length 74

65(64). Oval, convex, dark-colored beetles, 5–10 mm in length, with head deflexed and not visible from above (Figure 281); front coxae transverse .. .. **Býrrhidae** p. 388

65′. Size, shape, and color variable, but if oval and convex then front coxae are not transverse .... **Chrysomélidae** p. 418

66(61′). Body extremely flattened, elongate and more or less parallel-sided, 2–12 mm in length .... **Cucùjidae** p. 401

66′. Body not unusually flattened; size variable 67

67(66′). A pair of ocelli present near compound eyes (Figure 253 C); elytra with rows of large square punctures; brownish beetles, 3–6 mm in length (*Laricòbius*) .... **Derodóntidae*** p. 395

67′. Ocelli absent; elytra, color, and size variable 68

68(67′). Head scarcely or not at all visible from above; body shape variable 69

68′. Head easily visible from above; body usually elongate 77

69(68). Elongate, cylindrical, dark-colored beetles, usually less than 12 mm in length (one western species is about 50 mm in length); pronotum tuberculate, sometimes with blunt hornlike processes; elytra usually with ridges or punctures (Figure 296); tarsi actually 5-5-5, but fourth segment very small and difficult to see .... **Bostríchidae** p. 398

69′. Oval, convex beetles, not as above; usually less than 5 mm in length 70

70(69′). Antennal club relatively abrupt, and 3-segmented 71

70′. Antennae more gradually enlarged distally, the club with more than 3 segments 76

71(70). Abdomen with 6 visible sterna, the first very long; the 2 basal antennal segments enlarged .... **Corylóphidae** p. 404

71′. Abdomen with 5 (rarely 6) visible sterna, the first not unusually long...72

72(71′). Front coxae flattened, oval, and nearly contiguous; length 3 mm or less .... **Georýssidae*** p. 376

72′. Front coxae conical, or if small and flat then separated 73

73(72′). Front coxae conical and prominent; beetles often capable of tucking the head and prothorax under the body and rolling into a ball .. **Leiòdidae*** p. 378

73′. Front coxae round, flat, or transverse; beetles not capable of rolling into a ball 74

74(64′, 73′). Front coxae transverse; hind coxae separated; oval convex beetles less than 2 mm in length (*Cybocéphalus*) .... **Nitidùlidae*** p. 400

74′. Front coxae oval or rounded; hind coxae usually contiguous or nearly so; length 5 mm or less 75

75(74′). Abdomen with 6 visible sterna, the first very long; head usually not visible from above; length 0.5–5.0 mm .... **Corylóphidae** p. 404

75′. Abdomen with 5 visible sterna, the first not unusually long; head usually visible from above; length 1–3 mm .... **Phalácridae** p. 403

76(70′). Front coxae conical and prominent; beetles often capable of tucking the head and prothorax under the body and rolling into a ball .. **Leiòdidae*** p. 378

76′. Front coxae transverse, and separated .... **Býrrhidae** p. 388

77(68′). Abdomen with 6 visible sterna, the first very long; the two basal antennal segments enlarged .... **Corylóphidae** p. 404

77′. Abdomen with 5 visible sterna 78

78(77′). Antennae 10-segmented with a 1- or 2-segmented club; slender beetles 79

78′. Antennae 8- to 11-segmented, the club of at least 3 segments 81

79(78). Head and eyes prominent; length 6 mm or less 80

79′. Head small and partly retracted into prothorax, the eyes usually more or less concealed; length 1–18 mm .... **Colydìidae** p. 406

80(35, 52′, 79). Front coxae rounded or transverse .... **Rhizophágidae** p. 400

80′. Front coxae conical and prominent (*Phyllobaènus, Isohydnócera*) .... **Cléridae** p. 400

81(78′). Mandibles large, prominent, and strong; length 7–28 mm; mostly western United States (Psoìnae) (see also couplet 129) .... **Bostríchidae** p. 398

81′. Mandibles small and inconspicuous; size variable; widely distributed 82

82(81′). Front coxae transverse 83

82′. Front coxae rounded 84

83(82). Pronotum rather widely separated from elytra except at attachment point in center (Figure 298); tarsi actually 5-segmented, but first segment very short and difficult to see .... **Trogosítidae** p. 399

83′. Pronotum contiguous with base of elytra completely across body; tarsi actually 4-segmented; oval, convex beetles, less than 2 mm in length (*Cybocéphalus*) .... **Nitidùlidae*** p. 400

84(82′). Tarsi actually 5-segmented, but fourth segment small and difficult to see; anterior margin of pronotum not produced forward at sides .. **Erotýlidae** p. 402

84′. Tarsi actually 4-segmented; anterior margin of pronotum produced forward at sides (Mycetaeinae) (see also couplet 84″) .... **Endomýchidae** p. 404

84″. Tarsi actually 4-segmented; anterior margin of pronotum only slightly concave (see also couplets 53 and 79′) .... **Colydìidae** p. 406

85(60′). Third tarsal segment more or less lobed beneath 86

85′. Third tarsal segment slender or small, not lobed beneath 94

86(85). Antennal club distinct, of 3 or fewer segments 87

86′. Antennal club less distinct, composed of more than 3 segments 91

87(86). Head produced anteriorly into a broad muzzle; base of protonum as wide as base of elytra; gular sutures present or absent 88

87′. Head not produced anteriorly into a broad muzzle; width of pronotum variable; gular sutures present 89

88(87). Pronotum posteriorly with keel-like lateral margins and usually a transverse ridge; gular sutures absent; labrum separated from face by a suture; tibiae without apical spurs; length 0.5–11.0 mm .... **Anthríbidae** p. 424

88′. Pronotum rounded laterally; gular sutures present; labrum not separated from face by a suture; tibiae with 2 small movable apical spurs; length 3–5 mm (Cimberìnae) .... **Curculiónidae** p. 425

89(87′). Lateral margins of pronotum toothed (Figure 302 B); length less than 3 mm (*Oryzaéphilus*) .... **Cucùjidae** p. 401

89′. Lateral margins of pronotum not toothed; length usually over 3 mm... 90

90(89′). Base of pronotum as wide as and contiguous with base of elytra; front coxae more or less transverse; usually uniformly colored beetles, generally less than 5 mm in length (Figure 305 B) .... **Bytùridae** p. 405

90′. Base of pronotum usually narrower than, and slightly separated from, base of elytra; front coxae somewhat conical, rarely transverse; often brightly patterned, 3–24 mm in length (Figure 299) .... **Cléridae** p. 400

91(86′). Head produced anteriorly into a rather broad muzzle; pygidium exposed; first tarsal segment very long; oval, usually grayish or brownish beetles .... **Brúchidae** p. 417

91′. Head not as above; pygidium covered or exposed, but if exposed then the body is elongate and nearly parallel-sided 92

92(91′). Oval, convex, usually dark-colored beetles, with head deflexed and scarcely or not at all visible from above (Figure 281); front coxae transverse .... **Býrrhidae** p. 388

92′. Body elongate and nearly parallel-sided; head not deflexed, usually conspicuous from above; front coxae usually conical, rarely transverse...93

93(92′). Sides of pronotum serrate (Figure 302 B); length less than 3 mm (*Oryzaéphilus*) .... **Cucùjidae** p. 401

93′. Sides of pronotum not serrate (Figure 299); length 5 mm or more .... **Cléridae** p. 400

94(85′). Oval, convex beetles, 2 mm in length or less, often capable of deflecting the head and prothorax and rolling into a ball; hind coxae dilated into broad plates that conceal hind legs in repose; antennae with 10 or fewer segments, and with a 2-segmented club; hind wings fringed with long hairs .... **Clámbidae*** p. 380

94′. Not exactly fitting the above description 95

95(94′). The first 3 or 4 visible abdominal sterna more or less fused together... 96

95′. All abdominal sterna freely movable 98

96(95). Apical segment of maxillary palps needlelike, much more slender than preceding segments (*Cérylon, Philothérmus*) .... **Cerylónidae** p. 403

96′. Apical segment of maxillary palps not needlelike, its diameter as great as or greater than that of preceding segments 97

97(96′). Antennae 10-segmented, with a solid 2-segmented club, usually received in cavities beneath front corners of thorax; front coxae enclosed behind by mesosternum; oval beetles, 1.5 mm in length or less .... **Cerylónidae** p. 403

97′. Antennae usually 11-segmented, the club 2- or 3-segmented; front coxae usually distant from mesosternum; body generally elongate and cylindrical, but if oval then usually over 1.5 mm in length and with front corners of pronotum produced forward (see also couplet 53) .... **Colydìidae** p. 406

98(95′). Head scarcely or not at all visible from above 99

98′. Head easily visible from above 102

99(98). Antennal club compact, 3- or 4-segmented; elongate-cylindrical beetles 100

99′. Antennal club not very compact, and usually of 5 or more segments; oval, convex beetles 101

100(99). Length 3 mm or less; first 3 tarsal segments short, the fourth long; front coxae separated .... **Cìidae** p. 405

100′. Length usually over 3 mm; first tarsal segment longer; front coxae contiguous .... **Bostríchidae** p. 398

101(99′). Length 5–10 mm; eighth antennal segment about the same size as seventh and ninth; front coxae transverse .... **Býrrhidae** p. 388

101′. Length 2–5 mm; eighth antennal segment smaller than seventh or ninth; front coxae large and prominent, conical or quadrate .... **Leiòdidae*** p. 378

102(98′). Elongate, cylindrical, uniformly colored beetles (Figure 295 B); antennae with an abrupt 2- (rarely 3-) segmented club; head slightly constricted behind eyes and about as wide as pronotum .... **Lýctidae** p. 399

102′. Elongate-oval, often patterned beetles; antennal club less abrupt, composed of 3–5 segments; head not constricted behind eyes, and narrower than pronotum 103

103(102′). Pronotum truncate anteriorly (Figure 305 A); tibiae with apical spurs .... **Mycetophágidae** p. 405

103′. Pronotum excavated anteriorly, the sides produced forward (Figure 303 C); tibiae without apical spurs (Mycetaeìnae) .... **Endomýchidae** p. 404

104(43′). Hind tarsi 3- or 4-segmented 105

104′. All tarsi 5-segmented 106

105(104). Oval, convex, shiny beetles, 1–6 mm in length; antennae with a 3-to 5-segmented club; 6 (rarely 5) visible abdominal sterna; pronotum margined laterally, and as broad at base as base of elytra; tarsi 5-5-4; beetles often capable of tucking head and prothorax under body and rolling into a ball .... **Leiòdidae*** p. 378

105′. Not exactly fitting the above description 151

106(104′). Antennae lamellate (Figure 250 C–G) or flabellate (Figure 250 B), the terminal segments expanded on one side to form a lopsided club 107

106′. Antennae not lamellate or flabellate, the club usually symmetrical ... 113

107(106). First tarsal segment very small and difficult to see; pronotum rather widely separated from base of elytra except at attachment point in center (Figure 298); length 5–20 mm .... **Trogosítidae** p. 399

107′. First tarsal segment of normal size 108

108(107′). Antennae flabellate, the terminal 5 or more segments expanded laterally into long, thin, parallel-sided tonguelike lobes (as in Figure 250 B) ... 109

108′. Antennae lamellate, the terminal 3 or 4 segments expanded laterally into oval or elongate lobes capable of being united into a compact ball (Figure 205 C, D, G) (see also 108″) .... **Scarabaèidae** p. 381

108″. Antennae with the terminal (or intermediate) segments expanded laterally into rounded and flattened lobes that are not capable of being united into a compact ball (Figure 250 E, F) 111

109(108). Front tibiae dilated, flattened, and coarsely scalloped or toothed along outer edge; ventral surface of body clothed with long hair; stout-bodied, striped (*Polyphylla*) or unicolorous (*Pleócoma*) beetles, 17–43 mm in length; western United States .... **Scarabaèidae** p. 381

109′. Not exactly fitting the above description 110

110(109′). Tarsi with a hairy projection between claws, and the first 4 segments with lobes beneath (Figure 251 F); mandibles large and projecting forward; antennae not received in grooves on front; 16–24 mm in length (Figure 271) .... **Rhipicéridae** p. 380

110′. Tarsi not as above; mandibles small and inconspicuous; antennae often received in transverse grooves on front; usually less than 16 mm in length .... **Eucnèmidae** p. 394

111(108″). Last tarsal segment long, nearly as long as the preceding segments combined, with long claws (as in Figure 251 H); length 6 mm or less; generally aquatic beetles .... **Dryópidae** p. 389

111′. Last tarsal segment and claws not so lengthened; length over 7 mm ... 112

112(111′). Mentum deeply emarginate (Figure 253 A); head with a short, dorsal, anteriorly directed horn (Figure 253 B); first antennal segment not greatly lengthened (Figure 250 F); pronotum with a deep median groove, and elytra with longitudinal grooves; shining black beetles, 30–40 mm in length (Figure 272 C) .... **Passálidae** p. 381

112′. Mentum entire (Figure 252 A); head usually without such a horn; first antennal segment greatly lengthened (Figure 250 E); pronotum without a median groove and elytra often smooth; brown or black beetles, 8–40 mm in length .... **Lucànidae** p. 380

113(106′). A pair of ocelli present near compound eyes (Figure 253 C); elytra with rows of punctures (*Derodóntus*) or polished dark spots (*Peltástica*); lateral margins of pronotum toothed (*Derodóntus*, Figure 292) or thin and entire (*Peltástica*); brownish beetles, 3–6 mm in length .... **Derodóntidae*** p. 395

113′. Ocelli absent; other characters variable 114

114(113′). Dorsum with rows of short hair tufts (easily abraded) and not particularly shiny; tibiae dilated and flat; first 4 tarsal segments short, the fifth about as long as the others combined; black, oval, convex beetles, 4–6 mm in length, usually found in tree wounds .... **Nosodéndridae*** p. 396

114′. Not exactly fitting the above description 115

115(114′). Antennae short, scarcely reaching beyond anterior edge of pronotum, with a large compact club; front tibiae with a series of teeth externally, or prolonged distally into a stout spur; more or less cylindrical beetles, 9 mm in length or less 116

115′. Not exactly fitting the above description 117

116(16′, 115). Tarsi very slender, the first segment as long as the next 3 combined (Figure 251 K); head as broad as or broader than pronotum; eyes round and prominent; body slender and cylindrical (Figure 337) .... **Platypódidae** p. 438

116′. First tarsal segment not as long as the next 3 combined (Figure 251 G); head not broader than pronotum; eyes oval, emarginate, or divided, and not prominent; body stouter, cylindrical to slightly oval (Figure 338) .... **Scolýtidae** p. 438

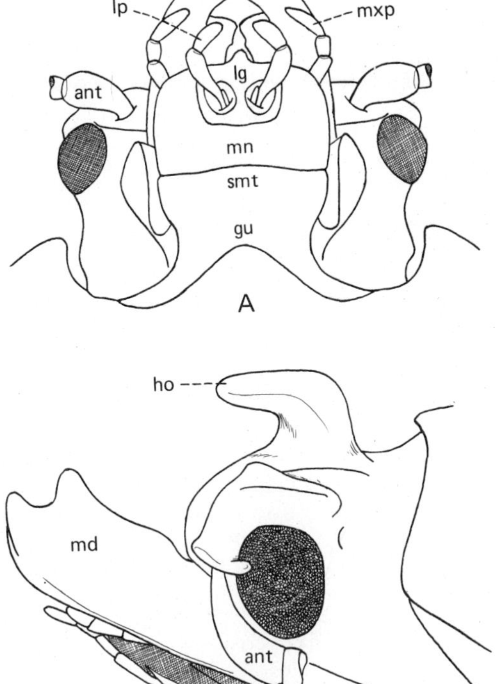

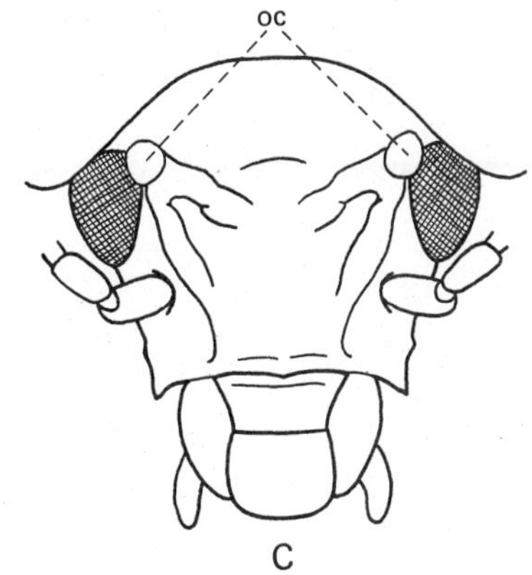

Figure 253. Heads of Coleóptera. A, ventral view, and B, lateral view of *Popílius disjúnctus* (Illiger) (Passálidae); C, *Derodóntus* (Derodóntidae). *ant,* base of antenna; *gu,* gula; *ho,* horn; *lg,* ligula; *lp,* labial palp; *md,* mandible; *mn,* mentum; *mxp,* maxillary palp; *oc,* ocelli; *smt,* submentum.

117(115′). Last tarsal segment very long, with long claws (as in Figure 251 H); first 3 visible abdominal sterna usually more or less fused together; elongate or oval beetles, 1–8 mm in length, usually aquatic or shore-inhabiting .. 186

117′. Tarsi and abdominal sterna not as above; mostly terrestrial beetles .. 118

118(117′). Elytra distinctly pubescent 119

118′. Elytra bare, or with only a few scattered hairs 133

119(118). Hind corners of pronotum prolonged backward into points that tightly embrace base of elytra; front coxae rounded or oval, and separated; prosternum prolonged backward into a median process that is received by mesosternum; oblong-oval, slightly flattened, black or brownish beetles, 2–5 mm in length .... **Thróscidae** p. 393

119′. Not exactly fitting the above description 120

120(119′). Head narrowed behind eyes into a narrow neck; femora usually clavate; body antlike, brown or black, 1–5 (usually less than 3) mm in length (Figure 267 B) .... **Scydmaènidae*** p. 379

120′. Head and body not as above; femora usually not clavate; size variable 121

121(120′). Head scarcely or not at all visible from above 122

121′. Head prominent, easily visible from above 126

122(121). Antennae clavate, club not abrupt; front coxae transverse and separated; hind coxae large, extending to lower edge of elytra; oval, convex, usually dark-colored beetles, 5–10 mm in length (Figure 281) .... **Býrrhidae** p. 388

122′. Antennae usually with a distinct club of 3–5 segments; coxae variable 123

123(122′). Front coxae conical and prominent 124

123′. Front coxae small, usually rounded, and not prominent 125

124(123). Antennal club of about 5 segments, the club not abrupt; tarsal segments subequal; oval, uniformly colored beetles, 2–5 mm in length... **Leiòdidae*** p. 378

124′. Antennal club abrupt, 3-segmented; last tarsal segment longer than the others; oval or elongate beetles, uniformly colored or patterned, 1–12 mm in length (Figure 293) .... **Derméstidae** p. 396

125(123′). Tibiae with apical spines or spurs; hind coxae not grooved for the reception of the femora; elytra often with apical spines or teeth; pronotum often tuberculate; length usually 3–10 mm (one western species reaches a length of about 50 mm) .... **Bostríchidae** p. 398

125′. Tibial spurs very small or lacking; hind coxae grooved for the reception of the femora; elytra without apical spines or teeth; pronotum not tuberculate; length 1–9 mm .... **Anobìidae** p. 396

126(121′). Front coxae conical and prominent 127

126′. Front coxae rounded, oval, or transverse, not prominent 128

127(126). Brownish, oval, uniformly colored beetles, 2–5 mm in length; base of pronotum as wide as base of elytra; found in nests of small mammals or ground-nesting bees, or on mountain beavers .... **Leptìnidae*** p. 378

127′. Elongate or elongate-oval beetles, not particularly flattened, usually brightly colored, 3–24 mm in length (Figure 299); base of pronotum usually narrower than base of elytra; not found in the situations listed above .... **Cléridae** p. 400

128(126′). First visible abdominal sternum longer than any other; front coxae oval or globose; elongate-oval, usually yellowish brown beetles, 1–5 mm in length, with a silky pubescence .... **Cryptophágidae** p. 402

128′. First visible abdominal sternum not unusually long; coxae and size variable 129

129(128′). Antennae with 10 or fewer segments; first tarsal segment shorter than second; front coxae small, about as long as wide, the front coxal cavities open behind; head including eyes wider than pronotum; length 7–28 mm; mostly western united States (Psoìnae) (see also couplet 81) .... **Bostríchidae** p. 398

129′. Antennae nearly always 11-segmented; other characters variable 130

130(129′). Front coxae nearly always transverse 131

130′. Front coxae globose or oval 132

131(130). Tarsi slender, the segments not lobed, and the first segment very short; body pubescence sparse; pronotum often separated from base of elytra except at attachment point in center (Figure 298); length 5–20 mm... **Trogosítidae** p. 399

131′. Some tarsal segments dilated or lobed beneath, the first segment not unusually short; body densely pubescent; pronotum contiguous with base of elytra; length less than 5 mm (Figure 305 B) (see also 131″).. **Bytùridae** p. 405

131″. The 3 basal tarsal segments about the same size and with a brush of hairs beneath, the fourth smaller and without the brush of hairs; body pubescence sparse; oval, somewhat flattened beetles (Figure 301 C) .... **Nitidùlidae** p. 400

132(130′). Elongate-oval, somewhat flattened beetles; head narrower than pronotum; first visible abdominal sternum short, visible only in angle between hind coxae; Quebec (*Lendòmus*) .... **Mycetophágidae*** p. 405

132′. Elongate, parallel-sided, more or less cylindrical beetles; head nearly as wide as pronotum (Figure 295 B); first visible abdominal sternum longer; widely distributed (see also 132″) .... **Lýctidae** p. 399

132″. Elongate, parallel-sided, flattened beetles, the head nearly as wide as pronotum (Figure 302 A, B); first visible abdominal sternum longer;

widely distributed (Silvanìnae) .... **Cucùjidae** p. 401

133(118′). Body oval and convex; head much narrower than pronotum 134

133′. Body elongate, or if oval then more or less flattened; head width variable 138

134(133). Front coxae conical and prominent; pronotum margined laterally; length 1–5 mm; usually capable of tucking head and prothorax under body and rolling into a ball .... **Leiòdidae*** p. 378

134′. Front coxae globose or transverse, usually not prominent; pronotum and size variable 135

135(134′). Maxillary palps long, nearly as long as antennae; antennae 8- or 9-segmented, with a pubescent club; head visible from above; dung-inhabiting beetles, 1–7 mm in length (Sphaeridiìnae) .... **Hydrophílidae** p. 375

135′. Maxillary palps much shorter than antennae; antennae 11-segmented 136

136(135′). Length 5–10 mm; antennae clavate, the club not abrupt; hind coxae large, extending to lower edge of elytra .... **Býrrhidae** p. 388

136′. Length 1–6 mm; antennal club abrupt, 3-segmented 137

137(136′). Length 1–3 mm; first 3 tarsal segments broad, the fourth small; pygidium covered by elytra .... **Phalácridae** p. 403

137′. Length about 6 mm; tarsi slender; pygidium exposed .... **Sphaerìtidae*** p. 376

138(133′). Head not visible from above; elongate, cylindrical, dark-colored beetles, usually less than 12 mm in length (one western species reaches a length of about 50 mm); pronotum tuberculate, sometimes with blunt hornlike processes .... **Bostríchidae** p. 398

138′. Head prominent and easily visible from above; size, shape, and pronotum variable 139

139(138′). Body very flat, the dorsal and ventral surfaces flat and parallel; fourth tarsal segment usually small; elongate, generally parallel-sided, usually reddish or brownish beetles, 2–12 mm in length (Figure 302 A) .... **Cucùjidae** p. 401

139′. Body not so flat, the dorsal surface slightly convex; fourth tarsal segment generally not unusually small 140

140(139′). Front coxae conical or quadrate, and projecting prominently; usually 6 visible abdominal sterna; antennae with a 3- or 4-segmented club, the last 3 segments pubescent; flattened, oval, usually blackish beetles (Figure 268), 1.5–16.0 mm in length. .... **Sílphidae** p. 378

140′. Front coxae usually globose or transverse, not prominently projecting; 5 visible abdominal sterna; other characters variable 141

141(140′). Antennae with 10 or fewer segments, and a 3-segmented club; first tarsal segment much shorter than second; front coxal cavities open behind; length 7–28 mm; western United States (*Psòa*) .... **Bostríchidae** p. 398

141′. Antennae 11-segmented (if 10-segmented, then body length is less than 4 mm) 142

142(141′). Front coxae transverse 143

142′. Front coxae globose 146

143(142). Antennae 10-segmented, with a 2-segmented club; length 3 mm or less; southern United States (*Smícrips*) .... **Nitidùlidae*** p. 400

143′. Antennae nearly always 11-segmented, the club with at least 3 segments; usually over 3 mm in length 144

144(143′). The 3 basal tarsal segments about the same size and with a dense brush of hairs beneath, the fourth segment smaller and without the brush of hairs 145

144′. The 4 basal tarsal segments with long hairs below, the fourth segment as large as the third, and the first segment short (Ostomìnae)... **Trogosítidae** p. 399

145(144). Oval or elongate, 1.5–12.0 mm in length; pronotum more or less quadrate, at most only slightly wider than head; elytra sometimes short and exposing tip of abdomen .... **Nitidùlidae** p. 400

145′. Oval or elongate-oval, 3–20 mm in length; pronotum more or less trapezoidal, narrower anteriorly, at base distinctly wider than head; elytra covering entire abdomen .... **Erotýlidae** p. 402

146(142′). Body oval to elongate-oval; head distinctly narrower than pronotum; pronotum margined laterally; often marked with red, yellow, or orange; length 3–20 mm .... **Erotýlidae** p. 402

146′. Body elongate, parallel-sided; head about as wide as pronotum 147

147(146′). Pygidium exposed; first visible abdominal sternum about as long as sterna 2–4 combined; length 4 mm or less (Figure 300 B) ...... **Rhizophágidae** p. 400

147′. Pygidium concealed; first visible abdominal sternum not as long as sterna 2–4 combined; length usually over 5 mm 148

148(147′). Fourth tarsal segment very small, the first of normal size; antennae with a 4-segmented club; usually black beetles, with the pronotum yellowish or reddish (Figure 302 D), 5.5–12.0 mm in length .... **Langurìidae** p. 402

148′. First tarsal segment very small, the fourth of normal size; antennae with a 2-(rarely 3-) segmented club; uniformly colored, black or brownish beetles, 2–20 mm in length 149

149(148′). Blackish beetles, 10–20 mm in length; western United States (*Polýcaon*) .... **Bostríchidae** p. 398

149′. Usually brownish beetles, 2–7 mm in length; widely distributed .. **Lýctidae** p. 399

150(40′). Tarsi 5-5-4 (rarely appearing 4-4-3) 151

150′. Tarsi apparently 3-3-3, 4-4-4, or 5-5-5 (4-5-5 in male *Cóllops,* family Melridae) 176

151(24′,105′,150). Front coxal cavities closed behind 152

151′. Front coxal cavities open behind 159

152(151). Tarsal claws pectinate (Figure 247 B); elongate-oval, pubescent, usually black or brown beetles, 4–12 mm in length (Figure 306 B)...**Allecùlidae** p. 408

152′. Tarsal claws not pectinate; size and color variable 153

153(152′). Last antennal segment lengthened, as long as the preceding 3 or 4 segments combined, the antennae filiform (Figure 308 B); head and pronotum narrower than elytra; elongate, dark-colored, shiny beetles, 6–15 mm in length .... **Lagrìidae** p. 408

153′. Last antennal segment not so lengthened (or the antennae clubbed); size, shape, and color variable 154

154(153′). Five visible abdominal sterna, with the suture separating the 2 basal segments poorly defined, so that these segments appear as one large segment; coxae widely separated; apical tarsal segment longer than the others combined; eyes small, round, and protruding; blackish, shiny beetles, 2–4 mm in length, living in rock cracks below the high tidemark along the Pacific Coast (Aegialitìnae) .... **Salpíngidae*** p. 408

154′. Not exactly fitting the above description 155

155(154′). Antennae 11-segmented (rarely 10-segmented), and arising beneath a frontal ridge; antennae filiform, moniliform, or slightly clubbed, only rarely capitate or flabellate; eyes often emarginate; shape and color variable (Figure 307); length 2–35 mm; a large and widely distributed group .... **Tenebriónidae** p. 406

155′. Antennae 10- or 11-segmented, with a distinct club, and not arising beneath a frontal ridge; eyes round 156*

156(155′). Antennae 11-segmented, moniliform or with a 3-segmented club .. 157*

156′. Antennae 10-segmented, the club of 1 or 2 segments; length less than 5 mm 158*

157(156). Antennae with a 3-segmented club; often with a mottled coloration; eyes large and prominent; body not particularly flattened; insects resembling tiger beetles .... **Othnìidae*** p. 408

157′. Antennae moniliform; straw-colored; eyes not particularly prominent; body very flat, the insect resembling a cucujid (*Hemipéplus*)...**Myctéridae*** p. 409

158(156′). Elongate slender beetles; elytra bare or nearly so; pygidium exposed (some males) .... **Rhizophágidae*** p. 400

158′. Oblong convex beetles; elytra pubescent, and covering pygidium .... **Sphíndidae*** p. 401

159(151′). Oval, black, somewhat flattened beetles, 5–12 mm in length (Figure 306 A); antennae with an abrupt club of 2 or 3 segments, and received in grooves on underside of prothorax; legs retractile .... **Monómmidae** p. 405

159′. Not exactly fitting the above description 160

160(159′). Pronotum with sharp lateral margins 161

160′. Pronotum with rounded lateral margins 164

161(160). Body elongate and very flat, the dorsal and ventral surfaces flat and parallel .... **Cucùjidae** p. 401

161′. Body not so flattened 162

162(161′). Body somewhat wedge-shaped, as high as or higher than wide, humpbacked, the head bent down, and the abdomen pointed apically (Figure 310); length 14 mm or less, usually less than 8 mm .... **Mordéllidae** p. 409

162′. Not exactly fitting the above description 163

163(162′). Antennae with a distinct 3-segmented club; pronotum without dents or depressions near posterior margin; first segment of hind tarsi not greatly lengthened; length 1–5 mm .... **Cryptophágidae** p. 402

163′. Antennae filiform or nearly so; pronotum with 2 dents or depressions near posterior margin (Figure 308 A); first segment of hind tarsi elongate, much longer than any other segment; length 3–20 mm .... **Melandrỳidae** p. 409

164(160′). Tarsal claws pectinate, with a large pad beneath each claw; head elongate and somewhat diamond-shaped, gradually narrowing behind eyes to a narrow neck; pronotum narrow anteriorly, about as wide as base of elytra posteriorly, somewhat bell-shaped; yellowish to brownish beetles, 8–20 mm in length .... **Cephalòidae*** p. 406

164′. Not exactly fitting the above description 165

165(164′). Pronotum with 2 dents or depressions near posterior margin (Figure 308 A), at base about as wide as base of elytra; first segment of hind tarsi much longer than any other segment 166

165′. Pronotum without such dents or depressions; other characters variable 167

166(165). Front of head distinctly prolonged anterior to eyes (somewhat as in Figure 329 G); bases of antennae distant from eyes; eyes round (Mycterìnae) .... **Myctéridae** p. 409

166′. Front of head only slightly projecting anterior to eyes; bases of antennae very close to eyes; eyes elongate-oval .... **Melandrỳidae** p. 409

167(165′). Penultimate segment of hind tarsi dilated and with a dense brush of hairs beneath; middle coxae conical and prominent, and contiguous; pronotum widest in anterior half, at base narrower than elytra; elongate, soft-bodied beetles, 3.5–20.0 mm in length (Figure 309 A) .... **Oedeméridae** p. 409

167′. Not exactly fitting the above description 168

168(167′). Antennae usually pectinate, flabellate, or plumose, rarely serrate 169

168′. Antennae (at least terminal segments) filiform 171

169(168). Length 3 mm or less; eyes emarginate; penultimate tarsal segment very small, the tarsi sometimes appearing 4-4-3 (*Emelìnus*) ...... **Euglénidae*** p. 411

169′. Length 4 mm or more; eyes usually not emarginate; penultimate tarsal segment not unusually small, the tarsi distinctly 5-5-4 170

170(169′). Pronotum as wide at base as base of elytra, and dark-colored; body somewhat wedge-shaped, higher than wide; elytra often tapering to a point posteriorly; length 4–15 mm .... **Rhipiphòridae** p. 410

170′. Pronotum distinctly narrower than base of elytra, often reddish or yellowish; body dorsoventrally flattened; elytra rounded apically, and usually widest behind middle; length 6–20 mm (Figure 309 B) ... **Pyrochròidae** p. 408

171(168′). Head abruptly narrowed behind eyes to form a narrow neck 172

171′. Head not constricted behind eyes 175

172(171). Tarsal claws cleft to base (Figure 247 C), or toothed; abdomen with 6 visible sterna; length 3–30 mm .... **Melòidae** p. 410

172′. Tarsal claws simple; abdomen usually with 5 visible sterna; length 12 mm or less 173

173(172′). Length over 6 mm; hind coxae contiguous; head constricted well behind eyes; body elongate (Figure 313 B) .... **Pedìlidae** p. 411

173′. Length less than 6 mm; hind coxae contiguous or separated; head constricted just behind eyes 174

174(173′). Eyes oval; pronotum sometimes with an anterior hornlike process extending forward over head (Figure 313 A); penultimate tarsal segment easily visible, the tarsi distinctly 5-5-4; first 2 visible abdominal sterna not fused; length 2–4 mm .... **Anthícidae** p. 411

174′. Eyes emarginate; pronotum without an anterior hornlike process; penultimate tarsal segment very small, the tarsi sometimes appearing 4-4-3; first 2 visible abdominal sterna more or less fused together; length 1.5–3.0 mm .... **Euglénidae*** p. 411

175(171′). Elytra long, covering entire abdomen; body not particularly flattened; pronotum widest in middle, narrower at base and apex (Figure 306 C); length 2–15 mm .... **Salpíngidae** p. 408

175′. Elytra short, exposing 2 or more abdominal segments; body strongly flattened; pronotum triangular, very narrow at base, widest anteriorly; length 6 mm or less .... **Inopéplidae*** p. 409

176(150′). Tarsi apparently 3-3-3; elongate-oval, more or less convex, pubescent beetles, 0.5–11.0 mm in length (Figure 328 B) .... **Anthríbidae** p. 424

176′. Tarsi apparently 4-4-4 (see also 176″) 177

176″. Tarsi 5-5-5 (rarely 4-5-5 in some males) 184

177(176′). Head produced anteriorly into a broad muzzle; antennae serrate or pectinate; elytra pubescent; oval, brownish or yellowish beetles, mostly 5 mm in length or less, with tip of abdomen exposed (Figure 320)... **Brùchidae** p. 417

177′. Not exactly fitting the above description 178

178(177′). Head scarcely or not at all visible from above; antennae of male pectinate, with long processes arising from segments 4–10, antennae of female serrate; scutellum heart-shaped, notched anteriorly; third tarsal segment lobed beneath; length 4–6 mm .... **Ptilodactýlidae** p. 388

178′. Either head easily visible from above, or otherwise not fitting the above description 179

179(178′). Oval, convex, usually dark-colored beetles, with the head scarcely or not at all visible from above (Figure 281); pronotum rounded laterally; length 5–10 mm .... **Býrrhidae** p. 388

179′. Head easily visible from above, or if concealed then pronotum is margined laterally 180

180(179′). Body elongate and very flat, the dorsal and ventral surfaces flat and parallel; generally reddish or brownish beetles, 2–12 mm in length (Figure 302 A) .... **Cucùjidae** p. 401

180′. Body not so flat, the dorsal surface more or less convex... 181

181(180′). Body very pubescent, the pubescence of long erect hairs; antennae rarely extending much beyond base of pronotum; base of pronotum narrower than base of elytra; length 3–24 mm (Figure 299) .... **Cléridae** p. 400

181′. Elytra short-pubescent or bare; other characters variable 182

182(181′). Gular sutures absent; pronotum posteriorly with keellike lateral margins and usually a transverse ridge; antennae more than half as long as body; head produced anteriorly into a broad muzzle, and somewhat retracted into thorax; no tibial spurs; elytra with rows of punctures; 0.5–11.0 mm in length .... **Anthríbidae** p. 424

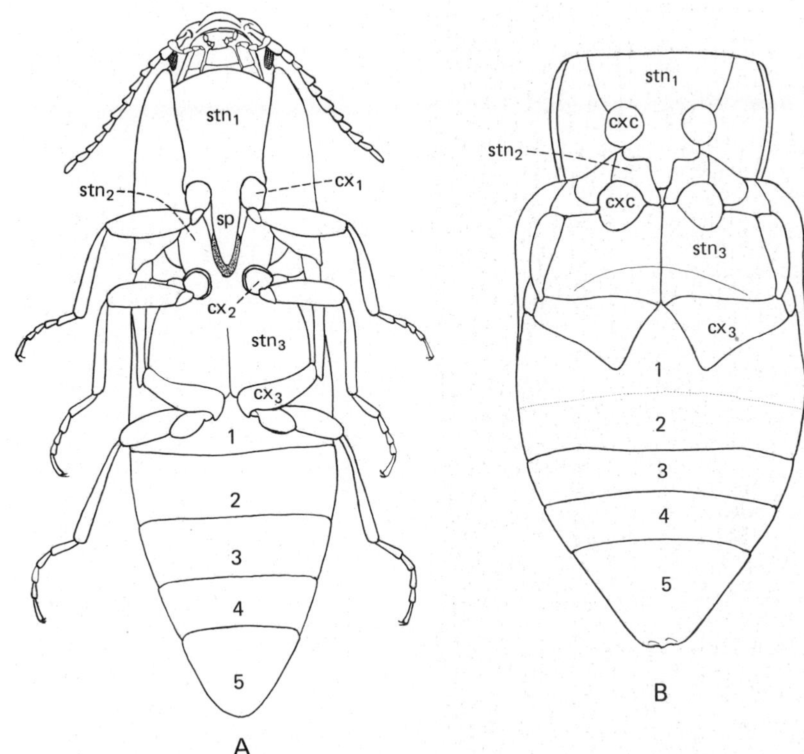

Figure 254. A, ventral view of a click beetle (*Agriòtes*); B, ventral view of the thorax and abdomen of a metallic wood-boring beetle (*Chrysóbothris*). *cx*, coxa; *cxc*, coxal cavity; *sp*, prosternal spine; *stn₁*, prosternum; *stn₂*, mesosternum; *stn₃*, metasternum; *1–5*, abdominal sterna.

182′. Gular sutures present; pronotum not as above; other characters variable 183

183(28′, 182′). Antennae usually more than half as long as body, inserted on frontal prominences, their insertions often partly surrounded by eyes (Figure 252 D); eyes often emarginate (rarely completely divided); first antennal segment at least 5 times as long as second; body usually elongate and parallel-sided; length 3–73 mm, usually over 12 mm .... **Cerambýcidae** p. 412

183′. Antennae usually less than half as long as body, and not inserted on frontal prominences; eyes usually entire; body generally oval; small beetles, usually less than 12 mm in length .... **Chrysomélidae** p. 418

184(176″). The first 3 visible abdominal sterna more or less fused together; tarsi long, with long claws (Figure 251 H); length 8 mm or less; mostly aquatic beetles 185

184′. The first 3 visible abdominal sterna not fused (rarely the first 2 are fused); tarsi not as above; size variable; usually terrestrial 188

185(184). Abdomen with 6 or 7 (rarely 5) visible sterna; oval, flattened, dark-colored, finely pubescent beetles, 4–6 mm in length (Figure 282 C) ... **Psephènidae** p. 388

185′. Abdomen with 5 visible sterna; body oval or elongate, convex or more or less cylindrical; length 1–8 mm 186

186(117, 185′). Antennae 10- or 11-segmented, the first 2 segments relatively long, the remaining segments short and broad; elytra distinctly pubescent; front

	coxae transverse; oval, convex beetles, 1–4 mm in length... **Limníchidae***	p. 389
186′.	Antennae 7- to 11-segmented, the segments generally not as above; elytra pubescent or bare; front coxae variable; elongate-oval beetles, 1–8 mm in length 187	
187(186′).	Front coxae transverse; elytra bare or pubescent. .... **Dryópidae**	p. 389
187′.	Front coxae globose or oval; elytra bare .... **Elmidae**	p. 389
188(184′).	Abdomen with 7 or 8 visible sterna; elytra usually soft 189	
188′.	Abdomen with 5 or 6 visible sterna; elytra variable 194	
189(188).	Ocelli present on front or vertex 190*	
189′.	Ocelli absent 191	
190(189).	Two ocelli on vertex between eyes; second visible abdominal sternum with a transverse ridge along front edge; length 2.5–7.5 mm (Omaliìni) .... **Staphylìnidae***	p. 377
190′.	Only 1 ocellus present, on front of head between eyes; a large, hairy, median swelling on first visible abdominal sternum; pale, straw-colored beetles, about 2.5 mm in length, with long slender antennae (males of *Thylódrias*) .... **Derméstidae***	p. 396
191(189′).	Middle coxae separated; elytra usually with reticulate sculpturing; flattened beetles, usually widest in posterior half, often brightly colored, and 5–18 mm in length (Figure 291 A) (some species, chiefly western, have the head prolonged into a prominent snout) .... **Lỳcidae**	p. 395
191′.	Middle coxae contiguous or nearly so; elytra not reticulate; elongate, usually parallel-sided beetles 192	
192(38′,191′).	Head more or less concealed by pronotum and usually not visible from above (Figure 290 A); mesal margins of metepisterna straight or nearly so (Figure 255 A); abdomen often with luminescent organs (yellowish areas on underside); length 5–20 mm .... **Lampýridae**	p. 394
192′.	Head not concealed by pronotum and easily visible from above (Figure 290 B); mesal margins of metepisterna variable; abdomen without luminescent organs; size variable 193	
193(192′).	Mesal margins of metepisterna more or less curved (Figure 255 B); antennae 11-segmented, and filiform or serrate (rarely pectinate); elytra usually broadly rounded apically; length 18 mm or less .... **Canthàridae**	p. 395
193′.	Mesal margins of metepisterna straight; antennae 12-segmented, and pectinate or plumose; elytra narrowed and more or less pointed apically (Figure 291 B); length 10–30 mm .... **Phengòdidae***	p. 394
194(188′).	The first 2 visible abdominal sterna partly fused together, the suture between them very weak (Figure 254 B); hard-bodied, usually metallic (especially ventrally) .... **Bupréstidae**	p. 390
194′.	All visible abdominal sterna separated by equally distinct sutures; soft- or hard-bodied, seldom metallic 195	
195(194′).	Head scarcely or not at all visible from above; oval or elongate-oval, usually convex beetles, generally 10 mm in length or less 196	
195′.	Head prominent from above; size and shape variable 207	
196(195).	Hind corners of pronotum prolonged backward into points that tightly embrace base of elytra; front coxae small and rounded; prosternum prolonged backward as a process that fits into mesosternum 197	
196′.	Hind corners of pronotum not prolonged backward as points; other characters variable 198	
197(196).	Oblong-oval beetles, widest in middle of body; usually brownish in color, and 2–5 mm in length; antennae usually not received in prosternal grooves .... **Thróscidae**	p. 393
197′.	Elongate, more or less cylindrical beetles, parallel-sided; brownish to black, and generally over 5 mm in length (Figure 289 D); antennae often received in prosternal grooves .... **Eucnèmidae**	p. 394

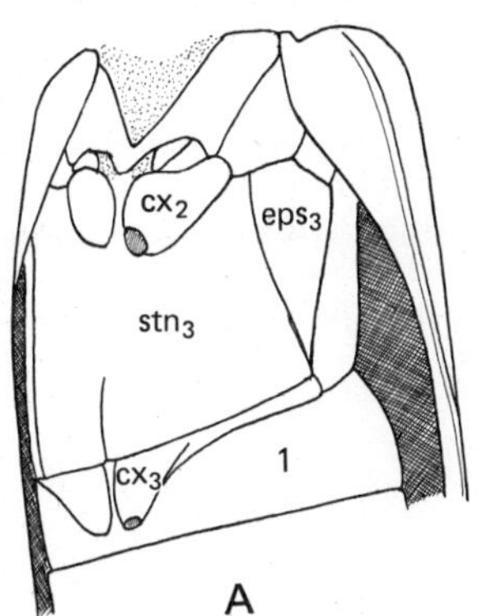

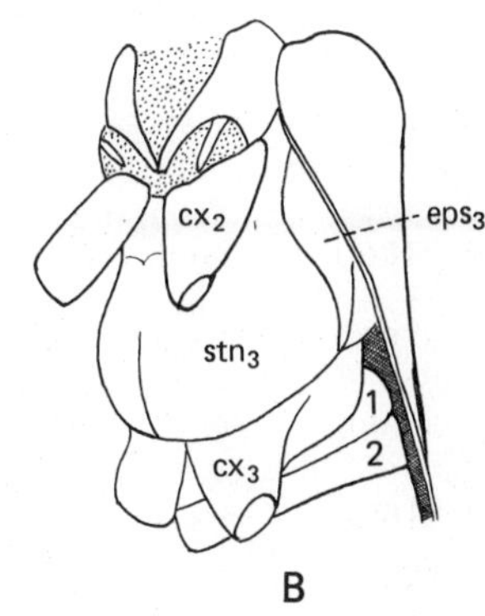

Figure 255. Lateroventral views of thorax and base of abdomen. A, *Photùris* (Lampýridae); B, *Chauliógnathus* (Canthàridae). cx, coxa; eps_3, metepisternum; stn_3, metasternum; *1–2*, abdominal sterna.

198(196′). Oval, convex beetles, 4–5 mm in length, with head completely ventral and retracted into prothorax, partly concealing eyes; basal antennal segment small, completely concealed, second and third segments much larger, flattened, and situated tightly in a groove in prosternum, remaining segments flattened, serrate, and exposed (extending along mesosternum); middle coxae widely separated; hind coxae grooved for reception of femora; legs strongly retractile; posterior margin of pronotum sinuate, with a row of large punctures; southeastern United States .... **Chelonarìidae*** p. 388

198′. Not exactly fitting the above description 199

199(198′). Third tarsal segment conspicuously lobed beneath, the fourth very small and difficult to see; scutellum heart-shaped, notched anteriorly; antennae serrate (females) or pectinate (some males); pale brown or tan, more or less elongate beetles, 4–6 mm in length .... **Ptilodactýlidae** p. 380

199′. Not exactly fitting the above description 200

200(199′). At least one tarsal segment with prominent lobes beneath 201

200′. Tarsal segments slender, without lobes beneath 203

201(200). Hind coxae grooved for reception of femora; length 4–10 mm 202

201′. Hind coxae not grooved for reception of femora; length 2–4 mm (see also couplet 229) .... **Helòdidae** p. 380

202(201). Antennae long, slender, moniliform, extending posteriorly to middle of elytra or beyond; tarsi with segments 2–4 lobed beneath, with fourth segment very short; elongate pubescent beetles; 4.0–7.5 mm in length .... **Artematòpidae** p. 388

202′. Antennae stout, clavate, and short, seldom extending much beyond base of pronotum; tarsi variable; oval, convex beetles; 5–10 mm in length (Figure 281) .... **Býrrhidae** p. 388

203(200′). Hind trochanters quadrate; front coxae contiguous 204

203′. Hind trochanters triangular; front coxae variable 205*

204(203). Hind coxae grooved for reception of femora; antennae usually with last 3 segments elongate (Figure 249 C), rarely pectinate, flabellate, or filiform; short-legged, not spiderlike; 1.1–9.0 mm in length (Figure 294) .... **Anobìidae** p. 396

204′. Hind coxae not grooved; antennae filiform, the last 3 segments not elongated (*Gnóstus*, occurring in ant nests in Florida, has the antennae 3-segmented); long-legged, brownish, spiderlike beetles; 2–4 mm in length (Figure 295 A) .... **Ptìnidae** p. 397

205(203′). Hind coxae dilated into broad oblique plates that extend to elytra and cover most of first visible abdominal sternum; tarsal segments decreasing in length distally; oval convex beetles; 3 mm in length or less (Figure 270 A) .... **Eucinètidae*** p. 380

205′. Hind coxae not dilated into broad oblique plates; size and shape variable 206*

206(205′). Oval, convex beetles; 2–5 mm in length .... **Leiòdidae*** p. 378

206′. Elongate beetles; 3–14 mm in length .... **Dascíllidae*** p. 380

207(196′). Middle and hind trochanters very long, hind trochanters nearly as long as femora; pronotum wider than long, but a little narrower at base than base of elytra, the hind angles pointed but not projecting backward beyond level of middle of rear edge of pronotum; elongate, slightly flattened, black beetles; 6.0–8.5 mm in length; Pennsylvania and California .... **Cerophýtidae*** p. 394

207′. Middle and hind trochanters of normal size; other characters usually not as above 208

208(207′). Antennae serrate, pectinate, or flabellate 209

208′. Antennae filiform or moniliform 218

209(208). Posterior corners of pronotum prolonged backward as sharp points... 210

209′. Posterior corners of pronotum not prolonged backward, base of pronotum straight, sinuate, or somewhat convex 214

210(209). Front coxae conical and prominent; prosternum not prolonged backward as a spinelike process 211

210′. Front coxae small and rounded; prosternum prolonged backward as a spinelike process 212

211(210). Mandibles large and prominent, apical half sharply bent, apices acute; length over 10 mm; southeastern United States .... **Callirhípidae** p. 389

211′. Mandibles short, not prominent, with blunt apices; length 5–6 mm; Texas, Utah, and California .... **Brachypséctridae*** p. 389

212(210′). Prothorax firmly attached to mesothorax and not movable; front coxae partly covered by the prosternal spine; oblong-oval beetles, usually brownish, 2–5 mm in length .... **Thróscidae** p. 393

212′. Prothorax loosely attached to mesothorax and movable; front coxae laterad of prosternal spine; beetles usually able to click and jump 213

213(212′). Labrum fused to front; antennae arising well in front of eyes, often received in grooves on front and prosternum; prosternum not lobed in front, its anterior margin straight or nearly so; more or less cylindrical beetles; usually 15 mm in length or less (*Palaeóxenus dòhrni* Horn, from southern California, brilliant orange and black, is 15–20 mm in length) (Figure 289 D) .... **Eucnèmidae** p. 394

213′. Labrum distinct; antennae usually arising near eyes, above base of mandibles, and usually not received in grooves on front (but sometimes received in grooves on prosternum); prosternum usually lobed in front (its anterior margin usually arcuate); somewhat flattened beetles; size variable, up to about 35 mm in length (Figure 289 A, C)... **Elatéridae** p. 391

214(209′). Elongate, slender, cylindrical beetles, 9.0–13.5 mm in length, brown or black with yellow appendages; antennae short, not extending beyond middle of prothorax, and filiform or serrate; head about as wide as pronotum, somewhat narrowed behind eyes; tarsal segments slender, without lobes beneath, as long as or longer than tibiae; elytra with short pubescence; maxillary palps of male flabellate; eastern United States .... **Lymexylónidae** p. 400

214′. Not exactly fitting the above description 215

215(214′). Pronotum quadrate or somewhat oval, the posterior corners rounded, the posterior margin straight or convex; body pubescence long; often brightly colored beetles 231

215′. Pronotum more or less trapezoidal in shape, the posterior corners angulate, the posterior margin sinuate; body pubescence when present usually short 216

216(215′). Length usually less than 10 mm; front coxae transverse; elytral pubescence moderate to dense; usually brownish; antennae 11-segmented .... **Dascíllidae** p. 380

216′. Length more than 10 mm; front coxae conical and prominent; elytral pubescence when present fine, short; brown to black beetles; antennae 11- or 12-segmented 217

217(216′). Length 16–24 mm; tarsi lobed beneath (Figure 251 F); widely distributed .... **Rhipicéridae** p. 380

217′. Length 11–18 mm; tarsi not lobed beneath; southeastern United States .. .. **Callirhípidae** p. 389

218(208′). Body antlike; head narrowed behind eyes to a narrow neck, and pronotum and elytra oval in dorsal view; length 6 mm or less 219*

218′. Body not antlike; size variable 220

219(218). Abdomen with 6 visible sterna; pronotum long-pubescent; femora clavate (Figure 267 B); widely distributed .... **Scydmaènidae*** p. 379

219′. Abdomen with 5 visible sterna; pronotum bare; femora slender; northeastern United States and California (Brathinìnae) .... **Staphylìnidae*** p. 377

220(218′). Body very flat, the dorsal and ventral surfaces flat and parallel ... **Cucùjidae** p. 401

220′. Body not so flat, the dorsal surface more or less convex ... 221

221(220′). Posterior corners of pronotum prolonged backward as sharp points; prosternum prolonged backward as a spinelike process that fits into a cavity in mesosternum (Figure 254 A) 222

221′. Posterior corners of pronotum not prolonged backward as sharp points, *or* prosternum not as above 224

222(221). Labrum distinct, separated from front of head by a suture; prosternum usually lobed in front (its anterior margin usually arcuate), extending forward under mouth parts (Figure 254 A); antennae arising near eyes, above base of mandibles; body somewhat flattened; union of prothorax and mesothorax loose, the beetles able to click and jump; length 3–35 mm .... **Elatéridae** p. 391

222′. Labrum usually not distinct, the suture separating it from front of head indistinct or absent; prosternum not, or but slightly, lobed in front, its anterior margin straight or nearly so; antennae arising well in front of eyes; body more or less cylindrical; union of prothorax and mesothorax not very loose, the beetles sometimes able to click and jump; length 3–20 mm 223

223(222′). Tarsal claws pectinate; mandibles large and usually prominent .... **Perothópidae*** p. 394

223′. Tarsal claws simple; mandibles small and inconspicuous .... **Eucnèmidae** p. 394

224(221′). Body very pubescent, the hairs long; mandibles long, bent, hooklike, and extending forward from head; eyes round, bulging; pronotum trapezoidal, about as wide as head anteriorly, narrower than base of elytra posteriorly; tibiae dilated apically, with 2 long apical spurs; tarsi long and slender, longer than tibiae; abdomen with 6 visible sterna; light brown beetles, 20–25 mm in length; southern United States .... **Cebriónidae*** p. 391

224′. Not exactly fitting the above description 225

225(224′). Length nearly always more than 10 mm; elytra bare, brown, and shining (*Párandra*) or black and punctate (*Spóndylis* and *Scaphìnus*) .... **Cerambýcidae** p. 412

225′. Length variable, but if more than 10 mm then elytra are pubescent ... 226

226(225′). Elongate, slender, cylindrical beetles, 9.0–13.5 mm in length, brown or black with yellow appendages; antennae short, not extending beyond middle of prothorax; head about as wide as pronotum, and somewhat narrowed behind eyes; pronotum margined laterally; tarsal segments slender, without lobes beneath, the tarsi as long as or longer than tibiae; maxillary palps of male flabellate; eastern United States .... **Lymexylónidae** p. 400

226′. Not exactly fitting the above description 227

227(226′). Brownish oval beetles, usually less than 3 mm in length, found in nests of small mammals or ground-nesting bees, or on mountain beavers; abdomen with 6 visible sterna; front coxae globular; eyes usually reduced; tip of abdomen exposed beyond elytra .... **Leptìnidae*** p. 378

227′. Size and color variable; not found in the situations listed above, but if found in somewhat similar situations then there are only 5 visible abdominal sterna and the elytra cover the entire abdomen; eyes well developed; front coxae variable, but usually not globular 228

228(227′). Hind trochanters quadrate, as long as or longer than wide; pronotum distinctly narrower than elytra at their widest point, the elytra oval and convex, bare or pubescent; legs long, the femora sometimes swollen or clavate; small, brownish, spiderlike beetles, 2–4 mm in length (*Gnóstus*, occurring in ant nests in Florida, has the antennae 3-segmented) .... **Ptìnidae** p. 397

228′. Hind trochanters small and triangular; elytra pubescent; shape usually not as above 229

229(228′). Oval or elongate-oval, convex beetles, 2–4 mm in length; hind femora often swollen; pronotum more or less quadrate, about twice as wide as long, its posterior margin sinuate; 5 visible abdominal sterna; front coxae conical; usually found near water, as the larvae are aquatic ... **Helòdidae** p. 380

229′. Elongate or elongate-oval, convex or flattened beetles, usually more than 4 mm in length; pronotum trapezoidal, quadrate, or oval, usually as long as or longer than wide, its posterior margin sinuate, straight, or convex; 5 or 6 visible abdominal sterna; front coxae variable; habitats variable ... 230

230(229′). Pronotum quadrate or trapezoidal, its posterior margin sinuate; body usually convex, more or less cylindrical; usually brownish beetles, 3–14 mm in length .... **Dascíllidae** p. 380

230′. Pronotum quadrate or oval, its posterior margin straight or convex; body somewhat flattened; often brightly colored beetles, 3–24 mm in length 231

231(39′, 215, 230′). Middle coxae rounded, not prominent; hind coxae flat or oval, projecting but slightly below ventral surface of abdomen; pronotum usually rounded laterally; eyes often emarginate.............................. **Cléridae** p. 400

231′. Middle coxae conical and prominent; hind coxae prominent, extending ventrally below ventral surface of abdomen; pronotum margined laterally; eyes round 232

232(231′). Elytra short, exposing at least 3 abdominal segments; antennae usually slightly clavate .... **Staphylìnidae** p. 377

232′. Elytra longer, not more than 2 abdominal segments exposed; antennae filiform or slightly serrate 233

233(232′). Antennae 10- or 11-segmented, and inserted on front above base of mandibles, the sockets facing anteriorly; hind coxae transverse; body pubescence usually long and erect; length 5–10 mm .... **Melýridae** p. 400

233′. Antennae 11-segmented, and inserted between eyes and distant from base of mandibles, the sockets facing dorsally; hind coxae triangular and prominent; body pubescence usually short and recumbent; length 1–15 mm .... **Canthàridae** p. 395

234(1′). Tarsi with 1 claw; head almost completely retracted into prothorax; body elongate and cylindrical, more than 10 mm in length, and often over 20 mm in length; often with a luminous area on each side of most segments .... **Phengòdidae*** p. 394

234′. Tarsi with 2 claws; head prominent, not retracted into thorax 235*

235(234′).	Body oval, dorsoventrally flattened, straw-colored, and 3 mm in length or less (*Thylódrias*) .... **Derméstidae***	p. 396
235′.	Body narrow and somewhat laterally flattened; usually over 3 mm in length .... **Rhipiphòridae***	p. 410

SUBORDER **Archostémata:** Coleopterists do not agree on the relationships of the two families here considered as representing the suborder Archostémata. The Cupédidae are considered by most authorities as being a very primitive group meriting subordinal rank, but some (for example, Arnett, 1968) would place the Micromálthidae in the suborder Polýphaga because they lack notopleural sutures. The two families in this suborder are small (only six North American species) and seldom encountered.

Family **Cupédidae**—Reticulated Beetles: This is a small and little known group, with only five species occurring in the United States. All are densely scaly, with the elytra reticulate and the tarsi distinctly 5-segmented. The prosternum extends backward as a narrow process that fits into a groove in the mesosternum, much as in click beetles. The common species in the eastern United States, *Cùpes cóncolor* Westwood, is 7–10 mm in length and brownish gray in color; in the Rocky Mountains and the Sierra Nevada the most common species is *Priácma serràta* LeConte, which is gray with faint black bands across the elytra. These beetles are usually found under bark.

Family **Micromálthidae:** This family includes a single rare species, *Micromálthus débilis* LeConte, which has been taken in several localities in the eastern United States. The adults are 1.8–2.5 mm in length, elongate and parallel-sided, dark, shiny, with yellowish legs and antennae; the tarsi are 5-segmented. This insect has a remarkable life cycle, with paedogenetic larvae; the larvae are able to reproduce (both oviparously and viviparously) parthenogenetically. These beetles have been found in decaying logs, principally oak and chestnut logs.

SUBORDER **Adéphaga:** The members of this suborder have the hind coxae dividing the first visible abdominal sternum (Figure 248 A); the posterior margin of this sternum does not extend completely across the abdomen, but is interrupted by the hind coxae. Nearly all the Adéphaga have filiform antennae and 5-5-5 tarsi, they have notopleural sutures, and most of them are predaceous.

Family **Rhysòdidae**—Wrinkled Bark Beetles: The members of this group are slender, brownish beetles 5.5–7.5 mm in length with three fairly deep longitudinal grooves on the pronotum and with the antennae moniliform (Figure 256). The pronotal grooves are complete in *Rhysòdes,* but are present on only about the posterior third of the pronotum in *Clinídium*. These beetles are usually found under the bark of decaying beech, ash, elm, or pine. Four species occur in the United States, one of each genus in the East, and another of each genus in the West.

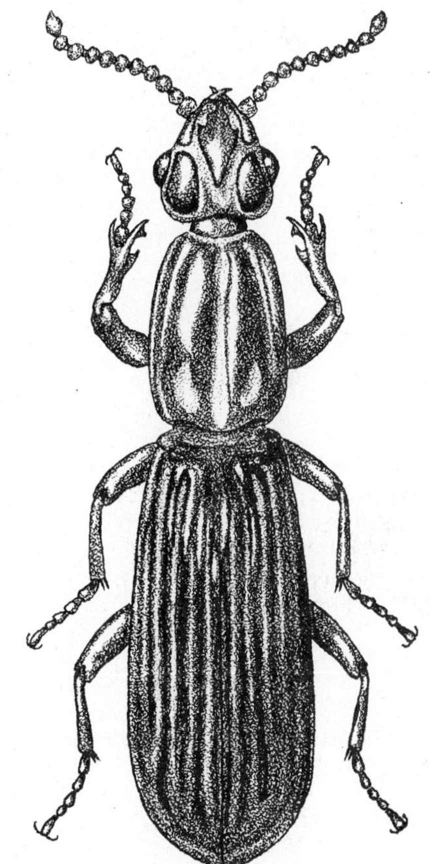

Figure 256. A wrinkled bark beetle, *Clinídium scúlptilus* Newman, 14 ×. (Courtesy of Arnett.)

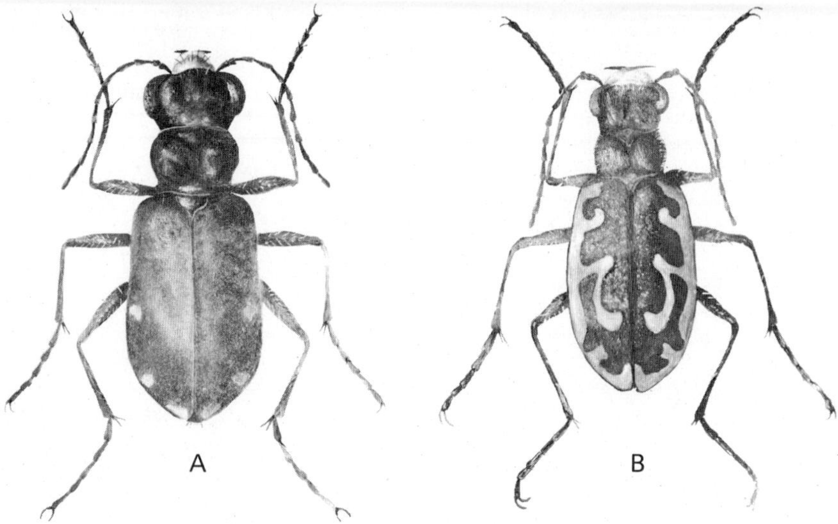

Figure 257. Tiger beetles. A, *Cicindèla sexguttàta* (Fabricius), 4 ×; B, *C. hirticóllis* Say, 3½ ×.

Family **Cicindèlidae**—Tiger Beetles: The tiger beetles are active, usually brightly colored insects found in open sunny situations; they are often common on sandy beaches. They can run or fly rapidly and are very wary and difficult to approach. When approached, they take flight quickly, sometimes after running a few feet, and usually alight some distance away facing the pursuer. They are predaceous and feed on a variety of small insects, which they capture with their long sicklelike mandibles; when handled, they can sometimes administer a painful bite.

The larvae are predaceous and live in vertical burrows in the soil in dry paths or fields or in sandy beaches. They prop themselves at the entrance of their burrow, with the traplike jaws wide apart, waiting to capture some passing insect. The larva has a hooklike spine on the fifth abdominal tergum with which it can anchor itself in its burrow and thus avoid being pulled out when it captures a large prey. After the prey is subdued, it is dragged to the bottom of the burrow, often a foot (0.3 m) underground, and eaten.

Adult tiger beetles are usually metallic or iridescent in color and often have a definite color pattern. They can usually be recognized by their characteristic shape (Figure 257), and most of them are 10–20 mm in length. Most of our tiger beetles belong to the genus *Cicindèla.*

Family **Caràbidae**—Ground Beetles: This is the second largest family of beetles in North America, with some 2500 species in our area; its members exhibit considerable variation in size, shape, and color. Most species are dark, shiny, and somewhat flattened, with striate elytra (Figure 258).

Ground beetles are commonly found under stones, logs, leaves, bark, debris, or running about on the ground; when disturbed, they run rapidly, but seldom fly. Most species hide during the day and feed at night; a few are attracted to lights. Nearly all are predaceous on other insects, and many are very beneficial. The members of a few genera (for example, *Scaphinòtus,* Figure 258 B) feed on snails. The larvae are also predaceous and occur in burrows in the soil, under bark, or in debris.

The largest and most brilliantly colored ground beetles belong to the genus *Calosòma;* these are often called caterpillarhunters, since they feed chiefly on caterpillars, particularly those that attack trees and shrubs. Most of these beetles are 25 mm or more in length. When handled, they give off a very disagreeable odor. *C. sycophánta* L., a brilliant greenish beetle with a dark-blue pronotum, was introduced from Europe to aid in the control of the gypsy moth. These beetles are attracted to lights.

The species in the genus *Bráchinus* are called bombardier beetles because of their habit of ejecting from the anus what looks like a puff of smoke. This is a glandular fluid that is ejected with a popping sound and which vaporizes into a cloud when it comes in contact with the air; the dis-

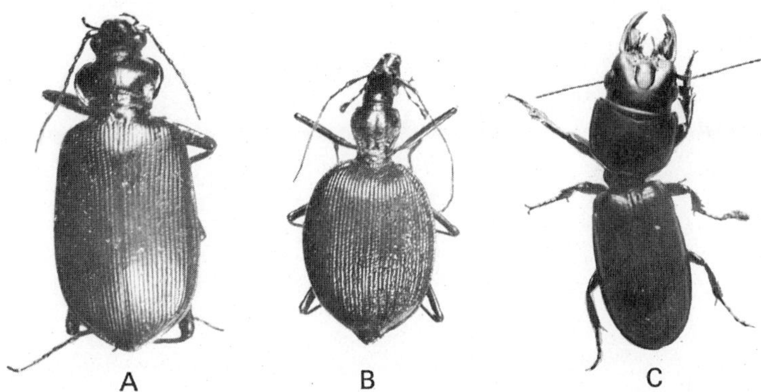

Figure 258. Ground beetles. A, *Calosòma scrutàtor* (Fabricius); B, *Scaphinòtus guyòti* (LeConte); C, *Scarìtes subterràneus* (Fabricius). All figures slightly enlarged. (C, courtesy of the Illinois Natural History Survey.)

charge of some species may irritate tender skin. This habit apparently serves both as a means of protection and of offense.

The members of the genus *Ómophron,* called round sand beetles (and formerly placed in a separate family, the Omophrónidae), differ from other carabids in having the scutellum concealed. They are small (5–8 mm in length), oval convex beetles that occur in wet sand along the shores of lakes and streams. They may be found running over the sand or burrowing in it (particularly under stones), and may occasionally be found running over the surface of the water. They run when disturbed and seldom fly. Adults and larvae are predaceous, but the larvae occasionally feed on seedlings of crops planted in moist soil.

Family **Amphizòidae**—Trout-Stream Beetles: This family contains five species in the genus *Amphizòa,* four occurring in western North America and one in eastern Tibet. These beetles are oval and dark-colored, and 11.0–15.5 mm in length. Adults and larvae of most species occur in the cold water of mountain streams, where they crawl about on submerged objects or on driftwood; one species occurring near Seattle lives in relatively warm quiet water. The larvae do not have gills and must obtain oxygen at the water surface; they frequently crawl out of the water onto twigs or floating objects; when dislodged, they float until they can grasp another object, as they apparently do not swim. The adults swim very little. Both adults and larvae are predaceous, feeding largely (if not entirely) on stonefly nymphs.

Family **Halíplidae**—Crawling Water Beetles: The haliplids are small, oval, convex beetles 2.5–4.5 mm in length, which live in or near water. They are usually yellowish or brownish with black spots (Figure 259 A) and may be distinguished from similar aquatic beetles by their very large and platelike hind coxae (Figure 259 B). They are fairly common in and about ponds; they swim or move about rather slowly. They frequently occur in masses of vegetation on or near the surface of the water. The adults feed chiefly on algae and other plant materials; the larvae (Figure 263 B) are predaceous. The two common eastern genera in this group can be separated by the presence or absence of two black spots at the base of the pronotum; these spots are present in *Peltódytes* (Figure 259 A) and absent in *Háliplus.*

Family **Dytíscidae**—Predaceous Diving Beetles: This is a large group of aquatic beetles that are usually very common in ponds and quiet streams. The body is smooth, oval and very hard, and the hind legs are flattened and fringed with long hairs to form excellent paddles. These beetles obtain air at the surface of the water, but can remain submerged for long periods because they carry air in a chamber under the elytra. They often hang head downward from the surface of the water. These insects may leave the water at night and fly to lights.

The dytiscids are very similar to another group of beetles common in fresh water, the Hydrophílidae. The adults of these two groups may be distinguished by the structure of the antennae and the maxillary palps, and sometimes by the structure of

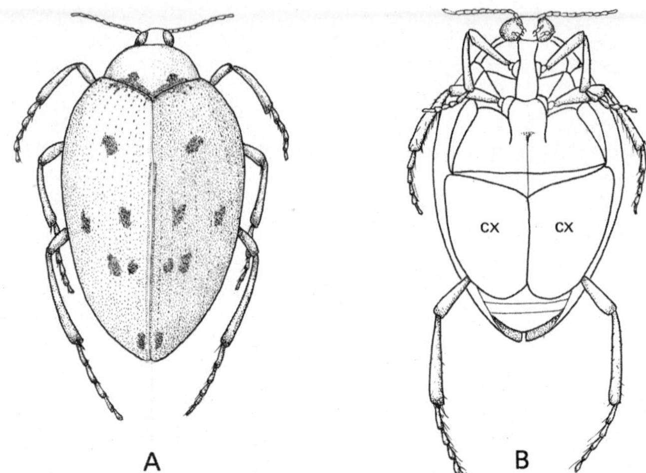

Figure 259. A crawling water beetle, *Peltódytes edéntulus* (LeConte), 11 ×. A, dorsal view; B, ventral view. *cx*, hind coxa.

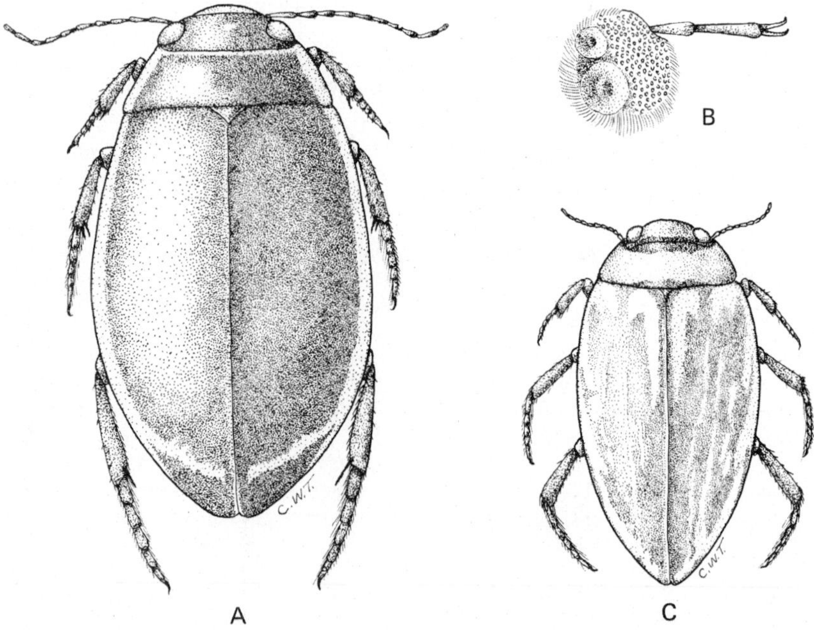

Figure 260. Predaceous diving beetles. A, *Dytíscus verticàlis* (Say), female, 2 ×; B, same, front tarsus of male; C, *Coptótomus interrogàtus* (Fabricius), 7 ×.

the metasternum. The dytiscids have long filiform antennae and very short maxillary palps (Figure 260), whereas the antennae of the hydrophilids are short and clubbed, and the maxillary palps are as long as or longer than the antennae (Figure 264). The metasternum in many hydrophilids is

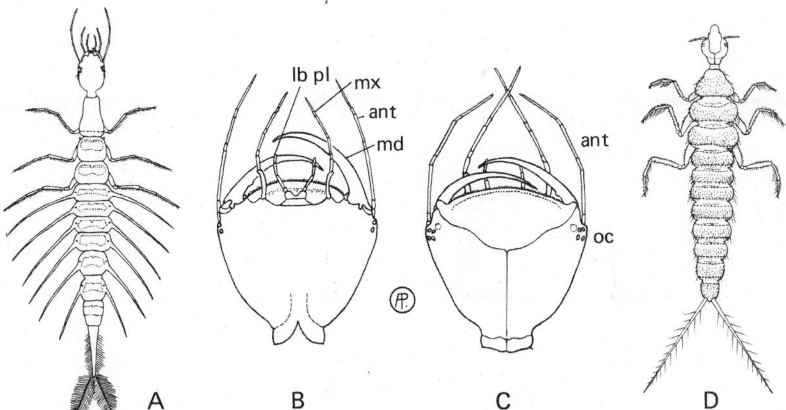

Figure 261. Larvae of Dytíscidae. A, *Coptótomus;* B, head of *Dytíscus,* ventral view; C, same, dorsal view; D, *Hydróporus. ant,* antenna; *lbpl,* labial palp; *md,* mandible; *mx,* maxilla; *oc,* ocelli. (Courtesy of Peterson. Reprinted by permission.)

prolonged posteriorly in a long spine (Figure 264 B). An excellent field character for separating these two groups is their method of swimming; the dytiscids move the hind legs simultaneously, like oars, whereas the hydrophilids move the hind legs alternately, as though they were running through the water.

Both adults and larvae of the dytiscids are highly predaceous and feed on a variety of small aquatic animals, including small fish. The larvae (Figure 261) are often called water tigers; they have long sicklelike jaws, which are hollow, and when they attack a prey they suck out its body fluids through the channels in the jaws. These larvae are very active and will not hesitate to attack an animal much larger than themselves.

Adult dytiscids vary in length from 3 to 40 mm; most of them are brownish, blackish, or greenish. The males of some species (Figure 260 B) have peculiar front tarsi that bear large suction discs; these discs are used in holding the smooth slick elytra of the female at the time of mating. Some of the larger species have a pale yellow band along the lateral margins of the pronotum and elytra (Figure A). A few members of this group have the tarsi appearing 4-4-5.

Family **Notéridae**—Burrowing Water Beetles: These beetles are very similar to the dytiscids, but have the scutellum hidden and have two equal claws on the hind tarsi. They are broadly oval, smooth, brownish to black beetles, 1.2–5.5 mm in length, and are similar to the dytiscids in habits. The common name of this group refers to the larvae, which burrow into the mud around the roots of aquatic plants.

Family **Gyrìndae**—Whirligig Beetles: The gyrinids are oval black beetles that are commonly seen swimming in endless gyrations on the surface of ponds and quiet streams. They are equally at home on the surface of the water or beneath the surface. They are extremely rapid swimmers, swimming principally by means of the strongly flattened middle and hind legs; the front legs are elongate and slender (Figure 262). These insects are peculiar in having each compound eye divided; they have a pair of compound eyes on the upper surface of the head and another pair on the ventral surface (Figure 252 C). The antennae are very short, somewhat clubbed, and have the third segment greatly expanded and somewhat earlike (Figure 249 E).

Both larvae and adults are predaceous. The adults feed chiefly on insects that fall onto the surface of the water; the larvae (Figure 263 A) feed on a variety of small aquatic animals and are often cannibalistic. Many of the adults when handled give off a characteristic fruity odor. The adults are often gregarious, forming large swarms on the surface of the water.

The eggs of whirligig beetles are laid in clusters or rows on the undersides of the leaves of aquatic plants, particularly water lilies and pondweed; pupation occurs in mud cells on the shore or on aquatic plants.

All but three of our 51 species of whirligig beetles belong to the genera *Gyrìnus* and *Dineù-*

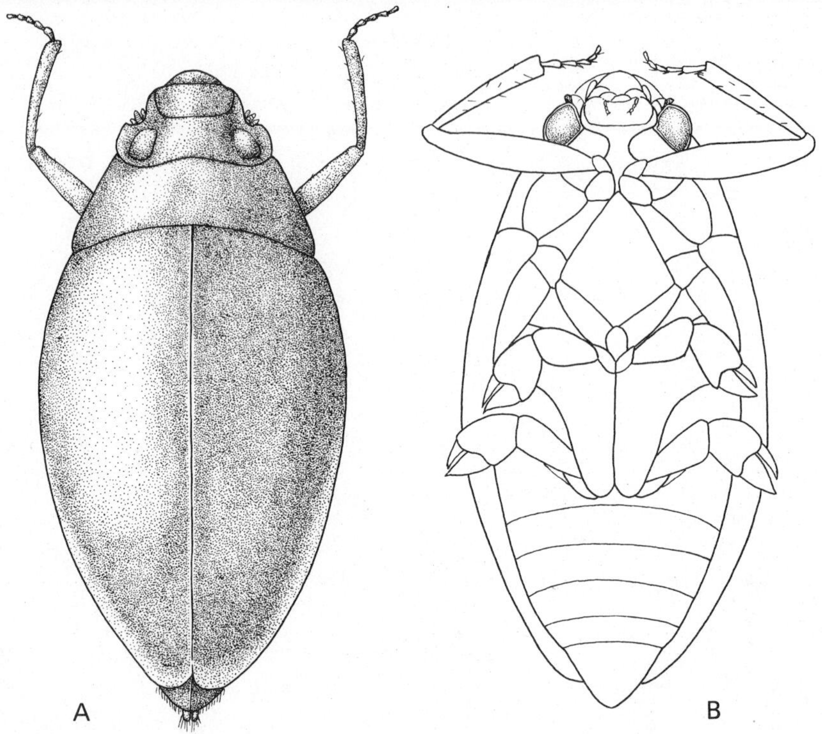

Figure 262. A whirligig beetle, *Dineùtus americánus* (Say), 7 ×. A, dorsal view; B, ventral view.

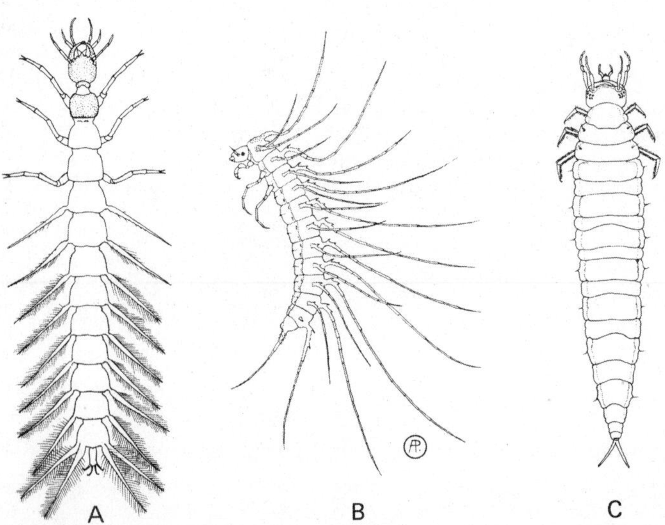

Figure 263. Larvae of aquatic beetles. A, *Dineùtus* (Gyrìnidae); B, *Peltódytes* (Halíplidae), lateral view; C, *Hydróphilus triangulàris* (Say) (Hydrophílidae). (Courtesy of Peterson. Reprinted by permission.)

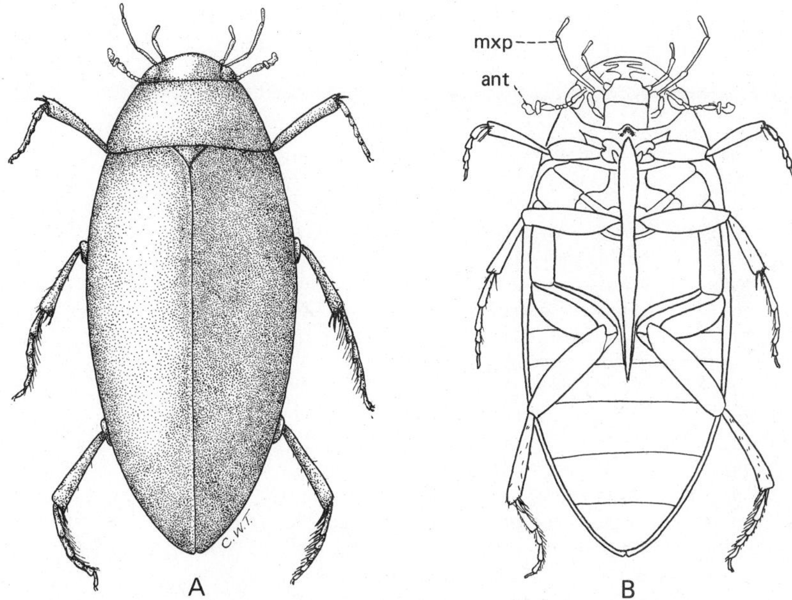

Figure 264. A water scavenger beetle. *Hydróphilus triangulàris* Say. A, dorsal view; B, ventral view. *ant,* antenna; *mxp,* maxillary palp.

tus. The species of *Gyrìnus* are less than 8 mm in length and have the scutellum visible and distinct; the species of *Dineùtus* are 10–15 mm in length and the scutellum is hidden (Figure 262 A).

SUBORDER **Myxóphaga:** This suborder contains two small families of tiny beetles that occur in water or wet places and apparently feed on filamentous algae (to which the suborder name refers). The Myxóphaga are distinguished by the character of the wings and mouth parts, and by the presence of notopleural sutures; all have 3-segmented tarsi and clubbed antennae. The two families of Myxóphaga are usually keyed out on the basis of their having notopleural sutures, and we have so keyed them (from couplet 11 in the key); the Sphaèridae are very tiny and the notopleural sutures may be very difficult to see, so we have also keyed out this family from couplet 11′ (notopleural sutures lacking).

Family **Sphaèridae**—Minute Bog Beetles: The sphaerids are tiny (0.5–0.75 mm in length), oval, convex, shining, blackish beetles that are found in mud and under stones near water, among roots of plants, and in moss in boggy places. They differ from other similarly shaped beetles found in these situations in having 3-segmented tarsi, and in the character of the abdomen (see key, couplet 45). The group is represented in this country by two or three species that occur in Texas, southern California, and Washington.

Family **Hydroscáphidae**—Skiff Beetles: The skiff beetles are about 1.5 mm in length, with 3-segmented tarsi and short elytra, and are similar in general appearance to rove beetles; the antennae are 9-segmented, with a 1-segmented club. They occur in the filamentous algae growing on rocks in streams. The group is represented in the United States by a single species, *Hydróscapha nàtans* LeConte, which occurs in southern California, southern Nevada, and Arizona.

SUBORDER **Polýphaga:** The members of this suborder differ from most other beetles in that the first visible abdominal sternum is not divided by the hind coxae, and its posterior margin extends completely across the abdomen; the hind trochanters are usually small, not large and offset toward the midline as in the Adéphaga (Figure 248 B), and notopleural sutures are lacking. This suborder includes the remaining families of beetles, which vary greatly in the form of the antennae, the tarsal formula, and in other characters.

Family **Hydrophílidae**—Water Scavenger Beetles: The hydrophilids are oval, somewhat convex beetles that can be recognized by the short clubbed antennae and the long maxillary palps (Figure 264). Most species are aquatic and are very similar in general appearance to the Dytíscidae. The aquatic species are generally black in color, and they vary in length from a few millimeters up to about 40 mm. The metasternum in many species is prolonged posteriorly as a sharp spine (Figure 264 B); this spine may be jabbed into the fingers of a person who is careless in handling one of these insects.

The water scavenger beetles differ somewhat from the dytiscids in habits. They rarely hang head downward from the surface of the water, as the dytiscids frequently do, and they carry air with them below the water in a silvery film over the ventral side of the body. In swimming, the hydrophilids move their legs alternately, whereas the dytiscids move the legs simultaneously, like a frog. The adults are principally scavengers, as the name implies, but the larvae are usually predaceous. The larvae of the water scavenger beetles (Figure 263 C) differ from those of the predaceous diving beetles in that they have only a single tarsal claw (dytiscid larvae have two), and the mandibles are usually toothed. The larvae are very voracious and feed on all sorts of aquatic animals.

The hydrophilids are common insects in ponds and quiet streams. A large and common species, *Hydróphilus triangulàris* Say, is shining black and about 1½ inches (38 mm) in length (Figure 264). Most hydrophilids are aquatic, but a few (subfamily Sphaeridiìnae) are terrestrial and occur in dung; these differ from the aquatic hydrophilids in having the first segment of the hind tarsi rather long, and the maxillary palps are usually shorter than the antennae. The most common dung-inhabiting species is *Sphaerídium scarabaeòides* (L.), which has a faint red spot and a fainter yellow spot on each elytron. Some of the aquatic species are attracted to lights at night. The aquatic species lay their eggs in silken cases, which are usually attached to aquatic plants. The full-grown larvae leave the water to pupate in earthen cells underground.

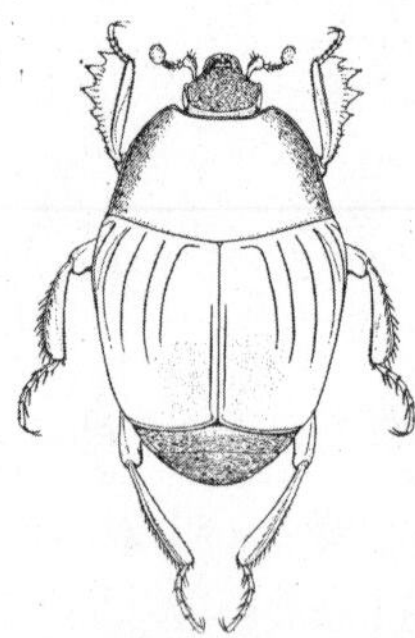

Figure 265. A hister beetle, *Geomysáprinus góffi* (Ross), 6 ×. (Courtesy of Ross and the Entomological Society of America.)

Family **Hydraènidae**—Minute Moss Beetles: These beetles are similar to the hydrophilids, but differ in having six or seven sterna (only five in the Hydrophílidae). They are elongate or oval, dark-colored beetles 1.2–1.7 mm in length, and occur in matted vegetation along stream margins, in wet moss, and along the seashore; they are probably scavengers.

Family **Georýssidae**—Minute Mud-Loving Beetles: This group includes two small and rare species, one occurring in the East and the other in the West. The eastern species, *Georýssus pusíllus* LeConte, is about 1.7 mm in length, black, and broadly oval in shape. These beetles occur in the mud along the banks of lakes and streams.

Family **Histéridae**—Hister Beetles: Hister beetles are small (0.5–10.0 mm in length), broadly oval beetles that are usually shining black in color; the elytra are cut off square at the apex, exposing one or two apical abdominal segments (Figure 265). The antennae (Figure 249 I) are elbowed and clubbed. The tibiae are dilated, and the anterior ones are usually toothed or spined. Hister beetles are generally found in or near decaying organic matter such as dung, fungi, and carrion, but are apparently predaceous on other small insects living in these materials. Some species, which are very flat, occur under the loose bark of stumps or logs; a few live in the nests of ants or termites. A few species are elongate and cylindrical; these live in the galleries of wood-boring insects. When disturbed, the hister beetles usually draw in their legs and antennae and become motionless. The appendages fit so snugly into shallow grooves on the ventral side of the body that it is often difficult to see them, even with considerable magnification.

Family **Sphaerìtidae**—False Clown Beetles: This group is represented in North America by a single species that occurs in carrion, manure, and decaying fungi from Alaska to northern Idaho and California. This species, *Sphaerìtes polìtus* Mannerheim, is 4.5–5.5 mm in length and black with a metallic bluish luster. It is very similar to some of the hister beetles, but the antennae are not elbowed, the tibiae are less expanded and lack teeth externally, and only the last abdominal segment is exposed beyond the elytra.

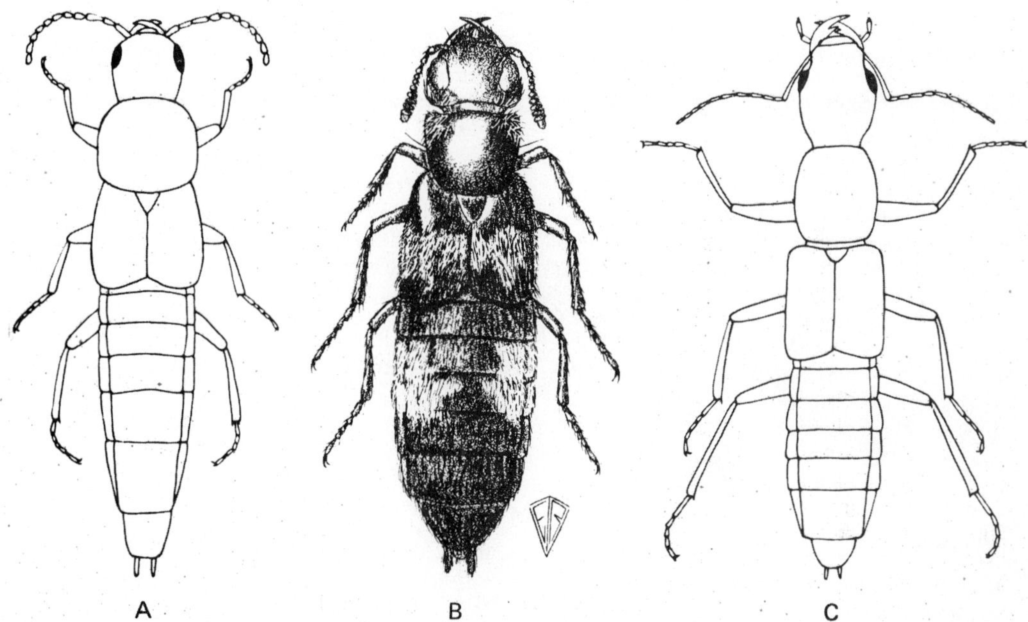

Figure 266. Rove beetles. A, *Quèdius peregrìnus* (Gravenhorst), 7½ ×. B, *Platycràtus maculòsus* (Gravenhorst), 4 ×. C, *Hesperòbium cribràtum* (LeConte), 7½ ×. (B, Courtesy of Arnett.)

Family **Staphylìnidae**—Rove Beetles: The rove beetles are slender and elongate, and can usually be recognized by the very short elytra; the elytra are usually not much longer than their combined width, and a considerable portion of the abdomen is exposed beyond their apices (Figure 266). The hind wings are well developed, and when at rest are folded under the short elytra. Rove beetles are active insects, and run or fly rapidly. When running, they frequently raise the tip of the abdomen, much as do scorpions. The mandibles are very long, slender, and sharp, and usually cross in front of the head; some of the larger rove beetles can inflict a painful bite when handled. Most of these beetles are black or brown in color; they vary considerably in size, but the largest are about 25 mm in length.

This is our largest family of beetles, with nearly 2900 North American species. These beetles occur in a variety of habitats, but are probably most often seen about decaying materials, particularly dung or carrion; they also occur under stones and other objects on the ground, along the shores of streams and the seashore, in fungi and leaf litter, and in the nests of birds, mammals, ants, and termites. Most species appear to be predaceous. The larvae usually occur in the same places and feed on the same things as the adults; a few are parasites of other insects.

Family **Pseláphidae**—Short-Winged Mold Beetles: The pselaphids are small yellowish or brownish beetles, 0.5–5.5 (mostly about 1.5) mm in length, and most of them are found under stones and logs, in rotting wood, and in moss; a few occur in ant, termite, and mammal nests. These beetles have short truncate elytra and resemble rove beetles, but have only 3 tarsal segments (most rove beetles have more), the pronotum is narrower than the elytra, and the antennae are abruptly clubbed (Figure 267 A). This group is a large one, with about 500 species occurring in North America.

The members of one subfamily of pselaphids, the Clavigerìnae, are peculiar in having the antennae 2-segmented and the tarsi with only one claw. These beetles occur in ant nests, where they are "milked" by the ants of a secretion on which the ants feed.

Family **Ptilìidae**—Feather-Winged Beetles: This family includes some of the smallest beetles known; few exceed 1 mm, and many are less than 0.5 mm in length. The body is oval, the hind wings bear a long fringe of hairs that often extends

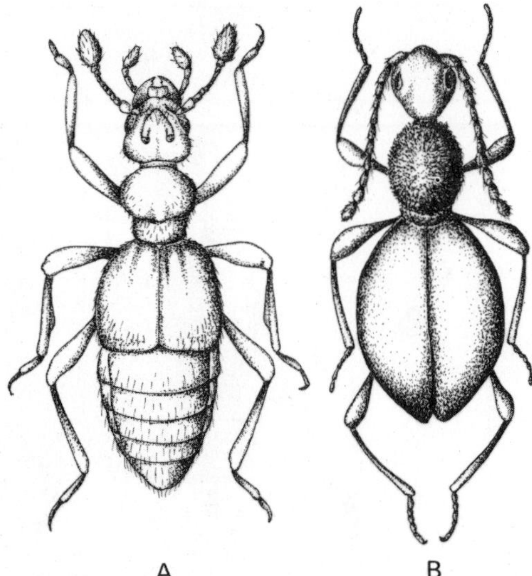

Figure 267. A, a short-winged mold beetle, *Trimiomélba dùbia* (LeConte), 30 ×; B, an antlike stone beetle, *Eucónnus clávipes* (Say), 18 ×. (Redrawn from Arnett.)

out from beneath the elytra, and the antennae bear whorls of long hairs. These beetles occur in rotting wood, dung, and in leaf litter, and feed chiefly on fungus spores.

Family **Limulòdidae**—Horseshoe Crab Beetles: The limulodids are usually a millimeter or less in length and are somewhat similar to horseshoe crabs in general appearance. They are oval in shape, with the elytra short and the abdomen somewhat tapering, and yellowish to brownish in color. Hind wings and compound eyes are absent. These beetles are found in ant nests, where they usually ride on the ants, feeding on exudations from the bodies of the ants. The group is a small one (four species in the United States), but is widely distributed.

Family **Dasycéridae:** This family includes the genus *Dasýcerus,* which was formerly placed in the family Lathridìidae; it includes only two species in our area, one in North Carolina and Georgia, and the other in California. These beetles differ from the Lathridìidae in having the front coxal cavities open behind and the front coxae contiguous. Their habits are similar to those of the Lathridìidae.

Family **Leptìnidae**—Mammal-Nest Beetles and Beaver Parasites: The leptinids are brownish, oblong-oval, louselike beetles, 2–3 mm in length. The species of *Leptìnus* (two in North America) occur in the nests and fur of mice, shrews, and moles, and occasionally in the nests of ground-nesting Hymenóptera. The species of *Leptinéllus* (two in North America) occur in the nests and fur of beavers, one species on the common beaver (*Cástor*) and the other on the mountain beaver (*Aplodóntia*). The single species of *Platypsýlla, P. cástoris* Ritsema, is an ectoparasite of the common beaver.

Family **Leiòdidae**—Round Fungus Beetles: The leiodids are a variable group that was formerly divided into at least two families. The Leiodìnae are convex, shiny, oval beetles, 1.5–6.5 mm in length, and brown to black in color; many species when disturbed tuck the head and prothorax under the body and roll into a ball, thus concealing all the appendages. These beetles occur in fungi, under bark, in decaying wood, and in similar places. The Catopìnae (formerly placed in the family Leptodíridae) are elongate-oval, somewhat flattened, brownish to black, pubescent, and 2–5 mm in length; they often have faint cross striations on the elytra and pronotum, and most of them have the eighth antennal segment shorter and smaller in diameter than the seventh and ninth segments. Most of these beetles occur in carrion, but some are found in fungi and others in ant nests.

Family **Sílphidae**—Carrion Beetles: The common species in this group are relatively large and often brightly colored insects that occur about the bodies of dead animals. The body is soft and somewhat flattened, the antennae are clubbed (clavate or capitate), and the tarsi are 5-segmented. Silphids range in length from 1.5 to 35.0 mm, but most species are over 10 mm.

Two common genera in this group are *Sílpha* and *Nicróphorus* (= *Necróphorus*). In *Sílpha* (Figure 268 A) the body is broadly oval and flattened, 10–24 mm in length, and the elytra are rounded or acute at the apex and almost cover the abdomen. In some species (for example, *S. americàna* L.) the pronotum is yellowish with a black spot in the center. In *Nicróphorus* (Figure 268 B) the body is more elongate, the elytra are short and truncate apically, and most species are red and black in color. The beetles of the genus *Nicróphorus* are often known as burying beetles; they excavate beneath the dead body of a mouse or other small animal, and the body sinks into the ground. These beetles are remarkably strong; a pair may move an animal as large as a rat several

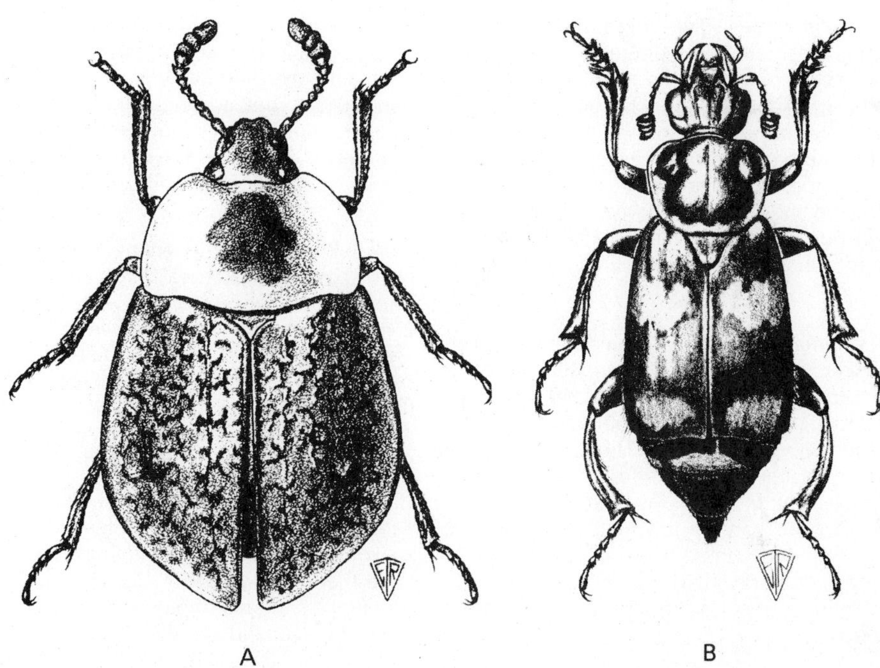

Figure 268. Carrion beetles. A, *Sílpha americàna* L.; B, *Nicróphorus sàyi* Laporte, 3 ×. (Courtesy of Arnett.)

feet to get it to a suitable spot for burying. After the body is buried, the eggs are laid on it. Both adults and larvae feed on carrion and are usually found beneath the bodies of dead animals.

Other species of silphids occur in various types of decaying animal matter; some occur in fungi, and a few occur in ant nests. A few are predaceous on maggots and other animals that occur in decaying organic matter. In some species (for example, *Nicróphorus*) the newly hatched larvae are fed carrion that is regurgitated by the parent beetles.

Family **Scydmaènidae**—Antlike Stone Beetles: The members of this group are antlike in shape (Figure 267 B), long-legged, brownish, somewhat hairy beetles, 1–5 mm in length; the antennae are slightly clavate, and the femora are often clavate (Figure 267 B). They occur under stones, in moss and leaf litter, and in ant nests. These beetles are secretive in habit, but sometimes fly about in numbers at twilight.

Family **Scaphidìidae**—Shining Fungus Beetles: The scaphidiids are oval, convex, blackish (sometimes with red spots), and shining beetles, 2–7 mm in length; the elytra are truncate apically, exposing the pointed terminal abdominal segment (Figure 269). These beetles occur in fungi, rotting wood, under bark, and in leaf litter.

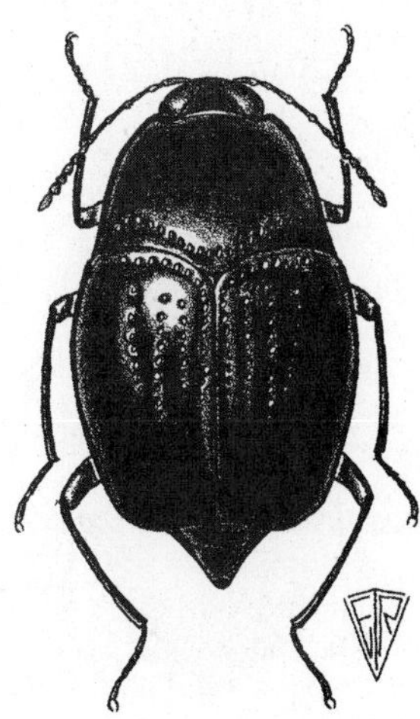

Figure 269. A shining fungus beetle, *Scaphídium quadriguttàtum pìceum* Melsheimer, 7 ×. (Courtesy of Arnett.)

Family **Eucinètidae**—Plate-Thigh Beetles: The eucinetids are small (2.5–3.0 mm in length), oval, convex beetles that have the head deflexed and not visible from above (Figure 270 A); there are six visible abdominal sterna, and the hind coxae are dilated into broad plates that extend to the elytra and cover most of the first visible abdominal sternum (hence the common name). Eight species occur in our area (in the East and in California), and they are generally found under bark or in fungi.

Family **Clâmbidae**—Fringe-Winged Beetles: The clambids are minute (about 1 mm in length), oval, convex, brownish to black beetles that are capable of tucking the head and prothorax under the body and rolling into a ball. They resemble the leiodids in this respect, but differ from leiodids in being pubescent, in having the hind coxae dilated into broad plates, and in having a fringe of long hairs on the hind wings. These beetles occur in decaying plant material. The group is small (nine North American species), and its members are not often encountered.

Family **Helòdidae**—Marsh Beetles: The helodids are oval beetles, 2–4 mm in length (Figure 270 B), and occur on vegetation in swampy places and in damp rotting debris. Some have enlarged hind femora and are active jumpers. The larvae, which have long slender antennae, are aquatic.

Family **Dascíllidae**—Soft-Bodied Plant Beetles: The dascillids are oval to elongate, soft-bodied, pubescent beetles, 3–14 mm in length; the head is usually visible from above, and some species have relatively large and conspicuous mandibles (Figure 270 C). They are most likely to be found on vegetation near water, but are not very common. This group contains 16 North American species, in two subfamilies (Dascillìnae and Eubriìnae).

Family **Rhipicéridae**—Cedar Beetles: The cedar beetles are elongate-oval, brownish beetles with orange antennae, 16–24 mm in length (Figure 271); the antennae are flabellate in the male and serrate to pectinate in the female. These beetles superficially resemble June beetles, and are good fliers; the larvae are parasites of cicada nymphs. This group is small (five North American species of *Sándalus*) but is widely distributed.

Family **Lucànidae**—Stag Beetles: The lucanids are sometimes called pinchingbugs because of the large mandibles of the males (Figure 272 A). In some males the mandibles are half as long as the body or longer and are branched like the antlers of a stag (hence the name "stag" beetles). Stag beetles are closely related to the Scarabaèidae, but the terminal segments of the antennae cannot be held tightly together as in the scarabs (Figure 250 F). The larger stag beetles are $1\frac{1}{2}$ inches (38 mm) or more in length.

These insects are usually found in woods; some species occur on sandy beaches. The adults are often attracted to lights at night. The larvae are found in decaying wood and are similar to the

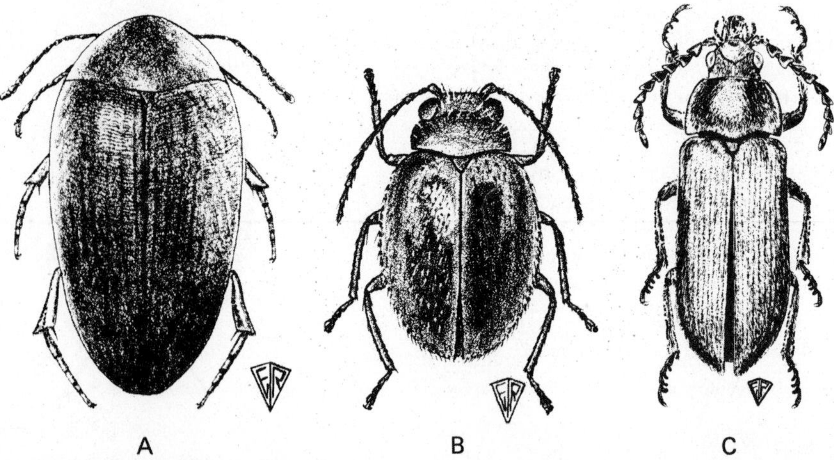

Figure 270. A, a plate-thigh beetle, *Eucinètus terminàlis* LeConte, 16 ×; B, a marsh beetle, *Prionocỳphon limbàtus* LeConte, 6 ×; C, a soft-bodied plant beetle *Dascíllus dàvidsoni* LeConte, 3 ×. (Courtesy of Arnett.)

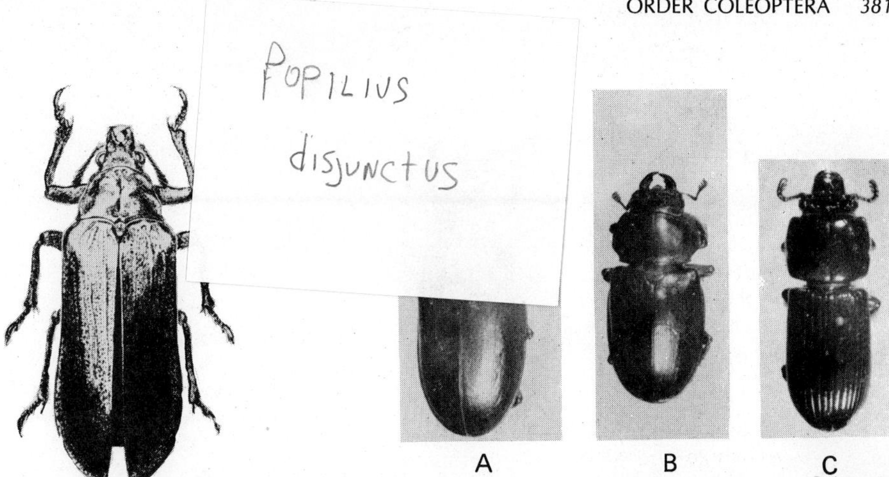

Figure 271. A cedar beetle, *Sándalus petrophỳa* Knoch, female, 3 ×. (Courtesy of Arnett.)

Figure 272. A, male, and B, female, of a stag beetle, *Pseudolucànus caprèolus* (L.); C, a bessbug, *Popílius disjúnctus* (Illiger). About natural size.

white grubs that are found in grassy soil; they feed on the juices of decaying wood.

Family **Passálidae**—Bess Beetles: These beetles are called by a variety of names—bessbugs, bessie-bugs, betsy-beetles, patent-leather beetles, and horned passalus beetles. Three species occur in the United States, only one of which occurs in the East. The eastern species, *Popílius disjúnctus* (Illiger) (Figure 272 C), is a shining black beetle, 32–36 mm in length, with longitudinal grooves in the elytra and a characteristic horn on the head (Figure 253 B). This family is closely related to the Lucànidae, but differs in that the mentum of the labium is deeply notched. The western species of the family occur in southern Texas.

The passalids are somewhat social, and their colonies occur in galleries in decaying logs. The adults are able to produce a squeaking sound by rubbing roughened areas on the underside of the wings across similar areas on the dorsal side of the abdomen. This sound is produced when the insect is disturbed; normally it probably serves as a means of communication. The adults prepare food (decaying wood) with their salivary secretions and feed it to the young. The passalids are fairly common insects.

Family **Scarabaèidae**—Scarab Beetles: This group contains about 1300 North American species, and its members vary greatly in size, color, and habits. The scarabs are heavy-bodied, oval or elongate, usually convex beetles, with the tarsi 5-segmented (rarely, the front tarsi are absent), and the antennae 8- to 11-segmented and lamellate. The last three (rarely more) of the antennal segments are expanded into platelike structures that may be spread apart (Figure 250 C) or united to

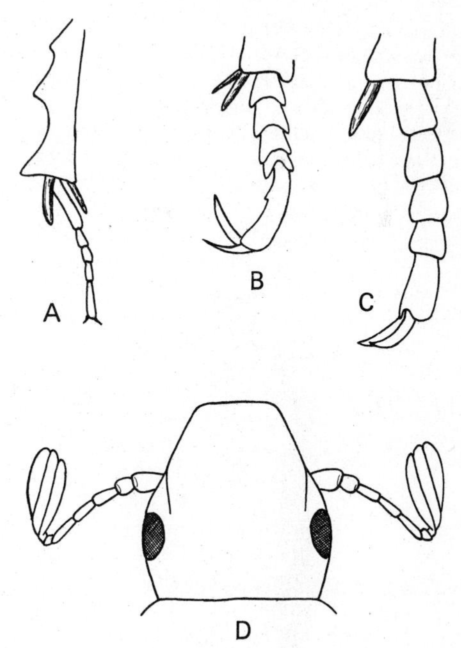

Figure 273. Characters of Scarabaèidae. A, hind tibia and tarsus of *Aphòdius* (Aphodiìnae); B, hind tarsus of *Popíllia* (Rutelìnae); C, hind tarsus of *Cánthon* (Scarabaeìnae); D, head of *Macrodáctylus* (Melolonthìnae), dorsal view.

form a compact terminal club (Figure 250 D). The front tibiae are more or less dilated, with the outer edge toothed or scalloped.

The scarabs vary considerably in habits. Many are dung feeders, or feed on decomposing plant materials, carrion, and the like; some live in the nests or burrows of vertebrates, or in the nests of ants or termites; a few feed on fungi; many feed on plant materials such as grasses, foliage, fruits, and flowers, and some of these are serious pests of lawns, golf greens, or various agricultural crops.

Key to the Subfamilies of the Scarabaèidae

1. Second antennal segment arising from apex of first (Figure 250 C, D); elytra smooth or with longitudinal ridges or small punctures; abdomen with 5 or 6 visible sterna 2

1′. Second antennal segment arising from a point proximad of apex of first (Figure 250 G); elytra rough, with irregular ridges and elevations; abdomen with 5 or fewer visible sterna .... **Trogìnae** p. 385

2(1). Middle and hind tibiae thickened and greatly dilated, their front edges finely toothed or with numerous, minute, bristlelike spines; tarsi with long fine hairs on underside; antennae 11-segmented; body capable of being contracted into a ball-like mass; 5–6 mm in length, blackish and shining .... **Acanthocerìnae** p. 385

2′. Middle and hind tibiae not as above; antennae 8- to 11-segmented; body not capable of being contracted into a ball-like mass; length 5–60 mm... 3

3(2′). Antennae 11-segmented 4

3′. Antennae 8- to 10-segmented 5

4(3). Antennal club 3-segmented, with at least some club segments pubescent; elytra striate; widely distributed .... **Geotrupìnae** p. 384

4′. Antennal club 5- to 7-segmented, the club segments bare or only sparsely hairy; elytra not striate; rare western beetles (*Pleocòma, Benedíctia*) .... **Pleocomìnae** p. 385

5(3′). Elytra tapering posteriorly, their tips distinctly separated and short, exposing 2 or 3 abdominal terga; body very hairy; brownish in color and 13–18 mm in length; rare beetles .... **Glaphyrìnae** p. 385

5′. Not exactly fitting the above description 6

6(5′). Antennae 10-segmented with a 3-segmented club, the basal segment of the club hollowed out and receiving next segment (which is largely concealed in repose); blackish beetles, glabrous and shining, about 7 mm in length; hind legs arising about middle of body (as in Figure 274 B); southern and western United States .... **Hybosorìnae** p. 384

6′. Not exactly fitting the above description 7

7(6′). Hind legs situated far back on body, usually nearer tip of abdomen than middle legs (Figure 274 A); abdominal spiracles covered by elytra; segments of antennal club usually hairy; dung feeders 8

7′. Hind legs usually situated at about middle of body, closer to middle legs than to tip of abdomen (Figure 274 B); at least 1 (often more) of the abdominal spiracles not covered by elytra; segments of antennal club smooth or only sparsely hairy; plant feeders 11

8(7). Hind tibiae with 1 apical spur (Figure 273 C); pygidium partly exposed; middle coxae widely separated; scutellum small and usually not visible .... **Scarabaeìnae** p. 384

8′. Hind tibiae usually with 2 apical spurs (Figure 273 A); pygidium usually covered by elytra; middle coxae approximate (Figure 274 A); scutellum well developed and visible 9

9(8′). Antennae 9-segmented; size and color variable 10

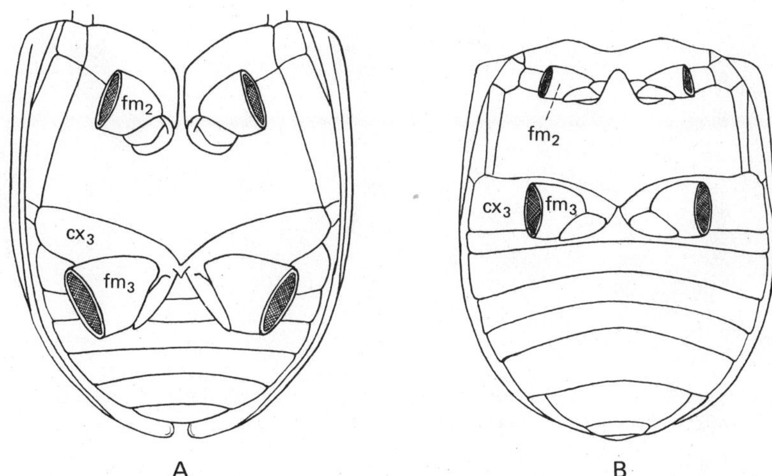

Figure 274. Ventral views of thorax and abdomen of Scarabaèidae. A, a dung-feeding scarab (*Aphòdius,* Aphodiìnae); B, a plant-feeding scarab (*Pelidnòta,* Rutelìnae). cx_3, hind coxa; fm_2, middle femur; fm_3, hind femur.

9′. Antennae 10-segmented; reddish brown beetles, 5–6 mm in length .... **Ochodaeìnae** p. 384

10(9). Clypeus expanded, the mandibles not visible from above, and usually notched at apex .... **Aphodiìnae** p. 384

10′. Mandibles not concealed by clypeus, and visible from above; clypeus not notched at apex .... **Aegialiìnae** p. 384

11(7′). Tarsal claws (at least on hind legs) of unequal size, the outer claw larger (Figure 273 B); hind tibiae with 2 apical spurs; pygidium exposed; often brightly colored beetles .... **Rutelìnae** p. 385

11′. Tarsal claws, at least on hind legs, of equal size (except in some males of the Dynastìnae, which have horns on the head or pronotum, and in *Hóplia,* subfamily Melolonthìnae, 6–9 mm in length, which has only 1 simple claw on the hind legs), or hind tibiae without apical spurs ... 12

12(11′). Tarsal claws usually toothed or bifid; clypeus not emarginate laterally, the bases of the antennae usually not visible from above; generally only 1 pair of abdominal spiracles exposed below edges of elytra ... **Melolonthìnae** p. 385

12′. Tarsal claws simple; clypeus variable, generally emarginate laterally, so that bases of antennae are visible from above; usually at least 2 pairs of abdominal spiracles exposed below edges of elytra 13

13(12′). Front coxae transverse; body usually convex above; mandibles bent, expanded and leaflike, and generally visible from above; males often with large horns on head or pronotum (Figure 278); lateral margins of elytra without a shallow emargination behind humeri; length 20–60 mm .... **Dynastìnae** p. 386

13′. Front coxae conical and more or less prominent; body convex or flattened above; mandibles not bent and leaflike, and usually not visible from above; no horns on head or pronotum; lateral margins of elytra often with a shallow emargination behind humeri (Figure 279); size variable ... 14

14(13′). Body flattened above; lateral margins of elytra usually with a shallow emargination behind humeri (Figure 279); size and color variable, but if 7 mm in length or less (*Válgus*), then elytra are truncate apically and do not cover entire abdomen, the hind coxae are widely separated, and the color is usually dark; widely distributed .... **Cetoniìnae** p. 387

A

B

C

D

Figure 275. Scarab beetles. A, an earth-boring dung beetle, *Geotrùpes spléndidus* (Fabricius); B, a skin beetle, *Tróx scabròsus* Beauvois; C, male, and D, female, of a dung beetle, *Phanaèus víndex* MacLachlan, 1½ ×.

14′. Body convex above; lateral margins of elytra without a shallow emargination behind humeri; 4–7 mm in length, light brown in color; elytra not truncate at apex, and covering entire abdomen; hind coxae approximated; rare western beetles (*Acòma*) .... **Pleocomìnae** p. 385

Subfamily **Scarabaeìnae (=Coprìnae)**—Dung Beetles and Tumblebugs: These beetles are robust, 5–30 mm in length, and feed chiefly on dung. Most of them are dull black, but some are metallic green in color. The tumblebugs (principally *Cánthon* and *Deltochìlum*) are black, about 25 mm in length or less, with the middle and hind tibiae rather slender, and there are no horns on the head or pronotum. Other genera in this subfamily have the middle and hind tibiae swollen at the tip, and often have a horn on the head. In *Phanaèus* (Figure 275 C, D), which is usually a little less than 25 mm in length, the body is a brilliant green with the pronotum golden, and the males have a long horn on the top of the head. The dung beetles in the genera *Còpris* and *Dichotòmius* (= *Pinòtus*) are black, with conspicuous striae on the elytra; *Còpris*, about 18 mm in length or less, has 8 striae on each elytron, and *Dichotòmius* (about 25 mm long and very robust) has 7. Other genera in this subfamily are generally less than 10 mm in length.

The tumblebugs are usually common in pastures and are interesting insects to watch. They chew off a piece of dung, work it into a ball, and roll this ball a considerable distance; they usually work in pairs, one pushing and the other pulling, rolling the ball with their hind legs. The ball is then buried in the soil, and the eggs are laid in the ball. The larvae are thus assured a food supply, and the location of the ball provides protection.

The sacred scarab of ancient Egypt, *Scarabaèus sàcer* L., is a member of this group, and has habits similar to those of the tumblebugs. In Egyptian mythology the ball of dung represented the earth and its rotation.

Subfamily **Aphodiìnae**—Aphodian Dung Beetles: This is a fairly large group of small dung beetles, and some are quite common, particularly in cow dung. They are usually black, or red and black.

Subfamily **Aegialiìnae:** The members of this group are similar to the Aphodiìnae, but have the mandibles visible from above. The group is a small one, and most of its members (including all the eastern species) belong to the genus *Aegiàlia*.

Subfamily **Ochodaeìnae:** This is a small group, and most of its members occur in the western states; one species, *Ochodaèus músculus* (Say), a reddish-brown oval beetle, 5–6 mm in length, with striate elytra, occurs in the northern states.

Subfamily **Hybosorìnae:** These beetles are about 7 mm in length, brownish black to black in color, and are shaped a little like a miniature June beetle. Three rare species occur in the United States, one in the southeastern states and the other two in Arizona and California.

Subfamily **Geotrupìnae**—Earth-Boring Dung Beetles: These beetles are very similar to some of the other dung-feeding scarabs, but have the antennae 11-segmented. They are stout-bodied, convex, oval beetles that are black or dark brown in color (Figure 275 A). The elytra are usually grooved or striate, the tarsi are long and slender, and the front tibiae are broadened and toothed or scalloped on the outer edges. The elytra completely cover the abdomen. These beetles vary in length from 5 to 25 mm, and are found beneath cow dung, horse manure, or carrion; some occur in logs or in decaying fungi. The larvae occur in or beneath dung or carrion; they feed on this material and hence are of value to man as scavengers.

Subfamily **Pleocomìnae:** The members of this group are western in distribution and are relatively rare beetles. The larvae live in the soil and feed on the roots of plants, and the adults live in burrows in the ground, usually coming out only at dusk or after a rain. The members of the genus *Pleocòma* are stout-bodied, relatively large (about 25 mm in length), and rather pubescent. The burrows of *P. fimbriàta* LeConte are about 25 mm in diameter and up to 2 feet (0.6 m) or more in depth. The members of the genus *Acòma* are much smaller, 4–7 mm in length, and light brown in color.

Subfamily **Glaphyrìnae:** The members of this group are elongate, brownish, and have the body very hairy. The elytra are short, exposing two or three abdominal terga; they taper posteriorly, and are separated at the apex. These beetles are 13–18 mm in length. Our species belong to the genus *Lichnánthe;* some occur in the Northeast, and some in the West; all are quite rare.

Subfamily **Acanthocerìnae:** These beetles are round, blackish, 5–6 mm in length, with the middle and hind tibiae greatly dilated and bearing rows of spines along their entire length. When disturbed, these beetles draw in their legs and antennae and form a hemispherical mass, and in this position they remain motionless. They occur under bark, in rotten logs and stumps, and occasionally on flowers. Three species occur in the United States: two species of *Cloeòtus,* which are widely distributed throughout the East, and *Acanthócerus aèneus* MacLeay, which occurs in Georgia and Florida.

Subfamily **Trogìnae**—Skin Beetles: The members of this group have the dorsal surface of the body very rough, and the second antennal segment arises before the tip of the first instead of from its apex (Figure 250 G). These beetles are oblong, convex, dark brown in color (and often covered with dirt), and are shaped much like June beetles (Figure 275 B). They are usually found on old, dry animal carcasses, where they feed on the hide, feathers, hair, or the dried tissues on the bones. They represent one of the last stages in the successions of insects living in animal carcasses. Some species occur in owl pellets, beneath bark, or on roots. When disturbed, these beetles draw in their legs and lie motionless, resembling dirt or rubbish, and are often overlooked. They overwinter as adults beneath leaves and in debris. Two genera occur in the United States: *Tróx* (widely distributed) and *Glarèsis* (western United States).

Subfamily **Melolonthìnae**—June Beetles, Chafers, and Others: This is a large and widely distributed group, and all its members are plant feeders; many species are of considerable economic importance. The best-known beetles in this group are the June beetles or May beetles, sometimes called junebugs, which are usually brown in color and are common around lights in the spring and early summer (Figure 276 A). Most of them belong to the genus *Phyllóphaga* (= *Lachnostérna*), which contains nearly a hundred eastern species. The adults feed at night on foliage and flowers. The larvae (Figure 277) are the well-known white grubs that feed in the soil on the roots of grasses and other plants. White grubs are very destructive insects and do a great deal of damage to pastures, lawns, and such crops as corn, small grains, potatoes, and strawberries. The life cycle usually requires two or three years to complete. The greatest damage to field crops occurs when fields are rotated from grass or meadow to corn.

This subfamily also contains the chafers (*Macrodáctylus*). The rose chafer, *M. subspinòsus* (Fabricius), is a slender, tan, long-legged beetle that feeds on the flowers and foliage of roses, grapes, and various other plants; it often feeds on peaches and other fruits. The larvae are small white grubs that occur in light soil and often do serious damage to roots. Poultry that eat these beetles become extremely ill and quite often are killed.

Most of the other beetles in this subfamily are robust, oval, and brownish, and resemble June beetles (though most are smaller); the beetles in the genus *Dichelónyx* are elongate and slender, with the elytra greenish or bronze in color, and the tarsal claws are simple.

Subfamily **Rutelìnae**—Shining Leaf Chafers: The larvae of these beetles feed on plant roots, and the adults feed on foliage and fruits. Many of the adults are very brightly colored. A number of important pest species are included in this subfamily.

One of the most serious pests in this group is the Japanese beetle, *Popíllia japónica* Newman

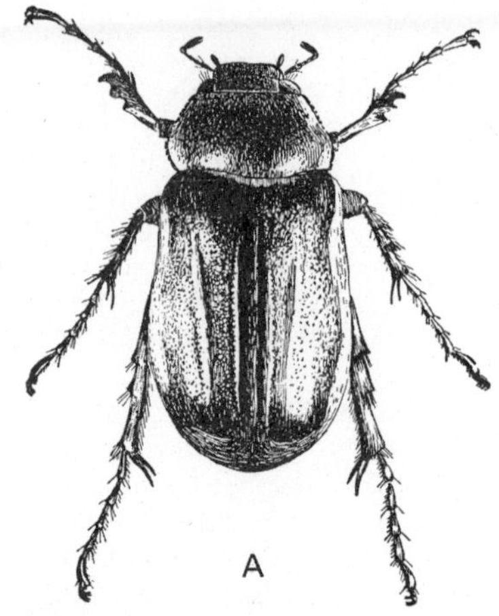

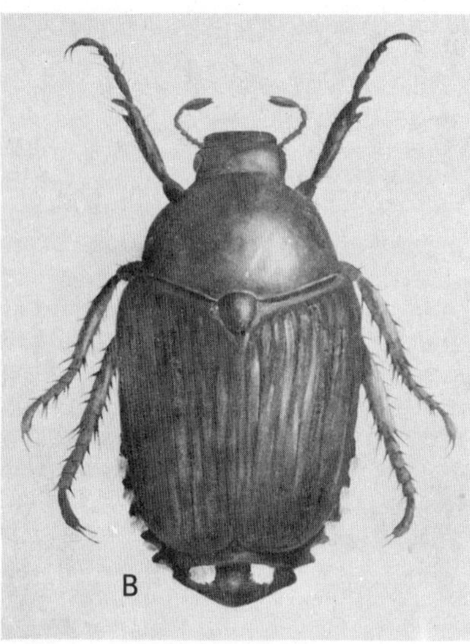

Figure 276. Plant-feeding scarabs. A, a June beetle, *Phyllóphaga portoricénsis* Smythe, 1½ ×; B, Japanese beetle, *Popíllia japónica* Newman, 4½ ×. (A, courtesy of Wolcott and the *Journal of Agriculture* of the University of Puerto Rico.)

(Figure 276 B). This species was introduced into the eastern United States on nursery stock from Japan about 1916. Since then, it has spread over a large part of the eastern United States, where it is a serious pest on lawns, golf courses, fruits, and shrubbery. The adult is a very pretty insect; the head and thorax are bright green, the elytra are brownish tinged with green on the edges, and there are white spots along the sides of the abdomen. This species has one generation a year and overwinters in the larval stage in the soil.

Figure 277. White grubs (*Phyllóphaga* sp.). (Courtesy of the Ohio Agricultural Research and Development Center.)

Another rather common and destructive species is the grape pelidnota, *Pelidnòta punctàta* (L.). The adult is 25 mm or more in length and looks a little like a large June beetle, but is yellowish with three black spots on each elytron (Figure 280 B). Most of the damage done by this species is done by the adult; the larvae feed chiefly in rotting wood.

The members of the genus *Cotálpa* are usually large beetles, uniform green or yellowish above and dark beneath; the larvae do considerable damage to the roots of berries, corn, and grass. One distinctive species in this genus is *C. lanígera* (L.), 20–26 mm in length, and entirely yellow with a metallic luster; it occurs on or near catalpa trees.

From Baja California to Utah the common members of the Rutelìnae are the black and reddish brown members of the genus *Paracotálpa* (= *Pocálta*). In Texas and Arizona are found the real jewels of this subfamily, species belonging to the genus *Plusiòtis*. These large scarabs are a brilliant green, sometimes with added longitudinal lines of metallic golden color; they are favored items among collectors.

Subfamily **Dynastìnae**—Rhinoceros Beetles, Hercules Beetles, and Elephant Beetles: This group contains some of the largest North American beetles, a few of which may reach a length of 2½ inches (64 mm). The dorsal surface of the body is rounded and convex, and the males usually have horns on the head and/or pronotum (Figure 278); the females lack these horns.

The largest Dynastìnae are the Hercules beetles (*Dynástes*), which occur principally in the southern states. *D. títyus* (L.), the eastern species, is 2.0–2.5 inches (50–64 mm) in length, greenish-gray mottled with large black areas, and the pronotal horn of the male extends forward over the head (Figure 278). The western species, *D. gránti* Horn, is similar, but is slightly larger and has a longer pronotal horn. The elephant beetles

Figure 278. Eastern hercules beetle, *Dynástes títyus* (L.); male at left, female at right. About natural size.

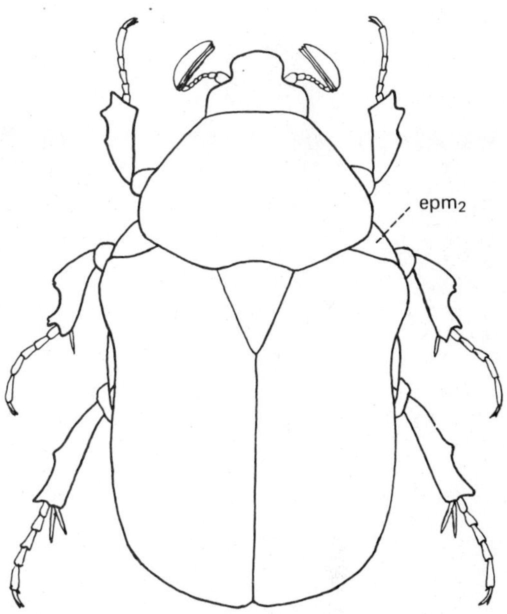

Figure 279. A bumble flower beetle, *Euphòria índa* (L.) (Cetoniìnae), 5 ×. *epm₂*, mesepimeron.

(*Stratègus*) are big brown scarabs, 1.5–2.0 inches (38–50 mm) in length), that occur from Rhode Island to Kansas and Texas; they have three horns on the head but none on the pronotum. In the rhinoceros beetle, *Xyloryctes jamaicénsis* (Drury), a dark brown scarab a little over 25 mm in length, the males have a single large upright horn on the head (the females have a small tubercle instead of a horn); the larva of this species feeds on the roots of ash trees. The rhinoceros beetle occurs from Connecticut to Arizona. The members of the genus *Phileùrus,* which are about 25 mm long and have two horns on the head, occur in the southern and southwestern states.

The smaller members of this subfamily, particularly the species in the genera *Lígyrus* and *Euetheòla,* are often serious pests of corn, sugarcane, and cereal crops; both adult and larval stages cause damage.

Subfamily **Cetoniìnae**—Flower Beetles and Others: The members of this group are principally pollen feeders and are common on flowers; many occur under loose bark or in debris, and a few occur in ant nests. The larvae feed on organic matter in the soil; some species damage the roots of plants. This subfamily includes the goliath beetles of Africa, which are among the largest insects known; some species reach a length of 4 inches (100 mm) or more.

Several genera in this subfamily (including *Cótinis, Euphòria,* and *Cremastocheìlus*) have the mesepimera visible from above, between the hind angles of the pronotum and the humeri of the elytra (Figure 279). The members of the genus *Cótinis* are over 18 mm in length, and have the scutellum small and covered by a median backward-projecting lobe of the pronotum. Those of *Euphòria* and *Cremastocheìlus* are smaller and have the scutellum large and exposed (Figure 279). The green June beetle, *Cótinus nítida* (L.), is a common dark-green beetle nearly 25 mm long; the adults feed on grapes, ripening fruits, and young corn, and the larvae often seriously damage lawns, golf courses, and various crops. The beetles in the genus *Euphòria* are somewhat bumblebeelike, and are often called bumble flower beetles; they are brownish yellow and black, very pubescent, and act much like bumblebees. These beetles do not extend their elytra in flight; the hind wings are extended through shallow emarginations at the sides of the elytra (Figure 279).

Perhaps the least known and most interesting members of this subfamily are those in the genus *Cremastocheìlus*. These beetles, which are 9–15 mm in length, are kept captive in ant nests to provide the ants with a nutritive fluid. The ants cling to the beetle's thorax and gnaw at pubescent glandular areas on the exposed mesepimera. Over 30 species belonging to this genus are known in the United States.

In the other common genera of Cetoniìnae the mesepimera are not visible from above. The hermit flower beetle, *Osmodérma eremícola* Knoch, is a brownish-black insect about 25 mm in length,

Figure 280. Plant-feeding scarabs. A, hermit flower beetle, *Osmodérma eremícola* Knoch (Cetoniìnae), slightly enlarged; B, grape pelidnota, *Pelidnòta punctàta* (L.) (Rutelìnae), 1½ ×; C, a flower beetle, *Trichiotìnus texànus* (Horn) (Cetoniìnae), 4 ×.

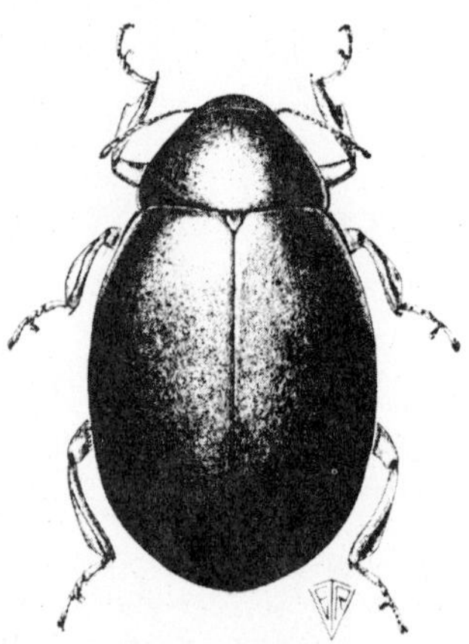

Figure 281. A pill beetle, *Amphicýrta déntipes* Erichson, 5 ×. (Courtesy of Arnett.)

with the elytra longer than wide (Figure 280 A); the larvae feed in decaying wood, and the adults are frequently found under dead bark or in tree cavities. The adults emit a very disagreeable odor when disturbed. In *Válgus* and *Trichiotìnus* the elytra are about as long as wide; the members of *Válgus* are small, less than 7.5 mm in length, and are brown in color and covered with scales; those of *Trichiotìnus* are brightly colored and pubescent (Figure 280 C). The adults of these two genera occur on various types of flowers, and the larvae live in decaying wood.

Family **Býrrhidae**—Pill Beetles: The pill beetles (Figure 281) are oval, convex, 5–10 mm in length, with the head bent downward and concealed from above, and with wide hind coxae that extend to the elytra. These insects usually occur in sandy situations, such as lake shores, where they may be found under debris. When disturbed, they draw in their legs and remain motionless.

Family **Psephènidae**—Water-Penny Beetles: These beetles derive their common name from the peculiar shape of the larvae (Figure 282 A, B). The larvae (called water pennies) are very flat and almost circular, and occur on the undersides of stones or other objects in streams and wave-swept shores. A single species, *Psephènus hérricki* (DeKay), occurs in the East; the adult is a somewhat flattened blackish beetle, 4–6 mm in length (Figure 282 C), which may be found in the vegetation bordering streams or in the water where the larvae occur. Some other species occur in the West.

Family **Ptilodactýlidae:** The members of this group are elongate-oval in shape, brownish in color, and 4–6 mm in length, and the head is generally not visible from above. The antennae are serrate in the female and pectinate in the male (segments 4–10 each bear a slender basal process about as long as the segment). The ptilodactylids occur on vegetation chiefly in swampy places; some larvae are aquatic and others occur in moist dead logs.

Family **Chelonarìidae:** Only one rare species of chelonariid occurs in the United States, *Chelonàrium lecóntei* Thomson, which occurs from North Carolina to Florida. This insect is oval, convex, 4–5 mm in length, and is black with patches of white pubescence on the elytra; the legs are retractile. The basal antennal segments are situated in a prosternal groove and the remaining segments extend back along the mesosternum. The larvae of these beetles are aquatic, and the adults are found on vegetation.

Family **Artematópidae:** This is a small family (eight North American species) formerly placed in the Dascíllidae (subfamily Dascillìnae), which they strongly resemble. They are elongate pubes-

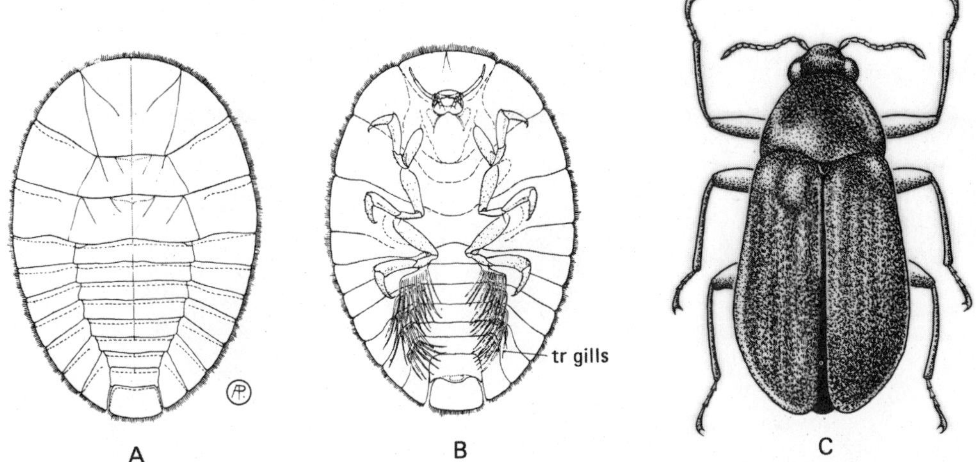

Figure 282. Psephènidae. A, dorsal view, and B, ventral view, of a water penny, the larva of, *Psephènus hérricki* (DeKay); C, adult water penny beetle, *Psephènus hérricki* (DeKay), 8 ×. *tr gills,* tracheal gills. (A and B, courtesy of Peterson; C, courtesy of Arnett.)

cent beetles, 4.0–7.5 mm in length, with the head deflexed and with long filiform antennae; the tarsi usually have the fourth segment small and segments 2–4 lobed. Species of *Eurypògon* are frequently taken by sweeping vegetation.

Family **Callirhípidae:** The only North American species in this family is *Zénoa pìcea* (Beauvois), an elongate, dark brown, shiny beetle, 11–15 mm in length; the antennae are short flabellate in both sexes. This is a rare beetle found under logs and bark, and is known from Ohio, Indiana, Pennsylvania, and Florida.

Family **Brachypséctridae:** This family is represented in the United States by a single very rare species, *Brachypséctra fúlva* LeConte, a yellowish brown beetle 5–6 mm in length, which is sometimes referred to as the Texas beetle. It resembles a click beetle in general appearance, but does not have the prosternal spine and mesosternal fossa characteristic of the Elatéridae. This insect is known from Texas, Utah, and California.

Family **Heterocéridae**—Variegated Mud-Loving Beetles: The heterocerids are a group of flattened, oblong, pubescent beetles (Figure 283 A) that live in mud or sand along the banks of streams of lakes; they superficially resemble a small scarab. Most of them are blackish or brownish with bands or spots of dull yellow, and 4.0–6.5 mm in length. The front and middle tibiae are greatly dilated and spiny, and are used in burrowing. These beetles may often be forced to leave their burrows in the stream bank by flooding the shore with water splashed up from the stream.

Family **Limníchidae**—Minute Marsh-Loving Beetles: The members of this and the two following families have the tarsal claws quite long (as in Figure 251 H), the first three visible abdominal sterna more or less fused together, and the larvae of most species (and usually also the adults) are aquatic. The limnichids are small (1–4 mm in length), oval, convex beetles that have the body clothed with fine pubescence. The most common limnichids (*Lutròchus*) have 11 antennal segments. These beetles are usually found in the wet sand or soil along the margins of streams.

Family **Dryópidae**—Long-Toed Water Beetles: The dryopids are elongate-oval, 1–8 mm in length, dull gray or brown, with the head more or less withdrawn into the prothorax (Figure 283 B); some species have the body covered with a fine pubescence. The antennae are very short, with most segments broader than long, and are concealed beneath the prosternal lobe. These beetles are usually found crawling about on the bottoms of streams, or along the shores; the adults may leave the stream and fly about, especially at night. Most known larvae are vermiform and live in soil or decaying wood (rather than in water).

Family **Élmidae**—Riffle Beetles: These beetles generally occur on the stones or debris in the

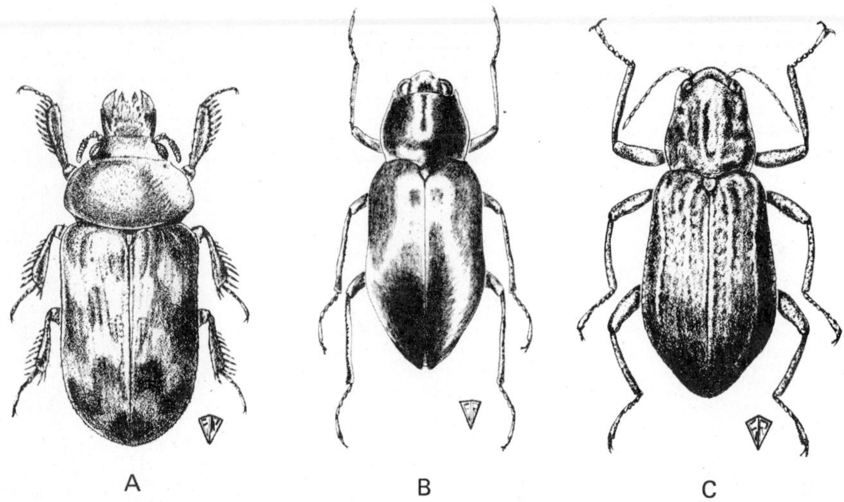

Figure 283. A, a variegated mud-loving beetle, *Neoheterócerus pállidus* (Say), 9 ×; B, a long-toed water beetle, *Hélichus lithóphilus* (Germar), 8 ×; C, a riffle beetle, *Stenélmis crenàta* (Say), 8 ×. (Courtesy of Arnett.)

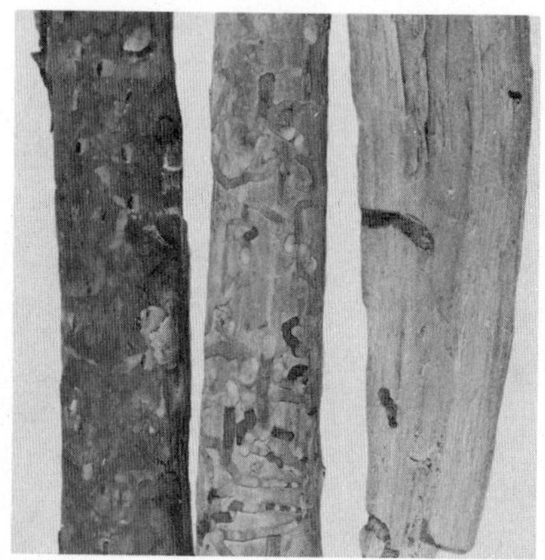

Figure 284. Galleries of buprestid larvae. (Courtesy of Davidson.)

riffles of streams; a few species occur in ponds or swamps, and a few are terrestrial. Riffle beetles are somewhat cylindrical in shape, with the elytra very smooth or somewhat ridged (Figure 283 C), and most of them are 3.5 mm in length or less. The larvae of most species, which occur in the same situations as the adults, are long and slender; those of *Phanócerus* are somewhat flattened and elliptical.

Family **Buprèstidae**—Metallic Wood-Boring Beetles: Most buprestid larvae bore under bark or in wood, attacking either living trees or newly cut or dying logs and branches; many do serious damage to trees and shrubs. The eggs are usually laid in crevices in the bark; the larvae, on hatching, tunnel under the bark, and some species eventually bore into the wood. The galleries under the bark are often winding and filled with frass; the galleries in the wood are oval in cross-section and usually enter the wood at an angle (Figure 284). Pupation occurs in the galleries. Buprestid larvae usually have the anterior end expanded and flattened (Figure 286), and are often known as flatheaded borers. The larvae of some species make winding galleries under the bark of twigs (Figure 285 B), others make galls (Figure 285 A), and one species girdles twigs.

The adults of this group are often rather metallic—coppery, green, blue, or black—especially on the ventral side of the body and on the dorsal surface of the abdomen. They are hard-bodied and compactly built, and usually have a characteristic shape (Figures 287 and 288). Many adult buprestids are attracted to dead or dying trees and logs and to slash; others occur on the foliage of trees and shrubs. These beetles run or fly rapidly and are often difficult to catch; some are colored like the bark and are very inconspicuous when they remain motionless. Many of the larger beetles in this group are common in sunny situations.

The larvae of *Chrysóbothris femoràta* (Olivier) attack a number of trees and shrubs and frequently do serious damage to fruit trees. The larvae of dif-

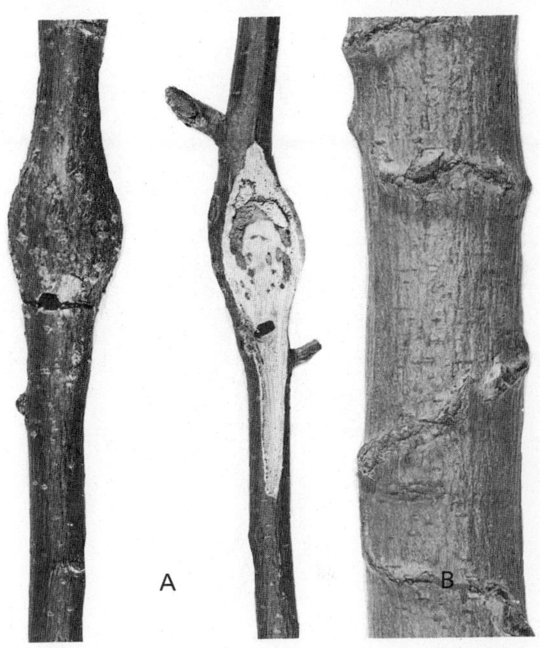

Figure 285. A, galls of *Ágrilus champlàini* Frost, in ironwood (*Ostrỳa*); B, the work of *Ágrilus bilineàtus carpìni* Knull on blue beech (*Carpìnus*). (Courtesy of Knull.)

ferent species of *Ágrilus* attack raspberries, blackberries, and other shrubs; *Ágrilus champlàini* Frost makes galls in ironwood (Figure 285 A), and *A. ruficóllis* (Fabricius) makes galls in raspberry and blackberry; *A. arcuàtus* (Say) is a twig-girdler. The adults of the genus *Ágrilus* are rather long and narrow (Figure 288 C); most are dark-colored with metallic shades, and some have light markings. The larvae of the species of *Bráchys* (Figure 287 D) are leaf miners. Most buprestids fly when disturbed, but the beetles in the genus *Bráchys* draw up their legs, "play dead," and fall off the foliage onto the ground. These smaller buprestids are usually found on foliage.

Family **Cebriónidae:** The cebrionids are elongate brownish beetles, 15–25 mm in length, with the body quite hairy and the mandibles hooklike and extending forward in front of the head. The larvae and females live in the ground; the males are excellent fliers and are largely nocturnal.

Family **Elatéridae**—Click Beetles: The click beetles constitute a large group (about 840 North American species), and many species are quite common. These beetles are peculiar in being able to "click" and jump; in most of the related groups, the union of the prothorax and mesothorax is such that little or no movement at this point is possible. The clicking is made possible by the flexible union of the prothorax and mesothorax, and a prosternal spine that fits into a groove on the mesosternum (Figure 254 A).

If one of these beetles is placed on its back on a smooth surface, it is usually unable to right itself by means of its legs. It bends its head and prothorax backward, so that only the extremities of the body are touching the surface on which it

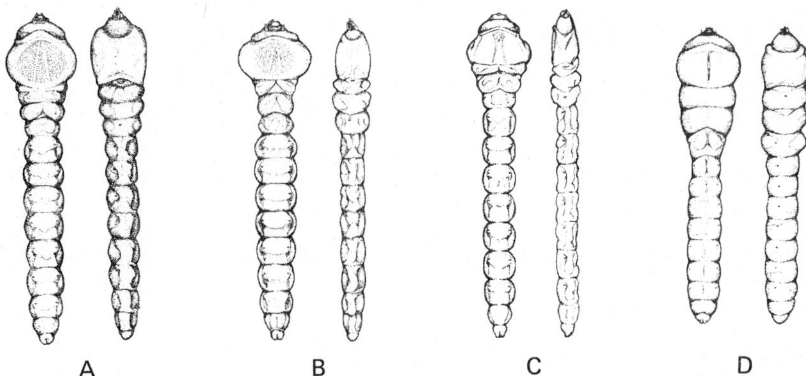

Figure 286. Larvae of Buprestidae. A, *Chrysóbothris trinérva* (Kirby); B, *Melanóphila drúmmondi* (Kirby); C, *Dicérca tenebròsa* (Kirby); D, *Ácmaeodèra prórsa* Fall. Dorsal view at left in each figure, lateral view at right. (Courtesy of USDA.)

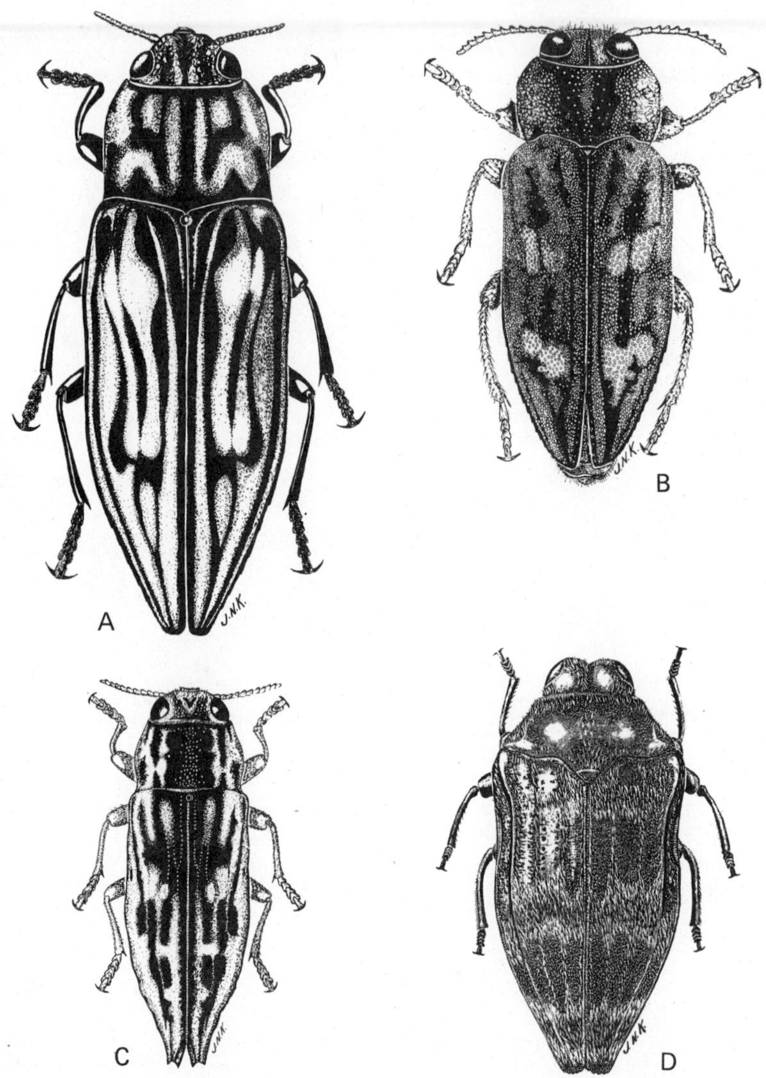

Figure 287. Metallic wood-boring beetles. A, *Chalcóphora fórtis* LeConte, which breeds in dead white pine; B, *Chrysóbothris floricola* Gory, which breeds in pine; C, *Dicérca lépida* LeConte, which breeds in dead ironwood and hawthorn; D, *Bráchys ovàtus* Weber, which mines in oak leaves. (Courtesy of Knull.)

rests; then, with a sudden jerk and clicking sound, the body is straightened out; this movement snaps the prosternal spine into the mesosternal groove and throws the insect into the air, spinning end over end. If the insect does not land right side up, it continues snapping until it does.

The click beetles can usually be recognized by their characteristic shape (Figure 289 A, C). The body is elongate, usually parallel-sided, and rounded at each end. The posterior corners of the pronotum are prolonged backward into sharp points or spines. The antennae are usually serrate (occasionally filiform or pectinate). Most of these beetles are between 12 and 30 mm in length, but a few exceed these limits. The largest and most easily recognized species is the eyed click beetle,

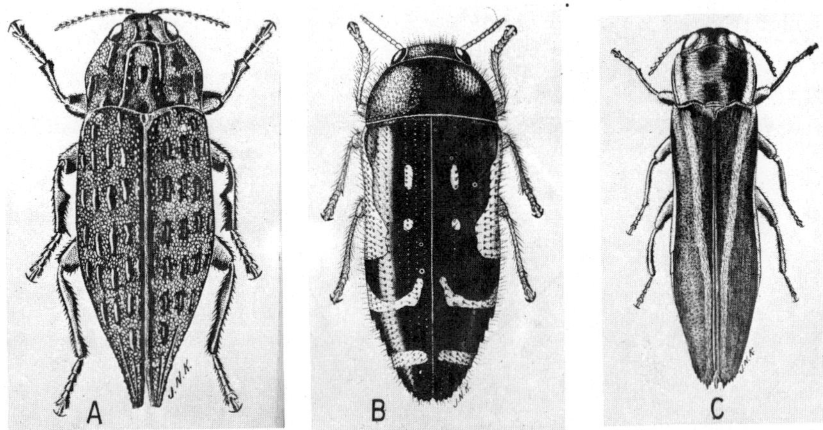

Figure 288. Metallic wood-boring beetles. A, *Dicérca tenebròsa* (Kirby), 3½ ×; B, *Ácmaeodèra pulchélla* (Herbst), 6 ×; C, *Ágrilus bilineàtus* (Weber), 6 ×. (Courtesy of Knull.)

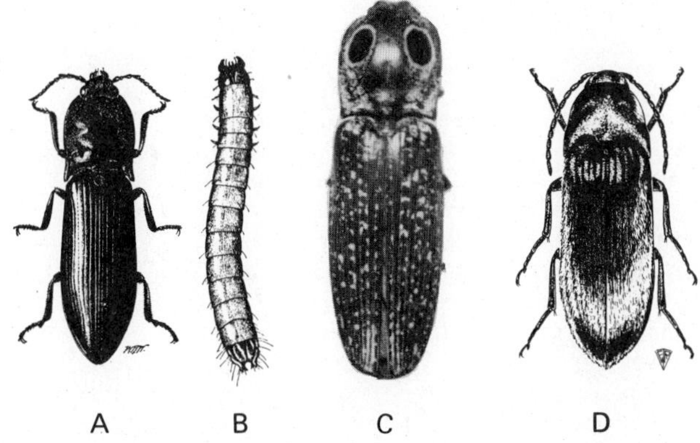

Figure 289. A, adult, and B, larva of a click beetle, *Ctenícera nóxia* (Hyslop) (slightly enlarged); C, eyed click beetle, *Álaus oculàtus* (L.) (about natural size); D, a false click beetle, *Anelástes drùryi* Kirby, 3 ×. (A and B, courtesy of USDA; D, courtesy of Arnett.)

Álaus oculàtus (L.), a mottled-gray beetle with the pronotum bearing two large black eyelike spots (Figure 289 C). This species may reach about 1½ inches (38 mm) or more in length. Most elaterids are inconspicuously colored with black or brown.

Adult click beetles are phytophagous and occur on flowers, under bark, or on vegetation. The larvae are slender, hard-bodied, and shiny, and are commonly called wireworms (Figure 289 B). The larvae of many species are very destructive, feeding on newly planted seed and the roots of beans, cotton, potatoes, corn, and cereals. Many elaterid larvae occur in rotting logs; some of these feed on other insects. Pupation occurs in the ground, under bark, or in dead wood.

Species of *Pyróphorus* in the southern states and in the tropics have two light-producing spots on the posterior edge of the prothorax and one on the abdomen. The light is much stronger than that of the lampyrids, and a large number flying about at night is a striking sight.

Family **Thróscidae:** The throscids are brown or black in color, oblong-oval in shape, and 5 mm in length or less. They are similar to elaterids, but have the prothorax firmly attached to the mesothorax and they do not "click." The prosternum is lobed anteriorly and almost conceals the mouth parts. These beetles occur chiefly on flowers, particularly those of milkweed, dogwood, and May apple.

Family **Cerophýtidae:** This group includes two very rare species of *Cerópytum,* one occurring in the East and the other in California. These beetles are elongate-oblong in shape, somewhat flattened, 7.5–8.5 mm in length, and brownish to black in color. The hind trochanters are very long, nearly as long as the femora. These beetles occur in rotten wood and under dead bark.

Family **Perothópidae:** These beetles are similar to the Eucnèmidae, but have the prothorax free and the tarsal claws pectinate. They are 10–18 mm in length, brownish in color, and are found on the trunks and branches of old beech trees. Three species of *Pérothops* occur in the United States from Pennsylvania to Florida, and in California.

Family **Eucnèmidae**—False Click Beetles: This family is very closely related to the Elatéridae. Its members are relatively rare beetles usually found in wood that has just begun to decay, chiefly in beech and maple. Most of them are brownish in color and about 10 mm in length or less (Figure 289 D). The pronotum is quite convex above, and the antennae are inserted rather close together on the front of the head, and there is no distinct labrum. These beetles quiver their antennae almost constantly, a habit not occurring in the Elatéridae. Some, like the click beetles, can click and jump.

Family **Telegeùsidae:** The Telegeùsidae are represented in North America by three species of small, rare beetles that occur in Arizona and California. Their most distinctive character is the form of the maxillary and labial palps, which have the terminal segment tremendously enlarged. The tarsi are 5-segmented, the antennae are serrate, and the seven or eight abdominal segments are less than half covered by the short elytra. The telegeusids are slender, 5–6 mm in length, and resemble small rove beetles; the hind wings do not fold, but extend back over the abdomen beyond the tips of the elytra.

Family **Phengòdidae**—Glow-Worms: This is a small group of relatively uncommon beetles closely related to the Lampýridae. Most of them are broad and flat, with the the elytra short and pointed, and the posterior part of the abdomen covered only by the membranous hind wings (Figure 291 B). The antennae are usually serrate, but in some males they may be pectinate or plumose. These insects vary in length from 10 to 30 mm and are found on foliage or on the ground. The adult females of many species are wingless and luminescent, as in the Lampýridae, and look much like larvae. The larvae are predaceous.

Family **Lampýridae**—Lightningbugs or Fireflies: Many members of this common and well-known group possess a "tail light"—segments near the end of the abdomen with which the insects are able to produce light. These luminous segments can be recognized, even when they are not glowing, by their yellowish-green color. During certain seasons, usually early summer, these insects fly about in the evenings and are conspicuous by their blinking yellow lights.

The lampyrids are elongate and very soft-bodied beetles in which the pronotum extends forward over the head so that the head is largely or entirely concealed from above (Figure 290 A). The elytra are soft, flexible, and rather flat except for the epipleurae. Most of the larger members of this group have luminescent organs, but many of the smaller ones do not.

The light emitted by these insects is unique in being cold; nearly 100 percent of the energy given off appears as light. In the electric arc light, only 10 percent of the energy is light, and the other 90 percent is given off as heat. The light given off by a firefly is produced by the oxidation of a substance called luciferin, which is produced in the cells of the light-producing organs. These organs have a rich tracheal supply, and the insect controls the emission of light by controlling the air supply to the organs. When air is admitted, the luciferin (in the presence of an enzyme called luciferinase) is almost instantly oxidized, releasing the energy as light. The flashing of fireflies is probably a mating response, and each species has a characteristic flashing rhythm; an expert can identify species by the length of the flashes and the interval between flashes. In some tropical species in this group, large numbers of individuals congregate and flash in unison.

During the day the lampyrids are usually found on vegetation. The larvae are predaceous and feed on various smaller insects and on snails. The females of many species are wingless and look very much like larvae. These wingless females and most lampyrid larvae are luminescent and are often called "glow-worms."

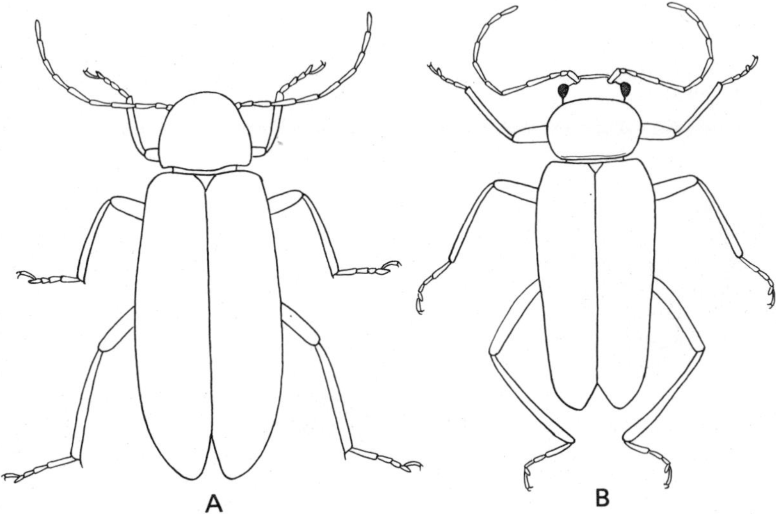

Figure 290. A, a lightningbug (*Photùrus*); B, a soldier beetle (*Chauliógnathus*), 3¾ ×.

Family **Canthàridae**—Soldier Beetles: The cantharids are elongate, soft-bodied beetles that are very similar to the lightningbugs (Lampýridae) but the head protrudes forward beyond the pronotum and is visible from above (not concealed by the pronotum as in the Lampýridae). These beetles do not have light-producing organs, and they have the fourth tarsal segment lobed beneath.

Adult soldier beetles are usually found on flowers; the larvae are predaceous on other insects. One common species, *Chauliógnathus pennsylvánicus* (De Geer) (Figure 290 B), about 13 mm in length, has each elytron yellowish with a black spot or stripe; members of other genera are yellowish, black, or brown in color.

Family **Lỳcidae**—Net-Winged Beetles: The lycids are elongate soft-winged beetles somewhat similar to the soldier beetles and fireflies, but may be readily recognized by the peculiar network of raised lines on the elytra (Figure 291 A). Some western species (*Lỳcus*) have a distinct snout. The elytra in some species are slightly widened posteriorly. The adults occur on foliage and tree trunks, usually in wooded areas; they feed on the juices of decaying plant materials and occasionally on other insects. The larvae are predaceous.

One of the more common members of this group is *Calópteron reticulàtum* (Fabricius), 11–19 mm in length; the elytra are yellow, with the posterior half and a narrow crossband in the anterior part black; the pronotum is black, margined with yellow. Most of the lycids are brightly colored, with red, black, or yellow. They are apparently distasteful to predators, and their coloration is mimicked by other beetles (certain Cerambýcidae) and some moths (for example, certain Ctenùchidae, Figure 413 C).

Family **Derodóntidae**—Tooth-Necked Fungus Beetles: The derodontids are small, usually brownish beetles less than 4 mm in length (Figure

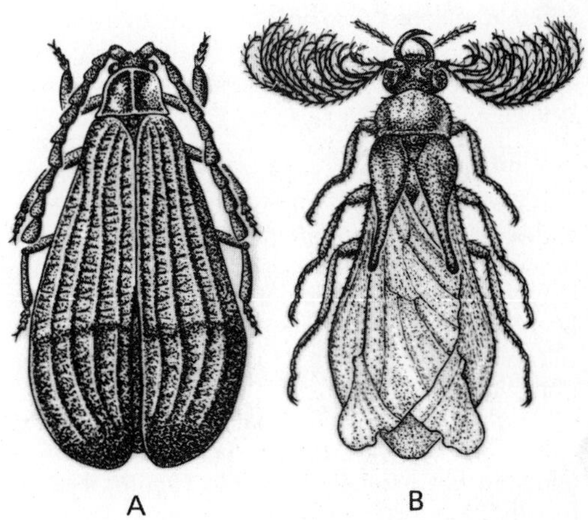

Figure 291. A, a net-winged beetle, *Calópteron terminàle* (Say); B, adult male of a glow-worm, *Phengòdes plumòsa* Olivier. 4 ×. (Courtesy of Arnett.)

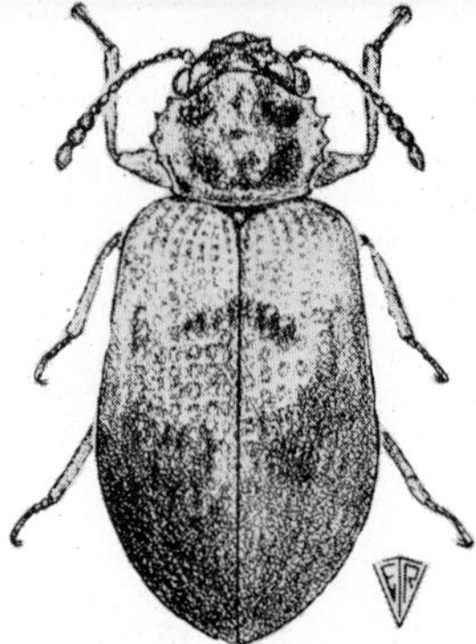

Figure 292. A tooth-necked fungus beetle, *Derodóntus maculàtus* Melsheimer, 15 ×. (Courtesy of Arnett.)

292), and have a pair of ocelli on the head near the inner margins of the compound eyes (Figure 253 C). The members of the genus *Derodóntus* have three or four strong teeth or notches along the lateral margins of the pronotum; other genera lack these teeth. The elytra completely cover the abdomen, and each bears many rows of large square punctures or polished dark spots. These beetles occur in woody fungi and under the bark of rotting logs.

Family **Nosodéndridae:** This family includes two species of *Nosodéndron,* one occurring in the East and the other in the West. The eastern species, *N. unicólor* Say, is an oval, convex, black beetle 5–6 mm in length, and occurs under the bark of dead logs and in debris. The nosodendrids are similar to the Býrrhidae, but have the head visible from above and the elytra bear rows of short yellow hair tufts.

Family **Derméstidae** – Dermestid or Skin Beetles: This group contains a number of very destructive and economically important species. The dermestids are mostly scavengers and feed on a great variety of plant and animal products, including leather, furs, skins, museum specimens, woolen or silk materials, rugs, stored food materials, and carrion. Most of the damage is done by the larvae.

Adult dermestids are small, oval or elongate-oval, convex beetles with short clubbed antennae, and they vary in length from 2 to 12 mm; they are usually hairy or covered with scales (Figure 293 A–C). They may be found in the materials mentioned above, and many feed on flowers. Some are black or dull-colored, but many have a characteristic color pattern. The larvae are usually brownish and are covered with long hairs (Figure 293 D–F).

The larger dermestids belong to the genus *Derméstes.* The larder beetle, *D. lardàrius* L. is a common species in this genus; it is a little over 6 mm in length and is black with a light-brown band across the base of the elytra. It feeds on a variety of stored foods, including meats and cheese, and occasionally damages the specimens in insect collections.

Some of the smaller dermestids are often common in houses and may do serious damage to carpets, upholstery, and clothing. Two common species of this type are the black carpet beetle, *Attagènus megátoma* (Fabricius), and the carpet beetle, *Anthrènus scrophulàriae* (L.); the former is a grayish black beetle, 3.5–5.0 mm in length (Figure 293 B), and the latter is a pretty little black-and-white patterned species, 3–5 mm in length (Figure 293 A). Most of the damage done by these species is done by the larvae; the adults are often found on flowers.

This is one group of insects that every entomology student will sooner or later encounter. All he has to do to get some dermestids is to make an insect collection and not protect it against these pests; the dermestids will eventually find the collection and ruin it. Many species in this group are serious pests in homes, markets, and food-storage places.

This group contains one of the worst stored-products pests in the world, the Khapra beetle, *Trogodérma granàrium* Everts. A native of India, this beetle is frequently intercepted at ports of entry into this country, and in 1953 it became established in California, Arizona, and New Mexico. It is now apparently eradicated in the United States.

While many of the dermestids are serious pests, they are nevertheless of value as scavengers, aiding in the removal of dead organic matter. Some of the species that feed on carrion, notably, *Derméstes canìnus* Germar, have been used by vertebrate zoologists to clean skeletons for study.

One species in this family, *Thylódrias contráctus* Motschulsky, is unusual in having the antennae filiform and the female wingless and larviform.

Family **Anobìidae:** The anobiids are cylindrical to oval, pubescent beetles, 1.0–9.0 mm in length; the head is deflexed and is usually concealed from above by the hoodlike pronotum. Most of them have the last three antennal segments enlarged

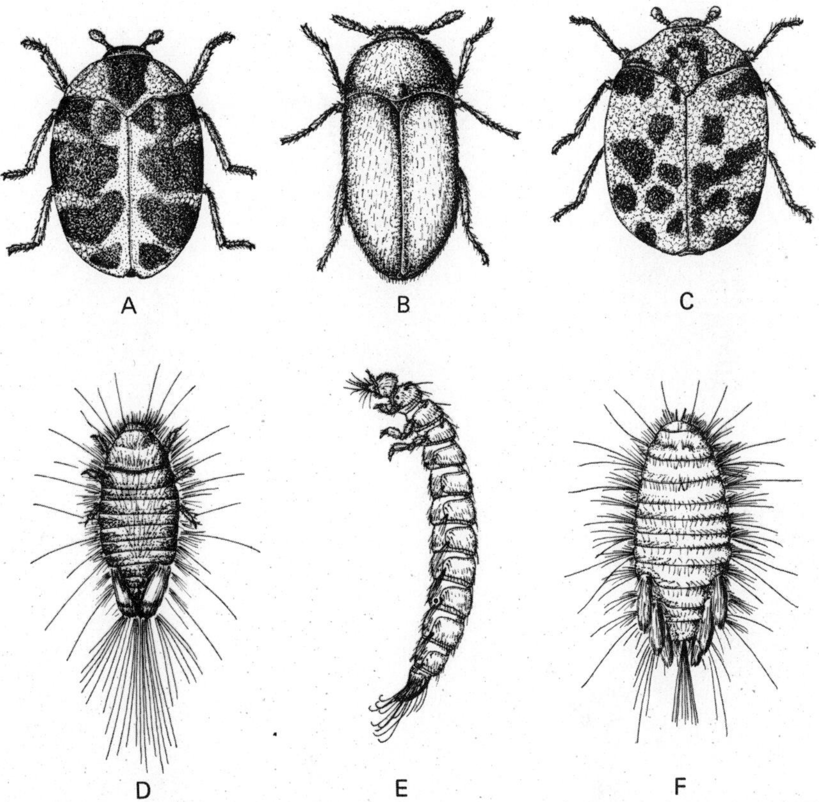

Figure 293. Dermestid beetles. A, carpet beetle, *Anthrènus scrophulàriae* (L.), adult; B, black carpet beetle, *Attagènus megátoma* (Fabricius), adult; C, furniture carpet beetle, *Anthrènus flávipes* LeConte, adult; D, larva of *A. scrophulàriae* (L.), dorsal view; E, larva of *A. megátoma* (Fabricius), lateral view; F, larva of *A. flávipes* LeConte, dorsal view. (E, courtesy of Peterson; other figures, courtesy of the Cornell University Agricultural Experiment Station.)

and lengthened (Figures 249 C, and 294 B, D–F); a few have these segments lengthened but not enlarged, and a few have the antennae serrate or pectinate. About 260 species occur in North America.

Most anobiids live in dry vegetable materials such as logs and twigs or under the bark of dead trees; others pass the larval stage in fungi or in the seeds and stems of various plants. Some species, such as *Xestòbium rufovillòsum* (De Geer) (Figure 294 F), are called death-watch beetles because they make a ticking sound as they bore through wood.

Some of the anobiids are common and destructive pests. The drugstore beetle, *Stegòbium paníceum* (L.) (Figure 294 E), infests various drugs and cereals; the cigarette beetle, *Lasiodérma serricórne* (Fabricius) (Figure 294 C), is common in dried tobacco, museum specimens, and insect collections. Some wood-boring species, such as the furniture beetle, *Anòbium punctàtum* (De Geer) (Figure 294 B), bore in timbers, woodwork, and furniture.

Family **Ptìnidae**—Spider Beetles: The ptinids are long-legged beetles, 1–5 mm in length, that have the head and pronotum much narrower than the elytra, and are somewhat spiderlike in appearance (Figure 295 A). Many species are minor pests of stored grain products; some feed on both plant and animal products and are known to attack museum specimens; one species is known to pass its larval stages in rat droppings, and another (*Ptìnus califòrnicus* Pic) feeds on the pollen provisions in nests of solitary bees.

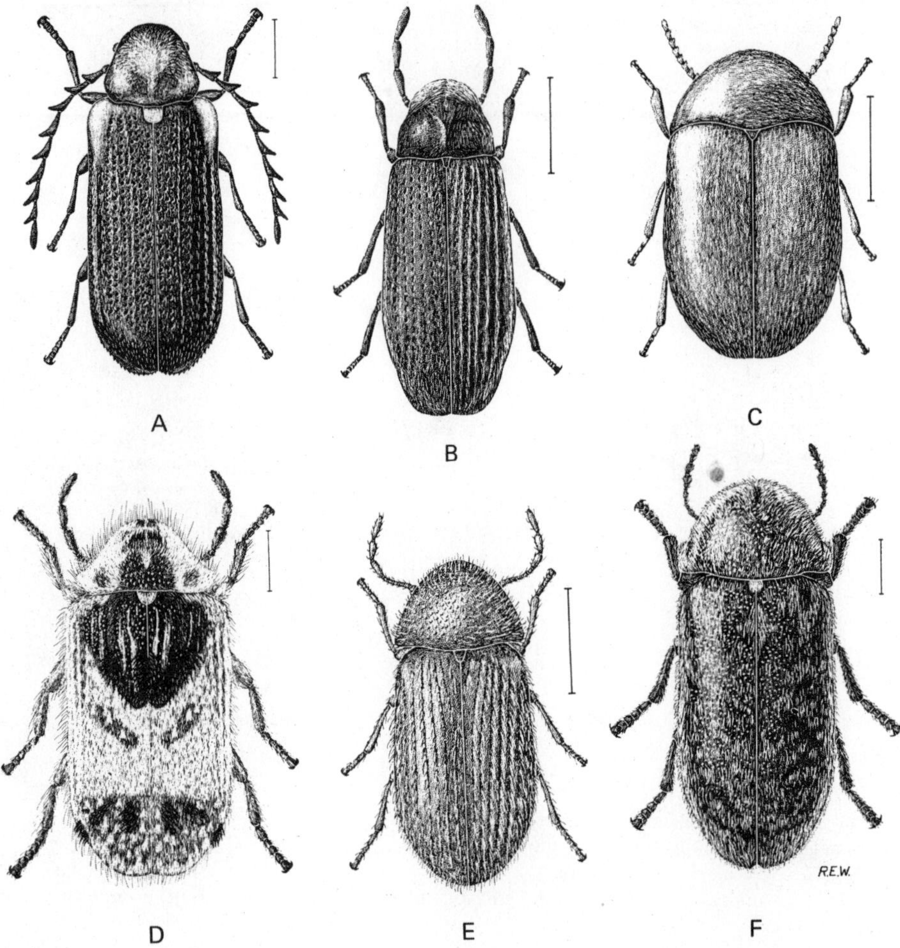

Figure 294. Anobiid beetles. A, *Eucràda humeràlis* (Melsheimer); B, furniture beetle, *Anòbium punctàtum* (De Geer); C, cigarette beetle, *Lasiodérma serricòrne* (Fabricius); D, *Trichodésma gibbòsa* (Say); E, drugstore beetle, *Stegòbium paníceum* (L.); F, a death-watch beetle, *Xestòbium rufovillòsum* (De Geer). The lines represent 1 mm. (Courtesy of White and the Ohio Biological Survey.)

Family **Bostríchidae**—Branch and Twig Borers: Most of the beetles in this group are elongate, somewhat cylindrical, and the head is bent down and scarcely visible from above (Figure 296). Most species vary in length from 3.5 to 12.0 mm, but one western species, *Dinápate wrìghti* Horn, which breeds in palms, reaches a length of 52 mm. Most species in this group are wood-boring and attack living trees, dead twigs and branches, or seasoned lumber. The apple twig borer, *Amphícerus bicaudàtus* (Say), attacks the twigs of apple, pear, cherry, and other trees.

One species in this family that occurs in the West, *Scobícia déclivis* (LeConte), is rather unusual in that adults often bore into the lead sheathing of telephone cables. This insect normally bores in the wood of oak, maple, and other trees; it apparently does not feed as it bores into the cables. The beetles make holes in the sheathing about 2.5 mm in diameter; these holes allow moisture to enter the cable, causing a short-circuiting of the wires and a consequent interruption of service. This insect is commonly known as the lead-cable borer or short-circuit beetle.

The bostrichids in the subfamily Psoìnae, which occur principally in the West, differ from other bostrichids in that the head is large and easily visible from above, and the mandibles are large and strong. The members of the genus *Polýcaon* are 14–28 mm long, brown or black in color, and

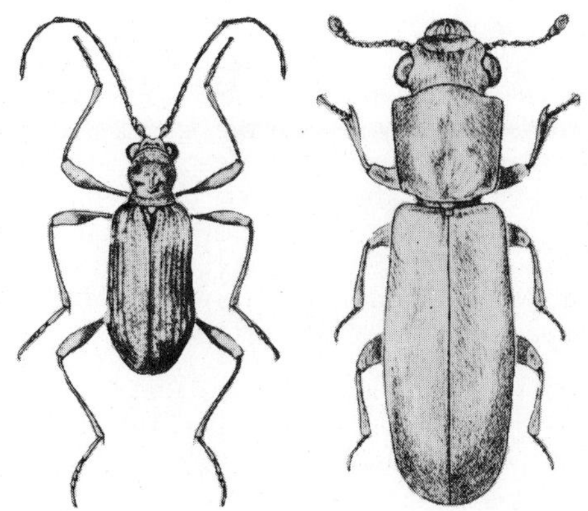

Figure 295. A, a spider beetle, *Ptìnus fúr* (L.), 5 ×; B, a powder-post beetle, *Trogoxỳlon parallelopípedum* (Melsheimer), 10 ×. (Courtesy of Arnett.)

Figure 296. A bostrichid beetle, *Ápate mónacha* Fabricius. (Courtesy of Wolcott and the *Journal of Agriculture* of the University of Puerto Rico.)

often cause great damage to orchards in California and Oregon by severely pruning the trees. The larvae tunnel through the heartwood of these trees, but the adults seldom enter the wood. *Psòa maculàta* (LeConte), 6 mm long, is the "spotted limb borer" of California; it breeds only in dead twigs of trees or shrubs and is usually bluish black or greenish with dense gray hair and with a few large lighter spots on the elytra.

Family **Lýctidae**—Powder-Post Beetles: These beetles derive their name from the fact that they bore into dry and seasoned wood and reduce it to a powder. Species of *Lýctus* may completely destroy furniture, wooden beams (particularly in barns and cabins), tool handles, and hardwood floors. They live beneath the surface for months, and timbers from which the adults have emerged may be peppered with tiny holes, as though fine shot had been fired into them (Figure 297). These beetles do not enter wood that is painted or varnished. The powder-post beetles are slender and elongate (Figure 295 B), uniformly colored brown to black, and 2–7 mm in length; the head is prominent from above and slightly constricted behind the eyes.

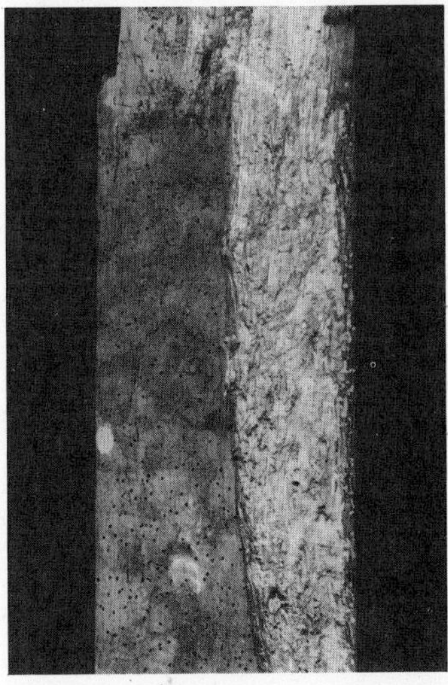

Figure 297. A board damaged by powder-post beetles, and showing exit holes of the beetles.

Family **Trogosítidae**—Bark-Gnawing Beetles: This group contains two subfamilies that differ rather markedly in shape: the Tenebroidìnae are elongate, with the head about as wide as the pronotum, and with the pronotum rather widely separated from the base of the elytra (Figure 298); the Ostomìnae are oval or elliptical, with the head

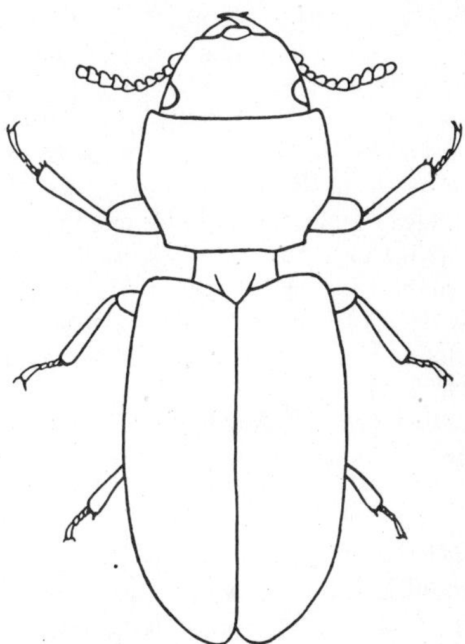

Figure 298. A trogositid beetle, *Tenebriòides* sp., 7½ ×.

only about half as wide as the pronotum, and the pronotum is rather closely joined to the base of the elytra. The Ostomìnae are very similar to some nitidulids (for example, Figure 301 C), but may be separated by the characters given in the key (couplet 144); most Ostomìnae have long erect hairs on the elytra, while the similarly shaped nitidulids have the elytra bare or short-pubescent.

Trogositids are 2.6–22.0 mm in length, and most are blackish, bluish, or greenish; the majority are predaceous. The cadelle, *Tenebròides mauritánicus* (L.) (Figure 298), occurs commonly in granaries; it is believed to feed on both other insects in the grain and on the grain itself. *Temnochìla viréscens* (Fabricius), a rather common and widely distributed species, is a bright blue-green beetle about 20 mm in length; it can administer a vicious bite with its powerful mandibles. Adults and larvae of trogositids are generally found under bark, in woody fungi, and in dry vegetable matter.

Family **Cléridae**—Checkered Beetles: The clerids are elongate, very pubescent beetles 3–24 (mostly 5–12) mm in length, and many are brightly colored. The pronotum is narrower than the base of the elytra, and sometimes narrower than the head (Figure 299). The tarsi are 5-segmented, but in many species the first or the fourth segment is very small and difficult to see.

The majority of the checkered beetles are predaceous both as adults and larvae. Many are common on or within tree trunks and logs, where they prey on the larvae of various woodboring insects (chiefly bark beetles); others occur on flowers and foliage. A few (for example, *Trichòdes,* Figure 299 E) are pollen feeders in the adult stage and sometimes also in the larval stage; *Trichòdes* larvae sometimes develop in the egg pods of grasshoppers or in the nests of bees and wasps.

Some of the clerids, which have the fourth tarsal segment very small and difficult to see, have been placed by some authorities in a separate family, the Corynètidae. These beetles are similar in general appearance and habits to the other clerids. One species in this group, *Necròbia rùfipes* De Geer (Figure 299 D), the redlegged ham beetle, is occasionally destructive to stored meats.

Family **Melýridae**—Soft-Winged Flower Beetles: The members of this family are elongate-oval, soft-bodied beetles 10 mm in length or less; many are brightly colored with brown or red and black (Figure 300 A). Some melyrids (Malachiìnae) have peculiar orange-colored structures along the sides of the abdomen, which may be everted and saclike or withdrawn into the body and inconspicuous. Some melyrids have the two basal antennal segments greatly enlarged. Most adults and larvae are predaceous, but many are common on flowers. Our most common species belong to the genus *Cóllops* (Malachiìnae); *C. quadrimaculàtus* (Fabricius) is reddish, with two bluish black spots on each elytron.

Family **Lymexylónidae**—Ship-Timber Beetles: This group is represented in the United States by two rare species that occur under bark and in dead logs and stumps; they cause much of the pin-hole damage in chestnut. These beetles are long and narrow and 9.0–13.5 mm in length; the head is bent down and narrowed behind the eyes to form a short neck; the antennae are filiform to serrate; the tarsi are 5-segmented; and the maxillary palps in the males are long and flabellate. These beetles are called ship-timber beetles because one European species has been very destructive to ship timbers. One of our two species, *Hylecoètus lùgubris* Say, is commonly called the sapwood timberworm.

Family **Nitidùlidae**—Sap Beetles: The members of this family vary considerably in size, shape, and habits. Most of them are small, 12 mm in length or less, elongate or oval, and in a few the elytra are short and expose the terminal abdominal segments (Figure 301). Most nitidulids are found where plant fluids are fermenting or souring; for example, around decaying fruits or melons, flowing sap, and some types of fungi. A few occur on or near the dried carcasses of dead animals, and several occur in flowers. Others are very common beneath the loose bark of dead stumps and logs, especially if these are damp enough to be moldy.

Family **Rhizophágidae**—Root-Eating Beetles: These beetles are small, slender, dark-colored, 1.5–3.0 mm in length (Figure 300 B), and usually occur under bark or in rotten wood; a few species live in ant nests. The antennae are 10-segmented with a 1- or 2-segmented club, the last tarsal segment is elongate and the other segments are short, the tip of the abdomen is exposed beyond the elytra, and the first and fifth abdominal sterna are longer than the others. One subfamily, the Monotomìnae (sometimes given family rank), has the head abruptly constricted into a narrow neck a little way behind the eyes, and the body is covered with short dense pubescence (to which dirt often adheres).

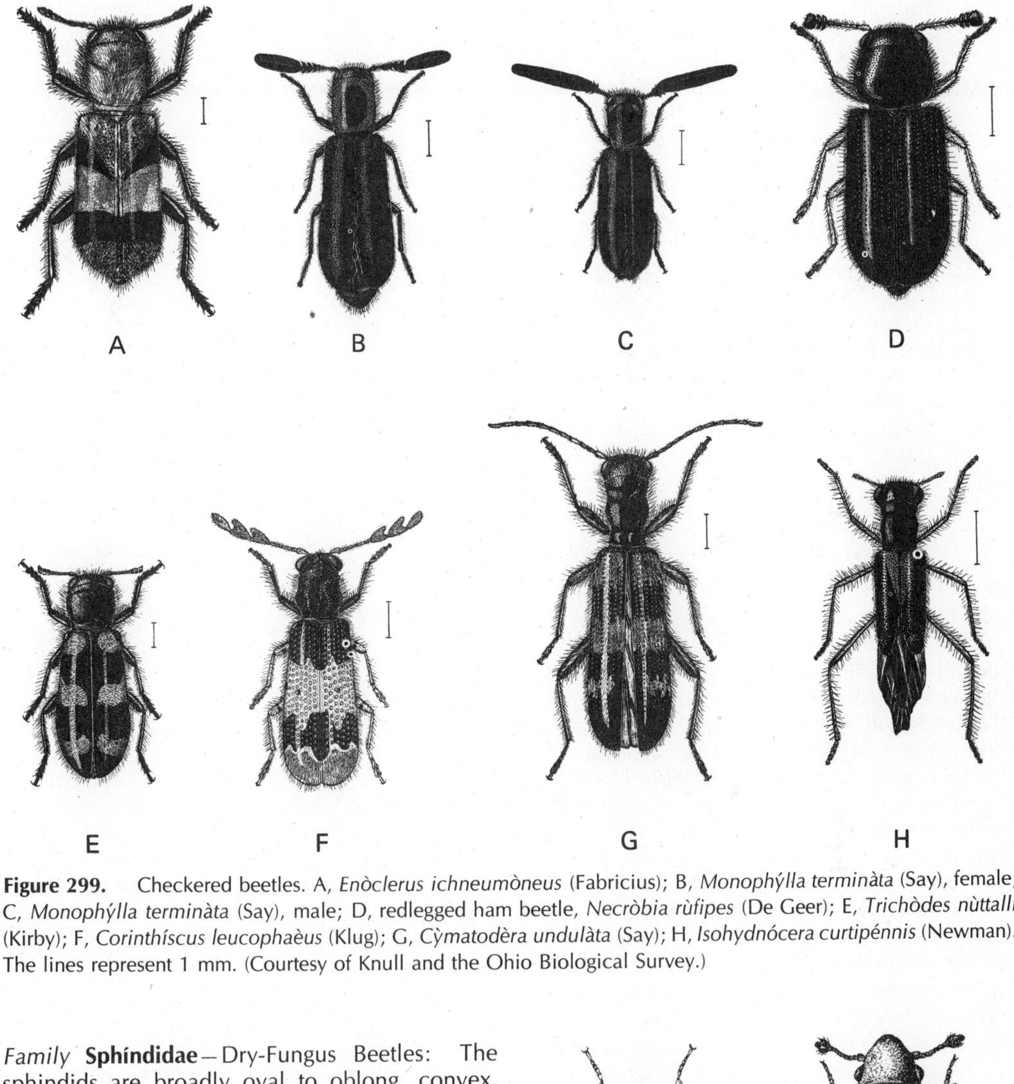

Figure 299. Checkered beetles. A, *Enòclerus ichneumòneus* (Fabricius); B, *Monophýlla terminàta* (Say), female; C, *Monophýlla terminàta* (Say), male; D, redlegged ham beetle, *Necròbia rùfipes* (De Geer); E, *Trichòdes nùttalli* (Kirby); F, *Corinthíscus leucophaèus* (Klug); G, *Cỳmatodèra undulàta* (Say); H, *Isohydnócera curtipénnis* (Newman). The lines represent 1 mm. (Courtesy of Knull and the Ohio Biological Survey.)

Family **Sphíndidae**—Dry-Fungus Beetles: The sphindids are broadly oval to oblong, convex, dark brown to black beetles, 1.5–3.0 mm in length. They have a 5-5-4 tarsal formula, and the 10-segmented antennae terminate in a 2- or 3-segmented club. The sphindids occur in dry fungi, such as the shelf fungi on tree trunks. Six relatively rare species occur in the United States.

Family **Cucùjidae**—Flat Bark Beetles: The beetles in this group are extremely flat, and are either

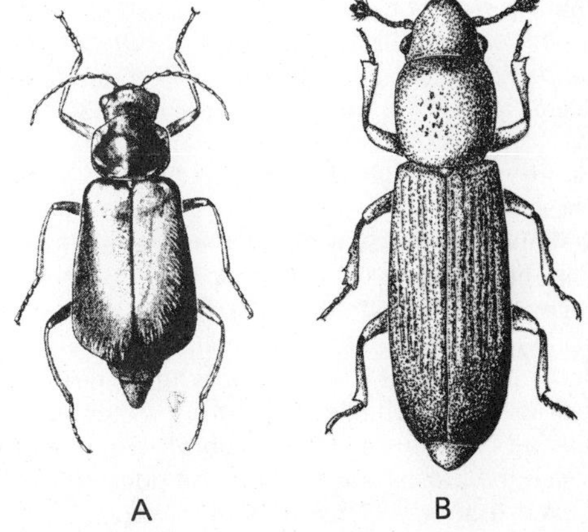

Figure 300. A, a soft-winged flower beetle, *Maláchius aèneus* (L.), 5 ×; B, a root-eating beetle, *Rhizóphagus bipunctàtus* (Say), 18 ×. (Redrawn from Arnett.)

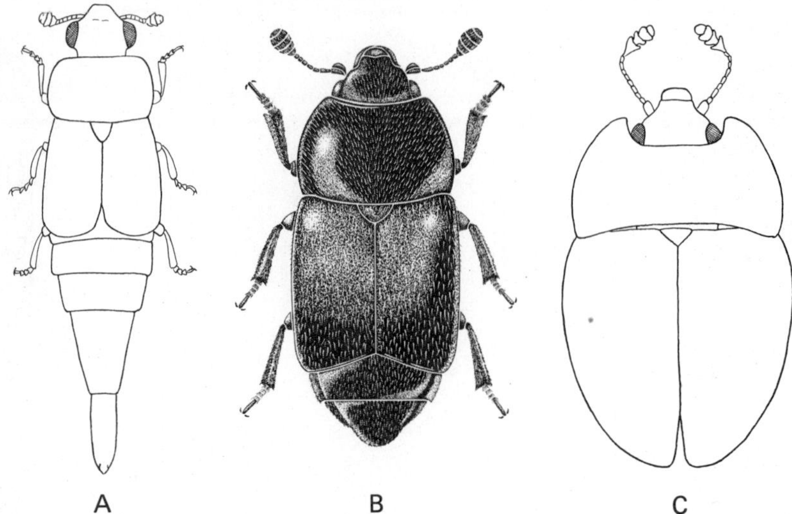

Figure 301. Representative Nitidùlidae. A, *Conótelus obscùrus* Erichson, 15×; B, *Carpóphilus lùgubris* Murray, 15×; C, *Lobìopa* sp., 7½ ×.

reddish, brownish, or yellowish in color. Most cucujids are found under the bark of freshly cut logs, chiefly maple, beech, elm, ash, and poplar. The largest cucujids, which belong to the genera *Cucùjus* and *Catogènus,* reach a length of about 13 mm. Our only species of *Cucùjus, C. clávipes* Fabricius, is uniform red in color (Figure 302 A); a common species of *Catogènus, C. rùfus* (Fabricius), is brown and has the elytra grooved.

Most of the cucujids are predaceous on mites and small insects, which they find under bark. Some species, including those of *Catogènus,* are parasitic in the larval stage on species of Cerambýcidae and Bracónidae, and undergo a hypermetamorphosis. A few species feed on stored grain or meal; one of the most important of these is the saw-toothed grain beetle, *Oryzaéphilus surinaménsis* (L.), so called because of the toothed lateral margins of the pronotum (Figure 302 B).

Family **Cryptophágidae**—Silken Fungus Beetles: These beetles are 1–5 mm in length, elongate-oval in shape, and yellowish brown and covered with a silky pubescence. They feed on fungi, decaying vegetation, and similar materials, and usually occur in decaying vegetable matter; some species occur in the nests of wasps or bumble bees.

Most cryptophagids have the prosternum extending back to the mesosternum; two genera in which the prosternum is short and does not reach the mesosternum (*Anchòrius* and *Diplocoèlus*) are sometimes placed in a separate family, the Biphýllidae.

Family **Languriidae**—Lizard Beetles: The lizard beetles are narrow and elongate, 5–10 mm in length, and usually have the pronotum reddish and the elytra black (Figure 302 D). The adults feed on the leaves and pollen of many common plants, including goldenrod, ragweed, fleabane, and clover. The larvae are stem borers; the larvae of the clover stem borer (*Langùria mozárdi* Latreille) attack clover and sometimes cause considerable damage.

Family **Erotýlidae**—Pleasing Fungus Beetles: The erotylids are small to medium-sized, oval, and usually shiny beetles that are found on fungi or may be attracted to sap; they often occur beneath the bark of dead stumps, especially where rotting fungus abounds. Some of the erotylids are brightly patterned with orange or red and black. The species in this group that have the tarsi distinctly 5-segmented are by some authorities placed in a separate family, the Dácnidae; the largest species of dacnids (*Megalodácne*) are about 20 mm in length and are black with two orange-red bands across the elytra (Figure 302 C). In other erotylids the fourth tarsal segment is very small, so that the tarsi appear 4-segmented; these beetles are smaller, 8 mm in length or less. Some erotylids are fairly common insects.

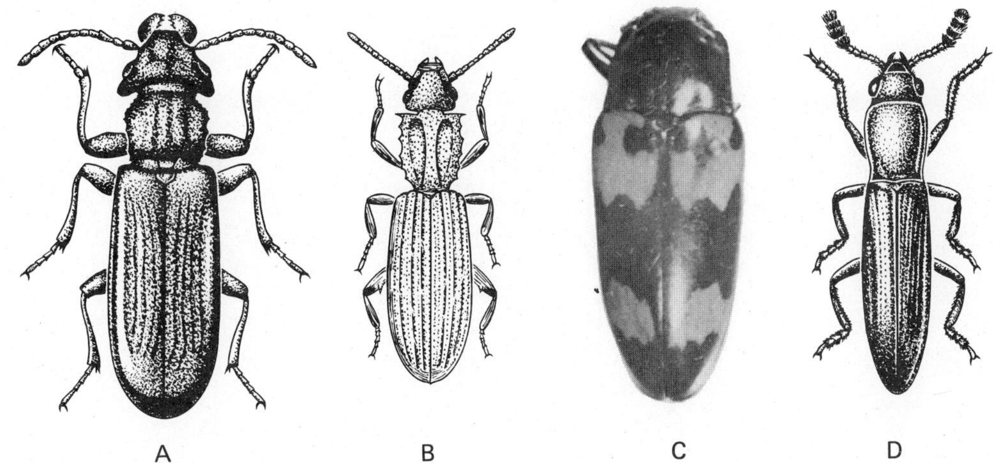

Figure 302. A, a flat bark beetle, *Cucùjus clávipes* Fabricius, 4 ×; B, saw-toothed grain beetle, *Oryzaéphilus surinaménsis* (L.), 17 ×; C, a pleasing fungus beetle, *Megalodácne hèros* (Say), 2½ ×; D, adult of the clover stem borer, *Langùria mozárdi* Latreille, 6 ×. (A, courtesy of Arnett; B and D, courtesy of USDA.)

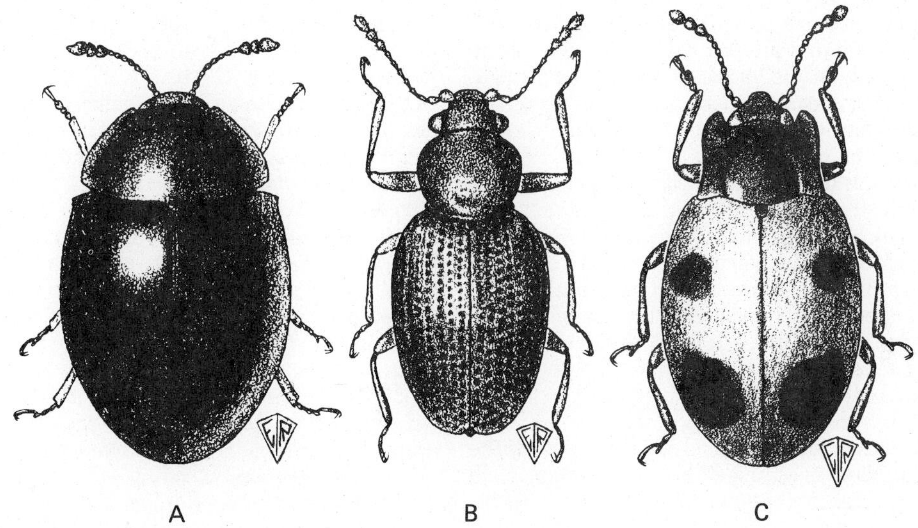

Figure 303. A, a shining flower beetle, *Phálacrus polìtus* Melsheimer, 25 ×; B, a minute brown scavenger beetle, *Melanophthálma americàna* Mannerheim, 26 ×; C, a handsome fungus beetle, *Endómychus biguttàtus* Say, 12½ ×. (Courtesy of Arnett.)

Family **Phalácridae**—Shining Flower Beetles: The phalacrids are oval, shining, cōnvex beetles, 1–3 mm in length (Figure 303 A), and are usually brownish in color. They are sometimes quite common on the flowers of goldenrod and other composites; the larvae develop in the heads of these flowers.

Family **Cerylónidae:** This family includes a group of genera formerly placed in the Colydìidae

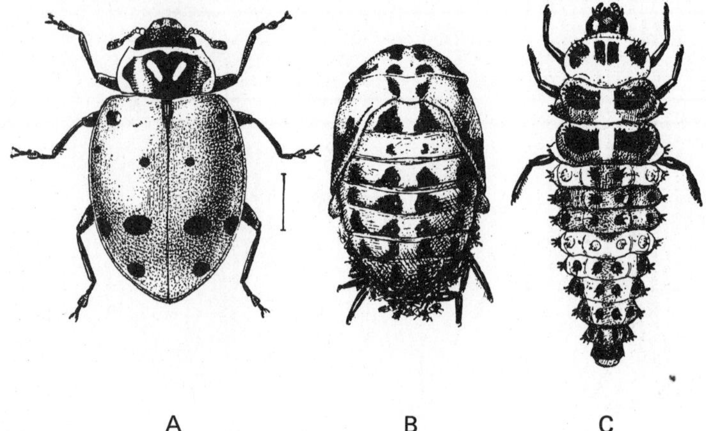

Figure 304. A ladybird beetle, *Hippodàmia convérgens* Guérin-Méneville. A, adult; B, pupa; C, larva. The line at the right of the adult indicates actual size. (Courtesy of USDA.)

(*Cérylon, Philothérmus, Euxéstus,* and five genera in the subfamily Murmidiìnae); they are somewhat more oval and flattened than most colydiids, the antennae are 10-segmented with a 2-segmented club and are received in a cavity of the prothorax, and the coxae are widely separated. The 15 North American species in this group are widely distributed, but are not common.

Family **Corylóphidae**—Minute Fungus Beetles: These beetles are rounded or oval and generally less than 1 mm in length; the tarsi are 4-segmented, but the third segment is small and concealed in a notch of the bilobed third segment, and the tarsi appear 3-segmented; the antennae are clubbed, and the club is usually 3-segmented. The hind wings are fringed with hairs. These beetles occur in decaying vegetable matter and in debris.

Family **Coccinéllidae**—Ladybird Beetles: The ladybird beetles are a well-known group of small, oval, convex, and often brightly colored insects. They may be distinguished from the chrysomelids, many of which have a similar shape, by the three distinct tarsal segments (chrysomelids appear to have four tarsal segments). Most of the ladybird beetles are predaceous, both as larvae and adults, and feed chiefly on aphids; they are frequently quite common, particularly on vegetation where aphids are numerous. Ladybirds hibernate as adults, frequently in large aggregations, under leaves or in debris.

The larvae of ladybird beetles (Figure 304 C) are elongate, somewhat flattened, and covered with minute tubercles or spines. They are usually spotted or banded with bright colors. These larvae are usually found in aphid colonies.

Two fairly common phytophagous species in this group are serious garden pests, the Mexican bean beetle, *Epiláchna varivéstis* Mulsant, and the squash beetle *E. boreàlis* (Fabricius). The Mexican bean beetle is yellowish, with eight spots on each elytron; the squash beetle is pale orange-yellow, with three spots on the pronotum and a dozen or so large spots arranged in two rows on the elytra, plus a large black dot near the tip of the elytra. These two species are the only large ladybird beetles in this country that are pubescent. The larvae of these species are yellow, oval in shape, with forked spines on the body. Both larvae and adults are phytophagous, and they are often very destructive.

Except for the two species of *Epiláchna,* the ladybird beetles are a very beneficial group of insects. They feed on aphids, scale insects, and other injurious insects. During serious outbreaks of aphids or scale insects, large numbers of ladybird beetles are sometimes imported into the infested areas to serve as a means of control: the cottony cushion scale, *Icérya púrchasi* Maskell, a pest of citrus in California, has been kept under control for a number of years by means of a ladybird beetle, *Rodòlia cardinàlis* (Mulsant), imported from Australia.

Family **Endomýchidae**—Handsome Fungus Beetles: These are small oval beetles, mostly 3–8 mm in length; they are smooth and shiny and usually brightly colored. They are somewhat similar to the Coccinéllidae, but have the head easily

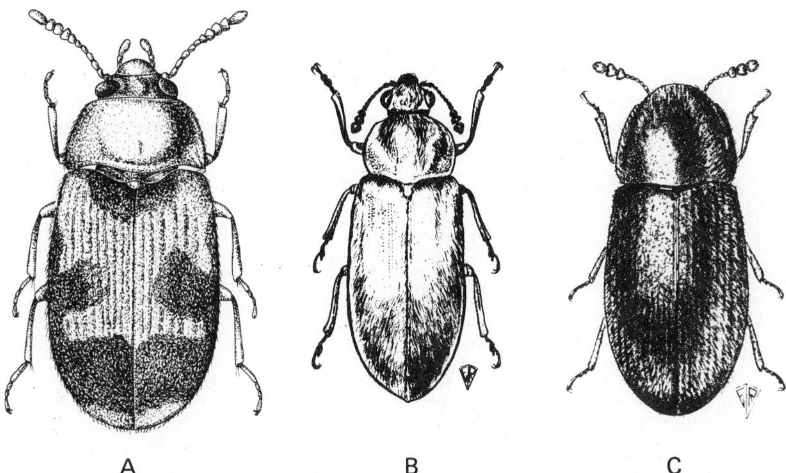

Figure 305. A, a hairy fungus beetle, *Mycetóphagus punctàtus* Say, 8 ×; B, a fruitworm beetle, *Bytùrus bàkeri* Barber, 8 ×; C, a minute tree-fungus beetle, *Cís fùscipes* Mellie, 14 ×. (Courtesy of Arnett.)

visible from above, the pronotum is broadly excavated with the sides produced forward (Figure 303 C), and the tarsal claws are simple. Some members of this group (the Mycetaeìnae, with 15 North American species) have the tarsi appearing 4-segmented, with the third segment easily visible; the others (21 North American species, in four subfamilies) have the third tarsal segment very small and the tarsi appear 3-segmented. Most of the endomychids occur under bark, in rotting wood, in fungi, or in decaying fruits, and feed on fungus and mold; a few of the Mycetaeìnae are found on flowers. One species, *Mycetaèa hírta* (Marsham), is occasionally a pest in granaries and warehouses because it spreads mold infection.

Family **Lathridìidae**—Minute Brown Scavenger Beetles: The lathridiids are elongate-oval, reddish brown beetles, 1–3 mm in length (Figure 303 B); the pronotum is narrower than the elytra, and each elytron bears six or eight rows of punctures. The tarsi are 3-segmented (Figure 251 I), or (males) 2-3-3 or 2-2-3. These beetles are found in moldy material and debris, and sometimes on flowers.

Family **Bytùridae**—Fruitworm Beetles: The byturids are small, oval, hairy beetles, pale brown to orange in color and mostly 3.5–4.5 mm in length, with clubbed antennae (Figure 305 B). The second and third tarsal segments are lobed beneath. The group is a small one, with only five species in the United States; the only common eastern species is *Bytùrus rùbi* Barber, a reddish yellow to blackish beetle 3.5–4.5 mm in length, which feeds on the flowers of raspberry and blackberry; the larvae, which are often called raspberry fruitworms, sometimes do serious damage to berries.

Family **Mycetophágidae**—Hairy Fungus Beetles: The mycetophagids are broadly oval, flattened, rather hairy beetles, 1.5–5.5 mm in length (Figure 305 A); they are brown to black in color, and often brightly marked with reddish or orange. These beetles occur under bark, in shelf fungi, and in moldy vegetable material.

Family **Cìidae**—Minute Tree-Fungus Beetles: The ciids are brownish to black beetles, 0.5–6.0 mm in length, and are similar in appearance to the Scolýtidae and Bostríchidae (Figure 305 C). The body is cylindrical, the head is deflexed and not visible from above, the tarsi are 4-segmented (with the first three segments short and the fourth long), and the antennae terminate in a 3-segmented club. These beetles occur under bark, in rotting wood, or in dry woody fungi, often in considerable numbers; they feed on fungi.

Family **Monómmidae:** The monommids (Figure 306 A) are black oval beetles, 5–12 mm in length, and are flattened ventrally and convex dorsally. They have a 5-5-4 tarsal formula with the first segment relatively long: the anterior coxal cavities are open behind, and the antennae terminate in a 2- or 3-segmented club and are received in

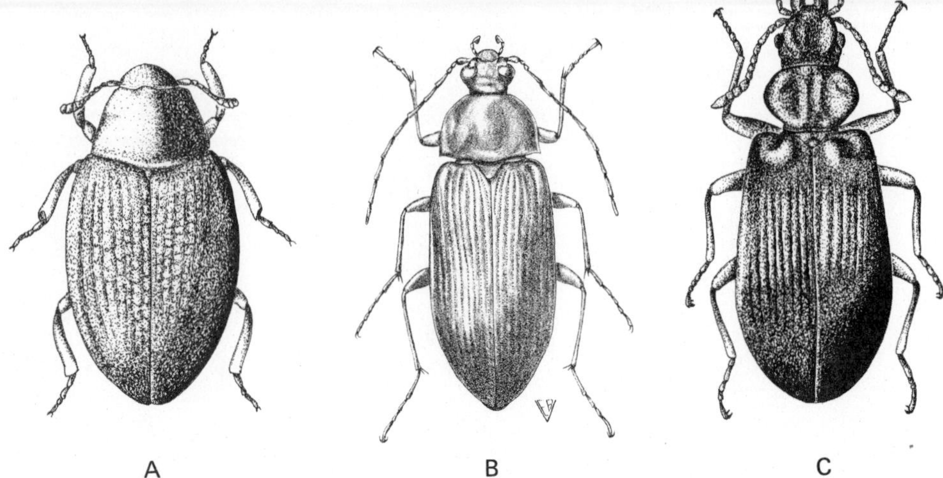

Figure 306. A, a monommid beetle, *Hypóphagus opúntiae* Horn, 3½ ×; B, a comb-clawed beetle, *Capnóchroa fuliginòsa* (Melsheimer), 4½ ×; C, a narrow-waisted bark beetle, *Pỳtho nìger* Kirby, 4 ×. (Courtesy of Arnett.)

grooves on the underside of the prothorax. The adults are found in leaf litter, and the larvae live in rotten wood. The group is a small one, with the five United States species occurring in the southern states from Florida to southern California.

Family **Colydìidae**—Cylindrical Bark Beetles: The colydiids are hard-bodied, shiny beetles 1–18 mm in length; most species are elongate and cylindrical, but some are oval or oblong and somewhat flattened. The antennae are 10- or 11-segmented, and terminate in a 2- or 3-segmented club, and the tarsi are 4-segmented. These beetles occur under dead bark, in shelf fungi, or in ant nests; many species are predaceous, others are plant feeders, and a few species (in the larval stage) are ectoparasites of the larvae and pupae of various wood-boring beetles.

Family **Cephalòidae**—False Longhorn Beetles: These beetles are elongate, convex, and somewhat similar to a cerambycid in shape (hence the common name). They are brownish to dark in color, 8–20 mm in length, and the head is somewhat diamond-shaped, narrowed behind the eyes to form a slender neck. They have a 5-5-4 tarsal formula, the tarsal claws are pectinate, and there is a long pad under each claw. The group is a small one, with ten species known from North America; little is known of their habits except that the adults are sometimes found on flowers.

Family **Tenebriónidae**—Darkling Beetles: The tenebrionids are a large and varied group, but can be distinguished by the 5-5-4 tarsal formula, the front coxal cavities closed behind (Figure 245 B), the eyes usually notched (Figure 252 B), the antennae nearly always 11-segmented and either filiform or moniliform, and five visible abdominal sterna. Most tenebrionids are black or brownish (Figure 307), but a few (for example, *Diapèris,* Figure 307 B) have red markings on the elytra. Many are black and smooth and resemble ground beetles. Some of the species that feed on the bracket fungi are brownish and rough-bodied and resemble bits of bark; one such species, *Bolitothèrus cornùtus* (Panzer), has two hornlike protuberances extending forward from the pronotum (Figure 307 I). The fungus-inhabiting members of the genus *Diapèris* are somewhat similar in general appearance to the ladybird beetles (Figure 307 B). Some of the tenebrionids are very hard-bodied.

Throughout the arid regions of the United States these beetles take over the ecological niche that is occupied by the Carábidae in the more verdant areas, being very common under stones, rubbish, beneath loose bark, and even being attracted to lights at night.

The most distinctive habit of the members of the extremely large genus *Eleòdes* (Figure 307 G) is the ridiculous position they assume when running from possible danger; the tip of the abdomen is elevated to an angle of about 45 degrees from

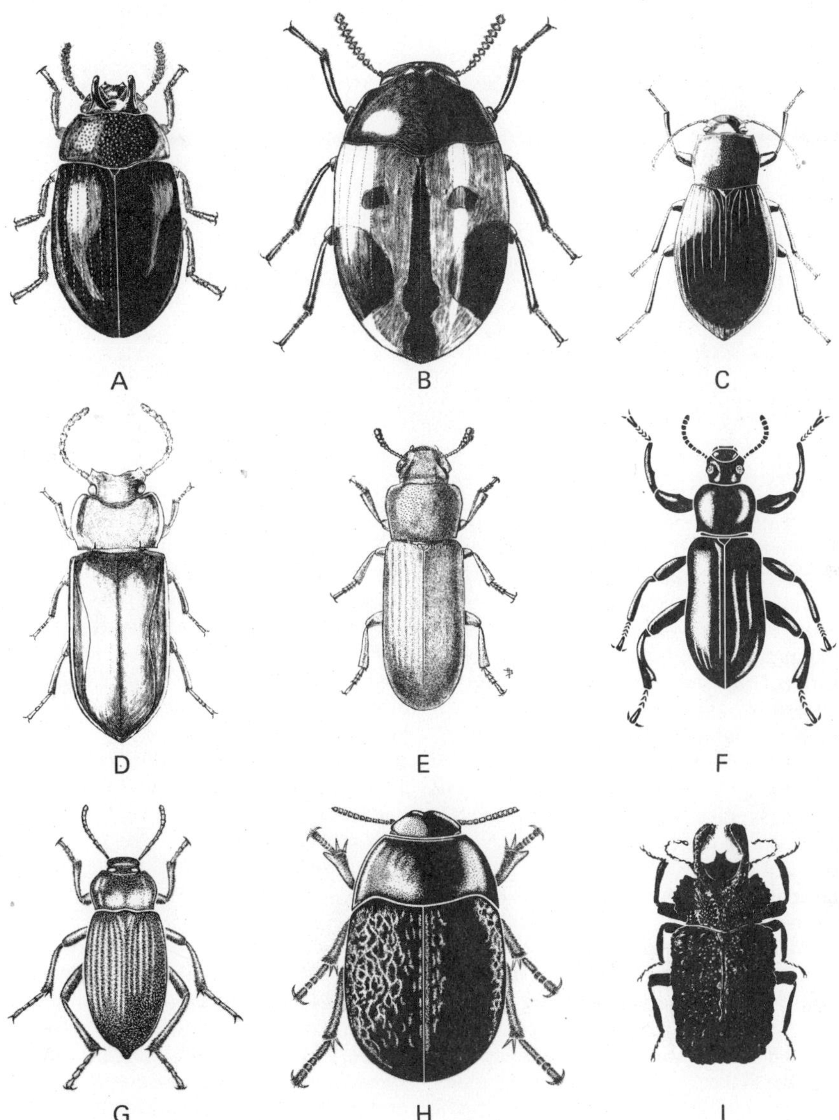

Figure 307. Darkling beetles. A, *Neomìda bicòrnis* (Fabricius), 8 ×; B, *Diapèris maculàta* (Olivier), 6 ×; C, *Hèlops aèreus* Germar, 4 ×; D, *Adelìna plàna* (Say), 7 ×; E, confused flour beetle, *Tribòlium confùsum* du Val, 10 ×; F, *Merìnus laèvis* (Olivier), 1¼ ×; G, *Eleòdes suturàlis* (Say), ¾ ×; H, *Eusáttus pòns* Triplehorn, 3 ×; I, *Bolitothèrus cornùtus* (Panzer), male, 3 ×. (E, courtesy of USDA; I, courtesy of Liles.)

the ground, and the beetles almost seem to be standing on their head as they run. When disturbed or picked up, they emit a black fluid with a very disagreeable odor.

Most tenebrionids feed on plant materials of some sort. A few are common pests of stored grain and flour and are often very destructive. The beetles in the genus *Tenèbrio* are black or dark

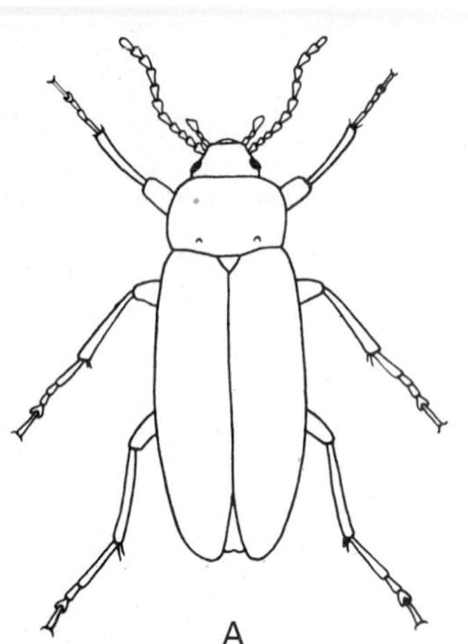

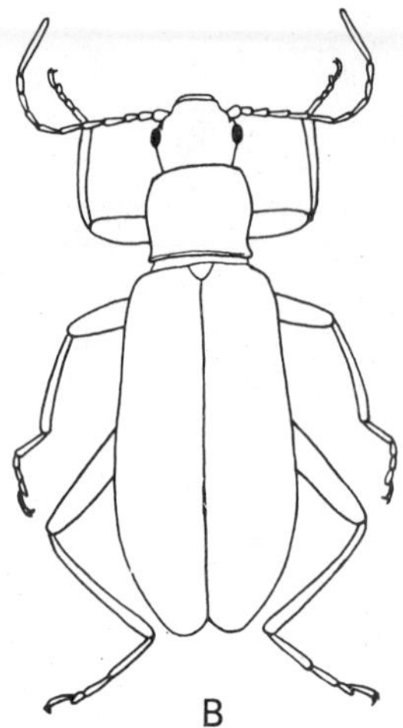

Figure 308. A, a melandryid, *Émmesa labiàta* (Say); B, a lagriid, *Arthrómacra* sp. 4 ×.

brown, 13–17 mm in length, and feed on grain products in both larval and adult stages; the larvae are commonly called mealworms and are quite similar to wireworms. The members of the genus *Tribòlium* are oblong brown beetles, 5 mm or less in length (Figure 307 E); both adults and larvae commonly occur in flour, corn meal, dog food, cereals, dried fruits, and similar materials.

This is the fifth largest family of beetles, with upwards of 1400 North American species, and many of its members are common insects. The majority of our species are western; only about 140 species occur in the East.

Family **Lagrìidae**—Long-Jointed Beetles: The lagriids are slender beetles that can usually be recognized by their characteristic shape (Figure 308 B), their 5-5-4 tarsal formula, and the elongate apical antennal segment (Figure 249 D). They are 10–15 mm in length and dark metallic in color. The adults are found on foliage or occasionally under bark; the larvae breed in plant debris and under the bark of fallen trees.

Family **Allecùlidae**—Comb-Clawed Beetles: The members of this family are small beetles, 4–12 mm in length, elongate-oval, and usually brownish or black with a somewhat glossy or shiny appearance due to the pubescence on the body (Figure 306 B). They can be distinguished from related groups by the pectinate tarsal claws (Figure 247 B). The adults are found on flowers and foliage, fungi, and under dead bark; the larvae resemble wireworms and live in rotting wood, plant debris, or fungi.

Family **Salpíngidae**—Narrow-Waisted Bark Beetles: The common name of this group refers to the fact that some of the larger species (for example, *Pỳtho* and *Lecóntia,* 10–30 mm in length) have the pronotum narrowed basally, causing them to superficially resemble ground beetles (Figure 306 C). Most salpingids are black, elongate, and somewhat flattened. The adults and larvae are predaceous; the adults occur under rocks and bark, in leaf litter, and on vegetation. The species of *Aegialìtes,* which occur along the Pacific coast from California to Alaska, live in rock cracks below the high tidemark along the seacoast; these beetles are elongate-oval, 3–4 mm in length, and black with a metallic luster.

Family **Pyrochròidae**—Fire-Colored Beetles: The pyrochroids are 6–20 mm in length, and are usually black, with the pronotum reddish or yellowish. The head and pronotum are narrower than the elytra, and the elytra are somewhat broader posteriorly. The antennae are serrate to pectinate, and in the males almost plumose (Figure 309 B), with long slender processes on segments 3–10. The eyes are often quite large. The adults are found on foliage and flowers and sometimes under bark; the larvae occur under the bark of dead trees.

Family **Othnìidae**—False Tiger Beetles: These beetles are superficially similar to tiger beetles, but have a 5-5-4 tarsal formula and the antennae terminate in a 3-segmented club. They are brown to dark in color, often mottled, and 5–9 mm in length. The adults are found on the leaves of trees and on cacti, and the larvae live in rotting leaves or under bark. Five species of *Elacàtis* occur in the United States; one has been reported from Virginia, while the others occur in the western states.

Family **Inopéplidae:** The inopeplids are small brownish beetles, 6 mm in length or less, that resemble a very flat rove beetle. The elytra are short, and the pronotum is triangular (narrowed posteriorly). The 12 United States species, all in the genus *Inopéplus,* occur in the southeastern states from Maryland to Florida and Texas.

Family **Myctéridae:** Some members of this family (*Hemipéplus,* two species, found in Florida and Georgia) strongly resemble cucujids; they are elongate, slender, very flat, yellowish beetles, 8–12 mm in length, with the front coxal cavities closed. These beetles are found under bark. Other mycterids (Mycterìnae) have the front coxal cavities open, and some of them (for example, *Mýcterus,* about 10 mm in length) have the head extended anteriorly, much like the broadnosed weevils; the body is more robust, and not at all flattened. These beetles are generally found under rocks or in debris, or on vegetation; both adults and larvae are said to be predaceous. The Mycterìnae have been placed in the Salpíngidae, but differ from them in having the penultimate tarsal segment lobed (this segment is slender and similar to the other segments in the Salpíngidae).

Family **Oedeméridae**—False Blister Beetles: The oedemerids are slender, soft-bodied beetles, 5–20 mm in length (Figure 309 A). Many are black with an orange pronotum, while others are pale with blue, yellow, red, or orange markings; a common eastern oedemerid is yellowish brown with the tips of the elytra black. These beetles have a 5-5-4 tarsal formula, and the penultimate tarsal segment is dilated and densely hairy beneath (Figure 251 C). The pronotum is somewhat narrowed posteriorly and narrower than the base of the elytra, and the eyes are often emarginate. The adults are usually found on flowers or foliage, and are attracted to lights at night; the larvae live in moist decaying wood, especially driftwood.

Family **Melandrỳidae**—False Darkling Beetles: The members of this group are elongate-oval, somewhat flattened beetles usually found under bark or logs; some species occur on flowers and foliage. They are mostly dark-colored and 3–20 mm in length; they can be usually recognized by the 5-5-4 tarsal formula and the two dents or impressions near the posterior border of the pronotum (Figure 308 A). The most common melandryids are the oval, black, eastern members of *Pénthe,* which are 5–15 mm long and are common under old dead bark; *P. pimèlia* (Fabricius) is entirely black, and *P. obliquàta* (Fabricius) has a bright orange scutellum. Some members of this family, which have the head strongly and abruptly constricted just behind the eyes, have by some authorities been placed in a separate family, the Scraptíidae.

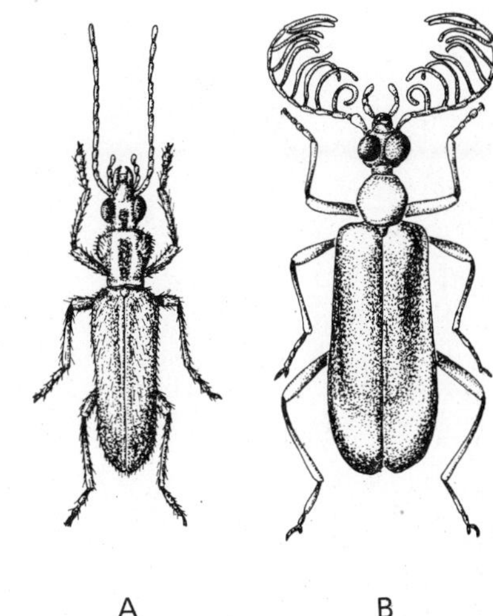

Figure 309. A, a false blister beetle, *Óxacis trimaculàta* Champion, 3 ×; B, a fire-colored beetle, *Dendròides canadénsis* LeConte, 3 ×. (Courtesy of Arnett.)

Family **Mordéllidae**—Tumbling Flower Beetles: These beetles have a rather characteristic body shape (Figure 310); the body is somewhat wedge-shaped, humpbacked, the head is bent down, and the abdomen is pointed apically and extends beyond the tips of the elytra. Most mordellids are black or mottled gray in color, and the body is covered with a dense pubescence. Most of them are 3–7 mm in length, but some reach a length of 14 mm. These beetles are common on flowers, especially the composites. They are quite active and run or fly quickly when disturbed; their common name is derived from the tumbling movements they make in attempting to escape capture.

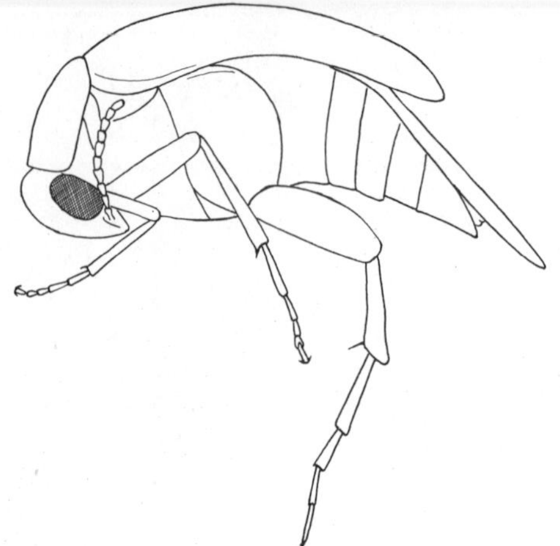

Figure 310. A tumbling flower beetle, *Mordélla marginàta* Melsheimer, 15 ×.

The larvae live in decaying wood and in plant pith; some are predaceous.

Family **Rhipiphòridae**—Wedge-Shaped Beetles: These beetles are similar to the Mordéllidae, but have the abdomen blunt instead of pointed at the apex. The elytra are more or less pointed apically and usually do not cover the tip of the abdomen; in some species the elytra are quite short. The antennae are pectinate in the males and serrate in the females. These beetles occur on flowers, particularly goldenrod, but they are not very common; they are sometimes found in the burrows of halictid bees. The larval stages are parasitic on various wasps (Véspidae, Scolìidae, and Tiphìidae) and bees (Halíctidae and Anthophorìnae); they undergo a hypermetamorphosis similar to that in the Melòidae. Some females in this family are wingless and larviform.

Family **Melòidae**—Blister Beetles: The blister beetles are usually narrow and elongate, the elytra are soft and flexible, and the pronotum is narrower than either the head or the elytra (Figure 311). These beetles are called blister beetles because the body fluids of the commoner species contain cantharadin, a substance that often causes blisters when applied to the skin. This substance is extracted from the bodies of a common European species (*Lýtta vesicatòria* (L.), called the spanishfly) and used as a drug; in medical practice, this drug is used to stimulate certain internal organs.

Several species of blister beetles are important pests, feeding on potatoes, tomatoes, and other plants. Two of these are often called the "old-fashioned potato bettles," *Epicàuta vittàta* (Fabricius) (with orange and black longitudinal stripes) and *E. marginàta* (Fabricius) (black, with the margins of the elytra and the sutural stripe gray, Figure 311 C); these beetles are 12-20 mm in length. The black blister beetle, *E. pennsylvánica* (De Geer), is a common black meloid, 7-13 mm in length, that is usually found on the flowers of goldenrod.

The larvae of most blister beetles are considered beneficial, for they feed on grasshopper eggs. A few live in bee nests in the larval stage, where they feed on bee eggs and on the food stored in the cells with the eggs.

The life history of blister beetles is rather complex; these insects undergo a hypermetamorphosis, with the different larval instars being quite different in form (Figure 312). The first larval instar is an active, long-legged form called a triungulin; it seeks out a grasshopper egg or a bee nest, and then molts. In the species that develop in bee nests, the triungulin usually climbs upon or hatches on a flower and attaches itself to a bee that visits the flower; the bee carries the triungulin to the nest, whereupon the triungulin attacks the bee's eggs. The second instar is somewhat similar to the triungulin, but the legs are shorter. In the third, fourth, and fifth instars the larva becomes thicker and somewhat scarabaeiform. The sixth instar has a darker and thicker exoskeleton and lacks functional appendages; this instar is usually known as the coarctate larva or pseudopupa, and it is the instar that hibernates. The seventh instar is small, white, and active (though legless), but apparently does not feed and soon transforms to the true pupa.

The members of the genus *Méloe,* some of which are about 25 mm in length, have very short elytra that overlap just behind the scutellum, and the hind wings are lacking; these insects are dark blue or black in color (Figure 311 A). They are sometimes called oil beetles, for they often exude an oily substance from the joints of the legs when disturbed.

The blister beetles in the genus *Nemógnatha* are unique in having the galeae prolonged into a sucking tube as long as or longer than the body. These beetles are usually brownish in color (sometimes blackish, or brown and black), and 8–15 mm in length; they are widely distributed.

Most of the blister beetles are elongate and somewhat cylindrical, but the species of *Cysteodèmus,* which occur in the Southwest from Texas to southern California, have the elytra broadly oval and very convex (Figure 311 D);

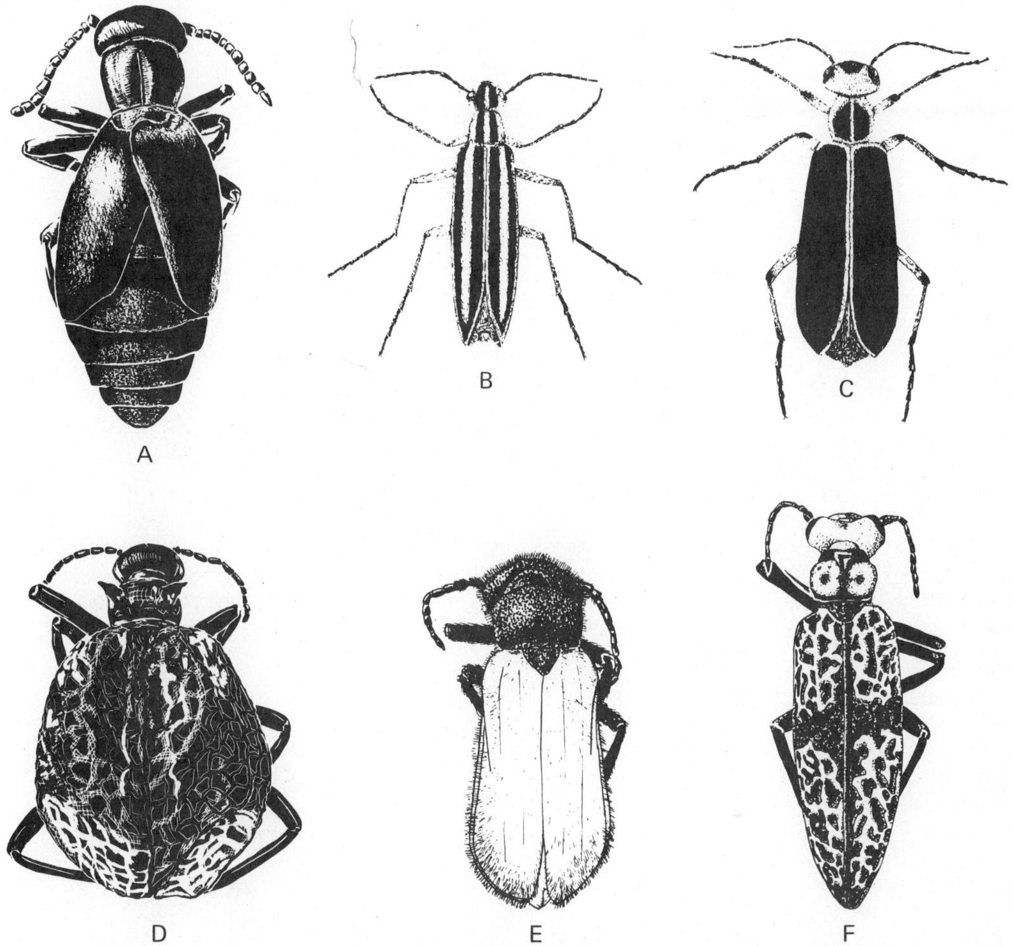

Figure 311. Blister beetles. A, an oil beetle, *Melòe laèvis* Leach, 2 ×; B, three-striped blister beetle, *Epicaùta lemniscàta* (Fabricius), 2 ×; C, *Epicaùta marginàta* (Fabricius), 2 ×; D, *Cysteodèmus armàtus* LeConte, 2½ ×; E, *Tricrània stánsburyi* (Haldeman), 4 ×; F, *Tegrodèra eròsa alòga* (Skinner), 2 ×. (B and C, courtesy of Baerg and the Arkansas Agricultural Experiment Station; others, courtesy of Noller and the Arizona Agricultural Experiment Station.)

these beetles are black, often with bluish or purplish highlights, and about 15 mm in length.

Family **Anthícidae**—Antlike Flower Beetles: These beetles are 2–6 mm in length and somewhat antlike in appearance, with the head deflexed and strongly constricted behind the eyes, and with the pronotum oval. The pronotum in many species (*Notóxus*, Figure 313 A, and *Mecinotársus*) has an anterior hornlike process extending forward over the head. Anthicids generally occur on flowers and foliage, some occur under stones and logs and in debris, and a few occur on sand dunes.

Family **Pedìlidae:** The pedilids are similar to the anthicids and euglenids, but are larger (7–13 mm in length), elongate and somewhat cylindrical (Figure 313 B), and not particularly antlike in appearance. The pronotum is oval or rounded, and the head is constricted some distance behind the eyes. Some species occur on vegetation in damp areas; others, particularly in the western states, occur in dry sandy areas.

Family **Euglénidae**—Antlike Leaf Beetles: The euglenids are reddish yellow to dark in color and 1.5–3.0 mm in length; they are very similar to the anthicids, but may be separated by the characters

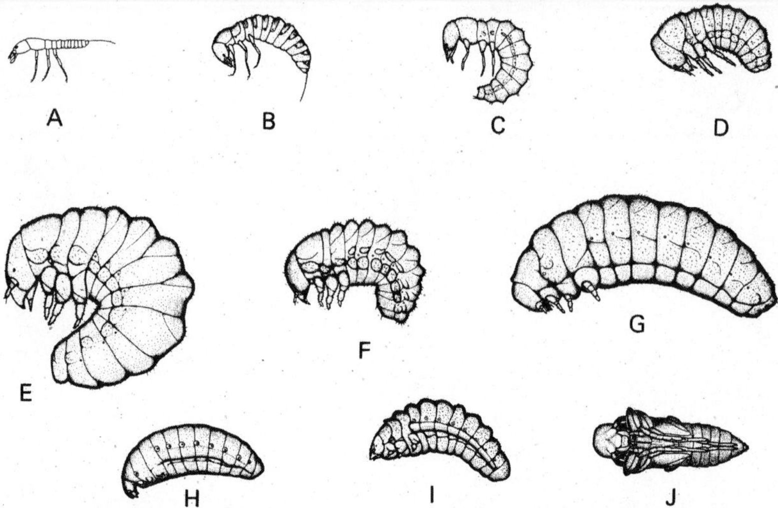

Figure 312. Larval and pupal instars of the black blister beetle, *Epicaùta pennsylvánica* (De Geer), showing hypermetamorphosis. A, newly hatched first instar, or triungulin; B, fully fed first instar; C, second instar; D, third instar; E, fourth instar; F, newly molted fifth instar; G, gorged fifth instar; H, sixth instar (coarctate larva or pseudopupa); I, seventh instar; J, pupa. (Courtesy of Horsfall and the Arkansas Agricultural Experiment Station.)

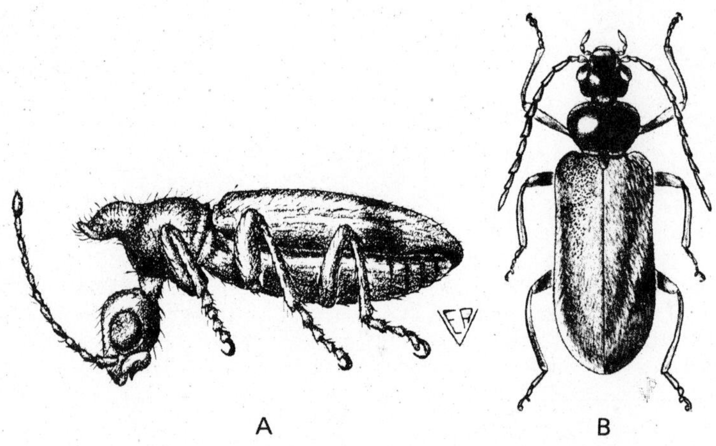

Figure 313. A, an antlike flower beetle, *Notóxus mónodon* Fabricius, 12 ×; B, a pedilid beetle, *Pedìlus lùgubris* Say, 5 ×. (Courtesy of Arnett.)

given in the key (couplet 174). They are found on foliage and flowers.

Family **Cerambýcidae**—Long-Horned Beetles: This family is a large one, with over 1200 species occurring in this country, and its members are all phytophagous. Most of the long-horns are elongate and cylindrical with long antennae, and many are brightly colored. The tarsi appear 4-segmented with the third segment bilobed, but are actually 5-segmented; the fourth segment is small and concealed in the notch of the third, and is often very difficult to see (Figure 251 A). Both the Cerambýcidae and Chrysomélidae have this type

Figure 314. Galleries of the poplar borer, *Sapérda calcaràta* Say. (Courtesy of the Ohio Agricultural Research and Development Center.)

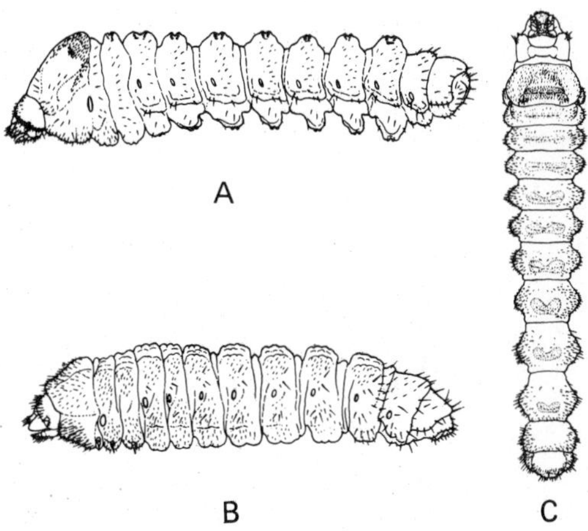

Figure 315. Cerambycid larvae. A, dogwood twig borer, *Obèrea tripunctàta* (Swederus), lateral view; B, twig pruner, *Elaphidionòides villòsus* (Fabricius), lateral view; C, linden borer, *Sapérda véstita* Say, dorsal view. (Courtesy of Peterson.)

of tarsal structure, and these groups are sometimes difficult to separate; they can usually be separated by the characters given in the key (couplet 183).

Most adult cerambycids, particularly the brightly colored ones, feed on flowers. Many, usually not brightly colored, are nocturnal in habit and during the day may be found under bark or resting on trees or logs; some of these make a squeaking sound when picked up.

Most of the Cerambýcidae are wood-boring in the larval stage, and many species are very destructive to shade, forest, and fruit trees, and to freshly cut logs. The adults lay their eggs in crevices in the bark, and the larvae bore into the wood. The larval tunnels in the wood (Figure 314) are circular in cross section (thereby differing from most buprestid tunnels, which are oval in cross section) and usually go straight in a short distance before turning. Different species attack different types of trees and shrubs. A few will attack living trees, but most species appear to prefer freshly cut logs, or weakened and dying trees or branches. A few girdle twigs and lay their eggs just above the girdled band. Some bore into the stems of herbaceous plants. The larvae (Figure 315) are elongate, cylindrical, whitish and almost legless, and differ from the larvae of the Bupréstidae in that the anterior end of the body is not broadened and flattened; they are often called roundheaded borers, to distinguish them from the flatheaded borers (larvae of Bupréstidae).

This family is divided into several subfamilies, which can generally be separated by the following key.

Key to the Subfamilies of Cerambýcidae

1. Tarsi distinctly 5-segmented, the fourth segment plainly visible (Figure 316 E); antennae short, rarely surpassing base of pronotum, the second segment more than half as long as third 2

1′. Tarsi appearing 4-segmented, the fourth segment very small and concealed in a notch of the dilated third segment, which has pubescent pads beneath (Figure 251 A); antennae variable in length, but usually surpassing base of pronotum, the second segment rarely half as long as the third 3

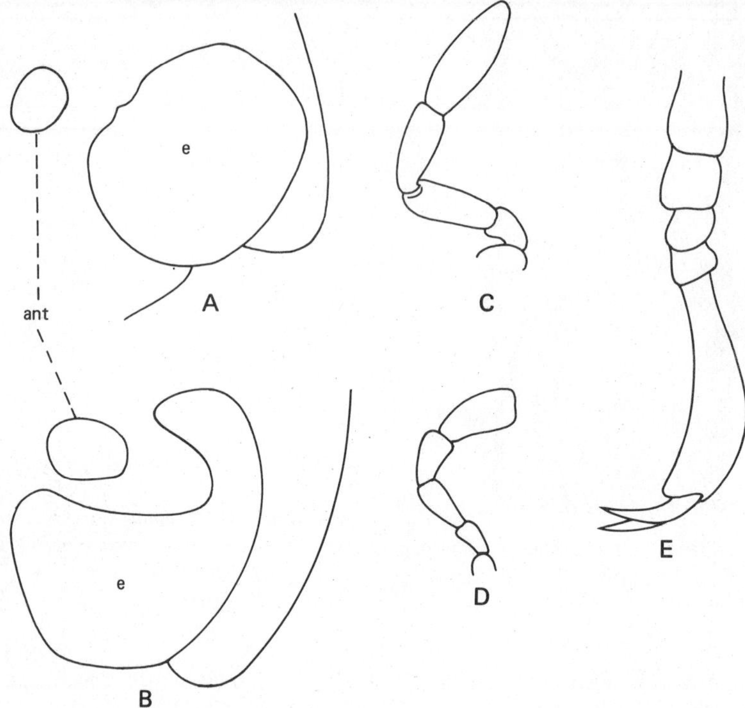

Figure 316. Characters of Cerambýcidae. A and B, dorsolateral views of the left compound eye and the base of the antenna: A, base of antenna not surrounded by eye (*Toxòtus,* Lepturìnae), B, base of antenna partly surrounded by eye (*Elaphídion,* Cerambycìnae); C and D, maxillary palps: C, *Monochàmus* (Lamiìnae), D, *Anoplodèra* (Lepturìnae); E, hind tarsus of *Párandra* (Parandrìnae). *ant,* base of antenna; *e,* compound eye.

2(1). Pronotum margined laterally; third tarsal segment entire or feebly emarginate; shining brown (Figure 319 F); widely distributed .... **Parandrìnae** p. 415

2′. Pronotum rounded laterally; third tarsal segment deeply bilobed; blackish; mostly southeastern and western United States .... **Spondylìnae** p. 415

3(1′). Pronotum margined laterally; front coxae transverse .... **Prionìnae** p. 415

3′. Pronotum rounded laterally (sometimes with a lateral spine or tubercle); front coxae usually globular or conical, rarely transverse 4

4(3′). Last segment of maxillary palps pointed apically (Figure 316 C); face vertical or slanting backward .... **Lamiìnae** p. 416

4′. Last segment of maxillary palps blunt or truncate apically (Figure 316 D); face slanting forward or subvertical 5

5(4′). Second antennal segment longer than broad, nearly half as long as third segment; head short, not narrowed behind eyes; front coxae somewhat globular; rather flattened, usually brownish beetles, with relatively short antennae .... **Asemìnae** p. 416

5′. Second antennal segment usually very short, not much longer than broad, and much less than half as long as third; other characters variable 6

6(5′). Front coxae conical; head somewhat elongate, narrowed behind eyes; base of antennae usually not surrounded by eyes (Figure 316 A); often with a broad-shouldered appearance, the elytra narrowing posteriorly (Figures 317 D and 319 A–D, H) .... **Lepturìnae** p. 416

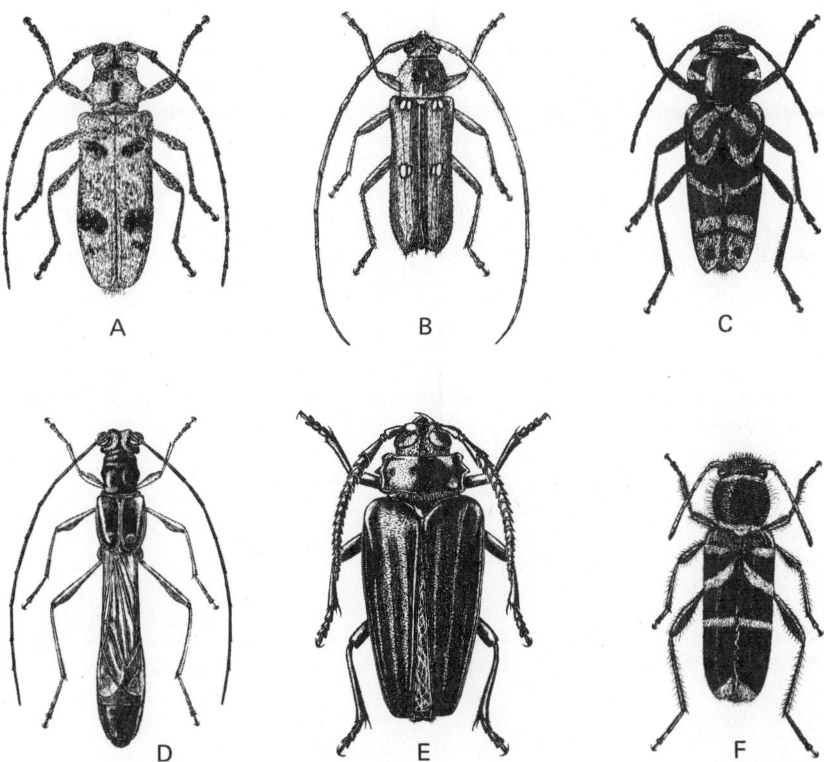

Figure 317. Long-horned beetles. A, *Gòes tigrìnus* (De Geer) (Lamiìnae), 1¼ ×; B, *Ebùria quadrigeminàta* (Say) (Cerambycìnae), 1¼ ×; C, sugar maple borer, *Glycòbius speciòsus* (Say) (Cerambycìnae) (natural size); D, *Necýdalis méllita* (Say) (Lepturìnae), 2 ×; E, *Priònus imbricòrnis* (L.) (Prionìnae) (natural size); F, *Clỳtus marginicóllis* Castelnau (Cerambycìnae), 3 ×. (Courtesy of Knull and the Ohio Biological Survey.)

6′. Front coxae variable, but usually not conical; head generally short and not narrowed behind eyes; base of antennae usually partly surrounded by eyes (Figure 316 B) (if not, then front coxae are globose or transverse); elytra generally parallel-sided in anterior two thirds of their length (Figures 317 B, C, F, and 319 E) .... **Cerambycìnae** p. 417

Subfamilies **Parandrìnae** and **Spondylìnae:** These beetles differ from other cerambycids in having the fourth tarsal segment plainly visible and the tarsi obviously 5-segmented (Figure 316 E). The Subfamily Parandrìnae contains three species in the genus *Párandra;* these beetles are elongate-oval, somewhat flattened, bright reddish brown, and 9–18 mm in length (Figure 319 F); they look a little like small lucanids. They live under the bark of dead pine trees; the larvae burrow in dry dead wood of logs and stumps. The subfamily Spondylìnae contains two species, *Spóndylis upifórmis* Mannerheim and *Scaphìnus mùticus* (Fabricius); *S. upifórmis* occurs from the Great Lakes westward, and *S. mùticus* occurs in the Southeast. These beetles are black, not particularly shiny, and 8–20 mm in length; their habits are similar to those of *Párandra*.

Subfamily **Prionìnae:** This group contains our largest cerambycids, some of which may reach a length of about 3 inches (76 mm). The Prionìnae differ from the two preceding families in having the tarsi appearing 4-segmented, and from the following subfamilies in having the pronotum margined laterally; most of them have spines or teeth along the margins of the pronotum, and some have the antennae serrate and containing 12 or more segments. The most common eastern species in this group belong to the genus *Priònus;*

Figure 318. Northeastern sawyer beetle, *Monochàmus notàtus* (Drury), female at left, male at right. About ½ ×. (Courtesy of Knull.)

these beetles (Figure 317 E) are broad and somewhat flattened, blackish-brown in color, with three broad teeth on the lateral margins of the pronotum, and 17–60 mm in length (some western members of this genus are even larger); the antennae contain 12 or more segments, and are serrate in the female. The members of the genus *Ergàtes,* which occur in the West, are also dark brown but have eight or ten small spines on each side of the pronotum, and the eyes are deeply emarginate; they are 35–65 mm in length. *Orthosòma brùnneum* (Forster), a fairly common eastern species, is long and narrow, light reddish brown, and 24–48 mm in length; it has two or three teeth on the lateral margins of the pronotum.

Subfamily **Asemìnae:** The members of this group are elongate, parallel-sided, somewhat flattened beetles, usually black (sometimes with the elytra brownish), mostly 10–20 mm in length, with relatively short antennae (Figure 319 G). Most of them have the eyes deeply emarginate (the eyes are completely divided in *Tetròpium*) and partly surrounding the bases of the antennae. The larvae of these beetles attack principally dead pine trees and pine stumps.

Subfamily **Lamiìnae:** The members of this subfamily can be recognized by the pointed terminal segment of the maxillary palps (Figure 316 C), and the rather vertical face. They are elongated, parallel-sided, and usually somewhat cylindrical, with the pronotum often a little narrower than the base of the elytra (Figure 317 A and 318). This group is a large one, and many species are of considerable economic importance.

The beetles in the genus *Monochàmus* (Figure 318) are often called sawyer beetles. They are usually over 25 mm in length and are either black or a mottled gray in color; the first antennal segment has a scarlike area near the tip. The antennae of the males are sometimes twice as long as the body; they are about as long as the body in the females. The larvae feed on evergreens, usually on freshly cut logs, but they may sometimes attack living trees. The holes made by the larvae are at least as large in diameter as a lead pencil, and those of some species are nearly 13 mm in diameter.

The genus *Sapérda* contains a number of important pest species. These beetles are about 25 mm in length and are sometimes strikingly colored. *S. cándida* Fabricius is white, with three broad, brown longitudinal stripes on the back; the larva bores in apple and other trees, and is commonly called the roundheaded apple tree borer. Other important species in this genus are the poplar borer, *S. calcaràta* Say, and the elm borer, *S. tridentàta* Olivier.

The species in the genus *Obèrea* are very slender and elongate. The raspberry cane borer, *O. bimaculàta* (Olivier), is black, with the pronotum yellow and bearing two or three black spots; the larvae are often serious pests in canes of raspberries and blackberries.

The species of *Tetraòpes* are about 13 mm in length and are red with black spots. The compound eyes are divided so that there are apparently two compound eyes on each side of the head. *T. tetraophthálmus* (Forster) is a common species feeding on milkweed, and is called the red milkweed beetle.

The twig girdler, *Oncíderes cingulàta* (Say), lays its eggs under the bark near the tips of living branches of hickory, elm, apple, and other deciduous trees. Before the egg is deposited, the beetle gnaws a deep groove around the twig, girdling it; the twig eventually dies and drops to the ground, and the larva completes its development in the twig.

Subfamily **Lepturìnae:** The long-horns in this group resemble those in the Cerambycìnae in having the terminal segment of the maxillary palps blunt or truncate at the apex (Figure 316 B); they differ from the Cerambycìnae in having the front

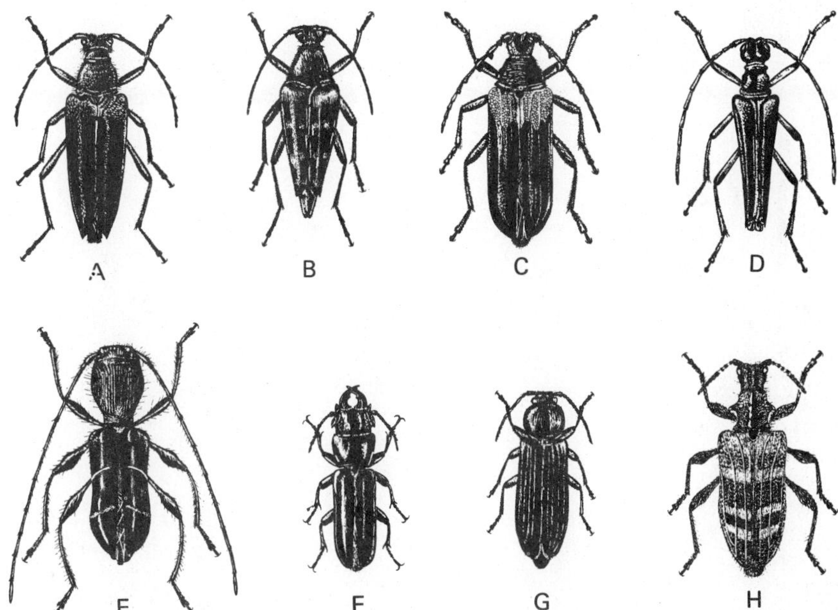

Figure 319. Long-horned beetles. A, *Anoplodèra canadénsis* (Olivier) (Lepturìnae); B, *Typócerus decéptus* Knull (Lepturìnae); C, *Desmócerus palliàtus* (Forster) (Lepturìnae); D, *Toxòtus cylindricóllis* (Say) (Lepturìnae); E, *Eudérces pìni* (Olivier) (Cerambycìnae); F, *Párandra polìta* Say (Parandrìnae); G, *Ásemum striàtum* (L.) (Asemìnae); H, *Rhàgium inquísitor* (L.) (Lepturìnae). (Courtesy of Knull and the Ohio Biological Survey.)

coxae conical, and the bases of the antennae are usually not surrounded by the eyes (Figure 316 E). Many Lepturìnae have the elytra tapering posteriorly, and/or the pronotum narrower than the base of the elytra, giving them a rather broad-shouldered appearance.

A striking eastern species in this group is the elderberry long-horn, *Desmócerus palliàtus* (Forster) (Figure 319 C). This is a dark-blue beetle about 25 mm long, with the basal third of the elytra orange yellow, and with segments 3–5 of the antennae thickened at the tips. The adult occurs on the flowers and foliage of elderberry, and the larva bores in the pith of this plant. Several other species of *Desmócerus* occur on elderberry in the western states; they are similar in general coloration, with the males having brilliant scarlet elytra and a black pronotum; the females have very dark-green elytra bordered narrowly with red along the outer margin.

This subfamily contains many species found on flowers; in most of them the elytra are broadest at the base and narrowed toward the apex (Figure 319 A, B, D, H). Some common genera are *Anoplodèra, Typócerus, Toxòtus,* and *Stenócorus.* Most of these beetles are brightly colored, often with yellow and black bands or stripes; in many cases the elytra do not cover the tip of the abdomen. All are excellent fliers.

Subfamily **Cerambycìnae:** This group is a large one, and its members vary considerably in size and general appearance. One of the most strikingly marked species in this subfamily is the locust borer, *Megacyllène robíniae* (Forster), the larva of which bores into the trunks of black locust. The adult is black with bright-yellow markings, and is relatively common on goldenrod in late summer. Another easily recognized species in this group is *Ebùria quadrigeminàta* (Say), a brownish species 14–24 mm in length, which has two pairs of elevated ivory-colored swellings on each elytron (Figure 317 B). The members of some genera in this group (*Smòdicum* and others) are somewhat flattened and have relatively short antennae; others (for example, *Eudérces,* Figure 319 E) are small, less than 9 mm in length, and somewhat antlike in appearance.

Family **Brùchidae**—Seed Beetles: The members of this family are short, stout-bodied beetles,

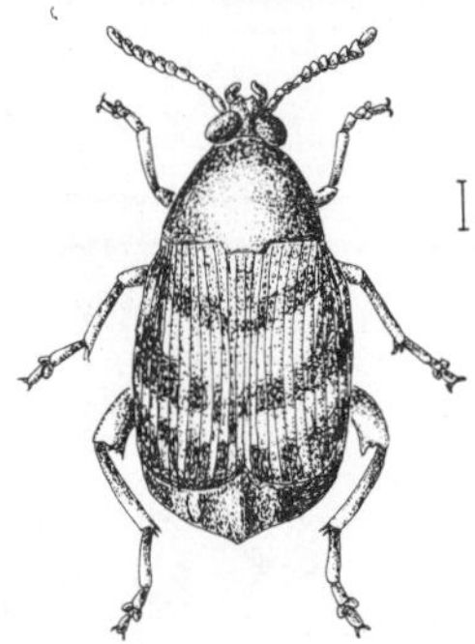

Figure 320. Bean weevil, *Acanthoscélides obtéctus* (Say). Line at the right represents actual length. (Courtesy of USDA.)

mostly less than 5 mm in length, with the elytra shortened and not covering the tip of the abdomen. The body is often somewhat narrowed anteriorly (Figure 320), and is usually dull grayish or brownish in color. The head is produced anteriorly into a short broad snout.

The larvae of most bruchids feed inside various seeds and pupate in the seeds. The adults generally oviposit on seeds that are fully developed or nearly so, but some oviposit on the flowers or young fruits. Some species develop in stored dry seeds. Some of the seed beetles, particularly those attacking leguminous plants, are serious pests.

Two common species in this family are the bean weevil, *Acanthoscélides obtéctus* (Say) (Figure 320), and the pea weevil, *Brùchus pisòrum* (L.). These beetles lay their eggs on the pods of beans or peas, and the larvae bore into the seeds; the adults emerge through little round holes cut in the seed. The bean weevil may breed indoors throughout the year in stored dried beans, but the pea weevil attacks the peas only in the field and does not oviposit on dried peas. These insects cause serious damage in stored seeds that are not protected. The housewife frequently sees bean weevils for the first time when they try to escape through the windows, and does not account for their appearance until she later empties a sack of dried beans and finds them full of holes.

Family **Chrysomélidae**—Leaf Beetles: The leaf beetles are closely related to the Cerambýcidae; both groups have a similar tarsal structure (Figure 251 A), and both are phytophagous. The leaf beetles usually have much shorter antennae and are smaller and more oval in shape than the cerambycids. The chrysomelids in the United States are all less than 13 mm in length; most of the cerambycids are larger. Many are brightly colored.

Adult leaf beetles feed principally on flowers and foliage. The larvae are phytophagous, but vary quite a bit in appearance and habits; some larvae are free feeders on foliage, some are leaf miners, some feed on roots, and some bore in stems. Many members of this family are serious pests of cultivated plants. Most species overwinter as adults.

The family Chrysomélidae is divided into a number of subfamilies, and those occurring in North America may be separated by the key below. Groups in this key marked with an asterisk are relatively rare, or are unlikely to be taken by the general collector.

Key to the Subfamilies of Chrysomélidae

1. Head largely or entirely concealed under prothorax; prothorax and elytra widened; body oval or circular, and convex; elytra smooth (Figure 322 B, E); mouth located posteriorly on ventral side of head, the mouth parts directed caudad (Figure 321 A) .... **Cassidìnae** p. 420

1′. Body not as above, or if oval and convex then the mouth parts are located anteriorly and are directed ventrad or forward 2

2(1′). Mouth parts located ventrally on head, and directed ventrally or caudad (as in Figure 321 A); body flattened dorsally, usually narrower anteriorly and widest posteriorly; elytra roughened by ridges or rows of punctures (Figure 323) .... **Hispìnae** p. 420

2′. Mouth parts located anteriorly on head, and directed ventrad or forward; elytra usually not as above 3

3(2′). Pygidium prominent, not covered by elytra; robust, subcylindrical beetles, mostly less than 6 mm in length; head buried in prothorax to eyes (Figure 321 C); elytra sometimes tuberculate 4

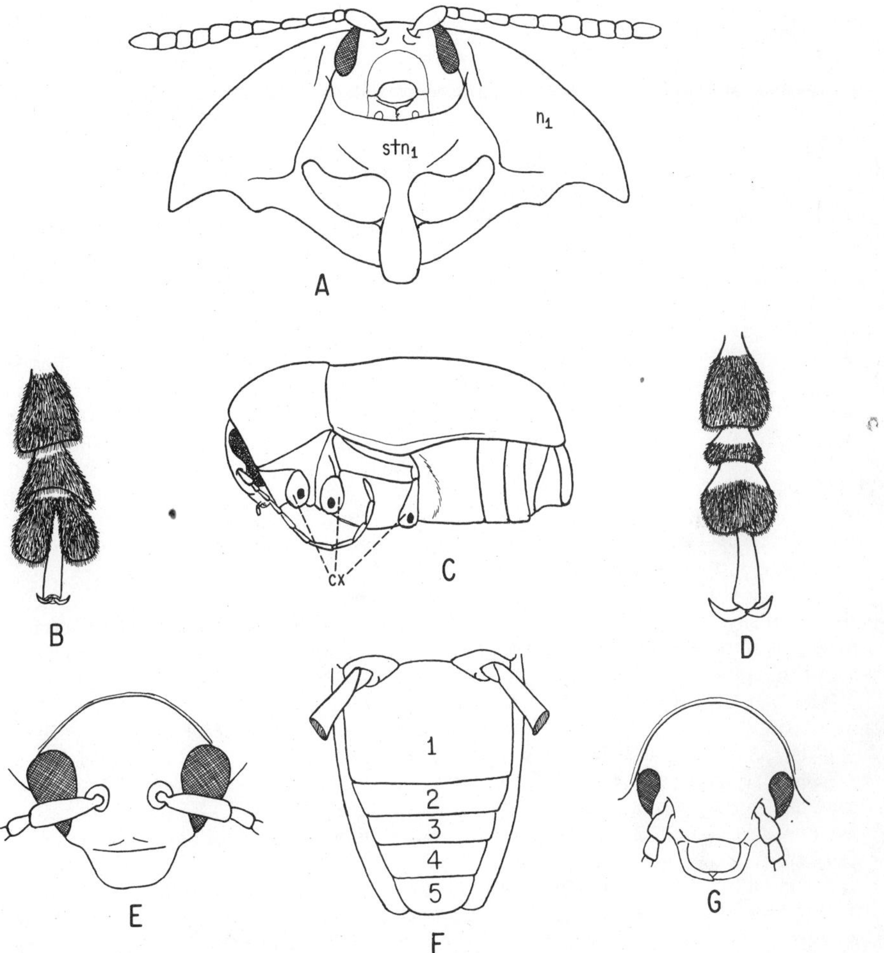

Figure 321. Characters of Chrysomélidae. A, head and prothorax of *Chelymórpha* (Cassidìnae), ventral view; B, tarsus of *Diabrótica* (Galerucìnae), ventral view; C, body of *Cryptocéphalus* (Cryptocephalìnae), lateral view; D, tarsus of *Leptinotársa* (Chrysomelìnae), ventral view; E, head of *Diabrótica* (Galerucìnae), anterior view; F, abdomen of *Donàcia*, ventral view; G, head of *Chrýsochus* (Eumolpìnae), anterior view. *cx*, coxae; n_1, pronotum; stn_1, prosternum; *1–5*, abdominal sterna.

3′.	Pygidium usually covered by elytra; oval or elongate beetles; size variable; elytra not tuberculate 8	
4(3).	Prosternum with lateral antennal grooves; legs retractile; elytra tuberculate .... **Chlamisìnae**	p. 421
4′.	Prosternum without lateral antennal grooves; legs not retractile; elytra not tuberculate 5	
5(4′).	Antennae filiform or slightly clavate 6	
5′.	Antennae serrate or pectinate 7	
6(5).	Base of pronotum narrower than base of elytra; southern Texas .... **Megascelìnae***	p. 421
6′.	Base of pronotum as wide as base of elytra, or nearly so; widely distributed .... **Cryptocephalìnae**	p. 421

7(5′).	Head more or less constricted behind eyes; eyes usually large and deeply emarginate .... **Zeugophorìnae***	p. 422
7′.	Head usually not constricted behind eyes; eyes usually not large or deeply emarginate .... **Clytrìnae**	p. 421
8(3′).	Pronotum margined laterally 9	
8′.	Pronotum rounded laterally 13	
9(8).	Antennae widely separated at base, farther apart than length of first antennal segment (Figure 321 G) 10	
9′.	Antennae close together at base, closer than length of first antennal segment (Figure 321 E) 12	
10(9).	Base of pronotum narrower than base of elytra; southwestern United States .... **Aulacoscelìnae***	p. 421
10′.	Base of pronotum about as wide as base of elytra; widely distributed...11	
11(10′).	Front coxae oval or transverse; third tarsal segment, seen from beneath, entire apically or with a slight median notch (Figure 321 D) .... **Chrysomelìnae**	p. 422
11′.	Front coxae rounded; third tarsal segment, seen from beneath, distinctly bilobed (Figure 321 B) .... **Eumolpìnae**	p. 424
12(9′).	Hind femora slender; elytra soft .... **Galerucìnae**	p. 424
12′.	Hind femora swollen; elytra usually firm .... **Alticìnae**	p. 422
13(8′).	First abdominal sternum very long (Figure 321 F); antennae long, usually about half as long as body (Figure 324), and close together at base; elongate, metallic coppery or blue-black, semiaquatic beetles .... **Donaciìnae**	p. 422
13′.	First abdominal sternum not unusually long; antennae shorter, less than half as long as body, and widely separated at base (Figure 321 G); color variable 14	
14(13′).	Base of pronotum narrower than base of elytra; body elongate and more or less parallel-sided 15	
14′.	Base of pronotum about as wide as base of elytra; body round or oval, convex, and usually shining 16	
15(14).	Punctures of elytra in rows; elytra not pubescent; pronotum without lateral teeth .... **Criocerìnae**	p. 422
15′.	Punctures of elytra not in rows, or if in rows then pronotum has small lateral teeth and elytra have scattered pubescence .... **Orsodacnìnae**	p. 422
16(14′).	Prosterum with lateral antennal grooves; small, round or oval, convex beetles, shining blue, green, or bronze; Florida and California .... **Lamprosomatìnae***	p. 421
16′.	Prosternum without lateral antennal grooves; color variable; widely distributed .... **Eumolpìnae**	p. 424

Subfamily **Cassidìnae**—Tortoise Beetles: The tortoise beetles are broadly oval or circular, with the elytra wide and the head largely or entirely covered by the pronotum. Some of them are shaped very much like ladybird beetles. Many of the smaller tortoise beetles (5–6 mm in length) are very brilliantly colored, often with golden color or markings; the mottled tortoise beetle, *Delòyola guttàta* (Olivier), has black markings on a reddish-gold background, and the golden tortoise beetle, *Metriòna bicólor* (Fabricius), is brilliant gold or bronzy without the black markings. Our largest member of this subfamily is the argus tortoise beetle, *Chelymórpha cassìdea* (Fabricius), which is 9.5–11.5 mm in length and is shaped very much like a box turtle; it is red with six black spots on each elytron and one black spot along the suture overlapping both elytra (Figure 322 B).

The larvae of tortoise beetles are elongate-oval, somewhat flattened, and very spiny. At the posterior end of the body is a forked process that is usually bent upward and forward over the body; to this process are attached cast skins and excrement, which form a parasol-like shield over the body (Figure 322 A). The larvae and adults of tortoise beetles feed principally on morning-glories and related plants.

Subfamily **Hispìnae**—Leaf-Mining Leaf Beetles: These beetles are 4–7 mm in length, elongate, and

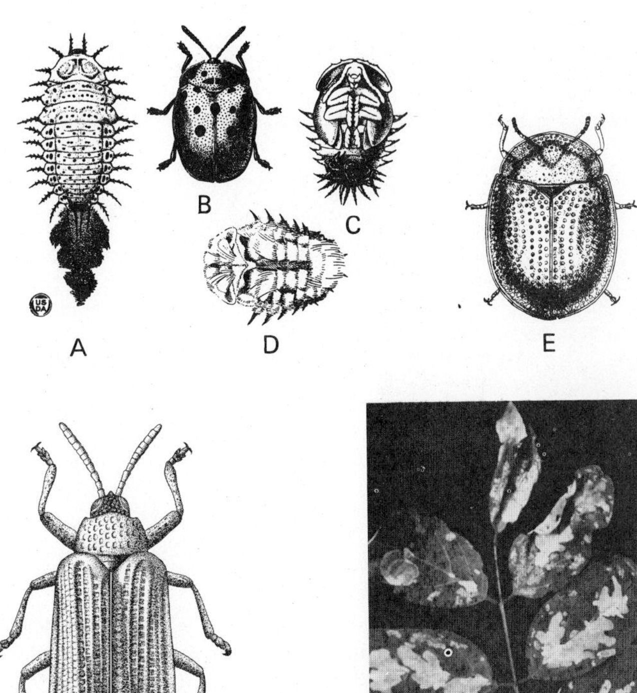

Figure 322. Tortoise beetles. A–D, argus tortoise beetle, *Chelymórpha cassídea* (Fabricius), 1½ ×; E, eggplant tortoise beetle, *Cássida pallídula* Boheman, 5 ×. A, larva, with anal fork (covered with fecal material) extended; B, adult; C, pupa, ventral view; D, pupa, dorsal view. (Courtesy of USDA.)

Figure 323. Locust leafminer, *Xenochálepus dorsàlis* (Thunberg). A, adult beetle, 7 ×; B, mines of larvae in black locust. (Courtesy of the Ohio Agricultural Research and Development Center.)

peculiarly ridged (Figure 323 A). Most of them are leaf-mining in the larval stage, and some are rather serious pests. The locust leafminer, *Xenochálepus dorsàlis* (Thunberg), an orange-yellow beetle with a broad black stripe down the middle of the back (Figure 323 A), is a serious pest of black locust; its mines are oval or irregular areas in the leaves, and a tree may be defoliated when these insects are numerous.

Subfamilies **Clytrìnae, Cryptocephalìnae, Chlamisìnae** (= **Chlamysìnae** or **Chlamydìnae**), and **Lamprosomatìnae**—Case-Bearing Leaf Beetles: The members of these groups are small, robust, somewhat cylindrical beetles that have the head buried in the prothorax almost to the eyes (Figure 321 C). When disturbed, they draw in their legs and fall to the ground and remain motionless. Most of these beetles are dark-colored, often with reddish or yellowish markings. The larvae are small fleshy grubs that crawl about dragging a small protective case, usually made of their own excrement; these cases are shorter than the body, and the posterior portion of the larva is bent downward and forward in the case. The larvae of most case-bearing leaf beetles feed on leaves; the larvae of some Chlamisìnae live in ant nests, where they feed on vegetable debris. Pupation in these beetles occurs within the case.

The members of these four subfamilies can be separated by the characters given in the key. The first three of these subfamilies are large and widely distributed groups; the Lamprosomatìnae are represented in the United States by only two species, one occurring in Florida and the other in California.

Subfamily **Aulacoscelìnae** (**Sagrìnae** in part): This group is represented in the United States by three rare species, which occur in New Mexico, Arizona, and California; the adults are leaf feeders, and the larvae are unknown.

Subfamily **Megascelìnae:** This is a tropical group that is represented in the United States by a single

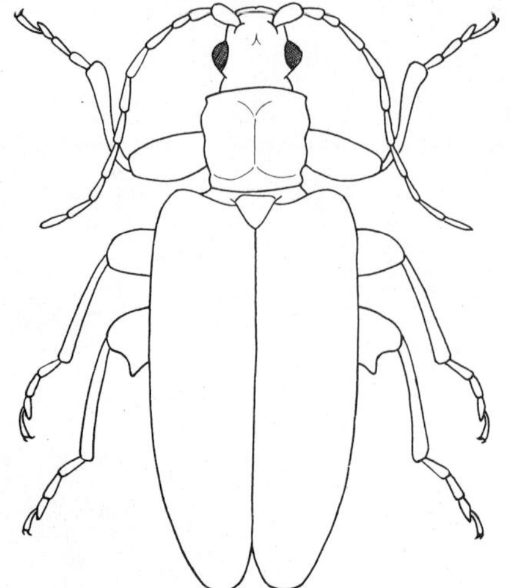

Figure 324. A long-horned leaf beetle, *Dònàcia* sp., 7½ ×.

species, *Megascèlis texàna* Linell, which has been recorded from the Brownsville area of Texas.

Subfamily **Zeugophorìnae:** This is a small group, represented in the United States by eight species of *Zeugóphora;* the adults are 3–4 mm in length and occur chiefly on poplar, hickory, and oak.

Subfamily **Donaciìnae**—Long-Horned Leaf Beetles: These beetles are elongate and slender and have long antennae (Figure 324). They are dark-colored and metallic, 5.5–12.0 mm in length, usually black, greenish, or coppery. They are active, fast-flying beetles, and in this respect resemble the tiger beetles. The long-horned leaf beetles are seldom seen far from water; the adults are generally found on the flowers or foliage of water lilies, pondweed, and other aquatic plants. The eggs are usually laid on the undersides of the leaves of water lily, in a whitish crescent-shaped mass near a small circular hole cut in the leaf by the adult. The larvae feed on the submerged parts of aquatic plants and obtain air through the plant stems; they pupate in cocoons that are fastened to vegetation below the water surface.

Subfamily **Alticìnae (Halticìnae)**—Flea Beetles: The flea beetles are small jumping leaf beetles that have the hind femora greatly enlarged. Most of them are blue or greenish, but many are black or black with light markings (Figure 325). A number of the flea beetles are very important pests of garden and field crops. *Épitrix hirtipénnis* (Melsheimer) attacks tobacco, *E. cucùmeris* (Harris) feeds on potatoes and cucumbers, and *E. fúscula* Crotch feeds on eggplant and tomatoes; these are small blackish beetles about 2 mm in length. *Áltica chalýbea* Illiger, a blue-black beetle 4–5 mm in length, feeds on the buds and leaves of grape. Adult flea beetles feed on the leaves of the food plant and eat tiny holes in them; the leaves of a heavily infested plant look as if small shot had been fired into them. The larvae usually feed on the roots of the same plant.

Subfamily **Criocerìnae:** The members of this subfamily have the head narrowed behind the eyes to form a slender neck, and the punctures of the elytra are arranged in rows. Three genera occur in the United States, *Crióceris, Oulèma,* and *Lèma;* some of these beetles are important pests.

The genus *Crióceris* includes two eastern species, both imported from Europe, which attack asparagus and often cause serious damage. Both species are about 7 mm in length; the striped asparagus beetle, *C. aspáragi* (L.), has a red prothorax and light yellow markings on the bluish-green elytra (Figure 326 A); the spotted asparagus beetle, *C. duodecimpunctàta* (L.), is brownish, with six large black spots on each elytron. Adults and larvae of *C. aspáragi* feed on the new shoots and cause damage to the growing plant; the larvae of *C. duodecimpunctàta* feed inside the berries and do not injure the shoots.

Our only species of *Oulèma* is the cereal leaf beetle, *O. melánopus* (L.), which is blue-black with a red pronotum and about 6 mm in length (Figure 326 B). This is a serious pest of various grains in some sections of the Midwest (chiefly Michigan, Ohio, and Indiana); both adults and larvae feed on the grain (and on various grasses).

Twenty-three species of *Lèma* occur in the eastern and southern United States. The most important species is probably the three-lined potato beetle, *L. trilineàta* (Olivier), which feeds on potato and related plants. This beetle is 6–7 mm in length, and reddish yellow with three broad black stripes on the elytra.

Subfamily **Orsodacnìnae** (including **Synetìnae**): This group is a small one, and the only species in it of much economic importance is the western fruit beetle, *Synèta álbida* LeConte, which damages the buds of many kinds of fruit trees along the North Pacific Coast. The only eastern genera are *Orsodácne* (7–8 mm in length and found chiefly on willow and dogwood flowers) and *Synèta*.

Subfamily **Chrysomelìnae:** Most of the members of this large subfamily are oval, convex, and

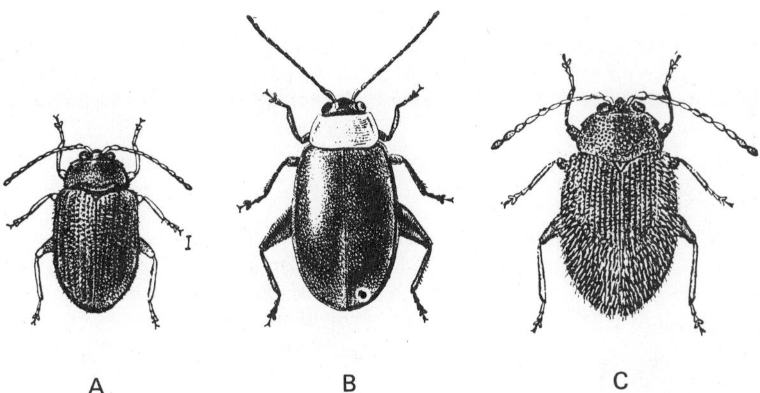

Figure 325. Flea beetles. A, potato flea beetle, *Épitrix cucùmeris* (Harris); B, spinach flea beetle, *Disonýcha xanthómelas* (Dalman); C, eggplant flea beetle, *Épitrix fùscula* Crotch. (Courtesy of USDA.)

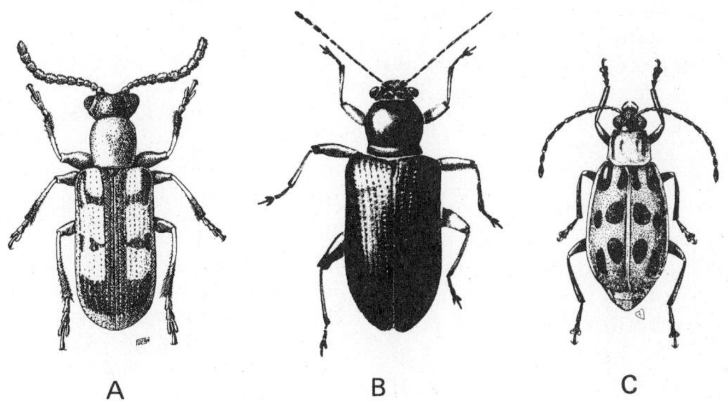

Figure 326. A, striped asparagus beetle, *Crióceris aspáragi* (L.); B, cereal leaf beetle, *Oulèma melánopus* (L.); C, spotted cucumber beetle, *Diabrótica undécimpunctàta howardi* Barber. (A, courtesy of the Utah State Agricultural College; B, courtesy of the Ohio Agricultural Research and Development Center; C, courtesy of USDA.)

brightly colored, 3.5–12.0 mm in length, and have the head sunk into the prothorax almost to the eyes. The Colorado potato beetle, *Leptinotársa decemlineàta* (Say), is the best known and most important species in this group. This is a large, yellow beetle striped with black (Figure 327), and is a very serious pest of potato plants over most of the country. Before the introduction of the potato into the United States, this species was confined to Colorado and neighboring states, where it fed on various wild species of nightshade (*Solànum*); since the introduction of the potato, this beetle has spread throughout the United States (except California and Nevada), and has been transported to Europe, where it is also a serious pest. This group includes the genus *Chrysolìna,* species of which

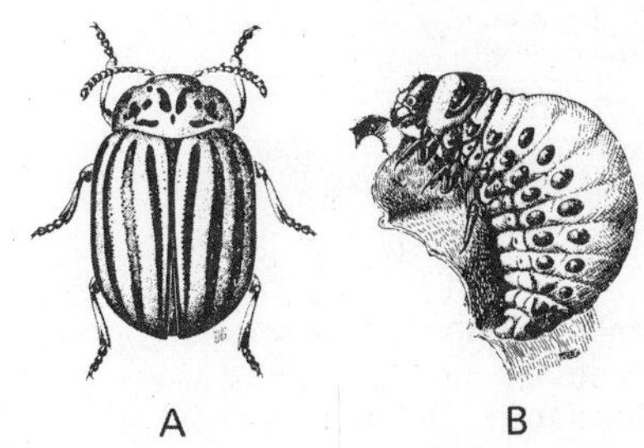

Figure 327. Colorado potato beetle, *Leptinotársa decemlineàta* (Say). A, adult; B, larva. (Courtesy of the Utah Agricultural Experiment Station.)

were introduced into California from Europe to control Klamath weed (see page 705).

Most of the other species in this subfamily feed on various wild plants and are of little economic importance. Species of *Labidómera* (relatively large red-and-black beetles) feed on milkweed; *Phyllodécta* (metallic blue or purple) feed on willow and poplar; and *Callígrapha* (whitish, with dark streaks and spots) feed on willow, alder, and other plants.

Subfamily **Galerucìnae:** The members of this group are small soft-bodied beetles, 2.5–11.0 mm in length, and most of them are yellowish with dark spots or stripes. The spotted cucumber beetle, *Diabrótica undécimpunctàta howardi* Barber (Figure 326 C), and the striped cucumber beetle, *Acalýmma vittàta* (Fabricius), feed on cucumbers and related plants; these beetles do serious damage to cucurbits by their feeding and they act as vectors of cucurbit wilt. The wilt bacilli pass the winter in the alimentary tract of the beetles; new plants are inoculated when the beetles begin to feed on them in the spring. The larvae of these two species are small, white, and soft-bodied, and feed on the roots and underground stems of cucurbits; the larva of the spotted cucumber beetle also feeds on the roots of corn and other plants, and is sometimes called the southern corn rootworm.

Two other corn rootworms—the northern corn rootworm, *Diabrótica longicòrnis* (Say), and the western corn rootworm, *D. virgífera* LeConte—are serious pests of corn in the midwest. Both adults and larvae cause damage, the larvae by feeding on the roots, and the adults by feeding in the silk; the latter activity prevents pollination and consequent kernel development.

The elm leaf beetle, *Pyrrhálta lutèola* (Müller), is another important pest species in this group; it is a greenish yellow beetle with a few black spots on the head and pronotum and a black stripe down the outer margin of each elytron.

Subfamily **Eumolpìnae:** These are usually oblong convex beetles that are either metallic in color or are yellowish and spotted. The dogbane beetle, *Chrýsochus auràtus* (Fabricius), which occurs on dogbane and milkweed, is one of the most brilliantly colored of the leaf beetles; it has an iridescent blue-green color with a coppery tinge, and is 8–11 mm in length. A closely related species, *C. cobaltìnus* LeConte, occurs in the Far West; it is darker and bluer than *C. auràtus,* and is 9–10 mm in length.

The western grape rootworm, *Adóxus obscùrus* (L.), causes serious damage to grape crops from Alaska to New Mexico, and also occurs in Europe and Siberia. Similar species found on grapes in the East belong to the genus *Fídia,* and are small, oval, hairy, and dark brown to black in color.

SUPERFAMILY **Curculionòidea:** The members of this group are sometimes called snout beetles, as most of them have the head more or less prolonged anteriorly into a beak or snout; this term is less appropriate (and is seldom used) for the Platypódidae and Scolýtidae, as the snout is scarcely developed in these two families. The Curculionòidea were formerly placed in a subdivision of the order called the Rhynchóphora.

Certain other characters besides the development of a snout distinguish the Curculionòidea from the beetles already described. The gular sutures are nearly always confluent, or lacking with no gula developed (Figure 244 C) (they are short but widely separated in the Cimberìnae). Prosternal sutures are lacking (except in the Anthríbidae), and in most of them the palps are rigid or invisible and the labrum is absent (Figure 244 A, B). The mouth parts are small and more or less hidden in most of these beetles; the mandibles, located at the tip of the snout, are usually the only mouth part structures easily visible without dissection. The tarsi are 5-segmented, but usually appear 4-segmented (the fourth segment is generally very small).

This is a large and important group of beetles, with more than 3100 species occurring in North America. Practically all feed on plant materials, and most of the larvae are burrowing in habit, infesting nuts, twigs, and the like. The larvae are whitish, **C**-shaped, more or less cylindrical, and usually legless. A great many are of considerable economic importance as pests of field or garden crops, forest, shade, and fruit trees, or of stored products.

There are differences of opinion regarding the classification of the beetles in this superfamily. The Bréntidae, Anthríbidae, Scolýtidae, and Platypódidae are almost universally recognized as distinct families, but the rest are arranged in different numbers of families by different authorities; we follow here the arrangement of Kissinger (1964), who places the remaining snout beetles in a single family, the Curculiónidae.

Family **Anthríbidae**—Fungus Weevils: The anthribids are elongate-oval, 0.5–30.0 (usually

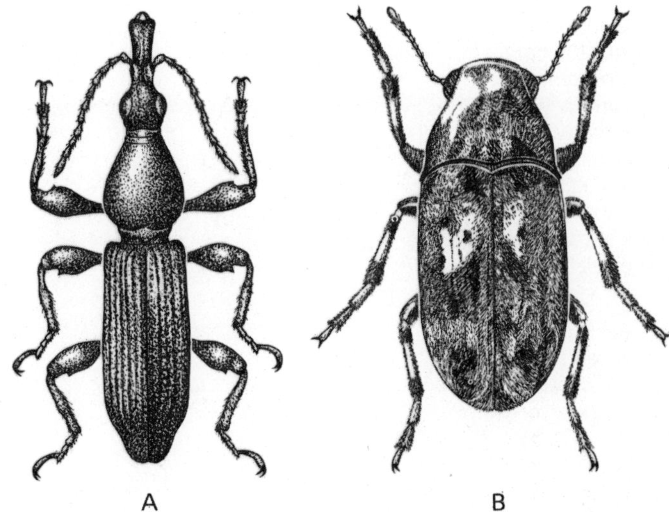

Figure 328. A, a straight-snouted weevil, *Arrhenòdes minùtus* (Drury), 4 ×; B, a fungus weevil, *Eupàrius marmòreus* (Olivier), 6½ ×. (A, courtesy of Arnett; B, courtesy of Pierce and the U.S. National Museum.)

less than 10.0) mm in length, with the beak short and broad and the antennae not elbowed (Figure 328 B). Some species have slender antennae that may be longer than the body (hence they look a little like some Cerambýcidae), and others have short antennae with a 3-segmented club. The adults of this group are usually found on dead twigs or beneath loose bark. The larvae vary in habits; some breed in woody fungi, some breed in the fungi of certain crops (for example, corn smut), some feed in seeds, and a few bore in dead wood. The introduced coffee bean weevil, *Araècerus fasciculàtus* (De Geer), is an important pest of seeds, berries, and dried fruits.

Family **Bréntidae**—Straight-Snouted Weevils: The brentids are narrow, elongate, cylindrical beetles, 10–30 mm in length, usually reddish or brownish and shining, with the snout projecting straight forward (Figure 328 A). The snout is generally longer and more slender in the female than in the male (Figure 329 G, H). This group is principally tropical, and only six species occur in North America. The only common eastern species is *Arrhenòdes minùtus* (Drury), which usually occurs under the loose bark of dead oak, poplar, and beech trees; the larvae are wood-boring, and sometimes attack living trees.

Family **Curculiónidae**—Snout Beetles: The members of this family are by far the most commonly encountered Curculionòidea, and are to be found almost everywhere; nearly 2500 species occur in North America. They show considerable variation in size, shape, and the form of the snout. The snout is fairly well developed in most species, with the antennae arising about the midlength of the snout (Figure 244 B); in some of the nut weevils (Figure 331 C) the snout is long and slender, as long as the body or longer.

All snout beetles (except a few occurring in ant nests) are plant feeders, and many are serious pests. Almost every part of a plant may be attacked, from the roots upward: the larvae usually feed inside the tissues of the plant, and the adults drill holes in fruits, nuts, and other plant parts.

Most snout beetles, when disturbed, will draw in their legs and antennae, fall to the ground, and remain motionless. Many are colored like bits of bark or dirt, and when they remain motionless they are very difficult to see. Some snout beetles (for example, *Conotrachèlus,* subfamily Cryptorhynchìnae) are able to stridulate by rubbing hardened tubercles on the dorsum of the abdomen against filelike ridges on the underside of the elytra; these sounds in *Conotrachèlus* are extremely weak, and usually can be heard only by holding the insect to one's ear.

Key to the Subfamilies of Curculiónidae

This key should serve to identify the vast majority of the specimens the general collector is likely to encounter. We follow here the arrangement of Kissinger (1964), who divides the Curculiónidae into 42

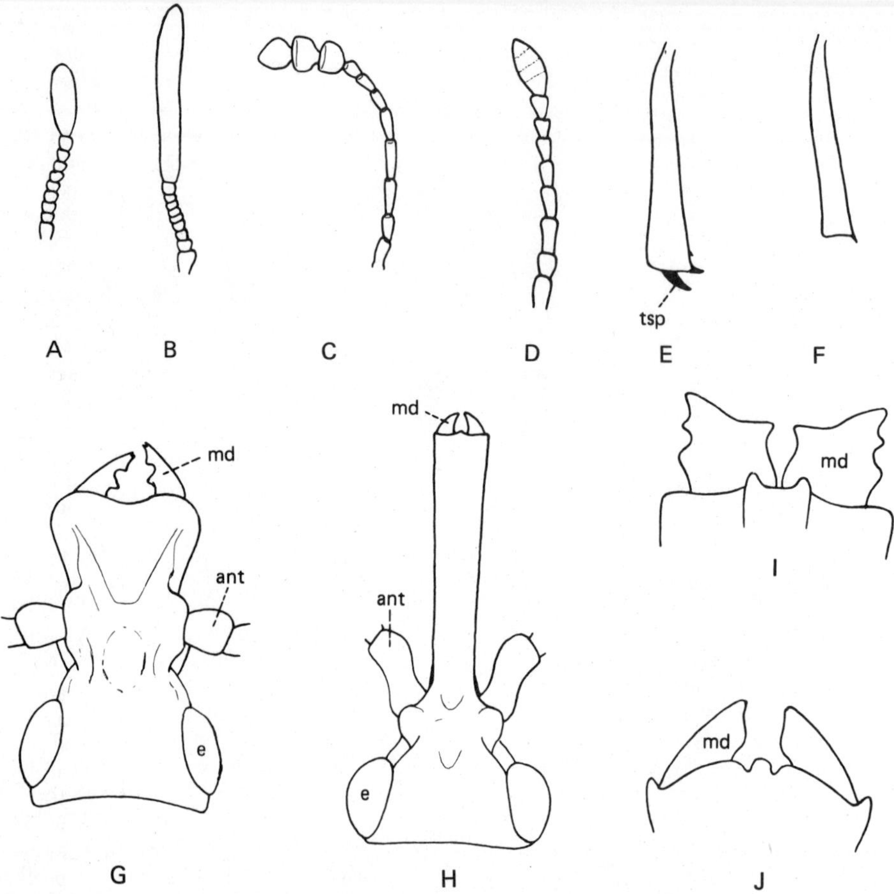

Figure 329. Characters of snout beetles. A–D, antennae; E–F, tibiae; G–H, heads; I–J, tip of snout. A, *Cỳlas,* female (Cyladìnae); B, same, male; C, *Rhynchìtes* (Rhynchitìnae); D, *Ithýcerus* (Ithycerìnae); E, *Attélabus* (Attelabìnae); F, *Rhynchìtes* (Rhynchitìnae); G, *Arrhenòdes,* male (Bréntidae); H, same, female; I, *Rhynchìtes* (Rhynchitínae); J, *Attélabus* (Attelabìnae). *ant,* antennae; e, compound eye; *md,* mandible; *tsp,* tibial spur.

subfamilies, but have omitted the Raymondionymìnae (three species, California), Cholìnae (three species, one in Arizona and two introduced into orchid houses), Petalochilìnae (one species, Florida), Cionìnae (one species introduced from Europe into Louisiana and Canada), Trachodìnae (five species, California and Alaska), and Alophìnae (nine species, northern North America).

1. Maxillary palps normal, segmented and flexible; labrum present; gular sutures distinct and separate; 3.0–4.5 mm in length .... **Cimberìnae** p. 438

1′. Maxillary palps rigid, the segments usually invisible, and the palpi often concealed; gular sutures usually fused; size variable 2

2(1′). Trochanters elongate, the femora attached at their apices and thus removed from the coxae (Figure 246 C); small, pear-shaped beetles, usually black, and 4.5 mm in length or less 3

2′. Trochanters short and triangular, the femora attached at their sides and contiguous with or closely adjacent to the coxae (Figure 246 D); size, shape, and color variable 4

3(2). Antennae elbowed, segments 6 and 7 of funiculus as wide as club .... **Nanophyìnae** p. 434

3′. Antennae not elbowed; segments 6 and 7 of funiculus narrower than club .... **Apionìnae** p. 432

4(2′). Antennae elbowed; beak usually with antennal scrobes 5

4′. Antennae not elbowed; beak usually lacking antennal scrobes 44

5(4). Tarsi slender, the third segment not bilobed; tarsal claws simple; beak short and broad, at rest fitting into a cavity in front of front coxae; prosternum a triangular plate in front of front coxae .... **Thecesternìnae** p. 434

5′. Third tarsal segment usually strongly bilobed; tarsal claws variable; beak variable in size and shape, either not fitting into a cavity in front of front coxae, the prosternum not a triangular plate in front of front coxae, or beak extending beyond front coxae 6

6(5′). Beak stout, quadrate, usually shorter than prothorax, often expanded laterally toward apex and with 1 or more longitudinal grooves; mandibles relatively large, with an apical projection or cusp that is deciduous and leaves a round or oval scar when it falls off (Figure 330 H, *scr*), or with many fine scales and/or setae laterally (the broad-nosed weevils) 7

6′. Beak usually slender and longer than prothorax, if shorter than lacking a median longitudinal groove; mandibles usually small, lacking a deciduous cusp or scar, and glabrous or with a few minute setae laterally 11

7(6). Anterior margin of prothorax with postocular lobes (Figure 330 F, *pol*) that sometimes partly cover the eyes; eyes more or less transverse 8

7′. Anterior margin of prothorax without postocular lobes; eyes more or less rounded, and usually well in front of prothorax 9

8(7). Mandibles with 3 large setae .... **Eremnìnae** p. 434

8′. Mandibles with 4 or more large setae .... **Leptopiìnae** p. 434

9(7′). Prothorax with a group of long fine hairs extending anteriorly from anterior margin behind eyes (Figure 330 D) .... **Tanymecìnae** p. 434

9′. Prothorax without such hairs 10

10(9′). Antennal scrobe vaguely defined posteriorly; scape usually passing above middle of eye when retracted next to head .... **Brachyrhinìnae** p. 434

10′. Antennal scrobe fairly well defined posteriorly, bent ventrally, and scape passing below eye when retracted next to head (Figure 330 G) .... **Thylacitìnae** p. 434

11(6′). Scape of antennae arising near eye, usually extending past posterior margin of eye, and not fitting into the short scrobe (Figure 330 E); funiculus 6-segmented; basal two thirds or more of antennal club dark, shining, and not annulated, the rest pale and not shining (Figure 330 E); third tarsal segment usually not bilobed; pygidium generally exposed.. **Rhynchophorìnae** p. 434

11′. Scape of antennae usually arising more apically, fitting into scrobe, and not extending beyond posterior margin of eye; antennal club either not as above, or if first segment of club is glabrous then funiculus is 7-segmented or the prosternum has an apical channel; third tarsal segment usually bilobed; pygidium generally covered 12

12(11′). Beak at rest fitting into a median channel in prosternum 13

12′. Beak at rest not fitting into a median channel in prosternum 17

13(12). Eyes partly covered by postocular lobes of prothorax when beak is in repose 14

13′. Eyes not covered when beak is in repose; eyes elongate-oval, pointed ventrally .... **Zygopìnae** p. 434

14(13). Pygidium covered by elytra; tibiae with an uncus (as in Figure 331 G, I) 15

14′. Pygidium exposed; tibiae without an uncus, but often mucronate (as in Fig-

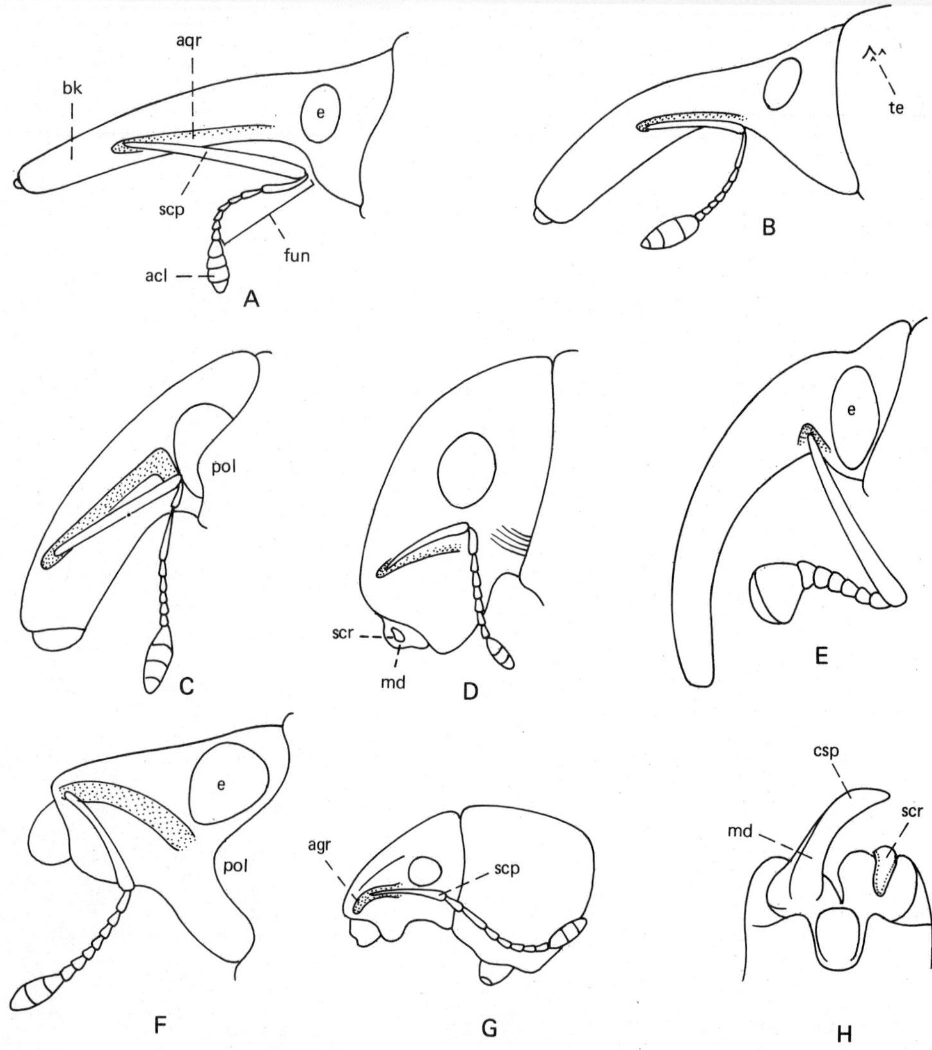

Figure 330. Characters of snout beetles. A–G, heads, lateral view; H, tip of snout, ventral view. A, *Anthónomus* (Anthonomìnae); B, *Mágdalis* (Magdalìnae); C, *Listronòtus* (Cylindrorhinìnae); D, *Pandeleteìus* (Tanymecìnae). E, *Rhodobaènus* (Rhynchoporìnae); F, *Eudiagògus* (Leptopiìnae); G, H, *Pantómorus* (Thylacitìnae). *acl,* antennal club; *agr,* scrobe; *bk,* beak or snout; *csp,* cusp of mandible; e, compound eye; *fun,* funiculus (antennal segments between scape and club); *md,* mandible; *pol,* postocular lobe of prothorax; *scp,* scape, basal antennal segment; *scr,* scar left on mandible where cusp has broken off; *te,* teeth on prothorax.

ure 331 H, I) .... **Ceutorhynchìnae** p. 434

15(14). Antennal club nearly evenly pubescent; hind tibiae with an apical comb of setae 16

15′. First segment of antennal club nearly glabrous; hind tibiae without an apical comb of setae; tarsi narrow, the third segment not bilobed .... **Cryptorhynchìnae** p. 435

16(15). Body with a dense varnishlike coating; third tarsal segment often no wider than first two segments; front coxae contiguous; tarsal claws simple and

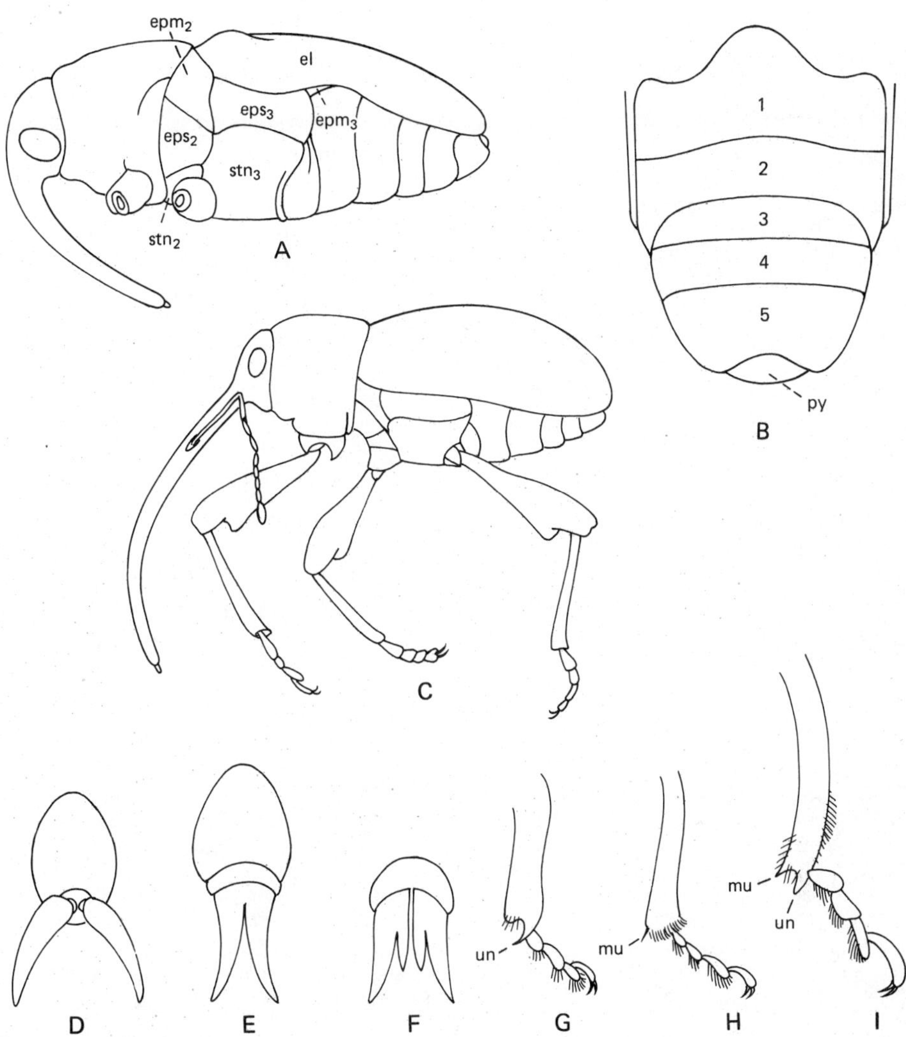

Figure 331. Characters of snout beetles. A, lateral view of body of *Odontocorŷnus* (Baridìnae); B, ventral view of abdomen of *Miccotrògus* (Tychiìnae); C, a nut weevil, *Curcùlio* sp., lateral view; D–F, tarsal claws: D, claws free and simple (*Ophriástes,* Leptopiìnae), E, claws connate (*Clèonus,* Cleonìnae), F, claws toothed (*Rhyssemàtus,* Cryptorhynchìnae); G–I, tibia and tarsus: G, tibia uncinate (*Laemosáccus,* Magdalìnae), H, tibia mucronate (*Tŷchius,* Tychiìnae), I, tibia mucronate and uncinate (*Erethístes,* Cholìnae). *el,* elytron; *epm*$_2$, mesepimeron; *eps*$_2$, episternum; *eps*$_3$, metepisternum; *mu,* mucro; *py,* pygidium; *stn*$_2$, mesosternum; *stn*$_3$, metasternum; *un,* uncus; *1–5,* abdominal sterna.

	free (as in Figure 331 D) (Bagoìni) .... **Erirhinìnae**	p. 436
16′.	Body without a dense varnishlike coating; third tarsal segment bilobed, usually wider than first two segments; front coxae separated, or tarsal claws toothed or connate .... **Cryptorhynchìnae**	p. 435
17(12′).	Mesepimera extending upward, sometimes visible in dorsal view between prothorax and elytra (Figure 331 A); elytra not produced anteriorly over base of prothorax 18	

17′. Mesepimera not as above, not visible in dorsal view 19

18(17). Funiculus 6-segmented; tarsal claws simple or toothed **Ceutorhynchìnae** p. 434

18′. Funiculus 7-segmented; tarsal claws simple, free or connate, or with a single claw .... **Baridìnae** p. 435

19(17′). Front coxae separated by a piece of the prosternum; second abdominal sternum about as long as or longer than third and fourth together; tarsal claws usually simple 20

19′. Front coxae contiguous 24

20(19). Eyes separated by a distance not greater than the maximum diameter of antennal club; front femora toothed, sometimes strongly so; pygidium concealed or exposed 21

20′. Eyes separated by a distance greater than the maximum diameter of antennal club, or lacking; front femora not toothed; pygidium concealed...22

21(20). Base of elytra produced over base of prothorax; elytra black, usually with a reddish area; pygidium exposed; beak more or less cylindrical (*Laemosáccus*) .... **Magdalìnae** p. 436

21′. Base of elytra not produced over base of prothorax; elytra unicolorous; pygidium exposed (*Piazorhìnus*) or more or less concealed (*Odóntopus*); beak slightly flattened apically .... **Prionomerìnae** p. 435

22(20′). Outer surface of apex of hind tibiae with an apical comb of setae laterad of base of uncus; scutellum minute or not visible; dorsal margin of scrobe directed toward lower half of eye .... **Hylobiìnae** p. 435

22′. Outer surface of apex of hind tibiae without an apical comb of setae laterad of base of uncus 23

23(22′). Hind tibiae with an apical dorsal comb of setae, the comb about as long as width of tibia at apex; beak usually about as long as prothorax .... **Pissodìnae** p. 435

23′. Hind tibiae without an apical comb of setae; beak usually shorter than prothorax .... **Cossonìnae** p. 436

24(19′). Suture between second and third abdominal sterna strongly produced backward laterally, reaching or surpassing the suture between third and fourth sterna (Figure 331 B); hind coxae distant from margin of elytra; beak tapered apically .... **Tychiìnae** p. 436

24′. Suture between second and third abdominal sterna straight, or at most only slightly produced backward laterally, not reaching suture between third and fourth sterna 25

25(24′). Tarsal claws connate at base (Figure 331 E) 26

25′. Tarsal claws free at base (as in Figure 331 D) (*Brachybàmus*, Erirhinìnae, has only 1 tarsal claw) 29

26(25). Funiculus 5-segmented; pygidium exposed .... **Gymnaetrìnae** p. 436

26′. Funiculus 7-segmented 27

27(26′). Elytra with an acute lateral tubercle behind humeri; tibiae angulate on inner surface near middle (*Stérnechus*)............................ **Hylobiìnae** p. 435

27′. Elytra without such lateral tubercles; tibiae not angulate on inner surface near middle 28

28(27′). Eyes distant from anterior margin of prothorax; anterior margin of prothorax with long postocular hairs and not produced into postocular lobes .... **Cleonìnae** p. 436

28′. Eyes partly concealed by postocular lobes on anterior margin of prothorax; prothorax without long postocular hairs (Smicronychìni, western United States) .... **Erirhinìnae** p. 436

29(25′). Tarsal claws simple (*Brachybàmus*, Erirhinìnae, has only 1 tarsal claw); second abdominal sternum longer than third, usually as long as third and fourth together 30

29′. Tarsal claws with a basal tooth or process (as in Figure 331 F); abdominal sterna 2–4 usually about equal in length 37

30(29). Hind tibiae uncinate, the uncus more than half as long as tarsal claws (Figure 331 G, I) 31

30′. Hind tibiae unarmed apically, or mucronate with mucro not more than half as long as tarsal claws (as in Figure 331 H) 34

31(30). Metepimera visible, their vestiture and sculpturing similar to that of metepisterna 32

31′. Metepimera normally covered by elytra, their vestiture and sculpturing finer than that on metepisterna 33

32(31). Uncus on hind tibiae projecting from slightly behind anterior margin of tibia; body usually without scales dorsally but with stellate scales ventrally .... **Magdalìnae** p. 436

32′. Uncus on hind tibiae projecting from anterior margin of tibia; body clothed dorsally and ventrally with narrow elongate scales (*Lépyrus*) . **Cleonìnae** p. 436

33(31′). Dorsal surface of body covered with round scales and usually with a varnishlike coating on top of scales; frons usually at least as wide as base of beak in dorsal view; hind coxae separated by a distance equal to or greater than the greatest diameter of the coxae .... **Erirhinìnae** p. 436

33′. Dorsal surface of body with narrow scales, or elongate and fairly broad scales, and without a varnishlike coating; frons much narrower than base of beak in dorsal view; hind coxae separated by a distance distinctly less than the greatest diameter of the coxae .... **Hylobiìnae** p. 435

34(30′). Dorsal margin of scrobe directed toward dorsal margin of eye, and bent abruptly downward in front of eye (Figure 330 C); prothorax with postocular lobes .... **Cylindrorhinìnae** p. 436

34′. Dorsal margin of scrobe not reaching dorsal margin of eye, and not bent downward in front of eye; prothorax lacking postocular lobes, or if such lobes are present then beak is more slender than greatest width of middle femora 35

35(34′). Front coxae much closer to hind margin of prosternum than to front margin .... **Erirhinìnae** p. 436

35′. Front coxae about equidistant from anterior and posterior margins of prosternum 36

36(35′). Eyes nearly round; beak slender, longer than prothorax, rather glabrous, its width in profile at base of antennae much less than width of eye .... **Anthonomìnae** p. 436

36′. Eyes transversely oval; beak stout, densely and rather uniformly setose .... **Hyperìnae** p. 436

37(29′). Front coxae about equidistant from anterior and posterior margins of prosternum 38

37′. Front coxae much closer to hind margin of prosternum than to front margin 41

38(37). Prothorax longer than wide, and wider in middle than at base; hind tibiae with a small uncus .... **Myrmecìnae** p. 436

38′. Prothorax wider than long 39

39(38′). Hind tibiae uncinate, the uncus longer than tarsal claws (Figure 331 G); first tarsal segment longer than fourth; eyes transversely oval .... **Magdalìnae** p. 436

39′. Hind tibiae unarmed or mucronate, or if apparently uncinate the uncus is distinctly shorter than tarsal claws; first tarsal segment shorter than fourth 40

40(39′). Hind tibiae with an apical comb of setae perpendicular to long axis of tibia; hind tibiae not narrowed apically; hind femora not much stouter than middle femora .... **Anthonomìnae** p. 436

40′. Apical comb of setae on hind tibiae oblique, and ascending for a distance greater than width of tibia at apex; hind tibiae narrowed apically; hind femora stouter than middle femora .... **Rhynchaenìnae** p. 437

41(37′). Pronotum with anterolateral toothlike projections (Figure 330 B) .... **Magdalìnae** p. 436

41′. Pronotum without such projections 42

42(41′). Prothorax oval, longer than wide, and narrowed at base; hind tibiae uncinate; antennal scrobes located more ventrally; body nearly glabrous .... **Myrmecìnae** p. 436

42′. Prothorax wider than long, and not wider in middle than at base; hind tibiae unarmed or mucronate; antennal scrobes located laterally 43

43(42′). Femora with a stout triangular tooth; elytra with slender elongate scales; beak slender, often as long as body or longer (Figure 331 C) .... **Curculionìnae** p. 437

43′. Femora without such a tooth; elytra with inconspicuous, short fine setae .... **Erirhinìnae** p. 436

44(4′). Pronotum margined laterally; elytra short and rounded apically, exposing parts of about 3 abdominal segments; oval, slightly flattened, metallic indigo-blue beetles, 2.8–3.2 mm in length; eastern North America .... **Pterocolìnae** p. 433

44′. Pronotum rounded laterally; elytra longer; other characters variable, but color usually not as above 45

45(44′). Antennae 10-segmented, the last segment elongate and swollen (Figure 329 A, B); pronotum narrowed posteriorly; body antlike, 5–6 mm in length, with the pronotum reddish and the elytra blue-black (Figure 332); southern United States .... **Cyladìnae** p. 432

45′. Antennae 11-segmented, club usually 3-segmented; pronotum not narrowed posteriorly 46

46(45′). Hind femora short and very broad, their upper margins slightly crenulate; beak long, slender, and decurved; hind coxae separated; length 3.5–4.2 mm; southern Florida .... **Oxycorynìnae** p. 433

46′. Hind femora slender or somewhat clavate, their upper margins not crenulate; beak and size variable 47

47(46′). Segments of antennal club usually separate and forming a loose club (Figure 329 C); length usually less than 7 mm 48

47′. Segments of antennal club firmly united, forming a compact club (Figure 329 D); size variable 49

48(47). Mandibles flat and toothed on inner and outer edges (Figure 329 I); beak long, nearly parallel-sided; tibiae with a short, straight terminal spur (Figure 329 F) .... **Rhynchitìnae** p. 433

48′. Mandibles stout, pincers-shaped, not toothed on outer edge (Figure 329 J); beak short, widened distally; tibiae with 2 large, curved terminal spurs (Figure 329 E) .... **Attelabìnae** p. 433

49(47′. Hind femora long and spiny; body broadly oval, 3 mm in length or less .... **Tachygonìnae** p. 433

49′. Hind femora clavate, not spiny; body elongate, 12–18 mm in length .... **Ithycerìnae** p. 433

Subfamily **Cyladìnae:** The only member of this group occurring in the United States is the sweetpotato weevil, *Cỳlas formicàrius elegántulus* (Summers); this is an introduced species and occurs principally in the southern states. This beetle is slender, elongate, antlike, and 5–6 mm in length; the pronotum is reddish brown and the elytra are blue-black (Figure 332). The larvae are often called sweetpotato root borers. This insect is a serious pest of sweet potatoes because the larvae bore in the vines and roots, and the plants are often killed. The larvae may continue to burrow through the tubers after they are harvested, and adults may emerge after the sweet potatoes are in storage or on the market.

Subfamily **Apionìnae:** The members of this group are small (4.5 mm in length or less) and somewhat pear-shaped, usually blackish in color, and the antennae are not elbowed. Most of our 127 species occur on legumes, where the larvae bore into the seeds, stems, and other parts of the plant. One species, the pine gall weevil, *Podàpion gallícola* Riley, forms galls on the twigs of pine trees.

Subfamily **Pterocolìnae:** This group is represented in North America by a single species, *Pterócolus ovàtus* (Fabricius), which occurs in the East. This beetle is broadly oval, indigo-blue in color, and 2.8–3.2 mm in length; the pronotum is margined laterally, and the elytra are short, rounded apically, and expose the central part of the last two or three abdominal segments. The larvae develop in the leaf rolls of *Attélabus* (see below, subfamily Attelabìnae); the female enters the leaf roll and destroys the *Attélabus* egg before ovipositing.

Subfamily **Oxycorynìnae:** Only one species in this subfamily occurs in the United States, *Rhopalótria slóssoni* (Schaeffer), which occurs in southern Florida; the adults and larvae feed on arrowroot (*Zàmia*). The adults have the elytra black, with an elongate reddish yellow mark near each humerus.

Subfamily **Rhynchitìnae**—Tooth-Nosed Snout Beetles: These beetles are so named because of the teeth on the edges of the mandibles (Figure 329 I). They are 1.5–6.5 mm in length, and usually occur on low vegetation. A common species in this group is the rose curculio, *Rhynchìtes bìcolor* (Fabricius), which occurs on roses. The adult is about 6 mm in length and is red, with the snout and the ventral side of the body black, and it has a broad-shouldered appearance; the larvae feed in rose fruits. Other species in this group breed in buds, fruits, and nuts.

Subfamily **Attelabìnae**—Leaf-Rolling Weevils: These beetles are short and robust, 3–6 mm in length, and are somewhat similar to the Rhynchitìnae; most of them are black, reddish, or black with red markings. The most interesting characteristic of this group is their method of laying eggs, from which their common name is derived. When a female is ready to oviposit, she cuts two slits near the base of the leaf, from each edge to the midrib, and rolls the part of the leaf beyond these cuts into a neat and solid ball; a single egg is laid near the tip of the leaf, usually on the underside, before the leaf is rolled up. She then gnaws the midrib of the leaf (at the end of the basal cuts) partly in two, and the leaf roll eventually drops to the ground. The larva feeds on the inner portion of this leaf roll, and pupates either in the roll or in the ground.

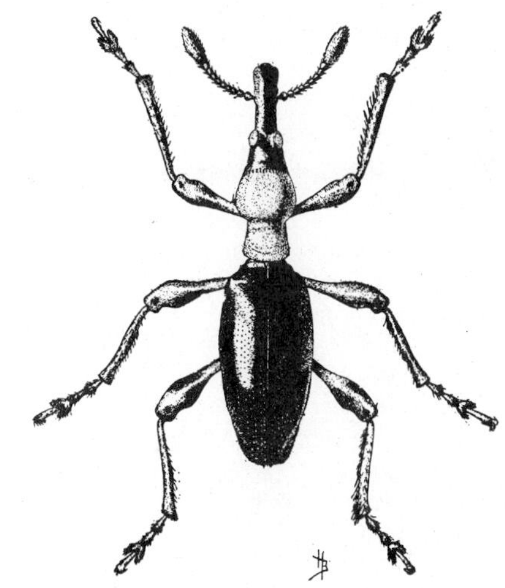

Figure 332. Sweetpotato weevil, *Cỳlas formicàrius elegántulus* (Summers), female. (Courtesy of USDA.)

The eight species of leaf-rolling weevils in the United States belong to the genus *Attélabus*. Most species occur on oak, hickory, or walnut, but one species (*A. nígripes* LeConte, red and 3.5–4.5 mm in length) feeds on sumac, and another (*A. rhòis* Boheman, 4.5–5.5 mm in length and dark reddish to black) feeds on alder and hazelnut.

Subfamily **Tachygonìnae**—Toad Weevils: These weevils are usually found on the foliage of oak, elm, or locust; the larvae are leaf miners in these trees. Adults at rest usually hang downward from the leaves, hanging by means of their spiny hind femora; they frequently walk about on the underside of the leaves. This group is represented in the United States by nine species of *Tachygònus*, which occur from the East to Arizona; they are not common.

Subfamily **Ithycerìnae (Belìnae):** This subfamily includes a single species, the New York weevil, *Ithýcerus noveboracénsis* (Forster), which occurs in eastern North America west to Nebraska and Texas. This beetle is shiny black, clothed with patches of gray and brown pubescence, and has the scutellum yellowish; it is 12–18 mm in length. This beetle occurs principally on the limbs and foliage of hickory, oak, and beech trees; the larvae are unknown.

Subfamily **Thecesternìnae**—Bison Snout Beetles: This group includes seven United States species, one of which occurs in the East. The eastern species, *Thecestérnus áffinis* LeConte, is a dull black beetle covered with brownish yellow scales, and 6.5–9.0 mm in length. When at rest the head and beak are completely withdrawn into a large cavity in the front of the prothorax. The Thecesternìnae occur under stones or dried cow dung; they are not common.

Subfamily **Nanophyìnae:** These weevils are similar to the Apioninae, but have the antennae elbowed. They are represented in our area by four species of *Nanophỳes,* which are widely distributed but are not common.

Subfamily **Eremnìnae:** The members of this and the four following subfamilies are commonly called the broad-nosed weevils, because of the character of the beak (see key to subfamilies, couplet 6); most of them are flightless because the elytra are grown together along the suture and the hind wings are vestigial. Only three species of Eremnìnae occur in North America. The most common species in the East is the Asiatic oak weevil, *Cyrtepístomus castàneus* (Roelofs), a species introduced from Japan and found on the foliage of oaks and other trees. This weevil is about 6 mm in length, dark brown, covered with light green scales (especially laterally).

Subfamily **Leptopiìnae:** This is a large group, with 153 North American species; most species are western, and some are brightly colored. The larvae feed chiefly on various herbaceous plants and shrubs.

Subfamily **Tanymecìnae:** This is a smaller group (41 North American species), mostly western. The larvae feed on a variety of herbaceous plants, shrubs, and trees. One species of importance in the Southeast is the citrus root weevil, *Pachnaèus lìtus* (Germar).

Subfamily **Thylacitìnae (Brachymerìnae):** This is a large and widely distributed group (nearly 100 North American species) containing some important pests. The most important species in this group are the whitefringed beetles (three species of *Graphógnathus*), which are serious agricultural pests in the southern states. These beetles are about 12 mm in length, with the edges of the elytra whitish and with two longitudinal white stripes on the head and pronotum (Figure 336 A). The whitefringed beetles are parthenogenetic; no males are known. Another injurious species in this group is the Fuller rose weevil, *Pantómorus cervìnus* (Boheman), 7–9 mm in length, which is especially common in the Far West. It attacks roses and many greenhouse plants, as well as citrus and other fruit trees. The larvae live in the soil and feed on the roots of the host plant, and the adults feed on the leaves. Members of the genus *Sitòna* (mostly pale in color and 4–5 mm in length) attack and seriously damage clovers.

Subfamily **Brachyrhinìnae:** This is a large and widely distributed group of broad-nosed weevils, with about 100 North American species; most of them are small (generally 6 mm in length or less). Members of the genus *Brachyrhìnus* are very common and feed on a variety of plants; *B. ovàtus* (L.) often causes serious injury to strawberries.

Subfamily **Rhynchophorìnae**—Billbugs and Grain Weevils: These beetles are stout-bodied and cylindrical and are of varying size; some of our largest snout beetles belong to this group. The antennae arise close to the eyes, and the scape extends posterior to the eye (Figure 330 E); the basal two thirds or more of the antennal club is smooth and shining. One of the largest of the billbugs is *Rhynchóphorus cruentàtus* (Fabricius), which is 20–30 mm in length and occurs on palms. The cocklebur weevil, *Rhodobaènus tredécimpunctàtus* (Illiger), a common eastern billbug, is 7–11 mm in length; it is reddish with small black spots on the elytra. The genus *Sphenóphorus* (Figure 333) includes the corn billbugs, which occur on various grasses including timothy and corn; the adults feed on the foliage and the larvae bore into the stalks. Among the most important pests in this group are the granary weevil, *Sitóphilus granàrius* (L.), and the rice weevil, *S. orỳzae* (L.). These are small brownish insects, 3–4 mm in length, that attack stored grain (wheat, corn, rice, and so forth); both adults and larvae feed on the grain, and the larvae develop inside the grains.

Subfamily **Zygopìnae:** This is a widely distributed group that is represented in North America by 40 species, which feed on various herbaceous plants and trees (including conifers).

Subfamily **Ceutorhynchìnae:** This is a large and widely distributed group (145 North American species), and includes some important pests. The grape curculio, *Crapònius inaequàlis* (Say), a blackish, very broadly oval beetle about 3 mm in length, feeds on the foliage of grape; the larvae develop in the grape berries. The iris weevil,

Monónychus vulpéculus (Fabricius), attacks iris; the larvae develop in the seed pods, and the adults feed in the flowers. The cabbage curculio, *Ceutorhýnchus ràpae* Gyllenhal, is a pest of cabbage.

Subfamily **Cryptorhynchìnae:** Many members of this large group (187 North American species) have the elytra rough and tuberculate; when at rest the beak is usually drawn back into a groove in the prosternum. The most important pest species in this group is the plum curculio, *Conotrachèlus nénuphar* (Herbst) (Figure 334), which attacks plum, cherry, peach, apple, and other fruits. The females lay their eggs in little pits they eat in the fruit, and then cut a crescent-shaped incision beside the pit containing the egg. The larvae develop in the fruit, and pupate in the soil. The adult is about 6 mm in length, dark-colored, and has two prominent tubercles on each elytron. The genus *Conotrachèlus* is a large one (62 North American species), and its members are widely distributed; the larvae develop in various fruits.

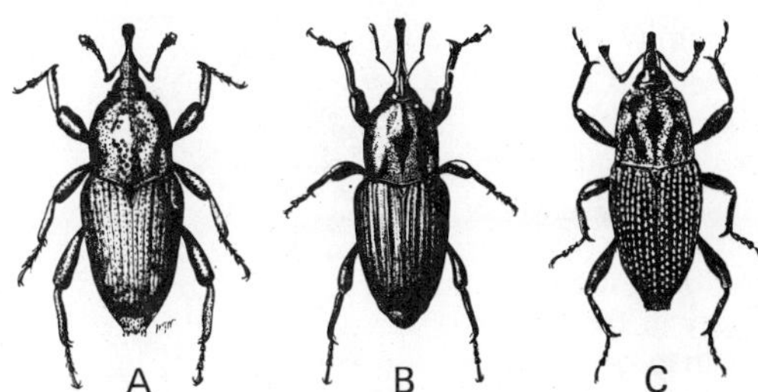

Figure 333. Billbugs (Rhynchophorìnae), 2 ×. A, curlewbug, *Sphenóphorus callòsus* (Olivier); B, maize billbug, *S. màidis* Chittenden; C, timothy billbug, *S. zèae* (Walsh). (Courtesy of USDA.)

Subfamily **Baridìnae:** This is the largest subfamily of the Curculiónidae, with about 500 North American species. These beetles are small and stout-bodied (Figure 336 B), and can generally be recognized by the upward-extending mesepimera, which are sometimes visible from above (Figure 331 A). Most species feed on various herbaceous plants; a few attack cultivated plants. The potato stalk borer, *Trichobàris trinotàta* (Say), attacks potato, eggplant, and related plants; the larvae bore in the stems and the adults feed on the leaves. *T. mucòrea* (LeConte) damages tobacco in the same way. The grape cane gallmaker, *Ampeloglýpter sesóstris* (LeConte), a stout-bodied reddish-brown beetle, 3–4 mm in length, makes galls on the shoots of grape.

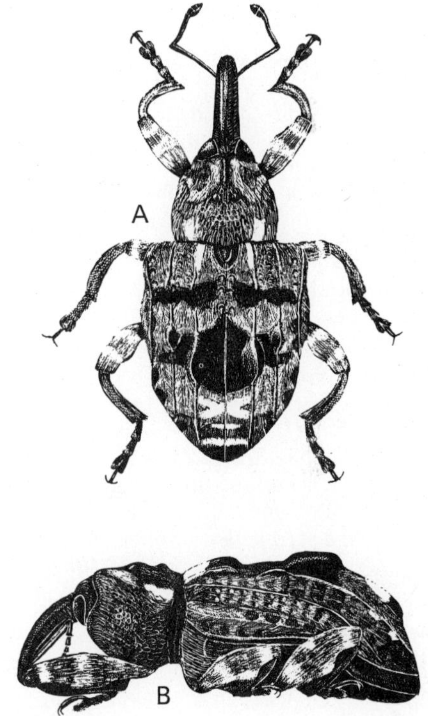

Figure 334. Plum curculio, *Conotrachèlus nénuphar* (Herbst). A, dorsal view; B, lateral view of an individual feigning death. (Courtesy of Rings and the Ohio Agricultural Research and Development Center.)

Subfamily **Prionomerìnae:** The five North American species in this group occur in the East; the larvae are leaf miners in sassafras, tulip tree, and oak.

Subfamily **Hylobiìnae:** Most members of this group are dark-colored and of moderate size (Figure 335). Several species (especially species of *Hylòbius*) are important pests of pine and other conifers. The bean stalk weevil, *Stérnechus paludàtus* (Casey) (Figure 336 E) is a member of this subfamily.

Subfamily **Pissodìnae**—Pine Weevils: The members of this group are usually brownish and cylindrical, and most are 8–10 mm in length (Figure 336 F). Many species are important pests of conifers; the larvae tunnel in the terminal leader of a young tree and kill it, and one of the lateral branches becomes the terminal leader, giving rise to a tree with a bend partway up the trunk; such a tree is of little value as a source of lumber. The

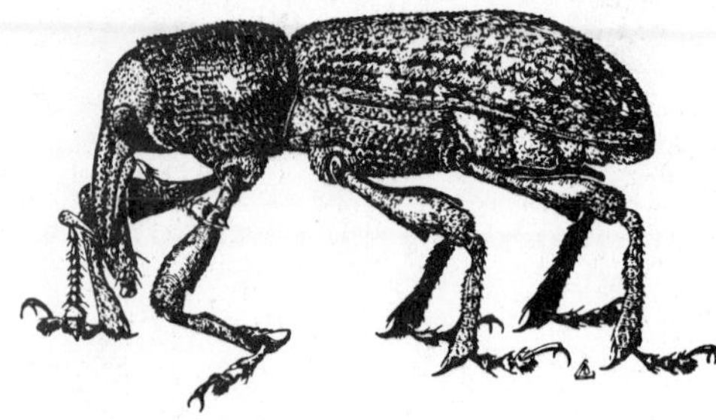

Figure 335. Pales weevil, *Hylòbius pàles* (Herbst) (Hylobiìnae), 5 ×. (Courtesy of USDA.)

white pine weevil, *Pissòdes stròbi* (Peck), is a common species attacking white pine; other species of *Pissòdes* attack other conifers.

Subfamily **Cossonìnae** – Broad-Nosed Bark Beetles: The Cossonìnae can usually be recognized by the broad short beak and the long curved spine at the apex of each front tibia. These beetles are 1.5–6.5 mm in length, and most of them occur under the loose dead bark of trees and under logs and stones; a few occur under driftwood and debris along the seacoast.

Subfamily **Tychiìnae:** The larvae of most Tychiìnae feed on the seeds of various legumes, and the adults occur on the flowers. The clover seed weevil, *Miccotrògus piciróstris* (Fabricius), is an important pest of clover in the Northwest.

Subfamily **Gymnaetrìnae:** Only seven species in this subfamily occur in North America, but some of these are fairly common insects. Some species develop in the seed pods of mullein (*Verbáscum*), some develop in the seed pods of *Lobèlia,* and another develops in galls at the base of plantain (*Plantágo*).

Subfamily **Cleonìnae:** The most common beetles in this group are those in the genus *Líxus,* which are elongate and cylindrical, 10–15 mm in length, with the curved beak nearly as long as the prothorax; they usually occur on weeds near water. *L. concàvus* Say, which breeds in the stems of dock, sunflower, and occasionally rhubarb, is commonly called the rhubarb curculio; the adult is blackish, covered with gray pubescence. Over 100 species of Cleonìnae occur in North America, 69 of them in the genus *Líxus*.

Subfamily **Cylindrorhinìnae:** Most members of this group breed in aquatic or subaquatic plants, and the adults are found near water; a few are pests of vegetables. The vegetable weevil, *Listróderes costiróstris oblìquus* (Klug), attacks many different vegetables, and is an important pest in the Gulf States and in California; the carrot weevil, *Listronòtus oregonénsis* (LeConte), is a pest of carrots and other vegetables in the East.

Subfamily **Erirhinìnae:** This is a large and widely distributed group, with 179 species reported from North America. The adults are usually found near water, as the larvae of many species develop in various aquatic plants.

Subfamily **Hyperìnae** – Clover Weevils: Most members of this small group (seven North American species, in the genus *Hỳpera*) feed on various clovers and are important clover pests. The alfalfa weevil, *H. pòstica* (Gyllenhal) (Figure 336 D), and the clover leaf weevil, *H. punctàta* (Fabricius), feed on the growing tips of the plant and skeletonize the leaves; *H. mèles* (Fabricius) feeds in the clover heads. These beetles are dark-colored and 3–8 mm in length.

Subfamily **Anthonomìnae:** Nearly 200 species of Anthonomìnae occur in North America (over 100 in the genus *Anthónomus*), and several are important pests of cultivated plants: the adults usually feed on fruits and lay their eggs in some of the feeding pits; the larvae develop inside the fruits. The boll weevil, *Anthónomus grándis* Boheman, is a well-known and serious pest of cotton in the southern states. It entered the United States from Mexico about 1800, and has since spread over most of the cotton-growing sections of this country. The adults are about 6 mm in length, yellowish to brown in color, with a slender snout about half as long as the body. They feed on the seed pods or bolls and flower buds, and lay their eggs in the holes made in feeding; the larvae feed inside the bolls and eventually destroy them. Other species of economic importance in this group are the strawberry weevil, *A. signàtus* Say, the cranberry weevil, *A. músculus* Say, and the apple curculio, *Tachypteréllus quadrigíbbus* (Say).

Subfamily **Myrmecìnae** – Antlike Weevils: These small shiny weevils have the prothorax oval and narrowed at the base, and are somewhat antlike in appearance (Figure 336 C). Some species develop in cynipid galls on oak. This group is a small one, and its members are not very common.

Subfamily **Magdalìnae:** These small cylindrical weevils can usually be recognized by the toothlike processes on the anterior corners of the pro-

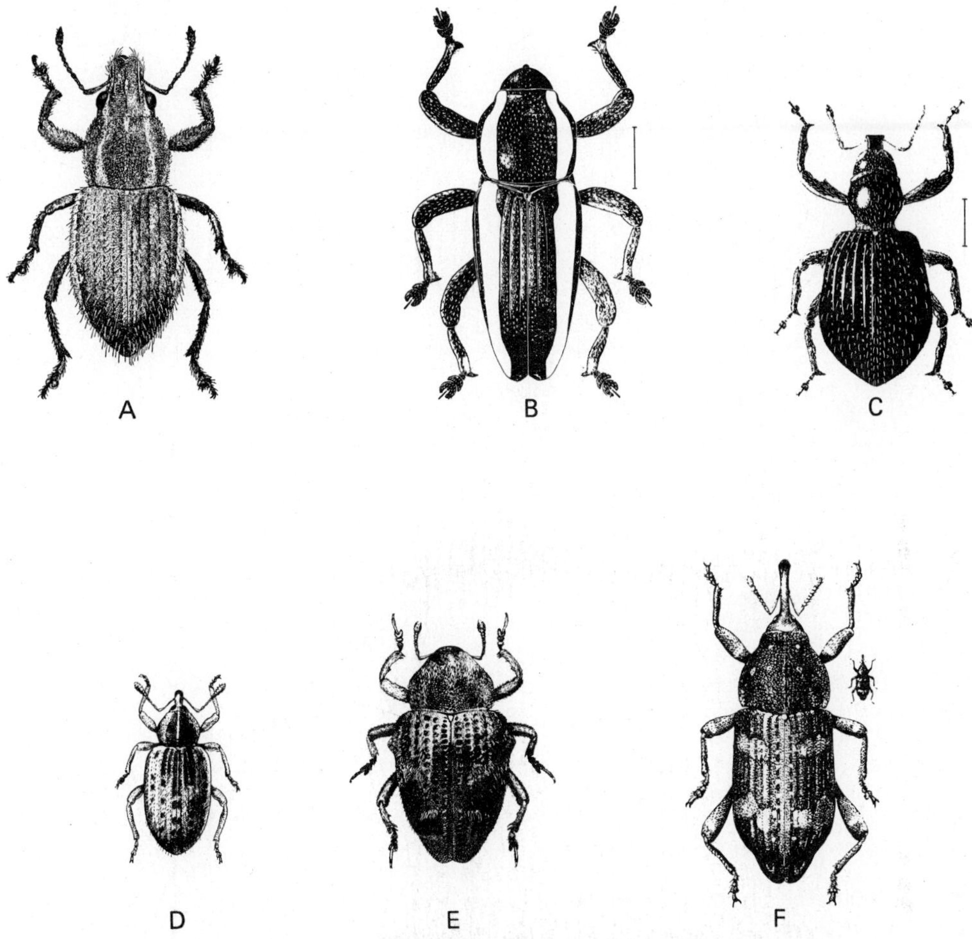

Figure 336. Snout beetles. A, a whitefringed beetle, *Graphógnathus leucolòma* (Boheman), 3½ × (Thylacitìnae); B, *Barìnus bivittàtus* (LeConte) (line = 1 mm) (Baridìnae); C, an antlike weevil, *Mýrmex subglàber* (Schaeffer) (line = 1 mm) (Myrmecìnae); D, alfalfa weevil, *Hýpera pòstica* (Gyllenhal) (Hyperìnae), 5 ×; E, bean stalk weevil, *Stérnechus paludàtus* (Casey) (Hylobiìnae); F, white pine weevil, *Pissòdes stròbi* (Peck) (insert is about natural size) (Pissodìnae). (A, D, E, and F, courtesy of USDA; B and C, courtesy of Sleeper.)

notum (Figure 330 B, *te*). The larvae attack trees, usually tunneling in the twigs or under the bark; a few are pests of orchard or shade trees.

Subfamily **Rhynchaenìnae**—Flea Weevils: These weevils are so called because of their jumping habits; the hind femora are relatively stout. The larvae are leaf miners and mine in the leaves of willow, elm, alder, cherry, and apple. The group is widely distributed, and is represented in our area by 16 species of *Rhynchaènus*.

Subfamily **Curculionìnae**—Acorn and Nut Weevils: These weevils are usually light brown in color, and have a very long and slender snout that may be as long as the body or longer (Figure 331 C). The adults bore into acorns and nuts with their long snouts and lay their eggs in some of these feeding holes; the larvae develop inside the nut. Our species (44 in North America) belong to the genus *Curcùlio*. *C. nàsicus* Say and *C. cáryae* (Horn) attack hickory nuts and pecans, and *C. occidentàlis* (Casey) attacks hazelnuts.

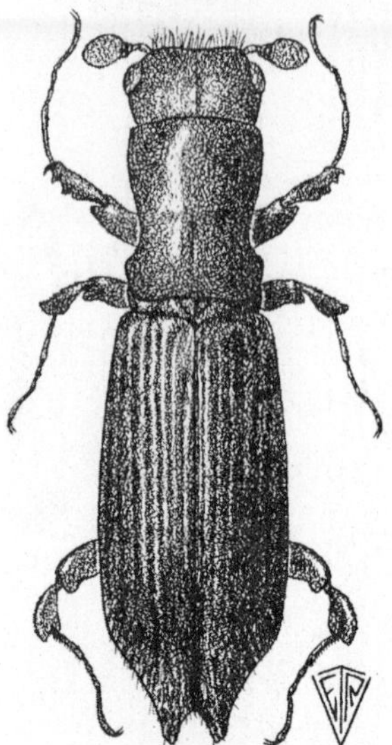

Figure 337. A pinhole borer, *Plátypus wílsoni* Swaine, 12 ×. (Courtesy of Arnett.)

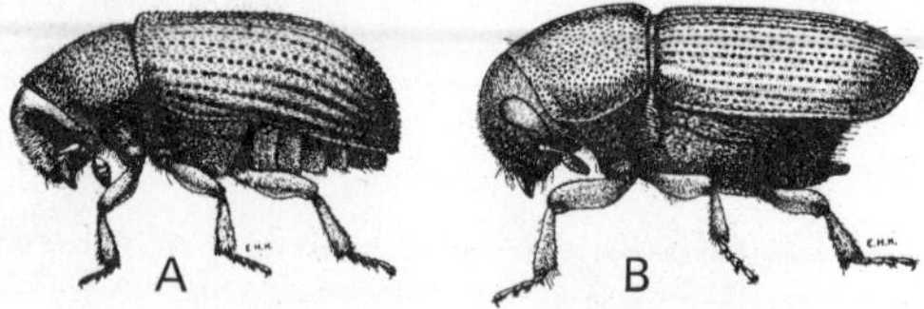

Figure 338. Elm bark beetles (Scolýtidae), 12 ×. A, native elm bark beetle, *Hylurgopìnus rùfipes* (Eichhoff); B, smaller European elm bark beetle, *Scólytus multistriàtus* (Marsham.) (Courtesy of Kaston and the Connecticut Agricultural Experiment Station.)

Subfamily **Cimberìnae (Nemonychìnae, Rhinomacerìnae)**—Pine-Flower Snout Beetles: This is a small group, with only seven species occurring in North America. These beetles are 3.0–4.5 mm in length, with the snout about as long as the prothorax and somewhat flattened and narrowed at the base; they differ from other subfamilies of Curculiónidae in having the labrum distinct and the palps flexible. The larvae of these beetles develop in the staminate flowers of various conifers; adults are usually found on conifers, but may occasionally be found on plum or peach trees.

Family **Platypódidae**—Pin-Hole Borers: The beetles in this group are elongate, slender, and cylindrical, with the head slightly wider than the pronotum; they are brownish in color and 4–6 mm in length (Figure 337). The tarsi are very slender, with the first segment longer than the remaining segments combined (Figure 251 K). Our only genus is *Plátypus*.

These beetles are wood-boring and bore in living trees, but they seldom attack a healthy tree; they generally attack deciduous trees. The larvae feed on fungi that are cultivated in their galleries.

Family **Scolýtidae**—Bark or Engraver Beetles, and Ambrosia or Timber Beetles: The scolytids are small cylindrical beetles, rarely over 6 or 8 mm in length and usually brownish or black in color, that feed in the inner bark or wood of trees. The family contains two groups, the bark or engraver beetles and the ambrosia or timber beetles; these groups are very similar in appearance (Figure 338), but the bark beetles have a large spine or projection at the apex of the front tibiae.

The bark or engraver beetles live beneath the bark of trees, mining on the surface of the hardwood but not entering it. Both adults and larvae mine under the bark. The adults enter first and excavate a characteristic gallery or group of galleries in which the eggs are laid. These brood galleries may be made by a single pair, or a male may have a harem of two or more females, each of which excavates a brood gallery. The eggs are laid in little notches at intervals along the sides of the brood galleries. When the eggs hatch, the larvae excavate tunnels leading away from the brood gallery; these tunnels get larger as the larva gets farther from the brood gallery, and they form a characteristic pattern under the bark (Figure 339). The pattern of these tunnels varies in different species. These scolytids are often called engraver beetles because of the elaborate patterns they excavate beneath the bark. When the larvae complete their growth, they pupate at the ends of their tunnels, and emerge through a round hole eaten through the bark. These numerous emergence holes resemble the holes that would be made by a charge of small lead shot.

Different species of bark beetles attack different species of trees; some attack only recently cut or dead logs or branches, while others attack living trees. Those that attack living trees, which are chiefly pests of evergreens, may tunnel under the bark to such an extent that the tree is girdled and dies.

Most of the bark beetles attacking pine belong to genera *Íps* and *Dendróctonus;* the latter contains some of the largest scolytids. Some of the bark beetles are important in the transmission of tree diseases: Dutch elm disease is transmitted chiefly by the smaller European elm bark beetle, *Scólytus multistriàtus* (Marsham) (Figure 338 B), a species imported from Europe. These beetles have already caused the death of thousands of American elm trees east of Illinois, and in 1950 were collected by the hundreds in San Jose, California, having previously been recorded no farther west than Iowa. The clover root borer, *Hylastìnus obscùrus* (Marsham), often causes serious damage to clover; the larvae tunnel in the roots of the clover and kill them.

The ambrosia or timber beetles bore into the hardwood of trees and feed on fungi that they cultivate in their galleries. They do not eat the wood, but do considerable damage by tunneling through it. The larvae develop in small cells adjoining the main galleries, and in most species the larvae are fed by the adults. Each species usually feeds on one particular type of fungus; when the females emerge and fly to another tree, they carry conidia of the fungus from the natal gallery to the new host and introduce the fungus into the gallery they excavate. After the eggs hatch, the females usually care for the larvae until they are full grown and pupate. To do this, they must keep the larval burrows supplied with fresh fungus, or "ambrosia," and they keep the galleries clean by carrying away the feces of the larvae.

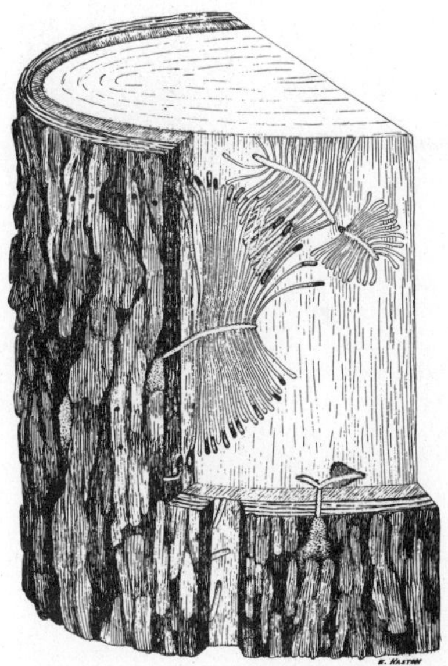

Figure 339. Semidiagrammatic drawing of a portion of a log containing galleries of bark beetle (Scolýtidae). The bark is cut through two entrance galleries, each with its accumulation of fine frass near the outside opening of the gallery. Three sets of galleries of different age are shown. In the one at the left the larvae are full grown and some have already pupated, and there is one empty pupal cell with its exit hole at the lower left corner of the cut-away section. Another entrance hole is evidenced by the frass accumulation on the bark at the left. (Courtesy of Kaston and the Connecticut Agricultural Experiment Station.)

COLLECTING AND PRESERVING COLEÓPTERA

Since this is such a large and varied group, most of the methods discussed in Chapter 34 for collecting and preserving insects are applicable here. Several general collecting procedures, however, may be noted: (1) many species may be taken by sweeping in a variety of situations; (2) many species, often strikingly colored, may be taken on flowers; (3) a number of species, such as the carrion beetles and others, may be obtained by means of suitably baited traps; (4) a number of species are attracted to lights at night, and may be collected at lights or in a light trap; (5) beetles of many groups are to be found under bark, in rotting wood, under stones, and in similar situations; (6) many species may be obtained by sifting debris or leaf litter; and (7) many beetles are aquatic and may be collected by the various aquatic equipment and methods described in Chapter 34.

Most beetles are preserved pinned (through the right elytron) or on points. When a beetle is mounted on a point, it is important that it be mounted so that the ventral side of the body and the legs are visible; the tip of the point may be bent down and the specimen attached to this bent-down tip by the right side of the thorax. It may sometimes be desirable to mount two specimens on the same point (when one is sure they are the same species), one dorsal side up and the other ventral side up. Many of the more minute beetles must be preserved in alcohol (70–80 percent) and mounted on a microscope slide for detailed study.

References on the Coleóptera

Arnett, R. H., Jr. 1958. A list of beetle families. *Coleop. Bull.*, 12:65–72.

Arnett, R. H., Jr. 1967. Recent and future systematics of the Coleoptera in North America. *Ann. Ent. Soc. Amer.*, 60(1):162–170; 2 f.

Arnett, R. H., Jr. 1968. *The Beetles of the United States (a Manual for Identification).* Ann Arbor, Mich.: The American Entomological Institute. xii + 1112 pp.; illus. This work originally appeared 1960–1962, published in loose-leaf sections (fascicles) by the Catholic University of America Press, Washington, D.C. The 1968 edition is essentially a reprinting of the original work bound in a single volume, with the same pagination (the indexes to individual fascicles are omitted, but their page numbers are retained) but with some changes in the introductory sections and some errors in the original work corrected.

Blatchley, W. S. 1910. *An Illustrated and Descriptive Catalogue of the Coleoptera or Beetles (Exclusive of the Rhynchophora) Known to Occur in Indiana*. Indianapolis, Ind.: Nature Publ. Co., 1385 pp., 590 f.

Blatchley, W. S., and C. W. Leng. 1916. *Rhynchophora or Weevils of Northeastern North America*. Indianapolis, Ind.: Nature Publ. Co., 682 pp., 155 f.

Böving, A. G., and F. C. Craighead. 1930. An illustrated synopsis of the principal larval forms of the order Coleoptera. *J. Ent. Soc. Amer.*, 11(1):1–351; 125 pl.

Bradley, J. C. 1930. *A Manual of the Genera of Beetles of America North of Mexico*. Ithaca, N.Y.: Daw, Illiston, 360 pp.

Brues, C. T., A. L. Melander, and F. M. Carpenter. 1954. Classification of insects. *Harvard Univ., Mus. Compar. Zool. Bull.*, 73; v + 917 pp., 1219 f.

The Coleopterists Bulletin. A quarterly journal containing papers on the Coleoptera, published by The Coleopterists Society (present address: Gainesville, Fla.).

Crowson, R. A. 1955. *The Natural Classification of the Families of Coleoptera*. London: Nathaniel Lloyd, 187 pp., 212 f.

Crowson, R. A. 1960. The phylogeny of the Coleoptera. *Ann. Rev. Ent.*, 5:111–134.

Dillon, E. S., and L. S. Dillon. 1961. *A Manual of Common Beetles of Eastern North America*. Evanston, Ill.: Row, Peterson, viii + 884 pp., 85 pl. (4 in color), 544 textf.

Edwards, J. G. 1949. *Coleoptera or Beetles East of the Great Plains*. Ann Arbor, Mich.: J. W. Edwards, 181 pp., 23 pl.

Edwards, J. G. 1950. *A Bibliographical Supplement to Coleoptera or Beetles East of the Great Plains, Applying Particularly to Western United States*, pp. 182–212. Published by the author, San Jose State College, San Jose, Calif.

Hatch, M. H. 1927. A systematic index to the keys for the determination of the nearctic Coleoptera. *Jr. N.Y. Ent. Soc.*, 35(3):279–306.

Hatch, M. H. 1953. *The Beetles of the Pacific Northwest. Part I: Introduction and Adephaga*. Seattle, Wash.: Univ. Washington Press, vii + 340 pp., 37 pl., 2 textf.

Hatch, M. H. 1957. The beetles of the Pacific Northwest. Part II: Staphyliniformia. *Univ. Wash. Publ. Biol.*, 16:1–384; illus.

Hatch, M. H. 1961. The beetles of the Pacific Northwest. Part III: Pselaphidae and Diversicornia I. *Univ. Wash. Publ. Biol.*, 16:i–ix, 1–503; 66 pl.

Hatch, M. H. 1965. The beetles of the Pacific Northwest. Part IV: Macrodactyles, Palpicornes, and Heteromera. *Univ. Wash. Publ. Biol.*, 16:i–viii, 1–268; 28 pl.

Hatch, M. H. 1973. *The Beetles of the Pacific Northwest. Part V: Rhipiceroidea, Sternoxi, Phytophaga, Rhynchophora, and Lamellicornia*. Seattle, Wash.: Univ. Washington Press, 650 pp.; illus.

Jaques, H. E. 1953. *How to Know the Beetles*. Dubuque, Iowa: Wm. C. Brown, iii + 372 pp., 865 f.

Kissinger, D. G. 1964. *Curculionidae of America North of Mexico. A Key to the Genera*. South Lancaster, Mass.: Taxonomic Publ., v + 143 pp., 59 f.

Leech, H. B., and H. P. Chandler. 1956. Aquatic Coleoptera. In *Aquatic Insects of California*, R. L. Usinger (Ed.). Berkeley, Calif.: Univ. California Press, pp. 293–371, 61 f.

Leech, H. B., and M. W. Sanderson. 1959. Coleoptera. In *Fresh-Water Biology*, W. T. Edmondson (Ed.). New York: Wiley, pp. 981–1023, 94 f.

Leng, C. W., *et al.* 1920–1948. *Catalogue of the Coleoptera of America North of Mexico*. Mt. Vernon, N.Y.: John D. Sherman. Original Catalogue, 1920: x + 470 pp. First Supplement, 1927, by C. W. Leng and A. J. Mutchler, 78 pp. Second and Third Supplements, 1933, by C. W. Leng and A. J. Mutchler, 112 pp. Fourth Supplement, 1939, by R. E. Blackwelder, 146 pp. Fifth Supplement, 1948, by R. E. Blackwelder and R. M. Blackwelder, 87 pp.

Linsley, E. G. 1961–1964. The Cerambycidae of North America. *Univ. Calif. Publ. Ent.* Part I, Introduction; 18:1–135; 16 f., 35 pl. (1961). Part II, Taxonomy and classification of the Parandrinae, Prioninae, Spondylinae, and Aseminae; 19:1–103; 34 f., 1 pl. (1962). Part III, Taxonomy and classification of the subfamily Cerambycinae, tribes Opsimini through Megaderini; 20:1–188; 56 f. (1962). Part IV, Taxonomy and classification of the subfamily Cerambycinae, tribes Elaphidionini through Rhinotragini; 21:1–165; 52 f. (1963). Part V, Taxonomy and classification of the subfamily Cerambycinae, tribes Callichromini through Ancylocerini; 22:1–197; 60 f. (1964).

Linsley, E. G., and J. A. Chemsak. 1972. Cerambycidae of North America. Part VI, No. 1. Taxonomy and classification of the subfamily Lepturinae. *Univ. Calif. Publ. Ent.*, 69:1–138; 2 pl., 41 textf.

Peterson, A. 1951. *Larvae of Insects. Part II. Coleoptera, Diptera, Neuroptera, Siphonaptera, Mecoptera, Trichoptera*. Ann Arbor, Mich.: Edwards Bros., v + 416 pp., 104 f.

Reichert, H. 1973. A critical study of the suborder Myxophaga, with a taxonomic revision of the Brazilian Torridincolidae and Hydroscaphidae (Coleoptera). *Arquivos de Zoology (São Paulo)*, 24(2): 73–162; 8 pl.

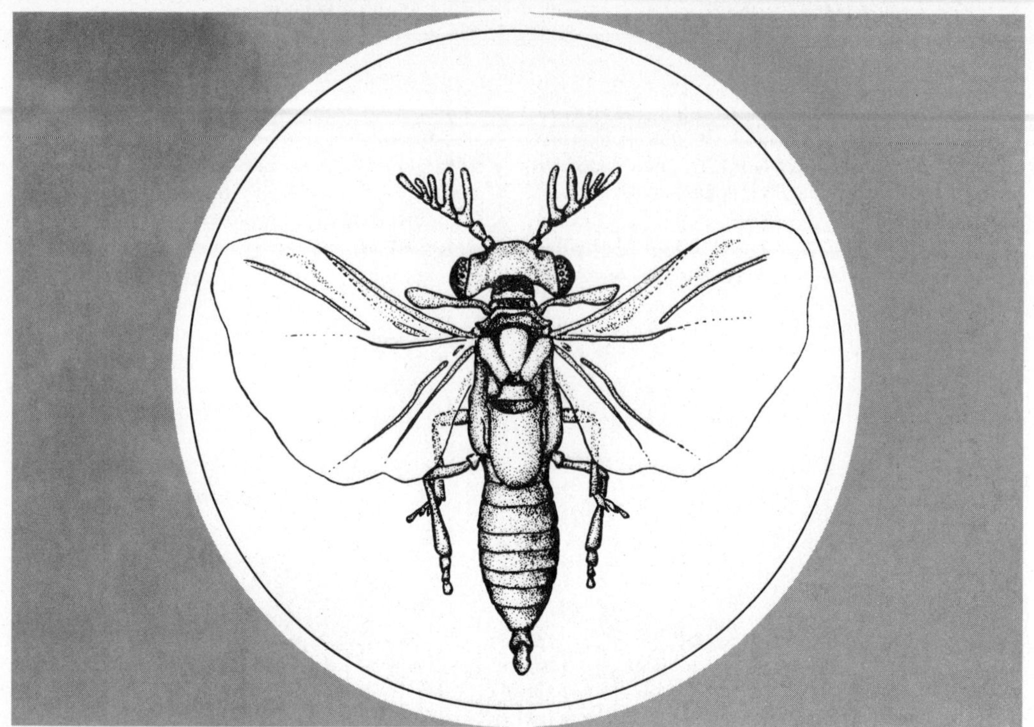

26: ORDER STREPSÍPTERA[1]
TWISTED-WINGED PARASITES

The Strepsíptera are minute insects, most of which are parasitic on other insects. The two sexes are quite different; the males are free-living and winged, while the females are wingless, often legless, and in the parasitic species, do not leave the host.

Male Strepsíptera (Figure 340 A–D) are somewhat beetlelike in appearance, with protruding eyes, and the antennae often have elongate processes on some segments; the front wings are reduced to clublike structures that resemble the halteres of the Díptera; the hind wings are large and membranous, fanlike, and have a reduced venation. The adult females of the free-living species (Figure 340 E) have a distinct head, with simple 4- or 5-segmented antennae, chewing mouth parts, and compound eyes. The females of the parasitic species usually lack eyes, antennae, and legs, the body segmentation is very indistinct, and the head and thorax are fused (Figure 340 G). The metamorphosis is complete.

The life history of the parasitic forms in this order is rather complex and involves hypermetamorphosis. A male, on emerging, seeks out and mates with a female, which never leaves its host. The female produces large numbers—up to several thousand—of tiny larvae, which escape from her body and the body of the host to the soil or to vegetation. These larvae, which are called

[1] Strepsíptera: *strepsi,* twisted; *ptera,* wings.

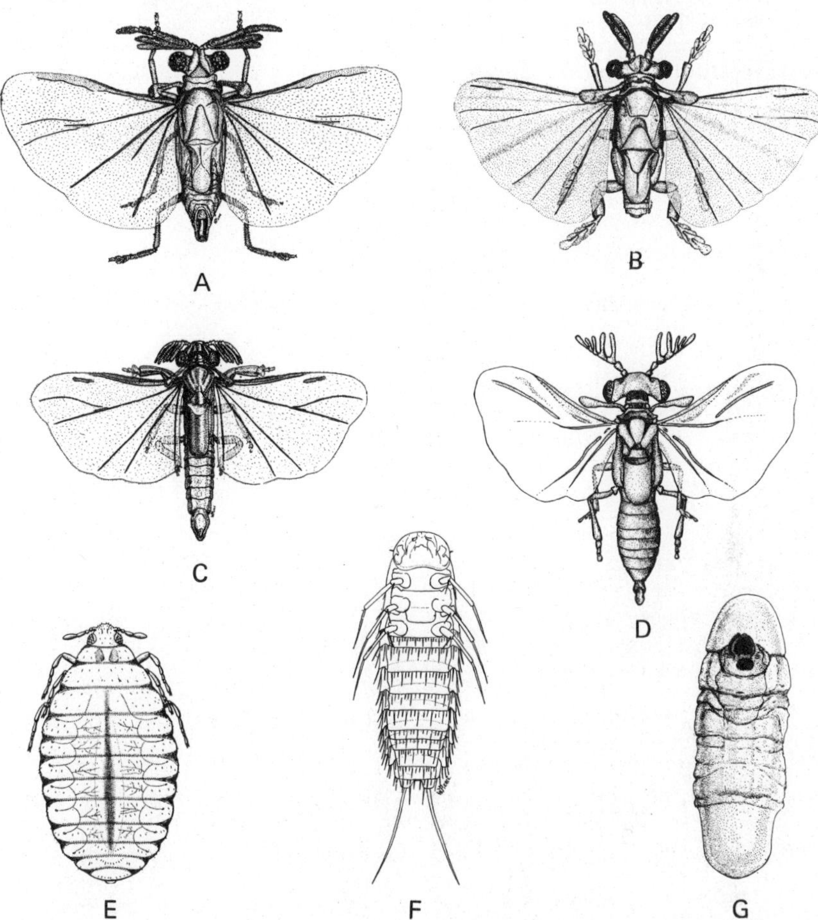

Figure 340. Strepsíptera. A, *Triozócera mexicàna* Pierce (Mengèidae), male; B, *Neostỳlops shánnoni* Pierce (Stylópidae), male; C, *Halictóphagus oncometòpiae* (Pierce) (Halictophágidae), male; D, *Halictóphagus serràtus* Bohart (Halictophágidae), male; E, *Eoxènos laboulbénei* Peyerimhoff (Mengèidae), female; F, *Stỳlops califòrnica* Pierce (Stylópidae), triungulin, ventral view; G, *Halictóphagus oncometòpiae* (Pierce) (Halictophágidae), female, ventral view. (A–C, F, and G, courtesy of Pierce; D, courtesy of Bohart; E, courtesy of Parker and Smith; A–C, courtesy of the U.S. National Museum; D–E, courtesy of the Entomological Society of America; F–G, courtesy of the U.S. National Museum.)

triungulins, have well-developed eyes and legs (Figure 340 F) and are fairly active insects; they locate and enter the body of the host. Once there, the larva molts into a legless wormlike stage that feeds in the host's body cavity. After several molts, it pupates inside the last larval skin. The male, on emerging, leaves its host and flies about; the female remains in the host, with the anterior part of its body protruding between the abdominal segments of the host; after the young are produced, it dies.

Various species of Orthóptera, Hemíptera, Homóptera, Hymenóptera, and Thysanùra serve as the hosts of Strepsíptera. The host is not always killed, but may be injured; the shape or color of the abdomen may be changed, or the sex organs may be damaged. The developing male strepsipteran usually causes more damage to its host than the female.

Many entomologists place the Strepsíptera in the order Coleóptera (usually as a single family, the Stylópidae), largely because of the similarity in life history (hypermetamorphosis) between these insects and the Melòidae and Rhipiphòridae. The status of the Strepsíptera is controversial; we follow Pierce (1964), who presents convincing evidence that they should be treated as a separate order.

Key to the Families of Strepsíptera (Males)

1. Tarsi 5-segmented, with 2 claws (Figure 340 A) .... **Mengèidae** p. 444
1′. Tarsi with 4 or fewer segments, and without claws (Figure 340 B–D) 2
2(1′). Tarsi 4-segmented; antennae 4- or 6-segmented (Figure 340 B) .... **Stylópidae** p. 444
2′. Tarsi 2- or 3-segmented; antennae 4- or 7-segmented (Figure 340 C, D) 3
3(2′). Tarsi 2-segmented; antennae 4-segmented .... **Elénchidae** p. 444
3′. Tarsi 3-segmented; antennae 7-segmented, the third, fourth, and fifth segments prolonged laterally, and the seventh segment elongate (Figure 340 C, D) .... **Halictophágidae** p. 444

Family **Mengèidae:** This group includes species that are free-living as adults, with the immature stages parasitizing Thysanùra; the adults are usually found under stones. No females of this group have been found in this country, but males of one species have been taken in Texas.

Family **Stylópidae:** This is the largest family in the order. Most of its members are parasitic on bees (Andrènidae, Halíctidae, and Hylaeìnae), but some are parasitic on wasps (Polistìnae, Eumenìnae, and Sphecìnae).

Family **Elénchidae:** The members of this small (two North American species) but widely distributed group are parasites of planthoppers (Fulgoròidea).

Family **Halictophágidae:** This is the second largest family in the order, with about 14 North American species. Its members are parasites of leafhoppers, planthoppers, treehoppers, and pygmy grasshoppers.

COLLECTING AND PRESERVING STREPSÍPTERA

The most satisfactory way to collect Strepsíptera is to collect parasitized hosts and rear out the parasites. Bees, wasps, leafhoppers, planthoppers, and other insects may harbor Strepsíptera. The parasitized hosts can often be recognized by the distorted abdomen, and one end of the parasite sometimes protrudes from between two of the abdominal segments. Some Strepsíptera occur under stones, and a few (males) may be attracted to lights. Males of *Stỳlops* are attracted to virgin females in hosts (bees) that are placed in screen cages and may be collected on or flying about the cages (MacSwain, 1949).

Strepsíptera should be preserved in alcohol, and for detailed study should be mounted on microscope slides.

References on the Strepsíptera

Bohart, R. M. 1936–1937. A preliminary study of the genus *Stylops* in California. *Pan-Pac. Ent.*, 12(1):9–18; 1 pl. (1936). 13(1–2):49–57; 1 pl. (1937).

Bohart, R. M. 1941. A revision of the Strepsiptera with special reference to the species of North America. *Calif. Univ. Pub. Ent.*, 7(6):91–160; f. A–H.

Bohart, R. M. 1943. New species of *Halictophagus* with a key to the genus in North America (Strepsiptera, Halictophagidae). *Ann. Ent. Soc. Amer.*, 36(3): 341–359; 47 f.

MacSwain, J. W. 1949. A method for collecting male *Stylops*. *Pan-Pac. Ent.*, 25(2):89–90.

Pierce, W. D. 1909. A monographic revision of the twisted-winged insects comprising the order Strepsiptera. *U.S. Natl. Mus. Bull.*, No. 66; xiii + 232 pp., 3 f., 15 pl., 1 map.

Pierce, W. D. 1918. The comparative morphology of the order Strepsiptera together with records and descriptions of insects. *Proc. U.S. Natl. Mus.*, 54(2242):391–501; pl. 64–78.

Pierce, W. D. 1964. The Strepsiptera are a true order, unrelated to Coleoptera. *Ann. Ent. Soc. Amer.*, 57(5):603–605.

Sylvestri, F. 1942. Nuove osservazione sulla *Mengenilla parvula* Silvestri (Insecta Strepsiptera). *Pontif. Acad. Sci. Acta Rome,* 6:95–96.

Ulrich, W. 1966. Evolution and classification of the Strepsiptera. *Proc. 1st. Internat. Congr. Parasitol.*, 1:609–611.

27: ORDER MECÓPTERA[1]

SCORPIONFLIES

The scorpionflies are medium-sized, slender-bodied insects with a long-faced appearance (Figure 341). The mouth parts, which are of the chewing type, are prolonged ventrally to form a beaklike structure; this peculiar head shape (Figure 342) is one of the most characteristic features of the scorpionflies. Most of the Mecóptera have four long and narrow membranous wings; the front and hind wings are similar in size and shape and have a similar venation (Figure 344). The venation is rather generalized, with numerous cross veins. The metamorphosis is complete, and the larvae (Figure 343) are usually eruciform (scarabaeiform in *Bòreus*).

Most of the scorpionflies are from 18 to 25 mm in length, and are usually found in woods, ravines, and similar areas of dense vegetation. The eggs are generally laid in the ground, and the larvae live either in or on the surface of the soil, feeding chiefly on dead insects and other animal matter. The common name for these insects is derived from the structure of the male genitalia in the family Panórpidae, which are bulbous and recurved and look a little like the sting of a scorpion (Figure 341). Unlike scorpions, however, these insects are quite harmless to man.

[1] Mecóptera: *meco,* long; *ptera,* wings.

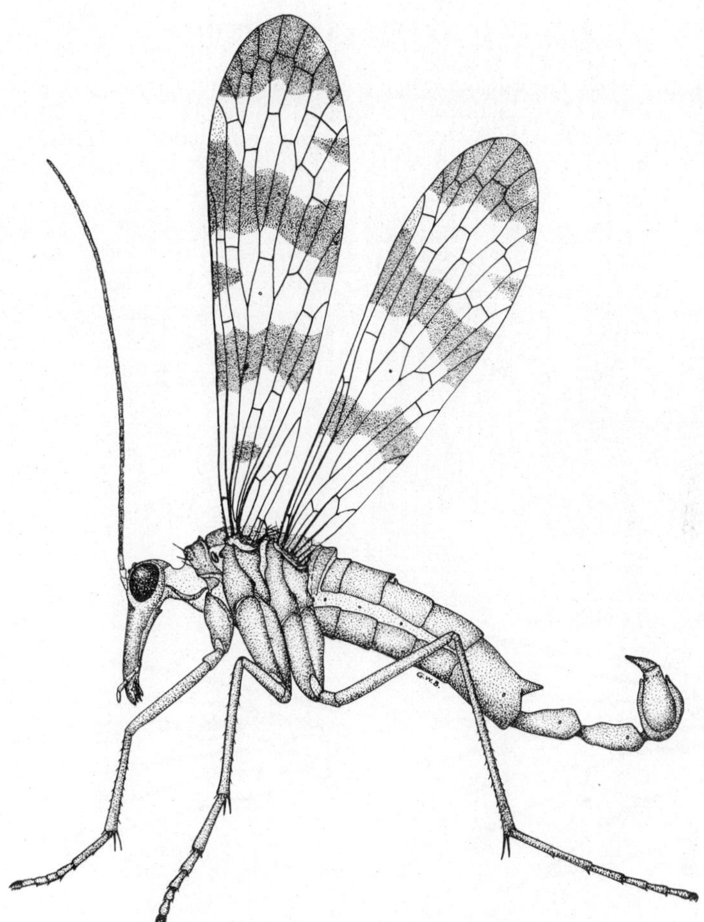

Figure 341. A male scorpionfly, *Panórpa hélena* Byers.

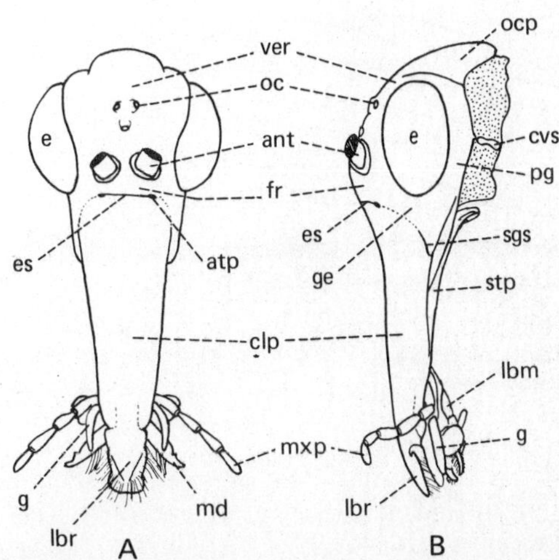

Figure 342. *(left)* Head of *Panórpa*. A, anterior view; B, lateral view. *ant*, antenna; *atp*, anterior tentorial pit; *clp*, clypeus; *cvs*, cervical sclerite; e, compound eye; *es*, epistomal suture; *fr*, frons; g, galea; *ge*, gena; *lbm*, labium; *lbr*, labrum; *md*, mandible; *mxp*, maxillary palp; *oc*, ocelli; *ocp*, occiput; *pg*, postgena; *sgs*, subgenal suture; *stp*, stipes; *ver*, vertex. (Redrawn from Ferris and Rees.)

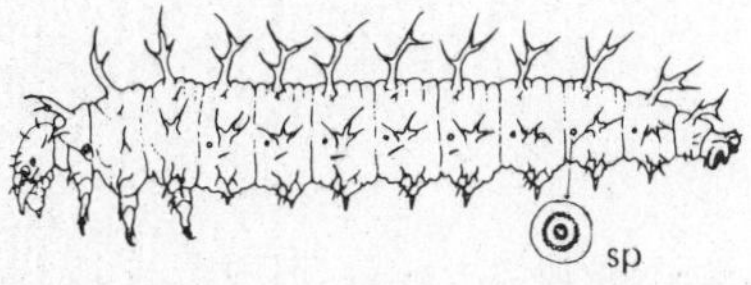

Figure 343. Larva of a scorpionfly (*Bíttacus*). *sp*, spiracle. (Courtesy of Peterson. Reprinted by permission.)

Key to the Families of Mecóptera

1. Wings reduced, bristlelike in male and scalelike in female (Figure 346); tarsi with 2 claws; dark-colored insects, 2–5 mm in length .... **Borèidae** p. 449

1′. Wings nearly always well developed, if reduced (females of *Brachypanórpa,* family Panórpidae) not bristlelike or scalelike or if absent

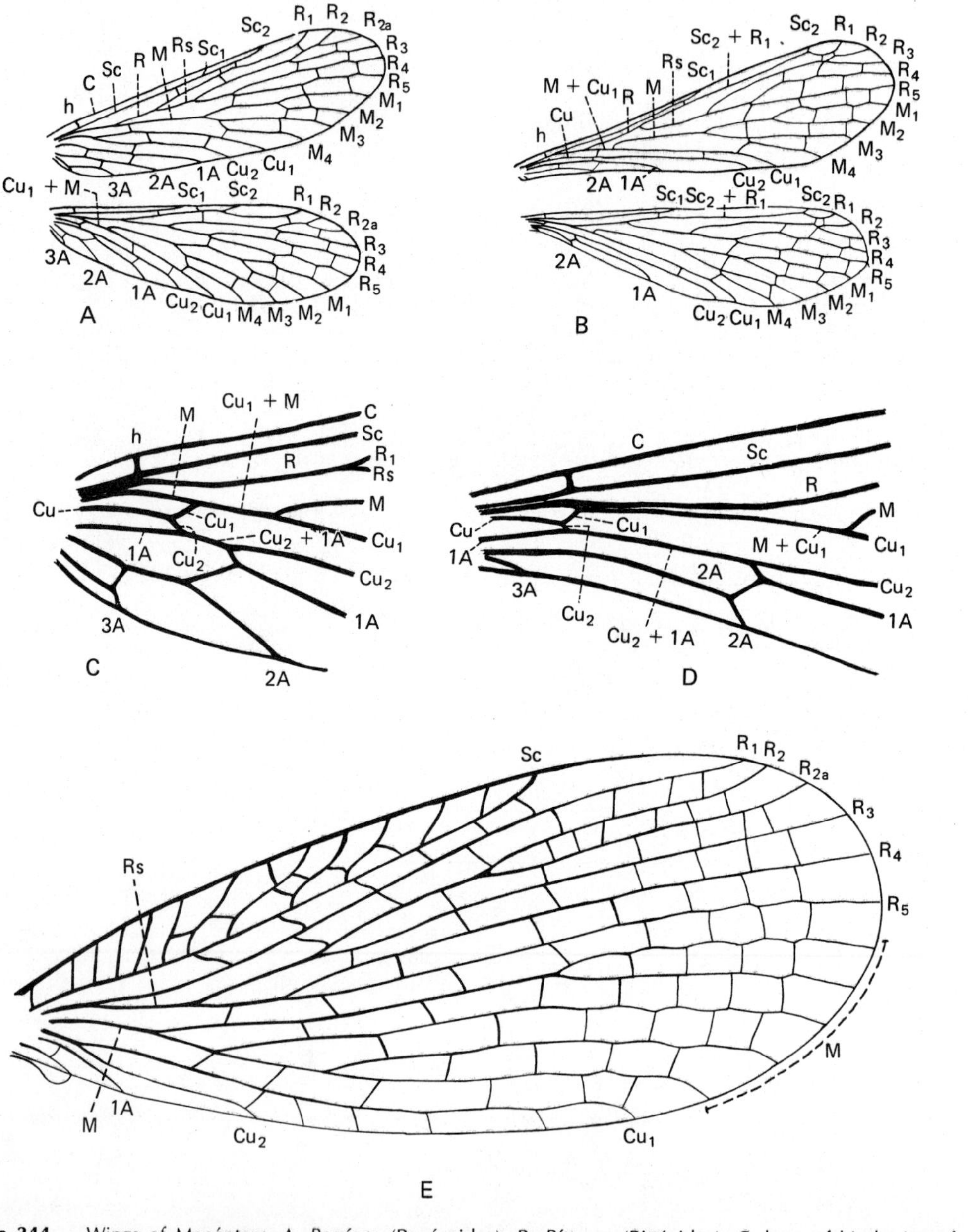

Figure 344. Wings of Mecóptera. A, *Panórpa* (Panórpidae); B, *Bíttacus* (Bittácidae); C, base of hind wing of *Panórpa;* D, base of hind wing of *Bíttacus;* E, front wing of *Mérope* (Meropèidae).

(*Apterobíttacus,* western United States, family Bittácidae) the tarsi have only one claw 2

2(1′ . Tarsi with 1 claw (Figure 345 B); fifth tarsal segment capable of being folded back on fourth; Rs 4-branched .... **Bittácidae** p. 450

2′. Tarsi with 2 claws (Figure 345 A); fifth tarsal segment not capable of being folded back on fourth; Rs usually with 5 or more branches 3

3(2′). Wings relatively broad, M with more than 4 branches (Figure 344 E), and the wings not patterned; male with a pair of forcepslike claspers at apex of abdomen (Figure 345 C); ocelli absent; a single rare species occurring in the eastern United States .... **Meropèidae** p. 449

3′. Wings narrower, M with only 4 branches, and the wings often patterned (Figures 341 and 344 A); male without claspers as described above, but with genitalia bulbous and recurved (Figure 341); ocelli present; a large and widely distributed group .... **Panórpidae** p. 449

Family **Borèidae**—Snow Scorpionflies: These insects are usually found in moss, on which they apparently feed; they are often found on the snow in the winter. The reduced and bristlelike wings of the male are used in grasping the female at the time of mating. This group is represented in North America by 14 species of *Bòreus,* two occurring in the East and 12 in the West; the two eastern species are *B. brumàlis* Fitch (Figure 346), a shiny black species, and *B. nivoriúndus* Fitch, a dull brown species. Hinton (1958) puts this family in a separate order, the Neomecóptera.

Family **Meropèidae**—Earwigflies: This group is represented in the United States by a single species, *Mérope tùber* Newman; this insect is dull brownish, somewhat flattened, with relatively broad wings (Figure 344 E), and 10–12 mm in length; the male has a pair of long forcepslike claspers at the apex of the abdomen (Figure 345 C). This species has been taken in the eastern United States and Ontario, south to northern Georgia, and west to the upper Mississippi Valley and Missouri (Byers, 1973); it is quite rare, and most specimens have been taken at lights or in traps.

Family **Panórpidae**—Common Scorpionflies: The male genitalia in this group are bulbous and recurved, and resemble the sting of a scorpion (Fig-

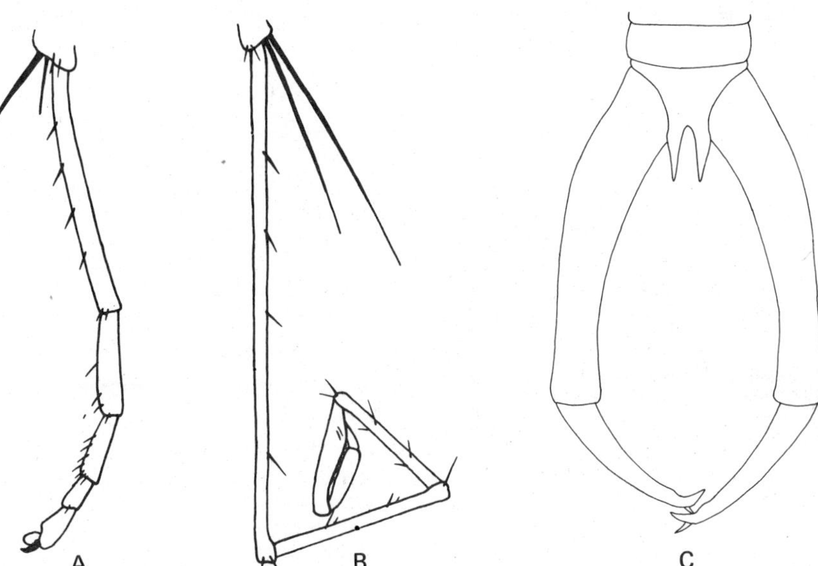

Figure 345. A, tarsus of *Panórpa* (Panórpidae); B, tarsus of *Bíttacus* (Bittácidae); C, anal appendages of a male *Mérope* (Meropèidae).

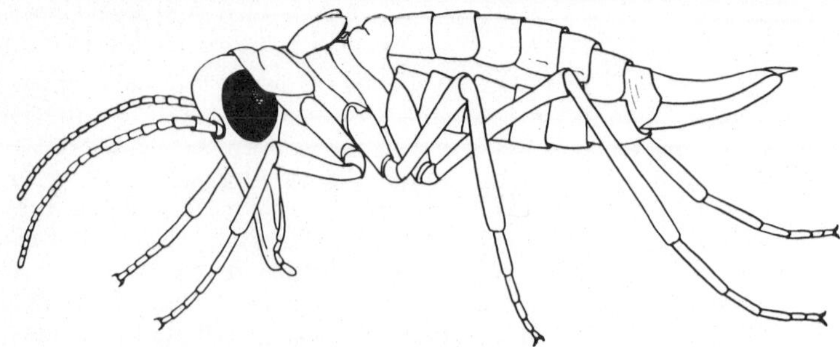

Figure 346. A snow scorpionfly, *Bòreus brumàlis* Fitch, female.

ure 341). These scorpionflies are usually yellowish brown in color with spotted or banded wings. The adults feed principally on dead insects. Two genera occur in the United States, *Panórpa* and *Brachypanórpa* (the latter is sometimes placed in a separate family, the Panorpódidae). *Panórpa* is widely distributed throughout the central and eastern states, and is represented by over 40 species. *Brachypanórpa,* which has a short face and Rs 4-branched, is represented by one species occurring in the southern Appalachian Mountains from Virginia to northern Georgia, and two species in the mountains of Oregon and Montana; the females in this genus have very short wings and are flightless.

Family **Bittácidae** – Hanging Scorpionflies, Hangingflies: The bittacids are yellowish brown and long-legged, about 25 mm in length or less, and look very much like crane flies. The wings are much narrower at the base than are those of the Panórpidae (Figure 344). One species occurring in California, *Apterobíttacus ápterus* (MacLachlan), is wingless. These insects spend most of their time hanging by their front legs from leaves and twigs. The adults are predaceous and capture their prey (while hanging) with their hind legs; the prey consists of small insects such as flies, aphids, caterpillars, and occasionally spiders. In captivity, bittacids are often cannibalistic.

Only a single genus, *Bíttacus,* with about half a dozen species, occurs in the eastern United States and California. *B. apicàlis* Hagen, which has dark wing tips, hangs with its wings outstretched; the other species hang with the wings folded back over the abdomen.

References on the Mecóptera

Barnes, J. W. 1956. Notes on Minnesota Mecoptera. *Ent. News,* 57(7):191–192.

Byers, G. W. 1954. Notes on North American Mecoptera. *Ann. Ent. Soc. Amer.,* 47(3):484–510; 17 f.

Byers, G. W. 1963. The life history of *Panorpa nuptialis* (Mecoptera: Panorpidae). *Ann. Ent. Soc. Amer.,* 56(2):142–149; 6 f.

Byers, G. W. 1965. Families and genera of Mecoptera. *Proc. 12th Int. Congr. Ent. London* (1964): 123.

Byers, G. W. 1973. Zoogeography of the Meropeidae (Mecoptera). *J. Kan. Ent. Soc.,* 46(4):511–516; 2 f.

Carpenter, F. M. 1931a. Revision of Nearctic Mecoptera. *Bull. Harvard Univ. Mus. Comp. Zool.,* 72:205–277; 5 pl.

Carpenter, F. M. 1931b. The biology of the Mecoptera. *Psyche,* 38(2):41–55.

Cooper, K. W. 1972. A southern California *Boreus, B. notoperates* n. sp. I. Comparative morphology and systematics (Mecoptera: Boreidae). *Psyche,* 79(4):269–283; 11 f.

Cooper, K. W. 1974. Sexual biology, chromosomes, development, life histories and parasites of *Boreus,* especially of *B. notoperates,* a southern California *Boreus.* II (Mecoptera: Boreidae). *Psyche,* 81(1):84–120; 4 f.

Hinton, H. E. 1958. The phylogeny of the panorpoid orders. *Ann. Rev. Ent.,* 3:181–206.

Setty, L. R. 1940. Biology and morphology of some North American Bittacidae. *Amer. Midl. Nat.,* 23(2):257–353; 178 f.

Tillyard, R. J. 1935. The evolution of the scorpion-flies and their derivatives (Order Mecoptera). *Ann. Ent. Soc. Amer.,* 28(1):1–45; 24 f., 2 tab.

28: ORDER TRICHÓPTERA[1]
CADDISFLIES

The caddisflies are small to medium-sized insects, somewhat similar to moths in general appearance. The four membranous wings are rather hairy (and occasionally bear scales also) and are usually held rooflike over the abdomen at rest. The antennae are long and slender. Most caddisflies are rather dull-colored insects, but a few are conspicuously patterned. The mouth parts are of the chewing type, with the palps well developed but with the mandibles much reduced; the adults feed principally on liquid foods. Caddisflies undergo complete metamorphosis, and the larvae are aquatic.

Caddisfly larvae are caterpillarlike, with a well-developed head and thoracic legs, and a pair of hooklike appendages at the end of the abdomen; the abdominal segments bear filamentous gills (Figure 353). Caddisfly larvae occur in various types of aquatic habitats; some occur in ponds or lakes, and others occur in streams. Some larvae are case makers, others construct nets under water, and a few are free-living.

The cases of the case-making larvae are made of bits of leaves, twigs, sand grains, pebbles, or other materials, and are of various shapes (Figure 352); each species builds a very characteristic type of case, and in some species the young larvae build a case different from that made by older larvae. The materials used in making the case are fastened together with silk, or they may be cemented together. Case-making larvae are plant feeders. The nets of the net-making species (found in streams) are made of silk spun from modified

[1] Trichóptera: *tricho,* hair; *ptera,* wings.

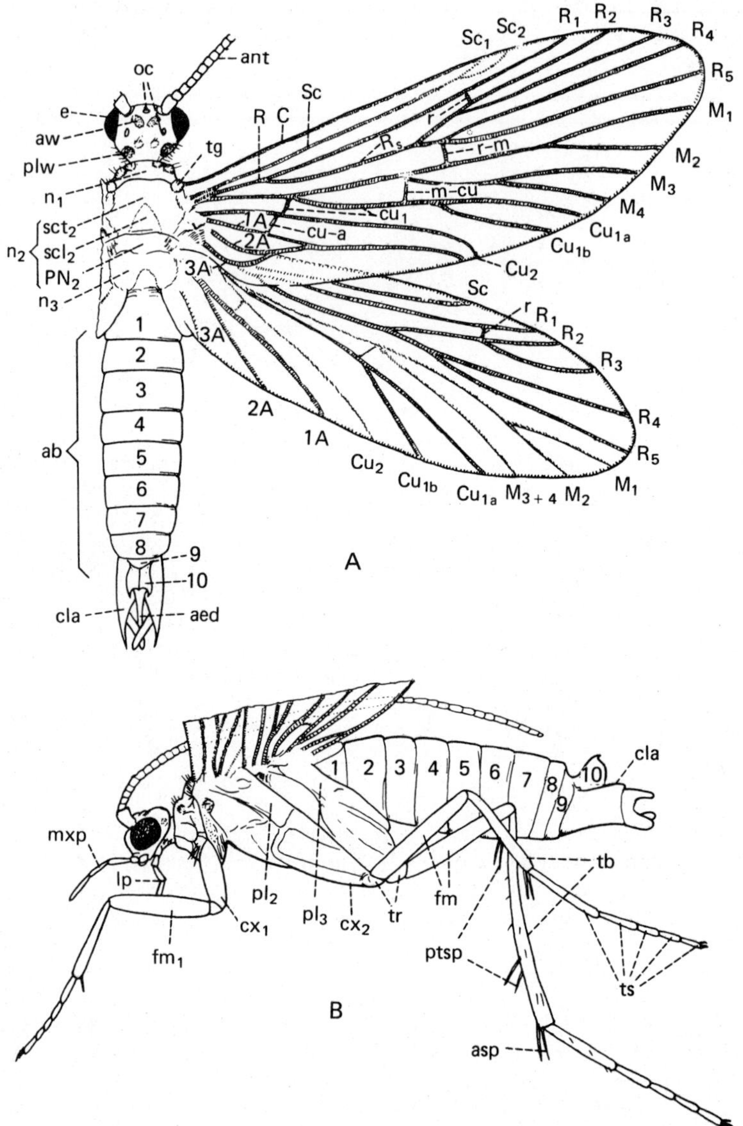

Figure 347. Structure of a caddisfly. A, dorsal view; B, lateral view. *ab,* abdomen; *aed,* aedeagus; *ant,* antenna; *asp,* apical spur; *aw,* anterior wart; *cla,* clasper; *cx,* coxa; e, compound eye; *fm,* femur; *lp,* labial palp; *mxp,* maxillary palp; n_1, pronotum; n_2, mesonotum; n_3, metanotum; *oc,* ocelli; pl_2, mesopleuron; pl_3, metapleuron; *plw,* posterolateral wart; PN_2, postnotum of mesothorax; *ptsp,* preapical tibial spur; scl_2, mesoscutellum; sct_2, mesoscutum; *tb,* tibia; *tg,* tegula; *tr,* trochanter; *ts,* tarsus; *1–10,* abdominal segments. (Redrawn from Ross.)

salivary glands, and may be trumpet-shaped, finger-shaped, or cup-shaped, with the open end facing upstream; they are often attached to the downstream side of a rock or other object over which the water flows. The larvae spend their time near these nets (often in a crevice or retreat of some sort), and feed on the materials caught in the nets. The free-living caddisfly larvae, which construct neither cases nor nets, are generally predaceous.

The larvae fasten their cases to some object in the water when they have completed their growth, seal the opening (or openings) in the case, and pupate in the case. When the pupa is fully developed, it cuts its way out of the case with its mandibles (which are well developed in this stage), swims to the surface, crawls out of the water onto a stone, stick, or similar object, and the adult emerges.

The wing venation of caddisflies (Figure 347 A) is rather generalized, and there are few cross veins. The subcosta is usually 2-branched, the radius 5-branched, the media 4-branched in the front wing and 3-branched in the hind wing, and the cubitus is 3-branched. The anal veins in the front wing usually form two **Y** veins near the base of the wing. Most species have a characteristic wing spot in the fork of R_{4+5}. Cu_2 in the hind wing usually fuses basally with 1A for a short distance. In naming the cubital and anal veins in this order we follow the interpretation of Ross and others rather than that of Comstock; the veins we call Cu_{1a} and Cu_{1b} are called Cu_1 and Cu_2, respectively, by Comstock, who considers the remaining veins to be anal veins. In some groups (for example, Figure 347 A), the basal part of Cu_1 in the front wing appears like a cross vein, and what looks like the basal part of Cu_1 is really a mediocubital cross vein (this cross vein is termed M_5 by Tillyard and others).

The majority of the caddisflies are rather weak fliers. The wings are vestigial in the females of a few species. The eggs are laid in masses or strings of several hundred, either in the water or on objects near the water. The adult in many species enters the water and attaches its eggs to stones or other objects. The eggs usually hatch in a few days, and in most species the larva requires nearly a year to develop. The adults usually live about a month. Adult caddisflies are frequently attracted to lights.

The chief biological importance of this group lies in the fact that the larvae are an important part of the food of many fish and other aquatic animals.

CLASSIFICATION OF THE TRICHÓPTERA

The arrangement of families followed here is that of Ross (1944), who recognizes 17 families in our area. These families are sometimes arranged in two or more groups, but Ross does not recognize any suborders in this order. The characters used in separating families of adult caddisflies are principally those of the thoracic warts, the ocelli, the maxillary palps, and spurs and spines on the legs, and the wing venation.

The thoracic warts, which are of considerable value in separating families, are wartlike or tuberclelike structures on the dorsum of the thorax, and are often more hairy than the surrounding areas; they vary in size, number, and arrangement, and some of these variations are shown in Figure 350. These warts are very difficult to interpret in pinned specimens, since they are often destroyed or distorted by the pin; for this and other reasons, caddisflies should be preserved in alcohol rather than on pins.

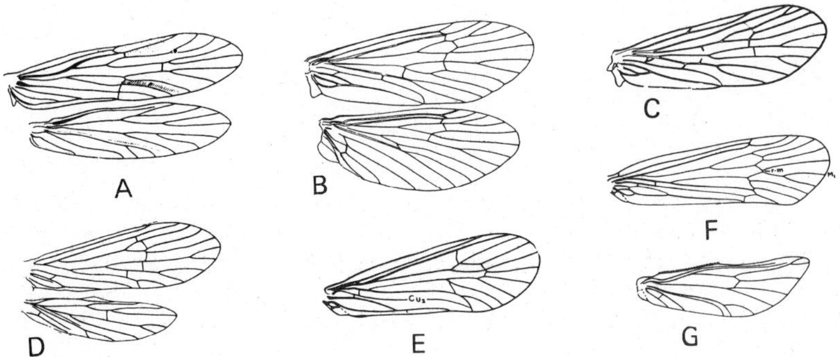

Figure 348. Wings of Trichóptera. A, *Dibùsa angàta* Ross (Hydroptílidae); B, *Aphropsỳche àprilis* Ross (Hydropsỳchidae); C, front wing of *Trentònius distínctus* (Walker) (Philopotámidae); D, *Psychomỳia nómada* (Ross) (Psychomyìidae); E, front wing of *Sericóstoma crassicórnis* (Walker) (Sericostomátidae); F, front wing of *Phanocèlia canadénsis* (Banks) (Limnephílidae); G, hind wing of *Helicopsỳche boreàlis* (Hagen) (Helicopsỳchidae). (Courtesy of Ross and the Illinois Natural History Survey.)

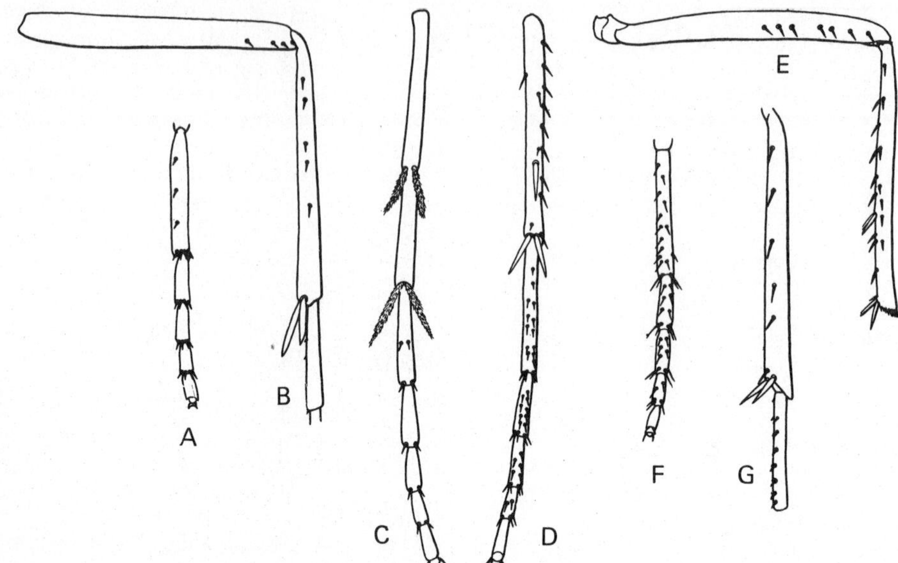

Figure 349. Legs of Trichóptera. A, middle tarsus of *Beraèa górteba* Ross (Beraèidae); B, middle leg of *Beraèa górteba* Ross; C, middle tibia and tarsus of *Theliopsỳche coròna* Ross (Lepidostomátidae); D, middle tibia and tarsus of *Brachycéntrus numeròsus* (Say) (Brachycéntridae); E, middle leg of *Molánna unióphila* Vorheis (Molánnidae); F, middle tarsus of *Sericóstoma crassicórnis* (Walker) (Sericostomátidae); G, middle tibia of *Sericóstoma crassicórnis* (Walker). (Courtesy of Ross and the Illinois Natural History Survey.)

The maxillary palps are nearly always 5-segmented in females, but may contain fewer segments in the males of some groups; the size and form of particular segments may differ in different families (Figure 351). Some variation in the spination of the legs is shown in Figure 349; the most important variations are in the number of tibial spurs, which may vary up to a maximum of four—two apical and two near the middle of the tibia. Wing venation is not a very important character in separating the families of caddisflies.

Key to the Families of Trichóptera

Families marked with an asterisk in this key are small and unlikely to be encountered by the general collector. Keys to larvae are given by Denning (1956), Krafka (1915), Pennak (1953), and Ross (1944, 1959).

1.	Mesoscutellum with posterior portion forming a flat triangular area with steep sides, and mesoscutum without warts; front tibiae never with more than 1 spur; some wing hairs clubbed; antennae short (Figure 354 F); length 6 mm or less .... **Hydroptílidae**	p. 458
1′.	Either mesoscutellum evenly convex, without a triangular portion set off by steep sides, or mesoscutum with warts; tibial spurs variable; no wing hairs clubbed; antennae usually as long as or longer than wings; length 5–40 mm 2	
2(1′).	Ocelli present 3	
2′.	Ocelli absent 8	
3(2).	Maxillary palps 3-segmented; males .... **Limnephílidae**	p. 459
3′.	Maxillary palps 4- or 5-segmented 4	

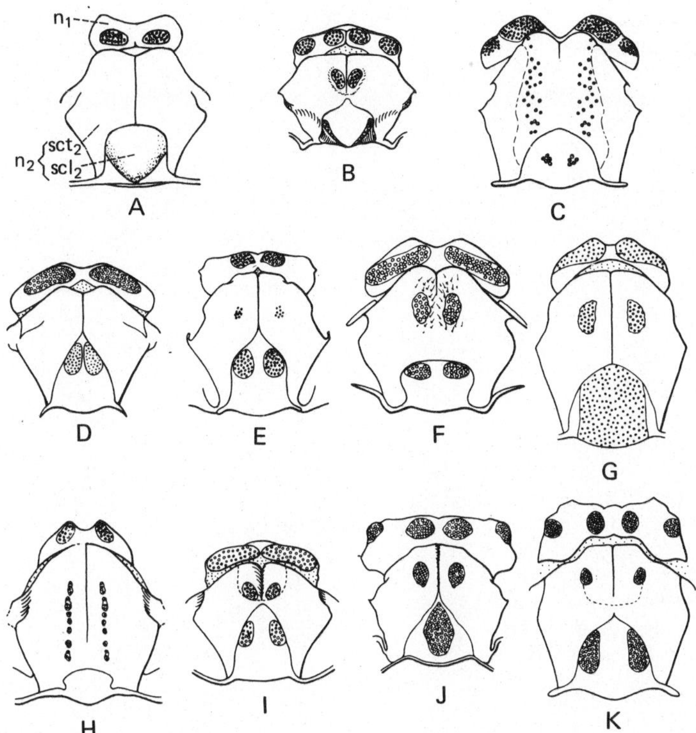

Figure 350. Pro- and mesonota of Trichóptera. A, *Hydropsỳche símulans* Ross (Hydropsỳchidae); B, *Psychomỳia flávida* Hagen (Psychomyìidae); C, *Anthripsòdes tarsi-punctàtus* (Vorheis) (Leptocéridae); D, *Beraèa górteba* Ross (Beraèidae); E, *Brachycéntrus numeròsus* (Say) (Brachycéntridae); F, *Helicopsỳche boreàlis* (Hagen) (Helicopsỳchidae); G, *Psilotrèta frontàlis* Banks (Odontocéridae); H, *Ganonèma americànum* (Walker) (Calamocerátidae); I, *Sericóstoma crassicórnis* (Walker) (Sericostomátidae); J, *Goèra calcaràta* Banks (Goèridae); K, *Theliopsỳche* sp. (Lepidostomátidae). n_1, pronotum; n_2, mesonotum; scl_2, mesoscutellum; sct_2, mesoscutum. (Courtesy of Ross and the Illinois Natural History Survey.)

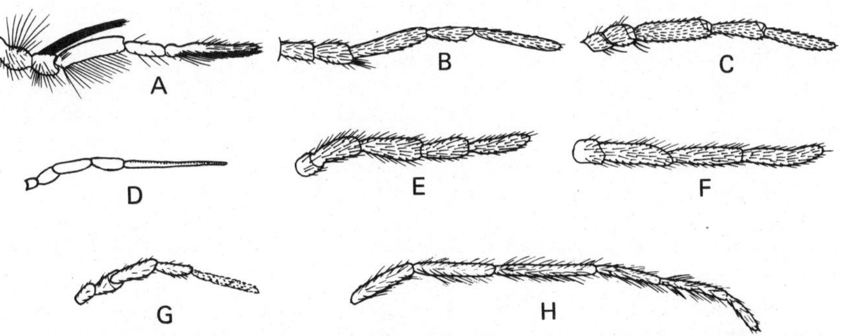

Figure 351. Maxillary palps of Trichóptera. A, *Psilotrèta* sp., male (Odontocéridae); B, *Dolóphilus shawnee* Ross, male (Philopotámidae); C, *Rhyacóphila lobífera* Betten, male (Rhyacophílidae); D, *Macronèmum zebràtum* (Hagen) (Hydropsỳchidae); E, *Banksìola selìna* Betten, female (Phryganèidae); F, *Banksìola selìna* Betten, male (Phryganèidae); G, *Cyrnéllus marginàlis* (Banks) (Psychomyìidae); H, *Triaenòdes tárda* Milne, male (Leptocéridae). (Courtesy of Ross and the Illinois Natural History Survey.)

4(3′).	Maxillary palps 4-segmented (Figure 351 F); males .... **Phryganèidae**	p. 459
4′.	Maxillary palps 5-segmented 5	
5(4′).	Maxillary palps with fifth segment 2 or 3 times as long as fourth (Figure 351 B) .... **Philopotámidae**	p. 457
5′.	Maxillary palps with fifth segment not more than $1\frac{1}{3}$ times as long as fourth (Figure 351 C) 6	
6(5′).	Maxillary palps with second segment short, subequal to first (Figure 351 C); labrum evenly rounded and fairly wide; males and females .... **Rhyacophílidae**	p. 457
6′.	Maxillary palps with second segment much longer than first; labrum with a wide basal portion set off by a crease from a long tonguelike apex; females 7	
7(6′).	Front tibiae with 2 or more spurs; middle tibiae with 4 spurs (as in Figure 349 C) .... **Phryganèidae**	p. 459
7′.	Front tibiae with 1 spur or none; middle tibiae with 2 or 3 spurs .... **Limnephílidae**	p. 459
8(2′).	Maxillary palps with 5 or more segments 9	
8′.	Maxillary palps with less than 5 segments 11	
9(8).	Terminal segment of maxillary palps much longer than the preceding segment and with close suturelike cross striae that are not possessed by the other segments (Figure 351 G) 10	
9′.	Terminal segment of maxillary palps without such striae and similar in general structure to the preceding segment and usually of the same length, or some segments with long hair brushes (Figure 351 A) 11	
10(9).	Mesoscutum without warts (Figure 350 A); R_{2+3} forked in front wing, often also forked in hind wing .... **Hydropsỳchidae**	p. 458
10′.	Mesoscutum with a pair of small warts (Figure 350 B); R_{2+3} not forked in either wing .... **Psychomyìidae**	p. 457
11(8′, 9′).	Middle tibiae without preapical spurs and with a row of black spines (Figure 349 B) 12	
11′.	Middle tibiae with preapical spurs, and with or without a row of spines (Figure 349 C–E) 16	
12(11).	Pronotum with a lateral pair of erect platelike warts separated by a wide mesal excavated collar that is usually hidden by the produced angulate margin of the mesonotum (Figure 350 C); mesonotum with the scutellum short and with the scutal warts represented by a long irregular line of setate spots; antennae very long and slender .... **Leptocéridae**	p. 461
12′.	Pronotum with warts much closer together, not platelike, and usually prominent; mesonotum with scutal warts either small or absent; antennae relatively stout, or not longer than body 13	
13(12′).	Anterior margin of hind wing cut away beyond the middle, and with a row of hamuli along the straight basal portion of the margin (Figure 348 G) .... **Helicopsỳchidae**	p. 461
13′.	Anterior margin of hind wing straight or evenly rounded 14	
14(13′).	Middle and hind tarsi with a crown of 4 black spines at apex of each segment, and only a few preapical spines arranged in a single row on basal tarsal segment (Figure 349 A); apical spurs of middle tibiae nearly half as long as basal tarsal segment (Figure 349 B) .... **Beraèidae***	p. 459
14′.	Middle and hind tarsi with apical spines more separated and not forming a crown, and with numerous preapical spines on all segments, arranged in a double row on the basal tarsal segment (Figure 349 F); apical spurs of middle tibiae not more than one third as long as basal tarsal segment (Figure 349 G) 15	
15(14′).	Mesoscutum with a deep anteromesal fissure, and with scutal warts near	

the meson (Figure 350 I); head with posterior warts diagonal and teardrop-shaped; front wing with a long cross vein between R_1 and R_2 and with Cu_2 joining apex of Cu_{1b} directly (Figure 348 E) .... **Sericostomátidae*** p. 461

15′. Mesonotum with only a shallow anteromesal crease, and with scutal warts some distance from the meson (Figure 350 E); head with posterior warts linear and transverse; front wing without a cross vein between R_1 and R_2 and with Cu_2 connected to apex of Cu_{1b} by a cross vein .... **Brachycéntridae** p. 461

16(11′). Middle femora with a row of 6 to 10 black spines on anteroventral face (Figure 349 E) .... **Molánnidae** p. 459

16′. Middle femora with 2 or no black spines on anteroventral face 17

17(16′). Mesoscutellum small and rectangular; mesoscutal warts represented by a linear area of small setate spots extending full length of scutum (Figure 350 H) .... **Calamocerátidae** p. 461

17′. Mesoscutellum longer and pointed; mesoscutal warts oval or lanceolate and short 18

18(17′). Mesoscutellum with a single large oval or round wart that extends the full length of the scutellum and may occupy almost the entire scutellum (Figure 350 G, J) 19

18′. Mesoscutellum with 2 warts that are smaller and confined to the anterior half of the scutellum (Figure 350 E, K) 20

19(18). Mesoscutellum round and distinctly domelike, the wart appearing to occupy most of the sclerite (Figure 350 G); mesoscutum with mesal line only faintly indicated; tibial spurs not hairy; maxillary palps of males 5-segmented .... **Odontocéridae** p. 459

19′. Mesoscutellum triangular, only slightly convex, the wart elongate and occupying only the mesal portion of the sclerite (Figure 350 J); mesoscutum with a distinct mesal depression; tibial spurs hairy; maxillary palps of males 3-segmented .... **Goèridae*** p. 461

20(18′). Middle tibiae with an irregular row, middle tarsi with a long double row of spines; preapical spurs of tibiae bare, short, and situated about two thirds of the distance from base of tibiae (Figure 349 D) ...... **Brachycéntridae** p. 461

20′. Middle tibiae without spines, their tarsi with only a scattered few in addition to apical ones; preapical spurs of tibiae hairy, long, and situated at middle of tibiae (Figure 349 C) .... **Lepidostomátidae*** p. 461

Family **Rhyacophílidae**—Primitive Caddisflies: The adults in this group are usually brownish with the wings more or less mottled, and vary in length from 3 to 13 mm; the antennae are short, and the maxillary palps (Figure 351 C) are 5-segmented in both sexes. The larvae occur in rapid streams. This family is divided into two subfamilies, which differ in larval habits; the larvae of the Rhyacophilìnae (Figure 353 B) are predaceous and do not make cases, while the larvae of the Glossosomatìnae are not predaceous and make saddlelike or turtle-shaped cases. The cases of the Glossosomatìnae (Figure 352 A) are oval; the dorsal side is convex and composed of relatively large pebbles, and the ventral side is flat and composed of smaller pebbles and sand grains. When these larvae pupate, the ventral side of the case is cut away and the upper part is fastened to a stone.

Family **Philopotámidae**—Finger-Net Caddisflies or Silken-Tube Spinners: These caddisflies vary in length from 6 to 9 mm and have the last segment of the maxillary palps elongate (Figure 351 B); they are usually brownish with gray wings. Most females of *Trentònius distínctus* (Walker) have the wings vestigial. The larvae live in rapid streams and construct finger-shaped or tubular nets that are attached to stones. These tubes have a large opening at the upstream end and a smaller one at the other end. Many such nets are frequently attached close together. The larva stays in the net and feeds on the food caught there; pupation occurs in cases made of pebbles and lined with silk.

Family **Psychomyìidae** (including **Polycentrópidae**)—Tube-Making and Trumpet-Net Cad-

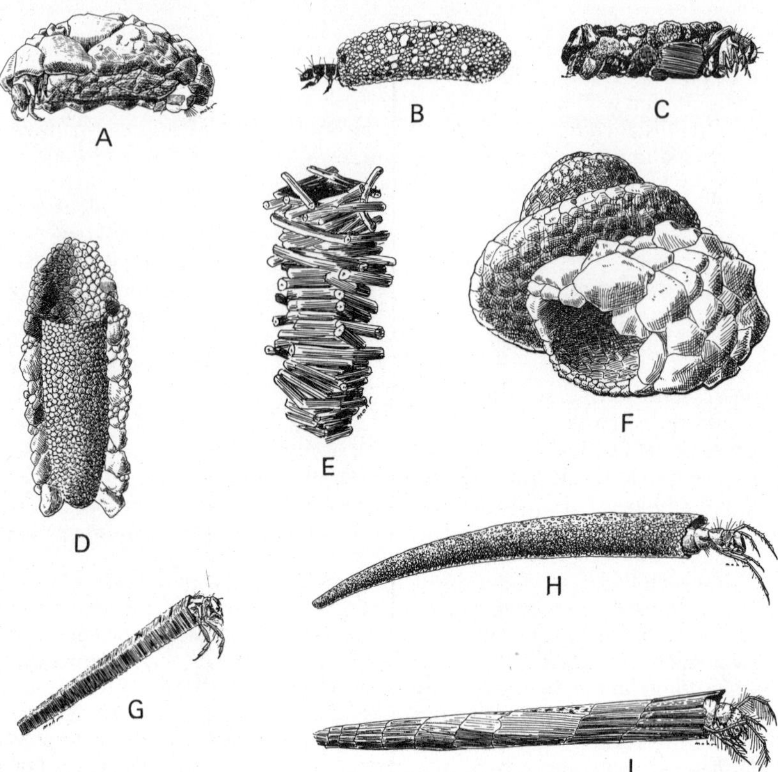

Figure 352. Cases of caddisfly larvae. A, *Glossosòma intermèdium* (Klapálek) (Rhyacophílidae); B, *Ochrotríchia ùnio* (Ross) (Hydroptílidae); C, *Limnéphilus rhómbicus* (L.) (Limnephílidae); D, *Molánna unióphila* Vorheis (Molánnidae); E, *Oecètis cineráscens* (Hagen) (Leptocéridae); F, *Heliocopsỳche boreàlis* (Hagen) (Helicopsỳchidae); G, *Brachycéntrus numeròsus* (Say) (Brachycéntridae); H, *Leptocélla álbida* (Walker) (Leptocéridae); I, *Triaenòdes tárda* Milne (Leptocéridae). (Courtesy of Ross and the Illinois Natural History Survey.)

disflies: These caddisflies vary in length from 4 to 11 mm; most of them are brownish with mottled wings. The larvae occur in a variety of aquatic situations; some occur in rapid streams, some in rivers, and others in lakes. Some (for example, *Polycéntropus*) construct trumpet-shaped nets which collapse rather rapidly when removed from the water; others (for example, *Phylocéntropus*) construct tubes in the sand at the bottoms of streams and cement the walls of these tubes to make a fairly rigid structure.

Family **Hydropsỳchidae**—Net-Spinning Caddisflies: This group is a large one, and many species are fairly common in small streams. The adults of both sexes have the maxillary palps 5-segmented with the last segment elongate (Figure 351 D), ocelli are absent, and the mesoscutum lacks warts (Figure 350 A). Most species are brownish, with the wings more or less mottled. The larvae occur in the parts of the stream where the current is strongest; they construct a caselike retreat of sand, pebbles, or debris, and near this retreat construct a cup-shaped net with the concave side of the net facing upstream. The larva feeds on materials caught in the net, and pupation occurs in the caselike retreat. These larvae are quite active, and if they are disturbed while feeding in the net, they back into their retreat very rapidly.

Family **Hydroptílidae**—Micro-Caddisflies: The members of this group vary in length from 1.5 to 6.0 mm; they are quite hairy (Figure 354 F), and

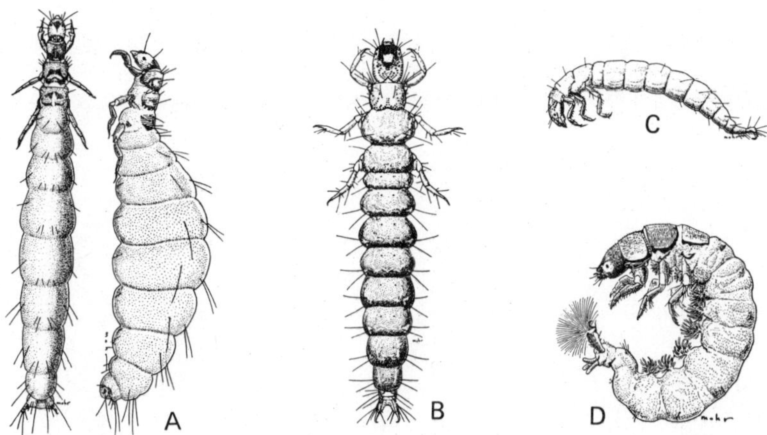

Figure 353. Caddisfly larvae. A, *Hydróptila waubesiàna* Betten (Hydroptílidae), dorsal view at left, lateral view at right; B, *Rhyacóphila fenéstra* Ross (Rhyacophílidae); C, *Polycéntropus interrúptus* (Banks) (Psychomyìidae); D, *Hydropsỳche símulans* Ross (Hydropsỳchidae). (Courtesy of Ross and the Illinois Natural History Survey.)

most of them have a salt-and-pepper mottling. The larvae of most species occur in small lakes. These insects undergo a sort of hypermetamorphosis; the early instars are active and do not construct cases, while the later instars are case-making; the anal hooks are much larger in the active instars than in the later instars. The case is usually somewhat purse-shaped, with each end open (Figure 352 B).

Family **Phryganèidae**—Large Caddisflies: The adults in this group are fairly large caddisflies (14–25 mm in length), and the wings are usually mottled with gray and brown (Figure 354 B, E); the maxillary palps are 4-segmented in the males (Figure 351 F) and 5-segmented in the females (Figure 351 E). The larvae occur chiefly in marshes or lakes; only a few are found in streams. The larval case is usually long and slender and composed of narrow strips glued together in a spiral.

Family **Limnephílidae**—Northern Caddisflies: This family is one of the largest in the order, with some 200 species in 20 genera occurring in North America; most species are northern in distribution. The adults vary in length from 7 to 23 mm, and most species are brownish with the wings mottled or patterned (Figure 354 A); the maxillary palps are 3-segmented in the males and 5-segmented in the females. The larvae occur principally in ponds and slow-moving streams; the cases are made of a variety of materials, and in some species the cases made by the young larvae are quite different from those made by older larvae. The larval stages of one species in this family, *Philocàsia démita* Ross, which occurs in Oregon, live in moist leaf litter.

Family **Molánnidae:** This group is small, and the known larvae live on the sandy bottoms of streams and lakes. The larval cases are shieldshaped and consist of a central cylindrical tube with lateral expansions (Figure 352 D). The adults, which are 10–16 mm in length, are usually brownish gray with the wings somewhat mottled, and have the palps 5-segmented in both sexes. The adults at rest sit with the wings curled about the body, and the body is held at an angle to the surface on which the insect rests.

Family **Beraèidae:** This family contains a single genus, *Beraèa,* with two North American species, one reported from Long Island, and the other from Georgia. The adults are brownish in color, and about 5 mm in length. Very little is known of the habits of the larvae.

Family **Odontocéridae:** The adults in this group are about 13 mm in length, the body is blackish, and the wings are grayish brown with light dots. The larvae live in the riffles of swift streams, where they construct cylindrical cases of sand. When ready to pupate, large numbers attach their cases to stones, with the cases close together and parallel.

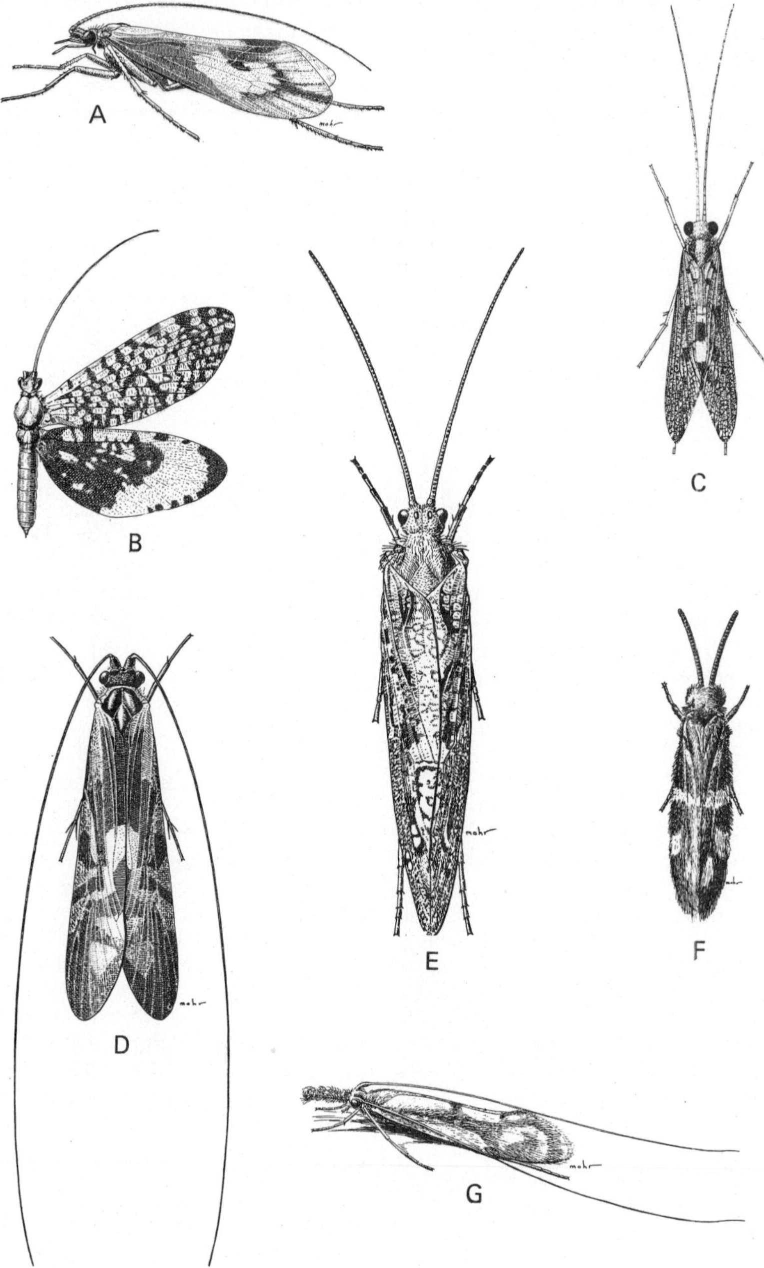

Figure 354. Adult caddisflies. A, *Platycéntropus radiàtus* (Say), male (Limnephílidae); B, *Eubasilíssa pardàlis* (Walker), female (Phryganèidae); C, *Hydropsỳche símulans* Ross, male (Hydropsỳchidae); D, *Macronèmum zebràtum* (Hagen), male (Hydropsỳchidae); E, *Phrygànea cinèrea* Walker, male (Phryganèidae); F, *Hydróptila hamàta* Morton, male (Hydroptílidae); G, *Triaenòdes tárda* Milne, male (Leptocéridae). (Courtesy of Ross and the Illinois Natural History Survey.)

Family **Calamocerátidae:** The adults of this group are orange-brown or brownish black, with the maxillary palps 5- or 6-segmented. The larvae occur in both still and rapidly flowing water; their cases are cylindrical and are made of sand or small pebbles. Two species in this family occur in the eastern states.

Family **Leptocéridae**—Long-Horned Caddisflies: These caddisflies are slender, often pale-colored, 5–17 mm in length, and have long slender antennae that are often nearly twice as long as the body (Figure 354 G). The larvae occur in a variety of habitats, and there is considerable variation in the types of cases they make. Some species make long, slender, tapering cases (Figure 352 H, I), some construct cases of twigs (Figure 352 E), and some construct cornucopia-shaped cases of sand grains.

Family **Goèridae:** This group is represented in North America by three genera, *Goèra, Goerìta,* and *Pseudogoèra*. The maxillary palps are 3-segmented in the males and 5-segmented in the females. The larvae occur in streams and construct cases of small pebbles with a larger pebble glued to each side to act as ballast.

Family **Lepidostomátidae:** This group contains two American genera, *Lepidóstoma* and *Theliopsỳche*. The females have 5-segmented maxillary palps, and the maxillary palps of the males are either 3-segmented or have a curiously modified 1-segmented structure. The larvae occur principally in streams or springs.

Family **Brachycéntridae:** This family contains two genera, *Brachycéntrus* and *Micrasèma*. The young larvae of *Brachycéntrus* occur near the shores of small streams where they feed principally on algae; older larvae move to midstream and attach their cases (Figure 352 G) to stones, facing upstream, and feed on both algae and small aquatic insects. The adults are 6–11 mm in length, and dark brown to black with the wings often tawny and checkered; the maxillary palps are 3-segmented in the males and 5-segmented in the females.

Family **Sericostomátidae:** This group contains the single genus *Sericóstoma,* the larvae of which occur in both lakes and streams. The habits of the larvae are not well known, as no nearctic species have been reared.

Family **Helicopsỳchidae**—Snail-Case Caddisflies: This family contains the single genus *Helicopsỳche,* the adults of which can usually be recognized by the short mesoscutellum with its narrow transverse warts (Figure 350 F), and the hamuli on the hind wings (Figure 348 G). The adults are 5-7 mm in length and are somewhat straw-colored, with the wings mottled with brownish color. The larvae construct cases of sand that are shaped like a snail shell (Figure 352 F). During development the larvae occur on sandy bottoms, and when ready to pupate, they attach their cases in clusters on stones. The cases are about 6 mm wide.

COLLECTING AND PRESERVING TRICHÓPTERA

Caddisfly adults are usually found near water. The habitat preferences of different species differ; hence one should visit a variety of habitats to get a large number of species. The adults can be collected by sweeping in the vegetation along the margins of and near ponds and streams, by checking the underside of bridges, and by collecting at lights. The best way of collecting the adults is at lights; blue lights seem more attractive than lights of other colors.

Caddisfly larvae can be collected by the various methods of aquatic collecting discussed in Chapter 34. Many can be found attached to stones in the water; others will be found among aquatic vegetation; still others can be collected with a dip net used to scoop up bottom debris or aquatic vegetation.

Both adult and larval caddisflies should be preserved in 80 percent alcohol. Adults may be pinned, but this frequently damages the thoracic warts that are used in separating families, and most dried specimens are more difficult to identify as to species than are specimens preserved in alcohol. When collecting at lights (for example, automobile headlights), large numbers can be easily collected by placing a pan containing about 6 mm of alcohol (or water containing a detergent) directly below the light; the insects will eventually fly into the alcohol and be caught. Specimens attracted to lights may also be taken directly into a cyanide jar and then transferred to alcohol, or they may be picked off the light by dipping the index finger in alcohol and scooping up the insect rapidly but gently on the wet finger. An aspirator is a useful collecting device for the smaller species.

References on the Trichóptera

Betten, C. 1934. The caddis flies or Trichoptera of New York State. *N.Y. State Mus. Bull.*, 292; 570 pp., 61 textf., 67 pl.

Denning, D. G. 1956. Trichoptera. In *Aquatic Insects of California*, R. L. Usinger (Ed.). Berkeley, Calif.: Univ. California Press, pp. 237–270; 37 f.

Krafka, J., Jr. 1915. A key to the families of trichopterous larvae. *Can. Ent.*, 47(7):217–225; 37 f.

Lloyd, J. T. 1921. The biology of North America caddis fly larvae. *Lloyd Libr. Bot., Pharm. and Materia Med. Bull.*, 21 (Ent. Ser. No. 1); 124 pp., 197 f.

Pennak, R. W. 1953. *Fresh-Water Invertebrates of the United States*. New York: Ronald Press, ix + 769 pp., 470 f.

Ross, H. H. 1944. The caddis flies or Trichoptera of Illinois. *Ill. Nat. Hist. Surv. Bull.*, 23(1):1–326; 961 f.

Ross, H. H. 1956. *Evolution and Classification of the Mountain Caddisflies*. Urbana, Ill.: Univ. Illinois Press, vi + 213 pp., 45 charts.

Ross, H. H. 1959. Trichoptera. In *Fresh-Water Biology*, W. T. Edmondson (Ed.). New York: Wiley, pp. 1024–1049; 17 f.

Ross, H. H. 1967. The evolution and past dispersal of the Trichoptera. *Ann. Rev. Ent.*, 12:169–206; 14 f.

Schmid, F. 1970. Le genre *Rhyacophila* et la famile des Rhyacophilidae (Trichoptera). *Mem. Soc. Ent. Canada*, No. 66; 230 pp., 52 pl., 39 textf.

Smith, S. D. 1968. The Arctopsychinae of Idaho (Trichoptera: Hydropsychidae). *Pan-Pac. Ent.*, 44(2):102–112; 6 f.

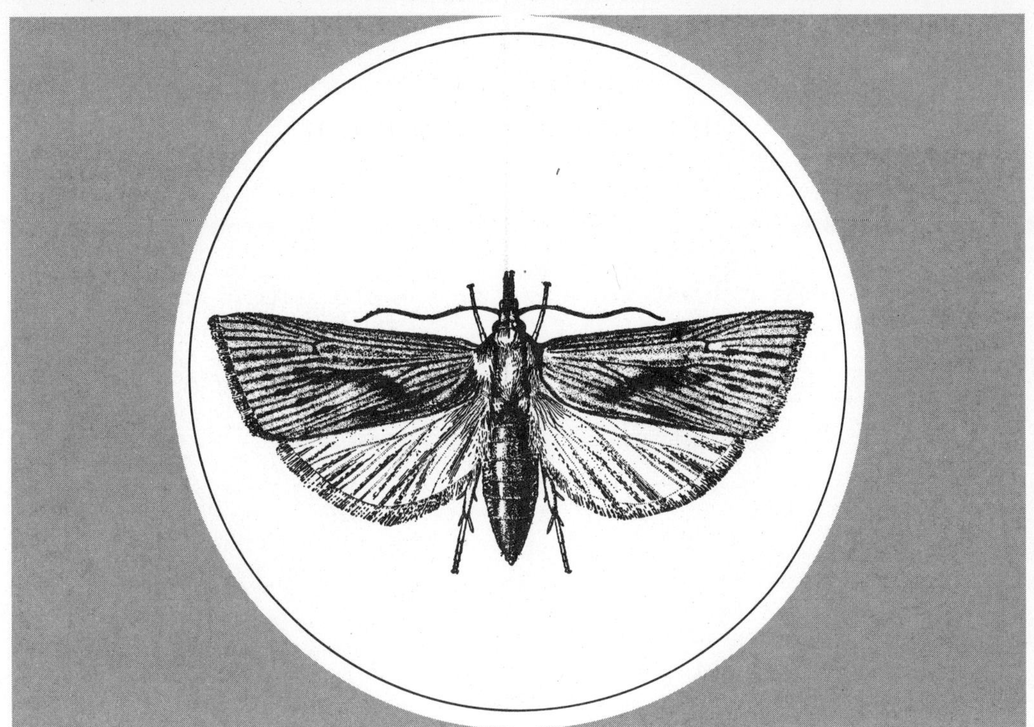

29: ORDER LEPIDÓPTERA[1]

BUTTERFLIES AND MOTHS

The butterflies and moths are common insects and well known to everyone. They are most readily recognized by the scales on the wings (Figure 355), which come off like dust on one's fingers when the insects are handled; most of the body and legs are also covered with scales. This order is a large one, with about 11,000 species occurring in the United States and Canada; its members are to be found almost everywhere, often in considerable numbers.

The Lepidóptera are of considerable economic importance. The larvae of most species are phytophagous, and many are serious pests of cultivated plants; a few feed on various fabrics, and a few feed on stored grain or meal. On the other hand, the adults of many species are beautiful and are much sought after by collectors, and many serve as the basis of art and design. Natural silk is the product of a member of this order.

The mouth parts of a butterfly or moth are usually fitted for sucking; a few species have vestigial mouth parts and do not feed in the adult stage, and the mouth parts in one family (the Micropterýgidae) are of the chewing type. The labrum is small and is usually in the form of a narrow transverse band across the lower part of the face, at the base of the proboscis. The mandibles are nearly always lacking. The proboscis, when present, is formed by the appressed, longitudinally grooved galeae of the maxillae and is usually long and coiled. The maxillary palps are generally small or lacking, but the labial palps are nearly always well developed and usually extend forward in front of the face (Figure 356 B).

[1] Lepidóptera: *lepido,* scale; *ptera,* wings.

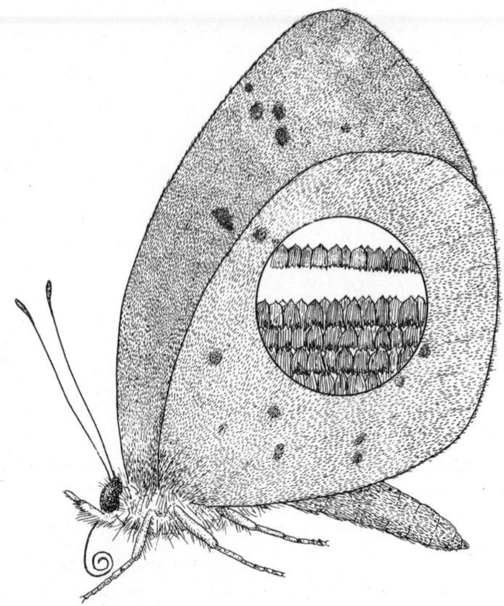

Figure 355. Butterfly with a section of the wing enlarged to show the scales.

The compound eyes of a butterfly or moth are relatively large and composed of a large number of facets. Most moths have two ocelli, one on each side close to the margin of the compound eye.

The members of this order undergo complete metamorphosis, and their larvae, usually called caterpillars, are a familiar sight. Many lepidopterous larvae have a grotesque or ferocious appearance, and some people are afraid of them, but the vast majority are quite harmless when handled. Only a few give off an offensive odor, and only a very few have stinging body hairs; the ferocious appearance is merely camouflage.

The larvae of Lepidóptera are usually eruciform (Figure 357), with a well-developed head and a cylindrical body of 13 segments (3 thoracic and 10 abdominal). The head usually bears six ocelli on each side just above the mandibles, and a pair of very short antennae. Each of the thoracic segments bears a pair of legs, and abdominal segments 3–6 and 10 usually bear a pair of prolegs. The prolegs are somewhat different from the thoracic legs; they are more fleshy and have a different segmentation, and they usually bear at their apex a number of tiny hooks called crochets. Some larvae, such as the measuringworms and loopers, have fewer than five pairs of prolegs, and some lycaenids have neither legs nor prolegs. The only other eruciform larvae likely to be confused with those of the Lepidóptera are the larvae of sawflies. Sawfly larvae (Figure 554) have only one ocellus on each side, the prolegs do not bear crochets, and there are generally more than five pairs of prolegs; most sawfly larvae are 25 mm in length or less, whereas many lepidopterous larvae are considerably larger than this.

Most butterfly and moth larvae feed on plants, but different species feed in different ways. The larger larvae generally feed at the edge of the leaf and consume all but the larger veins; the smaller larvae skeletonize the leaf or eat small holes in it. Many larvae are leaf miners and feed inside the

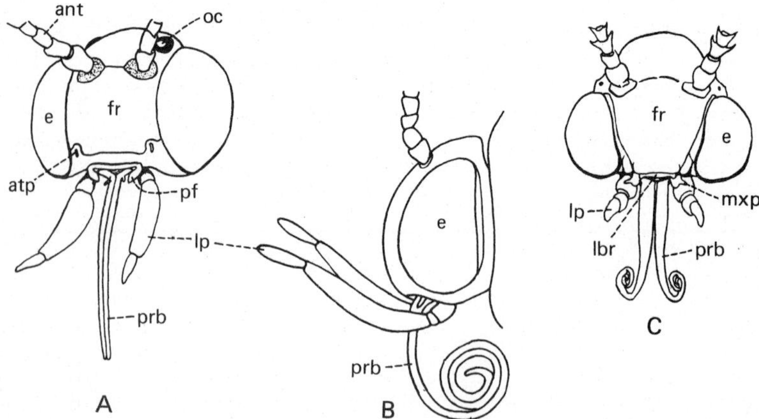

Figure 356. Head structure in Lepidóptera. A, *Sanninòidea* (Sesìidae), anterior view; B, same, lateral view; C, *Hyphántria* (Arctìidae). *ant,* antenna; *atp,* anterior tentorial pit; *e,* compound eye; *fr,* frons; *lbr,* labrum; *lp,* labial palp; *mxp,* maxillary palp; *oc,* ocellus; *pf,* pilifer; *prb,* proboscis. (Redrawn from Snodgrass.)

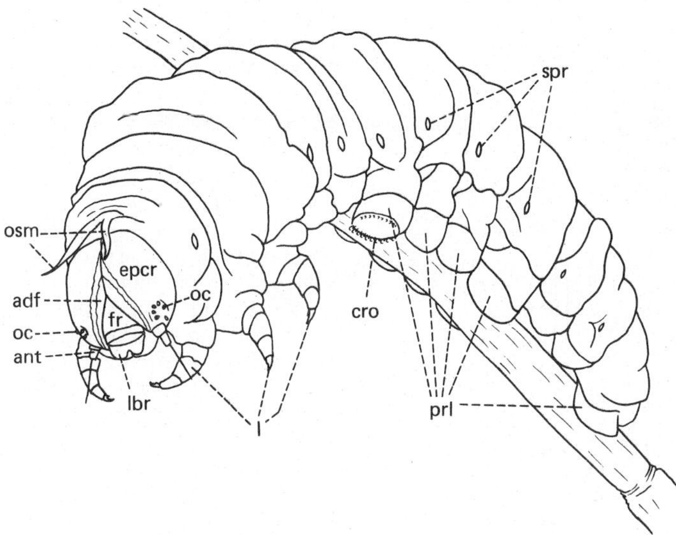

Figure 357. Larva of *Papílio* (Papiliónidae). *adf,* adfrontal area; *ant,* antenna; *cro,* crochets; *epcr,* epicranium; *fr,* frons; *l,* thoracic legs; *lbr,* labrum; *oc,* ocelli; *osm,* osmeterium (scent gland); *prl,* prolegs; *spr,* spiracles.

leaf; their mines may be linear, trumpet-shaped, or blotchlike. A few are gall makers, and a few bore in the fruit, stems, wood, or other parts of the plant. A very few are predaceous on other insects.

The larvae of Lepidóptera have well-developed silk glands, which are modified salivary glands that open on the lower lip. Many larvae use this silk in making a cocoon, and some use it in making shelters. Leaf rollers and leaf folders roll or fold up a leaf, tie it in place with silk, and feed inside the shelter so formed; other larvae tie a few leaves together and feed inside this shelter. Some of the gregarious species, such as the tent caterpillars and webworms, make a large shelter involving many leaves or even entire branches.

Pupation occurs in various situations. Many larvae form an elaborate cocoon and transform to the pupa inside it; others make a very simple cocoon, and still others make no cocoon at all. Many larvae pupate in some sort of protected situation. The pupae (Figure 358) are usually of the obtect type, with the appendages firmly attached to the body; moth pupae are usually brownish and relatively smooth, while butterfly pupae are variously colored and are often tuberculate or sculptured. Most of the butterflies do not make a cocoon, and their pupae are often called chrysalids (singular, chrysalis). The chrysalids of some butterflies (Danàidae, Nymphálidae, Satýridae, and Libythèidae) are attached to a leaf or twig by the cremaster, a spiny process at the posterior end of the body, and hang head downward (Figure 358 B); in other cases (Lycaènidae, Piéridae, Riodínidae, Papiliónidae, and Parnassìidae) the chrysalis is attached by the cremaster, but is held in a more or less upright position by a silken girdle about the middle of the body (Figure 358 A).

Most of the Lepidóptera have one generation a year, usually overwintering as a larva or pupa; a few species have two or more generations a year, and a few require two or three years to complete a generation. Many species overwinter in the egg stage, but relatively few overwinter as adults.

CLASSIFICATION OF THE LEPIDÓPTERA

Most authorities in this country divide the Lepidóptera into two suborders, the Jugàtae and the Frenàtae, on the basis of wing venation and the method of union of the two wings on each side. The Jugàtae have the front and hind wings similar in venation, and the two wings on each side are usually united by a small lobe at the base of the front wing, the jugum (Figure 359, *j*). The Frenàtae have the hind wing smaller than the front wing and with a reduced venation, and the two wings on each side are united by a frenulum (Figure 360, *f*) or by an expanded humeral angle of the hind wing (Figures 362–368). The Jugàtae are a small and relatively rare group; the vast majority of the Lepidóptera belong to the Frenàtae.

There are a number of other classifications of this order, but perhaps the ones most often encountered are (1) a division of the order into two

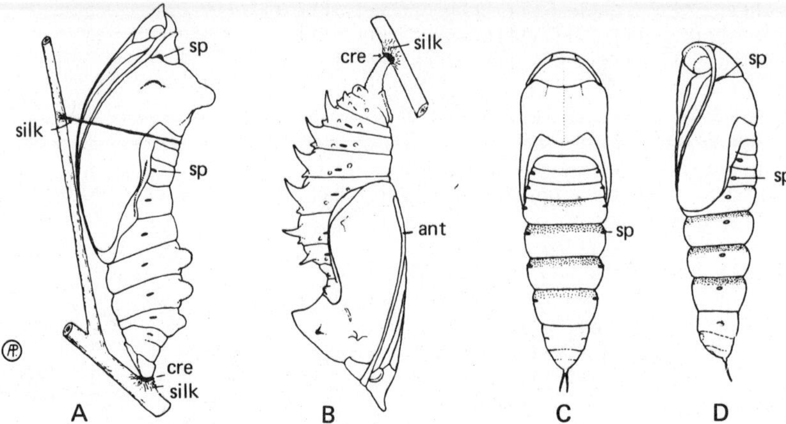

Figure 358. Pupae of Lepidóptera. A, *Papílio* (Papiliónidae); B, *Nýmphalis* (Nymphálidae); C, *Helìothis* (Noctùidae), dorsal view; D, same, lateral view. *cre,* cremaster; *sp,* spiracle. (Courtesy of Peterson. Reprinted by permission.)

suborders, Rhopalócera and Heterócera, and (2) a division into three suborders, Zeuglóptera, Monotrỳsia, and Ditrỳsia. The Rhopalócera, which have knobbed antennae, include the butterflies and skippers; the Heterócera, which have antennae of various sorts (usually not knobbed), include the moths (the rest of the order). The Rhopalócera lack a frenulum, and are generally slender-bodied and day-flying; the Heterócera usually have a frenulum, and are generally stout-bodied and night-flying. The Zeuglóptera include the Lepidóptera with functional mandibles, the Micropterýgidae. The Monotrỳsia and Ditrỳsia differ principally in genital characters; the Monotrỳsia include the families Eriocranìidae, Hepiálidae, Nepticùlidae, Incurvarìidae, Heliozèlidae, Opostégidae, and Tischerìidae, and the Ditrỳsia include the rest of the order.

The Frenàtae are divided into a series of superfamilies on the basis of wing venation, the presence or absence of a frenulum, and other characters. These superfamilies are grouped in two divisions, the Macrolepidóptera and Microlepidóptera. As the names of these divisions indicate, the Macrolepidóptera are mainly large insects and the Microlepidóptera are smaller, but there are other characters better than size (see key) for distinguishing these two groups.

A synopsis of the North American Lepidóptera is given below. This synopsis follows the arrangement of McDunnough (1938–1939) and Forbes (1923–1960), with a few changes based on more recent studies. Other names for the various groups are given in parentheses. The families marked with an asterisk are relatively rare or are unlikely to be taken by a general collector.

- Suborder Jugàtae (Homoneùra) — jugate moths
    - *Micropterýgidae (Eriocephálidae, Zeuglóptera) — mandibulate moths
    - *Eriocranìidae — eriocraniid moths
    - *Hepiálidae — ghost moths and swifts
- Suborder Frenàtae (Heteroneùra) — frenates
    - Division Microlepidóptera
        - Superfamily Zygaenòidea (Psychodòidea)
            - Limacòdidae (Euclèidae, Cochlidìidae) — slug caterpillars and saddleback caterpillars
            - *Megalopỳgidae (Lagòidae) — flannel moths
            - *Dalcéridae (Acrágidae) — dalcerid moths
            - *Epipyrópidae — planthopper parasites
            - *Pyromórphidae (Zygaènidae) — smoky moths
        - Superfamily Pyralidòidea
            - *Thyrídidae (Thỳridae) — window-winged moths

Pyrálidae (Pyralídidae) – snout moths, grass moths, and others
Pterophòridae (including Agdístidae) – plume moths
*Alucítidae (Orneòdidae) – many-plume moths
Superfamily Tortricòidea
Olethreùtidae – codling moth, oriental fruit moth, and others
Tortrícidae – leaf rollers, leaf tyers
*Phalonìidae (Conchỳlidae) – webworms
Cóssidae (including Hypóptidae and Zeuzéridae) – carpenter moths and leopard moths
Superfamily Carposinòidea
*Carposìnidae – carposinid moths
Superfamily Gelechiòidea
*Cosmopterýgidae (Lavérnidae) – cosmopterygid moths
*Walshìidae (Cosmopterýgidae in part) – walshiid moths
*Mómphidae (Cosmopterýgidae in part) – momphid moths
*Epermenìidae (Yponomeùtidae in part) – epermeniid moths
Gelechìidae – gelechiid moths
Oecophòridae (Depressarìidae) – oecophorid moths
*Blastobàsidae – blastobasid moths
*Stenòmidae (Stenomátidae, Xyloríctidae, Uzùchidae) – stenomid moths
*Ethmìidae (Oecophòridae in part) – ethmiid moths
Superfamily Yponomeutòidea
*Glyphipterýgidae (Choreùtidae, Hemerophílidae) – glyphipterygid moths
Sesìidae (Aegerìidae) – clear-winged moths
*Heliodínidae (Tinaegerìidae) – heliodinid moths
*Plutéllidae (including Acrolepìidae) – diamondback moths
Yponomeùtidae (including Argyresthìidae) – ermine moths
*Scýthridae (Scythrídidae) – scythrid moths
Superfamily Cycnodiòidea (Elachistòidea)
*Heliozèlidae – shield bearers, leaf miners
*Douglasìidae – leaf miners
*Elachístidae (Cycnodìidae) – grass miners
Superfamily Tineoìdea
Coleophòridae – casebearers
Gracilarìidae (including Phyllocnístidae) – leaf blotch miners
*Opostégidae – opostegid moths
*Lyonetìidae – lyonetiid moths
*Tischerìidae (Tinèidae in part) – the apple leaf miner and others
*Oinophílidae (Oenophílidae) – oinophilid moths
Psỳchidae (including Talaeporìidae) – bagworms
*Acrolóphidae (Tinèidae in part) – burrowing webworms
Tinèidae (including Amydrìidae and Setomórphidae) – clothes moths and others
Superfamily Nepticulòidea
*Nepticùlidae (Stigméllidae) – leaf miners
Superfamily Incurvariòidea
Incurvarìidae (including Prodóxidae and Adèlidae) – yucca moths, fairy moths, and others
Division Macrolepidóptera
Superfamily Uraniòidea
*Epiplèmidae – epiplemid moths
Superfamily Geometròidea
Geométridae – measuringworms, geometers, cankerworms, and others
Superfamily Drepanòidea
*Thyatíridae (Cymatophòridae) – thyatirid moths
Drepánidae – hook-tip moths
Superfamily Mimallonòidea
*Mimallónidae (Lacosòmidae, Perophòridae) – sack-bearers

Superfamily Noctuòidea
Ctenùchidae (Amátidae, Syntómidae, Euchromìidae)—wasp moths, scape moths, ctenuchas, and others
*Nòlidae—nolid moths
Arctìidae (including Lithosìidae)—tiger moths, footman moths
Agarístidae—forester moths
Noctùidae (Phalaènidae; including Plusìidae and Hyblaèidae)—noctuid moths: underwings, cutworms, dagger moths, owlet moths, and others
*Pericópidae (Nycteméridae; including Hýpsidae)—pericopid moths
*Dióptidae—oakworms
Notodóntidae (Cerùridae)—prominents
Lipàridae (Lymantrìidae)—tussock moths, gypsy moth, and others
*Manidìidae (Semantùridae)—manidiid moths
Superfamily Bombycòidea
*Apatelòdidae (Zanólidae, Eupterótidae)—apatelodid moths
*Bombýcidae—silkworm moths
Lasiocámpidae—tent caterpillars and lappet moths
Saturnìidae (including Citheronìidae = Ceratocámpidae)—giant silkworm moths and royal moths
Superfamily Sphingòidea
Sphíngidae (Smerínthidae)—sphinx or hawk moths, hornworms
Superfamily Hesperiòidea—skippers
Hesperìidae—skippers
*Megathỳmidae—giant skippers
Superfamily Papilionòidea—butterflies
Lycaènidae (Cupidínidae, Rurálidae)—gossamer-winged butterflies: blues, coppers, hairstreaks, and harvesters
*Riodínidae (Erycínidae, Lemonìidae)—metalmarks
Piéridae (Ascìidae)—whites, sulphurs, and orange-tips
Papiliónidae—swallowtails
Parnassìidae (Papiliónidae in part)—parnassians
*Libythèidae (Nymphálidae in part)—snout butterflies
Danàidae (Lymnádidae; Nymphálidae in part)—milkweed butterflies
Satýridae (Agapétidae; Nymphálidae in part)—satyrs, wood nymphs, arctics
Heliconìidae (Nymphálidae in part)—heliconians
Nymphálidae (Aegyrèidae)—brush-footed butterflies: fritillaries, checker-spots, crescent-spots, anglewings, mourningcloaks, admirals, purples, and others

CHARACTERS USED IN IDENTIFYING LEPIDÓPTERA

The identification of adult Lepidóptera by means of keys is not easy, and as a result the beginning student is likely to identify most of his specimens by comparing them with pictures. Most of the larger and more common species of moths, and practically all the American species of butterflies, are illustrated in color in Holland's *Moth Book* and *Butterfly Book,* and these books are practically a "must" for students seriously interested in this order; Klots' field guide (1951) is an excellent reference on the butterflies. The identification of many of the moths from pictures is difficult and often inaccurate, for moths in different groups are often superficially very similar; the serious student should be able to run a member of this order through a key.

The principal characters used in keying adult Lepidóptera to family are those of the wing venation; other characters used include the character of the antennae, ocelli, method of wing union, mouth parts, legs, and abdomen. It is often necessary to bleach the wings in order to see the venation; sometimes one may carefully scrape a few scales from the underside of the wing to see critical venational characters.

WING VENATION

The wing venation in this order is relatively simple because there are few cross veins and rarely extra branches of the longitudinal veins, and the vena-

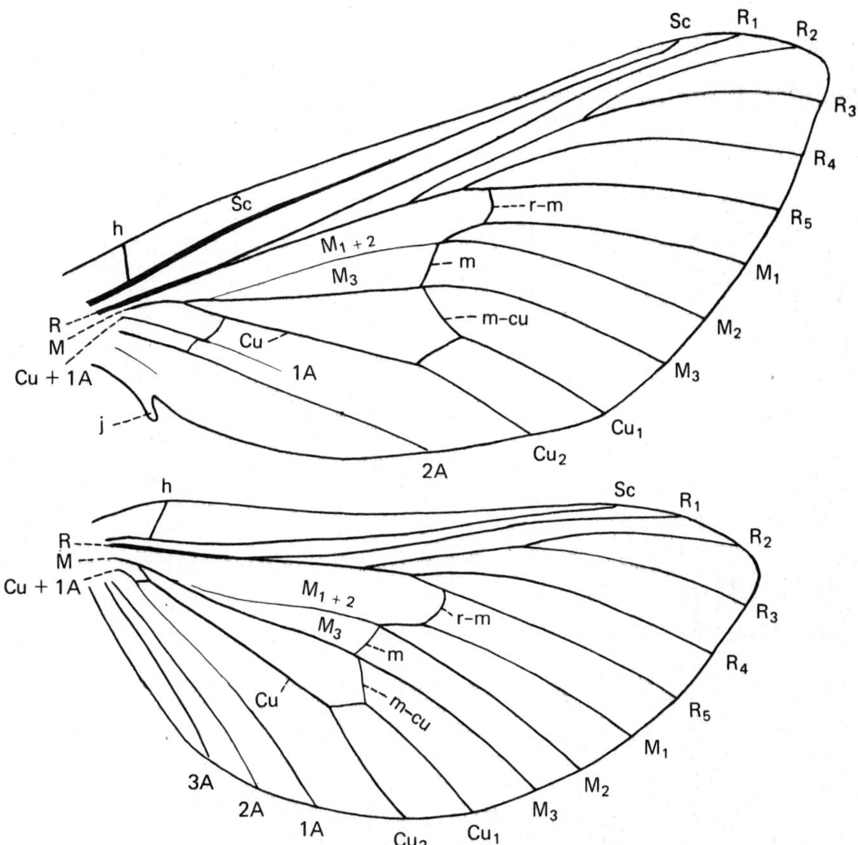

Figure 359. Venation of a jugate moth, *Sthenòpis* (Hepiálidae). *j*, jugum.

tion is reduced in some groups. There are differences of opinion regarding the interpretation of certain veins in the lepidopterous wing; we follow here the interpretation of Comstock.[2]

The most generalized venation in the Lepidóptera is to be found in the suborder Jugàtae, in which the venation of the front and hind wings is similar. The members of this suborder have the subcosta simple or 2-branched; the radius 5-branched (occasionally 6-branched); the media 3-branched; the cubitus 2-branched; and there are usually three anal veins (Figure 359).

The Frenàtae have the venation in the hind wing reduced; the radius of the front wing usually has five branches (occasionally fewer), but in the hind wing the radial sector is unbranched and R_1 is usually fused with the subcosta. The basal portion of the media is atrophied in most of the Frenàtae, with the result that a large cell is formed in the central portion of the wing; this cell is commonly called the discal cell. The first anal vein in the front wing of many Frenàtae is atrophied. A somewhat generalized frenate wing venation is shown in Figure 360. The veins may fuse in various ways in the Frenàtae, and this fusing or stalking is used in the key. The subcosta in the front wing is nearly always free of the discal cell and lies between it and the costa. The branches of the radius arise from the anterior side of the discal cell or from its anterior apical corner. Two or more branches of the radius are frequently stalked, that is, fused for a distance beyond the discal cell. Certain radial branches occasionally fuse again beyond their point of separation, thus forming accessory cells (for example, Figure 371

[2] The medio-cubital cross vein of the Comstock terminology is called M_4 by some authorities; the three branches of the media according to Comstock are M_1, M_2, and M_3. According to these other authorities, Comstock's Cu_1 and Cu_2 are Cu_{1a} and Cu_{1b}, his 1A is Cu_2, his 2A is 1A, and his 3A is 2A.

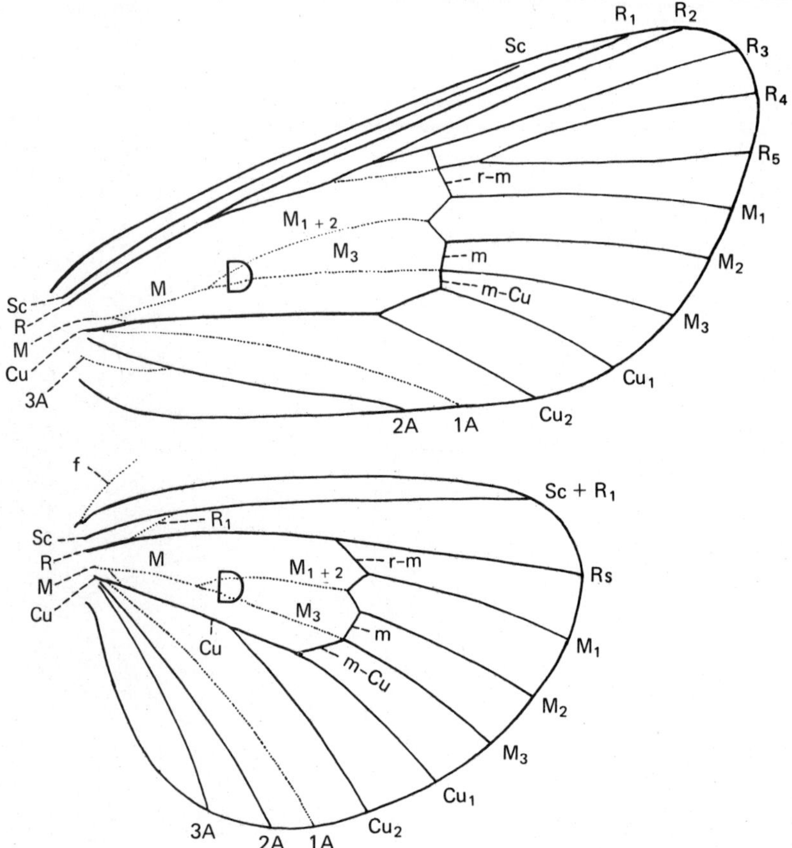

Figure 360. Venation of a frenate (generalized). The veins shown by dotted lines are atrophied or lost in some groups in the suborder. *D*, discal cell; *f*, frenulum.

A, *acc*). The three branches of the media usually arise from the apex of the discal cell in both wings, though M_1 may be stalked with a branch of the radius for a distance beyond the apex of the discal cell (Figure 367). The point of origin of M_2 from the apex of the discal cell is an important character used in separating different groups; when it arises from the middle of the apex of the discal cell, as in Figure 374, or anterior to the middle, the vein (Cu) forming the posterior side of this cell appears 3-branched; when M_2 arises nearer to M_3 than to M_1 (Figures 377–382), then the cubitus appears 4-branched.

Variations in the venation of the hind wing in the Frenàtae involve principally the nature of the fusion of $Sc + R_1$ and Rs, and the number of anal veins. In the lower families, R is separate from Sc at the base of the wing, and R_1 appears as a cross vein between Rs and Sc somewhere along the anterior side of the discal cell (Figure 371 B). R_1 also fuses with Sc eventually, and judging from the pupal tracheation, the vein reaching the wing margin is Sc (the R_1 trachea is always small); however, this vein at the margin is usually called $Sc + R_1$. In many cases Sc and R are fused basally, or they may be separate at the base and fuse for a short distance along the anterior side of the discal cell (Figures 380 and 381).

OTHER CHARACTERS USED IN THE KEY

Another wing character used in the identification of the Lepidóptera is the nature of the wing union on each side. In the suborder Jugàtae there is a small lobe at the base of the front wing (the jugum), which overlaps the base of the anterior edge of the hind wing (Figure 359, *j*). In most of

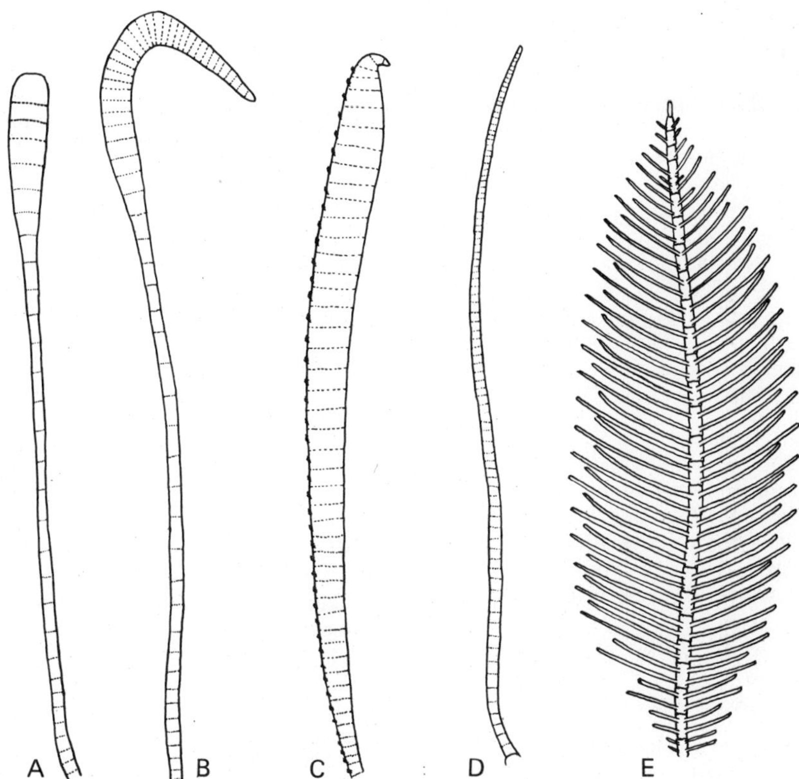

Figure 361. Antennae of Lepidóptera. A, *Còlias* (Piéridae); B, *Epargỳreus* (Hesperìidae); C, *Hémaris* (Sphíngidae); D, *Drastèria* (Noctùidae); E, *Callosàmia* (Saturnìidae).

the moths of the suborder Frenàtae the wings are united by a frenulum; the frenulum is a large bristle (males), or group of bristles (most females), arising from the humeral angle of the hind wing and fitting under a group of scales near the costal margin (on the lower surface) of the front wing (Figure 360, *f*). There is no frenulum in the butterflies and in some of the moths; the humeral angle of the hind wing is usually expanded in such forms, and fits up under the posterior margin of the front wing.

A few of the Microlepidóptera (for example, the Nepticulòidea and the Incurvariòidea) have minute hairlike spines under the scales of the wing; these are termed aculeae. The aculeae can be seen when the scales are bleached or removed; they are not movable at the base.

The head characters used are principally those of the antennae, ocelli, and mouth parts. The antennae of butterflies (Figure 361 A, B) are slender and knobbed at the tip; those of moths (Figure 361 C–E) are usually filiform, setaceous, or plumose. The basal segment of the antennae in some of the Microlepidóptera is enlarged, and when the antenna is bent down and back, this segment fits over the eye; such an enlarged basal antennal segment is called an eye cap (Figure 383 B). Most of the moths have a pair of ocelli located on the upper surface of the head close to the margins of the compound eyes; these can often be seen only by separating the hairs and scales. The form of the maxillary or labial palps is frequently used to separate the families of the Microlepidóptera.

The leg characters of value in identification include the form of the tibial spurs and the tarsal claws, the presence or absence of spines on the legs, and occasionally the structure of the epiphysis. The epiphysis is a movable pad on the inner side of the front tibia; it is probably used in cleaning the antennae. The front legs are very much reduced in some of the butterflies, particularly the Nymphálidae.

STUDYING WING VENATION IN THE LEPIDÓPTERA

It is often possible to make out venational details in a butterfly or moth without any special treatment of the wings, or in some cases venational details may be seen by putting a few drops of alcohol, ether, or chloroform on the wings, or by carefully scraping off a few of the wing scales. In many cases, however, it is necessary to bleach the wings in order to study all details of wing venation. A method of bleaching and mounting the wings of Lepidóptera is described below.

The materials needed for clearing and mounting lepidopterous wings are as follows:

1. Three watch glasses, one containing 95 percent alcohol, one containing 10 percent hydrochloric acid, and one containing equal proportions of aqueous solutions of sodium chloride and sodium hypochlorite (Clorox serves fairly well in place of this mixture)
2. A preparation dish of water, preferably distilled water
3. Slides (preferably 50 by 50 mm), masks, and binding tape
4. Forceps and dissecting needle

The procedure in clearing and mounting the wings is as follows:

1. Remove the wings from one side of the specimen, being careful not to tear them or to break any connections such as frenulum between the front and hind wings. The frenulum is less likely to be broken if the front and hind wings are removed together.
2. Dip the wings in 95 percent alcohol for a few seconds to wet them.
3. Dip the wings in 10 percent hydrochloric acid for a few seconds.
4. Place the wings in the mixture of sodium chloride and sodium hypochlorite (or Clorox), and leave them there until the color is removed. This usually requires only a few minutes. If the wings are slow in clearing, dip them in the acid again and then return them to the bleaching solution.
5. Rinse the wings in water to remove the excess bleach.
6. Place the wings on the slide, centered and properly oriented (preferably with the base of the wings to the left); this is most easily done by floating the wings in water (for example, in a preparation dish) and bringing the slide up from underneath. The wings should be oriented on the slide while they are wet.
7. Allow the slide and wings to dry. If all the bleach has not been removed and some is deposited on the slide, place the slide again in water, carefully remove the wings, clean the slide, and remount the wings.
8. Place the mask on the slide around the wings (data, labeling, and the like should be put on the mask), put on the cover slide, and bind. Care should be taken before the slide is bound to make sure the wings are dry and that both slides are perfectly clean.

Such a slide, and the specimen from which the wings are removed, should always be labeled so that they can be associated. A wing slide of this sort will keep indefinitely and can be studied under the microscope or can be projected on a screen for demonstration. In the case of wings 13 mm in length or less, it is better not to use a mask, as the mask may be thicker than the wings and the wings may slip or curl after the slide is bound. The labeling can be put on a small strip of paper that is attached to the outside of the slide with cellophane tape.

Key to the Families of Lepidóptera

This key is designed primarily for the advanced student. Since it is based to a considerable extent on wing venation, it may be sometimes necessary to bleach the wings of a specimen in order to run it through the key. For the sake of brevity the two anterior veins in the hind wing are referred to as Sc and Rs, though most of the first vein is usually $Sc+R_1$, and the base of the second vein may be R. A few families of the Microlepidóptera are separated only by characters of the male genitalia, and since we have not used such characters in our key these families key out at the same point. Keys to the larvae are given by Forbes (1923–1960) and Peterson (1948). The groups marked with an asterisk are relatively uncommon or are unlikely to be encountered by the general collector.

1. Wings present and well developed 2
1′. Wings absent or vestigial (females only) 113
2(1). Front and hind wings similar in venation, and usually also in shape; Rs in

hind wings 3- or 4-branched (Figures 359 and 388 B); front and hind wings usually united by a jugum; no coiled proboscis (suborder Jugàtae) 3*

2′. Front and hind wings dissimilar in venation and usually also in shape; Rs in hind wing unbranched; no jugum, the front and hind wings united by a frenulum or by an expanded humeral angle of the hind wing; mouth parts usually in the form of a coiled proboscis (suborder Frenàtae) 5

3(2). Wingspread 25 mm or more .... **Hepiálidae*** p. 496

3′. Wingspread 12 mm or less 4

4(3′). Functional mandibles present; middle tibiae without spurs; Sc in front wings forked near its middle (Figure 388 B) .... **Micropterýgidae*** p. 496

4′. Mandibles vestigial or absent; middle tibiae with 1 spur; Sc in front wings forked near its tip .... **Eriocranìidae*** p. 496

5(2′). Antennae threadlike, and swollen or knobbed at tip (Figure 361 A, B); no frenulum; ocelli absent (butterflies and skippers) 6

5′. Antennae of various forms, but usually not knobbed at tip (Figure 361 C–E); if antennae are somewhat clubbed, then a frenulum is present; ocelli present or absent (moths) 18

6(5). Radius in front wing 5-branched, with all the branches simple and arising from discal cell (Figure 362); antennae widely separated at base and usually hooked at tip (Figure 361 B); hind tibiae usually with a middle spur; stout-bodied insects (Hesperiòidea) 7

6′. Radius in front wing 3- to 5-branched, if 5-branched then with some branches stalked beyond discal cell (Figures 363–368); antennae close

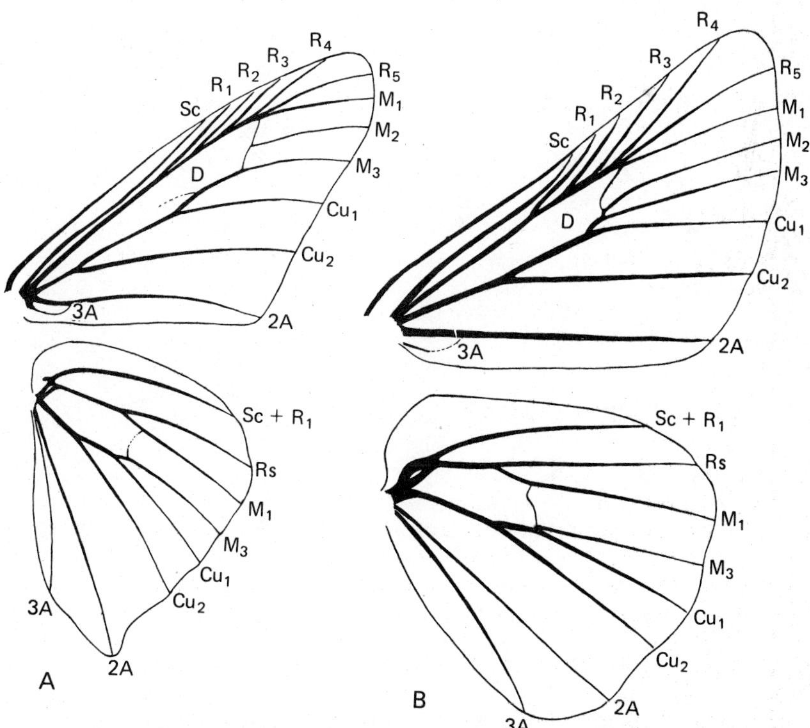

Figure 362. Wings of Hesperìidae. A, *Epargýreus* (Pyrgìnae); B, *Pseudocopaeòdes* (Hesperiìnae). *D*, discal cell.

together at base and never hooked at tip (Figure 361 A); hind tibiae never with a middle spur (Papilionòidea) 8

7(6). Either antennal club drawn out at tip and recurved (Figure 361 B), or wingspread less than 30 mm; head as wide as or wider than thorax; middle tibiae with apical and preapical spurs; widely distributed .... **Hesperìidae** p. 524

7′. Antennal club not drawn out at tip and recurved; wingspread 40 mm or more; head narrower than thorax; middle tibiae with only apical spurs; southern and western United States .... **Megathỳmidae*** p. 525

8(6′). Cubitus in front wing apparently 4-branched (Figure 363); 1 anal vein in hind wing; front legs of normal size, and tibiae with an epiphysis 9

8′. Cubitus in front wing apparently 3-branched (Figures 364–368); 2 anal veins in hind wing; front legs of normal size or reduced, tibiae without an epiphysis 10

9(8). Radius in front wing 5-branched (Figure 363 A); usually with one or more taillike prolongations on rear side of hind wing; large, usually dark-colored butterflies (Figure 434); widely distributed .... **Papiliónidae** p. 528

9′. Radius in front wing 4-branched (Figure 363 B); hind wing without taillike prolongations; medium-sized butterflies, usually white or gray with dark markings (Figure 435); western United States .... **Parnassìidae** p. 529

10(8′). Labial palps very long, longer than thorax, and thickly hairy (Figure 431 C) .... **Libythèidae*** p. 529

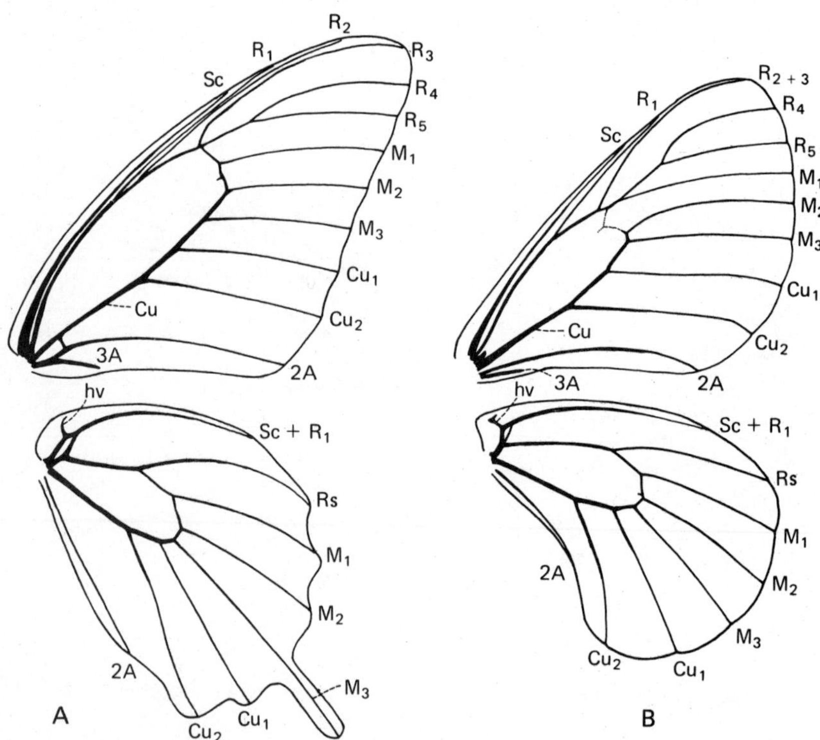

Figure 363. Wings of Papilionòidea. A, *Papílio* (Papiliónidae); B, *Parnássius* (Parnassìidae). *hv*, humeral vein.

10′. Labial palps of normal size, shorter than thorax 11

11(10′). Radius in front wing 5-branched (Figures 364–366 and 367 A); front legs usually reduced in size 12

11′. Radius in front wing 3- or 4-branched (Figures 367 B, 368, and 432); front legs usually of normal size 16

12(11). Third anal vein in front wing present but short, 2A appearing forked at base (Figure 364 A); antennae not scaled above; relatively large, brownish butterflies (Figure 436 A) .... **Danàidae** p. 530

12′. Third anal vein in front wing lacking, 2A not appearing forked at base (Figures 364 B, 365, 366 A, 367 A); antennae usually scaled above 13

13(12′). Some veins in front wing (especially Sc) greatly swollen at base (Figure 364 B); front wings more or less triangular; antennae swollen apically but not distinctly knobbed; small butterflies, usually brownish or grayish with eye spots in wings (Figure 437) .... **Satýridae** p. 530

13′. Generally with no veins in front wing greatly swollen at base (Sc in front wing is slightly swollen in some Nymphálidae); wing color and shape, and antennae, usually not as above 14

14(13′). M_1 in front wing stalked with R (Figure 367 A); front legs normal, or only slightly reduced, their tarsal claws bifid; small butterflies, usually white with black and/or orange markings (orange-tips) .... **Piéridae** p. 528

14′. M_1 in front wing not stalked with R; front legs much reduced and without tarsal claws, not used in walking; usually medium-sized to large butterflies, and not colored as above 15

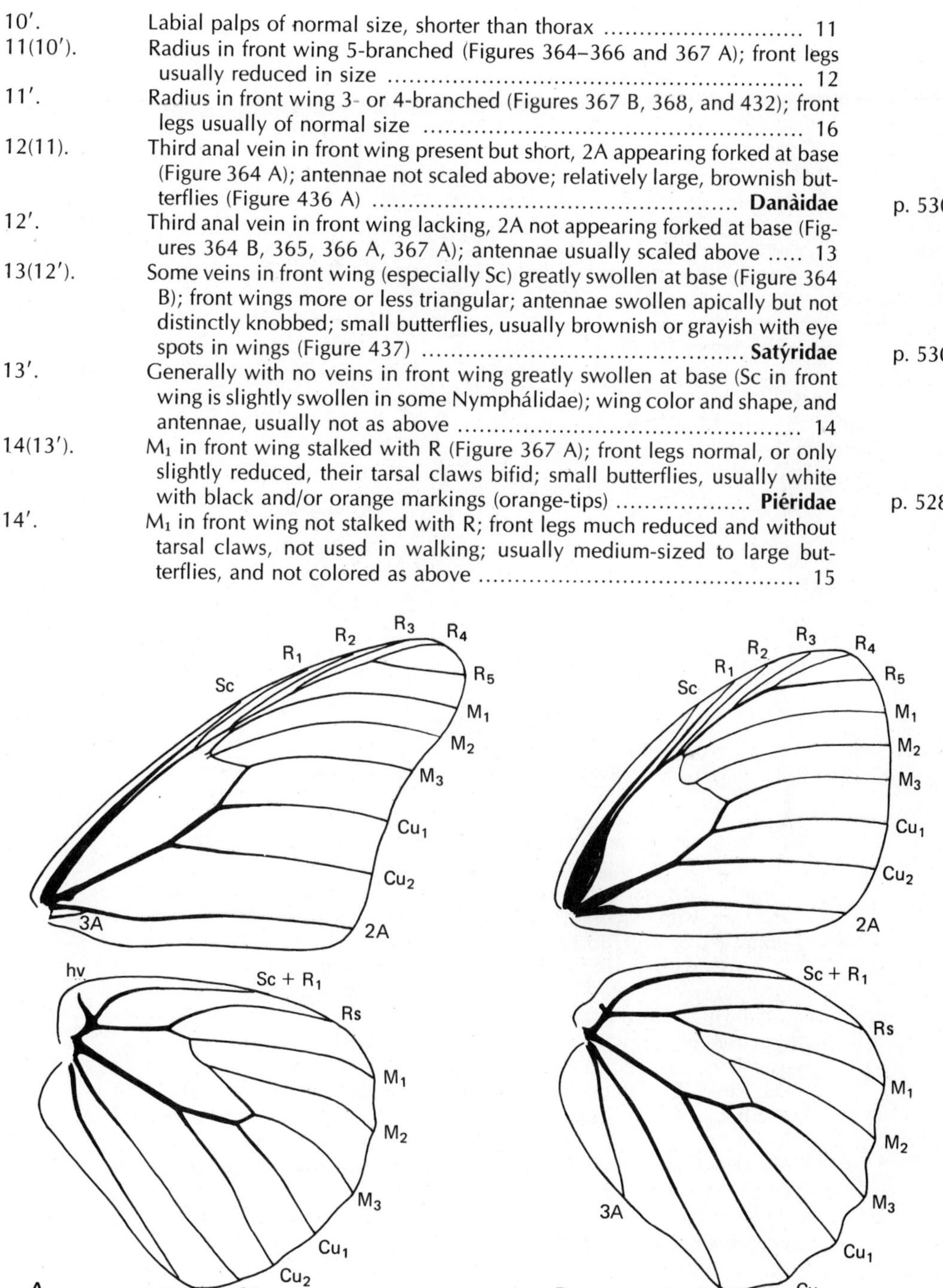

Figure 364. Wings of butterflies. A, *Danàus* (Danàidae); B, *Cercỳonis* (Satýridae). *hv,* humeral vein.

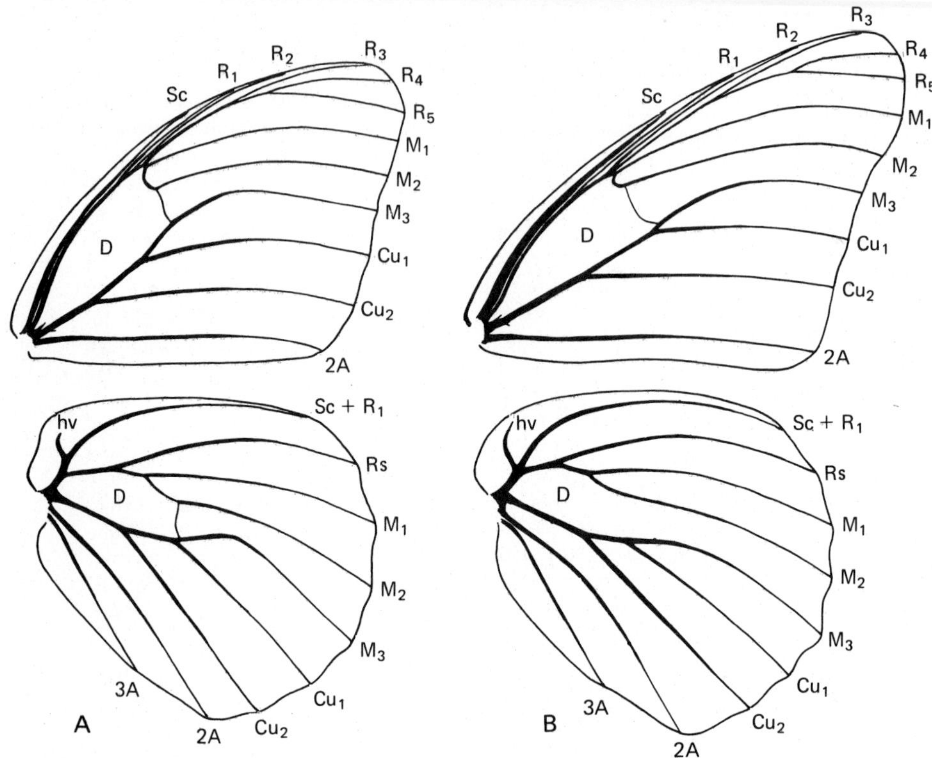

Figure 365. Wings of Nymphálidae. A, *Speyéria* (discal cell in the hind wing closed by a vestigial vein); B, *Limenìtis* (discal cell in the hind wing open). *D,* discal cell; *hv,* humeral vein.

15(14′).	Hind wing with humeral vein usually extending forward or bent distad (Figure 365); front wings more or less triangular (Figure 439); widely distributed	**Nymphálidae**	p. 532
15′.	Hind wing with humeral vein bent basad (Figure 366 A); front wings more elongate (Figure 438); mostly tropical	**Heliconìidae**	p. 530
16(11′).	M_1 in front wing stalked with R beyond discal cell (Figure 367 B); small to medium-sized butterflies, with white, yellow, or orange coloration, usually marked with black (Figure 433)	**Piéridae**	p. 528
16′.	M_1 in front wing usually not stalked with R beyond discal cell (Figure 368); usually not colored as above	17	
17(16′).	Hind wing with C thickened out to humeral angle, and Sc with a basal spur (the humeral vein) (Figure 368 A)	**Riodínidae***	p. 527
17′.	Hind wing with C not thickened at base, and without a humeral vein (Figures 366 B and 368 B)	**Lycaènidae**	p. 526
18(5′).	Wings, especially hind wings, deeply cleft or divided into plumelike divisions (Figure 394); legs long and slender, with long tibial spurs ...	19	
18′.	Wings entire, or front wings only slightly cleft	20	
19(18).	Each wing divided into 6 plumelike lobes	**Alucítidae***	p. 500
19′.	Front wings divided into 2–4 lobes, and hind wings divided into 3 lobes (Figure 394)	**Pterophòridae**	p. 500
20(18′).	A large part of the wings, especially the hind wings, devoid of scales (Figure 402); front wings long and narrow, at least 4 times as long as wide (Figure 401); hind margin of front wings and costal margin of hind wings with a		

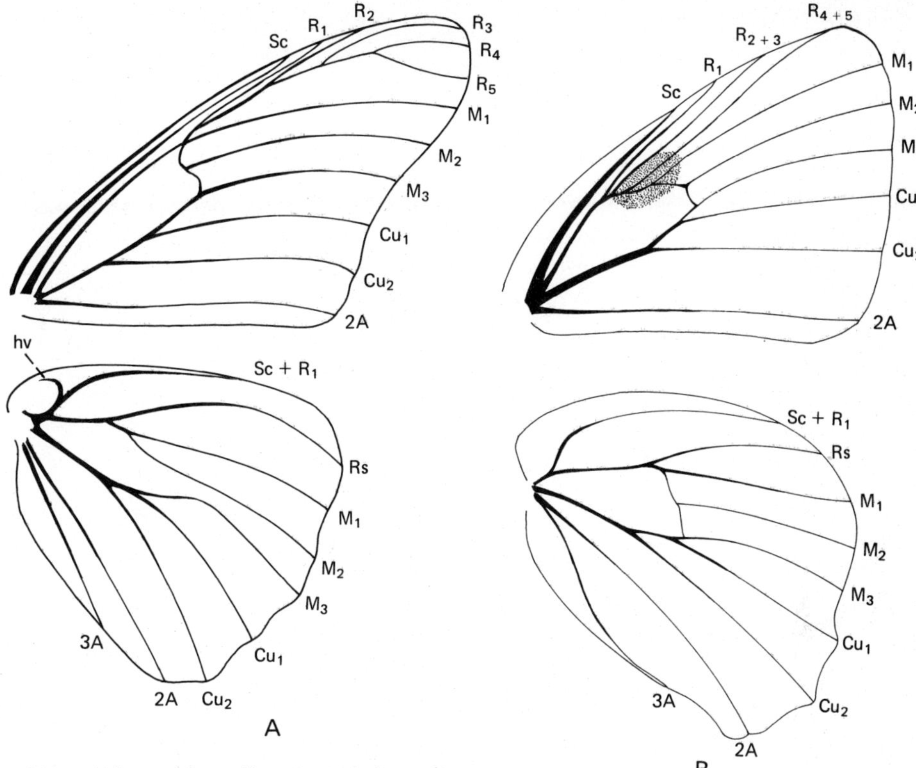

Figure 366. Wings of butterflies. A, *Agràulis* (Heliconìidae); B, *Thécla,* male (Lycaènidae). *hv,* humeral vein. The dark spot in the wing of B, near the end of the discal cell, is a scent gland.

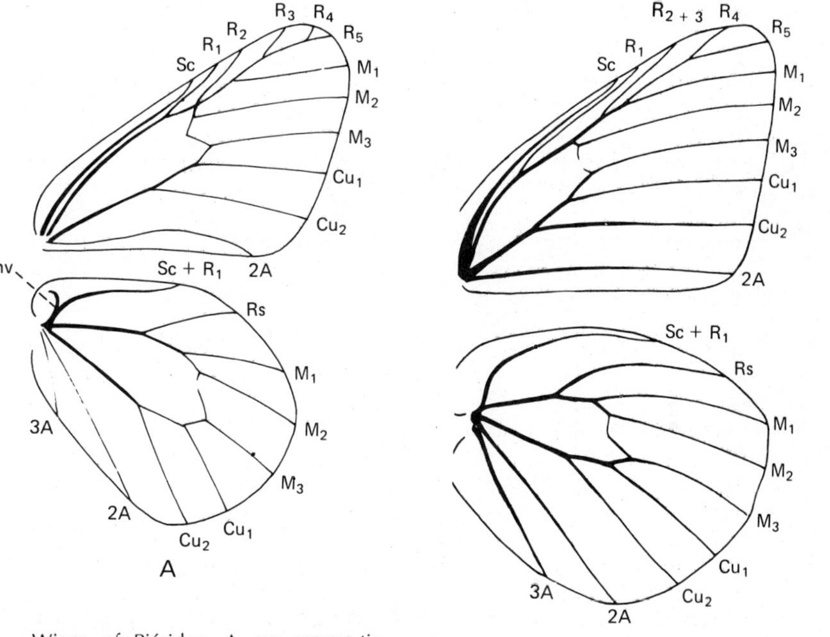

Figure 367. Wings of Piéridae. A, an orange-tip (*Eùchloe*); B, a sulphur (*Còlias*). *hv,* humeral vein.

	series of recurved and interlocking spines; wasplike day-flying moths ... . **Sesìidae**	p. 505
20′.	Wings scaled throughout, or if with clear areas then front wings are more triangular; wings without such interlocking spines 21	
21(20′).	Hind wings much broader than their fringe, and usually wider than front wings, never lanceolate; tibial spurs variable, often short or absent 22	
21′.	Hind wings with a fringe as wide as wings or wider, the wings usually no wider than front wings, often lanceolate (Figure 398); tibial spurs long, more than twice as long as width of tibia (Microlepidóptera) 63	
22(21).	Hind wing with 3 anal veins (mostly Microlepidóptera) 23	
22′.	Hind wing with 1 or 2 anal veins 33	
23(22).	Hind wing with Sc and Rs fused for a varying distance beyond apex of discal cell, or separate but very closely parallel (Figure 369); Sc and R in hind wings separate along front of discal cell, or base of R atrophied .... **Pyrálidae**	p. 498
23′.	Hind wing with Sc and Rs widely separate beyond apex of discal cell, and base of R usually well developed 24	
24(23′).	Sc and Rs in hind wing fused to near end of discal cell, or at least fused beyond middle of cell (Figure 370) 25*	
24′.	Sc and Rs in hind wing separate from base, or fused for a short distance along basal half of discal cell (Figures 371 and 372) 26	
25(24).	Wings largely or wholly blackish, and thinly scaled; R_5 in front wing arising from discal cell (Figure 370 A) .... **Pyromórphidae***	p. 498
25′.	Wings largely yellowish or white, and densely clothed with soft scales and	

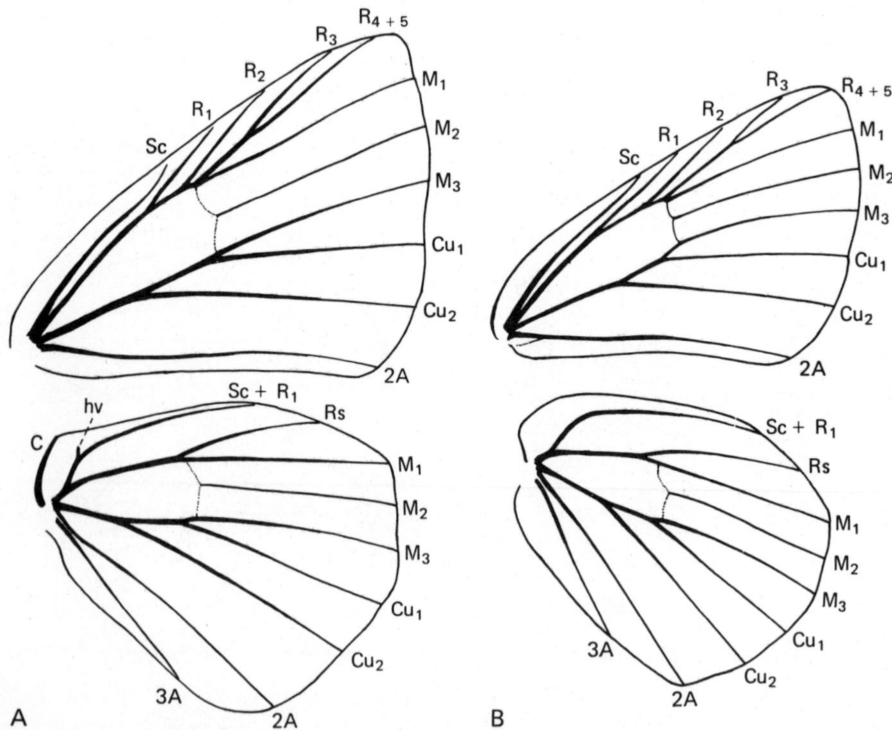

Figure 368. A, wings of *Lephilísca* (Riodínidae); B, wings of *Lycaèna* (Lycaènidae). *hv,* humeral vein.

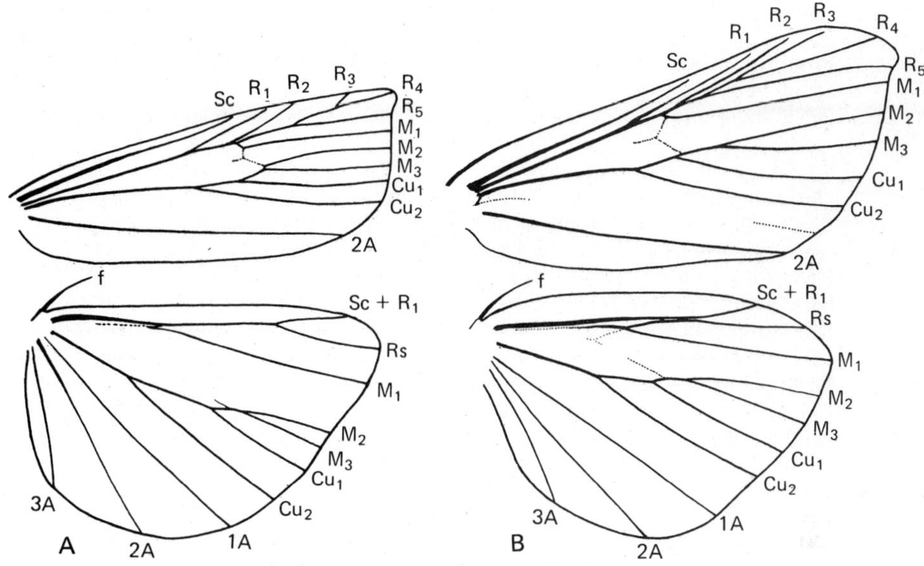

Figure 369. Wings of Pyrálidae. A, *Crámbus* (Crambìnae); B, *Pýralis* (Pyralìnae). *f,* frenulum.

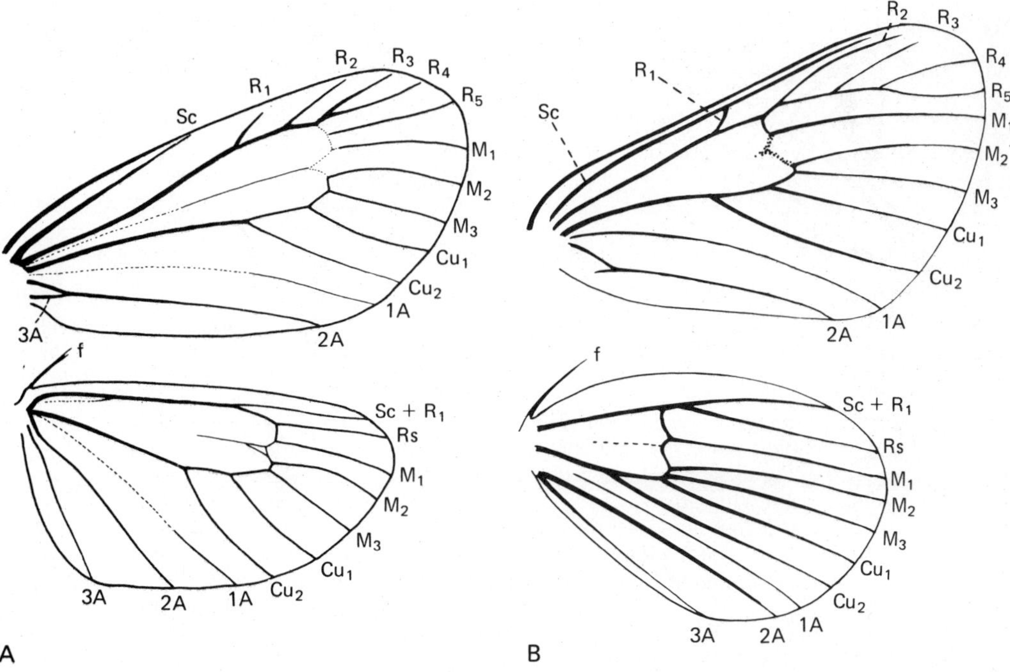

Figure 370. A, wings of *Málthaca* (Pyromòrphidae); B, wings of *Megalopỳge* (Megalopỳgidae). *f,* frenulum.

	hair; R_5 in front wing stalked beyond discal cell (Figure 370 B) .... **Megalopýgidae***	p. 497
26(24′).	Front wing with an accessory cell (Figure 371 A, *acc*) 27	
26′.	Front wing without an accessory cell (Figure 372) 30	
27(26).	Tibial spurs short, no longer than width of tibia; mouth parts often vestigial 28	
27′.	Tibial spurs long, more than twice width of tibia; mouth parts usually well developed, the proboscis scaled (Microlepidóptera) 63	
28(27).	Front wing with some branches of R stalked, and accessory cell extending beyond discal cell (Figure 371 A) 29	
28′.	Front wing with no branches of R stalked, and accessory cell not extending beyond discal cell; antennae bipectinate; small moths ... **Epipyrópidae***	p. 498
29(28).	Front wings subtriangular, about one half longer than wide; wings densely clothed with soft scales and hair; Arizona .... **Dalcéridae***	p. 498
29′.	Front wings more elongate, at least twice as long as wide; wings more thinly scaled; widely distributed .... **Cóssidae**	p. 502

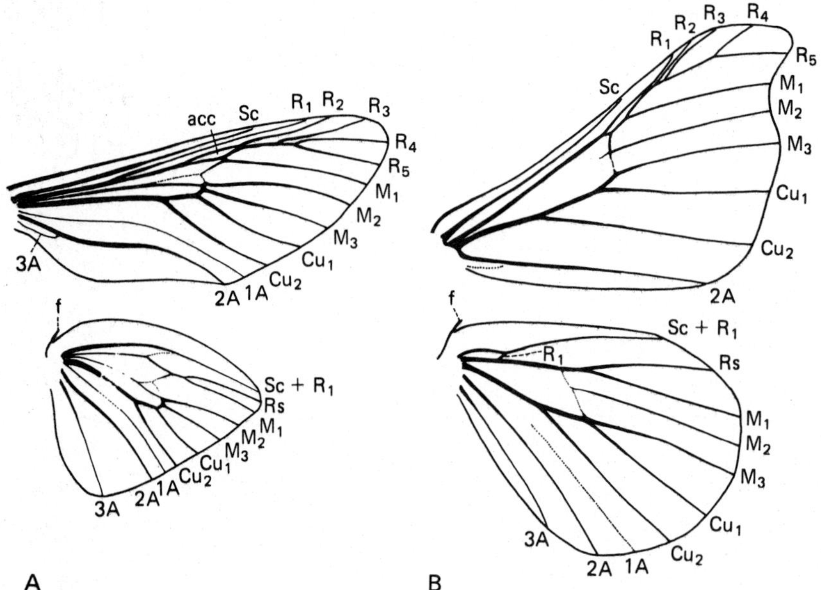

Figure 371. A, wings of *Prionoxýstus* (Cóssidae); B, wings of *Bómbyx* (Bombýcidae). *acc*, accessory cell; *f*, frenulum.

30(26′).	M_2 in front wing arising about midway between M_1 and M_2, or closer to M_1, the cubitus appearing 3-branched (Figures 371 B and 372 B); frenulum present or absent 31*	
30′.	M_2 in front wing arising closer to M_3 than to M_1, the cubitus appearing 4-branched; frenulum well developed (Figure 372 A) .... **Limacòdidae**	p. 497
31(30).	M_3 and Cu_1 in front wing stalked for a short distance beyond apex of discal cell; frenulum well developed; California (see also couplet 43) .... **Dióptidae***	p. 517
31′.	M_3 and Cu_1 in front wing not stalked beyond discal cell; frenulum small or absent; widely distributed 32*	

32(31′). Front wing with R_{2+3} and R_{4+5} stalked independently of R_1, and Sc and Rs in hind wing not connected by a cross vein (Figure 372 B) .... **Mimallónidae*** p. 513

32′. Front wing with R_2, R_3, R_4, and R_5 united on a common stalk, and Sc and Rs in hind wing connected basally by a cross vein (R_1) (Figure 371 B) .... **Bombýcidae*** p. 519

33(22′). Front wing with 2 distinct and separate anal veins (*Harrisìna*) .... **Pyromórphidae*** p. 498

33′. Front wing with a single complete anal vein (Figures 373 B and 374–382), or with 1A and 2A fusing near tip or connected by a cross vein (Figure 373 A) 34

34(33′). Front wing with a single complete anal vein (2A), 1A at most represented by a fold, and 3A absent or meeting 2A basally so that 2A appears forked at base (Figures 373 B and 374–382) 35

34′. Front wing with 1A and 2A fusing near tip (Figure 373 A) or connected by a cross vein .... **Psỳchidae** p. 508

35(34). Antennae thickened, spindle-shaped (Figure 361 C); Sc and Rs in hind wing connected by a cross vein near middle of discal cell, the two veins closely parallel to end of discal cell or beyond (Figure 373 B); stout-bodied, often large moths (wingspread 2 inches (50 mm) or more), with narrow wings (Figure 429) .... **Sphíngidae** p. 522

35′. Antennae variable, rarely spindle-shaped; Sc and Rs in hind wing usually not connected by a cross vein, or if such a cross vein is present then the two veins are strongly divergent beyond the cross vein 36

36(35′). M_2 in front wing arising about midway between M_1 and M_3, the cubitus appearing 3-branched (Figures 374–376), or (rarely) with M_2 and M_3 absent and the cubitus appearing to have fewer than 3 branches 37

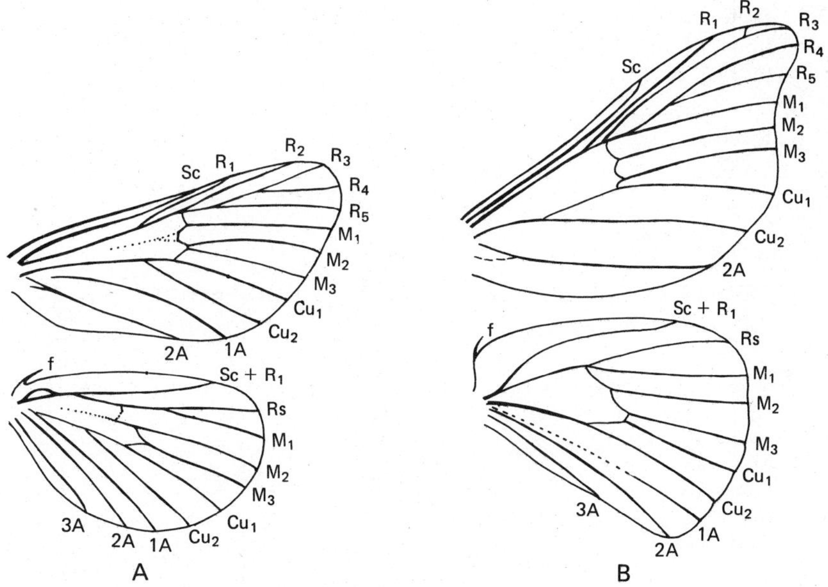

Figure 372. A, wings of *Euclèa* (Limacòdidae); B, wings of *Cicínnus* (Mimallónidae). *f*, frenulum.

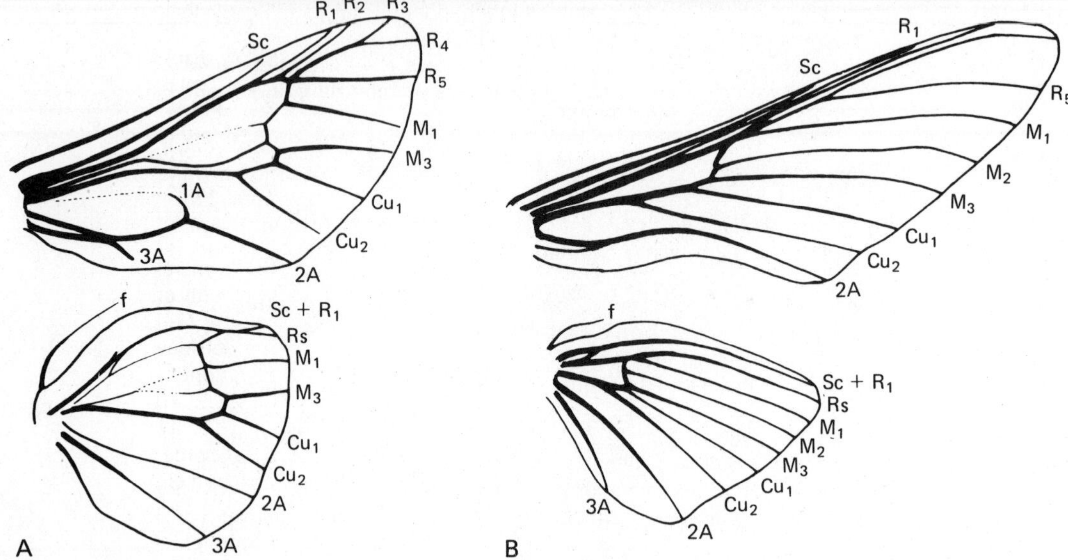

Figure 373. A, wings of *Thyridópteryx* (Psỳchidae); B, wings of *Hémaris* (Sphíngidae). *f*, frenulum.

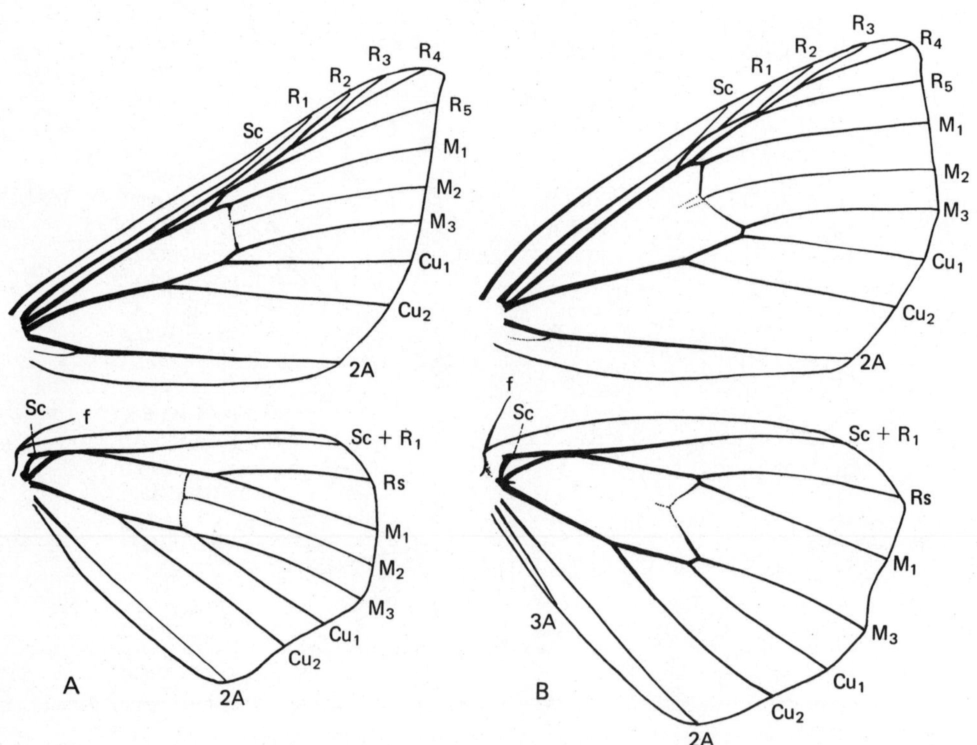

Figure 374. Wings of Geométridae. A, *Haemátopis;* B, *Xanthótype*. *f*, frenulum.

36′. M_2 in front wing arising closer to M_3 than to M_1, the cubitus appearing 4-branched (Figures 377–382) 49

37(36). Sc and Rs in hind wing swollen at base, fused to beyond middle of discal cell, then diverging; M_2 and M_3 in front wing sometimes absent; small slender moths (Lithosiìnae) .... **Arctìidae** p. 513

37′. Sc and Rs in hind wing not fused at base, though they may be fused farther distad or connected by a cross vein 38

38(37′). Antennae dilated apically; eyes hairy; Arizona .... **Manidìidae*** p. 519

38′. Antennae not dilated apically, or if so then eyes are bare; widely distributed 39

39(38′). Sc in hind wing strongly angled at base, and usually connected to humeral angle of wing by a strong brace vein; beyond the bend Sc fuses with or comes close to Rs for a short distance along discal cell (Figure 374) .... **Geométridae** p. 510

39′. Sc in hind wing straight or slightly curving at base, not of the above conformation 40

40(39′). Frenulum well developed; Sc and Rs in hind wing variable 41

40′. Frenulum vestigial or absent; Sc and Rs in hind wing never fused, but sometimes touching at a point beyond base, or connected by a cross vein 46

41(40). Sc in hind wing widely separated from Rs from near base of wing; M_1 in front wing stalked with R_5, which is well separated from R_4 .... **Epiplèmidae*** p. 510

41′. Sc in hind wing close to Rs at least to middle of discal cell, often farther 42

42(41′). M_2 in hind wing arising nearer to M_3 than to M_1, the cubitus appearing 4-branched; M_1 in hind wing arising from discal cell, not stalked with Rs beyond cell .... **Thyatíridae*** p. 511

42′. M_2 in hind wing absent, or arising midway between M_1 and M_3, or nearer to M_1, the cubitus appearing 3-branched; M_1 in hind wing stalked with Rs for a short distance beyond discal cell (Figure 375) 43

43(42′). M_3 and Cu_1 in both wings stalked for a short distance beyond discal cell; slender, butterflylike moths; California .... **Dióptidae*** p. 517

43′. Not exactly fitting the above description 44

44(43′). Slender-bodied moths; a tympanic hood at base of abdomen; Sc sinuous or swollen at base .... **Geométridae*** p. 510

44′. Stout-bodied moths; no tympanic hood at base of abdomen 45

45(44′). Sc and Rs in hind wing close together and parallel along almost entire length of discal cell (Figure 375 B); proboscis usually present; front wings fully scaled; tarsal claws with a blunt tooth at base .... **Notodóntidae** p. 517

45′. Sc and Rs in hind wing separating near middle of discal cell (Figure 375 A); proboscis lacking; front wings with 1 or 2 small clear spots near tip; tarsal claws simple .... **Apatelòdidae*** p. 519

46(40′). Sc and Rs in hind wing connected by a cross vein (Figure 371 B); white moths of medium size .... **Bombýcidae*** p. 519

46′. Sc and Rs in hind wing not connected by a cross vein (Figures 372 B, 375 A); color variable, but not white; size medium to large 47

47(46′). Sc and Rs in hind wing separating near middle of discal cell, at the end of a long narrow basal areole; Rs and M_1 in hind wing stalked beyond discal cell (Figure 375 A) .... **Apatelòdidae*** p. 519

47′. Sc and Rs in hind wing separating at base of wing; Rs and M_1 in hind wing not stalked beyond discal cell (Figures 372 B, 376) 48

48(47′). Yellowish moths with a wingspread of about 25 mm and outer margin of front wings somewhat scalloped (*Lacosòma*), or brownish moths with a

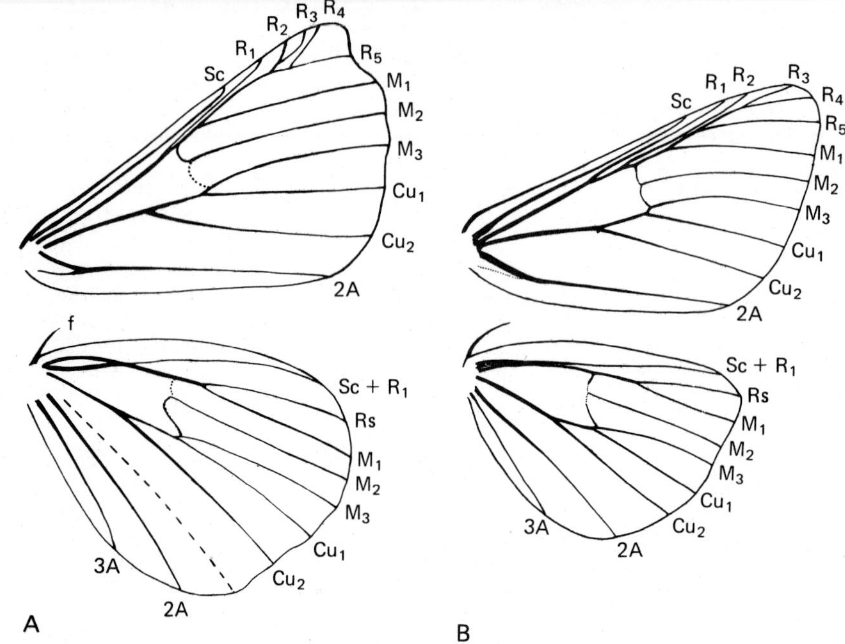

Figure 375. A, wings of *Apatelòdes* (Apatelòdidae); B, wings of *Datàna* (Notodóntidae). *f*, frenulum.

wingspread of about 1½ inches (38 mm) and a narrow blackish band across both front and hind wings (*Cicínnus*) (Figure 411 B); antennae closely scaled on upper side .... **Mimallónidae*** p. 513

48′. Color variable; wingspread 1–6 inches (25–150 mm); outer margin of front wings not scalloped (Figures 426 and 427) .... **Saturnìidae** p. 520

49(36′). All branches of R and M in front wing arising separately from the usually open discal cell (Figure 377 A); wings generally with clear spots .... **Thyrídidae*** p. 498

49′. Front wing with some branches of R and/or M fused beyond discal cell (Figures 377 B and 378–382) 50

50(49′). Hind wing with humeral veins and without a frenulum; Cu_2 in front wing arising in basal half or third of discal cell (Figure 377 B) .... **Lasiocámpidae** p. 519

50′. Hind wing without humeral veins, and usually with a frenulum; Cu_2 in front wing arising in distal half of discal cell 51

51(50′). Frenulum absent or vestigial; Sc and Rs in hind wing approximated, usually parallel along discal cell, or fusing beyond middle of cell (Figure 378 A); apex of front wings usually sickle-shaped .... **Drepánidae** p. 513

51′. Frenulum well developed; Sc and Rs in hind wing not as above; apex of front wings usually not sickle-shaped 52

52(51′). Antennae swollen apically; Sc in hind wing fused with Rs for only a short distance at base of discal cell (Figure 378 B); ocelli present; moths with a wingspread of about 25 mm, usually black with white or yellow spots in wings (Figure 416) .... **Agarístidae** p. 514

52′. Antennae usually not swollen apically; Sc in hind wing variable; ocelli present or absent 53

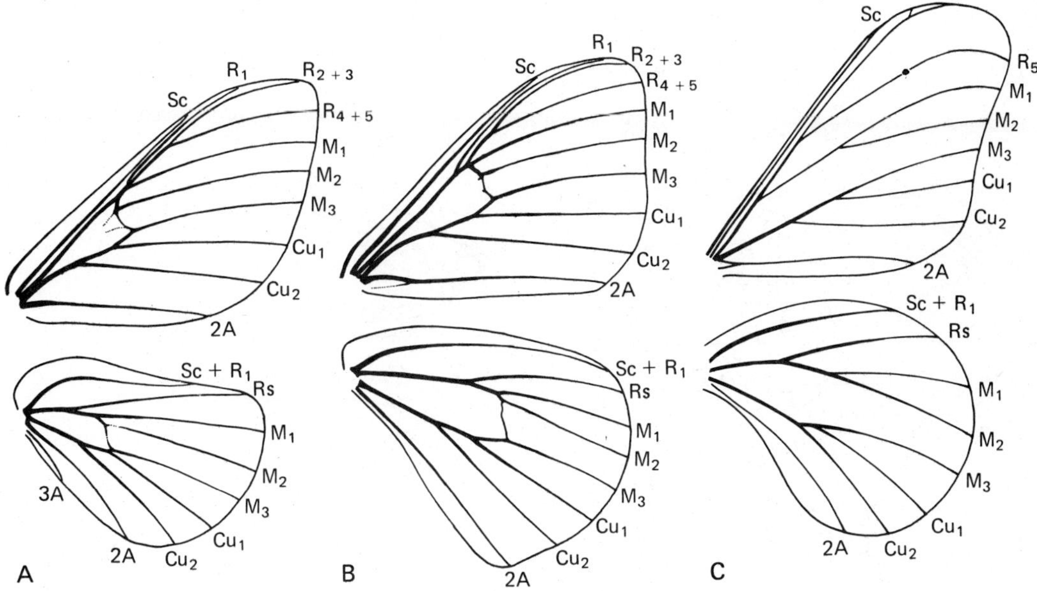

Figure 376. Wings of Saturnìidae. A, *Anisòta* (Citheroniìnae); B, *Autómeris* (Hemileucìnae); C, *Callosàmia* (Saturniìnae).

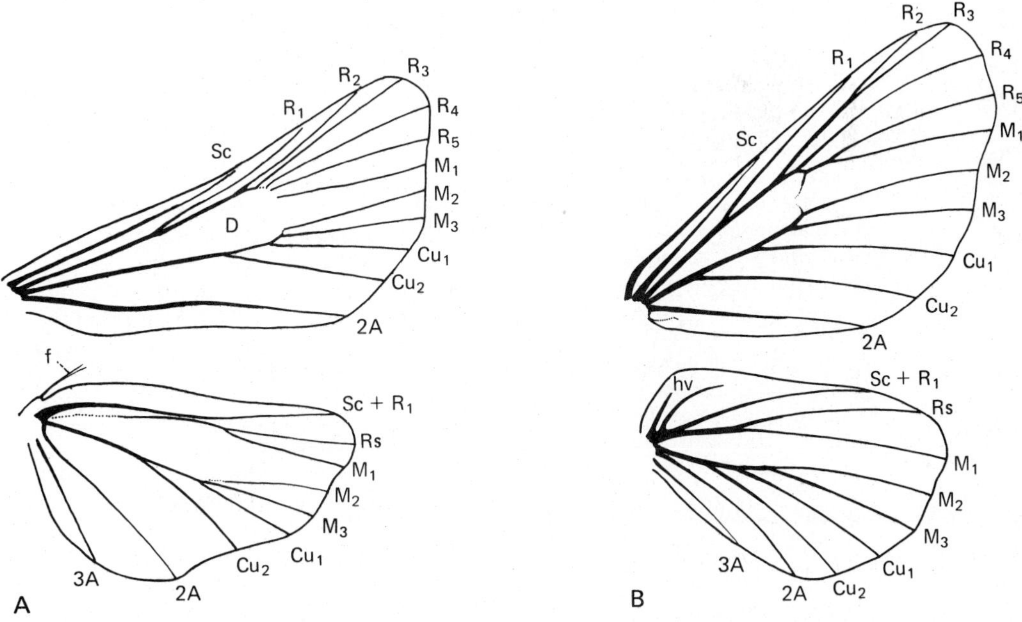

Figure 377. A, wings of *Thỳris* (Thyrídidae); B, wings of *Malacosòma* (Lasiocámpidae). *f*, frenulum; *hv*, humeral veins.

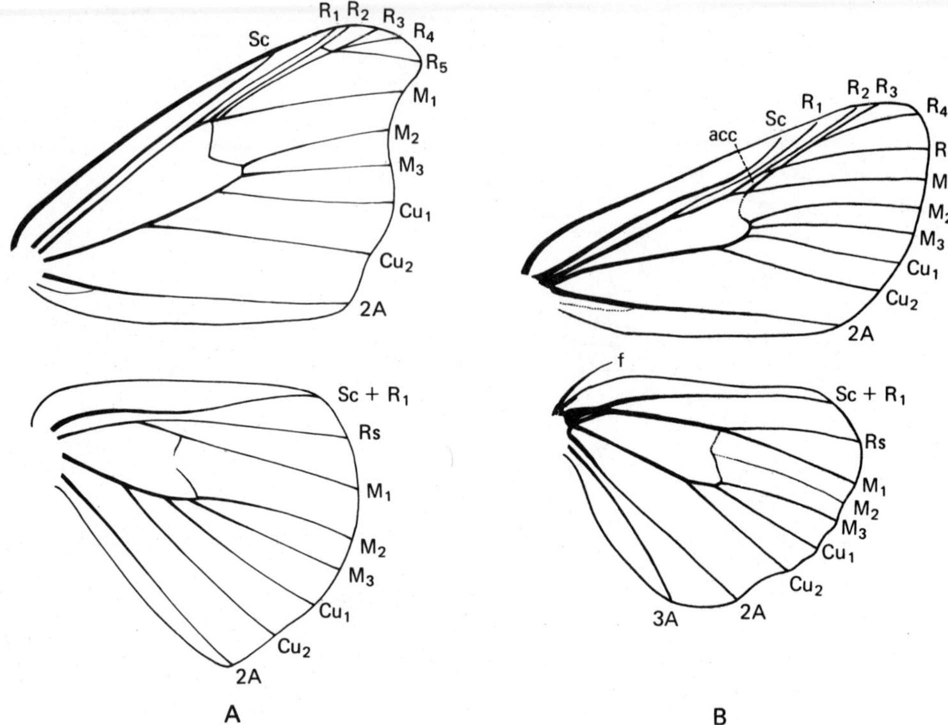

Figure 378. A, wings of *Orèta* (Drepánidae); B, wings of *Alýpia* (Agarístidae). *acc,* accessory cell; *f,* frenulum.

53(52′). Sc in hind wing apparently absent (Figure 379 A); day-flying moths (Figure 413) .... **Ctenùchidae** p. 513

53′. Sc in hind wing present and well developed 54

54(53′). Sc and Rs in hind wing fused for a varying distance beyond discal cell, or separate but very closely parallel (Figure 369); Sc and Rs in hind wing separate along front of discal cell, or base of Rs atrophied 55*

54′. Hind wing with Sc and Rs widely separate beyond discal cell, and base of Rs usually well developed 56

55(54). Front wings at least twice as long as wide, their costal margin often irregular or lobed (if straight, M_2 and M_3 are usually stalked); separation of Sc and Rs in hind wing generally well beyond discal cell; color variable, rarely white (Chrysaugìnae) .... **Pyrálidae*** p. 498

55′. Front wings less than twice as long as wide, their costal margin straight; M_2 and M_3 not stalked; separation of Sc and Rs in hind wing about opposite end of discal cell; white moths (*Eudeilínea*) .... **Drepánidae*** p. 513

56(54′). Apex of front wing sickle-shaped (Figure 378 A); Sc and Rs in hind wing separate and more or less parallel along anterior side of discal cell (as in Figure 378 A) (*Drépana*) .... **Drepánidae** p. 513

56′. Apex of front wing not sickle-shaped; Sc and Rs in hind wing not as above (Figures 379 B, 380–382) 57

57(56′). Ocelli present 58

57′. Ocelli absent 60

58(57). M_3 and Cu_1 in hind wing stalked (Figure 379 B); black or brownish moths with white or yellow spots or bands in wings, sometimes with metallic tints; the Gulf States and western United States .... **Pericópidae*** p. 517

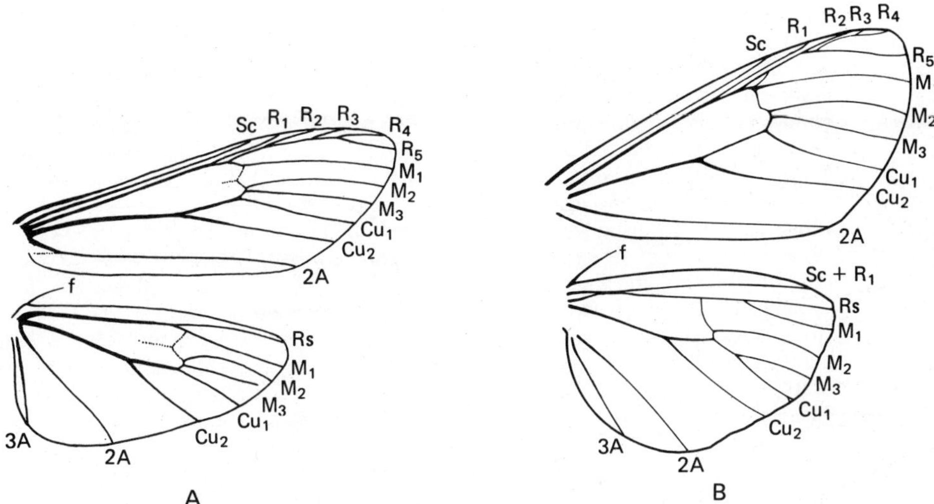

Figure 379. A, wings of *Scépsis* (Ctenùchidae); B, wings of *Gnophaèla* (Pericópidae). *f,* frenulum.

58′. M_3 and Cu_1 in hind wing not stalked; color variable; widely distributed 59

59(58′). Hind wing with Sc and Rs separating well before middle of discal cell, and Sc not noticeably swollen at base; cubitus in hind wing appearing 3- or 4-branched (Figure 381); labial palps extending to middle of front or beyond; usually dark-colored moths .... **Noctùidae** p. 514

59′. Hind wing with Sc and Rs usually fused (beyond a small basal areole) to middle of discal cell, or if not then Sc is swollen at base; cubitus in hind wing appearing 4-branched (Figure 380); labial palps not exceeding middle of front; usually light-colored moths .... **Arctìidae** p. 513

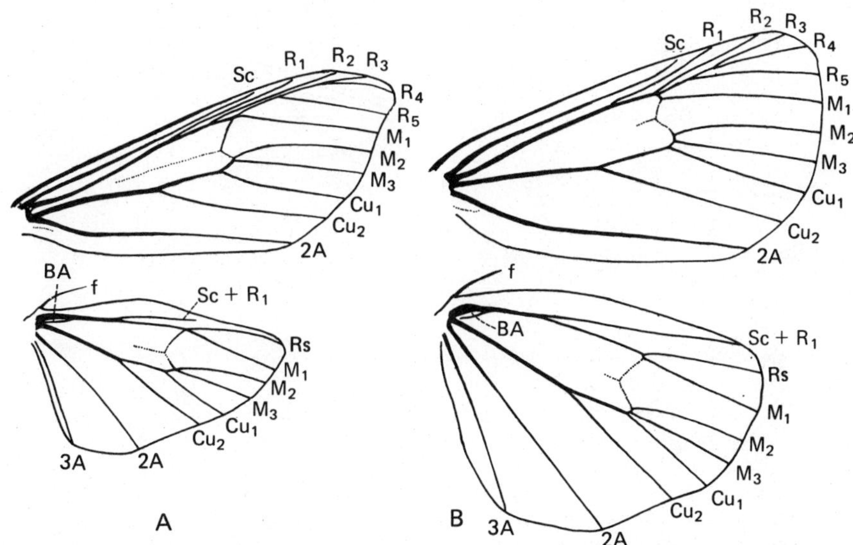

Figure 380. Wings of Arctìidae (Arctiìnae). A, *Halisidòta;* B, *Apántesis. BA,* basal areole; *f,* frenulum.

60(57′). Front wings with tufts of raised scales; Sc and Rs in hind wing fused (beyond a small basal areole) to near middle of discal cell; small moths .... **Nòlidae*** p. 513

60′. Front wings smoothly scaled; Sc and Rs in hind wing not as above .. 61

61(60′). Hind wing with a relatively large basal areole, and Sc and Rs fused for only a short distance at end of areole (Figure 382) .... **Lipàridae** p. 518

61′. Hind wing with a very small basal areole or none, and Sc and Rs fused for a varying distance along discal cell, at most to middle of cell 62

62(61′). Labial palps short, usually not exceeding middle of face; size variable, up to a wingspread of about 40 mm; often brightly colored, reddish, yellowish, or whitish (Lithosiìnae) .... **Arctìidae** p. 513

62′. Labial palps longer, extending to middle of front or beyond; wingspread 20 mm or less; dull-colored moths (Hypenodìnae) .... **Noctùidae*** p. 514

63(21′, 27′). Basal segment of antennae enlarged and concave beneath, forming an eye cap (Figure 383 B) 64

63′. Basal segment of antennae not forming an eye cap (Figure 383 A) 68

64(63). Maxillary palps well developed and conspicuous, folded in a resting position (as in Figure 383 D); wing membrane aculeate (with minute spines under the scales) 65*

64′. Maxillary palps vestigial, or projecting forward in a resting position; wing membrane not aculeate 66

65(64). Front wing with only 3 or 4 unbranched veins; wingspread usually over 3 mm .... **Opostégidae*** p. 508

65′. Front wing with branched veins (Figure 384 A); wingspread 3 mm or less .... **Nepticùlidae*** p. 510

66(64′). Labial palps minute and drooping, or absent; ocelli absent .... **Lyonetìidae*** p. 508

66′. Labial palps of at least moderate size, upcurved or projecting forward; ocelli present or absent 67

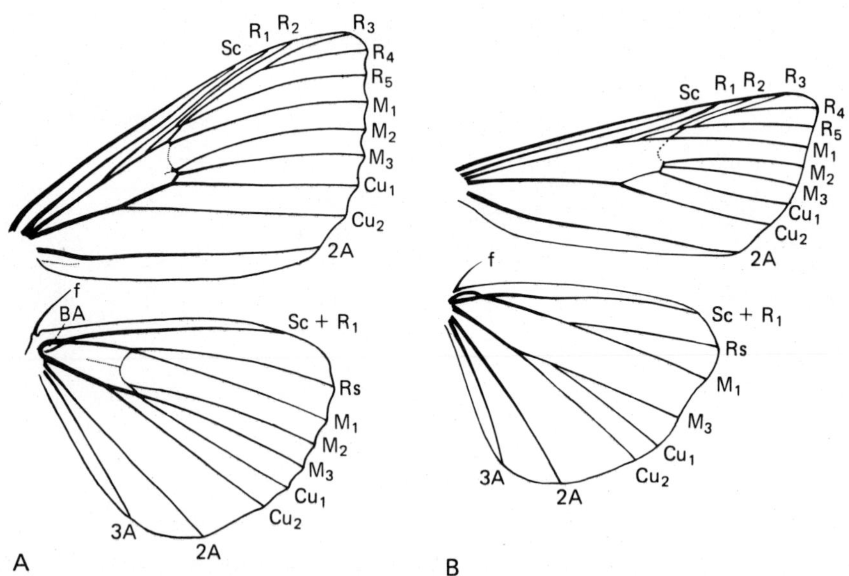

Figure 381. Wings of Noctùidae, with M_2 in hind wing present and Cu appearing 4-branched (A), and M_2 in hind wing absent and Cu appearing 3-branched (B). *BA*, basal areole.

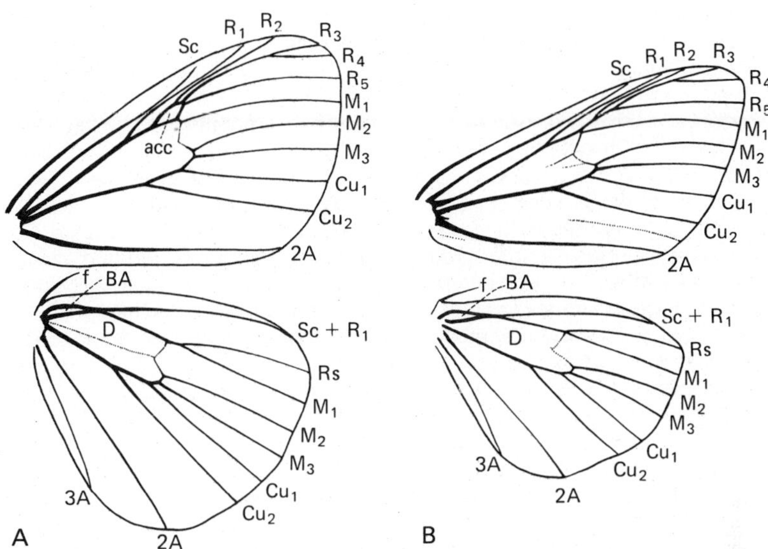

Figure 382. Wings of Lipáridae. A, *Hemerocámpa;* B, *Porthètria. BA,* basal areole; *D,* discal cell; *f,* frenulum.

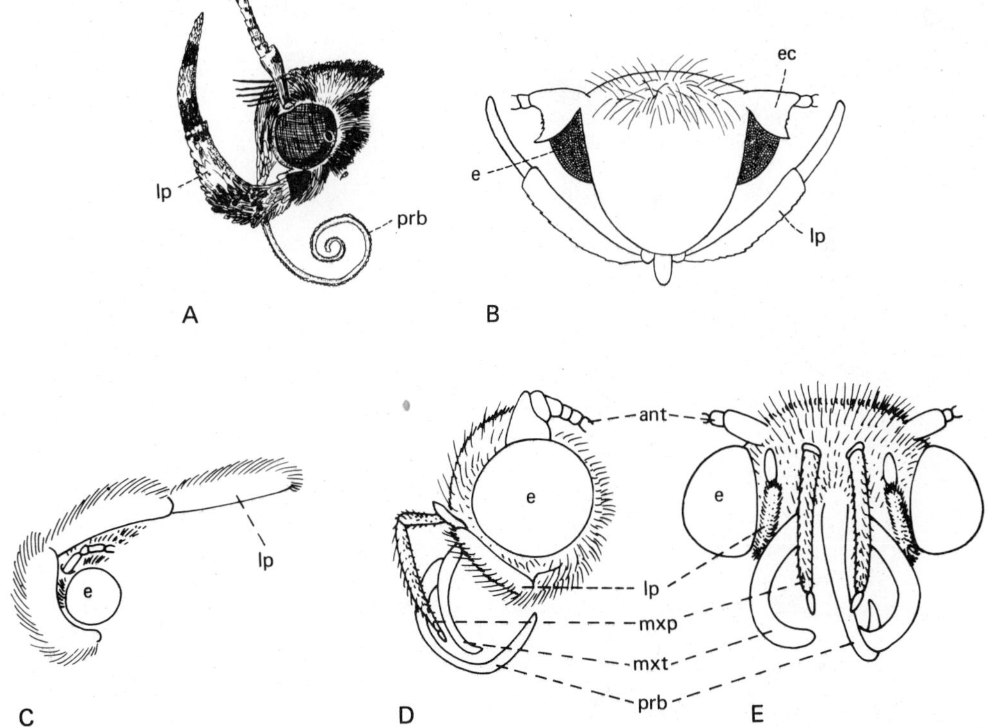

Figure 383. Head structure in Microlepidóptera. A, *Pectinóphora* (Gelechìidae), lateral view; B, *Zenodòchium* (Blastobàsidae), anterior view; C, *Acrólophus* (Acrolóphidae), lateral view; D, lateral, and E, anterior, views of *Tegetícula* (Incurvarìidae, Prodoxìnae). *ant,* antenna; *e,* compound eye; *ec,* eye cap; *lp,* labial palp; *mxp,* maxillary palp; *mxt,* maxillary tentacle; *prb,* proboscis. (A, redrawn from Busck; B, redrawn from Dietz.)

67(66′). Wings pointed at apex; hind wing without a discal cell; veins beyond discal cell in front wing diverging; no stigmalike thickening in front wing between C and R_1 (*Phyllocnístis,* etc.) .... **Gracilarìidae** p. 507

67′. Wings more or less rounded at apex; hind wing usually with a closed discal cell; veins beyond discal cell in front wing nearly parallel; front wing with a stigmalike thickening between C and R_1 (as in Figure 384 B) (*Calosìma*) .... **Blastobàsidae*** p. 504

68(63′). Maxillary palps well developed, folded in a resting position (Figure 383 D) 69

68′. Maxillary palps vestigial, or projecting forward in a resting position .. 72

69(68). Head smooth-scaled; R_5 when present extending to costal margin of wing; strongly flattened moths; Louisiana and Mississippi .... **Oinophílidae*** p. 508

69′. Head tufted, at least on vertex, or R_5 extending to outer margin of wing; widely distributed 70

70(69′). R_5 in front wing extending to costal margin of wing, or absent 71

70′. R_5 in front wing extending to outer margin of wing; head with a few erect hairs (*Acrolèpia*) .... **Plutéllidae*** p. 506

71(70). Wing membrane aculeate (see couplet 64); antennae smooth, often very long; female with a piercing ovipositor (Incurvariìnae and Prodoxìnae) .... **Incurvarìidae** p. 510

71′. Wing membrane not aculeate; antennae usually rough, with a whorl of erect scales on each segment; ovipositor membranous, retractile .... **Tinèidae** p. 509

72(68′). First segment or labial palps as large as second, or larger (Figure 383 C), or if smaller, then labial palps are recurved back over head and extend over most of thorax; eyes usually hairy; ocelli absent .... **Acrolóphidae*** p. 509

72′. First segment of labial palps smaller than second (Figure 383 A), and labial palps never extending past anterior portion of thorax; eyes usually bare; ocelli present or absent 73

73(72′). Distal margin of hind wings concave, apex produced (Figure 385 C) .... **Gelechìidae** p. 503

73′. Hind wings with distal margin rounded or trapezoidal and anal region well

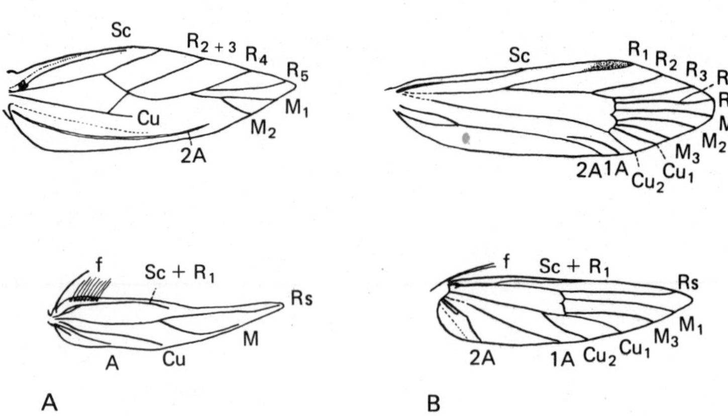

Figure 384. Wings of Microlepidóptera. A, *Obrússa* (Nepticùlidae); B, *Holcócera* (Blastobàsidae). *f,* frenulum. (A, redrawn from Braun; B, redrawn from Comstock, after Forbes, by permission of Comstock Publishing Co.)

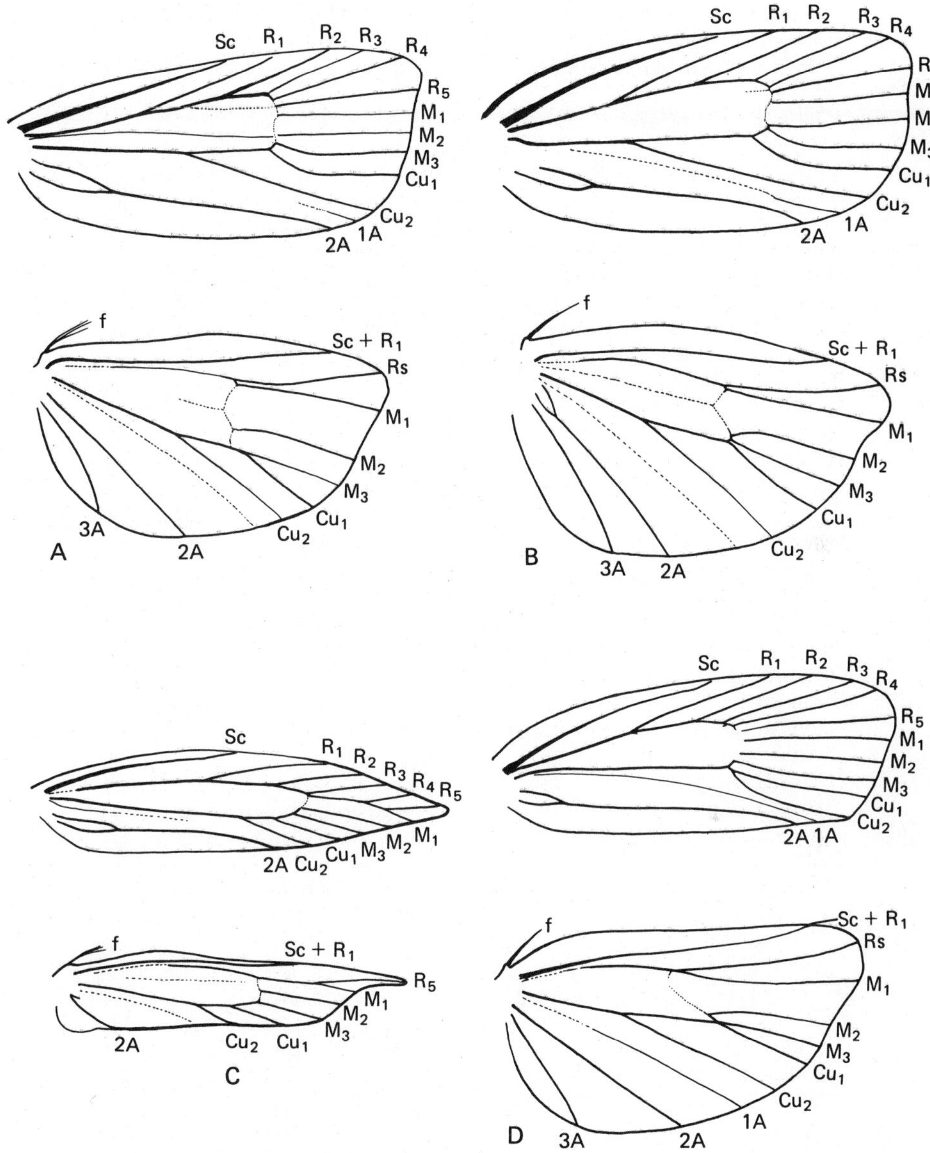

Figure 385. Wings of Microlepidóptera. A, Olethreùtidae (*Laspeyrèsia*); B, Tortrícidae; C, Gelechìidae; D, Stenòmidae (*Stenòma*). *f*, frenulum.

developed, venation complete or nearly so (Figures 385 A, B, D and 386) (see also 73″) 74

73″. Hind wings lanceolate or linear, pointed at apex, the anal region and venation often reduced (Figures 387 and 388 A) 90

74(73′). Hind wing with only 1 or 2 branches of M; 1A lacking in front wing .... **Carposìnidae*** p. 502

74′. Hind wing with 3 (rarely only 2) branches of M; 1A in front wing present or absent 75

75(74′). Cu_2 in front wing arising in basal three fourths of discal cell (Figure 385 A, B) 76

75′. Cu_2 in front wing arising in distal fourth of discal cell (Figure 385 D), or if not there is no fringe on base of Cu 77

76(75). Upper side of Cu in hind wing with a fringe of long hairs, or if this fringe is lacking (*Laspeyrèsia*) M_1 and M_2 in front wing are close together at tip; front wing with R_4 and R_5 separate, or M_2, M_3, and Cu_1 strongly convergent distally .... **Olethreùtidae** p. 500

76′. Upper side of Cu in hind wing without a fringe of long hairs; R_4 and R_5 in front wing often stalked or fused; M_2, M_3, and Cu_1 in front wing divergent or parallel .... **Tortrícidae** p. 501

77(75′). Labial palps and proboscis vestigial (*Solenòbia*) .... **Psỳchidae*** p. 508

77′. Labial palps and proboscis well developed 78

78(77′). 1A lacking in front wing 79*

78′. 1A present in front wing, at least at margin 81

79(78). Third segment of labial palps short and blunt, the palps beaklike; R_5 in front wing rarely stalked with R_4, and usually extending to outer margin of wing .... **Phaloniìdae*** p. 502

79′. Third segment of labial palps long and slender, usually tapering, the palps upturned to middle of front or beyond (Figure 383 A); R_5 in front wing stalked with R_4, and extending to costal margin of wing (Figure 385 C) 80*

80(79′). Hind wing with discal cell open, M_3 and Cu_1 stalked, and M_2 stalked with M_3 and Cu_1 (*Triclonélla*) .... **Cosmopterýgidae*** p. 502

80′. Hind wing with discal cell usually closed, M_3 and Cu_1 stalked or separated, and M_2 usually arising from discal cell .... **Gelechìidae*** p. 503

81(78′). Vertex and upper part of face tufted with dense bristly hairs 82

81′. Upper part of face (and usually also vertex) smooth, with short scales 83

82(81). Wing membrane aculeate (see couplet 64); antennae long, often longer than body; female with a piercing ovipositor (Adelìnae) .... **Incurvarìidae*** p. 510

82′. Wing membrane usually not aculeate; antennae generally short; female with the ovipositor membranous and retractile .... **Tinèidae** p. 509

83(81′). Rs and M_1 in hind wing arising close together, stalked, or fused (Figure 385 D) 84*

83′. Rs and M_1 in hind wing well separated at their origin, at least half as far apart as at wing margin Figure 386) 85

84(83). Front wings narrowly rounded or pointed apically (*Ceróstoma*) .... **Plutéllidae*** p. 506

84′. Front wings broadly rounded or blunt apically (Figure 385 D) .... **Stenòmidae*** p. 504

85(83′). Ocelli very large and conspicuous .... **Glyphipterýgidae*** p. 505

85′. Ocelli small or absent 86

86(85′). R_4 and R_5 in front wing stalked 87

86′. R_4 and R_5 in front wing not stalked 89

87(86). Front wing with a stigmalike thickening between C and R_1 (Figure 384 B); hind wings narrower than front wings .... **Blastobàsidae*** p. 504

87′. Front wing without such a stigmalike thickening; hind wings usually as wide as front wings (Figure 386 A) 88

88(87′). M_2 in hind wing arising closer to M_1 than to M_3 .... **Ethmìidae*** p. 505

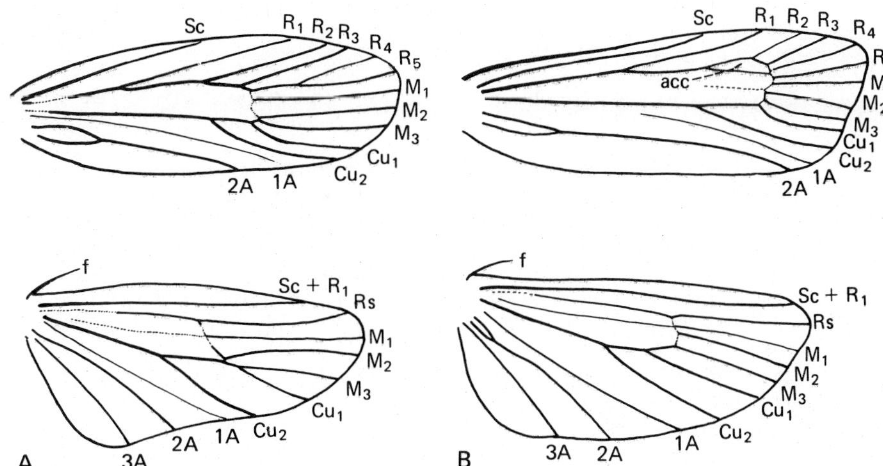

Figure 386. Wings of Microlepidóptera. A, *Depressària* (Oecophòridae); B, *Átteva* (Yponomeùtidae). *acc*, accessory cell; *f*, frenulum.

88′. M_2 in hind wing arising closer to M_3 than to M_1 (Figure 386 A) .... **Oecophòridae** p. 504

89(86′). M_1 and M_2 in hind wing stalked (*Plutélla*) .... **Plutéllidae*** p. 506

89′. M_1 and M_2 in hind wing not stalked .... **Yponomeùtidae** p. 506

90(73″). Face and vertex with long bristly hairs; antennae usually rough, with 1 or 2 whorls of erect scales on each segment; ocelli absent .... **Tinéidae** p. 509

90′. Face smooth-scaled; antennae variable; ocelli present or absent 91

91(90′). Front wing without a closed discal cell 92*

91′. Front wing with a closed discal cell 93

92(91). Front wings linear, with only 3 or 4 veins (*Cycloplàsis*) .... **Heliodínidae*** p. 506

92′. Front wings lanceolate, with 7 veins reaching margin (*Coptodísca*) .... **Heliozèlidae*** p. 507

93(91′). Hind wing without a discal cell, and with the R stem near middle of wing (well separated from Sc) and with a branch extending to C at about two fifths the wing length (Figure 387 B); R_5 in front wing free from R_4 but stalked with M_1; labial palps stout and drooping .... **Douglasìidae*** p. 507

93′. Not exactly fitting the above description 94

94(93′). Discal cell in front wing somewhat oblique, its apex closer to hind margin of wing than to front margin, and the branches of Cu very short (Figures 384 B and 387 C) 95

94′. Discal cell in front wing not oblique, its apex not much closer to hind margin of wing than to front margin, and the branches of Cu longer (Figures 384 B, 387 D, F, and 388 A) 97*

95(94). Front wing with a stigmalike thickening between C and R_1 (Figure 384 B); scape of antenna with a row of long hairs .... **Blastobàsidae*** p. 504

95′. Front wing without such a thickening; scale of antenna variable 96

96(95′). Front tibiae slender, epiphysis apical or absent; antennae turned forward at rest .... **Coleophòridae** p. 507

96′. Front tibiae stout, epiphysis well developed and at middle of tibia; antennae turned backward at rest (*Blastodácna, Batráchedra,* etc.) .... **Mómphidae*** and **Cosmopterýgidae*** p. 502

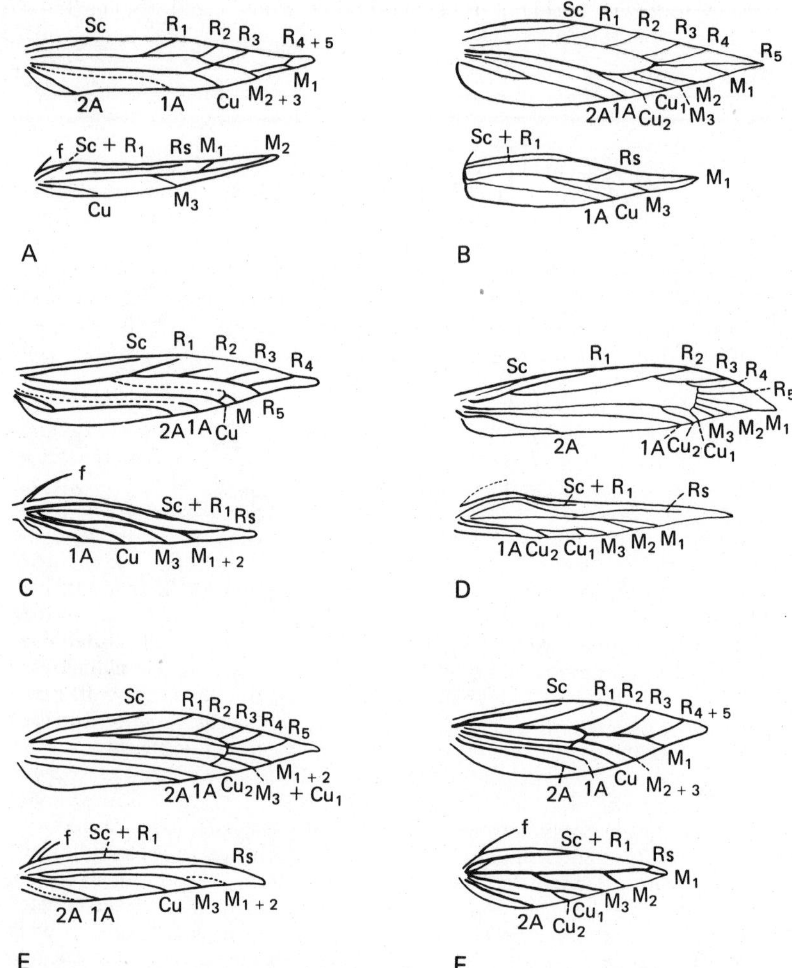

Figure 387. Wings of Microlepidóptera. A, *Bedéllia* (Lyonetìidae); B, *Tinágma* (Douglasìidae); C, *Coleóphora* (Coleophòridae); D, *Gracilària* (Gracilarìidae); E, *Tischèria* (Tischerìidae); F, *Antìspila* (Heliozèlidae). *f,* frenulum. (Redrawn from Comstock by permission of Comstock Publishing Co.; A, after Clemens; E and F, after Spuler.)

97(94′). Front wing with 5 veins reaching costal margin beyond Sc 98*

97′. Front wing with 4 or fewer veins reaching costal margin beyond Sc .. 106*

98(97). Accessory cell in front wing large, at least half as long as discal cell (Figure 387 E); vertex with a flat tuft covering base of antennae .. **Tischerìidae*** p. 508

98′. Accessory cell in front wing smaller, less than half as long as discal cell, or absent; vertex usually not as above 99*

99(98′). Vertex more or less tufted, or with rough bristly hair (*Parórnix*) .... **Gracilarìidae*** p. 507

99′. Vertex smooth-scaled 100*

100(99′). R_1 in front wing arising basad of middle or discal cell, usually at about basal third (Figure 387 D, E) 101*

100′. R_1 in front wing arising at or beyond middle of discal cell (Figures 384 B, 387 F, and 388 A) 103*

101(100). Front wing with a stigmalike thickening between C and R_1 (Figure 384 B); R_4 and R_5 stalked .... **Blastobàsidae*** p. 504

101′. Front wing without such a stigmalike thickening; R_4 and R_5 in front wing usually not stalked (Figure 387 D) 102*

102(101′). Third segment of labial palps pointed; maxillary palps folded over base of proboscis (*Limnàceia, Eteobàlea, Anóncia*) .... **Cosmopterýgidae*** p. 502

102′. Third segment of labial palps usually blunt; maxillary palps projecting forward, or rudimentary, or absent .... **Gracilarìidae*** p. 507

103(100′). Hind tarsi with more or less distinct groups of bristles near ends of segments; labial palps usually short, sometimes drooping .... **Heliodínidae*** p. 506

103′. Hind tarsi without such bristles; labial palps long, upcurved, the third segment long and tapering 104*

104(103′). R_4 and R_5 in front wing stalked 105*

104′. R_4 and R_5 in front wing not stalked (*Hélice, Theísoa,* etc.) .. **Gelechìidae*** p. 503

105(104). Hind wings lanceolate, with complete venation (*Borkhausénia*) .... **Oecophòridae*** p. 504

105′. Hind wings usually linear, with the venation reduced .... **Walshìidae*** and **Cosmopterýgidae*** p. 502

106(97′). Venation of front wing reduced, with 7 or fewer veins reaching wing margin from discal cell (Figure 387 F) 107*

106′. Venation of front wing complete or nearly so, with 8–10 veins reaching wing margin from discal cell 108*

107(106). Vertex rough-scaled (*Cremastobombýcia, Lithocólletis*) .... **Gracilarìidae*** p. 507

107′. Head entirely smooth-scaled .... **Heliozèlidae*** p. 507

108(106′). Vertex tufted; M_1 and M_2 in hind wing long-stalked (*Argyrésthia*) .... **Yponomeùtidae*** p. 506

108′. Vertex smooth; usually no branches of M in hind wing stalked 109*

109(108′). R_1 in front wing arising at about two thirds the length of discal cell; 9 veins in front wing reaching margin from discal cell .... **Scýthridae*** p. 507

109′. R_1 in front wing usually arising near middle of discal cell, or more basad; 8–10 veins in front wing reaching margin from discal cell 110*

110(109′). Labial palps long and upturned (as in Figure 383 A); venation of front wing usually complete, with 10 veins reaching margin from discal cell 111*

110′. Labial palps shorter, of moderate size or small, slightly upturned; venation of front wing somewhat reduced, with only 8 or 9 veins reaching margin from discal cell 112*

111(110). Hind tibiae stiffly bristled, usually in tufts at the spurs; ocelli absent .... **Epermenìidae*** p. 502

111′. Hind tibiae without such bristles; ocelli present or absent .... **Mómphidae*** and **Cosmopterýgidae*** p. 502

112(110′). Front wing with only 1 or 2 veins arising from apex of discal cell; hind wing with a forked vein at apex (Figure 388 A) .... **Elachístidae*** p. 507

112′. Front wing with at least 3 veins arising from apex of discal cell; hind wing without a forked vein at apex .... **Heliodínidae*** p. 506

113(1′). Moth developing in, and usually never leaving, a sac or case constructed and carried about by the larva .... **Psýchidae** p. 508

113′. Moth not developing in a sac or case constructed by the larva 114

114(113′). Ocelli present 115*

114′. Ocelli absent 116

115(114). Proboscis absent or vestigial; maxillary palps large; wings very small; aquatic moths (*Acéntropus*) .... **Pyrálidae*** p. 498

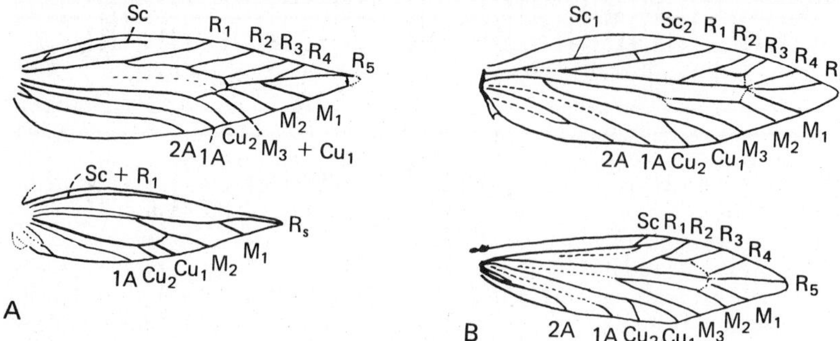

Figure 388. Wings of Lepidóptera. A, *Elachísta* (Elachístidae); B, *Micrópteryx* (Micropterýgidae). (Redrawn from Comstock by permission of Comstock Publishing Co.)

115′. Proboscis present; maxillary palps short, almost concealed ... **Tortrícidae*** p. 501

116(114′). Stout-bodied, short-legged, and densely woolly; proboscis absent or vestigial .... **Lipàridae** p. 518

116′. Slender-bodied, long-legged, and hairy or scaly; proboscis present .... **Geométridae** p. 510

SUBORDER **Jugàtae:** Jugate moths usually have a small basal lobe on the posterior margin of the front wing, the jugum (Figure 359, *j*), with which the front and hind wings are held together. The venation in the front and hind wings is very similar; Rs usually has as many branches in the hind wing as in the front wing. This is a small group (less than 30 North American species), and its members are seldom encountered.

Family **Micropterýgidae:** The Micropterýgidae are small moths that differ from all other Lepidóptera in that they have well-developed and functional mandibles; this family is sometimes placed in a separate order, the Zeuglóptera. They differ from the Eriocranìidae in that the subcosta in the front wing is forked near the middle. This group contains only three North American species, one of which (*Micrópteryx auricrinélla* Walsingham) occurs in the East. The larvae whose habits are known feed on mosses and liverworts.

Family **Eriocranìidae:** The Eriocranìidae are small moths that are somewhat similar to clothes moths in general appearance. The subcosta of the front wing is forked near its tip, and the mandibles are vestigial. One of the best known eastern species in this family is *Mnemónica auricyánea* Walsingham. The larvae make blotch mines in oak and chestnut and overwinter as pupae in the soil.

Family **Hepiálidae**—Ghost Moths and Swifts: The Hepiálidae are medium-sized to large moths, with wingspreads of from 1 to 3 inches (25–76 mm). Most of them are brown or gray with silvery spots on the wings. The jugum in this group is fingerlike and is reinforced by a branch of the third anal vein. The name "swift" refers to the fact that some of these moths have an extremely rapid flight; they superficially resemble some of the Sphíngidae. The larvae feed on the roots and woody tissues of plants. The smaller moths in this family, with a wingspread of 25–50 mm, belong to the genus *Hepìalus*; the larger moths belong to the genus *Sthenòpis*. The larva of *S. argenteomaculàtus* Harris (Figure 389) bores in the stems of alder, and the larva of *S. thùle* Strecker bores in willow.

SUBORDER **Frenàtae:** Frenates usually have the hind wing smaller than the front wing and with a reduced venation; Rs in the hind wing is never branched. The two wings on each side are held together by a frenulum, or by an expanded humeral angle of the hind wing. This suborder includes the vast majority of the Lepidóptera.

DIVISION **Microlepidóptera:** This group includes a variety of moths that vary in size and shape. Most of them are small, with a wingspread of 20 mm or less, but a few are larger (up to a wingspread of about 2 inches (50 mm) in some Cóssidae). Some have the wings relatively broad (the front wings more or less triangular, the hind wings as wide as or wider than the front wings), while others have both front and hind wings narrow and pointed apically. The wing venation is

Figure 389. A hepialid moth, *Sthenòpis argenteomaculàtus* Harris, 1.3 ×.

variable, but the broad-winged forms usually have two anal veins in the front wing and three in the hind wing. Many have long tibial spurs, and many have a broad fringe on the rear margin of the hind wings. This group makes up about half of the order.

Family **Limacòdidae**—Slug Caterpillars: These insects are called slug caterpillars because the larvae are short, fleshy, and sluglike. The thoracic legs are small and there are no prolegs, and the larvae move with a creeping motion. Many of the larvae are curiously shaped or conspicuously marked. The cocoons are dense, brownish, and oval, and have at one end a lid that is pushed out by the emerging adult. The adult moths (Figure 390 A) are small to medium-sized, robust, and hairy, and are usually brownish and marked with a large irregular spot of green, silver, or some other color.

One of the most common species in this group is the saddleback caterpillar, *Sibìne stimùlea* (Clemens). The larva (Figure 390 B) is green with a brown saddlelike mark on the back. These larvae have stinging hairs and can cause severe irritation to the skin. They feed principally on various trees.

Family **Megalopỳgidae**—Flannel Moths: These moths have a dense coat of scales mixed with fine curly hairs, which give the insect a somewhat woolly appearance. They are medium-sized to small, and usually brownish in color. The larvae are also hairy, and in addition to the usual five pairs of prolegs, they have two additional pairs that are suckerlike and lack crochets. The larvae have stinging spines under the hairs and can cause

A

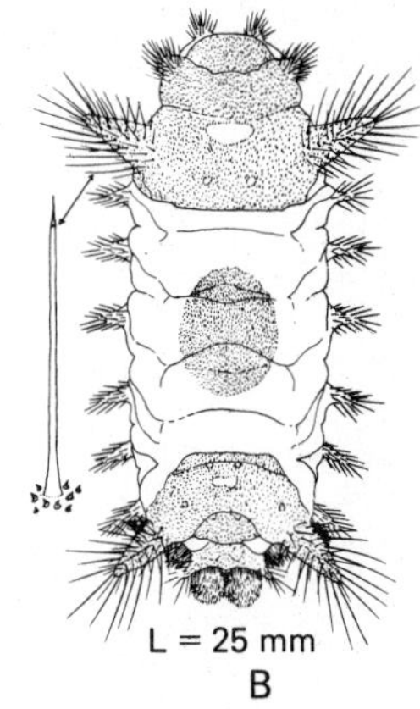

B

Figure 390. Adult (A) and larva (B) of the saddleback caterpillar, *Sibìne stimùlea* (Clemens). A, 3 ×. (B, courtesy of Peterson. Reprinted by permission.)

even more irritation than the saddleback caterpillars. The cocoons are tough and are provided with a lid as in the Limacòdidae; they are usually formed on twigs. The crinkled flannel moth, *Megalopỳge crispàta* (Packard), is a common eastern species; it is a yellowish moth with brownish spots or bands on the wings and has a wingspread of a little over 25 mm. The larva feeds on blackberry, raspberry, apple, and other plants.

Family **Dalcéridae:** This family is represented in the United States by two species that have been reported from Arizona. The moths are rather woolly and resemble flannel moths. The more common species, *Dalcérides ingénita* (Edwards), is an orange-yellow moth without markings and with a wingspread of about 25 mm; its larva is unknown.

Family **Epipyrópidae**—Planthopper Parasites: These moths are unique in that the larvae are parasites of planthoppers (Fulgoròidea) and other Homóptera. The moth larva feeds on the dorsal surface of the abdomen of the planthopper, under the wings. These moths are relatively rare, and only two species are known from the United States.

Family **Pyromórphidae**—Smoky Moths: The smoky moths are small, gray or black moths, usually with the prothorax reddish and often with other bright markings. The larvae have tufted hairs, and the commoner species feed on grape or Virginia creeper. The grapeleaf skeletonizer, *Harrisìna americàna* (Guérin), is a common species in this group. The adult is a small, narrow-winged, smoky moth with a reddish collar, and the larvae are yellow with black spots. A number of these larvae will feed on the same leaf, lined up in a row and backing up as they skeletonize the leaf.

Family **Thyrídidae**—Window-Winged Moths: The thyridids are small and dark-colored and have clear spaces in the wings. All branches of the radius are present, and they arise from the usually open discal cell (Figure 377 A). Some larvae burrow in twigs and stems and cause gall-like swellings; others feed on flowers and seeds. The most common eastern species is probably *Dysòdia oculatàna* Clemens, which occurs in the Ohio Valley.

Family **Pyrálidae**—Snout and Grass Moths: This family is the second largest in the order, with over 1230 species occurring in the United States and Canada. Most of the pyralids are small and rather delicate moths. The front wings are elongate or triangular, with the cubitus appearing 4-branched and the hind wings usually broad. Veins Sc and R in the hind wing are usually close together and parallel opposite the discal cell (the base of R is usually atrophied), and are fused or closely parallel for a short distance beyond the discal cell (Figure 369). Since the labial palps are often projecting, these moths are sometimes called snout moths.

The members of this family exhibit a great deal of variation in appearance, venation, and habits. The family is divided into a number of subfamilies, only a few of which can be mentioned here.

Subfamily **Pyraustìnae:** This subfamily is a large group (over 300 North American species), and many of its members are relatively large and conspicuously marked. The most important species in this subfamily is the European corn borer, *Ostrínia nubilàlis* (Hübner), which was introduced into the United States about 1917 and has since spread over a large part of the central and eastern states. The larvae live in the stalks of corn and other plants and frequently do a great deal of damage. This species has one or two generations a year; it overwinters in the larval stage. The adult moths (Figure 391) have a wingspread of a little over 25 mm, and are yellowish brown with darker markings. The grape leaffolder, *Désmia funeràlis* (Hübner), is a black moth with two white spots in the front wing and one white spot in the hind wing; the larva feeds on grape leaves, folding the leaf over and fastening it with silk. The melonworm, *Diaphània hyalinàta* (L.), is a glistening white moth with the wings bordered with black; the larva feeds on the foliage and burrows in the stems of melons and related plants. Other important species in this subfamily are the pickleworm, *Diaphània nitidàlis* (Stoll), and the garden webworm, *Loxóstege rantàlis* (Guenée).

Subfamily **Nymphulìnae:** The larvae of most Nymphulìnae are aquatic, breathing by means of gills, and feeding on aquatic plants. The waterlily leafcutter, *Sýnclita obliteràlis* (Walker), lives on greenhouse water plants, in cases made of silk.

Subfamily **Pyralìnae:** This subfamily is a small group of small moths; the larvae of most species feed on dried vegetable matter. One of the most important species in this subfamily is the meal moth, *Pýralis farinàlis* (L.); the larva feeds on cereals, flour, and meal, and makes silken tubes in these materials. The larvae of the clover hayworm,

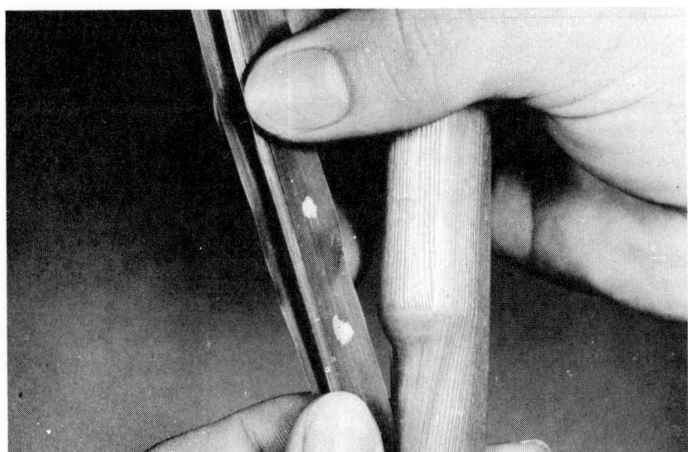

Figure 391. European corn borer, *Ostrínia nubilàlis* (Hübner). Top, egg masses on corn; center, larva; bottom, adults (male at left, female at right), 2 ×. (Courtesy of the Illinois Natural History Survey.)

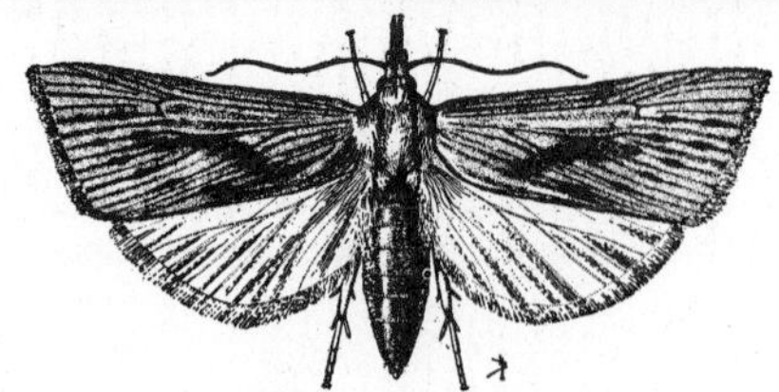

Figure 392. Sugarcane borer, *Diatraèa saccharàlis* (Fabricius) (Pyrálidae, Crambìnae), 2 ×. (Courtesy of USDA.)

Hypsopỳgia costàlis (Fabricius), occur in old stacks of clover hay.

Subfamily **Crambìnae**—Close-Wings or Grass Moths: These are common moths in meadows, where the larvae (known as sod webworms) bore into the stems, crowns, or roots of grasses. Most of them feed about the base of grasses, where they construct silken webs. The moths are usually whitish or pale yellowish brown, and when at rest, hold the wings close about the body (hence the name close-wing). An important pest species in this subfamily is the sugarcane borer, *Diatraèa saccharàlis* (Fabricius) (Figure 392), the larva of which bores in the stalks of sugarcane. Most of the species in this group belong to the genus *Crámbus*.

Subfamily **Galleriìnae:** The best-known member of this subfamily is the bee moth or wax moth, *Gallèria mellonélla* (L.). The larva occurs in bee hives, where it feeds on wax; it often does considerable damage. The adult has brownish front wings and has a wingspread of about 25 mm.

Subfamily **Phycitìnae:** The subfamily Phycitìnae is a large group (about 360 North American species), most of the members of which have long narrow front wings and broad hind wings; the larvae vary considerably in habits. The best known species in this subfamily are those that attack stored grain, the Indian meal moth, *Plòdia interpunctélla* (Hübner), and the Mediterranean flour moth, *Anagásta kuehniélla* (Zeller). The former is a gray moth with the apical two thirds of the front wings dark brown, and the latter (Figure 393) is uniformly gray; both moths are rather small. The larvae of the Indian meal moth feed on cereals, dried fruits, meal, and nuts, and spin webs over these materials; they often cause enormous losses in stored food supplies. The Mediterranean flour moth attacks all types of grain products and is an important pest in granaries, warehouses, markets, and homes.

Figure 393. Mediterranean flour moth, *Anagásta kuehniélla* (Zeller), 4 ×. (Courtesy of the Ohio Agricultural Research and Development Center.)

To this subfamily also belongs a moth that has been used for the deliberate destruction of plants: the cactus moth, *Cactoblástis cactòrum* (Berg), has been introduced into Australia to control the prickly pear cactus; this moth has successfully destroyed the dense cactus growth over many square miles of territory in New South Wales and Queensland (see page 705).

Another interesting species in this subfamily is the coccid-eating pyralid, *Laetília coccidívora* Comstock, the larva of which is predaceous on the eggs and young of various scale insects.

Family **Pterophòridae**—Plume Moths: These moths are small, slender, usually gray or brownish, and have the wings split into two or three featherlike divisions (Figure 394). The front wing usually has two divisions, and the hind wing, three. The legs are relatively long. When at rest, the front and hind wings are folded close together and are held horizontally, at right angles to the body. The larvae of plume moths are leaf rollers and stem borers, and some may occasionally do serious damage. The grape plume moth, *Pteróphorus periscelidáctylus* Fitch, is common on grape vines; the larvae tie together the terminal portions of the leaves and feed inside this shelter.

Family **Alucítidae**—Many-Plume Moths: The alucitids are similar to the pterophorids, but have the wings split into six plumelike divisions. Only one species in this family occurs in the United States, *Alùcita hùebneri* (Wallen); the adults have a wingspread of about 13 mm. This species, which was introduced, occurs in the northeastern states.

Family **Olethreùtidae:** These moths are small and brownish or gray in color, often with bands or

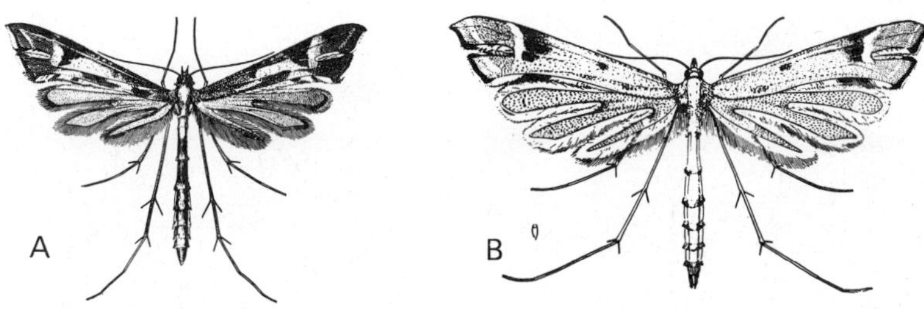

Figure 394. Plume moths (Pterophòridae). A, *Platyptília bàuri* Lange, female; B, *P. grándis* (Walsingham), female, 2 ×. (Courtesy of Lange and *Hilgardia.*)

mottled areas on the wings, and the front wings are rather square-tipped. Most species can be recognized as Olethreùtidae by the fringe of long hairs on the basal part of the cubitus in the hind wing. The larvae usually feed on foliage, fruits, or nuts. This family is a large one, with over 700 species in North America.

One of the most important pest species in this family is the codling moth, *Laspeyrèsia pomonélla* (L.), a pest of apples and other fruits. This species was introduced into the United States from Europe and is now widely distributed. The front wings are gray with brownish cross lines and a large coppery-brown spot across the apical portion of the wings (Figure 395). The adults appear in late spring and lay their eggs, which are flattened and transparent, on the surface of leaves. The young larvae crawl to young apples and chew their way into the fruit, usually entering by the blossom end. They are light-colored with a dark head. They complete their development in the fruit and pupate on the ground, under bark, or in similar protected situations. In the eastern portion of the United States there is a second generation in the latter part of the summer, with the full-grown larvae overwintering in cocoons under the bark of apple trees or in other protected places.

Figure 395. Codling moth, *Laspeyrèsia pomonélla* (L.), 3 ×. (Courtesy of the Ohio Agricultural Research and Development Center.)

The oriental fruit moth, *Graphólitha molésta* (Busck), is an oriental species that is widely distributed in this country; it is a serious pest of peaches and other fruits. It has several generations a year; the larvae of the first generation bore into the young green twigs, and the later generations of larvae bore into the fruit very much as does the codling moth. The winter is passed as a full-grown larva in a cocoon.

A number of other species in this family are occasionally destructive to various crops. The grape berry moth, *Paralobèsia viteàna* (Clemens) (Figure 396 B), feeds in the larval stage in the berries of grapes; it has two generations a year. The strawberry leafroller, *Áncylis comptàna fragàriae* (Walsh and Riley), attacks the foliage of strawberry and often does severe damage. The black-headed fireworm, *Rhopóbota naevàna* (Hübner), is a serious pest of cranberry plantings in the eastern states. The clover head caterpillar, *Graphólitha interstictàna* (Clemens), is a common pest that feeds in the heads of clover, destroying unopened buds and decidedly reducing the crop of seed; this insect has three generations a year and passes the winter as a pupa.

A species in this family, which is something of a curiosity, is the Mexican jumping-bean moth, *Laspeyrèsia sáltitans* (Westwood). The larva lives in the thin-walled seeds of *Sebastiàna,* and after consuming the inside of the seed, throws itself forcibly against the thin wall, causing the jumping movements of the seed.

Family **Tortrícidae:** The tortricids are small moths, usually gray, tan, or brown with spots or mottled coloration, and they have the front wings rather square-cut at the tip; when at rest, the wings are held rooflike over the body. The larvae vary in

Figure 396. A, adult of the fruittree leafroller, *Árchips argyrospìlus* (Walker), 2 × (Tortrícidae); B, adult of the grape berry moth, *Paralobèsia viteàna* (Clemens), 4 × (Olethreùtidae).

habits, but many species are leaf rollers or leaf tyers; they may pupate in these leaf nests, or they may spin cocoons in debris or under bark. Most species feed on perennial plants. The adults usually differ from those of the preceding family in lacking the long fringe of hairs on the cubitus of the hind wing.

The fruittree leafroller, *Árchips argyrospìlus* (Walker) (Figure 396 A) is a rather common tortricid that makes an unsightly leaf nest in fruit and forest trees and often causes serious defoliation. The spruce budworm, *Choristoneùra fumiferàna* (Clemens), is a very serious pest of spruce, fir, balsam, and other evergreens, and may completely defoliate and kill thousands of trees.

Family **Phaloniìdae:** This family includes a number of species whose larvae are web spinners and borers; most of them attack herbaceous plants. The adults are similar to those of the two preceding families, but the vein 1A is completely lacking in the front wing, and Cu_2 in the front wing arises in the apical fourth of the discal cell; M_1 in the hind wing is usually stalked with Rs. *Phalònia rutilàna* Hübner attacks juniper, tying the leaves together to form a tube in which the larva lives. The adult of this species has a wingspread of about 25 mm, and the front wings are orange marked with four brownish crossbands.

Family **Cóssidae**—Carpenter Moths and Leopard Moths: The cossids are wood-boring in the larval stage; the adults are medium-sized and heavy-bodied, and the wings are usually spotted or mottled. The carpenterworm, *Prionoxýstus robiniae* (Peck), is a common species that attacks various trees; the adult (Figure 397 A) is a mottled gray and has a wingspread of about 2 inches (50 mm); these insects may sometimes seriously damage trees. The leopard moth, *Zeùzera pyrìna* (L.), a slightly smaller moth with the wings pale and marked with large black dots (Figure 397 B), has similar habits. These moths require two or three years to complete their life cycle.

Family **Carposìnidae:** The moths in this group have relatively broad wings with raised scale tufts on the front wings, and M_2 (and usually also M_1) in the hind wings is lacking. The group is a small one, with only 13 species in our area. The larvae whose habits are known bore into fruits, plant shoots, and in the gummy enlargements of fruit trees. The larvae of the currant fruitworm, *Carposìna fernaldàna* Busck, feeds on the fruits of the currant; the infested fruit eventually drops, and the larvae pupate in the soil.

Families **Cosmopterýgidae, Walshìidae,** and **Mómphidae:** These families are separated mainly by the structure of the male genitalia (Hodges, 1962), and some of them will not key to family in our key (which is based principally on wing venation). These moths are small, with the wings long and narrow and usually sharply pointed at the apex (Figure 398 B); some species are rather brightly colored.

Most of these moths are leaf miners in the larval stage. The larvae of the cattail moth, *Lymnaècia phragmitélla* Stainton (Cosmopterýgidae), feed in the heads of cattails. The pink scavenger caterpillar, *Sathrobròta rìleyi* (Walsingham) (Cosmopterýgidae) (Figure 398 B), feeds in cotton bolls. The palm leaf skeletonizer, *Homáledra sabalélla* (Chambers) (Mómphidae), occurs in the southern states, where the larvae feed on the upper surface of the leaves of the saw palmetto; a group of larvae make a delicate silken cover over the injured portion of the leaf and cover it with their droppings.

Family **Epermeniìdae:** The Epermeniìdae are a small group of moths that were formerly placed in the family Scýthridae. The larvae of *Epermènia pimpinélla* Murtfeldt form puffy mines on *Pim-*

Figure 397. Cossid moths. A, carpenter moth, *Prionoxýstus robíniae* (Peck), 1½ ×; B, leopard moth, *Zeùzera pyrìna* (L.), 1⅓ ×.

pinélla integérrima Benth and Hook, a species of parsley. The pupa is enclosed in a rather frail cocoon on the under side of a leaf or in an angle of a leaf stalk.

Family **Gelechìidae:** This family is one of the largest of the Microlepidóptera (about 580 North American species), and many species are fairly common; the moths are all rather small. The labial palps are long and upcurved, and the terminal segment is long and pointed (Figures 383 A and 398 A). Veins R_4 and R_5 in the front wing are stalked at the base (rarely, they are fused for their entire length), and 2A is forked at the base. The hind wing usually has the outer margin somewhat curved (Figure 385 C). Gelechiid larvae vary in habits; some are leaf miners, a few form galls, many are leaf rollers or leaf tyers, and one species is a serious pest of stored grain.

The Angoumois grain moth, *Sitotròga cerealélla* (Olivier), is an important pest of stored grain. The larva feeds in the kernels of corn, wheat, and other grains, and the emerging adult leaves a conspicuous emergence hole at one end of the kernel (Figure 399). The grain may become infested with this insect, either in the milk stage of the growing grain or in storage; stored grain may be completely destroyed by it. The adult moth is light grayish brown with a wingspread of about 13 mm.

The pink bollworm, *Pectinóphora gossypiélla* (Saunders) (Figure 398 A), is a serious pest of cot-

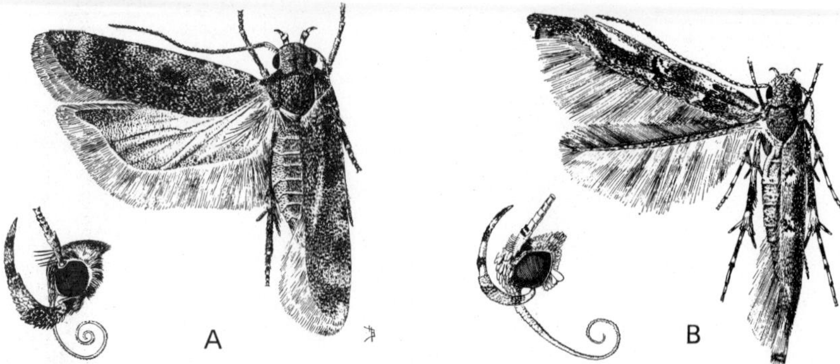

Figure 398. A, pink bollworm, *Pectinóphora gossypiélla* (Saunders) (Gelechìidae); B, *Sathrobròta rìleyi* (Walsingham) (Cosmopterýgidae), 4 ×. Inserts, lateral views of heads. (Courtesy of Busck and the USDA *Journal of Agricultural Research.*)

ton in the South and Southwest; the larvae attack the bolls, and losses up to 50 percent of the crop are not uncommon in fields that are infested with this insect.

Many species in the genus *Gnorimoschèma* form galls in the stems of goldenrod, different species attacking different species of goldenrods. The galls are elongate and spindle-shaped, and rather thin-walled (Figure 400). The larva pupates in the gall, but before pupating it cuts an opening (not quite completely through the wall) at the upper end of the gall; when the adult emerges, it can easily push out through this opening. Pupation occurs in mid- or late summer, and the adults emerge and lay their eggs on old goldenrod plants in the fall; the eggs hatch during the following spring.

Phthorimaèa operculélla (Zeller), the potato tuberworm, is a pest of potatoes and related plants; the larvae mine in the leaves and bore into the tubers.

Family **Oecophòridae:** The Oecophòridae are small and somewhat flattened moths, usually brownish in color, with the wings relatively broad and rounded apically. The venation (Figure 386 A) is complete, with 1A preserved in the front wing, R_4 and R_5 in the front wing stalked or coalesced throughout their length, and Rs and M_1 in the hind wing separate and parallel. The parsnip webworm, *Depressària pastinacélla* (Duponchel), attacks parsnips, celery, and related plants; the larvae web together and feed on the unfolding blossom heads and burrow into the hollow stem to pupate; the adults appear in late summer and hibernate in protected situations.

Family **Blastobàsidae:** The Blastobàsidae are small moths in which the hind wings are somewhat lanceolate and narrower than the front wings (Figure 384 B); the membrane of the front wing is slightly thickened along the costa. The larva of the acorn moth, *Valentínia glandulélla* Riley, feeds inside acorns that have been hollowed out by the larvae of acorn weevils. The larvae overwinter in the acorns, and the adults appear in the following summer. The larvae of *Zenodóchium coccivorélla* Chambers are internal parasites of female gall-like coccids of the genus *Kérmes*; this species has been found in Florida.

Family **Stenòmidae:** The Stenòmidae are larger than most of the Microlepidóptera, and the wings (Figure 385 D) are relatively broad. The larvae live

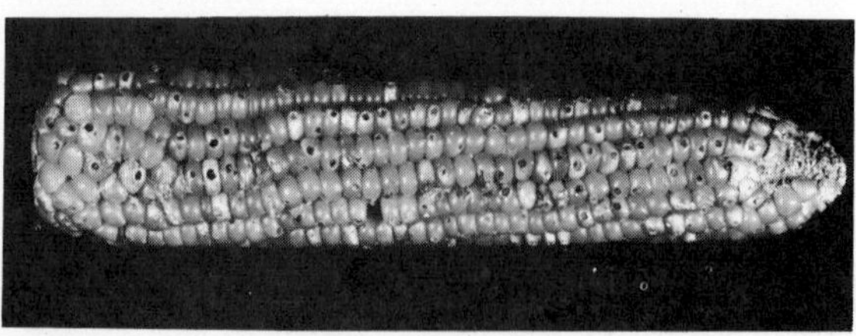

Figure 399. Injury to corn by the Angoumois grain moth. (Courtesy of Davidson.)

in webs on the leaves of oaks and other trees. *Stenòma schlaègeri* (Zeller) is a fairly common eastern species. The adult has a wingspread of about 30 mm; the wings are grayish white with dark markings, and when at rest, the moth resembles bird excrement.

Family **Ethmìidae:** The ethmiids are relatively broad-winged moths somewhat similar to the Oecophòridae; a few are rather plain-colored, but most are rather brightly patterned, often black and white. The larvae feed principally on the leaves and flowers of plants in the borage and waterleaf families (Boraginàceae and Hydrophyllàceae). Most of the 48 nearctic species occur in the West.

Family **Glyphipterýgidae:** The Glyphipterýgidae are small moths, some of which are similar in general appearance to the Tortrícidae. In the front wings, R_4 and R_5 are separate and Cu_2 arises near the apex of the discal cell; in the hind wing, 2A is forked at the base. These moths have large ocelli. The larvae are generally leaf tyers.

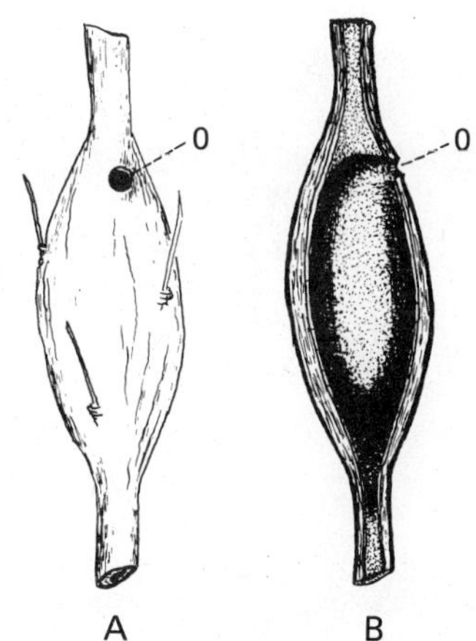

Figure 400. Gall of the goldenrod gall moth, *Gnorimoschèma* (Gelechìidae), A, exterior view; B, a gall cut open. *o,* opening cut by the larva before pupating, through which the emerging adult escapes.

Family **Sesìidae**—Clear-Winged Moths: The greater part of one or both pairs of wings in this family is devoid of scales, and many species bear a very striking resemblance to wasps (Figure 402). The front wings are long and narrow with the anal veins reduced, and the hind wings are broad with the anal area well developed (Figure 401). Many species are brightly colored, and most of them are active during the day. The two sexes are often differently colored, and in some cases they differ in the amount of clear area in the wings. The larvae bore in the roots, stems, canes, or trunks of plants or trees and often cause considerable damage.

The peachtree borer, *Sanninòidea exitiòsa* (Say), is one of the most important species in this family. The females lay their eggs on the trunks of peach trees near the ground, the larvae bore into the tree just below the surface of the ground; they often girdle the tree. There is one generation a year, and the larvae overwinter in their burrows in the tree. The female has the front wings fully scaled, and the abdomen is marked with a broad orange band; the male has both the front and hind wings largely clear, and the abdomen is ringed with several narrow yellow bands (Figure 402). The adults are active through the summer. The lesser peachtree borer, *Synánthedon píctipes* (Grote and Robinson), has similar habits, but the larvae generally bore into the trunk and the larger branches; both sexes resemble the male of *S. exitiòsa*.

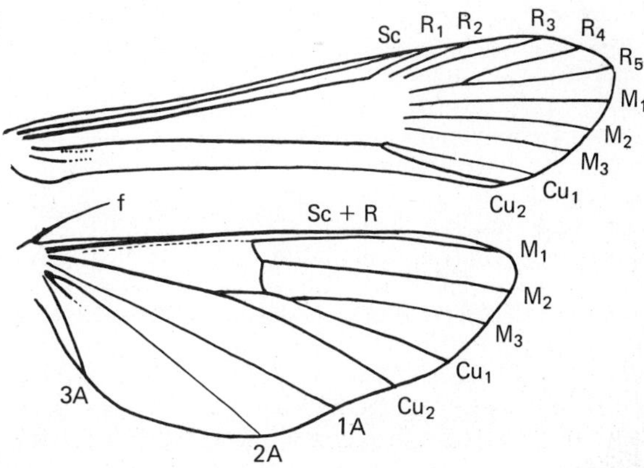

Figure 401. Wings of *Synánthedon* (Sesìidae). *f,* frenulum.

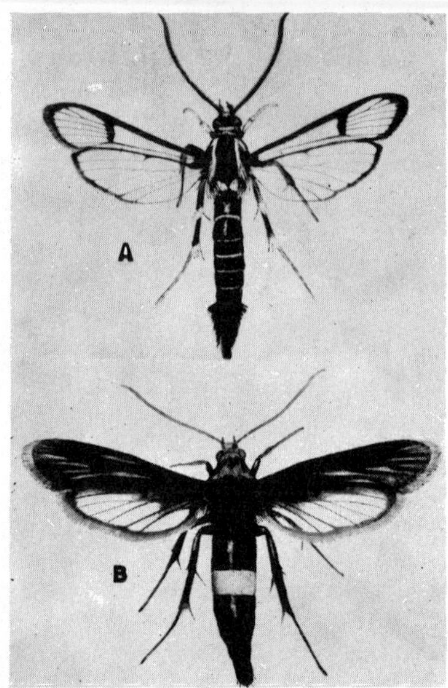

Figure 402. Peachtree borer, *Sanninòidea exitiòsa* (Say) (Sesìidae), 1½ ×. A, male; B, female. (Courtesy of the Ohio Agricultural Research and Development Center.)

Figure 403. An ermine moth, *Átteva* sp. (Yponomeùtidae), 2½ ×. (Courtesy of the Ohio Agricultural Research and Development Center.)

The squash vine borer, *Melíttia cucúrbitae* (Harris), is a serious pest of squash and related plants; the larvae bore into the stems and often destroy the plant. This species overwinters as a pupa in the soil. The adults are a little larger than those of the peach tree borer and have the front wings olive green and the hind wings clear; the hind legs are heavily clothed with a long fringe of orange-colored scales.

The currant borer, *Synánthedon tipulifórmis* (Clerck), is a small moth with a wingspread of about 18 mm. The larva bores in the stems of currants, and pupation occurs in the stems; the adults appear in early summer.

Family **Heliodínidae:** The Heliodínidae are small moths that have the hind wings very narrow and lanceolate and with a broad fringe; the adult at rest usually holds the hind legs elevated above the wings. The family is a small one, and the known larvae vary in habits. The larvae of *Cycloplàsis panicifoliélla* Clemens mine in the leaves of panic grass, forming at first a linear mine that is later enlarged to a blotch. When full grown, the larva cuts a circular piece from the leaf, folds this piece over to make a case, then drops to the ground and pupates in the case. The larvae of *Schreckensteìnia* feed on sumac and species of *Rùbus. Eucleménsia bassettélla* Clemens is an internal parasite of female gall-like coccids of the genus *Kérmes*.

Family **Plutéllidae**—Diamondback Moths: The Plutéllidae are similar to the Yponomeùtidae, but hold their antennae forward when at rest, and M_1 and M_2 in the hind wing are stalked. *Plutélla xylostélla* (L.) is a pest of cabbage and other cruciferous plants; its larvae eat holes in the leaves and pupate in silken cocoons attached to the leaves. The name "diamondback" refers to the fact that the male wings when folded show a series of three yellow diamond-shaped marks along the line where the wings meet.

Family **Yponomeùtidae**—Ermine Moths: The ermine moths are small and usually brightly patterned moths with rather broad wings (Figure 403). The branches of the main veins in the front wings are generally separate, and R_5 extends to the outer margin of the wing; Rs and M_1 in the hind wing are separate (Figure 386 B). The moths of the genus *Yponomeùta* have the front wings white dotted with black; the larvae of *Y. padélla* (L.) feed in a common web on apple and cherry. The larvae of the ailanthus webworm, *Átteva punctélla* (Cramer), live in a frail silken web on the leaves of ailanthus and feed on the leaves; the pupae are suspended in loose webs. The front wings of the adult are bright yellow, marked with four transverse bands of lead-blue, each enclosing a row of yellow spots (Figure 403). The larvae of the arborvitae leafminer, *Argyrésthia thuiélla* (Packard), feed on the leaves of cedar; the adults are white moths with the narrow front wings spotted with brown, and have a wingspread of about 8 mm.

Family **Scýthridae:** The family Scýthridae is closely related to the Yponomeùtidae, and it contains the single genus *Scýthris*. The larvae of *S. magnatélla* Busch feed on willow herbs (*Epilòbium*), folding over a portion of the leaf for an individual cell.

Family **Heliozèlidae**—Shield Bearers: The heliozelids are small moths with lanceolate wings; the hind wings have no discal cell (Figure 387 F). The larvae of the resplendent shield bearer, *Coptodísca splendoriferélla* (Clemens), are both leaf miners and casebearers; the larvae make a linear mine in apple, wild cherry, and related plants, and this mine is later widened. When full grown, the larva makes a case from the walls of its mine, lines it with silk, and attaches it to a limb or to the trunk of the tree. There are two generations a year, with the larvae of the second generation overwintering in the cases. The front wings of the adult are dark gray at the base, with the outer portion bright yellow with brown and silver markings.

Family **Douglasìidae:** The Douglasìidae are leaf miners in the larval stage, and the adults are small moths with lanceolate hind wings that lack a discal cell (Figure 387 B). Rs in the hind wing separates from the media near the middle of the wing. The ocelli are large. Only four species of douglasiids occur in this country. The larvae of *Tinágma obscurofasciélla* Chambers mine in the leaves of plants in the family Rosàceae.

Family **Elachístidae:** The Elachístidae are mainly leaf miners in grasses. The adults have lanceolate hind wings that have a well-formed discal cell; the venation is but slightly reduced (Figure 388 A). The larvae make blotch mines in grasses; the larvae of some species leave the mines and pupate in suspended webs. Most of the species in this small family belong to the genus *Elachísta*.

Family **Coleophòridae**—Casebearers: The moths in this family are small, with very narrow, sharply pointed wings. The discal cell of the front wing is oblique, and veins Cu_1 and Cu_2 (when present) are very short. There are no ocelli or maxillary palps. About a hundred species of casebearers, all belonging to the genus *Coleóphora,* occur in this country. The larvae are usually leaf miners when young and casebearers when they become larger.

The pistol casebearer, *Coleóphora malivorélla* Riley, is a common pest of apple and other fruit trees. The larvae construct pistol-shaped cases composed of silk, bits of leaves, and excrement, which they carry about; by protruding their heads from these cases they eat holes in the leaves. They overwinter as larvae in the cases, and the moths appear in midsummer.

Figure 404. Larvae (in their cases) of the cigar casebearer, *Coleóphora serratélla* (L.), on an apple leaf. (Courtesy of the Ohio Agricultural Research and Development Center.)

The cigar casebearer, *C. serratélla* (L.), also attacks apple and other fruit trees (Figure 404). This species is similar to the preceding casebearer except that the young larvae are miners in the leaves for two or three weeks before making their cases.

Family **Gracilarìidae**—Leaf Blotch Miners: This is a large group of small to minute moths with lanceolate wings. The front wing usually lacks an accessory cell, and the hind wing in some species has a hump along the costal margin near the base (Figure 387 D). The adult moths at rest have the anterior part of the body elevated, and the wing tips touch the surface on which the moth rests. The larvae usually make blotch mines, and the leaf is often folded.

The white oak leafminer, *Lithocollètis hamadryadélla* Clemens, is a common eastern species that feeds on various types of oak. The mines are on the upper surface of the leaves, and each mine contains a single larva; many mines may occur on a single leaf (Figure 405 A). The larvae are flat-

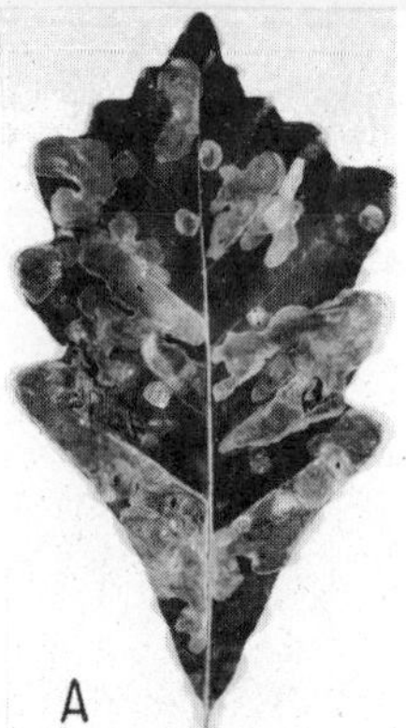

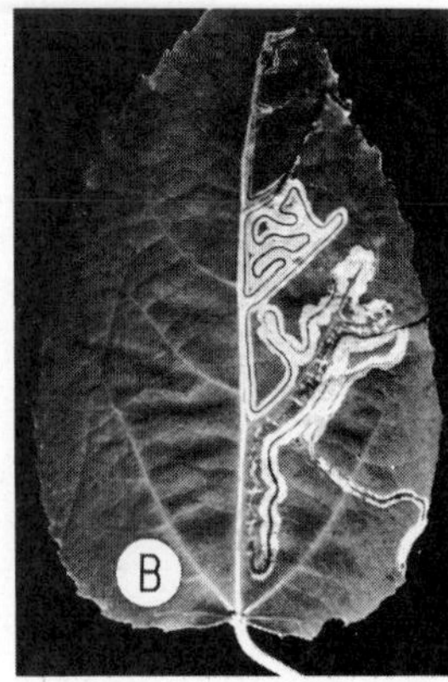

Figure 405. Leaf mines of Gracilarìidae. A, white oak leafminer, *Lithocollètis hamadryadélla* Clemens; B, aspen leafminer, *Phyllocnístis* sp. (A, courtesy of the Ohio Agricultural Research and Development Center.)

tened, with only rudiments of legs, and with the prothoracic segment enlarged. The larva pupates in a delicate cocoon inside the mine; it overwinters as a larva in dry leaves. The adult moth is white with broad irregular bronze bands on the front wings.

Some species of *Phyllocnístis* make winding serpentine mines in aspen leaves (Figure 405 B). The larva usually starts near the tip of the leaf, mines toward the base, and often has to go out toward the edge of the leaf in order to get across a large vein. It pupates in a silken cocoon at the end of the mine, usually at the basal edge of the leaf.

Family **Opostégidae:** The Opostégidae are small moths with linear hind wings and with the radius, media, and cubitus of the front wings unbranched; the first segment of the antenna forms a large eye cap. The larvae are miners. This is a small group and contains the single genus *Opóstega*.

Family **Lyonetìidae:** The Lyonetìidae are small moths with very narrow wings; the hind wings are often linear, with Rs extending through the center of the wing (Figure 387 A). Ocelli and maxillary palps are usually lacking. The larvae are leaf miners or live in webs between the leaves. The apple bucculatrix, *Bucculàtrix pomifoliélla* Clemens, overwinters in rows of white, longitudinally ribbed cocoons on the twigs of apple; the adults emerge in the spring and oviposit on the lower surface of the leaves. The larvae enter the leaf and make a serpentine mine on the upper surface. Silken molting cocoons are made on the surface of the leaf before the pupal cocoons on the twigs are formed.

Family **Tischerìidae:** The Tischerìidae are small moths in which the costal margin of the front wing is strongly arched and the apex is prolonged into a sharp point; the hind wings are long and narrow with a reduced venation (Figure 387 E). The maxillary palps are small or absent. The larvae of most species make blotch mines in the leaves of oak or apple trees and blackberry or raspberry bushes. The appleleaf trumpet miner, *Tischèria malifoliélla* Clemens, is a common species in the East, and often does considerable damage; the larva makes a trumpet-shaped mine in the upper surface of the leaf, overwinters in the mine, and pupates in the spring; there are two or more generations a year.

Family **Oinophílidae:** The family Oinophílidae is represented in the United States by a single species, *Phaeòses sabinélla* Forbes, which occurs in Louisiana and Mississippi. The adult is very flattened, shining gray-brown in color, and has a wingspread of about 9 mm. The larva feeds on decaying vegetable matter and fungi.

Family **Psỳchidae**—Bagworm Moths: These moths are so named because of the characteristic bags or cases that are made and carried about by the larvae; these bags are easily seen on trees during the winter after the leaves have fallen (Figure 406). The bags are composed of silk and portions of leaves and twigs; the larvae pupate in the bags, and most species overwinter as eggs in the bags. When the larvae hatch in the spring, they construct their cases and carry them about as they feed; when full grown, they attach the case to a twig, close it, and pupate inside it.

The adult males of this group are small, with well-developed wings, but the females are wingless, legless, and wormlike, and usually never leave the bag in which they pupate. The males on emergence fly about and locate a bag containing a female; mating takes place without the female leaving the bag. The eggs are later laid in the bag.

Thyridópteryx ephemeraefórmis (Haworth) is a common species of bagworm, the larvae of which attack chiefly red cedar and arborvitae. The adult males are small, dark-colored, heavy-bodied moths with large clear areas in the wings.

Figure 406. Bags of bagworm, *Thyridópteryx ephemeraefórmis* (Haworth). (Courtesy of the Ohio Agricultural Research and Development Center.)

Family **Acrolóphidae**—Burrowing Webworms: The acrolophids are medium-sized moths that resemble the noctuids. The first segment of the labial palps is as large as the second, or larger (Figure 383 D); the eyes are usually hairy; and the venation is complete, with three anal veins in both front and hind wings. The 48 species in this family are all placed in the genus *Acrólophus*. The larvae make a tubular web in the ground, sometimes extending as deep as 2 feet (0.6 m), into which they retreat when disturbed. They feed on the roots of grasses and also web in the blades at the surface. These insects often destroy entire young corn plants.

Family **Tinèidae**—Clothes Moths and Their Relatives: This is a large group of small moths. The wing venation is rather generalized in most species, but in some it is reduced. The maxillary palps are usually large and folded, and the labial palps are short. The larvae of many species are casebearers; some are scavengers or feed on fungi, and some feed on woolen fabrics. Of the more than 130 species of tineids in the United States, three species that attack clothes and woolens are of considerable economic importance.

The most common clothes moth is the webbing clothes moth, *Tinèola bisselliélla* (Hummel). The adult is straw-colored, without dark spots on the wings, and has a wingspread of 12–16 mm. The larvae feed on hair fiber, woolens, silks, felt, and similar materials, and do not form cases. The larva when full grown forms a cocoon of fragments of its food material fastened together with silk.

Second in importance among the clothes moths is the casemaking clothes moth, *Tínea pellionélla* (L.) (Figure 407), which forms a case from silk and fragments of its food material. This case is tubular and open at each end; the larva feeds from within the case and pupates in it. The adult is brownish, with three dark spots on each front wing.

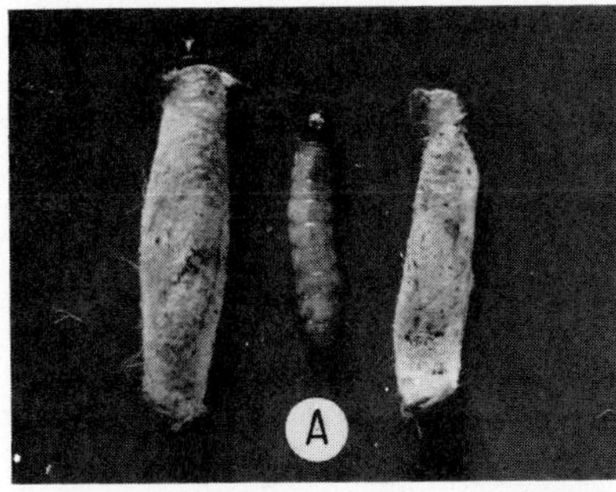

Figure 407. Case-making clothes moth, *Tínea pellionélla* (L.). A, Larvae and cases; B, adult, 2½ ×. (Courtesy of the Ohio Agricultural Research and Development Center.)

The clothes moth of least importance in the United States is the carpet moth, *Trichóphaga tapetzélla* (L.), which builds rather long silken tubes or galleries to go through certain fabrics which it may not feed upon. These tubes often have fragments of cloth woven in the silk. Where this species is found, it is quite destructive. The adult has a wingspread of 12–24 mm, and the front wings are black at the base and white in the apical portion.

Family **Nepticùlidae:** The Nepticùlidae are minute moths, some species of which have a wingspread of only 3 mm. The wing venation is somewhat reduced, and the surface of the wings bears spinelike hairs or aculeae. The basal segment of the antennae is enlarged to form an eye cap, the maxillary palps are long, and the labial palps are short. The male has a well-developed frenulum, but the frenulum of the female consists of only a few small bristles. Most species in this group are leaf miners in trees or shrubs; the mines are linear when the larvae are young, and are often broadened when the larvae become fully developed. The larvae usually leave the mines to pupate, spinning cocoons in debris on the surface of the soil. A few species in the genus *Ectoedèmia* are gall makers.

Family **Incurvarìidae:** The incurvariids are small moths with the wing venation very little reduced and the wing surface aculeate. The females have a piercing ovipositor. This family contains three subfamilies, which by some authorities are considered families.

Subfamily **Incurvariìnae:** These moths are dark-colored, and have the maxillary palps conspicuous, with the folded part about half as long as the width of the head. The larvae of the maple leafcutter, *Paracleménsia acerifoliélla* (Fitch), are leaf mining when young and become casebearers when older. The older larvae cut out two circular portions of the leaf and put these together to form the case. When the larva moves about, it carries this case with it and appears somewhat turtlelike. The winter is passed as a pupa inside the case. The adult moth is a brilliant steel blue or bluish green with an orange-colored head.

Subfamily **Prodoxìnae:** The moths in this group are white, and the folded part of the maxillary palps is about two thirds as long as the width of the head (Figure 383 E, *mxp*). The best known moths in this group are the yucca moths (*Tegetícula*), of which four species are known. The yucca is pollinated solely by these insects. The female moth collects pollen from the yucca flowers by means of long, curled, spinelike maxillary tentacles (palps), and then inserts her eggs into the ovary of another flower; after ovipositing, she thrusts the pollen she has collected onto the stigma of the flower in which the eggs have been laid. This ensures fertilization and the development of the yucca seeds on which the larvae feed; the perpetuation of the yucca is assured, as more seeds are developed than are needed for the larvae. The bogus yucca moths of the genus *Prodóxus* lack the maxillary tentacles and cannot pollinate yuccas; their larvae feed in the stems or fruit of these plants.

Subfamily **Adelìnae**—Fairy Moths: These are tiny moths in which the antennae of the males are extremely long and delicate; the antennae may be twice as long as the wings. The larvae are leaf miners when young and live in cases when older; they are found on herbaceous plants and shrubs. Most of the species in this subfamily belong to the genus *Adèla*.

DIVISION **Macrolepidóptera:** The members of this group vary in size, but most have a wingspread of 25 mm or more. The front wings are more or less triangular and the hind wings are rounded (never with a long fringe); the wings are never long, narrow, and pointed apically, as in some of the Microlepidóptera. There is generally only one anal vein in the front wing (2A), and one or two (2A, or 2A and 3A) in the hind wing.

Family **Epiplèmidae:** The Epiplèmidae are a small group of moths that are similar in size and general appearance to the Geométridae, but differ in wing venation; they have Sc + R and Rs in the hind wing widely separated from near the base of the wing. The cubitus in the front wing appears 3-branched, and the veins M_1 and R_5 are stalked and well separated from R_4. The larvae are sparsely hairy and have five pairs of prolegs. Five species of this group occur in the United States. The moths are plain-colored and have a wingspread of about 20 mm.

Family **Geométridae**—Measuringworms, Geometers: This family is the third largest in the order, with some 1200 species occurring in the United States and Canada. The moths in this group are mostly small, delicate, and slender-bodied; the wings are usually broad and are often marked with fine wavy lines. The two sexes are often different in color, and in a few species the females are wingless or have only rudimentary wings. The geometers are principally nocturnal and are often attracted to lights. The most characteristic feature of the wing venation is the form of the subcosta in the hind wing (Figure 374); the basal part of this vein makes an abrupt bend into the humeral angle and is usually connected by a brace vein to the humeral angle. The cubitus in the front wing appears 3-branched.

The larvae of geometers are the familiar caterpillars commonly called inchworms or measuringworms (Figure 408). They have two or three pairs of prolegs at the posterior end of the body and none in the middle; locomotion is accomplished by placing the posterior end of the body near the thoracic legs and then moving the anterior end of the body, thus progressing in a characteristic looping fashion. Many measuringworms, when disturbed, stand nearly erect on the posterior prolegs and remain motionless, resembling small twigs.

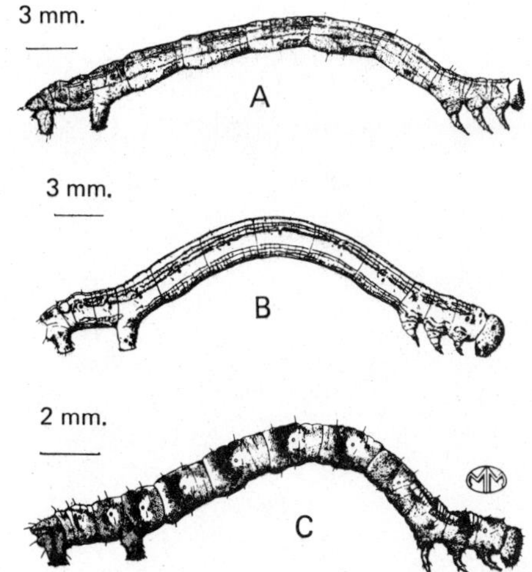

Figure 408. Larvae of Geométridae. A, *Pèro morrisonàrius* (Hy. Edwards); B, *Nepŷtia canosària* (Walker); C, *Protoboármia porcelària indicatòria* Walker. (Courtesy of McGuffin and MacKay, and *The Canadian Entomologist*.)

This group contains the cankerworms, which feed on the foliage of various deciduous trees and often cause serious defoliation. The two common species are the spring cankerworm, *Paleácrita vernàta* (Peck), and the fall cankerworm, *Alsóphila pometària* (Harris) (Figure 409). The spring cankerworm overwinters in the pupal stage, and the female lays its eggs in the spring; the fall cankerworm overwinters in the egg stage. The larvae of the spring cankerworm have two pairs of prolegs; the larvae of the fall cankerworm have three pairs. The adult females of both species are wingless.

Many of the geometers are common moths, but only a few can be mentioned here. The chickweed geometer, *Haemátopis gratària* (Fabricius), is a reddish-yellow moth with the margins of the wings and two bands near the margins pink (Figure 410 B); it has a wingspread of about 25 mm or less; the larva feeds on chickweed. One of the largest moths in this family is the notch-wing geometer, *Ennomos magnàrius* Guenée; it has a wingspread of $1\frac{1}{2}$ to 2 inches (35–50 mm), and the wings are reddish yellow, with small brown spots and shade to brown toward the outer margin (Figure 410 A); the larvae feed on various trees. Many of the geometers are light green in color. One of the common species of this type is the bad-wing, *Dŷspteris abortivària* Herrich-Schäffer (Figure 410 D); the front wings are large and triangular, and the hind wings are small and rounded. This moth has a wingspread of a little less than 25 mm; the larva rolls and feeds on the leaves of grape.

Family **Thyatíridae:** The Thyatíridae are similar to the Noctùidae, but have the cubitus in the front wings appearing 3-branched; in the hind wings, the veins $Sc + R_1$ and Rs are more or less parallel along the anterior margin of the discal cell. The

Figure 409. Fall cankerworm, *Alsóphila pometària* (Harris). A, adult female laying eggs; B, adult male. Natural size. (Courtesy of the Ohio Agricultural Research and Development Center.)

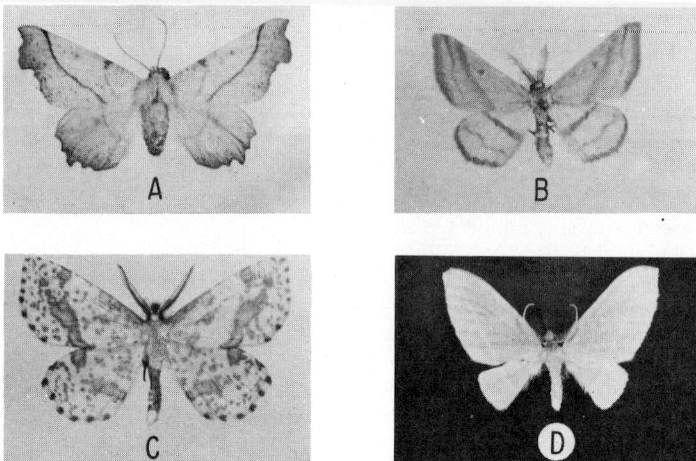

Figure 410. Geometer moths. A, notch-wing geometer, *Énnomos magnàrius* Guenée; B, chickweek geometer, *Haemátopis gratària* (Fabricius); C, crocus geometer, *Xanthótype sóspeta* Drury; D, bad-wing, *Dýspteris abortivària* Herrich-Schäffer. A, slightly reduced; B and D, slightly enlarged; C, about natural size.

Figure 411. A, a hook-tip moth, *Drépana arcuàta* Walker, 2 ×; B, an apatelodid moth, *Apatelòdes torrefácta* Abbott and Smith, 1½ ×.

Figure 412. Sack-bearer moths (Mimallónidae). A, *Lacosòma chiridòta* Grote, 2½ ×; B, *Cicínnus melsheìmeri* Harris, 1½ ×.

larvae of this small group feed on various trees and shrubs.

Family **Drepánidae**—Hook-Tip Moths: These moths are small, slender-bodied, and usually dull-colored, and can generally be recognized by the sickle-shaped apex of the front wings. The cubitus in the front wings appears 4-branched; in the hind wing $Sc + R_1$ and Rs are separated along the discal cell; the frenulum is small or absent. The larvae feed on the foliage of various trees and shrubs. The most common species in this group is *Drépana arcuàta* Walker, a dirty white moth marked with dark brownish lines and with a wingspread of about 25 mm (Figure 411 A); it occurs in the Atlantic states.

Family **Mimallónidae**—Sack-Bearers: These insects are called sack-bearers because the larvae make cases from leaves and carry them about. The group is a small one, with three species in two genera, *Lacosòma* and *Cicínnus*. The moths in the genus *Lacosòma* are yellowish in color, about 25 mm in wingspread, with the distal margin of the front wings deeply scalloped (Figure 412 A). Those in the genus *Cicínnus* are reddish gray peppered with small black dots and with a narrow dark line across the wings, a wingspread of about 32 mm, and the distal margin of the front wings evenly rounded (Figure 412 B). The larvae of mimallonids feed on oak.

Family **Ctenùchidae**—Ctenuchas and Wasp Moths: The ctenuchids are small day-flying moths, some of which are wasplike in appearance (but not so wasplike as the Sesìidae). They can usually be recognized by the venation of the hind wings (Figure 379 A); the subcosta is apparently absent.

Ctenùcha virgínica (Charpentier), a common species in the Northeast, has brownish-black wings, a brilliant metallic bluish body, and an orange head (Figure 413 B). The larva is a woolly yellowish caterpillar that feeds on grasses; the cocoon is formed largely of the body hairs of the caterpillar. The yellow-collared scape moth, *Scépsis fulvicóllis* (Hübner), is somewhat smaller than the ctenucha, with narrower wings, and with the central portion of the hind wings lighter; the prothorax is yellowish (Figure 413 A). The larva of this species feeds on grasses, and the adults frequent goldenrod flowers. The lichen moth, *Lycomórpha phòlus* (Drury), is a small blackish moth with the base of the wings yellowish (Figure 413 C); it looks a little like some of the lycid beetles. These moths occur in rocky places and the larvae feed on the lichens that grow on the rocks.

Figure 413. Ctenuchid moths. A, yellow-collared scape moth, *Scépsis fulvicóllis* (Hübner), 1½ ×; B, Virginia ctenucha, *Ctenùcha virgínica* (Charpentier), natural size; C, lichen moth, *Lycomórpha phòlus* (Drury), 1⅓ ×.

Family **Nòlidae:** The family Nòlidae contains small moths that have ridges and tufts of raised scales on the front wings. *Célama ovílla* (Grote) is fairly common in Pennsylvania on the trunks of beeches and oaks; the larva feeds on the lichens growing on the tree trunks. *Nigétia formosàlis* Walker is a rather pretty mottled moth that is fairly common in southern Indiana. The larva of *Célama triquetràna* (Fitch), a gray moth with a wingspread of 17–20 mm, feeds on apple, but is seldom numerous enough to do much damage. The larva of the sorghum webworm, *C. sorghiélla* (Riley), is a pest of sorghum.

Family **Arctìidae**—Tiger Moths and Footman Moths: The arctiids are small to medium-sized

Figure 414. Tiger moths (Arctiinae). A, virgin tiger moth, *Apántesis vírgo* (L.), ¾ ×; B, adult of saltmarsh caterpillar, *Estígmene acraèa* (Drury), 1½ ×.

moths, most of which are conspicuously and brightly spotted or banded. The wing venation is very similar to that in the Noctùidae, but Sc and Rs in the hind wing are usually fused to about the middle of the discal cell (Figure 380). The moths are principally nocturnal, and when at rest, hold the wings rooflike over the body. The larvae are usually hairy, sometimes very much so; the so-called woollybear caterpillars belong to this group. The cocoons are made largely from the body hairs of the larvae.

This family is divided into two subfamilies, the Lithosiìnae and the Arctiìnae; ocelli are present in the Arctiìnae and absent in the Lithosiìnae.

Subfamily **Lithosiìnae**—Footman Moths: The footman moths are small and slender-bodied, and most of them are rather dull-colored. The larvae of most species feed on lichens. The striped footman moth, *Hypoprèpia miniàta* (Kirby), is a beautiful insect; it has the front wings pinkish with three gray stripes, and the hing wings are yellow and broadly margined with gray.

Subfamily **Arctiìnae**—Tiger Moths: This subfamily contains the majority of the species in the family, and many of them are very common insects; a few are occasionally rather destructive to trees and shrubs.

The tiger moths in the genus *Apántesis* have the front wings black with red or yellow stripes, and the hind wings are usually pinkish with black spots. One of the largest and most common species in this genus is *A. vírgo* (L.), which has a wingspread of about 2 inches (50 mm) (Figure 414 A); the larva feeds on pigweed and other weeds, and winters in the larval stage.

Estígmene acraèa (Drury) is another common tiger moth. The adults are white, with numerous small black spots on the wings, and the abdomen is pinkish with black spots (Figure 414 B); the male has the hind wings yellowish. The larva feeds on various grasses and is sometimes called the saltmarsh caterpillar.

One of the best known of the woollybear caterpillars is the banded woollybear, *Ísia isabélla* (J. E. Smith); this caterpillar is brown in the middle and black at each end, and the adult is yellowish brown with three rows of small black spots on the abdomen. These caterpillars are often seen scurrying across the highways in the fall; they overwinter as larvae and pupate in the spring. The larva feeds on various weeds. The amount of black in this larva in the fall is thought by some to vary proportionately with the severity of the coming winter.

The larvae of some of the tiger moths feed on trees and shrubs and may often do serious damage. The fall webworm, *Hyphántria cùnea* (Drury), is a common species of this type. The larvae build large webs, often enclosing a whole limb of foliage, and feed within the web. These webs are common on many types of trees in late summer and fall. The adults are white with a few dark spots and have a wingspread of about 25 mm. The larvae of the hickory tussock moth, *Halisidòta cáryae* (Harris) (Figure 415 B), feed on hickory and other trees; the larva is somewhat similar to that of the tussock moths in the genus *Hemerocámpa*; the adults (Figure 415 A) are light brown with white spots on the front wings.

Family **Agarístidae**—Forester Moths: The foresters are usually black with two whitish or yellowish spots in each wing, and they have a wingspread of about 25 mm; the antennae are slightly clubbed. The wing venation (Figure 378 B) is similar to that of the Noctùidae. The eight-spotted forester, *Alýpia octomaculàta* (Fabricius), is a common species in this group (Figure 416); the larvae feed on grape and Virginia creeper and sometimes defoliate them.

Family **Noctùidae:** The Noctùidae is the largest family in the order, with some 2700 species in the United States and Canada. These moths are mostly nocturnal in habit, and the majority of the

Figure 415. (*left*) Hickory Tussock moth, *Halisidòta càryae* (Harris) (Arctìidae). A, adult, 1½ ×; B, larva. (Courtesy of Knull.)

Figure 416. Eight-spotted forester, *Alýpia octomaculàta* (Fabricius), 1½ ×.

moths that are attracted to lights at night belong to this group. The noctuids vary greatly in size and color, but most of them are of medium size (1–2 inches (25–50 mm) in wingspread) and dull color.

The noctuids are mostly heavy-bodied moths with the front wings somewhat narrowed and the hind wings broadened (Figure 418). The labial palps are usually long, the antennae are generally hairlike (sometimes brushlike in the males), and in some species there are tufts of scales on the dorsum of the thorax. The wing venation (Figure 381) is rather characteristic: M_2 in the front wing arises closer to M_3 than to M_1, and the cubitus appears 4-branched; the subcosta and radius in the hind wing are separate at the base but fuse for a very short distance at the base of the discal cell; M_2 in the hind wing may be present or absent.

Noctuid larvae are usually smooth and dull-colored (Figure 417), and most of them have five pairs of prolegs. The majority feed on foliage, but some are boring in habit and some feed on fruits. A number of species in this group are serious pests of various crops.

The largest noctuid occuring in the United States is the black witch, *Érebus òdora* (L.), a blackish species with a wingspread of 4 or 5 inches (100 or 130 mm) (Figure 418 D). It breeds in the southern states, where the larva feeds on various leguminous trees; the adults sometimes appear in the northern states in late summer.

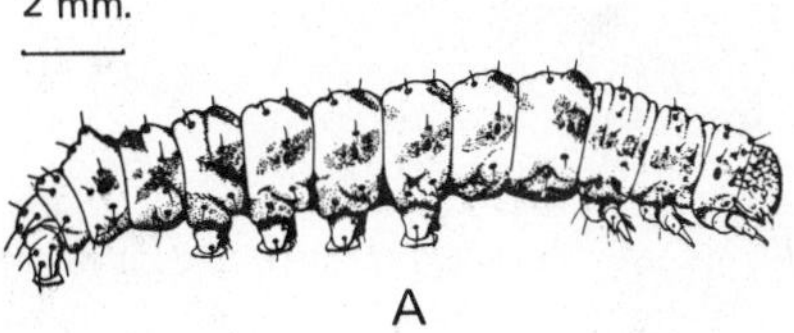

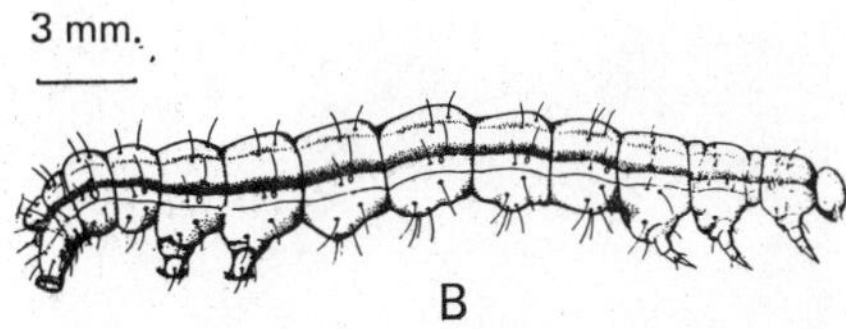

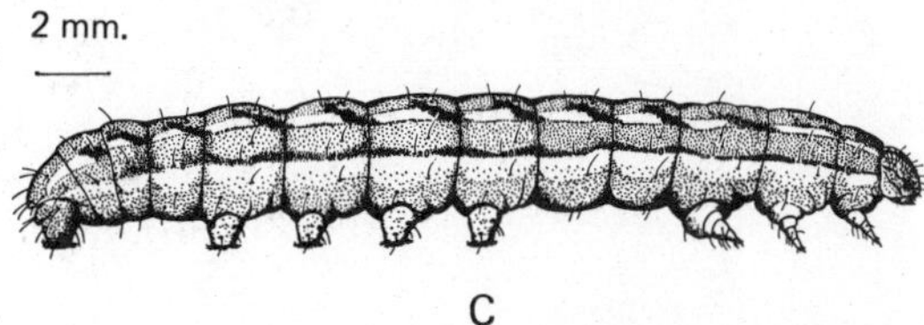

Figure 417. Noctuid larvae. A, *Pálthis angulàlis* Hübner; B, *Autógrapha selécta* Walker (a looper; note the reduced number of prolegs); C, *Anomogỳna elimàta* Guenée. (Courtesy of Brown, McGuffin, MacKay, and *The Canadian Entomologist.*)

Figure 418. Noctuid moths. A, adult of cabbage looper, *Trichoplùsia nì* (Hübner); B, *Séptis árctica* Freyer; C, *Eùxoa éxcellens* Grote (the adult of one of the cutworms); D, black witch, *Érebus òdora* (L.); E, *Euthisanòtia gràta* Fabricius; F, darling underwing, *Catocàla càra* Guenée. D, ⅓ ×; E, slightly enlarged; F, slightly reduced; other figures approximately natural size.

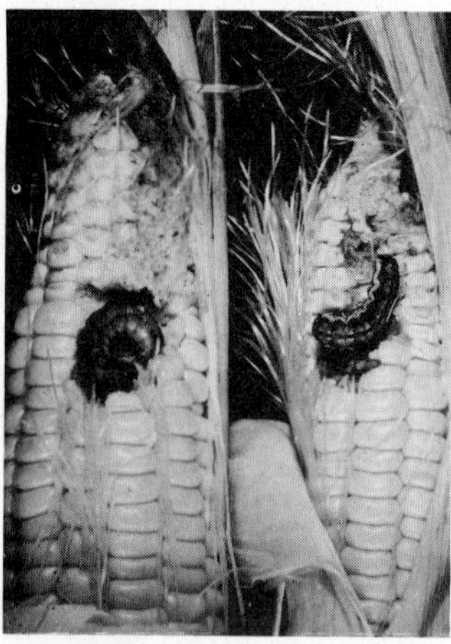

Figure 419. Larvae of corn earworm, *Helìothis zèa* (Boddie). (Courtesy of the Ohio Agricultural Research and Development Center.)

The armyworm, *Pseudalètia unipúncta* (Haworth), feeds on various grasses and frequently does serious damage to wheat and corn. The common name of this insect refers to the fact that the larvae frequently migrate in large numbers to a new feeding area. The moths are light brown with a single white spot in the middle of each front wing.

The corn earworm, *Helìothis zèa* (Boddie), is another serious pest; the larva feeds on a number of plants, including corn, tomato, and cotton, and is sometimes called the tomato fruitworm or the cotton bollworm. When feeding on corn (Figure 419), the larva enters the end of the corn ear on the silks and eats the kernels from the tip of the cob; it burrows in the fruit of tomatoes and into the bolls of cotton. This is a very important pest species. The adults are light yellowish in color and exhibit some variation in their markings.

A few species in this group are called loopers because they have only three pairs of prolegs (Figure 417 B) and move like measuringworms. The cabbage looper, *Trichoplùsia nì* (Hübner), is a serious pest of cabbage, and the celery looper, *Anágrapha falcífera* (Kirby), attacks celery. The adults are dark brown with a wingspread of about $1\frac{1}{2}$ inches (38 mm) and have a small elongate silvery spot in the middle of each front wing (Figure 418 A).

The underwings (*Catocàla*) are relatively large and strikingly colored moths. They are forest or woodland species, and the larvae feed on the foliage of various trees. The hind wings are usually brightly colored with concentric bands of red, yellow, or orange (Figure 418 F). When at rest, the hind wings are concealed and the front wings are colored much like the bark of the trees on which these moths usually rest.

The larvae of many species in this group are commonly called cutworms because they feed on the roots and shoots of various herbaceous plants, and the plant is often cut off at the surface of the ground. The cutworms are nocturnal in habit, and during the day hide under stones or in the soil. The more important cutworms belong to the genera *Agròtis, Hadèna, Perídroma, Féltia, Nephelòdes, Prodènia,* and *Eùxoa.*

The noctuids have a pair of tympanal auditory organs located at the base of the abdomen (such organs are present in many other families of moths, but not in all families). These organs are capable of detecting frequencies from 3 to over 100 kHz,[3] and they appear to function in the detection and evasion of bats. Bats are able to detect prey (and obstacles) in complete darkness by means of a sort of sonar; they emit very high-pitched clicks (sometimes as high as 80 kHz), and locate objects from the echoes of these clicks.

[3] Three kilohertz is in the top octave of the piano; the average upper limit of hearing in man is about 15 kilohertz.

Family **Pericópidae:** The Pericópidae are medium-sized moths that are usually black with large white areas in the wings; these moths occur chiefly in the South and West. *Compòsia fidelíssima* Herrich-Schäffer, a dark-blue moth marked with red and white, is found in southern Florida. Species in the genus *Gnophaèla* occur in western and southwestern United States.

Family **Dióptidae**—Oakworms: This family is represented in the United States by a single species, the California oakworm, *Phryganídia califórnica* Packard, which occurs in California. The adults are slender moths, pale brown with dark veins, and have a wingspread of 25–35 mm; the larvae feed on oak and often do serious damage.

Family **Notodóntidae**—Prominents: The prominents are usually brownish or yellowish moths that are similar to the Noctùidae in general appearance. The family name (*not*, back; *odont*, tooth) refers to the fact that in some species there are backward-projecting tufts on the hind margin of the wings, which protrude when the wings are folded (they are usually folded rooflike over the body when at rest), and the larvae have conspicuous tubercles on the dorsal surface of the body. The notodontids may be readily distinguished from the Noctùidae by the venation of the front wing (Figure 375 B); in the Notodóntidae, M_2 arises from the middle of the apex of the discal cell, and the cubitus appears 3-branched, whereas in the Noctùidae, M_2 in the front wing arises closer to M_3, and the cubitus appears 4-branched (Figure 381).

Notodontid larvae feed on various trees and shrubs and are usually gregarious. When disturbed, they often elevate the anterior and posterior ends of the body and "freeze" in this position, remaining attached by the four pairs of prolegs in

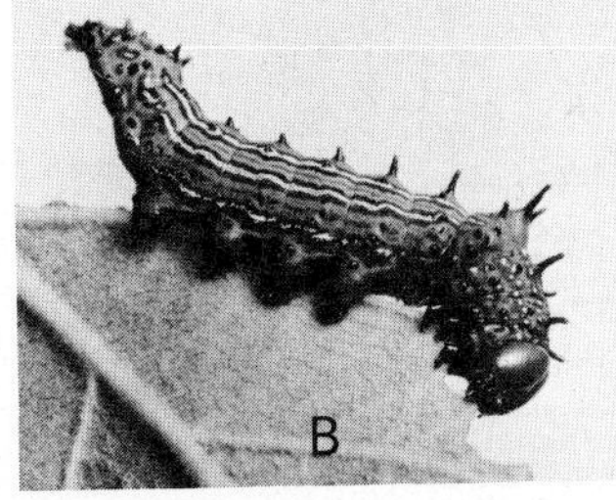

Figure 420. Notodóntidae. A, *Datàna minístra* (Drury); B, redhumped caterpillar, *Schizùra concínna* (J. E. Smith). Natural size. (B, courtesy of the Ohio Agricultural Research and Development Center.)

the middle of the body. The anal pair of prolegs is often rudimentary or modified into spinelike structures.

In this group, most of the brownish moths that have narrow dark lines across the front wings belong to the genus *Datàna*; these are sometimes called handmaid moths (Figure 420 A). The larvae are blackish with yellow longitudinal stripes. The yellownecked caterpillar, *D. minístra* (Drury), feeds on apple and other trees; the walnut caterpillar, *D. integérrima* Grote and Robinson, feeds principally on walnut and hickory.

The redhumped caterpillar, *Schizùra concínna* (J. E. Smith), is a fairly common species in this group. The larva is black with yellow stripes, with the head and a hump on the first abdominal segment red (Figure 420 B). The adult has a wingspread of a little over 25 mm; the front wings are gray with brown markings, and the hind wings are white with a small black spot along the rear edge. The larva feeds on apple and other orchard trees, and on various shrubs.

Family **Lipàridae**—Tussock Moths and Their Relatives: The liparids are medium-sized moths that are similar to the Noctùidae, but differ in that they lack ocelli and have the basal areole in the hind wing larger (Figure 382); in most species (Figure 382 A), M_1 in the hind wing is stalked with Rs for a short distance beyond the apex of the discal cell. The larvae are rather hairy and feed chiefly on trees. The tussock moths and the gypsy and browntail moths are serious pests of forest and shade trees; the tussock moths are native species, whereas the two latter were introduced from Europe.

The whitemarked tussock moth, *Hemerocámpa leucostígma* (J. E. Smith) (Figure 421), is a common species throughout most of North America. The males are gray, with lighter hind wings and plumose antennae, and the females are wingless. The eggs are laid on tree trunks or branches, usually near the cocoon from which the female emerged, and the species overwinters in the egg stage. The larva (Figure 421 A) may be recognized by the characteristic tufts or brushes of hairs.

The gypsy moth, *Porthètria díspar* (L.), was introduced from Europe into Massachusetts about 1866; since then, it has become widely distributed throughout New England and has caused widespread damage to forest trees. The females are white with black markings, and the males are gray (Figure 422). The females have a wingspread of about 1½ to 2 inches (38–50 mm), and the males are a little smaller. The eggs are laid on tree trunks

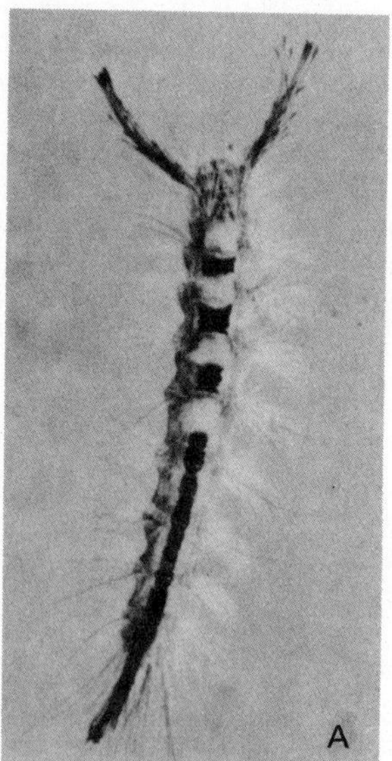

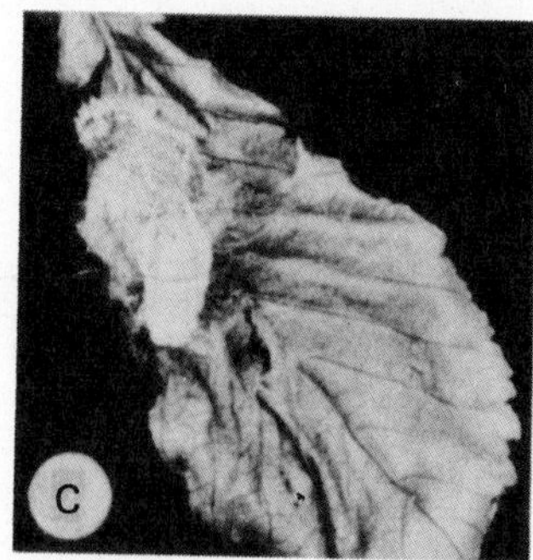

Figure 421. Whitemarked tussock moth, *Hemerocámpa leucostígma* (Abbott and Smith). A, larva; B, adult male; C, adult female. Slightly enlarged. (A, C, Courtesy of the Ohio Agricultural Research and Development Center; B, photographed by Carl W. Albrecht.)

or similar places, in a mass of the body hairs from the female; they overwinter and hatch the following spring. The females are very weak fliers and seldom travel very far from the cocoon from which they emerge; the dispersal of the species is accomplished largely by the young larvae.

The browntail moth, *Nýgmia phaeorrhoèa* (Donovan), is another serious pest of forest and shade trees and was introduced from Europe; it first appeared near Boston in the early 1890s, and has since spread throughout New England. The adults are white, have a wingspread of 25–38 mm, and have brownish hairs at the end of the abdomen; the males are a little smaller than the females. This species passes the winter as a larva in a leaf shelter. Both sexes are winged. The hairs of the larva, when blown onto the skin of man, cause an irritating rash.

The satin moth, *Stilpnòtia sálicis* (L.), is a more recent introduction from Europe and may prove to be an important pest species.

Family **Manidìidae:** This family is represented in the United States by a single species, *Anurápteryx crenulàta* Barnes and Lindsey, which occurs in Arizona.

Family **Apatelòdidae:** The Apatelòdidae are represented in North America by three species in the genus *Apatelòdes*. These moths are similar to the Notodóntidae, but usually have windowlike dots near the apex of the front wings; they have a wingspread of 1½ to 2 inches (38–50 mm) (Figure 411 B). The larvae feed on various shrubs and trees and pupate in the ground.

Family **Bombýcidae**—Silkworm Moths: This family contains a single species, *Bómbyx mòri* (L.), a native of Asia that is sometimes reared in this country. This insect has long been reared for its silk, and it is one of the most important beneficial insects. After centuries of domestication it is now a domestic species and probably does not exist in nature. Many different varieties of silkworms have been developed by breeding.

The adult moth is creamy white with several faint brownish lines across the front wings and has a wingspread of about 2 inches (50 mm). The body is heavy and very hairy. The adults do not feed, they rarely fly, and usually they live only a few days. Each female lays 300–400 eggs. The larvae are naked, have a short anal horn, and feed principally on the leaves of mulberry; they become full grown and spin their cocoons in about six weeks. When used for commercial purposes, the pupae are killed before they emerge, since the emergence of the moth breaks the fibers in the cocoon. Each cocoon is composed of a single thread about 1000 yards (914 m) long; about 3000 cocoons are required to make a pound of silk.

Figure 422. Gypsy moth, *Porthétria díspar* (L.). Male above, female below, ⅔ ×.

Sericulture is practiced in Japan, China, Spain, France, and Italy. The silk has a commercial value of from $200 to $500 million annually.

Family **Lasiocámpidae**—Tent Caterpillars and Lappet Moths: These moths are medium-sized and stout-bodied, with the body, legs, and eyes hairy. The antennae are somewhat feathery in both sexes, but the teeth of the antennae are longer in the male. There is no frenulum, and the humeral angle of the hind wing is expanded and provided with humeral veins (Figure 377 B). Most of these moths are brown or gray in color. The larvae feed on the foliage of trees, often causing serious damage; pupation occurs in a well-formed cocoon.

The eastern tent caterpillar, *Malacosòma americànum* (Fabricius) (Figure 423), is a common member of this group in eastern North America. The adults are yellowish brown and appear in midsummer; they lay their eggs in a bandlike cluster around a twig, and the eggs hatch the following spring. The young that hatch from a given egg cluster are gregarious and construct a tentlike nest of silk near the eggs (Figure 424); this tent is used as a shelter, with the larvae feeding during the day in nearby branches. The larvae feed on a number of different trees, but seem to prefer cherry. The larvae are black and somewhat hairy and have a yellow stripe down the middle of the back. When full grown they wander off and spin their cocoons in sheltered places.

Figure 423. Eastern tent caterpillar, *Malacosòma americànum* (Fabricius). Left, egg mass; center, larvae; right, adult female, ½ ×. (Courtesy of the Ohio Agricultural Research and Development Center.)

Figure 424. Tents of tent caterpillar. (Courtesy of Ohio Agricultural Research and Development Center.)

The forest tent caterpillar, *Malacosòma dísstria* Hübner, is widely distributed, but is probably more common in the South and Southwest, where it sometimes defoliates large areas. The caterpillars differ from those of the eastern caterpillar in that they have a row of keyhole-shaped spots (rather than a stripe) down the middle of the back; the adults are somewhat paler than those of the eastern tent caterpillar.

The lappet moths (*Tólype*) are bluish gray with white markings; the common name refers to the fact that the larvae have a small lobe or lappet on each side of each segment. The larvae of *T. véllida* (Stoll) feed on apple, poplar, and syringa, and those of *T. láricis* (Fitch) feed on larch.

Family **Saturnìidae**—Giant Silkworm Moths and Royal Moths: This family includes the largest moths in our area; some have a wingspread of 6 inches (150 mm) or more. It includes some of the largest lepidopterans in the world; some species of *Áttacus* have a wingspread of about 10 inches (250 mm). The smallest members of this family (in our area) have a wingspread of a little over 25 mm. Many are conspicuously or brightly colored, and many have transparent eye spots in the wings. The antennae are bipectinate or feathery for half or all their length, and are larger in the male than in the female. The mouth parts are reduced, and the adults do not feed.

The larvae of saturniids (Figures 425 and 427 B) are large caterpillars, and many are armed with conspicuous tubercles or spines. Most of them (Saturniìnae and Hemileucìnae) spin silken cocoons, which are attached to the twigs or leaves of trees and shrubs, or are formed among leaves on the ground; some (Citheroniìnae) pupate in the ground without forming a cocoon. Most species overwinter in the pupal stage and have one generation a year. A few species in this group have been used for the production of commercial silk; some of the Asiatic species have provided a silk that makes strong and long-wearing fabrics, but none of the North American species has proved satisfactory for commercial silk production.

The 69 North American species in this family are arranged in three subfamilies, the Saturniìnae, Hemileucìnae, and Citheroniìnae.

Subfamily **Saturniìnae**—Giant Silkworm Moths: The members of this group have one anal vein in the hind wing, the discal cell in the front wing may be open (Figure 376 C) or closed, M_1 in the front wing is not stalked with R, and the antennae of the male are pectinate to the tip.

The largest saturniine in this country is the cecropia moth, *Platysàmia cecròpia* (L.); most individuals have a wingspread of 5 or 6 inches (130 or 150 mm). The wings are reddish brown, crossed in the middle with a white band; in the middle of each wing is a crescent-shaped white spot bordered with red (Figure 426 D). The larva (Figure 425 A) is a greenish caterpillar that reaches

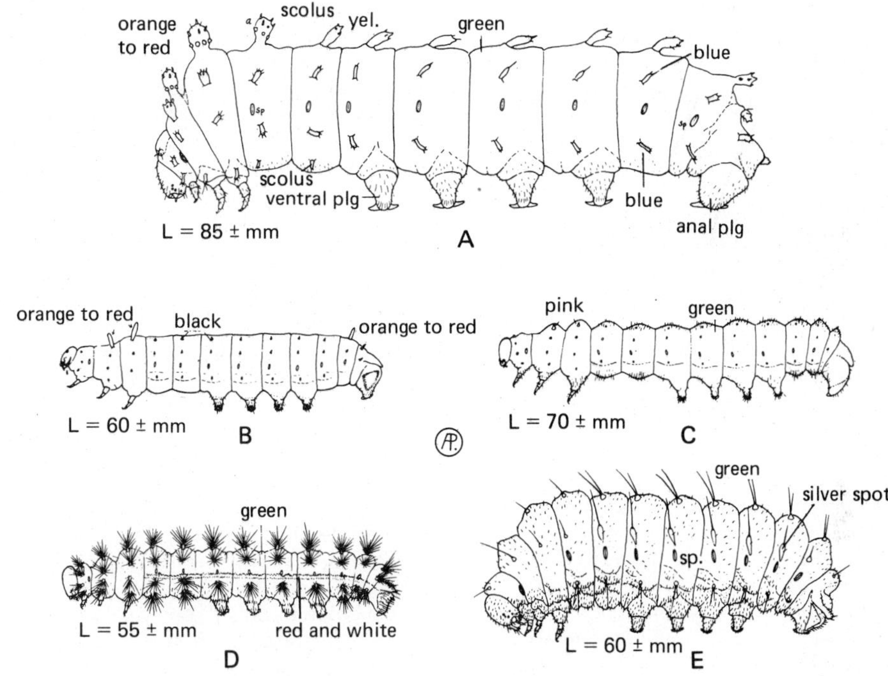

Figure 425. Larvae of Saturnìidae. A, cecropia, *Platysàmia cecròpia* (L.); B, promethea, *Callosàmia promèthea* (Drury); C, luna, *Áctias lùna* (L.); D, io, *Autómeris ìo* (Fabricius); E, polyphemus, *Antheraèa polyphèmus* (Cramer). *plg,* proleg. (Courtesy of Peterson. Reprinted by permission.)

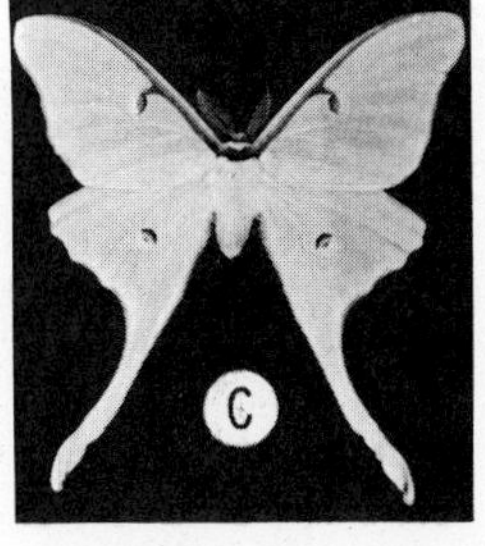

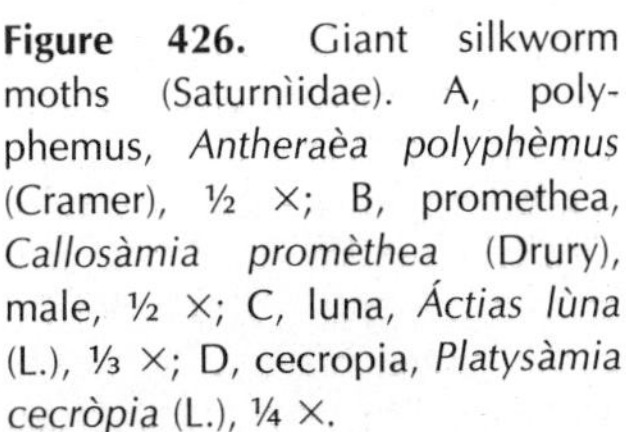

Figure 426. Giant silkworm moths (Saturnìidae). A, polyphemus, *Antheraèa polyphèmus* (Cramer), ½ ×; B, promethea, *Callosàmia promèthea* (Drury), male, ½ ×; C, luna, *Áctias lùna* (L.), ⅓ ×; D, cecropia, *Platysàmia cecròpia* (L.), ¼ ×.

a length of about 4 inches (100 mm); it has two rows of yellow tubercles down the back, and two pairs of large red tubercles on the thoracic segments. The cocoons are formed on twigs.

The promethea moth, *Callosàmia promèthea* (Drury), is sometimes called the spicebush silk moth because its larva feeds on spicebush, sassafras, and related plants. This moth is considerably smaller than the cecropia. The female is patterned a little like the cecropia, with the basal part of the wings dark brown and bordered by a white line; the outer portion of the wing is light brown. The male (Figure 426 B) is much darker, with a narrow marginal band of yellowish on the wings. Males often fly about during the day, and when on the wing look a little like a large mourningcloak butterfly. The cocoon is formed in a leaf, which is prevented from falling off the twig by the petiole of the leaf being securely fastened with silk.

One of the most beautiful moths in this group is the luna, *Áctias lùna* (L.), a light green moth with long tails on the hind wings and with the costal margin of the front wings narrowly bordered by dark brown (Figure 426 C). The larva (Figure 425 C) is greenish and feeds on walnut, hickory, and other trees, and the cocoon is formed in a leaf on the ground.

Another common moth in this group is the polyphemus, *Antheraèa polyphèmus* (Cramer), a large yellowish brown moth with a windowlike spot in each wing (Figure 426 A). The larva (Figure 425 E) is similar to that of the luna and feeds on various trees; its cocoon is formed in a leaf on the ground.

Subfamily **Hemileucìnae:** Some members of this group (*Autómeris*) have one anal vein in the hind wing, and others (*Colorádia, Hemileùca*) have two; the discal cell in the front wing is usually closed (Figure 376 B), M_1 in the front wing is usually not stalked with R, and the antennae of the male are pectinate to the tip. Most moths in this group have a wingspread of about 2 inches (50 mm).

The io moth, *Autómeris ìo* (Fabricius), is one of the most common (and the largest) in this group; it has a wingspread of about 2–3 inches (50–76 mm) and is yellow with a large eyespot in each wing. The female is usually larger than the male, and its front wings are reddish brown. The larva is a spiny green caterpillar with a narrow reddish stripe, edged below with white, extending along each side of the body (Figure 425 D). This larva should be handled with care, for the spines sting.

The buck moth, *Hemileùca màia* (Drury), is a little smaller than the io, and is blackish with a narrow yellow band through the middle of each wing; it occurs throughout the East, but is not common. It is largely diurnal in habit, and its larva (which has stinging hairs) pupates in the ground.

The pandora moth, *Colorádia pandòra* Blake, is a western species, a little smaller than the io, and is gray with lighter hind wings; it has a small dark spot near the center of each wing.

Subfamily **Citheroniìnae**—Royal Moths: The members of this group have two anal veins in the hind wings, the discal cell in the front wings is closed, M_1 in the front wing is stalked with R for a short distance (Figure 376 A), and the antennae of the male are pectinate in the basal half only. The larvae are armed with horns or spines and pupate in the ground.

Our largest species in this group is the regal moth, *Citherònia regàlis* (Fabricius) (Figure 427 A), which sometimes has a wingspread of 5 or 6 inches (130 or 150 mm). The front wings are gray or olive-colored spotted with yellow, and with the veins reddish brown; the hind wings are orange-red spotted with yellow; the body is reddish brown with yellow bands. The larva (Figure 427 B) is often called the hickory horned devil; when full grown it is 4 or 5 inches (100 or 130 mm) long and has curved spines in the anterior part of the body; though quite ferocious in appearance, this caterpillar is entirely harmless. It feeds principally on walnut, hickory, and persimmon.

The imperial moth, *Èacles imperiàlis* (Drury), is a large yellowish moth with dark peppered spots; each wing has a pinkish brown diagonal band near the margin (Figure 427 C). The larva feeds on various trees and shrubs. The moths in the genus *Anisòta* are small, with a wingspread of about $1\frac{1}{2}$ inches (38 mm); most of them are brownish in color, but one species, *A. rubicúnda* (Fabricius), the rosy maple moth, is pale yellow banded with pink (Figure 427 D).

Family **Sphíngidae**—Sphinx or Hawk Moths, Hornworms: The sphinx moths are medium-sized to large, heavy-bodied moths with long narrow front wings (Figure 429); some have a wingspread of 5 inches (130 mm) or more. The body is somewhat spindle-shaped, tapering, and pointed both anteriorly and posteriorly. The antennae are slightly thickened in the middle or toward the tip. The subcosta and radius in the hind wing are connected by a cross vein (R_1) about opposite the

Figure 427. Citheroniine moths. A, adult, and B, larva, of the regal moth, *Citherònia regàlis* (Fabricius), ½ ×; C, imperial moth. *Èacles imperiàlis* (Drury), ½ ×; D, rosy maple moth, *Anisòta rubicúnda* (Fabricius), slightly enlarged.

middle of the discal cell (Figure 373 B). The proboscis in many species is very long, sometimes as long as the body or longer.

These moths are strong fliers and fly with a very rapid wing beat; some are dayfliers, but most of them are active at dusk or twilight. Most of them feed much like hummingbirds, hovering in front of a flower and extending their proboscis into it; these moths are sometimes called hummingbird moths, and in many species the body is about the size of a hummingbird. Some species (for example, *Hémaris*) have large areas in the wings devoid of scales, and are called clear-winged moths; these are not to be confused with the clear-winged moths of the family Sesìidae, which are smaller and more slender and have the front wings much more elongate (compare Figures 429 B and 402).

The name "hornworm" is derived from the fact that the larvae of most species have a conspicuous horn or spinelike process on the dorsal surface of the eighth abdominal segment (Figure 428 A); the name "sphinx" probably refers to the sphinxlike position that some of these larvae occasionally assume. The larvae of most species pupate in the ground, in some cases forming pitcherlike pupae (the proboscis of the pupa looks like a handle); some species form a sort of cocoon among leaves on the surface of the ground.

One of the most common species in this group is the tomato hornworm, *Mandùca quinquemaculàta* (Haworth); the larva (Figure 428 A) is a

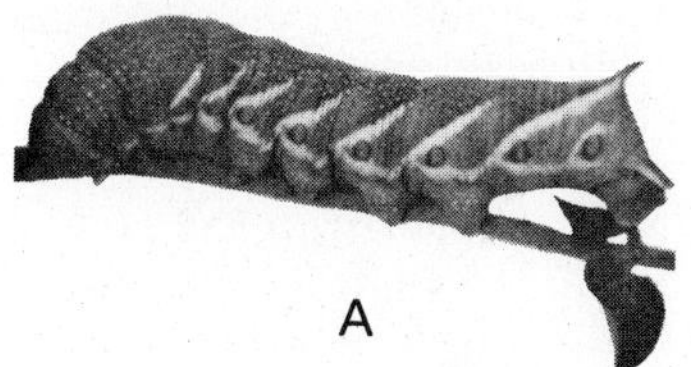

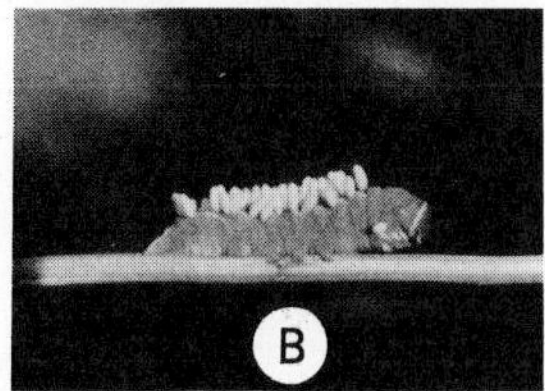

Figure 428. A, tomato hornworm, *Mandùca quinquemaculàta* (Haworth); B, a parasitized hornworm; the white objects on the back of the larva are cocoons of braconid parasites. (A, courtesy of the Ohio Agricultural Research and Development Center.)

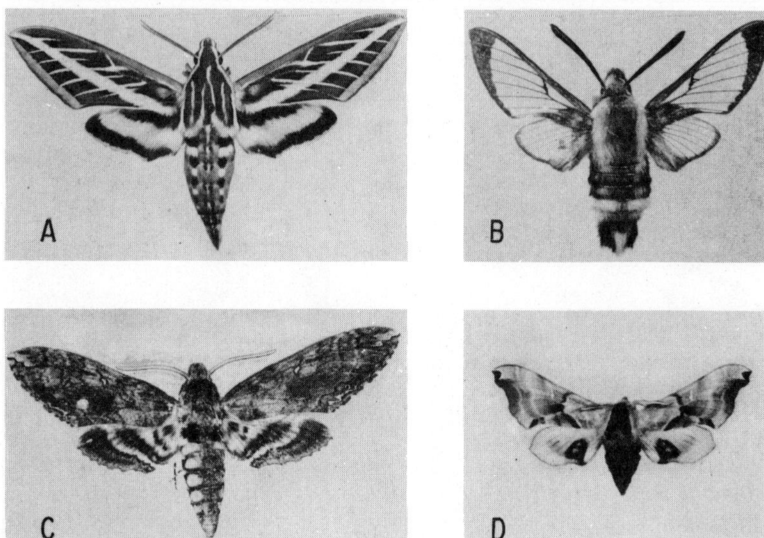

Figure 429. Sphinx or hawk moths. A, whitelined sphinx, *Hýles lineàta* (Fabricius); B, a clear-winged sphinx, *Hémaris díffinis* (Boisduval); C, adult of the tobacco hornworm, *Mandùca séxta* (L.); D, twin-spot sphinx, *Smerínthus jamaicénsis* (Drury). A, C, and D, ½ ×; B, about natural size.

large green caterpillar that feeds on tomato, tobacco, and potato. The larva of a similar species, *M. séxta* (L.), feeds on tobacco and other plants. The adults of these two species are large gray moths with a wingspread of about 4 inches (100 mm); the hind wings are banded, and there are five (*quinquemaculàta*) or six (*séxta*) orange-yellow spots along each side of the abdomen (Figure 429 C). These hornworms often do considerable damage to the plants on which they feed. Hornworms are often attacked by braconid parasites, which form small, white, silken cocoons on the outside of the caterpillar (Figure 428 B).

Family **Hesperìidae**—Skippers: The skippers are for the most part small and stout-bodied butterflies, and get their name from their fast and erratic flight. They differ from other butterflies (except the Megathỳmidae) in having none of the five R branches in the front wings stalked, and all arise from the discal cell (Figure 362); the antennae are widely separated at the base, and the tips are usually recurved or hooked. Most skippers at rest hold the front and hind wings at a different angle. The larvae are smooth, with the head large and the neck constricted; they usually feed inside a leaf shelter, and pupation occurs in a cocoon made of leaves fastened together with silk. Most species overwinter as larvae, either in leaf shelters or in cocoons.

Over 200 species of skippers occur in the United States; most of these (including all the eastern species) belong to two subfamilies, the Pyrgìnae (Hesperiìnae of some authors) and the Hesperiìnae (Pamphilìnae of some authors); a third subfamily, the Pyrrhopygìnae, occurs in the Southwest.

Subfamily **Pyrgìnae:** In the front wings of the Pyrgìnae the discal cell is usually at least two thirds as long as the wing, and M_2 arises midway between M_1 and M_3 and is not curved at the base (Figure 362 A); the middle tibiae lack spines. The males of some species have a costal fold, a long slitlike pocket near the costal margin of the front wing; this serves as a scent organ. Some species have scale tufts on the tibiae. Most of the skippers in this group are relatively large grayish or blackish insects (Figure 430 A, E, F). The larvae feed principally on legumes.

One of the largest and most common species in this subfamily is the silverspotted skipper, *Epargỳreus clàrus* (Cramer); it is dark brown with a large yellowish spot in the front wing and a silvery spot on the underside of the hind wing (Figure 430 A); the larva feeds on black locust and related plants; the species overwinters as a pupa.

Subfamily **Hesperiìnae**—Tawny Skippers: These skippers have the discal cell in the front wings less

Figure 430. Skippers (Hesperìidae). A, silverspotted skipper, *Epargỳreus clàrus* (Cramer) (Pyrgìnae), underside of wings, natural size; B, least skipper *Ancylóxipha nùmitor* (Fabricius) (Hesperiìnae), 1½ ×; C, Hobomok skipper, *Poànes hóbomok* (Harris) (Hesperiìnae), 1⅓ ×; D, Peck's skipper, *Polìtes péckius* (Kerby) (Hesperiìnae), 1¾ ×; E, checkered skipper, *Pýrgus commùnis* (Grote) (Pyrgìnae), 1½ ×; F, northern cloudy wing, *Thórybes pylàdes* (Scudder) (Pyrgìnae), slightly enlarged.

than two thirds as long as the wing; M_2 in the front wings is usually curved at the base and arises nearer to M_3 than to M_1 (Figure 362 B), and the middle tibiae are often spined. The tawny skippers (Figure 430 B–D) are usually brownish, with an oblique dark band (often called the stigma or brand) across the wing of the males; this dark band is composed of scales that serve as outlets for the scent glands. The larvae are chiefly grass feeders.

Subfamily **Pyrrhopygìnae:** These skippers are similar to the Pyrgìnae in wing venation, but have the antennal club wholly reflexed. The group is principally tropical, but one species, *Pyrrhopỳge aráxes* (Hewitson), occurs in southern Texas and Arizona; it is a large (wingspread a little over 25 mm), dark-colored skipper with light spots on the front wings, and the wings are held horizontally when at rest.

Family **Megathỳmidae**—Giant Skippers: These skippers have a wingspread of 1½ inches (38 mm) or more; they occur in the South and West. The antennal club is large, and the tip is not recurved as in many of the Hesperìidae. These skippers are

Figure 431. A, American copper, *Lycaèna phlaèas americàna* Harris (Lycaènidae); B, harvester, *Feníseca tarquínius* (Fabricius) (Lycaènidae); C, a snout butterfly, *Libytheàna bachmánii* (Kirtland) (Libythèidae); D, northern metalmark, *Lephelísca boreàlis* (Grote and Robinson) (Riodínidae). A, B, and D, slightly enlarged; C, about natural size.

stout-bodied, fast-flying, and when at rest the wings are held vertically above the body. The larvae bore in the stems and roots of yucca and related plants; maguey worms (Figure 609) are the larvae of a megathymid.

Family **Lycaènidae**—Gossamer-Winged Butterflies: These are small, delicate, and often brightly colored butterflies, and some are quite common. The body is slender, the antennae are usually ringed with white, and there is a line of white scales encircling the eyes. The radius in the front wings is 3- or 4-branched (3-branched in the Theclìnae, 4-branched in the other subfamilies). M_1 in the front wings arises at or near the anterior apical angle of the discal cell (except in the Gerydìnae; see Figure 432 A), and there is no humeral vein in the hind wings (Figures 366 B and 368 B). The front legs are normal in the female, but are shorter and lack tarsal claws in the male. Lycaenid larvae are flattened and sluglike; many secrete honeydew, which attracts ants, and some live in ant nests. The chrysalids are fairly smooth and are attached by the cremaster, with a silken girdle about the middle of the body. The adults are rapid fliers. Our lycaenids are arranged in four subfamilies, the Theclìnae, Lycaenìnae (=Chrysophanìnae), Plebeiìnae (=Lycaenìnae), and Gerydìnae (=Spalgìnae).

Subfamily **Theclìnae**—Hairstreaks: The hairstreaks are usually dark gray or brownish, with delicate striping on the underside of the wings, and usually with small reddish spots in the posterior part of the hind wings; there are usually two or three hairlike tails on the hind wings. There are only three branches of R in the front wing, and the last one is simple (Figure 366 B). These butterflies have a swift, darting flight, and are commonly found in meadows, along roadsides, and in other open areas.

One of the most common eastern species is the gray hairstreak, *Strỳmon mélinus* (Hübner); the larva bores in the fruits and seeds of legumes, cotton, and other plants. The great purple hairstreak, *Átlides hálesus* (Cramer), is the largest eastern species, with a wingspread of a little over 25 mm; it is brilliantly colored—blue, purple, and black—and quite iridescent; it occurs in the southern states. The elfins (*Incisàlia*) are small, brownish, early spring species which lack tails, but have the edges of the hind wings scalloped.

Subfamily **Lycaenìnae**—Coppers: The coppers are small butterflies that are orange-red or brown

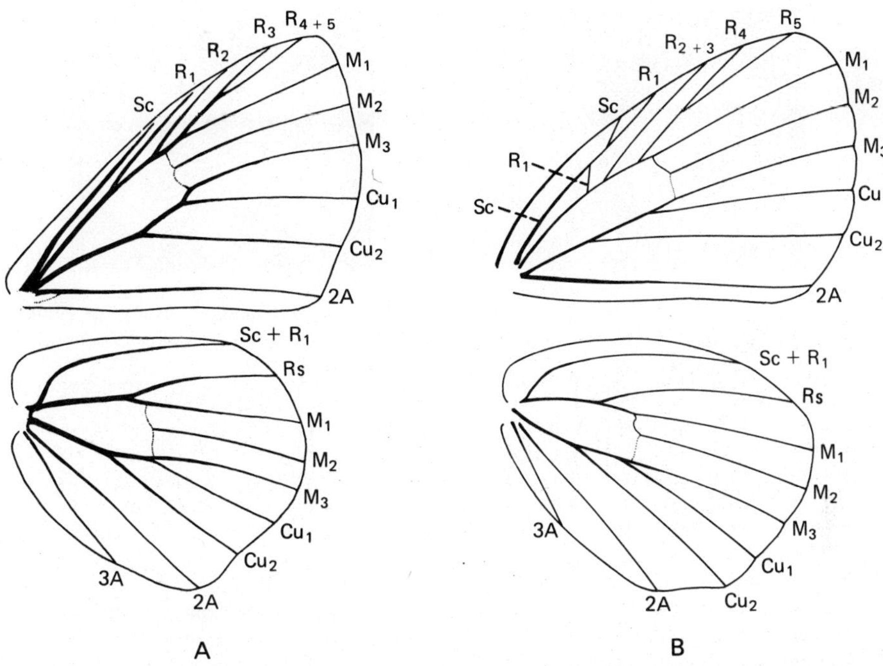

Figure 432. Wings of Lycaènidae. A, harvester (Gerydìnae); B, blue (Plebeiìnae).

(often with a coppery tinge) with black markings. The last branch of R in the front wings (R_{3-5}) is forked (with the branches R_3 and R_{4+5}) and arises at the anterior apical angle of the discal cell (Figure 368 B). These butterflies generally occur in open areas such as marshes and meadows and along roadsides.

The American copper, *Lycaèna phlaèas americàna* Harris (Figure 431 A), is one of the most common species in this group; the adults are quite pugnacious, and often "buzz" other butterflies (and even collectors!); the larva feeds on dock (*Rùmex*).

Subfamily **Plebeiìnae**—Blues: The blues are small, delicate, slender-bodied butterflies with the upper surface of the wings blue. The females are usually darker than the males, and some species occur in two or more color forms. The last branch of R in the front wing is forked (as in the coppers), but arises a little proximad of the anterior apical angle of the discal cell (Figure 432 B). Many larvae secrete honeydew, to which ants are attracted.

One of the most common and widespread species in this group is the spring azure, *Lycaenópsis argìolus* (L.); this species exhibits considerable geographic and seasonal variation in size and coloring. The tailed blues (*Evères*) have delicate taillike prolongations on the hind wings.

Subfamily **Gerydìnae**—Harvesters: The harvesters differ from the other lycaenids in having M_1 in the front wings stalked with a branch of R for a short distance beyond the discal cell (Figure 432 A). The wanderer or harvester, *Feníseca tarquínius* (Fabricius), is the only member of this group occurring in the United States; it is a brownish butterfly with a wingspread of about 25 mm (Figure 431 B). The larva is predaceous on aphids, and is one of the few predaceous lepidopterous larvae. This species is rather local and uncommon, and (in spite of its name) does very little wandering.

Family **Riodínidae**—Metalmarks: The riodinids are small, dark-colored butterflies that are somewhat similar to some of the lycaenids. They differ from the lycaenids in having the costa of the hind wing thickened out to the humeral angle, and in having a short humeral vein in the hind wing (Figure 368 A). Most species in this group are tropical or western, and only two occur in the East. The little metalmark, *Lephelísca virginiénsis* (Guérin), with a wingspread of about 20 mm, occurs in the

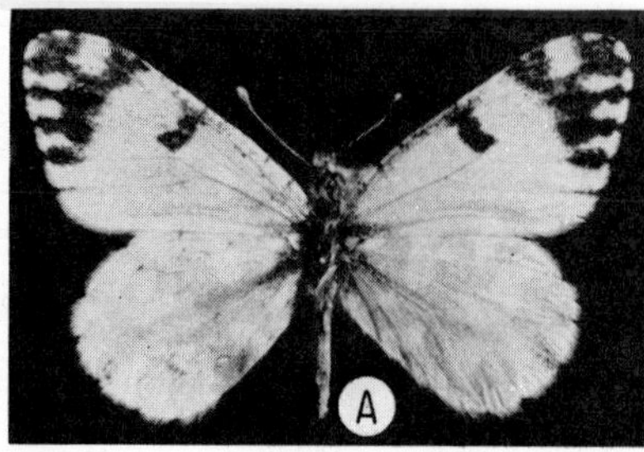

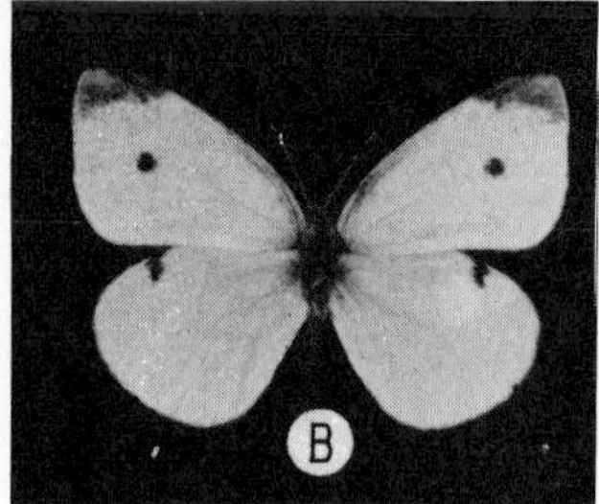

Figure 433. Pierid butterflies. A, an orange-tip, *Eùchloe creùsa lótta* Beutenmüller; B, cabbage butterfly, *Pìeris ràpae* (L.). A, slightly enlarged; B, slightly reduced.

southern states, and the northern metalmark, *L. boreàlis* (Grote and Robinson) (Figure 431 D), with a wingspread of 25–30 mm, occurs as far north as New York and Ohio; the little metalmark is fairly common in the South, but the northern metalmark is quite rare. The larvae feed on ragwort, thistle, and other plants.

Family **Piéridae**—Whites, Sulphurs, and Orange-Tips: The pierids are medium-sized to small butterflies, usually white or yellowish in color, with black marginal wing markings, and with the radius in the front wing usually 3- or 4-branched (rarely 5-branched in some orange-tips). The front legs are well developed, and the tarsal claws are bifid. The chrysalids are elongate and narrow and are attached by the cremaster and by a silken girdle around the middle of the body. Many pierids are very common and abundant butterflies, and are sometimes seen in mass migrations. The members of this family are divided into three groups: the whites, the sulphurs or yellows, and the orange-tips.

The whites are white with black markings. One of the most common species in this group is the cabbage butterfly, *Pìeris ràpae* (L.) (Figure 433 B), the larva of which often does considerable damage to cabbage and related plants; it has two or more generations a year, and overwinters as a chrysalis.

The sulphurs or yellows are yellow or orange in color and have the wings margined with black; rarely, they may be white with black wing margins. Many species occur in two or more seasonal color forms. A common butterfly in this group is the orange sulphur or alfalfa butterfly, *Còlias eurýtheme* Boisduval; most individuals of this species are orange with black wing margins, but some females are white. The larva feeds on clovers and related plants and often does serious damage to clover crops. The common or clouded sulphur, *C. philódice* Godart, is yellow with black wing margins; it often occurs in large numbers around muddy pools along roadsides. The larva feeds on clovers. The females of these sulphurs have the black marginal band on the wings broader than in the males, and there are light spots in this band, particularly in the front wings.

The orange-tips are small white butterflies with dark markings (Figure 433 A); the underside of the wings is mottled with greenish, and the front wings of many species are tipped with orange. These butterflies are mainly western; only two species occur in the East, and they are relatively rare. The larvae feed on cruciferous plants.

Family **Papiliónidae**—Swallowtails: These butterflies get their name from the fact that there is usually a tail-like prolongation on the hind wing; a few species have two or three such prolongations. The swallowtails differ from all the other butterflies, except the parnassians, in having only one anal vein in the hind wing and in having Cu in the front wing appearing 4-branched (Figure 363 A).

Swallowtail larvae are usually smooth-bodied and possess an eversible scent gland, or osmeterium (Figure 357, *osm*); this gland is everted from the upper part of the prothorax when the larva is disturbed, and gives off a disagreeable odor. The chrysalis is attached to various objects by the cremaster, and is held more or less upright by means of a silken girdle about the middle of the body (Figure 358 A). The winter is passed as a chrysalis.

This group contains the largest and some of the most beautifully colored of our butterflies. In many species the two sexes are somewhat dif-

Figure 434. Swallowtail butterflies. A, zebra swallowtail, *Gràphium marcéllus* (Cramer); B, tiger swallowtail, *Papílio glàucus* L.; C, black swallowtail, *Papílio polýxenes astérius* Stoll, male; D, giant swallowtail, *Papílio cresphóntes* Cramer. About one third natural size.

ferently colored. Several species are fairly common in the eastern states. The black swallowtail, *Papílio polýxenes astérius* Stoll (Figure 434 C), is largely black, with two rows of yellow spots around the margin of the wings; the female has quite a bit of blue between the two rows of yellow spots in the hind wings. The larva feeds on carrots, parsley, and related plants. The tiger swallowtail, *Papílio glàucus* L. (Figures 434 B and 632), is a large yellow swallowtail with black stripes in the front wings and black wing margins; in some individuals the wings are almost entirely dark. The larva feeds on cherry, birch, poplar, and various other trees and shrubs. The spicebush swallowtail, *Papílio tròilus* L., is blackish, with a row of small yellowish spots along the margins of the front wings and extensive blue-gray areas in the rear half of the hind wings; the larva feeds on spice-bush and sassafras. The zebra swallowtail, *Gràphium marcéllus* (Cramer) (Figure 434 A), is striped with black and greenish white and has relatively long tails; the larva feeds on papaw. This species shows considerable variation, with the adults that emerge at different seasons differing slightly in their markings. The pipevine swallowtail, *Báttus phílenor* (L.), is largely black, with the hind wings shading into metallic green posteriorly; the larva feeds on the Dutchman's-pipe. The giant swallowtail or orangedog, *Papílio cresphóntes* Cramer (Figure 434 D), is a large dark-colored butterfly with rows of large yellow spots on the wings; the larva feeds largely on citrus in the South and on prickly ash in the North.

Family **Parnassìidae**—Parnassians: The parnassians are medium-sized butterflies that are usually white or gray with dark markings on the wings (Figure 435); most of them have two small reddish spots in the hind wings. These butterflies pupate in the ground, among fallen leaves, in loose cocoonlike structures. Parnassians are principally montane and boreal in distribution.

Family **Libythèidae**—Snout Butterflies: These are small brownish butterflies with long projecting palps. The males have the front legs reduced, with only the middle and hind legs used in walking, while the females have the front legs longer and use them in walking. One species, *Libytheàna bachmánii* (Kirtland), occurs in the eastern states; this is a reddish-brown butterfly with white spots in the apical part of the front wings, and with the outer margin of the front wings rather deeply notched (Figure 431 C); the larva feeds on hackberry.

Figure 435. A parnassian, *Parnássius clòdius báldur* Edwards. About two thirds natural size.

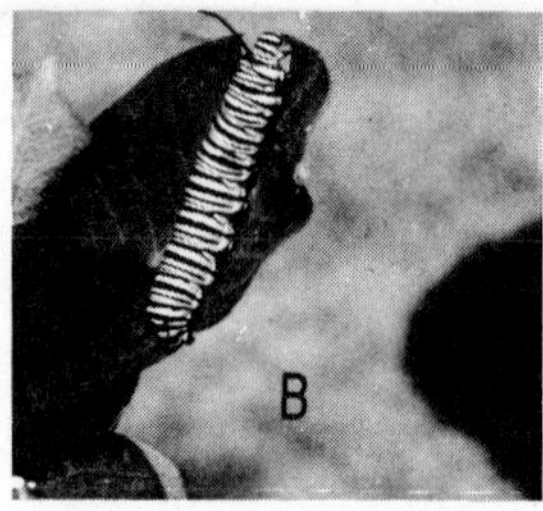

Figure 436. The Monarch, *Dánaus plexíppus* (L.). A, adult male; B, larva. About one half natural size.

Family **Danàidae**—Milkweed Butterflies: The danaids are large and brightly colored butterflies, usually brownish with black and white markings; the front legs are very small, without claws, and are not used in walking. The radius in the front wing is 5-branched, the discal cell is closed by a well-developed vein, and there is a short third anal vein in the front wing (Figure 364 A). The larvae feed on milkweed. The chrysalids are hung by the cremaster to leaves or other objects. The adults are "protected" by distasteful body fluids, and are seldom attacked by predators (see page 64).

The most common species in this group is the monarch butterfly, *Dánaus plexíppus* (L.), which occurs throughout the United States and a large part of the remainder of the world. The monarch is a reddish-brown butterfly with the wings bordered by black; in most of the black marginal band, there are two rows of small white spots (Figure 436 A). The caterpillar is yellowish green banded with black, with two threadlike appendages at either end of the body (Figure 436 B); the chrysalis is pale green spotted with gold.

The monarch is one of the few butterflies that migrate; large numbers migrate south in the fall, and the species reappears in the North the following spring. The longest flight known for an adult monarch (based on a tagged individual) is over 1800 miles (2900 km), from Ontario to Mexico (see page 60). The butterflies that migrate south in the fall overwinter in the South, and usually start back north the following spring. They may reproduce in their wintering grounds or after a short northward flight in the spring; the butterflies that arrive in the northern part of the country in the summer are not the same individuals that left there the preceding fall, but are the offspring of individuals that reproduced in the wintering grounds or en route north (see Urquhart, 1960).

The queen, *Dánaus gilíppus* (Cramer), a common species in the southeastern states, is similar to the monarch but is darker, and lacks the dark lines along the veins; its larva also feeds on milkweed.

Family **Satýridae**—Satyrs, Wood Nymphs, and Arctics: These butterflies are small to medium-sized, usually grayish or brown, and they generally have eyelike spots in the wings. The radius of the front wings is 5-branched, and some of the veins in the front wings (particularly Sc) are considerably swollen at the base (Figure 364 B). The larvae feed on grasses. The chrysalis is usually attached by the cremaster to leaves and other objects.

One of the most common species in this group is the wood nymph, *Cercýonis pégala* (Fabricius), a dark brown, medium-sized butterfly with a broad yellowish band across the apical part of the front wing; this band contains two black and white eyespots (Figure 437 A). Another common species is the little wood satyr, *Euptýchia cýmela* (Cramer), a brownish gray butterfly with prominent eyespots in the wings and with a wingspread of about 25 mm (Figure 437 C). The pearly eye, *Lèthe portlándia* (Fabricius) (Figure 437 D), a brownish butterfly with a row of black eyespots along the border of the hind wings, is a woodland species with a quick flight and a habit of alighting on tree trunks. Among the most interesting species in this group are the arctics or mountain butterflies (*Oenèis*), which are restricted to the Arctic region and the tops of high mountains. A race of the melissa arctic, *O. melíssa semídea* (Say), is restricted to the summits of the White Mountains in New Hampshire, and a race of the polixenes arctic, *O. políxenes katáhdin* (Newcomb), occurs on Mt. Katahdin in Maine. The jutta arctic, *O. jútta* (Hübner) (Figure 437 B), is a wide-ranging circumpolar species that occurs farther south than do most other arctics; it may be found in the sphagnum bogs of Maine and New Hampshire.

Family **Heliconìidae**—Heliconians: The heliconians are tropical butterflies with narrow and elongate front wings. As are the Danàidae, these

Figure 437. Satyrid butterflies. A, wood nymph, *Cercỳonis pégala* (Fabricius); B, jutta arctic, *Oenèis jútta* (Hübner); C, little wood satyr, *Euptỳchia cỳmela* (Cramer); D, pearly eye, *Lèthe portlándia* (Fabricius). A, slightly reduced; C, slightly enlarged; B and D, about natural size.

Figure 438. Heliconian butterflies. A, zebra butterfly, *Helicònius charitònius* (L.); B, gulf fritillary, *Agraùlis vanillae* (L.). Slightly reduced.

butterflies are "protected" by distasteful body fluids and are therefore avoided by predators. The larvae feed on various species of passion flowers. Only a few species in this group occur in the southern states. Our most common heliconian is the zebra butterfly, *Helicònius charitònius* (L.), a black butterfly striped with yellow (Figure 438 A); this species occurs in the Gulf States, but is most common in Florida. The chrysalis, when disturbed, wriggles about in a characteristic manner and produces a creaking sound. A heliconian that occurs over a large part of southeastern United States, extending as far north as New Jersey and Iowa, is the gulf fritillary, *Agràulis vanillae* (L.); this butterfly is bright orange-brown with black markings (Figure 438 B).

Figure 439. Brush-footed butterflies (Nymphálidae). A, viceroy, *Limenìtis archíppus* (Cramer); B, great spangled fritillary. *Speyéria cýbele* (Fabricius); C, pearl crescent-spot, *Phyciòdes thàros* Drury; D, mourningcloak, *Nýmphalis antìopa* (L.); E, red admiral, *Vanéssa atalánta* (L.); F, comma, *Polygònia cómma* (Harris). C, about natural size; the others slightly reduced.

Family **Nymphálidae**—Brush-Footed Butterflies: The members of this family have the front legs much reduced, without claws, and only the middle and hind legs are used in walking. This character also occurs in the Danàidae, Satýridae, Heliconìidae, and Libythèidae, and these groups are included in the Nymphálidae by some authorities. The radius in the front wing is 5-branched, and in most species the discal cell of the hind wing is either open or closed by a very weak vein. The chrysalids are usually suspended by the cremaster. This is a large group, and many of its members are common butterflies.

The fritillaries are brownish butterflies with numerous black markings consisting principally of short wavy lines and dots; the underside of the wings is usually marked with silvery spots. The larger fritillaries belong to the genus *Speyéria* (Figure 439 B); *Speyéria* larvae are nocturnal and feed on violets. The smaller fritillaries, 25–38 mm in wingspread, belong principally to the genus *Bolòria;* their larvae also feed on violets.

The crescent-spots (*Phyciòdes*) are small brownish butterflies with black markings, and the wings (particularly the front wings) are usually margined with black (Figure 439 C). The larvae feed principally on various asters.

The anglewings (*Polygònia*) are small to medium-sized and brownish with black markings, and the wing margins are very irregularly notched and often bear taillike prolongations (Figure 439 F); the underside of the wings is darker and looks much like a dead leaf, and there is usually a small **C**-shaped silvery spot on the underside of the hind wing. The larvae feed principally on nettles, elm, hop-vine, and other Urticàceae.

The red admiral, *Vanéssa atalánta* (L.) (Figure 439 E), is a very common and widely distributed butterfly; the larva feeds principally on nettles, feeding in a shelter formed by tying a few leaves together. There are usually two generations a year.

Two very similar and fairly common species, the painted lady, *Cýnthia cárdui* (L.), and Hunter's butterfly (or the painted beauty), *C. virginiénsis* (Drury), are orange-brown and brownish black above, with white spots in the front wings. The painted lady has four small eyespots on the underside of each hind wing, while Hunter's butterfly has two large eyespots on the underside of each hind wing. The larva of the painted lady feeds chiefly on thistles, while that of Hunter's butterfly feeds on everlastings.

The mourningcloak, *Nýmphalis antìopa* (L.), is a common butterfly that is brownish black with yellowish wing margins (Figure 439 D); the larvae are gregarious and feed chiefly on willow, elm, and poplar. This is one of the few butterflies that overwinter in the adult stage, and the adults appear early in the spring.

The admirals or sovereigns are medium-sized butterflies in which the antennal club is long and the humeral vein in the hind wing arises at the point of separation of $Sc + R_1$ and Rs (Figure 365 B). The viceroy, *Limenìtis archíppus* (Cramer), is a common species in this group and looks very much like the monarch; it differs in that it is slightly smaller, has a narrow black line across the hind wings, and has only a single row of white spots in the black marginal band of the wings (Figure 439 A). The resemblance of the viceroy to the monarch is a good example of protective (or Batesian) mimicry; the monarch is "protected" by distasteful body fluids and is seldom attacked by predators, and the viceroy's resemblance to the monarch is believed to provide it with at least some protection from predators. The larva of the viceroy, a rather grotesque-looking caterpillar, feeds on willow, poplar, and related trees; it overwinters in a leaf shelter formed by tying a few leaves together with silk. The red-spotted purple, *L. astỳanax* (Fabricius), another common species in this group, is a blackish butterfly with pale bluish or greenish spots, and with reddish spots on the underside of the wings. The larva, which is similar to that of the viceroy, feeds on willow, cherry, and other trees; it overwinters in a leaf shelter. A similar butterfly, the banded purple, *L. árthemis* (Drury), occurs in the northern states; it has a broad white band across the wings.

COLLECTING AND PRESERVING LEPIDÓPTERA

The order Lepidóptera contains many large and showy insects, and many students begin their collecting with these insects. Lepidóptera are generally fairly easy to collect, but are more difficult to mount and preserve in good condition than insects in most other groups. Specimens must always be handled with great care because the scales, which give the specimens their color, are easily rubbed off, and in many species the wings are easily torn or broken.

Lepidóptera may be collected with a net, or they may be gotten directly into a killing jar without the use of a net. A net for collecting these insects should be of a fairly light mesh, light enough that the specimen can be seen through the net. Once netted, a specimen should be gotten into a killing jar or stunned as quickly as possible so that it will not damage its wings by fluttering and attempting to escape. Many collectors prefer to insert the killing jar into the net to get the specimen into the jar, without handling the specimen directly; the killing agent in the jar should be of sufficient toxic strength to stun the insect quickly. If the specimen is removed to the killing jar by hand, it should be grasped carefully through the net by the body, pinched slightly to stun it, and then placed in the killing jar.

Many moths can be taken directly into a killing jar without the use of a net. A wide-mouthed jar is simply placed over the specimen when it is resting on some flat surface. The jar should be strong enough to stun the insect quickly, before it can flutter about too much inside and damage its wings.

The best place to collect most Lepidóptera is on or near the plant on which the larva feeds. Many species, particularly butterflies, frequent flowers and may be collected while feeding. To obtain a large number of species, one must visit a variety of habitats and collect at all seasons; many species occur only in certain types of habitats, many have a short adult life and are on the wing only a short time each year.

Many of the moths are most easily collected at lights. They may be collected by traps, but specimens so collected are often in poor condition. Better specimens can be collected at lights if there is some flat white surface near the light on which the insect will land; the specimen can be taken from such a surface directly into the killing jar. Many interesting species can be obtained by sugaring (see Chapter 34).

One must take precautions to prevent the specimens from becoming damaged after they are placed in the killing jar. The jar should be strong enough to stun a specimen quickly. Large and heavy-bodied specimens should not be placed in a jar along with small and delicate ones. The jar should not be allowed to become too crowded; it is advisable to remove the specimens soon after they have been stunned and then to place them in paper envelopes.

The best way to obtain good specimens of many species is to rear them, either from larvae or from pupae. Suggestions for rearing are given in Chapter 34. By rearing, the collector not only obtains good specimens, but also can become acquainted with the larval stages of different species and the plants on which the larvae feed.

Specimens of Lepidóptera can be preserved in a collection in three ways, in paper envelopes (as in the case of Odonàta and some other groups), spread and pinned, or spread and mounted under glass (in Riker or glass mounts). Envelopes are useful for temporary storage or in cases where the collection is large and space is not available for large numbers of spread specimens. If one desires to display his collection, the best type of mount is a Riker or glass mount. The best collections of Lepidóptera have the specimens spread and pinned.

All Lepidóptera that are pinned or mounted under glass should be spread. The beginning student or the person interested principally in displaying his collection is advised to spread his specimens in an upside-down position (Figure 623), and mount them in a glass or Riker mount; the advanced student or the person making a large collection of Lepidóptera should pin them or keep them in envelopes. Methods of spreading and mounting Lepidóptera are described in Chapter 34 and need not be given here. It takes a little practice to become proficient in spreading these insects, and some of the smaller specimens will tax the skill and patience of the collector, but the resulting collection will be worth the effort.

In a large collection of pinned Lepidóptera, space can be saved by putting the pins into the bottom of the box at an angle, and overlapping the wings of adjacent specimens. A collection must be protected against museum pests by having naphthalene or some similar repellent in the boxes; it should be kept in the dark, for many specimens will fade if exposed to light for long periods.

References on the Lepidóptera

Davis, D. R. 1964. Bagworm moths of the western hemisphere (Lepidoptera: Psychidae). *U.S. Natl. Mus. Bull.*, 244; v + 233 pp., 385 f., 12 maps.

Davis, D. R. 1967. A revision of the moths of the subfamily Prodoxinae (Lepidoptera: Incurvariidae). *U.S. Natl. Mus. Bull.*, 255; 170 pp., 153 f.

Davis, D. R. 1968. A revision of the American moths of the family Carposinidae (Lepidoptera: Carposinoidea). *U.S. Natl. Mus. Bull.*, 289; 105 pp., 122 f.

Duckworth, W. D. 1964. North American Stenomidae (Lepidoptera: Gelechioidea). *Proc. U.S. Natl. Mus.*, 116:23–72; illus.

Ehrlich, P. R. 1958. The comparative morphology, phylogeny and higher classification of the butterflies (Lepidoptera: Papilionoidea). *Univ. Kan. Sci. Bull.*, 39(8):305–370; 64 f.

Ehrlich, P. R., and A. H. Ehrlich. 1961. *How to Know the Butterflies*. Dubuque, Iowa: W. C. Brown, 262 pp., 525 f.

Field, W. D. 1971. Butterflies of the genus *Vanessa* and of the resurrected genera *Basaris* and *Cynthia* (Lepidoptera: Nymphalidae). *Smiths. Contrib. to Zool.*, No. 84; 105 pp., 160 f.

Forbes, W. T. M. 1923–1960. Lepidoptera of New York and neighboring states. *Mem. Cornell Univ. Agric. Expt. Sta.* Part I: Primitive forms, Microlepidoptera; Mem. 68 (1923); 729 pp., 439 f. Part II: Geometridae, Sphingidae, Notodontidae, Lymantriidae; Mem. No. 274 (1948); 263 pp., 255 f. Part III: Noctuidae; Mem. No. 329 (1954); 433 pp., 290 f. Part IV: Agaristidae through Nymphalidae including butterflies; Mem. No. 371 (1960); 188 pp., 188 f.

Ford, E. B. 1955. *Moths*. London: Collins, xix + 266 pp., 56 pl. (32 in color), 12 maps.

Fracker, S. B. 1930 (2nd ed.). The classification of lepidopterous larvae. *Contrib. Ent. Lab., Univ. Illinois*, No. 43; 161 pp., 112 f.

Grote, A. R. 1971. *Noctuidae of North America*. London: E. W. Classey, 85 pp., 4 col. pl.

Hardwick, D. F. 1970. A generic revision of the North American Heliothidinae (Lepidoptera: Noctuidae). *Mem. Ent. Soc. Can.*, No. 73; 59 pp., 114 f.

Hardwick, D. F. 1970. The genus *Euxoa* (Lepidoptera:

Noctuidae) in North America. I. Subgenera *Orosagrotis, Longivesica, Chorizagrotis, Pleonoctopoda,* and *Crassivesica*. *Mem. Ent. Soc. Can.*, No. 67; 177 pp., 326 f. (255–326 in color).

Hodges, R. W. 1962. A revision of the Cosmopterygidae of America north of Mexico, with a definition of the Momphidae and Walshiidae (Lepidoptera). *Ent. Amer.*, 42:1–171; 199 f.

Hodges, R. W. 1964. A review of the North American moths in the family Walshiidae (Lepidoptera: Gelechioidea). *Proc. U.S. Natl. Mus.*, 115(3485):289–330; 66 f.

Holland, W. J. 1931 (rev. ed.). *The Butterfly Book*. New York: Doubleday, xii + 424 pp., 198 f., 77 col. pl.

Holland, W. J. 1968. *The Moth Book*. New York: Dover, xxiv + 479 pp., 263 f., 48 col. pl. (A reprinting of a book published in 1903 by Doubleday, Page and Co.)

Klots, A. B. 1951. *A Field Guide to the Butterflies*. Boston: Houghton Mifflin, xvi + 349 pp., 8 textf., 40 pl. (some in color).

Klots, A. B. 1958. *The World of Butterflies and Moths*. New York: McGraw-Hill, 207 pp.; illus.

Lindsey, A. W., E. L. Bell, and R. C. Williams. 1931. Hesperioidea of North America. *J. Sci. Labs. Denison Univ.*, 26:1–142; 33 pl.

MacKay, M. R. 1968. The North American Aegeriidae (Lepidoptera): a revision based on late-instar larvae. *Mem. Ent. Soc. Can.*, No. 58; 112 pp., 50 f.

MacNeill, C. D. 1964. The skippers of the genus *Hesperia* in western North America, with special reference to California (Lepidoptera: Hesperiidae). *Univ. Calif. Publ. Ent.*, 35:1–230; 8 pl., 28 f., frontis. (color).

Macy, R. W., and H. H. Shepard. 1941. *Butterflies. A Handbook of the Butterflies of the United States Complete for the Region North of the Potomac and Ohio Rivers and East of the Dakotas*. Minneapolis: Univ. Minnesota Press, vii + 247 pp., 4 col. pl., 7 f., 38 photos, 2 maps.

McDunnough, J. 1938–1939. Check list of the Lepidoptera of Canada and the United States of America. *So. Calif. Acad. Sci. Mem.* Part I (1938), Macrolepidoptera; 274 pp. Part II (1939), Microlepidoptera; 171 pp.

McGuffin, W. C. 1967. Guide to the Geometridae of Canada (Lepidoptera). I. Subfamily Sterrhinae. *Mem. Ent. Soc. Can.*, 50:3–67; illus.

Mosher, E. 1916. A classification of the Lepidoptera based on characters of the pupa. *Bull. Ill. Nat. Hist. Surv.*, 12(2): 15–159; pl. 19–27.

Moths of America North of Mexico. 1972–1973. Fascicle 13, Part 1a: Pyralidae: Scopariinae and Nymphulinae; by E. G. Munroe; 134 pp. (1972). Fascicle 13, Part 1b: Pyralidae: Odontiinae and Glaphyriinae; by E. G. Munroe; 116 pp. (1972). Fascicle 20, Part 1: Mimallonoidea and Bombycoidea (in part: Apatelodidae, Lasiocampidae, and Bombycidae); by J. G. Franclemont; viii + 86 pp., 11 color pl., 22 f. (1973). Fascicle 20, Part 2a: Bombycoidea: Saturniidae (in part) (Citheroniinae; Hemileucinae, in part); by D. C. Ferguson; 153 pp., 11 color pl., 19 f. (1972). Fascicle 20, Part 2b: Bombycoidea: Saturniidae (conclusion) (Hemileucinae, in part, and Saturniinae); by D. C. Ferguson; xxi + 121 pp., 11 color pl., 11 f (1972). Fascicle 21: Sphingoidea: Sphingidae; by R. W. Hodges; xii + 158 pp., 16 pl. (14 in color), 8 halftones, 19 f. (1971). London: E. W. Classey and R. B. D. Publ. (Additional fascicles are currently in preparation.)

Munroe, E. 1970. Revision of the Midilinae (Lepidoptera: Pyralidae). *Mem. Ent. Soc. Can.*, No. 74; 94 pp., 118 f.

Passos, C. F. dos. 1964. A synonymic list of nearctic Rhopalocera. *The Lepidopterists' Soc. Mem.*, No. 1; v + 145 pp.

Peterson, A. 1948. *Larvae of Insects. Part I. Lepidoptera and Plant Infesting Hymenoptera*. Ann Arbor, Mich.: J. W. Edwards, 315 pp.; illus.

Powell, J. A. 1964. Biological and taxonomic studies on tortricine moths, with reference to the species in California. *Univ. Calif. Pub. Ent.*, 32:1–317; 8 pl., 108 f.

Powell, J. A. 1973. A systematic monograph of New World ethmiid moths (Lepidoptera: Gelechioidea). *Smiths. Contrib. to Zool.*, No. 120; 302 pp., 294 f., 22 pl., 68 maps.

Scudder, S. H. 1889. *Butterflies of Eastern United States and Canada*. 3 vol., 1958 pp., 74 pl. Cambridge, Mass.

Tietz, H. M. 1973. *An Index to the Described Life Histories, Early Stages and Hosts of the Macrolepidoptera of the Continental United States and Canada*. Middlesex, England: E. W. Classey, iv + 1042 pp.; 2 vol.

Tilden, J. W. 1965. *Butterflies of the San Francisco Bay Region*. Berkeley, Calif.: Univ. California Press, 88 pp.; illus. (incl. 8 col. pl.).

Urquhart, F. A. 1960. *The Monarch Butterfly*. Toronto: Univ. Toronto Press, xxiv + 361 pp., 79 f.

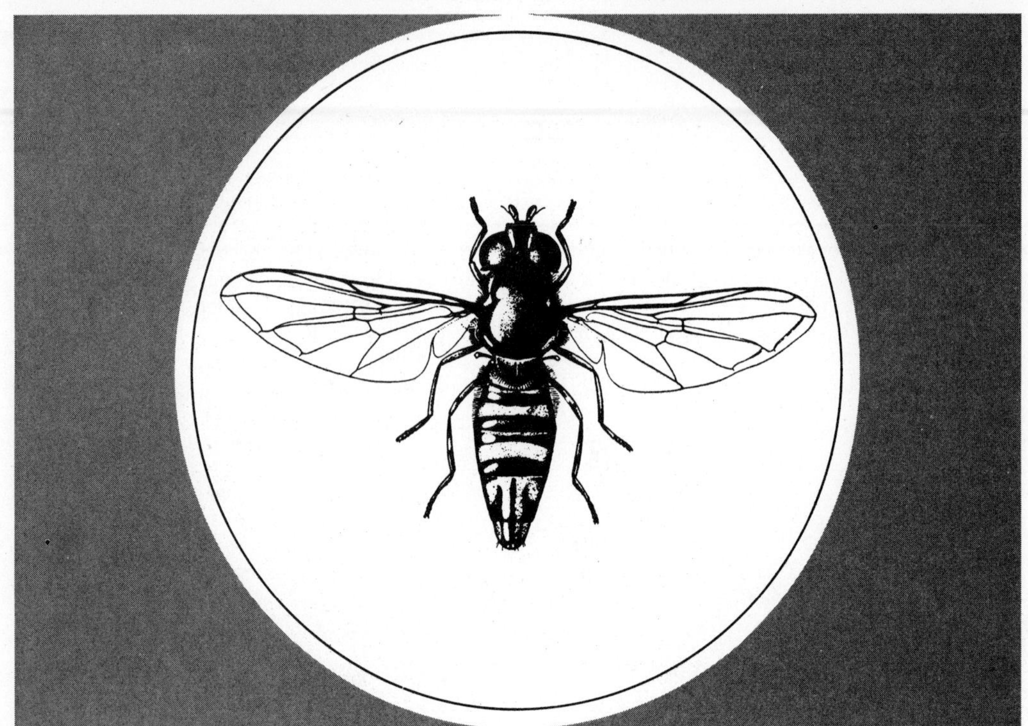

30: ORDER DÍPTERA[1]
FLIES

The Díptera constitute one of the largest orders of insects, and its members are abundant in individuals and species almost everywhere. Most of the Díptera can be readily distinguished from other insects to which the term "fly" is applied (sawflies, stoneflies, caddisflies, dragonflies, and others) by the fact that they possess only one pair of wings; these are the front wings, and the hind wings are reduced to small knobbed structures called halteres, which function as organs of equilibrium. There are occasional insects in a few other orders that have only one pair of wings (some mayflies, some beetles, male scale insects, and others), but none of these, except male scale insects, has the hind wings reduced to halteres. The Díptera are sometimes spoken of as the two-winged flies, to distinguish them from the "flies" in other orders. In the common names of Díptera, the "fly" of the name is written as a separate word, whereas in the common names of "flies" in other orders, the "fly" of the name is written together with the descriptive word.

The majority of the Díptera are relatively small and soft-bodied insects, and some are quite minute, but many are of great economic importance. The mosquitoes, black flies, punkies, horse flies, stable flies, and others are blood-sucking and are serious pests of man and animals. Many of the blood-sucking flies, and some of the scavenging

[1] Díptera: *di,* two; *ptera,* wings.

flies such as the house flies and blow flies, are important vectors of disease; the causative organisms of malaria, yellow fever, filariasis, dengue, sleeping sickness, typhoid fever, dysentery, and other diseases are carried and distributed by Díptera. Some flies, such as the Hessian fly and the apple maggot, are important pests of cultivated plants. On the other hand, many flies are useful as scavengers, others are important predators or parasites of various insect pests, others aid in the pollination of useful plants, and some are enemies of noxious weeds.

The mouth parts of the Díptera are of the sucking type, but there is considerable variation in mouth-part structure within the order. In many flies, the mouth parts are piercing, in others they are sponging or lapping (pages 15–19), and in a few flies, the mouth parts are so poorly developed as to be nonfunctional.

The Díptera undergo complete metamorphosis, and the larvae of many are called maggots. The larvae are generally legless and wormlike; in the primitive families (Nematócera) the head is usually well developed and the mandibles move laterally; in the higher families (Brachýcera and Cyclórrhapha) the head is reduced and the mouth hooks move in a vertical plane. In some families (Brachýcera) the head of the larva is sclerotized and more or less retractile, while in others (Cyclórrhapha) there is no sclerotization of the head at all (except for the mouth parts). The pupae of the Nematócera are of the obtect type, while those of other Díptera are coarctate, that is, the pupal stage is passed inside the last larval skin, which is called a puparium.

Dipterous larvae occur in many kinds of habitats, but a large proportion of them live in water—in all sorts of aquatic habitats including streams, ponds, lakes, temporary puddles, and brackish and alkaline water. The larvae that feed on plants generally live within some tissue of the plant, as leaf miners, gall insects, stem borers, or root borers. The predaceous larvae live in many different habitats—in water, in the soil, under bark or stones, or on vegetation. Many species feed during the larval stage in decaying plant or animal matter. Some fly larvae live in rather unusual habitats; one species (*Helaeomỳia petròlei* (Coquillett), family Ephýdridae) lives in pools of crude petroleum; other ephydrids breed in the Great Salt Lake.

Adult Díptera feed on various plant or animal juices, such as nectar, sap, or blood; most species feed on nectar, but many are blood-sucking, and many are predaceous on other insects.

CLASSIFICATION OF THE DÍPTERA

The classification of the Díptera followed in this book is that used in the *Catalog of the Diptera of America North of Mexico* (Stone et *al.*, 1965), except for the Baeonòtidae and Leptogástridae, which have been recognized since 1965. This arrangement is outlined below, with alternate names, spellings, and arrangements in parentheses. The groups marked with an asterisk are relatively rare or are unlikely to be taken by a general collector.

Suborder Nematócera (Nemócera; Orthórrhapha in part)—long-horned flies
- Superfamily Tipulòidea
  - *Trichocéridae (Trichocerátidae, Petaurístidae)—winter crane flies
  - Tipùlidae—crane flies
- Superfamily Psychodòidea
  - *Tanydéridae—primitive crane flies
  - Psychòdidae—moth flies and sand flies
  - Ptychoptéridae (Liriopèidae)—phantom crane flies
  - *Nymphomyìidae—nymphomyiid flies
- Superfamily Culicòidea
  - *Blepharicéridae (Blepharocéridae, Blepharocerátidae)—net-winged midges
  - *Deuterophlebìidae—mountain midges
  - Díxidae—dixid midges
  - Chaobòridae (Corèthridae; Culícidae in part)—phantom midges
  - Culícidae—mosquitoes
  - *Thaumalèidae (Orphnephílidae)—solitary midges
  - Ceratopogónidae (Helèidae)—biting midges, punkies, no-see-ums
  - Chironómidae (Tendipédidae)—midges
  - Simulìidae (Melusínidae)—black flies or buffalo gnats

Superfamily Anisopodòidea
Anisopódidae (Rhỳphidae, Silvicólidae, Phrynèidae; including Mycetobìidae) — wood gnats
Superfamily Bibionòidea
Bibiónidae — march flies
*Pachyneùridae (Anisopódidae in part) — pachyneurid gnats
Superfamily Mycetophilòidea
Mycetophílidae (Fungivòridae in part) — fungus gnats
Sciáridae (Lycorìidae; Fungivòridae in part) — dark-winged fungus gnats, root gnats
*Hyperoscelídidae (Hyperoscélidae, Corynoscelídidae; Scatópsidae in part) — hyperoscelidid gnats
Scatópsidae — minute black scavenger flies
Cecidomyìidae (Cecidomỳidae, Itonídidae) — gall midges or gall gnats
Superfamily Uncertain
*Baeonòtidae — baeonotid gnats
Suborder Brachýcera (Orthórrhapha in part) — short-horned flies
Superfamily Tabanòidea
Xylophágidae (Erínnidae) — xylophagid flies
Xylomỳidae (Xylomyìidae; Xylophágidae in part) — xylomyid flies
Stratiomỳidae (Stratiomyìidae; including Chiromỳzidae) — soldier flies
*Pelecorhýnchidae (Tabánidae in part) — pelecorhynchid flies
Tabánidae — horse flies and deer flies
Rhagiónidae (Léptidae) — snipe flies
*Hilarimórphidae (Rhagiónidae in part) — hilarimorphid flies
Superfamily Asilòidea
Therévidae — stiletto flies
*Scenopínidae (Omphrálidae) — window flies
*Apiocéridae (Apiocerátidae) — flower-loving flies
Mỳdidae (Mydàidae, Mydásidae) — mydas flies
Asìlidae — robber flies
Leptogástridae (Asìlidae in part) — grass flies
*Nemestrínidae — tangle-veined flies
*Acrocéridae (Acrocerátidae, Cýrtidae, Henópidae, Oncòdidae) — small-headed flies
Bombylìidae — bee flies
Superfamily Empidòidea
Empídidae (Émpidae) — dance flies
Dolichopódidae (Dolichópidae) — long-legged flies
Suborder Cyclórrhapha (Brachýcera in part) — circular-seamed flies
Division Aschìza — Cyclórrhapha without a frontal suture
Superfamily Lonchopteròidea
Lonchoptéridae (Musidóridae) — spear-winged flies
Superfamily Phoròidea
Phòridae — humpbacked flies
*Platypèzidae (Clythìidae) — flat-footed flies
Superfamily Syrphòidea
Pipuncùlidae (Dorilàidae, Dorylàidae) — big-headed flies
Sýrphidae — syrphid flies or flower flies
Conópidae — thick-headed flies
Division Schizóphora (including Pupípara) — muscoid flies
Section Acalyptràtae — acalyptrate muscoid flies
Superfamily Micropezòidea
Micropèzidae (including Tỳlidae and Calobátidae = Trepidarìidae) — silt-legged flies
*Nerìidae — cactus flies
Superfamily Nothybòidea
*Diópsidae — stalk-eyed flies

        Psìlidae—rust flies
        *Tanypèzidae (Micropèzidae in part)—tanypezid flies
    Superfamily Tephritòidea
        *Richardìidae (Otítidae in part)—richardiid flies
        Otítidae (Ortálidae, Ortalídidae)—picture-winged flies
        Platystomátidae (Otítidae in part)—picture-winged flies
        *Pyrgòtidae—pyrgotid flies
        Tephrítidae (Trypétidae, Trupanèidae, Trypanèidae, Euribìidae)—fruit flies
    Superfamily Sciomyzòidea
        *Helcomỳzidae (Dryomỳzidae in part)—seabeach flies
        *Ropaloméridae (Rhopaloméridae)—ropalomerid flies
        Coelòpidae (Phycodròmidae)—seaweed flies
        *Dryomỳzidae—dryomyzid flies
        Sépsidae—black scavenger flies
        Sciomỳzidae (Tetanocéridae, Tetanocerátidae)—marsh flies
    Superfamily Lauxaniòidea
        Lauxanìidae (Sapromỳzidae)—lauxaniid flies
        Chamaemyìidae (Chamaemỳidae, Ochthiphílidae)—aphid flies
        *Periscelídidae (Periscélidae)—periscelidid flies
    Superfamily Pallopteròidea
        Piophílidae—skipper flies
        *Thyreophòridae—thyreophorid flies
        *Neottiophílidae—neottiophilid flies
        *Palloptéridae (Sapromỳzidae in part)—pallopterid flies
        Lonchaèidae (Sapromỳzidae in part)—lonchaeid flies
    Superfamily Milichiòidea
        Sphaerocéridae (Sphaerocerátidae, Borbòridae, Cypsélidae)—small dung flies
        *Braùlidae (Pupípara in part)—bee lice
        *Tethìnidae (Opomỳzidae in part)—tethinid flies
        Milichìidae (Phyllomỳzidae; including Cárnidae)—milichiid flies
        *Canacèidae—beach flies
    Superfamily Drosophilòidea
        Ephỳdridae (Hydréllidae, Notiophílidae)—shore flies
        *Curtonòtidae (Cyrtonòtidae; Drosophílidae in part)—curtonotid flies
        Drosophílidae—pomace flies, vinegar flies, small fruit flies
        *Diastátidae (Drosophílidae in part)—diastatid flies
        *Camíllidae (Drosophílidae in part)—camillid flies
    Superfamily Chloropòidea
        Chlorópidae (Oscínidae, Titanìidae)—chloropid flies
    Unplaced Families of Acalyptràtae
        *Odinìidae (Odínidae; Agromỳzidae in part)—odiniid flies
        Agromỳzidae (Phytomỳzidae)—leafminer flies
        Clusìidae (Clusiòdidae, Heteroneùridae)—clusiid flies
        *Acartophthálmidae (Clusìidae in part)—acartophthalmid flies
        Heleomỳzidae (Helomỳzidae)—heleomyzid flies
        *Trixoscelídidae (Trixoscélidae, Trichoscélidae; Chyromỳidae in part)—trixoscelidid flies
        *Rhinotòridae—rhinotorid flies
        Anthomỳzidae (Opomỳzidae in part)—anthomyzid flies
        *Opomỳzidae (Geomỳzidae)—opomyzid flies
        *Chyromỳidae (Chyromyìidae)—chiromyid flies
        *Aulacigástridae (Aulacigastéridae; Drosophilidae in part)—aulacigastrid flies
        *Asteìidae (Astìidae)—asteiid flies
        *Cryptochètidae (Chamaemyìidae in part, Agromỳzidae in part)—cryptochetid flies
Section Calyptràtae—calyptrate muscoid flies

Superfamily Muscòidea
- Anthomyìidae (Anthomỳidae; Múscidae in part; including Scatomỳzidae = Scatophágidae = Scopeumátidae = Cordylùridae) — anthomyiid flies
- Múscidae (including Glossìnidae and Fannìidae) — muscid flies: house fly, face fly, horn fly, stable fly, tsetse flies, and others
- *Gasterophílidae (Gastrophílidae) — horse bot flies
- *Hippobóscidae (Pupípara in part) — louse flies
- *Stréblidae (Pupípara in part) — bat flies
- *Nycteribìidae (Pupípara in part) — bat flies

Superfamily Oestròidea
- Calliphòridae (Metopìidae in part) — blow flies
- Sarcophágidae (Stephanosomátidae; Metopìidae in part) — flesh flies
- Tachínidae (Larvaevòridae; including Phasìidae=Gymnosomátidae, Dexìidae, and Rhinophòridae) — tachinid flies
- *Cuterébridae — robust bot flies
- *Oéstridae (including Hypodermátidae) — warble flies and bot flies

CHARACTERS USED IN THE IDENTIFICATION OF DÍPTERA

The principal characters used in the identification of Díptera are those of the antennae, legs, wing venation, and chaetotaxy (the arrangement of the bristles, chiefly on the head and thorax). Occasionally various other characters are used, such as the presence or absence of certain sutures, the shape of the head or abdomen, the form of the mouth parts, and the presence or absence of ocelli.

ANTENNAE The antennae vary quite a bit between families, and to some extent within a single family. In the suborder Nematócera the antennae are many-segmented (Figure 440 A, B) and the segments (except possibly the two basal ones) are similar. In the suborders Brachýcera and Cyclórrhapha the antennae are generally 3-segmented (Figure 440 C–H) with the two basal segments small and the third segment larger. In some of the Brachýcera the third segment of the antennae is annulated, that is, it is divided into subsegments (Figure 440 C, D, F). This annulation is sometimes difficult to see unless the antenna is properly illuminated; it may often be difficult to decide whether such antennae are 3-segmented or many-segmented, but the divisions of the third segment in such flies are never so marked as the divisions between the three principal segments. Many of the Brachýcera bear an elongate process called a style at the end of the antenna (Figure 440 E). The Cyclórrhapha and some Brachýcera bear a large bristlelike structure, the arista, on the third segment (Figure 440 G, H); the arista may be a simple bristle or it may be plumose. In some of the Cyclórrhapha the form of the second or third segment may serve to separate different groups; for example, the calyptrate and acalyptrate groups of muscoid flies differ in the structure of the second antennal segment.

LEGS The principal leg characters used in separating families of flies are the structure of the empodium and the presence or absence of tibial spurs. The empodium (Figure 441, *emp*) is a structure arising from between the claws on the last tarsal segment; it is bristlelike or absent in most flies, but in a few families (Figure 441 B) it is large and membranous and resembles the pulvilli in appearance. The pulvilli are pads at the apex of the last tarsal segment, one at the base of each claw (Figure 441, *pul*). A fly may thus have two pads (the pulvilli), three pads (the pulvilli and a pulivilliform empodium), or no pads (pulvilli absent) on the pretarsus. Tibial spurs are spinelike structures, usually located at the distal end of the tibia (Figure 446, *tsp*). In some muscoid flies (Figure 463 B), there are bristles on the outer surface of the tibia just proximad from the apex; such bristles are spoken of as preapical tibial bristles (*ptbr*).

The body of most flies is more or less cylindrical, with the coxae situated very close together; in a few families the body is flattened and leathery, and the coxae are well separated (Figure 453 A). The coxae are generally short, but in some groups (for example, the fungus gnats, Figure 446) they are about as long as the femora.

WING VENATION Considerable use is made of venational characters in the identification of flies,

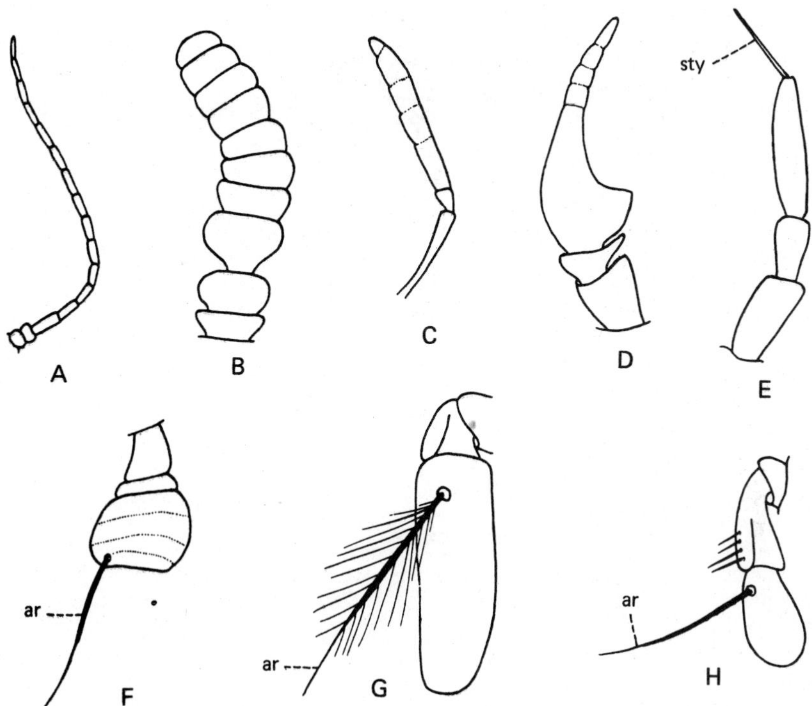

Figure 440. Antennae of Díptera. A, Mycetophílidae (*Mycomỳa*); B, Bibiónidae (*Bíbio*); C, Stratiomỳidae (*Stratìomys*); D, Tabánidae (*Tabànus*); E, Asìlidae (*Asìlus*); F, Stratiomỳidae (*Ptécticus*); G, Calliphóridae (*Callíphora*); H, Tachínidae (*Epálpus*). *ar*, arista; *sty*, style.

and it is often possible to identify a fly to family or beyond on the basis of wings alone. The wing venation in this order is relatively simple, and the tendency in the higher families is toward a reduction in the number of veins.

There are two different terminologies of wing venation commonly used in this order. Most authorities use the Comstock–Needham system of naming the veins and cells (Figure 442 A), but not all agree with the Comstock–Needham interpretation of the venation. This interpretation has the media 3-branched; some authorities (Tillyard and others) say it is 4-branched, and label Cu_1 of the Comstock–Needham system as vein M_4; according to Tillyard, the Comstock–Needham Cu_2 is Cu_1, 1A is Cu_2, 2A is 1A, and 3A is 2A. All authorities do not agree in naming the branches of the radius. Many use terms of the older system (Figure 442 B), particularly for certain wing cells.

A closed cell is one that does not reach the wing margin (for example, the anal or 1A cell in Figure 442). When the thickening of the anterior

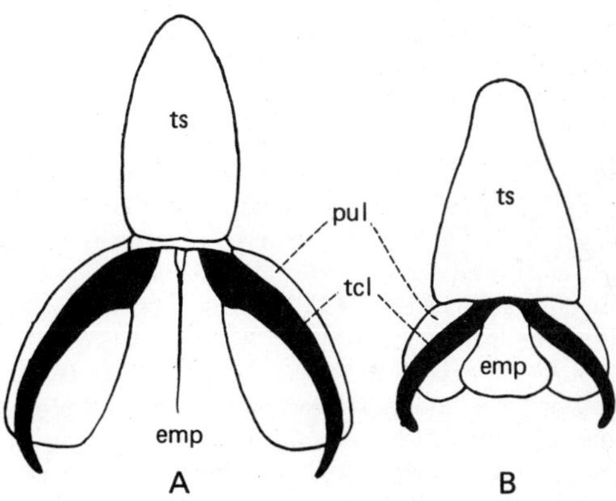

Figure 441. Tip of tarsus, dorsal view. A, robber fly, with the empodium bristlelike; B, horse fly, with the empodium pulvilliform. *emp*, empodium; *pul*, pulvilli; *tcl*, tarsal claw; *ts*, last tarsal segment.

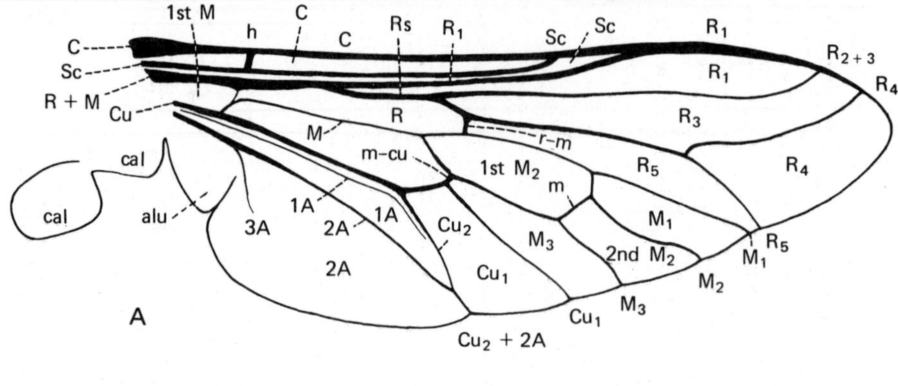

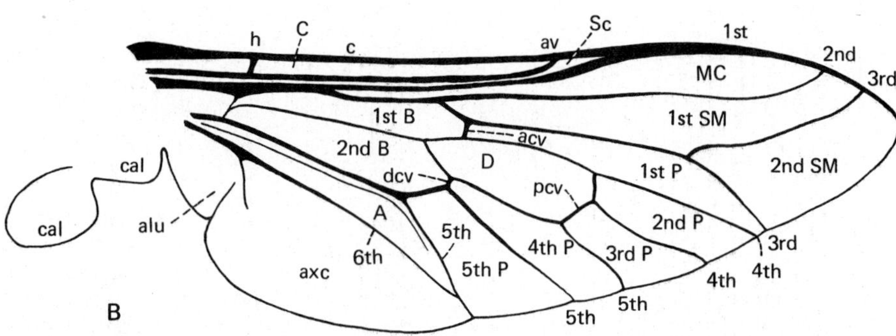

Figure 442. Wing of a horse fly (*Tabànus*), showing venational terminologies. A, Comstock-Needham system (for key to lettering, see p. 24); B, older system, in which the longitudinal veins are numbered. Labeling in B: *A*, anal cell; *acv*, anterior cross vein; *alu*, alula; *av*, auxiliary vein; *axc*, axillary cell; *B*, basal cells (first and second); *C*, costal cell; *c*, costal vein; *cal*, calypteres or squamae (the basal one is usually called the lower calypter, and the one next to the alula, the upper calypter); *D*, discal cell; *dcv*, discal cross vein; *h*, humeral cross vein; *MC*, marginal cell; *P*, posterior cells; *pcv*, posterior cross vein; *Sc*, subcostal cell; *SM*, submarginal or apical cells (first and second).

edge of the wing (the costa) ends near the wing tip (as in Figure 445 B–F, J), the costa is said to extend only to the wing tip; where there is no abrupt thinning of the anterior margin of the wing near the wing tip (as in Figure 445 G–I), the costa is said to continue around the wing.

Some flies have one or two lobes at the base of the wing, on the posterior side, which fold beneath the base of the wing when the wing is folded back over the abdomen; these lobes are the calypteres (also called squamae) (Figure 442, *cal*). The size of the calypteres is frequently used to distinguish families or groups of families.

Many of the muscoid flies have one or two points in the costa where the sclerotization is weak or lacking, or the vein appears to be broken; such points are termed costal breaks, and may occur near the end of R_1 and/or the humeral cross vein (Figures 459 B and 460 C–E, *cbr*). Costal breaks are best seen with transmitted light. A few muscoids have a series of long hairs or bristles along the costa beyond the end of R_1 (Figure 459 A, H); the costa in such cases is said to be spinose.

CHAETOTAXY In the identification of certain flies, particularly the muscoid groups, much use is made of the number, size, position, and arrangement of the larger bristles on the head and thorax. The terminology used in the chaetotaxy of flies is illustrated in Figures 443 and 444. The frontal

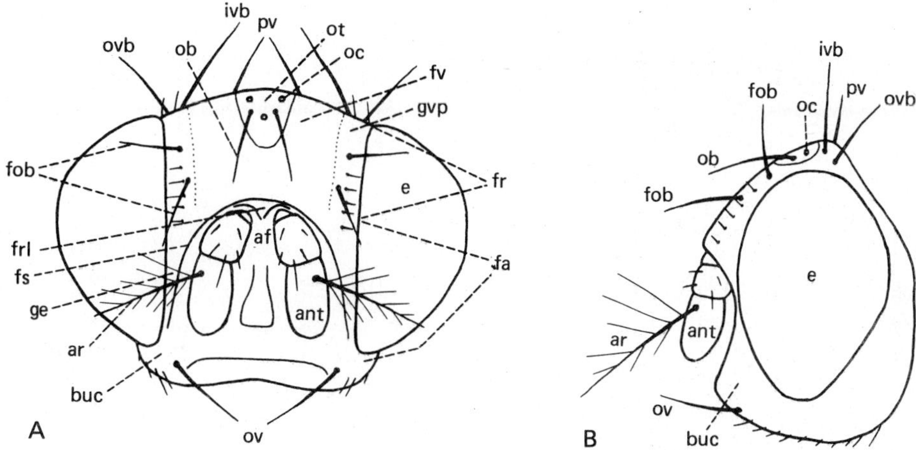

Figure 443. Areas and chaetotaxy of the head of a drosophilid fly. A, anterior view; B, lateral view. *af,* antennal fossa; *ant,* antenna; *ar,* arista; *buc,* bucca; e, compound eye; *fa,* face; *fob,* fronto-orbital bristles; *fr,* frons; *frl,* frontal lunule; *fs,* frontal suture; *fv,* frontal vitta; *ge,* gena; *gvp,* genovertical or orbital plate; *ivb,* inner vertical bristle; *ob,* ocellar bristle; *oc,* ocellus; *ot,* ocellar triangle; *ov,* oral vibrissae; *ovb,* outer vertical bristle; *pv,* postvertical bristles.

bristles (not shown in Figure 443) are located in the middle of the front, between the ocellar triangle and the frontal suture.

HEAD AND THORACIC SUTURES The principal head suture used in the identification of flies is the frontal suture (Figure 443, *fs*). This suture is usually in the shape of an inverted **U**, extending from above the bases of the antennae lateroventrad toward the lower margins of the compound eyes. This suture is commonly called the "frontal suture" by dipterists, but it is not the same as the frontal sutures in Figure 5. It is actually a ptilinal suture and marks the break in the head wall through which the ptilinum was everted at the time of the fly's emergence from the puparium (see page 588).

Between the apex of the **U** and the bases of the antennae is a small crescent-shaped sclerite called the frontal lunule (*frl*). The presence of a frontal suture distinguishes the muscoid flies (division Schizóphora of the suborder Cyclórrhapha) from other flies. In cases where the complete suture is difficult to see, the flies possessing it can be recognized by the presence of a frontal lunule above the bases of the antennae.

A transverse suture across the anterior part of the mesonotum (Figure 444, *trs*) separates most of the calyptrate from the acalyptrate muscoids. The calyptrate muscoids usually have sutures in the lateroposterior portions of the mesonotum, which separate the postalar calli (Figure 444, *pc*); these sutures are lacking in the acalyptrate muscoids.

SIZE In the keys and descriptions in this chapter, "medium-sized" means about the size of a house fly or blue-bottle fly; "small" means smaller, and "large" means larger than this size. "Very small" or "minute" means less than 3 mm in length, and "very large" means 25 mm or more in length.

Key to the Families of Díptera

Families in the following key marked with an asterisk are relatively rare or unlikely to be taken by a general collector. Some difficulty may be encountered with small or minute specimens, and a microscope of considerable magnification (90–120 ×) may be necessary in examining such specimens. Keys to larvae are given by Hennig (1948–1952) and Peterson (1951).

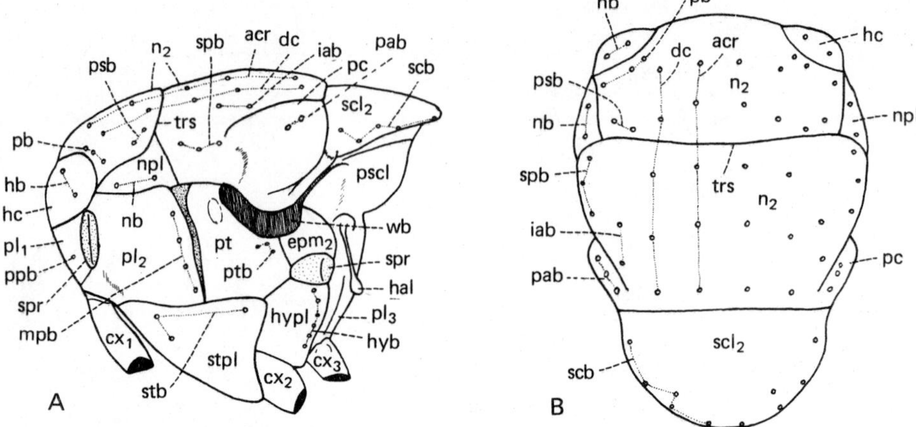

Figure 444. Areas and chaetotaxy of the thorax of a blow fly. A, lateral view; B, dorsal view. *acr*, acrostichal bristles; *cx*, coxae; *dc*, dorsocentral bristles; epm_2, mesepimeron; *hal*, halter; *hb*, humeral bristles; *hc*, humeral callus; *hyb*, hypopleural bristles; *hypl*, hypopleuron; *iab*, intra-alar bristles; *mpb*, mesopleural bristles; n_2, mesonotum; *nb*, notopleural bristles; *npl*, notopleuron; *pab*, postalar bristles; *pb*, posthumeral bristles; *pc*, postalar callus; pl_1, propleuron; pl_2, mesopleuron; pl_3, metapleuron; *ppb*, propleural bristle; *psb* presutural bristles; *pscl*, postscutellum; *pt*, pteropleuron; *ptb*, pteropleural bristles; *scb*, scutellar bristles; scl_2, mesoscutellum; *spb*, supra-alar bristles; *spr*, spiracle; *stb*, sternopleural bristles; *stpl*, sternopleuron; *trs*, transverse suture; *wb*, base of wing.

1. Wings present and well developed 2

1′. Wings absent or greatly reduced 128*

2(1). Antennae composed of 6 or more freely articulated segments (Figure 440 A, B), in some males very long-plumose (Figures 469 B, D and 474 C); Rs 1- to 4-branched, if 3-branched it is nearly always R_{2+3} that is forked 3

2′. Antennae composed of 5 or fewer (usually 3) freely articulated segments, the third occasionally annulated (appearing divided into subsegments, but these are not as distinct as the three main antennal segments), and often bearing a style or arista (Figure 440 C–H), never long-plumose; Rs 2- or 3-branched (rarely unbranched), if 3-branched it is nearly always R_{4+5} that is forked 29

3(2). Mesonotum with a **V**-shaped suture; legs long and slender (Figure 464 A) 4

3′. Mesonotum without a **V**-shaped suture; legs variable 7

4(3). Ocelli present; 2A usually short and curved abruptly into anal margin of wing .... **Trichocéridae*** p. 567

4′. Ocelli absent; 2A usually long, not as above 5

5(4′). R 5-branched, all 5 branches reaching wing margin; sometimes (*Protoplàsa*) with a cross vein in the M_3 cell (Figure 465 C); 1 anal vein .... **Tanydéridae*** p. 568

5′. R with 4 or fewer branches reaching wing margin; M_3 cell without a cross vein; 1–2 anal veins 6

6(5′). Only 1 anal vein reaching wing margin; R 4-branched; no closed discal cell (Figure 465 A); pulvilli present .... **Ptychoptéridae** p. 568

6′. Two anal veins reaching wing margin; R 2- to 4-branched; a closed discal cell usually present (Figure 465 B); pulvilli absent .... **Tipùlidae** p. 567

7(3′). Wings large, broadest in basal fourth, densely covered with fine hairs; true veins almost absent, but a fanlike development of folds present; antennae very long, in male at least 3 times as long as body, and 6-segmented;

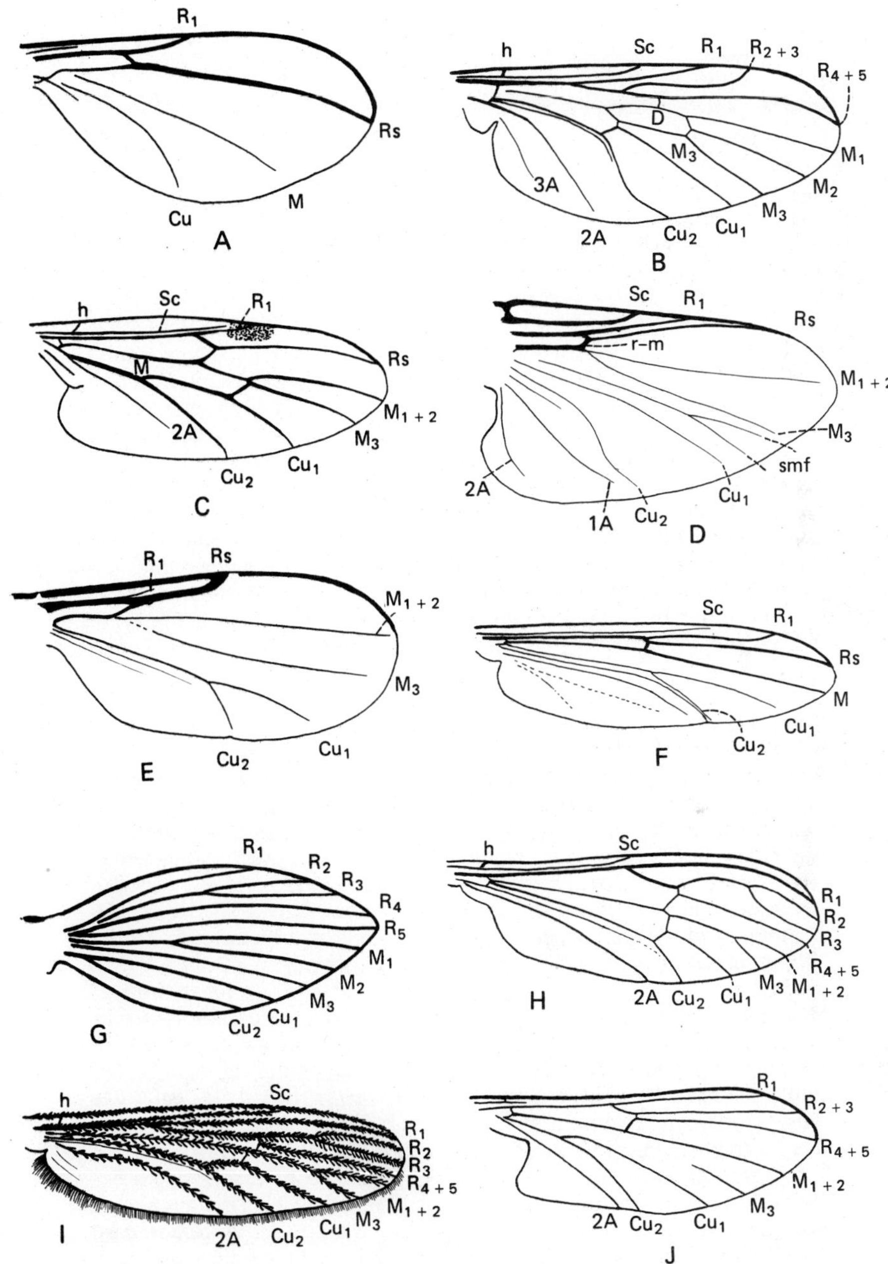

Figure 445. Wings of Nematócera. A, Cecidomyìidae; B, Anisopódidae (*Silvícola*); C, Bibiónidae (*Bíbio*); D, Simulìidae (*Simùlium*); E, Ceratopogónidae; F, Chironómidae; G, Psychòdidae (*Psychòda*); H, Díxidae (*Díxa*); I, Culícidae (*Psoróphora*); J, Blepharicéridae (*Blepharícera*). D, discal cell; *smf*, submedían fold.

ocelli and mouth parts absent; western United States .... **Deuterophlebìidae*** p. 569

7′. Not exactly fitting the above description 8

8(7′). Ocelli present 9

8′. Ocelli absent 21

9(8). A closed discal cell present 10

9′. No closed discal cell present 12

10(9). Fourth posterior (M_3) cell open 11

10′. Fourth posterior cell closed; medium-sized, elongate flies resembling sawflies (*Rachícerus*) .... **Xylophágidae*** p. 580

11(10). The two branches of Rs connected by a cross vein; antennae 16-segmented; Oregon to British Columbia (*Cramptonomỳia*) .. **Pachyneùridae*** p. 577

11′. The two branches of Rs not connected by a cross vein (Figure 445 B); antennae with 12–16 segments; widely distributed (Anisopodìnae) .... **Anisopódidae** p. 575

12(9′). Venation reduced, with 7 or fewer longitudinal veins reaching wing margin (Figure 445 A); antennae usually long and slender; costa usually continuing around wing, though weakened behind; minute delicate flies .... **Cecidomyìidae** p. 578

12′. Venation not so reduced, usually with more than 7 longitudinal veins reaching wing margin; antennae variable; costa ending near or before wing tip; size and shape variable 13

13(12′). Legs long and slender, the insect resembling a crane fly; anal angle of wing projecting (Figure 445 J); sometimes with a network of delicate lines between the veins; tibial spurs reduced or lacking .... **Blepharicéridae*** p. 569

13′. Either legs not long and slender and the insect not resembling a crane fly, or anal angle of wing not projecting, or tibial spurs present; wings without a network of delicate lines between the veins 14

14(13′). Tibiae with apical spurs 15

14′. Tibiae without apical spurs 19

15(14). Pulvilli present; antennae usually shorter than thorax, rather stout, and arising low on face, below compound eyes; second basal (M) cell present (Figure 445 C); anal angle of wing usually well developed .... **Bibiónidae** p. 575

15′. Pulvilli absent or very minute; antennae variable, but usually longer than thorax and arising about middle of compound eyes or higher; second basal cell and wing shape variable 16

16(15′). Rs 3-branched, with R_2 appearing much like a cross vein extending from R_{2+3} to about the end of R_1 (Figure 447 D) (*Axymỳia*) .... **Pachyneùridae*** p. 577

16′. Rs simple or 2-branched, with no cross vein between the branches of Rs when it is 2-branched 17

17(16′). Eyes meeting above bases of antennae (except males of *Pnỳxia*); Rs unbranched, and r-m in line with Rs (Figure 480 C, D) .... **Sciáridae** p. 577

17′. Eyes not meeting above bases of antennae; Rs simple or 2-branched, if simple the r-m cross vein is not quite in line with Rs 18

18(17′). Basal cells confluent and closed distally by r-m and m-cu; Rs forked opposite r-m; Sc complete, ending in costa; 2A reaching wing margin (Figure 447 C) (*Mycetòbia*) .... **Anisopódidae*** p. 575

18′. Basal cells variable; Rs simple or forked, if forked the fork is distad of r-m or r-m is obliterated by the fusion of Rs and M; Sc and 2A variable; a large and widespread group .... **Mycetophílidae**[2] p. 577

---

[2] *Hesperòdes jóhnsoni* Coquillet, reported from Massachusetts and New Jersey, lacks ocelli; it is 12 mm in length, a member of the subfamily Keroplatìnae, and has a wing venation similar to that shown in Figure 480 B.

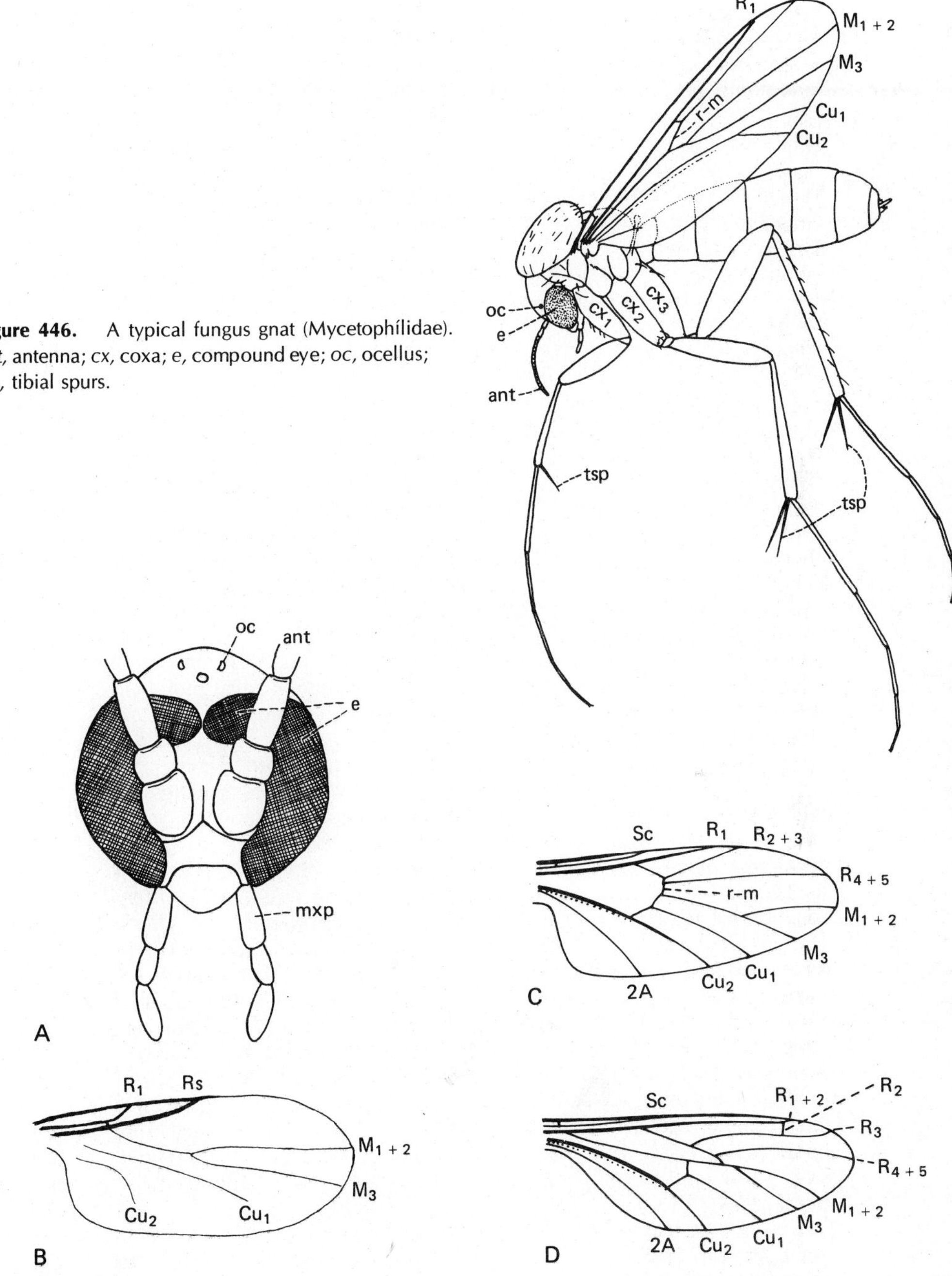

Figure 446. A typical fungus gnat (Mycetophílidae). *ant,* antenna; *cx,* coxa; e, compound eye; *oc,* ocellus; *tsp,* tibial spurs.

Figure 447. A, head of *Sciara* (Sciáridae), antero-dorsal view; B, wing of a scatopsid; C, wing of *Mycetòbia* (Anisopódidae); D, wing of *Axỳmyia* (Pachyneùridae). *ant,* antenna; e, compound eye; *mpx,* maxillary palp; *oc,* ocellus.

19(14′). Antennae long, usually half as long as body or longer; legs usually long and slender; veins in anterior part of wing (R_1 and Rs) not noticeably thicker than the others .... **Cecidomyìidae** p. 578

19′. Antennae short, not reaching beyond middle of thorax; legs usually short and stout; veins in anterior part of wing noticeably thicker than the others 20

20(19′). Rs forked; costa extending beyond end of R_{4+5} and almost to wing tip; palps 3- or 4-segmented; antennae 12-segmented .... **Hyperoscelídidae*** p. 578

20′. Rs not forked (Figure 447 B); costa extending only to end of Rs and, at most, only about three fourths of the wing length; palps 1-segmented; antennae 7- to 12-segmented .... **Scatópsidae** p. 578

21(8′). Costa ending at or near wing tip (Figure 445 D–F) 22

21′. Costa continuing around wing tip, though often weaker along hind margin of wing (Figure 445 G, I) 24

22(21). Wings broad, the posterior veins weak (Figure 445 D); antennae about as long as head; dark-colored flies, rarely over 3 mm in length, with a somewhat humpbacked appearance and short thick legs (Figure 476) .... **Simulìidae** p. 575

22′. Wings narrower, the posterior veins usually stronger (Figure 445 E, F) 23

23(22′). M nearly always forked (Figure 445 E); head rounded behind; metanotum rounded, without a median furrow or keel; legs of moderate length, the hind pair the longest; pulvilli absent; antennae usually 15-segmented; mouth parts with mandibles, and fitted for piercing ... **Ceratopogónidae** p. 573

23′. M not forked (Figure 445 F); head flattened behind; metanotum generally with a median furrow or keel; legs long, the front legs usually the longest; pulvilli present or absent; antennae 7- to 16-segmented; mouth parts without mandibles, not fitted for piercing .... **Chironómidae** p. 574

24(21′). Wings short, broad, pointed apically, usually densely hairy and held rooflike over body when at rest; Rs usually 4-branched; no cross veins except near base of wing (Figure 445 G) .... **Psychòdidae** p. 568

24′ Wings usually long and narrow, or if broad then not pointed apically (Figure 445 H, I); wings held flat over abdomen when at rest; wings not densely hairy, though there may be scales along the wing veins or the wing margin; Rs with 3 or fewer branches 25

25(24′). Venation much reduced, with 7 or fewer veins reaching wing margin 26

25′. Venation not reduced, with at least 9 veins reaching wing margin (Figure 445 H, I) 27

26(25). Wings with 7 longitudinal veins; antennae about as long as head, with the 2 basal segments thick and globose, the 10 remaining segments bristlelike; small, bare, reddish yellow or brownish flies .... **Thaumalèidae*** p. 572

26′. Wings usually with fewer than 7 longitudinal veins (Figure 445 A); antennae usually very long, at least in species with 7 longitudinal veins, and with 10–36 similar segments .... **Cecidomyìidae** p. 578

27(25′). Rs and its branches somewhat arched (Figure 445 H); wing veins and wing margin not fringed with scales; body and legs not scaly .... **Díxidae** p. 569

27′. Rs and its branches straight or nearly so; wing margin, and usually also wing veins, fringed with scales (Figure 445 I) 28

28(27′). Proboscis long, extending far beyond clypeus (Figure 469); scales present on wing veins and wing margin, and usually also on body ... **Culícidae** p. 569

28′. Proboscis short, extending little beyond clypeus; scales, when present, mostly confined to wing margin .... **Chaobòridae** p. 569

29(2′). Empodia pulvilliform, the tarsi with 3 pads (Figure 441 B) 30

29′. Empodia bristlelike or absent, the tarsi with not more than 2 pads (Figure 441 A) 38

30(29). Third antennal segment annulated (Figure 440 C, D, F) 31
30′. Third antennal segment not annulated (Figure 440 E, G, H), and usually bearing an elongate style (Figure 440 E) or arista (Figure 440 G, H) 35
31(30). Calypteres large and conspicuous; R_4 and R_5 divergent, enclosing wing tip (Figure 442) 32
31′. Calypteres small or vestigial; R_4 and R_5 variable 33
32(31). Anal vein (2A) slightly sinuate, the anal cell open; hind tibiae with apical spurs; abdomen of female posterior to fourth segment modified into a slender retractile postabdomen; face swollen below antennae, the antennae arising above middle of head; eyes densely hairy; Pacific Coast .... **Pelecorhýnchidae*** p. 581
32′. Anal vein straight or gently curved, the anal cell closed at or before wing margin; hind tibiae with or without apical spurs; abdomen of female robust, not as above; antennae usually arising below middle of head; eyes usually bare; widely distributed .... **Tabánidae** p. 581
33(31′). At least middle tibiae with apical spurs; Rs usually arising distinctly proximad of base of discal cell; branches of R not crowded together near costal margin (Figure 484) .... 34[3]
33′. Tibial spurs lacking or, at most, middle tibiae with a slight apical spur; Rs arising opposite base of discal cell; branches of R more or less crowded together near costal margin (Figure 448 A); R_5 (or R_{4+5} when it is not forked) ending before wing tip; M_3 cell open .... **Stratiomýidae**[3] p. 580
34(33). M_3 cell closed (Figure 484 C); front tibiae without apical spurs .... **Xylomýidae** p. 580
34′. M_3 cell open (Figure 484 A, B); front tibiae with an apical spur .... **Xylophágidae** p. 580
35(30′). Calypteres very large; head very small and placed low down, and composed almost entirely of eyes; body appearing humpbacked (Figure 494); costa extending only to wing tip .... **Acrocéridae*** p. 585
35′. Calypteres small or vestigial; head of normal size, the face or front broad; costa variable 36
36(35′). Costa usually ending at wing tip; venation peculiar, with many veins ending before wing tip (Figure 448 I); tibiae without apical spurs .... **Nemestrínidae*** p. 585
36′. Costa continuing around wing tip; venation normal (Figure 448 B); middle and hind tibiae usually with apical spurs 37
37(36′). Antennae with a short 2-segmented style that is shorter than third segment; length 2–3 mm (*Bolbomýia*) .... **Xylophágidae*** p. 580
37′. Antennae with a long terminal style that is longer than the three antennal segments combined (Figure 488); length usually over 3 mm .... **Rhagiónidae** p. 582
38(29′). Wings rounded apically, with strong veins anteriorly and weak oblique veins posteriorly (Figure 449 G); antennae apparently 1-segmented, with a long arista; hind legs long, the femora flattened laterally; small or minute flies with a humpbacked appearance (Figure 498) .... **Phòridae** p. 589
38′. Wings with normal venation or pointed at apex; antennae not as above .. 39
39(38′). Wings pointed at apex and with no cross veins except at base (Figure 449 H); third antennal segment rounded, with a terminal arista; small, slender, brownish or yellowish flies, 2–5 mm in length .... **Lonchoptéridae** p. 589
39′. Wings rounded at apex, almost always with cross veins beyond base of

---

[3] The Pantophthálmidae, large robust flies that are tropical but may occur in the extreme southern United States, would key to couplet 33; they lack tibial spurs, but do not have the branches of R crowded anteriorly as in the Stratiomýidae, R_4 and R_5 are divergent, enclosing the wing tip (much as in the Tabánidae, Figure 442), and the M_3 and anal cells are closed.

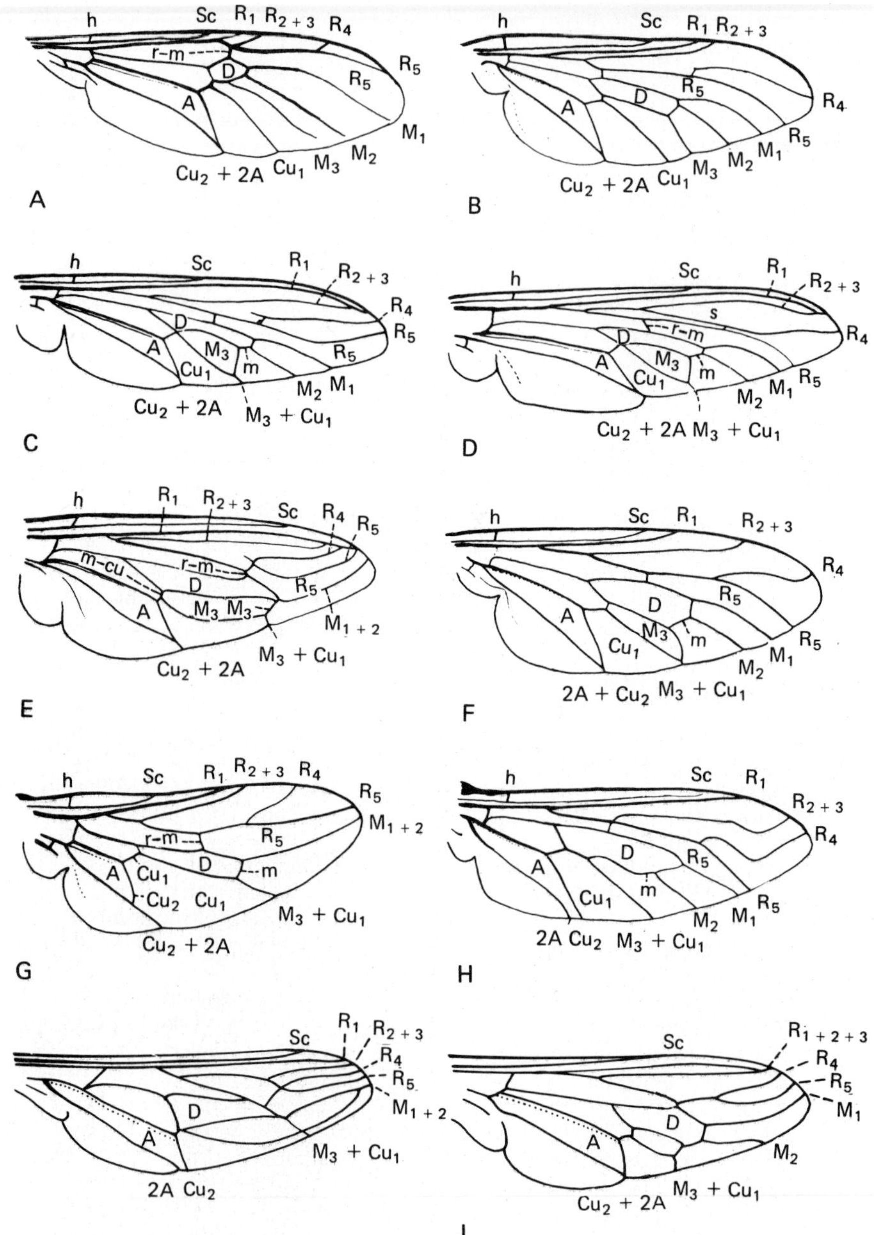

Figure 448. Wings of Brachýcera. A, Stratiomỳidae; B, Rhagiónidae; C, Asìlidae (*Effèria*); D, Asìlidae (*Prómachus*); E, Mỳdidae (*Mỳdas*), F, Therévidae; G, Scenopínidae; H, Bombylìidae; I, Nemestrínidae (*Neorhynchocéphalus*); J. Apiocéridae (*Apiócera*). *A*, anal (1A) cell; *D*, discal (first M_2) cell.

wing (Figures 448 G–H, J, 449 B–F, 450, 455, 459, 460); antennae, size, and color variable 40

40(39′). R_{4+5} forked (Figure 448), or at least the radius appearing 4-branched (Figure

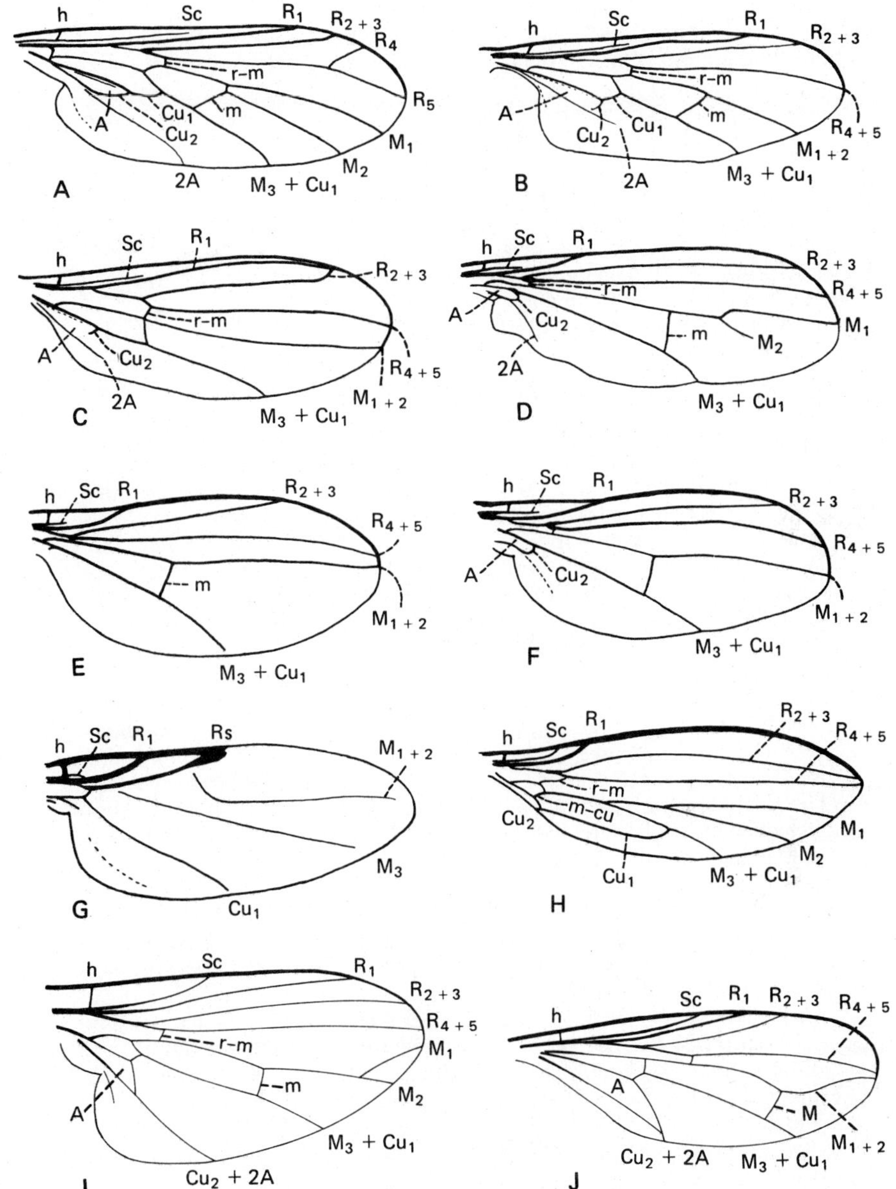

Figure 449. Wings of Brachýcera and Cyclórrhapha (Aschìza). A–C, Empídidae; D–F, Dolichopódidae; G, Phòridae; H, Lonchoptéridae, female; I, Platypèzidae; J, Pipuncùlidae. *A*, anal (1A) cell.

448 D) 41

40′. R_{4+5} not forked, the radius with not more than 3 branches (Figures 449 B–F, I, J, 450, 455, 459, 460) 49

41(40). Vertex sunken, the top of the head concave and the eyes bulging as seen in anterior view (Figure 492 D) 42

41′. Vertex little or not at all sunken, eyes not bulging 44

42(41). With 3 ocelli; antennae usually appearing 3-segmented; M_1 not ending in front of wing tip (Figure 448 C, D); size variable 43

42′. With 1 ocellus or none; antennae 4-segmented; M_1 curved forward and ending in front of wing tip (Figure 448 E); large flies (Figure 491) .... **Mỳdidae** p. 584

43(42). Abdomen very slender and elongate (Figure 493); alulae absent, wings narrowed basally; maxillary palps 1-segmented; R_1 cell open .... **Leptogástridae** p. 585

43′. Abdomen not so slender, tapering or oval (Figure 492); alulae usually present; maxillary palps 1- or 2-segmented; R_1 cell open or closed .... **Asìlidae** p. 584

44(41′). Five posterior cells (Figure 448 F, J); m-cu present, and M_3 and Cu_1 separate or fused at apex only; abdomen long and tapering 45

44′. Four or fewer posterior cells (Figures 448 G, H and 449 A), or if with 5 (some *Caenòtus,* family Bombylìidae, Figure 489 C), then m-cu absent and M_3 and Cu_1 fused basally; abdomen usually oval or oblong 46

45(44). R_5 and M_1 curving forward and ending in front of wing tip (Figure 448 J); rare flies occurring in the arid regions of the West .... **Apiocéridae*** p. 584

45′. R_5 and M_1 not curving forward, and ending behind wing tip (Figure 448 F); widely distributed .... **Therévidae** p. 583

46(44′). M_1 ending at or in front of wing tip; costa not continuing beyond wing tip; 3 posterior cells (Figure 448 G) .... **Scenopínidae*** p. 583

46′. M_1 ending behind wing tip; costa usually continuing beyond wing tip; 3 or 4 posterior cells (Figures 448 H and 449 A) 47

47(46′). Anal cell open (Figure 448 H), or closed near wing margin and apex acute; body often hairy and robust 48

47′. Anal cell closed far from wing margin (Figure 449 A) or absent, or if closed very near wing margin then the apex is not acute; body rarely hairy and usually not robust .... **Empídidae** p. 586

48(47). A closed discal cell present; usually over 5 mm in length .. **Bombylìidae** p. 585

48′. No closed discal cell present; 2.5–5.0 mm in length .. **Hilarimórphidae*** p. 583

49(40′). Hind tarsi nearly always expanded and/or flattened (Figure 463 C); wings relatively broad basally, the anal angle well developed; anal cell closed and pointed apically, usually closed some distance from wing margin (Figure 449 I); M_{1+2} often forked apically; Sc complete, reaching costa; no frontal suture; males holoptic, the upper facets larger than lower ones; arista terminal; small, usually black flies, less than 10 mm in length .... **Platypèzidae*** p. 589

49′. Not exactly fitting the above description 50

50(49′). Anal cell elongate, longer than second basal cell, usually pointed apically and narrowed or closed near wing margin (Figures 449 J and 450); no frontal suture (Figure 451); head bristles usually lacking 51

50′. Anal cell usually shorter, closed some distance from wing margin, or lacking (Figures 449 C–F, 455, 459, 460); if anal cell is elongate and pointed apically (Figure 459 C), then a frontal suture is present; head bristles usually present 55

51(50). Proboscis longer than head, slender, stiff, and often folding; face broad, with grooves below antennae; abdomen clavate, bent downward at apex (Figure 502); R_5 cell closed and pointed apically (Figure 450 D) .... **Conópidae** p. 591

51′. Proboscis small, rarely elongated; face narrow, without grooves below antennae; abdomen and R_5 cell variable 52

52(51′). R_5 cell closed; usually a spurious vein crossing r-m between R_{4+5} and M_{1+2} (Figure 450 A–C) .... **Sýrphidae** p. 590

52′. R_5 cell open, though sometimes narrowed apically; no spurious vein ... 53

53(52′). Head very large, hemispherical, the face very narrow (Figures 451 B and

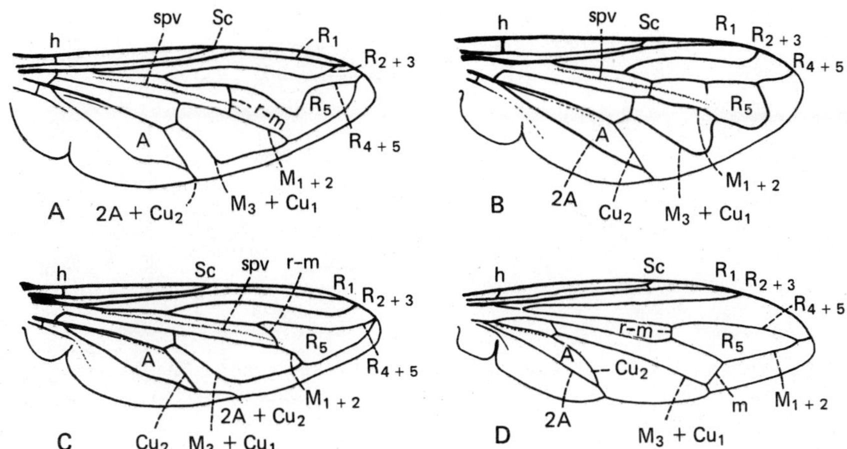

Figure 450. Wings of Sýrphidae (A–C) and Conópidae (D). A, *Erístalis;* B, *Mìcrodon;* C, *Spilomỳia;* D, *Physocéphala. A,* anal (1A) cell; *spv,* spurious vein.

499); Sc complete, ending in costa; proboscis small and soft .... **Pipuncùlidae** p. 589

53′. Head not unusually large, face normal; Sc more or less reduced and not reaching costa; proboscis slender and rigid 54

54(53′). R_{2+3} usually very short and ending in R_1, rarely lacking, or ending in costa beyond end of R_1; anal cell long, extending to wing margin and narrowly open, or closed near wing margin; minute flies, 1.2–4.0 mm in length, rather stocky in build with a humpbacked appearance, and usually brownish or grayish in color; mostly western (Platypygìnae and Mythicomyiìnae) .... **Bombylìidae** p. 585

54′. R_{2+3} ending in costa well beyond end of R_1; anal cell short (rarely lacking) and no longer than second basal cell, if long and closed near wing margin (Hybotìnae) the insect is relatively slender and usually black in color; size variable; widely distributed .... **Empídidae** p. 586

55(50′). Frontal suture absent (Figure 451) 56

55′. Frontal suture present (Figures 443 A, 461, 462) 58

56(55). Head very large, hemispherical, face very narrow (Figures 451 B and 499

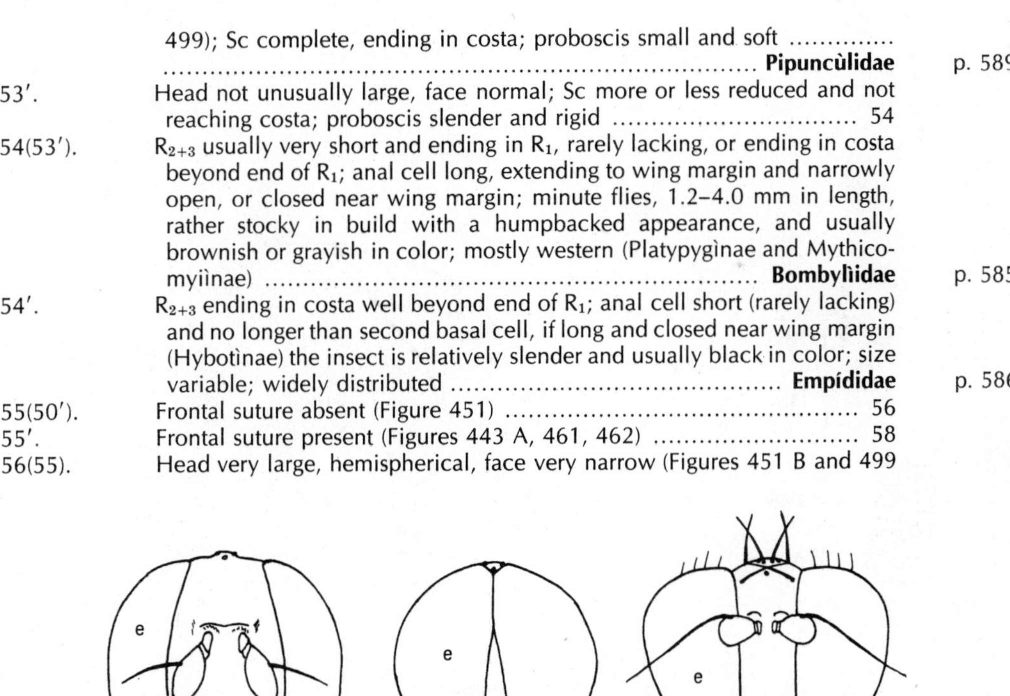

Figure 451. Heads of Díptera, anterior view. A, Sýrphidae (*Metasỳrphus*); B, Pipuncùlidae (*Pipúnculus*); C, Dolichopódidae (*Dolíchopus*). e, compound eye.

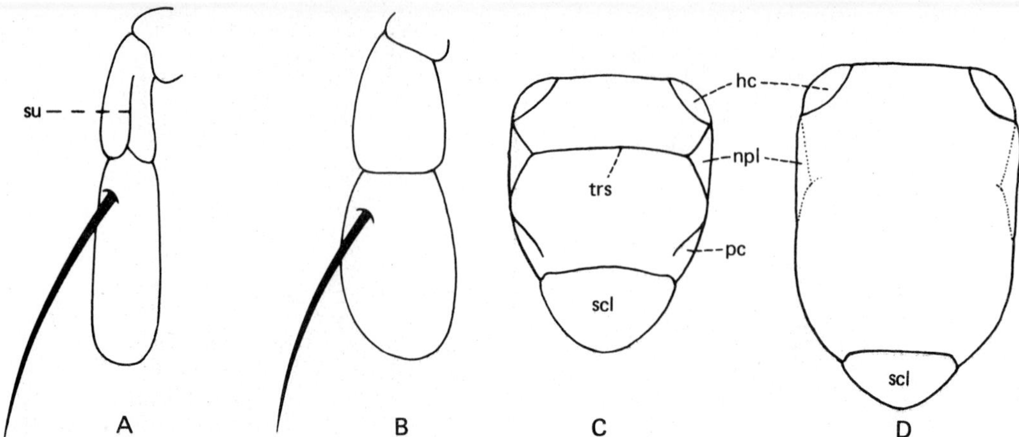

Figure 452. Antennae (A, B) and mesonota (C, D) of muscoid flies. A, calyptrate, showing suture (*su*) on second segment; B, acalyptrate, which lacks a suture on the second segment; C, calyptrate; D, acalyptrate. *hc*, humeral callus; *npl*, notopleuron; *pc*, postalar callus; *scl*, scutellum; *su*, suture; *trs*, transverse suture.

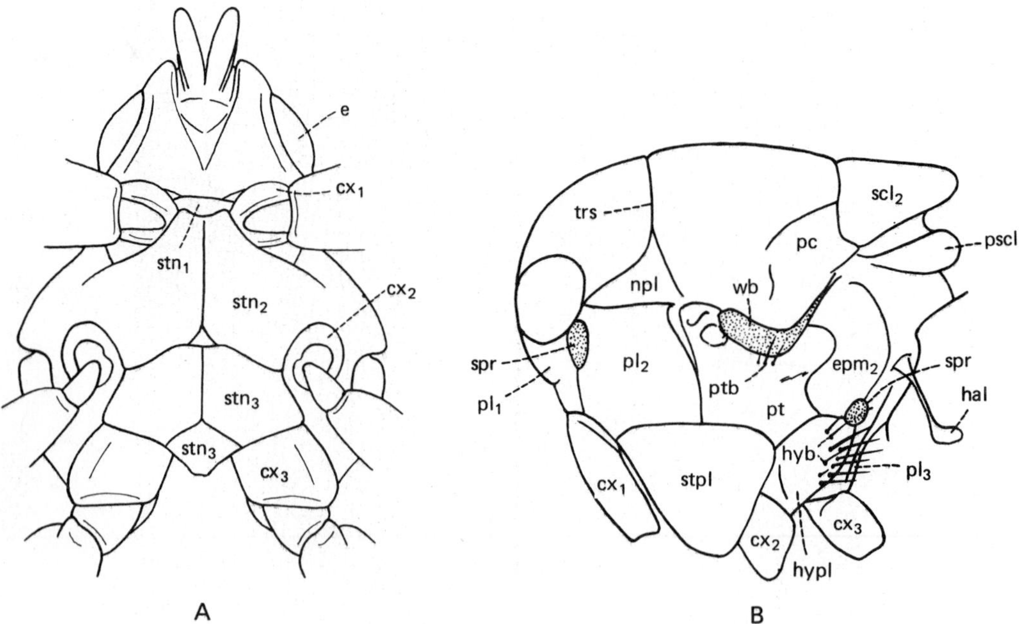

Figure 453. Thorax structure in muscoids. A, thorax of a hippoboscid (*Lýnchia*), ventral view; B, thorax of a tachinid (*Ptilodéxia*), lateral view. *cx*, coxa; e, compound eye; *epm*$_2$, mesepimeron; *hal*, halter; *hc*, humeral callus; *hyb*, hypopleural bristles; *hypl*, hypopleuron; *npl*, notopleuron; *pc*, postalar callus; *pl*$_1$, propleuron; *pl*$_2$, mesopleuron; *pl*$_3$, metapleuron; *pscl*, postscutellum; *pt*, pteropleuron; *ptb*, pteropleural bristles; *scl*$_2$, mesoscutellum; *spr*, spiracle; *stn*$_1$, prosternum; *stn*$_2$, mesosternum; *stn*$_3$, metasternum; *stpl*, sternopleuron; *trs*, transverse suture; *wb*, base of wing. Only the hypopleural and pteropleural bristles are shown in B.

	(*Chálarus*) .... **Pipuncùlidae**	p. 589
56′.	Head not unusually large; face variable 57	
57(56′).	The r-m cross vein located beyond basal fourth of wing; fork of Rs usually not swollen (Figure 449 B, C); male genitalia terminal, not folded forward under abdomen (Figure 496); body not metallic .... **Empídidae**	p. 586
57′.	The r-m cross vein located in basal fourth of wing, or absent; fork of Rs usually swollen (Figure 449 D–F); male genitalia often folded forward under abdomen (Figure 497); body usually metallic .... **Dolichopódidae**	p. 587
58(55′).	Coxae widely separated, legs attached lateroventrally (Figure 453 A); body somewhat flattened; ectoparasites of birds, mammals, or bees 59*	
58′.	Coxae close together (ventral aspect), legs attached ventrally; body not particularly flattened; not ectoparasitic in habit 60	
59(58).	Palps slender and elongate, forming a sheath for the proboscis; wings with anterior veins strong and crowded forward, the posterior veins weak or absent; tarsal claws often toothed; eyes well developed, oval; ectoparasites of birds and mammals .... **Hippobóscidae***	p. 602
59′.	Palps broader than long, projecting leaflike in front of head; wings uniformly veined; tarsal claws simple; eyes small or vestigial; mostly ectoparasites of bats .... **Stréblidae***	p. 602
60(58′).	Mouth opening small, the mouth parts vestigial or lacking (Figure 454 A); body hairy but not bristly, the insect beelike in appearance; R_5, and sometimes also M_{1+2}, ending before wing tip (bot and warble flies) 61*	
60′.	Mouth opening normal, mouth parts well developed and functional; body usually with bristles; R_5 and M_{1+2} variable 63	
61(60).	M_{1+2} nearly straight, the R_5 cell widened toward wing margin (Figure 523 A); second antennal segment without a longitudinal suture on outer side .... **Gasterophílidae***	p. 601
61′.	M_{1+2} bent forward distally, ending before wing tip, the R_5 cell narrowed or closed distally (Figure 523 B–D); second antennal segment with a longitudinal suture on outer side (as in Figure 452 A) 62*	
62(61′).	Scutellum extending far beyond base of metanotum, and postscutellum not developed (Figure 454 C); head with a deep groove on ventral side, palps not visible; arista bare or plumose .... **Cuterébridae***	p. 605
62′.	Scutellum very short, and postscutellum usually well developed (Figure 454 B); head apparently closed on ventral side, palps usually large; arista bare .... **Oéstridae***	p. 605
63(60′).	Second antennal segment with a longitudinal suture on outer side (Figure 452 A); thorax usually with a complete transverse suture (Figure 452 C); lower (innermost) calypter usually large (calyptrate muscoid flies, except *Loxócera*, family Psìlidae) 64	
63′.	Second antennal segment without such a suture (Figure 452 B); thorax usually without a complete transverse suture (Figure 452 D); lower calypter usually small or rudimentary (acalyptrate muscoid flies) 69	
64(63).	Hypopleura and pteropleura with bristles (Figure 453 B); R_5 cell narrowed or closed distally 65	
64′.	Hypopleura usually without bristles; if hypopleural bristles are present, then there are no pteropleural bristles, or the proboscis is rigid and fitted for piercing, or the R_5 cell is not narrowed distally 67	
65(64).	Postscutellum developed (Figure 453 B, *pscl*); abdominal terga usually with strong bristles, and their edges overlapping sterna; arista usually bare .... **Tachínidae**	p. 603
65′.	Postscutellum not developed (Figure 444 A); abdominal terga variable; arista usually plumose, at least in part 66	
66(65′).	Hindmost posthumeral bristle located laterad of presutural bristle, and usually 2 (rarely 3) notopleural bristles (Figure 456 A); arista usually	

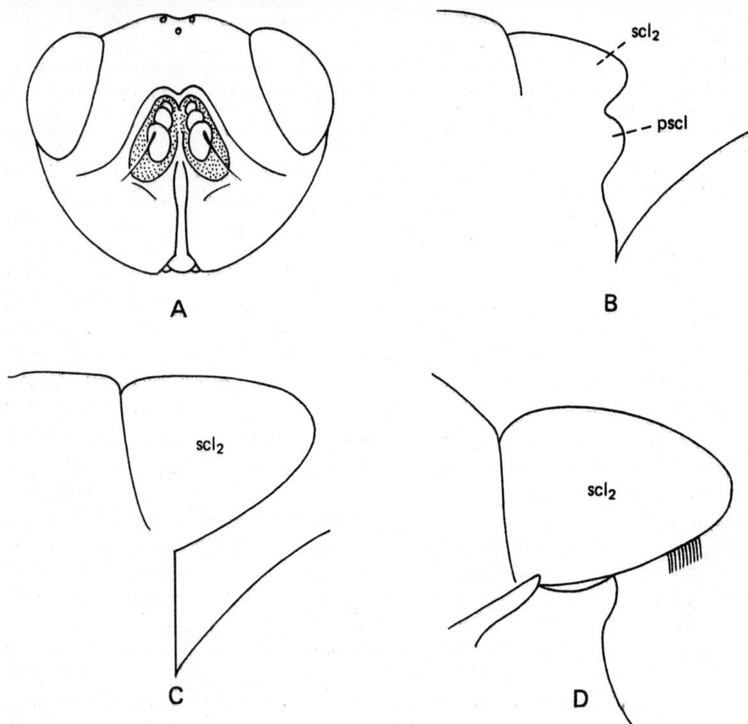

Figure 454. Characters of muscoid flies. A, head of horse bot fly (*Gasteróphilus*), anterior view; B–D, posterior part of thorax, lateral view: B, *Hypodérma* (Oéstridae); C, a cuterebrid; D, an anthomyiid. *pscl*, postscutellum; scl_2, mesoscutellum.

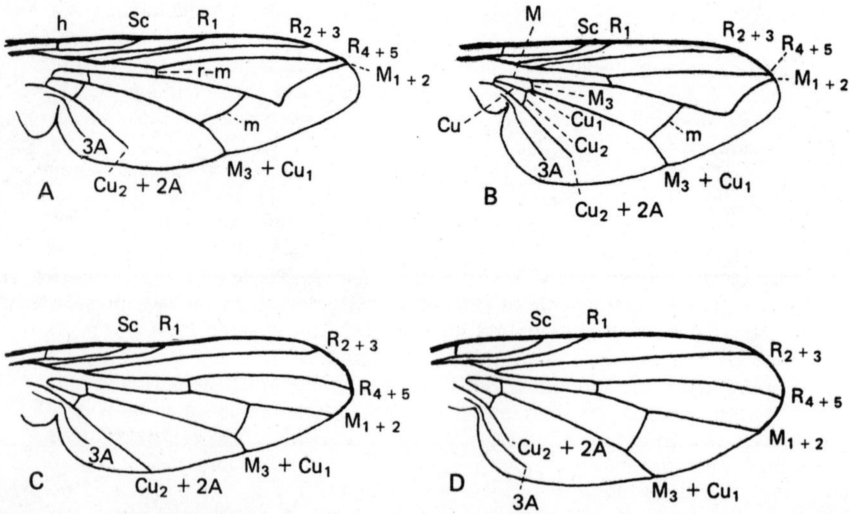

Figure 455. Wings of calyptrate muscoid flies. A, Tachínidae; B, Múscidae (*Músca*); C, Anthomyìidae (Scatophagìnae); D, Múscidae (*Fánnia*).

plumose beyond basal half; propleura usually pubescent; body often metallic .... **Calliphòridae** p. 602

66′. Hindmost posthumeral bristle located even with or mesad of presutural bristle, and usuálly 4 notopleural bristles (Figure 456 B); arista generally plumose only in basal half; propleura bare; body not metallic .... **Sarcophágidae** p. 603

67(64′). Third antennal segment longer than arista (Figure 457); oral vibrissae absent; mesonotum without bristles except above wings (*Loxócera*) .... **Psìlidae** p. 592

67′. Third antennal segment not so lengthened; oral vibrissae present; mesonotum with bristles 68

68(67′). Sixth vein (Cu_2 + 2A) reaching wing margin, at least as a fold (Figure 455 C); 1 sternopleural bristle (Figure 458 A, *stb*) or undersurface of scutellum with fine erect hairs (Figure 454 D) (a few exceptions); arista never pectinate on upper side only .... **Anthomyìidae** p. 600

68′. Sixth vein never reaching wing margin (Figure 455 B, D); usually more than 1 sternopleural bristle; undersurface of scutellum usually without fine erect hairs; arista variable, but may be pectinate on upper side only .... **Múscidae** p. 601

69(63′). Sc complete, or nearly so, ending in costa or just short of it, and free from R_1 distally (Figures 459 and 460 F); anal cell present 70

69′. Sc incomplete, not reaching costa, often fusing with R_1 distally (Figure 460 A–E); anal cell present or absent 105

70(69). Palps vestigial; posterior spiracle of thorax with at least 1 bristle (Figure 458 D, *spbr*); head spherical; abdomen elongate and usually narrowed at base (Figure 509) .... **Sépsidae** p. 595

70′. Palps generally well developed; posterior spiracle of thorax usually without bristles 71

71(70′). Dorsum of thorax flattened; legs and abdomen conspicuously bristly (Figure 508); seashore species .... **Coelòpidae** p. 594

71′. Dorsum of thorax convex, if rather flattened then the legs are not bristly 72

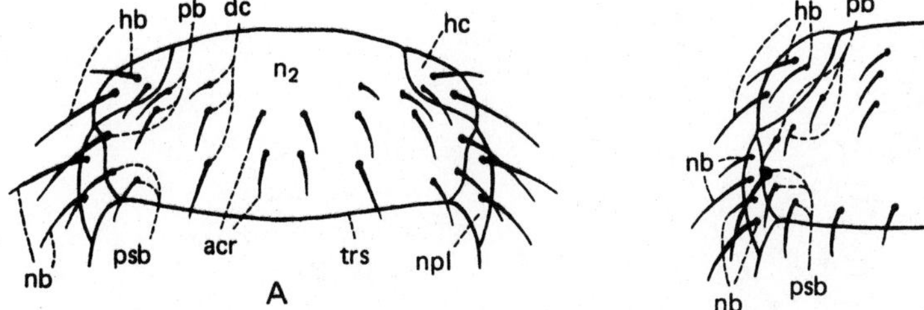

Figure 456. Anterior part of mesonotum of A, a blow fly (*Callíphora*), B, a flesh fly (*Sarcóphaga*). *acr*, acrostichal bristles; *dc*, dorsocentral bristles; *hb*, humeral bristles; *hc*, humeral callus; n_2, mesonotum; *nb*, notopleural bristles; *npl*, notopleuron; *pb*, posthumeral bristles; *psb*, presutural bristles; *trs*, transverse suture.

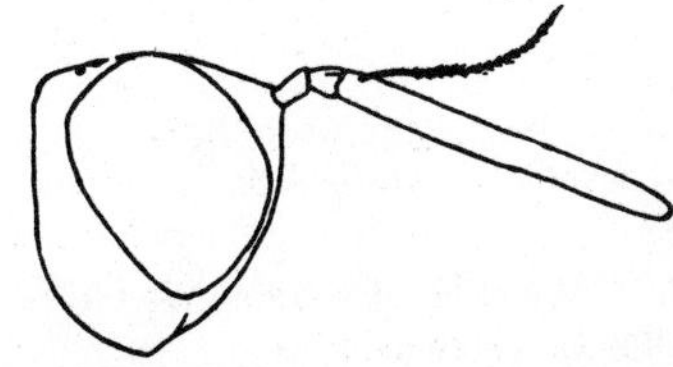

Figure 457. Head of *Loxócera* (Psìlidae) lateral view.

72(71′). Oral vibrissae present (Figure 461 A–C, *ov*) 73
72′. Oral vibrissae absent (Figure 461 F–I) 81
73(72). Costa spinose (Figure 459 A, H) 74
73′. Costa not spinose 77
74(73). Second basal and discal cells confluent (Figure 459 A, *B* + *D*); arista plumose .... **Curtonòtidae*** p. 597
74′. Second basal and discal cells separated (Figure 459 B, *B* and *D*); arista usually not plumose 75
75(74′). Postverticals diverging; anal vein (2A) reaching wing margin; 4–5 sternopleurals; 2 pairs of fronto-orbitals; ocellar triangle large .... **Neottiophílidae*** p. 596
75′. Postverticals converging 76

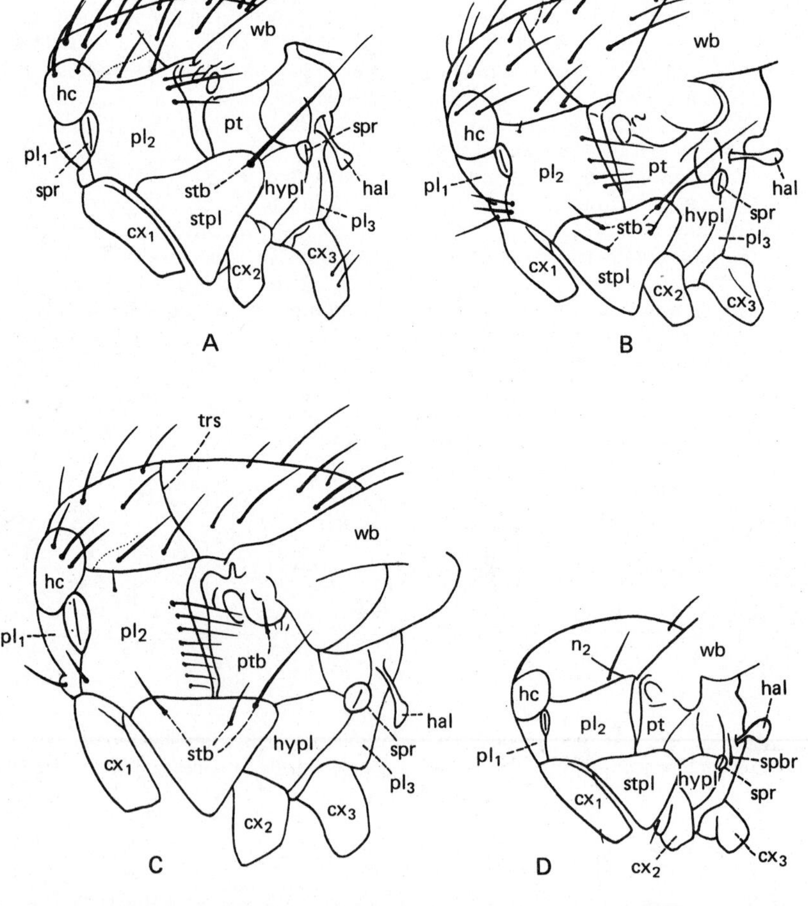

Figure 458. Thorax of muscoid flies, lateral view. A, Anthomyìidae (*Scatóphaga*); B, Anthomyìidae (*Anthomỳia*); C, Múscidae (*Músca*); D, Sépsidae (*Themìra*). *cx*, coxa; *hal*, halter; *hc*, humeral callus; *hypl*, hypopleuron; n_2, mesonotum; pl_1, propleuron; pl_2, mesopleuron; pl_3, metapleuron; *pt*, pteropleuron; *ptb*, pteropleural bristles; *spbr*, spiracular bristle; *spr*, spiracle; *stb*, sternopleural bristles; *stpl*, sternopleuron; *trs*, transverse suture; *wb*, base of wing.

76(75′). Orbital plates long, extending nearly to level of antennae; ocellar bristles laterad of median ocellus; 2–3 pairs of fronto-orbitals; 2A never reaching wing margin .... **Trixoscelídidae*** p. 599

76′. Orbital plates short, not reaching level of antennae (Figure 461 C); ocellar bristles between median and lateral ocelli (Figure 461 C); 1–2 pairs of fronto-orbitals; 2A variable, sometimes (Figure 459 H) reaching wing margin .... **Heleomỳzidae** p. 598

77(73′). Second basal and discal cells confluent (as in Figure 459 A, *B* + *D*); postverticals lacking; arista pubescent .... **Aulacigástridae*** p. 599

77′. Second basal and discal cells separated (Figure 459 B, *B* and *D*); postverticals present; arista variable 78

78(77′). 2–4 pairs of fronto-orbitals (Figure 461 A); second antennal segment usually with an angular projection on outer side (Figure 461 A); arista

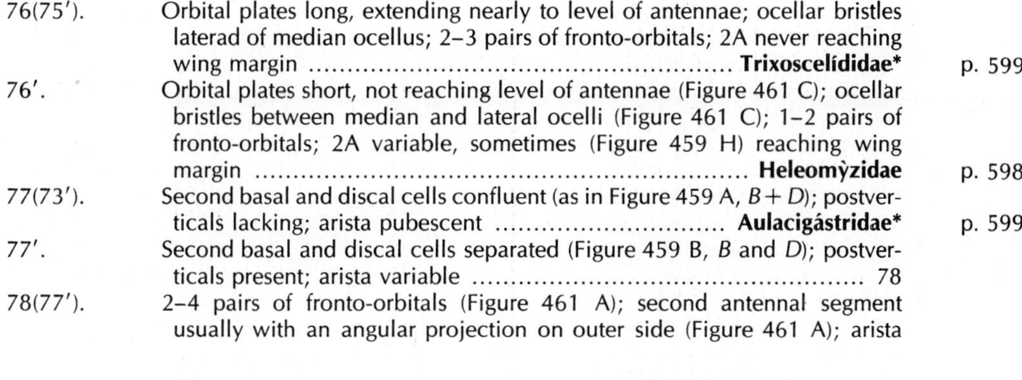

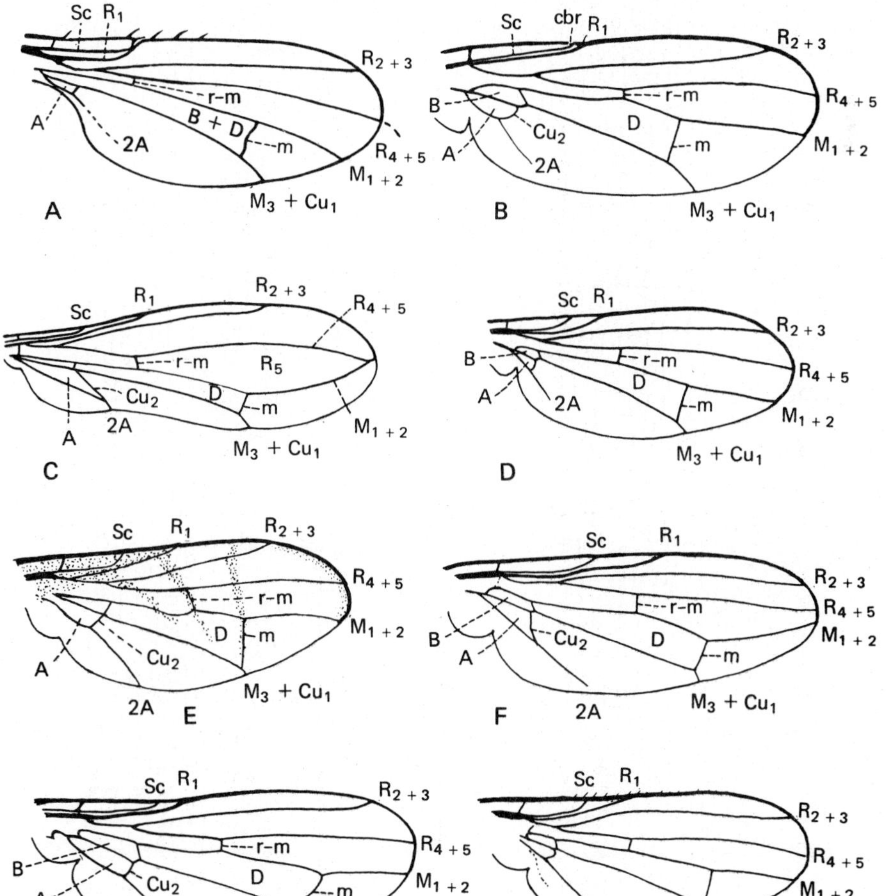

Figure 459. Wings of acalyptrate muscoid flies. A, Curtonòtidae (*Curtonòtum*); B, Piophílidae (*Pióphila*); C, Micropèzidae (*Taeniáptera*); D, Lauxanìidae (*Physegénua*); E, Platystomátidae (*Rivéllia*); F, Otítidae (*Acrostícta*); G, Sciomỳzidae (*Sépedon*); H, Heleomỳzidae (*Amoebalèria*). *A*, anal cell; *B*, second basal cell; *cbr*, costal break; *D*, discal (first M_2) cell.

	subapical .... **Clusìidae**		p. 598
78′.	At most 2 pairs of fronto-orbitals (Figure 461 B); second antennal segment without an angular projection on outer side; arista subbasal (Figure 461 B); small flies, rarely over 5 mm in length, usually shining black or metallic bluish 79		
79(78′).	Postverticals diverging; 2A not reaching wing margin (Figure 459 B) .... **Piophílidae**		p. 596
79′.	Postverticals converging; 2A variable 80*		
80(79′).	2A reaching wing margin; 1 pair of fronto-orbitals (*Borborópsis* and *Oldenbergiélla,* western Canada and Alaska) .... **Heleomỳzidae***		p. 598
80′.	2A not reaching wing margin; 2 pairs of fronto-orbital bristles; widely distributed .... **Chyromỳidae***		p. 599
81(72′).	Costa broken only near humeral cross vein; eyes with microscopic pubescence; postverticals widely separated and diverging... **Acartophthálmidae***		p. 598
81′.	Costa entire, broken only near end of Sc, or broken near end of Sc and near humeral cross vein; postverticals variable 82		
82(81′).	R_5 cell closed or much narrowed apically (Figure 459 C); legs usually long, slender, and stiltlike 83		
82′.	R_5 cell open and usually not narrowed distally, if narrower apically then the legs are not unusually long and slender 86		
83(82).	Proboscis long and slender, often elbowed; abdomen often clavate (Figure 502); anal cell long and pointed (except in *Stylogáster,* in which it is very short, and the ovipositor is slender and as long as the rest of the body)		

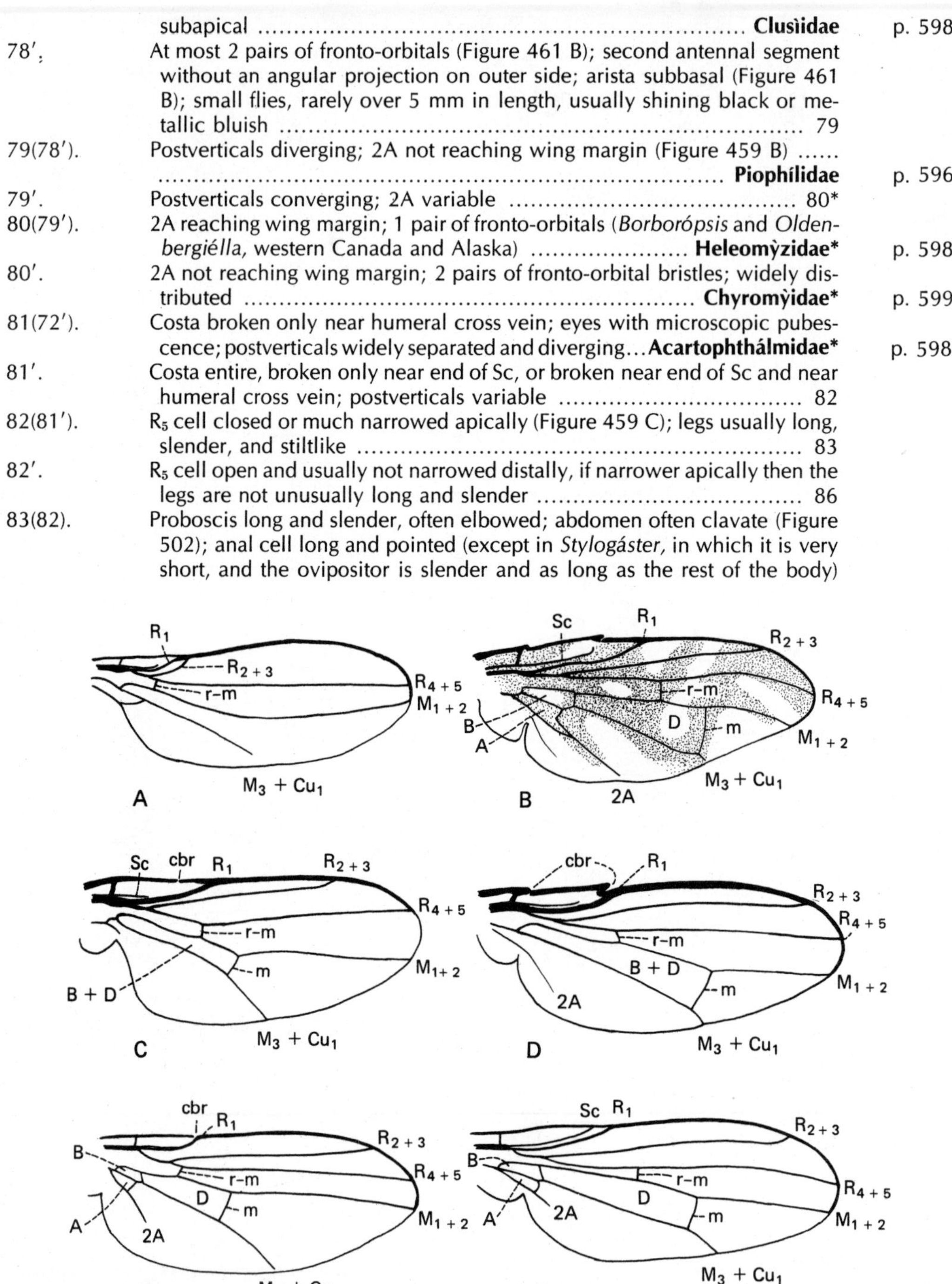

Figure 460. Wings of acalyptrate muscoid flies. A, Asteìidae (*Astèia*) (redrawn from Curran); B, Tephrítidae; C, Chlorópidae (*Epichlòrops*); D, Ephýdridae (*Éphydra*); E, Agromỳzidae (*Agromỳza*); F, Chamaemyìidae (*Chamaemỳia*). *A,* anal cell; *B,* second basal cell; *cbr,* costal break; *D,* discal (first M_2) cell.

	.... **Conópidae**	p. 591
83′.	Proboscis short, usually thick, not as above 84	
84(83′, 111).	Arista apical (Figure 461 I); southwestern United States .... **Nerìidae***	p. 592
84′.	Arista dorsal; widely distributed 85	
85(84′).	Head in profile higher than long; anal cell rounded apically; no sternopleural bristles .... **Tanypèzidae***	p. 592
85′.	Head in profile as long as or longer than high; anal cell square or pointed apically; 1 sternopleural bristle or none .... **Micropèzidae**	p. 592
86(82′).	Eyes prominently bulging, vertex sunken; femora sometimes enlarged;	

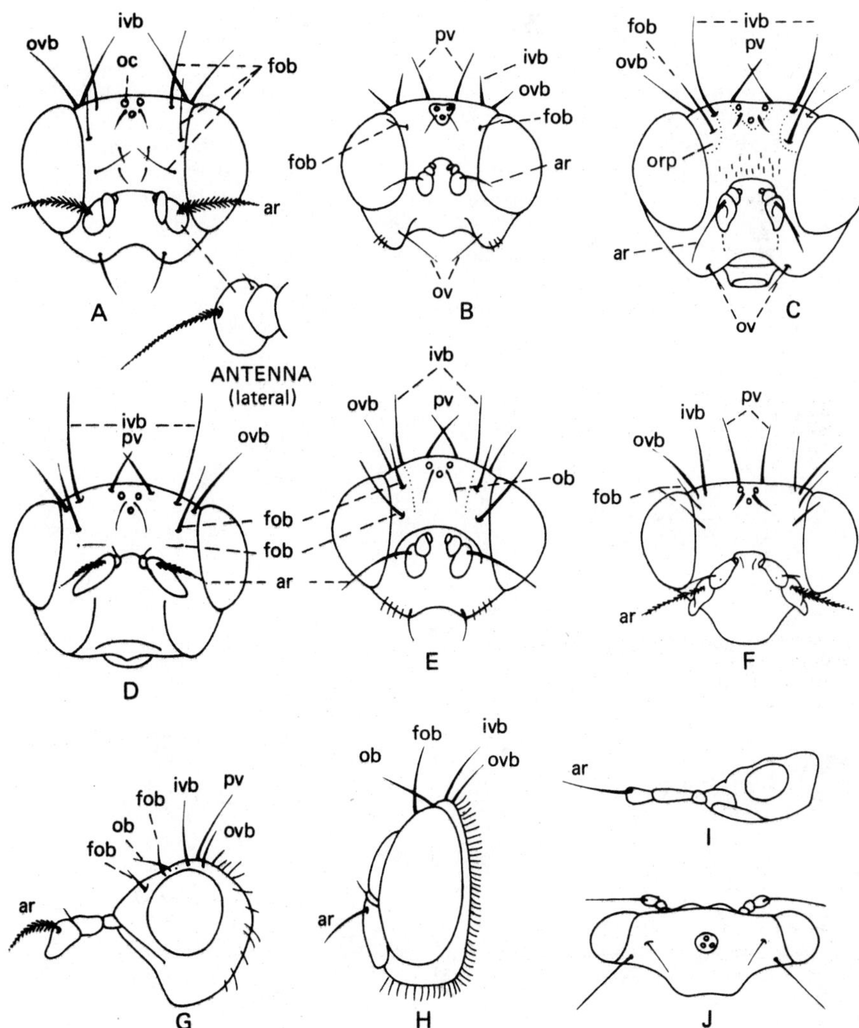

Figure 461. Heads of acalyptrate muscoid flies. A–F, anterior views; G–I, lateral views; J, dorsal view. A, Clusìidae (*Clùsia*); B, Piophílidae (*Pióphila*); C, Heleomỳzidae (*Heleomỳza*); D, Lauxanìidae (*Camptoprosopélla*); E, Chamaemyìidae (*Chamaemỳia*); F, G, Sciomỳzidae (*Tetanócera*); H, Lonchaèidae (*Lonchaèa*); I, Nerìidae (*Odontoloxòzus*); J, Diópsidae (*Sphyracéphala*). *ar,* arista; *fob,* fronto-orbial bristles; *ivb,* inner vertical bristles; *ob,* ocellar bristles; *oc,* ocellus; *orp,* orbital plate; *ov,* oral vibrissae; *ovb,* outer vertical bristles; *pv,* postvertical bristles.

medium-sized tropical flies, usually dark brown with yellowish markings 87*

86′. Eyes not prominently bulging, vertex not sunken; widely distributed ... 88

87(86). R_1 ending far beyond Sc; R_5 cell narrowed distally; no cross veins between R_{2+3} and costa; posterior spiracle of thorax with 1 or more bristles; Florida .... **Ropaloméridae*** p. 593

87′. R_1 ending close to Sc; R_5 cell not narrowed distally; a series of cross veins between R_{2+3} and costa (in our species); posterior spiracle of thorax without bristles; Arizona and New Mexico .... **Rhinotòridae*** p. 599

88(86′). Some or all tibiae with 1 or more preapical dorsal bristles (Figure 463 B); costa entire (Figure 459 D, G); body usually light-colored, at least in part 89

88′. Tibiae usually without preapical dorsal bristles; if such bristles are present then either the ovipositor is long and sclerotized, or R is setulose above, or the vein forming the distal end of the anal cell is bent (Figure 459 F); costa entire or broken near end of Sc 92

89(88). Postverticals converging (Figure 461 D); 2A short, not reaching wing margin (Figure 459 D); small flies, rarely over 6 mm in length .... **Lauxanìidae** p. 595

89′. Postverticals parallel, diverging, or absent; 2A reaching wing margin, at least as a fold 90

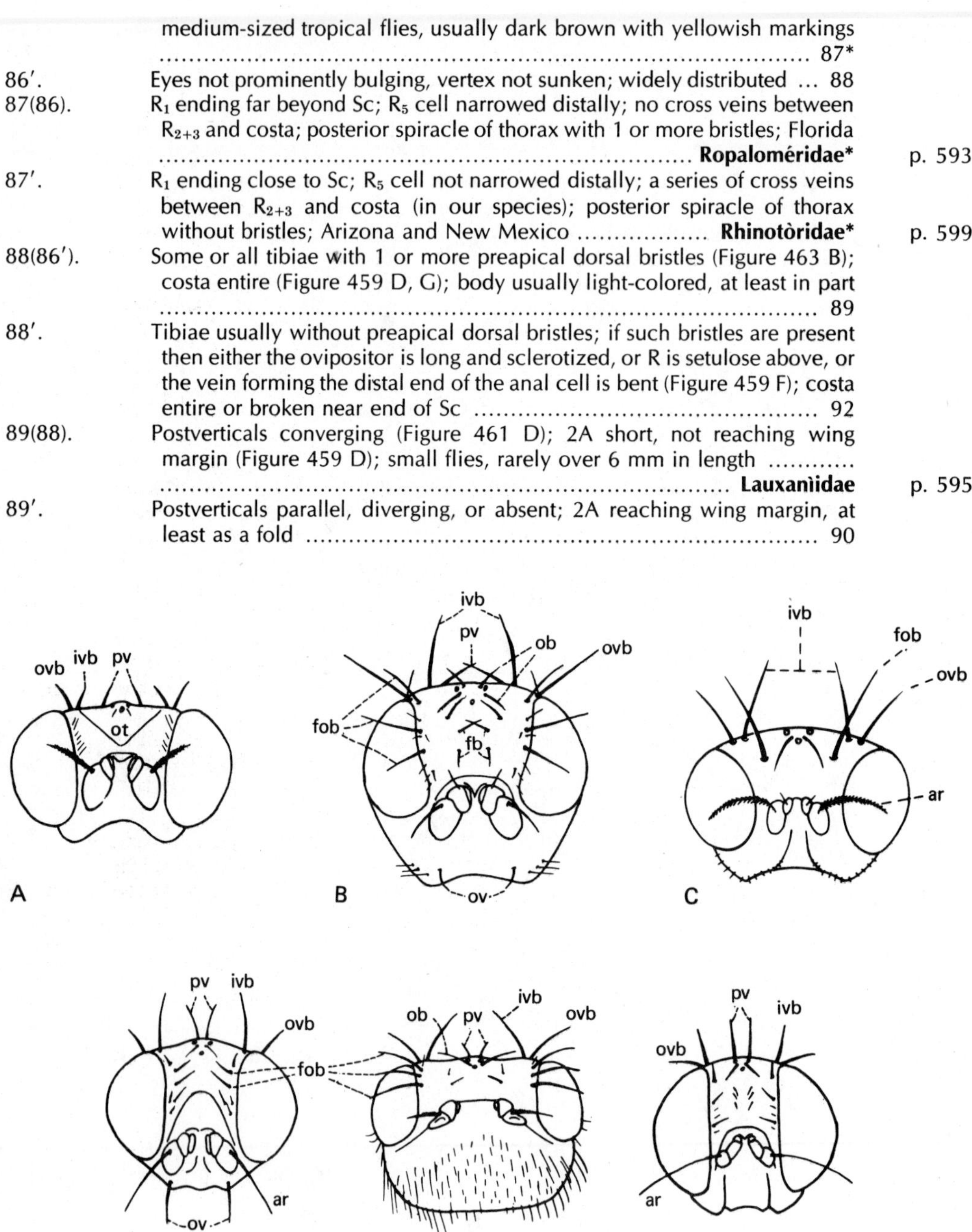

Figure 462. Heads of acalyptrate muscoid flies, anterior view. A, Chlorópidae (*Diplotóxa*); B, Tethínidae (*Tethìna*); C, Opomỳzidae (*Opomỳza*); D, Agromỳzidae (*Agromỳza*); E, Ephýdridae (*Éphydra*); F, Milichìidae (*Milíchia*). *ar,* arista; *fb,* frontal bristles; *fob,* fronto-orbital bristles; *ivb,* inner vertical bristles; *ob,* ocellar bristles; *ot,* ocellar triangle; *ov,* oral vibrissae; *ovb,* outer vertical bristles; *pv,* postvertical bristles.

90(89′). Femora with bristles, and a characteristic bristle usually present near middle of anterior face of middle femur (Figures 463 B and 510); R_1 ending at middle of wing (Figure 459 G); antennae usually projecting forward, and the face generally produced (Figure 461 G); mostly moderate-sized flies, brownish in color with patterned wings .... **Sciomỳzidae** p. 595

90′. Femoral bristles not developed; R_1 ending beyond middle of wing; antennae usually not projecting forward 91*

91(90′). Third antennal segment rounded (in profile); antennae separated; palps without apical bristles; oral margin not protruding .... **Helcomỳzidae*** p. 593

91′. Third antennal segment longer than wide (in profile), more or less flattened laterally; antennae not separated; palps with an apical bristle; oral margin protruding .... **Dryomỳzidae*** p. 595

92(88′). Head more or less produced laterally, in dorsal view at least 3 times as wide as long, with the antennae widely separated (Figure 461 J); scutellum bituberculate; front femora much swollen .... **Diópsidae*** p. 592

92′. Head not so produced laterally, the antennae close together; scutellum not bituberculate; femora usually not swollen 93

93(92′). Ocelli present 94

93′. Ocelli absent; medium-sized to large flies, often with considerable coloring in the wings (Figure 504) .... **Pyrgòtidae*** p. 592

94(93). Cu_2 bent distad in middle, anal cell with an acute distal projection posteriorly (Figures 459 F and 460 B); wings usually patterned 95

94′. Cu_2 straight or curved basad, anal cell without an acute distal projection posteriorly (Figure 459 E); wing color variable 96

95(94). Sc apically bent toward costa at almost a right angle, and usually ending before reaching costa (Figure 460 B); costa broken near end of Sc .... **Tephrítidae** p. 593

95′. Sc apically bent toward costa at a less abrupt angle and usually reaching costa (Figure 459 F); costa not broken near end of Sc .... **Otítidae** p. 592

96(94′). Costa broken near end of Sc 97

96′. Costa not broken near end of Sc (Figures 459 E, F and 460 F) 102

97(96). Sc apically bent toward costa at almost a right angle, and usually ending before reaching costa (Figure 460 B); wings usually patterned (Figures 505 A and 506) .... **Tephrítidae** p. 593

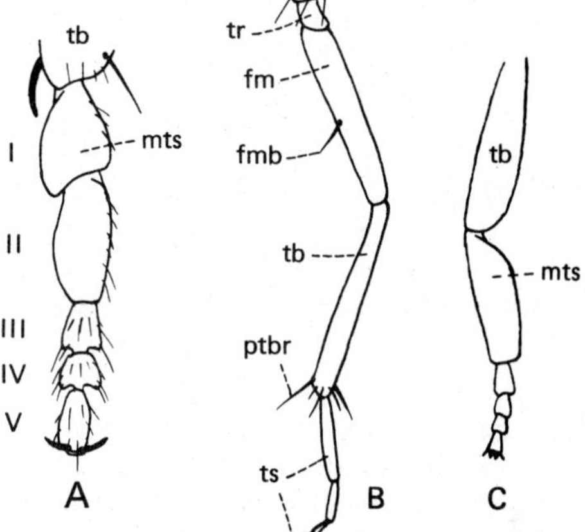

Figure 463. A, hind tarsus of *Copromỳza* (Sphaerocéridae); B, middle leg of *Tetanócera* (Sciomỳzidae); C, hind leg of *Agathomỳia* (Platypèzidae). *cx*, coxa; *fm*, femur; *fmb*, femoral bristle; *mts*, first tarsal segment; *ptbr*, preapical tibial bristles; *tb*, tibia; *tr*, trochanter; *ts*, tarsus; *I–V*, tarsal segments.

97′.	Sc apically bent toward costa at a less abrupt angle, and usually reaching costa 98	
98(97′).	Second abdominal segment usually with lateral bristles; femora often thickened and spinose; wings usually patterned .... **Richardìidae***	p. 592
98′.	Second abdominal segment without lateral bristles; femora not thickened 99	
99(98′).	Three to five pairs of fronto-orbitals; postverticals diverging; seashore species .... **Canacèidae***	p. 597
99′.	Only 1 pair of fronto-orbitals; postverticals parallel or diverging; widely distributed 100	
100(99′).	Head hemispherical in profile, eyes large and oval or semicircular (Figure 461 H); third antennal segment elongate (Figure 461 H); postverticals diverging; 2A usually sinuate; small, shining blackish flies .. **Lonchaèidae**	p. 596
100′.	Head more or less rounded in profile, eyes smaller and rounded or slightly oval; postverticals parallel or slightly divergent; 2A not sinuate; pale-colored flies, or with yellow or reddish markings 101*	
101(100′).	Costa spinose (as in Figure 459 A, H); eyes oval; Arizona and California .... **Thyreophòridae***	p. 596
101′.	Costa not spinose; eyes round; northern United States and Canada .... **Palloptéridae***	p. 596
102(96′).	Postverticals converging (Figure 461 E) or absent; R_1 bare above; small flies, usually gray in color .... **Chamaemyìidae**	p. 596
102′.	Postverticals diverging (sometimes very small and difficult to see); R_1 bare or setulose above; small to medium-sized flies, usually dark and shining 103	
103(102′).	Eyes horizontally oval, about twice as long as high; length 1.5–2.5 mm; grayish flies with yellowish markings on sides of thorax and abdomen and on front; recorded from New Mexico, Oregon, New Brunswick, and Newfoundland (*Cremifània*) .... **Chamaemyìidae***	p. 596
103′.	Not exactly fitting the above description 104	
104(103′).	Anal cell relatively long, its anterior side more than one fourth as long as posterior side of discal cell (Figure 459 E); sternopleural bristle lacking; propleural bristle weak or lacking; R_1 setulose above .... **Platystomátidae**	p. 592
104′.	Anal cell shorter, its anterior side usually less than one fourth as long as posterior side of discal cell; sternopleural bristles usually present; propleural bristle sometimes developed; R_1 bare or setulose above .... **Otítidae**	p. 592
105(69′).	Sc apically bent toward costa at almost a right angle, fading out beyond the bend (Figure 460 B); anal cell usually with an acute distal projection posteriorly; wings generally patterned (Figures 505 A and 506) .... **Tephrítidae**	p. 593
105′.	Sc and anal cell not as above; wing color variable 106	
106(105′).	Basal segment of hind tarsi short and swollen, shorter than second segment (Figure 463 A); small black or brown flies .... **Sphaerocéridae**	p. 596
106′.	Basal segment of hind tarsi normal, not swollen, and usually longer than second segment 107	
107(106′).	R_{2+3} short, ending in costa close to or with R_1 (Figure 460 A); postverticals diverging .... **Asteìidae***	p. 599
107′.	R_{2+3} longer, ending in costa beyond middle of wing (Figure 460 C–F); postverticals variable 108	
108(107′).	Third antennal segment large, reaching almost to lower edge of head; arista absent, but a short spine or tubercle at apex of third antennal segment; eyes large, vertically elongate; small, dark-colored flies, less than 2 mm in	

length; California .... **Cryptochètidae*** p. 600
108′. Arista present; third antennal segment not as above 109
109(108′). Costa entire (Figure 460 F); oral vibrissae absent 110
109′. Costa broken near end of Sc, sometimes also near humeral cross vein (Figure 460 D); oral vibrissae variable 112
110(109). Arista plumose; postverticals divergent .... **Periscelídidae*** p. 596
110′. Arista bare or pubescent; postverticals usually convergent 111
111(110′). R_5 cell narrowed apically; legs long and slender 84
111′. R_5 cell not narrowed apically; legs not unusually long and slender; length usually less than 7 mm .... **Chamaemyìidae** p. 596
112(109′). Costa broken only near end of Sc or R_1 (Figure 460 C, E) 113
112′. Costa broken near end of Sc or R_1, and also near humeral cross vein (Figure 460 D) 123
113(112). Anal cell absent (Figure 460 C); ocellar triangle large (Figure 462 A); postverticals converging or absent .... **Chlorópidae** p. 598
113′. Anal cell present (Figure 460 E); ocellar triangle and postverticals variable 114
114(113′). Costa spinose (as in Figure 459 A, H); oral vibrissae present; postverticals converging; orbital plates long, reaching nearly to level of antennae; usually with 2 pairs of fronto-orbitals that are reclinate or lateroclinate .... **Trixoscelídidae*** p. 599
114′. Costa not spinose; other characters variable 115
115(114′). Postverticals diverging; oral vibrissae present or absent 116
115′. Postverticals converging; oral vibrissae present but often weak (see also 115″) 120
115″. Postverticals and oral vibrissae absent 122
116(115). Ocellar triangle large and shining, reaching nearly to base of antennae (as in Figure 462 A); oral vibrissae present; small flies, not over 3.5 mm in length, occurring along seashore .... **Canacèidae*** p. 597
116′. Ocellar triangle short; other characters variable 117
117(116′). Oral vibrissae present (Figure 462 D), but sometimes weak 118
117′. Oral vibrissae absent .... **Psìlidae** p. 592
118(117). Wings strongly narrowed at base, anal angle not distinct (*Geomỳza*) .... **Opomỳzidae*** p. 599
118′. Wings not strongly narrowed at base, anal angle well developed 119
119(118′). Wings patterned; preapical tibial bristles usually present; 2 reclinate and 1 inclinate pairs of fronto-orbitals .... **Odinìidae*** p. 598
119′. Wings not patterned; preapical tibial bristles absent; fronto-orbitals usually not as above .... **Agromỳzidae** p. 598
120(115′). Wings strongly narrowed at base, anal angle not distinct (*Geomỳza*) .... **Opomỳzidae*** p. 599
120′. Wings not strongly narrowed at base, anal angle well developed 121
121(120′). All fronto-orbitals directed outward (Figure 462 B); presutural dorsocentrals present; mostly seashore species .... **Tethìnidae*** p. 597
121′. At least 1 pair of fronto-orbitals reclinate; presutural dorsocentrals absent .... **Anthomỳzidae** p. 599
122(115″). Sternopleural bristle present; sometimes with a spur on apical section of M_{1+2} extending into second posterior cell (*Opomỳza*) .... **Opomỳzidae*** p. 599
122′. Sternopleural bristle absent; M_{1+2} without a spur in apical section .. **Psìlidae** p. 592
123(112′). Anal cell lacking (Figure 460 D); postverticals small and diverging, or absent; oral vibrissae usually absent .... **Ephýdridae** p. 597
123′. Anal cell present; postverticals nearly always well developed and converging; oral vibrissae present and usually well developed 124
124(123′). A pair of lower fronto-orbitals bent inward (Figure 462 F); oral vibrissae

weakly differentiated .... **Milichìidae** p. 597

124′. No fronto-orbitals bent inward (Figure 443 A); oral vibrissae usually well differentiated 125

125(124′). Costa spinose (Figure 459 A); arista long-plumose; proclinate fronto-orbital in front of reclinate one, both remote from eye; mesopleura with bristles .... **Curtonòtidae*** p. 597

125′. Not exactly fitting the above description 126

126(125′). Mesopleura with bristles; arista usually short-plumose or pubescent; sternopleural bristles present or absent 127*

126′. Mesopleura without bristles; arista usually long-plumose (Figure 443 A); sternopleural bristle present .... **Drosophílidae** p. 597

127(126). Sternopleural bristle present; body not metallic .... **Diastátidae*** p. 597

127′. Sternopleural bristle absent; body metallic .... **Camíllidae*** p. 597

128(1′). Antennae 5-segmented, the third segment large, club-shaped, and annulated basally; head elongate, mouth parts vestigial; legs long, slender, and widely separated; wings probably vestigial (see page 568); length less than 2 mm; found in rapid streams in New Brunswick ..... **Nymphomyìidae*** p. 568

128′. Not exactly fitting the above description 129*

129(128′). Compound eyes consisting of a single facet; head and thorax small and well sclerotized; abdomen much enlarged, weakly sclerotized, and indistinctly segmented; antennae thick, 8-segmented; length 3.4 mm; occurring in forest leaf litter in Virginia .... **Baeonòtidae*** p. 580

129′. Compound eyes many-faceted, and otherwise not exactly fitting the above description 130*

130(129′). Coxae widely separated (Figure 453 A); abdominal segmentation sometimes obscure; ectoparasites of birds, mammals, or the honey bee ... 131*

130′. Coxae usually contiguous; abdomen distinctly segmented; usually not ectoparasitic 134*

131(130). Mesonotum short, resembling the abdominal segments; scutellum absent; antennae inserted in lateral grooves; parasitic on honey bees .... **Braùlidae*** p. 596

131′. Thorax and abdomen differentiated; scutellum present; parasitic on birds or mammals 132*

132(131′). Head small and narrow, folding back into a groove on mesonotum; spiderlike insects parasitic on bats .... **Nycteribìidae*** p. 602

132′. Head not folding back into a groove on mesonotum 133*

133(132′). Head fitting into an emargination of thorax; palps elongate and forming a sheath for the proboscis; eyes round .... **Hippobóscidae*** p. 602

133′. Head with a fleshy movable neck; palps broad, projecting leaflike in front of head; eyes vestigial or absent .... **Stréblidae*** p. 602

134(130′). Antennae consisting of 6 or more freely articulated segments; palps usually segmented 135*

134′. Antennae consisting of 3 or fewer segments; palps not segmented 140*

135(134). Mesonotum with a **V**-shaped suture (as in Figure 464); female with a long sclerotized ovipositor (*Chiònea, Limnóphila*) .... **Tipùlidae*** p. 567

135′. Mesonotum without a **V**-shaped suture; female without a sclerotized ovipositor 136*

136(135′). Halteres present 137*

136′. Halteres absent (females of *Pnýxia*) .... **Sciáridae*** p. 577

137(136). Eyes meeting above antennae; 2 or 3 ocelli present ...... **Cecidomyìidae*** p. 578

137′. Eyes not meeting above antennae; ocelli present or absent 138*

138(137′). Ocelli present; hind femora extending to about middle of abdomen 139*

138′.	Ocelli absent; hind femora extending to about end of abdomen (*Eretmóptera*, California) .... **Chironómidae***	p. 574
139(138).	Tibiae with apical spurs (female of *Baeopterogỳna*, Yukon Territory and Alaska) .... **Mycetophílidae***	p. 577
139′.	Tibiae without apical spurs (*Scatópse*, widely distributed) .. **Scatópsidae***	p. 578
140(134′).	Antennae apparently consisting of a single globular segment, more or less sunk in cavities in head; hind femora robust and laterally flattened .... **Phòridae***	p. 589
140′.	Antennae 2- or 3-segmented; hind femora not laterally flattened ... 141*	
141(140′).	Frontal suture present; third antennal segment more or less ovate, with a dorsal arista 142*	
141′.	Frontal suture absent; third antennal segment more or less tapering, without an arista (*Chersodròmia*) .... **Empídidae***	p. 586
142(141).	First segment of hind tarsi short and swollen, shorter than second segment (Figure 463 A); free-living, not parasitic on birds (some *Leptócera*) .... **Sphaerocéridae***	p. 596
142′.	First segment of hind tarsi not swollen, and longer than second segment; ectoparasitic on birds (*Cárnus*) .... **Milichìidae***	p. 597

SUBORDER **Nematócera:** This suborder contains a little less than one third of the North American species of flies, in 24 of the 107 families. Its members can be recognized by their many-segmented antennae, which are usually long; most nematocerans are small, slender, and long-legged, and are midgelike or mosquitolike in appearance. The wing venation varies from greatly reduced (in the Cecidomyìidae) to very complete (some crane flies); this suborder contains the only Díptera that have the radius 5-branched. The larvae have a well-developed head, with the mandibles moving laterally, and most of them live in water or in moist habitats; the pupae are of the obtect type.

This group contains many flies of economic importance. Many are blood-sucking and serious pests of man and animals (mosquitoes, punkies, black flies, and sand flies), and some of these serve as disease vectors. A few flies in this suborder (some Cecidomyìidae) are important pests of cultivated plants. The aquatic larvae of the Nematócera are an important item in the food of many freshwater fishes.

Family **Trichocéridae**—Winter Crane Flies: The members of this group are slender, medium-sized flies that are usually seen in the fall or early spring, and some may be seen on mild days in winter. They may be found in large swarms out-of-doors, or in cellars or caves. The larvae occur in decaying vegetable matter.

Family **Tipùlidae**—Crane Flies: This family is the largest in the order, with over 1450 species occurring in this country, and many of its members are common and abundant insects. Most of the tipulids resemble overgrown mosquitoes with extremely long legs, or daddy-long-legs with wings (Figure 464); the legs are very easily broken off. Some species are fairly large, reaching 25 mm or more in length, and have patterned wings. The members of this family differ from the Trichocéridae in that they lack ocelli; from the Tanydéridae

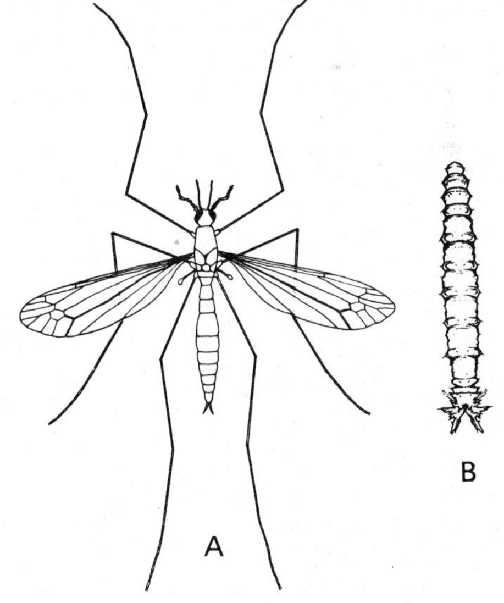

Figure 464. Crane fly (*Típula* sp., family Tipùlidae). A, adult; B, larva, 1½ ×. (B, courtesy of Johannsen and the Cornell University Agricultural Experiment Station.)

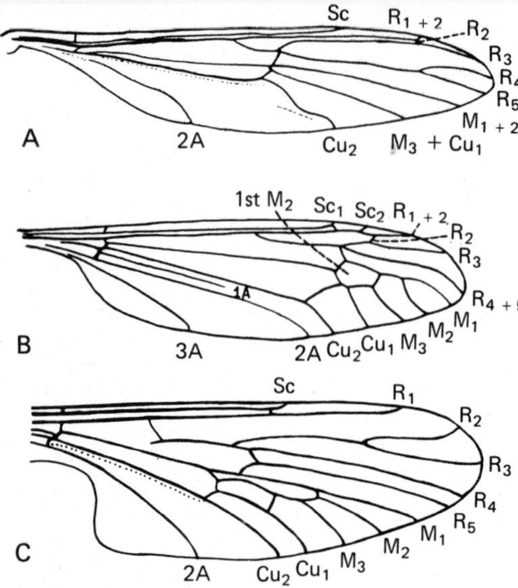

Figure 465. Wings of crane flies. A, *Bittacomórpha* (Ptychoptéridae); B, *Típula* (Tipùlidae); C, *Protoplàsa* (Tanydèridae).

in that they have fewer than five radial branches; and from the Ptychoptéridae in that they have two anal veins (Figure 465).

Crane flies occur chiefly in damp situations where there is abundant vegetation. The larvae of most species are aquatic or semiaquatic and feed on decaying vegetable matter; a few feed on living plant tissue and may damage cultivated plants, and a few are predaceous. Little is known of the feeding habits of the adults, but some possess a long slender proboscis and are known to feed on nectar. Crane flies do not bite man.

Three subfamilies of crane flies occur in North America: the Tipulìnae, Cylindrotomìnae, and Limoniìnae. The Tipulìnae have the terminal segment of the maxillary palps elongated and whiplashlike and the antennae usually 13-segmented, while the other two subfamilies have the terminal segment of the maxillary palps short and the antennae usually 14- to 16-segmented. The Tipulìnae are mostly large crane flies; most members of the other two subfamilies are medium-sized to small. The Cylindrotomìnae are a very small (nine North American species) group seldom encountered; the vast majority of the smaller crane flies (plus a few large ones) belong to the Limoniìnae.

Family **Tanydéridae**—Primitive Crane Flies: The tanyderids are represented in North America by four species, of which one, *Protoplàsa fítchii* Osten Sacken, occurs in the East. The tanyderids are medium-sized flies with banded wings, and their larval stages occur in wet, sandy soil at the margins of streams.

Family **Psychòdidae**—Moth Flies and Sand Flies: The psychodids are small to minute, usually very hairy, mothlike flies; the more common species (Psychodìnae) hold the wings rooflike over the body. The adults occur in moist shady places; they are sometimes extremely abundant in drains or sewers. The larvae occur in decaying vegetable matter, mud, moss, or water.

Most of the northern species in this family (for example, Psychodìnae) are harmless to man, but the species in the genus *Phlebótomus* (Phlebotomìnae), often called sand flies, are blood sucking; these occur in the southern states and in the tropics. Sand flies are known to act as vectors of several diseases in various parts of the world: pappataci fever (caused by a virus), which occurs principally in the Mediterranean region and in southern Asia; kala-azar and oriental sore (caused by leishmania organisms), which occur in South America, northern Africa, and southern Asia; espundia (caused by a leishmania), which occurs in South America; and oroya fever or verruga peruana (caused by a bartonella organism), which occurs in South America.

Family **Ptychoptéridae**—Phantom Crane Flies: A fairly common species in this family, *Bittacomórpha clávipes* (Fabricius), has the long legs banded with black and white, and the first segment of the tarsi is conspicuously swollen. These flies often drift with the wind, with the long legs extended. Other species in this family (for example, *Ptychóptera*) resemble large fungus gnats. The larvae of the phantom crane flies live in the decaying vegetable matter in marshes and swampy woods.

Family **Nymphomyìidae:** Our only representative of this family is *Palaeodípteron walkeri* Ide, which has been collected in a stream in New Brunswick. It is a pale, delicate insect, 1.4–1.7 mm long, with the wings represented by small scales (or the wings may have been broken off), the halteres well developed, and the body and legs long and slender. The eyes are separated dorsally and contiguous ventrally, and there is a

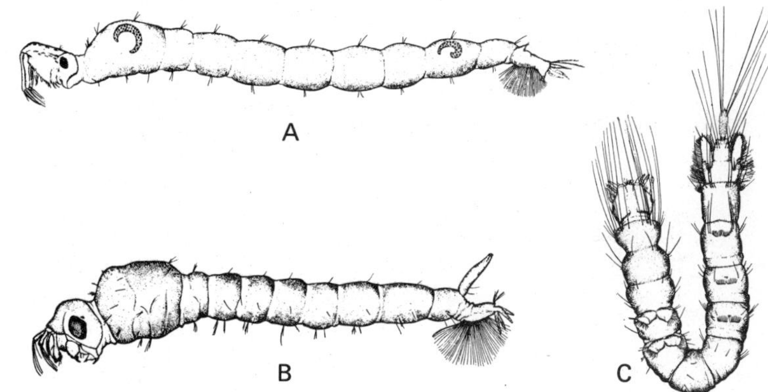

Figure 466. Larvae of phantom (A–B) and dixid (C) midges. A, *Chaóborus flávicans* (Meigen); B, *Mochlónyx cínctipes* (Coquillett); C, *Dixa alíciae* Johannsen. (Courtesy of Johannsen and the Cornell University Agricultural Experiment Station.)

single ocellus on each side of the head beneath the compound eye. The larvae are unknown, but are presumed to be aquatic.

Family **Blepharicéridae**—Net-Winged Midges: These midges are long-legged, mosquitolike insects that have the anal angle of the wing well developed (Figure 445 J), and sometimes have a network of fine lines between the wing veins. They are found near fast-flowing streams, but are not common. The larvae live in swift water, clinging to rocks by means of a series of ventral suckers.

Family **Deuterophlebìidae**—Mountain Midges: These midges are peculiar in having broad fanlike wings, and the males have extremely long antennae. Four species of *Deuterophlèbia* are known from the West (California to Alberta), where the larvae occur in swift-flowing mountain streams.

Family **Díxidae**—Dixid Midges: The dixids are small, long-legged, mosquitolike insects that are similar to mosquitoes in wing venation but lack the scales on the wings; the adults do not bite. The larvae (Figure 466 C) are aquatic and are somewhat similar to the larvae of *Anópheles* mosquitoes, but do not have the thorax enlarged; they usually feed at the surface of the water like anopheline larvae, but the usual position is with the body bent into a **U**, and they move by alternately straightening and bending the body. The larvae feed on algae.

Family **Chaobòridae**—Phantom Midges: These insects are very similar to mosquitoes, but differ in having a short proboscis and fewer scales on the wings; they do not bite. The larvae (Figure 466 A, B) are aquatic and predaceous and have the antennae modified into prehensile organs. The larvae of *Chaóborus* (Figure 466 A) are almost transparent, giving rise to the name "phantom midges" for this group. The larvae of some species (for example, *Mochlónyx,* Figure 466 B) have a breathing tube and are very similar to mosquito larvae in appearance; others (for example, *Chaóborus*) do not have a mosquitolike breathing tube. The larvae occur in various sorts of pools, and are sometimes very abundant; they frequently destroy large numbers of mosquito larvae. This group is a small one (18 North American species), but its members are fairly common insects.

Family **Culícidae**—Mosquitoes: This family is a large, abundant, well-known, and important group of flies. The larval stages are aquatic, and the adults can be recognized by the characteristic wing venation (Figure 445 I), the scales along the wing veins, and the long proboscis. Mosquitoes

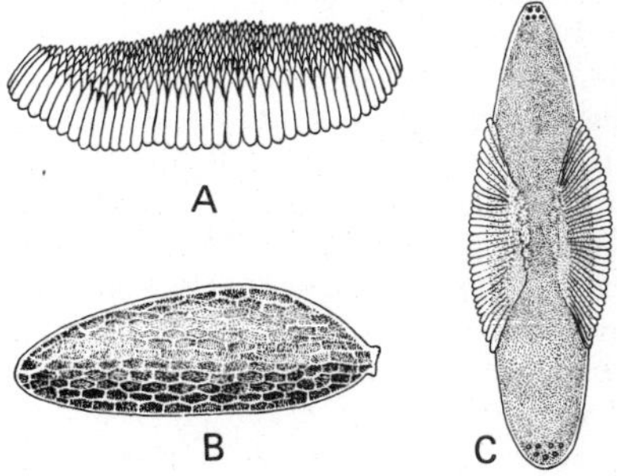

Figure 467. Eggs of mosquitoes. A, egg raft of *Cùlex réstuans* Theobald; B, egg of *Aèdes taeniorhýnchus* (Wiedemann); C, egg of *Anópheles quadrimaculàtus* Say, showing floats. (Courtesy of USDA, after Howard, Dyar, and Knab.)

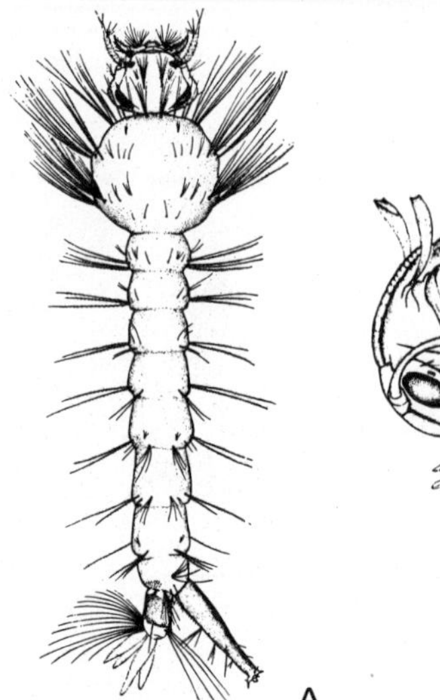

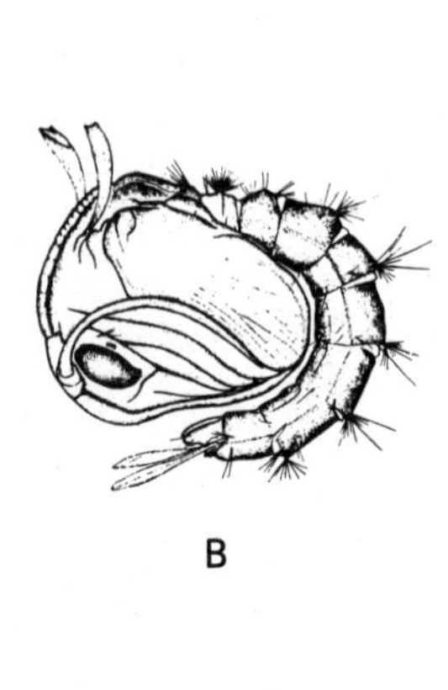

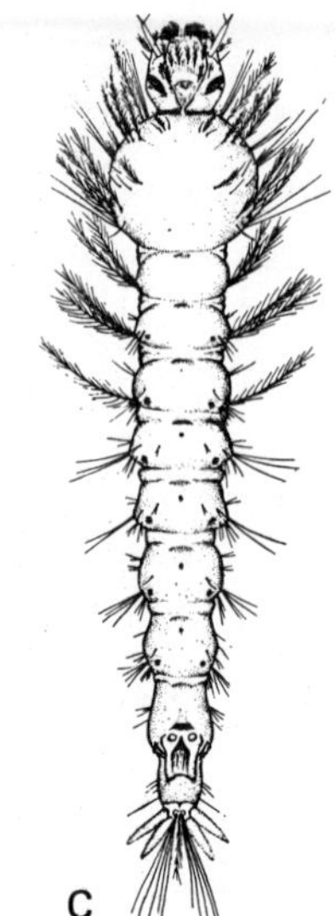

Figure 468. Larvae and pupa of mosquitoes. A, larva of *Cùlex pípiens* L.; B, pupa of *C. pípiens;* C, larva of *Anópheles punctipénnis* (Say). (After Johanssen, courtesy of the Cornell University Agricultural Experiment Station.)

are very important from the standpoint of human welfare because the females are blood-sucking, many species bite man, and they serve as vectors in the transmission of several important human diseases.

Mosquito larvae (Figure 468 A, C), or wrigglers, occur in a variety of aquatic situations—in ponds and pools of various sorts, in the water in artificial containers, in tree holes, and in other situations—but each species usually occurs only in a particular type of aquatic habitat. The eggs (Figure 467) are laid on the surface of the water, either in "rafts" (*Cùlex*) or singly (*Anópheles*), or near water (*Aèdes*). In the latter case the eggs usually hatch when flooded. The larvae of most species feed on algae and organic debris, but a few are predaceous and feed on other mosquito larvae. Mosquito larvae breathe principally at the suface. usually through a breathing tube at the posterior end of the body. The larvae of *Anópheles* lack a breathing tube and breathe through a pair of spiracular plates at the posterior end of the body.

Mosquito pupae (Figure 468 B) are also aquatic, and unlike most insect pupae, are quite active and are often called tumblers. They breathe at the surface of the water through a pair of small trumpetlike structures on the thorax.

Most adult mosquitoes do not travel far from the water in which they spent their larval stage. *Aèdes aegýpti* (L.), the vector of yellow fever and dengue, seldom travels more than a few hundred yards from where it emerges. Some species of *Anópheles* may range as far as a mile from where they emerge. On the other hand, some of the salt-marsh mosquitoes (for example, *Aèdes sollícitans* (Walker), Figure 472 A) may be found many miles from the larval habitat. Adult mosquitoes usually are active during the twilight hours or at night, or in dense shade; many spend the day in hollow trees, under culverts, or in similar resting places. Some adults overwinter in such places. Only the female mosquitoes are blood-sucking; the males (and occasionally also the females) feed on nectar and other plant juices.

The sexes of most mosquitoes can be easily determined by the form of the antennae (Figure 469); the antennae of the males are very plumose, while those of the females have only a few short hairs. In most mosquitoes other than *Anópheles* the maxillary palps are very short in the female (Figure 469 A), but are longer than the proboscis in the male (Figure 469 B); the maxillary palps are long in both sexes of *Anópheles,* but are clubbed in the male (compare Figure 469 C and D).

Most of our mosquitoes (119 of the 148 species recorded from North America) belong to four genera: *Anópheles, Aèdes, Psoróphora,* and *Cùlex.* These genera contain the species most important from man's point of view. Adults of *Anópheles* are rather easily distinguished; the maxillary palps are long in both sexes (Figure 469 C, D) and clubbed in the male (usually short in females of the other genera), the scutellum is evenly rounded (trilobed in the other genera), and the wings are usually spotted (not so in the other genera). The wing spotting in *Anópheles* is due to groups of differently colored scales on the wings. An *Anópheles* mosquito in a resting position has

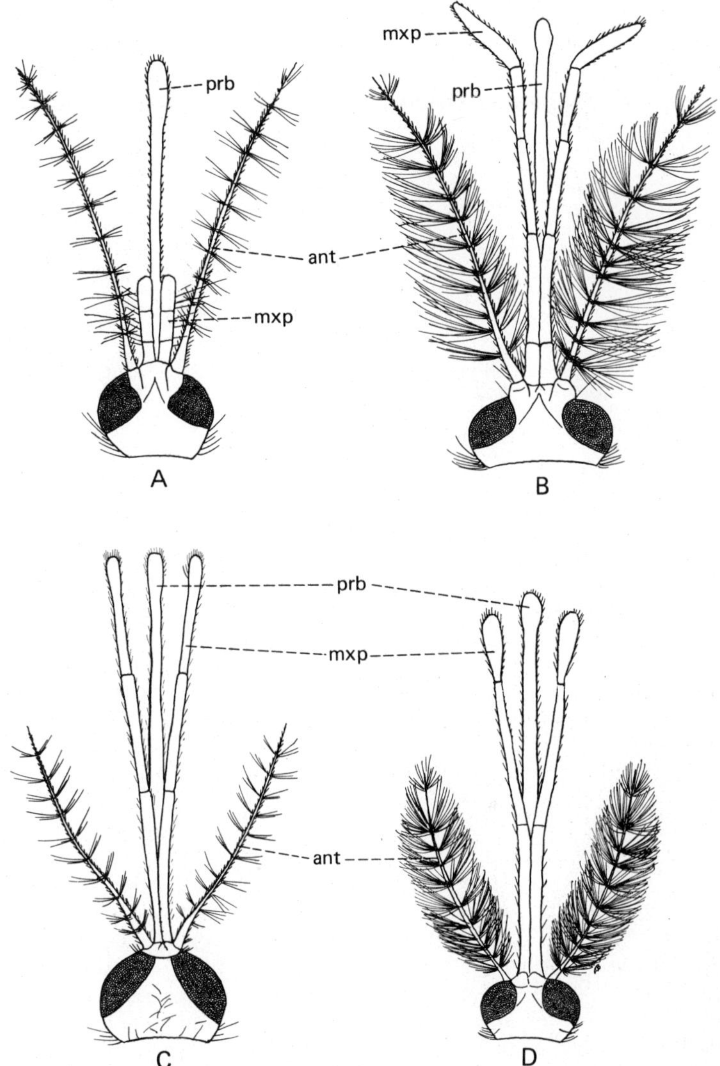

Figure 469. Head structure in mosquitoes, showing sex characters. A, *Aèdes,* female; B, same, male; C, *Anópheles,* female; D, same, male. *ant,* antenna; *mxp,* maxillary palp; *prb,* proboscis.

the body and proboscis in a straight line and at an angle to the surface on which the insect is resting (Figure 470 A, B). Some species seem almost to "stand on their head" in a resting position. Adults of the other genera have the body in a resting position more or less parallel to the surface, with the proboscis bent down (Figure 470 C). Adults of *Psoróphora* have a group of bristles (the spiracular bristles) immediately in front of the mesothoracic spiracle, while those of *Aèdes* and *Cùlex* lack spiracular bristles; *Psoróphora* mosquitoes are relatively large and have long erect scales on the hind tibiae. The best character to separate adults of *Aèdes* and *Cùlex* is the presence (*Aèdes*) or absence (*Cùlex*) of postspiracular bristles (a group of bristles immediately behind the mesothoracic spiracle). The tip of the abdomen of a female *Aèdes* is usually pointed, with the cerci protruding, and the thorax often has white or silvery markings; in *Cùlex* the tip of the female abdomen is generally blunt, with the cerci retracted, and the thorax is usually dull-colored.

The larvae of *Anópheles* differ from those of other mosquitoes in lacking a breathing tube (Figure 468 C), and when at rest they lie parallel to the surface of the water (Figure 471 A); the larvae of

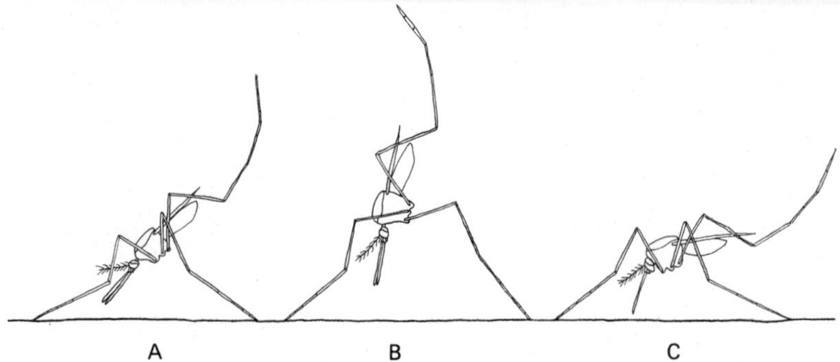

Figure 470. Resting positions of mosquitoes. A, B, *Anópheles;* C, *Cùlex*. (Redrawn from King, Bradley, and McNeel.)

Figure 471. Feeding positions of mosquito larvae. A, *Anópheles;* B, *Cùlex*. (Courtesy of USDA.)

the other three genera have a breathing tube (Figure 468 A), and when at rest have the body at an angle to the surface of the water (Figure 471 B). *Cùlex* larvae have several pairs of hair tufts on the breathing tube, and the tube is relatively long and slender; larvae of *Aèdes* and *Psoróphora* have only a single pair of hair tufts on the breathing tube. The larvae of *Aèdes* and *Psoróphora* usually differ in the sclerotization of the anal segment (the sclerotization going completely around the segment in *Psoróphora* but usually not complete in *Aèdes*). The breathing tube in *Aèdes* larvae is relatively short and stout.

Anópheles larvae occur chiefly in ground pools, marshes, and in places where there is considerable vegetation; the other mosquitoes breed in many places, but the most abundant *Aèdes* and *Psoróphora* mosquitoes breed in woodland pools and salt marshes, and *Cùlex* in artificial containers. The woodland species that are so troublesome early in the season are largely species of *Aèdes* and have a single brood a year. Many species that breed in large bodies of water, borrow pits, or in artificial containers may continue breeding through the season as long as weather conditions are favorable.

Mosquitoes act as vectors of several very important diseases of man: malaria, caused by Protozòa of the genus *Plasmòdium,* and transmitted by certain species of *Anópheles*; yellow fever, caused by a virus and transmitted by *Aèdes aegýpti* (L.); dengue, caused by a virus and transmitted by *Aèdes aegýpti* (L.) and other species of *Aèdes*; filariasis, caused by a filarial worm and transmitted chiefly by species of *Cùlex*; certain types of encephalitis, caused by a virus and transmitted by various species of mosquitoes (chiefly species of *Cùlex* and *Aèdes*).

Control measures against mosquitoes may be aimed at the larvae or at the adults. Measures aimed at the larvae may involve the elimination or modification of the larval habitats (for example, drainage), or may involve the treatment of the larval habitat with insecticides. Measures aimed at the adults may be in the nature of preventives (the use of protective clothing, screening, and the use of repellents), or insecticides (sprays or aerosols).

Family **Thaumalèidae**—Solitary Midges: The members of this group are small (3–4 mm in length), bare, reddish yellow or brownish flies, with the head small and situated low on the

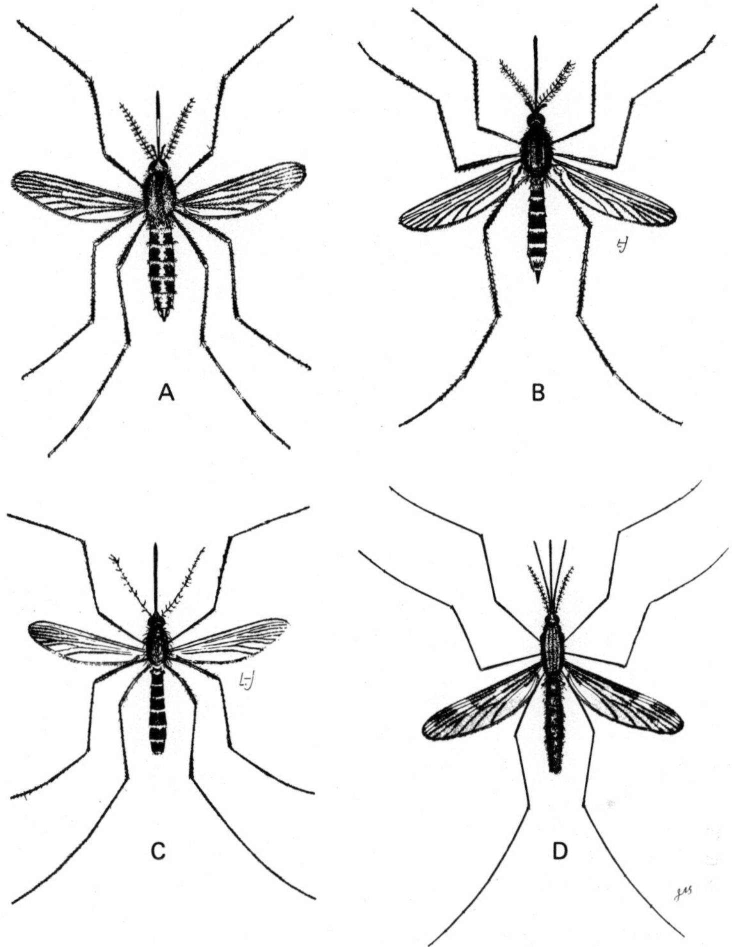

Figure 472. Common mosquitoes. A, saltmarsh mosquito, *Aèdes sollícitans* (Walker); B, a woodland mosquito, *Aèdes stímulans* (Walker); C, house mosquito, *Cùlex pípiens* L.; D, *Anópheles punctipénnis* (Say). (Courtesy of Headlee and the New Jersey Agricultural Experiment Station; after Smith.)

thorax. Only five species occur in North America, and they are quite rare; adults are usually found in the vegetation along streams in which the larvae occur.

Family **Ceratopogónidae**—Biting Midges, Punkies, or No-see-ums: These flies are very small, but are often serious pests because of their bloodsucking habits, particularly along the seashore or along the shores of rivers and lakes. Their small size is responsible for the name "no-see-ums," and their bite is all out of proportion to their size. Many species in this group attack other insects and suck blood from the insect host as an ectoparasite; punkies have been reported from mantids, walking sticks, dragonflies, alderflies, lacewings, certain beetles, certain moths, crane flies, and mosquitoes. Some of the larger species prey on smaller insects. Some species (Figure 473 B) have spotted wings. Most of the punkies that attack man belong to the genera *Culicòides* and *Leptocónops*. These insects apparently do not travel far from the place where the larvae occur, and one may often avoid punkie attacks by simply moving a few yards away.

Punkies are very similar to the midges (Chironómidae), but are generally stouter in build, with the wings broader and held flat over the ab-

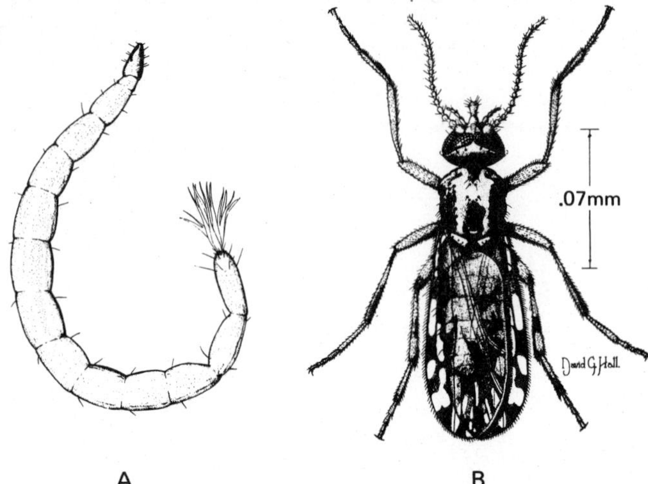

Figure 473. Little gray punkie, *Culicòides fùrens* (Poey) (Ceratopogónidae). A, larva; B, adult female; about 25 ×. (Courtesy of Dove, Hall, and Hull, and the Entomological Society of America.)

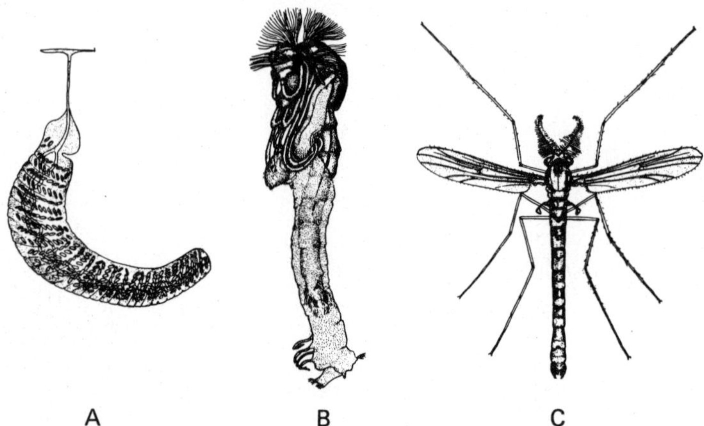

Figure 474. A midge, *Chirónomus plumòsus* (L.). A, egg mass; B, pupa, lateral view, with larval skin not completely shed; C, adult male. (Courtesy of Branch.)

domen at rest; the wings of midges are usually more elongate, and are held rooflike over the abdomen at rest.

The larvae of punkies are aquatic or semiaquatic, occurring in sand, mud, decaying vegetation, and the water in tree holes. Those occurring along the seashore apparently breed in the intertidal zone. The feeding habits of the larvae are not well known, but they are probably scavengers.

Family **Chironómidae**—Midges: These insects are to be found almost everywhere. They are small (some are very small), delicate, somewhat mosquitolike in appearance (Figure 474 C), and the males usually have the antennae very plumose. They often occur in huge swarms, usually in the evening, and the humming of such a swarm may be audible for a considerable distance. This group is large with about 670 North American species.

The larvae of most midges (Figure 475 B) are aquatic; a few occur in decaying matter, under bark, or in moist ground. Most of them are scavengers. Many of the aquatic forms live in tubes or cases. The larvae of some species are red in color, due to the presence of haemoglobin in the blood, and are known as bloodworms. Midge larvae swim by means of characteristic whipping movements of the body, something like the movements of mosquito larvae. Midge larvae are often very abundant and are an important item of food for many freshwater fish and other aquatic animals.

Family **Simulìidae**—Black Flies or Buffalo Gnats: The black flies are small, usually dark-colored insects with short legs, broad wings, and a humpbacked appearance (Figure 476). The females are blood-sucking. These insects are vicious biters and are serious pests in some sections of the country. The bites often cause considerable swelling and sometimes bleeding. Black flies sometimes attack livestock in such numbers and with such ferocity as to cause the death of the livestock, and there are records of human deaths caused by these insects. Black flies have a wide distribution, but are most numerous in the north temperate and subarctic regions; the adults usually appear in late spring and early summer.

Black fly larvae occur in streams, where they attach to stones and other objects by means of a disclike sucker at the posterior end of the body. The larvae (Figure 477 C, G) are somewhat club-shaped, swollen posteriorly, and move about like a measuringworm; their locomotion is aided by silk spun from the mouth. They pupate in cone-shaped cases (Figure 477 B, E) attached to objects in the water. These larvae are sometimes extremely abundant. The adults are most frequently encountered near the streams where the larvae occur, but may occur at considerable distances from streams.

The black flies in the United States are not known to be vectors of any disease of man, but in Africa, Mexico, and Central America certain species in this group act as vectors of onchocerciasis, a disease caused by a filarial worm and characterized by large subcutaneous swellings; in some cases the worms may get into the eyes and cause partial or complete blindness.

Family **Anisopódidae**—Wood Gnats: These gnats are usually found in moist places on foliage; some species occasionally occur in large swarms. The larvae live in or near decaying organic matter, fermenting sap, and similar materials, and the adults are often attracted to flowing sap. The most common species, which have faint spots on the wings, are in the genus *Silvícola*.

Family **Bibiónidae**—March Flies: The members of this group are small to medium-sized, usually dark-colored, stout-bodied flies with rather short

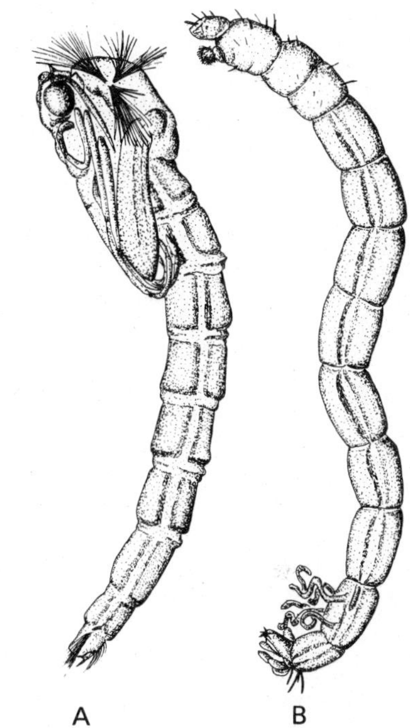

Figure 475. Pupa (A) and larva (B) of *Chirónomus téntans* Fabricius. (Courtesy of Johannsen and the Cornell University Agricultural Experiment Station.)

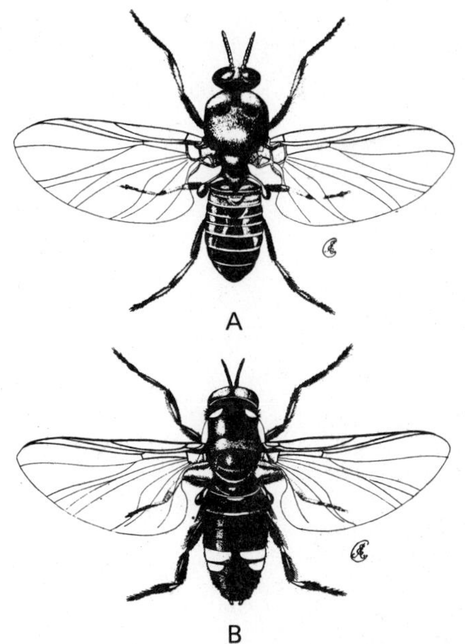

Figure 476. A black fly, *Simùlium nigricóxum* Stone. A, female; B, male. (Courtesy of Cameron and the Canadian Department of Agriculture.)

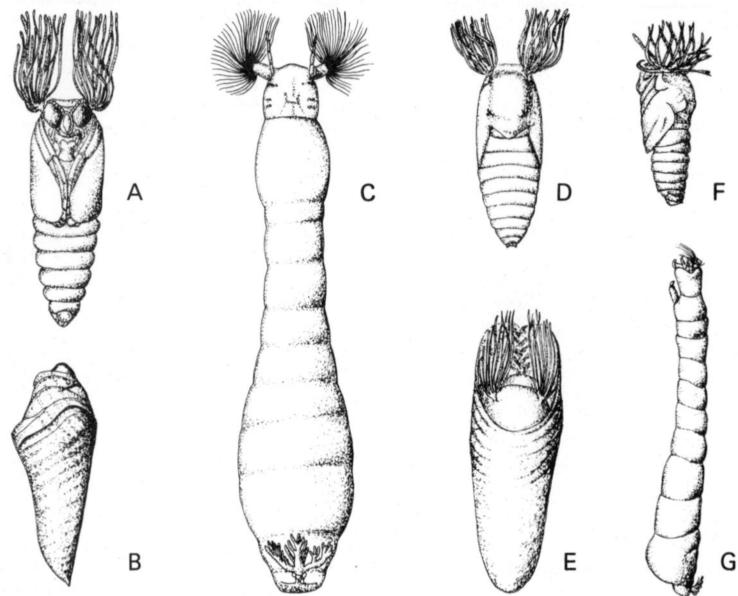

Figure 477. Immature stages of a black fly. A–E, *Simùlium nigricóxum* Stone; F–G, *S. pìctipes* Hagen. A, pupa, ventral view; B, pupal case; C, larva, dorsal view; D, pupa, dorsal view; E, pupa in pupal case; F, pupa, lateral view; G, larva, lateral view. (A–E, courtesy of Cameron and the Canadian Department of Agriculture; F, G, courtesy of Johannsen and the Cornell University Agricultural Experiment Station.)

Figure 478. A mating pair of "lovebugs," *Plècia neárctica* Hardy, a species of march fly. (Courtesy of Dwight Bennett.)

antennae (Figure 478); many have the thorax red or yellow. The wings often have a dark spot near the end of R_1 (Figure 445 C). The adults are most common in spring and early summer; they feed on flowers, and are sometimes numerous. The larvae feed in decaying vegetation and on plant roots.

One member of this family, *Plècia neárctica* Hardy (Figure 478), which occurs in the Gulf states, sometimes (usually in May and September) occurs in enormous swarms. Cars driving through such swarms become spattered with these insects, which may clog the radiator fins and cause the car to overheat, or spatter the windshield and obscure the driver's vision; if they are not soon cleaned off they damage the car's finish. Because pairs are often seen in copulo, these insects are commonly called "lovebugs." They are a particular problem in the northern part of peninsular Florida.

Family **Pachyneùridae:** Only two rare species of these gnats occur in the United States, *Axymỳia furcàta* McAtee (in the East) and *Cramptonomỳia spénceri* Alexander (in the Northwest). They have been variously classified—in the Anisopódidae, Bibiónidae, and Mycetophílidae—but do not fit well into any of these families. *A. furcàta* lacks a closed discal cell, it has two branches of M, and has a cross vein between R_1 and the anterior branch of Rs (Figure 447 D). *C. spénceri* has a closed discal cell, three branches of M, and has a cross vein between the two branches of Rs. *A. furcàta* has been taken in low vegetation along mountain streams.

Family **Mycetophílidae**—Fungus Gnats: The fungus gnats are slender, mosquitolike insects with elongated coxae and long legs (Figures 446 and 479). They are usually found in damp places where there is an abundance of decaying vegetation or fungi. The group is a large one, with over 600 North American species, and many of its members are common insects. Most fungus gnats are about the size of mosquitoes, but a few are 13 mm or more in length. The larvae of most species live in fungi, moist soil, or decaying vegetation; some species are pests in mushroom cellars. The larvae of the Keroplatìnae spin mucous webs; some of these are fungus feeders, and others are predaceous. Some of the predaceous larvae, such as *Orfèlia fúltoni* (Fisher) (Figure 479), are luminescent (see pages 67–68). Some adults of the Keroplatìnae, including some of our largest fungus gnats, feed on flowers.

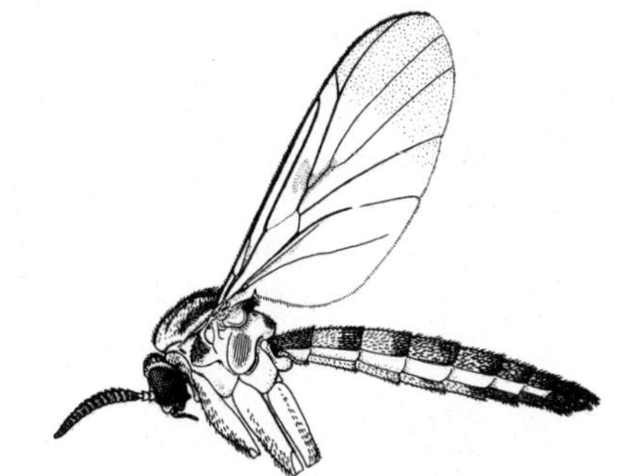

Figure 479. A fungus gnat, *Orfèlia fúltoni* (Fisher), 8 ×. (Courtesy of Fulton and the Entomological Society of America.)

Family **Sciáridae**—Dark-Winged Fungus Gnats, Root Gnats: These gnats are similar to the Mycetophílidae (Figure 481 A), but have the eyes meeting above the bases of the antennae (Figure 447 A) (except in *Pnýxia*), and the r-m cross vein is in line with and appears as a basal extension of Rs (Figure 480 C, D). The sciarids are usually blackish in-

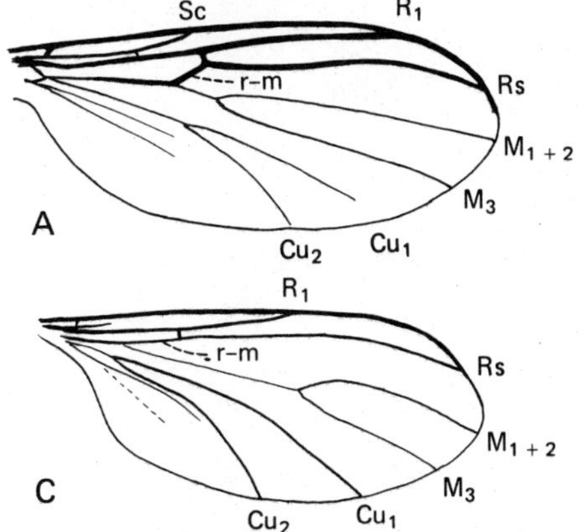

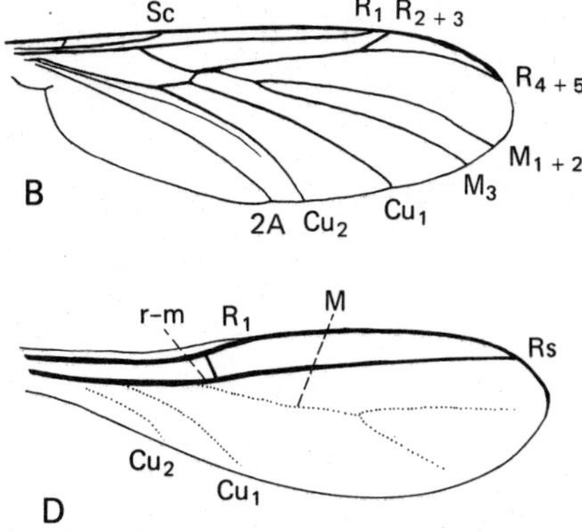

Figure 480. Wings of Mycetophílidae (A, B) and Sciáridae (C, D). A, Sciophilìnae; B, Keroplatìnae; C, *Scìara;* D, *Pnýxia,* male.

sects, and generally occur in moist shady places. The larvae of most species live in fungi, and some occasionally become pests in mushroom cellars. The larvae of a few species attack the roots of plants. One species, the potato scab gnat, *Pnýxia scàbiei* (Hopkins), attacks potatoes and serves as the vector of potato scab. The females of *P. scàbiei* have extremely short wings and no halteres. Sciarids are fairly common insects.

Family **Hyperoscelídidae:** This family, formerly considered a subfamily of the Scatópsidae, is represented in North America by a single rare species, *Synneùron annùlipes* Lundstrom, which has been recorded from Alaska, Washington, and Quebec.

Family **Scatópsidae**—Minute Black Scavenger Flies: These flies are black or brownish in color, 3 mm in length or less, and have short antennae. The veins near the costal margin of the wing (C, R_1, and Rs) are heavy, while the remaining veins are quite weak, and Rs ends in the costa at about one half to three fourths the wing length (Figure 447 B). The larvae breed in decaying material and excrement. The group is a small one (61 North American species), but its members are sometimes fairly abundant.

Family **Cecidomyìidae**—Gall Midges or Gall Gnats: Gall midges are minute, delicate flies with long legs and usually relatively long antennae, and with reduced wing venation (Figures 445 A, 481 B, 483). The larvae of about two thirds of the more than 1200 North American species cause galls on plants; most of the others are plant feeding (some living in galls formed by some other gall insect), but a few (for example, many Lestremiìnae) live in decaying organic matter, under bark, or in fungi, and a few are predaceous on aphids, scale insects, and other small insects.

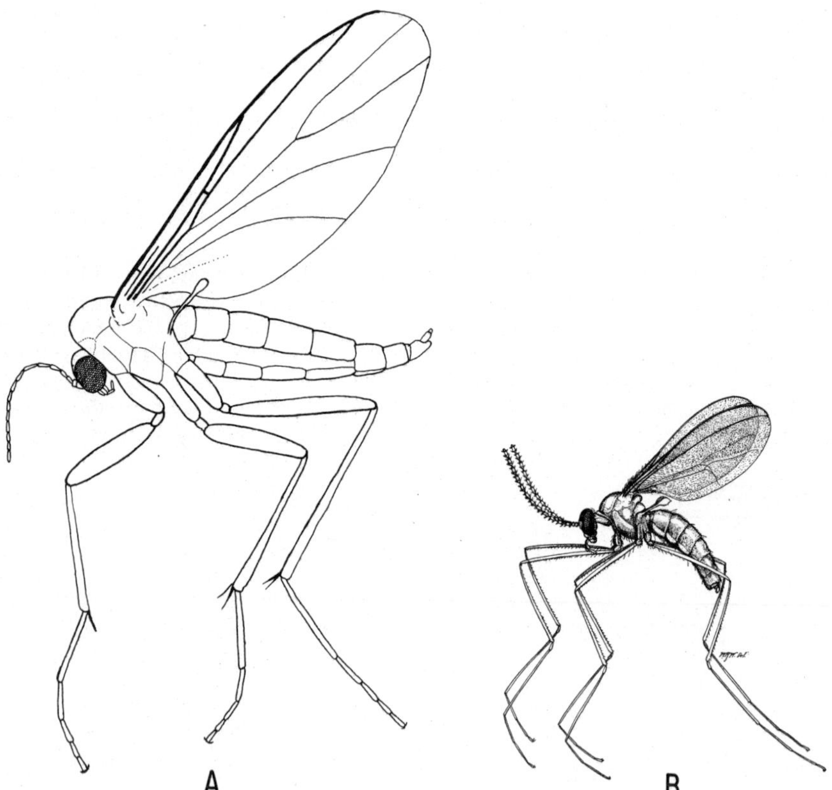

Figure 481. A, a dark-winged fungus gnat, *Sciàra* sp., 15 ×; B, a cecidomyiid, *Aphidoléstes meridionàlis* Felt (which is predaceous on aphids). (B, courtesy of USDA.)

The larvae of gall midges are tiny maggots, with the head small and poorly developed and the mouth parts minute. In the last larval instar of most species there is a characteristic **T**-shaped sclerite called the "breast bone" on the ventral side of the prothorax. Many of the larvae are brightly colored —red, orange, pink, or yellow.

The galls formed by gall midges occur on all parts of plants and are usually very distinctive. Many species of gall midges form a characteristic gall on a particular part of a particular species of plant. In some galls, such as the pine-cone willow gall and the maple leaf spot (Figure 482), only one larva develops; in others, such as the stem gall of willow, many larvae develop.

Paedogenesis (reproduction by larvae) occurs in several genera of gall midges. In *Miástor metralòas* Meinert, the larvae of which occur under bark, daughter larvae are produced inside a mother larva, and they eventually consume it and escape; these larvae may produce more larvae in a similar manner, through several generations, and the last larvae pupate.

One of the most important pest species in this group is the Hessian fly, *Mayetìola destrúctor* (Say), which is a serious pest of wheat (Figure 483). This insect overwinters as a full-grown larva in a puparium, under the leaf sheaths of winter wheat; the larvae pupate and the adults emerge in the spring. These adults oviposit on wheat, and the larvae feed between the leaf sheath and the stem, weakening the shoot or even killing it. The larvae pass the summer in a puparium, and the adults emerge in the fall and lay their eggs on the leaves of winter wheat. The damage to winter wheat can often be avoided by delaying the planting of wheat so that by the time the wheat has sprouted, the adult Hessian flies will have emerged and died.

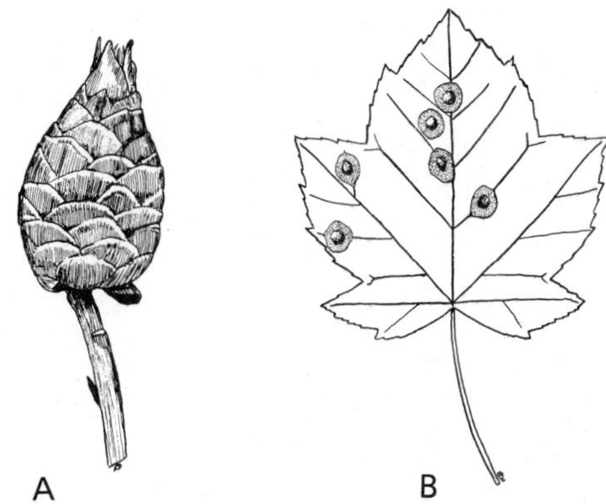

Figure 482. Galls of cecidomyiids, A, pine-cone willow gall, caused by *Rhabdóphaga strobilòides* (Osten Sacken); B, maple leaf spot, caused by *Cecidomỳia ocellàris* Osten Sacken. (Redrawn from Felt.)

Other species of economic importance in this family are the clover flower midge, *Dasineùra leguminícola* (Lintner), which is a serious pest of red clover throughout the country; the chrysanthemum gall fly, *Diarthronomỳia chrysánthemi* Ahlberg, a pest of chrysanthemums grown in greenhouses in various parts of the country; and the alfalfa gall midge, *Asphondỳlia wébsteri* Felt, which is sometimes a serious pest of alfalfa in the Southwest.

The North American gall midges are grouped in two subfamilies, the Lestremiìnae and Cecidomyiìnae. The Lestremiìnae have the first tarsal segment longer than the second, or have less than five tarsal segments; the Cecidomyiìnae have the tarsi 5-segmented and the first tarsal segment shorter than the second.

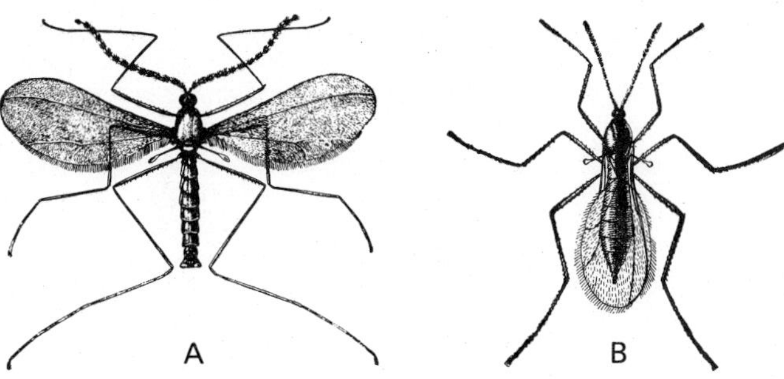

Figure 483. Hessian fly, *Mayetìola destrúctor* (Say). A, male; B, female. (Courtesy of USDA.)

Family **Baeonòtidae:** This family is known only from the female of *Baeonòtus mìcrops* Byers (Byers, 1969), which was collected in forest soil, beneath oak-leaf litter, in Virginia. This insect lacks wings and halteres, ocelli are absent and the compound eyes are single-faceted, and the abdomen is large and indistinctly segmented.

SUBORDER **Brachýcera:** Most of the flies in this group are relatively stout-bodied and medium-sized to large; our largest Díptera are in this suborder. The antennae have less than five segments (usually three), but the third segment is sometimes divided into subsegments; the antennae often bear a terminal style, but are seldom aristate. Most Brachýcera (all except the Dolichopódidae, many Empídidae, and some Stratiomỳidae, Bombylìidae, and Acrocéridae) have the radius 4-branched, with R_{4+5} forked (in a few Asìlidae it may appear that R_{2+3} is the branch that is forked; see Figure 448 D).

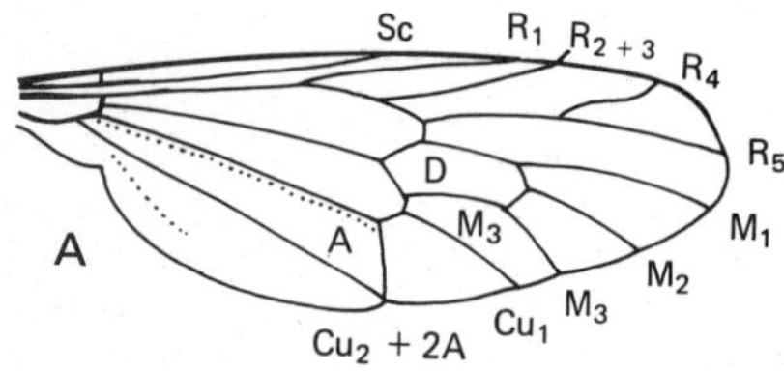

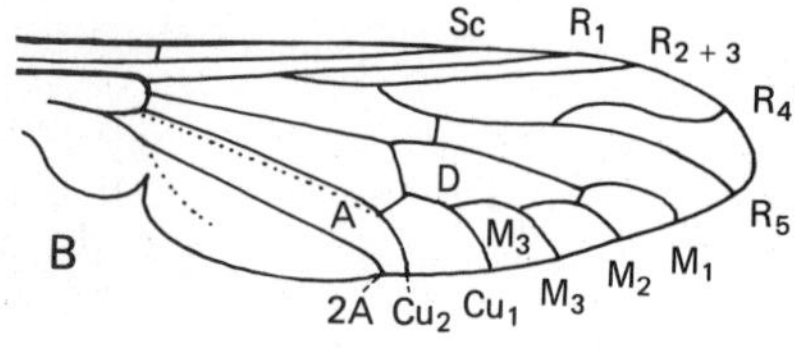

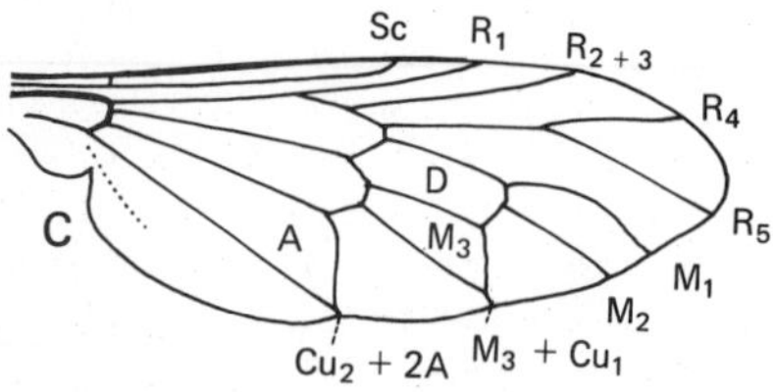

Figure 484. Wings of Xylophágidae (A, B) and Xylomỳidae (C). A, *Xylóphagus;* B, *Coenomỳia;* C, *Xylòmya.*

The adults of many Brachýcera are predaceous on other insects; most Brachýcera larvae are either parasites or predators. Brachyceran larvae have the head sclerotized, but more or less reduced and retractile; the mouth hooks move vertically. The pupae are of the coarctate type, and the adult emerges from a **T**-shaped opening in one end.

There are about 4650 North American species in this suborder, grouped in 18 families; about three fourths of these species are in four families (Asìlidae, Bombylìidae, Empídidae, and Dolichopódidae).

Family **Xylophágidae:** Xylophagids are relatively uncommon flies of medium to large size. They usually occur in wooded areas, and feed on sap or nectar. The larvae are predaceous or scavengers, and occur in the soil (*Coenomỳia*), under bark (*Xylóphagus*), or in decaying logs (*Rachícerus*). The flies in the genus *Xylóphagus* are slender and ichneumonlike; other xylophagids are more robust. The flies in the genus *Coenomỳia* are large (14–25 mm in length), usually reddish or brownish in color, with the eyes pubescent and the second to fifth posterior cells about as wide as long (Figure 484 B). The flies in the genus *Rachícerus* are peculiar in having the antennae many-segmented and serrate or somewhat pectinate; they have the fourth posterior (M_3) cell closed, the eyes emarginate just above the antennae, and are 5–8 mm in length. Other xylophagids are 10 mm in length or less, and quite rare.

Family **Xylomỳidae:** The most common flies in this small group (species of *Xylòmya*) are slender and ichneumonlike; they differ from the xylophagids in the genus *Xylóphagus* (which are very similar in appearance) in having the M_3 cell closed (Figure 484 C) and in lacking an apical spur on the front tibiae. The larvae occur in decaying wood or under bark, and are predaceous or scavengers.

Family **Stratiomỳidae**—Soldier Flies: Most of the soldier flies are medium-sized or larger and are usually found on flowers; many species are brightly colored and wasplike in appearance. The larvae occur in a variety of situations; some are aquatic and feed on algae, decaying materials, or on small aquatic animals; some live in dung or other decaying materials; some occur under bark; others are found in other situations.

In some species of soldier flies (for example, *Stratìomys*, Figure 485 A) the abdomen is broad

Figure 485. Soldier flies. A, *Stratìomys láticeps* Loew; B, *Hermètia illùcens* (L.). (B, courtesy of USDA.)

and flat, the wings at rest are folded back together over the abdomen, and the antennae (Figure 440 C) are long, with the third segment distinctly annulated. In other species (for example, in the genus *Ptécticus*) the abdomen is elongate, usually narrowed at the base, and the third antennal segment (Figure 440 F) appears globular, with an arista, and the annulations are very indistinct. Most soldier flies are dark-colored, with or without light markings, but some species are yellowish or light brown. The soldier flies are most easily recognized by their wing venation (Figure 448 A); the branches of the radius are rather heavy and are crowded together toward the costal margin of the wing, and the discal cell is small.

Family **Pelecorhýnchidae:** This group is represented in the United States by a single species, *Bequaertomỳia jònesi* (Cresson), which occurs in the Pacific Coast States. This insect is 13–15 mm in length and black with the wings smoky and the antennae and palps orange.

Family **Tabánidae**—Horse Flies and Deer Flies: Nearly 300 species of tabanids occur in North America, and many are quite common; they are medium-sized to large, rather stout-bodied flies. The females are blood-sucking and are often serious pests of livestock and man; the males feed chiefly on pollen and nectar and are often found on flowers. The two sexes are very easily separated by the eyes, which are usually contiguous in the males and separated in the females. The eyes are often brightly colored or iridescent. The larvae of most species are aquatic and predaceous, and the adults are generally encountered near swamps, marshes, ponds, and other situations where the larvae occur. Most horse flies are powerful fliers, and some species apparently have a flight range of several kilometers.

The two most common genera of tabanids, which include over half of the species in the family, are *Tabànus* and *Chrỳsops*. In *Tabànus* the hind tibia lack apical spurs, the head is somewhat hemispherical in shape (usually slightly concave on the posterior side in the female), and the third antennal segment (Figure 487 A) has a toothlike process near the base. *Tabànus* is a large genus, containing nearly a hundred North American species, and it includes some important pests. One of the largest flies in the genus is *T. atràtus* Fabricius, a black insect 25 mm or more in length (Figure 486 E). The so-called greenheads, flies about 13 mm in length with green eyes and a yellowish brown body, are often serious pests on bathing beaches. In *Chrỳsops* the hind tibiae have apical spurs, the head is more rounded, and the third antennal segment (Figure 487 B) is elongate and lacks a basal toothlike process. Most members of this genus are about the size of a house fly or a little larger, brown or black in color, with dark markings on the wings (Figure 486 A, B). These tabanids are called deer flies; they are usually encountered near marshes or streams and frequently buzz around one's head or get in one's hair.

The eggs of tabanids are usually laid in masses on leaves or other objects near or over water. Most species overwinter in the larval stage and pupate during the summer.

Some of the tabanids, particularly certain species of *Chrỳsops*, are known to serve as vectors of disease; tularemia and anthrax (and possibly other diseases) may be transmitted by tabanids in this

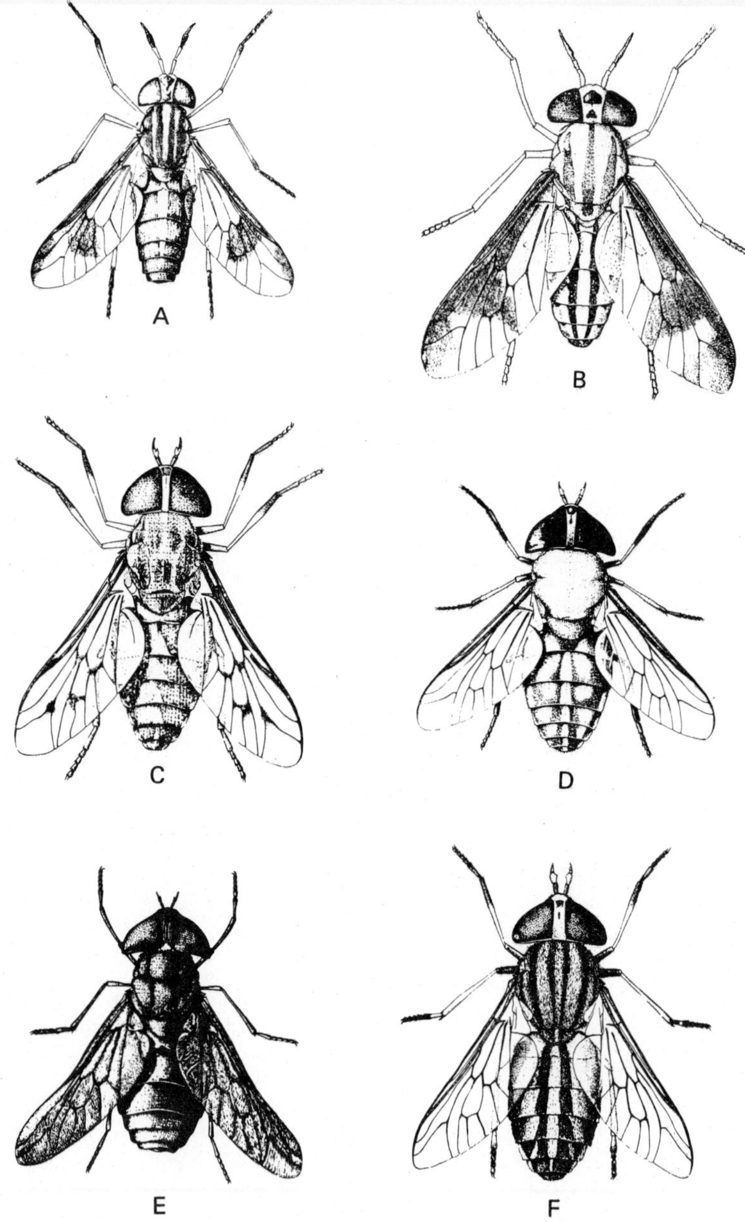

Figure 486. Horse flies and deer flies (Tabánidae). A, *Chrỳsops univittàtus* Macquart; B, *Chrỳsops pìkei* Whitney; C, *Tabànus súlcifrons* Macquart; D, *Tabànus quinquevittàtus* Wiedemann; E, *Tabànus atràtus* Fabricius; F, *Tabànus linèola* Fabricius. (Courtesy of Schwardt and Hall and the Arkansas Agricultural Experiment Station.)

country, and in Africa a disease caused by the filarial worm, *Lòa lòa* (Cobbold), is transmitted by deer flies.

Family **Rhagiónidae**—Snipe Flies: The snipe flies are medium-sized to large, with the head somewhat rounded, the abdomen relatively long and

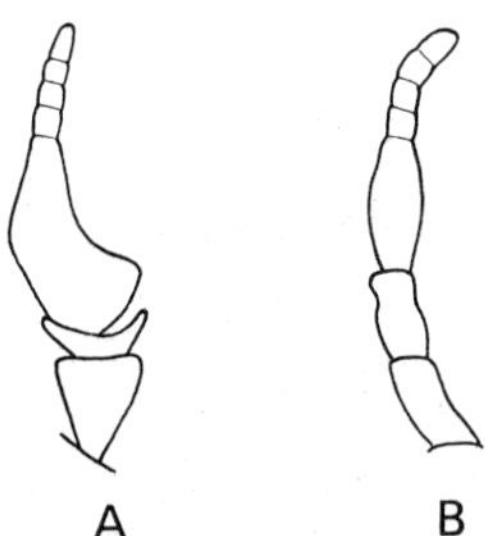

Figure 487. Antennae of tabanids. A, *Tabànus atràtus* Fabricius; B, *Chrỳsops fuliginòsus* Wiedemann.

tapering, and the legs rather long (Figure 488). Many species have spotted wings. The body may be bare or covered with short hair. Most snipe flies are brownish or gray, but some are black with spots or stripes of white, yellow, or green. They are common in woods, especially near moist places, and are usually found on foliage or grass. They are not particularly fast fliers. Both adults and larvae are predaceous on a variety of small insects. Most of the snipe flies do not bite, but several species of *Symphoromỳia* are common biting pests in the western mountains and coastal areas. Most snipe fly larvae occur in decaying vegetation or debris, where they prey upon various small insects. The larvae of the snipe flies in the genus *Athèrix* are aquatic; the adults lay their eggs in masses on twigs overhanging streams, into which the larvae fall after they hatch; the female remains on the egg mass and eventually dies there, and other females may lay their eggs on this mass until a ball of considerable size is formed, consisting of eggs and dead females.

Family **Hilarimórphidae:** The hilarimorphids are small flies, 2.5–5.0 mm in length, and dark brown to blackish in color. The group is represented in the United States by three species of *Hilarimórpha,* all of which are quite rare; they have been recorded in New Hampshire, Vermont, Illinois, Colorado, California, and Oregon.

Family **Therévidae**—Stiletto Flies: These flies are of medium size, usually somewhat hairy or bristly, and often have the abdomen pointed (Figure 489 A, B). They are superficially similar to some robber flies, but do not have the top of the head hollowed out between the eyes. Adults are not common, but are most likely to be found in dry open areas such as meadows and beaches. Little is known of the feeding habits of the adults, but they are probably plant feeders; the larvae are predaceous, and usually occur in sand or decaying wood.

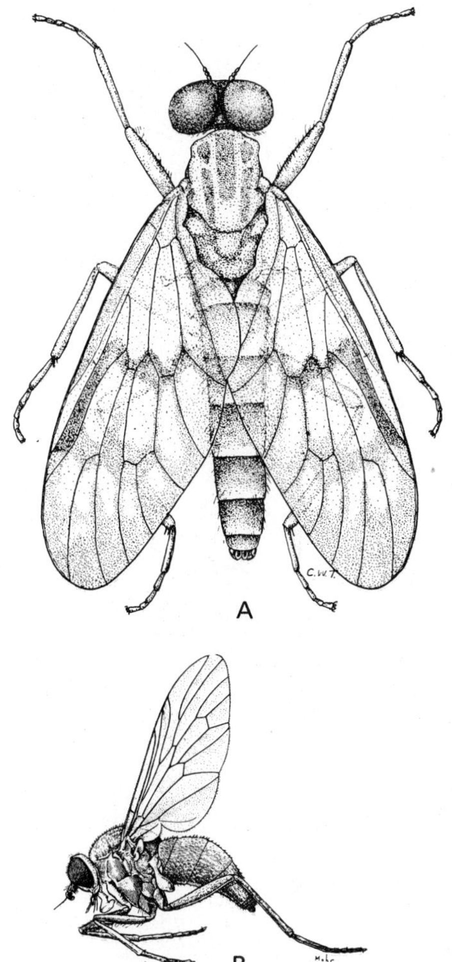

Figure 488. Snipe flies. A, a common snipe fly, *Rhàgio mystàceus* (Macquart); B, a blood-sucking snipe fly, *Symphoromỳia átripes* Bigot. (B, courtesy of Ross and the Entomological Society of America.)

Family **Scenopínidae**—Window Flies: The window flies are rather uncommon flies of medium or small size and are usually blackish in color. The common name is derived from the fact that one species, *Scenópinus fenestràlis* (L.) (Figure 490), is sometimes common on windows; the larva of this species is said to feed on the larvae of carpet

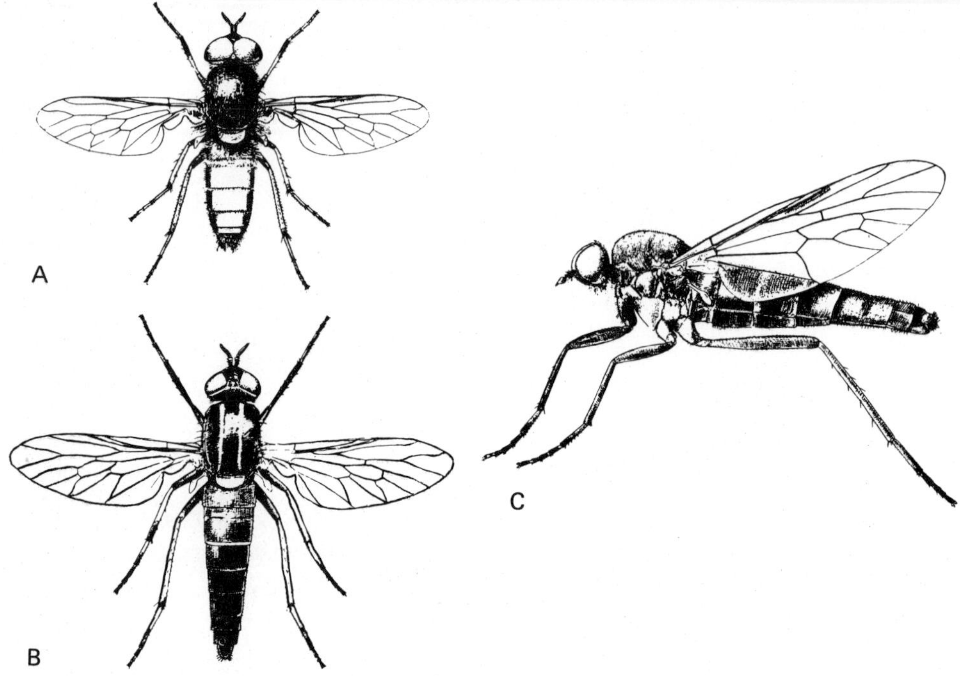

Figure 489. A, *Psilocéphala áldrichi* Coquillett, female (Therévidae); B, same, male; C, *Caenòtus inornàtus* Cole, female (Bombylìidae). (Courtesy of Cole and the U.S. National Museum.)

beetles. The larvae of other species occur in decaying wood and fungi.

Family **Apiocéridae**—Flower-Loving Flies: These are relatively large, elongate flies that resemble some of the robber flies (for example, Figure 492 B, C), but do not have the top of the head hollowed out between the eyes, and have a different wing venation (M_1 and the veins anterior to it ending in front of the wing tip; see Figure 448 J). This group is a small one (29 North American species), and its members are rather rare. They occur in the arid regions of the West, where they are often found on flowers.

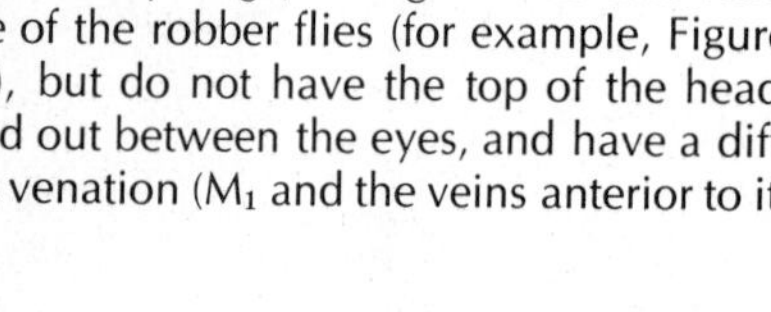

Figure 490. A window fly, *Scenópinus fenestràlis* (L.). (Redrawn from USDA.)

Family **Mỳdidae**—Mydas Flies: The mydas flies are very large and elongate, with long 4-segmented antennae. A Brazilian species, *Mỳdas hèros* Perty, which is 54 mm in length, is probably the largest dipteran known. *M. clavàtus* (Drury), a fairly common species in this country, is black, with the second abdominal segment yellowish or orange (Figure 491). Little is known of the habits of these flies, but the larvae occur in decaying wood and are predaceous; the adults are probably also predaceous.

Family **Asìlidae**—Robber Flies: This is a large group, with about 850 North American species, and many species are quite common. The adults are found in a variety of habitats, but each species usually occurs in a characteristic type of habitat. The adults are predaceous and attack a variety of insects, including wasps, bees, dragonflies, grass-

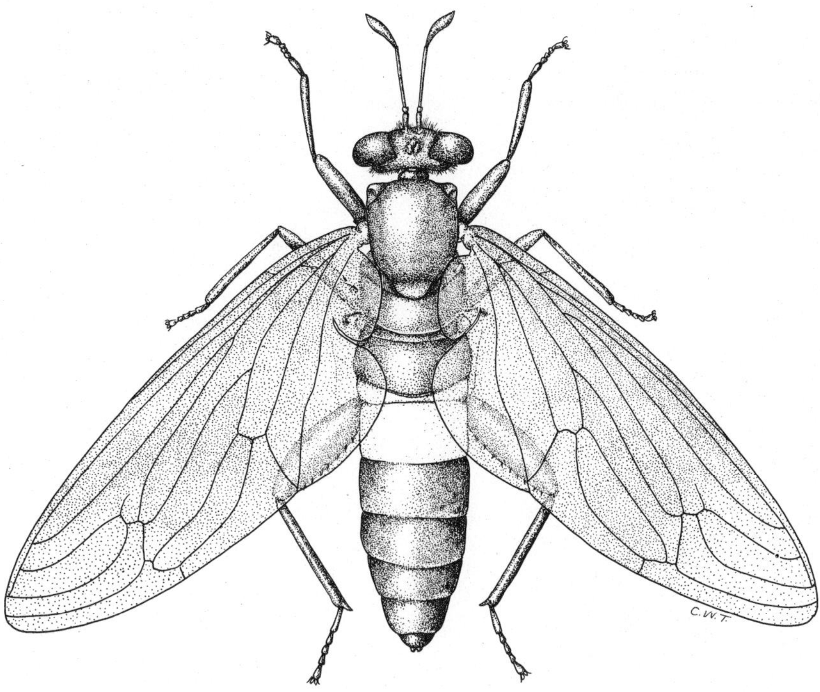

Figure 491. A mydas fly, *Mỳdas clavàtus* (Drury).

hoppers, and other flies, which they usually capture on the wing; they often attack an insect as large as or larger than themselves. Some of the larger robber flies can inflict a painful bite if carelessly handled.

Robber flies have the top of the head hollowed out between the eyes (Figure 492 D), the face more or less bearded, and they have a stout thorax with long, strong legs. Most of them are elongate, with the abdomen tapering (Figure 492 B, C), but some are stout-bodied and very hairy, and strongly resemble bumble bees or other Hymenóptera (Figure 492 A). The larvae live in soil, decaying wood, and similar places, and feed chiefly on the larvae of other insects.

Family **Leptogástridae**—Grass Flies: These flies are similar to the robber flies (with which they were formerly classified), but have the abdomen very slender and elongate (Figure 493). They generally occur in grassy areas, where they feed on small, soft-bodied, usually resting insects.

Family **Nemestrínidae**—Tangle-Veined Flies: These flies are of medium size, stout-bodied, and occur in open fields of fairly high vegetation; they hover persistently, and are very fast fliers. Some species occur on flowers. The group is small (only six North American species), and its members are relatively rare. Little is known of the larval stages, but two species are known to be parasites of grasshoppers.

Family **Acrocéridae**—Small-Headed Flies: These are rather rare flies of small to medium size with a somewhat humpbacked appearance and with the head very small (Figure 494). Some have a long, slender proboscis and feed on flowers; others have no proboscis, and apparently do not feed in the adult stage. The larvae are internal parasites of spiders. The eggs are laid in large numbers on vegetation, and hatch into tiny flattened larvae called planidia; the planidia eventually attach to and enter the body of a passing spider. Pupation occurs outside the host, often in the host's web.

Family **Bombylìidae**—Bee Flies: This is a large group (over 750 North American species) and its members are widely distributed; bee flies are fairly common insects, but are probably more common in the arid areas of the Southwest than elsewhere. Most of them are stout-bodied, densely

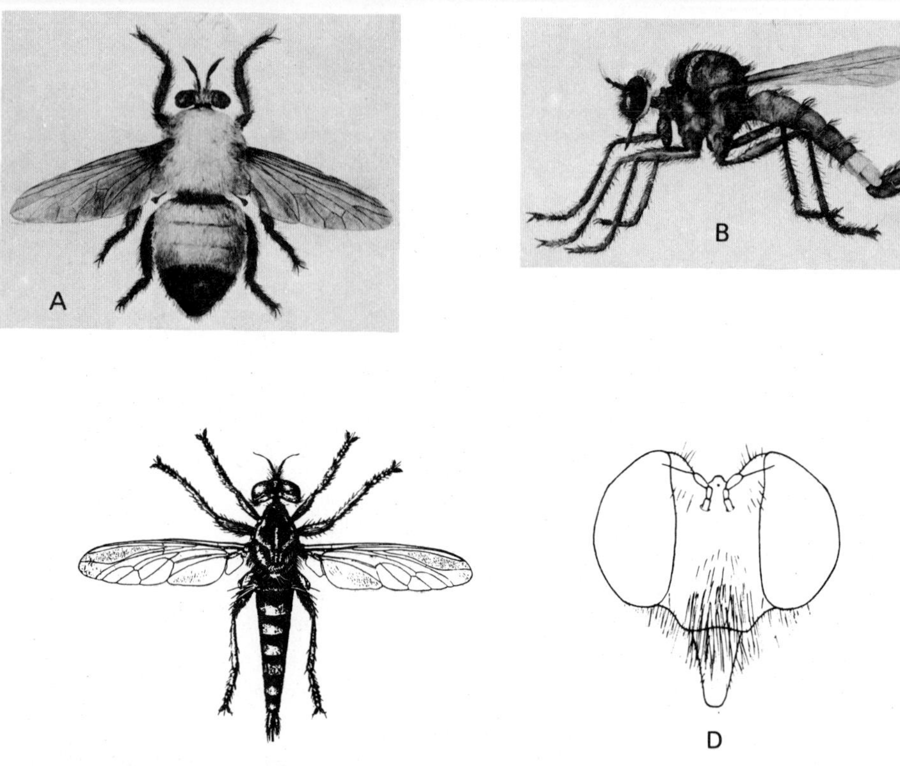

Figure 492. Robber flies. A, *Láphria làta* Macquart; B, *Effèria* sp.; C, *Prómachus vertebràtus* (Say); D, head of *Effèria,* anterior view. (C, courtesy of USDA.)

hairy flies of medium to large size, a few are slender and not very hairy, and a few are very small (some Mythecomyìinae are only 1.2 mm in length). Many have the proboscis long and slender. The adults are found on flowers or hovering over or resting on the ground or grass in open sunny places. They often visit water holes in arid regions. The wings at rest are usually held outstretched. Most species are very fast fliers, and when caught in an insect net, buzz much like a bee. Many have banded or spotted wings (Figure 495). The larvae, as far as known, are parasitic and attack caterpillars, grubs, hymenopterous larvae, and the eggs of grasshoppers. Some females hover over holes and crevices, dipping quickly to throw in an egg. The larvae crawl into the nest cell of a bee or wasp and wait until the host larva has completed its feeding before they consume it.

Family **Empídidae** – Dance Flies: The dance flies are so named because the adults sometimes occur in swarms, often over forest streams, flying with an up-and-down movement. This group is a large one (over 700 North American species), and many species are fairly common; all are small, and some are minute. The dance flies are found in a variety of situations, usually in moist places where there is an abundance of vegetation. They are predaceous on smaller insects, but occasionally frequent flowers. Most of them have a large thorax and a long tapering abdomen; the male genitalia are terminal and often are rather conspicuous (Figure 496).

Many species of dance flies have rather interesting mating habits. The males sometimes capture prey and use it to attract females. Some species of *Hílara* and *Émpis* that occur in the Northwest construct balloons which they carry about as a means of attracting females; these balloons may be made of silk (spun from the basal segment of the front tarsi) or of a frothy material from the anus, and they usually contain prey.

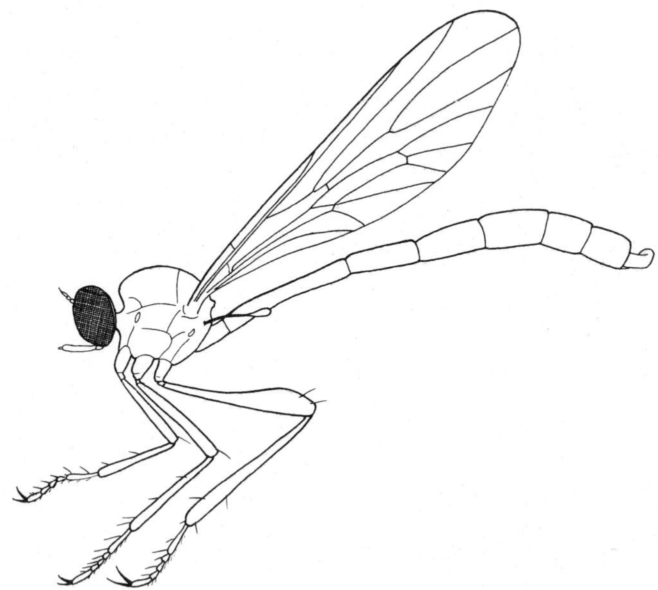

Figure 493. A grass fly, *Psilónyx annulàtus* (Say), 7½ ×.

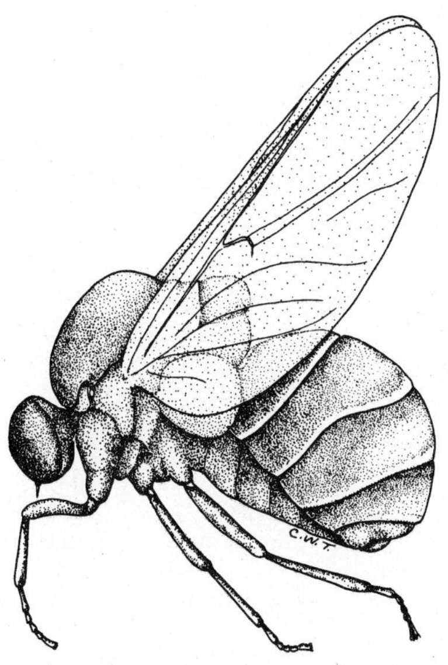

Figure 494. A small-headed fly, *Ogcòdes* sp.

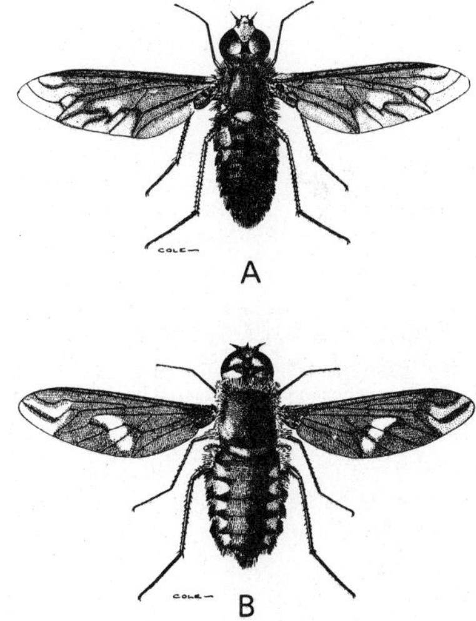

Figure 495. Bee flies. A, *Poecilánthrax álpha* (Osten Sacken); B, *Poecilánthrax signatipénnis* (Cole). (Courtesy of Cole and the New York Entomological Society.)

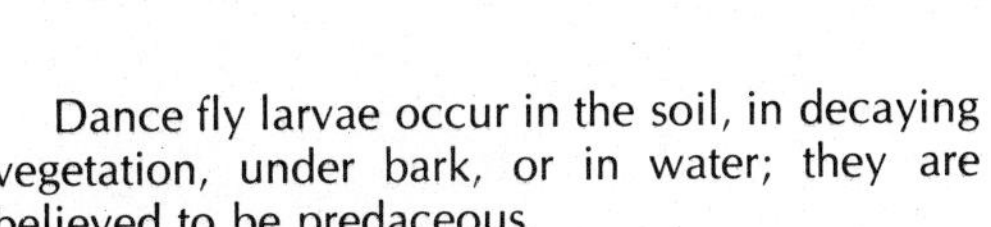

Dance fly larvae occur in the soil, in decaying vegetation, under bark, or in water; they are believed to be predaceous.

Family **Dolichopódidae**—Long-Legged Flies: The dolichopodids are small to minute flies that are usually metallic in color, greenish, bluish, or coppery. They are superficially similar to many of the muscoid flies (Schizóphora), but lack a frontal suture and have a rather characteristic wing venation (Figure 449 D–F): the r-m cross vein is very short or absent and is located in the basal fourth of

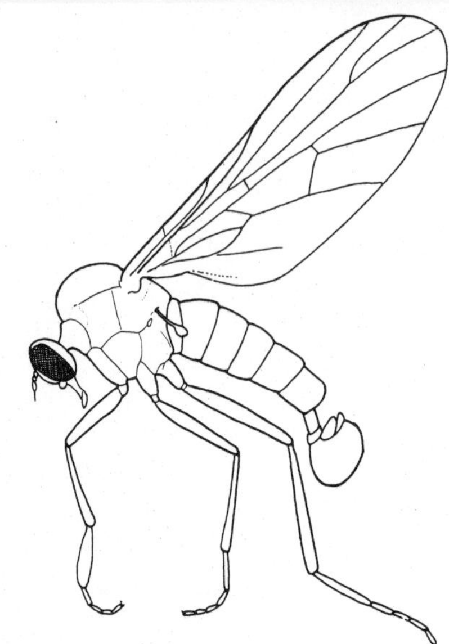

Figure 496. A dance fly (Empídidae), 10 ×.

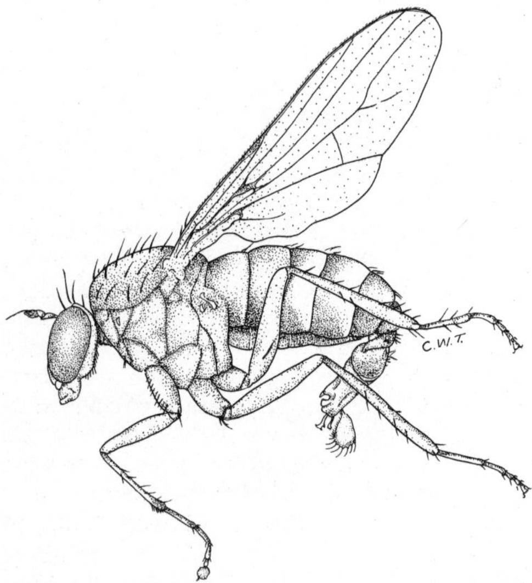

Figure 497. A long-legged fly, *Dolíchopus pugil* Loew, male.

the wing, and there is often a swelling of Rs where it forks. The male genitalia are usually large and conspicuous and folded forward under the abdomen (Figure 497); in the female the apex of the abdomen is pointed. The legs of the males are often peculiarly ornamented. Members of the genus *Melandèria,* which occur along the Pacific Coast, have the labellar lobes of the labium modified into mandiblelike structures.

This group is a large one (over 1230 North American species), and its members are abundant in many places, particularly near swamps and streams, in woodlands, and in meadows. Many species occur only in a particular type of habitat. The adults are predaceous on smaller insects. The adults of many species engage in rather unusual mating dances. The larvae occur in water or mud, decaying wood, grass stems, and under bark; not much is known of their feeding habits, but at least some are predaceous. The larvae of the genus *Medètera* live under bark and are predaceous on bark beetles.

SUBORDER **Cyclórrhapha:** The members of this suborder have the antennae 3-segmented and aristate, and the radius is always 3-branched. They range from minute to medium-sized, and most are relatively stout-bodied and bristly. The larvae lack a sclerotized head, and the mouth hooks move vertically.

An adult cyclorrhaphan emerges from the puparium through a circular opening at one end (it is from this character that the suborder gets its name). This opening is made by pushing out the end of the puparium with a structure called the ptilinum. The ptilinum is a saclike structure that is everted from the front of the head, above the bases of the antennae; after emergence the ptilinum is withdrawn into the head. In most of the Cyclórrhapha (the Schizóphora, or muscoid flies) the break in the head wall through which the ptilinum was everted is marked by the frontal suture; the Aschìza (six families, Lonchoptéridae through Conópidae) lack this suture.

The muscoid flies (Schizóphora, with 59 families and over 5600 North American species) make up about one third of the order, and are to be found almost everywhere. Many are small, and their identification is often difficult; identification is complicated by the fact that the division between some families is not very clear-cut, and many genera are placed in different families by different authorities. The muscoids fall into two principal groups, the acalyptrates (48 families, Micropèzidae through Cryptochètidae) and the calyptrates (11 families, Anthomyìidae through Oéstridae); these names refer to the development of the calypteres, which are large and well developed in most calyptrates and very small in the acalyptrates. These two muscoid groups also differ (with a few exceptions) in the structure of the second antennal segment (Figure 452 A, B) and the

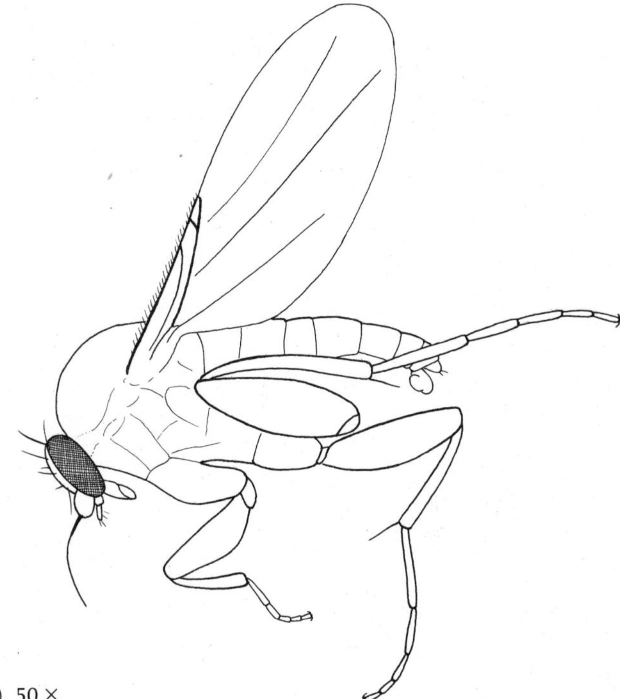

Figure 498. A humpbacked fly (Phòridae), 50 ×.

sutures on the dorsal surface of the thorax (Figure 452 C, D) (see key, couplet 63).

Family **Lonchoptéridae**—Spear-Winged Flies: The members of this group are slender, yellowish, or brownish flies less than 5 mm in length, with the wings somewhat pointed at the apex and with a characteristic venation (Figure 449 H). They are usually fairly common in moist, shady, or grassy places. The larvae occur in decaying vegetation. Males differ from females in venation; the M_3 cell is closed in the female (Figure 449 H) and open in the male. Males are extremely rare, and these flies are probably parthenogenetic. This family contains only four North American species, in the genus *Lonchóptera*.

Family **Phòridae**—Humpbacked Flies: The phorids are small or minute flies that are easily recognized by the humpbacked appearance (Figure 498), the characteristic venation (Figure 449 G), and the laterally flattened hind femora. The adults are fairly common in many habitats, but are most abundant about decaying vegetation. The habits of the larvae are rather varied; some occur in decaying animal or vegetable matter, some occur in fungi, some are internal parasites of various other insects, and some occur as parasites or commensals in the nests of ants or termites. A few of the species that occur in ant or termite nests (and some others as well) have the wings reduced or lacking. Nearly 300 species occur in our area.

Family **Platypèzidae**—Flat-Footed Flies: These flies are so named because of the peculiarly shaped hind tarsi, which are usually flattened or otherwise modified (Figure 463 C); the tarsi are generally more flattened in the females than in the males. The flat-footed flies are small, usually black or brown in color, and occur on low vegetation in wooded areas. The males frequently swarm in groups of up to 50 or more, the swarm dancing in midair one meter or more above the ground, with the hind legs hanging down. If disturbed (for example, by a swinging net), they scatter and reform a little higher up (out of net reach). Adults of the genus *Microsània* are attracted to smoke, apparently reacting to its odor. The larvae of flat-footed flies occur in fungi.

Family **Pipuncùlidae**—Big-Headed Flies: The members of this group are small flies with the

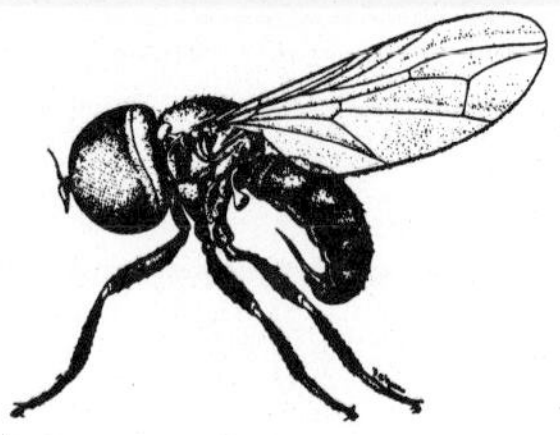

Figure 499. A big-headed fly, *Tomosvaryélla subviréscens* (Loew), female. (Courtesy of Knowlton and the Utah Agricultural Experiment Station.)

head very large and composed mostly of eyes (Figure 499), the wings are somewhat narrowed basally, and the anal cell is usually long and closed near the wing margin (Figure 449 J). The group is of moderate size (105 North American species), but its members are seldom common. The larvae are parasites of various hoppers, chiefly leafhoppers and planthoppers.

Family **Sýrphidae**—Syrphid Flies or Flower Flies: This is a large group (about 950 North American species), and many species are very abundant. Syrphids may be found almost everywhere, but different species occur in different types of habitats. The adults are often common about flowers and frequently do a great deal of hovering. Different species vary quite a bit in appearance (Figure 500), but (with a few exceptions) can be recognized by the spurious vein in the wing between the radius and the media (Figure 450 A–C, *spv*). Many are brightly colored and resemble various bees or wasps; some look much like honey bees, others like bumble bees, others like wasps, and the resemblance is often very striking. None of the syrphids will bite man.

Syrphid larvae vary considerably in habits and appearance (Figure 501). Many are predaceous on aphids, others live in the nests of social insects (ants, termites, or bees), others live in decaying vegetation or rotting wood, others live in highly polluted aquatic habitats, and a few feed on growing plants. The larvae of *Erístalis* (Figure 501 D, E),

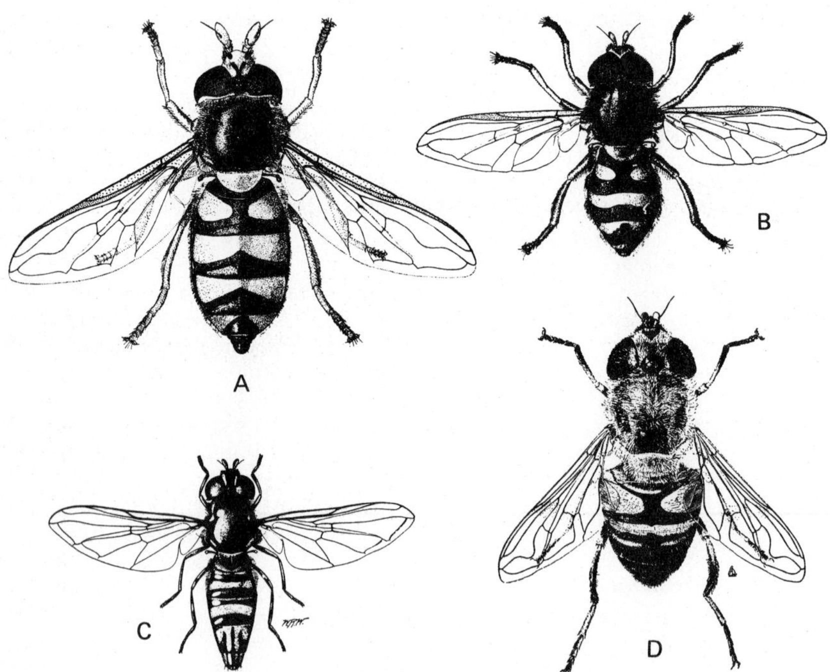

Figure 500. Syrphid flies. A, *Dídea fascìàta* Macquart; B, *Sýrphus tòrvus* Osten Sacken; C, *Allográpta oblìqua* (Say); D, *Erístalis ténax* (L.). (A, B, courtesy of Metcalf and the Maine Agricultural Experiment Station; C, D, courtesy of USDA.)

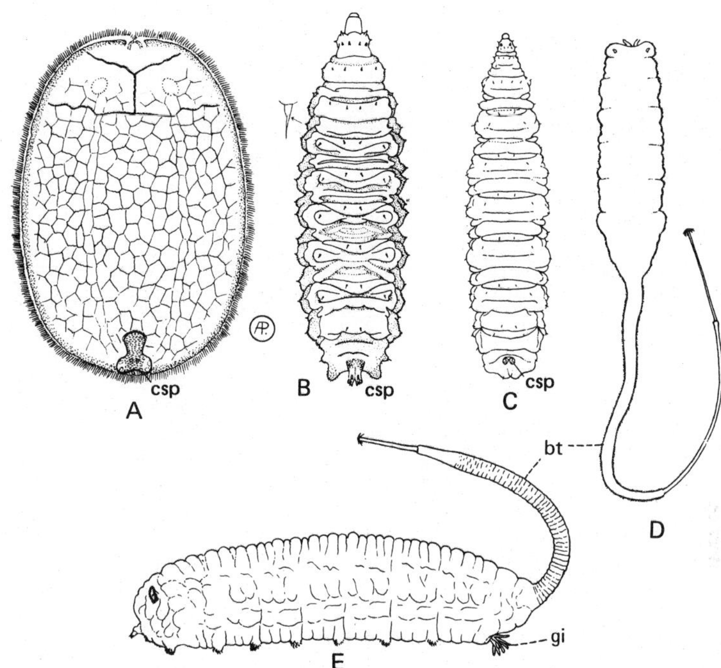

Figure 501. Larvae of syrphid flies. A, *Mìcrodon* sp., 50 ×; B, *Pipìza femoràlis* Loew, 50 ×; C, *Sýrphus víttafrons* Shannon, 3½ ×; D, E, *Erístalis* spp. (D, 2 ×; E, 3½ ×). *bt,* breathing tube; *csp,* caudal spiracle; *gi,* gills. (Courtesy of Peterson; reprinted by permission.)

which live in highly polluted water, have a very long breathing tube and are commonly called rat-tailed maggots; the adults of this genus (Figure 500 D) resemble bees. Rattailed maggots are sometimes responsible for intestinal myiasis in man.

Family **Conópidae**—Thick-Headed Flies: The conopids are medium-sized, brownish flies, many of which superficially resemble small thread-waisted wasps (Figure 502). The abdomen is usually elongate and slender basally, the head is slightly broader than the thorax, and the antennae are long. All species have a very long and slender proboscis; in some species the proboscis is elbowed. The wing venation is similar to that in the Sýrphidae (Figure 450), but there is no spurious vein; conopids may be distinguished from syr-

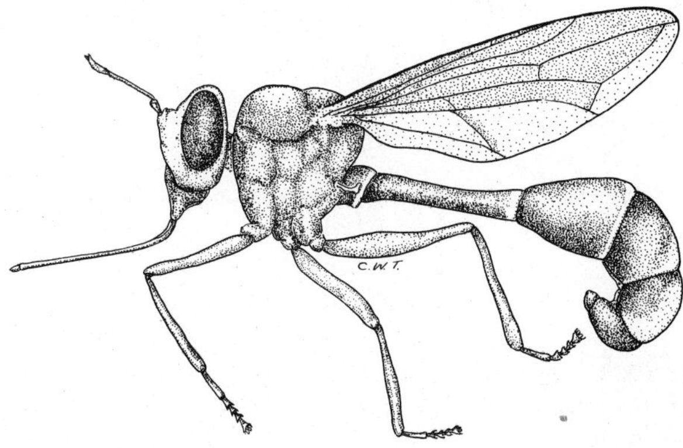

Figure 502. A thick-headed fly, *Physocéphala furcillàta* (Williston).

phids lacking a spurious vein by their long slender proboscis. In one genus (*Stylogáster*) the abdomen is slender, and in the female terminates in a very long ovipositor that is as long as the rest of the body. The adults are usually found on flowers. The larvae are endoparasites, chiefly of adult bumble bees and wasps, and the flies usually oviposit on their hosts during flight.

Family **Micropèzidae**—Stilt-Legged Flies: The members of this group are small to medium-sized elongate flies with very long legs. The first posterior (R_5) cell is narrowed apically, and the anal cell is often long and pointed (Figure 459 C). The adults are found near moist places. Only 31 species occur in North America, but the group is abundant in the tropics, where the larvae live in excrement.

Family **Nerìidae**—Cactus Flies: This group is represented in the United States by two species occurring in the Southwest. The most common species, *Odontoloxòzus longicòrnis* (Coquillett), ranges from southern Texas to southern California. It is slender, medium-sized, grayish with brown markings, and has long slender legs and long porrect antennae (Figure 461 I). The larvae breed in decaying cacti, and the adults are usually found only on such cacti.

Family **Diópsidae**—Stalk-Eyed Flies: This group is largely tropical, and only a single species, *Sphyracéphala brevicòrnis* (Say), occurs in North America. Most of the tropical species have the eyes situated at the ends of long stalks, but our species has relatively short eye stalks (Figure 461 J). Adults of our species are blackish, about 4.5 mm in length, with the front femora distinctly swollen. This species has been reared in the laboratory (from eggs laid by overwintered adults), but little is known of its life history in the field. The larvae feed on wet organic matter, and probably live in sphagnum bogs; adults are usually found in or near such habitats, often on skunk cabbage.

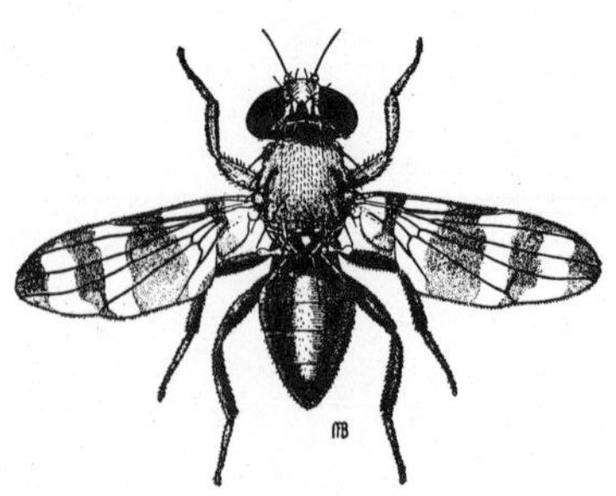

Figure 503. A corn-infesting otitid, *Euxésta stigmátias* Loew, 6 ×. (Courtesy of Wolcott and the *Journal of Agriculture* of the University of Puerto Rico.)

Family **Psìlidae**—Rust Flies: The psilids are small to medium-sized flies, usually rather slender, with long antennae. They have a peculiar ridge or weakening across the basal third of the wing. In the genus *Loxócera* the third antennal segment is very long and slender (Figure 457). The larvae live in the roots or galls of plants, and one species, *Psìla ròsae* Fabricius, the carrot rust fly, often does considerable damage to carrots, celery, and related plants.

Family **Tanypèzidae:** The Tanypèzidae are medium-sized flies with rather long and slender legs; they occur in moist woods and are quite rare. Only two species occur in the United States (in the Northeast), and nothing is known of their immature stages.

Family **Richardìidae:** This group is mainly neotropical, and only seven species occur in the United States; they are not common, and most adults have been taken in fruit-baited traps. Most species have patterned wings, and the larvae occur in decaying vegetation.

Families **Otítidae** and **Platystomátidae**—Picture-Winged Flies: The picture-winged flies are a large group of small to medium-sized flies that usually have the wings marked with black, brown, or yellowish, and the body is often shining and metallic (Figure 503). They are usually found in moist places, and are often very abundant. Little is known of their larval stages, but some are plant-feeding and occasionally damage cultivated plants (Figure 503), and some occur in decaying materials. These groups are most abundant in the tropics, but there are 128 species of Otítidae and 41 species of Platystomátidae in North America.

Family **Pyrgòtidae:** The Pyrgòtidae are rather elongate flies of medium to large size and often have considerable coloring in the wings; the head is prominent and rounded and there are no ocelli (Figure 504). The adults are mostly nocturnal and

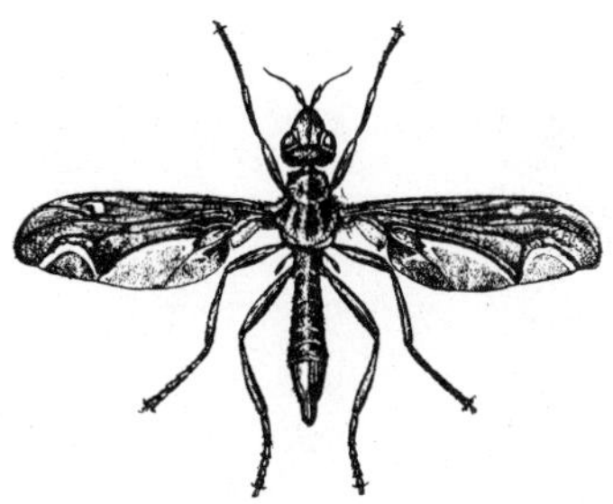

Figure 504. *Pyrgòta undàta* Wiedemann (Pyrgòtidae). (Courtesy of USDA.)

are frequently attracted to lights; the larvae are parasites of adult June beetles.

Family **Tephrítidae**—Fruit Flies: The members of this group are small to medium-sized flies that usually have spotted or banded wings, the spotting often forming complicated and attractive patterns (Figures 505 and 506). They can be recognized by the structure of the subcosta, which apically bends forward at almost a right angle and then fades out; in most species the anal cell has an acute distal projection posteriorly (Figure 460 B). The adults are found on flowers or vegetation. Some species have the habit of slowly moving their wings up and down while resting on vegetation, and are often called peacock flies. This group is a large one (239 North American species), and many species are quite common.

The larvae of most tephritids feed on plants, and some are rather serious pests. The larva of *Rhagóletis pomonélla* (Walsh), usually called the apple maggot, tunnels in the fruit of apple and other orchard trees (Figure 505); other species in this genus attack cherries. The Mediterranean fruit fly, *Cerátitis capitàta* (Wiedemann), attacks citrus and other fruits, and some years ago threatened to become a serious pest in the South; this species is now eradicated from the South. Species of the genus *Euróśta* form stem galls on goldenrod (Figure 507); the galls are rounded and thick-walled, with a single larva in the center. In the fall, the larva cuts a tunnel to the surface, overwinters as a larva in the gall, and pupates in the spring. A few of the tephritids are leaf miners in the larval stage.

Family **Helcomỳzidae**—Seabeach Flies: These flies are of medium size and are somewhat similar to the Sciomỳzidae, but lack femoral bristles and have R_1 ending beyond the middle of the wing. In profile the third antennal segment appears rounded, and the face is slightly concave below the antennae. Three species occur in North America, and they are found along the seashore from Oregon to Alaska. The larvae live in rotting seaweed.

Family **Ropaloméridae:** This is a small group of about a dozen tropical species, most of them occurring in Central and South America. They are of medium size, usually brownish or grayish in color, with the first posterior (R_5) cell narrowed

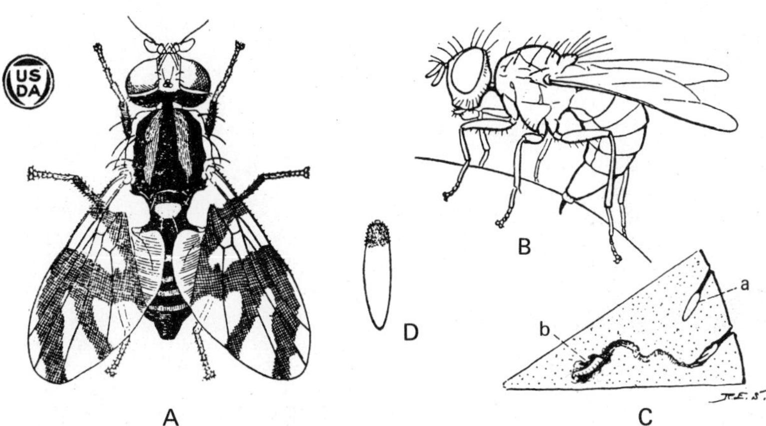

Figure 505. Apple maggot, *Rhagóletis pomonélla* (Walsh) (Tephrítidae). A, adult female, 7 ×; B, female puncturing skin of apple preparatory to depositing an egg; C, section of an apple showing an egg inserted at *a*, and a young maggot tunneling into the pulp at *b;* D, an egg (greatly enlarged). (Courtesy of USDA.)

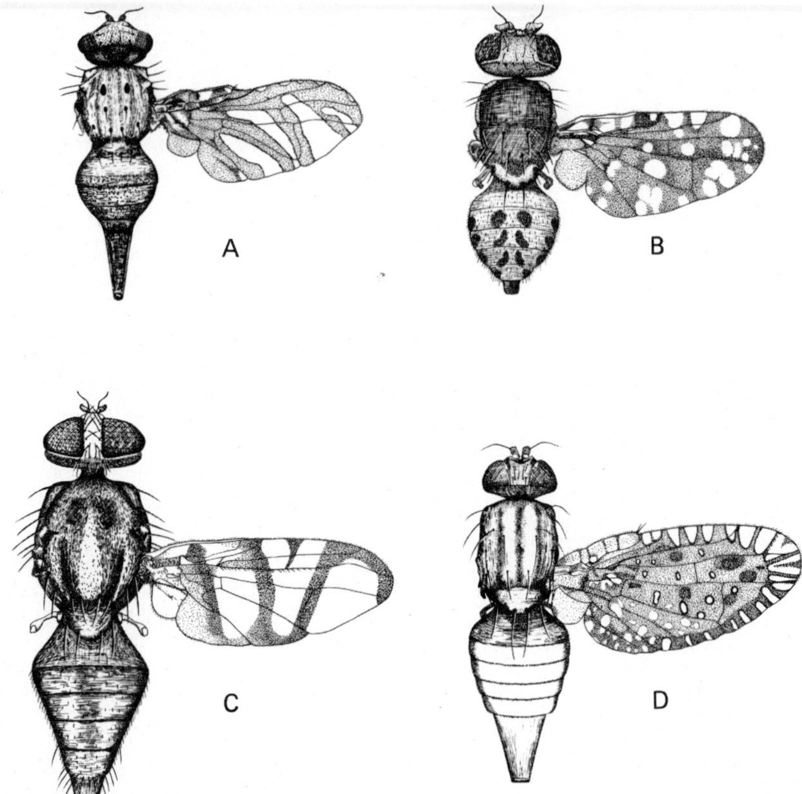

Figure 506. Fruit flies (Tephrítidae). A, *Peronỳma sarcinàta* (Loew); B, *Acidogòna melanùra* (Loew); C, *Zonosémata elécta* (Say); D, *Paracántha cúlta* (Wiedemann). (Courtesy of USDA.)

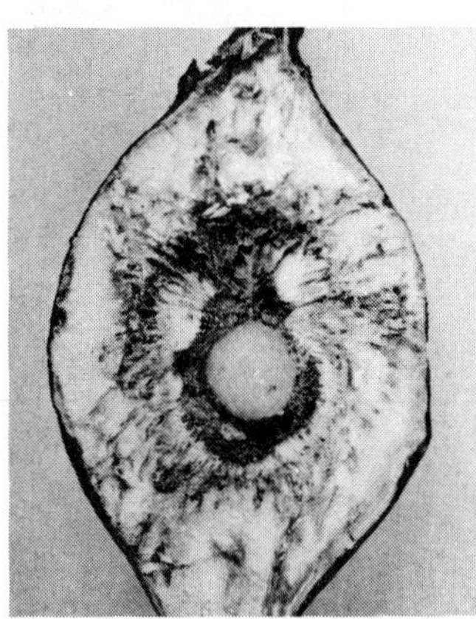

Figure 507. Gall of a goldenrod gall fly, *Eurósta* sp. (Tephrítidae), cut open to show the larva. (Courtesy of the Illinois Natural History Survey.)

apically, the femora thickened, and the hind tibiae often dilated. Our only species, *Rhỳtidops floridénsis* (Aldrich), occurs in Florida, where adults are usually found around fresh palm exudates.

Family **Coelòpidae**—Seaweed Flies: The members of this family are medium-sized to small flies, usually dark brown or black in color, and have the dorsum of the thorax conspicuously flattened and the body and legs very bristly (Figure 508). These flies occur along the seashore and are particularly abundant where various seaweeds have washed up. The larvae breed in the seaweed (chiefly kelp) in tremendous numbers, mainly just above the high-tide mark in seaweed that has begun to rot. The adults swarming over the seaweed often attract large numbers of shore birds, which feed on them. Seaweed flies feed on flowers, and sometimes cluster so thickly on the flow-

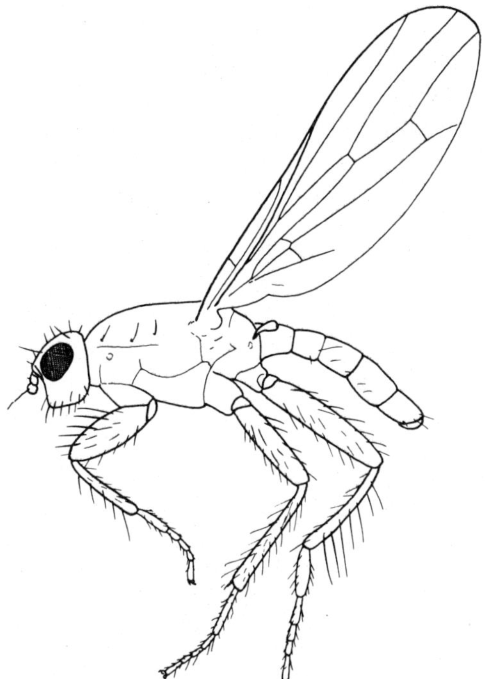

Figure 508. A seaweed fly, *Coelòpa* sp. (Coelòpidae), 10 ×.

ers near the shore that a single sweep of a net may yield a hundred or more individuals. Four of the five North American species occur along the Pacific Coast; the other, *Coelòpa frígida* (Fabricius), occurs along the Atlantic Coast from Rhode Island north.

Family **Dryomỳzidae:** This is a small (eight North American species) but widely distributed group resembling marsh flies. The adults are generally found in moist woods; the larval stages are unknown.

Family **Sépsidae**—Black Scavenger Flies: The sepsids are small, shining blackish flies (sometimes with a reddish tinge) that have the head spherical and the abdomen narrowed at the base (Figure 509); many species have a dark spot along the costal margin of the wing near the tip. The larvae live in excrement and various types of decaying materials. The adults are common flies, and are often found in considerable numbers near materials in which the larvae breed.

Family **Sciomỳzidae**—Marsh Flies: The marsh flies are small to medium-sized flies that are

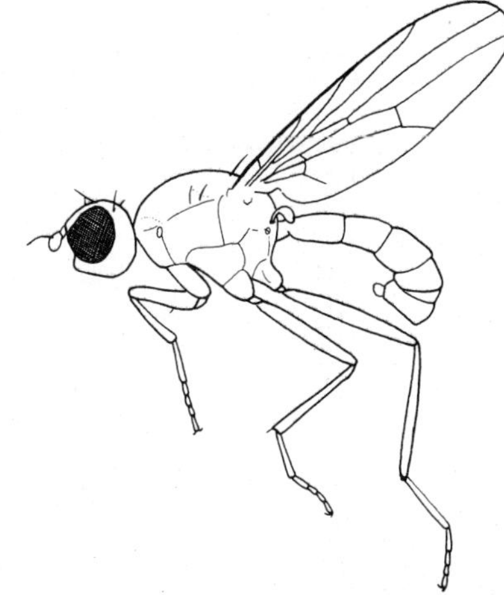

Figure 509. A black scavenger fly (Sépsidae), 15 ×.

usually yellowish or brownish, and have the antennae extending forward (Figure 510). Many species have spotted or patterned wings. They are common insects, and occur along the banks of ponds and streams, and in marshes, swamps, and woods. The larvae feed on snails, snail eggs, and slugs, generally as predators.

Family **Lauxanìidae:** Lauxaniids are small, relatively robust flies, rarely over 6 mm in length, and some have patterned wings; they vary considerably in color. They can usually be distinguished from other acalyptrate muscoids by the complete

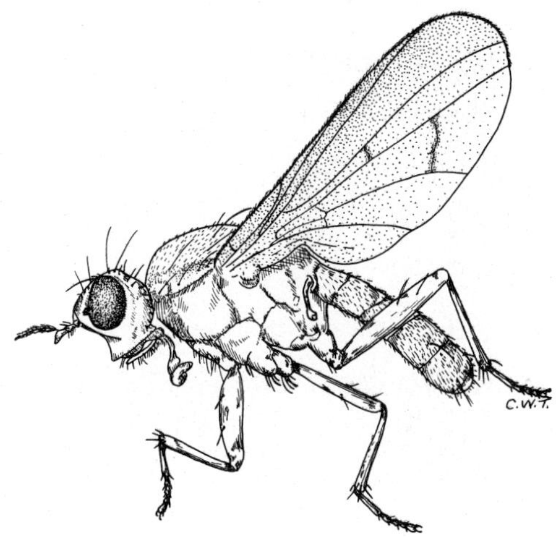

Figure 510. A marsh fly, *Tetanócera vícina* Macquart, 7½ ×.

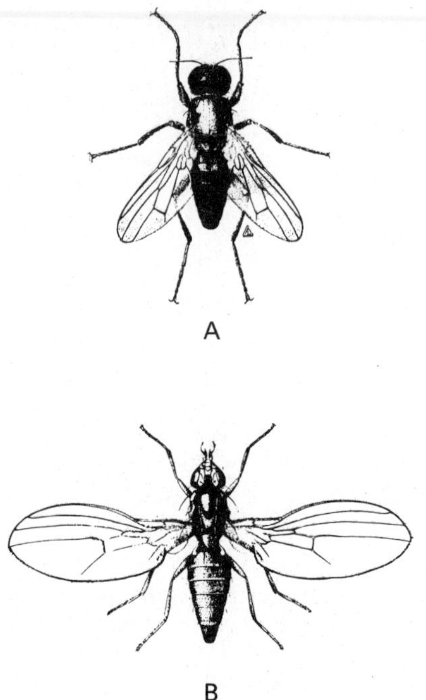

Figure 511. A, adult of cheese skipper, *Piópbila càsei* (L.) (Piophílidae); B, a leaf-miner fly, *Cerodóntha dorsàlis* (Loew) (Agromỳzidae). (Courtesy of USDA.)

subcosta, no oral vibrissae, and the postverticals converging. The group is a fairly large one (136 North American species), and its members are common in moist shady places; the larvae occur in decaying vegetation.

Family **Chamaemyìidae**—Aphid Flies: The chamaemyiids are small flies that are usually grayish in color with black spots on the abdomen. The larvae of most species are predaceous on aphids, scale insects, and mealybugs; one species has been reared from birds' nests.

Family **Periscelídidae:** The three North American species in this family are widely distributed but rare. They are usually found around the sap flowing from tree wounds; one species has been reared from fermenting oak sap.

Family **Piophílidae**—Skipper Flies: The skipper flies are usually less than 5 mm in length and are rather metallic black or bluish (Figure 511 A). The larvae are mostly scavengers, and some live in cheese and preserved meats. The larvae of the cheese skipper, *Pióphila càsei* (L.), are often serious pests in cheese and meats; the name "skipper" refers to the fact that the larvae can jump.

Family **Thyreophòridae:** This group is represented in the United States by two rare species of *Omomỳia,* which have been recorded from Arizona and California. These flies are 2.5–6.5 mm in length, and the males are densely hairy; there are deep grooves below the antennae, into which the antennae may be retracted. Little is known of the habits of these flies, but the California species, *O. hirsùta* Coquillett, has been collected from yucca.

Family **Neottiophílidae:** This principally European group is represented in North America by a single species, *Actenóptera hilarélla* (Zetterstedt), recorded from northern Quebec. The larva of a European species is an ectoparasitic blood-sucker on nestling birds.

Family **Palloptéridae:** Our nine species in this group are rare and poorly known; they are medium-sized flies that usually have pictured wings, and are found in moist shady places. The larvae of our species are unknown, but the larvae of European species are plant feeders in flower buds and stems, or occur under the bark of fallen trees where they prey on wood-boring beetle larvae.

Family **Lonchaèidae:** The lonchaeids are small, shining, blackish flies, with the abdomen in dorsal view oval and somewhat pointed apically; they occur chiefly in moist or shady places. The larvae are mostly secondary invaders of diseased or injured plant tissues; a few feed on pine cones, fruits, or vegetables. The group is a small one (38 North American species), and the adults are not very common.

Family **Sphaerocéridae**—Small Dung Flies: The sphaerocerids are very small, black or brown flies that can usually be recognized by the characteristic hind tarsi (Figure 463 A). They are found in swampy places near excrement, often in large numbers. The larvae live in excrement and refuse.

Family **Braùlidae**—Bee Lice: This family contains a single species, *Braùla coèca* Nitzsch, which occurs in various parts of the world but is quite rare in North America. It is wingless and 1.2–1.5 mm in length, and is found in bee hives, usually attached to the bees; the adults apparently feed on nectar and pollen at the bee's mouth.

Family **Tethìnidae:** Most tethinids are seashore species, occurring in beach grass, salt marshes, and around seaweed washed up on the shore; the majority are found along the Pacific Coast. The inland species occur mainly in alkaline areas.

Family **Milichìidae:** The milichiids are small flies, usually black or silvery in color, and are sometimes fairly common in open areas. The larvae generally live in decaying plant or animal materials; some are commensals of predaceous insects (riding on them, and feeding on exudates of their victims). One species, *Cárnus hemápterus* Nitzsch, which has rudimentary wings, is a bloodsucking ectoparasite of birds.

Family **Canacèidae**—Beach Flies: The canaceids are small flies that resemble the ephydrids in appearance and habits, but have only a single break in the costa, they have an anal cell, and the ocellar triangle is quite large (as in Figure 462 A). Adults of the five rare North American species occur along the seashore in the southeastern states and in California; the larvae live in the algae washed up on the shore.

Family **Ephýdridae**—Shore Flies: This is a large group (nearly 350 North American species), and some species are quite common. Shore flies are small to very small; most of them are dark colored, and a few have pictured wings. The adults are found in moist places—marshes, the shores of ponds and streams, and the seashore. The larvae are aquatic, and many species occur in brackish or even strongly saline or alkaline water; one western species, *Helaeomỳia petròlei* (Coquillett), breeds in pools of crude petroleum. These flies often occur in enormous numbers; pools along the seashore may sometimes be alive with the adults, which walk or cluster on the surface of the water (for example, *Éphydra ripària* Fallén, Figure 512). Along the shore of Great Salt Lake, ephydrids may arise from the ground in clouds, and a few sweeps of a net may yield a cupful. At one time the Indians gathered the puparia from the lake and ate them.

Family **Curtonòtidae:** This group is represented in North America by a single species, *Curtonòtum hélvum* (Loew), which occurs in the East. This species is about 6 mm in length, *Drosóphila*-like in appearance, and light yellowish brown with dark brown markings; it occurs in high grass in moist places. The larva is unknown.

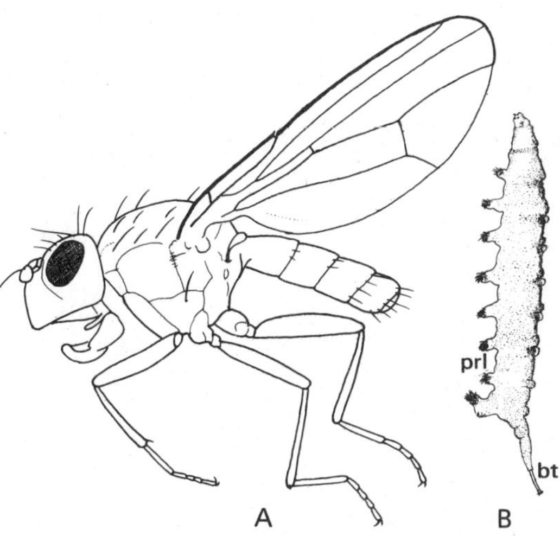

Figure 512. A shore fly, *Éphydra ripària* Fallén. A, adult, 10 ×; B, larva, 4 ×. *bt,* breathing tube; *prl,* prolegs. (B, courtesy of Peterson. Reprinted by permission.)

Family **Drosophílidae**—Pomace Flies or Small Fruit Flies: These flies are 3–4 mm in length and usually yellowish in color (Figure 513), and are generally found around decaying vegetation and fruit. This group is a large one (181 North American species), and many species are very common. The pomace flies are often pests in the household when fruit is present. The larvae of most species occur in decaying fruit and fungi. In the case of the larvae living in fruit, it has been shown that the larvae actually feed on the yeasts growing in the fruit. A few species are ectoparasitic (on caterpillars) or predaceous (on mealybugs and other small Homóptera) in the larval stage. Several species in this group, because of their short life span, giant salivary gland chromosomes, and ease of culturing, have been used extensively in studies of heredity.

Family **Diastátidae:** This is a small but widely distributed group whose members resemble the Drosophílidae and Curtonòtidae. Diastatids are relatively rare, and little is known of their habits.

Family **Camíllidae:** These flies resemble the Drosophílidae, but are metallic, lack sternopleural bristles, and have the anal cell open apically. One

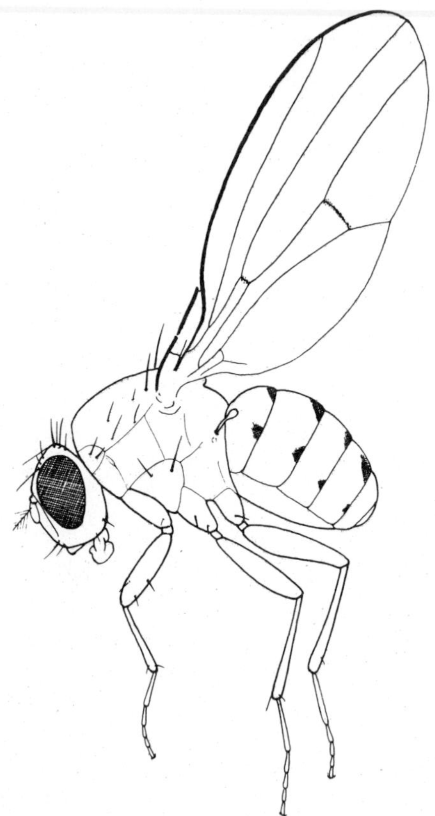

Figure 513. A pomace fly, *Drosóphila* sp., 20 ×.

species, *Camílla glàbra* (Fallén), has been recorded from Ontario; nothing is known of its biology.

Family **Chlorópidae:** The chloropids are small and rather bare flies, and some species are brightly colored with yellow and black. They are very common in meadows and other places where there is considerable grass, though they may be found in a variety of habitats. The larvae of most species feed in grass stems, and some are serious pests of cereals; a few are scavengers, and a few are parasitic or predaceous. Some of the chloropids (for example, *Hippélates*), which breed in decaying vegetation and excrement, are attracted to animal secretions and feed on pus, blood, and similar materials; they are particularly attracted to the eyes and are sometimes called eye gnats. These flies may act as vectors of yaws and pinkeye.

Family **Odinìidae:** This is a small group of uncommon flies, formerly placed in the family Agromỳzidae; they differ from the Agromỳzidae in having preapical tibial bristles and in having the wings patterned. The adults occur at fresh sap flows on trees, about woody fungi, on rotting tree trunks and stumps, and in similar places. Eleven species occur in the United States, most of them in the East.

Family **Agromỳzidae**—Leafminer Flies: These flies are small and usually blackish or yellowish in color (Figure 511 B). The larvae are leaf miners, and the adults occur almost everywhere. Most species are more easily recognized by their mines than by the insects themselves. *Phytomỳza aquilegívora* Spencer is a fairly common species that makes a serpentine mine in the leaves of wild columbine (Figure 514 B); *Agromỳza parvicòrnis* Loew makes a blotch mine in corn and several species of grasses; *Phytòbia clàra* (Melander) mines in the leaves of catalpa (Figure 514 A). Most agromyzids make serpentine mines, that is, narrow winding mines that increase in width as the larva grows.

Family **Clusìidae:** The clusiids are small (mostly 3–4 mm in length) and relatively uncommon flies in which the wings are often smoky or marked with brown, especially apically. The body color varies from pale yellow to black; some species have the thorax black dorsally and yellowish laterally. The larvae occur in decaying wood and under bark; they are able to jump, much like the larvae of skipper flies.

Family **Acartophthálmidae:** This family is represented in North America by two rare species that have been taken on rotten fungi and carrion from Massachusetts to Oregon and Alaska. One of these, *Acartophthálmus nigrìnus* (Zetterstedt), is about 2 mm long, and is black with the front coxae and halteres yellow.

Family **Heleomỳzidae:** The heleomyzids are a fairly large group (113 North American species) of small to medium-sized flies, most of which are brownish in color; many superficially resemble marsh flies (Sciomỳzidae), but they have well-developed oral vibrissae, the postvertical bristles are converging (Figure 461 C), the costa is spinose (Figure 459 H), and the antennae are smaller and less prominent. The adults are usually found in moist shady places; the larvae of most species live in decaying plant or animal matter, or in fungi.

Figure 514. Leaf mines of agromyzid flies. A, catalpa leafminer, *Phytòbia clàra* (Melander); B, columbine leafminer, *Phytomỳza aquilegívora* Spencer. (Courtesy of the Ohio Agricultural Research and Development Center.)

Family **Trixoscelídidae:** The members of this family are small flies, mostly 2–3 mm in length, with the body yellow or dark and the wings hyaline, spotted, or clouded. Thirty species are known in the United States, all but two occurring in the western states. *Spilochròa ornàta* (Johnson) (wings dark, with hyaline spots) occurs in Florida, and *Neóssos marylándica* Malloch (wings hyaline) has been reported from Maryland. These flies occur in grassy areas, woodlands, and deserts; *N. marylándica* Malloch has been reared from puparia found in the nests of various song birds.

Family **Rhinotòridae:** This is a small group of tropical flies, similar in general appearance and habits to the Ropaloméridae (page 593). Our only species, *Rhinotòra divérsa* Giglio-Tos, has been recorded in Arizona and New Mexico, where it was taken in banana-baited traps.

Family **Anthomỳzidae:** These flies are small and somewhat elongate, and occur in grass and low vegetation, especially in marshy areas; some species have pictured wings. The larvae live in marsh grasses and sedges.

Family **Opomỳzidae:** The opomyzids are small to minute flies that are usually found in grassy places; the known larvae feed in the stems of various grasses. Only 13 species have been reported from North America, and none of these is common; most of them occur in the West or in Canada.

Family **Chyromỳidae:** This is a small but widely distributed group of rather uncommon flies. Adults are usually taken on windows or on vegetation, and some species have been reared from birds' nests or rotting wood.

Family **Aulacigástridae:** This group is represented in the United States by a single species, *Aulacigáster leucopèza* (Meigen), which is widely distributed but rare. It is a small blackish fly, about 2.5 mm in length, with two light bands across the front above the antennae; the wings are slightly smoky. Adults occur on (and larvae breed in) sap flows from wounds in trees.

Family **Asteìidae:** This family contains small to minute flies (usually 2 mm in length or less), and can be recognized by the peculiar venation: R_{2+3} ending in the costa close to R_1 (Figure 460 A). Only 19 species occur in North America, and little is known of their habits.

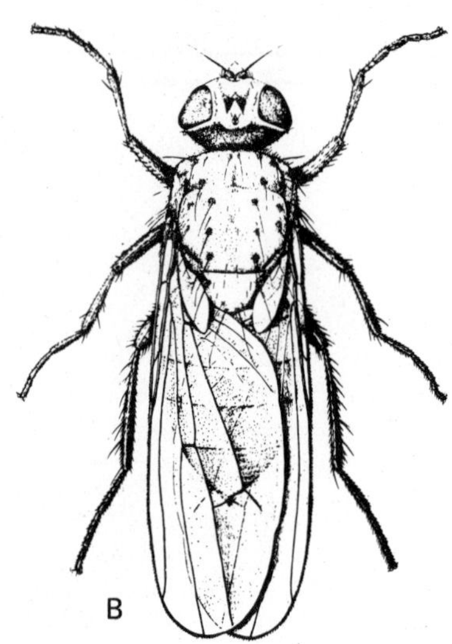

Figure 515. A, mines of spinach leafminer, *Pegomỳa hyoscỳami* (Panzer) (Anthomyìidae); B, adult female of seedcorn maggot, *Hylemỳa platùra* (Meigen), 8 × (Anthomyìidae). (A, courtesy of the Ohio Agricultural Research and Development Center; B, courtesy of USDA.)

Family **Cryptochètidae:** The flies in this group are somewhat similar to black flies (Simulìidae), and have habits similar to those of eye gnats (*Hippélates,* family Chlorópidae; see page 598). They can usually be recognized by the enlarged third antennal segment, which reaches nearly to the lower edge of the head, and which lacks an arista but bears at its apex a short spine or tubercle. As far as known, the larvae are parasites of scale insects in the family Margaròdidae. This is principally an Old World group of flies, and only one species, *Cryptochèta icéryae* (Williston), occurs in this country. *C. icéryae* was introduced into California from Australia in the 1880s to control the cottony cushion scale, *Icérya púrchasi* Maskell. This fly is about 1.5 mm in length, stout-bodied, with the head and thorax dark metallic blue and the abdomen shiny green. The introduction was a successful one; this fly is probably a more important natural enemy of the cottony cushion scale than the ladybird beetle *Rodòlia cardinàlis* (Mulsant), which was also introduced from Australia to control this scale insect.

Family **Anthomyìidae:** The members of this group are very similar to the Múscidae (in which family they are sometimes placed), but differ in having the anal vein ($Cu_2 + 2A$) reaching the wing margin, at least as a fold; most of them are dark-bodied and rather slender, and some (many Scatophagìnae) are quite hairy. This group is a large one, with some 560 North American species, and many are very common flies.

This family contains three subfamilies, the Scatophagìnae (which is sometimes given family rank), Fucelliìnae, and Anthomyiìnae. The Anthomyiìnae have fine erect hairs on the undersurface of the scutellum (Figure 454 D); these hairs are lacking in the other two subfamilies. The Fucelliìnae have cruciate frontal bristles and generally four sternopleural bristles, and the costa is spinose; the Scatophagìnae lack cruciate frontal bristles and generally have only one sternopleural bristle, and the costa is usually not spinose. Some of the more common Scatophagìnae are yellowish and quite hairy. The Scatophagìnae and Anthomyiìnae are large and widely distributed groups; the Fucelliìnae is a small group (only 18 North American species), and most of its members occur in the West and in Canada (some are common on Pacific Coast beaches).

The larval habits of anthomyiids are rather varied. Many of the Anthomyiìnae are plant feeders, in many cases feeding on the roots of the host

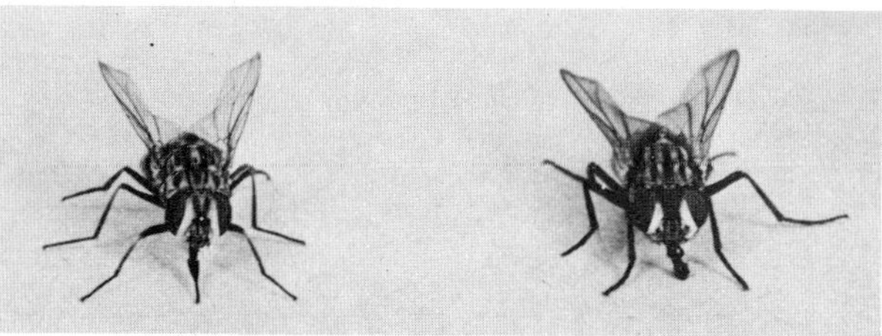

Figure 516. Two common muscids, showing the difference in the shape of the proboscis. Left, stable fly; right, house fly. (Courtesy of the Illinois Natural History Survey.)

plant; some of these (Figure 515) are serious pests of garden or field crops. Some of the Scatophagìnae are plant feeders (some of these are leaf miners), and some live in dung. The larvae of the Fucelliìnae are aquatic and predaceous.

Family **Múscidae:** This is a large group (over 700 North American species), and its members are to be found almost everywhere; many are important pests. The house fly, *Músca doméstica* L., breeds in filth of all kinds and is often very abundant; it is known to be a vector of typhoid fever, dysentery, yaws, anthrax, and some forms of conjunctivitis; it does not bite. The face fly, *Músca autumnàlis* De Geer, is an important pest of cattle; it gets its name from its habit of clustering on the face of cattle. The stable fly, horn fly, and tsetse flies are biting flies; unlike mosquitoes, horse flies, and others, both sexes bite. The stable fly, *Stomóxys cálcitrans* (L.) (Figure 517), is very similar to the house fly in appearance (Figure 516); it breeds chiefly in piles of decaying straw. The horn fly, *Haematòbia írritans* (L.), which is similar to the house fly in appearance but is smaller, is a serious pest of cattle; it breeds in fresh cow dung. The tsetse flies, *Glossìna* spp., do not occur in this country, but in Africa are vectors of the trypanosomes that cause sleeping sickness and similar diseases of man and various animals.

Fánnia and its relatives (subfamily Fanniìnae) differ from other muscids in having 3A curved outward distally, so that $Cu_2 + 2A$ if extended would meet it (Figure 455 D); this group is sometimes given family rank. These flies look very much like small house flies, and in some areas are a more important household pest than *M. doméstica;* the larvae breed in excrement and various types of decaying materials.

Family **Gasterophílidae**—Horse Bot Flies: These flies are somewhat similar to honey bees in general appearance. The larvae infest the alimentary tract of horses and are often serious pests. Three species occur commonly in this country, *Gasteróphilus intestinàlis* (De Geer), *G. nasàlis* (L.),

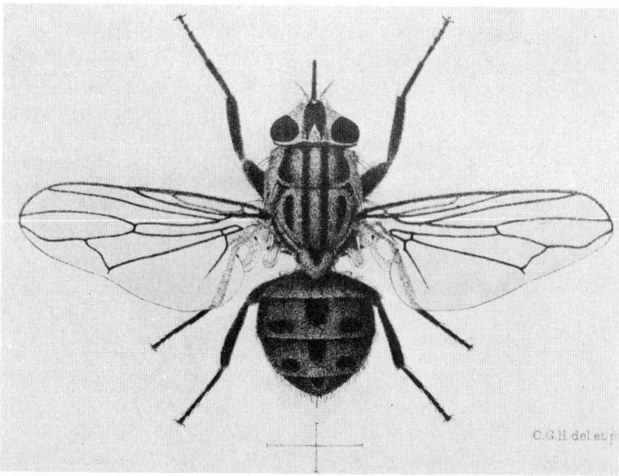

Figure 517. Stable fly, *Stomóxys cálcitrans* (L.). (Courtesy of the Illinois Natural History Survey.)

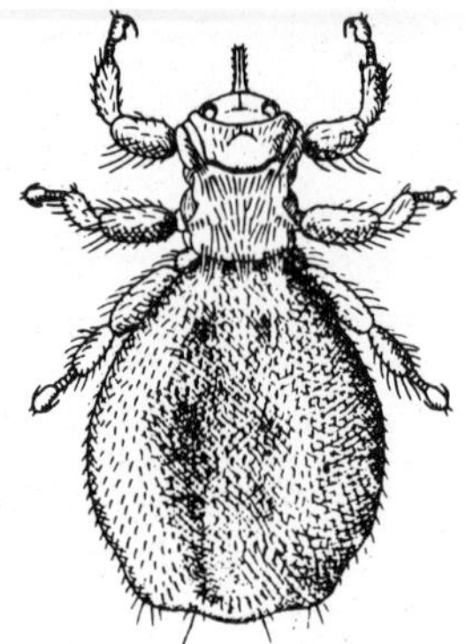

Figure 518. Sheep ked, or sheep-tick, *Melóphagus ovìnus* (L.). (Courtesy of Knowlton, Madsen, and the Utah Agricultural Experiment Station.)

Figure 519. A blow fly, *Lucília illústris* (Meigen).

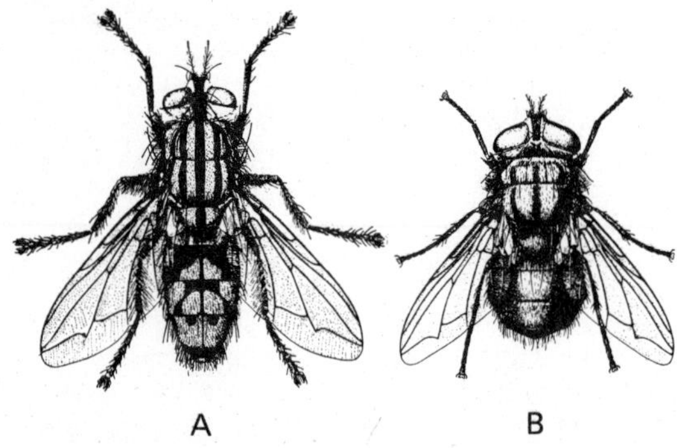

Figure 520. A, flesh fly, *Sarcóphaga haemorrhoidàlis* (Fallén); B, screwworm fly, *Cochliomỳia hominivòrax* (Coquerel) (Calliphòridae). (Courtesy of USDA.)

and *G. haemorrhoidàlis* (L.); a fourth species, *G. inérmis* Brauer, is very rare. In *G. intestinàlis* (Figure 523 A) the eggs are laid on the legs or shoulders of the horse and are taken into the mouth when the animal licks these parts. In *G. nasàlis* the eggs are usually laid on the underside of the jaw, and the larvae are believed to make their way through the skin into the mouth. In *G. haemorrhoidàlis* the eggs are laid on the lips of the horse. The larvae develop in the stomach (*intestinàlis*), duodenum (*nasàlis*), or rectum (*haemorrhoidàlis*); when ready to pupate, they pass out of the alimentary tract with the feces and pupate in the ground.

Family **Hippobóscidae**—Louse Flies: This group includes both winged and wingless forms. Most of the winged forms are dark brownish in color and somewhat smaller than house flies; they are most likely to be found on birds. These flies are easily recognized by their flat shape and leathery appearance; they are the only flies likely to be found on living birds. The sheep ked, *Melóphagus ovìnus* (L.) (Figure 518), is a fairly common wingless louse fly; it is about 6 mm in length, reddish brown in color, and is a parasite of sheep.

Families **Stréblidae** and **Nycteribìidae**—Bat Flies: These flies are ectoparasites of bats. Those in the family Stréblidae may be winged or wingless, or may have the wings reduced; there are no ocelli, and the compound eyes are small or absent. The bat flies in the family Nycteribìidae are small, wingless, and spiderlike, with the head folded back into a groove on the dorsum of the thorax; the compound eyes are small and 2-faceted. Only eleven species of bat flies occur in North America (six in the Stréblidae, five in the Nycteribiidae), and they are very seldom encountered; they occur in the South and West.

Family **Calliphòridae**—Blow Flies: Blow flies are to be found practically everywhere; many species are of considerable economic importance. Most blow flies are about the size of a house fly or a little larger, and many are metallic blue or green (Figure 519. Blow flies are very similar to flesh flies (Sarcophágidae), and some authorities put the two groups in a single family, the Metopìidae. Blow flies are often metallic in color and have the arista of the antenna plumose to the tip, whereas flesh flies are blackish with gray thoracic stripes (Figure 520 A), and have the arista bare or only the basal half plumose. In blow flies, the hindmost posthumeral bristle is usually more laterally located than is the presutural bristle, but in flesh flies the hindmost posthumeral bristle is either on a level with or is nearer the midline than the presutural bristle (Figure 456). Blow flies usually have two notopleural bristles and flesh flies usually have four.

Most blow flies are scavengers, the larvae living in carrion, excrement, and similar materials; the most common species are those that breed in carrion. These species lay their eggs on bodies of dead animals, and the larvae feed on the decaying tissues of the animal. To most people a dead animal teeming with maggots (mostly the larvae of blow flies) is a nauseating thing, but it should be remembered that these insects are performing a valuable service to man in helping to remove dead animals from the landscape. The larvae of some of the species that breed in carrion, particularly *Phaenícia sericàta* (Meigen) and *Phórmia regìna* (Meigen), when reared under aseptic conditions, have been used in the treatment of such diseases as osteomyelitis in man. On the other hand, many of these flies may act as mechanical vectors of various diseases; dysentery frequently accompanies high blow-fly populations.

Some blow flies lay their eggs in open sores of animals or man; in some cases the larvae feed only on decaying or suppurating tissue, but in other cases they may attack living tissue. The screwworm fly, *Cochliomỳia hominivòrax* (Coquerel) (Figure 520 B), is a species in the latter category; it lays its eggs in wounds or in the nostrils of its host, and its larvae may cause considerable damage. In recent years the number of screwworm flies in the South and Southwest has been greatly reduced by releasing large numbers of sterile male flies; the females mate only once, and if a female mates with a sterile male, its eggs fail to hatch.

Flies in this family are the "house flies" of the West, especially the Southwest; they are far more common than *Músca* in houses in that part of the country.

When fly larvae become parasitic on man or animals, the condition is spoken of as myiasis. The flies such as the screwworm may develop in surface wounds and cause cutaneous myiasis, or in the nasal cavities and cause nasal myiasis; a few other flies in this group have been known to develop in the intestine of man and cause intestinal myiasis. Myiasis in man is relatively rare in this part of the world and is probably a more or less accidental occurrence; in the South and Southwest it has been very important in domestic animals.

Family **Sarcophágidae**—Flesh Flies: Flesh flies are very similar to some blow flies, but are generally blackish with gray thoracic stripes (never metallic) (Figure 520 A). The adults are common insects and feed on various sugar-containing materials such as nectar, sap, fruit juices, and honeydew. The larvae vary considerably in habits, but nearly all feed on some sort of animal material; many are scavengers, feeding on dead animals; some are parasites of other insects (especially various beetles and grasshoppers); a few are parasites of vertebrates, usually developing in skin pustules, and some of these occasionally infest man; many species (most of the Miltogrammìnae) lay their eggs in the nests of various bees and wasps, where their larvae feed on the materials with which these nests are provisioned.

Family **Tachínidae:** This family is the second largest in the order (at least in North America), with over 1300 North American species, and its members are to be found almost everywhere. It is a very valuable group, as the larval stages are parasites of other insects, and many species aid in keeping pest species in check.

Tachinids are usually relatively easy to recognize. Both the hypopleural and pteropleural bristles are developed, and the postscutellum is prominent (Figure 453 B); the ventral sclerites of the abdomen are usually overlapped by the terga, and the abdomen generally has a number of very large bristles in addition to the smaller ones; the first posterior (R_5) cell is narrowed or closed distally; and most species have the arista bare. Many tachinids are very similar in general appearance to muscids and flesh flies (Figures 521 and 522 A); many are large, bristly, and beelike or wasplike in appearance.

Many different groups of insects are attacked by tachinids, and while most tachinids are more or less restricted to particular hosts, there are a few that may develop in a wide variety of hosts. Most tachinids attack the larvae of Lepidóptera, sawflies, or beetles, but some are known to attack Hemíptera, Orthóptera, and some other orders, and a few attack other arthropods. A number of tachinids have been imported into this country to aid in the control of introduced pests.

Most tachinids deposit their eggs directly on the body of their host, and it is not at all uncommon to find caterpillars with several tachinid eggs on them. Upon hatching, the tachinid larva usually burrows into its host and feeds internally (Figure 522); when fully developed, it leaves the host and pupates nearby. Some tachinids lay their

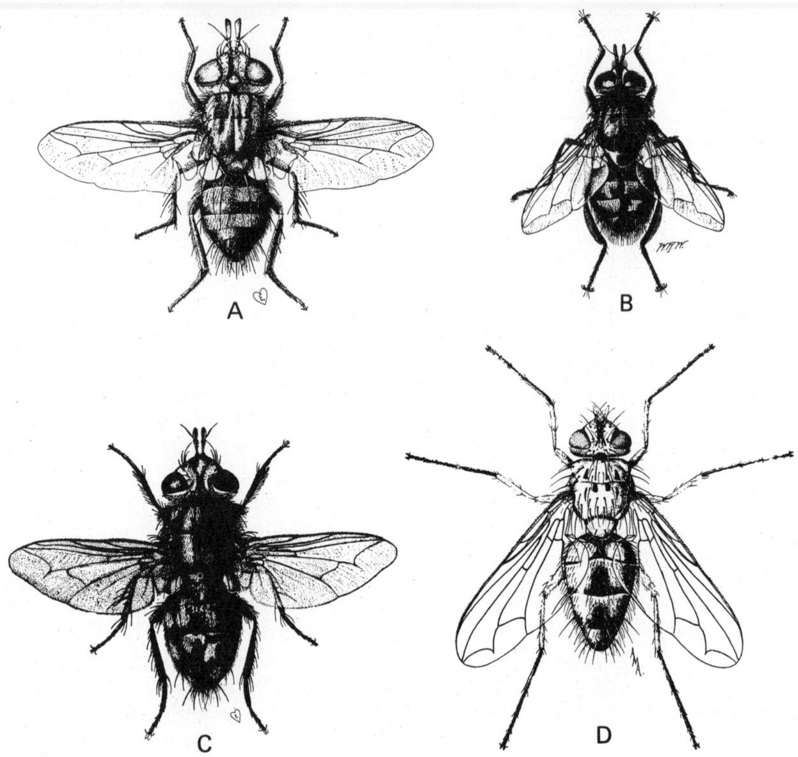

Figure 521. Tachinid flies. A, *Euphorócera claripénnis* (Macquart); B, *Winthèmia quadripustulàta* (Fabricius); C, *Árchytas marmoràtus* (Townsend); D, *Dexílla ventràlis* (Aldrich). (Courtesy of USDA.)

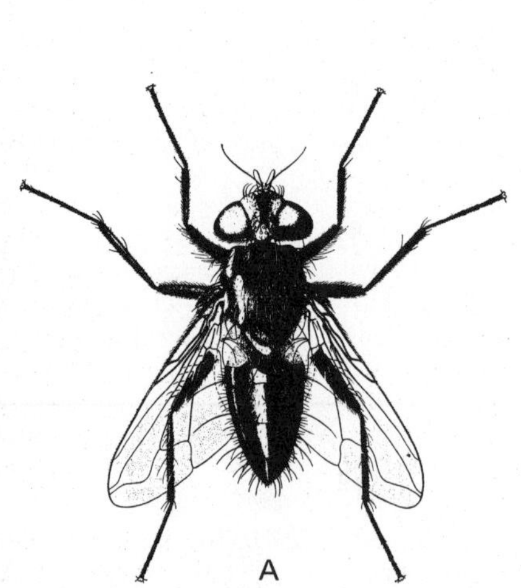

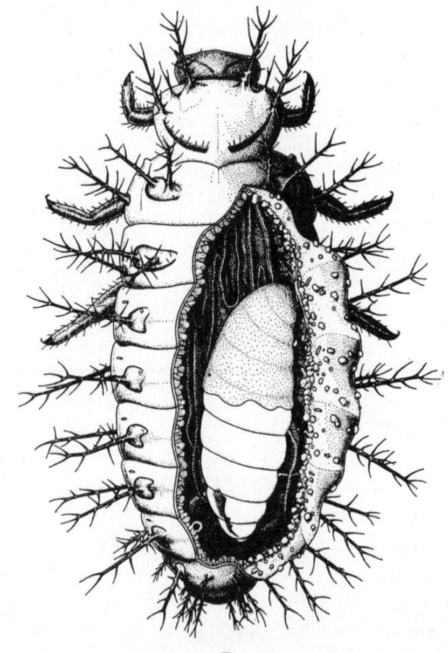

Figure 522. Bean beetle tachinid, *Aplomyiópsis epiláchnae* (Aldrich). A, adult; B, a bean beetle larva dissected to show a larva of this tachinid inside it. (Courtesy of USDA.)

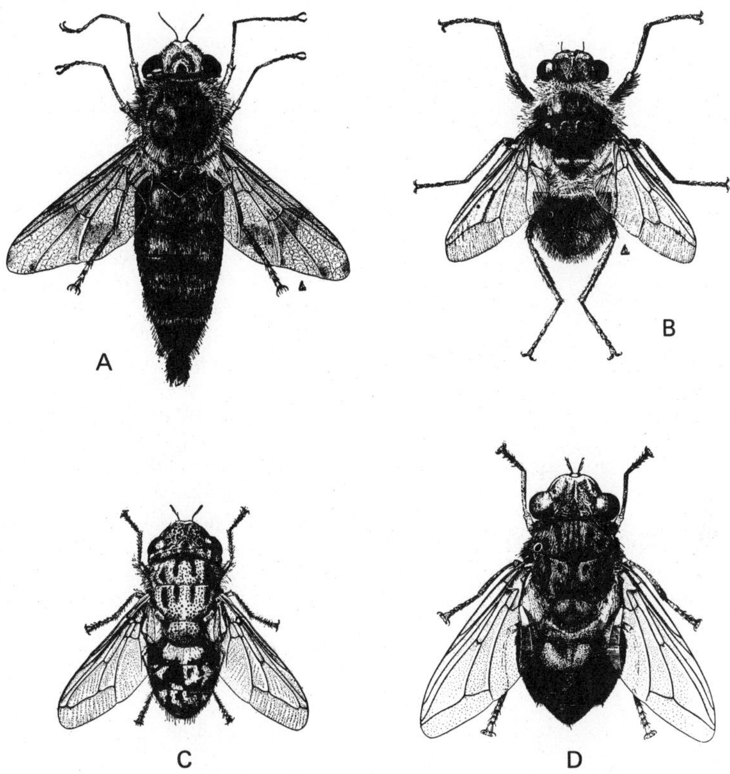

Figure 523. Bot and warble flies. A, horse bot fly, *Gasteróphilus intestinàlis* (De Geer), female; B, ox warble fly, *Hypodérma lineàtum* (de Villers), female; C, sheep bot fly, *Oéstrus òvis* L., female; D, human bot fly or torsalo, *Dermatòbia hóminis* (L., Jr.), female. (Courtesy of USDA.)

eggs on foliage; these eggs usually hatch into peculiar flattened larvae called planidia, which remain on the foliage until they can attach to a suitable host when it passes by. In other species that lay their eggs on foliage, the eggs hatch when they are ingested (along with the foliage) by a caterpillar; the tachinid larvae then proceed to feed on the internal organs of the caterpillar. An insect attacked by tachinids is practically always killed eventually.

Family **Cuterébridae**—Robust Bot Flies: The robust bot flies are large, stout-bodied, rather hairy flies that resemble bees; the larvae of most species are parasitic on rabbits and rodents. One tropical species, *Dermatòbia hóminis* (L., Jr.) (Figure 523 D), attacks livestock and occasionally man; this species lays its eggs on mosquitoes (principally mosquitoes in the genus *Psoróphora*), and the eggs hatch and the larvae penetrate the skin when the mosquito feeds on livestock or man. Stable flies and other muscids also serve as carriers of *D. hóminis* eggs to man.

Family **Oéstridae**—Warble Flies and Bot Flies: The members of this group are large, stout-bodied flies that resemble bees, and the larvae are endoparasites of various mammals. The sheep bot fly, *Oéstrus òvis* L. (Figure 523 C), is viviparous and deposits its larvae in the nostrils of sheep (rarely, also in man); the larvae feed in the frontal sinuses of the sheep. The ox warble flies, *Hypodérma bòvis* (L.) and *H. lineàtum* (de Villers) (Figure 523 B), are serious pests of cattle. The eggs of these species are usually laid on the legs of cattle, and the larvae penetrate the skin and migrate, often by way of the esophagus, to the back, where they develop in swellings or "warbles" just under the skin. When full grown, they escape through the skin and pupate in the ground. The adults of the ox warbles are very fast fliers, and although they do not bite or injure the cattle when they oviposit, they are very annoying to cattle. Ox warbles may seriously affect the health of cattle, and the holes made in the skin by the escaping larvae reduce the value of the hide when it is made into leather.

COLLECTING AND PRESERVING DÍPTERA

The general methods of collecting Díptera are similar to those of collecting other insects; to obtain a large variety, one must collect in a variety of habitats. Many of the smaller species can be best collected by sweeping, putting the entire catch into the killing bottle, and examining it carefully later. Traps such as that shown in Figure 617 A, using various types of baits, are useful collecting devices.

Most Díptera, particularly the smaller specimens, should be mounted as soon as possible after they are captured because they dry quickly and are likely to be damaged in mounting if they have dried out very much; it is best to mount them within a few hours after they are captured. Many of the smaller and more delicate specimens, such as midges, mosquitoes, and similar forms, should be handled very carefully in order to avoid rubbing off the minute hairs and scales; these are often important in identification, particularly if the specimen is ever identified to species. The only way to get good specimens of many of these delicate forms is to rear them and to get them into a killing jar without using a net.

The larger Díptera are preserved on pins, and the smaller specimens are mounted on points or microscopic slides. In pinning a fly, particularly the muscoids, it is important that the bristles on the dorsum of the thorax be kept intact; the pin should be inserted to one side of the midline. Most Díptera less than 6 mm in length, and some of the more slender forms longer than this, should be mounted on points, preferably on their side. Some of the more minute specimens (especially Nematócera) should be preserved on fluids, and must be mounted on microscope slides for detailed study.

References on the Díptera

Alexander, C. P. 1967. The crane flies of California. *Calif. Insect Surv. Bull.*, 8:1–269; 524 f.

Byers, G. W. 1969. A new family of nematocerous Diptera. *J. Kan. Ent. Soc.*, 42(4):366–371; 5 f. (Baeonotidae)

Carpenter, S. J., and W. J. LaCasse. 1955. *Mosquitoes of North America (North of Mexico).* Berkeley: Univ. California Press, vii + 360 pp., 127 pl.

Cole, F. R. 1969. *The Flies of Western North America.* Berkeley: Univ. California Press, xi + 693 pp., frontis. (col.) + 360 f.

Curran, C. H. 1934. *The Families and Genera of North American Diptera.* New York: published by the author, 512 pp.; illus. A reprint of this book has been published by Henry Tripp, Mt. Vernon, N.Y., 1965.

Diptera of Connecticut. 1942–1964. Guide to the insects of Connecticut. Part VI. The Diptera, or true flies of Connecticut. Bulletins of the Conn. State Geol. and Nat. Hist. Survey. First Fascicle, 1942, Bull. 64: External morphology; key to families; Tanyderidae, Ptychopteridae, Trichoceridae, Anisopodidae, and Tipulidae; by G. C. Crampton, C. H. Curran, C. P. Alexander, and R. B. Friend; x + 509 pp., 4 pl., 54 f. Second Fascicle, 1945, Bull. 68: Family Culicidae, the mosquitoes; by R. Matheson; ix + 48 pp., 6 pl., 16 f. Third Fascicle, 1946, Bull. 69; Asilidae; by S. W. Bromley; viii + 48 pp., frontis. + 39 f. Fourth Fascicle, 1950, Bull. 75: Family Tabanidae; by G. B. Fairchild; and family Phoridae; by C. T. Brues; vi + 85 pp., 1 pl. 8 f. Fifth Fascicle, 1952, Bull. 80: Tendipedidae (Chironomidae); by O. A. Johannsen and H. K. Townes; Heleidae (Ceratopogonidae); by O. A. Johannsen; and Fungivoridae (Mycetophilidae); by F. R. Shaw and E. G. Fisher; viii + 250 pp., 34 pl. (379 f.). Sixth Fascicle, 1958, Bull. 87: March flies and gall midges (Bibionidae); by D. E. Hardy; and Itonididae (Cecidomyiidae); by A. E. Pritchard and E. P. Felt; vi + 218 pp., 15 pl. Seventh Fascicle, 1960, Bull. 92: Psychodidae; by L. W. Quate; v + 54 pp., 7 pl. Eighth Fascicle, 1963, Bull. 93: Scatopsidae and Hyperoscelidae; by E. F. Cook; Blephariceridae and Deuterophlebiidae; by C. P. Alexander; and Dixidae; by W. R. Nowell; vi + 115 pp., 20 pl. Ninth Fascicle, 1964, Bull. 97: Simuliidae and Thaumaleidae; by A. Stone; vii + 126 pp., 81 f.

Felt, E. P. 1940. *Plant Galls and Gall Makers.* Ithaca, N.Y.: Comstock Publ., viii + 364 pp., 344 f., 41 pl.

Gillette, J. D. 1971. *Mosquitoes.* London: Weidenfeld and Nicolson, 274 pp., 22 f., 38 pl.

Hall, D. G. 1948. *The Blow Flies of North America.* Thomas Say Foundation, Publ. 4; v + 477 pp., 5 col. pl., 46 pl., 9 f.

Hennig, W. 1948–1952. *Die Larvenformen der Dipteren.* Berlin: Akademie-Verlag. Part 1, 1948; 185 pp., 63 f., 3 pl. Part 2, 1950; 458 pp., 276 f., 10 pl. Part 3, 1952; 628 pp., 338 f., 21 pl.

Huckett, H. C. 1965. *The Muscidae of Northern Canada, Alaska, and Greenland (Diptera).* Mem. Ent. Soc. Can. 42; 369 pp., 280 f.

Hull, F. M. 1962. *Robberflies of the world. The genera of the family Asilidae.* U.S. Natl. Mus. Bull. 224 (2 vol.); 907 pp., 2571 f.

Ide, F. P. 1965. A fly of the archaic family Nymphomyiidae (Diptera) from North America. *Can. Ent.,* 97(5):496–507; 21 f.

James, M. T. 1960. The soldier flies or Stratiomyidae of California. *Bull. Calif. Insect Surv.,* 6(5):79–122.

Johannsen, O. A. 1910–1912. The fungus gnats of North America. *Maine Agric. Expt. Sta. Bull.,* 172:209–279, 180:125–192, 196:249–327, 200:57–146; 19 pl.

Kessel, E. L., and E. A. Maggioncalda. 1968. A revision of the genera of Platypezidae, with descriptions of five new genera, and considerations of the phylogeny, circumversion, and hypopygia (Diptera). *Weismann J. Biol.,* 26(1):33–106; 57 f.

Maa, T. C. 1971. An annotated bibliography of batflies (Diptera: Streblidae, Nycteribiidae). *Pacific Insects Monog.,* 28:119–211.

Martin, C. H. 1968. The new family Leptogastridae (the grass flies) compared with the Asilidae (robber flies) (Diptera). *J. Kansas Ent. Soc.,* 41(1):70–100; 137 f.

Matheson, R. 1944. *Handbook of the Mosquitoes of North America.* Ithaca, N.Y.: Comstock Publ., viii + 314 pp., 41 f., 33 pl.

McAlpine, J. F. 1963. Relationships of *Cremifania* Czerny (Diptera: Chamaemyiidae) and description of a new species. *Can. Ent.,* 95(3):239–253; 12 f.

McFadden, M. W. 1972. The soldier flies of Canada and Alaska (Diptera: Stratiomyidae). I. Beridinae, Sarginae, and Clitellariinae. *Can. Ent.,* 104(4): 531–561.

Oldroyd, H. 1964. *The Natural History of Flies.* London: Weidenfeld and Nicolson, xiv + 324 pp., 40 f., 32 pl.

Pechuman, L. L. 1973. *Horse Flies and Deer Flies of Virginia (Diptera: Tabanidae).* Va. Polytech. Inst. and State Univ., Res. Div. Bull. 81; 92 pp., 50 f.

Peters, T. M., and E. F. Cook. 1966. The nearctic Dixidae (Diptera). *Misc. Pub. Ent. Soc. Amer.,* 5(5):231–278; 123 f.

Peterson, A. 1951. *Larvae of Insects.* Part II. *Coleoptera, Diptera, Neuroptera, Siphonaptera, Mecoptera, Trichoptera.* Ann Arbor, Mich.: Edwards Bros., v + 519 pp., 104 f.

Roback, S. D. 1951. A classification of the muscoid calyptrate Diptera. *Ann. Ent. Soc. Amer.,* 44(3):327–361; 2 f., 7 pl.

Spencer, K. A. 1969. *The Agromyzidae of Canada and Alaska.* Mem. Ent. Soc. Can. 64; 311 pp., 552 f.

Steffan, W. A. 1966. A generic revision of the family Sciaridae (Diptera) of America north of Mexico. *Univ. Calif. Pub. Ent.,* 44:1–77; 22 f.

Steyskal, G. C. 1967. A key to the genera of Anthomyiinae known to occur in America north of Mexico, with notes on the genus *Ganperda* (Diptera: Anthomyiidae). *Proc. Biol. Soc. Wash.,* 80:1–7; 6 f.

Stone, A. 1970. A synoptic catalog of the mosquitoes of the world, Supplement IV (Diptera: Culicidae). *Proc. Ent. Soc. Wash.,* 72(2):137–171.

Stone, A., *et al.* 1965. *A Catalog of the Diptera of America North of Mexico.* USDA Agric. Handbook, 276; 1969 pp.

Sublette, J. E. 1964. Chironomid midges of California. II. Tanypodinae, Podonominae, and Diamesinae. *Proc. U.S. Natl. Mus.,* 115:85–136.

Thompson, P. H. 1967. Tabanidae of Maryland. *Trans. Amer. Ent. Soc.,* 93(4):463–519; 6 f.

Vockeroth, J. R. 1969. *A revision of the genera of the Syrphini (Diptera: Syrphidae).* Mem. Ent. Soc. Can. 62; 176 pp., 100 f., 26 maps.

Wirth, W. W., and A. Stone. 1956. Aquatic Diptera. In *Aquatic Insects of California,* R. L. Usinger, Ed. Berkeley: Univ. California Press, pp. 372–482, 64 f.

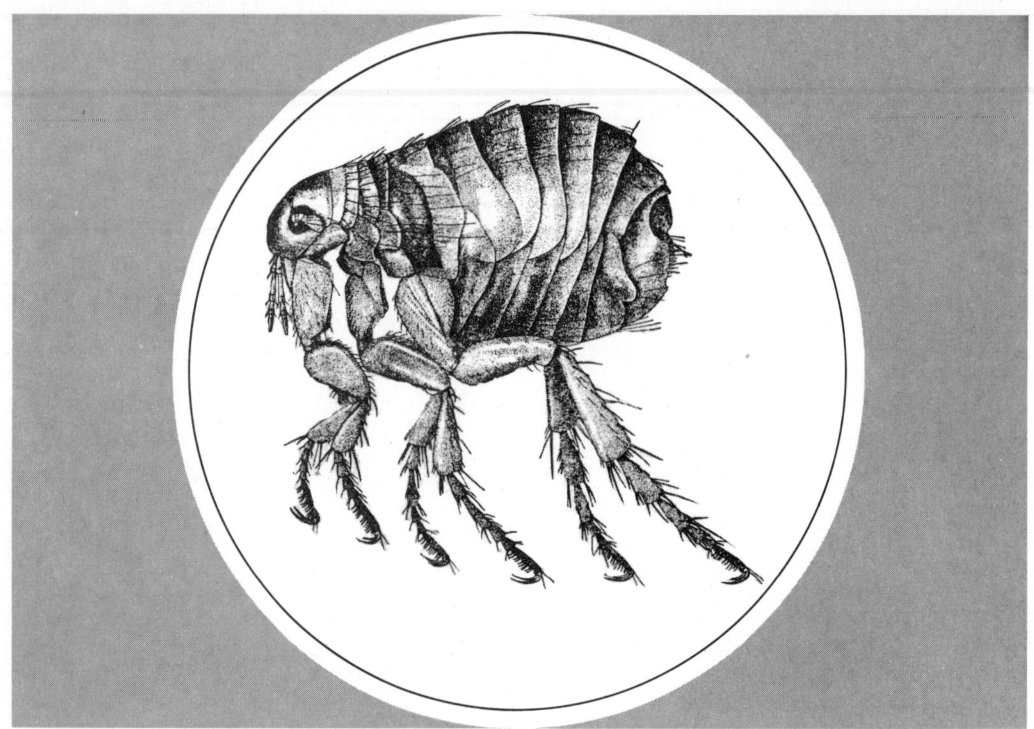

31: ORDER SIPHONÁPTERA[1]

FLEAS

The fleas are small wingless insects that feed as adults on the blood of birds and mammals. Many species are very annoying because of their bites, a few act as vectors of disease, a few serve as the intermediate host of certain tapeworms, and a few burrow into the skin of man or other animals.

The body of an adult flea (Figures 524 A and 526 D) is strongly flattened laterally and is provided with numerous backward-projecting spines and bristles. Fleas are jumping insects and have long legs with the coxae greatly enlarged. The antennae are short and lie in grooves in the head. The mouth parts (Figure 15) are of the sucking type, with three piercing stylets (the epipharynx and two maxillary stylets), and both maxillary and labial palps are well developed. Both sexes are blood-sucking. Eyes may be present or absent. The metamorphosis is complete.

Most fleas are active insects, moving freely over the body of their host, and frequently moving from one individual host to another. Many species, including those that attack man, are not very specific in their selection of a host and may feed on various animals. Many spend a large part of the time off the host. The adults are long-lived and may live a year or more; they are able to survive for several weeks off the host without feeding.

Fleas usually leave the host to lay their eggs, laying them in the dirt or in the nest of the host; the eggs may sometimes be laid on the host, but these eggs eventually fall off and develop on the

[1] Siphonáptera: *siphon*, a tube; *aptera*, wingless.

ground or in the host's nest. The eggs hatch into tiny, whitish, legless larvae, which are sparsely covered with bristly hairs and have a pair of tiny hooks on the last body segment (Figure 524 B); the head is well developed, and the mouth parts are of the chewing type. The larvae feed on organic debris, on their own cast skins, and on the feces of adult fleas; this latter item is an important part of the food of the larvae. When fully developed, the larva spins a silken cocoon and pupates; particles of dirt usually adhere to the cocoon.

FLEAS AND DISEASE The most important disease transmitted by fleas is plague, or black death, an acute infectious disease caused by the bacillus *Pasteurélla péstis* (Lehmann and Neumann). Three forms of plague occur in man, bubonic, pneumonic, and septicemic; the bubonic type is transmitted by fleas. Bubonic plague is a very serious disease because it often occurs in epidemic form and has a high mortality rate. Plague is primarily a disease of rodents and is spread from one rodent to another by fleas; rodents thus serve as a reservoir for the disease. The disease of wild rodents is often called sylvatic plague. Fleas may transmit plague in three ways: (1) by the regurgitation of the plague bacilli at the time of biting, due to a blocking of the digestive tract by clumps of the bacilli; (2) by infected feces of fleas being scratched into the skin; or (3) by the host ingesting an infected flea. Most plague transmission is by the first method.

Endemic typhus is a mild type of typhus caused by a *Rickéttsia;* it is primarily a disease of rodents (chiefly rats), but may be transmitted to man by fleas and to some extent by body lice.

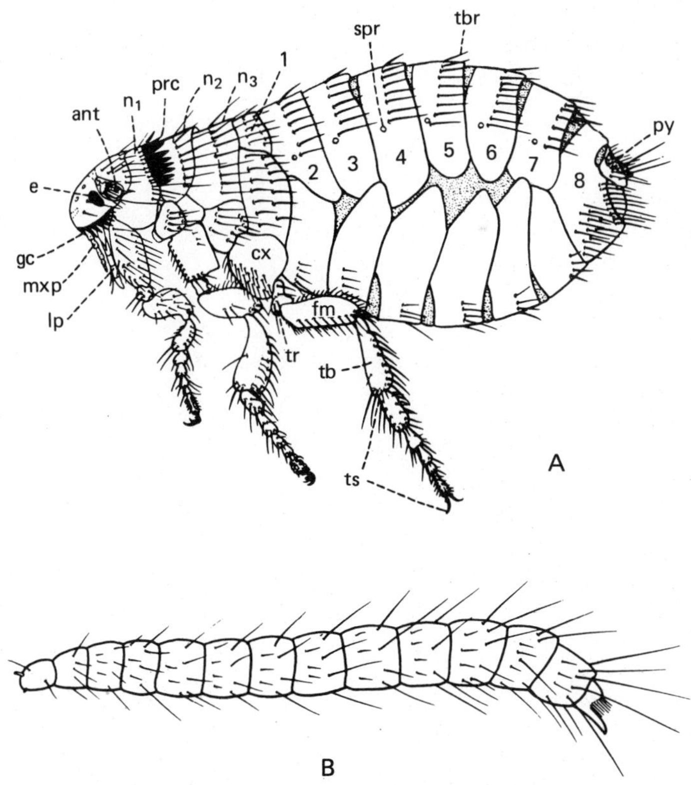

Figure 524. A, an adult cat flea, *Ctenocephálides fèlis* (Boúché); B, larva of a flea. *ant,* antenna; *cx,* coxa; *e,* eye; *fm,* femur; *gc,* genal comb; *lp,* labial palp; *mxp,* maxillary palp; n_1, pronotum; n_2, mesonotum; n_3, metanotum; *prc,* pronotal comb; *sn,* sensilium; *spr,* spiracle; *tb,* tibia; *tbr,* tergal or abdominal bristles; *tr,* trochanter; *ts,* tarsus; *1–8,* abdominal terga.

Fleas serve as the intermediate host of at least two species of tapeworms that occasionally infest man, *Dipylídium canìnum* (L.), usually a parasite of dogs, and *Hymenólepis diminùta* (Rudolphi), usually a parasite of rats. Larval fleas become infested with the tapeworm by ingesting the tapeworm eggs (which are passed in the feces of an infested host). Infection of the primary host (man, dog, or rat) follows the ingestion of a flea harboring the intermediate stage of the tapeworm.

CLASSIFICATION OF THE SIPHONÁPTERA

Several classifications of this order have been proposed in the past, but we follow here the classification of Lewis (1972–1975), which is much the same as that of Hopkins and Rothschild (1953, 1962). This arrangement puts the fleas of North America in seven families and is outlined below (with a list of the North American genera).

Pulícidae
- Tungìnae (Hectopsýllidae, Sarcopsýllidae)—chigoe flea (*Tùnga*)
- Pulicìnae
    - Archaeopsyllìni (Ctenocephálidae)—cat and dog fleas (*Ctenocephálides*)
    - Pulicìni (including Tungìnae in part)—sticktight flea (*Echidnóphaga*) and human flea and others (*Pùlex*)
    - Spilopsyllìni—fleas of various animals: *Actenopsýlla, Cediopsýlla, Euhoplopsýllus, Hoplopsýllus*
    - Xenopsyllìni—oriental rat flea (*Xenopsýlla*)

Rhopalopsýllidae—fleas of rodents and marsupials: *Polygènis, Rhopalopsýllus*

Vermipsýllidae—carnivore fleas: *Chaetopsýlla*

Hystrichopsýllidae
- Hystrichopsyllìnae—fleas of small rodents and insectivores: *Atyphlóceras, Hystrichopsýlla*
- Stenoponiìnae—fleas of small rodents: *Stenopònia*
- Neopsyllìnae
    - Neopsyllìni—fleas of ground squirrels and chipmunks: *Neopsýlla, Tamióphila*
    - Phalacropsyllìni—fleas of small rodents: *Catallàgia, Delotèlis, Epitédia, Maríngis, Phalacropsýlla*
- Anomiopsyllìnae
    - Jordanopsyllìni—fleas of mice: *Jordanopsýlla*
    - Anomiopsyllìni—fleas of rodents and their predators: *Anomiopsýllus, Callistopsýllus, Conorhinopsýlla, Megarthroglóssus, Stenistómera*
- Rhadinopsyllìnae
    - Corypsyllìni—fleas of insectivores: *Corypsýlla, Nearctopsýlla*
    - Rhadinopsyllìni—mostly fleas of rodents: *Paratyphlóceras, Rhadinopsýlla, Trichopsyllòides*
- Doratopsyllìnae—fleas of shrews: *Corrodopsýlla, Doratopsýlla*
- Ctenophthalmìnae
    - Carterettìni—fleas of small rodents: *Carterétta*
    - Ctenophthalmìni—fleas of moles and shrews: *Ctenophthálmus*

Ischnopsýllidae—bat fleas: *Myodopsýlla, Nycteridopsýlla, Sternopsýlla*

Leptopsýllidae
- Amphipsyllìnae
    - Amphipsyllìni—fleas of hares, etc.: *Amphipsýlla, Ctenophýllus, Odontopsýllus*
    - Dolichopsyllìni—*Dolichopsýllus* (on the mountain beaver)
    - Ornithophagìni—fleas of birds: *Ornithóphaga*
- Leptopsyllìnae—mouse fleas: *Leptopsýlla, Peromyscopsýlla*

Ceratophýllidae (Dolichopsýllidae in part)
- Ceratophyllìnae—mostly fleas of rodents: *Amphàlius, Ceratophýllus, Dasypsýllus, Diamànus, Jellisònia, Malàreus, Megábothris, Mioctenopsýlla, Monopsýllus, Nosopsýllus, Opisodàsys, Orchopèas, Oropsýlla, Pleochaètis, Tarsopsýlla, Thrássis*
- Foxellìnae—fleas of gophers, weasels, and lynxes: *Dactylopsýlla, Foxélla*

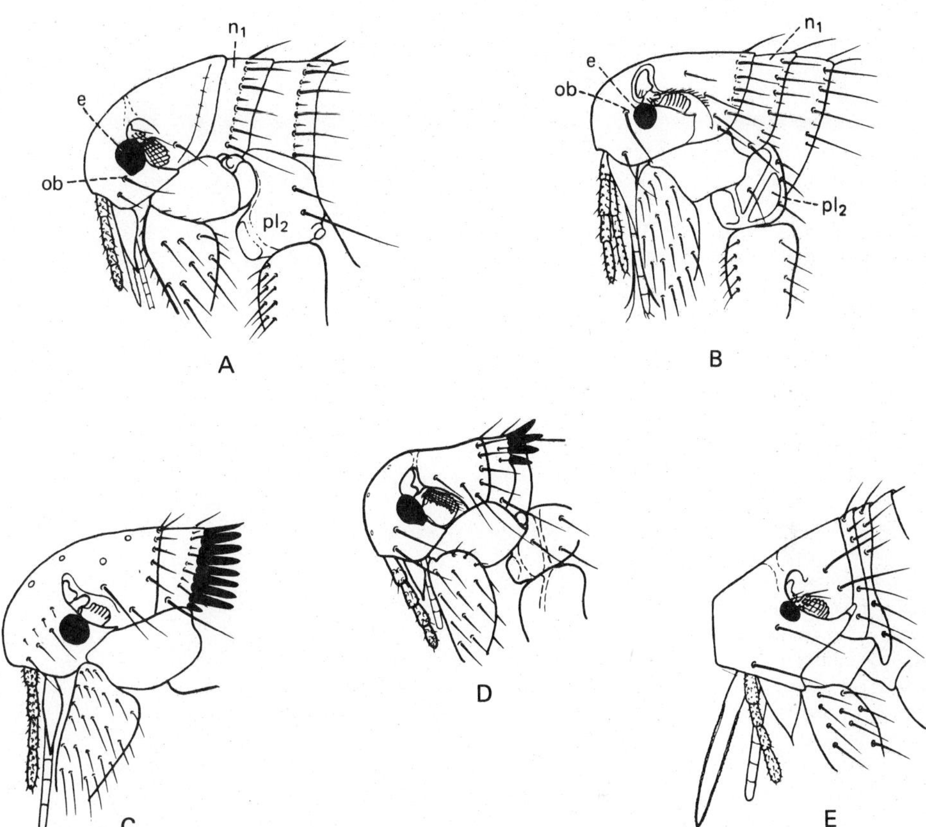

Figure 525. Head and prothoracic characters of Siphonáptera. A, human flea, *Pùlex írritans* L. (Pulícidae); B, oriental rat flea, *Xenopsýlla cheòpis* (Rothschild) (Pulícidae); C, northern rat flea, *Nosopsýllus fasciàtus* (Bosc) (Ceratophýllidae); D, rodent flea, *Hoplopsýllus anómalus* (Baker) (Pulícidae); E, sticktight flea, *Echidnóphaga gallinàcea* (Westwood) (Pulícidae). *e*, eye; n_1, pronotum; *ob*, ocellar bristle (below eye in A, in front of eye in B); pl_2, mesopleuron (with a **V**-shaped thickening in B which is absent in A).

CHARACTERS USED IN THE IDENTIFICATION OF SIPHONÁPTERA

The characters used to separate the families of fleas are best seen in specimens cleared and mounted on microscope slides. The sensilium (Figure 524 A, *sn*) is a plate (or pair of plates) located at the apex of the abdomen on the dorsal side of the body, just behind the last unmodified abdominal tergum; it has a group of rounded pits on each side. Spiniform bristles on the coxae are short stout bristles, usually located near the apex of the coxa. Internal ridges on the coxae are thickenings, usually apparent in a cleared specimen as a dark line extending the length of the coxa. The genal and pronotal combs (Figure 524 A, *gc* and *prc*) are rows of heavy bristles on the lower anterior margin of the head and the posterior margin of the pronotum. Antepygidial bristles are large bristles located just in front of the sensilium. The clypeal tubercle is located on the midline in the anterior part of the head; it is generally sunk in a groove and directed forward and upward (Figure 526 C, *clt*). The interantennal suture is a suture extending across the top of the head between the bases of the antennae (Figure 526 B, *ias*).

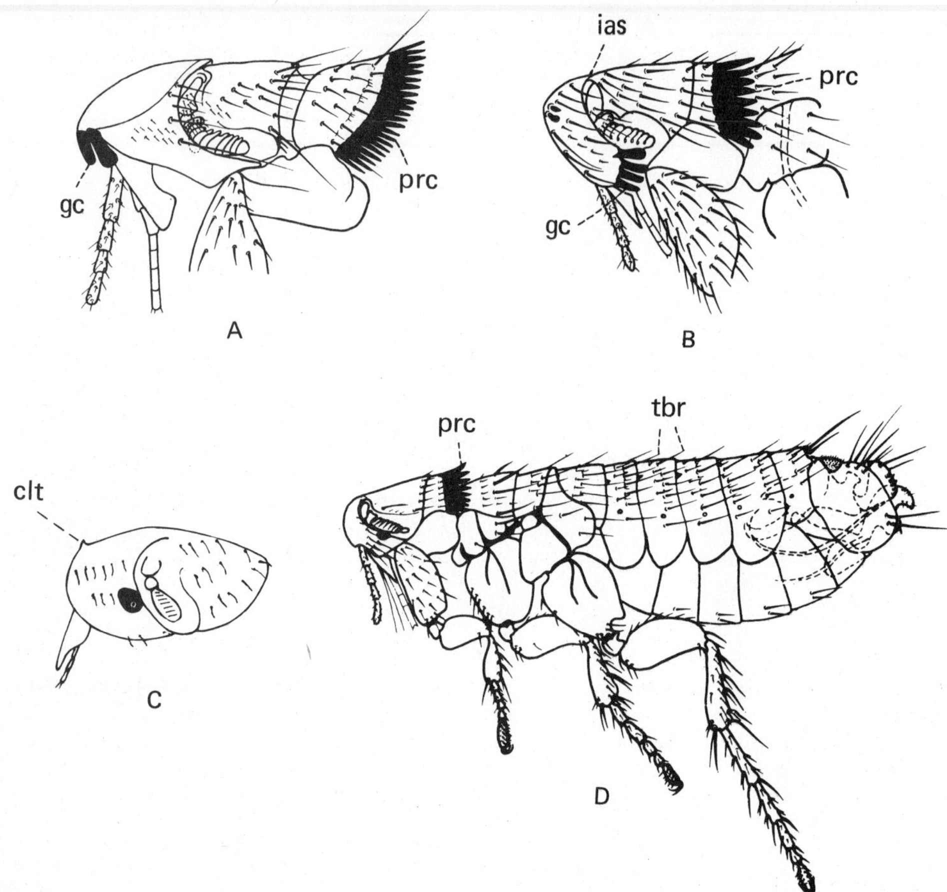

Figure 526. A, head and prothorax of a bat flea, *Myodopsýlla insígnis* (Rothschild) (Ischnopsýllidae); B, head and prothorax of a mouse flea, *Leptopsýlla ségnis* (Schönherr) (Leptosýllidae); C, head of *Rhopalopsýllus* (Rhopalopsýllidae); D, a rodent flea, *Orchopèas leucòpus* (Baker) (Ceratophýllidae). *clt,* clypeal tubercle; *gc,* genal comb; *ias,* interantennal suture; *prc,* pronotal comb; *tbr,* tergal bristles (2 rows on most terga).

Key to the Families and Subfamilies of Siphonáptera

1. The 3 thoracic terga together shorter than the first abdominal tergum (Figure 525 E) (sticktight and burrowing fleas) (family **Pulícidae,** in part) 2

1′. The 3 thoracic terga together longer than the first abdominal tergum (Figures 524 A, 525 A–D, 526 A, B, E) 3

2(1). Sensilium with 8 pits on each side; inner side of hind coxae without spiniform bristles .... subfamily **Tungìnae** p. 614

2′. Sensilium with 14 pits on each side; inner side of hind coxae with spiniform bristles (*Echidnóphaga*) .... subfamily **Pulicìnae** p. 614

3(1′). Abdominal terga 2–7 with at most 1 row of bristles (Figure 524 A); sensilium with 14 pits on each side; middle coxae without an internal ridge; hind tibiae with outer apex straight or rounded (family **Pulícidae**) .... subfamily **Pulicìnae** p. 614

3′. Abdominal terga 2–7 usually with 2 rows of bristles (Figure 526 D); sensilium with 14–16 (usually 16) pits on each side; middle coxae usually with an internal ridge; hind tibiae with a short, rounded or pointed tooth on outer apex 4

4(3′). The outer of the 2 dorsal apical bristles on front femora shorter than the inner; genal comb, pronotal comb, antepygidial bristles, and spiniform bristles on inner surface of hind coxae absent; parasites of large carnivores .... family **Vermipsýllidae** p. 614

4′. The outer of the 2 dorsal apical bristles on front femora longer than the inner; other characters variable 5

5(4′). Lower half of frons with a tubercle sunk in a groove and directed forward and upward (Figure 526 C); genal and pronotal combs lacking; 1 long antepygidial bristle on each side .... family **Rhopalopsýllidae** p. 614

5′. Without the above combination of characters 6

6(5′). Metanotum with marginal spines 7

6′. Metanotum without marginal spines (family **Hystrichopsýllidae**) 11

7(6). Interantennal suture present (Figure 526 B, *ias*) 8

7′. Interantennal suture absent 9

8(7). Genal comb present and consisting of 2 (rarely 3) broad lobes on each side (Figure 526 A); head elongated; eyes absent or vestigial; parasites of bats .... family **Ischnopsýllidae** p. 615

8′. Genal comb present or absent, but if present not as above; head usually not elongated; eyes often well developed; parasites of animals other than bats (family **Leptopsýllidae**) .... subfamily **Leptopsyllìnae** p. 615

9(7′). Genal comb present or absent; an arch of the tentorium visible in front of eye (family **Leptopsýllidae**) .... subfamily **Amphipsyllìnae** p. 615

9′. Genal comb absent; no arch of the tentorium visible in front of eye (family **Ceratophýllidae**) 10

10(9′). Eyes nearly always present and pigmented; preantennal region of the head usually without rows of bristles .... subfamily **Ceratophyllìnae** p. 615

10′. Eyes vestigial; preantennal region of head with 2 rows of bristles .... subfamily **Foxellìnae** p. 615

11(6′). Labial palps with at most 2 distinct segments; first abdominal tergum with a well developed comb .... subfamily **Stenoponiìnae** p. 614

11′. Labial palps with at least 4 distinct segments; first abdominal tergum generally without a distinct comb 12

12(11′). Antennal club distinctly 9-segmented; pleural ridge of metathorax complete 13

12′. Antennal club 7- or 8-segmented; pleural ridge of metathorax incomplete, short, or apparently absent .... subfamily **Rhadinopsyllìnae** p. 615

13(12). Genal comb, if present, consisting of 2 overlapping spines; dorsal margin of metasternum slanting downward from front to rear; basal abdominal sternum usually with a striarium (an area of close-set striae) .... subfamily **Neopsyllìnae** p. 614

13′. Genal comb not as above, or if absent then without the above combination of characters 14

14(13′). Fifth tarsal segment of all legs with 5 pairs of lateral bristles, and no bristles of similar size on plantar surface of segment; female with 2 spermathecae .... subfamily **Hystrichopsyllìnae** p.614

14′. Fifth tarsal segment of all legs with not more than 4 lateral bristles, the other pair(s) either lost or displaced onto plantar surface; female with only 1 spermatheca 15

15(14′). Genal comb almost always present; pronotum and abdominal terga 2–7 with at least 2 rows of bristles 16

15′. Genal comb absent; pronotum and abdominal terga 2–7 with only 1 row of bristles, the anterior row vestigial if present at all ....

Family **Pulícidae:** This is a small group (13 North American species) that is divided into two subfamilies.

Subfamily **Tungìnae:** The members of this group are more or less permanent parasites in the adult stage. They have a small thorax, short legs, and the abdomen of the female when full of eggs is greatly enlarged. The group is mainly tropical, but one species, the chigoe flea, *Túnga pénetrans* (L.), occurs in the southern states.

Males and virgin females of the chigoe flea live like other fleas, feeding on a variety of mammalian hosts, but after mating the female burrows into the skin of man or other animals, usually on the feet. Where the flea burrows into the skin a painful ulcerlike sore develops. In this location and nourished by the surrounding tissues of the host, the abdomen of the female swells (with the development of the eggs) and may get as large as a pea. The eggs are discharged to the outside and fall to the ground and develop. After all the eggs are discharged, the body of the female is usually expelled by the pressure of the surrounding tissues. These fleas generally burrow between the toes or under the toenails, and the sores if untreated may become gangrenous.

Subfamily **Pulicìnae:** This group contains only 12 North American species, but it contains most of the fleas that attack man and domestic animals. Most of these fleas are named after their principal host, but will usually attack a variety of hosts, including man.

The genus *Ctenocephálides* includes the cat flea, *C. fèlis* (Bouché), and the dog flea, *C. cànis* (Curtis). These fleas, which possess both genal and pronotal combs (Figure 524 A), are common pests of cats, dogs, and man, and frequently occur in and about buildings or homes where cats and dogs are kept. The dog flea serves as the intermediate host of the dog tapeworm, *Dipylídium canìnum* (L.).

The sticktight flea, *Echidnóphaga gallinàcea* (Westwood) (Figure 525 E), attacks domestic poultry and occasionally other birds and mammals. The adults tend to congregate in masses on the host, usually on the head, and often remain attached for several days or even weeks.

Both genal and pronotal combs are lacking in *Xenopsýlla* and *Pùlex* (Figure 525 A, B). The oriental rat flea, *X. cheòpis* (Rothschild), is a widespread and important species; it is the principal vector of bubonic plague (from rat to rat, and from rat to man), it serves as a vector of endemic typhus, and it may serve as the intermediate host of the tapeworm *Hymenólepis diminùta* (Rudolphi). The human flea, *P. írritans* L., has a worldwide distribution, and attacks man and various other animals; it is an important pest species.

Other genera in this subfamily are *Actenopsýlla* (recorded from the nest burrows of various sea birds along the Pacific Coast), *Cediopsýlla* (parasites of rabbits), *Euhoplopsýllus* (parasites of rabbits and their predators), and *Hoplopsýllus* (parasites of ground squirrels and hares).

Family **Rhopalopsýllidae:** This group is principally South and Central American in distribution, but three species occur in the southern states, from Florida to Texas; they are parasites of various small rodents and opossums.

Family **Vermipsýllidae**—Carnivore Fleas: This is a small group, with only five North American species (in the genus *Chaetopsýlla*); two occur in the East and three occur in the West and in Canada. These fleas are parasites of large carnivores, such as bears, wolves, foxes, and coyotes.

Family **Hystrichopsýllidae:** This is the second largest family of fleas, with 102 North American species. Most are parasites of small rodents and shrews; a few attack small carnivores. These fleas lack a row of spines on the posterior margin of the metanotum, and most of them have an interantennal suture, a pronotal comb, and two or three rows of bristles on the anterior part of the head.

Subfamily **Hystrichopsyllìnae:** Five species of *Hystrichopsýlla* and three species of *Atyphlóceras* occur in our area (one species in each genus in the East, and the remaining species in the West). They are parasites of small rodents and insectivores (moles and shrews).

Subfamily **Stenoponiìnae:** Two species of *Stenopònia* occur in our area, one in the East and one in the Southwest. Both are parasites of small rodents.

Subfamily **Neopsyllìnae:** This is a relatively large group (38 North American species), most of which occur in the West. Their hosts are chiefly various small rodents.

Subfamily **Anomiopsyllìnae:** Only one of our 25 species in this group (*Conorhinopsýlla stánfordi* Stewart, a parasite of flying squirrels) occurs in the East. The others occur in the West, where they are parasites of various small rodents, and occasionally rodent predators.

Subfamily **Rhadinopsyllìnae:** Most of the 23 North American species in this group are parasites of insectivores (moles and shrews) or small rodents; one occurs in the East, and the others occur in the West.

Subfamily **Doratopsyllìnae:** Our three species in this subfamily are parasites of moles and shrews. The group is widely distributed in this country.

Subfamily **Ctenophthalmìnae:** Our representatives of this group consist of two species of *Carterétta,* which occur in the West and parasitize small rodents, and one species of *Ctenophthálmus,* which occurs in the East and parasitizes moles and shrews.

Family **Ischnopsýllidae**—Bat Fleas: The members of this family, which are parasites of bats, can usually be recognized by the characteristic genal comb (Figure 526 A). They have a rather distinct interantennal suture on the dorsal surface of the head, and the eyes are vestigial. Eight species occur in this country, two in the East and six in the West.

Family **Leptopsýllidae:** This group is divided into two subfamilies, which are treated as families by some authorities; they differ in the presence of an interantennal suture, and parasitize different hosts.

Subfamily **Amphipsyllìnae:** The members of this group lack an interantennal suture, and have an arch of the tentorium visible in front of the eye in mounted specimens; some have a genal comb. Six of our eight species in this group (the Amphipsyllìni) are parasites of rabbits, small rodents, and lynxes (five of the six species occurring in the West). *Dolichopsýllus stylòsus* (Baker) is a parasite of the mountain beaver (*Aplodóntia*) and occurs from British Columbia to California; *Ornithóphaga anómala* Mikulin is a parasite of woodpeckers and owls in Utah.

Subfamily **Leptopsyllìnae:** This is a small group (eight North American species), and most of them are parasites of mice. They differ from the Amphipsyllìnae in having an interantennal suture, and they differ from the Hystrichopsýllidae in having a row of spines on the posterior margin of the metanotum. One species, *Leptopsýlla ségnis* (Schönherr), may serve as a vector of endemic typhus.

Family **Ceratophýllidae:** This is the largest family of fleas in North America (105 species), and most of its members are parasites of small rodents; a few are parasites of birds, and a few attack small carnivores. Most fleas with two rows of bristles on the abdominal terga, and without a genal comb or an interantennal suture, will belong to this family.

Subfamily **Ceratophyllìnae:** This is by far the larger of the two subfamilies (90 species), and its most important members are those that attack rodents, as some of these serve as vectors of plague from one rodent to another. The rat flea, *Nosopsýllus fasciàtus* (Bosc) (Figure 525 C), has been shown capable of transmitting plague from rodents to man, but is probably not an important vector. This flea may also transmit endemic typhus, and serve as the intermediate host of the tapeworm *Hymenólepis diminùta* (Rudolphi). Several species of *Ceratophýllus* attack birds, and some of these are pests of poultry. The European chicken flea, *C. gállinae* (Shrank), occurs in the northern United States as well as in Europe.

Subfamily **Foxellìnae:** This is a small group (15 North American species) whose members attack gophers, weasels, and lynxes.

COLLECTING AND PRESERVING SIPHONÁPTERA

Fleas can be most easily collected by capturing and examining the host; the methods suggested for collecting and preserving Mallóphaga (page 246) will also apply to the Siphonáptera.

Many species may be obtained from the nests or burrows of the hosts. In areas such as yards or buildings where fleas are particularly abundant, they may be collected by sweeping, or one may simply walk around in such an area and collect the fleas as they jump onto one's clothing; in the latter case, the fleas are most easily seen if one wears white clothing.

References on the Siphonáptera

Ewing, H. E., and I. Fox. 1943. *The Fleas of North America*. USDA Misc. Pub. 500; 128 pp., 10 pl.

Fox, I. 1940. *Fleas of Eastern United States*. Ames, Iowa: Iowa State College Press, vii + 191 pp., 166 f., 31 pl.

Holland, G. P. 1949. *The Siphonaptera of Canada*. Canada Dept. Agric. Pub. 817, Tech. Bull. 70; 306 pp., 350 f., 44 maps.

Holland, G. P. 1964. Evolution, classification, and host relationships of Siphonaptera. *Ann. Rev. Ent.*, 9:123–146, l f.

Hopkins, G. H. E., and M. Rothschild. 1953–1971. *An Illustrated Catalogue of the Rothschild Collection of Fleas* (Siphonaptera) *in the British Museum*. London: British Museum (Nat. Hist.). Vol. 1, 1953: *Tungidae and Pulicidae;* xv + 361 pp., 466 f., 45 pl. Vol. 2, 1956: *Coptopsyllidae, Vermipsyllidae, Stephanocircidae, Ischnopsyllidae, Hypsophthalmidae, and Xiphiopsyllidae;* xi + 445 pp., 708 f., 32 pl. Vol. 3, 1962: *Hystrichopsyllidae (Acedestiinae, Anomiopsyllinae, Hystrichopsyllinae, Neopsyllinae, Rhadinopsyllinae, and Stenoponiinae);* ix + 559 pp., 1050 f., 10 pl. Vol. 4, 1966: *Hystrichopsyllidae (Ctenophthalminae, Dinopsyllinae, Doratopsyllinae and Listropsyllinae);* viii + 549 pp., illus. Vol. 5, 1971: *Leptopsyllidae and Ancistropsyllidae;* viii + 530 pp., illus.

Hubbard, C. A. 1947. *Fleas of Western North America*. Ames, Iowa: Iowa State College Press, ix + 533 pp., 230 f.

Jellison, W. L., and N. E. Good. 1942. *Index to the Literature of Siphonaptera of North America*. U.S. Public Health Serv., Nat. Inst. Health Bull. 178; 193 pp.

Layne, J. N. 1971. Fleas (Siphonaptera) of Florida. *Fla. Ent.*, 54(1):35–51; 2 tab.

Lewis, R. E. 1972–1975. Notes on the geographic distribution and host preferences in the order Siphonaptera. Part 1. Pulicidae. *J. Med. Ent.*, 9(6):511–520 (1972). Part 2. Rhopalopsyllidae, Malacopsyllidae and Vermipsyllidae. *Op. cit.*, 10(2):255–260 (1973). Part 3. Hystrichopsyllidae. *Op. cit.*, 11(2):147–167 (1974). Part 4. Coptopsyllidae, Pygiopsyllidae, Stephanocircidae and Xiphiopsyllidae. *Op. cit.*, 11(4):403–413 (1974). Part 5. Ancistropsyllidae, Chimaeropsyllidae, Ischnopsyllidae, Leptopsyllidae, and Macropsyllidae. *Op. cit.*, 11(5):525–540 (1974). Part 6. Ceratophyllidae. *Op. cit.*, 11(6):658–676 (1975).

Snodgrass, R. E. 1946. The skeletal anatomy of fleas (Siphonaptera). *Smiths. Misc. Coll.*, 104(18):1–89; 21 pl., 8 textf.

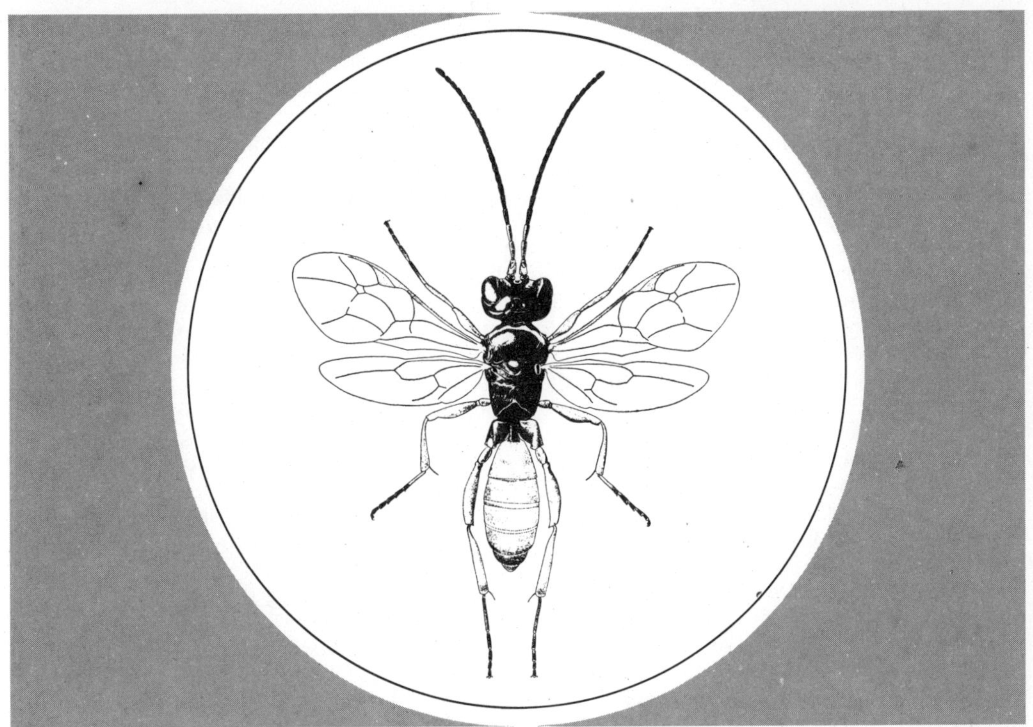

32: ORDER HYMENÓPTERA[1]

SAWFLIES, ICHNEUMONS, CHALCIDS, ANTS, WASPS, AND BEES

From man's standpoint, this order is probably the most beneficial in the entire insect class; it contains a great many insects that are of value as parasites or predators of various insect pests, and it contains the most important insects (the bees) that are involved in the pollination of plants. Biologically the Hymenóptera are a very interesting group, for they exhibit a great diversity of habits and complexity of behavior culminating in the social organization of the wasps, bees, and ants.

The winged members of this order have four membranous wings; the hind wings are smaller than the front wings and have a row of tiny hooks (hamuli) on their anterior margin by which the hind wing attaches to the front wing. The wings contain relatively few veins, and in some minute forms, there are almost no veins at all. The mouth parts are mandibulate, but in the higher forms, especially the bees, the labium and maxillae form a tonguelike structure through which liquid food is taken (see page 16 and Figure 8). The antennae usually contain ten or more segments and are generally fairly long. The tarsi are usually 5-segmented. The ovipositor is usually well developed; in the higher forms in the order, it is modified into a sting, which functions as an effective organ of offense and defense; only females can sting. The

[1] Hymenóptera: *hymeno,* god of marriage (referring to the union of front and hind wings by means of hamuli); *ptera,* wings.

metamorphosis is complete, and in most of the order, the larvae are grublike or maggotlike. The larvae of most of the sawflies and related forms (suborder Sýmphyta) are eruciform and differ from those of the Lepidóptera in that they have more than five pairs of prolegs that lack crochets and usually have only a single pair of ocelli. The pupae are of the exarate type and may be formed in a cocoon, in the host (in the case of parasitic species), or in special cells.

Sex in most Hymenóptera is determined by the fertilization of the egg; fertilized eggs develop into females, and unfertilized eggs usually develop into males.

CLASSIFICATION OF THE HYMENÓPTERA

The order Hymenóptera is divided into two suborders, each of which is further divided into superfamilies. In the suborder Sýmphyta the abdomen is broadly joined to the thorax, the trochanters are 2-segmented, and there are at least three closed cells at the base of the hind wing (Figure 527); nearly all the Sýmphyta are phytophagous. In the suborder Apócrita the basal segment of the abdomen is fused with the thorax and separated from the remainder of the abdomen by a constriction; the abdominal segment that is fused with the thorax is called the propodeum. The term "abdomen," when used in this chapter in speaking of the Apócrita, refers to that part of the body posterior to the propodeum. The trochanters appear 1- or 2-segmented in the Apócrita, and there are not more than two closed cells at the base of the hind wing (Figure 529).

A synopsis of the order Hymenóptera is given below; alternate spellings, synonyms, and other arrangements are given in parentheses. The groups marked with an asterisk are relatively rare or are unlikely to be taken by the general collector. The arrangement and names in this list are from the USDA Catalog of Hymenoptera and its two supplements (1951–1967), except for a few minor changes based on subsequent studies, and the superfamily placement of the families Trigonálidae, Formìcidae, and Pompílidae (which were not placed in any superfamily in the USDA Catlog and its supplements).

Suborder Sýmphyta (Chalastogástra)—sawflies and horntails
- Superfamily Megalodontòidea—primitive sawflies
  - *Xyèlidae—xyelid sawflies
  - *Pamphilìidae (Lỳdidae)—leaf-rolling and web-spinning sawflies
- Superfamily Tenthredinòidea—sawflies
  - *Pérgidae (Acordulecéridae)—pergid sawflies
  - Árgidae (Hylotómidae)—argid sawflies
  - Cimbícidae (Clavellarìidae)—cimbicid sawflies
  - *Dipriónidae (Lophýridae)—conifer sawflies
  - Tenthredínidae—common sawflies
- Superfamily Siricòidea—horntails and wood wasps
  - *Syntéxidae (Syntéctidae)—incense-cedar wood wasps
  - Sirícidae (Urocéridae)—horntails
  - *Xiphydrìidae—wood wasps
  - *Orússidae (Orýssidae)—parasitic wood wasps
- Superfamily Cephòidea—stem sawflies
  - Cèphidae—stem sawflies

Suborder Apócrita (Clistogástra, Petiolàta)
- Superfamily Ichneumonòidea—parasitic Hymenóptera
  - *Stephánidae—stephanids
  - Bracónidae—braconids
  - Ichneumónidae—ichneumons
- Superfamily Chalcidòidea—chalcids
  - *Mymàridae—fairyflies
  - *Trichogrammátidae—trichogrammatids
  - Eulóphidae (including Elásmidae)—eulophids
  - *Thysánidae (Encýrtidae in part; Signiphòridae)—thysanids
  - *Eutrichosomátidae (Encýrtidae in part)—eutrichosomatids
  - *Tanaostigmátidae (Encýrtidae in part)—tanaostigmatids

    - Eucharidae) — eucharitids
    - e — perilampids
    - gaonidae (Agaóntidae) — fig wasps
    - Torýmidae (Callimómidae; including Podagriónidae in part) — torymids
    - *Ormýridae — ormyrids
    - Pteromálidae (including Cleonýmidae in part and Miscogástridae) — pteromalids
    - Eurytómidae — eurytomids, seed chalcids
    - *Chalcedéctidae (Podagriónidae in part) — chalcedectids
    - Chalcídidae (Chálcidae) — chalcidids
    - *Leucospídidae (Leucóspidae) — leucospidids
- Superfamily Cynipòidea — gall wasps and others
    - *Ibalìidae — ibaliids
    - *Lioptéridae — liopterids
    - Figítidae — figitids
    - Cynípidae — gall wasps and others
- Superfamily Evaniòidea — parasitic Hymenóptera
    - Evanìidae — ensign wasps
    - Gasteruptìidae (Gasteruptiónidae) — gasteruptiids
    - Aulácidae (Gasteruptìidae in part) — aulacids
- Superfamily Pelecinòidea — parasitic Hymenóptera
    - Pelecìnidae — pelecinids
- Superfamily Proctotrupòidea — parasitic Hymenóptera
    - *Vanhornìidae — vanhorniids
    - *Roproniidae — roproniids
    - *Helòridae — helorids
    - Proctotrùpidae (Sérphidae) — proctotrupids
    - *Ceraphrónidae (Callicerátidae) — ceraphronids
    - Diaprìidae (including Belýtidae = Cinétidae) — diapriids
    - Scelionidae — scelionids
    - Platygastéridae (Platygástridae) — platygasterids
- Superfamily Bethylòidea — parasitic Hymenóptera
    - Chrysídidae (including Cléptidae) — cuckoo wasps
    - Bethýlidae — bethylids
    - Dryínidae (including Embolémidae) — dryinids
    - *Sclerogíbbidae — sclerogibbids
    - *Trigonálidae — trigonalids
- Superfamily Scoliòidea — parasitic wasps and ants
    - Tiphìidae (including Thýnnidae) — tiphiid wasps
    - *Sierolomórphidae — sierolomorphid wasps
    - Mutíllidae — velvet ants
    - *Rhopalosomátidae (Rhopalosómidae) — rhopalosomatid wasps
    - Scolìidae — scoliid wasps
    - *Sapýgidae — sapygid wasps
    - Formìcidae — ants
- Superfamily Vespòidea — vespoid wasps
    - Véspidae (including Euménidae) — paper wasps, potter wasps, and others
    - Pompílidae (Psammochàridae) — spider wasps
- Superfamily Sphecòidea — sphecoid wasps
    - Sphécidae (including Ampulícidae) — sphecid wasps
- Superfamily Apòidea — bees
    - Collètidae (including Hylaèidae) — plasterer and yellow-faced bees
    - Halíctidae — halictid bees
    - *Oxaèidae (Andrènidae in part) — oxaeid bees

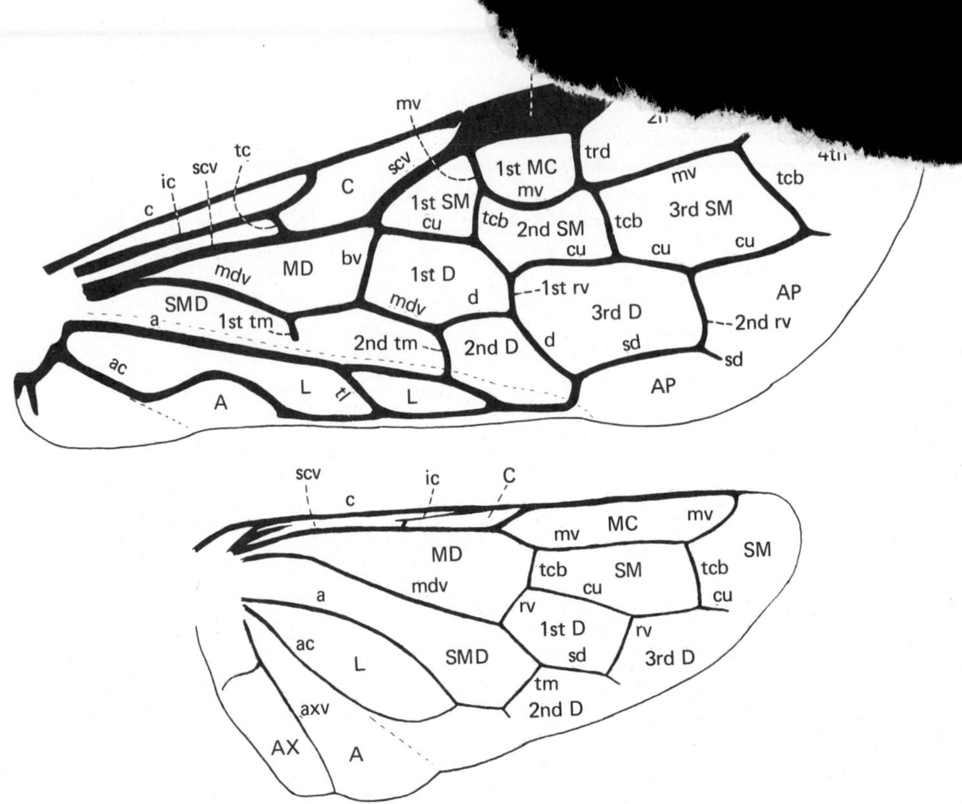

Figure 527. Wings of *Acanthólyda* (Pamphilìidae), showing the old system of terminology (veins are shown by small letters, cells by capitals). Veins: *a,* anal; *ac,* accessory, lanceolate, or subanal; *axv,* axillary; *bv,* basal; *c,* costal; *cu,* cubital; *d,* discoidal; *ic,* intercostal; *mdv,* median; *mv,* marginal or radial; *rv,* recurrent; *scv,* subcostal; *sd,* subdiscal or subdiscoidal; *st,* stigma; *tc,* transverse costal; *tcb,* transverse cubitals; *tl,* transverse lanceolate; *tm,* transverse median; *trd,* transverse radial or transverse marginal. Cells: *A,* anal; *AP,* apical or posterior; *AX,* axillary; *C,* costal; *D,* discoidal; *L,* lanceolate; *MC,* marginal; *MD,* median; *SM,* submarginal; *SMD,* submedian. The basal cells (hind wing) are *MD, SMD,* and *L.*

Andrènidae—andrenid bees
*Melíttidae—melittid bees
Megachìlidae—leafcutting bees
Anthophòridae (including Nomádidae, Eucéridae, Ceratìnidae, Xylocòpidae)—cuckoo bees, digger bees, and carpenter bees
Àpidae (including Bómbidae)—honey bees, bumble bees, and euglossine bees

CHARACTERS USED IN THE IDENTIFICATION OF HYMENÓPTERA

WING VENATION Venational characters are used a great deal to separate the various groups of Hymenóptera. There are not many veins or cells in the hymenopteran wings, but homologizing this venation with that in other orders has proved to be a problem. There are two basic terminologies in use for the venation of the Hymenótera, an old system (Figures 527 and 529) and that of Comstock (Figure 528 A); the latter has been modified by Ross (1936) (Figure 528 B). Ross's interpretation is better than that of Comstock, but it is often more convenient to use the old system; in our key we have used the terms of the old system.

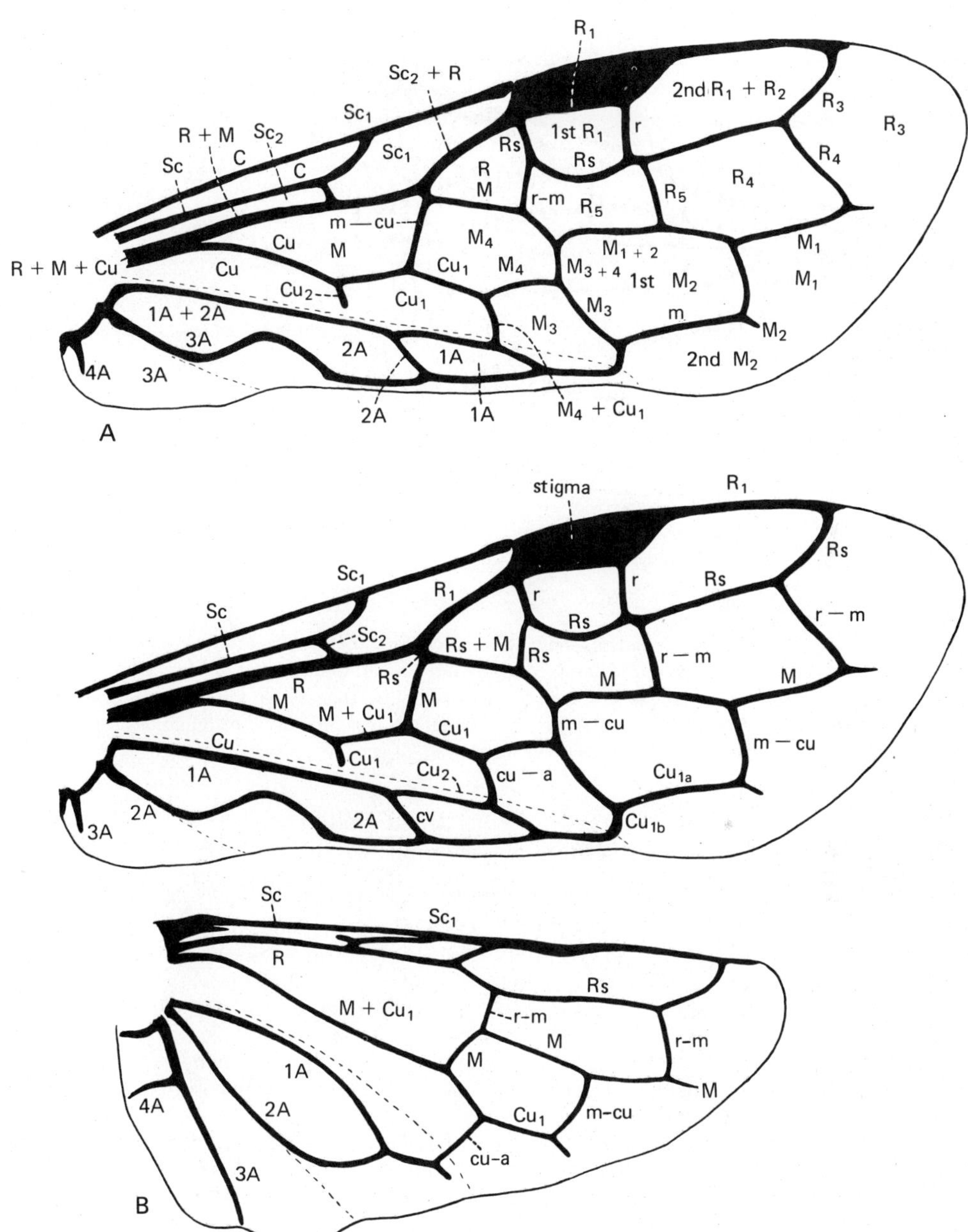

Figure 528. Wings of *Acanthólyda* (Pamphilìidae), showing (A) the Comstock terminology, and (B) the terminology of Ross.

LEG CHARACTERS The leg characters used in identification are chiefly the number of trochanter segments, the number and form of the tibial spurs, and the form of the tarsal segments. In the Sýmphyta and some superfamilies of the Apócrita there are two trochanter segments (Figure 550 A). The number and form of the apical spurs on the tibiae serve to separate families in several super-

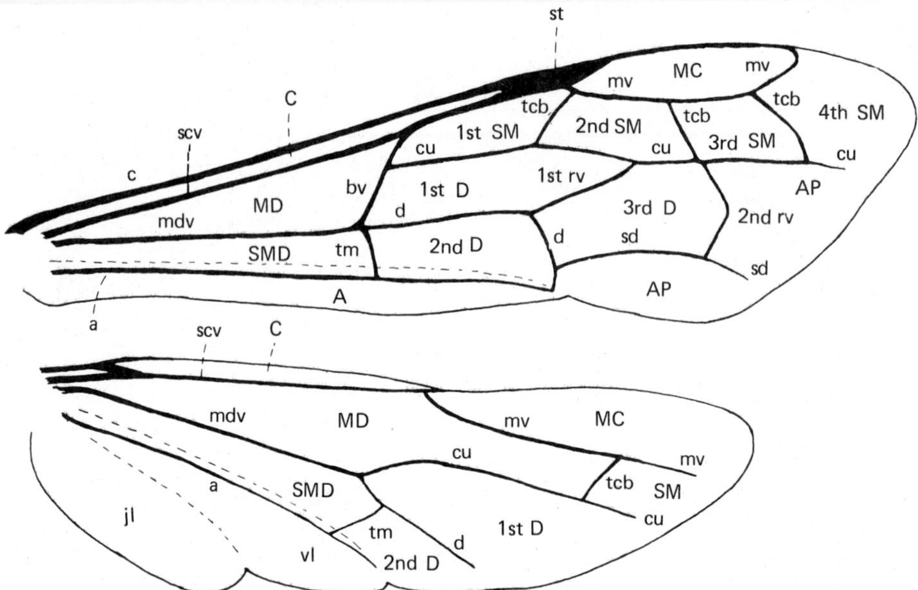

Figure 529. Wings of *Mỳzinum* (Tiphìidae), showing the old system of terminology (veins are shown by small letters, cells by capitals). Veins: *a*, anal; *bv*, basal; *c*, costal; *cu*, cubital; *d*, discoidal; *mdv*, median; *mv*, marginal or radial; *rv*, recurrent; *scv*, subcostal; *sd*, subdiscal or subdiscoidal; *st*, stigma; *tcb*, transverse cubitals; *tm*, transverse median. Cells: *A*, anal; *AP*, apical or posterior; *C*, costal; *D*, discoidal; *MC*, marginal; *MD*, median; *SM*, submarginal; *SMD*, submedian. The basal cells (hind wing) are *MD* and *SMD*. Lobes of hind wing: *jl*, jugal lobe; *vl*, vannal lobe.

families. In the bees (Apòidea) the first segment of the hind tarsi is usually much enlarged and flattened and may in some cases appear nearly as large as the tibia (Figure 536 B, C). In some superfamilies the size and shape of the hind coxae or the form of the tarsal claws may serve to separate families. Some of the Chalcidòidea have less than five tarsal segments.

ANTENNAL CHARACTERS The antennae of Hymenóptera vary in form, number of segments, and location on the face. In the higher Hymenóptera the number of antennal segments, and in some cases the form of the antennae, differ in the two sexes. In the bees and many of the wasps the male has 13 antennal segments and the female has 12; in the ants the antennae are much more distinctly elbowed in the queens and workers than in the males.

THORACIC CHARACTERS The thoracic characters used in identifying Hymenóptera involve principally the form of the pronotum and of certain mesothoracic sclerites and sutures. The shape of the pronotum as seen from above (Figure 533 A–D) serves to separate some families of Sỳmphyta, and its shape as seen from the side serves to separate superfamilies of Apócrita. The pronotum in the Apócrita may appear in profile more or less triangular and extending nearly or quite close to the tegulae (Figure 530 C: Ichneumonòidea, Cynipòidea, Evaniòidea, Pelicinòidea, Proctotrupòidea, and most Vespòidea), somewhat quadrate and not quite reaching the tegulae (Figure 530 A, B: Bethylòidea and Scoliòidea), or short and collarlike with a small rounded lobe on each side (Figure 530 D: Sphecòidea and Apòidea). Some Apócrita (for example, the Chalcidòidea) have a prepectus in the lateral wall of the thorax (Figure 530 A, *pp*). The presence or absence of parapsidal sutures or notauli (Figure 545, *ps*) and the form of the axillae (Figure 545, *ax*) often serve to separate related families.

ABDOMINAL CHARACTERS In the superfamilies Ichneumonòidea, Cynipòidea, and Chalcidòidea the ovipositor issues from the abdomen anterior to the apex, on the ventral side, and is not

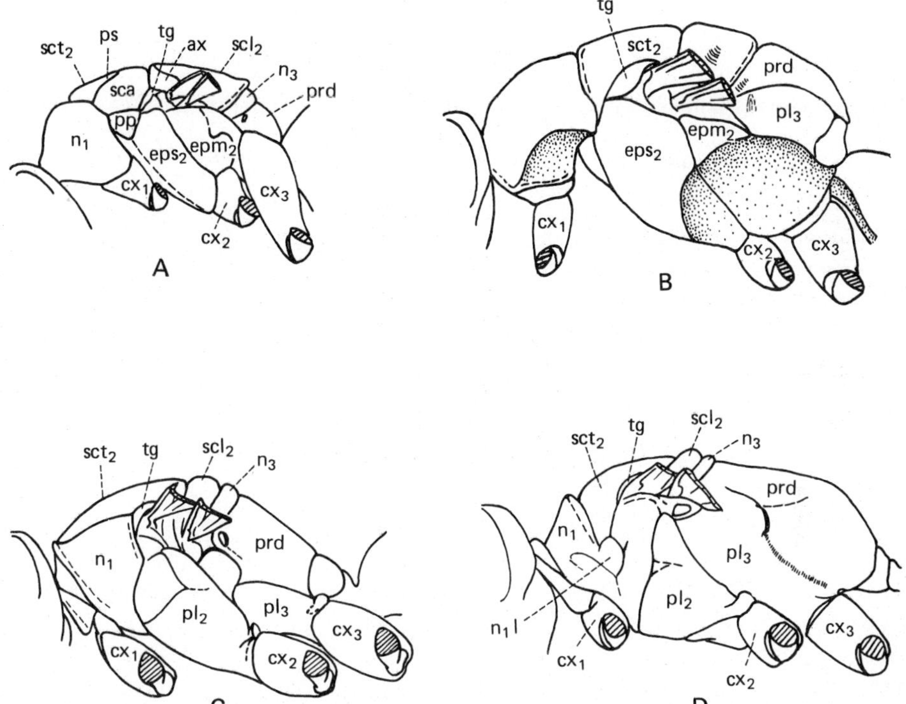

Figure 530. Thorax of Hymenóptera, lateral view. A, chalcid (Torýmidae); B, cuckoo wasp (Chrysídidae); C, paper wasp (Véspidae); D, thread-waisted wasp (Sphécidae). *ax*, axilla; *cx*, coxa; *epm*, epimeron; *eps*, episternum; *n*, notum; n_1l, pronotal lobe; *pl*, pleuron; *pp*, prepectus; *prd*, propodeum; *ps*, parapsidal suture; *sca*, scapula or parapsis; *scl*, scutellum; *sct*, scutum; *tg*, tegula.

withdrawn into the body when not in use (Figure 531 A). In most of the remaining Apócrita the ovipositor issues from the apex of the abdomen and is withdrawn into the body when not in use (Figure 531 B). The shape of the abdomen or of the abdominal petiole may serve to separate related groups in some superfamilies.

OTHER CHARACTERS In some of the wasps the shape of the compound eyes or ocelli differs in different families. The mouth-part structures used to separate groups of Hymenóptera are chiefly the form of the mandibles and the structure of the

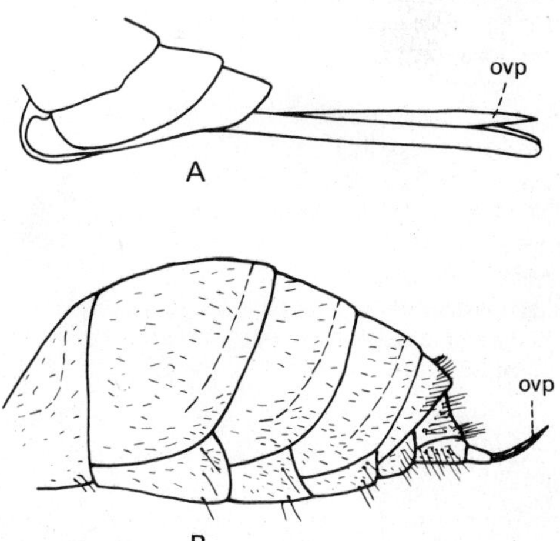

Figure 531. Position of the ovipositor in Hymenóptera. A, last sternite split ventrally, the ovipositor issuing from anterior to apex of abdomen (Ichneumónidae); B, last sternite not split ventrally, the ovipositor issuing from apex of abdomen (Sphécidae). *ovp*, ovipositor.

tongue (see Figure 8, page 16). The tongue provides some excellent characters for identification in the bees, but because it is usually folded up under the head in specimens of bees and is not easily studied, we have avoided the use of tongue characters as much as possible in our key. The head and thoracic characters that involve the form of sclerites and sutures are usually easy to see except when the specimen is very small or very hairy; in the latter case, it may be necessary to separate or remove the hairs to see the sutures. Characters such as the size, shape, or color of the insect provide easy means of identification in many groups. "Minute" means 2 mm in length or less; "small" means 2–7 mm in length.

The principal difficulties likely to be encountered in keying out a specimen in this order are those due to the small size of some specimens; the larger specimens should not cause a great deal of difficulty. We have included here a key to all the families of Hymenóptera represented in the United States, though we realize that the student is likely to have some difficulty in keying out the smaller specimens. Groups that are relatively rare are marked with an asterisk, and couplets containing such groups may often be skipped over by the beginning student. Reference to Table 4 (page 653) may enable the student to recognize the superfamily to which a specimen of the Apócrita belongs, and thus bypass a large part of the key.

Key to the Families of Hymenóptera

The old system of venational terminology (Figures 527 and 529) is used in this key and, unless otherwise indicated, all venational characters refer to the front wing. The number of marginal or submarginal cells refers to the number of *closed* cells. The groups marked with an asterisk are relatively rare or are unlikely to be taken by the general collector. No satisfactory keys are available for Hymenóptera larvae, but Peterson (1948) gives keys to the larvae of the Sýmphyta.

1. Base of abdomen broadly joined to thorax (Figures 555–558); trochanters 2-segmented; hind wings nearly always with at least 3 closed basal cells (*B* in Figure 532) (suborder Sýmphyta) 2

1′. Base of abdomen constricted, the abdomen more or less petiolate; trochanters 1- or 2-sgemented; hind wings with 2 or fewer closed basal cells (Figures 529, 538, 539, 541, 543, 549, 551, 581 A–C, 588, 589, 590) (suborder Apócrita) 13

2(1). Antennae inserted under a frontal ridge below eyes, just above mouth (Figure 533 E); 1 submarginal cell (Figure 532 D) .... **Orússidae*** p. 651

2′. Antennae inserted above base of eyes, near middle of face; 1–3 submarginal cells 3

3(2′). Front tibiae with 1 apical spur 4

3′. Front tibiae with 2 apical spurs 7

4(3). Pronotum in dorsal view wider than long, and shorter along midline than laterally (Figure 533 D); mesonotum with 2 diagonal furrows extending anterolaterally from anterior margin of scutellum (Figure 533 D); abdomen terminating in a dorsally located spearlike plate or spine .... **Sirícidae** p. 651

4′. Pronotum in dorsal view either **U**-shaped (Figure 533 B) or more or less trapezoidal (Figure 533 A, C); mesonotum without diagonal furrows; abdomen not terminating in a dorsally located spear or spine 5

5(4′). Pronotum in dorsal view **U**-shaped, posterior margin deeply curved, and very short along midline (Figure 533 B); costal cell and transverse costal vein present (Figure 532 B); abdomen cylindrical .... **Xiphydrìidae*** p. 651

5′. Pronotum in dorsal view not **U**-shaped, posterior margin straight or only slightly curved (Figure 533 A, C); costal cell present or absent; abdomen more or less flattened laterally 6

6(5′). Costal cell present and distinct; apical spur on front tibiae pectinate on inner margin; pronotum in dorsal view much wider than long (Figure 533 C); California and Oregon .... **Syntéxidae*** p. 651

6′. Costal cell absent or very narrow (Figure 532 A); apical spur on front tibiae

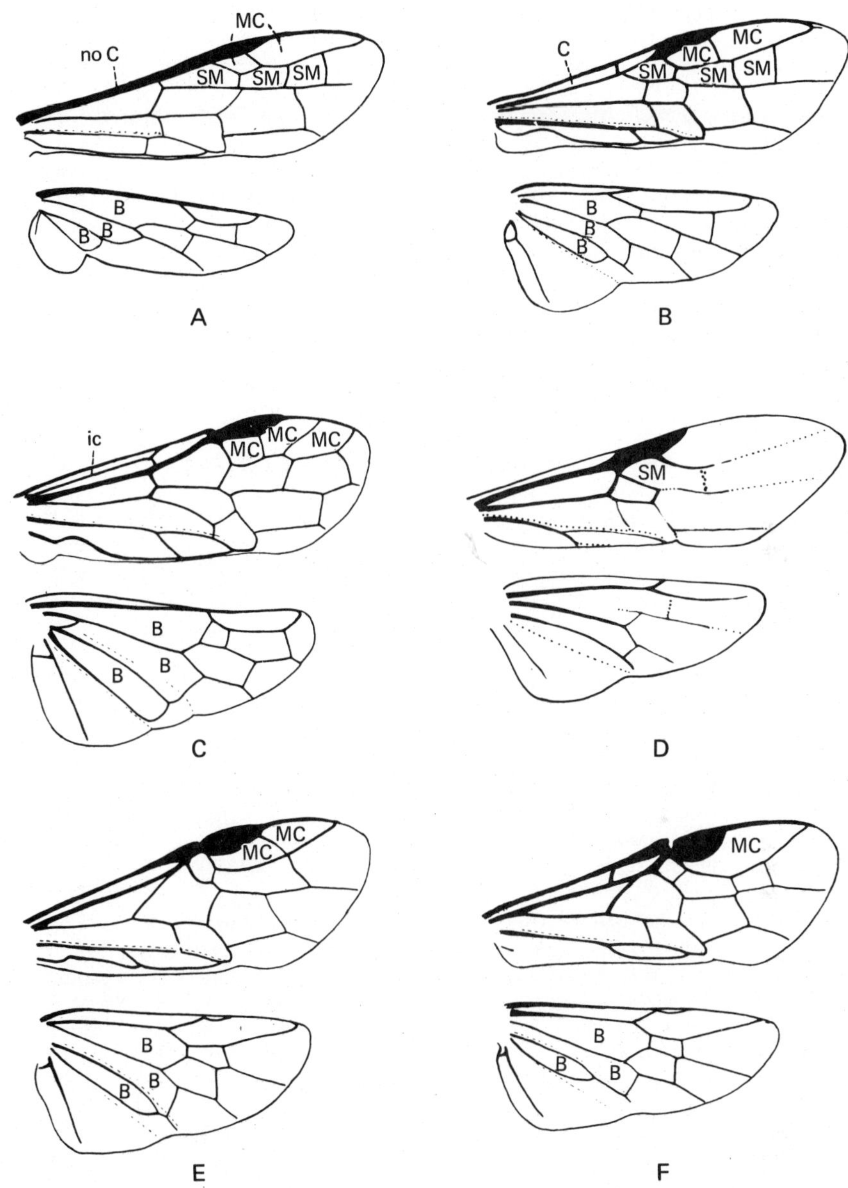

Figure 532. Wings of Sýmphyta. A, Cèphidae (*Cèphus*); B, Xiphydrìidae (*Xiphýdria*); C, Xyèlidae (*Macroxỳela*); D, Orússidae (*Orússus*); E, Tenthredínidae (*Dólerus*); F, Tenthredínidae (*Amauronématus*). *B,* basal cell; *C,* costal cell; *ic,* intercostal vein; *MC,* marginal cell; *SM,* submarginal cell.

not pectinate on inner margin; pronotum in dorsal view about as long as or longer than wide (Figure 533 A); widely distributed .... **Cèphidae** p. 651

7(3′). Antennae 3-segmented, third segment very long (Figure 534 E), sometimes **U**-shaped .... **Árgidae** p. 648

7′. Antennae with more than 3 segments 8

8(7′). Third antennal segment very long, longer than remaining segments com-

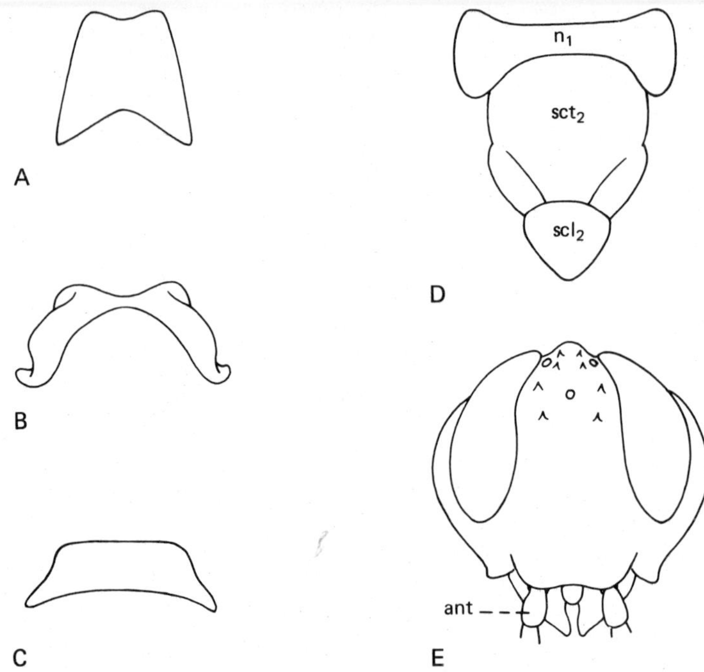

Figure 533. Head and thoracic characters of Sýmphyta. A–D, dorsal views; E, anterior view. A, pronotum of *Hartígia* (Cèphidae); B, pronotum of *Xiphýdria* (Xiphydrìidae); C, pronotum of *Syntéxis* (Syntéxidae); D, thorax of *Urócerus* (Sirícidae); E, head of *Orússus* (Orússidae). *ant,* base of antenna; n_1, pronotum; scl_2, mesoscutellum; sct_2, mesoscutum. (C, redrawn from Ross.)

bined (Figure 534 D); 3 (rarely 2) marginal cells and an intercostal vein (Figure 532 C) .... **Xyèlidae*** p. 648

8′. Third antennal segment short (Figure 534 A–C); 1 or 2 marginal cells (Figure 532 E, F); intercostal vein usually absent 9

9(8′). Antennae clubbed, and with 7 or fewer segments (Figure 534 A); large, robust sawflies resembling bumble bees (Figure 555 A) ...... **Cimbícidae** p. 649

9′. Antennae filiform (Figure 534 B), serrate, or pectinate (Figure 534 C), rarely slightly clubbed 10

10(9′). Antennae 6-segmented; anterior margin of scutellum more or less transverse .... **Pérgidae*** p. 648

10′. Antennae with more than 6 segments; anterior margin of scutellum **V**-shaped 11

11(10′). An intercostal vein and usually 2 transverse median veins present (Figures 527 and 528); antennae with 13 or more segments .... **Pamphilìidae*** p. 648

11′. No intercostal vein, and only 1 transverse median vein (Figure 532 E, F); antennae variable 12

12(11′). Antennae 7- to 10-segmented, and usually filiform (Figure 534 B); 1 or 2 marginal cells (Figure 532 E, F) .... **Tenthredínidae** p. 649

12′. Antennae with 13 or more segments, and either serrate or pectinate (Figure 534 C); 1 marginal cell .... **Dipriónidae*** p. 649

13(1′). First abdominal segment (sometimes the first 2 abdominal segments) bearing a hump or node, and strongly differentiated from rest of abdomen (Figures 535 and 579); antennae usually elbowed, at least in female, with first segment long .... **Formìcidae** p. 672

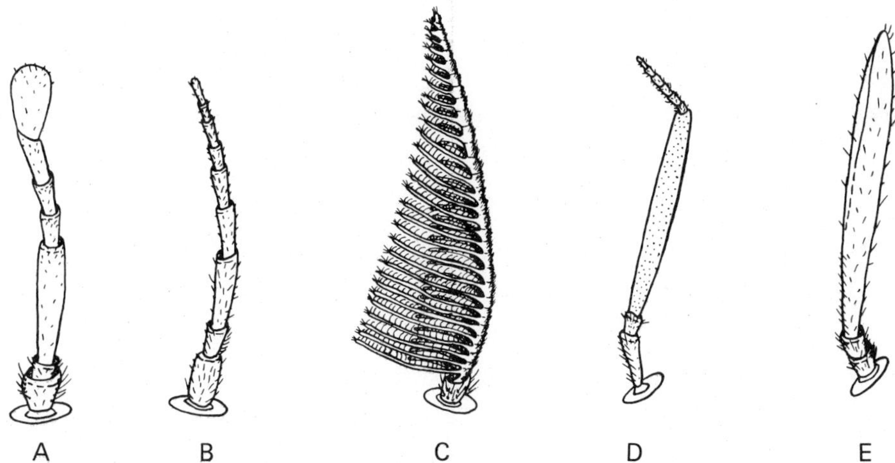

Figure 534. Antennae of Sýmphyta. A, Cimbícidae (*Címbex*); B, Tenthredínidae (*Leucopelmònus*); C, male Dipriónidae (*Neodíprion*); D, Xyèlidae (*Macroxỳela*); E, Argidae (*Árge*).

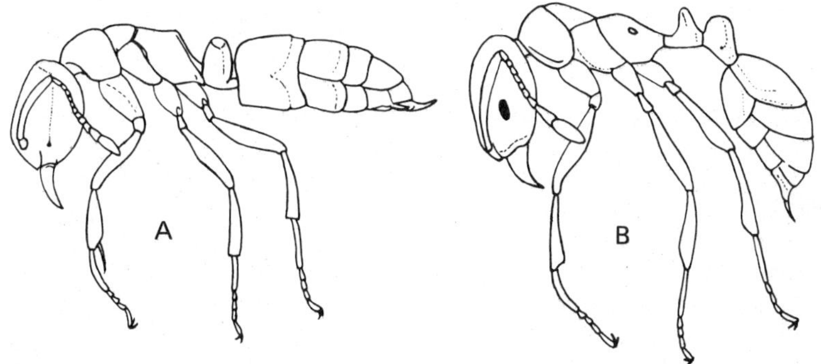

Figure 535. Ant workers. A, Ponerìnae (*Ponèra*); B, Myrmicìnae (*Solenópsis*).

13′. First abdominal segment not as above, or antennae not elbowed 14

14(13′). Wings well developed 15

14′. Wings vestigial or lacking 89

15(14). Pronotum with a rounded lobe on each side posteriorly that does not extend to the tegula (Figure 530 D); venation complete or nearly so (Figures 538, 539, 588–590) 16

15′. Pronotum without a rounded lobe on each side posteriorly, and sometimes extending to tegula (Figure 530 A–C); venation variable, sometimes reduced 26

16(15). First segment of hind tarsus slender, not broadened or thickened, usually shorter than remaining segments combined (Figure 536 A); all body hairs unbranched; abdomen often petiolate .... **Sphécidae** p. 681

16′. First segment of hind tarsi elongate, generally as long as or longer than remaining segments combined, usually thickened or flattened (Figure 536 B–D); some body hairs, especially those on thorax, branched or plumose; abdomen not petiolate (superfamily Apòidea) 17

17(16′). Jugal lobe in hind wing as long as or longer than submedian cell (Figure

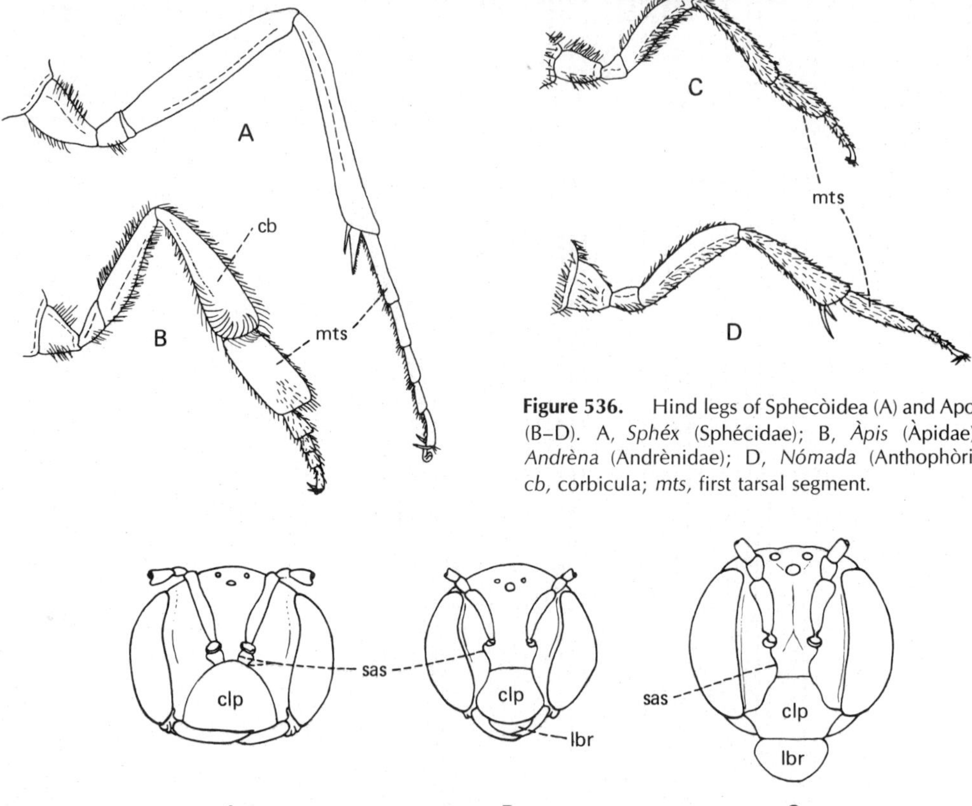

Figure 536. Hind legs of Sphecòidea (A) and Apoìdea (B–D). A, *Sphéx* (Sphécidae); B, *Àpis* (Àpidae); C, *Andrèna* (Andrènidae); D, *Nómada* (Anthophòridae). *cb,* corbicula; *mts,* first tarsal segment.

Figure 537. Heads of bees, anterior view. A, Andrènidae (*Andrèna*); B, Megachìlidae (*Ósmia*); C, Anthophòridae (*Triepèolus,* Nomadìnae). *clp,* clypeus; *lbr,* labrum; *sas,* subantennal suture.

538 A–E, *jl*); galeae and glossa short 18

17′. Jugal lobe in hind wing shorter than submedian cell, or lacking (Figures 538 F and 539); galeae and glossa usually long 23

18(17). Basal vein strongly arched, and usually 3 submarginal cells (Figure 538 C); glossa pointed (Figure 8 D); 1 subantennal suture below each antennal socket .... **Halíctidae** p. 693

18′. Basal vein straight or only slightly arched, and 2–3 submarginal cells (Figure 538 A, B, D, E); glossa pointed, truncate, or slightly bilobed; 1 or 2 subantennal sutures below each antennal socket 19

19(18′). With 2 submarginal cells 20

19′. With 3 submarginal cells 21

20(19). Apex of marginal cell pointed, and second submarginal cell smaller than first (Figure 538 E); glossa truncate or bilobed (Figure 8 C); 1 subantennal suture below each antennal socket; black bees, usually with white or yellow markings on face (Figure 601) (Hylaeìnae) .... **Collètidae** p. 692

20′. Apex of marginal cell more or less truncate (Figure 538 B) (Panurgìnae), or if pointed (a few Andrenìnae) then submarginal cells are equal in length; glossa pointed; 2 subantennal sutures below each antennal socket (Figure 537 A); color variable, but usually not as above .... **Andrènidae** p. 694

21(19′). Second recurrent vein sigmoid (Figure 538 D, *rv*); glossa truncate or

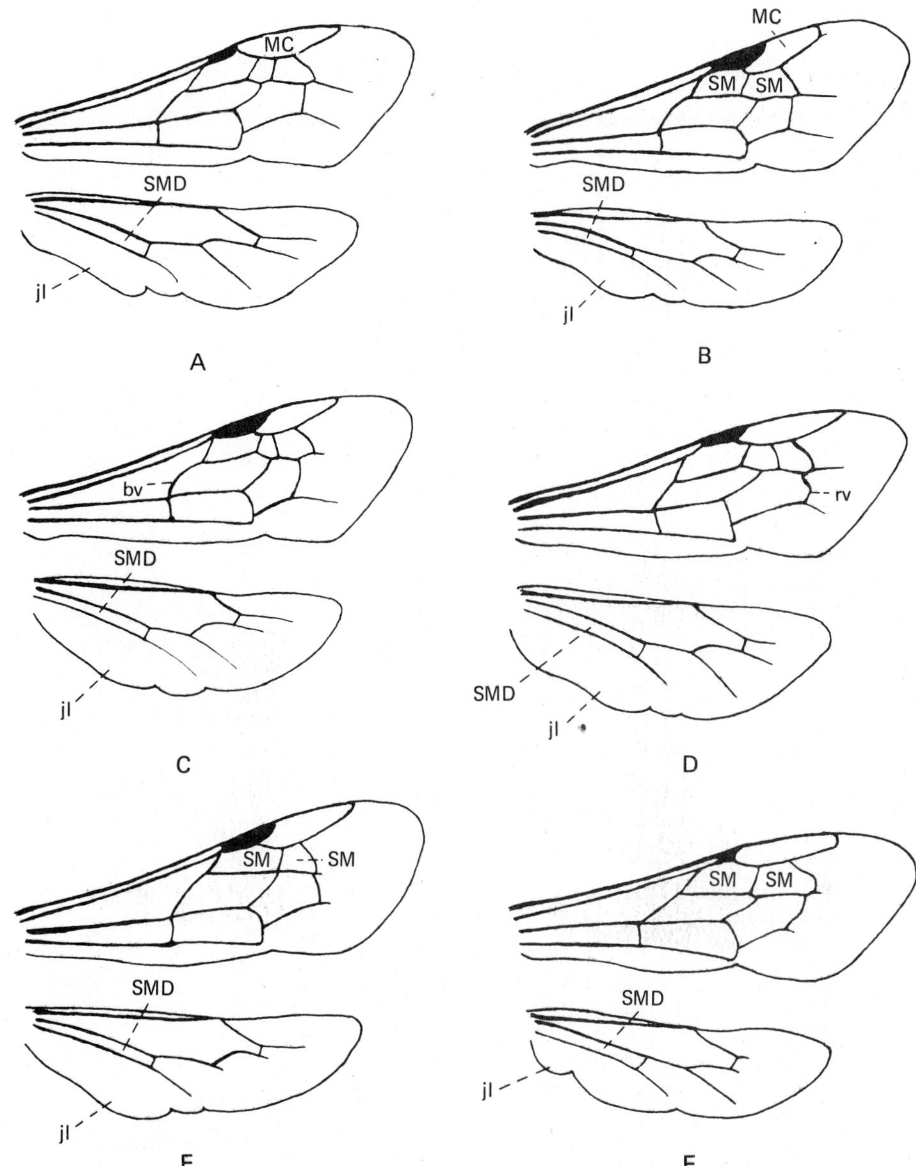

Figure 538. Wings of Apòidea. A, *Andrèna* (Andrènidae, Andrenìnae); B, *Panúrga* (Andrènidae, Panurgìnae); C, *Sphecòdes* (Halíctidae, Halictìnae); D, *Collètes* (Collètidae, Colletìnae); E, *Hylaèus* (Collètidae, Hylaeìnae); F. *Coelióxys* (Megachìlidae, Megachilìnae). *bv,* basal vein; *jl,* jugal lobe; *MC,* marginal cell; *rb,* second recurrent vein; *SM,* submarginal cells; *SMD,* submedian cell.

bilobed; 1 subantennal suture below each antennal socket (Colletìnae) .... **Collètidae** p. 692

21′. Second recurrent vein straight, not sigmoid (Figure 538 A); glossa pointed; 2 subantennal sutures below each antennal socket (Figure 537 A) ... 22

22(21′). Apex of marginal cell on costal margin of wing; stigma well developed; widely distributed (Andrenìnae) .... **Andrènidae** p. 694

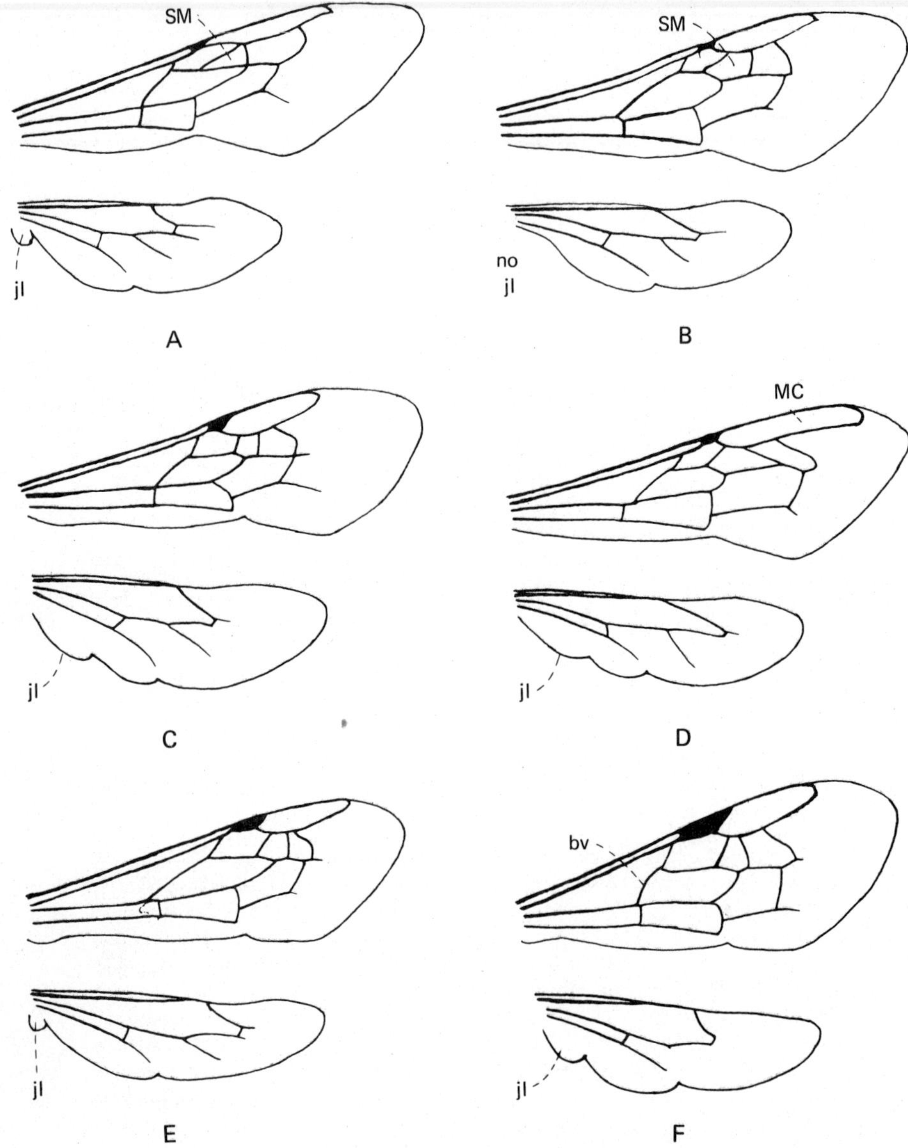

Figure 539. Wings of Apòidea. A, *Xylocòpa* (Anthophòridae, Xylocopinae); B, *Bómbus (Apidae, Bombinae); C, Melissòdes* (Anthophòridae, Anthophorìnae); D, *Àpis* (Àpidae, Apìnae); E, *Nómada* (Anthophòridae, Nomadìnae); F, *Ceratìna* (Anthophòridae, Xylocopìnae). *bv,* basal vein; *jl,* jugal lobe; *MC,* marginal cell; *SM,* second submarginal cell.

22′. Apex of marginal cell bent away from costal margin of wing; stigma very small or absent; southwestern United States .... **Oxaèidae*** p. 694

23(17′). Segments of labial palps similar and cylindrical (as in Figure 8 C); glossa short .... **Melíttidae*** p. 694

23′. First 2 segments of labial palps long and somewhat flattened (Figure 8 A); galeae elongate 24

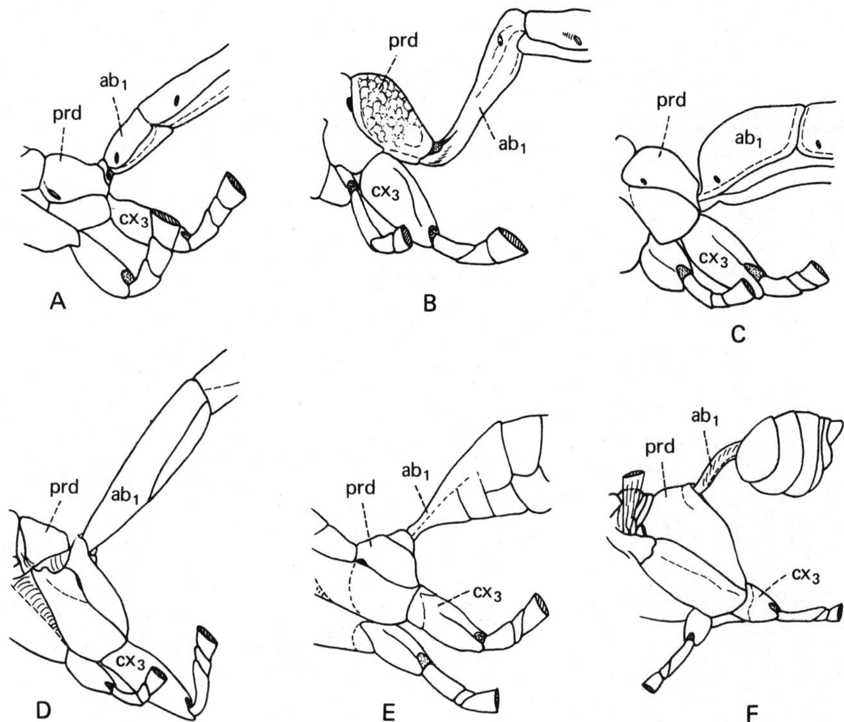

Figure 540. Base of abdomen in parasitic Hymenóptera. A, Ichneumónidae (Ephialtìnae); B, Ichneumónidae (Ophionìnae); C, Bracónidae; D, Gasteruptìidae; E, Aulácidae; F, Evanìidae. *ab,* first abdominal segment; *cx*₃, hind coxa; *prd,* propodeum.

24(23′). Two submarginal cells, the second nearly as long as the first (Figure 538 F); subantennal suture extending from outer margin of antennal socket (Figure 537 B) .... **Megachìlidae** p. 695

24′. Usually 3 submarginal cells (Figure 539); subantennal suture extending from middle of antennal socket (Figure 537 C) 25

25(24′). Hind tibiae without apical spurs (Apìnae), or if with apical spurs (Bombìnae and Euglossìnae) then jugal lobe of wing is absent; genae broad ... **Àpidae** p. 696

25′. Hind tibiae with apical spurs; a jugal lobe present in hind wing; genae very narrow .... **Anthophòridae** p. 695

26(15′). Venation slightly to considerably reduced, front wings usually with 5 or fewer closed cells, and hind wings usually without closed cells (Figures 541, 543, 549 G) 27

26′. Venation complete or nearly so, front wings usually with 6 or more closed cells and hind wings with at least 1 closed cell (Figures 549 A–F, H, and 551) 67

27(26). Pronotum in profile more or less triangular, and extending to tegulae or nearly so (Figure 530 C); hind wings nearly always without a jugal lobe 28

27′. Pronotum in profile more or less quadrate, and not quite reaching tegulae (Figure 530 A, B); forms with 3 or more closed cells in front wings usually have a jugal lobe in hind wings 44

28(27). Abdomen arising on propodeum between bases of hind coxae or only slightly above them (as in Figure 540 A–C); antennae variable 29

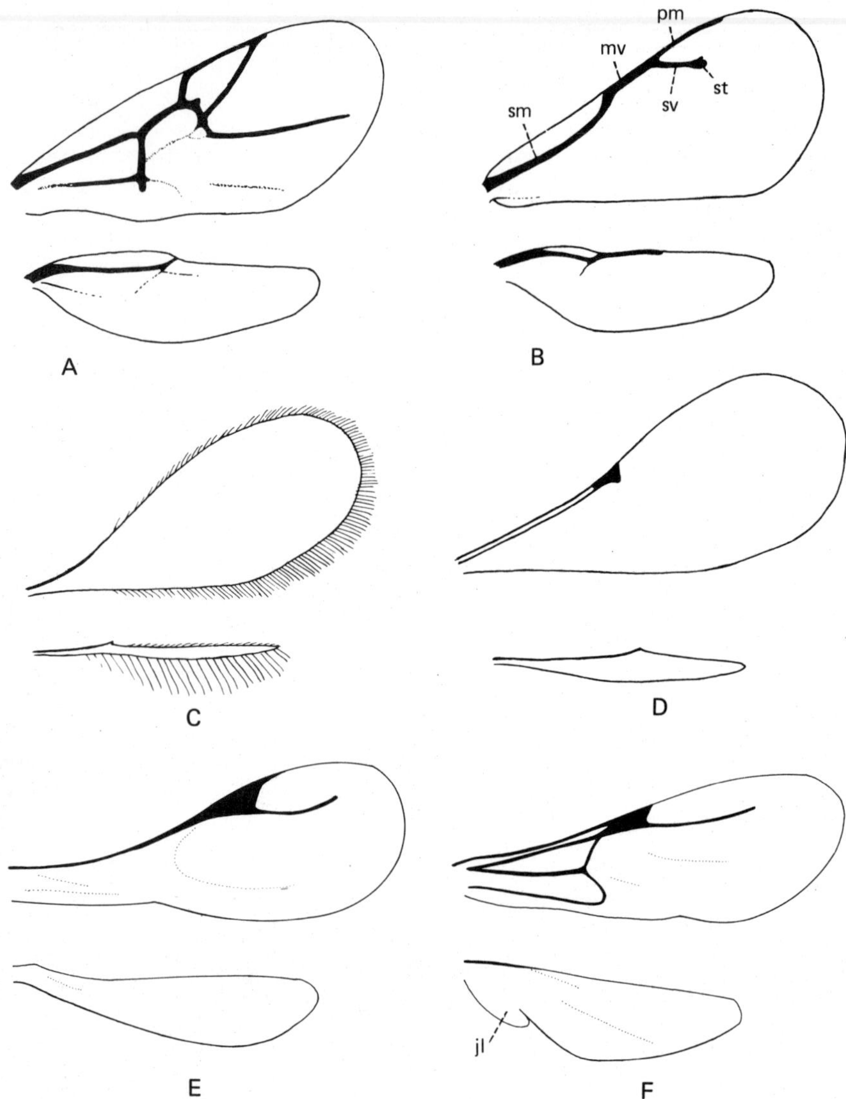

Figure 541. Wings of Hymenóptera. A, Cynípidae (Cynipìnae); B, Perilámpidae; C, Mymàridae; D, Diaprìidae (Diapriìnae); E, Ceraphrónidae; F, Bethýlidae. *jl,* jugal lobe; *mv,* marginal vein; *pm,* postmarginal vein; *sm,* submarginal vein; *st,* stigma; *sv,* stigmal vein.

28′. Antennae arising on propodeum far above bases of hind coxae (Figure 540 D–F); antennae 13- or 14-segmented 68

29(28). Ovipositor arising from anterior to apex of abdomen, and permanently extruded (Figures 531 A and 542 A); antennae filiform, with 11–16 segments; venation usually as in Figure 541 A or 543 E 30

29′. Ovipositor arising from apex of abdomen, and usually withdrawn into abdomen when not in use; antennae filiform or elbowed, with 7–23 seg-

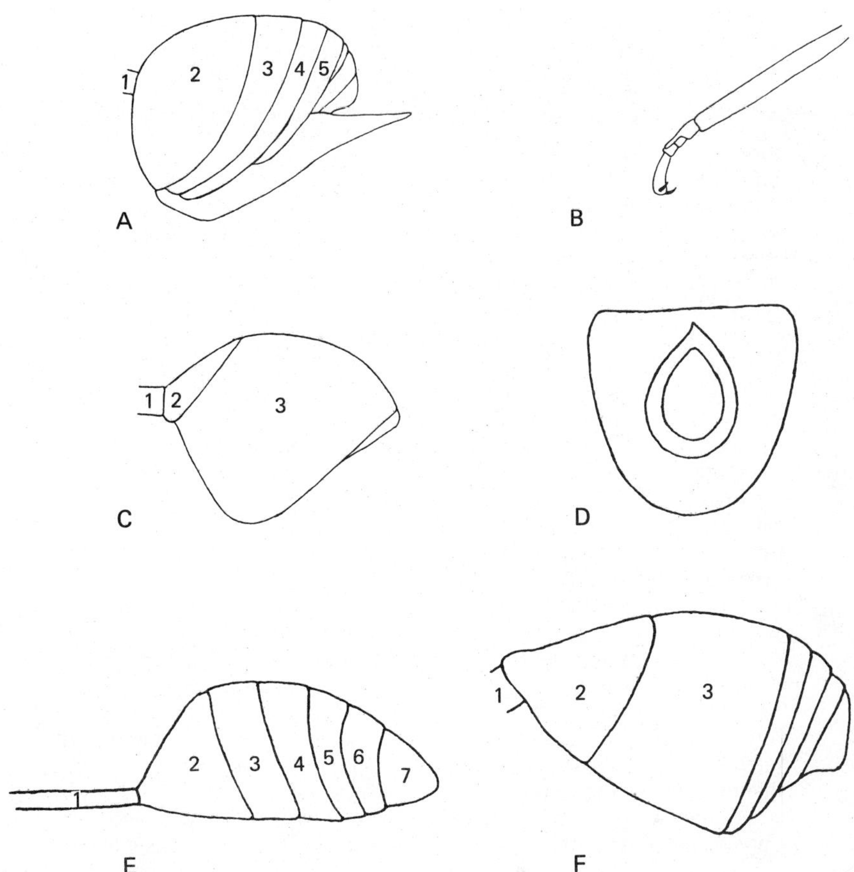

Figure 542. Characters of Cynipòidea. A, abdomen of *Diplólepis* (Cynipìnae, Cynípidae); B, hind tarsus of *Ibália* (Ibalìidae); C, abdomen of *Callaspídia* (Aspiceratìnae, Figítidae); D, scutellum of Eucoilìnae (Cynípidae); E, abdomen of *Anácharis* (Anacharitìnae, Figítidae); F, abdomen of Figitìnae (Figítidae). The abdominal tergites are numbered.

ments; venation usually as in Figure 543 A–D, F (superfamilies Pelecinòidea and Proctotrupòidea) 35

30(29). A costal cell present, the venation similar to that in Figure 541 A (superfamily Cynipòidea) 31

30′. Costal cell absent, the venation similar to that in Figure 543 E) .... **Bracónidae** p. 653

31(30, 97). First segment of hind tarsi twice as long as the other segments combined, the second segment with a long process on outer side extending to tip of fourth segment (Figure 542 B); abdomen compressed, longer than head and thorax combined; antennae 13-segmented in female and 15-segmented in male; 7–16 mm in length .... **Ibalìidae*** p. 665

31′. First segment of hind tarsi much shorter, second segment without a long process on outer side; antennae variable, but usually 13-segmented in female and 14-segmented in male; generally 8 mm in length or less .. 32

32(31′). Dorsal surface of scutellum with a rounded or oval elevation or keel in center (Figure 542 D); cubital vein arising from base of basal vein; second abdominal tergum longer than third; antennae 11- to 16-segmented, usually 13-segmented in female and 15-segmented in male (Eucoilìnae) .... **Cynípidae** p. 665

32′. Dorsal surface of scutellum not as above; venation, abdominal terga, and antennae variable 33

33(32′). Second abdominal tergum narrow, tongue-shaped, shorter than third (Figure 542 C); cubital vein arising from base of basal vein (Aspiceratìnae) .... **Figítidae*** p. 665

33′. Second abdominal tergum not tongue-shaped, or (some Cynipìnae) tongue-shaped but much longer than third 34

34(33′). Second abdominal tergum at least half as long as abdomen (Figure 542 A), or if shorter then the cubital vein arises from middle of basal vein (Charipìnae and Cynipìnae) .... **Cynípidae** p. 665

34′. Second abdominal tergum less than half as long as abdomen (Figure 542 E, F); cubital vein arising from base of basal vein, or lacking (Anacharitìnae and Figitìnae) .... **Figítidae*** p. 665

35(29′). Antennae arising far above clypeus on a frontal shelf or prominence (Figure 544 A); small or minute, usually black insects 36

35′. Antennae usually not arising on a frontal shelf or prominence, and arising either just above clypeus or near middle of face 37

36(35). Marginal cell small and incomplete, or absent; discoidal vein absent or incomplete; hind wings without a jugal lobe (Figures 541 D and 549 G); antennae 11- to 14-segmented, usually clubbed in female ...... **Diaprìidae** p. 668

36′. Marginal cell large, but not always completely closed; discoidal vein present; hind wings with a jugal lobe; antennae 10-segmented (Embolemìnae) .... **Dryínidae*** p. 669

37(35′). Antennae with 14 or more segments 38

37′. Antennae with 13 or fewer segments 40

38(37). First segment of hind tarsi much shorter than second; female with abdomen very long (about $1\frac{1}{2}$ inches (38 mm)) and slender (Figure 573); male (which is very rare) with abdomen shorter and clavate; black and shining insects .... **Pelecìnidae** p. 667

38′. First segment of hind tarsi longer than second; small or minute insects 39*

39(38′, 75′). Antennae 15-segmented; first discoidal cell small and triangular (Figure 543 H); abdomen not compressed, the petiolar segment narrowed apically; shining black, 4.5 mm in length (Figure 574) .... **Helòridae*** p. 668

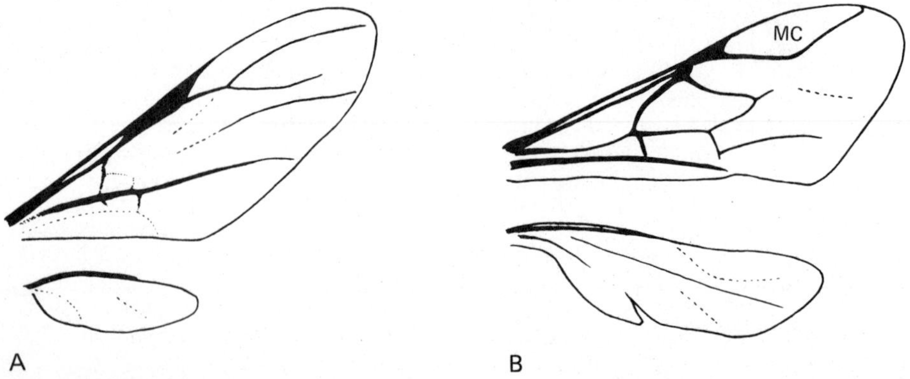

MC

A

B

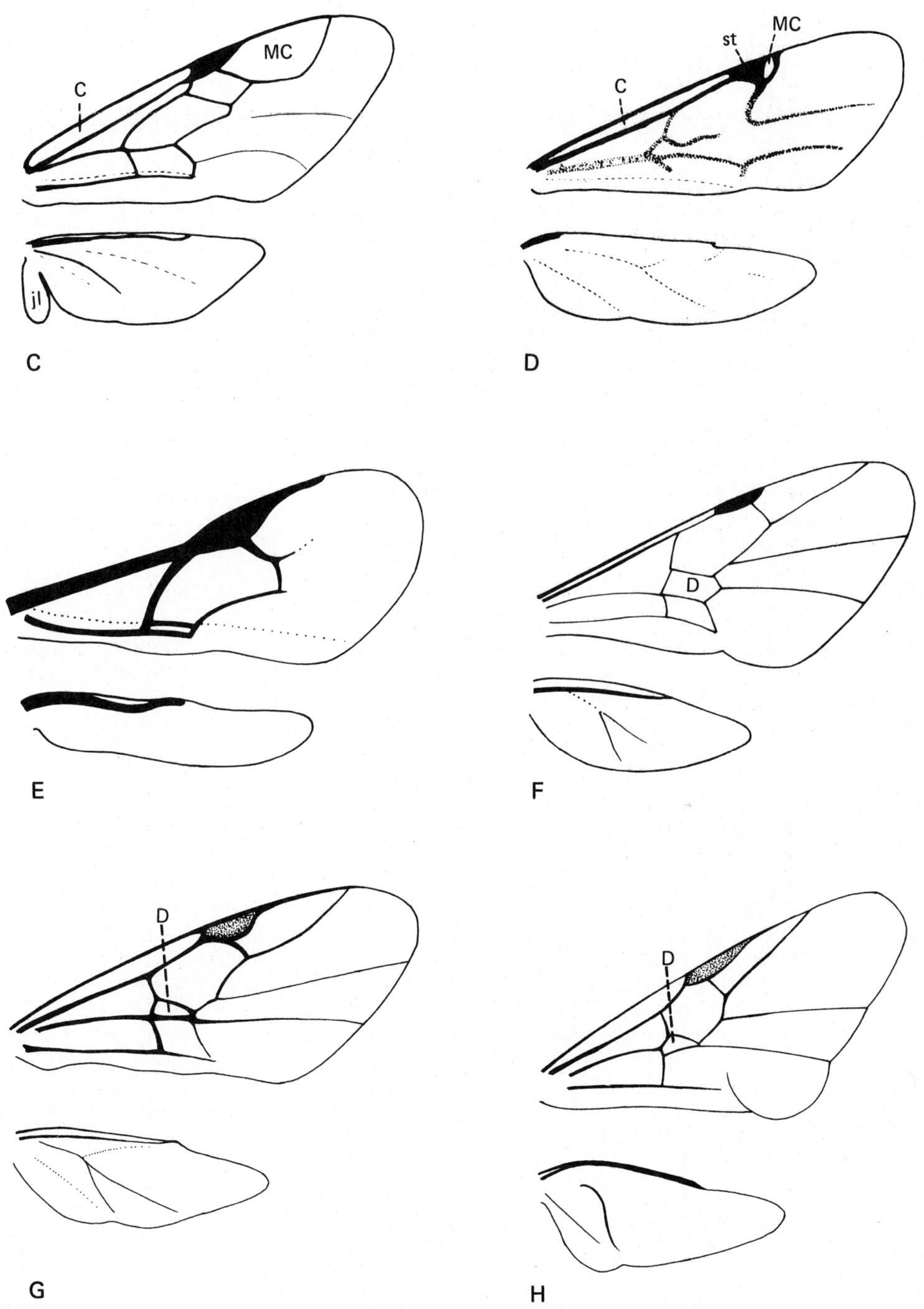

Figure 543. Wings of Hymenóptera. A, Pelecìnidae; B, Chrysídidae; C, Evanìidae; D, Proctotrùpidae; E, Bracónidae (Aphidiìnae); F, Ropronìidae; G, Vanhornìidae; H, Helòridae. *C,* costal cell; *D,* first discoidal cell; *jl,* jugal lobe; *MC,* marginal cell; *st,* stigma.

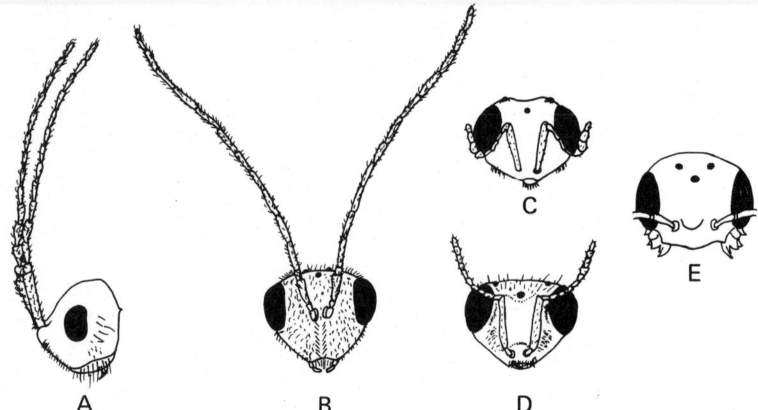

Figure 544. Head structure in the Proctotrupòidea. A, Diaprìidae; B, Proctotrùpidae; C, Platygastéridae; D, Sceliónidae; E, Vanhornìidae. A, lateral view; B–E, anterior views.

39′. Antennae 14-segmented; first discoidal cell more or less quadrate, 4- to 6-sided (Figure 543 F); abdomen strongly compressed; color variable; usually over 4.5 mm in length .... **Roproniidae*** p. 668

40(37′). Mandibles widely separated, not meeting when closed, and when open with the tips directed laterally (Figure 544 E); abdomen with 2 (females) or 4 (males) visible terga, the first covering most of abdomen; venation as in Figure 543 G .... **Vanhornìidae*** p. 668

40′. Mandibles normal, tips meeting when closed; venation usually more reduced than in Figure 543 G 41

41(40′). Antennae arising in middle of face, and 13-segmented (Figure 544 B); front wings with a broad stigma and a small marginal cell (Figure 543 D); abdomen with a short cylindrical petiole and the second segment much longer than the others .... **Proctotrùpidae** p. 668

41′. Antennae arising near margin of clypeus (Figure 544 C, D) 42

42(41′). Antennae 9- or 10-segmented; front wings with neither marginal nor stigmal veins, often without any venation; some individuals (females of *Inostémma,* Figure 575 C) with a long curved process arising from dorsum of first abdominal segment and extending forward over thorax .... **Platygastéridae** p. 668

42′. Antennae usually 11- or 12-segmented, if 7- or 8-segmented then the antennal club is unsegmented; marginal and stigmal veins generally present (Figure 541 E); abdomen without a curved process such as described above 43

43(42′). Abdomen rounded laterally .... **Ceraphrónidae*** p. 668

43′. Abdomen more or less keeled laterally, and dorsoventrally flattened .... **Sceliónidae** p. 668

44(27′). Venation greatly reduced (as in Figure 541 B), hind wings without an incision setting off a jugal or vannal lobe; antennae elbowed; thorax usually with a distinct prepectus (Figure 530 A, *pp*); trochanters generally 2-segmented (superfamily Chalcidòidea) 45

44′. Wings with more veins, hind wings usually with a lobe (jugal or vannal) set off by a distinct incision (Figures 541 F and 543 B); antennae usually not

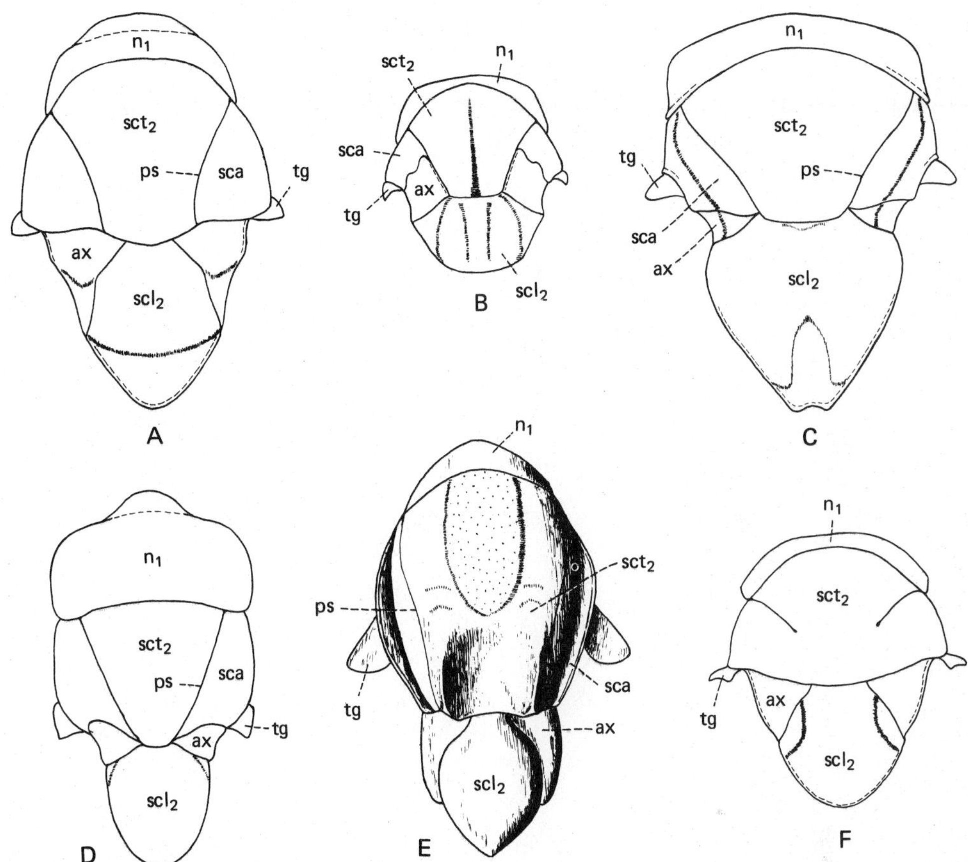

Figure 545. Thorax of Chalcidòidea, dorsal view. A, Torýmidae (*Tórymus*); B, Eulóphidae; C, Perilámpidae (*Perilámpus*); D, Eurytómidae (*Eurýtoma*); E, Eupélmidae; F, Pteromálidae (*Pterómalus*). *ax*, axilla; n_1, pronotum; *ps*, parapsidal suture; *sca*, scapula; scl_2, mesoscutellum; sct_2, mesoscutum; *tg*, tegula.

elbowed; trochanters usually 1-segmented (superfamily Bethylòidea) 64

45(44). Tarsi 3-segmented; wing pubescence often arranged in rows; very minute insects .... **Trichogrammátidae*** p. 659

45′. Tarsi 4- or 5-segmented; wing pubescence usually not arranged in rows; size variable 46

46(45′). Hind wings very narrow, linear, with a long stalk at base (Figure 541 C); wings with a long fringe, and front wings without a stigmal vein; antennal scape short and compressed, and without a ring segment; very minute insects .... **Mymàridae*** p. 659

46′. Hind wings not so narrow and without a long stalk at base; wing fringe usually short; antennal scape long, and usually with 1–3 minute ring segments 47

47(46′). Axillae extending cephalad to or beyond tegulae (Figure 545 B); apical spur of front tibia small and straight (Figure 546 A); tarsi usually 4-segmented;

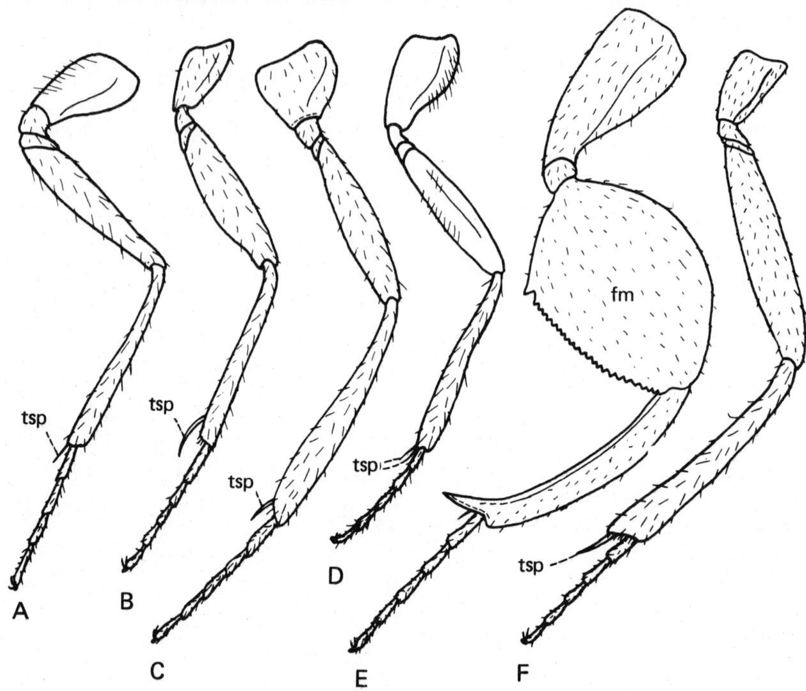

Figure 546. Legs of Chalcidòidea. A, front leg, Eulóphidae; B, front leg, Pteromálidae; C, hind leg, Pteromálidae; D, hind leg, Eurytómidae; E, hind leg, Chalcídidae; F, middle leg, Encýrtidae. *fm,* femur; *tsp,* tibial spur.

antennae generally with 9 or fewer segments .... **Eulóphidae** p. 659

47′. Axillae not extending cephalad to or beyond tegulae (Figure 545 A, C–E); apical spur of front tibia large and curved (Figure 546 B); tarsi usually 5-segmented; antennae variable 48

48(47′). Head long, oblong, with a deep longitudinal groove above (Figure 567 A); occipital margin usually with a small tubercle or spine; front and hind legs stout, tibiae much shorter than femora, middle legs slender (females) .... **Agaónidae*** p. 662

48′. Head and legs not as above 49

49(48′). Mesopleura large and convex, usually without a femoral groove (Figure 547 B, C); axillae usually meeting at their inner basal angles; apical spur on middle tibia generally very large and stout (Figure 546 F) 50

49′. Mesopleura with a groove for the reception of the femora (Figures 547 D and 548); apical spur of middle tibia not enlarged 54

50(49, 96′). Mesonotum more or less convex, parapsidal sutures lacking or indistinct 51

50′. Mesonotum rarely convex, usually flattened, parapsidal sutures present and usually distinct (Figure 545 E); marginal vein usually long 52

51(50). Marginal vein very long, as long as submarginal vein; scutellum very short and transversely linear; tibiae with lateral spurs .... **Thysánidae*** p. 659

51′. Marginal vein short, shorter than submarginal vein; scutellum never short or transversely linear; middle tibiae without lateral spurs; a large and widespread group .... **Encýrtidae** p. 659

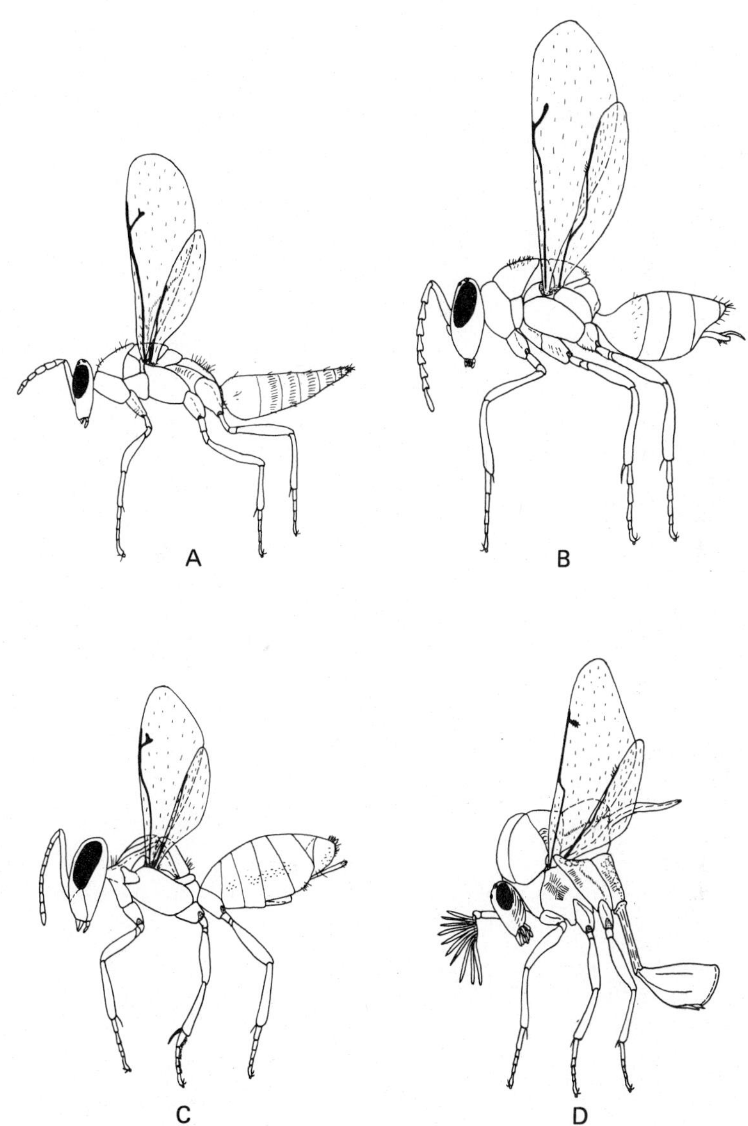

Figure 547. Chalcidòidea. A, Eulóphidae; B, Encýrtidae; C, Eupélmidae; D, Eucharítidae.

52(50′). Mesonotum of female flattened or slightly concave, with a median triangular elevation anteriorly (Figure 545 E), and parapsidal sutures often not sharply defined; mesonotum of male slightly convex, with the parapsidal sutures usually incomplete, not curved off laterally; a large and widespread group .... **Eupélmidae** p. 660

52′. Mesonotum convex in both sexes, parapsidal sutures complete and curved off laterally, scapulae short; Florida and western United States 53*

53(52′). First antennal segment of female slender, not dilated or compressed; flagellum of male antennae filiform, without branches; Texas and Mon-

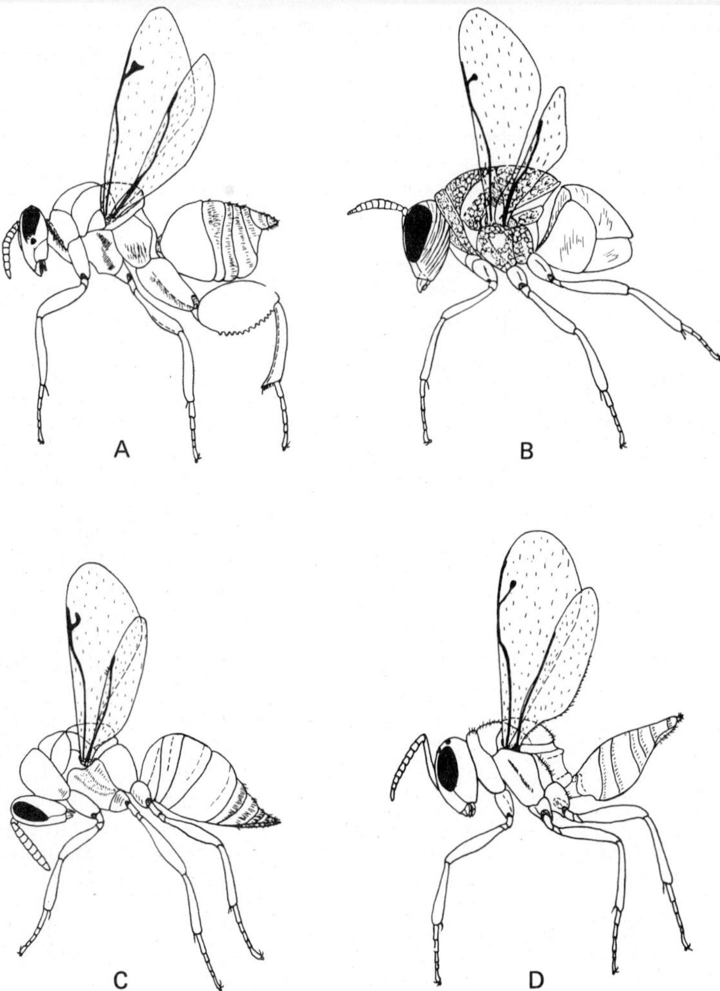

Figure 548. Chalcidòidea. A, Chalcídidae (*Brachymèria*); B, Perilámpidae (*Perilámpus*); C, Eurytómidae (*Eurý-toma*); D, Pteromálidae (*Pterómalus*).

	tana .... **Eutrichosomátidae***	p. 659
53′.	First antennal segment of female more or less dilated or compressed; flagellum of male antennae with 4 branches; Florida, Arizona, and California .... **Tanaostigmátidae***	p. 659
54(49′).	Mandibles sickle-shaped, with 1 or 2 teeth on inner side; thorax strongly elevated, pronotum with only an anterior face and not visible from above (Figure 547 D); axillae contiguous; scutellum large and produced posteriorly; abdomen compressed, the second segment very large; stigmal vein not developed .... **Eucharítidae***	p. 660
54′.	Mandibles stout, not sickle-shaped, and with 3 or 4 teeth at apex; thorax not elevated; axillae usually separated 55	
55(54′, 96).	Hind tibiae with 1 apical spur (Figure 546 C); pronotum in dorsal view more or less conical, narrowed anteriorly; hind coxae rarely larger than	

front coxae; ovipositor usually short, if long then stigma is small; mostly minute, black or metallic .... **Pteromálidae** p. 662

55′. Hind tibiae with 2 apical spurs (one of which may be small) (Figure 546 D); pronotum in dorsal view usually quadrate and not distinctly narrowed anteriorly; ovipositor generally long; color variable 56

56(55′). Hind femora greatly swollen, and usually toothed or denticulate beneath (Figure 546 E); hind tibiae usually arcuate 57

56′. Hind femora not or but slightly swollen, and either not toothed beneath or with only 1 or 2 teeth 60

57(56). Hind coxae considerably larger than front coxae 58

57′. Hind coxae little if any larger than front coxae .... **Chalcedéctidae*** p. 664

58(57). Hind coxae sharply ridged above 59*

58′. Hind coxae somewhat oval or rounded, not sharply ridged above .... **Chalcídidae** p. 665

59(58). Front wings folded longitudinally at rest; ovipositor usually long and curving upward and forward over dorsal side of abdomen; generally black and yellow insects, 10 mm or more in length .... **Leucospídidae*** p. 665

59′. Front wings not folded longitudinally at rest; ovipositor short and not upcurved; color usually black; mostly 7 mm in length or less (Podagrionìnae) .... **Torýmidae*** p. 662

60(56′). Hind coxae considerably larger than front coxae (Figure 568 B) 61

60′. Hind coxae little if any larger than front coxae (Figure 548 B–D) 62

61(60). Parapsidal sutures present (Figure 545 A); ovipositor exserted and usually very long (Figure 568 B); abdomen not pitted or punctured; body metallic .... **Torýmidae** p. 662

61′. Parapsidal sutures absent or very indistinct; ovipositor short and hidden; abdomen of female conical and elongate, of male oblong, and usually with rows of deep pits or punctures in both sexes .... **Ormýridae*** p. 662

62(60′). Pronotum more or less quadrate and as wide as mesonotum (Figure 545 C, D); mesonotum usually very coarsely sculptured 63

62′. Pronotum short, transversely linear, rarely as wide as mesonotum (Figure 545 F); mesonotum usually finely sculptured .... **Pteromálidae** p. 662

63(62). Pronotum short, much wider than long (Figure 545 C); abdomen of female subtriangular, second tergum (or fused second and third terga) covering most of its surface (Figure 548 B); thorax very robust; often metallic insects .... **Perilámpidae** p. 662

63′. Pronotum more or less quadrate, nearly as long as wide (Figure 545 D); abdomen of female rounded or ovate, more or less compressed, second tergum never very large (Figure 548 C); thorax of more normal proportions; black or yellowish insects, thorax not metallic .... **Eurytómidae** p. 663

64(44′). Antennae with 22 or more segments, and arising low on face; Arizona (males) .... **Sclerogíbbidae*** p. 670

64′. Antennae with 10–13 segments 65

65(64′). Antennae 10-segmented; front tarsi of female usually pincerlike .... **Dryínidae*** p. 669

65′. Antennae 12- or 13-segmented; front tarsi not pincerlike 66

66(65′). Abdomen with 3–5 visible terga, the last one often dentate apically; head not elongate; body usually metallic blue or green and coarsely sculptured .... **Chrysídidae** p. 669

66′. Abdomen with 6–7 visible terga; head usually oblong and elongate; body black .... **Bethýlidae*** p. 669

67(26′). Abdomen arising on propodeum far above bases of hind coxae (Figure 540 D–F) 68

67′. Abdomen arising on propodeum between bases of hind coxae, or only slightly above them (as in Figure 540 A–C) 71

68(28′, 67). Hind wings with a distinct jugal lobe (Figure 543 C); abdomen short, oval

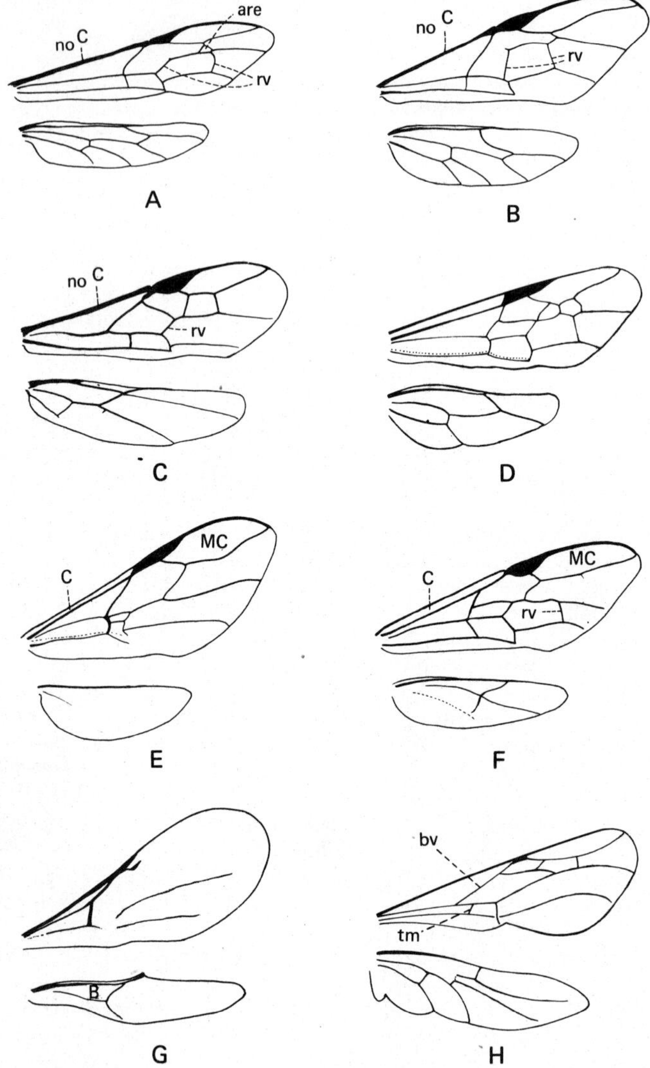

Figure 549. Wings of Hymenóptera. A, Ichneumónidae *(Megarhýssa);* B, Ichneumónidae *(Òphion);* C, Bracónidae; D, Trigonálidae; E, Gasteruptìidae; F, Aulácidae; G, Diaprìidae (Belytìnae); H, Rhopalosomátidae (*Rhopalosòma*). *are,* areolet; *B,* basal cell; *bv,* basal vein; *C,* costal cell; *MC,* marginal cell; *rv,* recurrent vein; *tm,* transverse median vein.

to circular and compressed, with a cylindrical petiole (Figure 572) .... **Evanìidae** p. 666

68′. Hind wings without a distinct jugal lobe (Figure 549 E, F); abdomen elongate 69

69(68′). Prothorax long and necklike; venation usually complete, front wings with a stigma (Figure 549 E, F); antennae 14-segmented; length over 8 mm; widely distributed 70

69′. Prothorax not long and necklike; venation reduced, much as in Figure 541

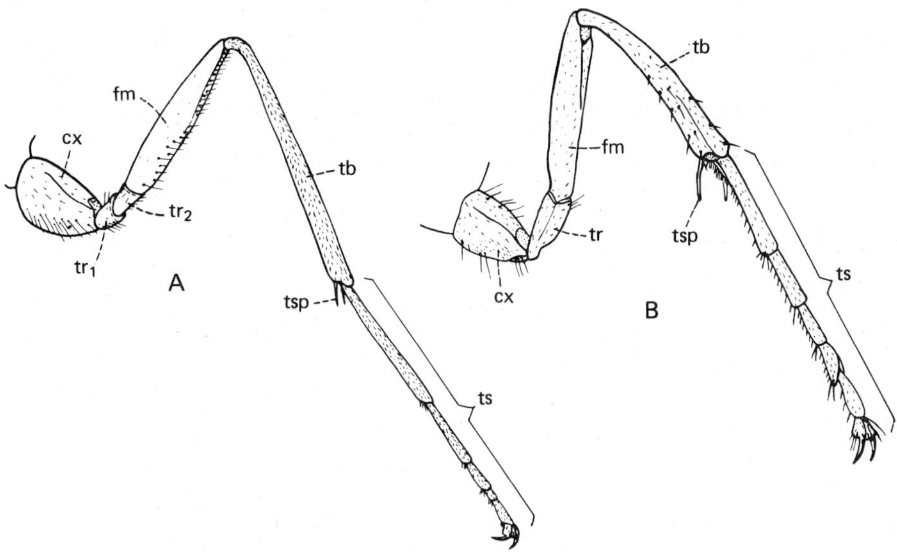

Figure 550. Legs of Hymenóptera. A, Ichneumónidae; B, Sphécidae. *cx,* coxa; *fm,* femur; *tb,* tibia; *tr,* trochanter; *ts,* tarsus; *tsp,* tibial spurs.

A, front wings without a stigma; antennae 13-segmented in female and 14-segmented in male; length less than 8 mm; Texas ...... **Lioptéridae*** p. 665

70(69). One recurrent vein or none, and 1 submarginal cell or none (Figure 549 E); usually black, with relatively short antennae .... **Gasteruptìidae** p. 666

70′. Two recurrent veins, and 1 or 2 submarginal cells (Figure 549 F); usually black with a reddish abdomen, and the antennae relatively long .... **Aulácidae** p. 667

71(67′). Hind trochanters 2-segmented (Figure 550 A), distal segment sometimes poorly defined, rarely the trochanters 1-segmented; antennae with 14 or more segments; hind wings usually without a jugal lobe (Figure 549 A–D); ovipositor variable, but sometimes long, half as long as abdomen or longer, and permanently exserted (Figure 531 A) 72

71′. Hind trochanters 1-segmented (Figure 550 B); antennae usually 12-segmented in female and 13-segmented in male; hind wings usually with a jugal lobe (Figure 551); ovipositor short, issuing from apex of abdomen (usually as a sting), and usually withdrawn into abdomen when not in use (Figure 531 B) 77

72(71). Head somewhat spherical, set out on a long neck, and bearing a crown of teeth; costal cell usually present but narrow; 1 submarginal cell or none; female with a long ovipositor; length usually over 10 mm .... **Stephánidae*** p. 652

72′. Head not as above; venation, size, and ovipositor variable 73

73(72′). Costal cell present (Figure 549 D); ovipositor very short 74

73′. Costal cell absent (Figure 549 A–C); ovipositor often long 76

74(73). Venation somewhat reduced, with not more than 1 submarginal cell; antennae 14- or 15-segmented 75*

74′. Venation not reduced, with 2 or 3 submarginal cells; antennae with 16 or more segments .... **Trigonálidae*** p. 670

75(74). Mandibles widely separated, not meeting when closed, and when open with the tips directed laterally (Figure 544 E); abdomen with 2 (females) or

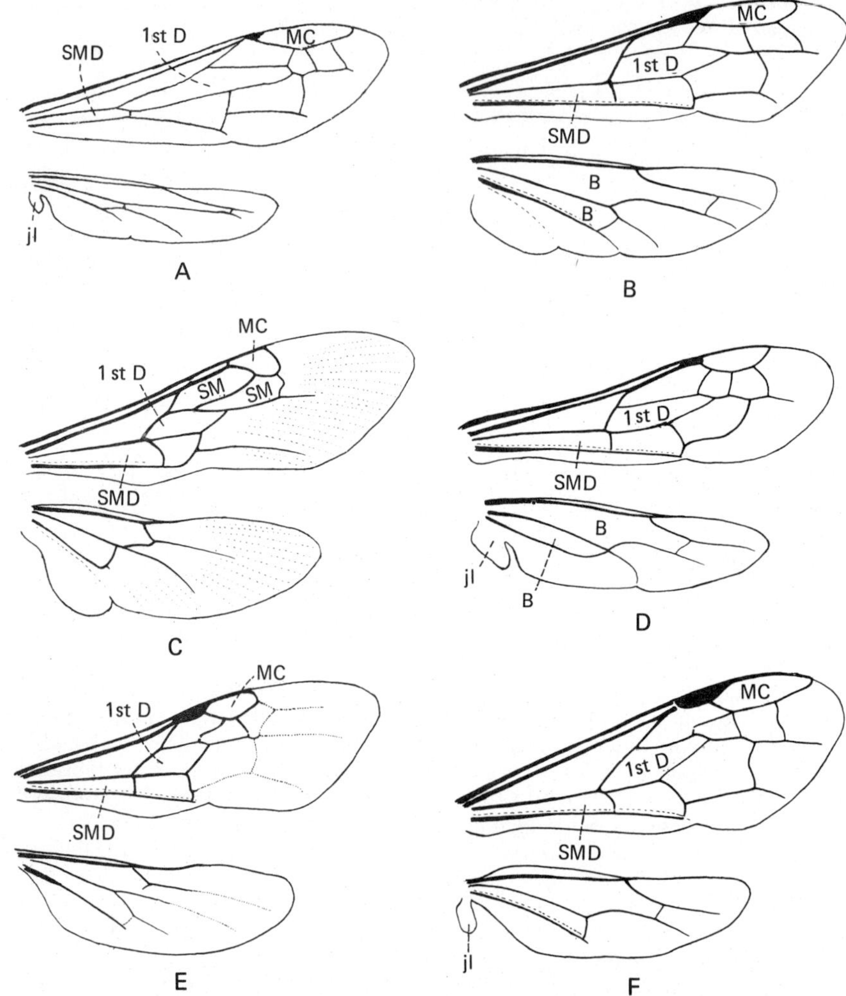

Figure 551. Wings of Vespòidea (A) and Scoliòidea (B–F). A, Véspidae (*Polístes*); B, Tiphìidae (*Mỳzinum*); C, Scolìidae *(Scòlia);* D, Pompílidae; E, Mutíllidae *(Dasymutílla);* F, Tiphìidae (Myrmosìnae). *B,* basal cell; *D,* discoidal cell; *jl,* jugal lobe; *MC,* marginal cell; *SM,* submarginal cell; *SMD,* submedian cell.

4 (males) visible terga, the first covering most of abdomen .... **Vanhornìidae*** 668

75′. Mandibles normal, tips meeting when closed 39*

76(73′). Two recurrent veins (Figure 549 A, B), or if with only 1 then with the abdomen 3 times as long as rest of body and with tip of propodeum prolonged behind hind coxae; first submarginal and first discoidal cells usually confluent; size variable, from a few mm up to 40 mm or more (excluding the ovipositor) .... **Ichneumónidae** 654

76′. One recurrent vein (Figure 549 C) or none; first submarginal and first discoidal cells usually separated; abdomen not greatly elongate; propodeum not prolonged behind hind coxae; mostly small insects, rarely over 15 mm in length .... **Bracónidae** 653

77(71′). First discoidal cell nearly always very long, much longer than submedian

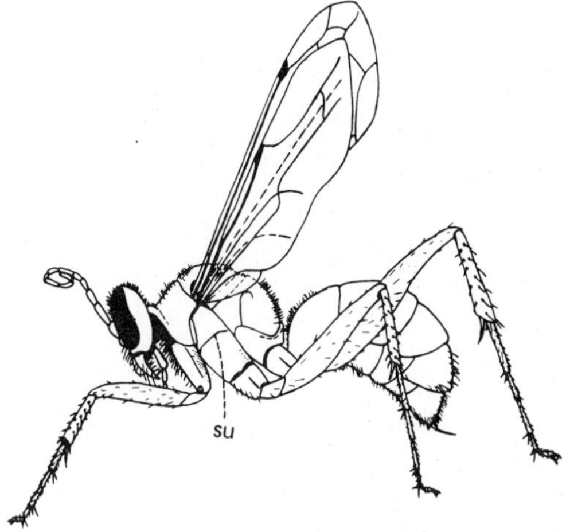

Figure 552. A spider wasp (Pompílidae), showing the transverse suture (*su*) across the mesopleuron.

cell (Figure 551 A); wings usually folded longitudinally at rest; 3 submarginal cells .... **Véspidae** 676

77′. First discoidal cell shorter than submedian cell (Figure 551 B–F); wings usually not folded longitudinally at rest; 2–3 submarginal cells 78

78(77′). Mesopleura with a transverse suture (Figure 552, *su*); legs long, hind femora usually extending to or beyond apex of abdomen .... **Pompílidae** 680

78′. Mesopleura without a transverse suture; legs shorter, hind femora usually not extending to apex of abdomen 79

79(78′). Mesosternum and metasternum together forming a plate divided by a transverse suture, and overlapping bases of middle and hind coxae, the hind coxae well separated (Figure 553 A); wing membrane beyond closed cells with fine longitudinal wrinkles (Figure 551 C); apex of abdomen of male with 3 retractile spines; large, usually brightly colored wasps ... **Scolìidae** 671

79′. Mesosternum and metasternum not forming such a plate, though there may be a pair of plates overlying bases of middle coxae (Figure 553 B); hind

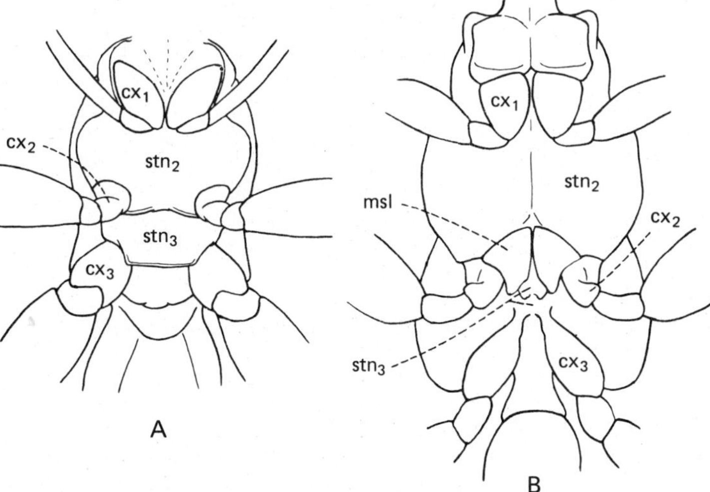

Figure 553. Thorax, ventral view. A, Scolìidae (*Scòlia*); B, Tiphìidae (*Típhia*). *cx*, coxae; *msl*, mesosternal lobe; *stn_2*, mesosternum; *stn_3*, metasternum.

coxae contiguous or nearly so; wing membrane beyond closed cells usually not wrinkled; apex of abdomen of male without 3 retractile spines; size and color variable 80

80(79′). Antennae clavate (Figure 581 D); 2 submarginal cells (Figure 581 A); length 10–20 mm; color usually black and yellow; western United States (Masarìnae) .... **Véspidae** p. 676

80′. Antennae not clavate; other characters variable 81

81(80′). Transverse median vein more than two thirds its length distad of basal vein (Figure 549 H); hind tarsi very long; flagellar segments of antennae long and slender, each with 2 apical spines; light brown wasps, 14–20 mm in length (*Rhopalosòma*) .... **Rhopalosomátidae*** p. 671

81′. Transverse basal vein opposite basal vein, or nearly so (Figure 551 E, F); tarsi not as above; flagellar segments of antennae without apical spines; size and color variable 82

82(81′). Mesosternum with 2 lobelike extensions behind, which project between and partly cover bases of middle coxae (Figure 553 B, *msl*); hind wings with a jugal lobe (Figure 529) (Brachycistidìnae, Tiphiìnae, Myzinìnae, Anthoboscìnae) .... **Tiphìidae** p. 671

82′. Mesosternum without such lobes, at most a pair of minute toothlike projections behind; hind wings with or without a jugal lobe 83

83(82′). Apex of second discoidal cell produced above, and jugal lobe in hind wings about half as long as submedian cell (Figure 581 C); length 6–7 mm; southwestern United States (Euparagiìnae) .... **Véspidae*** p. 676

83′. Not exactly fitting the above description 84

84(83′). Hind wings with a distinct jugal lobe (Figure 551 F) 85*

84′. Hind wings without a distinct jugal lobe (Figure 551 E) 88

85(84). Abdominal segments separated by strong constrictions; eyes usually not emarginate (males of Myrmosìnae and Methochìnae) .... **Tiphìidae*** p. 671

85′. Abdomen without such constrictions; eyes sometimes emarginate ... 86*

86(85′). Body bare, marked with yellow or white; eyes deeply emarginate (Sapygìnae) .... **Sapỳgidae*** p. 672

86′. Body usually very hairy; color and eyes variable 87*

87(86′). Second abdominal tergum with lateral submarginal "felt lines" (narrow longitudinal bands of relatively dense, closely appressed hairs); usually very pubescent (males of Apterogynìnae) .... **Mutíllidae*** p. 671

87′. Second abdominal tergum without lateral "felt lines"; body and legs clothed with long erect hair; males and females (*Fedtschénkia,* California) .... **Sapỳgidae*** p. 672

88(84′). Shining black, 4.5–6.0 mm in length; second abdominal tergum without felt lines (see couplet 87); males without spines at apex of abdomen; eyes not emarginate mesally; males and females .... **Sierolomórphidae*** p. 671

88′. Not shining black, but very hairy and often brightly colored; size variable but usually over 6 mm in length; second abdominal tergum usually with lateral submarginal "felt lines"; usually with 1 or 2 spines at apex of abdomen; eyes rounded (Sphaerophthalmìnae) or emarginate (Typhoctìnae and Mutillìnae) mesally; males .... **Mutíllidae** p. 671

89(14′). Tarsi 4-segmented; antennae elbowed; length less than 6 mm (see also couplet 47) .... **Eulóphidae*** p. 659

89′. Tarsi 5-segmented; antennae and size variable 90

90(89′). Antennae filiform, with 16 or more segments 91*

90′. Antennae filiform or elbowed, with 15 or fewer segments 93

91(90). Hind trochanters 1-segmented; ovipositor issuing from apex of abdomen, and usually withdrawn into abdomen when not in use; females; Arizona .... **Sclerogíbbidae*** p. 670

91′. Hind trochanters 2-segmented; ovipositor issuing from anterior to apex of abdomen, and permanently exserted; widely distributed 92*

92(91′). Abdomen petiolate, the petiole curved and expanded apically .... **Ichneumónidae*** p. 654

92′. Abdomen not petiolate, or if petiolate then the petiole is not curved or expanded apically .... **Bracónidae*** p. 653

93(90′). Hind trochanters 2-segmented; antennae elbowed and often clubbed (Figures 547 and 548); prepectus well developed and triangular (Figure 530 A, *pp*); pronotum in profile somewhat quadrate; ovipositor issuing from anterior to apex of abdomen, and permanently exserted (wingless chalcids) 94*

93′. Hind trochanters usually 1-segmented; antennae variable; prepectus, if present, elongate and less well differentiated; pronotum and ovipositor variable 97

94(93). Head with a deep triangular impression anteriorly; males 95*

94′. Head without such an impression 96*

95(94). Abdomen much drawn out to a point apically, or broadened at tip; antennae short and stout, 3- to 9-segmented (see also couplet 48) .... **Agaónidae*** p. 662

95′. Abdomen not pointed or enlarged apically .... **Torýmidae*** p. 662

96(94′). Mesopleura with an oblique femoral groove or impression (Figure 548) 55*

96′. Mesopleura large and convex, without a femoral groove (Figure 547 B, C) 50*

97(93′). Hind trochanters 2-segmented (Figure 550 A); ovipositor issuing from anterior to apex of abdomen and permanently exserted; petiole of abdomen cylindrical, abdomen compressed; antennae often swollen apically (wingless Cynipòidea) 31*

97′. Hind trochanters 1-segmented (Figure 550 B); ovipositor issuing from apex of abdomen, usually as a sting, and usually withdrawn into abdomen when not in use (Figure 531 B); abdomen not compressed; antennae variable 98

98(97′). Second abdominal tergum with lateral "felt lines" (see couplet 87); body usually very pubescent; antennae usually 12-segmented, rarely 11- or 13-segmented; females .... **Mutíllidae** p. 671

98′. Second abdominal tergum without lateral "felt lines" 99*

99(98′). Antennae arising on a frontal shelf or prominence (Figure 544 A); females 100*

99′. Antennae not arising on a frontal shelf or prominence 101*

100(99). First abdominal segment forming a distinct petiole; antennae 12- or 13-segmented .... **Diaprìidae*** p. 668

100′. First abdominal segment not forming a distinct petiole; antennae 10-segmented (Embolemìnae) .... **Dryínidae*** p. 669

101(99′). Abdomen with sharp lateral margins; antennae elbowed 102*

101′. Abdomen rounded laterally; antennae variable 103*

102(101). Antennae with 10 or fewer segments; males .... **Platygastéridae*** p. 668

102′. Antennae usually 11- or 12-segmented; females .... **Sceliónidae*** p. 668

103(101′). Antennae 10- or 11-segmented 104*

103′. Antennae 12- or 13-segmented 105*

104(103). Males with 10-segmented antennae; females with front tarsi pincerlike .... **Dryínidae*** p. 669

104′. Males with 11-segmented antennae; females with front tarsi not pincerlike .... **Ceraphrónidae*** p. 668

105(103′). Antennae arising in middle of face (Figure 544 B) 106*

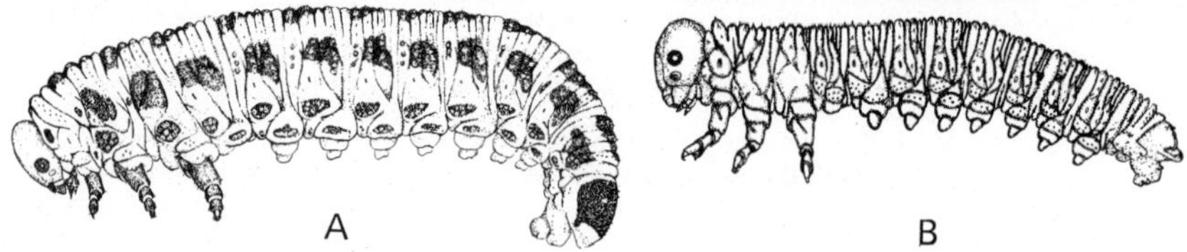

Figure 554. Sawfly larvae. A, *Neodíprion lecóntei* (Fitch) (Dipriónidae); B, *Allántus cintus* (L.) (Tenthredínidae). (Courtesy of USDA.)

105′.	Antennae arising low on face, near margin of clypeus 107*	
106(105).	Hind tarsi very long, nearly as long as tibiae and femora combined; first abdominal segment long and slender; wings present but very short (*Olíxon*) .... **Rhopalosomátidae***	p. 671
106′.	Tarsi and abdomen not as above, abdomen spindle-shaped .... **Proctotrùpidae***	p. 668
107(105′).	Head elongate, usually longer than wide; front femora usually thickened in middle; females .... **Bethýlidae***	p. 669
107′.	Head not elongate, usually oval and wider than high (females of Brachycistidìnae, Myrmosìnae, and Methochìnae) .... **Tiphìidae***	p. 671

SUBORDER **Sýmphyta:** The members of this suborder, except for the family Orússidae, are phytophagous, and the majority are external feeders on foliage. The larvae of the external feeders are eruciform (Figure 554) and differ from the larvae of the Lepidóptera in that they have more than five pairs of prolegs that lack crochets and usually have only one pair of ocelli. The larvae of a few species bore in stems, fruit, wood, or leaves (leaf miners); these larvae usually have the prolegs reduced or absent. All the Sýmphyta have a well-developed ovipositor, which is used in inserting the eggs into the tissues of the host plant. In the Tenthredinòidea the ovipositor is somewhat sawlike, hence the common name "sawflies" for the members of this group.

Most of the Sýmphyta have a single generation a year and overwinter as a fullgrown larva or as a pupa, either in a cocoon or in some sort of protected place. Most of the external feeders overwinter in a cocoon or cell in the soil, while boring species usually overwinter in their tunnels in the host plant. Some of the larger species may require more than a year to complete their development.

Family **Xyèlidae:** The Xyèlidae are medium-sized to small sawflies, mostly less than 10 mm in length, which differ from other sawflies in having three marginal cells (Figure 532 C) and the third antennal segment very long (longer than the remaining segments combined) (Figure 534 D). Unlike that of all other sawflies except the Pamphilìidae, the costal cell is divided by a longitudinal vein. The larvae of the xyelids feed on hickory, elm, and in the staminate flowers of pine. This group is a small one (33 North American species), and none of its members is of very great economic importance.

Family **Pamphilìidae**—Web-Spinning and Leaf-Rolling Sawflies: These sawflies are stout-bodied and usually less than 15 mm in length. The larvae tie leaves together with silk or roll up a leaf and feed in the shelter so formed. Members of this group are uncommon, and only a few are of much economic importance. One web-spinning species, *Neurótoma inconspícua* (Norton), feeds on plum; a leaf-rolling species, *Pamphílius pérsicum* MacGillivray, feeds on peach.

Family **Pérgidae:** The sawflies in this small group (13 North American species) occur from the eastern states west to Arizona, but are uncommon; their larvae feed on the foliage of oak and hickory. Our species belong to the genus *Acordulécera*.

Family **Árgidae:** The Árgidae are a small group (72 North American species) of medium-sized to small, stout-bodied sawflies, easily recognized by the characteristic antennae (Figure 534 E); males of a few species have the last antennal segment **U**-shaped or **Y**-shaped. Most of the argids are black

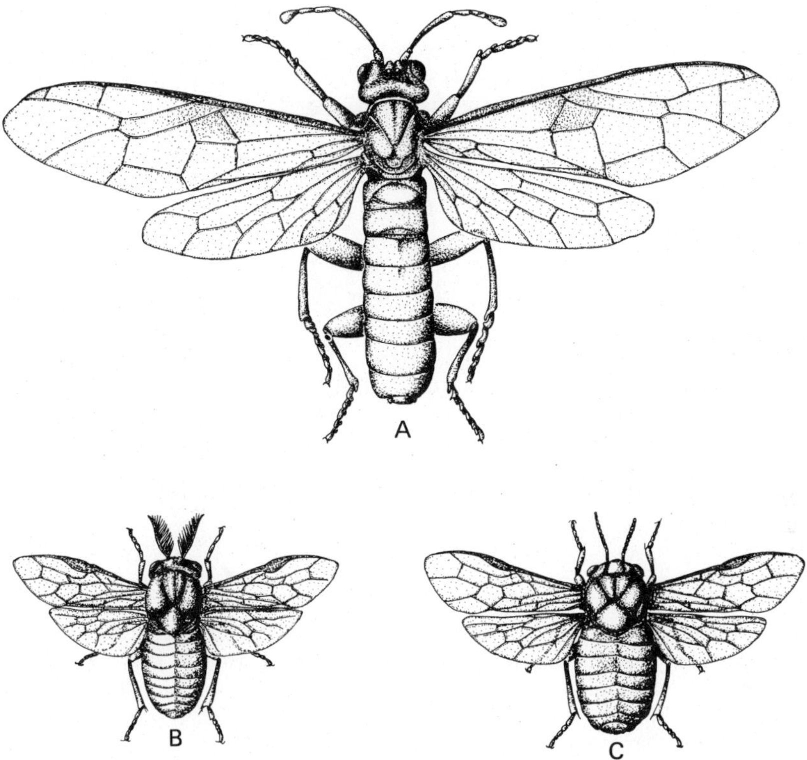

Figure 555. A, elm sawfly, *Címbex americàna* Leach, male (Cimbícidae); B, redheaded pine sawfly, *Neodíprion lecóntei* (Fitch), male (Dipriónidae); C, same, female. (B and C, Redrawn from USDA.)

or dark-colored. The larvae feed chiefly on various kinds of trees, but *Árge humeràlis* (Beauvois) feeds on poison ivy, *Sphacóphilus cellulàris* (Say) feeds on sweet potato, and *Schizocerélla pilicórnis* (Holmgren) mines leaves of *Portuláca*.

Family **Cimbícidae:** The Cimbícidae are large, robust sawflies with clubbed antennae. Some resemble bumble bees. The most common species is the elm sawfly, *Címbex americàna* Leach, a dark-blue insect 18–25 mm in length (Figure 555 A); the female has four small yellow spots on each side of the abdomen. The full-grown larva of this species is about 1½ inches (38 mm) long, with the diameter of a lead pencil, and is greenish yellow with black spiracles and a black stripe down the back. When at rest or when disturbed, it assumes a spiral position; often, when disturbed, it will eject a fluid, sometimes for a distance of several centimeters, from glands just above the spiracles. This species has one generation a year and overwinters as a full-grown larva in a cocoon in the ground; it pupates in the spring, and the adults appear in early summer. The larva feeds chiefly on elm and willow.

Family **Dipriónidae**—Conifer Sawflies: These are medium-sized sawflies with 13 or more antennal segments. The antennae are serrate in the female and pectinate or bipectinate in the male (Figures 534 C and 555 B, C). The larvae (Figure 554 A) feed on conifers and may sometimes do serious damage. These insects are relatively rare in the Midwest, but are fairly common elsewhere.

Family **Tenthredínidae**—Common Sawflies: This is a very large group (about 840 North American species),and probably nine out of ten of the sawflies the general collector is likely to encounter will belong to this family. The adults are wasplike insects, often brightly colored, and are usually found on foliage or flowers. They are medium-sized to small, rarely over 20 mm in length (Figure

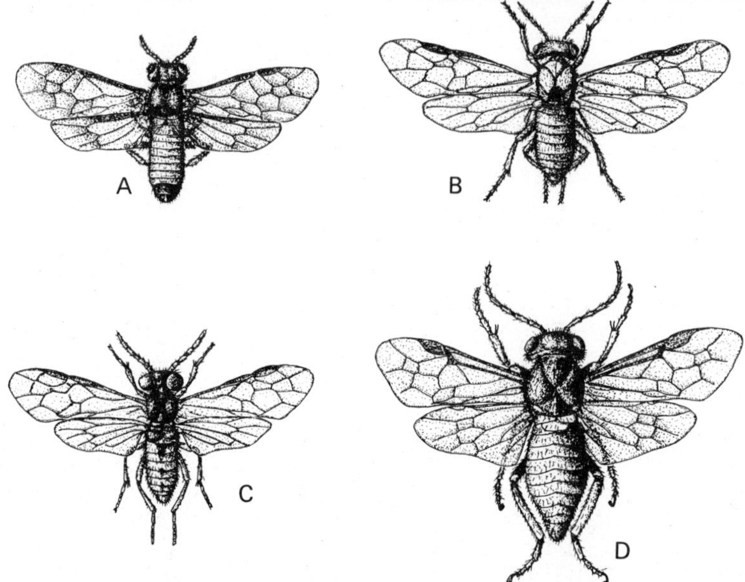

Figure 556. Common sawflies (Tenthredínidae). A, birch leafminer, *Fenùsa pusilla* (Lepeletier), male; B, cherry and hawthorn sawfly, *Profenùsa canadénsis* (Marlatt), female; C, same, male; D, raspberry leaf sawfly, *Prióphorus mòrio* (Lepeletier), female. (A, Redrawn from Friend and the Bulletin of the Connecticut Agricultural Experiment Station; B and C, Redrawn from Parrot and Fulton and the Bulletin of the Geneva, N. Y., Agricultural Experiment Station; D, Redrawn from Smith and Kido and *Hilgardia*.)

Figure 557. A, an adult horntail, *Trèmex colúmba* (L.); B, horntail pupa in the larval gallery. (A, courtesy of Knull; B, courtesy of the Ohio Agricultural Research and Development Center.)

556). The larvae (Figure 554 B) are eruciform, and most of them are external feeders on foliage; when feeding, they usually have the body (or the posterior part of it) coiled over the edge of the leaf. There is usually a single generation a year, and the insect overwinters in a pupal cell or cocoon, either in the ground or in a protected situation.

Sawfly larvae feed chiefly on various trees and shrubs, and some of them are very destructive. The larch sawfly, *Pristíphora erichsònii* (Hartig), is a very destructive pest of larch and, when numerous, may cause extensive defoliation over large areas. The imported currant-worm, *Nématus rìbesii* (Scopoli), is a serious pest of currants and gooseberries.

A few species in this group are gall makers, and a few are leaf miners. Species of the genus *Euùra* form galls on willow, one of the commonest being a small oval gall on the stem. The birch leafminer (Figure 556 A), *Fenùsa pusílla* (Lepeletier), which makes blotch mines in birch, is a serious pest in the northeastern states; it has two or three generations a year and pupates in the ground. The elm leaf miner, *Fenùsa úlmi* Sundevall, mines in elm leaves and frequently does quite a bit of damage.

The family Tenthredínidae is divided into eight subfamilies, chiefly on the basis of wing venation. The two sexes are differently colored in many species.

Family **Syntéxidae**—Incense-Cedar Wood Wasps: This family is represented in the United States by a single species, *Syntéxis libocèdrii* Rohwer, which occurs in California and Oregon. The adult female is black and 8 mm in length; the larva bores in the wood of the incense cedar.

Family **Sirícidae**—Horntails: Horntails are fairly large insects, usually 25 mm or more in length, and the larvae are wood-boring. Both sexes have a horny spearlike plate on the last abdominal tergite, and the female has a long ovipositor. The most common eastern species is *Trèmex colúmba* (L.), a brown and black insect about 1½ inches (38 mm) in length (Figure 557 A). The larvae burrow in maple, elm, beech, and other trees, but are seldom sufficiently numerous to do a great deal of damage. Pupation occurs in the burrow made by the larva (Figure 557 B).

Family **Xiphydrìidae**—Wood Wasps: The wood wasps are moderate-sized (12–20 mm in length) cylindrical insects, somewhat similar to the horntails, but they lack the horny plate at the apex of the abdomen. The larvae bore in the dead and decaying wood of deciduous trees. There are only six North American species, and none is very common.

Family **Orússidae**—Parasitic Wood Wasps: This is a small group of rare insects, the adults of which are somewhat similar to horntails but are considerably smaller (8–14 mm in length). The larvae as far as known are parasites of the larvae of metallic wood-boring beetles (Bupréstidae).

Family **Cèphidae**—Stem Sawflies: These are slender, laterally compressed sawflies (Figure 558); the larvae bore in the stems of grasses and berries. *Cèphus cínctus* Norton bores in the stems of wheat and is often called the wheat stem sawfly (Figure 558 C); the adult is about 9 mm in length, shining black, and banded and spotted with yellow. *C. cínctus* is an important wheat pest in the western states; *C. pygmaèus* (L.), a similar species, occurs in the East. *Jànus ínteger* (Norton) bores in the stems of currants; the adult is shining black and about 13 mm in length; there is a single generation a year, and the insect overwinters in a silken cocoon inside the plant in which the larva feeds.

SUBORDER **Apócrita:** The Apócrita differ from the Sýmphyta in having the base of the abdomen constricted, the thorax appearing 4-segmented (with the propodeum representing the first abdominal segment fused with the thoracic segments), and the hind wings with not more than two basal cells. The larvae are usually grublike or maggotlike, and vary in feeding habits; some are parasitic or predaceous on other insects, while others are plant feeders. The adults feed chiefly on flowers, sap, and other plant materials; some of the parasitic species occasionally feed on the body fluids of the host (Figure 564 B).

A great many species in this suborder are parasitic[2] in the larval stage on other insects (or other invertebrates), and because of their abundance are very important in keeping the populations of other insects in check. Most of the parasitic Apócrita lay their eggs on or in the body of the host, and many have a long ovipositor with which hosts in cocoons, burrows, or other protected situations may be reached. In some cases only a single egg is laid on a host; in others, several to many eggs may be laid on the same host. A single parasite attacking a host usually pupates inside that host; where there are many parasites in the same host, they may pupate inside it, on the outside of it (Figures 428 B and 561), or entirely away from it. Some species are parthenogenetic. Polyembryony occurs in a few species, that is, a single egg develops into many larvae. Some of the

[2] Most insects that are parasites of other insects are by some authorities termed *parasitoids*. According to this terminology, both parasites and parasitoids live in or on the body of another living animal (the host), at least during part of the life cycle; a parasite usually does not kill its host or consume a large part of the host tissues, while a parasitoid consumes all or most of the host's tissues and eventually kills it.

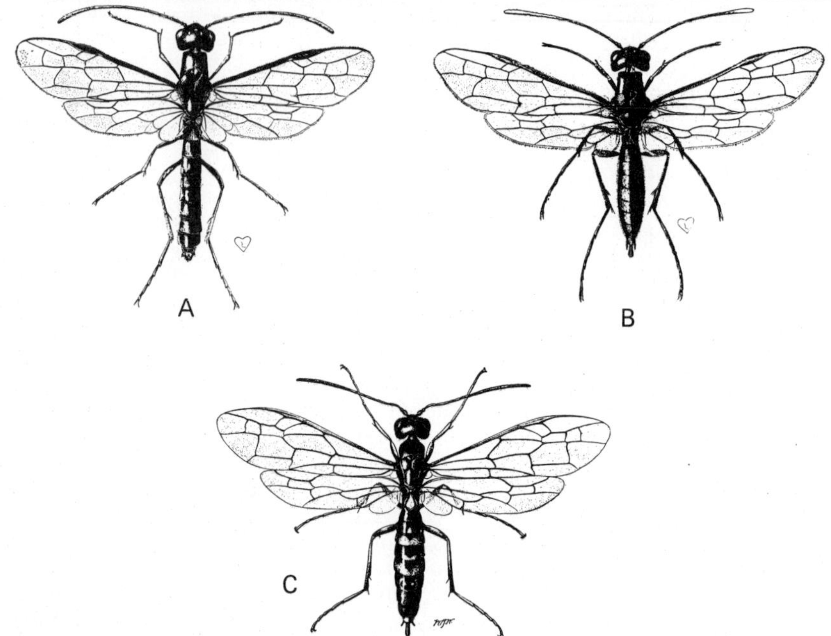

Figure 558. Stem sawflies (Cèphidae). A, *Tràchelus tábidus* (Fabricius), male; B, same, female; C, wheat stem sawfly, *Cèphus cínctus* Norton, female. (Courtesy of USDA.)

parasitic species are hyperparasites, that is, they attack an insect that is a parasite of another insect.

The superfamilies of Apócrita differ in the form of the pronotum, the character of the ovipositor and the antennae, the number of trochanter segments, and the wing venation; the principal characters of these superfamilies are summarized in Table 4. All members of the Ichneumonòidea, Evaniòidea, Pelecinòidea, Proctotrupòidea, and Bethylòidea, and some of the Chalcidòidea, Cynipòidea, and Scoliòidea, are parasites of insects (or other invertebrates). All Apócrita have a piercing ovipositor, but as a rule the females of the Ichneumonòidea, Chalcidòidea, Cynipòidea, Evaniòidea, Pelecinòidea, Proctotrupòidea, and Bethylòidea do not sting man. In the Scoliòidea, Vespòidea, Sphecòidea, and Apòidea, the ovipositor is modified into a sting, and females of these usually do sting man. These two groups of superfamilies are considered by some authors as the Divisions Parasítica (parasitic groups in which the females usually do not sting man) and Aculeàta (those with a sting). The term "wasp" is sometimes applied to all the Apócrita except the ants (Formìcidae) and bees (Apòidea); in this book we use it only (with a few exceptions) for the Scoliòidea (except ants), Vespòidea, and Sphecòidea.

This is by far the larger of the two suborders of Hymenóptera, with about 16,000 of the approximately 17,100 North American species in the order.

SUPERFAMILY **Ichneumonòidea:** This is a very large and important group, and its members are parasites of other insects or other invertebrate animals. These insects are wasplike in appearance, but (with rare exceptions) do not sting.

Family **Stephánidae:** The stephanids are a small group (six North American species) of rare insects which, as far as known, are parasites of the larvae of wood-boring beetles. The adults are 5–19 mm in length, slender, ichneumonlike, with a long ovipositor. The head is somewhat spherical, set out on a neck, and bears a crown of about five teeth around the median ocellus; the hind coxae are long, and the hind femora are swollen and

Table 4 CHARACTERS OF THE SUPERFAMILIES OF APÓCRITA

Character	Ichneumonòidea	Chalcidòidea	Cynipòidea	Evaniòidea	Pelecinòidea	Proctotrupòidea	Bethylòidea	Scoliòidea	Vespòidea	Sphecòidea	Apòidea
Pronotum[a]	C	A	C	C	C	C	A,B	A,B	C	D	D
Ovipositor[b]	A	A[e]	A	A	B	B	B	B	B	B	B
Sting	No[e]	No	No	No	No	No	Yes[e]	Yes[e]	Yes	Yes	Yes[e]
Number of Hind Trochanter Segments	2	2	1[e]	2	1	1–2	1[e]	1	1	1	1
Antennae[c]	F	E	F	F	F	E,F	F[e]	E,F	F	F	E,F
Number of Antennal Segments	16+[e]	5–13	13–16	13–14	14	7–15	10+	12–13	12–13	12–13	12–13
Venation[d]	N[e]	R	R	N[e]	R	N,R	N,R	N[e]	N	N	N
Key couplet to start with	72[f]	45	31[f]	68	38	35[f]	64,74	13,79	77	16	17

[a]Letters refer to drawings in Figure 530.
[b]Letters refer to drawings in Figure 531.
[c]E, elbowed; F, filiform.
[d]N, normal (front wings with 6 or more closed cells); R, reduced (front wings with 5 or fewer closed cells).
[e]Exceptions occur.
[f]A few will key out elsewhere in the key.

toothed beneath. Most of our six species occur in the West.

Family **Bracónidae:** This is a large (over 1700 North American species) and beneficial group of parasitic Hymenóptera. The adults are all relatively small (rarely over 15 mm in length), and a great many are more stout-bodied than the ichneumons, and the abdomen is about as long as the head and the thorax combined (Figures 559 and 560). They resemble ichneumons in lacking a costal cell, but differ in that they have not more than one recurrent vein (Figure 549 C). Many species in this family have been of considerable value in the control of insect pests.

The habits of the braconids are similar to those of the ichneumons. Unlike the ichneumons, however, many of them pupate in silken cocoons on the outside of the body of the host (Figure 561) and others spin silken cocoons entirely apart from the host (often many cocoons in a mass). Polyembryony occurs in a few species, chiefly in the genus *Macrocéntrus* (Figure 559 C, D); each egg of *M. grándii* Goidanich, a parasite of the European corn borer, develops into from 16 to 24 larvae.

The family Bracónidae is divided into 21 subfamilies, some of which may be mentioned here. The Macrocentrìnae, Agathidìnae, Chelonìnae, Microgasterìnae, and Rogadìnae (Rhogadìnae) are chiefly parasites of lepidopterous larvae. The gregarious forms of the Macrocentrìnae are polyembryonic. In the Chelonìnae the egg is laid in the host egg, and the parasite matures when the host reaches maturity. *Chélonus texànus* Cresson (Figure 560 B) is a parasite of the larvae of various noctuid moths; species of *Apánteles* (Microgasterìnae) (Figure 560 C–E) attack the corn borer and

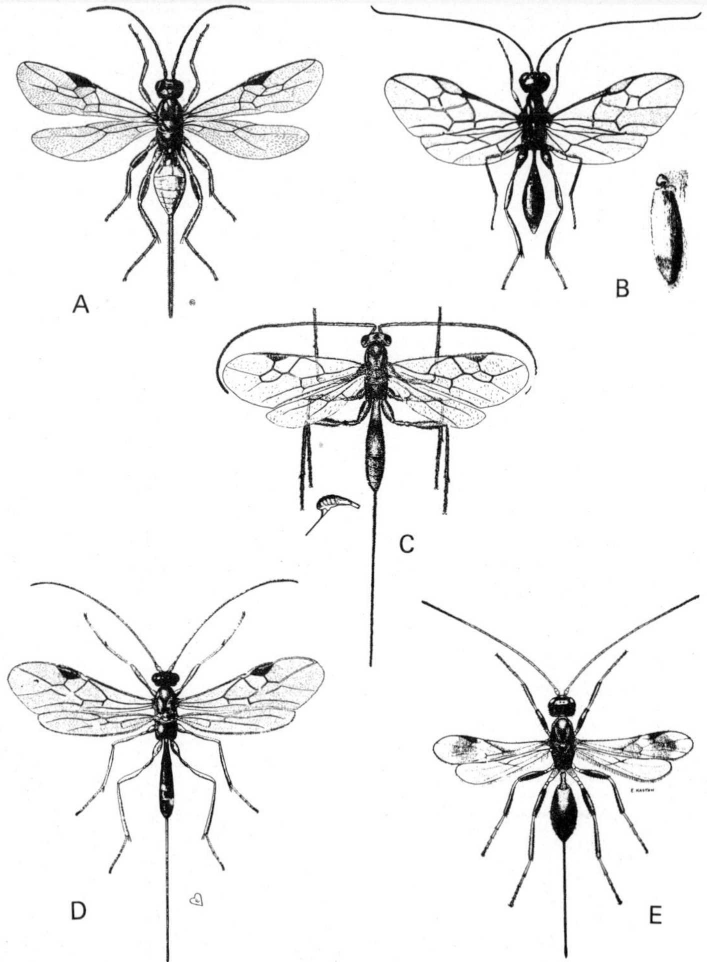

Figure 559. Bracónidae. A, *Coelòides dendróctoni* Cushman, female (Braconìnae), a parasite of bark beetles (Scolýtidae); B, *Metèorus nigricóllis* Thomson, male (Euphorìnae), a parasite of the European corn borer (insert shows cocoon); C, *Macrocéntrus ancylívorus* Rohwer, female (Macrocentrìnae) (insert, lateral view of abdomen), a parasite of various tortricid moths; D, *Macrocéntrus grándii* Goidanich, female, a parasite of the European corn borer; E, *Spàthius canadénsis* Ashmead, female, a parasite of bark beetles (Scolýtidae). (A, courtesy of DeLeon and the New York Entomological Society; B, courtesy of Parker and the Entomological Society of Washington; C and D, courtesy of USDA; E, courtesy of Kaston and the Connecticut Agricultural Experiment Station.)

similar pests; *Phanómeris phyllótomae* Muesebeck (Figure 560 F) attacks the birch leaf-mining sawflies. The Helconìnae, Spathiìnae, and Doryctìnae are parasites of beetle larvae, the Helconìnae attacking chiefly wood-boring beetles; *Spàthius canadénsis* Ashmead (Figure 559 E) attacks bark beetles (Scolýtidae). The Ichneutìnae attack sawflies; the Dacnusìnae, Alysiìnae, and Opiìnae attack Díptera; the Opiìnae attack chiefly flies in the families Tephrítidae and Agromỳzidae. Other braconids attack ants, bugs, or other insects.

Family **Ichneumónidae**—Ichneumons: This family is one of the largest in the entire class Insécta, with over 3100 species occurring in North America, and its members are to be found almost everywhere. The adults vary considerably in size, form, and coloration, but the majority resemble slender wasps (Figures 562 and 563). They differ

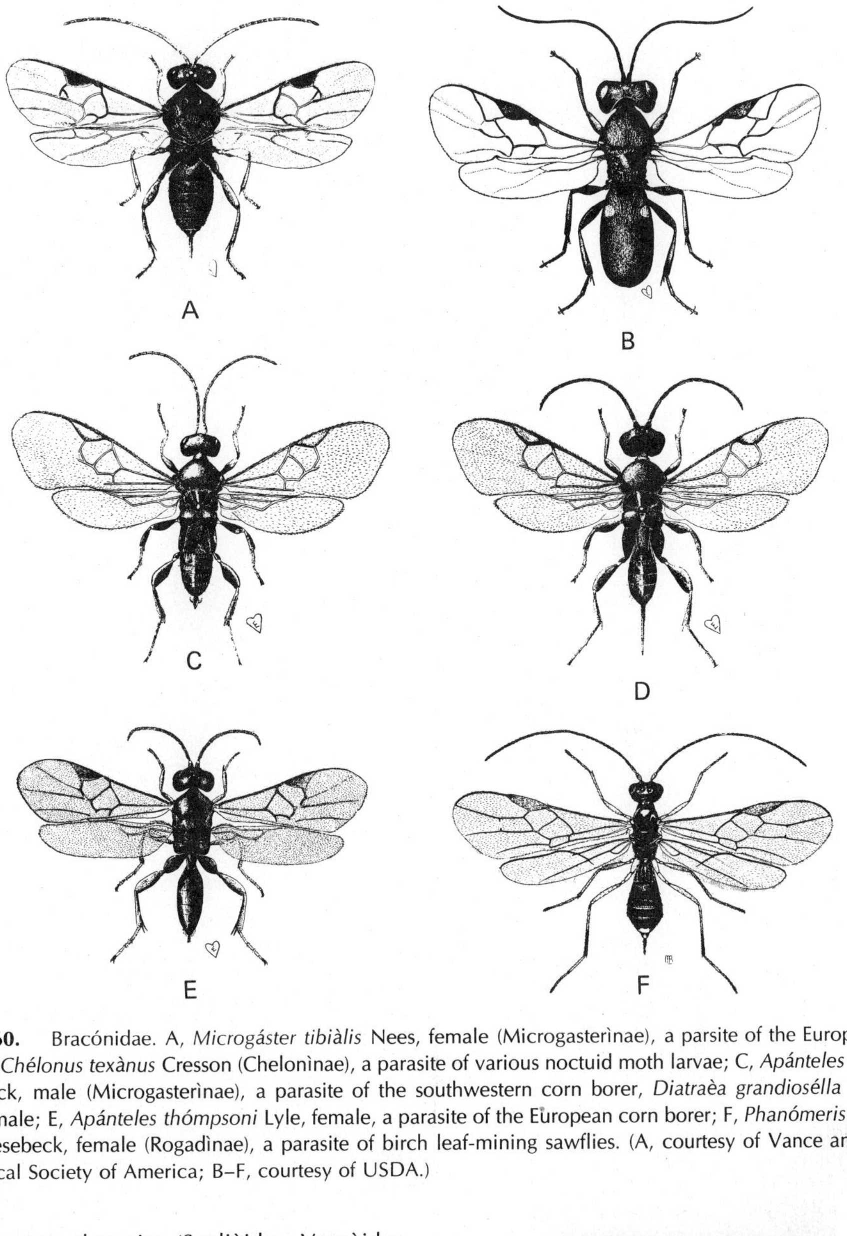

A B C D E F

Figure 560. Bracónidae. A, *Microgáster tibiàlis* Nees, female (Microgasterìnae), a parsite of the European corn borer; B, *Chélonus texànus* Cresson (Chelonìnae), a parasite of various noctuid moth larvae; C, *Apánteles diatraèae* Muesebeck, male (Microgasterìnae), a parasite of the southwestern corn borer, *Diatraèa grandiosélla* Dyar; D, same, female; E, *Apánteles thómpsoni* Lyle, female, a parasite of the European corn borer; F, *Phanómeris phyllótomae* Muesebeck, female (Rogadìnae), a parasite of birch leaf-mining sawflies. (A, courtesy of Vance and the Entomological Society of America; B–F, courtesy of USDA.)

from the wasps that sting (Scoliòidea, Vespòidea, and Sphecòidea) in that they have the antennae longer and with more segments (usually 16 or more antennal segments in ichneumons and 12 or 13 in wasps), the trochanters 2-segmented (1-segmented in the stinging wasps), and they lack a costal cell in the front wings. In many ichneumons (Figure 562 A) the ovipositor is quite long, often longer than the body, and it arises anterior to the tip of the abdomen and is permanently extruded;

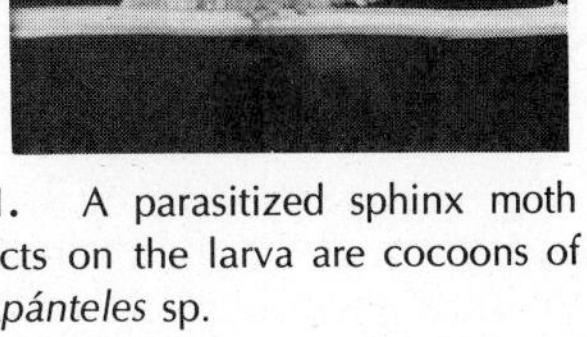

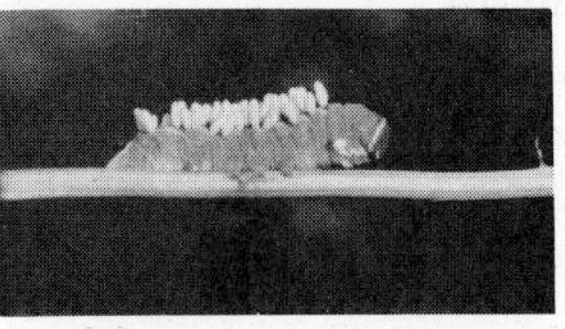

Figure 561. A parasitized sphinx moth larva; the white objects on the larva are cocoons of braconids, probably *Apánteles* sp.

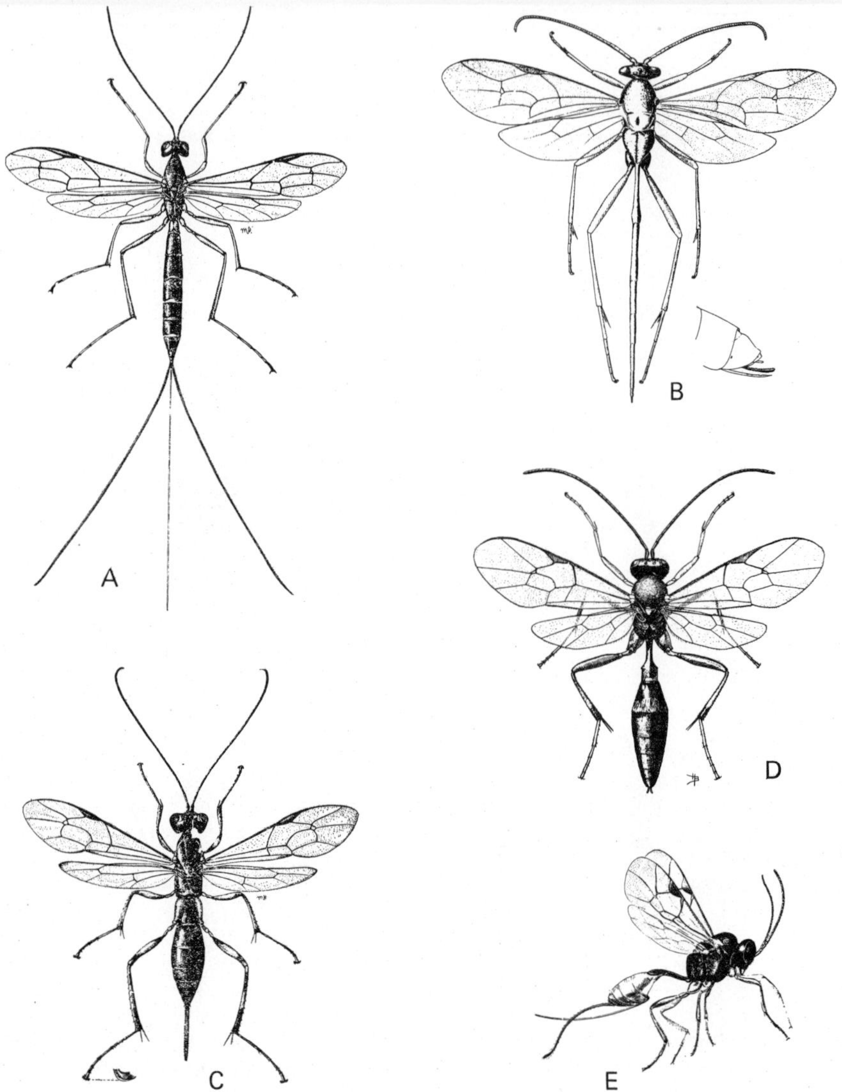

Figure 562. Ichneumónidae. A, *Rhyssélla nítida* (Cresson), female (Ephialtìnae, Rhyssìni); B, *Casinària texàna* (Ashmead), female (Porizontìnae) (insert shows tip of abdomen in lateral view); C, *Phytodiètus vulgàris* Cresson, female (Tryphonìnae); D, *Phobocámpe dísparis* (Viereck), female (Porizontìnae); E, *Tersílochus conotràcheli* (Riley), female (Tersilochìnae). (A and C, courtesy of Rohwer; B, courtesy of Walley; D and E, courtesy of USDA; A, courtesy of the U.S. National Museum; B, courtesy of *Scientific Agriculture;* C, courtesy of the U.S. National Museum.)

in the stinging wasps the ovipositor issues from the tip of the abdomen and is withdrawn into the abdomen when not in use. In most ichneumons the first discoidal and first submarginal cells in the front wing are confluent, owing to the loss of a part of the cubital vein, and the second submarginal cell, lying opposite the second recurrent vein, is often quite small (Figure 549 A, *are*); this small submarginal cell (called the areolet) is lacking in some ichneumons (Figure 549 B). The ichneumons differ from the braconids in having two recurrent veins; the braconids have only one or none (Figures 543 E and 549 C), and in having the abdomen longer than the head and thorax com-

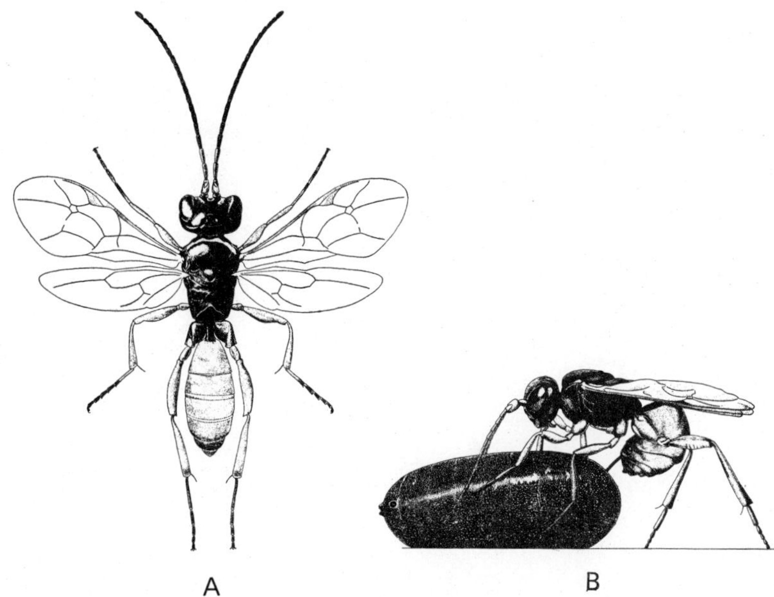

Figure 563. A hyperparasitic ichneumon, *Phygadeùon subfúscus* Cresson (Gelìnae). A, adult male; B, female ovipositing in puparium of host. The host of this ichneumon is a tachinid fly, *Aplomyiòpsis epiláchnae* (Aldrich), which is a parasite of the Mexican bean beetle, *Epiláchna varivéstis* Mulsant (see Figure 522). (Courtesy of USDA.)

bined. In many species there is a considerable difference in the appearance of the two sexes; they may differ in color, size, body form, or even in the presence of wings.

The ichneumons attack a great variety of hosts, though most species attack only a few types of hosts. There are few groups of insects that are not hosts of some ichneumon, and some species in this family attack spiders. Most ichneumons are internal parasites of the immature stages of the host. The parasite may complete its development in the stage of the host in which the egg is laid, or in a later stage.

The family Ichneumónidae is divided into 24 subfamilies; no attempt will be made here to distinguish these subfamily groups, since there are differences of opinion about the exact limits of some subfamilies and the names to be used for them. We only note some of the more important or striking types in the family, and follow the subfamily arrangement of Townes (1969).

The largest ichneumons in the United States belong to the tribe Rhyssìni of the subfamily Ephialtìnae; some of these may be $1\frac{1}{2}$ inches (38 mm) or more in body length, and the ovipositor may be twice as long as the body. These insects attack the larvae of horntails, wood wasps, and various wood-boring Coleóptera; the long ovipositor is used in getting the eggs of the ichneumon into the tunnels of the host, and the ovipositor may sometimes penetrate 13 mm or more of wood. It is a little difficult to imagine the hairlike ovipositor of these insects being pushed through wood, but the process takes place nevertheless. The genus *Megarhýssa* contains several species that attack horntails; *Rhyssélla nítida* (Cresson) (Figure 562 A) attacks wood wasps (Xiphydrìidae).

Some of the other Ephialtìnae are parasites of lepidopterous larvae, some (especially those in the tribe Polysphinctìni) attack spiders, and some attack wood-boring Coleóptera.

Most of the ichneumons in the subfamily Tryphonìnae are parasites of sawflies; *Phytodiètus vulgàris* Cresson (Figure 562 C) attacks tortricid moths. Some members of this subfamily carry their eggs on the ovipositor, attached by short stalks; when a suitable host is found, the eggs are attached to the skin of the host by a stalk, and if no host is found, the eggs may be discarded. The parasite larvae usually complete their development in the cocoon of the host.

The members of the subfamily Gelìnae are mostly external parasites of pupae in cocoons; a few attack wood-boring beetle larvae, a few attack dipterous larvae, and a few are hyperparasites of braconids or other ichneumons (Figure 563). The

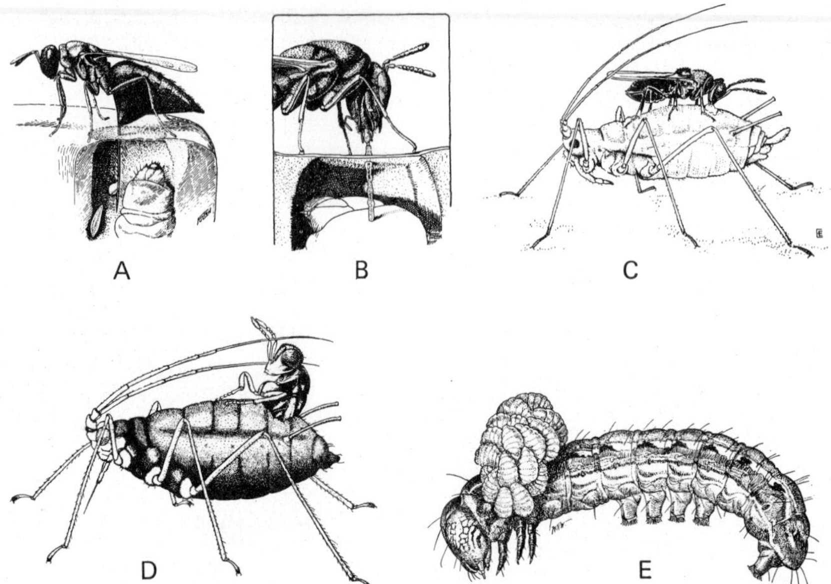

Figure 564. Feeding and emerging chalcids. A, *Habrócytus* (Pteromálidae) ovipositing; B, *Habrócytus* feeding at the tube made by her ovipositor; C, *Zarhópalus inquísitor* (Howard) (Encýrtidae) feeding at an oviposition puncture made in the abdomen of an aphid; D, adult of *Aphelìnus jucúndus* Gahan (Eulóphidae) emerging from an aphid; E, a colony of *Eupléctrus* larvae (Eulóphidae) feeding on a caterpillar. (A and B, courtesy of Fulton and the Entomological Society of America; C and D, courtesy of Griswold and the Entomological Society of America; E, courtesy of USDA.)

members of the subfamily Ichneumonìnae are internal parasites of Lepidóptera; they oviposit in either the host larva or pupa, but always emerge from the host pupa. Most species in this subfamily have the two sexes quite different in appearance. The Banchìnae are internal parasites of caterpillars; the Scolobatìnae are chiefly parasites of sawflies, ovipositing in the host larva and emerging from its cocoon; the Microleptìnae attack fungus gnats (Mycetophílidae and Sciáridae); the Diplazontìnae attack Sýrphidae, laying their eggs in the egg or young larva of the host and emerging from the puparium of the host. The Porizontìnae are parasites of lepidopterous larvae; *Casinària texàna* (Ashmead) (Figure 562 B) is a parasite of the saddleback caterpillar, and *Phobocámpe díspari*s (Viereck) (Figure 562 D) is a parasite of the gypsy moth. The Tersilochìnae are parasites of beetles; *Tersílochus conotràcheli* (Riley) (Figure 562 E) is a parasite of the plum curculio.

Females of the Ophionìnae (which are parasites of caterpillars) have a very compressed abdomen and a short, very sharp ovipositor. Most ichneumons when handled will attempt to sting by poking at one's fingers with their ovipositor, but in most cases this can scarcely be felt. The ovipositor of the Ophionìnae, on the other hand, can actually penetrate one's skin, and the effect is much like a sharp pin prick. Most of these ichneumons are yellowish to brownish in color, and about 25 mm in length. They often come to lights at night.

SUPERFAMILY **Chalcidòidea**—Chalcids: The chalcids constitute a large and important group of insects, with about 2200 North American species. Nearly all are very small, and some are quite minute; some of the Mymàridae, for example, are less than 0.5 mm in length. Chalcids are to be found almost everywhere, but because of their small size they are frequently overlooked—or discarded—by the beginning student. The majority of the chalcids are only about 2 or 3 mm in length, though a few (for example, some of the Leucospídidae) may reach a length of 10 or 15 mm. The members of this group occur in a variety of situations, chiefly on flowers and foliage, and it is seldom that one can sweep through vegetation without coming up with a few of them. They generally hold the wings flat over the abdomen when at rest, and many appear to jump when they take flight.

The chalcids can generally be recognized by the characteristic wing venation (Figure 541 B); the antennae are usually elbowed and never contain more than 13 segments; the pronotum is somewhat collarlike and does not reach the tegulae, and there is usually a prepectus present in the side of the thorax (Figure 530 A). Most of the chalcids are dark-colored, and many are metallic blue or green in color. Most species are clear-winged. There is a great deal of variation in body shape in this group (Figures 547, 548, 564–569), and some chalcids have rather peculiar, even grotesque, shapes. The wings are reduced or lacking in some of the chalcids.

Most of the chalcids are parasites of other insects, attacking chiefly the egg or larval stage of the host. Most of the hosts are in the orders Lepidóptera, Díptera, Coleóptera, and Homóptera, and since these orders contain most of the crop pests, it can be seen that the chalcids are a very beneficial group in that they aid in keeping pests in check. Many species have been imported into this country to act as a means of controlling various insect pests. A few chalcids are phytophagous, their larvae feeding inside seeds, stems, or galls.

This superfamily is divided into a number of families; some families consist of distinctive-looking insects and are easily recognized, but in most cases the separation of families is rather difficult. There are differences of opinion among entomologists about the limits of some of the families.

Family **Mymàridae**—Fairyflies: The fairyflies are very tiny insects, mostly less than a millimeter in length, with the hind wings linear (Figure 541 C). All attack insect eggs, and some species attack the eggs of aquatic insects. This group contains some of the smallest insects known; one species of *Aláptus* has a body length of 0.21 mm (about a hundredth of an inch).

Family **Trichogrammátidae:** The Trichogrammátidae are very tiny insects, 0.3–1.0 mm in length, and may be recognized by the 3-segmented tarsi, the microscopic hairs of the wings usually being arranged in rows, and the rather short head that is somewhat concave behind. The members of this group are parasites attacking eggs. Some species have been reared in large numbers to aid in the control of certain orchard pests.

Family **Eulóphidae:** The Eulóphidae are a large group (over 600 North American species) of rather small insects (1–3 mm in length); they are parasites of a wide variety of hosts, including a number of major crop pests (Figures 564 D, E and 565 A–D). They may be recognized by the 4-segmented tarsi (Figure 546 A) and the axillae extending forward beyond the tegulae (Figure 545 B). Many have a brilliant metallic coloring, and the males of many species have pectinate antennae.

Some of the eulophids are hyperparasites, and there are some interesting phenomena regarding hyperparasitism and sex in the eulophids that attack scale insects. In the genus *Coccóphagus,* the females develop as parasites of scale insects, while the males develop as hyperparasites attacking parasites of scale insects, often females of their own species!

Family **Thysánidae:** The thysanids are small, stout-bodied chalcids that attack scale insects, whiteflies, and other Homóptera, or are hyperparasites of the chalcids attacking Homóptera.

Family **Eutrichosomátidae:** This group is represented in the United States by two rare species, one occurring in Georgia and Texas, and the other from Maryland westward to New Mexica, Idaho, and Montana; the larvae attack snout beetles (Curculiónidae).

Family **Tanaostigmátidae:** Four rare species in this group have been recorded from Florida, Arizona, and California; the larvae appear to be gall makers.

Family **Encýrtidae:** The Encýritidae are a large and widespread group, with some 345 North American species. They are 1–2 mm in length and can usually be recognized by the broad convex mesopleura (Figure 547 B); in most of the chalcids the mesopleura have a groove for the femora, but this groove is lacking in the encyrtids (also lacking in the thysanids, eutrichosomatids, tanaostigmatids, and eupelmids). The encyrtids differ from the eupelmids in that they have the mesonotum convex and lack or have incomplete the parapsidal furrows. Most of the encyrtids are parasites of aphids (Figure 564 C, D), scale insects, and whiteflies, but the group contains species that attack insects in other orders (for example, *Ooencýrtus kuwánai* (Howard), Figure 565 F, is a parasite of the gypsy moth). A few are hyperparasites. Polyembryony occurs in a number of species, with

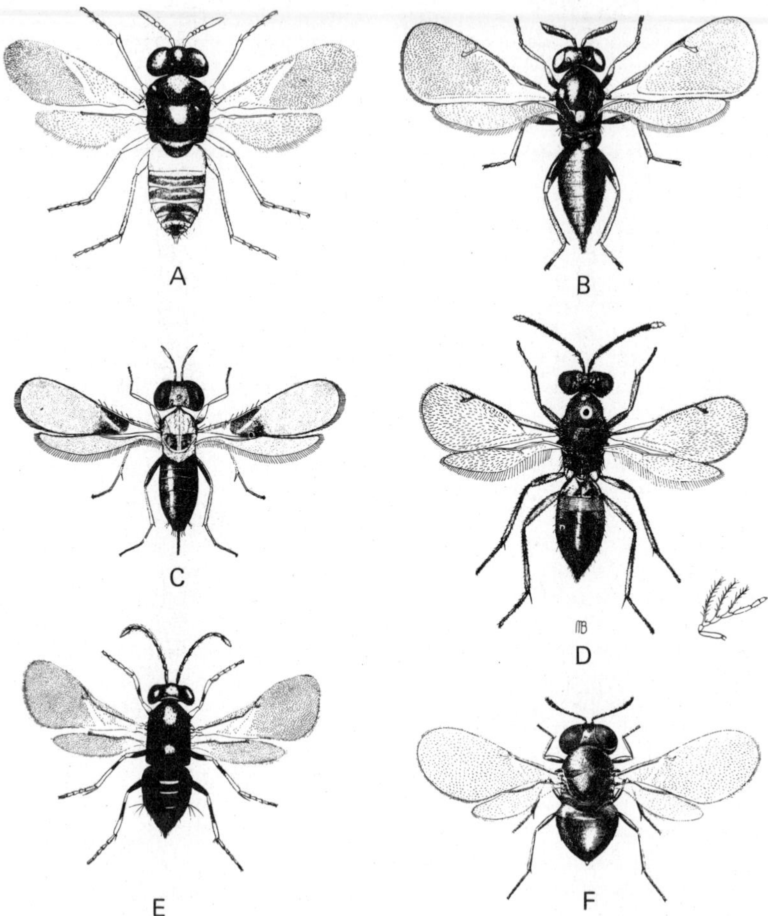

Figure 565. Chalcidòidea. A–D, Eulóphidae; E–F, Encýrtidae. A, *Aphelìnus jucúndus* Gahan, female, a parasite of aphids; B, *Tetrástichus bruchóphagi* Gahan, a parasite of the clover seed chalcid, *Bruchóphagus platýptera* (Walker); C, *Centródora speciosíssima* (Girault), female, a parasite of the cecidomyiids and chalcids that attack wheat; D, *Hemiptársenus aneméntus* (Walker), female, a parasite of leaf-mining sawflies; E, *Zarhópalus inquísitor* (Howard), male, a parasite of aphids and mealybugs; F, *Ooencýrtus kuwánai* (Howard), female, an imported parasite of the gypsy moth. (A and E, courtesy of Griswold and the Entomological Society of America; others, courtesy of USDA.)

from ten to over a thousand young developing from a single egg.

Family **Eupélmidae:** The Eupélmidae are a large group (88 North American species), and some species are fairly common. They are similar to the encyrtids, but have the mesonotum flatter and parapsidal furrows are present (Figure 566 A, B, E, F). Some of them are wingless or have very short wings (Figure 566 E, F). Many of the eupelmids are good jumpers and often tumble about after jumping, before gaining a foothold; their jumping seems to be aided by their ability to bend the head and abdomen up over the thorax, much as do the click beetles. The wingless or short-winged forms, when killed in a cyanide bottle, usually die with the head and abdomen bent up over the thorax. The members of this group attack a wide variety of hosts; a number of species are known to attack hosts in several different orders. A few are parasites of spiders.

Family **Eucharítidae:** The Eucharítidae, though not very common, are rather distinctive-looking

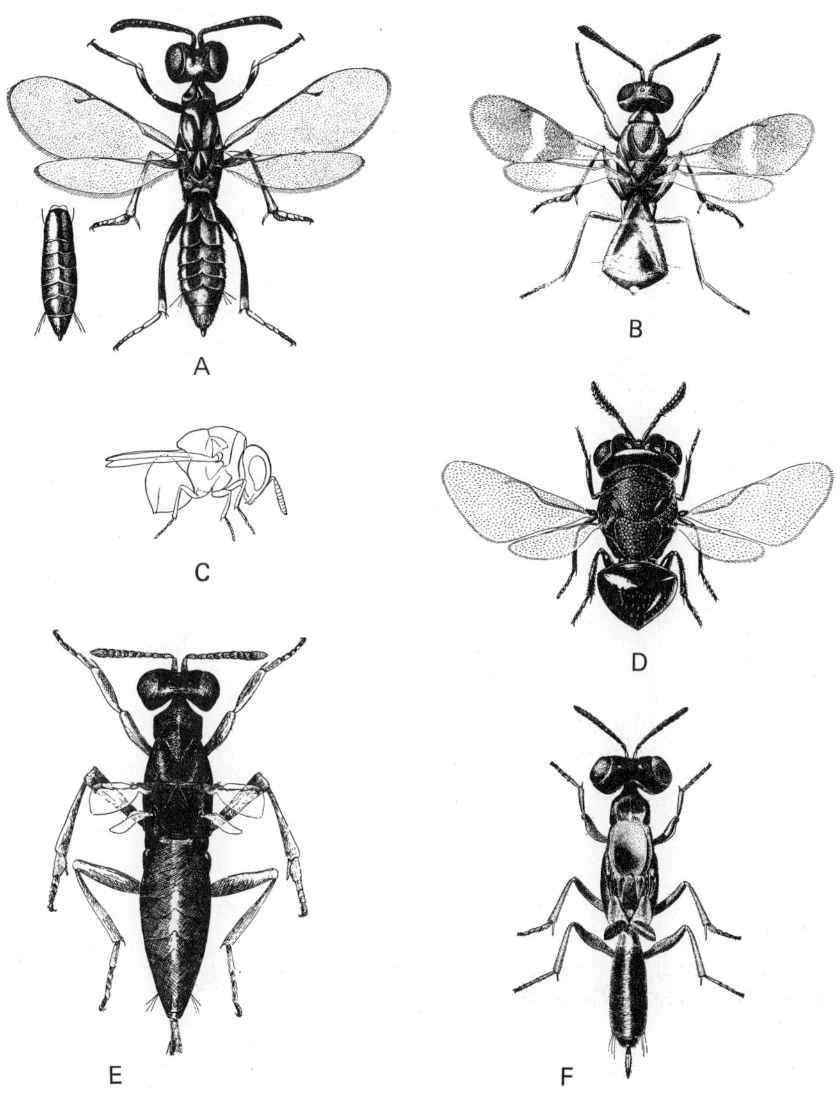

Figure 566. Chalcidòidea. A, B, E, F, Eupélmidae; C, D, Perilámpidae. A, *Eupélmus allýnii* (French), female (insert is abdomen of male), a parasite of the Hessian fly; B, *Anastàtus díspāris* Ruschka, an imported egg parasite of the gypsy moth; C, *Perilámpus platygáster* Say, a hyperparasite attacking *Metèorus dimidiàtus* (Cresson), a braconid parasite of the grape leaffolder, *Désmia funeràlis* (Hübner) (Pyrálidae), lateral view; D, same, dorsal view; E, *Eupélmus atropurpùreus* Dalman, female, a parasite of the Hessian fly; F, *Eupelmélla vesiculàris* (Retzius), female, which attacks insects in the orders Coleóptera, Lepidóptera, and Hymenóptera. (Courtesy of USDA.)

insects with very interesting habits. They are fair-sized (at least for a chalcid), black or metallic blue or green in color, with the abdomen petiolate and the scutellum often spined; the thorax often appears somewhat humpbacked (Figure 547 D). These chalcids are parasites of the pupae of ants. The eggs are laid, usually in large numbers, on leaves or buds and hatch into tiny flattened larvae called planidia. These planidia simply lie in wait on the vegetation or on the ground and attach to passing ants, which carry them to the ant nest. Once in the ant nest, the planidia leave the worker

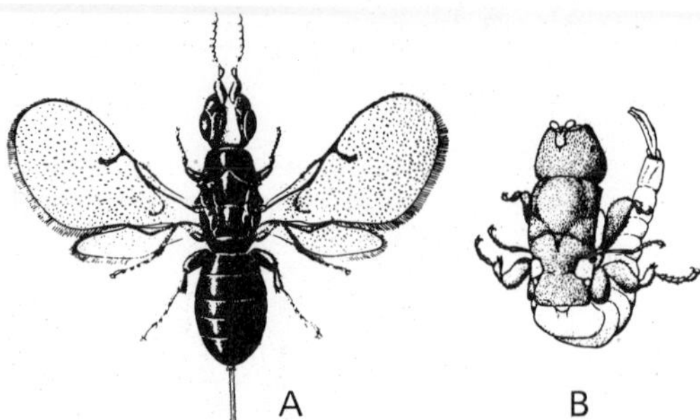

Figure 567. Fig wasp, *Blastóphaga psènes* (L.) A, female; B, male. (Courtesy of Condit and the California Agricultural Experiment Station.)

ant that brought them there and attach to ant larvae; they do little or no feeding on the larvae of the ant, but feed after the larva has pupated.

Family **Perilámpidae:** The Perilámpidae are stout-bodied chalcids with the thorax large and coarsely punctate, and the abdomen small, shiny, and triangular (Figures 548 B and 566 C, D). Some are metallic green in color and resemble cuckoo wasps (Chrysídidae), and others are black; they are frequently found on flowers. Most perilampids are hyperparasites, attacking the Díptera and Hymenóptera that are parasites of caterpillars; a few attack free-living insects in various orders. *Perilámpus platygáster* Say (Figure 566 C, D) is a hyperparasitic species; it attacks *Metèorus dimidiàtus* Cresson, a braconid parasite of the grape leaffolder. The perilampids, like the eucharitids, lay their eggs on foliage, and the eggs hatch into larvae of the planidium type (small, flattened, able to go without feeding for a considerable time); these planidia remain on the foliage and attach to a passing host (usually a caterpillar) and penetrate into its body cavity. If a hyperparasitic species enters a caterpillar that is not parasitized, it usually does not develop, but if the caterpillar is parasitized, then the perilampid larva usually remains inactive in the caterpillar until the caterpillar parasite has pupated, and then attacks the parasite. The perilampids generally attack the pupae of tachinids, braconids, or ichneumons.

Family **Agaónidae**—Fig Wasps: This group is represented in the United States by two species, *Blastóphaga psènes* (L.) and *Secundeisènia mexicàna* (Ashmead); the former occurs in California and Arizona, and the latter in Florida. *B. psènes* (Figure 567) was introduced into the United States to make possible the production of certain varieties of figs. The Smyrna fig, which is grown extensively in California, produces fruit only when it is pollinated with pollen from the wild fig, or caprifig, and the pollination is done entirely by fig wasps. The fig wasp develops in a gall in flowers of the caprifig. The blind and flightless males (Figure 567 B) emerge first, and may mate with females still in their galls. The female, on emerging from the gall, collects pollen from male flowers of the caprifig, and stores it in special baskets (corbiculae). The female pollinates figs of both types (Smyrna fig and caprifig), but oviposits successfully only in the shorter flowers of the caprifig. Fig growers usually aid in the process of Smyrna fig pollination by placing in their fig trees branches of the wild fig; when the fig wasps emerge from the wild fig, they are almost certain to visit flowers of the Smyrna fig and thus pollinate them.

Family **Torýmidae:** The torymids are somewhat elongate, metallic-green insects 2–4 mm in length, with a long ovipositor; the hind coxae are very large, and there are distinct parapsidal sutures on the thorax (Figures 545 A and 568 A–C). This group includes both parasitic and phytophagous species; the Torymìnae, Erimerìnae, and Monodontomerìnae attack gall insects and caterpillars; the Podagrionìnae attack mantid eggs; and the Idarnìnae and Megastigmìnae attack seeds.

Family **Ormýridae:** The Ormýridae are similar to the Torýmidae, but have the parapsidal sutures indistinct or lacking and have a very short ovipositor. They are parasites of gall insects.

Family **Pteromálidae:** The Pteromálidae are a large group (about 340 North American species) of minute black or metallic-green or bronze insects (Figures 548 D, 564 A, B, 569 A–H). These insects are parasitic and attack a wide variety of hosts; many are very valuable in the control of crop pests. The adults of many species feed on the body fluids of the host, which exude from the puncture made by the parasite's ovipositor (as in Figure 564 C). In the case of *Habrócytus cerealéllae* (Ashmead), which attacks larvae of the angoumois grain moth and in which the larvae are out of reach of the adult pteromalid (in the seed), a viscous fluid is secreted from the ovipositor and is formed into a tube extending down to the host larva. The body fluids of the host are sucked up through this tube by the adult (Figure 564 A, B).

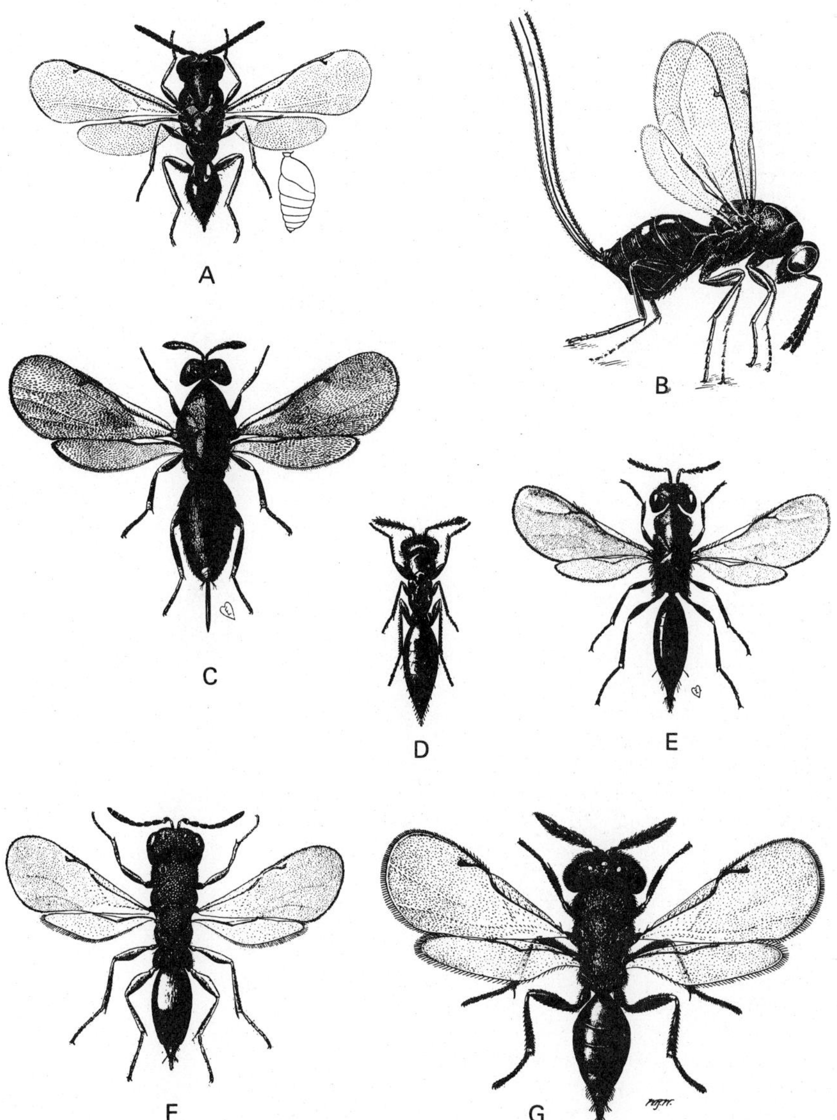

Figure 568. Chalcidòidea. A–C, Torýmidae; D–G, Eurytómidae. A, *Tórymus vàrians* (Walker), the apple seed chalcid, male (insert is a lateral view of the abdomen); B, same, female; C, *Liodontómerus perpléxus* Gahan, female, a parasite of the clover seed chalcid (G in this figure); D, *Harmólita grándis* (Riley), the wheat strawworm, a wingless female; E, *Harmólita trítici* (Fitch), female, the wheat jointworm; F, *Eurýtoma pachyneùron* Girault, female, a parasite of the Hessian fly and the wheat jointworm (E in this figure); G, *Bruchóphagus platýptera* (Walker), the clover seed chalcid. (Courtesy of USDA.)

Family **Eurytómidae**—Seed Chalcids: The eurytomids are similar to the perilampids in having the thorax coarsely punctate, but differ in that they have the abdomen rounded or oval and more or less compressed (Figures 548 C and 568 D–G). They are usually black, with the thorax, head, and antennae often rather hairy, and they are generally more slender in build than the perilampids. Eury-

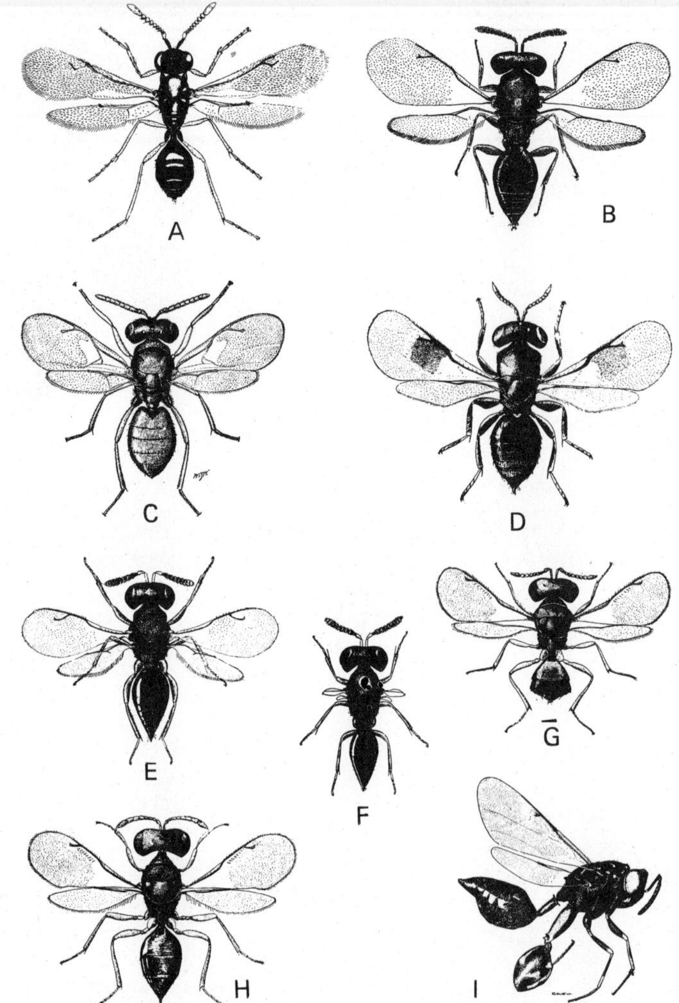

Figure 569. Chalcidòidea. A–H, Pteromálidae; I, Chalcídidae. A, *Ásaphes lùcens* (Provancher), male, a parasite of aphids; B, *Bubékia fállax* Gahan, female, a parasite of the Hessian fly; C, *Pterómalus eùrymi* Gahan, a parasite of the alfalfa caterpillar, *Còlias eurýtheme* Boisduval; D, *Merisóporus chalcidóphagus* (Walsh and Riley), female, a parasite of the Hessian fly; E, *Eupterómalus subápterus* (Riley), female, a parasite of the Hessian fly; F, same, a subapterous female; G. *Callítula bìcolor* Spinola, male, a parasite of various flies and platygasterids; H, same, female; I, *Spilachálcis flavopícta* (Cresson), a parasite of various Coleóptera, Lepidóptera, and Hymenóptera. (A, courtesy of Griswold and the Entomological Society of America; B–I, courtesy of USDA.)

tomids vary in habits; some are parasitic and some are phytophagous. The larvae of species in the genus *Harmólita* (Figure 568 D, E) feed in the stems of grasses, sometimes producing galls on the stems; some of these insects are often serious pests of wheat. The clover seed chalcid, *Bruchóphagus platýptera* (Walker) (Figure 568 G), infests the seeds of clover and other legumes. A few species in this group are hyperparasites.

Family **Chalcedéctidae:** The Chalcedéctidae are like the Chalcídidae and Leucospídidae in having the hind femora swollen and toothed, but differ in having the hind coxae little, if any, larger than the front coxae. This group is a small one and is represented in the United States by four species that occur in Texas and California; the larvae are parasites of buprestid beetles.

Family **Chalcídidae:** The Chalcídidae are fair-sized chalcids (2–7 mm in length) with the hind femora greatly swollen and toothed (Figures 546 E, 548 A, 569 I), and they differ from the leucospidids in having the ovipositor short and the wings not folded longitudinally when at rest. The chalcidids are parasites of various Lepidóptera, Díptera, and Coleóptera. Some are hyperparasitic, attacking tachinids or ichneumons.

Family **Leucospídidae:** The Leucospídidae are usually black-and-yellow insects, and they are parasites of various bees and wasps. They are rather rare, but may occasionally be found on flowers. They are stout-bodied and have the wings folded longitudinally at rest, and look a little like a small yellowjacket. The ovipositor is long and curves upward and forward over the abdomen, ending over the posterior part of the thorax. Like the chalcidids, the leucospidids have the hind femora greatly swollen and toothed on the ventral side.

SUPERFAMILY **Cynipòidea:** The members of this group are mostly small or minute insects with a reduced venation (Figure 541 A). Most species are black, and the abdomen is usually shiny and somewhat compressed. The antennae are filiform, the pronotum extends back to the tegulae, and the ovipositor issues from anterior to the apex of the abdomen. Of the more than 800 species in this group in the United States, some 640 (all in the subfamily Cynipìnae) are gall makers or gall inquilines; the others, as far as is known, are parasites.

Family **Ibalìidae:** The ibaliids are relatively large (7–16 mm in length) and have the abdomen somewhat elongate; they are parasites of horntails and are not very common.

Family **Lioptéridae:** These insects have the abdomen petiolate and attached far above the bases of the hind coxae. Three rare species occur in Texas and California; their immature stages are unknown.

Family **Figítidae:** The members of this group are parasites of the pupae of lacewings and Díptera. The family is divided into three subfamilies, primarily on the basis of the structure of the abdomen; the Anacharitìnae, which have the abdomen distinctly petiolate and the second tergum longer than the third (Figure 542 E) attack the cocoons of lacewings (Chrysòpidae); the Aspiceratìnae, in which the second abdominal tergum is narrow and much shorter than the third (Figure 542 C), attack the pupae of syrphid flies; the Figitìnae, in which the second tergum is only slightly shorter than the third (Figure 542 F), attack the pupae of various Díptera.

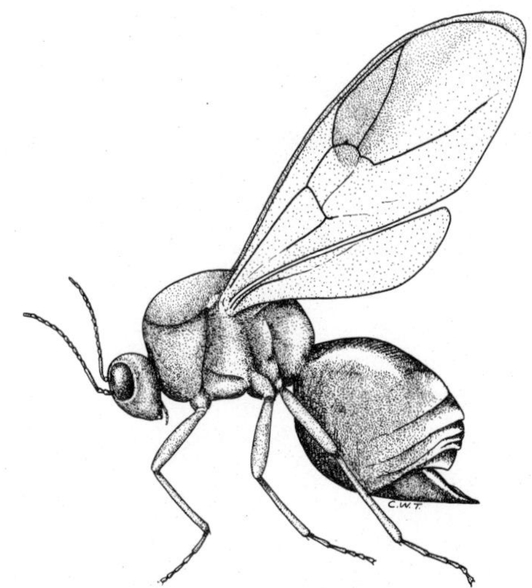

Figure 570. A gall wasp, *Diplólepis ròsae* (L.). This species develops in the mossy rose gall (Figure 571 D).

Family **Cynípidae**—Gall Wasps and Others: This family is divided into three subfamilies, of which two (the Eucoilìnae and Charipìnae) are parasitic and the third (Cynipìnae) are gall makers or gall inquilines; a little over a hundred species of the first two subfamilies occur in the United States, compared with some 640 Cynipìnae.

The Eucoilìnae can be recognized by the rounded elevation on the scutellum (Figure 542 D); they are parasites of the pupae of various flies. The Charipìnae are minute insects, 2 mm in length or less, with the thorax smooth; they are hyperparasites, attacking braconids parasitic in aphids.

The Cynipìnae, or gall wasps, are a large group, and many species are quite common. They are small to minute, usually black insects, which can be recognized by their characteristic shape (Figure 570) and wing venation (Figure 541 A). The abdomen is oval, somewhat compressed and shining, and the second tergum covers about half or more of the abdomen. The Cynipìnae differ

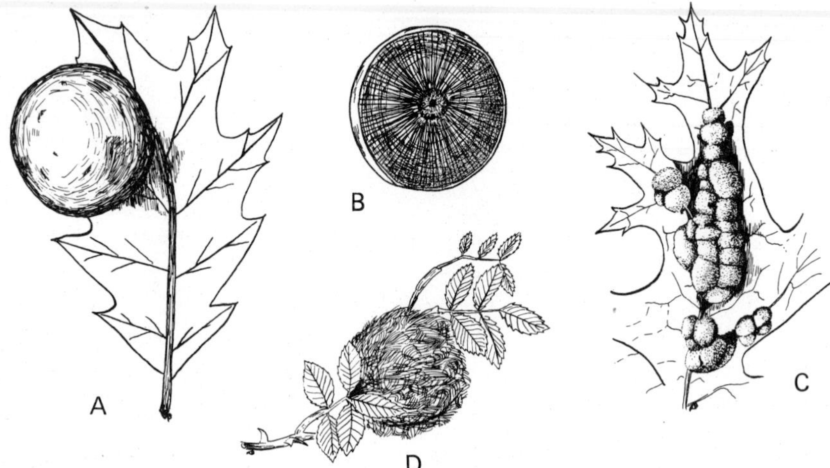

Figure 571. Galls of Cynípidae. A, an oak-apple gall, caused by *Amphíbolips* sp.; B, another oak-apple gall, cut open to show the interior and the central capsule in which the gall-wasp larva develops; C, wooly oak gall, caused by *Callirhỳtis lanàta* (Gillette); D, mossy rose gall, caused by *Diplólepis ròsae* (L.). (Redrawn from Felt.)

from the Charipìnae in that they are generally larger (up to 8 mm in length), and the thorax usually has coarse sculpturing.

Each species of gall maker forms a characteristic gall on a particular part of a particular plant (Figure 571); the galls are much more often noticed than are the insects. Many of the gall wasps form galls on oak. Some galls harbor a single insect, while many insects develop in others. The inquilines among the gall wasps live in galls made by some other gall insect. Most of the gall wasps are of little economic importance, but some of their galls have been used as a source of tannic acid and others have been used as a source of certain dyes.

Many gall wasps have a rather complex life history with two quite different generations a year. One generation, which develops during the summer in one type of gall, emerges in the fall and consists entirely of females that reproduce parthenogenetically. The eggs of this generation hatch and develop in a different type of gall and the adults that emerge in the early part of the following summer consist of males and females. Both the adult insects and the galls of these two generations may be quite different in appearance.

SUPERFAMILY **Evaniòidea:** The members of this group have the abdomen attached high above the hind coxae (Figure 540 D–F), the antennae filiform and 13- or 14-segmented, the trochanters 2-segmented, and the venation generally fairly complete in the front wings (front wings with a costal cell). Some (Gasteruptìidae and Aulácidae) superficially resemble ichneumons. All are parasites of other insects.

Family **Evanìidae**—Ensign Wasps: The ensign wasps are black, somewhat spiderlike insects 10–15 mm in length (Figure 572). The abdomen is very small and oval and is attached by a slender petiole to the propodeum considerably above the base of the hind coxae (Figure 540 F); it is carried almost like a flag (hence the common name for this family.) The ensign wasps are parasites of the egg capsules of cockroaches and are likely to be found in buildings or other places where cockroaches occur.

Family **Gasteruptìidae:** These insects resemble ichneumons, but have short antennae, a costal cell in the front wings, and the head is set out on a slender neck. They have one submarginal cell or none and one recurrent vein or none (Figure 549 E); they are black, and the ovipositor of the female is about as long as the body. Adults are fairly common, and are usually found on flowers, particularly wild parsnip, wild carrot, and related species. The larvae are parasites of solitary wasps and bees.

Figure 572. An ensign wasp, *Prosevània punctàta* (Brullé). A, male; B, female. (Courtesy of Edmunds.)

Family **Aulácidae:** The aulacids resemble the gasteruptiids, but are usually black with a reddish abdomen, the antennae are longer, and there are two recurrent veins in the front wings (Figure 549 F). These insects are parasites of the larvae of wood-boring beetles and xiphydriid wood wasps, and adults are usually found around logs in which the hosts occur.

SUPERFAMILY **Pelecinòidea:** This group is represented in North America by a single species, in the family Pelecìnidae.

Family **Pelecìnidae:** The only North American species in this group is *Pelecìnus polyturàtor* (Drury), which is a large and striking insect. The female is 2 inches (50 mm) or more in length, shining black, with the abdomen very long and slender (Figure 573); the male, which is extremely rare in this country, is about 25 mm long, and has the posterior part of the abdomen swollen. The females do not sting. This insect is a parasite of the larvae of June beetles.

SUPERFAMILY **Proctotrupòidea:** All the members of this superfamily are parasites, attacking the immature stages of other insects. Most of them are small or minute, black and often shiny, and are likely to be confused with cynipids, chalcids, or some of the scolioid or bethyloid wasps. The smaller members of this group have a much-reduced wing venation, similar to that of the chalcids, but may be distinguished from chalcids by the structure of the thorax and ovipositor; the pronotum in the proctotrupoids appears triangular in a lateral view and extends to the tegulae, and the ovipositor issues from the tip of the abdomen rather than from anterior to the tip. Many have the abdomen dorsoventrally flattened with the lateral edges rather sharp. Proctotrupoids are not so com-

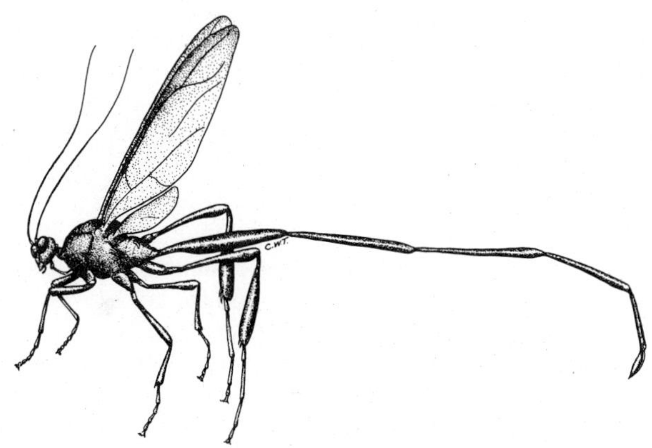

Figure 573. A pelecinid, *Pelecìnus polyturàtor* (Drury), female, 1½ ×.

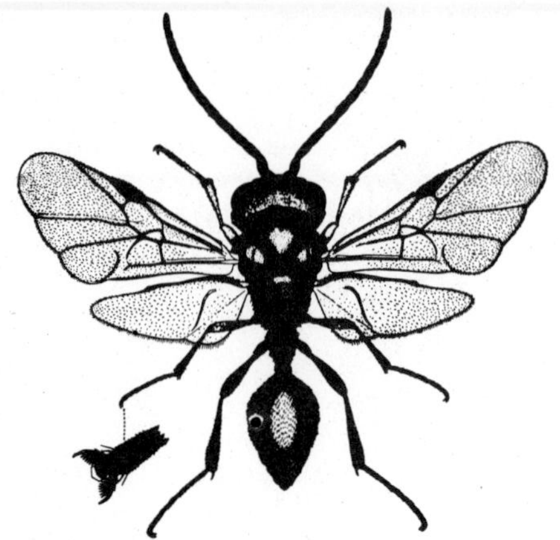

Figure 574. *Helòrus paradóxus* (Provancher), female (Helòridae), showing tarsal comb. (Courtesy of Clancy and the University of California.)

mon as the chalcids or ichneumonoids, and some are quite rare; approximately 930 species occur in North America.

Family **Vanhornìidae:** This group includes a single North American species, *Vanhòrnia eucnemídarum* Crawford, which is a parasite of the larvae of eucnemid beetles.

Family **Roproniìdae:** This family contains three rare North American species of *Roprònia.* The adults are 8–10 mm in length and have a laterally flattened, somewhat triangular and petiolate abdomen, and a fairly complete venation in the front wing (Figure 543 F). The immature stages are parasites of sawflies.

Family **Helòridae:** This family contains a single North American species, *Helòrus paradóxus* (Provancher), a black insect about 4 mm long with a fairly complete venation in the front wings (Figures 543 H, 574). This species is a parasite of the larvae of lacewings (Chrysòpidae), and the adult helorid emerges from the host cocoon.

Family **Proctotrùpidae:** Most of the Proctotrùpidae range in length from 3 to 6 mm (some are larger). They may be recognized by the large stigma in the front wing, beyond which is a very small marginal cell (Figure 543 D). Very little is known of their habits, but some are parasites of beetles, and a few attack flies.

Family **Ceraphrónidae:** The Ceraphrónidae are a fairly large group (104 North American species), and members of it have been reared from a variety of hosts. Some ceraphronids are hyperparasitic, attacking the braconid or chalcid parasites of aphids or scale insects. Wingless forms in this group can often be collected by sifting soil and leaf litter.

Family **Diaprìidae:** The diapriids are small to minute black insects, most of which are parasites of immature Díptera. They can usually be recognized by the form of the head; the antennae arise on a shelflike protuberance in about the middle of the face (Figure 544 A). The family contains four subfamilies, but all except about three of the approximately 300 North American species in the family belong to just two subfamilies, the Diapriìnae and Belytìnae (=Cinetìnae). The Diapriìnae are small to minute and have a very much reduced wing venation with no closed cell in the hind wings (Figure 541 D). The Belytìnae are usually larger and have a closed cell in the hind wings (Figure 549 G). These insects are usually collected by sweeping; the Belytìnae are most common in wooded areas, for they attack fungus gnats (Mycetophílidae) and other flies breeding in fungi.

Family **Sceliónidae:** The Sceliónidae are small insects that are parasites of insect or spider eggs; some of them have been successfully utilized in the control of crop pests. The females of some of the scelionids, particularly those that attack the eggs of grasshoppers or mantids, attach themselves to the female of the host species and ride on it until the host lays its eggs, whereupon the scelionid leaves the host and attacks the eggs. In a few such cases the female scelionid may do some feeding on the adult of the host, but usually the adult host merely serves as a means of transportation. This phenomenon of one insect attaching itself to another for transportation is called phoresy; it occurs also in the chalcid family Eucharítidae (page 660).

Family **Platygastéridae:** The Platygastéridae are minute, shining-black insects with reduced wing venation (Figure 575) (much as in chalcids). The antennae are usually 10-segmented and are attached very low on the face, next to the clypeus (Figure 544 C). Most of the platygasterids are parasites of the larvae of Cecidomyìidae; *Platygáster hiemàlis* Forbes (Figure 575 B) is an important

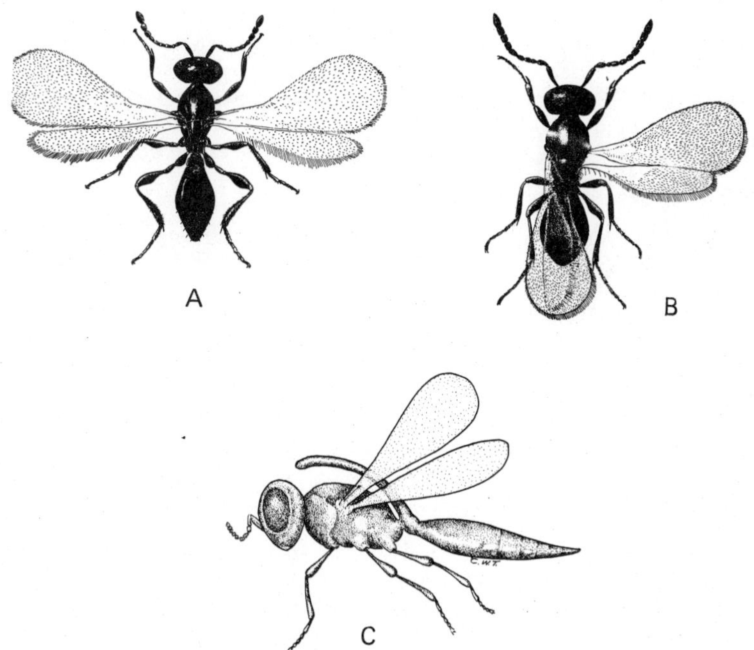

Figure 575. Platygastéridae. A, *Euxestonòtus érror* (Fitch), female; B, *Platygáster hiemàlis* Forbes, female; C, *Inostémma* sp. (A and B, courtesy of USDA.)

agent in the control of the Hessian fly. Polyembryony occurs in several species in this family, with as many as 18 young developing from a single egg.

Most of the platygasterids are normal-looking insects, but the females of the genus *Inostémma* are peculiar in that they have a long handlelike process arising from the dorsum of the first abdominal segment and extending forward over the thorax (Figure 575 C); this structure serves as a receptacle for the ovipositor when it is not in use.

SUPERFAMILY **Bethylòidea:** Most of the members of this group are parasites of other insects. The only commonly collected insects in this group are the cuckoo wasps (Chrysídidae); the others are quite rare.

Family **Chrysídidae**—Cuckoo Wasps: The cuckoo wasps are small insects, rarely over 12 mm in length, and are metallic green or blue in color and usually have the body coarsely sculptured. Some of the chalcids and bees are of a similar size and coloration, but the cuckoo wasps can be recognized by the wing venation (Figure 543 B)—a fairly complete venation in the front wing but no closed cells in the hind wing—and the structure of the abdomen. The abdomen consists of only three or four visible segments and is hollowed out ventrally. When a cuckoo wasp is disturbed, it usually curls up in a ball. Most of the cuckoo wasps are external parasites of full-grown wasp or bee larvae; the species in the genus *Cléptes* attack sawfly larvae, and those in *Mesitiópterus* attack the eggs of walking sticks.

Family **Bethýlidae:** The Bethýlidae are small to medium-sized, usually dark-colored wasps; the females of many species are wingless and antlike in appearance. In a few species, both winged and wingless forms occur in each sex. These wasps are parasites of the larvae of Lepidóptera and Coleóptera; several species attack moths or beetles that infest grain or flour. A few species will sting man.

Family **Dryínidae:** The Dryínidae are rare wasps, and in most species the two sexes are quite different in appearance. Some females are wingless and antlike. The antennae are 10-segmented, and the front tarsi of the female are usually pincerlike.

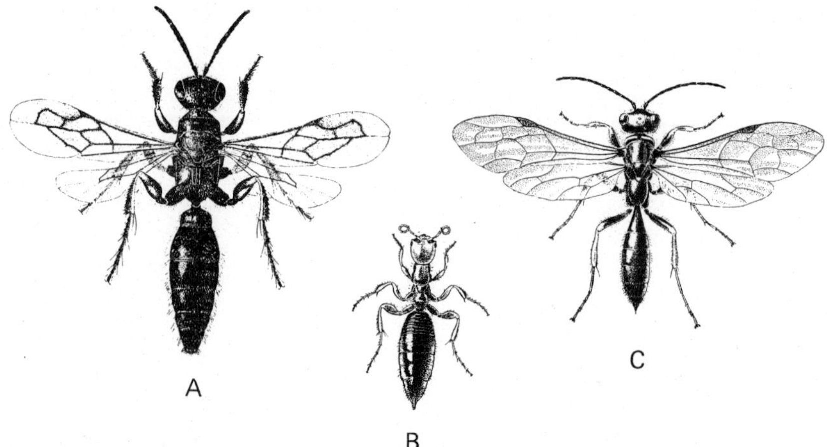

Figure 576. Tiphiid wasps. A, *Típhia popilliávora* Rohwer, male (Tiphiìnae); B, *Neozelobòria próximus* Turner, female (Brachycistidìnae); C, same, male. (A, courtesy of USDA; B and C, courtesy of Burrell and the New York Entomological Society.)

The peculiar front tarsi of some females in this family are used in holding the host during oviposition. The dryinids whose life histories are known are parasites of nymphs and adults of the homopterous groups Fulgoròidea, Cicadéllidae, and Membràcidae. Dryinid larvae feed internally on their host, although during most of their development a part of the body of the larva protrudes from the host in a saclike structure. The parasite, when full grown, leaves the host and spins a silken cocoon nearby. Polyembryony occurs in *Aphelòpus thèliae* Gahan, which attacks the treehopper *Thèlia bimaculàta* (Fabricius), with 40 to 60 young developing from a single egg.

Family **Sclerogíbbidae:** This family is represented in North America by a single, very rare species occurring in Arizona, *Probéthylus schwárzi* Ashmead. A few sclerogibbids (occurring in other parts of the world) are known to be parasites of Embióptera.

Family **Trigonálidae:** The trigonalids are a small group (five North American species) of rather rare insects; they are medium-sized, usually brightly colored, and rather stout-bodied; they look much like wasps, but have the antennae very long and many-segmented.

The trigonalids are parasites of social Véspidae or of the parasites of caterpillars. The very minute eggs are laid in considerable numbers on foliage. In the case of the species attacking caterpillar parasites, the eggs hatch when eaten by a caterpillar, and the trigonalid larva attacks the ichneumon, tachinid, or other parasite larva present in the caterpillar. In the species that attack vespid larvae, it is thought that the eggs are eaten by a caterpillar, which is in turn eaten by a vespid wasp, which in regurgitating the caterpillar and feeding it to its young transfers the trigonalid larvae from the caterpillar to the wasp larvae.

SUPERFAMILY **Scoliòidea:** We include in this group six families of wasps, and the ants (Formìcidae). The ants are not placed in any superfamily in the USDA Catalogue, but appear more closely related to the wasps in this superfamily than to the insects in other hymenopterous superfamilies. The ants differ from the wasps in this group in the form of the petiole of the abdomen (Figures 535 and 579) and the antennae (nearly always distinctly elbowed); and they differ in habits. Scolioid wasps are similar to vespoid wasps, but the pronotum is generally a little less triangular and usually does not quite reach the tegulae; the pronotum in sphecoid wasps is more collarlike, usually not particularly triangular in lateral view, and there is a rounded lobe on each side that does not reach the tegulae (Figure 530 D). The wasps in the superfamily Scoliòidea are parasites, much as those in the preceding superfamilies of Apócrita; the female lays its eggs on one host, and then goes on its way to lay eggs on others; the wasp larva feeds externally on its host. The wasps in this group usually do not construct a nest, as do the wasps in the Vespòidea and Sphecòidea.

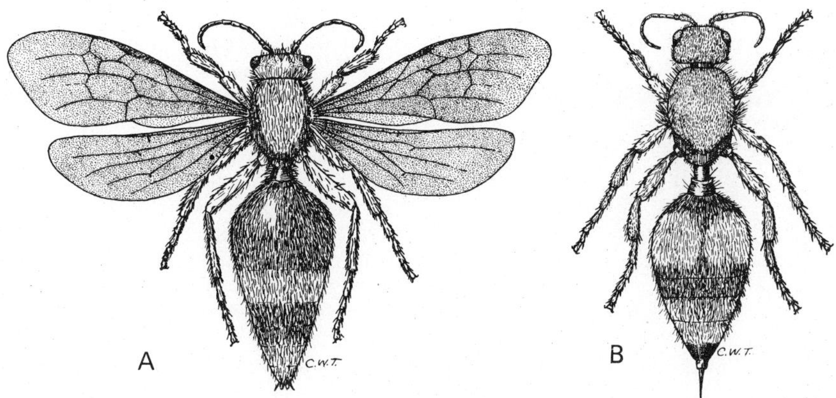

Figure 577. A velvet ant, *Dasymutílla occidentàlis* (L.). A, male; B, female.

Family **Tiphìidae:** This family is divided into six subfamilies, some of which are often considered as families. Both sexes are winged in the Tiphiìnae, Myzinìnae, and Anthoboscìnae, but the females are wingless in the Methochìnae, Myrmosìnae, and Brachycistidìnae (Figure 576). Most members of the Tiphiìnae are fair-sized, black, and somewhat hairy wasps with short legs (Figure 576 A); the Myzinìnae are brightly colored, black and yellow, and 25 mm or more in length. The Tiphiìnae and Myzinìnae attack the larvae of scarab beetles and are a very beneficial group; one species, *Típhia popilliávora* Rohwer (Figure 576 A), has been introduced into this country to aid in the control of the Japanese beetle. The Methochìnae and Myrmosìnae are small groups in which the females are wingless, antlike, and much smaller than the males (as in Figure 576 B, C). The Methochìnae attack the larvae of tiger beetles, and the Myrmosìnae attack various bees and wasps. The Brachycistidìnae and Anthoboscìnae are western, and little is known of their immature stages.

Family **Sierolomórphidae:** The Sierolomórphidae are a small (six North American species) but widely distributed group of shining black wasps 4.5–6.0 mm in length; they are quite rare, and nothing is known of their immature stages.

Family **Mutíllidae**—Velvet Ants: These wasps are so called because the females are wingless and antlike, and are covered with a dense pubescence (Figure 577). The males are winged and usually larger than the females, and are also densely pubescent. Most species have "felt lines" laterally on the second abdominal tergum: narrow longitudinal bands of relatively dense, closely appressed hairs. The females have a very painful sting. Some species can stridulate, and produce a squeaking sound when disturbed. Most of the mutillids whose life histories are known are external parasites of the larvae and pupae of various wasps and bees; a few attack certain beetles and flies. Mutillids are generally found in open areas. This group is a large one (about 475 North American species), and most species occur in the South and West, chiefly in arid areas.

Family **Rhopalosomátidae:** This group includes two rare species that occur in the East, *Rhopalosòma neárcticum* Brues and *Olíxon bánksii* (Brues). *R. neárcticum* is 14–20 mm or more in length, light brown in color, and superficially resembles ichneumons in the genus *Òphion,* but does not have the abdomen compressed, the antennae contain only 12 (female) or 13 (male) segments, and there is only one recurrent vein in the front wing (Figure 549 H). *O. bánksii* is about 6 mm long, and has greatly reduced wings that extend only to the tip of the propodeum. The larvae of these wasps attack crickets.

Family **Scolìidae:** The Scolìidae are somewhat similar to males of the Mutíllidae; they are large, hairy, and usually black with a yellow band (or bands) on the abdomen (Figure 578). Larvae of these wasps are external parasites of the larvae of scarabaeid beetles; the adults are commonly found on flowers. The females burrow into the

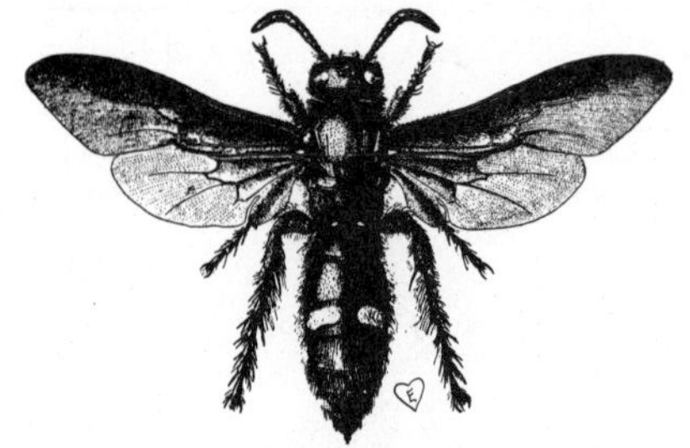

Figure 578. *Scòlia dùbia* Say (Scolìidae), a parasite of the green June beetle. (Courtesy of Davis and Luginbill and the North Carolina Agricultural Experiment Station.)

ground to locate a host; when they find a grub, they sting it and paralyze it, and then burrow deeper into the soil and construct a cell around the grub. Many grubs may be stung without the wasp ovipositing; such grubs usually do not recover.

Family **Sapỳgidae:** The Sapỳgidae are a small (17 North American species) and rare group; the adults are of moderate size, usually black spotted or banded with yellow, and with short legs. They are parasites of leafcutting bees (Megachìlidae) and wasps.

Family **Formìcidae**—Ants: This is a very common and widespread group, well known to everyone. The ants are probably the most successful of all the insect groups; they occur practically everywhere in terrestrial habitats and outnumber in individuals most other terrestrial animals. The habits of ants are often very elaborate, and a great many studies have been made of ant behavior.

Though most ants are easily recognized, there are a few other insects that strongly resemble ants, and some of the winged forms of ants resemble wasps. The most distinctive structural feature of ants is the form of the pedicel of the abdomen, which is 1- or 2-segmented and bears an upright lobe (Figures 535 and 579); the antennae are usually elbowed, and the first segment is often very long.

All ants are social insects, and most colonies contain three castes, queens, males, and workers (Figure 579).[3] The queens are larger than the members of the other castes and are usually winged, though the wings are shed after the mating flight. The queen usually starts a colony and does most of the egg laying in the colony. The males are winged and usually considerably smaller than the queens; they are short-lived and die soon after mating. The workers are sterile wingless females and make up the bulk of the colony. In the smaller ant colonies there are usually just the three types of individuals, but in many of the larger colonies there may be two or three types within each caste; these may vary in size, shape, or other characters.

Ant colonies vary greatly in size, from a dozen or more up to many thousands of individuals. Ants nest in all sorts of places; some nest in various types of cavities in plants (in stems, in nuts or acorns, in galls, and so on), some (for example, the carpenter ants) excavate galleries in wood, but perhaps the majority of ants nest in the ground. The ground nests of ants may be small and relatively simple, or they may be quite large and elaborate, consisting of a maze of tunnels and galleries. The galleries of some of the larger mound nests may extend several feet underground. Certain chambers in such underground nests may serve as brood chambers, others as chambers for the storage of food, and others may be used in some other way; most ants will shift their brood from one part of the nest to another when conditions change.

Males and queens in most ant colonies are produced in numbers at certain seasons; these emerge and engage in mating flights. Shortly after mating, the male dies, and the queen either starts a new colony or goes into an already established colony. This established colony may be of her own or of an alien species; in the latter case her offspring may be spoken of as temporary or permanent social parasites, as the case may be. The queen sheds her wings immediately after the mating flight, usually locates a suitable nesting site, makes a small excavation, and produces her first brood. This first brood is fed and cared for by the queen and consists of workers. Once the first workers appear, they take over the work of the colony—nest construction, caring for the young, gathering food, and the like—and henceforth the queen does little more than lay eggs. The queens of some species may live for several years. There may be more than one queen in some colonies. In some species of ants, certain castes or types of individuals may not be produced until the colony is several years old.

The feeding habits of ants are rather varied. Some are carnivorous, feeding on the flesh of

[3] In a few species there is no worker caste.

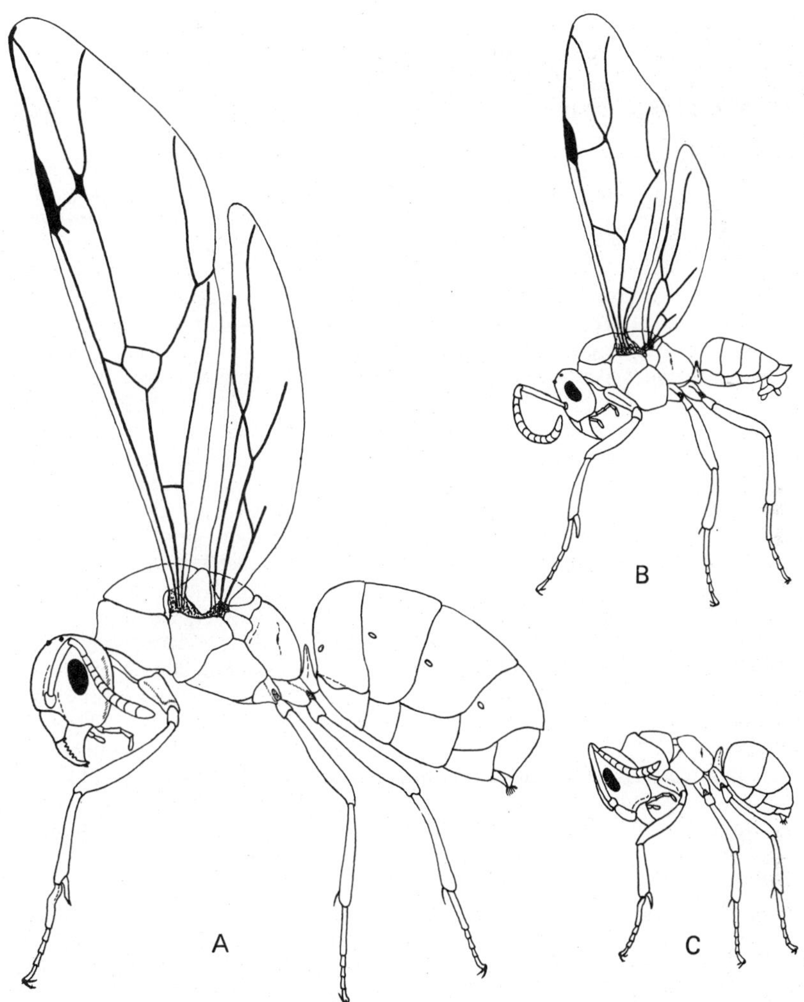

Figure 579. Castes of an ant (*Formìca* sp.). A, queen; B, male; C, worker.

other animals (living or dead), some feed on plants, some feed on fungi, and many feed on sap, nectar, honeydew, and similar substances. Ants in the nest often feed on the excretions of other individuals, and the exchange of food between individuals (trophallaxis) is a common occurrence. Many ants are serious pests in houses, greenhouses, and other places, owing to their feeding on foodstuffs, plants, and other materials.

Ants produce a number of secretions that function in offense, defense, and communication; these are produced by various glands and are discharged to the outside chiefly through the mouth, anus, or sting (Dolichoderìnae and Formicìnae lack a sting). The sting serves as the chief means of offense and defense; all ants may bite, and some can bite rather severely. Some ants give off or eject from the anus a foul-smelling substance that serves as a means of defense. Many ant secretions act as alarm substances, some stimulate group activity, and many (laid down by a foraging individual) serve as an odor trail that other individuals can follow. Some of these secretions appear to play a role in caste determination.

Key to the Subfamilies of Formìcidae (Workers)

Seven of the ten recognized subfamilies of ants, with about 560 species, occur in our area; the workers of these subfamilies may be separated by the following key.

1. Compound eyes absent or vestigial; ocelli absent (Figure 580 C); pedicel of 1 or 2 segments; frontal carinae short and vertical, not covering bases of antennae (Figure 580 C); antennae short; southern United States . **Dorylìnae** p. 674
1′. Without the above combination of characters 2
2(1′). Pedicel of abdomen 1-segmented 3
2′. Pedicel of abdomen 2-segmented 6
3(2). Gaster with a distinct constriction between first and second segments (Figure 535 A); sting well developed 4
3′. Gaster without a constriction between first and second segments; sting vestigial 5
4(3). With a pygidium bearing a row of spines on its lateral and posterior borders; slender, very rare ants, occurring in Texas and Arizona .... **Cerapachyìnae** p. 674
4′. Without a pygidium; widely distributed .... **Ponerìnae** p. 674
5(3′). Opening at posterior end of gaster terminal, circular, and usually surrounded by a fringe of hairs (Figure 580 A); petiole scalelike (Figure 579) .... **Formicìnae** p. 676
5′. Opening at posterior end of gaster ventral and slitlike (Figure 580 B); petiole usually not particularly scalelike .... **Dolichoderìnae** p. 675
6(2′). Frontal carinae usually close together, and not expanded laterally to cover bases of antennae (Figure 580 D); clypeus with upper margin rounded, and not prolonged upward between frontal carinae; southern United States .... **Pseudomyrmecìnae** p. 674
6′. Frontal carinae nearly always well separated, and expanded laterally to cover bases of antennae; clypeus usually prolonged upward between frontal carinae (Figure 580 E); widely distributed .... **Myrmicìnae** p. 674

Subfamily **Dorylìnae:** The Dorylìnae are the legionary ants or army ants; they are mostly tropical, but one genus (*Éciton*) occurs in the southern and southwestern sections of the United States. These ants are nomadic and often travel in distinct files or "armies"; they are highly predaceous. The queens in this group are wingless.

Subfamily **Cerapachyìnae:** This subfamily is represented in North America by only four very rare species occurring in Arizona and Texas. The colonies are usually small, consisting of a few dozen individuals or less. These ants are predaceous.

Subfamily **Ponerìnae:** In this subfamily the pedicel of the abdomen is 1-segmented, but there is a distinct constriction between the first and second segments of the gaster (that part of the abdomen posterior to the pedicel) (Figure 535 A). The only common genus in the East is *Ponèra*; the workers are 2–4 mm in length, and the queens are only a little larger. These ants form small colonies and nest in rotten logs or stumps, or in the soil beneath various objects. They feed on other insects; in the tropics ponerines are important predators of termites.

Subfamily **Pseudomyrmecìnae:** These ants are very slender, and nest in hollow twigs, galls, and other cavities in plants; they are largely arboreal in habit. Our seven species are restricted to the southern states.

Subfamily **Myrmicìnae:** This is the largest subfamily of ants (300 North American species), and its members can usually be recognized by the fact that the pedicel of the abdomen is 2-segmented (Figure 535 B). The members of this group are widely distributed, and vary considerably in habits. The ants in the genera *Pogonomýrmex* and

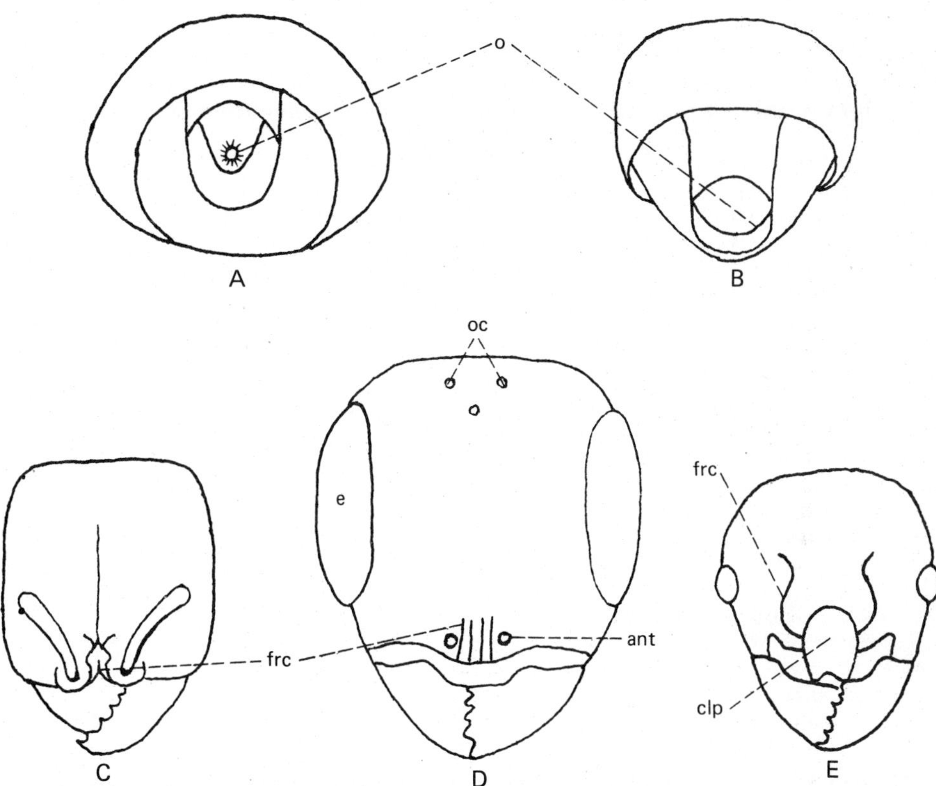

Figure 580. Characters of Formìcidae. A, apex of abdomen of *Formìca* (Formicìnae), terminal view; B, apex of abdomen of *Tapinòma* (Dolichoderìnae), ventroposterior view; C–E, heads, anterior view: C, *Éciton* (Dorylìnae); D, *Pseudomýrmex* (Pseudomyrmicìnae); E, *Myrmìca* (Myrmicìnae). *ant,* base of antenna; *clp,* clypeus; *e,* compound eye; *frc,* frontal carina; *o,* opening at posterior end of gaster (rounded in A, a transverse slit in B); *oc,* ocelli.

Pheidòle are often called harvester ants; they feed on seeds, and store seeds in their nests. The fungus ants of the genus *Trachymýrmex* feed on fungi which they cultivate in their nests. The leafcutting ants (*Átta*) cut pieces of leaves and carry them to their nest, and feed on a fungus grown on these leaves; *A. texàna* (Buckley) is common in some parts of the South and Southwest, and sometimes does considerable damage by its leaf-cutting activities. *Monomòrium pharaònis* (L.), the Pharaoh ant, is a small light yellowish ant that is a common pest in houses. Some of the ants in this group are parasites or inquilines; they live in the nests of other species and do not have a worker caste.

The imported fire ant, *Solenópsis saevíssima ríchteri* Forel, a species introduced into this country from South America, is an important pest in the South, from Georgia and Florida to Texas. It builds large mounds in open areas, and feeds on young plants and seeds, and it often attacks young animals. It has a painful sting, and the aftereffects of the sting are severe in some individuals. The workers are reddish to blackish in color and 3–6 mm in length. A related native species, *S. molésta* Say, the thief ant, is a common house-infesting species in the South and West. Ants of the genus *Solenópsis* may be distinguished from other myrmicine ants by the fact that the antennae are 10-segmented, with a 2-segmented club.

Subfamily **Dolichoderìnae:** In this and the following subfamily, the pedicel of the abdomen consists of a single segment, and there is no constriction between the first and second segments of the gaster (as in Figure 579). In the Dolichoderìnae the cloacal orifice is slitlike and is located ventrally. This is a small group (19 North American species), and most of its members occur in the southern part of the United States; most of them are rather small, the workers being less than 5 mm in length. These ants possess anal glands that secrete a foul-smelling fluid, which can sometimes be forcibly ejected from the anus for a distance of several centimeters. One species, the Argentine ant, *Iridomýrmex hùmilis* (Mayr), is a common household pest in the southern states.

Subfamily **Formicìnae:** This is the second largest subfamily of ants (184 North American species) and is widespread in distribution. It differs from the preceding subfamily in that the anal orifice is terminal and circular. There is considerable variation in habits in this group. The genus *Camponòtus* includes the carpenter ants, some of which are the largest ants in North America; *C. pennsylvánicus* (De Geer) is a large black ant that excavates a series of anastomosing galleries in wood for its nest. Unlike termites, the carpenter ants do not feed on the wood. The ants in the genus *Polyérgus* are slave makers and are entirely dependent on slaves. When a *Polyérgus* queen starts a new colony, she raids a nest of another species, usually a *Formìca,* kills the queen in that colony, and the *Formìca* workers usually adopt the *Polyérgus* queen. To maintain the colony, the *Polyérgus* ants make raids on *Formìca* colonies, killing the workers and carrying off the pupae.

The worker caste of *Polyérgus* is given to fighting, whereas the slaves take over the activities of nest building, brood rearing, foraging, and the like. The *Polyérgus* ants are often called amazons. *P. lùcidus* Mayr, a brilliant red species, is fairly common in the eastern United States. The genus *Làsius* contains a number of small field ants that make small mound nests and feed largely on honeydew; many of them tend aphids, storing the aphid eggs through the winter and placing the young aphids on their food plant in the spring.

Formìca is a very large genus, containing about 70 North American species. Many are mound-building; the mounds of *F. exsectòides* Forel, a common species in the eastern United States, are sometimes 2 or 3 feet (0.6–0.9 m) high and several feet (2 or more m) across. The United States varieties of *F. sanguínea* Latreille are slave makers, somewhat similar in habits to the amazons; they periodically raid the nests of other species of *Formìca* and carry off worker pupae. Some of these are eaten, but others are reared and take their place in the *sanguínea* colony. The honey ants of the genus *Myrmecocýstus,* which occur in the southwestern United States, are of interest in that some of the individuals (termed "repletes") serve as reservoirs for the honeydew collected by other workers.

SUPERFAMILY **Vespòidea:** Most of the Vespòidea can be recognized as wasps by the single-segmented trochanters, the ovipositor issuing from the apex of the abdomen, and the antennae 12- or 13-segmented; they differ from the sphecoid wasps in the form of the pronotum (Figure 530 C, D).

Adult wasps generally feed on nectar, sap, or similar materials, and the larvae are fed other insects or spiders. In most of the solitary vespoid wasps the adult constructs a nest of some sort, usually in the ground or in some natural cavity, or of mud, and then goes out and finds suitable prey, stings it and paralyzes it, brings it back to the nest, lays an egg on it, seals up the nest or cell, and then repeats the process until it has prepared a number of cells, each with food for a young. The social vespoids construct a nest of a papery material and feed the young during their growth. Some of the spider wasps attack a spider in its own cell or burrow and do not move it after stinging and ovipositing on it.

Family **Véspidae:** The members of this large group (over 300 North American species) can usually be recognized by the very long first discoidal cell in the front wings (Figure 551 A) and the fact that the wings are usually folded longitudinally when at rest. This family is divided into seven subfamilies, the Vespìnae, Polistìnae, and Polybiìnae are social wasps, while the remaining subfamilies consist of solitary wasps.

Key to the Subfamilies of Véspidae

1. Two submarginal cells (Figure 581 A); antennae rather strongly clavate (Figure 581 D); length 10–20 mm; western and southwestern United States .... **Masarìnae** p. 678

1′. Three submarginal cells; antennae only slightly or not at all clavate 2

2(1′). Apex of second discoidal cell produced above, and jugal lobe in hind wings about half as long as submedian cell (Figure 581 C); length 6–7

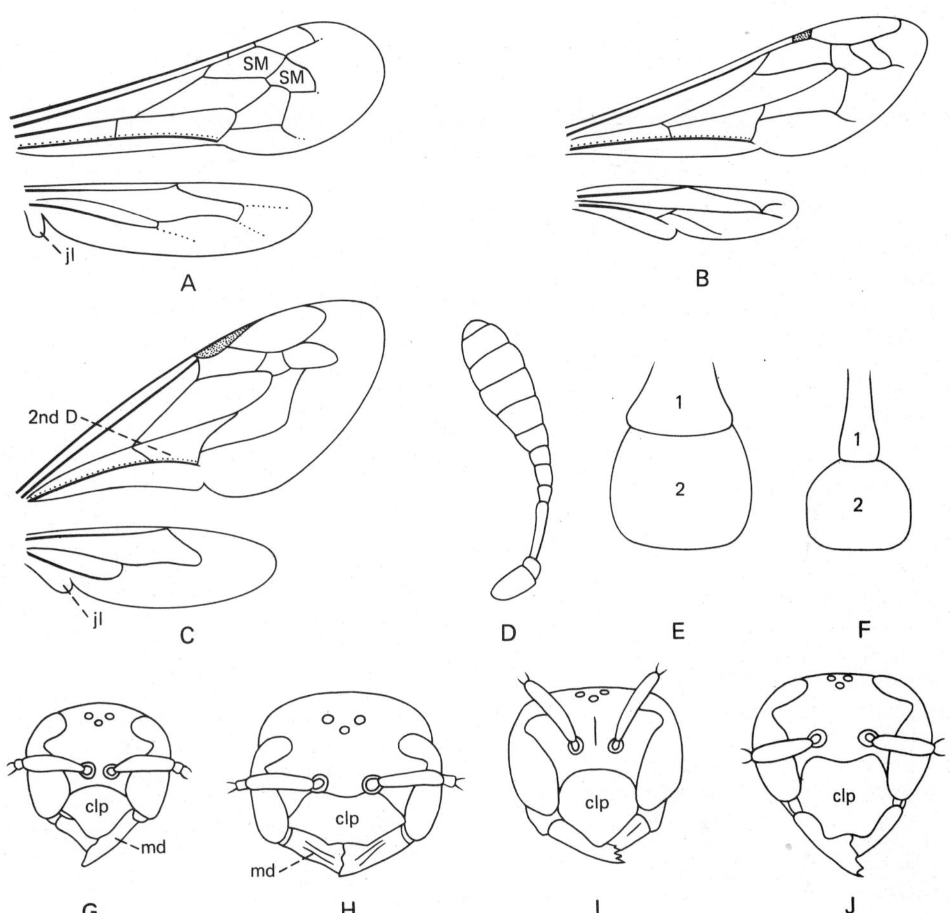

Figure 581. Characters of Véspidae. A, wings of *Pseudomásaris* (Masarìnae); B, wings of *Véspa* (Vespìnae); C, wings of *Euparàgia* (Euparagiìnae); D, antenna of *Pseudomásaris* (Masarìnae); E, basal abdominal segments of *Polístes* (Polistìnae), dorsal view; F, basal abdominal segments of *Mischocýttarus* (Polybiìnae), dorsal view; G–I, heads, anterior view: G, *Rýgchium* (Eumenìnae); H, *Zèthus* (Zethìnae); I, *Polístes* (Polistìnae); J, *Véspa* (Vespìnae). *clp*, clypeus; *D*, discoidal cell; *jl*, jugal lobe; *md*, mandible; *SM*, submarginal cells; *1, 2*, abdominal segments.

mm; southwestern United States .... **Euparagiìnae** p. 679

2′. Apex of second discoidal cell truncate, not produced above, and jugal lobe in hind wings short and rounded or absent 3

3(2′). Middle tibiae with 1 apical spur; tarsal claws toothed or bifid; solitary wasps 4

3′. Middle tibiae with 2 apical spurs; tarsal claws simple; social wasps 5

4(3). Mandibles short and broad, and clypeus wider than long (Figure 581 H); thorax narrowed in front of tegulae, narrower than head; abdomen petiolate; black wasps, about 25 mm in length; southeastern United States .... **Zethìnae** p. 678

4′. Mandibles elongate and knifelike, often crossing, and clypeus as long as or longer than wide (Figure 581 G); thorax not narrowed in front of tegulae, and about as wide as head; abdomen petiolate (Figure 585 A) or sessile

(Figure 585 C); size and color variable, but usually not as above; a large and widely distributed group .... **Eumenìnae** p. 680

5(3′). Hind wings without a jugal lobe (Figure 581 B); clypeus broadly truncate and more or less emarginate at apex (Figure 581 J) .... **Vespìnae** p. 678

5′. Hind wings with a jugal lobe (Figure 551 A); clypeus variable 6

6(5′). First abdominal segment stalklike, only slightly widened distally, and at apex much narrower than second segment (Figure 581 F) (*Mischocýttarus*, southern and western states), or abruptly widened and vespinelike, broadly sessile (*Brachygástra*, southern Texas and southern Arizona) .... **Polybìinae** p. 678

6′. First abdominal segment not stalklike, gradually widening distally, at apex nearly as wide as second segment (Figure 581 E); widely distributed .... **Polistìnae** p. 678

The social vespids, or paper wasps, include the yellowjackets and hornets, with which most people are familiar. As are other truly social insects, the individuals of a colony are of three castes; queens, workers, and males. Queens and workers are females and have a very effective sting, to which anyone who has ever gotten too familiar with these insects can testify. In some species there is very little difference between the queen and workers, and in a few parasitic species the worker caste is not differentiated.

The social vespids construct a nest out of a papery material that consists of wood or foliage chewed up and elaborated by the insect. The colonies in temperate regions exist for just a single season; only the queens overwinter, and in the spring each queen starts a new colony. The queen begins construction of a nest (or she may use a nest built in a previous year) and raises her first brood, which consists of workers. The workers then assume the duties of the colony, and thenceforth the queen does little more than lay eggs. The larvae are fed chiefly on insects and other animals.

Subfamily **Vespìnae:** Most of our species of Vespìnae belong to the genus *Véspula*; this group includes the insects commonly called yellowjackets. The nests of these wasps consist of several to many tiers of hexagonal paper cells, all enclosed in a papery envelope. Some species build their nests in the open, attached to branches, under a porch, or beneath any projecting surface; other species build their nests in the ground. The most common exposed nests, which may sometimes be nearly 0.3 m in diameter (Figure 583), are made by the baldfaced hornet, *Véspula maculàta* (L.), an insect that is largely black with yellowish-white markings (Figure 582 A). Most of the black-and-yellow paper wasps that are commonly called yellowjackets (Figure 582 B) nest in the ground.

Subfamily **Polistìnae:** The Polistìnae are elongate and slender with a spindle-shaped abdomen and are usually reddish or brown in color marked with yellow (Figure 584). Their nests (Figure 584 B) consist of a single more or less circular horizontal comb of paper cells, suspended from a support by a slender stalk. The cells are open on the lower side while the larvae are growing and are sealed when the larvae pupate. The North American species in this subfamily belong to the genus *Polístes*.

Subfamily **Polybìinae:** The most common wasps in this group (*Mischocýttarus*) resemble a small *Polístes* but have the basal abdominal segment narrower; they occur in the South and West, and their nests resemble those of *Polístes*. One species of *Brachygástra* occurs in southern Texas and southern Arizona; it has the abdomen sessile, and its nests are a little like those of a baldfaced hornet (Figure 583).

The solitary vespids vary considerably in their nesting habits, but most of them provision their nests with caterpillars. Some species utilize cavities in twigs or logs for a nest, others burrow in the ground, and others make a nest of mud or clay. Most of the solitary vespids are black marked with yellow or white, and they vary in size from about 10 to 25 mm in length.

Subfamily **Zethìnae:** The Zethìnae are black wasps, about 25 mm long, that have the abdomen petiolate (much as in Figure 585 A); they are not common. In some species several females may construct a colony of cells made of leaves or plant fibers pasted together. The food of the larvae consists of caterpillars.

Subfamily **Masarìnae:** The members of this group are black and yellow wasps, 10–20 mm in length, which differ from other vespids in having only two

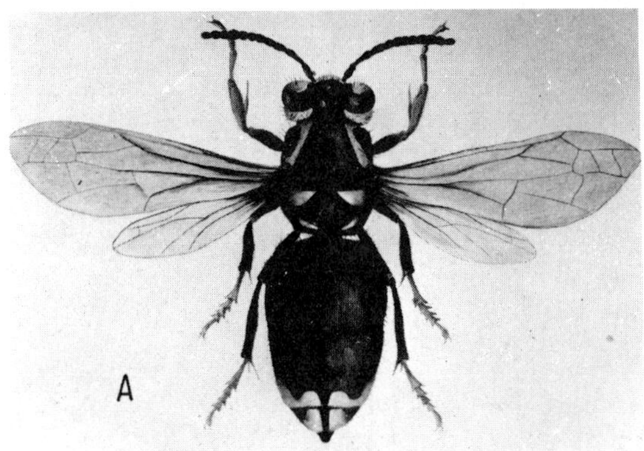

Figure 582. Paper wasps (Vespìnae). A, baldfaced hornet, *Véspula maculàta* (L.); B, a yellowjacket, *Véspula macùlifrons* (Buysson).

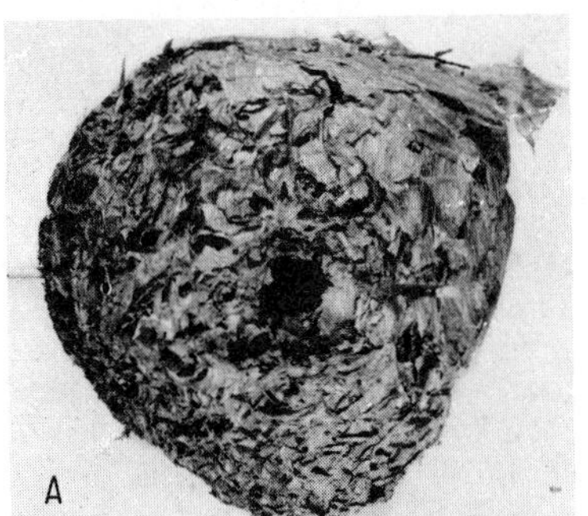

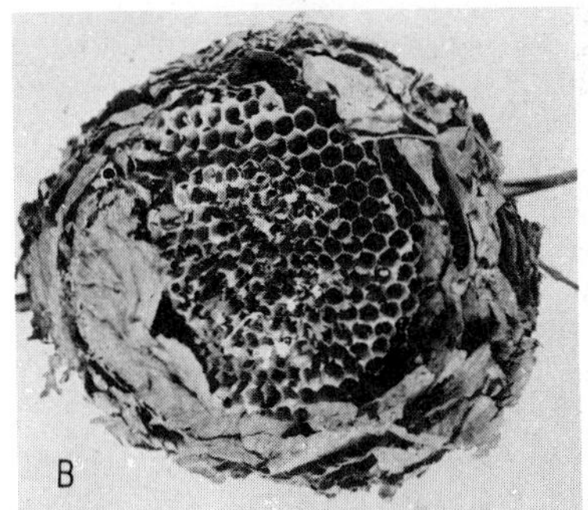

Figure 583. Nests of a baldfaced hornet, *Véspula maculàta* (L.). A, nest as seen from below, showing entrance opening; B, lower part of outer envelope removed to show a tier of cells.

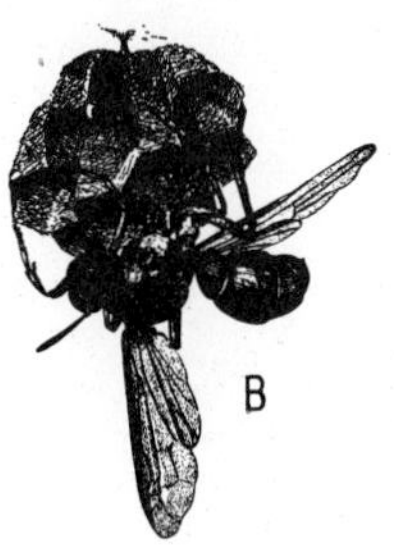

Figure 584. A paper wasp, *Polístes fuscàtus pállipes* Lepeletier. A, adult female; B, adult at nest. (B, courtesy of USDA.)

submarginal cells in the front wing (Figure 581 A) and in having clubbed antennae (Figure 581 D). They occur only in the West. They make nests of mud or sand attached to rocks or twigs, and provision their nests with pollen and nectar. This group is a small one, with only 14 species in North America.

Subfamily **Euparagiìnae:** These wasps occur only in the Southwest (Texas to Nevada and Califor-

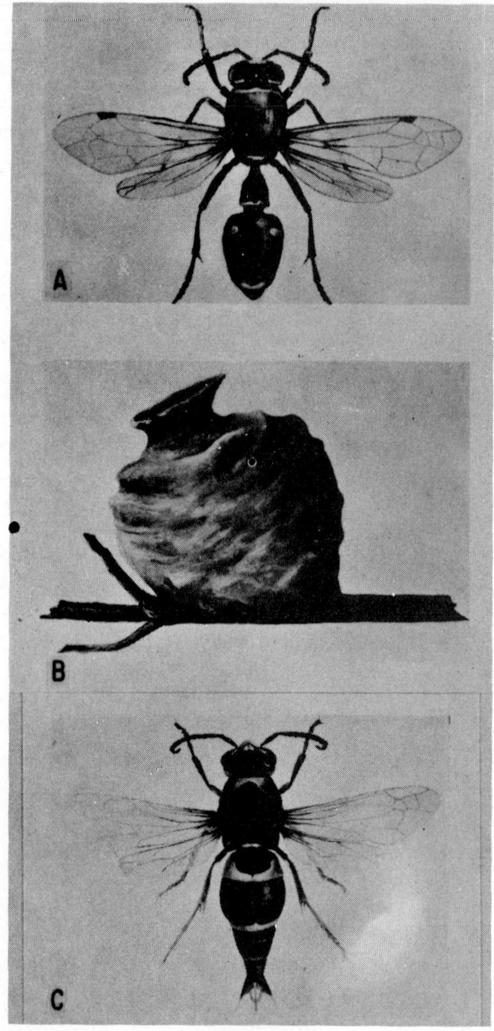

Figure 585. A, adult, and B, nest, of a potter wasp, *Eùmenes fratérnus* Say. C, a mason wasp, *Rýgchium dorsàle dorsàle* (Fabricius); this species nests in small colonies in vertical burrows in the ground.

nia), and are relatively rare; only seven species occur in our area. They are small (6–7 mm in length), rather stocky in build, and are usually black with light (light red, yellow, or ivory) markings. *Euparágia scutellàris* Cresson constructs nests in the ground with a curved turret at the surface; it provisions its nest with weevil larvae.

Subfamily **Eumenìnae**—Mason or Potter Wasps: This is a large (about 250 North American species) and widespread group, and many species are very common. The species in the genus *Eùmenes* construct juglike nests of mud, which are attached to twigs and are provisioned with caterpillars (Figure 585 A, B). The other species in this subfamily nest in various sorts of mud or clay nests, in burrows, in cavities in twigs or logs, or in the abandoned nests of other wasps. Most species provision their nests with caterpillars; some provision their nests with the larvae of chrysomelid beetles. Most of these wasps do not lay their eggs on the insects with which the cells are provisioned, but suspend their eggs on slender threads from the ceiling or side of the cells.

Family **Pompílidae**—Spider Wasps: The spider wasps are slender wasps with long spiny legs and a characteristic suture across the mesopleura (Figures 552 and 586). The more common members of this group are 15–25 mm in length, but some of the western spider wasps are about $1\frac{1}{2}$ inches (38 mm) or more in length. Most of them are dark-colored, with smoky or yellowish wings; a few are brightly colored. The adults are usually found on flowers or on the ground in search of prey. The larvae of most species feed on spiders (hence the common name), although these are not the only wasps that attack spiders. The spider wasps generally capture and paralyze a spider and then prepare a cell for it in the ground, in rotten wood, or in a suitable crevice in rocks. Some spider wasps construct a cell first, then hunt for a spider to store in the cell. A few species attack the spider in its own cell or burrow and do not move it after stinging and ovipositing on it; a few species oviposit on spiders that have been stung by another wasp. The spider wasps are fairly common insects, and the females have a very efficient sting.

SUPERFAMILY **Sphecòidea:** Sphecoid wasps can be distinguished from other wasps by the structure of the pronotum, which terminates laterally in a rounded lobe that does not reach the tegula (Figure 530 D). They differ from bees, which have a similar pronotum structure, by having all body hairs simple (some are branched or plumose in bees), and the basal segment of the hind tarsi is not particularly enlarged or flattened. Sphecoid wasps are relatively bare (many bees are quite hairy), and some have the abdomen distinctly petiolate.

There are differences of opinion about the taxonomic arrangement of the wasps in this group, and for some of the names to be used for them. We follow here the arrangement to be used in a forthcoming book, *Sphecid Wasps, a Generic*

Revision, by R. M. Bohart and A. S. Menke, to be published by the University of California Press.

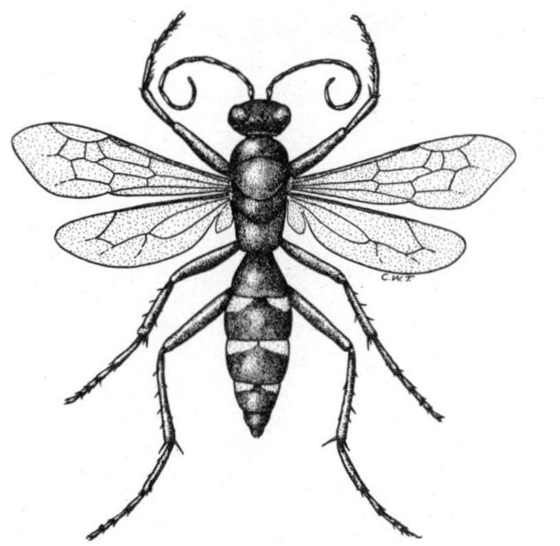

Figure 586. A spider wasp, *Episýron quinquenotàtus* (Say), 2½ ×.

Family **Sphécidae:** The members of this large group (over 1200 North American species) are solitary wasps, though large numbers of some of them (for example, Bembicìni) may nest in a small area. They nest in a variety of situations, but the majority nest in burrows in the ground, in various natural cavities, or construct cells of mud. Each group within the family is usually restricted to a particular type of prey as food for their larvae, and constructs a characteristic type of nest. A few are cleptoparasites,[4] or inquilines. The adults are often found on flowers.

This group contains a number of subfamilies and tribes that differ in appearance and habits, some of which are considered distinct families by some authorities. These groups may be separated by the following key.

[4] *Clepto,* meaning to rob or steal; a cleptoparasite is one that feeds on food stored for the host larvae.

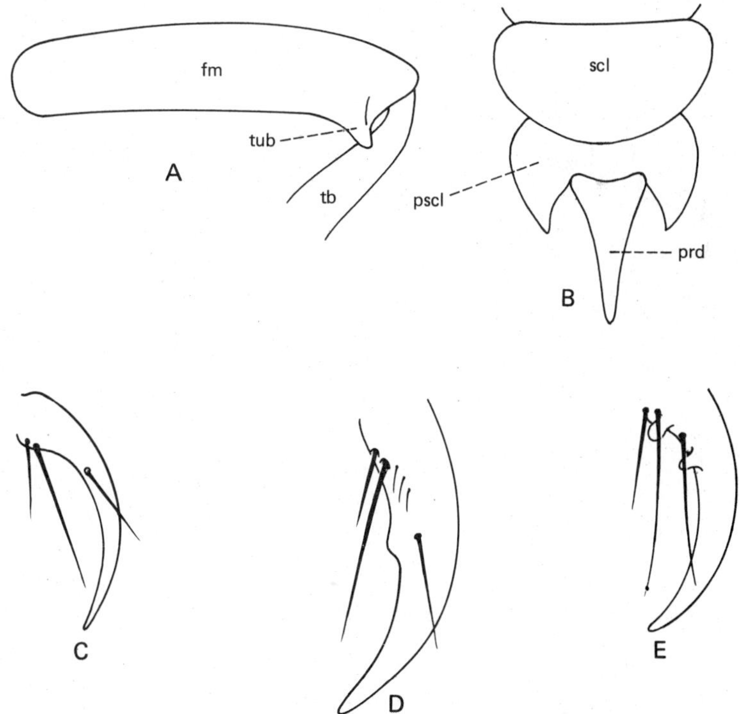

Figure 587. Characters of Sphécidae. A, a portion of the hind leg of Alyssonìni (Nyssonìnae); B, scutellum and postscutellum of *Oxýbelus* (Oxybelìni, Crabronìnae); C, tarsal claw of *Ammóphila* (Ammophilìni, Sphecìnae); D, tarsal claw of *Scéliphron* (Sceliphronìni, Sphecìnae); E, tarsal claw of *Sphéx* (Sphecìni, Sphecìnae). *fm,* femur; *prd,* propodeal spine; *pscl,* postscutellum; *scl,* scutellum; *tb,* tibia; *tub,* apical tubercle of the femur.

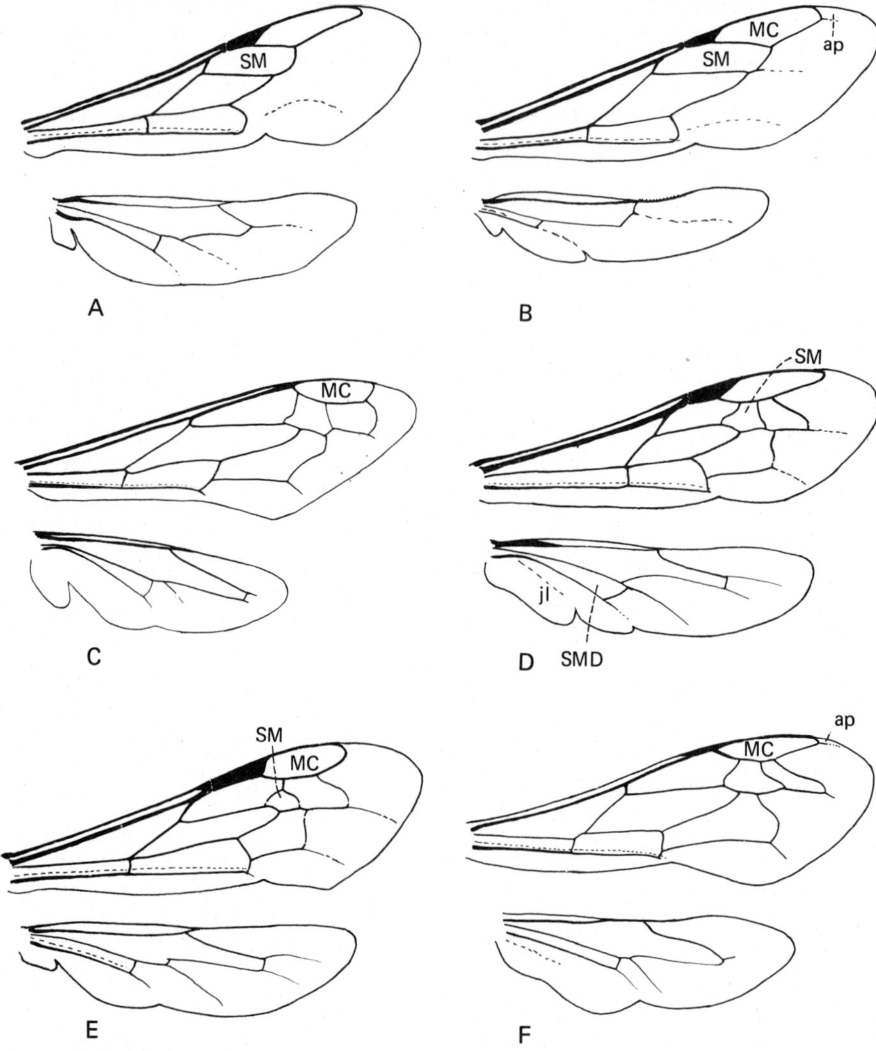

Figure 588. Wings of Sphécidae. A, *Trypóxylon* (Trypoxylonìni, Larrìnae); B, *Crábro* (Crabronìni, Crabronìnae); C. *Microbémbex* (Bembicini, Nyssonìnae); D, *Philánthus* (Philanthìni, Philanthìnae); E, *Cérceris* (Cercerini, Philanthìnae); F, *Táchysphex* (Larrìni, Larrìnae), *ap*, appendiculate marginal cell; *jl*, jugal lobe; *MC*, marginal cell; *SM*, submarginal cell; *SMD*, submedian cell.

Key to the Subfamilies and Tribes of Sphécidae

1. Parapsidal sutures usually distinct and complete; pronotum long, conically produced anteriorly, usually with a median groove (Figure 593); mesosternum usually produced into a forked process posteriorly; abdomen of male with 4–6 exposed terga .... **Ampulicìnae** p. 687

1′. Parapsidal sutures indistinct or absent; pronotum short, not as above; mesosternum not as above; abdomen of male usually with 7 exposed terga 2

2(1′). Postscutellum with 2 scalelike backward-projecting processes (Figure 587 B); propodeum with a median spine or forked process; base of cubital vein, between first submarginal and first discoidal cells, weak or lacking (Figure 590 C) (Oxybelìni) .... **Crabronìnae** p. 690

2′. Postscutellum, and usually also propodeum, simple and not as above; cubital vein well developed between first submarginal and first discoidal cells 3

3(2′). One submarginal cell (Figure 588 A, B), or if with more than one then the eyes are deeply emarginate 4

3′. Two or 3 submarginal cells (Figures 588 C–F, 589, 590 A–B, D–F); eyes not emarginate, or only slightly so 6

4(3). Eyes deeply emarginate (Figure 591 A); medium-sized, slender, black wasps (Figure 595 A) (Trypoxylonìni) .... **Larrìnae** p. 687

4′. Eyes not emarginate (Figure 591 E) 5

5(4′). Marginal cell appendiculate (Figure 588 B); head large and quadrate; antennae arising low on face (Figure 591 E); usually black wasps with yellow markings (Crabronìni) .... **Crabronìnae** p. 690

5′. Marginal cell not appendiculate (Pemphredonìni) .... **Pemphredonìnae** p. 688

6(3′). Middle tibiae with 1 apical spur (some Bembicìni may have one or more hairs at apex of middle tibiae that are nearly as large as the spur; these wasps have a large triangular labrum, Figure 591 B) 7

6′. Middle tibiae with 2 apical spurs; labrum never as large and triangular as in Figure 591 B 15

7(6). Labrum large, free, triangular, as long as or longer than wide (Figure 591 B); ocelli vestigial; marginal cell not appendiculate, and second submarginal cell receiving both recurrent veins (Figure 588 C) (Bembicìni) .. **Nyssonìnae** p. 689

7′. Labrum small, usually concealed by clypeus; ocelli and venation variable 8

8(7′). Abdomen not petiolate, and with a strong constriction, both dorsally and ventrally, between first and second segments (Figure 592 A, B); relatively robust wasps, usually black with yellow markings (Figure 597 C, D) .... **Philanthìnae** 9

8′. Abdomen either petiolate, or without a strong constriction between first and second segments 11

9(8). Hind femora reniform at apex; second submarginal cell more or less triangular, usually petiolate and not touching marginal cell (Figure 588 E) (Cercerìni) .... **Philanthìnae** p. 690

9′. Hind femora simple at apex, not reniform; second submarginal cell quadrate and touching marginal cell (Figure 588 D) 10

10(9′). Inner margins of eyes notched (Figure 591 C) (Philanthìni)...**Philanthìnae** p. 690

10′. Inner margins of eyes straight or nearly so (Aphilanthopsìni)...**Philanthìnae** p. 690

11(8′). Hind femora produced below at apex as a flattened tubercle overlying base of tibiae (Figure 587 A); second submarginal cell petiolate (as in Figures 588 E and 589 C); abdomen not petiolate (Alyssonìni) .... **Nyssonìnae** p. 689

11′. Hind femora simple at apex, not as above; second submarginal cell variable 12

12(11′). Marginal cell appendiculate (Figure 588 F), or if not then the mandibles are notched externally (Figure 591 D); abdomen not petiolate; color variable .... **Larrìnae** 13

12′. Marginal cell not appendiculate (Figure 589 A, B); mandibles not notched externally; abdomen often petiolate (Figures 592 D and 596 D); color usually black .... **Pemphredonìnae** 14

13(12). Lateral ocelli normal; inner margins of eyes nearly parallel; pronotum trilobed (Miscophìni) .... **Larrìnae** p. 687

13′. Lateral ocelli distorted or deformed; inner margins of eyes converging

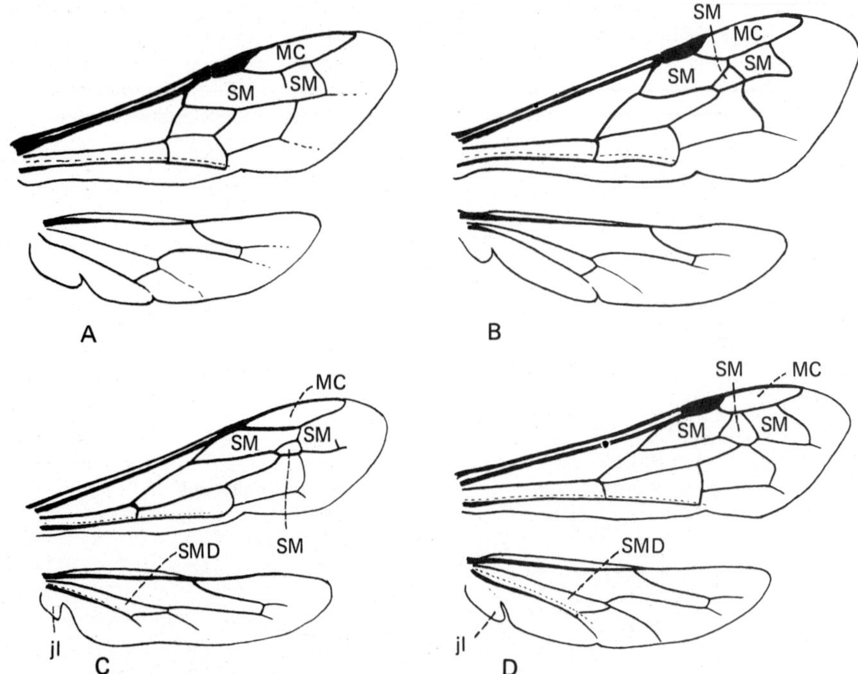

Figure 589. Wings of Sphécidae. A, *Pémphredon* (Pemphredonìni, Pemphredonìnae); B, *Psén* (Psenìni, Pemphredonìnae); C, *Nýsson* (Nyssonìni, Nyssonìnae); D, *Gorỳtes* (Gorytìni, Nyssonìnae). *jl,* jugal lobe; *MC,* marginal cell; *SM,* submarginal cell; *SMD,* submedian cell.

above; pronotum simple (Larrìni) .... **Larrìnae** p. 687

14(12′). One or 2 submarginal cells (Figure 589 A); antennae arising low on face, near base of eyes (Figure 591 F) (Pemphredonìni) ...... **Pemphredonìnae** p. 688

14′. Three submarginal cells (Figure 589 B); antennae arising near middle of face, above base of eyes (Figure 591 G) (Psenìni) ...... **Pemphredonìnae** p. 688

15(6′). Hind femora produced below at apex as a flattened tubercle overlying base of tibiae (Figure 587 A); second submarginal cell petiolate (as in Figures 584 E and 589 C); abdomen not petiolate (Alyssonìni) .... **Nyssonìnae** p. 689

15′. Hind femora simple at apex, not as above; second submarginal cell and abdomen variable 16

16(15′). Vannal lobe of hind wings large, strongly projecting posteriorly (Figure 590 A, B, E, F, *vl*); mesonotum not expanded laterally into laminae that overlie bases of tegulae 17

16′. Vannal lobe of hind wings smaller, not strongly projecting posteriorly (Figures 589 C, D and 590 D); mesonotum often expanded laterally into laminae that overlie bases of tegulae 20

17(16). Abdomen with a distinct, usually long, cylindrical petiole (Figure 592 E); marginal cell pointed or narrowly rounded apically, and not appendiculate (Figure 590 A, E, F); eyes widely separated .... **Sphecìnae** 18

17′. Abdomen not petiolate; marginal cell truncate at apex and appendiculate (Figure 590 B); eyes of male very large and contiguous above (Figure 591 H) .... **Astatìnae** p. 687

18(17). Tarsal claws without teeth on inner margin (Figure 587 C); second submarginal cell receiving both recurrent veins, and discoidal vein in hind

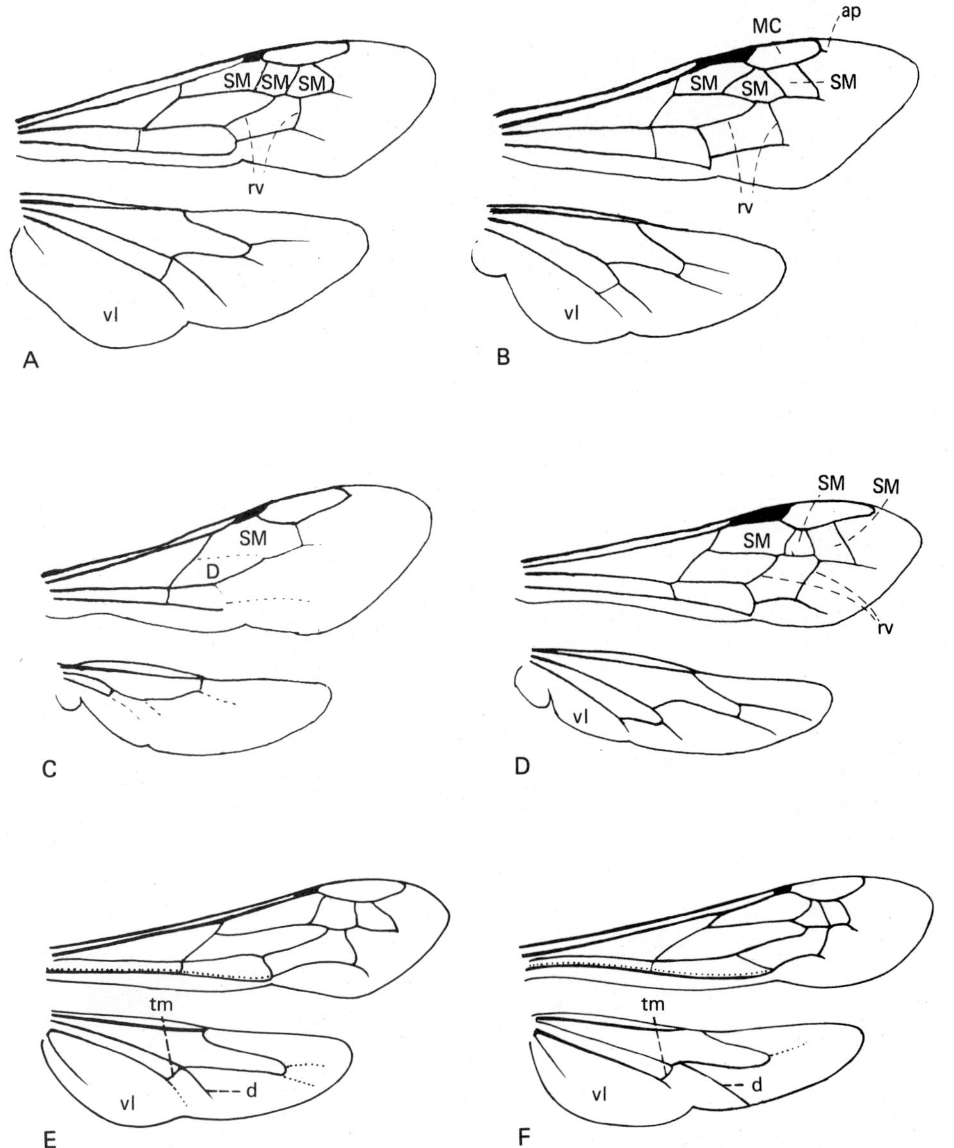

Figure 590. Wings of Sphécidae. A, *Sphéx* (Sphecìni, Sphecìnae); B, *Astàta* (Astatìnae); C, *Oxýbelus* (Oxybelìni, Crabronìnae); D, *Méllinus* (Mellinìni, Nyssonìnae); E, *Scéliphron* (Sceliphronìni, Sphecìnae); F, *Ammóphila* (Ammophilìni, Sphecìnae). *ap,* appendiculate marginal cell; *d,* discoidal vein; *D,* first discoidal cell; *MC,* marginal cell; *rv,* recurrent veins; *SM,* submarginal cell; *tm,* transverse median vein; *vl,* vannal lobe.

wings arising distinctly beyond anterior end of transverse median vein (Figure 590 F); petiole of abdomen usually 2-segmented (Figure 596 B) (Ammophilìni) .... **Sphecìnae** p. 688

18′. Tarsal claws of at least front and middle legs with 1 or more teeth on inner margin (Figure 587 D, E); second submarginal cell receiving 1 or both recurrent veins; discoidal vein in hind wing nearly always arising at anterior

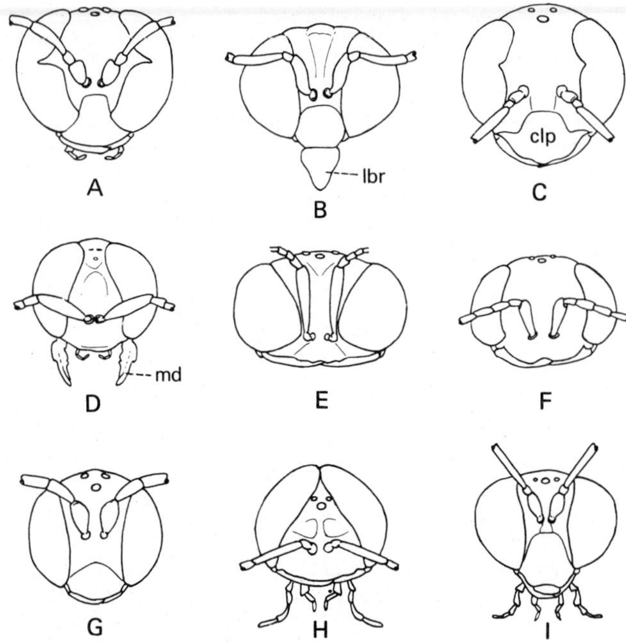

Figure 591. Heads of Sphécidae, anterior view. A, *Trypóxylon* (Trypoxylonìni, Larrìnae); B, *Microbémbex* (Bembicìni, Nyssonìnae); C, *Philánthus* (Philanthìni, Philanthìnae); D, *Líris* (Larrìni, Larrìnae); E, *Crábro* (Crabronìni, Crabronìnae); F, *Pémphredon* (Pemphredonìni, Pemphredonìnae); G, *Psén* (Psenìni, Pemphredonìnae); H, *Astàta*, male (Astatìnae); I, *Sphècius* (Gorytìni, Nyssonìnae). *clp*, clypeus; *lbr*, labrum; *md*, mandible.

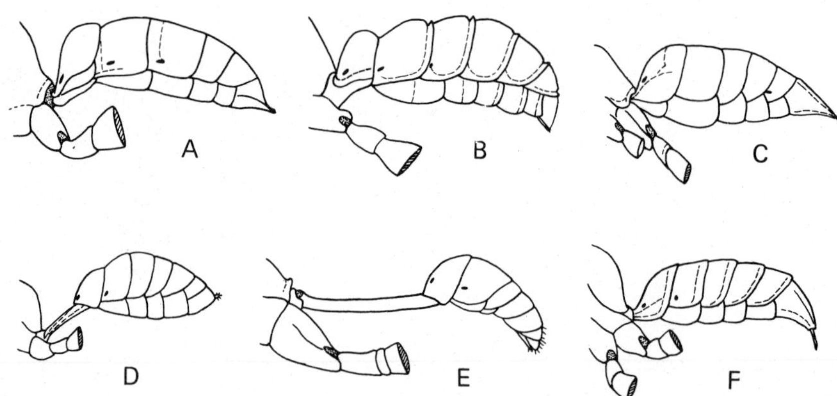

Figure 592. Abdominal structure in Sphécidae, lateral view. A, *Philánthus* (Philanthìni, Philanthìnae); B, *Cérceris* (Cercerìni, Philanthìnae); C, Larrìnae; D, *Psén* (Psenìni, Pemphredonìnae); E, *Scéliphron* (Sceliphronìni, Sphecìnae); F, *Sphècius* (Gorytìni, Nyssonìnae).

end of transverse median vein (Figure 590 E) 19

19(18′). Tarsal claws of front and middle legs with 2 or more teeth on inner margin (Figure 587 E); second submarginal cell receiving only 1 recurrent vein (Figure 590 A) (Sphecìni) .... **Sphecìnae** p. 688

19′.	Tarsal claws of front and middle legs with a single median (or rarely, subbasal) tooth on inner margin (Figure 587 D); second submarginal cell usually receiving both recurrent veins (Figure 590 E) (Sceliphronìni) .... **Sphecìnae**	p. 688
20(16′).	Second submarginal cell not receiving a recurrent vein (Figure 590 D); first abdominal segment long, slender, swollen apically, and separated from second by a distinct constriction (Mellinìni) .... **Nyssonìnae**	p. 689
20′.	Second submarginal cell receiving 1 or both recurrent veins; first abdominal segment stout, not particularly swollen apically, and separated from second segment by a less distinct constriction 21	
21(20′).	Basal vein distant from stigma by less, generally much less, than twice the distance from apex of marginal cell to apex of wing (Figure 589 C, D); last abdominal tergite of male simple, not trilobed 22	
21′.	Basal vein distant from stigma by 2 or more times the distance from apex of marginal cell to apex of wing (as in Figure 588 C); last abdominal tergite of male trilobed (Stizìni) .... **Nyssonìnae**	p. 689
22(21).	Second submarginal cell triangular and petiolate (Figure 589 C); propodeum with upper hind angles acute or produced as sharp spines; thorax coarsely punctate (Nyssonìni) .... **Nyssonìnae**	p. 689
22′.	Second submarginal cell not as above, usually quadrate (Figure 589 D); propodeum and thorax variable 23	
23(22′).	Jugal lobe in hind wings as long as submedian cell or longer (as in Figure 588 D); eyes widely separated, and clypeus with a median upward-projecting lobe (as in Figure 591 C); thorax coarsely punctate (Aphilanthopsìni) .... **Philanthìnae**	p. 690
23′.	Jugal lobe in hind wings not more than half as long as submedian cell (Figure 589 D); eyes closer together, and entire clypeus projecting upward (Figure 591 I); thorax smooth (Gorytìni) .... **Nyssonìnae**	p. 689

Subfamily **Ampulicìnae:** The ampulicine wasps are small (length 10 mm or less), black or black and reddish, rather rare wasps (Figure 593). They nest in twigs, under bark, and under leaf litter on the ground, and provision their nests with small cockroaches. Only four species occur in our area, two in the East, one in Texas, and one in southern California.

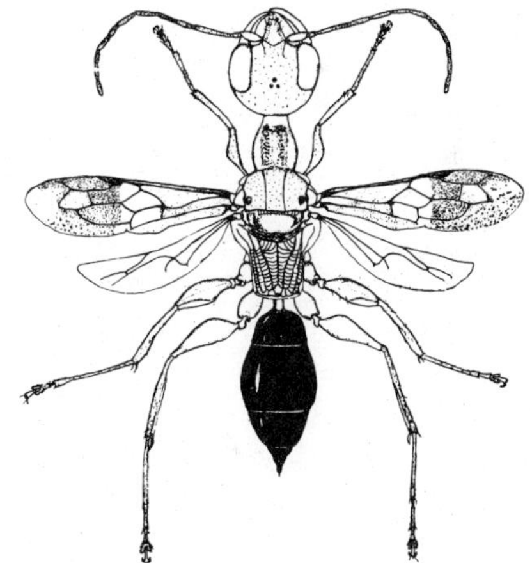

Figure 593. An ampulicine wasp, *Rhinópsis ferrugínea* Bradley. (Courtesy of Strandtmann and the Entomological Society of America.)

Subfamily **Astatìnae (Dimorphìnae)**—Vari-Colored Wasps: These wasps are rather stout-bodied, about 13 mm in length, and are either all black or black with the abdomen red. They nest in the ground and provision their nests with Hemíptera, especially Pentatómidae and Lygaèidae.

Subfamily **Larrìnae:** Most of the wasps in this group are dull-colored and of medium size, and nest in sandy places. The Miscophìni (Dinetìni, Nitelìni), which are small and rare insects, provision their nests with spiders, small Hemíptera, or small grasshoppers. The Larrìni include some relatively stout-bodied wasps (Figure 594) that nest in the ground in sandy places and provision their nests with various Orthóptera (chiefly grasshoppers or crickets). The Trypoxylonìni include the organ-pipe mud-daubers. These wasps are elongate, slender, usually shining black wasps with the inner margins of the eyes deeply emarginate (Figures 591 A and 595 A); most of them have only 1 submarginal cell (Figure 595 A).

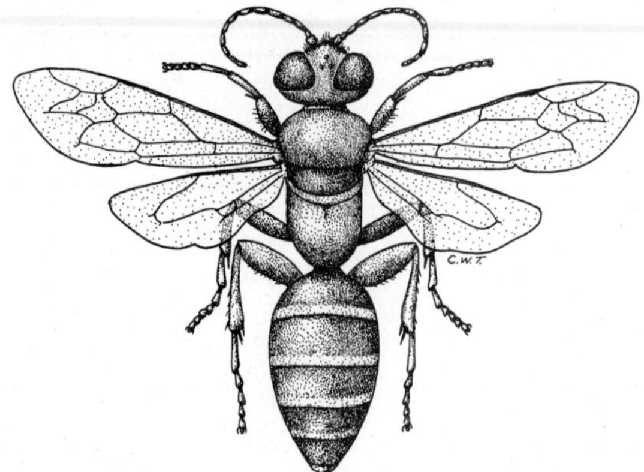

Figure 594. A larrine wasp, *Táchytes auruléntus* (Fabricius) (Larrìni, Larrìnae), 3 ×.

They vary in length from about 13 to 25 mm or more. Some species of organ-pipe mud-daubers make their nests of mud, with the cells arranged in the form of a long tube (Figure 595 B); other species nest in hollow twigs, abandoned wood-boring beetle galleries, or other similar cavities. The organ-pipe mud-daubers provision their nests with spiders.

Subfamily **Pemphredonìnae**—Aphid Wasps: The aphid wasps are small, slender, usually black wasps (Figure 596 D) that nest in cavities in twigs or logs (a few nest in the ground), and provision their nests with various Homóptera. Most of the Psenìni provision their nests with hoppers (Cercòpidae, Membràcidae, and Cicadéllidae); a few species in this tribe provision their nests with aphids or psyllids. Most of the Pemphredonìni nest in the ground and provision their nests with aphids or thrips.

Subfamily **Sphecìnae**—Thread-Waisted Wasps: These wasps are very common insects, and most of them are 25 mm or more in length; some of the largest sphecids are included in this subfamily. The common name refers to the very slender petiole of the abdomen. The wasps in the tribe Sphecìni (=Ammobiìni) differ from all other Sphecìnae (except *Chlorìon,* tribe Sceliphronìni) in having only one recurrent vein meeting the second submarginal cell in the front wings. These wasps nest in burrows in the ground and provision their nests with grasshoppers or crickets. A common species in this group is *Sphéx ichneumòneus* (L.), which is reddish brown with the tip of the abdomen black (Figure 596 C).

The wasps in the tribe Ammophilìni (=Sphecìni) are slender, and usually black with the basal half or two thirds of the abdomen yellowish or orange (Figure 596 B); they nest in the ground and provision their nests with caterpillars. There are two North American genera, *Ammóphila* (=*Sphéx*) and *Podalònia; Ammóphila* (common wasps) have the abdominal petiole 2-segmented, while *Podalònia* (less common) have the abdominal petiole 1-segmented.

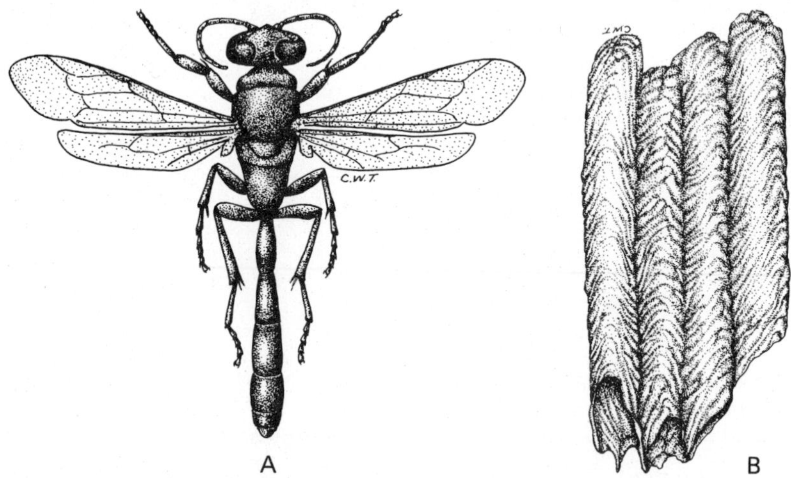

Figure 595. An organ-pipe mud-dauber. A, adult of *Trypóxylon clavàtum* Say, 3½ ×; B, nest of *T. polítum* Say, ½ ×.

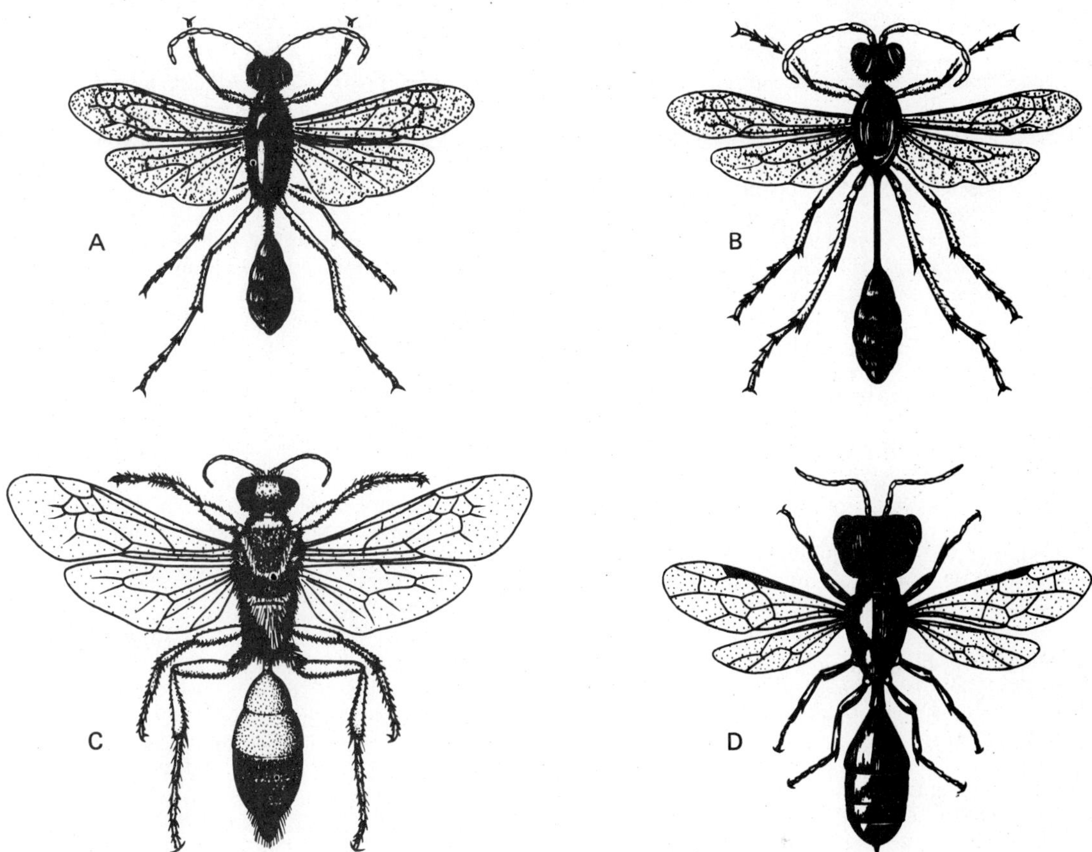

Figure 596. Sphecid wasps. A–C, thread-waisted wasps (Sphecìnae); D, an aphid wasp (Pemphredonìnae). A, *Chlorìon aeràrium* Patton; B, *Ammóphila nígricans* Dahlbom; C, *Sphéx ichneumòneus* (L.); D, *Pémphredon inornàtus* Say.

Two genera in the tribe Sceliphronìni, *Scéliphron* and *Chalýbion,* are commonly called mud-daubers; they construct nests of mud and provision them with spiders. Their nests usually consist of a number of cells, each about 25 mm long, placed side by side; these nests are common on ceilings and walls of old buildings. The two most common species of mud-daubers are *S. caementàrium* (Drury), which is blackish brown with yellow spots and yellow legs, and *C. califòrnicum* (Saussure), which is metallic blue with bluish wings. The other genera in this tribe are *Pòdium* and *Chlorìon*. The wasps in the genus *Pòdium,* which have the antennae inserted below the middle of the eyes, are mainly southern in distribution and are uncommon, and they provision their nests with cockroaches. The wasps in the genus *Chlorìon* (Figure 596 A), which are widely distributed but uncommon, have only one recurrent vein meeting the second submarginal cell in the front wings.

Subfamily **Nyssonìnae:** This is a large and varied group, and its members have been variously classified by different workers. Nearly all these wasps have the mesonotum expanded laterally into laminae that more or less overlie the bases of the tegulae, and the jugal lobe of the hind wing is shorter than the submedian cell; all except the Bembicìni have two apical spurs on the middle tibiae. This subfamily is divided into six tribes: the Alyssonìni (Alysonìni), Nyssonìni, Mellinìni, Gorytìni, Stizìni, and Bembicìni.

The Alyssonìni are rather rare, and little is known of their nesting habits, but some species nest in the ground and provision their nests with planthoppers. The Nyssonìni are a small and not very common group; most species are inquilines (or cleptoparasites) in the nests of other sphecid wasps. The Mellinìni are small and rather rare; they nest in the ground and provision their nests with adult flies.

Most of the Gorytìni are small wasps, about 13 mm long or less, with black and yellow markings; they nest in the ground and provision their nests with various Homóptera, chiefly Cercòpidae, Cicadéllidae, and Membràcidae. One species in this group, *Sphècius speciòsus* (Drury), commonly known as the cicada-killer, is a very large and striking insect (Figure 597 A); it varies in length from about 25 to 38 mm and is black or rusty in color with yellow bands on the abdomen. Cicada-killer wasps nest in burrows in the ground and provision their nests with cicadas.

The Stizìni are a small group; most species nest in the ground; some provision their nests with meadow grasshoppers and others with leafhoppers. The species in the genus *Stizòides* are "cuckoo" wasps or inquilines, laying their eggs on the grasshopper prey of certain thread-waisted wasps.

The Bembicìni, or sand wasps, are rather stout-bodied wasps of moderate size (Figure 597 B) which are most easily recognized by the elongate and triangular labrum (Figure 591 B). They nest in burrows in sandy areas and differ from most of the other sphecid wasps in that a great many burrows may be made in a small area, to form what amount to colonies, and in some species the adults continue to feed the larvae during their growth. The food of the larvae consists mainly of flies; a few species feed their young nymphal Hemíptera, adult Lepidóptera, or bees. *Microbémbex monodónta* (Say) is a common sand wasp occurring in the Northeast and along the seashore; it is mostly black with greenish white markings. *Stíctia carolìna* (Fabricius), an insect about 25 mm long and black with yellow markings, is fairly common in the South; it often hunts for flies near horses, and is called the "horse guard." Other sand wasps are black with yellow, white, or pale green markings.

Subfamily **Philanthìnae:** The Philanthìnae are digger wasps of medium size, usually black with yellow markings, which have a distinct constriction between the first and second abdominal segments. The Philanthìni (Figure 597 C) provision their nests with bees, the Apilanthopsìni provision their nests with ants, and the Cercerìni (Figure 597 D) provision their nests with various types of beetles (Chrysomélidae, Bupréstidae, and Curculiónidae). These wasps are fairly common.

Subfamily **Crabronìnae:** The Crabronìnae are another group of digger wasps. The Crabronìni, or square-headed wasps, are fairly common insects that vary in length from about 6 to 20 mm and are usually black with yellow markings (Figure 598 A). They are easily recognized by the large and quadrate head, with the inner margins of the eyes straight and converging ventrally (Figure 591 E), and the single submarginal cell (Figure 588 B). The square-headed wasps vary in their nesting habits; some nest in hollow stems or in abandoned galleries in wood (Figure 598 B), and others burrow in the ground. The principal prey utilized by these wasps is flies, but some species utilize various other types of insects. The adults are commonly found on flowers. The Oxybelìni, or spiny digger wasps, are a small group of rather uncommon wasps; they nest in sandy areas, and most species provision their nests with small flies; in some species the captured flies are carried impaled on the sting.

SUPERFAMILY **Apòidea**—Bees: Bees are common insects and are to be found almost everywhere, particularly on flowers; about 3500 species occur in North America. They differ from most of the wasps in that the young are fed honey and pollen rather than animal food; the honey is collected in the form of nectar from flowers and concentrated into honey by evaporation.

The bees resemble the sphecoid wasps in having the pronotum terminating laterally in rounded lobes that do not reach the tegulae. A distinctive feature that separates the bees from the wasps is the form of the body hairs; in the bees at least some of the body hairs, particularly those on the thorax, are branched or plumose, whereas the body hairs of wasps are simple and unbranched. The bees that are cleptoparasites, that is, which live as "cuckoos"[5] in the nests of other bees, are usually wasplike in appearance with relatively little body hair and without a pollen-transporting apparatus, and can be recognized as bees by their more flattened hind basitarsi, and the body hairs. The bees that are not parasitic, which construct a nest and collect pollen and have a pollen-transporting apparatus, are usually easily distinguished from wasps.

The distinctive features of the nonparasitic bees have to do largely with the transport of pollen (Figures 536 B and 599). Most bees are quite hairy, and as they visit flowers a certain

[5] The European cuckoo, like our cowbird, builds no nest, but lays its eggs in the nests of other birds, and its young are reared by the foster parents.

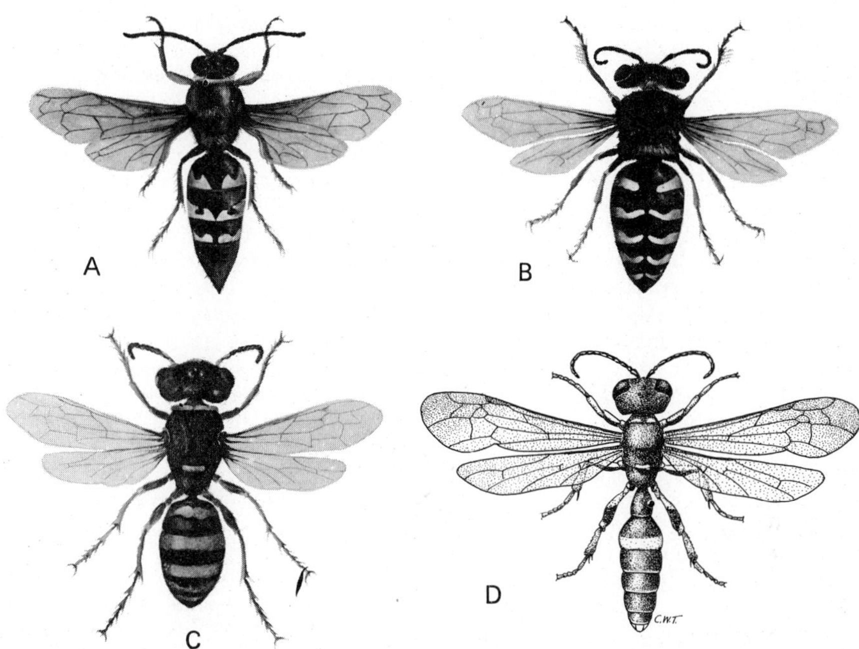

Figure 597. Sphecid wasps. A, cicada-killer wasp, *Sphècius speciòsus* (Drury) (Gorytìni, Nyssonìnae), about natural size; B, a sand wasp, *Bémbix americànus spinòlae* Lepeletier (Bembicìni, Nyssonìnae), slightly enlarged; C, a bee-killer wasp, *Philánthus ventrílabris* Fabricius (Philanthìni, Philanthìnae), 2 ×; D, a weevil wasp, *Cérceris clypeàta* Dahlbom (Cercerìni, Philanthìnae), 2 ×.

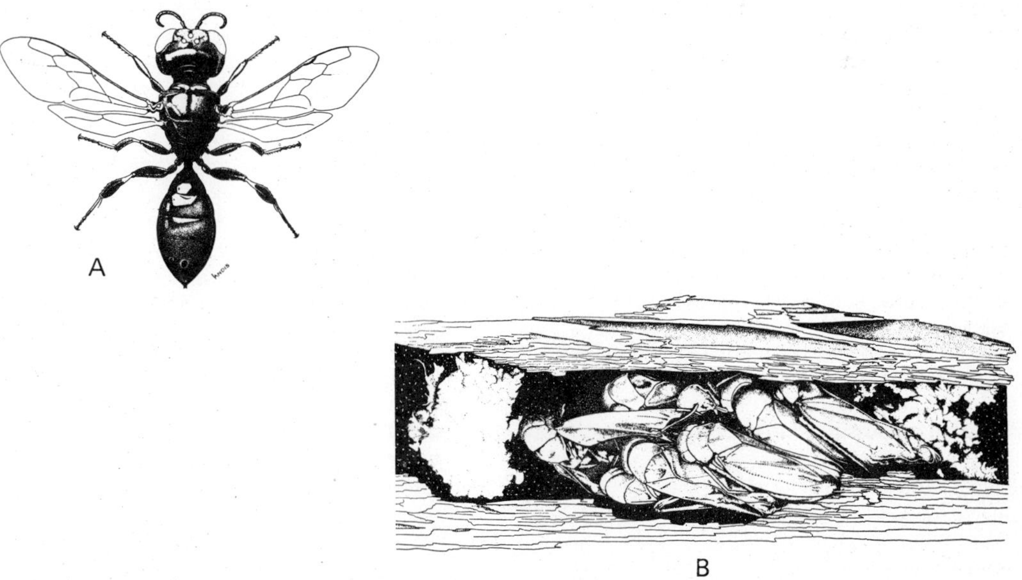

Figure 598. A square-headed wasp, *Crossócerus ambíguus* (Dahlbom). A, adult, 2 ×; B, a section of a rotting log in which this wasp has stored leafhoppers. (Courtesy of Davidson and Landis and the Entomological Society of America.)

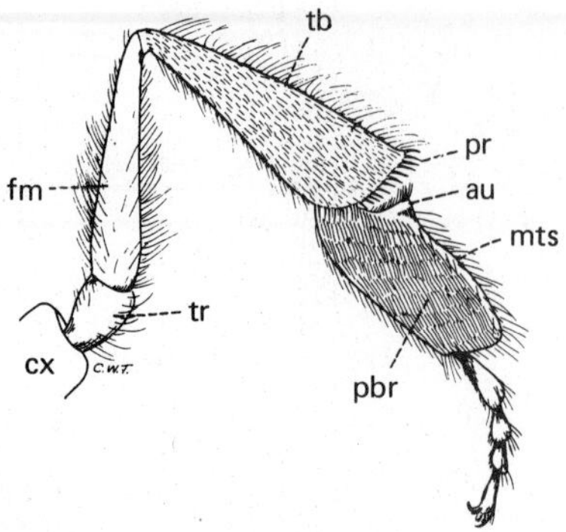

Figure 599. Hind leg of a honey bee, inner surface, showing the pollen-transporting apparatus. *au,* auricle; *cx,* coxa; *fm,* femur; *mts,* first tarsal segment; *pbr,* pollen brush; *pr,* pollen rake or pecten; *tb,* tibia; *tr,* trochanter. The pollen is collected off the body hairs by the front and middle legs and deposited on the pollen brushes (*pbr*) of the hind legs. The pollen on the pollen brush of one leg is raked off by the rake (*pr*) on the other, the pollen falling on the surface of the auricle (*au*); the closing of the tarsus on the tibia forces the pollen upward, where it adheres to the floor of the pollen basket or corbicula (which is on the outer surface of the tibia). As this process is repeated, first on one side and then on the other, the pollen is packed into the lower ends of the pollen baskets until both are filled (see Figure 600).

amount of pollen more or less accidentally sticks to their body hairs. This pollen is periodically combed off and transported on brushes of hairs called scopae (located on the ventral side of the abdomen in the Megachìlidae), or on corbiculae (the broad, shiny, slightly convex outer surfaces of the hind tibiae (Figure 536 B, *cb*), as in the social Apidae).

The maxillae and labium of bees form a tonguelike structure through which the insect sucks up nectar. There is some development of such a tongue in other Hymenóptera, but in most bees the tongue is elongate and the bee is thus able to reach the nectar in flowers with a deep corolla. The structure of the tongue differs considerably in different bees and provides characters that are used in classification.

The two sexes of bees differ in the number of antennal segments and abdominal tergites. The males have 13 antennal segments and 7 visible abdominal tergites; the females have only 12 antennal segments and 6 visible abdominal tergites.

The pollen-collecting bees play an extremely important role in the pollination of plants. Some of the higher plants are self-pollinating, but a great many are cross-pollinated, that is, the pollen of one flower must be transferred to the stigma of another. Crosspollination is brought about by two principal agencies, the wind and insects. Wind-pollinated plants include the grasses (such as the cereal grains, timothy, and the like), many trees (such as the willows, oaks, hickories, elms, poplars, and conifers), and many wild plants. The insect-pollinated plants include most of our orchard fruits, berries, many vegetables (particularly the cucurbits), many field crops (such as the clovers, cotton, and tobacco), and many flowers. Most of the pollination is done by bees, often chiefly honey bees and bumble bees, but a great deal of pollinating is done by certain solitary bees. Many growers, by bringing in hives of honey bees when the plants are in bloom, have been able to get greatly increased yields of orchard fruits, clover seed, and other crops that are dependent on bees for pollination. When it is realized that the annual value of the insect-pollinated crops in this country is about $6 billion, it will be apparent that the bees are extremely valuable insects.

The bees are very similar to the wasps in their nesting habits. Most species are solitary and nest in burrows in the ground, in cavities in plants, or in similar situations. The nests are always provisioned with nectar and pollen. A number of bees (the cuckoo bees) build no nest of their own, but lay their eggs in the nests of other bees; these are the parasitic bees. Two types of bees in the United States, honey bees and bumble bees, are highly social, and the colonies consist of a queen, workers, and drones (males). Some of our halictid bees (for example, some *Augochlorélla, Lasioglóssum,* and *Halíctus*) are primitively social.

There are differences of opinion about the classification of bees; the arrangement followed here is that of Michener (1974), in which the North American bees are classified in seven families.

Family **Collètidae**—Plasterer Bees and Yellow-Faced Bees: This is a rather primitive group of bees, with the tongue short and either truncate or bilobed at the apex (Figure 8 C). The family is divided into two subfamilies, the Colletìnae and the Hylaeìnae.

Subfamily **Colletìnae**—Plasterer Bees: These bees burrow into the ground to nest and line their burrows with a thin translucent substance. They

Figure 600. A honey bee collecting pollen. Note the large mass of pollen on the hind leg of this bee. (Courtesy of Teale.)

are of moderate size and are quite hairy, with bands of pale pubescence on the abdomen; there are three submarginal cells, and the second recurrent vein is sigmoid (Figure 538 D). These bees are not very common.

Subfamily **Hylaeìnae (Prosopìnae)**—Yellow-Faced Bees: The Hylaeìnae are small, black, very sparsely hairy bees, usually with yellowish markings on the face (Figure 601) and with only two submarginal cells (Figure 538 E). They are very wasplike in appearance, and the hind legs of the female do not have pollen brushes; pollen for larval food is carried to their nests in the crop, mixed with nectar, instead of on the body or legs. These bees nest in various sorts of cavities and crevices, in plant stems, or in burrows in the ground. North American species belong to the genus *Hylaèus,* and many are very common bees.

Family **Halíctidae:** The halictids are small to moderate-sized bees, often metallic, and can usually be recognized by the strongly arched basal vein (Figure 538 C). Most of them nest in burrows in the ground, either on level ground or in banks; the main tunnel is usually vertical, with lateral tunnels branching off from it and each terminating in a single cell. Larger numbers of these bees often nest close together, and many bees may use the same passageway to the outside. Nearly 500 species of halictids occur in our area.

Figure 601. A yellow-faced bee, *Hylaèus modéstus* Say, 10 ×.

Figure 602. Solitary bees. A, *Andrèna wilkélla* (Kirby) (Andrènidae); B, *Agapóstemon viréscens* (Fabricius) (Halíctidae).

Three subfamilies of halictids occur in the United States: the Halictìnae (the largest and most common of the three subfamilies), Nomiìnae, and Dufoureìnae. The Dufoureìnae, represented by the genus *Dufóurea,* differ from the other two subfamilies in that they have only two submarginal cells, and have the clypeus short, usually not longer than the labrum, and in profile strongly convex and protruding. The Nomiìnae, represented by the genus *Nòmia,* have the first and third submarginal cells about the same size; these bees are often of considerable importance in the pollination of plants. In the Halictìnae the third submarginal cell is shorter than the first; this group contains several genera of fairly common bees.

Subfamily **Halictìnae:** In *Agapóstemon* (Figure 602 B), *Augochloröpsis, Augochlorélla,* and *Augochlòra,* the head and thorax are a brilliant metallic greenish; these bees are small, 14 mm in length or less, and some of the bees in the genus *Augochlòra* are only a few millimeters in length. The other fairly common genera are *Halíctus, Lasioglóssum,* and *Sphecòdes*; these usually have the head and thorax black (in some species of *Halíctus* the head and thorax are metallic). In *Halíctus* the abdomen has apical bands of pale pubescence; in *Lasioglóssum* the abdomen lacks apical bands but often has basal bands of pale pubescence; and in *Sphecòdes* the abdomen is red. The bees in the genus *Sphecòdes* are rather wasplike in appearance, and are parasites (cleptoparasites) of other bees. Some members of the genus *Lasioglóssum* are frequently attracted to people who are perspiring, and are called sweat bees.

Family **Oxaèidae:** This group is chiefly tropical, and is represented in the United States by four species of *Protoxaèa* that occur in the Southwest. These bees are large and fast-flying, and nest in deep burrows in the soil.

Family **Andrènidae:** The andrenids are small to medium-sized bees that can be recognized by the two. subantennal sutures below each antennal socket (Figure 537 A). They nest in burrows in the ground, and their burrows are similar to those of the halictids; sometimes large numbers of these bees will nest close together, usually in areas where the vegatation is sparse.

The approximately 1285 species of andrenids in North America are arranged in two subfamilies, the Andrenìnae and Panurgìnae. The Andrenìnae have the apex of the marginal cell pointed or narrowly rounded and on the costal margin of the wing, and they usually have three submarginal cells (Figure 538 A). The Panurgìnae have the apex of the marginal cell truncate, and usually have only two submarginal cells (Figure 538 B). Most species of Andrenìnae (616 of our 670 species) belong to the genus *Andrèna* (Figure 602 A), and the majority of the Panurgìnae (448 species) belong to the genus *Pérdita*. The Panurgìnae are moderate-sized to minute, and many have yellow or other bright markings.

Family **Melíttidae:** The melittids are small, dark-colored, rather rare bees, similar in nesting habits to the Andrènidae. They differ from the bees in the preceding families in that they have the jugal lobe of the hind wing shorter than the submedian cell; they differ from the following families in that they

Figure 603. A leafcutting bee, *Megachìle latimànus* Say, 3 ×.

Figure 604. A cuckoo bee, *Triepèolus lunàtus* (Say) (Anthophòridae), 3 ×.

have the segments of the labial palps similar and cylindrical; the labial palps of the Megachìlidae, Anthophòridae, and Àpidae have the first two segments elongate and flattened. Our species nest in burrows in the soil.

Three subfamilies of Melíttidae occur in the United States: the Macropodìnae (with two submarginal cells and a very broad stigma), the Dasypodìnae (with two submarginal cells and a narrow stigma), and the Melittìnae (with three submarginal cells).

Family **Megachìlidae**—Leafcutting Bees: The leafcutting bees are mostly moderate-sized, fairly stout-bodied bees (Figure 603). They differ from most other bees in having two submarginal cells of about equal length (Figure 538 F), and the females of the pollen-collecting species carry the pollen by means of a scopa on the ventral side of the abdomen rather than on the hind legs. The common name of these bees is derived from the fact that in many species the nest cells are lined with pieces cut from leaves. These pieces are usually very neatly cut out, and it is not uncommon to find plants from which circular pieces have been cut by these bees. A few species in this family are parasitic. The nests are made in various places, occasionally in the ground but more often in some natural cavity, frequently in wood.

This family is divided into two subfamilies, the Lithurgìnae and the Megachilìnae. The former is represented in our area by a single genus, *Lithúrge* (with five species), which occurs chiefly in the South, and its members feed largely on cactus flowers; the Megachilìnae form a large group (over 630 North American species) of widespread distribution. Some of the more common genera of Megachilìnae are *Anthídium, Dianthídium, Stèlis, Herìades, Hóplitis, Ósmia, Megachìle,* and *Coelióxys*; the bees in the genera *Stèlis* and *Coelióxys* are parasitic. In *Coelióxys* the abdomen is somewhat conical and tapers posteriorly almost to a point. One introduced species of *Megachìle* is an important pollinator of alfalfa in the West.

Family **Anthophòridae**—Cuckoo Bees, Digger Bees, and Carpenter Bees: This family differs from the Àpidae (in which it was formerly classified) in having the hind tibiae with apical spurs, a jugal lobe in the hind wing, the genae very narrow, and the maxillary palps well developed. It is divided into three subfamilies, the Nomadìnae, Anthophorìnae, and Xylocopìnae.

Subfamily **Nomadìnae**—Cuckoo Bees: All the bees in this group are parasites in the nests of other bees; they belong to the tribes Neolarrìni, Townsendiellìni, Biastìni, Holcopasitìni, Ammobatìni, Nomadìni, Protepeolìni, and Epeoloidìni. They are usually wasplike in appearance and have relatively few hairs on the body. They lack a pollen-transporting apparatus, and have the clypeus somewhat protuberant, the front coxae lit-

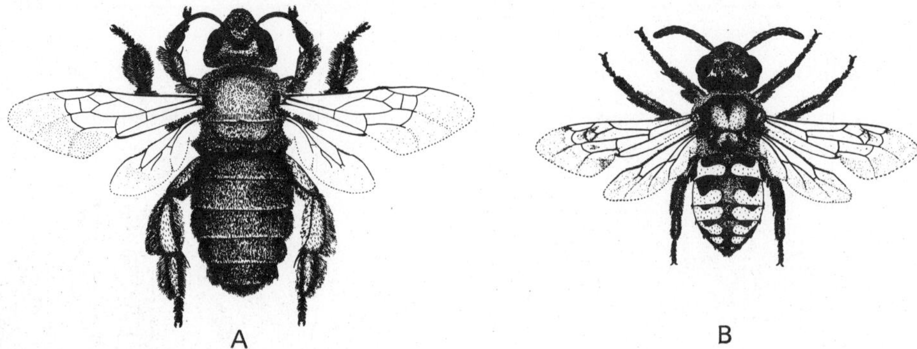

Figure 605. Anthophorid bees. A, a digger bee, *Anthóphora occidentàlis* Cresson, 2 ×; B, a cuckoo bee, *Melécta califórnica mirànda* Fox, 2 ×, an inquiline of *A. occidentàlis*. (Courtesy of Porter.)

tle broader than long, and the last abdominal tergite usually (at least in females) has a triangular platelike area. Some of these bees (for example, members of the genus *Nómada*) are usually reddish and of medium or small size; others (for example, *Epèolus* and *Triepèolus*) (Figure 604) are fair-sized (13–19 mm) and dark-colored, with small patches of pale pubescence.

Subfamily **Anthophorìnae**—Digger Bees: The digger bees resemble the Nomadìnae in the form of the clypeus, front coxae, and the tergal plate on the last abdominal segment, but are robust and hairy, and most of them are pollen-collecting. They nest in burrows in the ground or in banks, and the cells are lined with a thin wax or varnishlike substance. The pollen-collecting tribes in the subfamily are the Exomalopsìni, Melitomìni, Eucerìni, Anthophorìni, and Centridìni; the bees in the tribes Melectìni, Ctenoschelìni, and Rathymìni are mostly large hairy bees that lack a pollen transport apparatus, and are usually parasitic on their close relatives (for example, *Melécta* or *Anthóphora*, Figure 605).

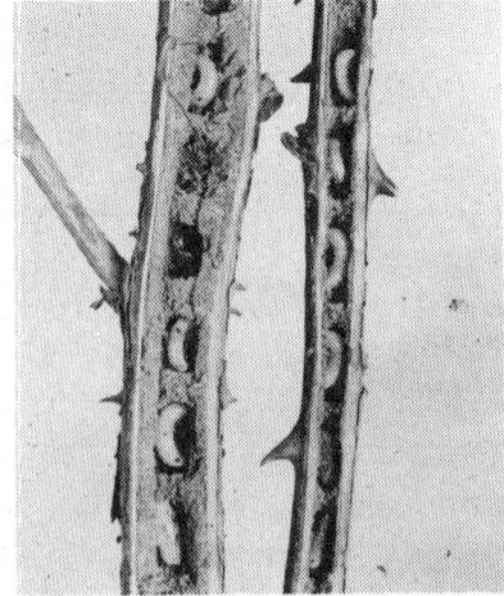

Figure 606. Nest of the small carpenter bee, *Ceratìna dùpla* Say.

Subfamily **Xylocopìnae**—Carpenter Bees: These bees do not have the clypeus protuberant, the front coxae are transverse, and the last abdominal tergite lacks a triangular platelike area. These bees make their nests in wood or in plant stems. The two genera in this group, *Ceratìna* and *Xylocòpa*, differ somewhat in habits, and their members differ considerably in size. The small carpenter bees (*Ceratìna*) are dark bluish green and about 6 mm in length; they are superficially similar to some of the halictids, particularly since the basal vein is noticeably arched, but may be distinguished from a halictid by the much smaller jugal lobe in the hind wings (compare Figures 538 C and 539 F). These bees excavate the pith from the stems of various bushes and nest in the tunnels so produced (Figure 606). The large carpenter bees (*Xylocòpa*) are robust bees about 25 mm in length, similar in appearance to bumble bees, but have the dorsum of the abdomen largely bare (Figure 607 A), and the second submarginal cell is triangular (Figure 539 A); these bees excavate galleries in solid wood.

Family **Àpidae**—Bumble Bees, Honey Bees, and Euglossine Bees: The Àpidae differ from the Anthophòridae in that they have the maxillary palps vestigial, the genal area broad, corbiculae on the hind legs, and they lack a pygidial plate; most Àpidae are social.

Figure 607. A, a large carpenter bee, *Xylocòpa virgínica* (L.) (Xylocopìnae); B, a bumble bee, *Bómbus pennsylvánicus* (De Geer) (Bombìnae). 1½ ×.

Figure 608. Honey bee, *Àpis mellífera* L., 5 ×.

Subfamily **Bombìnae**—Bumble Bees: Bumble bees can usually be recognized by their robust shape and black and yellow coloration (Figure 607 B); a few are marked with orange. They are relatively large bees, most of them being 20 mm or more in length. The hind wings lack a jugal lobe (Figure 539 B). Bumble bees are very common insects, and they are important pollinators of certain kinds of clover because of their very long tongues.

Most bumble bees nest in the ground, usually in a deserted mouse nest or bird nest or similar situation. The colonies are annual (at least in temperate regions), and only the fertilized queens overwinter. In the spring, the queen selects a nest site and begins construction of the nest; the first brood raised by the queen consists of workers. Once the workers appear, they take over all the duties of the colony except egg laying; they enlarge the nest, collect food and store it in little saclike "honey pots," and care for the larvae. Later in the summer, males and queens are produced, and in the fall all but these queens die.

Bumble bees in the genus *Psíthyrus* are parasites of other bumble bees (*Bómbus*). *Psíthyrus* females differ from those of *Bómbus* in having the outer surface of the hind tibiae convex and hairy (flat or concave and largely bare in *Bómbus*). These bees have no worker caste; the females invade the nests of other bumble bees and lay their eggs, leaving their young to be reared by the workers of the host nest. In the absence of a worker caste, the males of *Psíthyrus* can usually be readily distinguished in the field from females by their smaller size.

Subfamily **Apìnae**—Honey Bees: Honey bees may be recognized by their golden brown coloration and characteristic shape (Figures 600 and 608), the form of the marginal and submarginal cells in the front wing (Figure 539 D), and the absence of spurs on the hind tibiae. These bees are common and well-known insects, and they are the most important bees in the pollination of plants. They are extremely valuable insects, as they produce some $75 million worth of honey and beeswax annually, and their pollinating activities are worth 15 or 20 times this amount.

Only a single species of honey bee occurs in this country, *Àpis mellífera* L.; this is an introduced species, and most of its colonies are in man-made hives; escaped swarms usually nest in a hollow tree. The cells in the nest are in vertical combs, two cell layers thick. Honey bee colonies are perennial, with the queen and workers overwintering in the hive; a queen may live several years. Unlike the bumble bee queen, the honey bee queen is unable to start a colony by herself. As in most of the Hymenóptera, the sex of a bee is determined by the fertilization of the egg; fertilized eggs develop into females, and unfertilized eggs develop into males. Whether a larval honey bee destined to become a female becomes a worker or queen depends on the sort of food it is fed. There is normally only one queen in a honey bee colony; when a new one is produced, it may be killed by the old queen, or one of the queens (usually the old queen) may leave the hive in a swarm, along with a group of workers, and build a nest elsewhere. The new queen mates during a mating flight, and thereafter never leaves the nest except to swarm. The males serve only to fertilize the queen; they do not remain in the colony long, as they are eventually killed by the workers.

Honey bees have a very interesting "language," a means of communicating with one another (see Frisch, 1967, 1971). When a worker goes out and discovers a flower with a good nectar flow, she returns to the hive and "tells" the other workers about it—the type of flower, its direction from the hive, and how far away it is. The type of flower involved is communicated by means of its odor, either on the body hairs of the returning bee or in the nectar it brings back from the flower. The distance and direction of the flower from the hive are "told" by means of a peculiar sort of dance put on by the returning worker. Many social insects have a "language" or a means of communication, but its exact nature is known in relatively few cases.

Subfamily **Euglossìnae:** The euglossine bees are brilliant metallic, often brightly colored bees that are tropical in distribution. They have a very long tongue, they have apical spurs on the hind tibiae, they lack a jugal lobe in the hind wings, and the scutellum is produced backward over the abdomen. One species in this group has been recorded from Brownsville, Texas.

COLLECTING AND PRESERVING HYMENÓPTERA

Most of the general collecting methods described in Chapter 34 will apply to the insects in this order. Species of Hymenóptera are to be found almost everywhere, and to secure a large variety of species, one should examine all available habitats and use all available methods of collecting. Many of the larger and more showy Hymenóptera are common on flowers. The parasitic species may be reared from parasitized hosts, or they may be taken by sweeping. Many insects in this order are attracted to lights, malaise traps (Figure 617 C), or to various types of molasses baits.

Since many of the Hymenóptera sting, it is well to exercise a certain amount of care in removing them from the net. The simplest way is to get the insect into a fold of the net and stun it by pinching the thorax; then it may be transferred to the killing bottle. If one has a pair of forceps, he can grasp the insect through the net with the forceps and transfer it to the killing bottle. A third method, which is considerably slower, is to get the insect into a fold of the net and then put this fold into the killing jar until the insect is stunned. Some of the large ichneumons that have the abdomen laterally flattened (subfamily Ophionìnae) are able to "sting" by jabbing with their short sharp ovipositor; such insects should be grasped through the net by the *abdomen*; this way, since the insect cannot move its abdomen, it cannot jab with the ovipositor. Many stinging Hymenóptera feeding on flowers can be collected directly into a killing jar without the use of a net.

The smaller Hymenóptera should be mounted on their side on a point, or if they are extremely minute, they should be preserved in liquid or mounted on a microscope slide. It is usually necessary to mount the more minute forms on microscope slides for detailed study. Some of the best characters for the identification of bees are in the mouth parts; hence the mouth parts of these insects should be extended if possible. All specimens, whether pinned or mounted on points, should be oriented so that the leg and thoracic characters and venation can be easily seen. The Hymenóptera are generally harder-bodied than the Díptera and are less likely to be damaged in handling.

References on the Hymenóptera

Ashmead, W. H. 1904. Classification of the chalcid flies or the superfamily Chalcidoidea, with descriptions of new species in the Carnegie Museum. *Carnegie Mus. Mem.*, 1(4):225–551; illus.

Askew, R. R. 1971. *Parasitic Insects.* New York: American Elsevier, xx + 316 pp., 124 f.

Bischoff, H. 1927. *Biologie der Hymenopteren.* Berlin: Verlag Julius Springer, 598 pp., 224 f.

Bohart, R. M., and A. S. Menke, 1963. A reclassification of the Sphecinae, with a revision of the nearctic species of the tribes Sceliphronini and Sphecini (Hymenoptera: Sphecidae). *Univ. Calif. Pub. Ent.*, 30(2):91–182; 115 f.

Clausen, C. P. 1940. *Entomophagous Insects.* New York: McGraw-Hill, x + 688 pp., 257 f. (Hymenoptera, pp. 3–342, f. 2–156.)

Cole, A. C. 1968. *Pogonomyrmex Harvester Ants. A Study of the Genus in North America.* Knoxville: Univ. Tennessee Press, x + 222 pp., 201 f., 11 pl., 1 tab., 13 maps.

Creighton, W. S. 1950. *The ants of North America.* Harvard Univ., Mus. Comp. Zool. Bull. 104; 585 pp.; illus.

Dasch, C. E. 1964. *Ichneumon-flies of America north of Mexico. 5. Subfamily Diplazontinae.* Mem. Amer. Ent. Inst. 3; 304 pp., 153 f., 111 maps.

Duncan, C. D. 1939. A contribution to the biology of North American vespine wasps. *Stanford Univ. Pub., Univ. Ser. Biol. Sci.*, 8(1):1–272; 54 pl.

Eberhard, M. J. W. 1969. *The social biology of the polistine wasps.* Misc. Pub. Mus. Zool. Univ. Mich. 140; 101 pp., 23 f.

Eichwort, G. C. 1969. A comparative morphological study and generic revision of the augochlorine bees (Hymenoptera: Halictidae). *Kan. Univ. Sci. Bull.*, 48:325–524; 418 f., 4 tab.

Evans, H. E. 1963. *Wasp Farm.* Garden City, N.Y.: Natural History Press, viii + 178 pp., 25 pl., 16 f.

Evans, H. E., and M. J. W. Eberhard. 1970. *The Wasps.* Ann Arbor: Univ. Michigan Press, vii + 265 pp., 122 f.

Evans, H. E., and C. M. Yoshimoto. 1962. The ecology and nesting behavior of the Pompilidae (Hymenoptera) of the northeastern United States. *Misc. Pub. Ent. Soc. Amer.*, 3(3):65–120.

Felt, E. P. 1940. *Plant Galls and Gall Makers.* Ithaca, N.Y.: Comstock Publ., 364 pp., 344 f., 41 pl.

Frisch, K. von. 1967. *The Dance Language and Orientation of Bees.* Cambridge, Mass.; Belknap Press of Harvard Univ. Press, xv + 566 pp.; illus.

Frisch, K. von. 1971 (rev. ed.). *Bees, Their Vision, Chemical Senses, and Language.* Ithaca, N.Y.: Cornell Univ. Press, xviii + 157 pp., 76 f.

Gregg, R. E. 1963. *The Ants of Colorado, Their Taxonomy, Ecology, and Geographic Distribution.* Boulder, Colo.: Univ. Colorado Press, 792 pp., 26 tab., 24 pl., 16 maps, 163 additional charts, 1 col. vegetation map.

Grout, R. A. (Ed.). 1949. *The Hive and the Honey Bee.* Hamilton, Ill.: Dadant and Sons, xviii + 652 pp., 305 f.

Kinsey, A. C. 1930. The gall wasp *Cynips.* A study in the origin of species. *Indiana Univ. Stud.*, 16:1–577; 429 f.

Kinsey, A. C. 1936. *The origin of higher categories in Cynips.* Indiana Univ. Publ., Sci. Ser., Contrib. from Dept. Zoology, No. 242; 334 pp., 172 f.

Krombein, K. V. 1967. *Trap-Nesting Wasps and Bees.* Washington, D.C.: Smithsonian Press, 576 pp.; illus.

LaBerge, W. E., *et al.* 1967–1972. A revision of the bees in the genus *Andrena* of the western hemisphere. Part I (1967): *Callandrena; Bull. Univ. Nebr. State Mus.*, 7:1–316; 340 f., 4 tab. Part II (1969): *Plastandrena, Aporandrena, Charitandrena; Trans. Amer. Ent. Soc.*, 95(1):1–47; 38 f. Part III (by W. E. LaBerge and J. K. Bousman) (1970): *Tylandrena; Trans. Amer. Ent. Soc.*, 96(4):543–605; 75 f. Part IV (1971): *Scraptopsis, Xiphandrena,* and *Rhaphandrena; Trans. Amer. Ent. Soc.*, 97(3):441–520; 68 f. Part V (by W. E. LaBerge and D. W. Ribble) (1972): *Gonandrena, Geissandrena, Parandrena, Pelicandrena; Trans. Amer. Ent. Soc.*, 98(3):271–358; 76 f.

Lanham, U. N. 1951. Review of the wing venation of the higher Hymenoptera (suborder Clistogastra), and speculations on the phylogeny of the Hymenoptera. *Ann. Ent. Soc. Amer.*, 44(4):614–628; 27 f.

Malyshev, S. I. 1968. *Genesis of the Hymenoptera and the Phases of Their Evolution.* London: Methuen (translated from Russian), viii + 319 pp.; illus.

Marsh, P. M. 1963. A key to the nearctic subfamilies of the family Braconidae (Hymenoptera). *Ann. Ent. Soc. Amer.*, 56(4):522–527; 29 f.

Michener, C. D. 1944. Comparative external morphology, phylogeny, and a classification of the bees (Hymenoptera). *Amer. Mus. Nat. Hist. Bull.*, 82(6):151–326; 13 diag., 246 f.

Michener, C. D. 1974. *The Social Behavior of Bees. A Comparative Study.* Cambridge, Mass.: Belknap Press of Harvard Univ. Press, xii + 404 pp.; illus.

Michener, C. D., and M. H. Michener. 1951. *American Social Insects.* New York: Van Nostrand, xiv + 267 pp., 109 f.

Mitchell, T. B. 1960–1962. *Bees of eastern United States.* Vol. 1, Tech. Bull. 141, N.C. Agric. Expt. Sta., 1960; 538 pp., 134 f. Vol. 2, *op. cit.*, Bull. 152, 1962;

557 pp., 134 f.

Muesebeck, C. F. W., K. V. Krombein, H. K. Townes, *et al.* 1951–1967. Hymenoptera of America north of Mexico; synoptic catalog. USDA Agric. Monog. 2 (1951); 1420 pp. First Supplement to USDA Agric. Monog. 2 (1958); 305 pp. Second Supplement to USDA Agric. Monog. 2 (1967); 584 pp.

Peterson, A. 1948. *Larvae of Insects*. Part I. *Lepidoptera and Plant-Infesting Hymenoptera*. Ann Arbor, Mich.: Edwards Bros., 315 pp., 84 f.

Richards, O. W. 1956. Handbooks for the identification of British insects. Hymenoptera: Introduction and key to families. *Roy. Ent. Soc. London,* 6(1):1–94; 197 f., 22 pl. (Other papers in this series, by various authors, cover various groups of Hymenoptera.)

Ross, H. H. 1936. The ancestry and wing venation of the Hymenoptera. *Ann. Ent. Soc. Amer.,* 29(1):99–111; 2 pl.

Ross, H. H. 1937. A generic classification of nearctic sawflies (Hymenoptera, Symphyta). *Ill. Biol. Monog.,* 15(2):1–173; 1 chart, 424 f.

Schneirla, T. C. 1971. *Army Ants. A Study in Social Organization*. San Francisco: W. H. Freeman, xxii + 350 pp.; illus.

Smith, E. L. 1970. Evolutionary morphology of the external genitalia. 2. Hymenoptera. *Ann. Ent. Soc. Amer.,* 63(1):11–27; 15 f.

Smith, M. R. 1943. A generic and subgeneric synopsis of the male ants of the United States. *Amer. Midl. Nat.,* 30:273–321; 7 f.

Smith, M. R. 1947. A generic and subgeneric synopsis of the United States ants, based on workers (Hymenoptera, Formicidae). *Amer. Midl. Nat.,* 37:521–647; illus.

Spradbery, J. P. 1973. *Wasps. An Account of the Biology and Natural History of Social and Solitary Wasps*. Seattle: Univ. Washington Press, 416 pp., 135 f., 28 pl. (9 in color).

Townes, H. 1969. The genera of Ichneumonidae. *Mem. Amer. Ent. Inst.,* No. 11 (part 1), 300 pp., 134 f.; No. 12 (part 2), 537 pp., 311 f.; No. 13 (part 3), 307 pp., 185 f.

Townes, H., and V. K. Gupta. 1962. *Ichneumon-flies of America north of Mexico. 4. Subfamily Gelinae, tribe Hemigasterini*. Mem. Amer. Ent. Inst. 2; 305 pp., 116 f., 162 maps.

Viereck, H. L., *et al.* 1916. The Hymenoptera, or wasp-like insects, of Connecticut. *Bull. Geol. and Nat. Hist. Surv. State of Conn.,* 22:1–824; 15 f., 10 pl.

Weber, N. A. 1972. *Gardening ants, the attines*. Mem. Amer. Philos. Soc. 92, xx + 146 pp.; illus.

Wheeler, G. C., and J. Wheeler. 1972. The subfamilies of Formicidae. *Proc. Ent. Soc. Wash.,* 74(1):35–45; 10 f.

Wheeler, W. M. 1910. *Ants, Their Structure, Development, and Behavior*. New York: Columbia Univ. Press, xxvi + 663 pp., 286 f.

Wheeler, W. M. 1928. *The Social Insects, Their Origin and Evolution*. New York: Harcourt, Brace and World, xvii + 378 pp., 79 f.

Wilson, E. O. 1971. *The Insect Societies*. Cambridge, Mass.: Harvard Univ. Press, x + 548 pp.; illus.

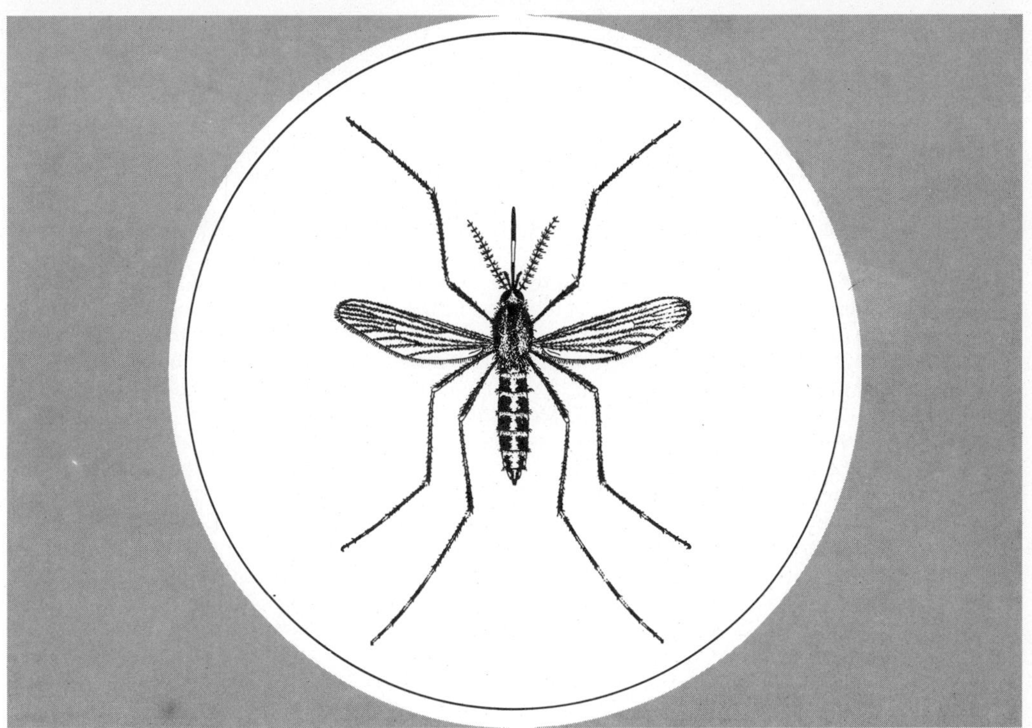

33: THE RELATION OF INSECTS TO MAN

On the basis of their relation to man, insects may be classified into two general groups, beneficial and injurious. Many insects may be considered neutral because their numbers are so small or their habits are such that no direct effects are felt by man.

Man benefits from insects in many ways; without them, human society could not exist in its present form. Without the pollinating services of bees and other insects, we would have few vegetables, few fruits, little or no clover (and hence much less beef, mutton, and wool), no coffee, no tobacco, few flowers—in fact, we should not have a great many of the things that are an integral part of our domestic economy and civilization. Insects provide us with honey, beeswax, silk, and many other useful products. Many species are parasitic or predaceous and are important in keeping the pest species under control; others help in the control of noxious weeds; and still others clean up refuse and make the world a little more pleasant. Insects are the sole or major item of food of many birds, fish, and other animals (including man in some parts of the world). Some species have been used in the treatment of certain diseases. The study of insects has helped scientists solve many problems in heredity, evolution, sociology, stream pollution, and other fields. Insects also have aesthetic value; artists, milliners, and designers have made use of their beauty, and many people derive a great deal of pleasure from the study of insects as a hobby.

On the other hand, many insects are obnoxious or destructive. They attack various growing plants, including plants of value to man, and feed on them, injure or kill them, or introduce disease into them. They attack man's possessions, including his home, his clothing, and his food stores, and destroy, damage, or contaminate them. They attack man and animals and are annoying because of their presence, odors, bites, or stings, and many are agents in the transmission of some of the most serious diseases that beset man and animals.

Most people are much more aware of the injurious insects and their effects than they are of the beneficial insects, and the injurious species are probably better known than the beneficial ones. In spite of the excessive attention paid to injurious insects by the public in general and entomologists in particular, we believe that the good done by the beneficial insects outweighs the harm done by the injurious ones.

BENEFICIAL INSECTS

It is difficult to estimate in terms of dollars and cents the value of insects to man. The pollinating services of insects are worth at least $6 billion annually, and commercial products derived from insects are worth about $175 million more. It seems safe to say that insects are worth nearly $7 billion annually.

INSECTS AND POLLINATION

Sexual reproduction in the higher plants is made possible by the process of pollination. This process consists of the pollen (the male germ cells) being transferred from the stamens to the stigma; from the stigma a pollen tube grows down the style to the female germ cell. This process must take place in practically every case before the flower will bear seed. As the seed develops, the tissues around it swell and form the fruit.

A few of the higher plants are self-pollinating, but the majority are cross pollinated, that is, the pollen of one flower must be transferred to the stigma of another. Pollen is transferred from one flower to another in two principal ways, by the wind and by insects. Wind-pollinated plants produce a large amount of dry pollen which is blown far and wide; such plants manage to reproduce because a few of the millions of pollen grains produced happen to land on the stigma of the right flower. Insect-pollinated plants produce smaller amounts of pollen, which is usually sticky and adheres to the bodies of insects that visit the flower; this pollen is later rubbed off the insect onto the stigma of another flower, in most cases more or less by accident as far as the insect is concerned.

Many flowers have peculiar features of structure that help to ensure pollination. Some, such as the iris, are so constructed that an insect cannot get to the nectar without collecting pollen on its body and cannot enter the next flower of this same kind without leaving some of the pollen on the stigma of that flower. Milkweeds have special pollen masses, the pollinia, which are arranged in such a way that when an insect alights on the edge of the flower, its legs slip into a fissure in the pollinia; the pollinia then become attached to the insect's leg and are carried to the next flower.

Some plants are dependent upon a single species or type of insect for pollination. Some of the orchids are pollinated only by certain long-tongued hawk moths. The Smyrna fig is pollinated by the fig wasp, *Blastóphaga psènes* (L.) (see page 622), and yuccas are pollinated solely by yucca moths (*Tegetícula*) (see page 510).

The plants that are wind-pollinated and hence not dependent upon insects include corn, wheat, rye, oats, timothy, and other grasses; trees such as the willows, oaks, hickories, elms, poplars, birches, and conifers; and many wild plants such as ragweed and pigweed. On the other hand, such orchard fruits as apples, pears, plums, cherries, citrus fruits, and nuts; strawberries, raspberries, blackberries, cranberries, and blueberries; such vegetables as melons, cucumbers, pumpkins, squash, cabbage, onions, and carrots; such field crops as the clovers and tobacco; and many flowers—all are dependent upon insects for pollination.

The rosaceous plants (apple, pear, cherry, blackberry, strawberry) are dependent chiefly upon honey bees for pollination; the clovers are dependent upon various bees, chiefly honey bees and bumble bees. Many plants with strongly scented and conspicuous nocturnal flowers, such as honeysuckle, tobacco, and petunias, are pollinated not only by bees but also by certain moths. Umbelliferous plants like carrots and parsnips are pollinated chiefly by various flies, bees, and wasps. Pond lilies, goldenrod, and some other flowers are pollinated by bees and certain beetles.

Clover is an important farm crop in many parts of the country and is used as hay and forage and to enrich the soil. The average annual crop of clover seed in Ohio (250,000 bushels) would plant some 3 million acres in clover; this acreage would yield about 4.5 million tons of hay (worth about $100 million) and add about 273 million pounds of nitrogen to the soil (worth about $60 million). Red clover and alsike are entirely dependent on insects for pollination and seed production, and sweet clover and alfalfa, though somewhat self-pollinated, depend on insect pollination for profitable seed yields. The job of pollinating clover is tremendous; an acre of red clover, for example, contains about 216 million individual flowers, and every one of these must be visited by an insect before it will produce seed. Under normal field conditions (at least in Ohio) about 82 percent of the pollinating of red clover is done by honey bees and 15 percent by bumble bees. The average seed yields of red clover and alsike in Ohio are about 1.0 and 1.6 bushels per acre, respectively; with a dense honey bee population in clover fields, these yields can be increased to 4 and 8 bushels per acre, and with maximum insect pollination, they can be increased to 12 and 20 bushels per acre.

Sheep may be raised on grasses that are wind-pollinated, but a practical sheep raiser prefers clovers. Some years ago the sheep growers in New Zealand imported red-clover seed to improve their pastures. The clover grew all right, but produced no seed for the next year's crop because there were no suitable insects in New Zealand to pollinate the clover. After bumble bees were introduced there and had become established, thus making possible the pollination of clover, there was continuous good grazing for New Zealand sheep.

Orchard fruits, with the possible exception of sour cherries and most peaches, are largely or entirely insect pollinated, and this job is done chiefly by bees. Experiments involving the use of cages over orchard trees have shown that if bees are excluded from the tree when it is in bloom, the set of fruit is usually less than 1 percent of the blooms; if a hive of bees is caged with a tree, the set of fruit is increased, in some cases to as high as 44 percent of the blooms. Such experiments indicate that the fruit yields in orchards can be greatly increased by the use of bees. Although many factors complicate the problem of orchard pollination, a large number of growers obtain considerably increased yields of fruit by placing hives of bees in their orchards when the trees are in bloom.

The value to man of the pollinating insects is enormous; the annual yields of insect-pollinated plants in this country are valued at about $6 billion. Of all the insects that pollinate plants, the most important is the honey bee; this insect is highly prized for its honey and wax, but for every dollar's worth of honey and wax it produces, 15 or 20 dollars' worth of pollinating services are rendered to agriculture.

COMMERCIAL PRODUCTS DERIVED FROM INSECTS

HONEY AND BEESWAX The production of honey is a very old industry, dating back to the time of the Pharaohs. Honey bees are not native to the United States, but were introduced into this country in about 1638. Several strains of this insect now occur here. Honey is used extensively as a food and in the manufacture of many products. Beeswax is used extensively by industry in making candles, sealing wax, polishes, certain types of inks, models of various kinds, dental impressions, cosmetics, and other products.

Beekeeping is a multimillion-dollar industry. Florida, which ranked first in the nation in honey production in 1972, had some 350,000 colonies, and a total honey production of 26,600,000 pounds (worth $10 to $15 million to the beekeeper). The several million colonies of bees in the United States produce about 240 million pounds of honey and about 4½ million pounds of wax annually, a production worth nearly $75 million.

SILK The silk industry is an ancient one, extending as far back as 2500 B.C. The rearing of silkworms and the processing and weaving of silk are principally an oriental industry, but they are practiced to some extent in a number of other countries, especially Spain, France, and Italy. Several types of silkworms have been utilized for the production of commercial silk, but the most important is *Bómbyx mòri* (L.), a domesticated species. Although silk is at the present time being replaced by various synthetic fibers, it is still a very important industry; the annual world production of silk is about 65 to 75 million pounds.

SHELLAC Shellac is produced from the secretions of the lac insect, *Láccifer lácca* (Kern), a type of scale insect occurring on fig, banyan, and other plants in India, Burma, Indo-China, Formosa, Ceylon, and the Philippine Islands. These insects form encrustations 6 to 13 mm thick on the twigs of the host plant. The twigs containing these encrustations are collected and ground; the "seed lac" so formed is melted and dried in sheets or flakes, which are shipped to a processing plant where the shellac is made. About $9 million worth of shellac is used annually in the United States.

DYES AND OTHER MATERIALS Several insects have been used in the manufacture of dyes. The cochineal insect, *Dactylòpius cóccus* Costa, a scale insect somewhat similar to the mealybugs, is used for the production of cochineal dyes. These insects feed on *Opúntia* cacti (prickly pear) in the southwestern states and Mexico. The dye obtained from these insects is crimson in color and is produced from the dried bodies of the insects. This dye is now largely replaced by aniline dyes. Dyes have also been made from other types of scale insects and from certain cynipid galls. Some of the cynipid galls have also been used as a source of tannic acid, which is used in the manufacture of ink and for other purposes. Certain drugs, such as cantharidin, which is made from the dried bodies of a European blister beetle, the spanishfly, *Lytta vesicatòria* L., have been made from insects. Many insects, such as hellgrammites and crickets, are often sold as fish bait.

ENTOMOPHAGOUS INSECTS

Insects have a high reproductive capacity and are potentially able to build up tremendous populations, but they seldom do so, largely because of the many animals that feed on them. A considerable proportion of these entomophagous, or insect-eating, animals are insects. The check exerted upon insect pests by entomophagous insects is a very important factor in keeping down the populations of pest species. Probably nothing that man can do in controlling insects by other methods will compare with the control exerted by entomophagous animals, yet the public has little knowledge or appreciation of this enormous benefit to man (see pages 62–63).

A classic example of the successful control of an insect pest by means of a predator is that of the cottony cushion scale, *Icérya púrchasi* Maskell, a serious pest of citrus in California, by a ladybird beetle. This scale was first found in California in 1868, and in 15 years threatened to destroy the citrus industry in southern California. In 1888–1889 a ladybird beetle, *Rodòlia cardinàlis* (Mulsant), was introduced from Australia (where it was thought the scale originated), and in less than two years the scale was under complete control.

While we have here classified predaceous and parasitic insects as beneficial to man, it should be understood that their economic importance is determined by the insect they attack; if the species attacked is injurious, the entomophagous insect is considered beneficial, but if it attacks a beneficial species, it is considered injurious.

INSECTS AS SCAVENGERS

The insect scavengers are those that feed on decomposing plants or animals or on dung. Such insects assist in converting these materials into simpler substances which are returned to the soil where they are available to plants; they also serve to remove unhealthful and obnoxious materials from man's surroundings. Insects such as the wood-boring beetles, termites, carpenter ants, and other wood feeders are important agents in hastening the conversion of fallen trees and logs to soil; the galleries of these insects serve as avenues of entrance for fungi and other decay organisms that hasten the breakdown of the wood. Dung beetles (Scarabaèidae, Histéridae, and others) and dung flies (principally various muscoids) hasten the decomposition of dung. Carrion-feeding insects such as blow flies, carrion beetles, skin beetles (Derméstidae and Trogìnae), and others are of considerable value in the removal of carrion from the landscape. The insect scavengers are essential to maintaining a balance in nature.

Some of the dung-feeding scarabs have been introduced into Australia to reduce fly populations in cattle areas. These beetles feed on cow dung, and they clean up the dung so quickly that the flies breeding in the dung do not have time to complete their development.

THE IMPORTANCE OF SOIL INSECTS

Many types of insects spend a part of or all their lives in the soil. The soil provides the insect a home or nest, protection, and often food; it is tunneled in such a way that it becomes more aerated, and it is enriched by the excretions and dead bodies of the insects. Soil insects improve the physical properties of the soil and add to its organic content.

Soil insects vary in feeding habits. Many feed on humus or decaying plant materials; some feed on the underground parts of growing plants (and may be injurious); many are scavengers. Many feed above ground and use the soil only as a nest site; some of these, such as ants, digger wasps, and bees, bring food into the soil in connection with feeding the young.

Soil insects are often very numerous; the populations of springtails alone may be many millions per acre. Ants are sometimes extremely abundant;

they generally nest in the soil and feed above ground. Other important soil-inhabiting insects are the mole crickets, cicadas (nymphal stages), termites, various burrowing bees and wasps, many beetles and flies (usually in the larval stage only), and some aphids.

INSECTS AS DESTROYERS OF UNDESIRABLE PLANTS

A large proportion of the insects feed on plants, but only a small number of these are considered pests; many of the others may be beneficial by destroying noxious weeds, cacti, or certain undesirable deciduous plants. It often happens that when a plant is introduced into a geographic area, it thrives to such an extent that it becomes a pest; in some cases plant-feeding insects have been introduced to bring this plant under control.

Prickly pear cacti (*Opúntia* spp.) were at one time introduced into Australia, and by 1925 had spread over some 25 million acres to form a dense, impenetrable growth. In 1925 a moth, *Cactoblástis cactòrum* (Berg), the larvae of which burrow in the cactus plants was introduced into Australia from Argentina. As a result of the feeding of this moth, the dense cactus growth is now reduced to about 1 percent of the area it occupied in 1925.

A European species of St. Johnswort, *Hypéricum perforàtum* L., was introduced about 1900 into northern California. It became particularly abundant in the vicinity of the Klamath River, and is commonly called Klamath weed or goatweed. By the middle 1940s it had spread over about $2\frac{1}{3}$ million acres of range land in California and over extensive acreage in other western states. This plant is considered a serious pest because it replaces desirable range plants and is poisonous to livestock. Attempts to control it by chemicals were expensive and not entirely effective. From 1944 to 1948 a few species of European beetles (chrysomelids and buprestids) were imported into California to control Klamath weed; one of the chysomelids, *Chrysolìna quadrigémina* (Rossi), proved particularly effective. The Klamath weed has now been reduced to about 1 percent of its former abundance, and more desirable plants on this range have increased.

Alligatorweed, *Alternánthera philoxeròides* (Martius) Grisebach, is an aquatic plant native to South America that first appeared in this country (in Florida) in 1894, and has subsequently spread throughout the Southeast, and westward to Texas and California. It is a plant that forms dense mats near the water surface, impeding boat traffic, blocking drainage canals, killing fish and other wildlife by crowding out desirable food plants, providing habitats for mosquitoes, and contributing to water pollution. The area infested with this plant in 1970 was estimated to be some 70,000 acres. Herbicides have not been successful in controlling this plant, and studies of its insect enemies in South America indicated that three species might help to control the plant in this country, a thrips, *Amỳnothrips ándersoni* O'Neill, a pyralid stem borer, *Vògtia málloi* Pastrana, and a flea beetle, *Agásicles* sp. These were brought to this country and released, the first introduction being in 1964. The flea beetle and thrips have become established, and are most abundant in Florida; the beetle, particularly, appears to be providing good control of the alligatorweed.

Three species of ragweeds (*Ambròsia* spp.) have recently been introduced into Eurasia from their native North America. In the U.S.S.R. they are fast becoming abundant agricultural weeds in pastures and orchards and on cultivated lands, and (as in North America) are important sources of allergenic pollen. A noctuid moth, *Tarachídia candefácta* Hübner, was introduced from California into the U.S.S.R. in 1968 to control the ragweeds. It was introduced into southwestern U.S.S.R., and has since become established as far north as Leningrad. This is the first species intentionally introduced from North America into Europe for weed control.

It should be noted in this connection that weed-feeding insects are not always beneficial. In some cases an insect may feed on weeds early in the season and later invade cultivated crops; sometimes weeds may provide food on which large populations may be built up, later to attack crop plants. In other cases an insect may change its host from a wild to a cultivated plant; the Colorado potato beetle, for example, originally fed on a wild species of *Solànum* (nightshade) and later changed to the potato.

INSECTS AS FOOD OF MAN AND ANIMALS

A great many animals utilize insects as food. Insectivorous animals may be important to man as food (for example, many fish, game birds, and mammals), they may have an aesthetic value (many birds and other vertebrates), or they may act as important agents in the control of insect pests. Man himself is sometimes insectivorous.

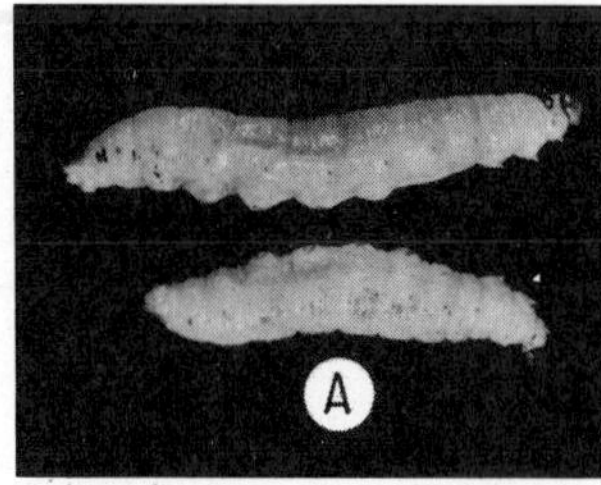

Figure 609. "Gusanos de Maguey," edible caterpillars canned and sold in Mexico.

Many freshwater fish feed to a large extent on insects, particularly on such aquatic forms as the mayflies, stoneflies, caddisflies, mosquito larvae, midge larvae, and the larvae of various aquatic beetles. Although certain species of game fish prey upon smaller fish or on other aquatic animals, the insects are a basic item in the food chains leading to these game fish.

The birds that feed largely or entirely upon insects have an aesthetic value because of their interesting habits, and they often have a practical value by acting as important predators of insect pests. Birds that feed on insects consume large quantities of them; nestlings will often eat their weight in insects daily. Many examples might be cited of cases where birds have been instrumental in checking insect outbreaks. A particularly striking case is that of gulls checking a mormon cricket outbreak in Utah some years ago, an event now commemorated by a monument in Salt Lake City.

Many other vertebrates are insectivorous, and some of these have been of value in controlling insect pests. Toads, frogs, lizards, bats, skunks, moles, and shrews feed largely or entirely on insects.

Insects are utilized as food by man in many parts of the world. The Arabs eat locusts (Acrididae); certain of the African natives eat ants, termites, beetle grubs, caterpillars, and grasshoppers; grasshoppers are frequently eaten by man in the Orient. In Mexico "Gusanos de Maguey" are considered a delicacy; these are the larvae of one of the giant skippers, which are collected from the fleshy leaves of the maguey plant. They are sold fresh in the market and are fried before eating; they may also be purchased in cans (Figure 609), already fried and ready to eat. The caterpillars are about $2\frac{1}{2}$ inches (64 mm) long when full grown. Cans of these and other edible insects are available in many places in the United States.

About the only insects eaten by man in this country are the few that are canned and sold in gourmet food shops (such as those shown in Figure 609), and relatively few people eat even these. On the other hand, we eat honey (which has been regurgitated by insects), and some close relatives of insects (lobsters, shrimp, and crabs), and consider these excellent foods. For most Americans, eating insects is strictly "for the birds" and definitely not for man. Any food containing the least trace of insects is considered contaminated, and unfit for human consumption; food processing companies spend millions of dollars each year to keep insects out of their products. On the other hand, for thousands of species of animals (including some primates) insects constitute the principal or sole items of their diet, which means that insects do have considerable food value. In these days of increasing population and decreasing food supply, "civilized" man may be missing a bet by passing up this important source of human food.

INSECTS IN MEDICINE AND SURGERY

Man has for centuries used insects or their products as therapeutic agents. Cantharidin, an extract from the bodies of blister beetles, has been used in the treatment of certain conditions of the urogenital system. Bee venom has been used in the treatment of arthritis. Malaria has been induced in patients suffering from paresis, to produce high body temperatures.

One of the most striking roles of insects in medicine is the use of blow fly larvae in treating conditions involving decaying tissues. For centuries military surgeons have noticed that severe wounds which remained untreated for several days and became infested with maggots healed better when dressed than similar wounds that had not been infested. After World War I, this fact was investigated experimentally, and it was found that the fly larvae fed on the decaying tissues of such wounds and secreted something into the wound which promoted the healing process. From this experimental work, there was developed a technique of treating diseases such as osteomyelitis with blow fly larvae. The larvae were reared under aseptic conditions to avoid introducing additional infection, and were placed in the decaying tissues of the patient; there they were allowed to feed, and when full grown, were replaced by younger larvae. This treatment resulted in a less conspicuous scar afterward, and there were fewer recurrences than in the operative treatment formerly used. After further study of this process it was discovered that the excretion of the larvae that produced the curative effect was allantoin. At present, allantoin is used in the treatment of osteomyelitis and other deep-seated wounds in which there is decaying tissue. Thus, fly larvae have been instrumental in developing a modern medical treatment for a condition that was previously very difficult to cure.

THE USE OF INSECTS IN SCIENTIFIC RESEARCH

Basic physiological processes, as well as such biological phenomena as inheritance, population dynamics, variation, and evolution, are essentially similar in all animals—and since many insects have a short life cycle and are relatively easy to maintain in the laboratory, they are frequently used in scientific studies of these processes.

Studies of insect physiology have advanced our knowledge of physiology generally. Extensive studies of insect nutrition, neuromuscular physiology, and hormones have contributed to our knowledge of these functions in other animals as well. Cockroaches, hornworms, silkworms, triatomid bugs, and house flies are most frequently used in these studies.

The little fruit flies, *Drosóphila* spp., which are easily reared in large numbers and whose larvae have giant salivary gland chromosomes have been used extensively in genetic studies. Much has been added to our knowledge of the basic principles of inheritance by the study of these flies.

Insects have often been used as the experimental animal in studies of behavior. Studies of social insects, for example, have provided much interesting and valuable information on social organization and behavior, thus increasing our understanding of human social behavior. Studies of the responses of insects to various environmental factors, such as temperature, moisture, and photoperiod, have increased our understanding of the action of these factors in other animals as well.

Insect populations are often used as an index of ecological conditions. In studies of stream or lake pollution, for example, the degree of pollution can be determined by the type and amount of insect life present. Insect populations may also serve as an index to successions; the length of time an animal has been dead can often be determined by its insect fauna.

THE AESTHETIC VALUE OF INSECTS

Insects become fascinating animals when one begins to study them carefully. There are a great many people for whom insect study provides a stimulating hobby, one just as interesting as the study of birds, flowers, or other natural objects.

The beauty of insects has been utilized for patterns by artists, jewelers, and designers. Some of the butterflies, moths, and beetles have provided basic patterns in many types of art. A brilliantly colored tropical leafhopper, *Cardioscárta pulchélla* (Guérin), has a black, white, and red pattern that is frequently used in Mexican and Central American art. Insects are used in making jewelry, either by the use of all or part of actual specimens, or by using them as designs. Bracelets, necklaces, necktie pins, and scatter pins are often made in the design of an insect. In some tropical countries the natives make necklaces of "ground pearls," the wax cysts of female scale insects of the genus *Margaròdes*. The wings of *Mórpho* butterflies, brilliant bluish butterflies occurring in South America, are often mounted under glass and made into trays, pictures, and certain types of jewelry. Showy insects mounted in plastic or under glass are sometimes made into paperweights, book ends, and the like.

INJURIOUS INSECTS

Man suffers tremendous losses from the feeding and other activities of insects. Many insects feed on plants that man cultivates; others feed on stored materials, clothing, or wood that are of value to man; still others feed on man and other animals directly.

The annual losses in the United States due to insects have been estimated at about $5 billion, which is less than the amount representing the benefits derived from insects. Thus, we may say that the good done by insects outweighs the harm they do, though the good is often less evident than the harm.

INSECTS ATTACKING CULTIVATED PLANTS

Most types of plants, including all sorts of growing crops, are attacked and injured by insects. The injury is caused by insects feeding or ovipositing on the plant or serving as agents in the transmission of plant diseases. This injury may vary from a reduction in crop yields to the complete destruction of the plant. The damage to plants by insects has been estimated to amount to about $3 billion annually in this country.

PLANT INJURY BY FEEDING The methods of feeding and types of damage done by insects feeding on plants have been discussed above (under "Phytophagous Insects," pages 61–62). Such feeding produces injury of various types, and the severity of the injury may vary all the way from only very slight damage to the death of the plant.

PLANT INJURY BY OVIPOSITION A few insects injure plants when they lay their eggs, particularly when they oviposit in stems or fruits. The periodical cicada, in laying its eggs in twigs, usually injures the twig so much that the terminal portion dies; or weakens it so that it is easily broken at the point of oviposition. Tree crickets, treehoppers, and certain leafhoppers injure twigs in a similar manner. Insects that lay their eggs in fruit often cause the fruit to become misshapen.

INSECTS AND PLANT DISEASE During recent years much has been learned of the role played by insects in the transmission of plant diseases. Some 200 plant diseases have been shown to have insect vectors. About three fourths of these diseases are caused by viruses. A summary of the more important plant diseases transmitted by insects is given in Table 5.

Table 5 PLANT DISEASES TRANSMITTED BY INSECTS AND OTHER ARTHROPODS

A. VIRUS DISEASES[a]

Disease	Vectors	Host	Method of Transmission
Sugarcane mosaic	Aphids: *Rhopalosìphum màidis* (Fitch), *Hysteroneùra setàriae* (Thomas), and *Toxóptera gráminum* (Rondani)	Sugarcane, sorghum, corn	By feeding
Alfalfa dwarf	Leafhopper: *Draeculacéphala minérva* Ball	Alfalfa	By feeding
Alfalfa witch's broom	Leafhopper: *Scaphytòpius acùtus* (Say)	Alfalfa	By feeding
Aster yellows (European)	Leafhoppers: *Aphròdes bicíncta* (Schrank), *Macrósteles quadripunctulàtus* (Kirschbaum), *M. laèvis* (Ribaut), and *M. sexnotàtum* (Fallén)	Aster, clover	By feeding
Aster yellows (Japanese)	Leafhopper: *Scleroràcus flavopíctus* (Ishihara)	Aster	By feeding
Aster yellows (N. American eastern strain)	Leafhopper: *Macrósteles fàscifrons* (Stål)	Aster	By feeding
Aster yellows (N. American western strain)	Leafhoppers: *Gyponàna hásta* DeLong, *Scaphytòpius acùtus* (Say), *S. delóngi* Young, *S. irroràtus* (Van Duzee), *Acinópterus angulàtus* Lawson, *Macrósteles fáscifrons* (Stål), *Éndria inímica* (Say), *Chlorotéttix símilis* DeLong, *Colladònus flavocapitàtus* (Van Duzee), *C. hòlmesi* (Bliven), *C. intricàtus*	Aster, celery, squash, cucumber, wheat, barley	By feeding

Disease	Vectors	Host	Method of Transmission
	(Ball), *C. kirkáldyi* (Ball), *C. rupinàtus* (Ball), *Euscelídius variegàtus* (Kirschbaum), *Exscultànus incurvàtus* (Osborn and Lathrop), *Paraphlépsius apertìnus* (Osborn and Lathrop), *Texanànus làthropi* (Baker), *T. látipex* Delong, *T. orégonus* (Ball), *T. pergràdus* DeLong, *T. spatulàtus* (Van Duzee)		
Clover phyllody	Leafhoppers: *Aphròdes álbifrons* (L.), *Scaphytòpius acùtus* (Say), *Macrósteles cristàta* (Ribaut), *M. fáscifrons* (Stål), *M. viridigríseus* (Edwards) *Eùscelis lineolàtus* (Brullé), *E. plébeja* (Fallén), *Pseudotéttix subfúsculus* (Fallén)	Clover	By feeding
Clover stunt	Leafhoppers: *Aphròdes bicíncta* (Schrank), *Macrósteles laèvis* (Ribaut), *Eùscelis plébeja* (Fallén)	Clover	By feeding
Corn stunt	Leafhoppers: *Dálbulus elimàtus* (Ball), *D. màidis* (DeLong and Wolcott), *Graminélla nígrifrons* (Forbes)	Corn	By feeding
Elm phloem necrosis	Leafhopper: *Scaphòideus luteòlus* Van Duzee	Elm	By feeding
Pierce's disease[a] of grape	Leafhoppers: *Cuérna costàlis* (Fabricius), *C. occidentàlis* Oman and Beamer, *C. yúccae* Oman and Beamer, *Homalodísca coagulàta* (Say), *H. laceràta* (Fowler), *Oncometòpia orbòna* (Fabricius), *Carneocéphala fláviceps* (Riley), *C. fúlgida* Nottingham, *C. triguttàta* Nottingham, *Draeculacéphala crassicórnis* Van Duzee, *D. minérva* Ball, *D. noveboracénsis* (Fitch), *D. portòla portòla* Ball, *Graphocéphala cythùra* (Baker), *Helochàra commùnis* Fitch, *Hòrdnia circellàta* (Baker), *Keonólla conflùens pacífica* (DeLong and Severin), *K. dolobràta* (Ball), *Neokólla séverini* DeLong, *Friscànus friscànus* (Ball), *Pagarònia confùsa* Oman, *P. furcàta* Oman, *P. tredecimpunctàta* Ball, *P. triunàta* Ball	Grape	By feeding
Peach X-disease (eastern)	Leafhoppers: *Gyponàna lámina* DeLong, *Scaphytòpius acùtus* (Say), *Colladònus clitellàrius* (Say), *Fieberiélla flòrii* (Stål), *Norvellìna*	Peach	By feeding

Disease	Vectors	Host	Method of Transmission
	seminùda (Say), *Paraphlépsius irroràtus* (Say)		
Peach X-disease (western)	Leafhoppers: *Keonólla conflùens pacífica* (DeLong and Severin), *Scaphytòpius acùtus* (Say), *Colladònus geminàtus* (Van Duzee), *C. montànus montànus* (Van Duzee), *Fieberiélla flòrii* (Stål)	Peach	By feeding
Phony peach disease	Leafhoppers: *Oncometòpia nígricans* (Walker), *O. orbòna* (Fabricius), *Homalodísca insólita* (Walker), *H. coagulàta* (Say), *Cuérna costàlis* (Fabricius), *Draeculacéphala portòla portòla* Ball, *Graphocéphala versùta* (Say)	Peach	By feeding
Potato yellow dwarf	Leafhoppers: *Aceratagállia longùla* (Van Duzee), *A. sanguinolénta* (Provancher), *A. curvàta* Oman, *A. obscùra* Oman, *Agallíópsis novélla* (Say), *Agállia constrícta* (Van Duzee), *A. quadripunctàta* (Provancher)	Potato	By feeding
Sugarbeet Argentine curly top	Leafhopper: *Agalliàna énsigera* Oman	Sugarbeet	By feeding
Sugarbeet curly top (Turkish strain)	Leafhoppers: *Circùlifer tenéllus* (Baker), *C. opacipénnis* (Lethierry)	Sugarbeet	By feeding
Sugarbeet yellow wilt	Leafhopper: *Paratànus exitiòsus* (Beamer)	Sugarbeet	By feeding
Tomato-Brazilian curly top	Leafhoppers: *Agállia álbida* (Uhler), *Agalliàna énsigera* Oman, *A. sticticóllis* (Stål)	Tomato	By feeding

B. BACTERIAL DISEASES

Disease	Pathogen	Vectors	Host	Method of Transmission
Stewart's disease	*Bactèrium stewarti* Smith	Corn flea beetle, *Chaetocnèma pulicària* Melsheimer, corn rootworms, *Diabrótica* spp., and seedcorn maggot	Corn	Pathogen winters in alimentary canal of vector, enters plant through feeding wounds
Cucurbit wilt	*Erwínia tracheíphila* (Erw. Smith)	Cucumber beetles, *Acalýmma vittàta* (Fabricius) and	Cucumber and other cucurbits	Pathogen winters in alimentary canal of beetle;

Disease	Pathogen	Vectors	Host	Method of Transmission
		D. undecimpunctàta howardi Barber		enters with feces in wounds
Fire blight	*Erwínia amyl-óvora* (Burrill)	Various insects, especially flies, bees, and leafhoppers	Pear, apple, quince	By nectar feeders, and from cankers to new growth by leafhoppers

[a]The exact nature of some of these pathogens is not known; some may be agents other than viruses. There is evidence (*Science*, 184:1375–1377; 1974) that Pierce's disease of grape, for example, may be caused by a bacterium.

There are three ways by which insects cause plant pathogens to enter the plant.

1. The pathogen may accidentally gain entrance through egg or feeding punctures or openings through which the insect has entered the plant tissue. Certain molds and rots enter in this fashion.
2. The pathogen may be transmitted on or in the body of the insect from one plant to another. Flies and bees pick up and spread the bacilli that cause fire blight in apple and pear. The fungus causing Dutch elm disease is transmitted in this fashion by the elm bark beetle.
3. The pathogen may remain in the body of the insect for a time, often for long periods, and be inoculated into the plant by the feeding or feces of the insect. In some cases the pathogen passes a part of its life cycle in the insect, and may reproduce there. Cucurbit wilt disease is transmitted in this way by the striped and spotted cucumber beetles. The pathogen overwinters in the beetles, and the plants are infected in the spring by infected feces of the insect being dropped on the leaves and washed into the wounds of the plant. Stewart's disease of corn is transmitted in a similar manner by the corn flea beetle. In a few cases, such as the streak disease of corn, the pathogen may pass from the insect (a leafhopper) to its offspring through the eggs.

The virus diseases are caused by organisms that are too small to be seen; consequently, it has been difficult to determine some phases of their life cycle. Some can apparently be transmitted by almost any insect that feeds on the diseased plant; in other cases the pathogens appear to be transmitted by only one species of insect. The virus diseases are transmitted principally by insects in the order Homóptera.

The damage done by insect feeding alone may be severe, but a disease vector can, by a small amount of feeding, inoculate a plant with a disease that may reduce its productivity or even kill it. Two sugarbeet leafhoppers per beet plant can cause in themselves comparatively little damage, but if they are carrying the pathogens of the curly-top disease, they may cause enormous losses.

INSECTS ATTACKING STORED PRODUCTS

After materials produced by plants and animals have been stored for use as food or clothing or have been utilized in buildings or fabrics, they may be attacked and damaged by insects. The damage is done by the insects feeding or tunneling in these materials, or contaminating them, and the possibility of insect attack greatly increases the expense of packing and storage. The annual insect damage to stored products in this country has been estimated to be about $1 billion.

PESTS OF WOOD All sorts of wooden structures, such as buildings, furniture, fence posts, utility poles, and materials such as pasteboard and paper, are subject to attack by insects. One of the most widespread and destructive pests of wood and wood products is the termite. Termites eat out the interior portions of beams, sills, floors, and joists, and often build tunnels over or through foundations to reach the wooden parts of buildings. Timbers attacked eventually collapse. Powder-post beetles and carpenter ants tunnel in dry posts and timbers and weaken them.

PESTS OF FABRICS AND CLOTHING Most materials made from animal fibers, such as furs, clothing, blankets, rugs, and upholstering, may be attacked and damaged by insects. The amount of material actually eaten may be small, but the value of the materials attacked may be greatly reduced. The most important fabric pests are dermestid beetles and clothes moths.

PESTS OF STORED FOODS Many types of stored foods, particularly meats, cheese, milk products, flour,meal, cereals, stored grain, nuts, and fruits, may be attacked by insects. Considerable damage may be done by the feeding or tunneling of the insects, or the actual damage may be slight and the effect of the insects mainly contamination. The important pests of this type are the Angoumois grain moth, Indian meal moth, Mediterranean flour moth, confused flour beetle, granary and rice weevils, Khapra beetle, saw-toothed grain beetle, and flour mites. Some of these attack whole grain, and others feed mainly on meal or flour. Bean and pea weevils tunnel in and may completely destroy stored beans and peas. Stored meats and cheese are attacked principally by the larder beetle, cheese skipper, and various mites. Drugstore beetles attack a variety of vegetable products, including chocolate, pepper, and tobacco.

INSECTS ATTACKING MAN AND ANIMALS

Insects affect man and animals directly in four principal ways: (1) they may be merely annoying, (2) they may inject venom by their bites or stings, (3) they may live in or on man or animals as parasites, or (4) they may serve as agents in the transmission of disease. These types of damage by insects have been estimated to cost about $670 million annually in the United States.

ANNOYANCE OF INSECTS Everyone has been bothered by insects that buzz around or crawl over one's body. Such effects are mainly psychological, but in some cases the "nuisance value" of annoying insects may be considerable. Bot flies and face flies, though they neither bite nor sting, cause great annoyance to cattle. Many insects annoy by their odors or secretions; others may get into one's eyes or ears.

VENOMOUS INSECTS Many arthropods inject into man and animals toxins that cause irritation, swelling, pain, and sometimes paralysis. Those that inject a venom by their bite include various biting flies, bugs, mites, ticks, centipedes, and spiders; the bites of some of these are very painful, they often result in swelling or (for example, in the case of certain spiders) a necrotic ulcer, and in some cases may cause death; some tick bites result in paralysis. Those that inject a venom by their sting include the bees, wasps, and scorpions; such stings may be very painful and often cause considerable swelling; the sting of some scorpions may be fatal. Many people are particularly sensitive to bee or wasp stings and may suffer anaphylactic shock or even death as a result; more people in this country are killed by wasp or bee stings than by the bites of venomous snakes. A few caterpillars, such as the saddleback, puss moth larvae, and the larvae of the io moth, have stinging hairs that produce a type of dermatitis. Some of the blister beetles have body fluids that are irritating to the skin. A few insects, such as rose chafers, are toxic when swallowed.

PARASITIC INSECTS Many insects and other arthropods live in or on the bodies of man or animals as parasites and cause irritation, damage to tissues, and in some cases even death. The chewing lice are external parasites of birds and mammals, and feed on hair, feathers, dermal scales, and other external structures; they cause considerable irritation and a general run-down condition in the animal attacked. The sucking lice are external parasites of mammals and are bloodsucking; they cause irritation, and bad sores often result from the rubbing or scratching brought on by their bites. Fleas, bed bugs, and other biting forms cause similar irritation. The mange and scab mites, which burrow into the skin of man and animals, are often extremely irritating.

Many flies pass their larval stage as internal parasites of man and animals, causing a condition known as myiasis; these insects may cause serious damage, even death, to the animal affected. The larvae of the ox warble flies live under the skin of the host; they produce a general run-down condition in cattle, reduce milk production, and lower the value of the hides for leather. The sheep bot fly larva burrows in the nasal passages of its host. The screwworm fly lays its eggs in wounds and other exposed tissues of man and animals, and the larvae feed on the living tissues of the host. The larvae of the horse bot flies develop in the alimentary tract of horses and cause irritation and damage to the mucous membranes there.

INSECTS AND DISEASE TRANSMISSION The insects that attack man and animals do their greatest damage when they act as disease vectors. The bites and stings of venomous insects and the disturbance caused by parasitic insects may be severe, but are rarely fatal; many insect-borne diseases have a high mortality rate. Insects act as agents in the transmission of disease in two general ways: they may serve as mechanical vectors of the pathogen, or they may act as biological vectors. In the latter case the insect serves as a host in the life cycle of the pathogen. There are some diseases, known to be transmitted by insects or other arthropods, in which the exact role played by the vector is not completely understood.

The insects of chief importance in the mechanical transmission of pathogenic organisms are the filth-inhabiting flies such as house flies and blow flies. These insects pick up the pathogens on their feet or on other parts of their body when feeding on fecal material or other wastes, or they may ingest the pathogens; later they contaminate man's food when they feed on it. The flies have the habit of regurgitating materials that were previously eaten, particularly on foods that are solid or semisolid, and so may contaminate human foods. Typhoid fever, cholera, and dysentery may be transmitted by flies in this way.

The arthropods that serve as a host of the pathogen as well as a vector are chiefly the bloodsucking forms; they pick up the pathogen when feeding on a diseased host and later infect another host. In such cases there is usually a period during which certain phases of the pathogen's life cycle are passed before the arthropod is capable of infecting another host. The host is usually infected either by the bite of the vector or by having the excretions or body fluids of the vector rubbed into the skin. In a few cases the vector must be swallowed before infection results.

MALARIA This disease is a typical example of those in which an insect serves both as vector and host of the pathogen. Millions of people throughout the world are affected by it. Malaria is a disease characterized by rather regularly recurring paroxysms of chills and fever, and in which the red blood cells are destroyed by the pathogen. It is caused by Protozòa in the genus *Plasmòdium* and is transmitted by certain species of mosquitoes in the genus *Anópheles*. Three types of malaria are common in man; benign tertian malaria, caused by *P. vìvax* (Grassi and Feletti), which has wide distribution; malignant tertian malaria, caused by *P. falcíparum* (Welch), which is principally tropical, and is the most dangerous type of malaria; and quartan malaria, caused by *P. malàriae* (Grassi and Feletti), which is the least common of the three types.

A person normally acquires malaria only through the bite of an infective female *Anópheles* mosquito which has previously obtained the plasmodia from a malaria patient. When such a mosquito bites a person, large numbers of tiny spindle-shaped bodies (the sporozoite stage of the *Plasmòdium*) are injected into the blood stream with the mosquito's saliva (Figure 610). These leave the blood stream within a period of 30 or 40 minutes and enter the parenchymal cells of the liver. After one or more generations (the number depending on the species of *Plasmòdium*) of asexual reproduction in the liver cells, they enter the red blood cells. In a red blood cell the *Plasmòdium* is an irregularly shaped stage called a trophozoite, which feeds on the blood cell. When the trophozoite matures, its nucleus begins to divide and the trophozoite becomes a schizont. By successive nuclear divisions of the schizont, some 10–24 daughter organisms are formed; these products of schizont division are called merozoites. The red blood cell soon ruptures, and the merozoites are released into the plasma; they enter other red blood cells, and the process of feeding and asexual reproduction (which is here called schizogony) continues. The asexual cycle of *Plasmòdium* in the blood stream of man is repeated every 24–72 hours, the interval depending on the species of *Plasmòdium;* the release of the merozoites into the plasma coincides with the paroxysms of the disease.

After several generations of merozoites have been produced, sexual forms called gametocytes appear; these are of two types, male and female. The gametocytes develop no further until they are ingested by a suitable *Anópheles* mosquito. If the *Anópheles* mosquito bites a malarial patient and does not pick up any gametocytes, it does not become infective; if it picks up gametocytes, the parasite continues its cycle of development in the mosquito. Once in the stomach of the mosquito, the gametocytes undergo certain changes; the male gametocyte throws off flagellated bodies, and the female gametocyte throws off some of its chromatin material. The fusion of a flagellated body with a modified female gametocyte constitutes fertilization and results in the formation of a zygote. The zygote soon becomes elongated and motile, and burrows into the stomach wall and forms a cystlike structure known as an oocyst. Successive nuclear divisions in the oocyst result in the formation of a large number of elongate spindle-shaped bodies, the sporozoites. After some 10–15 days, depending on the temperature, the oocyst ruptures and releases the sporozoites into the body cavity of the mosquito; the sporozoites (or at least some of them) travel to and enter the salivary glands of the mosquito. From this time on, until the mosquito dies or until it hibernates, it is capable of infecting a person with malaria.

Some of the most serious diseases of man and animals are transmitted by insects and other arthropods, and the principal vectors are the biting flies, sucking lice, fleas, bugs, mites, and ticks. A summary of the more important diseases transmitted by arthropods is given in Table 6. The arthropods listed as "vectors" sometimes play a passive role in the transmission of the disease.

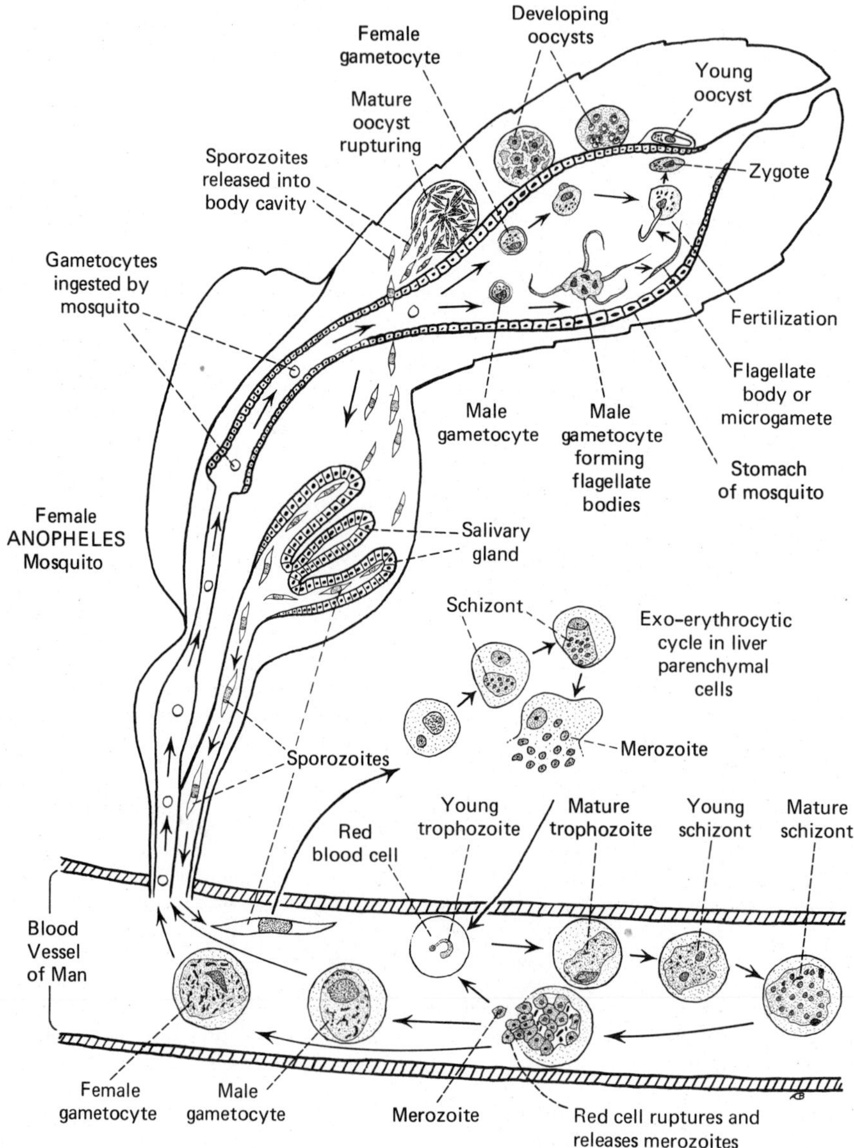

Figure 610. Life cycle (diagrammatic) of malarial parasite, *Plasmòdium vìvax* (Grassi and Feletti). For explanation, see text.

Table 6 DISEASES TRANSMITTED BY INSECTS AND OTHER ARTHROPODS

A. DISEASES CAUSED BY HELMINTHS (ROUNDWORMS AND FLATWORMS)

Disease	Pathogen	Vector	Host	Distribution
Tapeworms	*Dipylídium canìnum* (L.)	Dog flea, *Ctenocephálides cànis* (Curtis)	Dog and man	Worldwide
	Hymenólepis diminùta (Rudolphi)	Rat flea, *Xenopsýlla cheòpis* (Rothschild)	Rat and man	Worldwide
	Diphyllo-bóthrium látum (L.)	Water fleas (*Cỳclops* spp.) (Crustàcea)	Man and animals	Worldwide
	Thysanosòma ostiniòides Diesing	Psocids: *Liposcèlis* sp., *Rhyopsòcus* sp.	Sheep and other ruminants	North and South America
Lung fluke	*Paragònimus westermáni* (Kerbert)	Crabs and crayfish	Man	Far East, Africa, South and Central America, Mexico
Filariasis	*Wucherèria báncrofti* (Cobbold), and *Microfilària màlayi* (Brug)	Mosquitoes, principally in the genera *Aèdes, Cùlex, Anópheles,* and *Mansònia;* some biting midges *(Culicòides)*	Man	Worldwide in the tropics and subtropics
Onchocerciasis	*Onchocérca vólvulus* (Leuckart), a roundworm	Black flies, *Simùlium* spp.	Man	Mexico, Central America, equatorial Africa
Loaiasis	*Lòa lòa* (Cobbold), a roundworm	Deer flies, *Chrỳsops* spp.	Man	Africa
Guinea worm	*Dracúnculus medinénsis* (L.), a roundworm	Water fleas (*Cỳclops* spp.) (Crustàcea)	Man	Africa, southern Asia, East Indies

B. DISEASES CAUSED BY PROTOZÒA

Disease	Pathogen	Vector	Host	Distribution
Malaria	*Plasmòdium vìvax* (Grassi and Feletti), *P. falcíparum* (Welch), and *P. malàriae* (Grassi and Feletti)	Mosquitoes in the genus *Anópheles*	Man	Worldwide in tropical, subtropical, and temperate regions

~~C. DISEASES CAUSED BY BACTERIA~~

Disease	Pathogen	Vector	Host	Distribution
African sleeping sickness	*Trypanosòma gambiénse* Dutton and *T. rhodesiénse* Stephens and Fantham	Tsetse flies, *Glossìna* spp.	Man and animals	Equatorial Africa
Nagana	*Trypanosòma brùcei* Plimmer and Bradford	Tsetse flies, *Glossìna* spp.	Wild and domestic animals	Equatorial Africa
Chagas' disease	*Trypanosòma crùzi* Chagas	Assassin bugs, principally in the genera *Triátoma* and *Rhódnius*	Man and rodents	South America, Central America, Mexico, and Texas
Kala-azar	*Leishmània dónovani* (Laveran and Mesnil)	Sand flies, *Phlebótomus* spp.	Man	Mediterranean region, Asia, and South America
Espundia	*Leishmània braziliénsis* Vianna	Sand flies, *Phlebótomus* spp.	Man	South America, Central America, Mexico, North Africa, southern Asia
Oriental sore	*Leishmània trópica* (Wright)	Sand flies, *Phlebótomus* spp.	Man	Africa, Asia, South America
Texas cattle fever	*Babèsia bigémina* Smith and Kilbourne	Cattle tick, *Boóphilus annulàtus* (Say)	Cattle	Southern United States, Central and South America. South Africa, Philippines
Amoebic dysentery	*Endamoèba histolýtica* (Schaudinn)	House fly, *Músca doméstica* L., various blow flies and flesh flies	Man and animals	Worldwide

C. DISEASES CAUSED BY BACTERIA

Disease	Pathogen	Vector	Host	Distribution
Bubonic plague	*Pasteurélla péstis* (Lehmann and Newmann)	Various fleas, especially the rat flea, *Xenopsýlla cheòpis* (Rothschild)	Man and rodents	Worldwide
Tularemia	*Pasteurélla tularénsis* (McCoy and Chapin)	Deer flies (*Chrỳsops* spp.); ticks, principally *Dermacéntor* spp. and *Haemaphysàlis* spp.; fleas; and the body louse, *Pedículus h. humànus* L.	Man and rodents	United States, Canada, Europe, the Orient

C. DISEASES CAUSED BY BACTERIA

Disease	Pathogen	Vector	Host	Distribution
Anthrax	*Bacíllus anthràcis* Cohn	Horse flies, *Tabànus* spp.	Man and animals	Worldwide
Typhoid fever	*Eberthélla typhòsa* (Zopf)	House fly, *Músca doméstica* L., and various blow flies and flesh flies	Man	Worldwide
Bacillary dysentery	*Bacíllus* spp.			
Cholera	*Víbrio cómma* (Schroeter)			

D. DISEASES CAUSED BY SPIROCHAETES

Disease	Pathogen	Vector	Host	Distribution
Relapsing fever	*Borrèlia recurréntis* (Lebert) and *B. dúttonii* (Breinl)	Ticks (*Ornithódorus* spp.) and the body louse, *Pedículus h. humànus* L.	Man and rodents	Worldwide
Fowl spirochaetosis	*Borrèlia anserìna* (Sakharoff)	Fowl tick, *Árgas pérsicus* (Oken)	Chicken, turkey, goose	North America, Brazil, India, Australia, Egypt

E. DISEASES CAUSED BY BARTONELLA AND RICKETTSIA ORGANISMS

Disease	Pathogen	Vector	Host	Distribution
Verruga peruana or Oroya fever	*Bartonélla bacillifórmis* (Strong et *al.*)	Sand fly, *Phlebótomus* sp.	Man	Bolivia, Peru, Ecuador, Chile
Epidemic typhus	*Rickéttsia prowazékii* da Rocha-Lima	Body louse, *Pedículus h. humànus* L., rat flea, *Xenopsýlla cheòpis* (Rothschild) and rat mite, *Liponýssus bàcoti* (Hirst)	Man and rodents	Worldwide
Endemic or murine typhus	*Rickéttsia prowazékii mooseri* Monteiro	Rat flea, *Xenopsýlla cheòpis* (Rothschild), various other fleas, lice, mites, and ticks on rodents	Man and rodents	Worldwide
Scrub typhus ot tsutsugamushi disease	*Rickéttsia tsutsugamùshì* (Hayashi)	Harvest mites or chiggers, *Trombícula* spp.	Man and rodents	Japan, China, Formosa, India, Australia East Indies, and some South Pacific islands
Spotted fever	*Rickéttsia rickéttsii* (Wolbach)	Various ticks, mainly *Dermacéntor andersòni* Stiles and *D. variábilis* (Say)	Man and rodents	North and South America

C. DISEASES CAUSED BY BACTERIA

Disease	Pathogen	Vector	Host	Distribution
African tick fever Q fever	*Rickéttsia* spp.	Various ticks (Ixódidae)	Man	South Africa, Australia, western United States

F. DISEASES CAUSED BY VIRUSES

Disease	Pathogen	Vector	Host	Distribution
Yellow fever	A virus	Various mosquitoes, especially *Aèdes aegýpti* (L.)	Man, monkeys, and rodents	American and African tropics and subtropics
Dengue	A virus	Mosquitoes in the genus *Aèdes*, principally *A. aegýpti* (L.) and *A. albopíctus* Skuse	Man	Worldwide in tropics and subtropics
Encephalitis	Several virus strains	Various mosquitoes in the genera *Cùlex* and *Aèdes*	Man and horse	United States, Canada, South America, Europe, and Asia
Pappataci fever	A virus	Sand fly, *Phlebótomus papatàsii* (Scopoli)	Man	Mediterranean region, India, Ceylon
Colorado tick fever	A virus	Various ticks	Man	Western United States

References on the Relation of Insects to Man

Baker, E. W., T. M. Evans, D. J. Gould, W. B. Hull, and H. L. Keegan. 1956. *A Manual of Parasitic Mites of Medical and Economic Importance*. New York: National Pest Control Assoc., 170 pp., 59 f.

Beard, R. L. 1963. Insect toxins and venoms. *Ann. Rev. Ent.*, 8:1–18.

Bishopp, F. C., *et al.* 1952. *Insects*. USDA Yearbook, xix + 780 pp.; illus.

Black, L. M. 1959. Biological cycles of plant viruses in insect vectors. In *The Viruses;* 3 vol., F. M. Burnett and W. M. Stanley (Eds.). Vol. 2, pp. 157–185. New York: Academic Press.

Black, L. M. 1962. Some recent advances on leafhopper borne viruses. In *Biological Transmission of Disease Agents,* K. Maramorosch (Ed.). Pp. 1–9. New York: Academic Press.

Borror, D. J. 1947. *Insects and pollination*. Nat. Audubon Soc., Ser. 13, Bull. 9; 4 pp.; illus.

Borror, D. J. 1973. *How insects benefit man*. Audubon Nature Bull., set NB4; 4 pp.; illus.

Brittain, W. H. 1933. *Apple pollination studies*. Can. Dept. Agr., Bull. 162; 198 pp., 73 f.

Carter, W. 1973 (2nd ed.). *Insects in Relation to Plant Disease*. New York: Wiley, 759 pp.; illus.

Chandler, A. C., and C. P. Read. 1961 (10th ed.). *Introduction to Parasitology*. New York: Wiley, xii + 882 pp., 258 f.

Davidson, R. H., and L. M. Peairs. 1966 (6th ed.). *Insect Pests of Farm, Garden, and Orchard*. New York: Wiley, ix + 675 pp., 587 f.

Debach, P. 1974. *Biological Control by Natural Enemies*. New York: Cambridge Univ. Press, 325 pp., 49 pl., 7 graphs.

DeLong, D. M. 1960. Man in a world of insects. *Ohio J. Sci.*, 60(4):193–206.

Faust, E. C., P. C. Beaver, and R. C. Jung. 1962. *Animal Agents and Vectors of Human Disease*. Philadelphia: Lea and Febiger, 485 pp., 195 f.

Free, J. B. 1970. *Insect Pollination of Crops*. London: Academic Press, 544 pp.

Greenberg, B. 1973. *Flies and Disease*. 2 vol. Vol. 1: *Ecology, Classification, and Biotic Associations,* 856 pp. Vol. 2. *Biology and Disease Transmission,* 447 pp. Princeton, N.J.: Princeton Univ. Press.

Horsfall, W. R. 1962. *Medical Entomology. Arthropods and Human Disease*. New York: Ronald Press, ix + 467 pp., 90 f.

Huffaker, C. B. (Ed.). 1971. *Biological Control*. New

York: Plenum Press, 511 pp.

Hunter, G. W., III, W. W. Frye, and J. C. Swartzwelder. 1960 (3rd ed.). *A Manual of Tropical Medicine*. Philadelphia: W. B. Saunders, xxx + 892 pp.; illus.

James, M. T., and R. F. Harwood. 1969. *Herms's Medical Entomology* (6th ed.). New York: Macmillan, viii + 484 pp.; illus.

Markell, E. K., and M. Voge. 1958. *Diagnostic Medical Parasitology*. Philadelphia: W. B. Saunders, 276 pp., 115 f.

Mattingly, P. F. 1969. *The Biology of Mosquito-Borne Disease*. New York: American Elsevier, 184., 46 f., 12 pl.

Metcalf, C. L., and W. P. Flint. 1962 (4th ed., revised by R. L. Metcalf). *Destructive and Useful Insects*. New York: McGraw-Hill, xii + 1087 pp.; illus.

Nielson, M. W. 1968. The leafhopper vectors of phytopathogenic viruses (Homoptera, Cicadellidae). Taxonomy, biology, and virus transmission. *USDA Tech. Bull.* 1382; 386 pp., 108 f.

Snow, K. R. 1974. *Insects and Disease*. New York: Wiley, x + 208 pp.; illus.

Taylor, R. M. 1967. *Catalogue of Arthropod-Borne Viruses of the World*. Bethesda, Md.: National Institute of Allergy and Infectious Diseases, x + 898 pp.

Van den Bosch, R., and P. S. Messenger. 1973. *Biological Control*. New York: Intertext Press, xii + 180 pp.; illus.

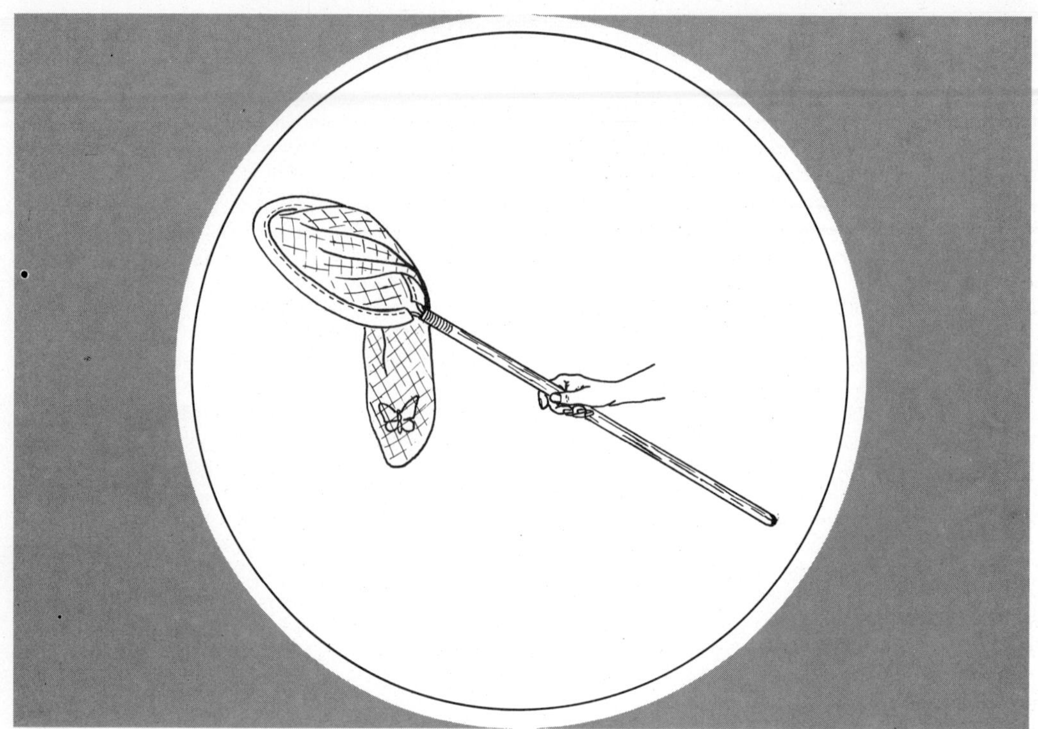

34: COLLECTING, PRESERVING, AND STUDYING INSECTS

One of the best ways to learn about insects is to go out and collect them; handling them and preparing collections will reveal to the student many things he will not get from textbooks. Many people find the collecting and study of insects an extremely interesting hobby, for it provides not only the satisfaction that comes from being in the field, but also the satisfaction of learning at first hand. The student will develop much more interest in insects by collecting and handling them than he will by merely looking at pictures or preserved specimens. He will have seen the specimens alive, and thus gain an insight as to their habitat, habits, and behavior—information often as valuable as morphological characters in determining their taxonomic position.

WHEN AND WHERE TO COLLECT

In collecting insects—as with hunting, fishing, bird-watching, or almost any activity—there is a direct correlation between time and effort expended and proficiency gained. The uninitiated person can go through habitats literally swarming with insects, and be totally unaware of their presence unless he is bitten or stung by them. There are few outdoor activities that will sharpen one's powers of observation and perception, test one's patience and skill, and provide a never-ending source of wonderment and pleasure than collecting insects.

Insects can be found practically everywhere and usually in considerable numbers; the more kinds of places in which one looks for them, the greater the variety he will be able to collect. The best time to collect is in the summer, but insects are active from early spring until late fall, and many can be found in hibernation during the winter. The adults of many species have a short seasonal range; hence one should collect throughout the year if he wishes to get the greatest variety. Since different species are active at different times of the day, at least some kinds of insects can be collected at any hour. Bad weather conditions, such as rain or low temperature, will reduce the activity of many insects, thus making it more difficult to find or collect them; but others are little affected and can be collected in any kind of weather. If one knows where to look, he can find insects in the average community at any hour of the day, any day in the year.

Many kinds of insects feed upon or frequent plants; hence plants provide one of the best places for collecting. Insects can be picked, shaken, or swept off the plant with a net. Different species feed on different kinds of plants; one should therefore examine all sorts of plants. Every part of the plant may harbor insects; the majority will probably be on the foliage or flowers, but others may be on or in the stem, bark, wood, fruit, or roots.

Various types of debris often harbor many kinds of insects. Some species can be found in the leaf mold and litter on the surface of the soil, particularly in woods or areas where the vegetation is dense; others can be found under stones, boards, bark, and similar objects; still others can be found in rotting or decaying material of all sorts, such as fungi, decaying plants or the bodies of dead animals, rotting fruits, and dung. Many of the insects in these situations can be picked up with the fingers or forceps; others can be obtained by sifting debris.

Many insects can be found in or around buildings, or on animals or human beings. Many use buildings, cavities under buildings, culverts, and similar places as a shelter, and some species are most easily collected in such situations. Other insects found in buildings feed on clothing, furniture, grain, food, and other materials. Insects that attack animals are usually to be found around those animals, and a person interested in collecting species that attack man can often get them with very little effort—by letting the insects come to him.

On warm evenings, insects from various sources are attracted to lights and can be collected at street or porch lights, on the windows or screens of lighted rooms, or at lights put up especially to attract them. This is one of the easiest ways of collecting many types of insects. Blue lights seem to be more attractive than red or yellow ones.

A great many insects—the immature stages only in some cases, and all stages in others—are found in aquatic situations. Different types of aquatic habitats harbor different species, and different insects can be found in different parts of any particular pond or stream. Some are to be found on the surface, others are free-swimming in the water, others occur on aquatic vegetation, others are attached to or are under stones or other objects in the water, and still others burrow in the sand or muck of the bottom. Many aquatic insects can be collected by hand or by means of forceps; others are most easily collected by various types of aquatic collecting equipment.

The adults of a great many species are best obtained by collecting the immature stages and rearing them. This involves collecting cocoons, larvae, or nymphs, and maintaining them in some sort of container until the adults appear. It is often possible to get better specimens by this method than by collecting adults in the field.

Many insects are nocturnal, but are not attracted to lights; the collector must search for them at night and capture them by hand. Examination of tree trunks, leaves and other vegetation, fallen logs, rock faces, and other habitats at night will reveal a sizeable arthropod fauna, one unsuspected by those who confine their collecting to the daylight hours. Flashlights and lanterns of various sorts are useful for night collecting, but the best sort of light is a headlamp; such a light not only leaves both hands free (insect collectors often wish they had three or four extra arms and hands), but its beam focuses the wearer's attention on smaller areas and sharpens his perception; the lamp illuminates only the area where the collector is looking. Excellent results may be obtained with a headlamp having an elastic headband and operated by a 6-volt battery attached to the wearer's belt.

COLLECTING EQUIPMENT

The minimum equipment necessary to collect insects is one's hands and some sort of container for the specimens collected. However, one can do much better with a net and killing jar, or better yet with some sort of shoulder bag containing some additional equipment. For general collecting it is best to have at least the following items:

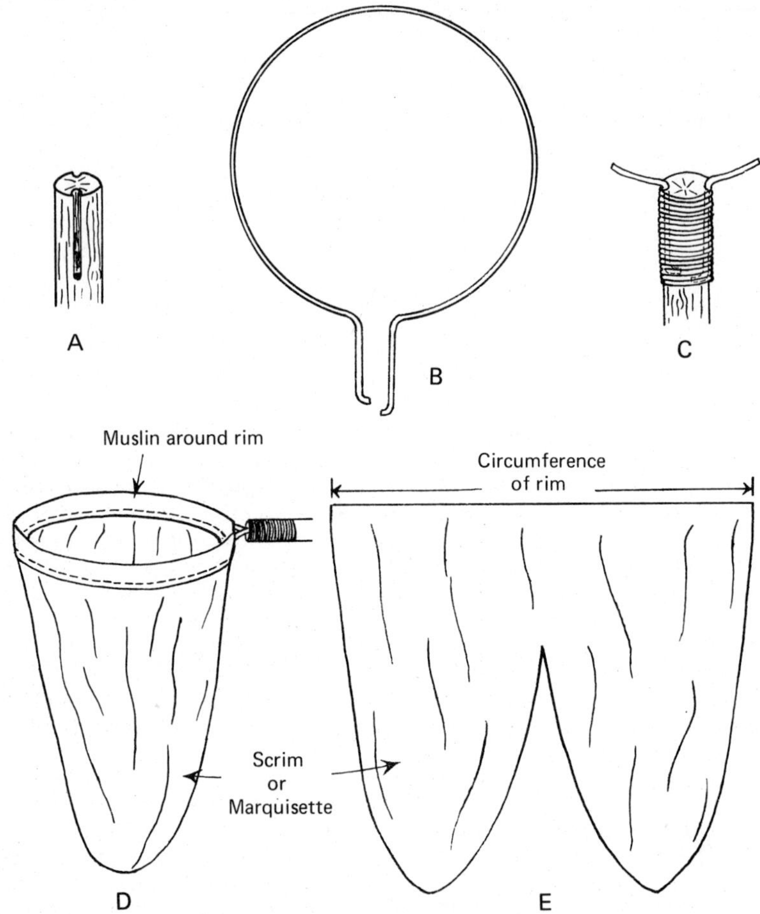

Figure 611. Homemade insect net. Grooves and holes are cut in the end of the handle, as in A; the wire for the rim is bent, as shown in B, fitted into the holes and grooves, and held there with heavy cord, wire, or friction tape. C. The material for the bag is cut as in E, and the finished net is shown in D.

1. Insect net
2. Killing jars
3. Pillboxes containing cleansing tissue
4. Envelopes, or paper for making envelopes
5. Vials of preservative
6. Forceps
7. Hand lens

These items, with the exception of the first, sixth, and seventh, are most easily carried in a shoulder bag; the forceps and hand lens can be attached to a string around one's neck and carried in a shirt pocket. Strictly speaking, a hand lens is not a means of collecting, but it is very useful for examining insects in the field.

Other items of value for some types of collecting are as follows:

8. Aspirator
9. Beating umbrella or sheet
10. Sifter
11. Traps
12. Aquatic collecting equipment
13. Headlamp (for night collecting)
14. Sheath knife

INSECT NET

Insect nets can be purchased from a supply house or can be homemade; homemade nets are fairly easy to make, and are much less expensive than supply house nets. A method of constructing an insect net is shown in Figure 611. The handle should be light and strong, and about a yard (1 m) long; the rim should be about 12 inches (0.3 m) in diameter and made of fairly heavy wire (no. 6 to no. 8 gauge). Grooves and holes are cut in one end of the handle (Figure 611 A); the wire for the rim is bent as shown in Figure 611 B, fitted into these holes and grooves, and fastened in place with heavy cord, fine wire, or friction tape, or a 50-mm length of metal tubing may be slipped over it.

The ideal shape for the bag is shown in Figure 611 D. The material for the bag (excepting the rim) can be made from a single piece of cloth cut as shown in Figure 611 E, and if the edges are sewed together with French seams the net can be used with either side out. The bag should be made of two types of cloth, a heavy band (muslin or canvas) around the rim and a lighter material for the main part of the bag; the choice of the latter material will depend on the type of collecting for which the net will be used. A net for general collecting should have a sufficiently open mesh that an insect can be seen through it; the best material is probably marquisette or scrim (cheese cloth is unsatisfactory because it snags too easily). With a more open mesh (for example, bobbinet) many smaller insects will escape through the meshes. A net used primarily for beating or sweeping should be made of muslin or fine-mesh bolting cloth, through which even the smallest insects cannot escape. The metal rim and handle of these nets are usually made of stronger material than in an aerial net used for general collecting.

Some people prefer an insect net that can be taken apart and carried inconspicuously. Such a net can be made from a collapsible frame known as a landing net, which can be bought from sporting-goods stores (Figure 612).

A net used with care will last a long time. It should be kept away from stout thorns and barbed wire (to avoid tearing), and it should be kept dry; insects caught in a wet net are seldom fit for a collection, and moisture eventually rots the net fabric.

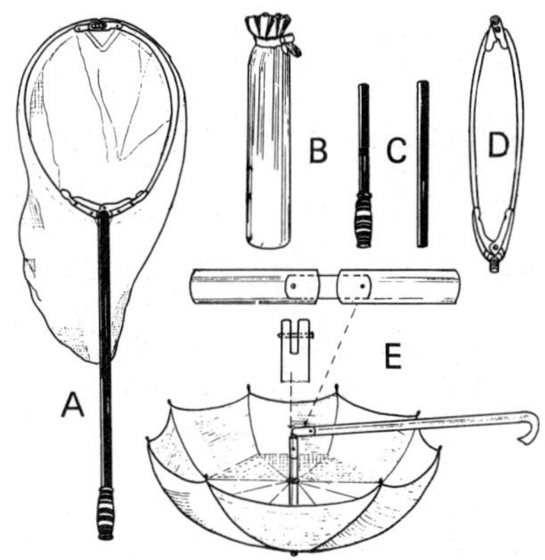

Figure 612. Collapsible net and beating umbrella. The net (A) may be collapsed (D), the handle removed and unjointed (C), and all these parts placed in a carrying bag (B). The beating umbrella (E) has a hinged joint in the handle and is held in the position illustrated when in use. (From DeLong and Davidson. Courtesy of the Ohio State University Press.)

When collecting insects with a net, one may look for particular insects and then swing at them, or one may simply swing the net through vegetation (sweeping). The former method is usually used for collecting the larger insects, and often demands a certain amount of speed and skill; the latter method will produce the greater quantity and variety of insects, but may damage some specimens. When one catches a particularly active insect, he must use certain precautions to prevent the insect from escaping before it can be transferred to the killing jar. The safest method is to fold the net over with the insect in the bottom of the net (Figure 613); the insect is then grasped

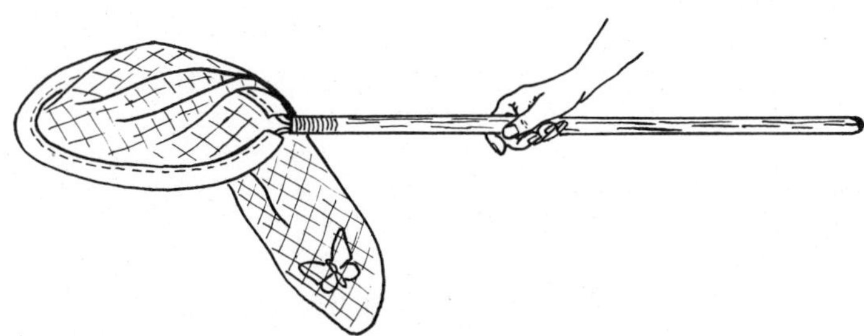

Figure 613. An insect net turned to prevent the escape of captured specimens.

through the net (provided it is not one that stings), and transferred to the killing bottle. If the insect is one that stings (when in doubt it is better to assume that it *does* sting), there are three methods of transferring it to the killing bottle. (1) The fold of the net containing the insect can be put into the killing bottle until the insect is stunned; then the insect can be picked out of the net and put into the bottle. (2) The insect can be grasped through the net with forceps, rather than with the fingers, and transferred to the bottle. (3) The insect may be gotten into a fold of the net and stunned by pinching (pinching the *thorax*), and then transferred to the killing bottle. The third method is the most efficient.

After sweeping, to make sure that no desired individuals escape, the insects can be shaken into the bottom of the net, and this part of the net placed in the killing jar (a large-mouthed jar is needed for this), which is then covered until the insects are stunned. The specimens desired, or the entire catch, can then be transferred to the killing jar.

Another method of getting the results of sweeping, or even individual insects, from the net to the killing jar is to insert the jar into the net. The insect(s) may be worked to the bottom of the net with a few swings, and the net pinched off just above them. Hold the tip of the net up (many insects tend to move upward to escape), and insert the killing jar into the net (with the lid removed), quickly move it past the pinched-off point, and work the insect(s) into the jar. The jar may be capped from the outside long enough to stun the insects, or it may be worked to the open end of the net (with the lid over the jar outside the net), then remove the lid from the outside and cap the jar. Some insects may escape with this method, but with a little experience losses will be minimized.

KILLING BOTTLES

If the insect is to be preserved after it is captured, it must be killed, and killed in such a way that it is not injured or broken; this calls for some sort of killing bottle. Bottles of various sizes and shapes may be used, depending on the type of insects involved, and various materials may be used as the killing agent. It is desirable when in the field to have two or three bottles of different sizes for insects of different types. A separate jar should always be used for Lepidóptera, because their delicate wings may be damaged by other insects (especially beetles), and because their wing scales will come off and adhere to other insects (making them look dusty). It is desirable to have at least one small bottle (perhaps an inch (25 mm) in diameter and 4–6 inches (100–150 mm) in length) for small insects, and one or more larger bottles for larger insects. Corked bottles are preferable to screw-capped bottles, but either type will do. Wide-mouthed bottles or jars are better than narrow-necked ones. All killing bottles, regardless of the killing agent used, should be conspicuously labeled "POISON," and all glass bottles should be reinforced with tape to prevent shattering in case of breakage.

Several materials can be used as the toxic agent in a killing bottle, but we prefer cyanide; such bottles kill quickly and last a long time, while most other materials kill more slowly and do not last so long. Cyanide is extremely poisonous, but with certain precautions bottles made with it can be as safe as bottles made with some other killing agent.

Cyanide bottles can be made in two general ways (Figure 614); those made with calcium cyanide have a plug of cotton and a piece of cardboard to hold the cyanide in the bottle, while those made with sodium or potassium cyanide have plaster of paris holding the cyanide in the bottle. Calcium cyanide may be preferred in small killing bottles made of a vial.

A calcium cyanide killing bottle is made as shown in Figure 614 A. The cotton and cardboard should be packed down tightly, and the cardboard should have some pinholes in it; the bottom and rim of the bottle should be reinforced with tape to reduce the hazards of breakage. If the killing bottle is capped with a large cork, it may be more convenient to put the cyanide in a hole in the bottom of the cork, and keep it there with a plug of cotton and a covering of cloth. Calcium cyanide is a dark gray powder that is often used as a fumigant; it is extremely poisonous and should be handled with great care, and only persons familiar with its properties should use it. This type of bottle is ready for use as soon as it is prepared.

A cyanide bottle made with plaster of paris takes longer to prepare but will last longer. A bottle made with calcium cyanide will last a month or two, whereas one made with sodium or potassium cyanide and plaster will last a year or two. The potassium (or sodium) cyanide should be in a finely granular or powdered form, and the bottle to be used should be clean and dry. The bottle is made as shown in Figure 614 B; after the wet plaster has been poured in, the bottle should be left

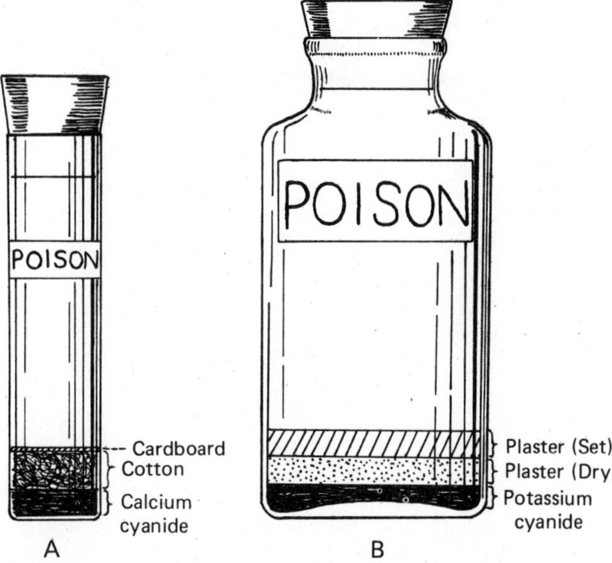

Figure 614. Cyanide bottles. A, a small bottle made up with calcium cyanide; B, a large bottle made up with plaster of paris.

uncorked, preferably outdoors, until the plaster has thoroughly set and dried (a day or two); then it is corked, the bottom is taped, a poison label is put on, and after another day or so it is ready for use.

Other materials that can be used as killing agents in insect bottles are ethyl acetate, carbon tetrachloride, and chloroform; ethyl acetate is the least dangerous of the three to use. Bottles using these materials are made by putting some sort of absorbing material in the bottle and soaking it with the killing agent. Cotton makes a good absorbent material, but if it is used it should be covered with a piece of cardboard or screen; otherwise, the insects become entangled in the cotton and are difficult or impossible to remove without damage. If ethyl acetate or carbon tetrachloride is used, the absorbent material can be plaster of paris, mixed with water and poured into the bottom of the bottle, and allowed to set and thoroughly dry. Killing bottles made with these materials do not last very long and must be recharged frequently. Carbon tetrachloride and chloroform are poisonous, and one should avoid breathing the fumes; ethyl acetate is relatively nontoxic to man (it is an ingredient of nail polish).

The efficiency of a killing bottle depends to a large extent on how it is used. It should never be left uncorked any longer than is necessary to put insects in or take them out; the escaping gas reduces its strength, and an uncorked bottle (particularly one made up with cyanide) is a hazard. The inside of the bottle should be kept dry; bottles sometimes "sweat," that is, moisture from the insects (and sometimes from the plaster) condenses on the inside of the bottle, particularly if it is exposed to bright sunlight. Such moisture will ruin delicate specimens. It is a good idea to keep a few pieces of cleansing tissue or other absorbent material in the bottle at all times, to absorb moisture and to prevent the insects from getting badly tangled up with one another. This material should be changed frequently, and the bottle should be wiped out periodically. A bottle that has been used for Lepidóptera should not be used for other insects unless it is first cleaned to remove scales that would get on new insects put into the bottle.

OTHER TYPES OF COLLECTING APPARATUS

Aerial nets such as those already described are standard collecting equipment for most work, but many other devices are useful in certain situations or for collecting certain types of insects. Some of the more important of these are described below. The collector who has a little ingenuity will be able to devise many others.

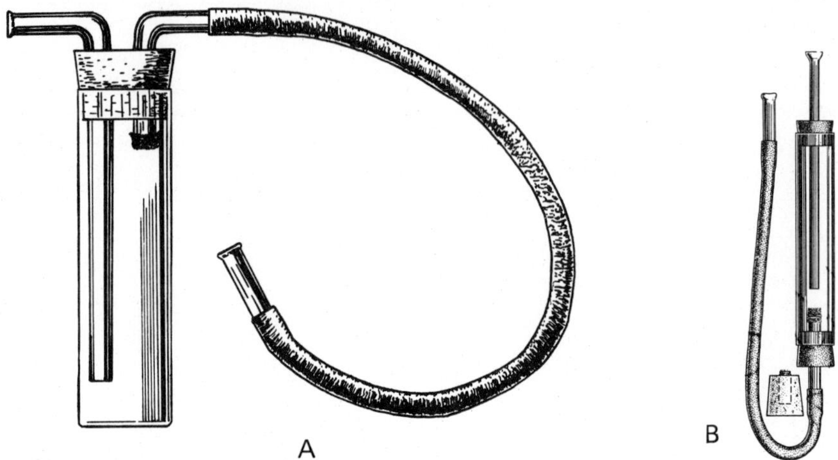

Figure 615. Aspirators. A, the vial type; B, the tube type. (B, from DeLong and Davidson. Courtesy of the Ohio State University Press.)

ASPIRATOR This is a very useful device for capturing small insects, particularly if one wishes to catch them and keep them alive. Two types of aspirators are shown in Figure 615; sucking through the mouthpiece will draw small insects into the vial (A) or tube (B), and a cloth over the inner end of the mouthpiece tube prevents the insects from being sucked into the mouth. If one has a series of these vials or tubes, an insect-filled one can be removed and replaced with an empty one.

BEATING UMBRELLA Many insects that occur on vegetation feign death by dropping off the plant when it is jarred slightly. The collector can take advantage of this habit by placing a collecting device underneath a plant and then jarring the plant with a stick; the insects that fall onto the collecting device beneath may be easily picked up. The best device for this sort of collecting is a beating umbrella (Figure 612 E), an umbrella frame covered with white muslin or light canvas. A white sheet, or even an open insect net, may also be used to catch insects jarred off a plant.

SIFTERS Many small and unusual insects that occur in trash and leaf litter are most easily collected by some sort of sifting device; the insects that occur in such materials can often be collected in no other way. The simplest collecting procedure is to take a handful of the material and sift it slowly onto a large piece of white cloth, oilcloth, or cardboard. The tiny animals falling onto the white surface will reveal themselves by their movement, and can be picked up with an aspirator or a wet brush. The material may also be sifted onto a white cloth from a small box with a screen bottom.

Perhaps the simplest way of getting the insects and other animals out of soil, debris, or leaf litter, is to use a Berlese funnel (Figure 616). A Berlese funnel is an ordinary (usually large) funnel containing a piece of screen or hardware cloth, with a killing jar or container of alcohol below it, and the material to be sifted placed on the screen. An electric light bulb is placed above the funnel and as the upper part of the material in the funnel dries, the insects and other animals move downward and eventually fall into the container below the funnel, where they are killed. A Berlese funnel is the best device for collecting debris-inhabiting insects, mites, pseudoscorpions, and small spiders.

Anyone using a Berlese funnel will notice that many of the animals collected (for example, the springtails and many of the mites) remain on the surface of the alcohol. The fact that many soil- and debris-inhabiting animals will float on alcohol or water makes it possible to get many of these animals out of such materials by putting the materials in water; many animals come to the surface of the water, where they can be removed and placed in alcohol.

TRAPS Traps are an easy and often very effective method of collecting many types of insects. A trap is any device, usually containing something to which the insects are attracted, which is so arranged that once the insects get into it they cannot get out. The attractant used and the general form of the trap will be determined by the type of insects one wants to collect. Space does not permit a description here of many types of traps, but a few can be mentioned; the ingenious collector should be able to devise any that are not described (see Peterson, 1953).

A trap or other device using light as the attractant frequently yields insects in a quantity and quality not obtained by any other type of collecting. Many types of bulbs may be used, some of which are more attractive to insects (or at least to certain types of insects) than ordinary incandescent bulbs. Black light, ultraviolet, and mercury vapor bulbs often attract more insects than ordinary light bulbs.

A light trap for insects may be made in such a way that the insects coming to the trap are diverted, by a series of baffles, into a cyanide jar or container of alcohol (Figure 617 D). Such a trap will catch a lot of insects, but the specimens taken may not always be in very good shape. One can get specimens in better condition by simply waiting at a light and getting desired insects directly into a killing bottle or aspirator as they settle on something near the light (for example, a wall, screen, or sheet).

Walk-in light traps are sometimes used at more or less permanent locations. Such a trap is simply a screened chamber with a light mounted at the top. Insects attracted to this light, instead of falling into a jar of cyanide or alcohol, settle on the floor or walls of the chamber, where they can be picked up by the operator.

A rather elaborate device which is gaining popularity among insect collectors is the Malaise trap, named for Dr. René Malaise of Sweden (Figure 617 C). Many modifications of this trap have been developed, but they are all essentially tentlike structures of fine netting into which flying insects wander. The underlying principle of this type of trap is that insects usually move upward in attempting to escape, and in the Malaise trap they eventually move into a collecting apparatus at the top of the trap, and are killed in a jar of alcohol or one charged with cyanide or ethyl acetate. Such traps often turn up rare, unusual, or elusive insects not taken by collectors using conventional methods. Directions for building Malaise traps are given by Townes (1962, 1972).

Traps of the type shown in Figure 617 B are useful for catching flies that are attracted to decaying materials such as meat and fruit; if the trap is visited frequently, the specimens it catches can be retrieved in good condition. Varying the bait will produce a more varied catch.

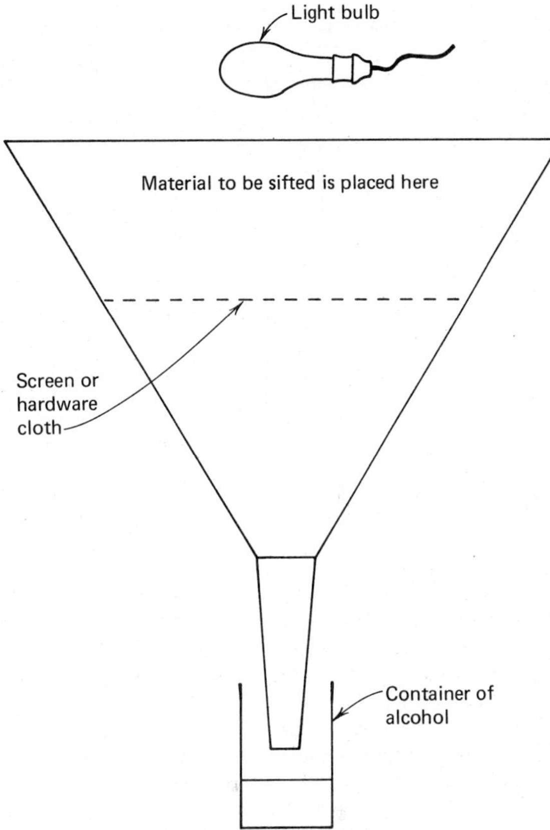

Figure 616. A Berlese funnel. The funnel can be supported by a ringstand, or by three or four legs attached near the middle of the funnel. The light bulb can be that of an ordinary gooseneck lamp, or it can be in a metal cylinder placed over the top of the funnel. The material to be sifted is placed on the screen.

Pitfall traps of the type shown in Figure 617 A are useful for catching carrion beetles and other insects that do not fly readily. Such a trap may be made of a large tin can, preferably with a few holes punched in the bottom to prevent water from accumulating in it, and with some sort of screen over the bait to permit easy removal of the insects caught. The can is sunk in the ground with its top at ground level. Most of the insects attracted by the bait will fall into the can and be unable to get out. The bait may be a dead animal, a piece of meat that will eventually decay, fruit, molasses, or some similar material. Here again, varying the bait will yield a more varied catch.

Household insects that do not fly, such as silverfish and cockroaches, can be trapped by

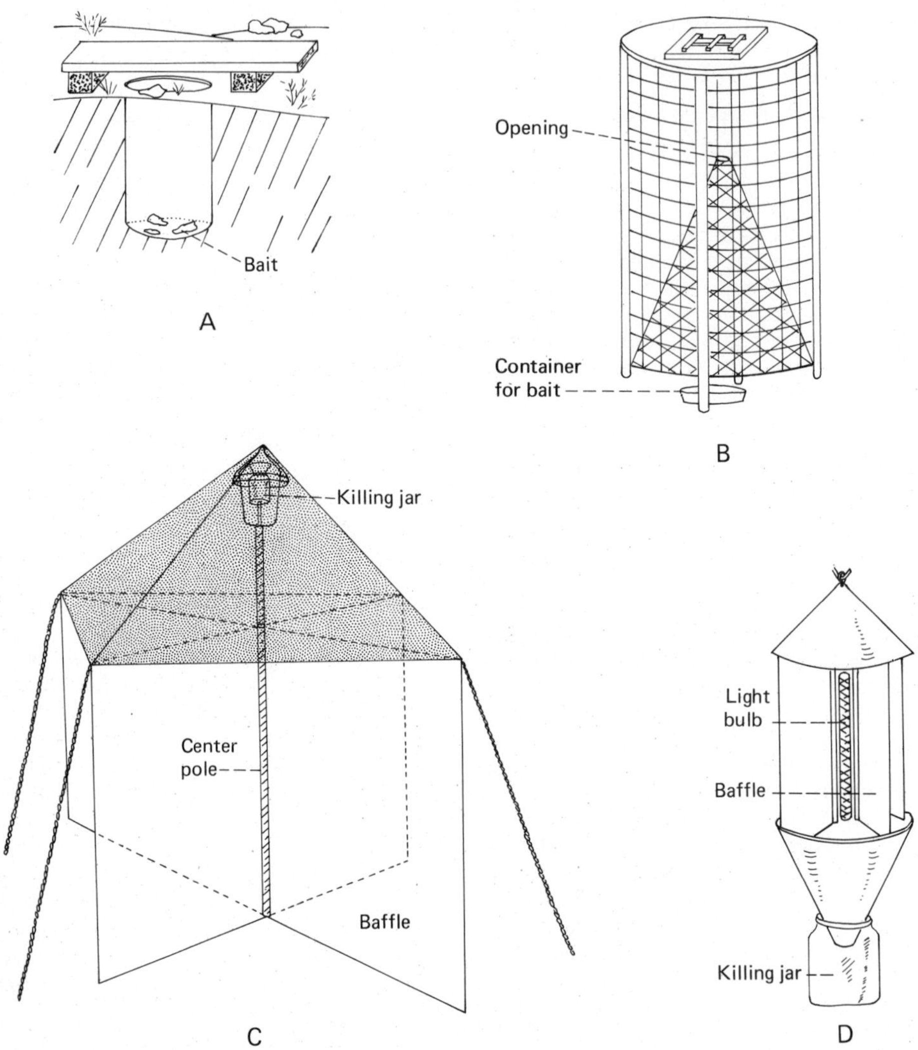

Figure 617. Insect traps. A, a pitfall trap, consisting of a can sunk in the ground; B, a fly trap, a cylindrical screen cage with a screen cone at the bottom; the bait is placed in a container below the center of the cone, and flies attracted to the bait eventually go through the opening at the top of the cone into the main part of the trap, from which they can be removed through the door at the top; C, a Malaise trap, a square tentlike structure supported by a central pole, with screen or cloth baffles across the diagonals, and a killing jar at the top; D, a light trap; specimens attracted to the light are funneled into the killing jar at the bottom.

means of an open-topped baited box. A box 4 or 5 inches deep is placed on the floor, provided with a ramp from the floor to the top of the box, and baited with dog biscuits, crackers, or some similar materials. If the upper 2 or 3 inches (50 to 75 mm) of the box sides are coated on the inside with petroleum jelly, the insects that get into the box will not be able to crawl out.

Many insects can be caught by "sugaring," that is, preparing a sugary mixture and spreading it on tree trunks, stumps, or fence posts. Various mixtures may be used, but one containing something that is fermenting is probably the best; it may be made with molasses or fruit juices and a little stale beer or rum.

AQUATIC COLLECTING EQUIPMENT Many aquatic insects can be collected with one's fingers or with forceps when one is examining plants, stones, or other objects in the water, but many more can be collected by using a dip net, strainer, dipper, or other device. A dip net can be made much like an aerial net, but should be shallower (no deeper than the diameter of the rim) and much stronger. The handle should be heavy, and the rim should be made of a 6- or 9-mm metal rod and securely fastened to the handle. The part of the bag that is attached to the rim should be of canvas, and it is desirable to have an apron of the same material extending down over the front of the bag. The rim need not be circular; many collectors prefer to have the rim bent in the form of the letter D. The bag may be made of heavy marquisette or bolting cloth. Strainers of the tea-strainer type, with a rim from 2 to 6 inches (50–150 mm) in diameter, are useful for aquatic collecting if they are not subjected to too hard use. Dip nets or strainers can be used to collect free-swimming forms, forms on vegetation, and forms burrowing in the sand or muck of the bottom. A good catch can often be obtained in streams by placing the net or strainer at a narrow place in the current and then turning over stones or disturbing the bottom upstream from the net. Retrieving insects from the muck and debris collected in a net or strainer is not always easy, for most of them are not noticed until they move. A good way to locate them is to dump the contents of the net into a large white pan with some water; against the white background, the insects can be more easily located and picked out. The best device for collecting small free-swimming forms such as mosquito larvae or midge larvae is a long-handled white enameled dipper; small larvae are easily seen against the white background of the dipper and can be removed with an eye dropper.

OTHER EQUIPMENT The collector will often need a large heavy knife for prying up bark, cutting open galls, or digging into various materials. A vial of insect pins is useful for pinning together mating pairs before they are put into the killing bottle. A notebook and pencil should always be a part of the collector's gear. The collecting of certain types of insects often requires special items of equipment; the amount and type of equipment a collector uses will depend entirely on the sort of collecting he expects to do.

HANDLING THE CATCH

The collector must learn by experience how long it takes his killing bottles to kill an insect. He will learn that some insects are killed very quickly, while others, even in the same bottle, are very resistant to the killing agent. A mosquito in a strong cyanide bottle will be killed in a few minutes, whereas some of the snout beetles may remain alive in the same bottle for an hour or two. The catch should be kept in the killing bottle until the specimens are killed, but not much longer. Many insects will become discolored if left in too long, particularly in a bottle containing cyanide. It is advisable to remove the insects within an hour or two after they are killed.

Specimens removed from the killing bottle in the field may be placed in pillboxes or paper envelopes for temporary storage. The pillboxes should contain some sort of absorbent material, such as cleansing tissue, which will reduce the bouncing around of the specimens during transportation and will absorb excess moisture. Paper envelopes, either ordinary letter envelopes or triangular envelopes like that shown in Figure 618, are excellent for the temporary storage of large-

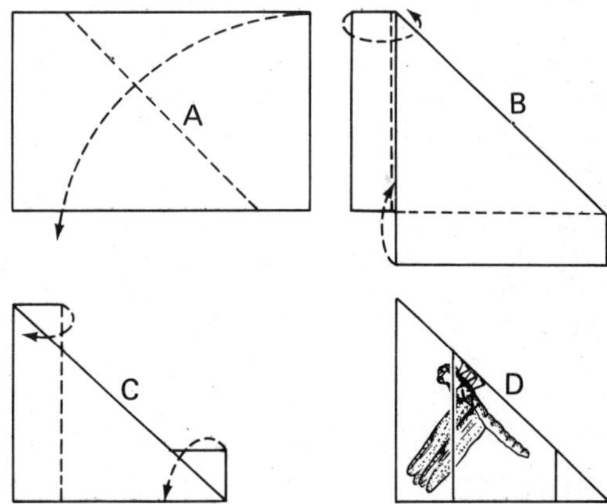

Figure 618. A method of folding triangular paper envelopes for insect specimens. The paper is folded as illustrated in A, B, and C to form the completed envelope D. (From DeLong and Davidson. Courtesy of the Ohio State University Press.)

winged insects such as butterflies, moths, or dragonflies. These triangular envelopes can be made quickly from a sheet of notebook paper, and specimens will remain in good condition in them; data on the collection can be written on the outside.

Many insects may be killed by dropping them directly into 70–90% ethyl or isopropyl alcohol, where they can be stored indefinitely. This method is used exclusively for many insects, such as very minute forms that are to be mounted on microscope slides for detailed study (springtails, lice, fleas, and some Coleóptera, Hymenóptera, and Díptera), and many soft-bodied insects that may shrivel when mounted dry (camel crickets, termites, mayflies, stoneflies, caddisflies, and others). On the other hand, adult Lepidóptera and Odonàta, and most Díptera and Hymenóptera, should not be placed in alcohol. Any collector will soon learn the best way to kill and preserve the various kinds of insects.

Each day's catch should be processed as soon as possible. If specimens are to be pinned in the field, this should be done before they become too stiff to handle without breaking off appendages; many small insects dry very quickly. Specimens to be preserved in alcohol should be put into alcohol as soon as possible after they are killed (or killed directly in alcohol). Insects that are to be stored in paper envelopes (such as Odonàta and Lepidóptera) should be processed while they are still soft enough to be folded (with the wings above the body).

It is extremely important to associate each lot of insects collected with a data slip indicating at least the place and date of the collection. A specimen without data may perhaps be better than no specimen at all—but not much! A specimen with incorrect data is even worse, and will create problems for later workers, especially taxonomists who place considerable importance on the data accompanying specimens. In most instances, such data can be supplied only by the collector, and the longer he waits to label his catch, the greater the chance for errors in the labeling.

MOUNTING AND PRESERVING INSECTS

Insects can be mounted and preserved in various ways. Most specimens are pinned, and once dried will keep indefinitely. Specimens too small to pin can be mounted on "points," on tiny "minuten" pins, or on microscope slides. Large and showy insects, such as butterflies, moths, grasshoppers, dragonflies, and others, may be mounted in various types of glass-topped display boxes. Soft-bodied forms (nymphs, larvae, and many adults) should be preserved in fluids.

RELAXING

All insects should be mounted as soon as possible after they have been collected; if they are allowed to dry they become brittle, and may be broken in the process of being mounted. Specimens stored in pill boxes or envelopes for a long time must be relaxed before they are mounted. Relaxing may be accomplished by means of a relaxing chamber, by means of a special relaxing fluid, or sometimes hard-bodied insects such as beetles can be relaxed enough to pin by dropping them in hot water for a few minutes.

A relaxing chamber can be made of any wide-mouthed can or jar that can be made airtight. The bottom of the jar is covered with wet sand or cloth (preferably with a little carbolic acid added to prevent mold), the insects are put in the jar in open shallow boxes, and the jar is tightly closed. Special jars for this purpose can also be obtained from supply houses. One must learn by experience how long it takes to relax an insect, but specimens are usually sufficiently relaxed to mount after a day or two in such a chamber.

Entire specimens, or parts thereof, can often be relaxed by dipping them in a relaxing fluid for several minutes. The formula for this fluid (sometimes known as Barber's fluid) is as follows:

95% ethyl alcohol	50 cm^3
Water	50 cm^3
Ethyl acetate	20 cm^3
Benzene	7 cm^3

Another method of relaxing a specimen is to inject tap water into it with a hypodermic syringe (with a 20 or 25 gauge needle); the needle is inserted into the thorax under the wings, and the thorax is completely filled with water. This method is particularly useful for Lepidóptera (except perhaps the very small ones) that have been kept in paper envelopes. After the injection the specimen is returned to the envelope for 5–20 minutes, then it should be relaxed enough to mount.

CLEANING SPECIMENS

It is seldom necessary to clean specimens, and it is often better not to do so; a little dirt is preferable to a damaged specimen. Cleaning specimens is most likely to be desirable when they have been collected from mud, dung, or a similar material, some of which has adhered to the specimens. The easiest way to remove this material is to put the specimen in alcohol, or in water to which a detergent has been added. If the material to be removed is greasy, cleaning fluid can be used.

Dust, lint, Lepidóptera scales, and the like may be removed by means of a camel's-hair brush dipped in ether, chloroform, acetone, or other cleaning fluid. This will also remove films of oil or grease that sometimes exude from pinned specimens. Recently ultrasonic cleaners are available which quickly and thoroughly clean specimens.

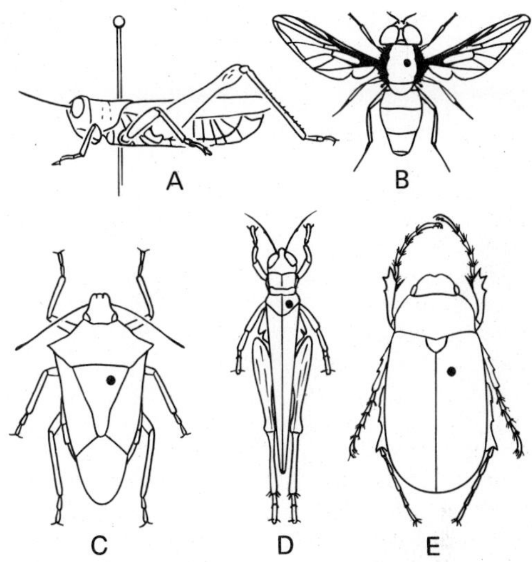

Figure 619. Methods of pinning insects. A, specimen in lateral view showing method of pinning grasshoppers; the black spots in the other figures show the location of the pin in the case of flies (B), bugs (C), grasshoppers (D), and beetles (E). (Courtesy of the Illinois Natural History Survey.)

PINNING

Pinning is the best way to preserve hard-bodied insects; pinned specimens keep well, retain their normal appearance, and are easily handled and studied. The colors often fade when the insect dries, but this is difficult to avoid; bright colors are generally better preserved if the specimens are dried rapidly.

Common pins are undesirable for pinning insects; they are usually too thick and too short, and they rust. Insects should be pinned with a special type of steel pin known as an insect pin. These pins are longer than common pins, they can be obtained in various sizes (thicknesses), and they do not rust. Insect-pin sizes range from 00 to 7; the smaller sizes (that is, smaller in diameter) are too slender for general use, for which sizes 2 and 3 are the best. These pins may be obtained from various supply houses (see list on page 765).

Insects are usually pinned vertically through the body as shown in Figures 619 and 620. Forms such as bees, wasps, flies, butterflies, and moths are pinned through the thorax between the bases of the front wings. With flies and wasps it is desirable to insert the pin a little to the right of the midline. Bugs are pinned through the scutellum (Figure 619 C), a little to the right of the midline if the scutellum is large. Grasshoppers are pinned through the posterior part of the pronotum, just to the right of the midline (Figure 619 D). Beetles should be pinned through the right elytron, about halfway between the two ends of the body (Figure 619 E); the pin should go through the metathorax and emerge through the metasternum (see Figure 243) so as not to damage the bases of the legs. Dragonflies and damselflies are best pinned horizontally through the thorax, with the left side uppermost; this reduces the space necessary to house the collection, and a specimen so pinned can be studied just as easily as one pinned vertically. If the specimen does not have the wings together above its back when it dies, the wings should be so placed and the specimen put into an envelope for a day or so until it has dried enough for the wings to remain in this position. Then it is carefully pinned through the upper part of the thorax, below the base of the wings.

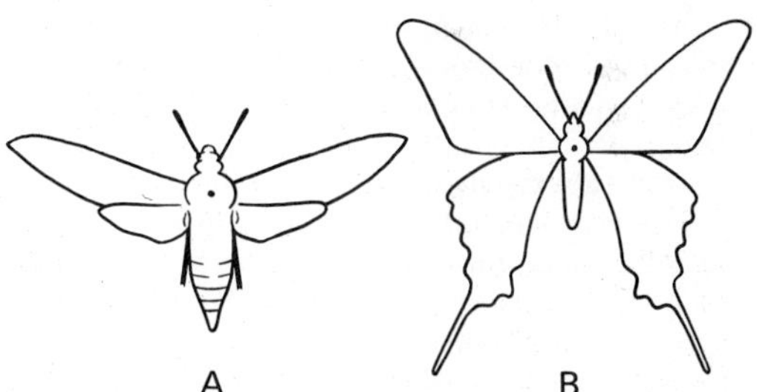

Figure 620. Method of pinning Lepidóptera. These insects are pinned through the center of the thorax, in both moths (A) and butterflies (B). (Courtesy of the Illinois Natural History Survey.)

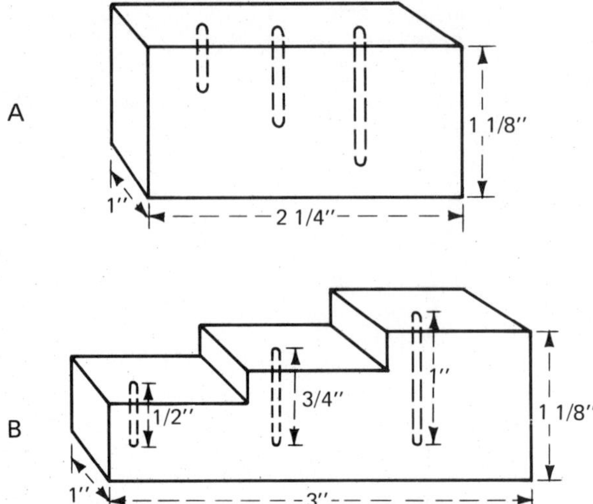

Figure 621. Pinning blocks. These may be a rectangular piece of wood containing holes drilled to different depths (A), or a block shaped like a stair step, with holes drilled to the bottom (B). The block of the type shown in A usually has the holes drilled to depths of 25, 16, and 9.5 mm. After a specimen or label is placed on the pin, the pin is inserted into the appropriate hole until it touches bottom—into the deepest hole for the specimen, the middle hole for the label bearing locality and date, and the last hole for any additional label. (From DeLong and Davidson. Courtesy of the Ohio State University Press.)

The easiest way to pin an insect is to hold it between the thumb and forefinger of one hand and insert the pin with the other. All specimens should be mounted at a uniform height on the pin, about 25 mm above the point. Uniformity (and this applies to the position of labels on the pin as well as to the position of the insect) can be obtained with a pinning block. Pinning blocks are of various types (Figure 621), but a common type (Figure 621 A) consists of a block of wood in which are drilled three small holes of different depths, usually 25, 16, and 9.5 mm, respectively.

If the abdomen sags when the insect is pinned, as it sometimes does, the pinned specimen may be stuck on a vertical surface with the abdomen hanging down, and left there until it dries. If the insect is pinned on a horizontal surface, a piece of stiff paper or cardboard may be placed on the pin beneath the insect to support it until it dries.

It is not necessary that the appendages of a pinned insect be in a lifelike position (though the appearance of the collection will be greatly improved if they are), but it is desirable to have them projecting out from the body slightly so that they can be easily examined. The legs should be extended enough so that all parts are easily visible, and the wings should be extended out from the body so that the venation can be seen. Pinned bees that have the tongue extended will be easier to identify than those with the tongue folded tightly against the underside of the head.

Various types of mounting boards are used by entomologists to position the appendages of insects while they dry. These may be made of balsa wood, cork, styrofoam, cardboard, or any soft material that allows a pin to be inserted deeply enough for the lower surface of the specimen to rest on a flat surface; pins can then be used to arrange the legs, antennae, or other parts in any position desired, and hold them there until the specimen dries. Once the student becomes familiar with the characters used in identification in various groups, he can arrange and prepare his specimens accordingly.

A sheet of cork, balsa wood, or other soft material is very useful for the temporary storage of pinned insects until they can be sorted and put into boxes.

SPREADING INSECTS

It does not greatly matter about the position of the legs or wings of most insects when the specimen is pinned, as long as all parts can be easily seen and studied. With moths and butterflies and possibly some other insects, and in the case of insects mounted in display boxes (see below), the wings should be spread before the insect is put into the collection. The method of spreading will depend on whether the specimen is mounted pinned or unpinned, and the position into which the wings should be put depends on the type of insect.

An insect that is to be a part of a pinned collection is spread on a spreading board (Figure 622). Spreading boards can be obtained from a supply house or they can be made at home. An insect to be mounted under glass, as in a Riker or glass mount, may be spread on any flat surface such as a piece of corrugated cardboard or a sheet of cork or balsa wood. An insect spread on a spreading board is ordinarily spread dorsal side up, and the pin is left in the insect; one spread on a flat surface for a Riker mount is spread in an upside-down position, and the pin is *not* left in the body of the insect.

There are certain standard positions for the wings of a spread insect. In the case of butterflies and moths (many figures in Chapter 29) and mayflies (Figure 92) the rear margins of the front wings should be straight across, at right angles to the body, and the hind wings should be far enough forward that there is no large gap at the side between the front and hind wings. With grasshoppers, dragonflies, damselflies, and most other insects, the front margins of the hind wings should be straight across, with the front wings far enough forward that they just clear the hind wings. The front and hind wings of a butterfly or moth are always overlapped, with the front edge of the hind wing *under* the rear edge of the front wing; in other insects the wings are usually not overlapped.

The actual process of spreading an insect is relatively simple, though it requires a little practice to acquire any degree of proficiency. One must be very careful not to damage the specimen in the spreading process. Butterflies and moths must be handled with particular care in order not to rub off the scales on the wings; these insects should always be handled with forceps. If the specimen is to be mounted on a spreading board, it is first pinned (like any other pinned insect), and the pin inserted in the groove of the spreading board until the wings are flush with the surface of the board. If the specimen is to be spread upside down on a flat surface, the pin is inserted into the thorax from underneath, and the insect is pinned on its back on some flat surface. It is often advisable to place a pin along each side of the body to prevent it from swinging out of line.

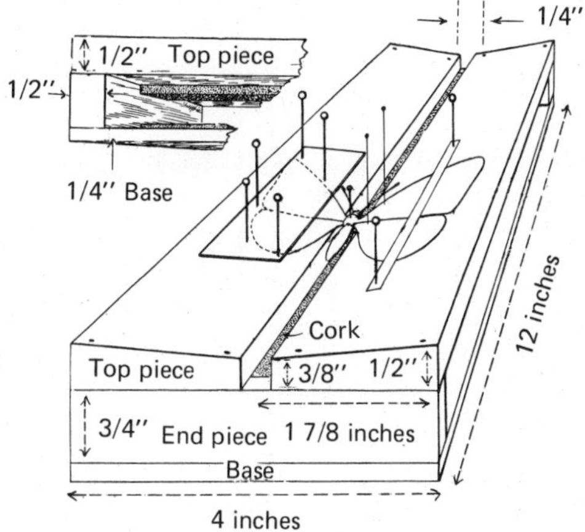

Figure 622. The spreading board, showing dimensions, details of construction (inset), and a spread specimen. The wings of the specimen may be held in place by a single broad strip of paper as shown on the left wings, or by a narrower strip and pins as shown on the right wings. (Courtesy of the Illinois Natural History Survey.)

The steps in spreading a butterfly are shown in Figure 623. The wings are moved into position by pins and held there by strips of paper or other material pinned to the board; and the antennae are oriented and held in position by means of pins. The wings should be maneuvered by pins from near the base of the wing, along the front margin; the veins are heavier at this point and there is less likelihood of tearing the wing. Do not put the pin through the wing if it can be avoided as this leaves a hole in the wing. The specimen should be fastened down securely, and it may sometimes be necessary to use more strips of paper than are shown in Figure 623. This figure illustrates a method of spreading an insect upside down on any flat surface, and the final step in this process is to hold the body down with forceps and carefully remove the pin (G); if the specimen is spread on a spreading board the steps are similar, but the pin is left in the specimen.

The length of time it takes a spread specimen to dry will depend on the size of the specimen and such other factors as temperature and humidity. No general statement of the time required can be made; the student will have to learn this by experience. To determine whether the specimen is ready to be removed from the spreading board, touch the abdomen gently with a needle; if the abdomen can be moved independently of the wings,

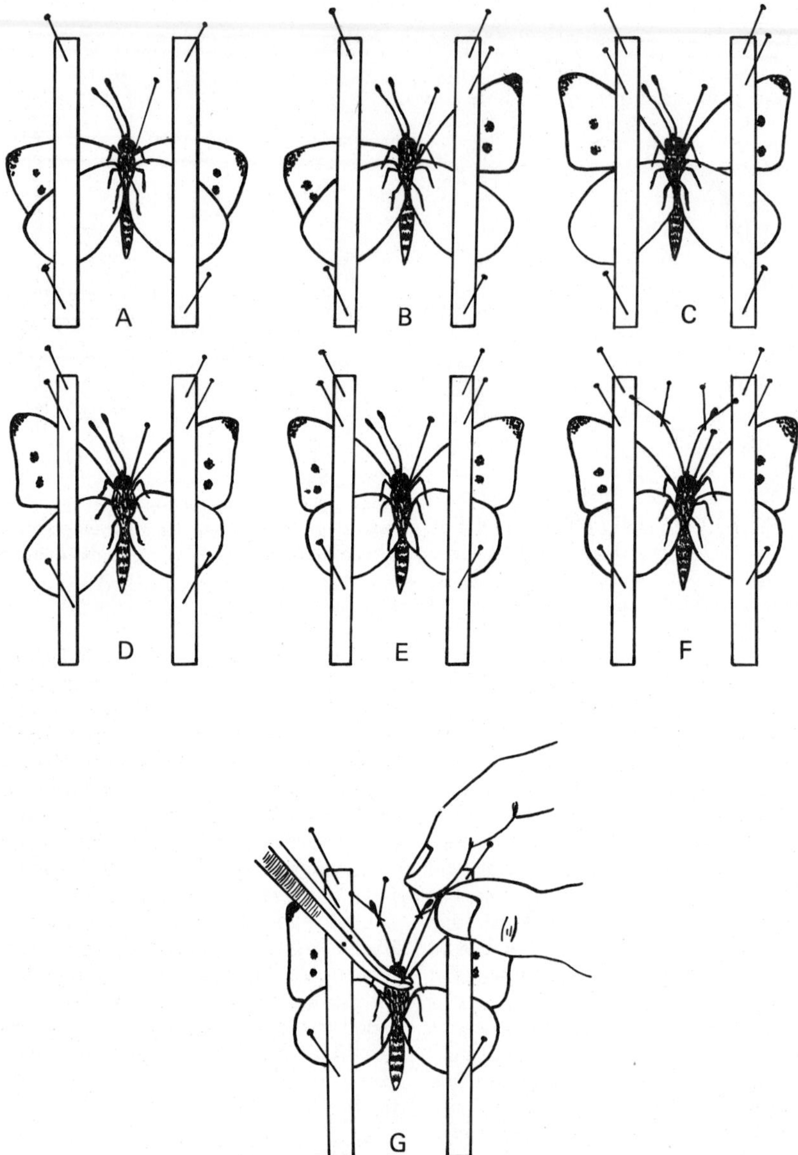

Figure 623. Steps in spreading a butterfly upside down on a flat surface. A, position before starting to raise the wings; B, front wing on one side raised; C, front wing on the other side raised, with hind margin of front wings in a straight line; D, hind wing on one side raised; E, hind wing on the other side raised; F, antennae oriented and held in position by pins; G, removing the pin from the body of the butterfly.

the specimen is not yet dry; if the body is stiff, the specimen can be removed. Some of the larger moths may take a week or more to dry thoroughly. In every case care should be taken that the data on the specimen not be lost; these data can be noted alongside the specimen when it is spread.

In camp work or in the lower school grades, for example, mounting in a Riker or similar mount is

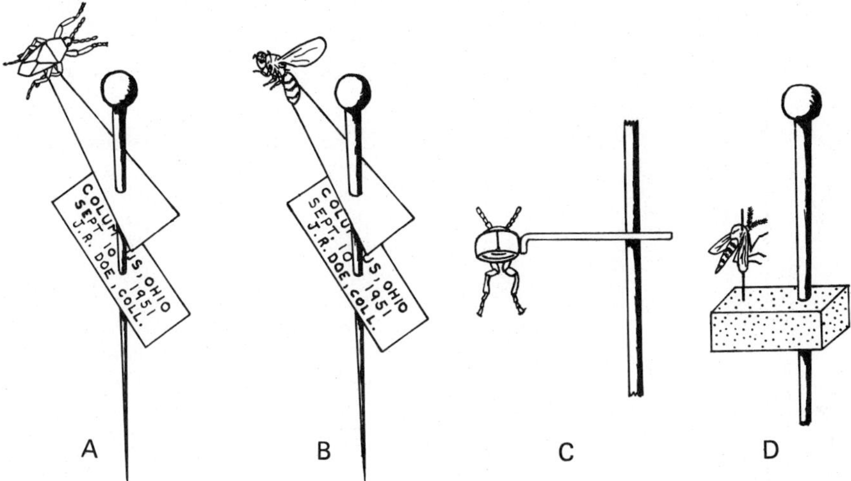

Figure 624. Methods of mounting minute insects. A, bug on point, dorsal side up; B, fly on point, left side up; C, beetle mounted dorsal side up, attached by its side to the bent-down tip of the point; D, mosquito mounted on a minuten pin.

preferable to spreading the specimen pinned; such specimens are more easily displayed and are less subject to breakage. On the other hand, spread specimens in good scientific collections are nearly always pinned. Circumstances will determine what type of spreading method is to be used.

MOUNTING SMALL INSECTS

Insects too small to pin may be mounted on a card point (Figures 624 A–C and 625), on a "minuten" pin (Figure 624 D), or on a microscope slide, or they may be preserved in liquid. Most small specimens are mounted on points.

Points are elongated triangular pieces of light cardboard or celluloid, about 8 or 10 mm long and 3 or 4 mm wide at the base. The point is pinned through the base, and the insect is glued to the tip of the point. Points can be cut with scissors, or they can be cut with a special type of punch (obtainable from supply houses).

Putting an insect on a point is a very simple process. The point is put on the pin, the pin is grasped by the pointed end, and the upper side of the tip of the point is touched to the glue and then touched to the insect. One should use as little glue as possible (so that body parts are not covered by it), and the specimen should be correctly oriented on the point. The standard positions of an insect mounted on a point are shown in Figure 624 A–C; if the insect is put on the point dorsal side up (A), the point should not extend beyond the middle of the body. It is important that body parts to be examined when the insect is being identified should not be embedded in glue. Beetles mounted on points should always have the ventral side of the body visible; flies, wasps, and other insects in which the wings are extended above the body are best mounted on their side (B).

The glue used in mounting insects on points should be quick-drying and should be quite hard when it sets. A good type of glue to use is a commercial glue (not paste or mucilage) or household cement. Glue is also useful in repairing broken specimens and replacing broken-off wings or legs.

DRYING SPECIMENS

Small specimens will dry quickly in the open air, but it may sometimes be desirable to artificially hasten the drying of larger insects. Large specimens will eventually dry in the open air, but it is not advisable to leave them exposed for very long because of the possibility of damage by dermestids, ants, or other pests. A chamber with one or more light bulbs can be used for rapid drying. A simple drying chamber can be made from a wooden box with a door on one side; slats may be

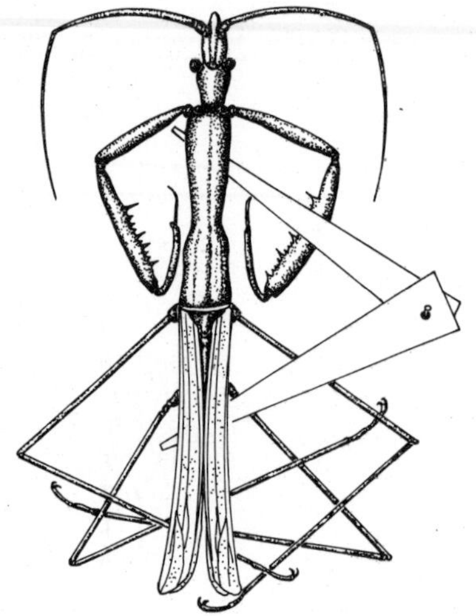

Figure 625. A method of mounting long slender insects that are too small to pin; such insects are mounted on two points.

placed on the sides of the box to allow mounting or spreading boards to be arranged at various distances from the heat source (the light bulbs). Such boxes should be vented with a few small holes in the side or top to allow moisture to escape.

Many soft-bodied arthropods (insect larvae, spiders, and others) can be dehydrated by freeze-drying or vacuum-drying. These techniques yield specimens that are not particularly fragile, showing no distortion and very little color loss, and they subsequently show no indication of reabsorption of water or decomposition. After dehydration they are pinned and stored like any other pinned insect. The equipment and procedures used in freeze-drying are described by Woodring and Blum (1963); those for vacuum-drying are described by Blum and Woodring (1963).

Another method of preserving larvae, which is often used for caterpillars, is by inflation. Inflated larvae are very fragile, but they show excellent color preservation and little or no distortion. The equipment and procedures used in inflating larvae are described by Peterson (1948:4–10) (see page 148 for reference).

PRESERVATION OF INSECTS IN FLUIDS

Any type of insect can be preserved in fluid. Insects may be preserved in fluid temporarily until one has an opportunity to pin them, and many collectors prefer to store their collection in fluid rather than dried in envelopes or pillboxes. However, specimens preserved in fluids are usually not so easily examined as those on pins or points, and in general any insect that *can* be preserved dry should be mounted on a pin or point.

The forms for which preservation in fluids is the standard means of preservation consist of the following: (1) soft-bodied insects (for example, mayflies, caddisflies, stoneflies, midges, and others), which would shrivel and become distorted if pinned and allowed to dry; (2) many very small insects, which are best studied in detail when mounted on a microscope slide (for example, lice, fleas, thrips, Collémbola, and others; (3) insect larvae and most insect nymphs; and (4) arthropods other than insects.

The fluid generally used for the preservation of insects and other arthropods is ethyl alcohol (70–80 per cent). The preservation is better for many forms if certain other substances are added to the alcohol; the most commonly used modifications of ethyl alcohol are the following:

Hood's Solution:
- 70–80% ethyl alcohol .... 95 cm^3
- Glycerine .... 5 cm^3

Kahle's Solution:
- 95% ethyl alcohol .... 30 cm^3
- Formaldehyde .... 12 cm^3
- Glacial acetic acid .... 4 cm^3
- Water .... 60 cm^3

Alcoholic Bouin's Solution:
- 80% ethyl alcohol .... 150 cm^3
- Formaldehyde .... 60 cm^3
- Glacial acetic acid .... 15 cm^3
- Picric acid .... 1 g

Ethyl alcohol (and the modifications of it mentioned above) can also be used as a killing agent for many insects and other arthropods, but it is unsatisfactory as a killing agent for insect larvae. The killing agents commonly used for larvae are the following:

KAAD Mixture:
- 95% ethyl alcohol .... 70–100 cm^3
- Kerosene .... 10 cm^3
- Glacial acetic acid .... 20 cm^3
- Dioxane .... 10 cm^3

XA Mixture:
- 95% ethyl alcohol .... 50 cm^3
- Xylene .... 50 cm^3

If KAAD is used, the amount of kerosene should be reduced for soft-bodied larvae such as maggots. Larvae killed in either of these mixtures are ready for transfer to alcohol for storage after ½ to 4 hours. In the case of insects killed in alcohol, the alcohol should be changed after the first few days, as it becomes diluted by the body fluids of the animals put in it. Any of these killing agents are likely to remove the bright colors of larvae, especially greens, yellows, and reds. All known killing and preserving fluids are likely to destroy some colors.

A problem always encountered when specimens are preserved in fluids is the evaporation of the fluid. The vials should be stoppered with rubber, neoprene, or polyethylene (not cork) stoppers, and it is advisable to use oversized stoppers that do not extend very far into the bottle. Screw-cap vials are satisfactory if the cap is tight-fitting. Procaine vials or tubes (usually available free from any dentist) make ideal temporary containers for many small forms. All containers should be well filled with fluid, and should be examined at least once or twice a year so that evaporated fluid can be replaced. Evaporation may be retarded by covering the stoppers with some sort of sealing material such as parafin; another method is to place a number of small stoppered vials in a large jar, fill the jar with alcohol, and seal the jar with a rubber gasket.

MOUNTING ON MICROSCOPE SLIDES

Many small arthropods (lice, fleas, thrips, midges, mites, and others), and often such isolated body parts as legs or genitalia, are best studied when mounted on microscope slides. Material so mounted is generally transferred to a slide from preserving fluid, and the mount may be temporary or permanent. "Temporary" mounts are used for material that is to be returned to the preserving fluid after study; such mounts may last anywhere from a few minutes to many months, depending on the mounting medium used. "Permanent" mounts are used for material that is not to be returned to the preserving fluid after study; such mounts do not last indefinitely, but may last for many years. Specimens mounted on microscope slides for class use are usually mounted as "permanent" mounts; specimens of particular taxonomic value, which one would like to keep indefinitely should be kept in fluids, and mounted for study only in temporary mounts.

Many small or soft-bodied specimens may be mounted directly in a mounting medium, but others (especially dark-colored or thick-bodied specimens, or such structures as genitalia) must be cleared before mounting; some mounting media have a clearing action. Several substances may be used as clearing agents, but the most commonly used ones are probably potassium hydroxide (KOH) and Nesbitt's solution. KOH can be used for almost any arthropod or arthropod structure; Nesbitt's solution is often used for clearing such small arthropods as mites, lice, and Collémbola. After clearing in KOH the specimen should be washed in water (preferably with a little acetic acid added) to remove any excess of the KOH; its subsequent treatment will depend on the type of medium in which it is mounted. Specimens cleared in Nesbitt's solution can be transferred directly to some mounting media, but with other media must be run through certain reagents first.

KOH used for clearing is a 10–15 percent solution; the formula for Nesbitt's solution is as follows:

Chloral hydrate	40 g
Concentrated HC1	2.5 cm³
Distilled water	25–50 cm³
(more for lightly sclerotized specimens)	

KOH can be used cold or warm, or the specimen may be boiled in it; boiling is faster but may sometimes distort the specimen. Clearing in cold KOH requires from several hours to a day or more; the same specimen may be cleared in a few minutes by boiling. Nesbitt's solution is usually used cold, and the clearing may require from a few hours to a few days.

Small specimens mounted on microscope slides can be mounted on a regular slide without any special support for the cover glass other than the mounting medium itself. Larger or thicker specimens should be mounted on a depression slide or with some sort of support for the cover glass, to keep it level and to prevent the specimen from being flattened. The support for a cover glass on an ordinary miscroscope slide may consist of small pieces of glass or a piece of fine wire bent into a loop. Some specimens are best studied in a depression slide or small dish without a cover glass so that the specimen can be maneuvered and examined from different angles. If a cover glass is added, most specimens are mounted dorsal side up. Fleas are usually mounted with the left side up, and many mites are commonly mounted ventral side up.

The media most often used for temporary slide mounts are water or alcohol, glycerine, and glycerine jelly. Water and alcohol evaporate rapidly, and mounts with these materials generally last only a few minutes unless more of the medium is added. Temporary slides made with glycerine or glycerine jelly are much better and last a relatively long time; they can be made semipermanent by "ringing" (putting a ring of asphaltum, nail polish, or a similar material around the edge of the cover glass). With glycerine jelly a bit of the jelly is put on the slide and liquefied by heat; then the specimen is added and oriented and a cover glass is put on; this material cools to a solid jelly. Specimens mounted in glycerine jelly can be unmounted by reversing the process. Specimens can be put into glycerine or glycerine jelly directly from water or alcohol.

The media used for permanent slide mounts are of two general types: those with a water base, and resins. Specimens can be mounted in water base media directly from water or alcohol; such mounts are somewhat less permanent than resin mounts, but their life can be prolonged by ringing. Specimens mounted in a resin must first be dehydrated (by running through successively increasing concentrations of alcohol: 70, 95, and 100 percent), and then through xylol and into the resin. The most commonly used resin is balsam. There are many water-base media, but the following is one of the best:

Hoyer's Chloral Hydrate (Berlese's Fluid):

Water	50 cm³
Gum arabic	30 g
Chloral hydrate	200 g
Glycerine	20 cm³

The gum arabic should be ground-up crystals or powder, not flakes; this mixture should be filtered through glass wool before use.

All permanent slide mounts take some time to dry; they should be kept horizontal (cover glass up) during drying, and are best stored in slide boxes in this same position.

It is sometimes desirable to stain an insect before it is mounted. A number of different stains are suitable for this purpose, but one very commonly used is acid fuchsin. The procedure to be followed in using this stain on scale insects is outlined on page 320.

STUDIES OF INSECT GENITALIA

Many taxonomic studies of insects involve a detailed study of the external genitalia (see page 26), particularly those of the male. The genitalia are sclerotized structures that can sometimes be studied in the dried insect without any special treatment of the specimen, but in most cases are partly or largely internal and must be removed and cleared for detailed study.

If the genitalia are to be removed and cleared, the abdomen of the insect (or the apical part of it) is removed and placed in a solution of KOH (about 15 percent). Clearing may be accomplished in a few minutes by boiling, or by leaving the genitalia in the KOH for a longer period at room temperature; in the latter case, clearing may require from a few hours to a few days, depending on how heavily sclerotized these structures are. Overclearing renders the genitalia transparent and difficult to study; such genitalia are more easily studied if stained with borax carmine after clearing.

After the genitalia are cleared, they are washed in water with a little acetic acid added (about 1 drop per 50 cm³ of water), and placed in small dishes of glycerine for study. They can be mounted on microscope slides, but this permits a study from only one angle; in small dishes they can be turned and studied from any angle desired.

After the study is completed, the genitalia are stored in microvials of glycerine (vials about 10–12 mm in length), and these vials are kept with the specimens from which the genitalia were removed. If the genitalia came from a pinned specimen, the vial is put on the pin (the pin going through the cork of the vial) below the specimen. Genitalia removed from a specimen must be handled in such a way that they can always be associated with the specimen from which they came.

LABELING

The scientific value of an insect specimen depends to a large extent on the information regarding the date and locality of its capture, and to a lesser extent on such additional information as the name of the collector and the habitat or food plant on which the specimen was collected. The beginning student may look upon such labeling as an unnecessary chore, but the time will always come when data on a specimen are indispensable. An insect collector should *always* label his specimens with date and locality; this is the minimum amount of data for a specimen; additional data are desirable, but optional.

The appearance of a collection of pinned insects is greatly influenced by the nature of the labels. Small, neat, and properly oriented labels add much to the collection. They should be on fairly stiff white paper, and preferably not larger than 6 by 19 mm in size. They should be at a uniform height on the pin, parallel to and underneath the insect. One label only is placed about 16 mm above the point of the pin, or if more than one label is used, the uppermost one should be at this distance above the point. The labels should be oriented so that all are read from the same side; we prefer that they be read from the right side (Figure 628), but most people prefer that they be read from the left side. In the case of specimens mounted on points, the label should extend parallel to the point (Figure 624 A, B) and be offset like the point. If the pinned specimens in the collection have the labels read from the right, specimens on points placed with them should have the point directed downward; if the pinned specimens have the labels read from the left, specimens on points placed with them should have the point directed upward (so that all labels can be read from the same side). If there are two or more labels on the pin (for example, one for locality, date and collector, as in Figure 626, and another for the host plant), the labels should be parallel and arranged to be read from the same side.

Labels indicating locality, date, and collector may be printed by hand with a fine-pointed pen or they may be obtained partly printed from a supply house (Figure 626). A number of labels may be typed on a sheet of plain paper and photographed, and the labels cut from a print made of the photograph; the size of the print will determine the size of the labels.

The discussion above applies to labels containing data concerning the locality, date, and collector, and not to labels identifying the insects. Identifying labels are discussed below, under "Housing, Arrangement, and Care of the Collection."

Labels for specimens preserved in fluids should be written on a good grade of rag paper with India or other waterproof ink, and placed inside the container with the specimen(s). Labels for specimens mounted on microscope slides are attached to the upper surface of the slide, on one or both sides of the cover glass.

HOUSING, ARRANGEMENT, AND CARE OF THE COLLECTION

The basic considerations in housing, arrangement, and care of an insect collection are the same whether the collection consists of a few cigar boxes of specimens or thousands of museum drawers containing millions of specimens. The specimens in a collection must be systematically

Columbus Columbus Columbus Columbus Columbus Columbus
O. O. O. O. O. O.
Columbus Columbus Columbus Columbus Columbus Columbus
O. O. O. O. O. O.
Columbus Columbus Columbus Columbus Columbus Columbus
O. O. O. O. O. O.
Columbus Columbus Columbus Columbus Columbus Columbus
O. O. O. O. O. O.
Columbus Columbus Columbus Columbus Columbus Columbus
O. O. O. O. O. O.

Lincoln Co., Lincoln Co., Lincoln Co., Lincoln Co., Lincoln Co.,
Me. Me. Me. Me. Me.
D.J. Borror D.J. Borror D.J. Borror D.J. Borror D.J. Borror
Lincoln Co., Lincoln Co., Lincoln Co., Lincoln Co., Lincoln Co.,
Me. Me. Me. Me. Me.
D.J. Borror D.J. Borror D.J. Borror D.J. Borror D.J. Borror
Lincoln Co., Lincoln Co., Lincoln Co., Lincoln Co., Lincoln Co.,
Me. Me. Me. Me. Me.
D.J. Borror D.J. Borror D.J. Borror D.J. Borror D.J. Borror

Figure 626. Two sheets of printed locality labels (actual size), each label with a space for writing in the date. Labels containing the name of a town are preferable to those containing the name of a county, particularly in sections of the country where the counties are large.

arranged, and protected from museum pests, light, and moisture. The general arrangement of a collection will depend principally on its size, the purpose for which it is intended, and the method used in preserving the specimens (whether they are pinned, in envelopes, in liquid, on slides, etc.).

Pinned insects should be kept in dust-proof boxes having a soft bottom that will permit easy pinning. Several types of insect boxes may be purchased from supply houses; the most commonly used type is made of wood, about 9 by 13 by 2½ inches (230 by 330 by 60 mm) in size, with a tight-fitting lid and an inner bottom of sheet cork, composition board, or foam plastic. Such boxes usually cost from \$3.50 to \$15.00; the better boxes of this type are called Schmitt boxes.

Satisfactory low-cost pinning boxes may be made of cigar boxes or heavy cardboard boxes by lining the bottoms with sheet cork, balsa wood, foam plastic, or soft corrugated cardboard. This bottom material should be glued in place, or cut so that it fits very tightly into the box. The enthusiastic beginner will soon find that he requires more than one box; he will initially wish to arrange his specimens by orders, and will probably have a separate box (or more than one box) for each order. As the collection grows he can add more boxes, so that he can expand with a minimum of rearranging or transferring specimens from box to box.

For a small collection that is housed in one or a few boxes, an arrangement similar to that shown

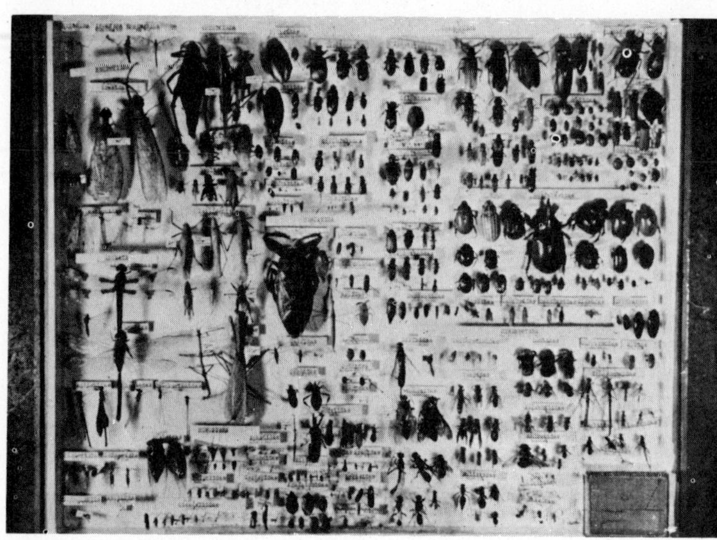

Figure 627. A synoptic insect collection.

in Figure 627 is suggested. It is unlikely that anyone except the specialist will have the specimens in his collection identified further than to family, and for many collectors, particularly the beginner, it will be difficult enough to carry the identification that far. The simplest arrangement, therefore, is to have the specimens arranged by order and family, with the order label (containing the order name and common name) on a separate pin, and the family label (containing family and common names) either on a separate pin or on the pin of the first insect in a row of specimens in that family.

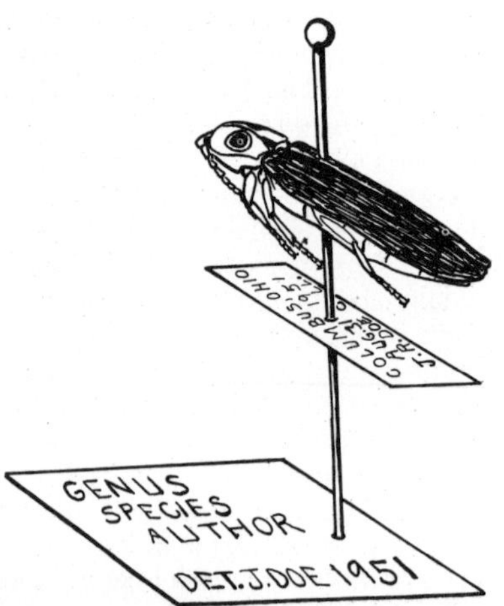

Figure 628. The identification label, giving the scientific name of the insect and the name of the person identifying the specimen.

There are various ways of arranging the specimens in a small collection, but the arrangement should be neat and systematic, and the labels should be easily seen.

Most large institutions and many private collectors house their collections in uniform glass-topped museum drawers which fit into steel cabinets. Specimens may be pinned directly into the cork or foam plastic bottoms in such drawers, but usually they are pinned in small unit trays of various sizes which fit snugly in the drawers (Figure 629). The unit tray system facilitates rapid expansion and rearrangement of the collection without the need of handling individual specimens, which is time-consuming and hazardous to the specimens. The unit trays are of a convenient size to fit under a dissecting microscope, so that unless it is necessary to examine the ventral surface of a specimen, the specimen can be examined without removing it from the tray, thus reducing the chance of breakage.

In larger collections, such as those of specialists or those in museums, where the specimens are identified to species, the species determination is usually put on a plain white or bordered label placed low on the pin against the bottom of the box. This label contains the complete scientific name (genus, species, subspecies if any, and the name of the describer), the name of the person making the determination, and the date (usually the year only) the determination was made (Figure 628). In large collections where each drawer contains a series of unit trays (Figure 629), each unit tray usually contains specimens of just one species.

Figure 629. A drawer of a large insect collection.

Many insect collectors eventually become interested in and concentrate their efforts on a particular order, family, or even genus. By contacts and exchanges with other collectors interested in that group a collector may build up a sizeable collection, and be in a position to contribute to our knowledge of that group by his publications. Some collectors prefer to specialize on insects from a particular habitat (aquatic insects, wood borers, flower-frequenting insects, gall insects, leaf miners, etc.), medically important insects, the insect pests of particular types of plants (Figure 630), beneficial insects, or those with particular habits (predators, parasites, scavengers, etc.). The possibilities are many.

We believe that everyone interested in entomology, regardless of the field in which he is primarily interested, should concentrate on a particular taxonomic group. A certain satisfaction comes with a thorough knowledge of even a small group of animals, and such a study can prove to be a very interesting hobby for a person whose major interest or occupation is in another field.

DISPLAY MOUNTING

Many collectors may wish to keep their collection in containers where the insects can be easily displayed. Several types of mounts are useful for this purpose. A pinned collection may be easily displayed if it is mounted in glass-topped boxes or in glass-doored wall cabinets; in the latter case the back of the cabinet should be covered with a material that will permit easy pinning. Butterflies, moths, and many other insects may be displayed in Riker mounts—boxes in which the insects are directly under the glass top and on cotton (Figure 631). Cases somewhat similar to Riker mounts, but without the cotton and with glass on the top and bottom (Figures 632 A and 633 A), are useful for displaying one or a few specimens (that is, one or a few in each mount). It is also possible to enclose specimens between sheets of plastic, or to embed specimens in plastic.

RIKER MOUNTS A Riker mount (Figure 631) is a cotton-filled cardboard box with most of the lid removed and replaced with glass, and with the glass top holding the insects in place on the cotton. Riker mounts may be of almost any size (12 by 16 inches (0.3 by 0.4 m) is about the largest size that is practical), and are about 19 to 25 mm deep. They can be purchased from supply houses, but they are very easily made at home; all that is required is a box, glass, cotton, and binding tape. Almost any sort of cardboard box may be used; if it is too deep, it can be cut down. Cardboard is most easily cut with a razor blade held in a holder; such holders can be purchased from any hardware store or "five-and-ten" for about 25 cents. A section of the lid is cut out, leaving a margin around the edge of the lid about 6 to 9 mm. A piece of glass (windowpane thickness will do) is then cut to fit on the inside of the lid. Anyone who can use a glass cutter can cut the glass himself, often from discarded pieces; otherwise,

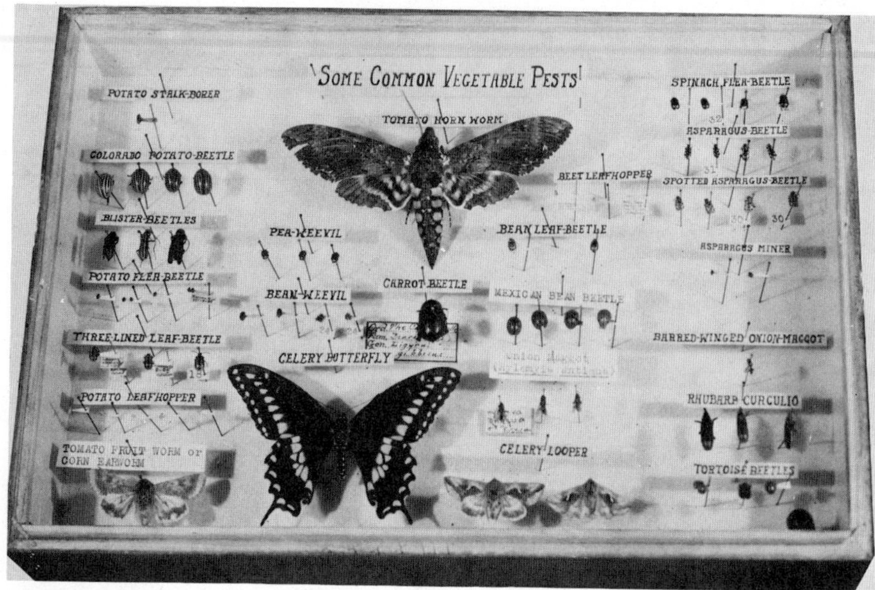

Figure 630. An illustrative collection showing some common insect pests of vegetables.

he can buy the glass and have it cut at a hardware store. Before the glass is put into the lid, it is well to cover the lid with binding tape. This will greatly improve the appearance of the box, particularly if the box originally had printing on it. Black tape makes the best-looking boxes. A little practice will enable one to cover a homemade box neatly. The glass is held in the lid with strips of gummed paper or masking tape on the four sides, each strip as long as that side of the glass. The cotton used should be of a good grade, with a smooth surface; it should be thick enough to extend a little way above the sides of the box before the lid is put on, and should be cut a little small and stretched to fit the box. If one wishes to hang up this sort of mount, two brass fasteners can be put into the bottom (from the underside, and reinforced on the inside with gummed paper) and a piece of string or wire tied between the two fasteners (Figure 631 B). One should be careful to place the insects in the box so that they will be right side up when the box is hung. When large-bodied insects are placed in a Riker mount, a little hole should be teased in the cotton with forceps for the body of the insect. After the specimens are in the box, the lid is put on and fastened with pins or tape.

It is sometimes desirable to mount individual insects in small Riker mounts. Such mounts may be made in any small box (for example, a pillbox), and if the box is not more than 2 or 3 inches (50 or 75 mm) wide, a sheet of plastic (which can be cut with scissors) can be used in place of glass.

GLASS MOUNTS Mounts similar to Riker mounts, but without the cotton and with glass on the top and bottom (Figures 632 A and 633 A), are excellent for displaying individual moths, butterflies, or other insects. They are made in two general ways: all glass (Figure 632) or with a cardboard frame (Figure 633). The size will depend on the size of the specimen(s) to be mounted. One should allow a margin on all four sides of the mount, and the mount should be deep enough to accommodate the body and legs of the specimen. Mounts for large-bodied insects such as sphinx moths will be fairly heavy if made entirely of glass, and for such insects a mount with a cardboard frame may be preferable; for smaller insects the all-glass mounts are preferable because they are easier to make.

The only materials needed to make an all-glass mount are glass, a transparent cement, and binding tape. One can obtain scrap window glass free at most hardware stores, and cut it himself. A commercial household cement, which is fast-drying and easily applied, is a suitable cement. Many tapes are suitable, but the best is probably an electrical tape (black, 19 mm wide).

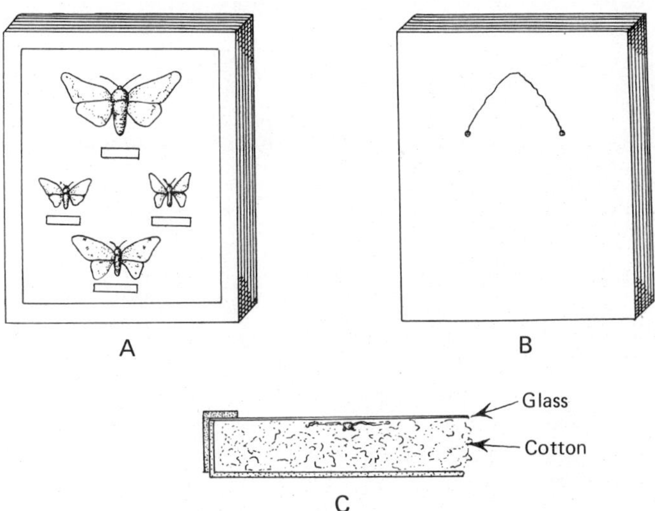

Figure 631. The Riker mount. A, front view; B, back view; C, sectional view showing a specimen in place under the glass on the cotton.

Glass cutting is easy to learn, safe, and much cheaper than having the glass cut professionally. One needs a glass cutter, a perfectly flat surface, a straightedge (for example, a yardstick or ruler), and some way of holding the straightedge firmly against the glass when using the cutter. The glass is scratched *with a single stroke* of the cutter; with practice, one can learn the pressure necessary to make this scratch. The glass is broken by pressing *away from* the scratch. Pieces can be broken in the hands or at the edge of a table; narrow pieces should be turned over and tapped firmly (with the reverse end of the cutter) along the scratch line until the glass breaks. The narrower the piece to be cut off, the more skill necessary to cut it evenly.

A glass cutter keeps its edge longer if the wheel is immersed in a light oil (for example, kerosene) when not in use. For a better cut, the cutter wheel should be oiled during use. If one measures the glass accurately and marks it with ink before each cut, he should be able to cut the glass to within 0.8 mm of the desired size.

To make an all-glass mount, proceed as follows:

1. Specimens to be displayed in glass mounts must first be spread upside down on a piece of sheet cork, balsa wood, corrugated cardboard, or other flat surface, with the wings and antennae in a standard position (see pages 732–734 and Figure 623). The legs should be pressed close to the body of the specimen to minimize its thickness.
2. Cut two identical pieces of single-weight window glass for the top and bottom of the mount, allowing at least 6 mm margin on all four sides of the spread specimen(s).
3. Cut enough supporting pieces of glass (single weight or double weight) to provide room for the body of the insect (Figure 632 B). These supporting pieces should all be the same size; their length should equal one dimension (usually the shorter) of the top and bottom pieces, and they should be separated in the center of the mount by a distance two or three times the width of the insect's body.
4. Clean all glass thoroughly, preferably with a commercial glass cleaner.
5. Place the bottom piece of glass on a clean flat surface, and remove the lint from it with a camel's-hair brush. Place a small drop of cement on the corners of one end. After removing the lint from one of the supporting pieces, press the piece down in place with the end of the brush handle, line it up with the edges of the bottom piece, and remove any excess cement that oozes out.
6. Continue building up needed thicknesses of supporting glass on each side, aligning each piece carefully, and allowing time for each to set before adding the next. Place the cement

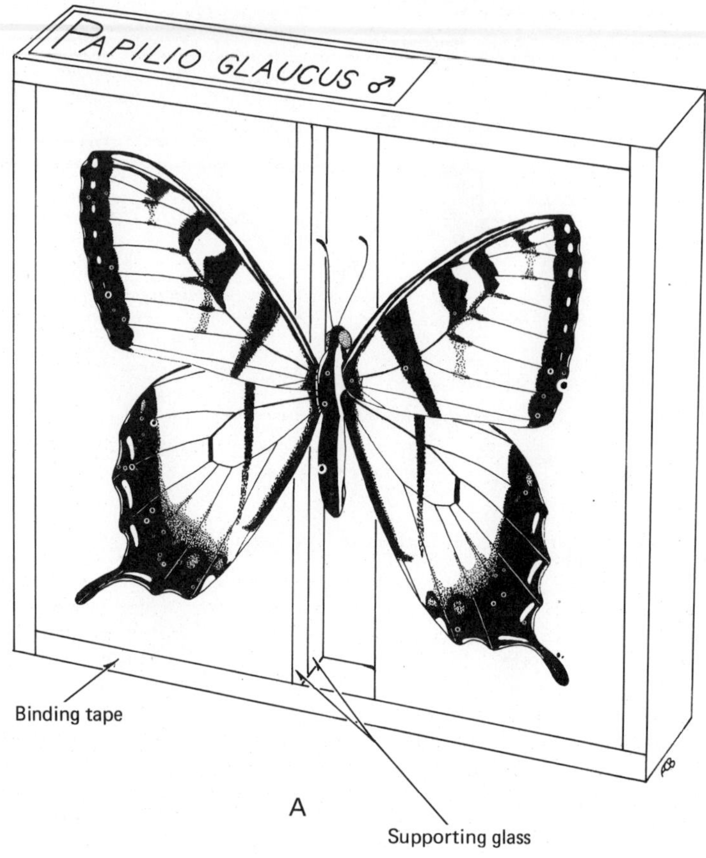

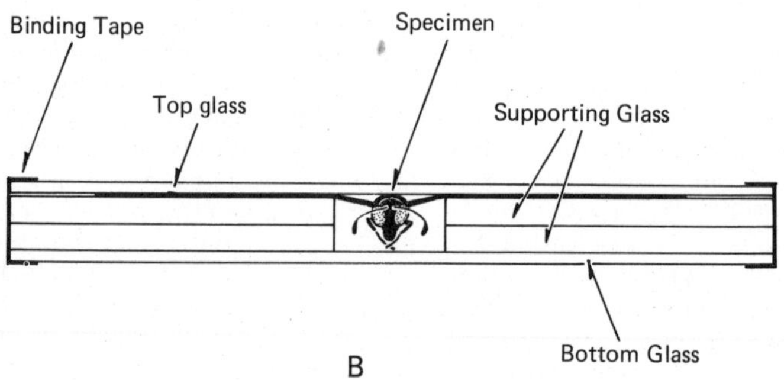

Figure 632. The all-glass mount. A, completed mount; B, sectional view of the mount.

only on the outer corners of the glass, and use only a small drop. Some cement may spread inward and be visible in the completed mount, but this will not be objectionable.

7. When the supporting pieces are cemented in position, place the specimen on the supporting pieces and center it. Put a small drop of cement on the four corners, and place the top

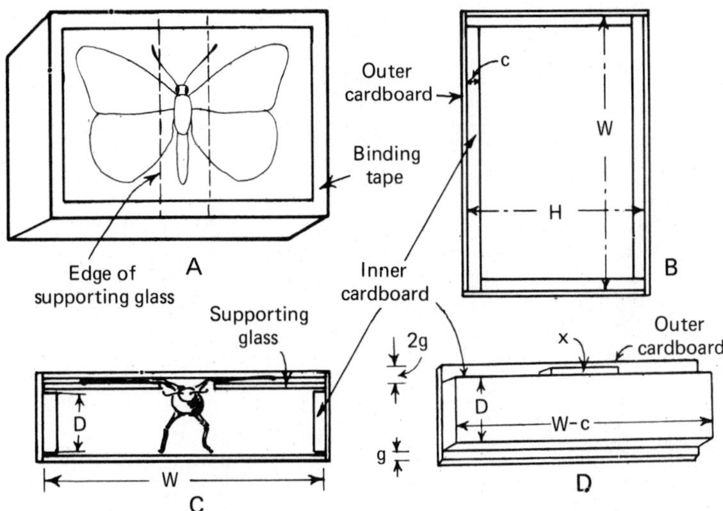

Figure 633. Construction of a glass mount. A, completed mount; B, top view of the frame, showing the construction of the corners; C, sectional view; D, view from inside of one side of the frame, showing how the two layers of cardboard are put together. *c*, thickness of inner cardboard; *D*, width of inner strip of cardboard; *g*, thickness of glass; *H*, height of case; *W*, width of case; x, a cardboard wedge to prevent the supporting glass from slipping sideways.

piece of glass in position, being careful not to move the specimen. Press the top down hard, and place a small weight on it. Leave this weight in place until the cement sets (15 minutes to an hour or more).

8. Tape the sides of the mount. The tape covers the sharp edges of the glass, seals the mount, and gives it a finished look.
9. Cement a label on the top edge, if desired (Figure 632 A).
10. Store in a dry place to discourage mold.

A glass mount with a cardboard frame (Figure 633) is very similar to the all-glass mount, but contains only one pair of supporting pieces of glass; the remaining thickness of the mount is made up by the frame. The sides of the mount are of two layers of cardboard; the outer layer may be thin, but the inner layer should be of very heavy cardboard such as that used in certain types of packing cases (*not* corrugated cardboard). The inner cardboard should be at least as thick as the glass; if such cardboard is not available, it can be made by cementing two or more thicknesses of ordinary cardboard together. The width of the cardboard strips forming the inner layer of the sides will determine the depth of the mount and the amount of space available for the body and legs of the insect. A good mount of this type requires considerable care in cutting and fitting the parts; the glass and cardboard must be measured and cut very exactly. Figure 633 shows how this type of glass mount is made.

If large numbers of glass mounts are to be made, the use of standard sizes will simplify glass cutting, displaying, and storing. Two or more specimens can be put in a mount by placing them in a vertical row (with two series or pieces of supporting glass), and (or) side by side (with at least three series or pieces of supporting glass, the lateral ones being narrower than the middle ones). Specimens mounted in a vertical row should be about the same thickness; if one is thicker, the thinner one may slip. The specimens are held in position by the top piece of glass; hence it is important that this piece be pressed down tightly against the specimen.

PLASTIC MOUNTS Butterflies, moths, and other insects may be mounted for display between two sheets of a fairly thick transparent plastic; each sheet is bulged out (the plastic can be so shaped when it is heated) where the body of the insect will be. The two sheets are put together, with the insect between, and sealed around the edges with acetone or some other sealing material. Such sheets can be obtained, all ready for use, from some supply houses.

Many types of insects may be embedded in Bioplastic. This is a rather involved process, and space does not permit describing it in detail here. The materials needed, together with instructions for their use, can be obtained from supply houses. Ward's Natural Science Establishment has prepared a booklet entitled, *How to Embed in Bioplastic,* which is a complete manual on the subject.

The mountings described above are only a few of the possible types useful for displaying insects; an ingenious collector should be able to devise many additional types.

PROTECTING THE COLLECTION

All insect collections are subject to attack by dermestid beetles, ants, and other museum pests, and if the collection is to last any length of time, certain precautions must be taken to protect it from these pests. Various materials may be used for this purpose, but one material commonly used is naphthalene (in flake or ball form). Naphthalene flakes can be put into a small cardboard pillbox that is firmly attached to the bottom of the insect box (usually in one corner), and has a few pin holes in it. Paradichlorobenzene can also be used, but it volatilizes more rapidly than naphthalene and must be renewed at more frequent intervals. A combination of equal parts of naphthalene and paradichlorobenzene will protect the specimens for a considerable time. To protect specimens in Riker mounts, napthalene flakes should be sprinkled under the cotton when the mount is being made. A collection should be checked periodically to make sure that plenty of repellent is present. If boxes or drawers are stored in tight cabinets that are not opened frequently, the repellent should last a long time.

Another method of protecting pinned insects from pests is to spray or paint the insides of the boxes with a solution of an insecticide that has a considerable residual effect, such as chlordane or DDT. Such treatment may be effective for many years.

It should be emphasized that paradichlorobenzene and naphthalene are only repellents, and while they will keep out potential pests, they will not kill pests already in the collection. If a box or drawer is found to be infested with pests, it should be fumigated (with carbon disulfide, ethylene dichloride, or methyl bromide) or heat-treated to destroy these pests. Heating boxes, cases, or mounts to 150° F or higher for several hours (if the boxes are such that the heat will not damage them) will destroy any dermestids or other pests they may contain. Many good collections have been ruined by pests because the collector failed to protect them.

PACKING AND SHIPPING INSECTS

A dried insect on a pin is such a fragile object that it would seem almost impossible to ship a box of pinned insects through the mails and have it arrive at its destination with the specimens intact. It can be done if a few simple rules are followed. The preparation of specimens for shipment is based largely on the treatment they are likely to receive in transit. They will be turned upside down, sideways, and subjected to severe and repeated jarring. Therefore, the two most important considerations are to make certain that all pins are firmly anchored so that they cannot work loose and bounce around and break specimens, and the box in which they are pinned must be placed in a larger box, surrounded by packing material to cushion the blows the package will invariably receive.

We are concerned here with the transporting or shipping of *dead* insects. Before transporting or shipping living insects, one should check with the quarantine officials and the postal authorities.

Pinned specimens should be inserted firmly into the bottom of the insect box, preferably with pinning forceps; the bottom of the box should be of a material that will hold the pins firmly. Large specimens should be braced with extra pins to prevent them from swinging around and damaging other specimens; long appendages, or a long abdomen, should be braced and supported by extra pins. A sheet of cardboard cut to fit the inside of the box (with a slot cut out along one side to facilitate removal) should be placed over the top of the pinned specimens, and the space between this and the lid of the box should be filled with cotton, cellucotton, or a similar material; this prevents the pins from being dislodged during shipment. One should *never* include in a box of pinned specimens vials of insects preserved in fluid, regardless of how firmly the vials may appear to be fastened in the box. The rough handling the average box gets when going through the mail may dislodge even the most "firmly" attached vial and ruin the specimens.

If a box of pinned insects contains specimens from which the genitalia (or other parts) have been removed and stored in a microvial on the pin below the insect (see page 738), special precautions must be taken to make sure these vials do not come loose and damage specimens in the box. Pins containing such vials should be inserted far enough so that the vial rests on the bottom of the box; the vial is then held in a fixed position by insect pins, one placed at the end of the vial and two others crossed over the middle of the vial.

When specimens preserved in fluids are to be shipped, measures should be taken to protect the specimens in the containers. The containers should be completely filled with fluid, and it is sometimes desirable to add cotton or some similar material in the container to prevent the specimens from bouncing about. Small and delicate larvae, such as mosquito larvae, should be in vials so completely filled with fluid that there is not even an air bubble in the vial. An air bubble in a vial can have the same effect on a specimen as a solid object in the vial would have. One method of accomplishing this is to use glass tubes stoppered with rubber stoppers, filling the vial containing the specimens to the brim, and then carefully inserting the stopper with a pin alongside it (to allow excess fluid to escape); when the stopper is in place, the pin is removed. Another way of getting the vial completely filled with liquid (without any air bubbles) is to fill the vial to the brim and insert the stopper with a hypodermic needle through it. The excess fluid comes out through the needle, and when the needle is removed the stopper seals (if the process is carefully done), and there is no air bubble inside the vial.

If two or more containers of insects in fluid are packed in the same box, they should be wrapped in wide strips of cellucotton or some similar soft material so that no two vials are in contact.

Insects in glass or Riker mounts can ordinarily withstand considerable jolting without damage, but care should be taken that the glass of these mounts does not get broken. Such mounts should be packed in an abundance of soft packing material, and no two of them should touch each other in the box.

Insect material mounted on microscope slides should be shipped in wooden or heavy cardboard slide boxes, preferably boxes in which the slides are inserted into grooves and are on edge in the box. Strips of a soft material should be placed between the slides and the lid of the box, so that the slides do not bounce about.

Dried specimens in envelopes or pillboxes should be packed in such a way that the specimens do not bounce around inside the box. Pillboxes should be padded inside with cellucotton to immobolize the specimens, and boxes containing envelopes should be filled with cotton or cellucotton.

Boxes containing pinned insects, insects in fluids, microscope slides, or dried insects in envelopes or pill boxes that are to be sent through the mail should be packed inside a larger box. The outer box should be selected so as to allow at least 2 inches (50 mm) of packing material (excelsior, shredded paper, cotton, and so forth) on all sides of the smaller box. This packing material should not be so loose as to allow the inner box to rattle around, or so tight that the cushion effect is lost.

Whenever material is shipped through the mail, an accompanying letter should be sent to the addressee, notifying him of the shipment. Packages of dead insects sent through the mail are usually marked "Dried (or Preserved) Insects for Scientific Study," and are sent by parcel post. It is well to mark such packages for gentle handling in transit, though this does not always ensure that they will not get rough treatment. Material shipped to points inside the United States should be insured, though it may be difficult to place an evaluation on some material. The statement "No Commercial Value" on a box shipped from one country to another will facilitate the box getting through customs.

WORK WITH LIVING INSECTS

Anyone studying insects who does nothing but collect, kill, and mount these animals and study the dead specimens will miss the most interesting part of insect study. The student who takes time to study *living* insects will find that they are fascinating and often amazing little animals. Living insects can be studied in the field or in captivity. Many are very easy to keep in captivity, where they can be studied more easily, and often at closer range, than in the field.

KEEPING LIVING INSECTS IN CAPTIVITY

Relatively little equipment or attention is required to keep an insect alive in captivity for a short period. Insects can be brought in from the field, kept in a cage of some sort for a day or so, and then released. On the other hand, rearing adult insects from their immature stages or maintaining cultures of insects through one or more generations usually requires more equipment and atten-

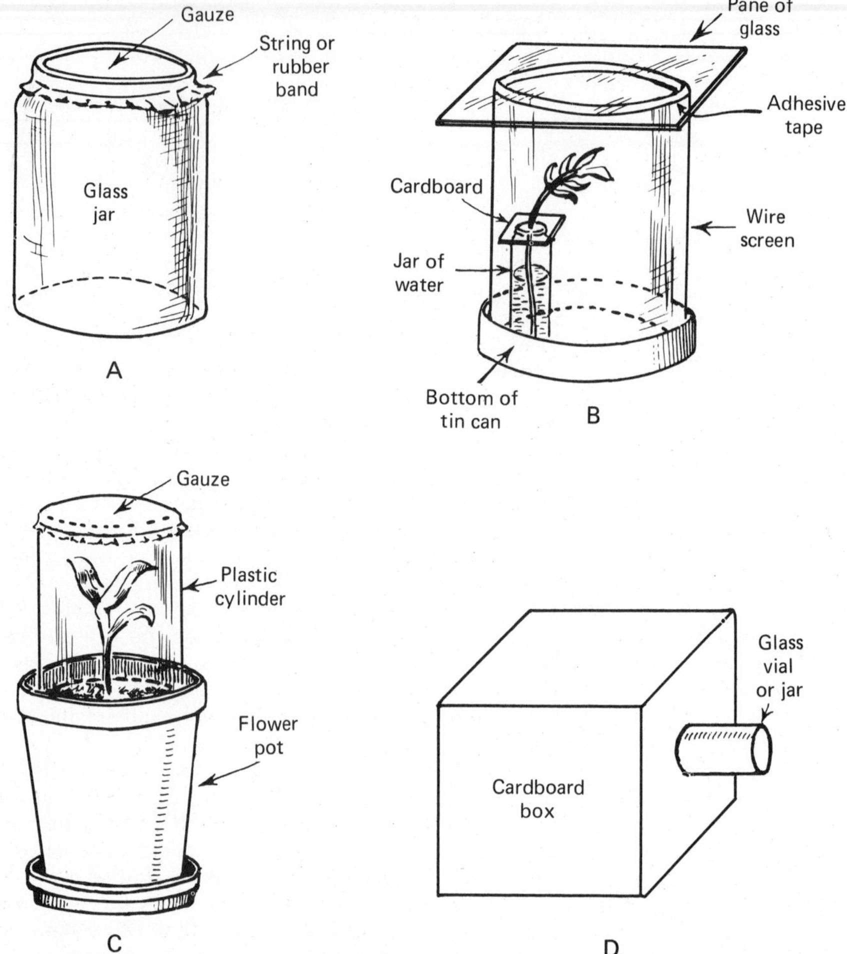

Figure 634. Some types of insect cages. A, jar cage; B, cylindrical screen cage; C, "flowerpot" cage; D, emergence box.

tion. However, there are many types of insects that are fairly easy to rear or culture.

Rearing adult insects from immature stages is an excellent way to learn about their habits and life histories. The activities of insects in cages can generally be more easily observed, and certainly observed to a greater extent, than insects in the field. Many insects collected as immatures and reared will be found to be parasitized, and the parasites will emerge rather than the host insect; this is particularly true of caterpillars.

CAGES FOR INSECTS Almost anything will serve as a suitable cage for keeping insects in captivity for a short time, or for rearing some types of insects. The simplest type of cage is a glass (or clear plastic) jar of some sort covered with gauze held in place with a string or rubber band (Figure 634 A). The jar may vary in size from a small vial up to a large (1-gallon (4-liter) or larger) jar, depending on the size and numbers of the insects. In some cases food, water, or other materials necessary to the well-being of the insects can simply be placed in the bottom of the jar. Such containers are also suitable for aquaria; mosquitoes, for example, can be reared in vials that hold only a few cubic centimeters of water.

Cages suitable for rearing some types of insects or for display can be made of cardboard, gauze,

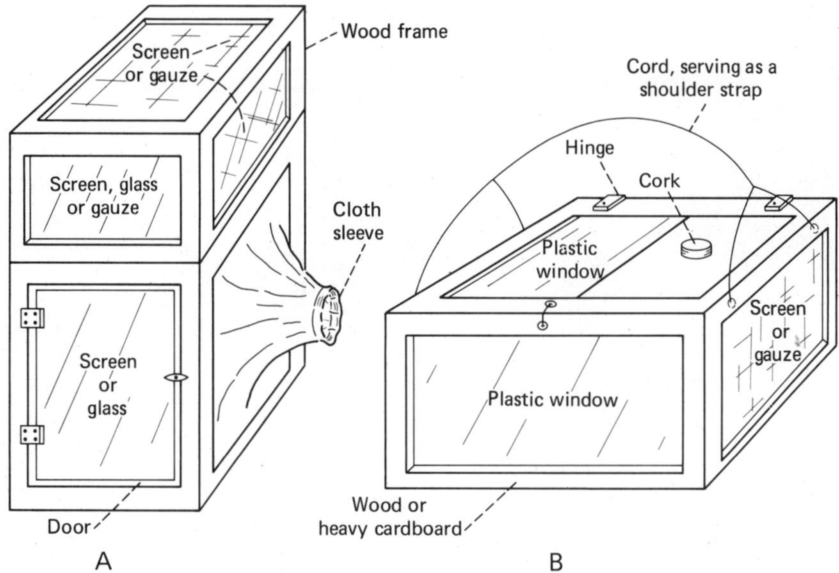

Figure 635. Insect cages. A, sleeve cage; B, a field carrying cage.

and clear plastic. Any small cardboard box can be used; its size will depend on the size of the insect it is to contain. Holes cut in the ends and covered with gauze will provide ventilation; clear plastic or glass in the front will provide visibility; the top may be covered with either glass, clear plastic, or an opaque lid.

A more permanent type of cage can be made of window screen with a wood or metal framework. The bottom 25 mm or so of a large tin can with a cylinder of screen inserted in it (Figure 634 B) makes a good cage. Cages of wood and screen can be made with the opening at the top, like a lid, or with a door on one side. If the cage is to be used for fairly active insects and it is necessary to get into the cage frequently, it should be provided with a sleeve (Figure 635 A).

When one is rearing a plant-feeding insect, and the plant upon which it feeds is not too large, the insect can be reared in a "flowerpot" cage (Figure 634 C). The plant is planted in a flowerpot or a large tin can, and a cylinder of glass, plastic, or screen is placed around the plant and covered at the top with gauze.

An emergence box such as that shown in Figure 634 D works well for rearing adults from larvae living in debris, soil, excrement, and other materials. The material containing the larvae is placed in the box, which is then closed tightly. When the adults emerge, they are attracted by the light coming into the box through the vial, and go into the vial.

The best way to rear some insects is to leave them in their habitat in the field and cage them there. Many types of cages can be constructed around an insect in the field. In the case of a plant-feeding insect, a cage consisting of a roll of clear plastic or fine screen, with gauze at each end, may be placed around that part of the plant containing the insect (Figure 636 B), or a cage made of window screen on a wooden framework may be built about part of the plant. Many plant-feeding insects can be confined on a certain part of a plant by means of barriers of some sort, such as tanglefoot bands (Figure 636 A). Aquatic insects can be reared in cages of screen submerged in their habitat; the screen should be fine enough to prevent the escape of the insect but coarse enough to allow food material to enter.

Cages made of heavy cardboard or wood, gauze, and plastic can easily be fitted with a shoulder strap and used to bring living material from the field into the laboratory or classroom. With a carrying cage such as the one shown in Figure 635 B, large materials can be put into the cage by lifting the lid, or single insects may be put into the box through the hole in the lid.

When one is rearing insects indoors, he must usually make sure that the conditions of temperature and humidity are satisfactory and that suf-

Figure 636. Methods of caging insects in the field. A, a tanglefoot barrier on a leaf, for small nonflying insects; B, a cage of plastic and gauze for caging insects on their food plant. (A, courtesy of Davidson.)

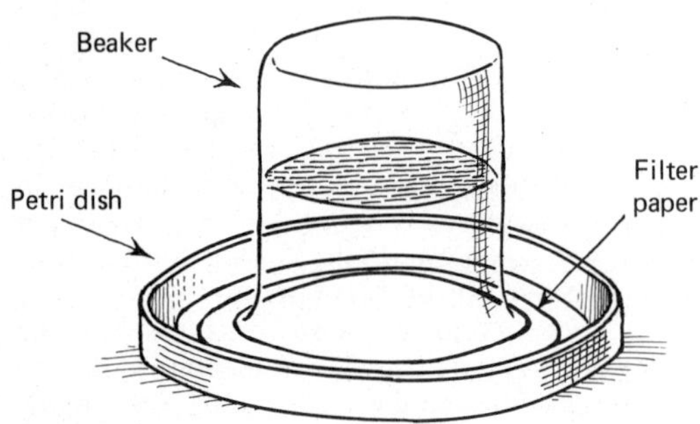

Figure 637. A method of providing water for caged insects.

ficient food and water is provided. Many insects, such as leaf-eating caterpillars, must be regularly provided with fresh food; this means adding fresh leaves every day or so, or having some way of keeping large amounts of foliage fresh in the cage for several days at a time. If the insect requires water, the water may be provided by means of a beaker inverted in a petri dish (Figure 637); by a vial full of water, plugged with cotton, and lying on its side in the cage; by a sponge soaked with water; or by some similar means.

Peterson (1953) describes a great variety of cages and other devices for rearing insects, both in the laboratory and in the field.

SOME INSECTS EASILY REARED Some of the easiest insects to rear indoors are those that normally live indoors, for example, the insects that attack flour, meal, or other stored food products. They may be kept and reared in the original container of the food material, or in a glass jar covered with fine gauze. It is usually not necessary to provide these insects with moisture. The various stages of the insect can be obtained by sifting the meal, and some of these can be added to fresh meal to keep the culture going.

Cockroaches are excellent insects for rearing, since they are fairly large and active, most people are familiar with them, and in most parts of the country they are abundant and easily obtained. A culture may be started by trapping some adults (page 727). Cockroaches can be reared in various types of containers, a large glass or plastic jar covered with gauze, or even an open box, provided the box is several centimeters deep and the upper 2 or 3 inches (50 or 75 mm) of the sides are smeared with vaseline so that the roaches cannot climb out. These insects are practically omnivorous, and many different types of material will serve as suitable food. Dog biscuits make a good food. Plenty of water should be provided.

Many types of insects that have aquatic immature stages can be reared easily from the immature to the adult stage. The type of aquarium needed will depend on the type of insect being reared.

Small forms feeding on organic debris or microorganisms can be reared in containers as small as vials; larger ones, particularly predaceous forms, require larger containers. Larvae or pupae of mosquitoes, for example, can be kept in small containers in some of the same water in which they were found, with a cover over the container to prevent the escape of the adults. When vials are used, the simplest cover is a plug of cotton. In many cases it is necessary to simulate the insect's habitat in the aquarium (for example, have sand or mud in the bottom and have some aquatic plants present), and in the case of predaceous insects, such as dragonfly nymphs, smaller animals must be provided as food. The water must be aerated for some aquatic types. In maintaining an aquarium, one should strive to keep all the conditions in the aquarium as near as possible to the conditions in the animal's normal habitat.

When one is attempting to maintain aquatic insects in the laboratory generation after generation, special provision must be made for the different life-history stages which frequently require special food, space, or other conditions. Some mosquitoes are relatively easy to maintain in culture in the laboratory, especially species that normally breed continuously through the warmer parts of the year, and in which the adults do not require a large space for their mating flights. The yellow fever mosquito, *Aèdes aegýpti* L., is easily cultured in the laboratory[1]; at a temperature of 85° F the development from egg to adult requires only 9–11 days. The females must obtain a blood meal before they will produce eggs; a person's arm can provide this meal, but a laboratory animal such as a rabbit (with the hair shaved from a portion of its body) is better. The adults are allowed to emerge in cages of about 1-ft^3 (0.028 m^3) capacity. A solution of honey in the cage will provide food for the males (which do not feed on blood) and for the females before their blood meal.

A small dish of water is placed in the cage for egg laying. If wooden blocks or paper are placed in this water, the eggs will be deposited on these at the margin of the water as it recedes. These eggs will usually hatch within 10 to 20 minutes after they are placed in water at room temperature, even after months of desiccation. If the larvae are reared in large numbers, they are best reared in battery jars; as many as 250 larvae can be reared in a 6-inch (150-mm) battery jar half filled with water. The larvae can be fed ground dog biscuit, which is sprinkled on the surface of the water daily; for first instar larvae, 30–35 milligrams should be used daily. This amount should be increased for successive instars up to 140–150 milligrams daily for fourth instar larvae. Pupation of the fourth instar larvae takes place 7–9 days after the eggs hatch, and the adults emerge about 24 hours later.

It is usually fairly easy to rear adult insects from galls; the important thing in rearing most gall insects is to keep the gall alive and fresh until the adults emerge. The plant containing the gall can be kept fresh by putting it in water, or the gall may be caged in the field. If the gall is not collected until the adults are nearly ready to emerge (as determined by opening a few), it can simply be placed inside a glass jar, in a vial of water, and the jar covered with gauze. This same procedure can be used to rear out adults of leaf miners that pupate in the leaf. If the leaf miner pupates in the soil (for example, certain sawflies), the plant containing the insect should be grown in a flowerpot cage.

Adults of some wood-boring insects are easily reared out. If the insect bores into drying or dried wood, the wood containing the larvae can be placed in an emergence box like that shown in Figure 634 D; if it bores only in living wood, the adults can be obtained by placing some sort of cage over the emergence holes (in the field).

Termite cultures are easily maintained in the laboratory and are of value in demonstrating the social behavior and the wood-eating and fungus-cultivating habits of these insects. Various types of containers can be used for a termite culture, but the best for demonstration purposes is either a battery jar or a glass-plate type of container. A termite colony will last quite a while without queens in either type of container, but will prove more interesting if queens or supplemental queens are present.

If a battery jar is used, 6 mm or so of earth is placed in the bottom of the jar and a sheet of wood is placed on either side of the jar; balsa wood is the best because the termites become established in it quickly. Thin, narrow strips of a harder wood are placed on each side between the balsa wood and the glass, and pieces are placed between the sheets of balsa wood to hold them in place. Termites placed in such a container become established in a few hours; they tunnel through the earth and the wood and build fungus

[1] Since this species is an important disease vector, special precautions should be taken to prevent the escape of any individuals reared.

Figure 638. A glass-plate type of container for rearing termites.

"gardens" (which are apparently an important source of nitrogen and vitamins) between the wood and the glass. The wood will be destroyed in a few weeks and must be replaced. Water must be added every few days. This can be done by thoroughly moistening a pad of cotton and putting it between the glass and the wood at the top on each side.

A glass-plate type of container is somewhat similar to the ant nest described below, but has a metal rather than a wood frame (Figure 638). The container should be about a foot (0.3 m) wide, a foot (0.3 m) high, and about $\frac{1}{2}$-inch (13 mm) thick, and should have a pan at the base to hold it upright. No earth need be used in this type of container. A piece of balsa wood is placed in the container, with narrow strips inserted between it and the two glass plates (front and rear). The termites are placed in the space between the wood and the glass. A thin pad of cotton batting is placed over the top of the wood, between the two glass plates, and this is thoroughly soaked with water about twice a week. The fungus gardens are maintained here as in the battery-jar culture.

The chief problem encountered in rearing caterpillars is that of providing suitable food. Many caterpillars feed only on certain species of plants; hence it is necessary to know the food plant of a caterpillar one wishes to rear. Caterpillars may be reared in almost any sort of cage, provided the cage is cleaned and fresh food is provided regularly. Plant food can be kept fresh longer if it is put in a small jar of water inside the cage; a cover on the top of the water jar, around the stem of the plant, will prevent the caterpillars from falling into the water (Figure 634 B). If the caterpillar is one that requires special conditions for pupation, the conditions must be provided. Butterfly larvae will usually pupate on the leaves or on the sides or top of the cage; most moth larvae will pupate in the corner of the cage or under debris of some sort. Some moth larvae (for example, the larvae of sphinx moths) pupate in the ground; they should be reared in a cage containing several centimeters of soil.

Many of the larger moths pupate in the fall and emerge as adults in the spring, and their cocoons can be collected in the fall. If these cocoons are brought indoors in the fall, they may dry out or the adults may emerge in the middle of the winter (though this may not be objectionable). The drying-out can be prevented by putting the cocoons in a jar that has 25 mm or so of dirt in the bottom, and sprinkling the dirt and cocoon with water about once a week. To keep the cocoons from emerging in the middle of winter, they may be kept in screen cages (preferably cages containing some dirt or debris) outdoors (for example, on the outside window sill of a room). If the emerging moth is a female and it emerges at a time when other moths of its kind are on the wing, it will often attract male moths from a considerable distance if kept in an outdoor cage.

Because of their social behavior, ants make very interesting animals to maintain in indoor cages. The simplest type of ant cage, particularly for display, is a narrow vertical cage with a wooden framework and glass sides (Figure 639). This is filled with an ant-dirt mixture obtained by digging up an ant hill, preferably a small one under a stone or board; this mixture should contain all stages and castes if possible. The queen can usually be recognized by her larger size. The glass sides of the cage should be darkened by covering them with some opaque material; otherwise all the tunnels the ants make will be away from the glass and not visible. Food and moisture must be provided. Food can be provided by putting a few insects into the cage from time to time, or by putting a few drops of diluted molasses or honey on a small sponge or wad of cotton in the cage. Moisture can be provided by keeping a wet sponge or wad of cotton on the underside of the lid or on top of the dirt.

An observation bee hive makes an excellent class demonstration. It can be set up inside a classroom window, and the bees can come and go at will, yet all that goes on inside the hive can be observed. Space does not permit a detailed description of how an observation bee hive is constructed, but Figure 640 shows what it is like. One

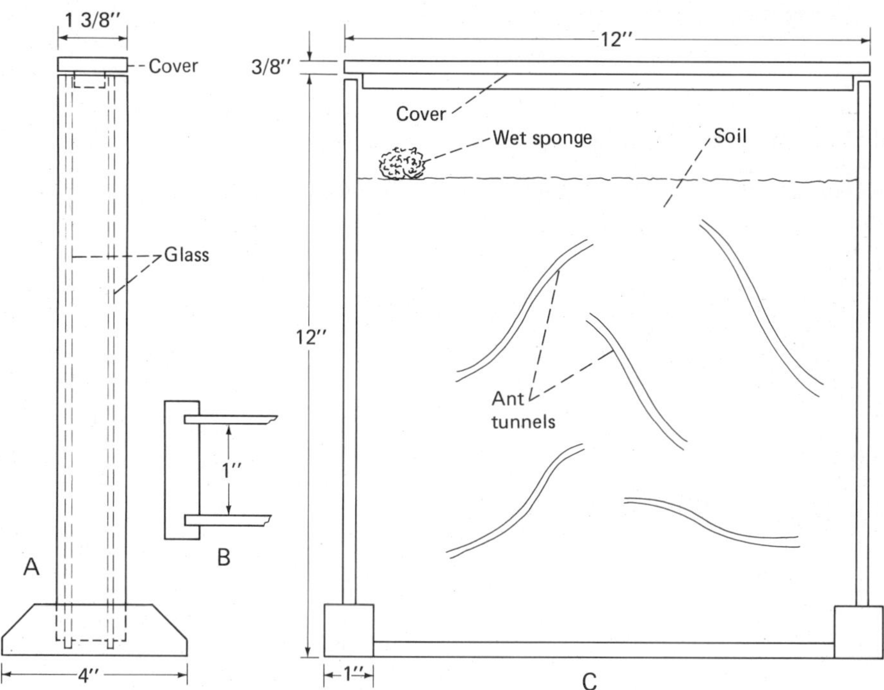

Figure 639. Vertical type of ant cage. A, end view; B, top view of one end showing cage construction; C, front view.

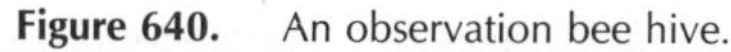

Figure 640. An observation bee hive.

who wishes to set up an observation bee hive should get in touch with a local beekeeper and ask for his help and suggestions.

There are a number of insects that will prove interesting to rear or maintain for a short time in captivity. Singing insects such as crickets, katydids, or cicadas may be kept caged for a time with relatively little difficulty. If case-making insects are caged, it will often be possible to observe how the cases are made, and perhaps special materials (such as colored bits of glass for caddisworms usually using sand grains) may be provided for the case. Caging predaceous insects with their prey (particularly mantids), or parasitic insects with their hosts, will demonstrate these interrelationships. With a little knowledge of a species' food habits and habitat requirements, the ingenious student can usually devise methods of rearing almost any type of insect.

MARKING INSECTS

The practice of marking animals so that individuals or groups can be subsequently recognized has been used in studies of many kinds of animals and has yielded a great deal of information about the animals marked, in some cases information that could not have been obtained by any other method. With larger animals such as birds (by banding), mammals (by tagging, tattooing, ear marking, and by other methods), and fish (by gill tagging), each animal is marked differently and can be individually recognized. With insects, some methods involve the marking of mass lots of individuals; others involve the marking of insects individually.

The small size of most insects makes it impractical to mark them with any sort of numbered tag; consequently most of the marking of insects, especially small insects, consists of marking mass lots of individuals. Flies that are live-trapped may be sprayed with various dyes (acid fuchsin, eosin, methylene green, and others) and released; the use of different colors serves to mark lots released from different points or at different times. Some insects can be marked with radioactive materials by feeding the adults or larvae with these materials; the marked individuals are identified by means of special instruments designed to detect radioactivity.

Some types of insects can be marked so that individuals can be recognized. Numbered tags have been used to mark Lepidóptera, and the largest program of marking Lepidóptera has been with the monarch butterfly (Urquhart, 1960). Many thousands of monarchs have been marked, using paper tags 17 by 7 mm in size (made of a specially treated paper and using a special adhesive) folded over the leading edge of the front wing near the body. The most distant recovery of a marked monarch was an individual marked in Ontario and recovered in Mexico (1870 miles (3010 km) away) about four months after it was marked.

Insects such as bees can be marked on the thorax with dots of different colored enamel, the color and position of each dot representing a particular digit. Insects such as dragonflies and damselflies can be marked with dots on the wing (Figure 641); the dots,of a fast-drying material like nail polish or India ink, are put on with a fine brush or pointed stick. Individual insects can also be marked by cutting off certain sections of certain legs, or by cutting characteristic notches in the wings.

A great deal can be learned about the habits and behavior of an insect by the use of marking techniques, for example, length of life, mating habits, territorial behavior, movements and flight range, and changes in color or habits with increasing age of the adult. With adequate data on the recaptures of marked individuals, it is sometimes possible to estimate populations and the rate of population turnover due to emergence and deaths or to movements of individuals into or out of a given study area.

The basic formula for calculating populations from the recaptures of marked individuals is relatively simple. If a sample consisting of M individuals is collected in a given area, marked, and released, then M/P of the population is marked (where P is the total population on the area). If this population is sampled again later, assuming that none of the marked individuals has died, that no new individuals have emerged, and that the marked individuals have become uniformly dispersed over the sampling area, then the proportion of the second sample that is marked is the same as it was when the marked individuals were first released. If the total number in the second sample is represented by C, and the number of marked individuals in this sample is represented by M^1, then the proportion of the second sample that is marked is M^1/C. Thus,

$$\frac{M}{P} = \frac{M'}{C}$$

Therefore,

$$P = \frac{M \times C}{M'}$$

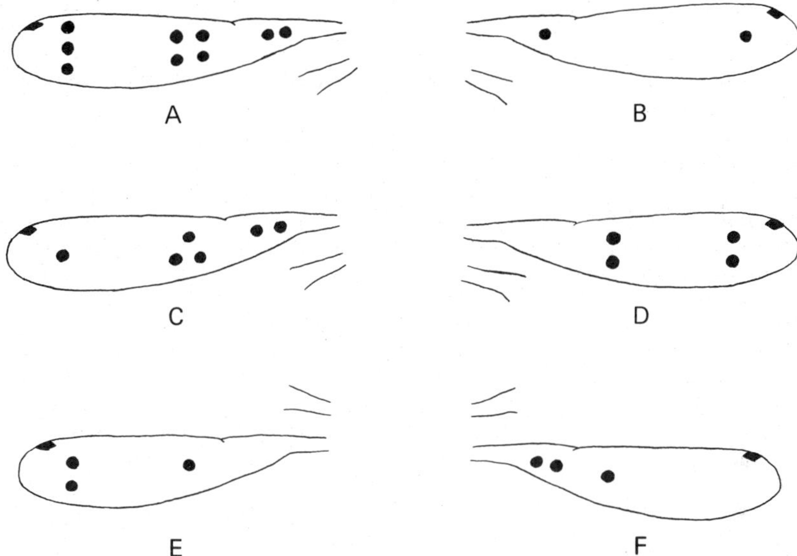

Figure 641. A method of marking damselfly wings. Dots may be placed at three locations on the wing, proximal to the nodus (one or two dots), just distal to the nodus (one to four dots), and just proximal to the stigma (one to three dots). Each insect marked has an identifying number consisting of two letters (indicating which wing is marked) and three digits (indicating the number of dots in each of the three locations on the wing). The specimens shown here are identified as follows: A, LF243; B, RF101; C, LF231; D, RF022; E, LH012; F, RH210 (Borror, 1934).

or,
Total population

$$= \frac{\text{(number marked) (total recaptured)}}{\text{number of marked individuals recaptured}}$$

In most ecological studies of a particular insect, some technique of marking can be used to advantage. A high school biology class, camp nature-study class, or a similar group might undertake a study involving marking as a group project. There are many insects in every neighborhood that could be marked either in mass lots or individually. Such a project would not only arouse considerable interest, since many people would be on the lookout for the marked insects, but a great deal of information about the insect might be obtained from the study.

CENSUSES OF INSECT POPULATIONS

It is seldom practical to make a census of an insect population in a field area by counting every insect; most field studies involve some method of estimating the population from samples. Sampling techniques can be designed to estimate the total population in a given area, or they can be designed to indicate comparative populations. The former involves making accurate counts on sample areas that are representative of the entire area studied, and the latter involves using some standard sampling procedure that, when used at different times or in different places, gives information on population trends or differences. The particular method used in any given case will depend on the nature of the area chosen for census and the species in which the investigator is interested.

In cases where the total population in an area such as a field is to be estimated, the insects in a number of small sample areas are collected and counted. A cylinder covering an area of about 1 ft^2 (0.093 m^2) is put down over the vegetation, and a fumigant is introduced into the cylinder to stun or kill the insects caught there. Then all the material inside the cylinder, together with the soil below it to some standard depth, is taken to the laboratory and examined, and the insects (and perhaps other animals as well) are carefully counted. The total population of the area is calculated from several such samples. The accuracy of this method depends on the number and the representativeness of the samples; the number of samples taken will usually depend on the amount of time the investigator has for this study.

Most of the methods used to estimate field populations, particularly in cases where the investigator is interested in only one or a few species, involve procedures designed to count a standard percentage of the population. This percentage may be unknown, but it is possible to determine population trends or to compare the populations of different areas by this method. The sampling techniques used will depend largely on the habits of the species concerned. A common method of sampling the populations on low vegetation is to take a given number of standard sweeps with an insect net and count the catch. For other insects the investigator may count the insects (or points of insect injury) on a certain number of plants, fruits, or leaves. Traps may be used in some cases to determine population trends or differences. Many different sorts of counting techniques may be used in studies of this sort, and in any given study, the technique must be adapted to the characteristics of the species being studied. The aim in each case is to count a uniform percentage of the population.

In some cases it may be possible to obtain a fairly accurate estimate of the total population of a given species in a given area by means of marking. This technique was discussed in the preceding section.

PHOTOGRAPHING INSECTS

Photographing insects, especially in color, has become a common practice of both the professional entomologist and the layman. Insect photographs are used extensively to illustrate books, bulletins, or journal articles, for class use, and for illustrating public lectures. Many books (for example, Ross, 1953) have been written about the photography of insects and other natural history subjects, so we need not go into this subject in detail here.

A large assortment of lenses, filters, adapters, synchronized flash and other lighting equipment is currently available, so that the photographer can select almost anything he needs to photograph, either the entire insect or only a small part of it. Lenses are available for almost any size of magnification that may be desired.

Pictures of dead or mounted insects may be useful for some purposes, but pictures of living insects, or at least of insects that *look* alive and are in a natural pose, are far better. This is often a difficult problem, but may be solved in one of two general ways, (1) by using equipment permitting a very short exposure time, and getting as close as possible without disturbing the insect, or (2) stupefying the insect temporarily so that more time is available for making the photograph; various chemicals (for example, CO_2), or chilling the insect, may serve to condition it for this type of photographic exposure. It is often possible to get a good picture by training the camera on a spot where the insect will eventually alight and then waiting for the insect to alight there; many insects may be photographed by aiming the camera at a flower and photographing the insects when they come to the flower.

Photomicrographic equipment (camera, lighting, etc.) has been developed that can be attached to (or built into) a microscope; such equipment enables one to photograph very minute insects, or parts of insects, at high magnification. The scanning microscope is another recently developed piece of equipment with which one can secure pictures of very high magnification, often showing details that could not be seen with an ordinary microscope.

One can get pictures of considerable entomological interest without photographing any insects at all. Insect nests or cocoons, damaged leaves or other objects, wood borer tunnels, and similar objects make excellent photographic material, and are usually much easier to photograph than living insects.

Photographing insects has become a hobby with many naturalists and camera enthusiasts, who choose insects as well as flowers and birds because of their color patterns, or because they are intrigued by the habits and biology of these animals.

DRAWINGS OF INSECTS

The student will sooner or later have occasion to make drawings of insects or insect structures, either for his personal notes as a part of a laboratory exercise, or as part of a research report prepared for publication. One need not be a natural artist to prepare good drawings of insects. The aim of entomological drawing is accuracy rather than artistry, and simple line drawings often serve better than elaborately shaded or wash drawings.

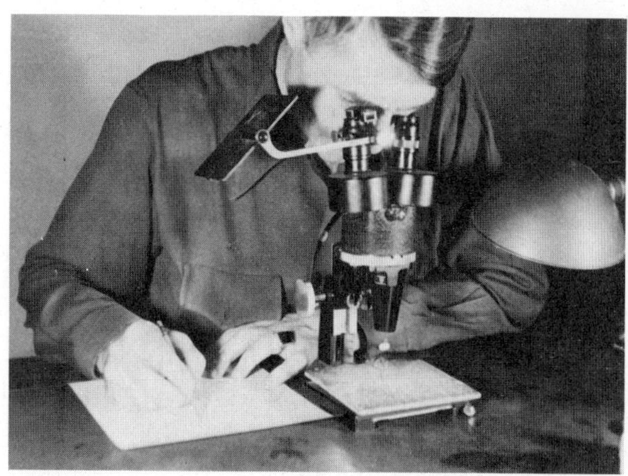

Figure 642. Camera lucida in use.

The student should strive primarily for accuracy in drawings of insects or insect structures. A gifted artist can make a freehand drawing that is fairly accurate, but most people require some sort of mechanical aid to obtain accuracy. There are several devices and techniques by which one can turn out an accurately proportioned drawing with a minimum of effort; these include the camera lucida, projection apparatus, the use of crosshatching, and careful measurements of the specimen to be drawn.

A camera lucida (Figure 642) is a device that fits over the eyepiece of a microscope. It contains a system of prisms and mirrors so arranged that, by looking through it, the observer sees both the object under the microscope and the paper on which the drawing is to be made, and can draw exactly what he sees through the microscope. It takes a little practice to learn how to use a camera lucida, but once one gets the knack of it, he can turn out accurate drawings rather rapidly. A camera lucida is a rather expensive piece of equipment and is likely to be available only in well-equipped university or research laboratories.

Any insect or insect structure that is fairly flat and translucent can be drawn by projection. The object to be drawn is projected by means of a photographic enlarger, projection lantern, or other projection apparatus onto a sheet of paper, and the drawing is traced over the projected image. This is the ideal method of making drawings of insect wings, which can be mounted between two glass slides. Elaborate projectors can be obtained which will give magnifications from four or five up to several hundred, but they are rather expensive. Photographic enlargers, projection lanterns, or microprojectors can be used if one does not want too much magnification.

The crosshatching principle can be used for making drawings from specimens and for copying drawings at a different scale. The object to be drawn is observed through a grid of crossed lines and drawn on coordinate paper, the detail of the object being put in one square at a time. For drawing a macroscopic object, a grid made of crossed threads can be set up in front of the object; for microscopic objects, a transparent disk on which fine crosslines are scratched is put into the eyepiece of the microscope. For copying a drawing at a different scale, a grid of one scale is put over the drawing to be copied and the details of the drawing are copied one square at a time on coordinate paper that has a different scale.

A wall chart or any greatly enlarged drawing can be made from a text figure either by projection or by the crosshatching method. Text drawings can be projected by an opaque projector and traced, or they can be enlarged on a chart by using the grid principle described in the preceding paragraph.

If one does not have any of these mechanical aids, he can achieve a considerable degree of accuracy by carefully measuring the specimen to be drawn and then making the drawing agree with these measurements. Measurements of small objects should be made with dividers.

The simplest way to obtain a symmetrical drawing, when one is drawing an animal (or part of an animal) that is bilaterally symmetrical, is to make only the right or left half of the drawing from the specimen and then to trace the other half from the first half.

Whether or not a drawing should contain some sort of shading depends on what one wishes to show. Many drawings of insect structures (for example, most of the drawings in this book showing anatomical characters) will show what they are intended to show without any shading, or perhaps with a few well-placed lines. If one wishes to show contour and/or surface texture, as would be shown in a photograph, more elaborate shading will be necessary. This shading may be done by stippling (a series of dots, as in Figure 72), parallel or crossed lines (for example, the eyes in Figure 119), a series of dots and lines (for example, Figure 207), or by the use of a special type of drawing paper containing tiny raised aeas (stipple board, coquille board, Ross board, etc., which was used in preparing such drawings as those in Figures 294 and 307). There are press-on sheets of various types of shading, stippling, lines, crosshatching, and other patterns, which provide a quick yet satisfactory method of obtaining shading and texture in drawings. The best known of these is called "Craf-Tone" and can be obtained in most stores handling art supplies.

When one is preparing a drawing for publication, he should keep in mind the method by which his drawing will be reproduced and the character of the publication in which it will appear. Most printed illustrations are reproduced either by a zinc etching, a halftone, or by lithoprinting. The zinc process is used for line drawings; it reproduces only black and white, and the original must be made with India ink. Photographs are reproduced by means of halftones; a halftone plate is made by photographing through a screen the picture to be reproduced, and the printed illustration is made up of a series of tiny dots. The lithoprinting process involves making a plate, and the printed page is reproduced by offset printing; in this process, black-and-white drawings and photographs are reproduced about equally well. Fine lines in a black-and-white drawing are usually reproduced better by lithoprinting than by a zinc etching. Drawings prepared for publication are ordinarily made about twice the size at which they will be reproduced, sometimes larger. The subsequent reduction tends to eliminate minor irregularities in the original drawing. If the reduction is very great, particularly in a zinc reproduction, the fine lines will disappear or lines close together on the original drawing will appear run together in the printed drawing.

The student who wishes to learn how to prepare good drawings should study the better drawings in textbooks and research papers. By studying carefully the details of such drawings, he will learn some of the tricks of giving an effect of contour with a minimum of shading, and he will learn the methods of shading that best produce the desired effects. He will also learn something of the preferred style of arranging and labeling drawings.

THE PROJECTION OF INSECT MATERIALS

Any insect, or insect part, that is not too big or too opaque can be projected by means of an ordinary slide projector or microprojector; all that is necessary is to have the material on a slide, or in some form that can be put into the projector. Projected materials are very useful teaching devices, and while many slides for projection can be obtained from supply houses, many can be made by the student or teacher.

WING SLIDES

The insect parts that are the easiest to prepare for projection, and which often give a projection that is better than one made by photography, are the wings. Most insect wings are transparent or nearly so, and when projected show the venation beautifully. Most colored wings, when the coloring is in the wing membrane, show this color upon projection as well as or better than a colored photographic transparency. Wings that are thick and opaque, such as the elytra of beetles, do not project very well unless they are first cleared (see page 737); wings of Lepidóptera must be cleared or bleached before they are mounted if the projection is designed to show the venation; the procedures involved in this process have been discussed above (page 472).

Most insect wings mounted for projection can be broken off a dried insect and mounted (dry) between two 2- by 2-inch (50- by 50-mm) glass slides; this process generally takes only a few minutes, and the mounted wings will last indefinitely. If the wings removed from a dried insect are folded (for example, as in Orthóptera, Plecóptera, and some other insects), they must be unfolded and flattened before being mounted; to do this they must first be softened or relaxed, or attempts to unfold them will only result in the wings being torn. Such wings can usually be relaxed with a few drops of alcohol or relaxing fluid (see page 730); after the wing is flattened out (on one 2- by 2-inch slide), it should be allowed to dry before the cover slide is added and the slide bound.

Wings mounted for projection between 2-by 2-inch slides should be oriented in a standard fashion, as shown in the wing drawings in this book. The slide is labeled on the outside, generally on the binding tape.

SLIDES OF OTHER INSECT PARTS

Almost any insect part that is more or less flattened and not too opaque can be mounted between 2- by 2-inch slides, or on a microscope slide, and projected—for example, mouth parts, legs, antennae, genitalia, or other parts. Structures that are particularly opaque should be cleared (in KOH) before they are mounted.

Insects or insect parts that are mounted on microscope slides can be projected with a microprojector, or by means of a 2- by 2-inch slide projector if a special carriage is made for the slide (Figure 643). The projection of a microscope slide with a 2- by 2-inch slide projector is generally not very satisfactory unless the specimen on the slide is at least 6 mm long.

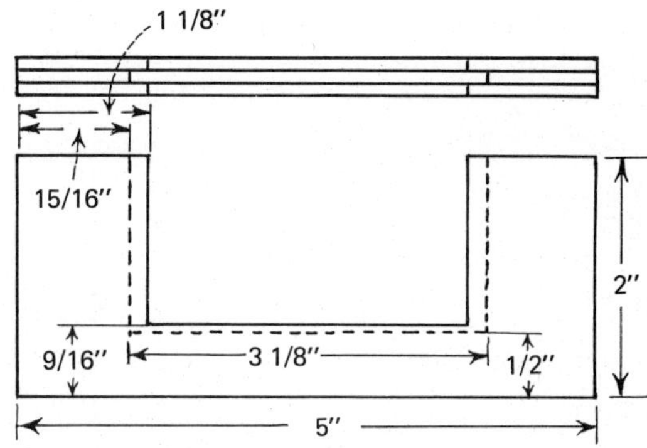

Figure 643. Carriage for microscope slides, for projection in a lantern-slide projector.

Elaborate and expensive microprojectors for projecting minute organisms on microscope slides are available from supply houses handling optical equipment, but a fairly satisfactory microprojector can be made with a microscope, a projection lantern with a strong bulb (300–500 watts), some opaque cloth, and a mirror. A diagram of such a microprojector is shown in Figure 644. The cloth is used over the space between the projector and the substage of the microscope and around the substage, to prevent the escape of light. Such a setup will give a fairly clear field up to 3 feet (0.9 m) or more in diameter, and in a well-darkened room magnifications up to 100 times can be used. A somewhat more elaborate homemade microprojector is described by H. S. Seifert in *Turtox News*, 29(1):30–33, 1951.

PROJECTION OF LIVING INSECTS

Small aquatic insects can be placed in a slide-sized water cell (Figure 645) and projected with almost any slide projector; the result is like a motion picture. The materials for making such a cell cost less than ten cents.

Such a cell can be made with two 2- by 2-inch (50- by 50-mm) slides which can be purchased at any photographic supply store, and narrow strips of single-weight window glass. These strips are cut $\frac{5}{16}$ inch (8 mm) wide, with the strips at the bot-

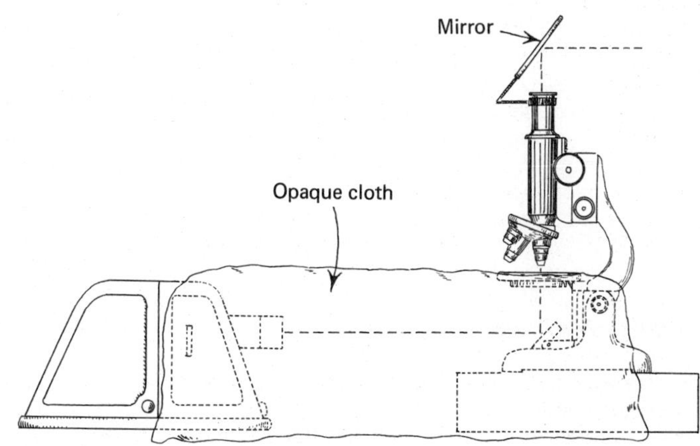

Figure 644. Diagram of a homemade microprojector. The opaque cloth is fastened tightly around the projector and around the base of the microscope to prevent the escape of light.

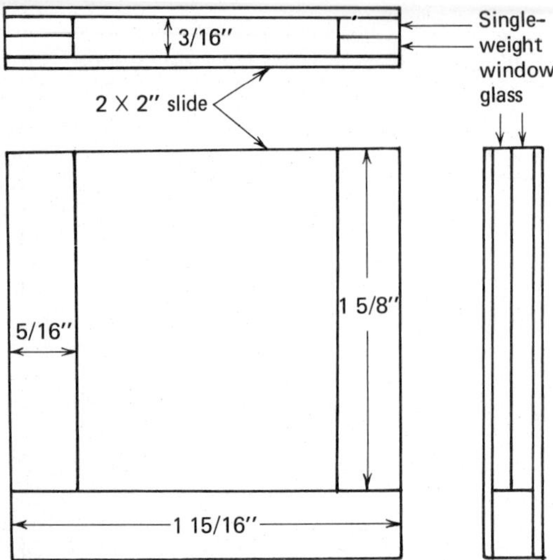

Figure 645. A water cell for the projection of small living aquatic insects by means of a lantern-slide projector.

tom $1\frac{15}{16}$ inches (50 mm) long and those at the sides $1\frac{5}{8}$ inches (42 mm) long. The sides and bottom of the cell are made of two thicknesses of this glass, making the inside of the cell $\frac{3}{16}$ inch (4.8 mm) thick. Any good waterproof cement (for example, household cement) may be used in putting the cell together. The trick in making a cell of this sort is to make it watertight; hence the pieces should be cemented together carefully. A strip of wood could be used in place of the strips of glass, or the entire cell could be made of plastic instead of glass, but glass is the preferred material.

If the slide carriage of the projector will not take this cell (and it probably won't), remove the carriage and insert a narrow strip of thin wood or heavy cardboard into the bottom of the slide carriage aperture; the cell will rest on this strip. The cell is filled to about 6 mm from the top with water, the organisms to be projected are added, and the cell is inserted into the projector. In some projectors this cell will heat up after 10 or 15 minutes of use; hence it is advisable to have one or two extra cells that can be used alternately, to avoid overheating. The image on the screen will be upside down, but this is a minor detail; if one desires it right side up, it can be inverted by means of mirrors.

SOURCES OF INFORMATION

Information on insects is available in the form of literature published by various federal and state organizations, from various private organizations such as supply houses, museums, and societies, and from a great mass of books and periodicals. Much of this literature will be available in a good library, and a good bit of it can be obtained at little or no cost to the student or teacher. Information is also available from contacts with other people who are interested in insects—amateurs and workers in universities, museums, and experiment stations. Materials such as entomological equipment or visual aids such as slides, movies, and exhibits are available from supply houses, museums, and often from various state or private agencies.

GOVERNMENT PUBLICATIONS

Many government publications are available to the public free of charge, and others can frequently be obtained free through a senator or congressman. The publications that are sold are sold at a nominal cost. There is a wealth of literature on insects available from the government.

Information on the publications of various governmental agencies can be obtained from the Division of Public Documents, Government Printing Office, Washington, D.C. 20402. This office publishes a number of lists of publications (one is on insects), which are available without cost. Most government publications on insects are published by the U.S. Department of Agriculture, and information on the publications of this department may be obtained from the following sources: (1) from List 11, *List of the Available Publications of the U.S. Department of Agriculture* (which is revised every year or so), available from the U.S. Department of Agriculture, Washington, D.C. 20250; (2) from various indexes published by the USDA; (3) from indexing journals, such as the *Agricultural Index* and *Bibliography of Agriculture;* and (4) from the *Monthly List of Publications and Motion Pictures,* formerly published monthly but now published every two months (this is available free from the USDA).

The federal government has many publications dealing wholly or in part with insects. These include several serial publications, such as the *Journal of Agricultural Research* (semimonthly, discontinued since 1949), *The Experiment Station Record* (monthly, discontinued since 1946), and *Bibliography of Agriculture* (monthly). Some publications, such as the USDA Yearbooks and various annual reports, appear once a year. Publications of a great many series appear irregularly;

among those that frequently deal with insects are the *Bulletins, Farmers' Bulletins, Technical Bulletins, Circulars,* and *Miscellaneous Publications* of the USDA, and the publications of the Smithsonian Institution and the U.S. National Museum.

STATE PUBLICATIONS

Many of the publications of state agencies are available free to residents of that state. In some states there are several agencies whose publications would be of interest to the student or teacher of entomology, particularly the state agricultural experiment station, the state extension service, the state departments of education and conservation, the state biological or natural history survey, and the state museum. Information on the publications available from these agencies can usually be obtained by writing to the agencies directly. The publications of various state agencies are listed in the *Monthly Check List of State Publications,* which is published by the Library of Congress.

Many state agricultural experiment stations are closely associated with the state agricultural college and are located in the same town; the state extension service is nearly always a part of the state agricultural college. State departments of education or conservation are usually located in the state capital; state museums are usually located either in the state capital or in the same town as the state university. Most state universities have museums that contain insect collections and which often publish papers on insects. State biological surveys are usually associated with the state university or the state agricultural college.

The locations of the state agricultural experiment stations and the state agricultural extension services in the fifty states are given in Table 7; zip codes are given in parentheses. Many states have one or more branch stations in addition to the principal experiment station; only the principal station is listed. The agricultural extension services in the various states are associated with the state university or state agricultural college.

Table 7 LOCATIONS OF THE STATE AGRICULTURAL EXPERIMENT STATIONS AND THE STATE EXTENSION SERVICES

State	Experiment Station	Extension Service
Alabama	Auburn (36830)	Ala. Polytechnic Inst., Auburn (36830)
Alaska	College (99735)	Univ. Alaska, College (99735)
Arizona	Tuscon (85721)	Univ. Arizona, Tuscon (85721)
Arkansas	Fayetteville (72701)	Univ. Ark., Fayetteville (72701)
California	Berkeley (94720)	Univ. Calif. Berkeley (94720)
Colorado	Fort Collins (80521)	Colo. State Univ., Fort Collins (80521)
Connecticut	New Haven (06504)	Univ. Conn., Storrs (06268)
Delaware	Newark (19711)	Univ. Delaware, Newark (19711)
Florida	Gainesville (32603)	Univ. Florida, Gainesville (32603)
Georgia	Experiment (30212)	Univ. Georgia, Athens (30601)
Hawaii	Honolulu (96822)	Univ. Hawaii, Honolulu (96822)
Idaho	Moscow (83843)	Univ. Idaho, Moscow (83843)
Illinois	Urbana (61803)	Univ. Illinois, Urbana (61803)
Indiana	Lafayette (47907)	Purdue Univ., Lafayette (47907)
Iowa	Ames (50010)	Iowa State Univ., Ames (50010)
Kansas	Manhattan (66504)	Kan. State Univ., Manhattan (66504)
Kentucky	Lexington (40506)	Univ. Kentucky, Lexington (40506)
Louisiana	Baton Rouge (70803)	La. State Univ., Baton Rouge (70803)
Maine	Orono (04473)	Univ. Maine, Orono (04473)

State	Experiment Station	Extension Service
Maryland	College Park (20742)	Univ. Maryland, College Park (20742)
Massachusetts	Amherst (01003)	Univ. Mass., Amherst (01003)
Michigan	East Lansing (48823)	Mich. State Univ., E. Lansing (48823)
Minnesota	St. Paul (55101)	Univ. Minnesota, St. Paul (55101)
Mississippi	State College (39762)	Miss. State Univ., State College (39762)
Missouri	Columbia (65202)	Univ. Missouri, Columbia (65202)
Montana	Bozeman (59715)	Mont. State Univ.; Bozeman (59715)
Nebraska	Lincoln (68503)	Univ. Nebraska, Lincoln (68503)
Nevada	Reno (89507)	Univ. Nevada, Reno (89507)
New Hampshire	Durham (03824)	Univ. N. Hampshire, Durham (03824)
New Jersey	New Brunswick (08903)	Rutgers Univ., New Brunswick (08903)
New Mexico	University Park (88070)	N. Mex. State Univ., University Park (88070)
New York	Ithaca (14850)	Cornell Univ., Ithaca (14850)
North Carolina	Raleigh (27607)	N. Carolina State Univ., Raleigh (27607)
North Dakota	Fargo (58103)	N. Dakota State Univ., Fargo (58103)
Ohio	Wooster (44691)	Ohio State Univ., Columbus (43210)
Oklahoma	Stillwater (74075)	Okla. State Univ., Stillwater (74075)
Oregon	Corvallis (97331)	Oregon State Univ., Corvallis (97331)
Pennsylvania	University Park (16802)	Penn. State Univ., University Park (16802)
Rhode Island	Kingston (02881)	Univ. Rhode Island, Kingston (02881)
South Carolina	Clemson (29631)	Clemson Univ., Clemson (29631)
South Dakota	Brookings (57007)	S. Dakota State Univ., Brookings (57007)
Tennessee	Knoxville (37901)	Univ. Tennessee, Knoxville (37901)
Texas	College Station (77843)	A. & M. College of Tex., College Station (77843)
Utah	Logan (84321)	Utah State Univ., Logan (84321)
Vermont	Burlington (05401)	Univ. Vermont, Burlington (05401)
Virginia	Blacksburg (24061)	Va. Polytechnic Inst., Blacksburg (24061)
Washington	Pullman (99163)	Wash. State Univ., Pullman (99163)
West Virginia	Morgantown (26506)	W. Va. Univ., Morgantown (26506)
Wisconsin	Madison (53706)	Univ. Wisconsin, Madison (53706)
Wyoming	Laramie (82071)	Univ. Wyoming, Laramie (82071)

MISCELLANEOUS AGENCIES

Biological supply houses are useful sources of equipment, material, and often of publications of interest to an entomologist. All supply houses publish catalogues, and their catalogues are sent free or at a nominal cost to teachers and schools. These catalogues are of value in indicating what can be obtained from the supply houses, and many of their illustrations will suggest to the ingenious student or teacher things that he can prepare himself.

A list of the supply houses handling entomological equipment and supplies is given on page 765. Some of these (for example, General Biological and Carolina Biological Supply) put out a monthly publication that is sent free to teachers. These publications often contain articles of a technical nature as well as suggestions for the teacher. General Biological Supply House also publishes a series of leaflets called Turtox Service Leaflets, which cover a variety of subjects, and many of them are of value to the student or teacher of entomology.

Many societies, museums, and research institutions publish material that is useful to the entomologist. Entomological societies (see below), state biological survey organizations, and organizations such as the National Audubon Society (950 Third Ave., New York, N.Y. 10022) will send lists of their publications on request.

DIRECTORIES OF ENTOMOLOGISTS

Anyone interested in insects will find it profitable to become acquainted with others who have similar interests. If he is located near a university or museum or experiment station, he should become acquainted with the workers there who are interested in insects. Persons throughout the country who are interested in various phases of entomology can often be located by consulting the membership lists of the various entomological societies, which are usually published at intervals in the societies' journals or various directories. Some of the most useful directories of people working in entomology and other biological fields are mentioned below; they are usually available in a good public or university library.

Directory of Zoological Taxonomists of the World. This was published by the Society of Systematic Zoology in 1961. It contains (1) a detailed classification of the animal kingdom, with a list of the specialists working on each group, and (2) an alphabetical list of the specialists, with their addresses. It is particularly valuable in locating someone who is an authority on a particular group of animals.

Naturalists' Directory. This is published every few years by PCL Publications Inc., P.O. Box 583, South Orange, N.J. The entries include the name, address, and special interests, and are arranged alphabetically under the various states, Canadian provinces, and many foreign countries.

Directories of the U.S. Department of Agriculture. *Directory of Organization and Field Activities of the U.S. Department of Agriculture;* USDA Agric. Handbook No. 76. *Professional Workers in State Agricultural Experiment Stations and Other Cooperating State Institutions;* USDA Agric. Handbook No. 305. These directories are revised every year or two, and are particularly useful for determining who is located at a particular university or experiment station.

American Men and Women of Science, 12th edition (1971); the entries are listed alphabetically and include a biographical sketch.

ENTOMOLOGICAL SOCIETIES

There are a great many entomological societies in this country, membership in which is generally open to anyone interested in entomology. The dues vary, but are generally $5.00 or more per year. Members receive the publications of the society, notices of meetings, and newsletters. The national societies usually have meetings only once a year; smaller local societies may have meetings at more frequent intervals.

A list of the entomological societies in the United States and Canada may be found in *Entomol. News,* 42(4):126–130 (1931), and a list of the entomological societies of the world may be found in *Bull. Ent. Soc. Am.,* 2(4):1–22 (1956). Some of the better known entomological societies in the United States and Canada, with their addresses and principal publications, are as follows:

American Entomological Society. Academy of Natural Sciences, Philadelphia, Pa. *Transactions of the American Entomological Society;* quarterly. *Entomological News;* monthly, except August and September.

Brooklyn Entomological Society. Brooklyn, N. Y. *Bulletin of the Brooklyn Entomological Society* (ceased publication in 1968); five times yearly. *Entomologica Americana;* quarterly.

Cambridge Entomological Club. Harvard University, Cambridge, Mass. *Psyche;* quarterly.

Entomological Society of America. 4603 Calvert Road, College Park, Md. 20740. *Annals of the Entomological Society of America;* quarterly. *Journal of Economic Entomology;* bimonthly. *Bulletin of the Entomological Society of America;* quarterly. *Environmental Entomology;* bimonthly.

Entomological Society of Canada. Ottawa, Ont. *Canadian Entomologist;* monthly. This journal was begun in 1868 by the old Entomological Society of Canada; from 1871 to 1951 it was published by the Entomological Society of Ontario; from 1951 to 1960 it was published jointly by the Entomological Society of Ontario and the new Entomological Society of Canada;

the latter society has published this journal since 1960.

Entomological Society of Washington. Washington, D.C. *Proceedings of the Entomological Society of Washington;* quarterly.

Florida Entomological Society. Gainesville, Fla. *The Florida Entomologist;* quarterly.

Kansas (Central States) Entomological Society. Manhattan, Kan. *Journal of the Kansas Entomological Society;* quarterly.

Michigan Entomological Society. East Lansing, Mich. *Michigan Entomologist* (since 1971 called *Great Lakes Entomologist*); published quarterly since July, 1966.

New York Entomological Society. New York. *Journal of the New York Entomological Society;* quarterly.

Pacific Coast Entomological Society. San Francisco, Calif. *The Pan-Pacific Entomologist;* quarterly.

GENERAL REFERENCES

Below is a list of the more important general references, usually available in a large library, which will help one to locate a particular book, periodical, or other reference on a zoological or entomological subject. Anyone planning to do a substantial amount of work in a large library should become familiar with the card catalog of that library, the method of cataloging the library's holdings, and the general layout of the library (including the location of the materials one is likely to use).

Zoological Record. This is a bibliography of the world literature on zoology and has been published annually since 1864. It contains titles of papers, books, and the like, arranged alphabetically under some 19 major sections. Each of the 19 sections contains a subject index and a systematic index (to orders, families, and so forth).

Biological Abstracts. This is an abstracting journal, published monthly, with the papers arranged in each issue under a number of major subject matter headings. Each volume is fully indexed. This is a very useful reference in all fields of biology.

Union List of Serials in the Libraries of the United States and Canada. This volume, with its supplements, contains a list of periodicals, with an indication of the various libraries in the United States and Canada that have each one, and the volumes each has. Supplements since 1950 are under the title *New Serial Titles.* These references are useful in determining where a particular periodical may be obtained (for example, through an interlibrary loan) if it is not present in one's local library.

Index to the Literature of American Economic Entomology. This was published from 1917 to 1962, the first several volumes about every five years, and more recent volumes yearly; Volume 18 (1962), which covers the literature of 1959, is the last in this series. This is a very valuable index for entomologists; the entries in each volume are arranged alphabetically by author and subject, and the subject classification is quite detailed. The more recent volumes cover the literature from North America, Hawaii, and the West Indies.

Review of Applied Entomology. This is published monthly in two series; A, agricultural entomology, and B, medical and veterinary entomology. It is an abstracting journal of the world literature on applied entomology. The entries are not arranged in any special sequence, but each volume contains an author and a detailed subject index.

Bibliography of Agriculture. This is published monthly; it lists references, alphabetically by subject, on subjects pertaining to agriculture from all over the world; it contains a section on entomology.

Agricultural Index. This index is published monthly; it is a detailed index, alphabetically arranged by subject, to some 150 American and English periodicals and to government publications.

Bibliography of the More Important Contributions to American Economic Entomology. Parts 1 to 5 were by S. Henshaw, 1890–1896, and Parts 6 to 8 were by N. Banks, 1898–1905.

Entomological Abstracts. This is published monthly, and each yearly volume contains about 9000 abstracts. The abstracts in each issue are arranged under a variety of headings, and each volume contains a subject index.

Apiculture Abstracts. This is published quarterly; the abstracts are arranged under a variety of headings in each issue, and each volume contains a subject and an author index.

The following references, usually available in a large library, are of a more general nature than those listed above, but are often of value to a zoologist or entomologist.

Document Catalogue. This is a journal, published monthly; it lists all government publications, alphabetically by author and subject, and is a comprehensive list of all government publications.

Monthly Checklist of State Publications. Publications are listed in this journal by states and departments, with an annual index by author, title, and subject. This reference is useful as a source of information on the publications of such state agencies as experiment stations, universities, wildlife departments, and the like.

The United States Catalogue and the Cumulative Book Index. This is published monthly, with cumulations at intervals. All books and pamphlets printed in English are listed alphabetically by author, title, and subject. This reference is a useful source of information on current or recent books.

Bibliographic Index. This is a journal, published quarterly; it is a bibliography of bibliographies classified by subjects arranged alphabetically.

A World Bibliography of Bibliographies. Four editions are now out, 1939–1940, 1947–1949, 1955, and 1965. This covers most separate bibliographic works published in European languages since 1740; it is general in scope and stronger in the humanities than in technical fields.

SOURCES OF ENTOMOLOGICAL SUPPLIES

Many of the materials needed for making an insect collection or working with insects can be home made, but some must be obtained from a supply house. The following are some of the leading biological supply houses in the United States.

American Biological Supply Co., 1330 Dillon Heights Ave., P.O. Box 3149, Baltimore, Md. 21228.

Arthropod Specialties Co., P.O. Box 1973, Sacramento, Calif. 95809. (This company is a good source of the plastic microvials used in genitalia studies.)

Bio Metal Associates, 316 Washington St., El Segundo, Calif. 90245. Eastern Office: BioQuip East, 1115 Rolling Rd., Baltimore, Md. 21228. Western Office: BioQuip West, P.O. Box 61, Santa Monica, Calif. 90406.

Carolina Biological Supply Co.: (1) Burlington, N.C. 27215; (2) Powell Laboratories Division, Gladstone, Ore. 97027.

Entomology Research Institute, Lake City, Minn. 55041.

Entomological Supplies, Inc., 5655 Oregon Ave., Baltimore, Md. 21227.

General Biological Supply House, Inc., 8200 S. Hoyne Ave., Chicago, Ill. 60620.

Ward's Natural Science Establishment, Inc., P.O. Box 1712, Rochester, N.Y. 14603. Ward's of California, P.O. Box 1749, Monterey, Calif. 93942.

A great many concerns throughout the country handle optical equipment such as microscopes, laboratory supplies, and scientific instruments. Each year the American Association for the Advancement of Science, in a special issue of *Science,* publishes a "Guide to Scientific Instruments." This guide gives information on where instruments and apparatus of various sorts can be obtained. The most recent of these was published Nov. 26, 1974 (*Science,* Vol. 186, No. 4165A). A few of the leading suppliers of laboratory equipment (many of whom also handle entomological supplies) are as follows:

Aloe Scientific, 1831 Olive St., St. Louis, Mo. 63103.

AO Instrument Co., Eggert & Sugar Rd., Buffalo, N.Y. 14215.

Bausch & Lomb Optical Co., 77466 Bausch St., Rochester, N.Y. 14602.

Central Scientific Co., 1700 Irving Park Rd., Chicago, Ill. 60613.

The Chemical Rubber Co., 18901 Cranwood Pkwy., Cleveland, Ohio 44128.

Clay-Adams Co., 141 E. 25th St., New York, N.Y. 10010.

Cole-Parmer Instrument Co., 7330 N. Clark St., Chicago, Ill. 60626.

Dennoyer-Geppert Co., 5235 Ravenswood Ave., Chicago, Ill. 60640.

Fisher Scientific Co., 711 Forbes Ave., Pittsburgh, Pa. 15219.

General Scientific Equipment Co., Limekiln Pike and Williams Ave., Philadelphia, Pa. 19150.

E. Leitz, Inc., 468 Park Ave. S., New York, N.Y. 10016.

Matheson Scientific, Inc., 1735 N. Ashland Ave., Chicago, Ill. 60622.

Welch Scientific Co., 7300 Linder Ave., Stokie, Ill. 60076.

Will Scientific, Inc., Box 1050, Rochester, N.Y. 14603.

References on Collecting, Preserving, and Studying Insects

Beirne, B. P. 1955. Collecting, preparing, and preserving insects. Can. Dept. Agric. Ent. Div. Pub. 932; 133 pp., 108 f.

Blaker, A. A. 1965. *Photography for Scientific Publication: A Handbook*. San Francisco: W. H. Freeman, xii + 158 pp., frontis. (color) + 20 pl., 34 f.

Blum, M. S., and J. P. Woodring. 1963. Preservation of insect larvae by vacuum dehydration. *J. Kan. Ent. Soc.*, 36(2):96–101; 3 f.

Borror, D. J. 1934. Ecological studies of *Argia moesta* Hagen (Odonata) by means of marking. *Ohio J. Sci.*, 34(2):97–108; 17 f., 2 graphs.

Borror, D. J. 1948. Analysis of repeat records of banded white-throated sparrows. *Ecol. Monog.*, 18(3):411–430; 4 f.

Borror, D. J. 1958. A projection cell for small aquatic organisms. *Turtox News*, 36(2):50–51; 1 f.

Borror, D. J., and A. C. Borror. 1961. Glass mounts for displaying Lepidoptera. *Turtox News*, 39(12):298–300; 2 f.

Byers, G. W. 1958. Individual identification labels for pinned insect specimens. *Ent. News*, 69(5):113–116.

Byers, G. W. 1959. A rapid method for making temporary insect labels in the field. *J. Lep. Soc.*, 13(2):96–98.

Cruickshank, A. D. (Ed.) 1957. *Hunting with the Camera*. New York: Harper and Row, 215 pp. frontis. (color) + 41 f. (Chap. 4, Insects, by E. S. Ross; pp. 108–134, f. 23–29.)

DeLong, D. M., and R. H. Davidson. 1936. *Methods of Collecting and Preserving Insects*. Columbus, Ohio: Ohio State Univ. Press, 20 pp., 11 f.

Edwards, J. G. 1963. Spreading blocks for butterfly wings. *Turtox News*, 41(1):16–19; 3 f.

Hillcourt, W. 1950. *Field Book of Nature Activities*. New York: G. P. Putnam's Sons, 320 pp.; illus.

Kalmus, H. 1960. *101 Simple Experiments with Insects*. Garden City, N.Y.: Doubleday, xii + 194 pp., 39 f.

Kinne, R. 1962. *The Complete Book of Nature Photography*. New York: A. S. Barnes, 191 pp.; illus.

Knudson, J. W. 1972. *Collecting and Preserving Plants and Animals*. New York: Harper and Row, 320 pp.

Levi, H. W. 1966. The care of alcoholic collections of small invertebrates. *Syst. Zool.*, 16(3):183–188.

Mansuy, M. C. 1929. Collection and preservation of insects for use in the study of agriculture. USDA Farmers' Bull. 1601; 19 pp., 18 f.

Miller, D. F., and G. W. Blaydes. 1962 (2nd ed.). *Methods and Materials for Teaching Biological Sciences*. New York: McGraw-Hill, x + 453 pp.; illus.

Needham, J. G., *et al.* 1937. *Culture Methods for Invertebrate Animals*. Ithaca, N.Y.: Comstock Publ., xxxii + 590 pp., 84 f.

Oldroyd, H. 1958. *Collecting, Preserving, and Studying Insects*. New York: Macmillan, 327 pp., 135 f., 1 map, 15 pl.

Oman, P. W., and A. D. Cushman. 1948. Collection and preservation of insects. USDA Misc. Pub. 601; 42 pp., 42 f.

Papp, C. S. 1968. *Scientific Illustration. Theory and Practice*. Dubuque, Iowa: Wm. C. Brown, xi + 318 pp., 1345 f.

Peterson, A. 1953 (7th ed.). *A Manual of Entomological Techniques*. Ann Arbor, Mich.: J. W. Edwards, v + 367 pp., 182 pl.

Post, R. L., D. G. Aarhus, H. F. Perkins, and G. L. Thomasson. 1969. Insect collecting manual. Dept. Ent., N. Dak. State Univ., N. Dakota Insect Ser. Pub. 8; 36 pp.; illus.

Ross, E. S. 1953. *Insects Close Up*. Berkeley: Univ. California Press, 79 pp., 125 f.

Sabrosky, C. W. 1971. Packing and shipping pinned insects. *Bull. Ent. Soc. Amer.*, 17(1):6–8.

Smith, R. C., and R. H. Painter. 1966. (7th ed.). *Guide to the Literature of the Zoological Sciences*. Minneapolis: Burgess, xiv + 238 pp.

Southwood, T. R. E. 1966. *Ecological Methods, with Particular Reference to the Study of Insect Populations*. London: Methuen, xviii + 391 pp.; illus.

Townes, H. 1962. Design for a Malaise trap. *Proc. Ent. Soc. Wash.*, 64(4):253–262; illus.

Townes H. 1972. A light-weight Malaise trap. *Ent. News*, 83:239–247; 3 f.

Urquhart, F. A. 1960. *The Monarch Butterfly*. Toronto: Univ. Toronto Press. xxiv + 361 pp., 79 f.

Valentine, J. M. 1942. On the preparation and preservation of insects, with particular reference to Coleoptera. *Smiths. Inst. Misc. Coll.*, 103(6):1–16; 5 f.

Wagstaffe, R., and J. H. Fidler (Eds.). 1955. *The Preservation of Natural History Specimens*. Vol. 1. *Invertebrates*. New York: Philosophical Library, xiii + 205 pp., 129 f.

Woodring, J. P., and M. Blum. 1963. Freeze-drying of spiders and immature insects. *Ann. Ent. Soc. Amer.*, 56(2):138–141; 2 f.

Zweifel, F. W. 1961. *A Handbook of Biological Illustration*. Chicago: Univ. Chicago Press, xv + 131 pp., 61 f.

GLOSSARY

The definitions given here apply primarily to the use of these terms in this book; elsewhere some terms may have additional or different meanings. Some terms not listed here may be found in the Index.

Abdòmen the posterior of the three main body divisions (Figure 1, *ab*).

Accéssory cell a closed cell in the front wing of Lepidóptera formed by the fusion of two branches of the radius, usually the R_2 cell (Figure 371, *acc*).

Accessory vein an extra branch of a longitudinal vein (indicated by a subscript *a;* for example, an accessory of M_1 is designated M_{1a}); the most posterior vein in the anal area of the front wing of certain Hymenóptera (Figure 527, *ac*).

Acróstichal bristles one or more longitudinal rows of small bristles along the center of the mesonotum (Díptera; Figure 444, *acr*).

Acùlea (pl., **aculeae**) minute spines on the wing membrane (Lepidóptera).

Acùleate with aculeae (Lepidóptera); with a sting (Hymenóptera).

Acùminate tapering to a long point.

Acute pointed; forming an angle of less than 90°.

Adfrontal areas a pair of narrow oblique sclerites on the head of a lepidopterous larva (Figure 357, *adf*).

Adventítious vein a secondary vein, neither accessory nor intercalary, usually the result of cross veins lined up to form a continuous vein.

Aèdeàgus the male intromittent organ; the distal part of the phallus: penis plus parameres.

Aestivation dormancy during a warm or dry season.

Agámic reproducing parthenogenetically, that is, without mating.

Alinòtum the notal plate of the mesothorax or metathorax of a pterygote insect (Figure 18, *AN*).

Álula (pl., **álulae**) a lobe at the base of the wing (Díptera; Figure 442, *alu*); calypter (see).

Ametábolous without metamorphosis.

Ànal pertaining to the last abdominal segment (which bears the anus); the posterior basal part (for example, of the wing).

Anal area of the wing the posterior portion of the wing, usually including the anal veins.

Anal cell a cell in the anal area of the wing; cell 1A (Díptera; Figure 442 B, *A*).

Anal crossing where A branches posteriorly from Cu+A (Odonàta; Figure 98, *Ac*).

Anal lobe a lobe in the posterior basal part of the wing.

Anal loop a group of cells in the hind wing of dragonflies, between Cu_2, 1A, and 2A, which may be rounded (Figure 100 B), elongate (Figure 100 C), or foot-shaped (Figure 98, *alp*).

Ánnulated with ringlike segments or divisions.

Anteàpical just proximad of the apex.

Anteapical cell a cell in the distal part of the wing (leafhoppers; Figure 198, table).

Anteclýpeus an anterior division of the clypeus (Figure 102, *aclp*).

Antecóxal sclerite a sclerite of the metasternum, just anterior to the hind coxae.

Anténna (pl., **antennae**) a pair of segmented appendages located on the head above the mouth parts, and usually sensory in function (Figure 6).

Anténnal club the enlarged distal segments of a clubbed antenna (Figure 244, *acl*).

Antennal fossa a cavity or depression in which the antennae are located (Figure 443, *af*).

Antennal groove a groove in the head capsule into which the basal segment of the antenna fits (Figure 244, *agr*).

Anténnule the first antennae of Crustàcea (Figure 66, *antl*).

Antenòdal cross veins cross veins along the costal border of the wing, between the base of the wing and the nodus, extending from the costa to the radius (Odonàta; Figure 98, *an*).

Antepenúltimate the second from the last.

Antepygídial bristle one or more large bristles on the apical margin of the seventh (next to the last) tergum (Siphonáptera).

Anterior front; in front of.

Anterior cross vein the r-m cross vein (Díptera; Figure 442 B, *acv*).

Anterodorsal in the front and at the top or upper side.

Anteromèsal in the front and along the midline of the body.

Anteroventral in the front and underneath or on the lower side.

Ànus the posterior opening of the alimentary tract (Figure 23, *ans*).

Àpical at the end, tip, or outermost part.

Apical cell a cell near the wing tip (Figure 198, table;

Figure 442 B, *SM;* Figures 527 and 529, *AP*).

Apical cross vein a cross vein near the apex of the wing (Plecóptera, Figure 143 D, *apc;* Homóptera, Figure 198, table).

Ápodeme an invagination of the body wall forming a rigid process that serves for muscle attachment and for the strengthening of the body wall (Figure 3, *apd*).

Apóphysis (pl., **apóphysès**) a tubercular or elongate process of the body wall, either external or internal (Figure 3, *apo*).

Appendículate marginal cell with the vein forming the posterior margin of the marginal cell extending a short distance beyond the apex of the cell (Hymenóptera; Figures 588 B, F, 590 B, *ap*).

Appendix a supplementary or additional piece or part (of the homopteran wing, see Figure 198, *ap*).

Ápterous wingless.

Aptérygote belonging to the subclass Apterygòta (see Chapter 9), primitively wingless.

Aquatic living in water.

Árcuate bent like a bow, or arched.

Árculus a basal cross vein between the radius and the cubitus (Odonàta; Figures 98–100, *arc*).

Àreole an accessory cell (see also *basal areole*).

Arèolet a small cell in the wing; in the Ichneumónidae, the small submarginal cell opposite the second recurrent vein (Figure 549, *are*).

Arísta a large bristle, usually dorsally located, on the apical antennal segment (Díptera; Figure 443, *ar*).

Arístate bristlelike; with an arista; aristate antenna (Figures 6 J and 452 A, B).

Aròlium (pl., **aròlia**) a padlike structure at the apex of the last tarsal segment, between the claws (Orthóptera; Figure 113 D, *aro*); a padlike structure at the base of each tarsal claw (Hemíptera; Figures 164 and 166 A, *aro*).

Articulation a joint, as between two segments or structures.

Aspirator a device with which insects may be picked up by suction (Figure 615).

Asymmetrical not alike on the two sides.

Àtrium (pl., **àtria**) a chamber; a chamber just inside a body opening.

Átrophied reduced in size, rudimentary.

Attenuated very slender and gradually tapering distally.

Auricle a small lobe or earlike structure (Hymenóptera; Figure 599, *au*).

Auxiliary vein the subcosta (Díptera; Figure 442, *av*).

Axílla (pl., **axíllae**) a triangular or rounded sclerite laterad of the scutellum, and usually just caudad of the base of the front wing (Hymenóptera; Figure 530, *ax*).

Áxillary cell a cell in the anal area of the wing (Díptera, Figure 442, *axc;* Hymenoptera, Figure 527, *AX*).

Axillary vein a vein in the anal area of the hind wing (Hymenóptera, Sýmphyta; Figure 527, *axv*).

Band a transverse marking broader than a line.

Bàsad toward the base.

Bàsal at the base; near the point of attachment (of an appendage).

Basal anal cell an anal cell near the wing base; a cell at the base of the wing between 1A and 2A (Plecóptera; Figure 142, *BA*).

Basal àreole a small cell at the base of the wing; the cell at the base of the wing between Sc and R (Lepidóptera; Figures 380–382, *BA*).

Basal cell a cell near the base of the wing, bordered at least in part by the unbranched portions of the longitudinal veins; in the Díptera, one of the two cells proximad of the anterior cross vein and the discal cell (Díptera, Figure 442 B, *B;* Hymenóptera, see Figures 527 and 529).

Basal vein a vein in about the middle of the front wing, extending from the median vein to the subcostal or cubital vein (Hymenóptera; Figures 527 and 529, *bv*).

Basement membrane a noncellular membrane underlying the epidermal cells of the body wall (Figures 2 and 3, *bm*).

Basistérnum that part of a thoracic sternum anterior to the sternacostal suture.

Beak the protruding mouth-part structures of a sucking insect; proboscis (Figures 10–11, 13–14, *bk*).

Bìfid forked, or divided into two parts.

Bilateral symmetry (see *symmetry*).

Bilobed divided into two lobes.

Bipectinate having branches on two sides like the teeth of a comb.

Biràmous with two branches; consisting of an endopodite and an exopodite (Crustàcea).

Bisexual with males and females.

Bituberculate with two tubercles or swellings.

Bivalved with two valves or parts, clamlike.

Blastoderm the peripheral cell layer in the insect egg following cleavage (Figure 36 C, *bl*).

Book gill the leaflike gills of a horseshoe crab (Figure 44, *bg*).

Book lung a respiratory cavity containing a series of leaflike folds (spiders).

Borrow pit a pit formed by an excavation, where earth has been "borrowed" for use elsewhere.

Boss a smooth lateral prominence at the base of a chelicera (spiders).

Brace vein a slanting cross vein; in Odonàta, a slanting cross vein just behind the proximal end of the stigma (Figure 100 F, *bvn*).

Brachýpterous with short wings that do not cover the abdomen.

Bridge cross vein a cross vein anterior to the bridge vein (Odonàta; Figure 98, *bcv*).

Bridge vein the vein that appears as the basal part of the radial sector, between M_{1+2} and the oblique vein (Odonàta; Figure 98, *brv*).

Brood the individuals that hatch from the eggs laid by one mother, individuals that hatch at about the same time and normally mature at about the same time.

Bùcca (pl., **bùccae**) a sclerite on the head below the compound eye and just above the mouth opening (Díptera; Figure 443, *buc*).

Bùccula (pl., **bucculae**) one of two ridges on the underside of the head, on each side of the beak (Hemíptera; Figures 10 and 164, *buc*).

Caècum (pl., **caèca**) a saclike or tubelike structure, open at only one end.

Calamístrum one or two rows of curved spines on the metatarsus of the hind legs (spiders; Figure 59, *clm*).

Calcària movable spurs at the apex of the tibia (Figure 113 J–K, *clc*).

Cállus (pl., **cálli**) a rounded swelling.

Calýpter (pl., **calýpteres**) one of two small lobes at the base of the wing, located just above the halter (Díptera; Figure 442, *cal*). (Also called *squama*.)

Camera lùcida a device enabling one to make accurate drawings of objects seen through a microscope; when it is attached to the eyepiece of a microscope (Figure 642), the observer can see the object under the microscope and his drawing paper at the same time.

Campániform sensíllum a sense organ consisting of a dome-shaped cuticular area into which the sensory cell process is inserted like the clapper of a bell (Figure 29 B).

Campodèiform larva a larva shaped like the dipluran *Campòdea* (Figure 89), that is, elongate, flattened, with well developed legs and antennae, and usually active.

Cannibalistic feeding on other individuals of the same species.

Capitate with an apical knoblike enlargement; capitate antennae (Figure 6 F).

Càrapace a hard dorsal covering consisting of fused dorsal sclerites (Crustàcea; Figure 66, *crp*).

Cardo (pl., **cardines**) the basal segment or division of a maxilla (Figure 7 A, *cd*); one of two small laterobasal sclerites in the millipede gnathochilarium (Figure 74 B, *cd*).

Carìna (pl., **carìnae**) a ridge or keel.

Càrinate ridged or keeled.

Carnivorous feeding on the flesh of other animals.

Caste a form or type of adult in a social insect (termites, see Figure 134; ants, see Figure 579).

Caterpillar an eruciform larva; the larva of a butterfly (Figure 357), moth, sawfly, or scorpionfly.

Caudad toward the tail, or toward the posterior end of the body.

Caudal pertaining to the tail or posterior end of the body.

Caudal filament a threadlike process at the posterior end of the abdomen.

Cell a unit mass of protoplasm, surrounded by a cell membrane and containing one or more nuclei or nuclear material; a space in the wing membrane partly (an open cell) or completely (a closed cell) surrounded by veins.

Céphalad toward the head or anterior end.

Cephálic on or attached to the head; anterior.

Cephalothòrax a body region consisting of head and thoracic segments (Crustàcea and Aráchnida; Figure 57, *cph*).

Cércus (pl., **cerci**) one of a pair of appendages at the posterior end of the abdomen (Figure 1, *cr*).

Cervical pertaining to the neck or cervix.

Cervical sclerite a sclerite located in the lateral part of the cervix, between the head and the prothorax (Figure 6, *cvs*).

Cérvix the neck, a membranous region between the head and prothorax (Figure 18, *cvx*).

Chaètotáxy the arrangement and nomenclature of the bristles on the exoskeleton (Díptera; Figures 443 and 444).

Cheek the lateral part of the head between the compound eye and the mouth (see *gena*).

Chèlate pincerlike, having two opposable claws.

Chelícera (pl., **chelícerae**) one of the anterior pair of appendages in arachnids (Figure 57, *ch*).

Chèliped a leg terminating in an enlarged pincerlike structure (Crustàcea; Figure 66, *chp*).

Chìtin a nitrogenous polysaccharide with the formula $(C_8H_{13}NO_5)_n$, occurring in the cuticle of arthropods.

Chordotònal organ a sense organ, the cellular elements of which form an elongate structure attached at both ends to the body wall.

Chrýsalis (pl., **chrýsalids** or **chrysálides**) the pupa of a butterfly (Figure 358 A, B).

Class a subdivision of a phylum or subphylum, containing a group of related orders.

Clàval suture the suture of the front wing separating the clavus from the corium (Hemíptera; Figure 164, *cls*).

Claval vein a vein in the clavus (Hemíptera, Homóptera; Figure 202, *clv*).

Clávate clublike, or enlarged at the tip; clavate antenna, Figure 6 D, E.

Clàvus the oblong or triangular anal portion of the front wing (Hemíptera and Homóptera; Figures 164 and 167, *cl*).

Claw tuft a dense tuft of hairs below the claws (spiders; Figure 59 D, *clt*).

Cleft split or forked.

Cleptoparasite a parasite that feeds on food stored for the host larvae.

Closed cell a wing cell bounded on all sides by veins, and not reaching the wing margin.

Closed coxal cavity one bounded posteriorly by a sclerite of the same thoracic segment (front coxal cavities, Coleóptera, Figure 245 B), or one completely surrounded by sternal sclerites and not touched by any pleural sclerites (middle coxal cavities, Coleóptera, Figure 245 D).

Clubbed with the distal part (or segments) enlarged; clubbed antennae (Figure 6 D–F, L, M).

Clýpeus a sclerite on the lower part of the face, between the frons and the labium (Figure 5, *clp*).

Coárctate larva a larva somewhat similar to a dipterous puparium, in which the skin of the preceding instar is not completely shed but remains attached to the caudal end of the body; the sixth instar of a blister beetle, also called a pseudopupa (Figure 297 H).

Coarctate pupa a pupa enclosed in a hardened shell formed by the next to the last larval skin (Díptera; Figure 43 F).

Cocoon a silken case inside which the pupa is formed.

Cóllophore a tubelike structure located on the ventral side of the first abdominal segment (Collémbola; Figure 88, *co*).

Cóllum the tergite of the first body segment (Diplópoda; Figure 74 A, *colm*).

Còlon the large intestine; that part of the hindgut between the ileum and the rectum (Figure 23, *cn*).

Cólulus a slender pointed structure lying just anterior to the spinnerets (spiders).

Commensalism a living together of two or more species, none of which is injured thereby, and at least one of which is benefited.

Compound eye an eye composed of many individual elements or ommatidia, each of which is represented externally by a facet; the external surface of such an eye consists of circular facets that are very close together, or of facets that are in contact and more or less hexagonal in shape (Figure 1, *e*, and Figure 30 C, D).

Compressed flattened from side to side.

Cóndyle a knoblike process forming an articulation.

Cónnate fused together or immovably united.

Constricted narrowed.

Contiguous touching each other.

Convergent becoming closer distally.

Corbícula (pl., **corbículae**) a smooth area on the outer surface of the hind tibia, bordered on each side by a fringe of long curved hairs, which serves as a pollen basket (bees).

Còrium the elongate, usually thickened, basal portion of the front wing (Hemíptera; Figure 167, *cor*).

Cornea the cuticular part of an eye (Figure 30, *cna*).

Cornicle one of a pair of dorsal tubular structures on the posterior part of the abdomen (aphids; Figure 201 C, *crn*).

Cornículi (sing., **cornículus**) urogomphi (see).

Coronal suture a longitudinal suture along the midline of the vertex, between the compound eyes (Figure 5, *cs*).

Corpus allàtum (pl., **corpora allàta**) one of a pair of small structures immediately behind the brain (Figure 28, *ca*).

Costa a longitudinal wing vein, usually forming the anterior margin of the wing (Figure 20, *C*).

Costal area the portion of the wing immediately behind the anterior margin.

Costal break a point on the costa where the sclerotization is weak or lacking, or the vein appears to be broken (Díptera; Figures 459 A, B, and 460 C–E, *cbr*).

Costal cell the wing space between the costa and the subcosta.

Coxa (pl., **coxae**) the basal segment of the leg (Figure 19, *cx*).

Coxópodite the basal segment of an arthropod appendage.

Crawler the active first instar of a scale insect (Figure 224 B).

Cremáster a spinelike or hooked process at the posterior end of the pupa, often used for attachment (Lepidóptera; Figure 358, *cre*).

Crénulate wavy, or with small scallops.

Cribéllum a sievelike structure lying just anterior to the spinnerets (spiders; Figure 58 B, *crb*).

Crochets (pronounced *croshàys*) hooked spines at the tip of the prolegs of lepidopterous larvae (Figure 357, *cro*).

Crop the dilated posterior portion of the foregut, just behind the esophagus (Figure 23, *cp*).

Cross vein a vein connecting adjacent longitudinal veins.

Crùciate crossing; shaped like a cross.

Ctenídium (pl., **ctenídia**) a row of stout bristles like the teeth of a comb (Psocóptera, Figure 151 F, *ct;* Siphonáptera, Figure 524, *gc, prc*).

Cùbito-anal cross vein a cross vein between the cubitus and an anal vein (Figure 20, *cu-a*).

Cùbitus the longitudinal vein immediately posterior to the media (Figure 20, *Cu*).

Cùneus a more or less triangular apical piece of the corium, set off from the rest of the corium by a suture (Hemíptera; Figure 167, *cun*).

Cursorial fitted for running; running in habit.

Cùticle (or **cutícula**) the noncellular outer layer of the body wall of an arthropod (Figures 2 and 3, *cut*).

Cyst a sac, vesicle, or bladderlike structure.

Deciduous having a part or parts that may fall off or be shed.

Decumbent bent downward.

Deflexed bent downward.

Dentate toothed, or with toothlike projections.

Dentículate with minute toothlike projections.

Depressed flattened dorsoventrally.

Deùtonymph the third instar of a mite (Figure 55 D).

Diapause a period of arrested development and reduced metabolic rate, during which growth, differentiation, and metamorphosis cease; a period of dormancy not immediately referable to adverse environmental conditions.

Dichóptic the eyes separated above (Díptera).

Dièćious having the male and female organs in different individuals, any one individual being either male or female.

Dilated expanded or widened.

Discal cell a more or less enlarged cell in the basal or central part of the wing (Homóptera, the R cell, Figure 163; Lepidóptera, Figure 360, *D;* Díptera, Figure 442 B, *D*).

Discal cross vein a cross vein behind the discal cell (Díptera; Figure 442 B, *dcv*).

Discoidal cell a cell near the middle of the wing (Hymenóptera; Figures 527 and 529, *D*).

Discoidal vein the vein forming a continuation of the median vein beyond the end of the transverse median vein, and extending along the posterior margin of the first discoidal cell (Hymenóptera; Figures 527 and 529, *d*).

Distad away from the body, toward the end farthest from the body.

Distal near or toward the free end of an appendage; that part of a segment or appendage farthest from the body.

Diurnal active during the daytime.

Divaricate extending outward and then curving inward toward each other distally (divaricate tarsal claws, Figure 251 A).

Divergent becoming more separated distally.

Dormancy a state of quiescence or inactivity.

Dorsad toward the back or top.

Dorsal top or uppermost; pertaining to the back or upper side.

Dorsocentral bristles a longitudinal row of bristles on the mesonotum, just laterad of the acrostichal bristles (Díptera; Figure 444, *dc*).

Dorsolateral at the top and to the side.

Dorsomésal at the top and along the midline.

Dorsoscutéllar bristles a pair of bristles on the dorsal portion of the scutellum, one on each side of the midline (Díptera).

Dorsoventral from top to bottom, or from the upper to the lower side.

Dorsum the back or top (dorsal) side.

Écdysis (pl., **écdyses**) molting; the process of shedding the exoskeleton.

Eclòsion hatching from the egg.

Ectoparasite a parasite that lives on the outside of its host.

Ejaculatory duct the terminal portion of the male sperm duct (Figure 27 B, *ejd*).

Elatériform larva a larva resembling a wireworm, that is, slender, heavily sclerotized, with short thoracic legs, and with few body hairs (Figure 289 B).

Elbowed antenna an antenna with the first segment elongated and the remaining segments coming off the first segment at an angle (Figure 6 N).

Élytron (pl., **élytra**) a thickened, leathery, or horny front wing (Coleóptera, Dermáptera, some Homóptera; Coleóptera, Figure 242, *el*).

Emárginate notched or indented.

Embòlium a narrow piece of the corium, along the costal margin, separated from the rest of the corium by a suture (Hemíptera; Figure 167 C, *emb*).

Emergence the act of the adult insect leaving the pupal case or the last nymphal skin.

Empòdium (pl., **empòdia**) a padlike or bristlelike structure at the apex of the last tarsal segment, between the claws (Díptera; Figure 441, *emp*).

Endite the basal segment of the spider pedipalp, which is enlarged and functions as a crushing jaw (Figure 57 B, *cx*).

Endocùticle (or **endocutícula**) the innermost layer of the cuticle (Figure 2, *end*).

Endoparasite a parasite that lives inside its host (for example, Figure 522 B).

Endópodite the mesal branch of a biramous appendage.

Endoptérygote having the wings developing internally; with complete metamorphosis.

Endoskeleton a skeleton or supporting structure on the inside of the body.

Entire without teeth or notches, with a smooth outline.

Entomóphagous feeding on insects.

Epicrànium the upper part of the head, from the face to the neck (Lepidóptera; Figure 357, *epcr*).

Epicùticle (or **epicutícula**) the very thin, nonchitinous, external layer of the cuticle (Figure 2, *epi*).

Epidérmis the cellular layer of the body wall which secretes the cuticle (Figures 2 and 3, *ep*).

Epigastric furrow a transverse ventral suture near the anterior end of the abdomen, along which lie the openings of the book lungs and the reproductive organs (spiders; Figure 57 B, *ef*).

Epígynum the external female genitalia of spiders (Figure 57 B, *epg*).

Epimèron (pl., **epimèra**) the area of a thoracic pleuron posterior to the pleural suture (Figure 18, *epm*).

Epinòtum the thoracic dorsum posterior to the mesonotum, consisting of the metanotum and propodeum (ants).

Epiphàrynx a mouth-part structure on the inner surface of the labrum or clypeus; in chewing insects a median lobe on the posterior (ventral) surface of the labrum.

Epíphysis (pl., **epíphysès**) a movable pad or lobelike process on the inner surface of the front tibia (Lepidóptera).

Épiphyte an air plant, one growing nonparasitically upon another plant or upon a nonliving object.

Epipleùra (pl., **epipleùrae**) the bent-down lateral edge of an elytron (Coleóptera).

Epipleùrite a small sclerite in the membranous area between the thoracic pleura and the wing bases (Figure 18, *epp*).

Épiproct a process or appendage situated above the anus and appearing to arise from the tenth abdominal segment; actually, the dorsal part of the eleventh abdominal segment (Figure 1, *ept*).

Epistérnum (pl., **epistérna**) the area of a thoracic pleuron anterior to the pleural suture (Figure 18, *eps*).

Epístomal suture the suture between the frons and the clypeus (Figure 5, *es*), and connecting the anterior tenitorial pits.

Épistome the part of the face just above the mouth; the oral margin (Díptera).

Erùciform larva a caterpillar; a larva with a more or less cylindrical body, a well developed head, and with thoracic legs and abdominal prolegs (Figure 357).

Esóphagus the narrow portion of the alimentary tract immediately posterior to the pharynx (Figure 23, *eso*).

Eustérnum the ventral plate of a thoracic segment, exclusive of the spinasternum.

Evagination an outpocketing, or saclike structure on the outside.

Eversible capable of being everted or turned outward.

Exarate pupa a pupa in which the appendages are free and not glued to the body (Figure 43 C–E).

Excavated hollowed out.

Exocùticle (or **exocutícula**) the layer of cuticle just outside the endocuticle, between the endocuticle and the epicuticle (Figure 2, *exo*).

Exópodite the outer branch of a biramous appendage.

Exoptérygote with the wings developing on the outside of the body, as in insects with simple metamorphosis.

Exoskeleton a skeleton or supporting structure on the outside of the body.

Exserted protruding or projecting from the body.

External the outside; that part away from the center (midline) of the body.

Exùviae (usually used only in the plural) the cast skin of an arthropod.

Eye, compound (see *compound* eye).

Eye, simple (see *ocellus*).

Eye cap a structure overhanging or capping the compound eye (Lepidóptera; Figure 383 B, *ec*).

Face the front of the head, below the frontal suture (Díptera; Figure 443, *fa*).

Facet the external surface of an individual compound-eye unit or ommatidium.

Family a subdivision of an order, suborder, or superfamily, and containing a group of related genera, tribes, or subfamilies. Family names end in *-idae*.

Fastígium the anterior dorsal surface of the vertex (grasshoppers).

Fèces excrement, the material passed from the alimentary tract through the anus.

Fèmur (pl., **fémora**) the third leg segment, located between the trochanter and the tibia (Figure 19, *fm*).

Filament a slender threadlike structure.

File a filelike ridge on the ventral side of the tegmen, near the base, a part of the stridulating mechanism in crickets and long-horned grasshoppers (Figure 111).

Filiform hairlike or threadlike; filiform antenna (Figure 6 B).

Flábellate with fanlike processes or projections; flabellate antenna (Figure 6 L).

Flabéllum (pl., **flabélla**) a fanlike or leaflike process (Hymenóptera; Figure 8, *flb*).

Flagéllum (pl., **flagélla**) a whiplike structure; that part of the antenna beyond the second segment (Figure 6 N, *fl*).

Foliàceous leaflike.

Follicle a minute cavity, sac, or tube.

Fontanélle a small, depressed, pale spot on the front of the head between the eyes (Isóptera; Figure 137, *fon*).

Foràmen magnum the opening on the posterior side of the head, through which pass the internal structures that extend from the head to the thorax (Figure 5, *for*).

Foregut the anterior portion of the alimentary tract, from the mouth to the midgut.

Fossorial fitted for or with the habit of digging.

Frass plant fragments made by a wood-boring insect, usually mixed with excrement.

Frénulum a bristle or group of bristles arising at the humeral angle of the hind wing (Lepidóptera; Figure 360, *f*).

Frons the head sclerite bounded by the frontal (or frontogenal) and epistomal sutures and including the median ocellus (Figure 5, *fr*).

Front that portion of the head between the antennae, eyes, and ocelli; the frons.

Frontal bristles bristles above the antennae, away from the edge of the compound eye (Díptera; Figure 462 B, *fb*).

Frontal carìna (pl., **frontal carìnae**) a longitudinal ridge on the face, mesad of the antennae (Figure 580, *frc*).

Frontal lùnule a small crescent-shaped sclerite located just above the base of the antennae and below the frontal suture (Díptera; Figure 443, *frl*).

Frontal suture one of two sutures arising at the anterior end of the coronal suture and extending ventrad toward the epistomal suture (Figure 5, *fs*); a suture shaped like an inverted **U**, with the base of the **U**

crossing the face above the bases of the antennae, and the arms of the **U** extending downward on each side of the face (Díptera; Figure 443, *fs;* actually a ptilinal suture).

Frontal vitta an area on the head between the antennae and the ocelli (Díptera; Figure 443, *fv*).

Frontogènal suture a more or less vertical suture on the front of the head, between the frons and the gena.

Fronto-orbital bristles bristles on the front next to the compound eyes (Díptera; Figure 443, *fob*).

Funículus (or **fùnicle**) the antennal segments between the scape and the club (Figure 332, *fun*).

Furca a fork or forked structure; a forked apodeme arising from a thoracic sternum (Figure 25, *fu*).

Furcula the forked springing apparatus of the Collémbola (Figure 88, *fur*).

Gàlea the outer lobe of the maxilla, borne by the stipes (Figure 7 A, *g*).

Gall an abnormal growth of plant tissues, caused by the stimulus of an animal or another plant.

Ganglion (pl., **ganglia**) a knotlike enlargement of a nerve, containing a coordinating mass of nerve cells (Figure 23, *gn*).

Gaster the rounded part of the abdomen posterior to the nodelike segment or segments (ants).

Gèna (pl., **gènae**) the part of the head on each side below and behind the compound eyes, between the frontal and occipital sutures (Figure 5, *ge*); the cheek.

Gènal comb a row of strong spines borne on the anteroventral border of the head (Siphonáptera; Figure 524, *gc*).

Generation from any given stage in the life cycle to the same stage in the offspring.

Genículate elbowed, or abruptly bent; geniculate antenna (Figure 6 N).

Genitàlia the sexual organs and associated structures; the external sexual organs (Figures 21 and 22).

Genovertical plate an area on the head above the antenna and next to the compound eye (Díptera; Figure 443, *gvp*), also called the orbital plate.

Gènus (pl., **génera**) a group of closely related species; the first name in a binomial or trinomial scientific name. Names of genera are latinized, capitalized, and when printed are italicized.

Gill evaginations of the body wall or hind gut, functioning in gaseous exchanges in an aquatic animal.

Glàbrous smooth, without hairs.

Glòbose, Glóbular spherical or nearly so.

Glossa (pl., **glossae**) one of a pair of lobes at the apex of the labium between the paraglossae (Figure 7 C, *gl*); in bees, see Figure 8.

Gnathochilàrium a platelike mouth-part structure in the Diplópoda, representing the fused maxillae and labium (Figure 74).

Gonapóphysis (pl., **gonapóphysès**) a mesal posterior process of a gonopod, in the female forming the ovipositor (see Figures 22 and 90).

Gonopod a modified leg that forms a part of the external genitalia.

Gonopore the external opening of the reproductive organs.

Gregarious living in groups.

Grub a scarabaeiform larva; a thick-bodied larva with a well developed head and thoracic legs, without abdominal prolegs, and usually sluggish (Figures 42 and 277).

Gùla a sclerite on the ventral side of the head between the labium and the foramen magnum (Figure 243, *gu*).

Gùlar sutures longitudinal sutures, one on each side of the gula (Figure 243, *gs*).

Gynándromorph an abnormal individual containing structural characteristics of both sexes (usually male on one side and female on the other).

Haèmocoele a body cavity filled with blood.

Hálter (pl., **haltères**) a small knobbed structure on each side of the metathorax, representing a hind wing (Díptera; Figure 81, *hal*).

Hámuli (sing., **hámulus**) minute hooks; a series of minute hooks on the anterior margin of the hind wing, with which the front and hind wings are attached together (Hymenóptera).

Haustellate formed for sucking, the mandibles not fitted for chewing (or absent).

Haustéllum a part of the beak (Díptera; Figures 13 and 14, *hst*).

Head the anterior body region, which bears the eyes, antennae, and mouth parts (Figure 1, *hd*).

Hemélytron (pl., **hemélytra**) the front wing of Hemíptera (Figure 167).

Hemimetábolous having simple metamorphosis like that in the Odonàta, Ephemeróptera, and Plecóptera (with the nymphs aquatic).

Herbívorous feeding on plants.

Hermáphroditic possessing both male and female sex organs.

Heterodynamic life cycle a life cycle in which there is a period of dormancy.

Heterógamy alternation of bisexual with parthenogenetic reproduction.

Heterómerous the three pairs of tarsi differing in the number of segments (Coleóptera, for example, with a tarsal formula of 5-5-4).

Hibernation dormancy during the winter.

Hindgut the posterior portion of the alimentary tract, between the midgut and the anus.

Holometábolous with complete metamorphosis.

Holóptic the eyes contiguous above (Díptera).

Homodynamic life cycle a life cycle in which there is continuous development, without a period of dormancy.

Hòmonym one and the same name for two or more different things (taxa).
Honeydew liquid discharged from the anus of certain Homóptera.
Hornworm a caterpillar (larva of Sphíngidae) with a dorsal spine or horn on the last abdominal segment (Figure 428).
Horny thickened or hardened.
Host the organism in or on which a parasite lives; the plant on which an insect feeds.
Hùmeral pertaining to the shoulder; located in the anterior basal portion of the wing.
Humeral angle the basal anterior angle or portion of the wing.
Humeral bristles bristles on the humeral callus (Díptera; Figure 444, *hb*).
Humeral callus one of the anterior lateral angles of the thoracic notum, usually more or less rounded (Díptera; Figure 444, *hc*).
Humeral cross vein a cross vein in the humeral portion of the wing, between the costa and subcosta (Figure 20, *h*).
Humeral suture the mesopleural suture (Odonàta; Figure 97, pls_2).
Humeral vein a branch of the subcosta that serves to strengthen the humeral angle of the wing (Neuróptera, Figure 232 C, *hv;* Lepidóptera, Figure 377 B, *hv*).
Hùmerus (pl., **hùmeri**) the shoulder; the posterolateral angles of the pronotum (Hemíptera).
Hỳaline like glass, transparent, colorless.
Hypermetamorphosis a type of complete metamorphosis in which the different larval instars represent two or more different types of larvae (Figure 312).
Hyperparasite a parasite whose host is another parasite.
Hypodermis the epidermis (see).
Hypógnathous with the head vertical and the mouth parts located ventrally (for example, as in Figure 5).
Hypopharynx a median mouth-part structure anterior to the labium (Figures 7, 11–14, *hyp*); the ducts from the salivary glands are usually associated with the hypopharynx, and in some sucking insects the hypopharynx is the mouth-part structure containing the salivary channel.
Hypopleùral bristles a more or less vertical row of bristles on the hypopleuron, usually directly above the hind coxae (Díptera; Figure 444, *hyb*).
Hypopleùron (pl., **hypopleùra**) the lower part of the mesepimeron; a sclerite on the thorax located just above the hind coxae (Díptera; Figure 444, *hypl*).
Hz hertz (cycles per second).

Íleum the anterior part of the hindgut (Figure 23, *il*).
Imàgo (pl., **imàgoes** or **imágines**) the adult or reproductive stage of an insect.
Inclinate bent toward the midline of the body.
Inferior appendage the lower one (Anisóptera) or two (Zygóptera) of the terminal abdominal appendages, used in grasping the female at the time of copulation (male Odonàta; Figure 97, *iap*).
Infraepistérnum a ventral subdivision of an episternum (Figure 97, *iep*).
Inner vertical bristles the more mesally located of the large bristles on the vertex, between the ocelli and the compound eyes (Díptera; Figure 443, *ivb*).
Ínquiline an animal that lives in the nest or abode of another species.
Instar the insect between successive molts, the first instar being between hatching and the first molt.
Instinctive behavior unlearned stereotyped behavior, in which the nerve pathways involved are hereditary.
Integument the outer covering of the body.
Intelligence the capacity to modify behavior as a result of experience.
Interantennal suture a suture extending between the bases of the two antennae (Siphonáptera; Figure 526, *ias*).
Intercàlary vein an extra longitudinal vein that develops from a thickened fold in the wing, more or less midway between two pre-existing veins (Ephemeróptera; Figures 95 and 96, ICu_1).
Intercostal vein the subcosta (Hymenóptera; Figure 527, *ic*).
Intersternite an intersegmental sclerite on the ventral side of the thorax; the spinasternum.
Interstitial situated between two segments (interstitial trochanter of Coleóptera; Figure 246 D, *tr*); coincident (the ends of two veins meeting).
Intima the cuticular lining of the foregut, hindgut, and trachae.
Intra-alar bristles a row of two or three bristles situated on the mesonotum above the wing base, between the dorsocentral and the supra-alar bristles (Díptera; Figure 444, *iab*).
Invagination an infolding or inpocketing.
Iteropàrous a type of life history in which the animal reproduces two or more times during its lifetime.

Johnston's organ a sense organ similar to a chordotonal organ, located in the second antennal segment of most insects; this organ functions in sound perception in some Díptera.
Joint an articulation of two successive segments or parts.
Jùgal lobe a lobe at the base of the wing, on the posterior side, proximad of the vannal lobe (Hymenóptera; Figures 538 and 539, *jl*).
Jùgum a lobelike process at the base of the front wing, which overlaps the hind wing (Lepidóptera; Figure 359, *j*); a sclerite in the head (Hemíptera and Homóptera; Figures 10 and 164, *j*).

Keeled with an elevated ridge or carina.

kHz kilohertz (kilocycles per second).

Labéllum the expanded tip of the labium (Díptera; Figures 13 and 14, *lbl*).

Làbial of or pertaining to the labium.

Labial palp one of a pair of small feelerlike structures arising from the labium (Figure 7 C, *lp*).

Labial suture the suture on the labium between the postmentum and the prementum (Figure 7 C, *ls*).

Làbium one of the mouth-part structures, the lower lip (Figures 5, *lbm*, and 7 C).

Làbrum the upper lip, lying just below the clypeus (Figure 5, *lbr*).

Labrum-epipharynx a mouth part representing the labrum and epipharynx.

Lacínia (pl., **lacíniae**) the inner lobe of the maxilla, borne by the stipes (Figure 7 A, *lc*).

Lamélla (pl., **laméllae**) a leaflike plate.

Lámellate with platelike structures or segments; lamellate antenna (Figures 6 M and 250 C, D).

Lámina linguàlis (pl., **láminae linguàles**) one of two median distal plates in the millipede gnathochilarium (Figure 74 B, *ll*).

Lanceolate spear-shaped, tapering at each end.

Lanceolate cell a cell in the anal area of the wing (Hymenóptera; Figure 527, *L*).

Larva (pl., **larvae**) the immature stage, between egg and pupa, of an insect having complete metamorphosis; the six-legged first instar of Àcari (Figures 54 B and 55 A); an immature stage differing radically from the adult.

Larviform shaped like a larva.

Laterad toward the side, away from the midline of the body.

Lateral of or pertaining to the side (that is, the right or left side).

Laterotérgite a tergal sclerite located laterally or dorsolaterally.

Lateroventral to the side (away from the midline of the body) and below.

Leaf miner an insect that lives in and feeds upon the leaf cells between the upper and lower surfaces of a leaf.

Lígula the terminal lobes (or lobe) of the labium, the glossae and paraglossae.

Linear linelike, long and very narrow.

Longitudinal lengthwise of the body or of an appendage.

Looper a caterpillar that moves by looping its body, that is, by placing the posterior part of the abdomen next to the thorax and then extending the anterior part of the body forward; a measuringworm.

Lòrum (pl., **lòra**) the cheek; a sclerite on the side of the head (Hemíptera and Homóptera; Figures 164 and 198, *lo*); the submentum in bees (Figure 8, *smt*).

Luminescent producing light.

Lunule, frontal (see *frontal lunule*).

Maggot a vermiform larva; a legless larva without a well developed head capsule (Díptera; Figure 42 A).

Malpighian tubules excretory tubes that arise near the anterior end of the hindgut and extend into the body cavity (Figure 23, *mt*).

Mandible jaw; one of the anterior pair of paired mouth-part structures (Figure 7, *md*).

Mandibulate with jaws fitted for chewing.

Marginal cell a cell in the distal part of the wing bordering the costal margin (Díptera, Figure 442 B, *MC;* Hymenóptera, Figures 527 and 529, *MC*).

Marginal vein a vein on or just within the wing margin; the vein forming the posterior side of the marginal cell (Hymenóptera; Figures 527, 529, and 541 B, *mv*).

Margined with a sharp or keel-like lateral edge.

Maxílla (pl., **maxíllae**) one of the paired mouth-part structures immediately posterior to the mandibles (Figure 7, *mx*).

Máxillary of or pertaining to the maxilla.

Maxillary palp a small feelerlike structure arising from the maxilla (Figure 7 A, *mxp*).

Maxílliped one of the appendages in Crustàcea immediately posterior to the second maxillae.

Mèdia the longitudinal vein between the radius and cubitus (Figure 20, *M*).

Mèdial cross vein a cross vein connecting two branches of the media (Figure 20, *m*).

Median in the middle; along the midline of the body.

Median cell a cell between the subcostal and median veins at the base of the wing (Hymenóptera; Figures 527 and 529, *MD*).

Medio-cubital cross vein a cross vein connecting the media and cubitus (Figure 20, *m-cu*).

Membrane a thin film of tissue, usually transparent; that part of the wing surface between the veins; the thin apical part of a hemelytron (Hemíptera; Figure 167, *mem*).

Mémbranous like a membrane; thin and more or less transparent (wings); thin and pliable (cuticle).

Mental setae setae on the mentum (Odonàta; Figure 104, *mst*).

Mentum the distal part of the labium, which bears the palps and the ligula (Figure 7 C, *mn*); a median, more or less triangular piece in the millipede gnathochilarium (Figure 74 B, *mn*).

Meropleùron (pl., **meropleùra**) a sclerite consisting of the meron (basal part) of the coxa and the lower part of the epimeron.

Mèsad toward the midline of the body.

Mèsal at or near the midline of the body.

Mesénteron the midgut, or middle portion of the alimentary tract (Figure 23, *mg*).

Mesepimèron (pl., **mesepimèra**) the epimeron of the mesothorax (Figures 18 and 243, epm_2).

Mesepistérnum (pl., **mesepistérna**) the episternum of the mesothorax (Figures 18 and 243, eps_2).

Mesínfraepistérnum a ventral subdivision of the mesepisternum (Odonàta; Figure 97, iep_2).

Mèson the midline of the body, or an imaginary plane dividing the body into right and left halves.

Mesonòtum the dorsal sclerite of the mesothorax (Figure 1, n_2).

Mesopleùral bristles bristles on the mesopleuron (Díptera; Figure 444, *mpb*).

Mesopleùron (pl., **mesopleùra**) the lateral sclerite(s) of the mesothorax; the upper part of the episternum of the mesothorax (Díptera; Figure 444, pl_2).

Mesoscutéllum the scutellum of the mesothorax (Figure 18, scl_2), usually simply called the scutellum.

Mesoscùtum the scutum of the mesothorax (Figure 18, sct_2).

Mesostérnum the sternum, or ventral sclerite, of the mesothorax.

Mesothorax the middle or second segment of the thorax (Figure 1, th_2).

Métamère a primary body segment (usually referring to the embryo).

Metamórphosis a change in form during development.

Metanòtum the dorsal sclerite of the metathorax (Figure 1, n_3).

Metapleùron (pl., **metapleùra**) the lateral sclerite(s) of the metathorax.

Metascutéllum the scutellum of the metathorax (Figure 18, scl_3).

Metastérnum the sternum, or ventral sclerite, of the metathorax.

Metatársus (pl., **metatársi**) the basal segment of the tarsus (Figure 57, *mts*).

Metathorax the third or posterior segment of the thorax (Figure 1, th_3).

Metazònite the posterior portion of a millipede tergum when the tergum is divided by a transverse groove.

Metepimèron (pl., **metepimèra**) the epimeron of the metathorax (Figure 18, epm_3).

Metepistérnum (pl., **metepistérna**) the episternum of the metathorax (Figure 18, eps_3).

Metínfraepistérnum a ventral subdivision of the metepisternum (Odonàta; Figure 97, ips_3).

Mìcropyle a minute opening (or openings) in the chorion of an insect egg, through which sperm enter the egg (Figure 36, *mcp*).

Midgut the mesenteron, or middle portion of the alimentary tract (Figure 23, *mg*).

Millimeter 0.001 meter, or 0.03937 inch (about 1/25 inch).

Minùte very small; an insect a few millimeters in length or less would be considered minute.

Molt a process of shedding the exoskeleton; ecdysis; to shed the exoskeleton.

Monècious possessing both male and female sex organs, hermaphroditic.

Moníliform beadlike, with rounded segments; moniliform antenna (Figure 6 C).

Morphology the science of form or structure.

Myìasis a disease caused by the invasion of dipterous larvae.

Mýriapod a many-legged arthropod; a centipede, millipede, pauropod, or symphylan.

Naìad an aquatic, gill-breathing nymph.

Nasùtus (pl., **nasùti**) an individual of a termite caste in which the head narrows anteriorly into a snoutlike projection (Figure 134 B).

Nocturnal active at night.

Node a knoblike or knotlike swelling.

Nòdiform in the form of a knob or knot.

Nòdus a strong cross vein near the middle of the costal border of the wing (Odonàta; Figures 98–100, *nod*).

Notàulix (pl., **notàulices**) parapsidal suture (see).

Notopleùral bristles bristles on the notopleuron (Díptera; Figure 444, *nb*).

Notopleùral suture a suture between the notum and the pleural sclerites (Figure 243, *npls*).

Notopleùron (pl., **notopleùra**) an area on the thoracic dorsum, at the lateral end of the transverse suture (Díptera; Figure 444, *npl*).

Nòtum (pl., **nòta**) the dorsal surface of a body segment (usually used when speaking of the thoracic segments).

Nymph an immature stage (following hatching) of an insect that does not have a pupal stage; the immature stage of Àcari that has eight legs.

Oblique vein a slanting cross vein; in Odonàta, where Rs crosses M_{1+2} (Figure 98, *obv*).

Obtect pupa a pupa in which the appendages are more or less glued to the body surface, as in the Lepidóptera (Figures 43 A, B and 358).

Occípital suture a transverse suture in the posterior part of the head which separates the vertex from the occiput dorsally and the genae from the postgenae laterally (Figure 5, *os*).

Ócciput the dorsal posterior part of the head, between the occipital and postoccipital sutures (Figure 5, *ocp*).

Océllar bristles bristles arising close to the ocelli (Díptera; Figure 443, *ob*).

Ocellar triangle a slightly raised triangular area in which the ocelli are located (Díptera; Figure 443, *ot*).

Océllus (pl., **océlli**) a simple eye of an insect or other arthropod (Figure 5, *oc*).

Ommatídium (pl., **ommatídia**) a single unit or visual section of a compound eye (Figure 30 D).

Onísciform larva a platyform larva (see).

Oothèca (pl., **oothècae**) the covering or case of an egg mass (Orthóptera).

Open cell a wing cell extending to the wing margin, not entirely surrounded by veins.

Open coxal cavity one bounded posteriorly by a sclerite of the next segment (front coxal cavities, Coleóptera; Figure 245 A), or one touched by one or more pleural sclerites (middle coxal cavities, Coleóptera; Figure 245 C).

Opérculum (pl., **opércula**) a lid or cover.

Opisthógnathous with the mouth parts directed backward.

Oral pertaining to the mouth.

Oral vibrissae a pair of stout bristles, one on each side of the face near or just above the oral margin, and larger than the other bristles on the vibrissal ridge (Díptera; Figure 443, *ov*).

Orbital plate an area on the head above the antenna and next to the compound eye (Díptera; Figure 461 C, *orp*), also called genovertical plate.

Order a subdivision of a class or subclass, containing a group of related superfamilies or families.

Osmetèrium (pl., **osmetèria**) a fleshy, tubular, eversible, usually **Y**-shaped gland at the anterior end of certain caterpillars (Papiliónidae; Figure 357, *osm*).

Óstiole a small opening.

Óstium (pl., **óstia**) a slitlike opening in the insect heart.

Outer fork the fork of R_{4+5} (Ephemeróptera; Figures 94 and 95 A, B, *of*).

Outer vertical bristles the more laterally located of the large bristles on the vertex, between the ocelli and the compound eyes (Díptera; Figure 443, *ovb*).

Ovàriole a more or less tubular division of an ovary (Figure 27, *ovl*).

Òvary the egg-producing organ of the female (Figures 23 and 27 A, *ovy*).

Òviduct the tube leading away from the ovary through which the eggs pass (Figures 23 and 27 A, *ovd*).

Ovíparous laying eggs.

Òviposit to lay or deposit eggs.

Ovipósitor the egg-laying apparatus; the external genitalia of the female (Figures 1, 22, 97 E, and 531, *ovp*).

Paèdogénesis the production of eggs or young by an immature or larval stage of an animal.

Palp a segmented process born by the maxillae or labium (Figure 7, *lp*, *mxp*).

Palpifer the lobe of the maxillary stipes which bears the palp (Figure 7 A, *plf*).

Palpiger the lobe of the mentum of the labium which bears the palp (Figure 7 C, *plg*).

Papílla a small nipplelike elevation.

Paraglóssa (pl., **paraglóssae**) one of a pair of lobes at the apex of the labium, laterad of the glossae (Figure 7 C, *pgl*).

Pàraproct one of a pair of lobes bordering the anus lateroventrally (Figures 1 and 97 A, *ppt*).

Parápsidal suture a longitudinal suture of the mesonotum separating the median area from the lateral area (Hymenóptera; Figures 530 and 545, *ps*). (Also called parapsidal furrow or notaulix.)

Parápsis (see *scapula*).

Parasite an animal that lives in or on the body of another living animal (its host), at least during a part of its life cycle, feeding on the tissues of its host; most entomophagous insect parasites kill their host (see *parasitoid*).

Parasitic living as a parasite.

Parasitoid an animal that feeds in or on another living animal for a relatively long time, consuming all or most of its tissues, and eventually killing it (also used as an adjective, describing this mode of life). Parasitoid insects in this book are referred to as parasites.

Parthenogénesis development of the egg without fertilization.

Patélla a leg segment between the femur and tibia (arachnids; Figure 57, *ptl*).

Paurometábolous with simple metamorphosis, the young and adults living in the same habitat, and the adults winged.

Pecten a comblike or rakelike structure.

Pectinate with branches or processes like the teeth of a comb; pectinate antenna (Figure 6 H); pectinate tarsal claw (Figure 247 B).

Pedicel the second segment of the antenna (Figure 6 N, *ped*); the stem of the abdomen, between the thorax and the gaster (ants).

Pedipalps the second pair of appendages of an arachnid (Figures 47 and 57, *pdp*).

Pelagic inhabiting the open sea; ocean-dwelling.

Penultimate next to the last.

Péristome the ventral margin of the head, bordering the mouth.

Peritròphic membrane a membrane in insects with chewing mouth parts, secreted by the cells lining the midgut; this membrane is secreted when food is present, and forms an envelope around the food; it usually pulls loose from the midgut, remains around the food, and passes out with the feces.

Pétiolate attached by a narrow stalk or stem.

Pétiole a stalk or stem; the narrow stalk or stem by which the abdomen is attached to the thorax (Hymenóptera); in ants, the nodelike first segment of the abdomen.

pH a measure of the acidity or alkalinity of a medium. A pH value of 7.0 indicates neutral; lower values indicate acid and higher values alkaline.

Phallus the male copulatory organ, including any processes that may be present at its base.

Pharynx the anterior part of the foregut, between the mouth and the esophagus (Figure 23, *phx*).

Phéromone a substance given off by one individual that causes a specific reaction by other individuals of the same species, such as sex attractants, alarm substances, etc.

Phrágma (pl., **phragmàta**) a platelike apodeme or invagination of the dorsal wall of the thorax (Figure 25, *ph*).

Phỳlum (pl., **phỳla**) one of the dozen or so major divisions of the animal kingdom.

Phytóphagous feeding on plants.

Pictured with spots or bands (pictured wings, Figure 506).

Pílifer one of a pair of lateral projections on the labrum (Lepidóptera; Figure 356, *pf*).

Pìlose covered with hair.

Planídium larva a type of first instar larva in certain Díptera and Hymenóptera which undergo hypermetamorphosis, a larva that is legless and somewhat flattened.

Platyform larva a larva that is extremely flattened, as the larva of Psephènidae (Figure 282). (Also called onisciform larva.)

Pleùral pertaining to the pleura, or lateral sclerites of the body; lateral.

Pleural suture a suture on a thoracic pleuron extending from the base of the wing to the base of the coxa, which separates the episternum and epimeron (Figures 1 and 18, *pls*).

Pleùrite a lateral or pleural sclerite.

Pleùron (pl., **pleùra**) the lateral area of a thoracic segment.

Pleurotérgite a sclerite containing both pleural and tergal elements.

Plùmose featherlike; plumose antenna (Figure 6 I).

Poikilothermous cold-blooded, the body temperature rising or falling with the environmental temperature.

Point a small triangle of stiff paper, used in mounting small insects (Figure 624).

Pollen basket (see *corbicula*).

Pollen brush a brush of short stiff hairs used in collecting pollen (bees; Figure 599, *pbr*).

Pollen rake a comblike row of bristles at the apex of the hind tibia of a bee (Figure 599, *pr*).

Polyembryony an egg developing into two or more embryos.

Porrect extending forward horizontally; porrect antennae (Figure 461 G, J).

Postabdomen the modified posterior segments of the abdomen, which are usually more slender than the anterior segments (Crustàcea, Figure 68 A, *pa;* see also the postabdomen in a scorpion, Figure 45).

Postalar callus a rounded swelling on each side of the mesonotum, between the base of the wing and the scutellum (Díptera; Figure 444, *pc*).

Posterior hind or rear.

Posterior cell one of the cells extending to the hind margin of the wing, between the third and sixth longitudinal veins (Díptera; Figure 442 B, *P*).

Posterior cross vein a cross vein at the apex of the discal cell (Díptera; Figure 442 B, *pcv*).

Postgèna (pl., **postgènae**) a sclerite on the posterior lateral surface of the head, posterior to the gena (Figure 5, *pg*).

Posthùmeral bristle a bristle on the anterolateral surface of the mesonotum, just posterior to the humeral callus (Díptera; Figure 444, *pb*).

Postmarginal vein the vein along the anterior margin of the front wing, beyond the point where the stigmal vein arises (Chalcidòidea; Figure 541 B, *pm*).

Postmentum the basal portion of the labium, proximad of the labial suture (Figure 7 C, *pmt*).

Postnodal cross veins a series of cross veins just behind the costal margin of the wing, between the nodus and stigma, and extending from the costal margin of the wing to R_1 (Odonàta; Figures 98 and 99, *pn*).

Postnòtum (pl., **postnòta**) a notal plate behind the scutellum, often present in wing-bearing segments (Figure 18, *PN*).

Postoccípital suture the transverse suture on the head immediately posterior to the occipital suture (Figure 5, *pos*).

Postócciput the extreme posterior rim of the head, between the postoccipital suture and the foramen magnum (Figure 5, *po*).

Postpétiole the second segment of a 2-segmented pedicel (ants).

Postscutéllum a small transverse piece of a thoracic notum immediately behind the scutellum; in Díptera, an area immediately behind or below the mesoscutellum (Figure 453 B, *pscl*).

Postvertical bristles a pair of bristles behind the ocelli, usually situated on the posterior surface of the head (Díptera; Figure 443, *pv*).

Preàpical situated just before the apex; preapical tibial bristle of Díptera (Figure 463 B, *ptbr*).

Prebasilàre a narrow transverse sclerite, just basal to the mentum, in the gnathochilarium of some millipedes (Figure 74 B, *pbs*).

Predàceous feeding as a predator.

Predator an animal that attacks and feeds on other animals (its prey), usually animals smaller or less powerful than itself. The prey is usually killed quickly, and mostly or entirely eaten; many prey individuals are eaten by each predator.

Pregenital anterior to the genital segments of the abdomen.

Prementum the distal part of the labium, distad of the labial suture, on which all the labial muscles have their insertions (Figure 7 C, *prmt*).

Preoral anterior to or in front of the mouth.

Prepéctus an area along the anteroventral margin of the mesepisternum, set off by a suture (Hymenóptera; Figure 530, *pp*).

Prepupa a quiescent stage between the larval period and the pupal period; the third instar of a thrips (Figure 160 B).

Presutural bristles bristles on the mesonotum immediately anterior to the transverse suture and adjacent to the notopleuron (Díptera; Figure 444, *psb*).

Pretarsus (pl., **pretarsi**) the terminal segment of the leg, typically consisting of a pair of claws and one or more padlike structures (Figure 19 B, D, *ptar*).

Probóscis the extended beaklike mouth parts (Figure 469, *prb*).

Pròclinate inclined forward or downward.

Proctodaèum the hindgut, or the hindmost of the three major divisions of the alimentary tract, from the Malpighian tubules to the anus.

Procuticle the inner portion of the cuticle, consisting of endocuticle and exocuticle.

Produced extended, prolonged, or projecting.

Proepimèron (pl., **proepimèra**) the epimeron of the prothorax (Figure 243, epm_1).

Proepistérnum (pl., **proepistérna**) the episternum of the prothorax (Figure 243, eps_1).

Profile the outline as seen from the side or in lateral view.

Prógnathous having the head horizontal and the mouth parts projecting forward.

Proleg one of the fleshy abdominal legs of certain insect larva (Figure 357, *prl*).

Prominence a raised, produced, or projecting portion.

Prominent raised, produced, or projecting.

Pronòtal comb a row of strong spines borne on the posterior margin of the pronotum (Siphonáptera; Figure 521, *prc*).

Pronòtum the dorsal sclerite of the prothorax (Figures 1 and 18, n_1).

Propleùral bristles bristles located on the propleuron (Díptera; Figure 444, *ppb*).

Propleùron (pl., **propleùra**) the lateral portion, or pleuron, of the prothorax (Figure 444, pl_1).

Propòdeum the posterior portion of the thorax, which is actually the first abdominal segment united with the thorax (Hymenóptera, suborder Apócrita; Figure 530, *prd*).

Propupa the instar preceding the pupa, in which the wing pads are present and the legs are short and thick (Thysanóptera; Figure 160 B). (Sometimes called the prepupa.)

Prosòma a term referring to the anterior part of the body, usually applied to the cephalothorax; the anterior part of the head or cephalothorax.

Prostérnum the sternum, or ventral sclerite, of the prothorax.

Prothorax the anterior of the three thoracic segments (Figure 1, th_1).

Protonymph the second instar of a mite (Figure 54 C).

Proventrículus the posterior portion of the foregut; the gizzard (Figure 23, *prv*).

Proximad toward the end or portion nearest the body.

Proximal nearer to the body, or to the base of an appendage.

Prozònite the anterior portion of a millipede tergum when the tergum is divided by a transverse groove.

Prùinose covered with a whitish waxy powder.

Pseudaròlium (pl., **pseudaròlia**) a pad at the apex of the tarsus, resembling an arolium.

Pseudocércus (pl., **pseudocérci**) a urogomphus (see).

Pseudocùbitus a vein appearing as the cubitus, but actually formed by the fusion of the branches of M and Cu_1 (Neuróptera; Figure 233 B, *pscu*).

Pseudomèdia a vein appearing as the media, but actually formed by the fusion of branches of Rs (Neuróptera; Figure 233 B, *psm*).

Pseudopupa a coarctate larva; a larva in a quiescent pupalike condition, one or two instars before the true pupal stage (Coleóptera, Melòidae; Figure 312 H).

Pteropleùral bristles bristles on the pteropleuron (Díptera; Figure 444, *ptb*).

Pteropleùron (pl., **pteropleùra**) a sclerite on the side of the thorax, just below the base of the wing, and consisting of the upper part of the mesepimeron (Díptera; Figure 444, *pt*).

Pterostigma a thickened opaque spot along the costal margin of the wing, near the wing tip (also called the stigma) (Odonàta, Figures 98 and 99, *st*).

Ptérygote winged; a member of the subclass Pterygòta.

Ptilìnum a temporary bladderlike structure that can be inflated and thrust out through the frontal (or ptilinal) suture, just above the bases of the antennae, at the time of emergence from the puparium (Díptera).

Pubéscent downy, covered with short fine hairs.

Pulvílliform lobelike or padlike; shaped like a pulvillus; pulvilliform empodium (Figure 441 B, *emp*).

Pulvíllus (pl., **pulvílli**) a pad or lobe beneath each tarsal claw (Díptera; Figure 441, *pul*).

Punctate pitted or beset with punctures.

Puncture a tiny pit or depression.

Pùpa (pl., **pùpae**) the stage between the larva and adult in insects with complete metamorphosis, a nonfeeding and usually an inactive stage (Figure 43).

Pupàrium (pl., **pupària**) a case formed by the hardening of the next to the last larval skin, in which the pupa is formed (Díptera; Figure 43 F).

Pupate transform to a pupa.

Pupíparous giving birth to larvae that are full grown and ready to pupate.

Pygídium the last dorsal segment of the abdomen.

Quadrangle a cell immediately beyond the arculus (Odonàta, Zygóptera; Figure 99, *q*).

Quadrate four-sided.

Radial cell a cell bordered anteriorly by a branch of the radius; the marginal cell (Hymenóptera; Figure 532, *MC*).

Radial cross vein a cross vein connecting R_1 and the branch of the radius immediately behind it (Figure 20, *r*).

Radial sector the posterior of the two main branches of the radius (Figure 20, *Rs*).

Radius the longitudinal vein between the subcosta and the media (Figure 20, *R*).

Raptorial fitted for grasping prey; raptorial front legs (Figures 113 F and 165).

Réclinate inclined backward or upward.

Rectum the posterior region of the hindgut (Figure 23, *rec*).

Recurrent vein one of two transverse veins immediately posterior to the cubital vein (Hymenóptera; Figures 527 and 529, *rv*); a vein at the base of the wing between the costa and subcosta, extending obliquely from the subcosta to the costa (Neuróptera; Figure 232 C, *hv*).

Recurved curved upward or backward.

Réniform kidney-shaped.

Retículate like a network.

Retina the receptive apparatus of an eye.

Retractile capable of being pushed out and drawn back in.

Rhabdom a rodlike light-sensitive structure formed of the inner surfaces of adjacent sensory cells in the ommatidium of a compound eye (Figure 30, *rh*).

Riker mount a thin, glass-topped exhibition case filled with cotton (Figure 631).

Rostrum beak or snout.

Rudimentary reduced in size, poorly developed, vestigial.

Rùgose wrinkled.

Saprόphagous feeding on dead or decaying plant or animal materials, such as carrion, dung, dead logs, etc.

Scape the basal segment of an antenna (Figure 6 N, *scp*).

Scápula (also called **parápsis**) (pl., **scápulae**) one of two sclerites on the mesonotum immediately lateral of the parapsidal sutures (Hymenóptera; Figure 530, *sca*).

Scarabaèiform larva a grublike larva, that is, one with the body thickened and cylindrical, with a well developed head and thoracic legs, without prolegs, and usually sluggish (Figures 42 and 277).

Scavenger an animal that feeds on dead plants or animals, on decaying materials, or on animal wastes.

Scent gland a gland producing an odorous substance.

Scientific name a latinized name, internationally recognized, of a species or subspecies. The scientific name of a species consists of the generic and specific names and the name of the describer of the species, and that of a subspecies consists of generic, specific, and subspecific names and the name of the describer of the subspecies. Scientific names (excluding authors' names) are always printed in italics.

Sclerite a hardened body wall plate bounded by sutures or membranous areas.

Sclerotized hardened.

Scòlytoid larva a fleshy larva resembling the larva of a scolytid beetle.

Scòpa (pl., **scòpae**) a pollen-transporting apparatus, either a corbicula (which see) or a brush of hairs on the hind legs or ventral side of the abdomen (bees).

Scópula (pl., **scópulae**) a small, dense tuft of hair.

Scraper the sharpened anal angle of the front wing (tegmen) of a cricket or long-horned grasshopper, a part of the stridulating mechanism.

Scròbe a groove or furrow; antennal scrobe (Figures 244 and 330, *agr*).

Scutéllum a sclerite of the thoracic notum (Figure 18, *scl*); the mesoscutellum, appearing as a more or less triangular sclerite behind the pronotum (Hemíptera, Homóptera, Coleóptera).

Scùtum the middle division of a thoracic notum, just anterior to the scutellum (Figure 18, *sct*).

Sebàceous glands glands secreting fatty or oily material.

Sectorial cross vein a cross vein connecting two branches of the radial sector (Figure 20, *s*).

Segment a subdivision of the body or of an appendage, between joints or articulations.

Semelpàrous a type of life history in which the animal reproduces only once during its lifetime.

Semiaquatic living in wet places, or partially in water.

Seminal vesicle a structure, usually saclike, in which the seminal fluid of the male is stored before being discharged, usually an enlargement of the vas deferens (Figure 27 B, *smv*).

Sense cone or **sense peg** a minute cone or peg, sensory in function (Figures 29, 153, and 162, *scn*).

Serrate toothed along the edge like a saw; serrate antenna (Figure 6 G).

Sessile attached or fastened, incapable of moving from place to place; attached directly, without a stem or petiole.

Sèta (pl., **sètae**) a bristle.

Setàceous bristlelike; setaceous antenna (Figure 6 A).

Sètate provided with bristles.

Sètulose bearing short, blunt bristles.

Sigmoid shaped like the letter **S**.

Simple unmodified, not complicated; not forked, toothed, branched, or divided.

Spátulate spoon-shaped; broad apically and narrowed basally, and flattened.

Species a group of individuals or populations that are similar in structure and physiology and are capable of interbreeding and producing fertile offspring, and which are different in structure and/or physiology from other such groups and normally do not interbreed with them.

Spermathèca (pl., **spermathècae**) a saclike structure in the female in which sperms from the male are received and often stored (Figure 27 A, *spth*).

Spermátophore a capsule containing sperm, produced by the males of some insects.

Spinastérnum an intersegmental sclerite of the thoracic venter which bears a median apodeme or spina, associated with or united with the sternal sclerite immediately anterior to it; also called the intersternite.

Spindle-shaped elongate and cylindrical, thickened in the middle and tapering at the ends.

Spine a thorn-like outgrowth of the cuticle.

Spinneret a structure with which silk is spun, usually fingerlike in shape (Figures 57 B and 58 B–E, *spn*).

Spinose beset with spines; spinose costa in Díptera (Figure 459 H).

Spiracle an external opening of the tracheal system; a breathing pore (Figures 1 and 26, *spr*).

Spirácular bristle a bristle very close to a spiracle (Díptera; Figure 458, *spbr*).

Spiracular plate a platelike sclerite next to or surrounding the spiracle.

Spur a movable spine (when on a leg segment, usually located at the apex of the segment).

Spùrious claw a false claw; a stout bristle that looks like a claw (spiders).

Spurious vein a veinlike thickening of the wing membrane between two true veins; an adventitious longitudinal vein between the radius and media, crossing the r-m cross vein (Díptera, Sýrphidae; Figure 450 A–C, *spv*).

Squáma (pl., **squámae**) a scalelike structure; a calypter; the palpiger (Odonàta; Figure 101, *plg*).

Stàdium (pl., **stàdia**) the period between molts in a developing arthropod.

Stalked with a stalk or stem; with a narrow stemlike base; of veins, fused together to form a single vein.

Stémmata (sing., **stémma**) the lateral ocelli of insect larvae.

Sternacóstal suture a suture of the thoracic sternum, the external mark of the sternal apophysis or furca, separating the basisternum from the sternellum.

Sternàuli (pl., **sternàulices**) a longitudinal furrow on the lower side of the mesopleuron (Hymenóptera).

Sternéllum the part of the eusternum posterior to the sternacostal suture.

Sternite a subdivision of a sternum; the ventral plate of an abdominal segment.

Sternopleùral bristles bristles on the sternopleuron (Díptera; Figure 444, *stb*).

Sternopleùron (pl., **sternopleùra**) a sclerite in the lateral wall of the thorax, just above the base of the middle leg (Díptera; Figure 444, *stpl*).

Sternum (pl., **sterna**) a sclerite on the ventral side of the body; the ventral sclerite of an abdominal segment (Figure 1, *stn*).

Stígma (pl., **stigmàta**) a thickening of the wing membrane along the costal border near the apex (Figures 98, 99, and 127, *st*).

Stigmal vein a short vein extending posteriorly from the costal margin of the wing, usually a little beyond the middle of the wing (Chalcidòidea; Figure 541 B, *sv*).

Stìpes (pl., **stípites**) the second segment or division of a maxilla, which bears the palp, the galea, and the lacinia (Figure 7 A, *stp*); lateral lobes of the millipede gnathochilarium (Figure 74 B, *stp*).

Stomodaèum the foregut.

Strìa (pl., **strìae**) a groove or depressed line.

Strìate with grooves or depressed lines.

Strídulate to make a noise by rubbing two structures or surfaces together.

Stripe a longitudinal color marking.

Stylate with a style; stylelike; stylate antenna (Figure 6 K).

Style a bristlelike process at the apex of an antenna (Figure 6 K, *sty*); a short, slender, fingerlike process (Figure 90, *sty*).

Stylet a needlelike structure; one of the piercing structures in sucking mouth parts.

Stylus (pl., **styli**) a short, slender, fingerlike process (Thysanùra; Figure 90, *sty*).

Subantennal suture a suture on the face extending ventrally from the base of the antenna (Figures 5 and 537, *sas*).

Subàpical located just proximad of the apex.

Subbasal located just distad of the base.

Subclass a major subdivision of a class, containing a group of related orders.

Subcosta the longitudinal vein between the costa and the radius (Figure 20, *Sc*).

Subcuticle the innermost part of the endocuticle, representing newly secreted cuticle (Figure 2, *scu*).

Subdiscal (or **subdiscoidal**) **vein** the vein forming the posterior margin of the third discoidal cell (Hymenóptera; Figures 527 and 529, *sd*).

Subequal approximately, or almost, equal in size or length.

Subesophágeal ganglion the knotlike swelling at the anterior end of the ventral nerve cord, usually just below the esophagus (Figures 23 and 28, *segn*).

Subfamily a major subdivision of a family, containing a group of related tribes or genera. Subfamily names end in *-inae*.

Subgènal suture the horizontal suture below the gena, just above the bases of the mandibles and maxillae, a lateral extension of the epistomal suture (Figure 5, *sgs*).

Subgenital plate a platelike sternite that underlies the genitalia.

Subgènus (pl., **subgénera**) a major subdivision of a genus, containing a group of related species. In scientific names, subgeneric names are capitalized and placed in parentheses following the genus name.

Subimàgo the first of two winged instars of a mayfly after it emerges from the water.

Submarginal cell one or more cells lying immediately behind the marginal cell (Hymenóptera; Figures 527 and 529, *SM*).

Submarginal vein a vein immediately behind and paralleling the costal margin of the wing (Chalcidòidea; Figure 541 C, *sm*).

Submedian cell the cell behind the median cell, in the basal posterior portion of the wing (Hymenóptera; Figures 527 and 529, *SMD*).

Submentum the basal part of the labium (Figure 7 C, *smt*).

Subocular suture a suture extending ventrally from the compound eye (Figure 5, *sos*).

Suborder a major subdivision of an order, containing a group of related superfamilies or families.

Subphỳlum (pl., **subphỳla**) a major subdivision of a phylum, containing a group of related classes.

Subquadrangle a cell immediately behind the quadrangle (Odonàta, Zygóptera; Figure 99, *sq*).

Subspecies a subdivision of a species, usually a geographic race. The different subspecies of a species are ordinarily not sharply differentiated and intergrade with one another and are capable of interbreeding. (For names of subspecies, see *scientific name*.)

Subtriangle a cell or group of cells proximad of the triangle (Odonàta, Anisóptera; Figure 98, *str*).

Successions groups of species that successively occupy a given habitat as the conditions of that habitat change.

Súlcate with a groove or furrow.

Súlcus (pl., **súlci**) a suture formed by an infolding of the body wall (the suture at the left in Figure 3); a groove or furrow.

Superfamily a group of closely related families. Superfamily names end in *-oidea*.

Superior appendage one of the two upper appendages at the end of the abdomen, a cercus (Odonàta; Figure 97, *sap*).

Supplement an adventitious vein formed by a number of cross veins being lined up to form a continuous vein, located behind and more or less parallel to one of the main longitudinal veins (Odonàta; Figure 98, *mspl, rspl*).

Supra-alar bristles a longitudinal row of bristles on the lateral portion of the mesonotum, immediately above the wing base (Díptera; Figure 444, *spb*).

Suture an external linelike groove in the body wall, or a narrow membranous area between sclerites (Figure 3, *su*); the line of juncture of the elytra (Coleóptera).

Swimmeret an abdominal appendage that functions as a swimming organ (Crustàcea; Figure 66, *sw*).

Sýmbiont an organism living in symbiosis with another organism.

Symbiòsis a living together, in a more or less intimate association, of two species, which benefits both.

Symmetry a definite pattern of body organization; bilateral symmetry, a type of body organization in which the various parts are arranged more or less symmetrically on either side of a median vertical plane, that is, where the right and left sides of the body are essentially similar.

Synonyms two or more names for the same thing (taxon).

Systematics taxonomy (see).

Taenídium (pl., **taenídia**) a circular or spiral thickening in the inner wall of a trachea.

Tandem one behind the other, the two connected or attached together.

Tarsal claw a claw at the apex of the tarsus (Figure 19, *tcl*).

Tarsal formula the number of tarsal segments on the front, middle, and hind tarsi, respectively.

Tarsomere a subdivision, or "segment," of the tarsus.

Tarsus (pl., **tarsi**) the leg segment immediately beyond the tibia, consisting of one or more "segments" or subdivisions (Figure 19, *ts*).

Táxis (pl., **taxès**) a directed response involving the movement of an animal toward or away from a stimulus.

Táxon (pl., **táxa**) a taxonomic category, for example, phylum, class, order, etc. (see list, page 86).

Taxonomy the science of classification into categories of varying rank, based on similarities and differences, and the describing and naming of these categories.

Tégmen (pl., **tégmina**) the thickened or leathery front wing of an orthopteran.

Tégula (pl., **tégulae**) a small scalelike structure overlying the base of the front wing (Figure 530, *tg*).

Télson the posterior part of the last abdominal segment (Crustàcea).

Tenáculum a minute structure on the ventral side of the third abdominal segment which serves as a clasp for the furcula (Collémbola).

Teneral a term applied to recently molted, pale, soft-bodied individuals.

Tentorial pits pitlike depressions on the surface of the head that mark the points of union of the arms of the tentorium with the outer wall of the head. There are usually two tentorial pits in the epistomal suture (Figures 5 and 24, *atp*), and one at the lower end of each postoccipital suture (Figures 5 and 24, *ptp*).

Tentorium the endoskeleton of the head, usually consisting of two pairs of apodemes (Figure 24).

Tergite (the *g* has the soft or *j* sound) a sclerite of the tergum.

Tergum (pl., **terga**) the dorsal surface of any body segment (Figure 1, *t*).

Terminal at the end; at the posterior end (of the abdomen); the last of a series.

Terrestrial living on land.

Testis (pl., **testes**) the sex organ in the male that produces sperm (Figure 27 B, *tst*).

Thorax the body region behind the head, which bears the legs and wings (Figure 1, *th*).

Tibia (pl., **tibiae**) the fourth segment of the leg, between the femur and tarsus (Figure 19, *tb*).

Tibial spur a large spine on the tibia, usually located at the distal end of the tibia.

Tonofibríllae the fine connective fibrils extending from the ends of the skeletal muscles into the cuticle.

Tórmogen cell an epidermal cell associated with a seta, which forms the setal membrane or socket (Figure 2, *tmg*).

Tóxicognath a poison jaw (centipedes, Figure 76, *pj*; a modified leg).

Tràchea (pl., **tràcheae**) a tube of the respiratory system, lined with taenidia, ending externally at a spiracle, and terminating internally in the tracheoles (Figure 26).

Tracheòles the fine terminal branches of the respiratory tubes.

Translucent allowing light to pass through, but not necessarily transparent.

Transverse across, at right angles to the longitudinal axis.

Transverse costal vein a cross vein in the costal cell (Hymenóptera; Figure 527, *tc*).

Transverse cubital vein a transverse vein connecting the marginal and cubital veins (Hymenóptera; Figures 527 and 529, *tcb*).

Transverse marginal vein a cross vein in the marginal cell (Hymenóptera; Figure 527, *trd*).

Transverse median vein a cross vein between the median or discoidal vein and the anal vein (Hymenóptera; Figures 527 and 529, *tm*).

Transverse radial vein a transverse marginal vein (see).

Transverse suture a suture across the mesonotum (Díptera; Figure 444, *trs*).

Triangle a small triangular cell or group of cells near the base of the wing (Odonàta, Anisóptera; Figures 98 and 100, *tri*).

Tribe a subdivision of a subfamily, containing a group of related genera. Names of tribes end in *-ini*.

Trichobóthria minute sensory hairs on the tarsi (spiders; Figure 59 B, *trb*).

Tríchogen cell the epidermal cell from which a seta develops (Figure 29, *trg*).

Trígonal brace a strong forked vein in the basal part of the wing, formed by the fork of Cu_1 in the front wing and M_{3+4} in the hind wing (Neuróptera, Myrmeleontòidea; Figure 234, *trbr*).

Trigonal vein the vein forming the anterior fork of the trigonal brace (Neuróptera, Myrmeleontòidea).

Tripectinate having three rows of comblike branches.

Triúngulin larva the active first instar larva of the Strepsíptera and certain beetles that undergo hypermetamorphosis (Figures 312 A and 340 F).

Trochánter the second segment of the leg, between the coxa and femur (Figure 19, *tr*).

Trochántin a small sclerite in the thoracic wall immediately anterior to the base of the coxa (Coleóptera; Figure 246 B, *tn*).

Trophalláxis the exchange of alimentary canal liquid among colony members of social insects and guest organisms, either mutually or unilaterally; trophallaxis may be stomodeal (from the mouth) or proctodeal (from the anus).

Tròpism the orientation of an animal with respect to a stimulus, either positive (turning toward the stimulus) or negative (turning away from the stimulus).

Truncate cut off square at the end.

Truss cell the cell immediately behind the point of fusion of Sc and R (Neuróptera, Myrmeleontòidea; Figure 234, *trc*).

Tùbercle a small knoblike or rounded protuberance.

Tỳlus the clypeal region of the head (Hemíptera; Figure 164, *ty*).

Týmbal a sclerotized plate in the sound-producing organ of a cicada (Figure 206, *tmb*).

Týmpanal hood one of a pair of tubercles or rounded prominences on the dorsal surface of the first abdominal segment (Lepidóptera).

Týmpanum (pl., **týmpana**) a vibrating membrane; an auditory membrane or eardrum (Figures 19 D and 206, *tym*).

Types forms designated, when a species or group is described, to be most representative or typical, to serve as the reference if there is any question about what that species or group includes. The type of a species or subspecies (the holotype) is a specimen, the type of a genus or subgenus is a species, and the type of a tribe, subfamily, family, or superfamily is a genus.

Unisexual consisting of or involving only females.

Urogómphi (sing., **urogómphus**) fixed or movable cerculike processes on the last segment of a beetle larva (also called pseudocerci or corniculi).

Ùropod one of the terminal pair of abdominal appendages, usually lobelike (Crustàcea; Figure 66, *ur*).

Vagìna the terminal portion of the female reproductive system, which opens to the outside (Figures 23 and 27 A, *vag*).

Válvifers the basal plates of the ovipositor, derived from the basal segment of the gonopods.

Válvulae the three pairs of processes forming the sheath and piercing structures of the ovipositor.

Vánnal lobe a lobe in the anal area of the wing immediately distad of the jugal lobe when a jugal lobe is present (Hymenóptera; Figure 591, *vl*).

Vás déferens (pl., **vàsa deferéntia**) the sperm duct leading away from a testis (Figure 27 B, *vd*).

Vás éfferens (pl., **vàsa efferéntia**) a short duct connecting a sperm tube in the testis with the vas deferens (Figure 27 B, *ve*).

Vein a thickened line in the wing.

Venter the ventral side.

Ventrad toward the ventral or underside of the body; downward.

Ventral lower or underneath; pertaining to the underside of the body.

Vermiform larva a legless wormlike larva, without a well developed head (Figure 42 A).

Vertex the top of the head, between the eyes and anterior to the occipital suture (Figure 5, *ver*).

Vésicle a sac, bladder, or cyst, often extensible.

Vestígial small, poorly developed, degenerate, nonfunctional.

Vibríssae, oral (see *oral vibrissae*).

Vítelline membrane the cell wall of the insect egg; a thin membrane lying beneath the chorion (Figure 36, *vm*).

Vítta (pl., **vittae**) a broad stripe.

Vivíparous giving birth to living young, not egg-laying.

Vulvar lamina the posterior margin (usually prolonged posteriorly) of the eighth abdominal sternite (female Anisóptera).

Wireworm an elateriform larva; a larva that is slender, heavily sclerotized, with few hairs on the body, with thoracic legs but without prolegs; the larva of a click beetle (Figure 279 B).

Y-vein two adjacent veins fusing distally, forming a **Y**-shaped figure (for example, the anal veins in the front wing, Figure 386).

Zoóphagous feeding on animals.

References

Borror, D. J. 1960. *Dictionary of Word Roots and Combining Forms.* Palo Alto, Calif.: National Press Books (now Mayfield Publ.), v + 134 pp.

Brown, R. W. 1954. *Composition of Scientific Words.* Washington, D.C.: published by the author, 882 pp.

Carpenter, J. R. 1938. *An Ecological Glossary.* London: Kegan Paul,Trench, Trubner, ix + 306 pp., 12 pp. of maps and tables.

Dorland, W. A. N. 1932 (16th ed.). *The American Illustrated Medical Dictionary.* Philadelphia: W. B. Saunders, 1493 pp.; illus.

Hanson, D. R. 1959. *A Short Glossary of Entomology with Derivations.* Los Angeles, Calif.: published by the author, 83 pp.

Henderson, I. F., and W. D. Henderson. 1939 (3rd ed., rev. by J. H. Kenneth). *A Dictionary of Scientific Terms.* London: Oliver and Boyd, xii + 383 pp.

Jaeger, E. C. 1955 (3rd ed.). *A Source Book of Biological Names and Terms.* Springfield, Ill.: C. Thomas, xxxv + 317 pp.

Jardine, N. K. 1913. *The Dictionary of Entomology.* London: West, Newman, ix + 259 pp.

Pennak, R. W. 1964. *Collegiate Dictionary of Zoology.* New York: Ronald Press, 583 pp.

Smith, J. B. 1906. *Explanation of Terms Used in Entomology.* Brooklyn, N.Y.: Brooklyn Ent. Soc. 154 pp., 3 pl.

Snodgrass, R. E. 1935. *Principles of Insect Morphology.* New York: McGraw-Hill, ix + 667 pp., 319 f.

Torre-Bueno, J. R. de la. 1937. *A Glossary of Entomology.* Lancaster, Pa.: Science Press, x + 336 pp., 9 pl. (1962 ed., with "Supplement A" is available from the Brooklyn Ent. Soc., N.Y.)

Tuxen, S. L. (ed.). 1970 (rev. ed.). *Taxonomist's Glossary of Genitalia in Insects.* Copenhagen: Ejnar Munksgaard, 359 pp.; illus.

Tweney, C. F., and L. E. C. Hughes (Eds.). 1940. *Chambers' Technical Dictionary.* New York: Macmillan, viii + 957 pp.

ABBREVIATIONS USED IN THE FIGURES

The following list includes all the abbreviations used in the original figures in Chapters 2 through 32. The abbreviations used on wing drawings for the veins and cells (using the Comstock–Needham terminology) are not listed in the figure legends, but are included in the following list. Subscript numerals are used to designate branches of the longitudinal veins. Such numerals are often used to designate the particular thoracic segment on which a structure is located (1, designating the prothorax; 2, the mexothorax; and 3, the metathorax). Subscript numerals are occasionally used to designate the particular abdominal segment on which a sclerite is located.

a, anal vein
A, anal vein; anal cell
ab, abdomen
ac, accessory vein
Ac, anal crossing
acc, accessory cell
acg, accessory gland
acl, antennal club
aclp, anteclypeus
acr, acrostichal bristles
acs, acrosternite
act, acrotergite
acv, anterior cross vein
adf, adfrontal area
aed, aedeagus
af, antennal fossa
agr, antennal groove; scrobe
al, anal lobe
alp, anal loop
alu, alula
am, axillary muscles
an, antenodal cross veins
AN, alinotum
anc, anal cleft
ancs, antecostal suture
anp, anal plate
anr, anal ring
ans, anus
ant, antenna
antc, antecosta
antl, antennule
ao, dorsal aorta
ap, appendix; appendiculate marginal cell
AP, apical or posterior cell
apc, apical cross vein
apd, apodeme
apo, apophysis
ar, arista
arc, arculus
are, areolet
aro, arolium
art, articulation
as, antennal suture
asc, antennal sclerite
ask, antennal socket
asp, apical spur
aspr, anterior spiracle
at, alimentary tract
ata, anterior tentorial arm
atb, anal tube
atp, anterior tentorial pit
au, auricle
av, auxiliary vein
aw, anterior wart
awp, anterior notal wing process
ax, axilla
AX, axillary cell
axc, axillary cell
axcr, axillary cord
axs, axillary sclerite
axv, axillary vein

B, basal cell
ba, basalare
BA, basal areole; basal anal cell
bc, bursa copulatrix
bcv, bridge cross vein
bg, book gill
bk, beak, rostrum
bl, blastoderm
bm, basement membrane
bms, basalar muscles
bp, brood pouch
br, brain
brv, bridge vein
buc, bucca; buccula
bv, basal vein
bvn, brace vein

c, costal vein
C, costa; costal cell
ca, corpus allatum
cal, calypter
cb, corbicula
cbr, costal break
cc, crystalline cone
cd, cardo
cec, circumesophageal connective
cg, cerebral ganglion
ch, chelicera
chp, cheliped
cl, clavus
cla, clasper
clc, calcaria
clm, calamistrum
clp, clypeus
cls, claval suture
clt, clypeal tubercle; claw tuft
clv, claval vein
cm, caecum
cn, colon
cna, cornea
cngc, corneagenous cells
co, collophore
colm, collum
com, commissural trachea
comn, tritocerebral commissure
con, connective
cor, corium
covd, common oviduct
cp, crop
cph, cephalothorax
cr, cercus

crb, cribellum
cre, cremaster
crl, crystalline lens
crn, cornicle
cro, crochet
crp, carapace
cs, coronal suture
csp, cusp
ct, ctenidium
cu cubital vein
Cu, cubitus; cubital cell
cun, cuneus
cut, cuticle
cvs, cervical sclerite
cvx, cervix
cx, coxa
cxc, coxal cavity
cxg, coxal groove
cxp, coxopodite

d, discoidal vein
D, discal cell; discoidal cell
dc, dorsocentral bristles
dcv, discal cross vein
dg, dorsal gonapophysis
dlm, dorsal longitudinal muscles
dm, dome
do, dorsal ostioles
dp, distal process
dta, dorsal tentorial arm
DSJ, disjugal furrow
dtra, dorsal trachea

e, compound eye
ec, eye cap
ef, epigastric furrow
eg, eggs
ejd, ejaculatory duct
el, elytron
emb, embolium
emp, empodium
end, endocuticle
endr, endodermal rudiments
ep, epidermis
epcr, epicranium
epg, epigynum
eph, epipharynx
epi, epicuticle
epm, epimeron
epp, epipleurite
epr, epistomal ridge
eps, episternum
ept, epiproct
es, epistomal suture
eso, esophagus
ex, exuvia
exm, extensor muscle
exo, exocuticle

f, frenulum
fa, face
fb, frontal bristles
fc, food channel
fcn, frontal ganglion connective
fg, frontal ganglion
fl, flagellum
flb, flabellum
flm, flexor muscle
fm, femur
fmb, femoral bristle
fn, fang
fob, fronto-orbital bristle
fon, fontanelle
for, foramen magnum
fr, frons or front
frc, frontal carina
frclp, frontoclypeus
frl, frontal lunule
fs, frontal suture
fu, furca
fun, funiculus
fur, furcula
fv, frontal vitta

g, galea
gc, genal comb
ge, gena
gen, genitalia
gi, gill
gl, glossa
glc, gland cell
gld, duct of gland cell
gls, gland spines
gn, ganglion
gna, gnathochilarium
gr, gill remnant
gs, gular suture
gu, gula
gvp, genovertical or orbital plate

h, humeral cross vein
hal, halter
hb, humeral bristles
hbr, hypostomal bridge
hc, humeral callus
hd, head
ho, horn
hp, humeral plate
hr, heart or heart chamber
hst, haustellum
hv, humeral vein
hyb, hypopleural bristles
hyp, hypopharynx
hypl, hypopleuron

iab, intra-alar bristles
iap, inferior appendage
iar, interantennal ridge
ias, interantennal suture
ic, intercostal vein
ICu, cubital intercalary vein
iep, infraepisternum
il, ileum
ism, intersegmental membrane
it, intercalated triangle
ivb, inner vertical bristles

j, jugum
jl, jugal lobe

l, leg
L, lanceolate cell
lba, labial articulation
lbl, labellum
lbm, labium
lbn, labial nerve
lbr, labrum
lbrn, labral nerve
lc, lacinia
lct, layer of cuticle
le, labrum-epipharynx
lg, ligula
lgp, lateral gonapophysis
ll, lamina lingualis
lo, lorum
lp, labial palp
LP, lateral plate
ls, labial suture
lst, lateral setae
ltra, longitudinal trachea

m, medial cross vein
M, media, medial cell
ma, mandibular articulation
MC, marginal cell
mcf, median caudal filament
mcp, micropyle
m-cu, medio-cubital cross vein
md, mandible
MD, median cell
mdn, mandibular nerve
mdp, median plate
mdu, microduct

mdv, median vein
mem, membrane
mf, fork of media
mg, midgut or mesenteron
mh, movable hook of palp
ml, median lobe
mm, marginal macroducts
mn, mentum
mo, mouth
mp, mouth parts
mpb, mesopleural bristles
mpo, marginal 8-shaped pores
ms, mesoderm
msl, mesosternal lobe
mspl, medial supplement
mst, mental setae
mt, Malpighian tubules
mts, metatarsus; first tarsal segment
mu, mucro
mv, marginal vein
mx, maxilla
mxa, maxillary articulation
mxl, maxillary lobe
mxn, maxillary nerve
mxp, maxillary palp
mxt, maxillary tentacle

n notum
nb, notopleural bristles
nc, ventral nerve cord
n_1l, pronotal lobe
nod, nodus
npl, notopleuron
npls, notopleural suture
nv, nerve

o, opening
ob, ocellar bristles
obv, oblique vein
oc, ocellus or simple eye
ocg, occipital ganglion
ocp, occiput
ocpd, ocellar pedicel
ocs, ocular suture
of, outer fork
og, optic ganglion
op, operculum
opl, optic lobe
orp, orbital plate
os, occipital suture
osm, osmeterium
ot, ocellar triangle
ov, oral vibrissae
ovb, outer vertical bristles
ovd, oviduct
ovl, ovariole
ovp, ovipositor
ovt, ovarian tubules
ovy, ovary

p, palp
P, posterior cell
pa, postabdomen
pab, postalar bristles
pb, posthumeral bristle
pbr, pollen brush
pbs, prebasalare
pc, postalar callus
pclp, postclypeus
pcn, pore canal
pcv, posterior cross vein
pdp, pedipalp
ped, pedicel
pf, pilifer
pg, postgena
pgc, pigment cell
pgf, pygofer
pgl, paraglossa
ph, phragma
phx, pharynx
pj, poison jaw
pl, pleuron
pla, plate
plap, pleural apophysis
plf, palpifer
plg, palpiger
plm, pleural membrane
pls, pleural suture
plw, posterolateral wart
pm, postmarginal vein
pmt, postmentum
pn, postnodal cross vein
PN, postnotum
pnwp, posterior notal wing process
po, postocciput
pol, postocular lobe
por, postoccipital ridge
pos, postoccipital suture
pp, prepectus
ppb, propleural bristles
ppt, paraproct
pr, pollen rake
prb, proboscis
prc, pronotal comb
prd, propodeum
prl, proleg
prmt, prementum
pro, prosoma
prv, proventriculus
ps, parapsidal suture
psb, presutural bristles
pscl, postscutellum
pscu, pseudocubitus
psl, paired second lobe
psm, pseudomedia
psp, posterior spiracle
pt, pteropleuron
ptar, pretarsus
ptb, pteropleural bristles
ptbr, preapical tibial bristles
ptl, patella
ptp, posterior tentorial pit
ptsp, preapical tibial spur
pul, pulvillus
pv, postvertical bristles
pvp, perivalvular pores
pwp, pleural wing process
py, pygidium

q, quadrangle

r, radial cross vein
R, radius; radial cell
rec, rectum
ret, retina
rh, rhabdom
r-m, radio-medial cross vein
Rs, radial sector
rspl, radial supplement
rv, recurrent vein

s, sectorial cross vein
sa, sensory area
sap, superior appendage
sas, subantennal suture
sb, subalare
sbm, subalar muscles
sc, salivary channel
Sc, subcosta; subcostal cell
sca, scapula
scb, scutellar bristles
scl, scutellum
scn, sense cone; sense peg
sco, scopula
scp, scape
scr, scar
sct, scutum
scu, subcuticle
scv, subcostal vein
sd, subdiscal or subdiscoidal vein
se, seta

sec, secretion of adult
segn, subesophageal ganglion
sgl, salivary or labial glands
sgo, scent gland opening
sgp, subgenital plate
sgr, subgenal ridge
sgs, subgenal suture
sh, shell
sl, suspensory ligament
sld, salivary duct
sm, submarginal vein
SM, submarginal cell
SMD, submedian cell
smf, submedian fold
smm, submedial macroducts
smml, submarginal macroducts
smt, submentum
smv, seminal vesicle
sn, sensilium
snc, sensory cell
sos, subocular suture
sp, spur or spine
spb, supra-alar bristles
spbr, spiracular bristle
spn, spinneret
spr, spiracle
spt, sperm tube
spth, spermatheca
spthg, spermathecal gland
spv, spurious vein
sq, subquadrangle
ss, setal socket
st, stigma
stb, sternopleural bristles
std, foregut or stomodaeum
stg, prosternal groove
stl, sternal lobe
stn, sternite or sternum
stns, prosternal suture
stp, stipes
stpl, sternopleuron
str, subtriangle
stra, spiracular trachea
strp, stridulatory pegs
sty, style, stylet, or stylus
stys, stylet sac
su, suture
sv, stigmal vein
sw, swimmeret

t, tergite or tergum
tb, tibia
tbr, tergal bristles
tc, transverse costal vein
tcb, transverse cubital vein
tcl, tarsal claw
te, teeth
tg, tegula
th, thorax
thap, thoracic appendages
tl, transverse lanceolate vein
tm, transverse median vein
tmb, tymbal
tmg, tormogen (socket forming) cell
tn, trochantin
tnt, tentorium
tr, trochanter
trb, trichobothria
trbr, trigonal brace
trc, truss cell
trd, transverse radial vein
trg, trichogen (seta-forming) cell
tri, triangle
trs, transverse suture
ts, tarsus
tsm, tergosternal muscles
tsp, tibial spur
tst, testis
ttb, tentorial bridge
tub, tubercle
ty, tylus
tym, tympanum

un, uncus
ur, uropod

va, valve
vag, vagina
vc, ventral circulus
vd, vas deferens
ve, vas efferens
ver, vertex
vf, valvifer
vg, ventral gonapophysis
vl, vannal lobe
vlv, valvula
vm, vitelline membrane
vtra, ventral trachea
vu, vulna

w, wing
wb, base of wing

x, connection between axillary sclerite and epipleurite

y, young

INDEX

Numbers in italics refer to pages bearing illustrations only; numbers in boldface indicate the most important page reference. Many items not in this index may be found in the Glossary (page 767).